PEOPLE
AND OUR
COUNTRY

NORMAN K. RISJORD, Senior Author
Professor of History
University of Wisconsin
Madison, Wisconsin

TERRY L. HAYWOODE
Instructor of Sociology
Baruch College, CUNY
New York, New York

HOLT, RINEHART AND WINSTON, PUBLISHERS
New York • Toronto • London • Sydney

NORMAN K. RISJORD is Professor of History at the University of Wisconsin in Madison. He received his B.A. degree from the College of William and Mary and his Ph.D. from the University of Virginia. Dr. Risjord taught for four years at DePauw University, Greencastle, Indiana, before moving to the University of Wisconsin. He has written three books and numerous articles on the revolutionary and early national periods of American history.

Dr. Risjord won the William H. Kiekhofer Distinguished Teaching Award in his first year at the University of Wisconsin. His classroom lectures were broadcast on the State Educational Radio Network in 1965–1966, 1972–1973, and 1978–1979. He was a Fulbright Lecturer at the University of Uppsala, Sweden, in 1968, and he served as Teaching Fellow at the University of Dundee, Scotland, in 1973–1974. He is a member of the University–High Schools Liaison Committee, and he has addressed social studies conferences throughout the country on the art of teaching history.

ACKNOWLEDGMENTS

Grateful acknowledgment is made to the following publishers and authors:

Crown Publishers, Inc., for "Photography on the Battlefield," adapted from *Mathew Brady* by James D. Horan. Copyright © 1955.

Joan Daves for excerpts from "I Have a Dream" by Martin Luther King, Jr. Copyright © 1963 by Martin Luther King, Jr.

Charles Scribner's, Sons, *Dictionary of American Biography* for adaptation of "Rosika Schwimmer and the Peace Movement."

Holt, Rinehart and Winston, Publishers, for "A Crisis of Conscience" and "A Family Divided," adapted from *In Search of America* by David Fowler et al. Copyright © 1972. For "Life in Spanish California," adapted from *America's Frontier Story* by Martin Ridge and Ray Allen Billington. Copyright © 1969.

Smithsonian Magazine (November 1976, vol. 7, #8) for adaptation of the "Aaron Burr–Alexander Hamilton Duel."

Photo credits are on page 840.

ISBN: 0-03-056942-7
  45 071 98765

CONSULTANTS AND REVIEWERS

Special Consultants

Savannah C. Jones
Specialist, Social Studies Education
Birmingham Board of Education
Birmingham, Alabama

Joseph D. Baca
Program Specialist/Social Studies
New Mexico Department of Education
Santa Fe, New Mexico

Reading Consultant

Everett T. Keach, Jr.
Professor, Social Science Education
University of Georgia
Athens, Georgia

Geography Consultant

Nicholas K. Sakellaris
Social Studies Teacher
Westover Senior High School
Fayetteville, North Carolina

Educational Consultant

Donald V. Salvucci
Chairman, Social Science Department
Brockton High School
Brockton, Massachusetts

Content Reviewers

Nancy F. Cott
Associate Professor of History and American Studies
Yale University
New Haven, Connecticut

Jane De Hart Mathews
Professor of History
University of North Carolina
Greensboro, North Carolina

Mary S. McAuliffe
Assistant Professor of History
Iowa State University
Ames, Iowa

Edwin A. Miles
Professor of History
University of Houston
Houston, Texas

Walter Nugent
Professor of History
Indiana University
Bloomington, Indiana

William L. O'Neill
Professor of History
Rutgers University
New Brunswick, New Jersey

Darrett B. Rutman
Professor of History
University of New Hampshire
Durham, New Hampshire

TABLE OF CONTENTS

UNIT 2
BUILDING A NATION

UNIT 4
AN EXPANDING NATION

UNIT 7

YEARS OF TRIAL AND HOPE

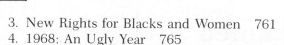

MAPS

CHARTS AND GRAPHS

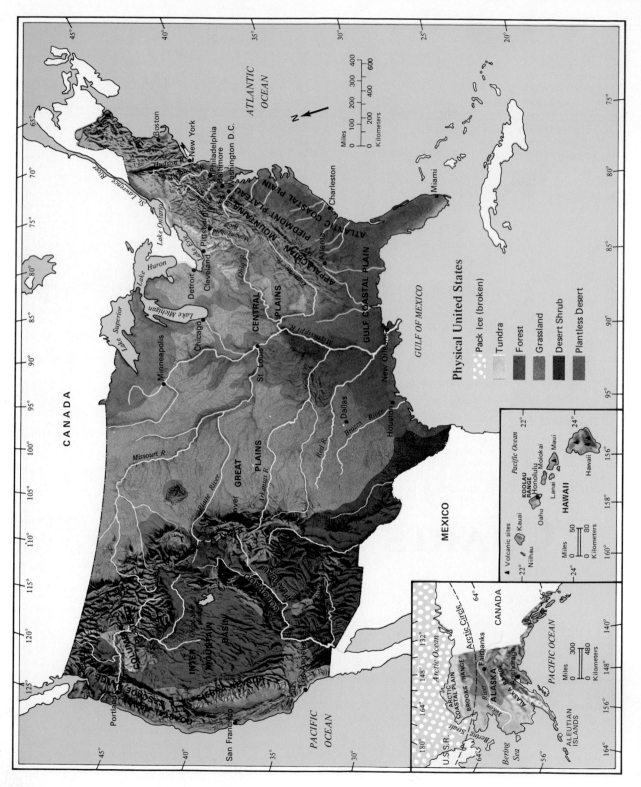

Physical United States

Pack Ice (broken)

Tundra

Forest

Grassland

Desert Shrub

Plantless Desert

CANADA

ATLANTIC
OCEAN

PACIFIC
OCEAN

GULF OF MEXICO

MEXICO

St. Lawrence River

Lake Ontario

Lake Erie

Lake Huron

Lake Superior

Lake Michigan

Hudson River

Ohio R.

Tennessee R.

Mississippi R.

Missouri R.

Platte River

Arkansas R.

Red R.

Brazos River

Colorado River

Snake River

Columbia River

Gila River

Boston

New York

Philadelphia

Baltimore

Washington D.C.

Charleston

Miami

Atlanta

Detroit

Cleveland

Pittsburgh

Chicago

Minneapolis

St. Louis

Dallas

Houston

New Orleans

Los Angeles

San Francisco

Portland

APPALACHIAN MOUNTAINS

PIEDMONT PLATEAU

ATLANTIC COASTAL PLAIN

GULF COASTAL PLAIN

CENTRAL PLAINS

GREAT PLAINS

COLORADO PLATEAU

INTERMOUNTAIN BASIN

SIERRA NEVADA

CASCADE RANGE

COAST RANGE

Miles
0 100 200 300 400

Kilometers
0 200 400 600

N

HAWAII

KOOLAU RANGE

Honolulu

Kauai

Niihau

Oahu

Molokai

Lanai

Maui

Hawaii

Pacific Ocean

▲ Volcanic sites

Miles
0   50

Kilometers
0   80

ALASKA

CANADA

Arctic Circle

Arctic Ocean

ARCTIC COASTAL PLAIN

BROOKS RANGE

ALASKA RANGE

ALEUTIAN ISLANDS

Bering Sea

Bering Strait

PACIFIC OCEAN

U.S.S.R.

Fairbanks

Anchorage

Yukon River

Miles
0   300

Kilometers
0   480

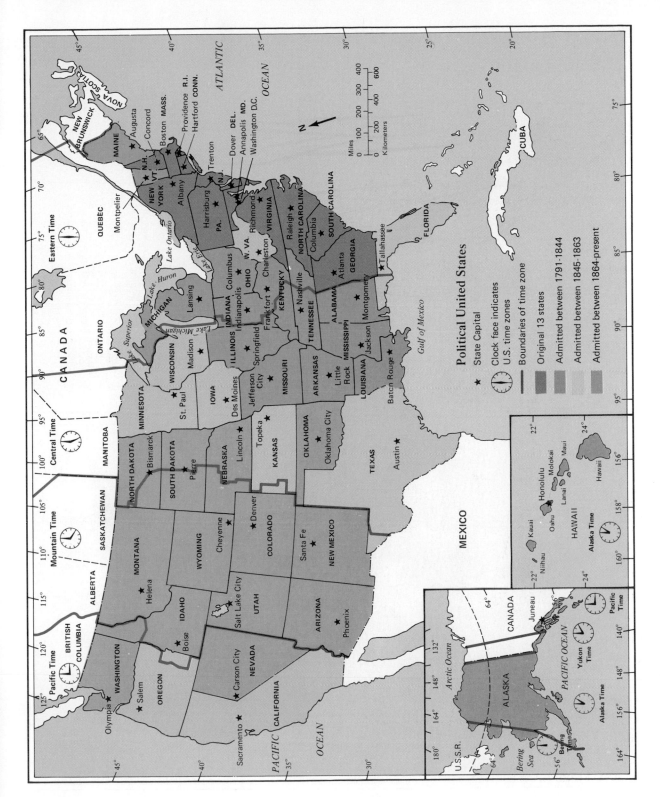

ATLANTIC OCEAN

CANADA

NOVA SCOTIA

NEW BRUNSWICK

QUEBEC

Montpelier

Eastern Time

MAINE
Augusta
Concord
N.H.
VT.
Boston MASS.
Providence R.I.
Hartford CONN.
Trenton N.J.
Dover DEL.
Annapolis MD.
Washington D.C.

ONTARIO

Lake Ontario
Lake Erie
Lake Huron
Lake Superior
Lake Michigan

NEW YORK
Albany
Harrisburg PA.
Richmond VIRGINIA
Raleigh
NORTH CAROLINA
Columbia
SOUTH CAROLINA

MICHIGAN
Lansing

WISCONSIN
Madison

Columbus OHIO
Indianapolis INDIANA
Charleston W. VA.
Frankfort KENTUCKY
Nashville TENNESSEE

Central Time

MINNESOTA
St. Paul

IOWA
Des Moines

ILLINOIS
Springfield

MISSOURI
Jefferson City

ARKANSAS
Little Rock

ALABAMA
Montgomery

MISSISSIPPI
Jackson

LOUISIANA
Baton Rouge

GEORGIA
Atlanta

Tallahassee
FLORIDA

Gulf of Mexico

MANITOBA

SASKATCHEWAN

NORTH DAKOTA
Bismarck

SOUTH DAKOTA
Pierre

NEBRASKA
Lincoln

KANSAS
Topeka

OKLAHOMA
Oklahoma City

TEXAS
Austin

Mountain Time

ALBERTA

BRITISH COLUMBIA

MONTANA
Helena

WYOMING
Cheyenne

COLORADO
Denver

NEW MEXICO
Santa Fe

UTAH
Salt Lake City

IDAHO
Boise

Pacific Time

WASHINGTON
Olympia

OREGON
Salem

NEVADA
Carson City

CALIFORNIA
Sacramento

ARIZONA
Phoenix

PACIFIC OCEAN

MEXICO

Miles
Kilometers
N

Political United States

★ State Capital
🕐 Clock face indicates
— U.S. time zones
Boundaries of time zone
Original 13 states
Admitted between 1791-1844
Admitted between 1845-1863
Admitted between 1864-present

HAWAII

Niihau
Kauai
Oahu
Honolulu
Molokai
Lanai
Maui
Hawaii

Alaska Time

ALASKA

U.S.S.R.
Bering Sea
Bering Strait
CANADA
Juneau

Arctic Ocean
PACIFIC OCEAN

Yukon Time
Alaska Time
Pacific Time

xv

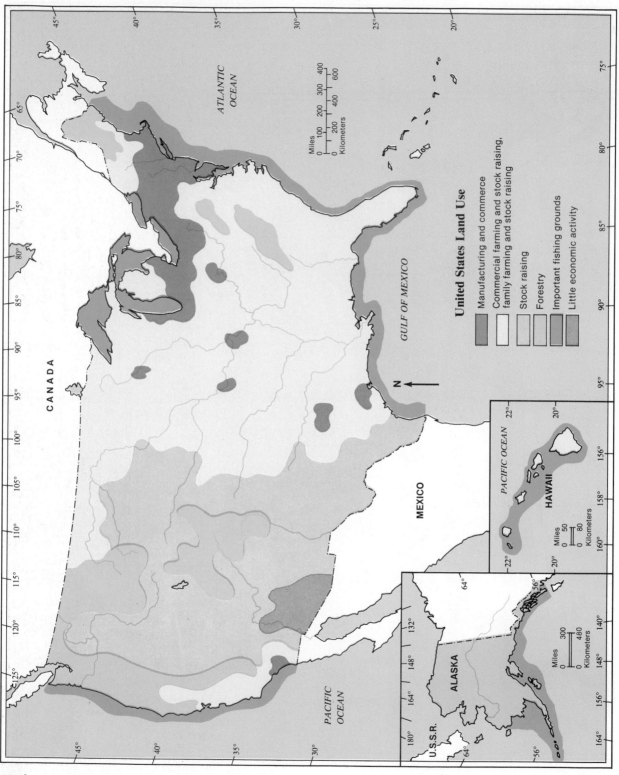

United States Land Use

- Manufacturing and commerce
- Commercial farming and stock raising, family farming and stock raising
- Stock raising
- Forestry
- Important fishing grounds
- Little economic activity

N

ATLANTIC OCEAN

GULF OF MEXICO

PACIFIC OCEAN

CANADA

MEXICO

Miles
0   100   200   300   400
Kilometers
0   200   400   600

HAWAII

PACIFIC OCEAN

Miles
0   50
Kilometers
0   80

ALASKA

U.S.S.R.

Miles
0   300
Kilometers
0   480

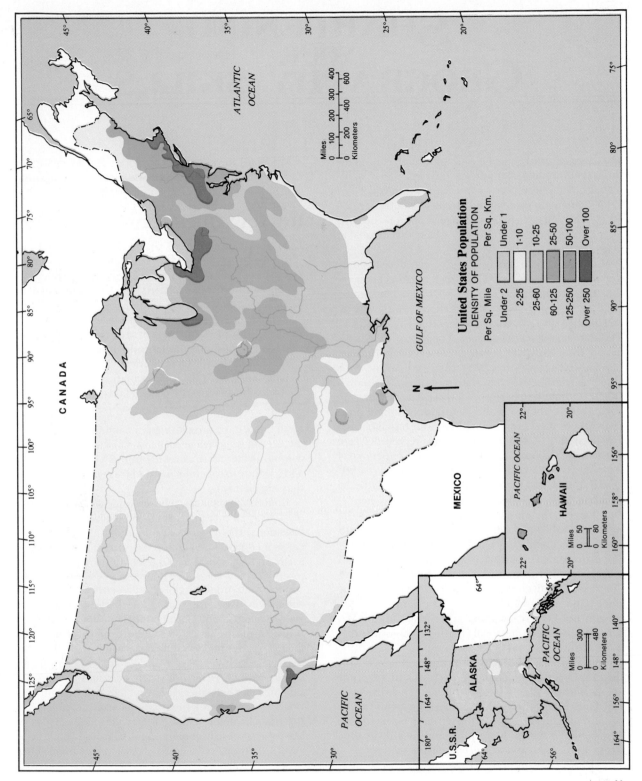

United States Population
DENSITY OF POPULATION

Per Sq. Mile		Per Sq. Km.
Under 2		Under 1
2-25		1-10
25-60		10-25
60-125		25-50
125-250		50-100
Over 250		Over 100

ATLANTIC OCEAN

GULF OF MEXICO

CANADA

MEXICO

PACIFIC OCEAN

N

Miles
0 100 200 300 400

Kilometers
0 200 400 600

PACIFIC OCEAN

HAWAII

Miles
0 50

Kilometers
0 80

ALASKA

U.S.S.R.

PACIFIC OCEAN

Miles
0 300

Kilometers
0 480

SHARPENING YOUR GEOGRAPHY SKILLS

You have probably used geographic and map skills throughout your social studies courses. These skills will also come into play as you work with *People and Our Country*. To understand the history of the United States, you will have to be able to read not only the written narrative but those parts of the story that are told in maps.

Mapmaking as a precise science was developed by the ancient Greeks. The first Greek mapmakers drew the earth as a disk floating in the ocean. Later mapmakers drew the earth as an oblong shape, which was divided into a grid system of intersecting coordinates—the latitude and longitude lines. The lines of longitude, drawn from north to south, were called *meridians*. Lines of latitude, drawn east to west, were called *parallels*. Since the Greeks knew that the earth was actually a sphere, although they pictured it on a flat surface as an oblong shape, they measured latitude and longitude in degrees. (As you know, a complete circle has 360°, and a half circle has 180°.) The equator represents zero degrees (0°) latitude. From the equator to either one of the poles is 90°. For instance, the North Pole is 90° north latitude, and the South Pole is 90° south latitude.

Although latitude lines are always parallel—hence, their name—the meridians of longitude that cross the equator at right angles and meet at the North and South poles are not completely parallel. For instance, the distance in a degree of latitude is about 109 kilometers (68 miles) whether it is measured at the equator or at one of the poles. The distance in a degree of longitude, on the other hand, is about 112 kilometers (70 miles) at the equator but becomes smaller and smaller toward the poles. At the poles a degree of longitude includes no distance at all.

Zero degrees longitude is the prime meridian. It runs through Greenwich, England. Distances in longitude are measured east and west of this line. The earth is divided into hemispheres (half circles, or spheres) at the equator (the dividing line of the northern and southern hemispheres) and at the prime meridian (the dividing line of the eastern and western hemispheres).

Any point in the world can be located by giving its latitude and longitude. All the maps include markings that indicate latitude and longitude lines.

Review Questions

1. Is your community in the eastern hemisphere or the western hemisphere? Explain your answer.
2. Is your community in the northern hemisphere or the southern hemisphere? Explain your answer.
3. Describe the exact location of your community in degrees of latitude and longitude.
4. Using the physical map of the United States on page xiv, describe the latitude of one of the Great Lakes and the Rio Grande River. Then describe the longitude of: the Appalachian Mountains, the Rocky Mountains, the Great Plains, and the Mississippi River.

All maps have three things in common: (1) they are pictures of the earth or its parts; (2) their purpose is to communicate information about the earth or its parts; and (3) they use various methods to represent the area they are picturing.

Modern mapmakers, whose professional title is *cartographer*, picture the earth in several ways. A globe is considered the most accurate picture of the earth because it comes closest to representing the shape of the earth. In fact, a globe is a model of the earth in miniature.

A flat map, unlike a globe, represents as flat what is actually curved—the earth. The earliest mapmakers tried to make up for this misrepresentation by transferring all the information on a globe to the flat surface of a map. They assumed that it was possible to do this. But they were mistaken. For example, imagine cutting an orange in half, removing the inside, and placing the rind on a piece of paper. You can't flatten it without cutting some of it, stretching and distorting the shape of the rind. In much the same way, flat maps distort or leave out some aspect of the earth that could have been shown correctly on a globe. To solve these and other

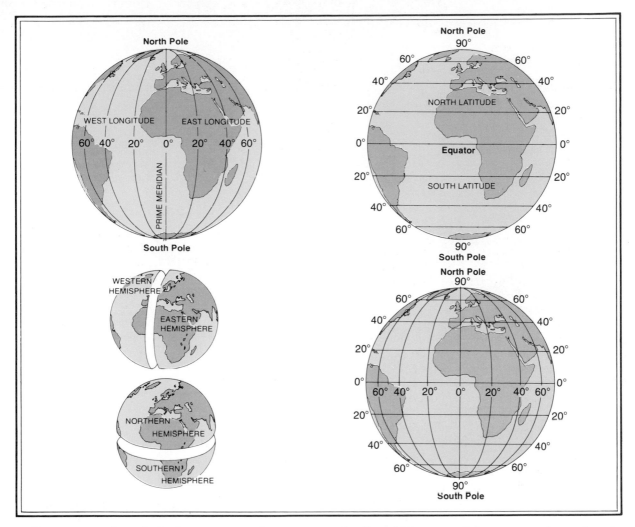

problems, mapmakers decided not to try to show too much information on a map. Instead, they created different kinds of maps for different purposes. These maps are called projections, after the method used to make them.

Imagine a glass globe with a light bulb inside. To make a map a mapmaker surrounds the lighted globe with a piece of paper onto which the outlines of land areas and the lines of latitude and longitude are projected. This information is then transferred to the paper, and the paper is removed from the globe and laid out flat. The mapmaker is ready to add information in order to complete the map.

There are several kinds of map projections. The two used in this book are the Mercator projection and the conical projection. The Mercator projection is named after Gerard Mercator, a Belgian geographer and mathematician who, in the 16th century, developed the method of using lines of latitude and longitude to determine distances.

A Mercator projection is made by wrapping a piece of paper around a globe until the ends meet to form a cylinder. Near the equator, where the paper and the globe touch, the continents and water areas are accurate. Near the poles, however, where the globe curves away from the paper, the land areas become distorted. For instance, in a Mercator projection, Greenland seems bigger than South America, although it is actually little more than one tenth the area.

A Mercator map shows direction correctly. A straight line drawn north and south on a Mercator map runs due north and due south in reality. Meridians of longitude

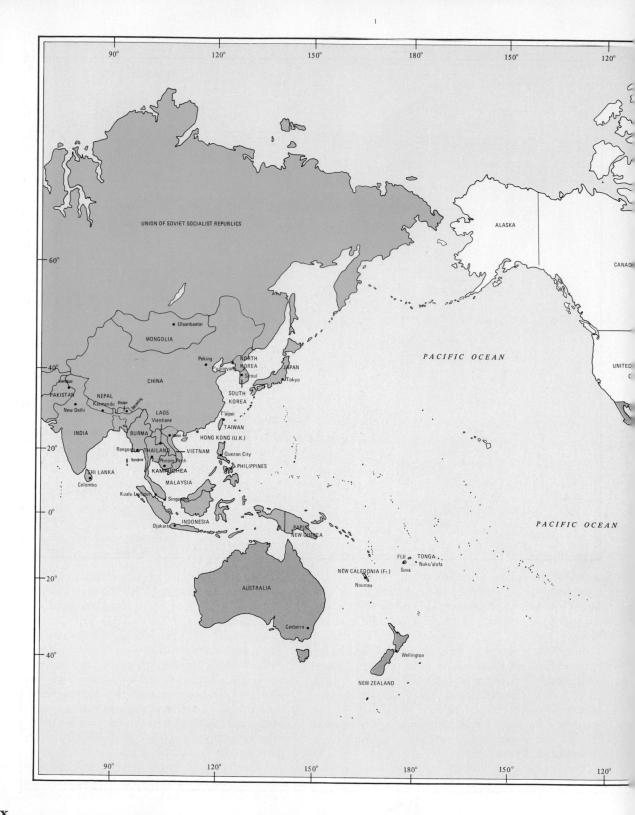

UNION OF SOVIET SOCIALIST REPUBLICS

ALASKA

CANADA

PACIFIC OCEAN

UNITED
S

CANADA

MONGOLIA

• Ulaanbaatar

CHINA

• Peking
P'yongyang
NORTH
KOREA
Seoul
SOUTH
KOREA

JAPAN
Tokyo

PAKISTAN

NEPAL
Kathmandu Bhutan
New Delhi

LAOS
Vientiane

T'aipei
TAIWAN

HONG KONG (U.K.)

INDIA

BURMA

Rangoon
THAILAND
Bangkok
Hanoi
VIETNAM

Quezon City
PHILIPPINES

SRI LANKA
Colombo

Phnom Penh
KAMPUCHEA

MALAYSIA

Kuala Lumpur
Singapore

INDONESIA
Djakarta

PAPUA
NEW GUINEA

PACIFIC OCEAN

FIJI
Suva
TONGA
Nuku'alofa

NEW CALEDONIA (Fr.)
Noumea

AUSTRALIA

Canberra

Wellington

NEW ZEALAND

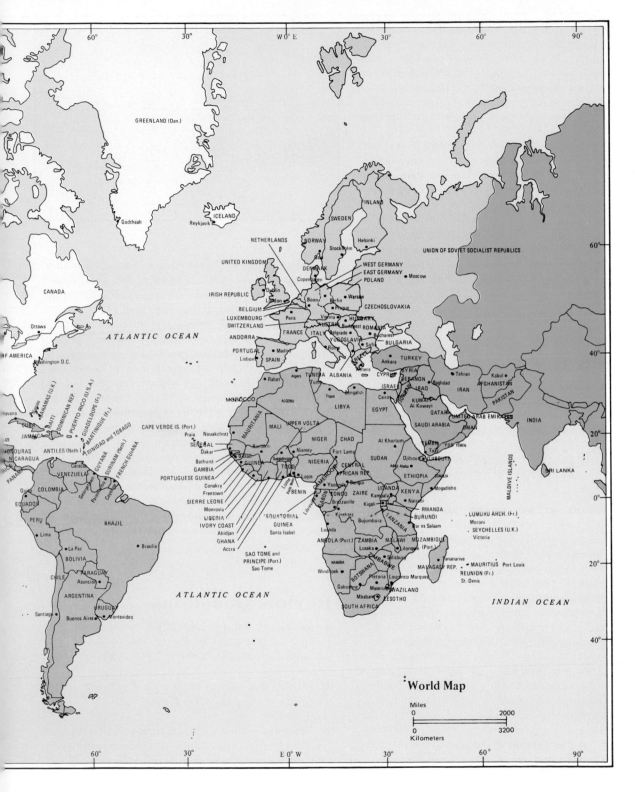

World Map

Miles
0 — 2000
0 — 3200
Kilometers

are distorted on a Mercator projection. They are shown as parallel lines, although they are not actually parallel. Furthermore, a Mercator map shows parallels of latitude of the same length everywhere. But in looking at the globe, you can see that parallels of latitude are actually large circles near the equator and small circles near the poles. The map of the world on pages xx and xxi is a Mercator projection.

A conical projection is made by placing a paper cone over a lighted globe. Lines of longitude are lines radiating from the peak of the cone. Lines of latitude are circles. The map on this page is a modified conical projection with one standard parallel, the one where the paper touches the globe. The standard parallel is the area of the map that shows the least distortion.

Conical projections are especially good for showing an area the size of the United States, the Soviet Union, or Europe. All maps in this book that show the 48 contiguous states of the United States are conical projections.

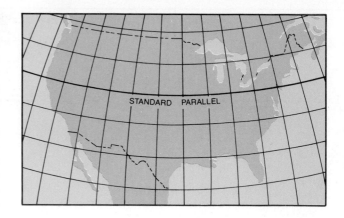

Review Questions

1. The world map on pages xx and xxi is a Mercator projection. The maps of the United States on pages xiv, xv, xvi, and xvii are conical projections. Describe the ways in which these pictures differ.

2. Which is larger, Greenland or South America? Which appears larger on a Mercator map? Why?

All information on a map is communicated through symbols. These symbols form what may be called map language. Like the language you speak and write, map language uses symbols to represent things.

A good symbol in map language is one that is clear, simple, easily distinguished from other symbols, and communicates information as effectively and as unambiguously as possible. Lines, patterns, colors, dots, asterisks, and other symbols are used. For example, water is usually represented by the color blue, hills and mountains by brown, and vegetation by green. Dots stand for cities and towns on most maps, and stars are frequently used for the capitals of states and nations. Political boundaries are represented by solid lines or dashes. Ideally, symbols should be understandable without the help of a key or a legend. But most maps include legends so that people reading the map know precisely what they are looking at.

Among the most important map symbols are those used to indicate scale. Scale on a map tells a map reader what distance on the earth is represented by a certain distance on the map. All the scales in this book indicate distance, both in kilometers and in miles.

Because map language uses symbols to represent things, it always refers to experience. As a result, the knowledge you derive from reading maps can be used to make references to, see relationships among, and improve your understanding of many areas of human activity. For instance, if you combine the data gathered by reading the physical map of the United States on page xiv with information in the text about colonization, you will improve your understanding of the task of settlement that confronted the earliest colonists. The maps will also help you explore relationships between resources and the development of the nation and see how rivers function as natural roads to unite people and how mountains function as natural boundaries to separate them.

Review Questions

1. Locate the natural boundaries that separated the Spanish colonizers of the Pacific coast from the English colonizers of the Atlantic coast.

2. Identify the natural roads that eventually tied together all the parts of the United States.

3. Determine which natural features made settlement of the United States difficult and which made it relatively easy.

SHARPENING YOUR READING SKILLS

One of the most basic forms of communication between two people is a conversation. In most conversational situations, people communicate through speech and bodily gestures. Such conversations, charged with the energy each person brings to the situation, are direct and immediate. A conversation can be indirect, too. An exchange of letters is a conversation between letter writers, and a book is a conversation between author and reader. These conversations are not as direct as face-to-face conversation. But each is no less charged with energy and no less compelling to the people involved.

As you read *People and Our Country,* you will be involving yourself in a conversation with the authors, Professors Risjord and Haywoode. They will be talking with you through the words they have used to recreate the world of American history. You will respond by recreating as vividly as possible in your own mind the world they describe in the text.

You will translate their words into an imaginative understanding of the experience these words describe. You will also relate these experiences to your own life experience in several ways.

Translating the written work into human experience involves three levels of reading skills. These skills will help you make the names, dates, places, events, and ideas you read become more meaningful. They are organized on three levels. As you move from one level to the next, you move from basic skills, such as recognizing synonyms and antonyms, to more complex skills, such as determining the relationship between facts and identifying the authors' point of view. The three levels of reading skills you will use are: literal understanding, interpretive understanding, and critical understanding.

Literal understanding of what you read is the most basic reading skill. It involves being able to: use a dictionary; figure out the meaning of something from its context; find clues to meanings in pictures, graphs, and maps; list events in chronological order; know when events form a sequence of cause and effect; recall specific facts; recognize people, places, events, and dates; and other basic reading skills.

Interpretive understanding is the next level. It involves an ability to use the skills you have developed on the first level in order to reach another, higher level of understanding. When you interpret what you read, you use the following kinds of skills: drawing inferences from ideas in the reading; judging the implications of what you have read; seeing the relationship between facts; forming conclusions; comparing ideas, events, developments, people, and so forth; and recognizing the main idea of a passage.

When you have mastered both literal and interpretive reading skills, you will be ready to read on the highest level, the level of critical understanding. Reading on this level means coming to terms with the authors. In your "conversation" with them, it is the level at which you and the authors are "face to face." Drawing on the skills you have developed by working on the literal and the interpretive levels, you will be able to: identify the authors' assumptions; distinguish between fact and opinion; recognize the authors' point of view; and evaluate the consistency of their arguments, the structure and the style of their narrative, and the way they have organized their presentation of American history. In other words, when you read on this level, you will be thinking about why something is said as well as what is said.

Review Questions

1. Turn to page 25, read the questions under Reading for Meaning, and label each question Level 1, Level 2, or Level 3. Explain why you labeled each question as you did.

2. Reread this information about reading skills. Then make up three questions about this material. One question should be on the literal level, one on the interpretive level, and one on the critical level.

3. In your own words, explain what you think is the relationship between the three levels of reading skills introduced in this section. Which level do you think is the most important? Why?

Wilderness Communities

For the Pueblo it started with corn, some 500 years before Columbus reached America. The Indian people living on the Colorado Plateau in western North America had learned how to cultivate fields and to grow crops. This steady food supply meant they could live closer together.

Communities of related families built mud-brick apartment houses on the cliffs and mesas of the Colorado Plateau. These units are called pueblos. The Pueblo civilization flourished between about 1000 and 1300 A.D.

There were many advantages to community living. Ideas and new techniques could be shared. Shortly after developing corn, the Pueblo people learned to grow cotton. They wove the cotton into cloth, and fashioned robes and blankets. Bows and arrows came into use, replacing the more primitive spears in the hunt.

Each family had a room of its own in the pueblo. The family consisted of a husband and a wife and the daughters and their husbands. Sons went off to live with their wives' families. Most of the pueblo was organized according to maternal relationships, even though females did not rule. The head of each clan was a man, and apparently only men participated in public decision making. In other respects, however, the pueblo was a democracy, for each family had an equal voice. Even today the descendants of the Pueblo people, the Hopi, have no police and no penal system. Religion, custom, and family hold the community together.

The climate of the American Southwest was wetter then than it is today. Trees grew on the mesas and water flowed in the rivers the year around. Thus, the Pueblo people could grow corn and cotton in the fertile valleys.

These life-giving rains came to an end quite suddenly. For 23 years (1276–1299) there was drought and the corn fields turned into desert. The weakened Pueblo people then came under attack from their neighbors, the Apache and the Navajo. The Pueblo culture faded, and the people moved away. Their descendants can be found today in parts of Arizona and New Mexico, and some live in new, brick pueblos. But the great apartment complexes of the Colorado Plateau stand empty, relics of a community that flourished and died before Columbus reached America.

Mesa Verde, Colorado

Chapter 1

The First Americans

prehistory-1620

She was a small, slim girl, scarcely more than 10 years old. And there she was, playing leapfrog with cabin boys from the English ships. Jamestown, only a few months old itself, had its first friendly visitor.

Pocahontas was the daughter of Powhatan, the dominant Indian leader in that part of Virginia. There had been friction between the races ever since the English had landed in April 1607. The Indians had naturally resented the intrusion on their lands. Both sides had engaged in petty thievery and had taken hostages. To recover some captives, Powhatan had sent a delegation into Jamestown, and he had sent Pocahontas along to give the mission a peaceful color.

An excellent choice she was. Still in youthful innocence, she was naturally friendly and open. Her father called her Matoaka, "Little Snow Feather," and it described her well.

Captain John Smith, one of the leaders of the colony, quickly recognized her value. Treating her as an uncle might a favored niece, Smith taught her some English words and learned from her some of the Indian language. When the food gave out in Jamestown, Pocahontas went to her relatives to borrow Indian corn. Smith later wrote that she was "the instrument" that saved the colony "from death, famine, and utter confusion."

She could not prevent hostility, however. Smith kept Powhatan off balance by mixing generosity with threats. After Smith left the colony in 1609, Powhatan declared war. To make sure the English got no further aid, Powhatan ordered his daughter to stay away from them. Reluctantly she obeyed. The fighting dragged on for years.

Then, in 1613 the Virginians kidnapped Pocahontas. They hoped to trade her for some captives Powhatan held, or perhaps even to persuade him to end the war. But Powhatan refused to make a deal. For the next year Pocahontas lived with a minister and his family. Eventually, she took the English name Rebecca. In 1614 she married a young Englishman, John Rolfe, who had recently introduced tobacco planting to the Virginia colony. Powhatan blessed the marriage and, in so doing, ended the war between the Pamunkeys and the English.

Pocahontas had fed the colony and had twice brought it peace. Yet, one more request was to be made of her. The Virginia settlement had always been in financial difficulty. Thus its directors had decided that if Pocahontas were to tour England, she would spread the fame of Virginia and attract investors. Pocahontas agreed. She sailed in the summer of 1616, with her husband and son and a dozen friends.

Her tour was an enormous success. She was introduced to the queen and was entertained by the rich. People who met her remarked on her natural dignity and noble character. The damp climate and hectic life proved too much for her, however. She died of tuberculosis in the spring of 1617, while waiting to go home.

The Virginians and the Pamunkeys were the first chapter in the story of the American frontier. But their quarrels would be reenacted over the next 200 years, as Europeans came into contact with American Indians. Europeans, possessing better tools and weapons, took over lands the Indians (the name given to American Indians by Columbus) had inhabited, cut down the forests, and wasted the game. Many American Indians welcomed the first Europeans and helped them adjust to the wilderness. But, like Powhatan, they soon became suspicious of European intentions and fearful of their numbers. Europeans, in turn, came to believe that the American Indians' way of life was inferior. They justified the seizure of Indian lands on the grounds that they could put the land to better use. In this centuries-long clash of peoples, Pocahontas was the first victim.

Chapter Objectives

After you have finished reading this chapter, you should be able to:
1. List the achievements and the characteristics of the life-style of the major groups of American Indians.
2. Identify major exploring nations and their explorers and discoveries.
3. Describe the pattern of English exploration and settlement in Virginia.

The peopling of the rich continent of North America is one of the most wondrous chapters in history. The story did not begin with the first English settlements or even with Columbus and the Spanish adventurers. It began over 10,000 years ago, when a slowly receding glacier left open a neck of land between Siberia and present-day Alaska. Soon the ocean waters, raised by the melting glacier, covered the sandy bridge once again.

Before that, waves of peoples had made their way into the forests of this northern continent. In time, some of them had built great cities and prosperous civilizations.

Long before the arrival of Columbus, the American continent was a mixture of peoples and cultures, a blend of different ways of living and thinking. Columbus's discovery in 1492 simply began a new wave of migration.

1. The Indians Discover America

THE EARLY SETTLERS. As the climate warmed, the ice sheet disappeared, leaving behind it raging rivers and crystalline lakes. Wandering hunters came across the Siberian land bridge and filtered across the mountains and *prairies* of what is now western Canada and the northwestern United States. After many years some of these people settled across the continent, in the eastern woodlands between the Great Lakes and the Atlantic Ocean. Because they lived by hunting and fishing, their villages were small and widely scattered. Such villages were made up of groups of related families, or clans. Clans that spoke the same language formed tribes, whose leaders met from time to time to discuss war or plan hunts.

Prairies are the flat grasslands of the Middle West. The word is French because French fur traders were the first Europeans to see the prairie.

Because these woodland tribes came to North America at about the same time, their languages were similar. Modern *anthropologists* think language is an important bond among peoples. They refer to these early tribes of the eastern woodlands as being Algonkian (al-GAHN-kee-un) speaking. Among these numerous and powerful tribes were such names as Massachuset, Ottawa, Wappinger, Delaware, Huron, and Shawnee. *Together, the Algonkian-speaking tribes ruled the forests between the St. Lawrence River and the Atlantic coast for many years.* (See map, page 6.)

Anthropologists study human culture and its development.

These early peoples occupied the eastern half of the continent. The Pequot (PEE-kwat) and the Narragansett fished along the New England coast. To the south along the Appalachian lowlands lived the Shawnee. And west to the Mississippi, the Sac and Fox tribes tended their patches of corn and squash. All used stone tools and hunted food with flint-tipped arrows. Dependent on wild game, most of them moved frequently and left few traces—not even trash deposits, which are rich sources of information for anthropologists. So, little is known about them. All that remain are the oral traditions passed down through the centuries.

THE FLOWERING OF INDIAN CULTURE: MAYA AND AZTEC. Some thousands of years later, other peoples began to move out of central Asia. Perhaps they, too, were driven by drought or cold or other harsh conditions. They spread over the rest of the North American continent, passing southward toward the isthmus that leads to South America. For hundreds of years they lived in the area now called Middle, or Central, America. *There the Maya built a brilliant civilization, creating great cities where once the jungles of Mexico stood.* (See map, page 6.) Many years before the Europeans arrived, the Maya had a civilization equal to any in the world.

About 1000 A.D., 500 years before Columbus and about the time the Vikings were venturing across the Atlantic toward Iceland and Greenland, a new civilization arose in what is now Mexico. These people were sun worshippers. *The most powerful of these people were the Aztec, who lived in the central valley of Mexico.* By the time Columbus and the Spanish explorers arrived, the Aztec had a flourishing civilization and fabulous wealth.

THE MISSISSIPPI CULTURE. The Aztec also influenced the peoples living to the north of them, along the lower Missis-

The ruins of Monte Albán are in south-central Mexico. The site is very elaborate. It includes plazas, pyramids, a game court, and extensive underground passageways.

sippi. These people also became sun worshippers, and they built mounds to house their dead. This Mississippi Culture, so called because its main villages were on the lower Mississippi River, spread its influence over the southern part of North America. Anthropologists refer to these tribes as the Muskogean (mus-KOE-gee-un) language group, named after the Muskogee (or Creek), who dwelt in the long-needled pine forests of the Southeast.

The Mississippians were one of a number of peoples who built mounds. Together, such cultures formed a larger group, which archeologists call the mound builders. The remains of their mounds have been found throughout the eastern and midwestern United States, from Maine to Minnesota, south to the Gulf of Mexico, and east to Florida. They were built not only in the shape of hills, but also in the shape of birds, serpents, rings, semicircular earthern ridges, and other things. Archeologists do not know what purposes these mounds served, but some think they might have been used as fortifications, ceremonial centers, and even stations from which astronomers could observe the skies.

The Mississippians were a sedentary people, who farmed the land and hunted only part of the time. By staying in one place, they were able to organize themselves better than their neighbors. ***They had rulers and priests, they used iron implements and clay pottery, and they wore clothing of woven fabric.*** Their traders roamed wide distances in search of goods. They drank out of conch shells from the Gulf of Mexico. Their jewelry contained obsidian (ahb-SID-ee-un)—a shiny, black, semiprecious stone from Wyoming.

The Mississippians developed outposts as protection from their more primitive neighbors, who were a constant threat.

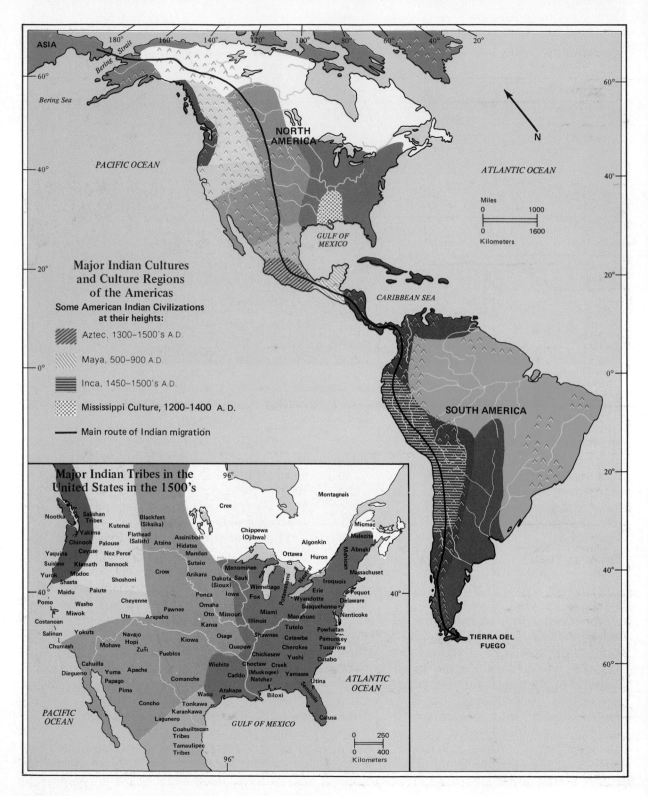

ASIA

180° Bering Strait 160° 140° 120° 100° 80° 60° 40° 20°

60°

Bering Sea

NORTH AMERICA

PACIFIC OCEAN

ATLANTIC OCEAN

40°

N

60°

40°

20°

GULF OF MEXICO

Miles
0   1000

0   1600
Kilometers

Major Indian Cultures and Culture Regions of the Americas

Some American Indian Civilizations at their heights:

Aztec, 1300–1500's A.D.

Maya, 500–900 A.D.

Inca, 1450–1500's A.D.

Mississippi Culture, 1200–1400 A.D.

Main route of Indian migration

CARIBBEAN SEA

0°

SOUTH AMERICA

20°

TIERRA DEL FUEGO

60°

Major Indian Tribes in the United States in the 1500's

96°

Cree

Montagnais

Nootka

Salishan Tribes

Kutenai

Blackfeet (Siksika)

Chippewa (Ojibwa)

Micmac

Malecite

Yakima

Flathead (Salish)

Atsina

Assiniboin

Algonkin

Abnaki

Chinook

Palouse

Hidatsa

Ottawa

Mahican

Cayuse

Nez Perce

Mandan

Huron

Yaquina

Bannock

Sutaio

Massachuset

Suislaw

Klamath

Crow

Arikara

Menominee

Iroquois

Modoc

Shoshoni

Dakota (Sioux)

Sauk

Winnebago

Erie

Pequot

Yurok

Shasta

Paiute

Ponca

Iowa

Fox

Wyandotte

Delaware

Maidu

Pomo

Washo

Cheyenne

Omaha

Missouri

Miami

Susquehanna

Nanticoke

Miwok

Ute

Arapaho

Oto

Illinois

Manahoac

Tutelo

Costanoan

Yokuts

Pawnee

Kansa

Shawnee

Catawba

Powhatan

Pamunkey

Salinan

Navajo

Hopi

Osage

Quapaw

Cherokee

Yuchi

Tuscarora

Chumash

Mohave

Zuñi

Pueblos

Chickasaw

Creek (Muskogee)

Cusabo

Cahuilla

Apache

Wichita

Choctaw

Natchez

Yamasee

Utina

Diegueno

Yuma

Papago

Comanche

Caddo

ATLANTIC OCEAN

Pima

Waco

Atakapa

Biloxi

Seminola

Concho

Tonkawa

Karankawa

Lagunero

Calusa

PACIFIC OCEAN

Coahuiltecan Tribes

GULF OF MEXICO

Tamaulipec Tribes

96°

0   250

0   400
Kilometers

40°

40°

Cultural Region and Occupation	INDIAN WAYS OF LIFE			
	Food	Housing	Tools	Clothing
Arctic—Fishers and Hunters	fish, seal walrus; berries in summer	igloos in winter; tents made of hide in summer	harpoons, bows	parkas, trousers, boots of hide
Subarctic—Hunters	elk, deer, freshwater fish, berries	hogans of bark, log "cabins"	spears, traps, fishhooks, canoes, toboggans, snowshoes	shirts, trousers, moccasins of hide
Northwest Coast—Fishers and Hunters	salmon, halibut, berries, deer	large villages of plank houses	fishhooks and nets, bows, dugout canoes, stone knives and axes, baskets	shirts and trousers of hide, wooden helmets
Eastern Woodlands—Hunters and Farmers	deer, fish, corn, beans, wild rice, melons, grapes	bark longhouses and round plank houses in villages	bows, spears, bark and dugout canoes	of hide; in south—woven cloth
Plains—Hunters	buffalo, deer, freshwater fish, fowl	hogans made of hide, log houses with sod roofs	bows, lances, clubs and shields, rawhide containers	of hide, ceremonial feather headdresses
California and Great Basin—Food Gatherers and Hunters	roots, berries, small game, fish	earth huts, caves	bows, spears, baskets of skins	of hide
Plateau—Food Gatherers and Hunters	roots, berries, small game, fish	earth huts, caves	bows, spears	of hide
Dry Southwest—Farmers and Hunters	corn, beans, small game, berries	adobe or stone "pueblos" in large villages; nomadic tribes used hogans, brush shelters	bows, throwing sticks, hoes	of woven cloth
Middle America—Farmers and City Dwellers	corn, squash, beans, tomatoes, peppers, melons, cocoa	stone houses, some two-storied, built around inner courts on streets in cities; temples, schools	stone knives, axes, chisels, copper knives	of woven cotton cloth, leather sandals, feathered headdresses
Caribbean—Hunters and Farmers	fish, beans, corn, peppers	large villages of thatched houses	spears, slings, clubs, bows	of woven cloth
Andean—Farmers and City Dwellers	beans, corn, potatoes, fish	village houses made of stone and adobe; city houses made of large stones	copper and bronze tools	of woven cloth, spun wool
Tropical Forest—Farmers and Hunters	cassava, beans, corn, small game	thatched roof shelters	spears, bows and arrows, blow guns	little clothing, body paints
Southern—Food Gatherers and Hunters	wild seeds, fruit, small game	simple shelters covered with mats and hides	bolas, bows and arrows, spears	little clothing, some garments made of hide

7

The nomadic tribes who lived on the plains to the west, as well as the woodland Algonkian tribes to the northeast, were jealous and suspicious of them. When Columbus reached America, the Mississippians were under attack and on the decline. Yet their influence lingered on. Among their descendants were the Indian tribes of the Southeast—Cherokee, Creek, Choctaw, Chickasaw. These peoples possessed well-developed farming methods and lived in highly organized village communities.

THE COMING OF THE IROQUOIS.

The Iroquois were another closely related group of tribes who spoke the same language. Coming somewhat later across the Siberian land bridge, they too settled in the northeastern forest, pushing aside the older Algonkian tribes. The most important group clustered in present-day New York State, but Iroquois-speaking tribes also lived in the Ohio valley (Wyandotte) and in the South (Tuscarora). Just about the time that Columbus was sailing for America, some Iroquois-speaking tribes came into contact with the declining Mississippians. Although these Iroquois-speaking tribes helped to destroy the Mississippi culture, they also learned from it. They learned how to raise corn and fashion metal tools. And they imitated the Mississippians' villages and tribal organization.

For a long time the Iroquois wasted their energies on tribal feuds. Then, according to legend, there came Hiawatha, a religious leader with a gift for politics. His strong religious faith won him a following, and he was able to end the feuds. Instead of seeking revenge, a person who was wronged could collect a fine. For murder the fine was 20 strings of shell beads, called wampum, if the victim was a man; 30 strings if a woman.

Iroquois masks were used for many purposes. The importance of the masks was their symbolism. They were worn by tribal members who showed prowess in a skill.

The Iroquois valued women highly. Women were the center of the social system and the heads of their families. A clan was formed from among the wife's relatives, rather than from the husband's.

Hiawatha's next step was to create political union among the Iroquois. He asked the women who headed each clan to appoint a representative, or *sachem*, to meet in a tribal council. Each of the five (later six) tribal nations then sent delegates to the Great Council Fire, which met at least every five years or more often if necessary. This was the first **federal system** of government in America, and it gave the Iroquois a political unity that matched their fighting ability.

By the time the Europeans arrived in North America, the Iroquois were the most powerful of the eastern woodland Indians. They were a much-desired ally in the battles between the English, the French, and the Dutch. But the Europeans, with their firearms and their diseases, brought about the Iroquois' downfall.

A **federal system** of government is one in which each unit (such as the Iroquois nations or our states) sends representatives to a central lawmaking body (the Iroquois' Great Fire or our Congress).

Section Review

1. Mapping: Look at the map on page 6. Using this map, explain how the early settlers migrated to the Americas.
2. Identify or explain: anthropologist, obsidian, sachem.
3. Name one major achievement of each of the following groups: Maya, Mississippians, Iroquois.
4. Who was Hiawatha, and how did he end the tribal feuds among the Iroquois people?
5. Why do you think anthropologists can find more information about sedentary peoples than about nomadic peoples?

2. The Awakening of Europe

THE VIKINGS. It was not long before others found their way to North America. Ferocious fighters and marvelous sailors, the Vikings left northern Europe in the ninth and tenth centuries, seeking first plunder and then good farmland. Their longboats pierced the fog of the north Atlantic, eventually touching Iceland, Greenland, and the coast of North America.

Some time around the year 1000, Leif Ericson sailed along the coast of North America, landing on the island that is now called Newfoundland. There, on the north shore, he and his crew found a sheltered bay and built a settlement. Why, we do not know. Perhaps they had planned to fish or farm or to use the settlement as a base for further exploration. What we do know is that their village lasted only a few years before being abandoned. The pines and hemlocks remained, but the longboats disappeared into the misty seas.

The Vikings now knew about America, but no one else seemed to care. Europe was not ready. The universe was mysterious, and the unknown was still deadly. There were no accurate maps, and the ships could not sail far from shore because they had few navigational instruments. Besides, European ships were not made for long trips. Coastal trade was carried on by the longboats propelled by oars. Such ships were called galleys. The sailing ships were clumsy and could sail only with the wind. People still had to develop the confidence that they could not only cross the vast Atlantic, but more importantly, that they could also find their way back.

THE REBIRTH OF EUROPE. A hundred years or so after Leif Ericson visited America, the pace of life in Europe seemed to quicken. *Beginning in Italy, a spiritual,*

9

intellectual, and artistic awakening— called the Renaissance (ren-ah-ZAHNTZ) —spread slowly across Europe. For centuries people had concentrated on religion and life after death. Now they became more concerned about their lives on earth—more curious about the world in which they were living. Prince Henry the Navigator of Portugal gathered mapmakers and sea captains at his court in the early 1400's. With Henry's financial backing the Portuguese explorers poked south along the coast of Africa, eventually reaching its tip about the time Columbus sailed for America.

The Crusades helped contribute to rebirth. Starting in 1096 and continuing for the next 200 years, the Christian rulers and nobles organized expeditions to recapture the Holy Land from the Muslims. Although they failed in their objective, they returned with tales of strange lands and many new products. Thus, merchants eventually pushed their way across the dry mountains of Persia to India. In 1271 the Italian merchant Marco Polo ventured to China, returning in 1295 with new tales of wealth in the East. (See map, pages 12–13.)

Trade between Europe and the East flourished until the middle of the 15th century, when the Ottoman Turks conquered Persia and Palestine, cutting off trade routes. The only alternative left was to reach the East by sea. The Portuguese, who had already explored the coast of Africa, showed the way. In 1488 Bartholomeu Dias reached the southern tip of Africa, which later adventurers would name the Cape of Good Hope. A decade later Vasco da Gama ventured around the Cape and crossed the Indian Ocean, finally landing at Calicut, India. When he returned with a shipful of spices and silks, interest in the East was aroused throughout Europe. Soon the Portuguese were making regular runs to India and the Spice Islands. As a result, Lisbon, the capital of Portugal, became the commercial center of Europe.

NEW DEVELOPMENTS IN NAVIGATION. *During these years of exploration, the Portuguese developed a new kind of ship, one that depended on sails rather than oars.* Called carracks (KAR-ukz), the first of these were stubby wooden tubs. Compared with later sailing ships, they were awkward and homely. But they were a great improvement over the oar-driven galleys. With them explorers could venture out of the sight of land for weeks, even months, at a time. Traders could even establish profitable businesses with distant lands.

The Portuguese also picked up knowledge about the earth as they moved slowly south along the coast of Africa. As they approached the equator, they saw the noonday sun climb higher and higher above the horizon, until at last it stood straight overhead. *Measuring the distance of the sun above the horizon enabled them to tell how far they were north or south of the equator, a position known as latitude.*

The Portuguese explorers also discovered changes in the winds that pushed their vessels. In Europe the winds usually came from the west, but off the coast of Africa they came from the southeast. Then at the equator the winds hardly blew at all; the hot air simply drifted upward.

Knowledge of these wind belts would later be of enormous use to cargo ships. For example, merchants who frequently crossed the Atlantic named the winds that came out of the southeast the trade winds. Rather than fight the so-called westerlies across the Atlantic, they would sail south to the Portuguese-owned islands off the coast of Africa (the Madeira Islands, the Cape Verde Islands, or the Canary Islands). From there the trade winds would blow them right into the islands of the West Indies.

COLUMBUS REACHES NORTH AMERICA. When the Turks cut off the overland route to India, the Portuguese took

The carrack was a major improvement in transportation that changed 15th-century life. What developments in transportation in this century have affected life today?

to the sea and sailed around the tip of Africa. But it occurred to others that if the world were truly round, it might be possible to reach the East by sailing west across the Atlantic Ocean. People who had read books knew the world was round. The ancient Egyptians had discovered that through their astronomy.

Renaissance scholars, eager for knowledge, pored through the Egyptian and Greek writings and spread the word. People who had had no schooling still thought the world was flat, but among intelligent ship captains and merchants, there was little doubt that it was round. (They might have suspected as much on a calm day at sea, when they could observe that only the tip of the sail on a distant ship was visible at first.)

Christopher Columbus was just such a person. An Italian who came from the busy seaport of Genoa, Columbus had sailed over many seas. He had even ventured as far as Iceland, halfway to America, on a fishing trip. *Columbus thought that if he sailed directly west, he could reach India more rapidly than by traveling around Africa.* Since Portugal was interested only in Africa, he took his idea to the rulers of Spain, Ferdinand and Isabella. They agreed to finance his venture. The three small carracks he

requested were not very expensive. And if he succeeded, it would be a good jab in the ribs to Spain's proud neighbor, Portugal.

But Columbus was wrong. In 1492, after a month at sea running before the trade winds, he came upon a palmy bit of land (part of what we now call the Bahamas) off the coast of Florida. Because he found no civilization there, he sailed on, reaching a somewhat larger island, which he gloriously named Hispañola, or Little Spain. Columbus found people living on this island (related to the other peoples who lived in North America), whom he called Indians, thinking he was in the East. *Instead, he had reached a continent unknown to Europe.*

Columbus persuaded a few natives to return with him to Spain. Although he had found neither silks nor spices to take back with him, the American Indians impressed Ferdinand and Isabella enough that they financed a much more elaborate voyage the next year and two more after that. Columbus eventually explored the coast of Central and South America without ever realizing he had found a land new to Europeans.

OTHER EXPLORERS IN THE AMERICAS. Although Columbus failed to find a route to India, Spain still came out ahead in its expeditions. The colony established on Hispañola became the center for further exploration. Other islands were colonized, including Puerto Rico, Jamaica, and Cuba. And explorers sailed along the coast of South America, the area first recognized by Amerigo Vespucci (ves-POO-chee), the explorer whose name was given to the continents. At last, in 1519 Ferdinand Magellan passed through the windy straits at the southern tip of the continent and entered the broad Pacific Ocean. After touching several island groups (at one—the Philippines—Magellan was killed by natives) the expedition rounded Africa and returned to Spain. Thereafter, only the most stubborn could doubt that the world was round.

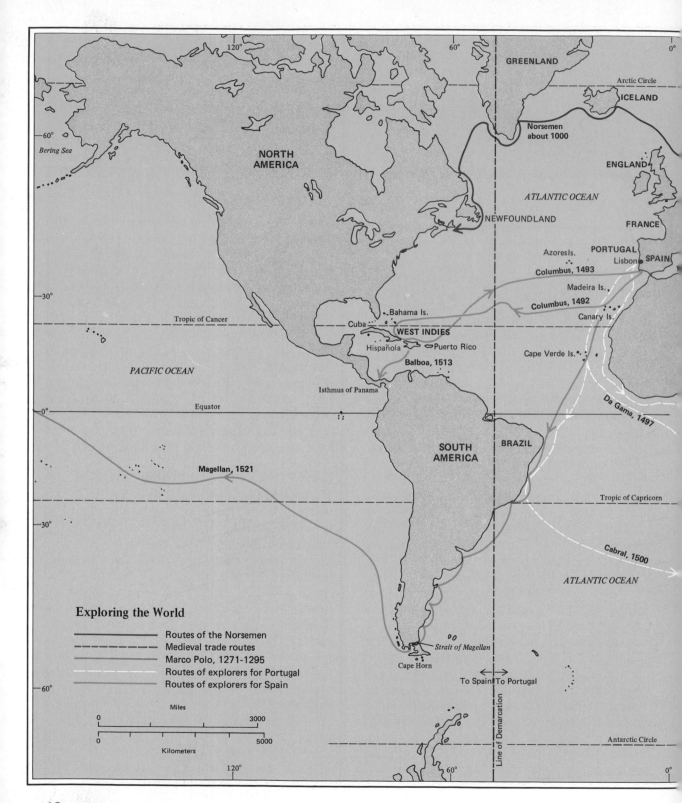

GREENLAND

Arctic Circle

ICELAND

Norsemen
about 1000

Bering Sea

NORTH
AMERICA

ENGLAND

ATLANTIC OCEAN

FRANCE

NEWFOUNDLAND

Azores Is.

PORTUGAL

Lisbon

SPAIN

Columbus, 1493

Madeira Is.

Columbus, 1492

Tropic of Cancer

•Bahama Is.

Canary Is.

Cuba

WEST INDIES

Hispañola

•Puerto Rico

Cape Verde Is.

PACIFIC OCEAN

Balboa, 1513

Da Gama, 1497

Isthmus of Panama

Equator

SOUTH
AMERICA

BRAZIL

Magellan, 1521

Tropic of Capricorn

Cabral, 1500

ATLANTIC OCEAN

Exploring the World

———————— Routes of the Norsemen
– – – – – – – – Medieval trade routes
———————— Marco Polo, 1271-1295
– – – – – – – – Routes of explorers for Portugal
———————— Routes of explorers for Spain

Strait of Magellan

Cape Horn

To Spain To Portugal

Miles

0 3000

0 5000

Kilometers

Line of Demarcation

Antarctic Circle

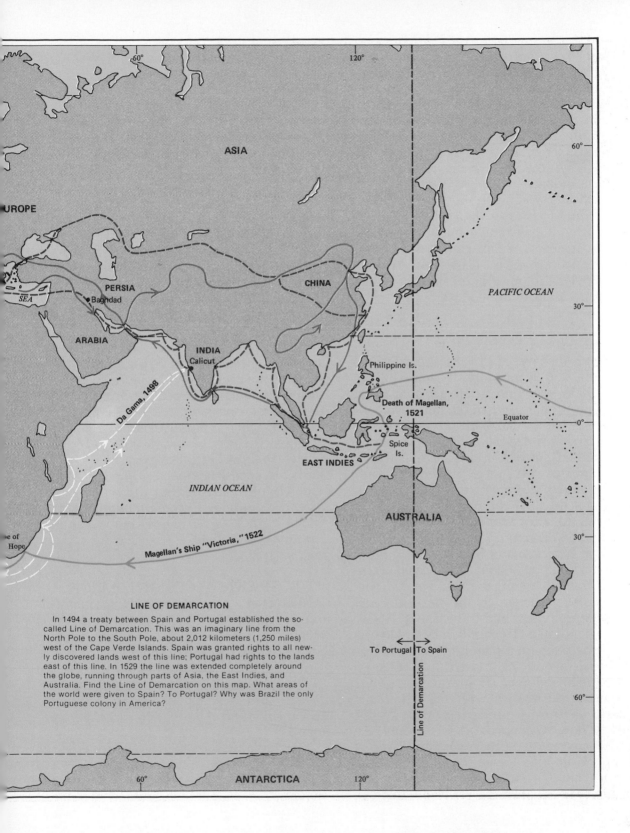

LINE OF DEMARCATION

In 1494 a treaty between Spain and Portugal established the so-called Line of Demarcation. This was an imaginary line from the North Pole to the South Pole, about 2,012 kilometers (1,250 miles) west of the Cape Verde Islands. Spain was granted rights to all newly discovered lands west of this line; Portugal had rights to the lands east of this line. In 1529 the line was extended completely around the globe, running through parts of Asia, the East Indies, and Australia. Find the Line of Demarcation on this map. What areas of the world were given to Spain? To Portugal? Why was Brazil the only Portuguese colony in America?

When they finally ventured inland, the Spaniards found wealth more fabulous than anything in the East. In 1519 Hernando Cortés landed on the coast of Mexico and marched inland to the city where the Aztec emperor Montezuma ruled. His metal-garbed soldiers slaughtered the Indians and took their gold. From 1531 to 1535 Francisco Pizarro (pih-ZAHR-oh) was in Peru and did the same to the peaceful, artistic Quechua (KECH-wah) of Peru. The Indians suffered and many were put into slavery. Nevertheless, Spain gained. Its armies scooped up American gold, and treasure ships carried it home. The center of power in Europe slipped from Portugal to Spain.

THE SEARCH FOR GOLD.

The fabulous riches discovered by Cortés and Pizarro inspired a search for more. It seemed likely that if there was gold in Mexico and Peru, there ought to be some in the northern continent as well. In 1528 Pánfilo de Narváez (day nahr-VAH-ez) landed with a small army on the coast of Florida. There, Narváez and some of his men waded through swamps and pine forests for three months looking for gold. By the time he returned to the coast, the crew that had been left on the ships had given him up for lost and had left for Cuba. Narváez and his remaining crew built rafts and paddled along the coast of the Gulf of Mexico, hoping to find a Spanish settlement. All perished in the sea but four, who eventually reached the coast of Texas.

Ten years later Hernando de Soto led another expedition on a search for gold in Florida. Cruel toward the Indians, like most of the Spanish explorers, de Soto and his group had many skirmishes with the American Indians as they wound their way across what is now Alabama and Mississippi. At last de Soto reached the Mississippi River—the first European to see the so-called "Father of Waters"—and crossed it, near the mouth of the Arkansas River. There, in present-day Arkansas he caught a fever and died. His people buried him in the mighty Mississippi, and they started for home.

The journey of de Soto's party took three years (1539–1542). During that time another expedition set out from Mexico to look for the cities of gold that de Vaca had heard about. Led by Francisco Coronado (kor-oe-NAH-doe), this expedition traveled into present-day Arizona (one of Coronado's lieutenants was the first White person to see the Grand Canyon) and across the plains of southwestern Kansas. Instead of golden cities, Coronado found a sea of grass populated with vast herds of buffalo.

Coronado's disappointing return ended the major thrust of the Spanish into the interior of North America. The Spaniards concentrated thereafter on the known riches of Mexico and Peru. Later, settlements were established in Santa Fe and California. In North America the Spanish set up defensive outposts on the Rio Grande frontier to protect themselves from the Plains Indians.

Horses, brought to America by the Spaniards, escaped from some of the early expeditions and flourished on the plains alongside the buffalo. Captured and tamed by Indians, they were of enormous value in hunting the buffalo.

THE SPANISH COLONIZATION OF AMERICA.

As early as 1493 Spanish colonists migrated with Columbus to the New World. St. Augustine, Florida, the first Spanish settlement in what is now the United States, was founded in 1565. In 1609 Spaniards settled at Santa Fe, New Mexico, but were driven out by the Pueblo Indians in 1680. The Pueblo were later conquered.

Throughout the following decades as many as 2,000 Spaniards arrived in North America each year. With them they brought not only horses, but also cattle, sheep, hogs,

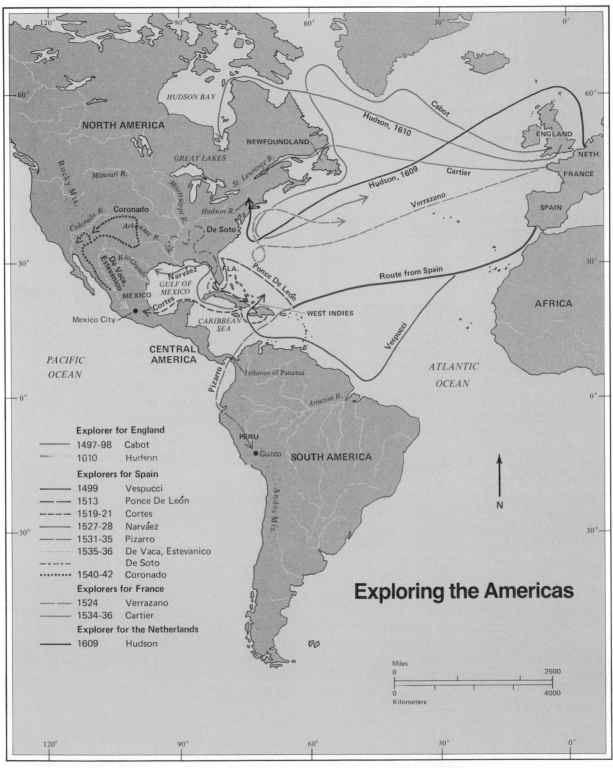

HUDSON BAY

NORTH AMERICA

Cabot

Hudson, 1610

NEWFOUNDLAND

ENGLAND

NETH.

GREAT LAKES

St. Lawrence R.

Hudson, 1609

Cartier

FRANCE

Rocky Mts.

Missouri R.

Mississippi R.

Hudson R.

Verrazano

SPAIN

Coronado

Colorado R.

Arkansas R.

De Soto

De Vaca,
Estevanico

Rio Grande

Narváez

FLA.

Ponce De León

Route from Spain

AFRICA

MEXICO

Cortes

GULF OF
MEXICO

Mexico City

CARIBBEAN
SEA

WEST INDIES

PACIFIC
OCEAN

CENTRAL
AMERICA

Vespucci

ATLANTIC
OCEAN

Pizarro

Isthmus of Panama

Amazon R.

PERU

Cuzco

SOUTH AMERICA

Andes Mts.

N

Explorer for England
— 1497-98 Cabot
········ 1010 Hudson

Explorers for Spain
— 1499 Vespucci
– – 1513 Ponce De León
- - - 1519-21 Cortes
— 1527-28 Narváez
– – 1531-35 Pizarro
— 1535-36 De Vaca, Estevanico
–·–· De Soto
········ 1540-42 Coronado

Explorers for France
– – 1524 Verrazano
— 1534-36 Cartier

Explorer for the Netherlands
— 1609 Hudson

Exploring the Americas

Miles
0 2500

0 4000
Kilometers

and European crops—all of which they introduced to the Indian cultures with whom they came into contact.

The Spanish settlements were either missions, *presidios* (pray-SID-ee-os), or *villas*.

The missions were run by Roman Catholic priests and inhabited by the priests and the Indians whom the Spanish either forced or persuaded to live there. Missions usually included workshops, mills, and farmlands,

Sidenote to History

The Adventures of Cabeza de Vaca

A chill November wind lashed the sea into huge waves, which crashed across the sandy beach. Through the breakers there came a small sailing craft, containing 20 exhausted Spaniards. So high were the waves that three men drowned trying to beach the vessel. Such was the beginning of the ordeal of Álvar Núñez Cabeza de Vaca. The year was 1528.

De Vaca and his fellows were the surviving remnant of the ill-fated Narváez expedition, which had set out a year before to explore the Gulf Coast of North America. The island where the castaways had landed was on the coast of Texas, not far from present-day Galveston. Indians there had given the explorers food and shelter and had helped them through the winter. In the spring the Spaniards had started south along the coast, hoping to reach settlements in Mexico. De Vaca, too ill to travel, had been left behind.

For the next four years Cabeza de Vaca lived among the coastal Indians. To learn more of the surrounding country, he became a trader, carrying shells and other relics of the sea to tribes in the interior. In 1533 he started south along the coast in search of his former comrades. Captured by hostile Indians, he was taken to a village, where he met two former members of his party and an African slave, Estévanico. His other men had been killed.

For more than a year, the four men lived as slaves of the Indians. Life in that arid, vacant land was a constant search for food. Spring rains brought deer and buffalo into that part of Texas, but the rest of the time survival depended on the availability of spiders, worms, caterpillars, lizards, snakes, and ant eggs. Beans of the mesquite tree, mashed and mixed with water, served as both bread and vegetable.

The four men practiced what little medicine they knew on their Indian masters and soon earned a reputation as healers. When they escaped at last in the summer of 1535, they were welcomed by neighboring tribes, who brought their children and the sick to be touched and cured. Finding the interior tribes friendlier than those on the coast, the four began moving west, crossing countless mountains and river valleys. Tales of gold and jewels also lured them on. As each tribe escorted them on to the next, their journey became a sort of traveling medical show.

In the spring of 1536, after a hike of more than 1,280 kilometers (800 miles), they again encountered the sea. But this time it was the Pacific Ocean, or rather an arm of it, known as the Gulf of California. There the lonely wandering ended. A mounted band of Spanish slave-catchers found them and took them to a nearby mission. A march of another 1,280 kilometers got them to Mexico City, the seat of the colonial government.

For eight years Cabeza de Vaca and his fellows wandered in the wilderness, traversing a continent. And the stories they brought back—stories of treasure they had never seen—inspired the later expeditions of Hernando de Soto and Francisco Coronado.

as well as a church and the living quarters of the priests and the Indians. Occasionally, a mission would grow enough grain that it could afford to export some to Europe. Or it would produce such goods as woven blankets, tanned animal hides, pottery, wine, and olive oil.

To protect the missions, the Spanish built *presidios,* or forts. In time these forts evolved into cities. The Spanish also established *villas,* or towns, such as San Antonio, Albuquerque, and Monterey. The towns formed the nucleus of a settled region of ranches, farms, and villages.

SPAIN BEGINS TO DECLINE. *By 1565 Spain had reached the peak of its power in Europe and was beginning to face difficulties.* Charles V, grandson of Ferdinand and Isabella, ruled over a domain larger than the world had ever seen. His empire extended from the North Sea to the Mediterranean Sea, from the plains of Germany to the mountains of Peru. And that was its flaw. It was too big to govern. Charles had to battle the Turks in the East and the periodic rebellions in western Europe. Also, the religious movement begun by Martin Luther in Germany had all of Europe in turmoil.

Charles eventually retired to a monastery, leaving the Spanish part of his empire and the Netherlands to his son Philip. But the empire continued to crumble. The Dutch rose up, crying for independence. And in America, Philip's treasure ships were being periodically stolen by the English. In 1588, angered by this piracy and by England's open suport of the Dutch rebellion, Philip sent his mighty Armada of 100 ships to conquer England.

This picture is a copy of a page from an Aztec manuscript. It shows Cortés and his companions fighting with the Aztecs. What kinds of things are shown that most likely helped the Spanish defeat the Aztecs?

The outnumbered English refused to battle the Spanish head-on. Instead, they hung along the flanks of the Spanish fleet, picking off stragglers. When the Spanish fleet was put into the harbor of Calais (kah-LAY), just across the channel from England, the English sailed fire ships into the harbor. In panic the Spanish cut their anchor ropes and sailed out in wild disorder. The English were able to pick off many of the Spanish ships. The remaining ones tried to escape by sailing all the way around Britain. But North Sea gales smashed many onto the rocky coast of Scotland. It was a sadly broken fleet that finally made its way back to Spain. *The defeat of the Spanish Armada marked the fall of Spain and the rise of a new star in Europe—England.* It changed the whole future of America, too.

Section Review

1. Mapping: **a)** Look at the map on pages 12–13. Find the equator, the Tropic of Cancer, the Tropic of Capricorn, and the Line of Demarcation. Describe the location of the trade-wind belt. **b)** Look at the map on page 15. Use the key to follow the routes taken by the different explorers. Which explorer traveled to Cuzco? Name one who visited the coast of Florida. Which one traveled along the St. Lawrence River?
2. Identify or explain: Henry the Navigator, Marco Polo, carracks, latitude, Ferdinand and Isabella, Montezuma, Estévanico.
3. What were the Crusades, and how did they contribute to the rebirth of Europe?
4. Name two events that contributed to the decline of Spain.
5. Name one important contribution the voyages of Magellan made to the development of an accurate understanding of the world's geography.

3. The Expansion of England

ENGLAND'S EARLY EXPLORATIONS. The Renaissance came late to England, but it had the same effect that it had had on southern Europe. Queen Elizabeth I was on the throne. The pace of life had picked up. Art and literature were flourishing. *The English had an intense curiosity about the New World and were eager for a share of its riches.* Since Spain seemed to have a monopoly on the southern half of the Americas, England turned its attention to North America.

As early as 1497 Elizabeth's grandfather, Henry VII, had employed an Italian sea captain, John Cabot, to explore the icy reaches of North America under the English flag. Cabot sailed along the coasts of Labrador and Newfoundland, and then south, perhaps as far as Chesapeake Bay. Because Spanish explorations of the interior had not yet begun, Cabot was the first European since Leif Ericson to see North America. This discovery gave England a solid claim to at least part of North America.

THE LOST COLONY. By the middle of the 16th century, English *sea dogs* were penetrating the frigid waters north of Hudson Bay, looking for a northerly passage to India. And with the secret support of Queen Elizabeth, they began raiding the Spanish treasure ships. The boldest of these Elizabethan sea dogs was Sir Francis Drake, a hero of the battle with the Spanish Armada.

Before war between England and Spain was declared officially, Drake sailed around South America to the Pacific Ocean, in order to attack the Spanish treasure ports on the coast of Peru. Loaded with booty and with the entire Spanish fleet searching for him, Drake sailed for home the long way around—the first adventurer to circle the globe since Magellan.

A *sea dog* is a species of small shark. During the late 1500's English pirates and privateers who raided Spanish towns and ships were called sea dogs.

Another Elizabethan sea dog, Sir Walter Raleigh, got the idea of having a permanent English settlement in the New World. Since Raleigh was willing to finance the venture out of his own pocket, Queen Elizabeth was agreeable. She granted him the entire seacoast north of Spanish Florida, which he named Virginia.

Raleigh's first shipload of colonists set out in 1585. They chose for their settlement a small, sandy island off the coast of what is now North Carolina. (See map below.) Because it was an island, Roanoke offered some protection from Indians. The shallow waters around it also protected the settlers from Spanish warships.

But the spot the settlers had chosen was too desolate. When Sir Francis Drake stopped by after one of his raids on Spanish treasure ships, the settlers went home with him. In 1587 Raleigh sent out another party of 150 colonists, but the war with Spain prevented him from contacting the settlement for four years. When a relief ship finally appeared at Roanoke in 1591, the colonists were gone. There were no bodies and no sign of violence, and only one clue existed—the word "Croatan," carved on a tree. The Croatan were neighboring Indians. Whether they attacked the settlement or whether the colonists gave up and went to live with the Indians, we do not know.

JAMESTOWN: FIRST ENGLISH FOOTHOLD. After the war with Spain ended in 1603, the English were able to resume their search for an empire. Elizabeth died in that year. Since she had no children, the throne passed to her cousin, James Stuart, King of Scotland. Although his accession to the throne of England as James I did not unite the two countries, they did end up

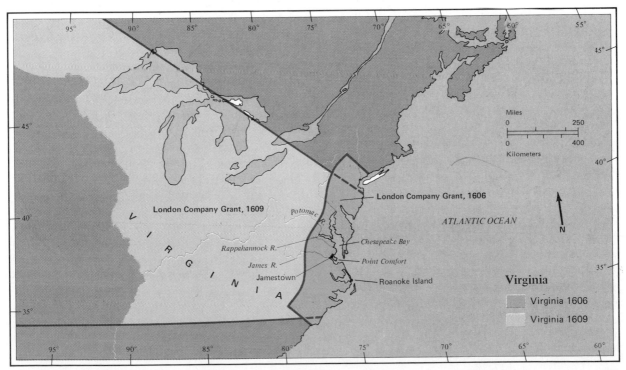

This engraving, from Captain John Smith's book, Generall Historie of Virginia, 1624, depicts Pocahontas saving Smith's life. According to Smith she took "his head in her armes, and laid her owne upon his to save him from death."

under the same monarch thereafter. (The United Kingdom of Great Britain was created by an Act of Union in 1707.)

Sir Walter Raleigh's experience with Roanoke proved that the financing of a colony was too much for one person. *So in 1606 a group of London merchants formed a company to undertake a new venture.* The London Company's charter, issued by the king, outlined the organization of the company and defined its powers. It also gave the company permission to set up a colony along the Atlantic coast known as Virginia.

Charter in hand, the company sent out three small shiploads of settlers in December 1606. All were men, for the colony was viewed as a trading post, not an agricultural community. The company would not make money sending people all the way to America to grow cabbages. *Basically the colony was set up to obtain gold, either by stealing it from the American Indians or by earning it in some trade.* The settlement could even serve as a way station when trading with China, if a northwest passage to the Pacific Ocean were ever found.

In the spring of 1607, coming from the south with the trade winds at their backs, the Virginia colonists sailed into the mouth of Chesapeake Bay, then up the broad river, which they named the James in honor of the king. They chose a site some 48 kilometers (30 miles) upriver (see map, page 19), far enough from the sea to allow ample warning of an attack. (Although there was peace with Spain, the Spanish still claimed the entire New World under the agreement of 1494.)

A DIFFICULT BEGINNING. *The Virginia settlers chose a small island on the edge of the river as a site for their town, which they named Jamestown after the king.* They hoped living on an island would give them some protection against Indians. It was not very good protection, as it turned out. In addition, the island was low and swampy. Malarial fevers plagued the colony, and the wells used for drinking water were easily polluted.

Many of the troubles of the Jamestown settlement were probably caused by the inexperience of the settlers. But the company also made mistakes. Instead of sending over a governor with adequate powers, it created a council of 12 to make decisions. This form of government did not work well in a wilderness community. As company employees, the settlers went to work only when ordered—and there was no one to give orders. Moreover, since the settlers believed the company would keep them supplied with crops, no one saw a need to plant them.

Nevertheless, the London Company probably had a difficult time recruiting people who were willing to risk their lives in a wilderness outpost. A measure of the quality of the recruits is that they lived near some of the finest oyster beds and fishing grounds in the world—and starved. When the settlers finally did send a small boat out to fish, it sailed for home.

20

CAPTAIN JOHN SMITH, AN EARLY HERO.

The governing council did contain one able leader, a professional soldier named John Smith. Smith might have brought some order to the confusion at Jamestown, except that he took literally the company's request for further exploration. Taking the colony's only vessel, he probed the broad *estuaries* of the Potomac and the Rappahannock, looking for a passage to the Pacific Ocean. That might sound odd today, but remember, the Spanish explorer Balboa had reached the Pacific after walking only a short distance across the Isthmus of Panama. Perhaps there were many places where the continent was that narrow. When questioned in sign language, the Indians talked of a vast sea to the northwest. How could Smith know it was only Lake Erie?

An *estuary* is an arm of the sea at the lower end of a river.

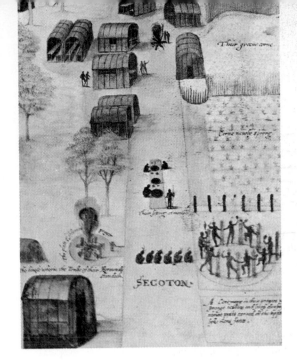

This illustration of a North Carolina Indian village is from a watercolor by John White, painted during his stay in Virginia in 1585. Compare this picture with the Pueblo village you examined earlier.

When he returned from his travels to find the colony floundering in semistarved confusion, Smith took command. He organized work parties, forcing some to build a fort, others to plant crops. His high-handed methods made enemies, however. Facing mutiny, he resigned from the council and took the next ship back to England. But Smith was not done with America. He returned a few years later to explore further, sailing along the northern coast, and to write on his map the name for the area that has remained—New England.

THE "STARVING TIME."

In 1609 the London Company won a new charter from the king, which reorganized the colony and more exactly defined its boundaries. From Old Point Comfort, where the James River meets Chesapeake Bay, the colony was to extend 320 kilometers (200 miles) north and 320 kilometers (200 miles) south. From the Atlantic Ocean it would extend west to "the South Sea" (Pacific Ocean). On the basis of this grant, Virginia claimed an empire, which included the Great Lakes and the Ohio Valley, territory disputed over with the Indians and later with the French, the Spanish, the English, and finally even with the American Congress.

Under the reorganization plan, the London Company named a governor and gave him full power. The company also made a huge investment in the colony. It sent over a large group of colonists, which for the first time included women. Unfortunately, an enormous storm scattered the fleet. Governor Gates was shipwrecked on the previously unknown island of Bermuda. When the rest of the fleet straggled into Jamestown with its weary and hungry passengers, it took the colony by surprise. Most of the fleet's food stores had been ruined by the sea. The colony, already short of food, was unprepared for such numbers.

That winter was the worst yet. Survivors called it the starving time. To stay alive, the colonists ate roots, insects, frogs, snakes, and other humans. The colony had about 500 people when the winter began. Scarcely 50 survived, and they were ready to give up. When the spring supply ship arrived, they piled aboard, and were actually sailing down the James when Governor Gates, who had built himself a ship in Bermuda, arrived.

Gates infused new life into the colony. He set up a strict set of rules and put everyone to work. About the year 1612, when the planter John Rolfe imported some tobacco seed from the West Indies, the colony at last found a source of profit. Until then the colony had sent home only lumber and barrel staves, a far cry from the London Company's early expectations. Since tobacco was becoming very popular in England, the company applauded the new crop. Virginians even took to planting tobacco with so much enthusiasm that they didn't bother to grow such food crops as corn. For some years the colony continued to import food.

BEGINNINGS OF SELF-GOVERNMENT.
As they became more comfortable physically, the Virginians became increasingly unhappy about the strict rule of their governors. Repeated complaints to London finally brought action. In 1618 the company sent over a new governor, Sir George Yeardley, with instructions to summon an assembly of the people. Yeardley asked each of the settlements, or boroughs (the English word for a town that had political rights), to elect two representatives to meet in a House of Burgesses in Jamestown. *The first assembly, which met on July 30, 1619, marked the beginnings of self-government in America.*

THE HEADRIGHT SYSTEM.
The company also instructed Governor Yeardley to make the colonists, previously considered servants of the company, financially independent. Thus, 20 hectares (50 acres) of land were given to every head of family in Virginia. Then, to stimulate immigration, the Governor offered 20 hectares (50 acres) to every person coming to the colony, and another 20 hectares (50 acres) for every "head" that person brought along.

The London Company, nearly bankrupt and weary of financing settlers who often died, hoped to populate its colony without expense by offering the one resource it had plenty of—land. This system, called the headright system, was largely responsible for Virginia's growth in the 17th century. It was, however, only a right to use the land, not a right to ownership. Landholders still had to pay the company a "quit rent" (so named because it "quit" the holder of any other obligation, such as military service). It was from these rents and the trade monopoly that the company hoped to make its profit.

As the Jamestown colony was finally getting established, another important development took place. *In 1619 the first Africans arrived in the colony.* At first they were regarded as indentured servants, but they were later freed after completing a specified term of labor. Some of them then acquired land. But by 1650 Africans were being brought to the English colonies as slaves. They were a cheap source of labor and could be forced to work long hours under poor conditions.

THE KING TAKES CHARGE.
The political and economic changes of 1619 solved most of Virginia's problems. Tobacco was in high demand and the colony was prospering. It had even survived an Indian attempt to wipe it out in 1622. But all this had done little to help the London Company. In constant financial trouble, the company by 1620 had run into problems with the king. James regarded London merchants as political enemies, and some of them were. He also objected to many of the London Company's ideas and actions. Then the Indian uprising, with the Virginians's frantic

This painting—called "Good Times in the New World (The Hope of Jamestown)"—was painted in 1841 by John Gadsby Chapman. What do you think the artist was trying to say about life in the new world?

calls for assistance, confirmed his attitudes.

In 1624 James not only began a suit in court to end the company's charter, but he took the land and its people back under his control. Virginia thereafter was a ***royal colony,*** meaning one owned and directed by the king or queen. Virginians themselves noted little difference, except that they had to pay their quit rents to the king instead of to the company. James wisely retained the assembly created in 1619, although he did appoint the governor. As the colony developed, a council was created to advise the governor and to serve as the colony's highest court of law. The king also named the members of the council, although usually on the suggestion of the governor. The governor's council also helped to form laws. By about the middle of the 17th century, it began meeting separately from the Burgesses. Thus began a two-house legislature. The council served as the upper house and the House of Burgesses served as the lower.

A ***royal colony*** was owned and ruled by the king or queen. A colony run by a joint stock company was a corporate colony. Most corporate colonies were taken over by the king or queen, as Virginia was. By the time of the Revolution, there were only two, Connecticut and Rhode Island. The third type of colony was called proprietary. Proprietary colonies will be discussed in the next chapter.

Virginia's system worked fairly well, and for its time, it was quite democratic. One had to be a landholder to sit in the House of Burgesses. But all free White men could vote, regardless of wealth or social standing. When other royal colonies were created later in the century, they were patterned on Virginia. The first English colony, then, became the model for most of the others.

Section Review

1. Mapping: Look at the map on page 19. Using the scale of kilometers and miles, decide the approximate length of the land grants of 1606 and 1609.
2. Identify or explain: Croatan, Sir Francis Drake, London Company, House of Burgesses, quit rent, royal colony.
3. Describe two ways in which the English sea dogs affected the exploration of America.

Chapter 1 Review

Bird's-Eye View

Over 10,000 years ago wandering hunters—the ancestors of the American Indians—crossed a sandy neck of land, which connects Siberia and present-day Alaska. In the course of centuries, they and their descendants filtered throughout North America. Some settled in one place, following a sedentary, agricultural way of life. Others led a nomadic life, hunting and gathering wild foods. Among the most outstanding Indian peoples were the Maya, Aztec, and Inca, who built brilliant civilizations in Central and South America; the Algonkian-speaking tribes of the eastern woodlands; the Iroquois, who developed the first federal system of government in the Americas; the Mississippians, who developed a complex culture in the Mississippi valley; and the Pueblo, Apache, and Navajo, whose different ways of life strongly influenced the Southwest.

The European exploration of the Americas was stimulated indirectly by the Crusades and directly by the inventions, discoveries, and ways of thinking that emerged in Europe during the Renaissance. Portugal took the lead in exploration by developing more seaworthy ships and by its better methods of navigating the seas. The Spanish followed and became, with Columbus, the second group of Europeans to reach North America. (The Vikings had settled Newfoundland briefly around 1000 A.D.) By 1565 Spain had become the greatest power in Europe. Thirty years later it was eclipsed by a new power—England.

The first English settlement in the New World, financed by Sir Walter Raleigh, was established on Roanoke Island in 1585. By 1591 both the settlement and the settlers had disappeared. The next settlement was established by the London Company in 1607 at Jamestown. It formed the basis of the colony of Virginia, whose representative government later served as a model for other English colonial governments in America.

Vocabulary

Define or identify each of the following:

sea dog	prairie	latitude
headright system	nomadic	House of Burgesses
royal colony	Coronado	indentured servant

Review Questions

1. Describe how the ancestors of the American Indians came to North America.
2. What were the characteristics of the Mississippi culture?
3. In what ways did the development of the carrack and the knowledge of latitude and wind belts help European exploration?
4. Name the Spanish explorers who looked for gold. Where did they search? What did they find?
5. What steps were taken by the English to establish a successful colony at Jamestown?
6. What political and economic changes established Virginia as a model for other colonies?

Reviewing Social Studies Skills

1. Name four maps in this chapter.
2. List four elements common to each map.
3. Using the map on page 6 and the chart on page 7, answer the following:
   a. Identify two tribes in the Mississippi culture region.
   b. Identify one tribe in the Northwest Coast culture region, and describe their tools.
   c. Which culture region had buffalo for food?
   d. On which ocean does the Dry Southwest border?
   e. Which culture region in the present-day United States occupies the largest area?
4. Maps can be used to show relationships of one thing to another. (New York is north of Miami; Denver is on the eastern slopes of the Rocky Mountains.) Using the maps in this chapter, describe the relationships between: the Hudson Bay and the Gulf of Mexico; Marco Polo's route to China and Columbus's route to America.
5. Using the index, list all the page references for Jamestown. Which pages have maps? Which page has a picture? Which one has a chart?

Reading for Meaning

1. One way to explain the meaning of a word is to give a synonym for it (fast/rapid). To explain the word's opposite meaning you would give an antonym (fast/slow). Choose two of the following words, and explain each one by giving either a synonym or antonym for it: nomadic, sedentary, primitive.
2. The words historians use influence the way we see the past. How do the italicized words in these passages influence the way you see the Vikings, the Indians of Peru, and Spanish soldiers:
   a. "*Ferocious* fighters and *marvelous* sailors, the Vikings. . ."
   b. ". . . the *peaceful artistic* Quechua of Peru. . ."
   c. "His *metal-garbed* soldiers *slaughtered* the Indians. . ."
3. Use the evidence presented in this chapter to answer the following question: How did the Renaissance in Europe set the stage for exploration of the Americas?

Bibliography

An interesting, well-written account of early Virginia is *Behold Virginia! The Fifth Crown,* by George Findlay Willison (Harcourt, Brace, Jovanovich, Inc.).

In the 19th century, Henry Wadsworth Longfellow wrote a poem about Hiawatha. This poem is called "The Song of Hiawatha" and may be found in many American literature books.

Prisoner of the Mound Builder, by Lloyd Harnishfeger, is the story of a handicapped young hunter who is captured by the Mound Builders, and survives to become the chief of the Ottawa (Lerner).

Chapter 2

1620-1735

The Atlantic Frontier

It was the 16th of March, 1621, and spring had come to New England. Spirits had risen in the warm sunshine, as people had begun realizing that the tiny Plymouth settlement had survived its first winter. That day a stranger had come to town. A tall Indian, dressed only in a bow and an arrow, had marched boldly down the street and up to the meetinghouse. While families had fled into their crude wood cabins, town leaders had intercepted the newcomer. "Welcome!" he had said in fair English. He told the settlers that Samoset (SAM-oe-set) was his name.

The astonished Pilgrims had lowered their weapons and begun asking questions. Samoset, they discovered, had learned English from people who had fished along the coast. In fact, he had a friend, Squanto, who had not only spoken English but had visited England three times! A world traveler was the last thing the Pilgrims had expected to find in the American woods. It seemed as though Samoset was ready for Plymouth, but Plymouth was unprepared for its Indian visitor.

Samoset, the Pilgrims soon discovered, also knew Massasoit (mas-uh-SOIT), the Indian leader in that part of New England. As the Pilgrims' most important neighbor, he was well worth knowing. Thus, they sent Samoset off to get his friends.

Samoset returned the following day with Squanto and several other friends, who brought beaver skins to trade. And so began a lasting friendship. Squanto remained with the Pilgrims to the end of his days. He guided them to the best fishing spots, and he showed them how to grow Indian corn, an American crop unknown in England.

Chapter Objectives

After you have finished reading this chapter, you should be able to:
1. Describe how England was affected by the Protestant Reformation.
2. List the reasons for establishing each of the New England colonies.
3. Define a proprietary colony.
4. Contrast the differences in English policy toward the colonies before and after the Glorious Revolution.

Thus, the Plymouth colony had a more promising beginning than did Jamestown. Although many Pilgrims sickened and died, those who remained proved more successful than the Virginians. The Pilgrims were fortunate in that no Indians had claimed their chosen site for settlement.

Another reason the Pilgrims fared better than the Virginians was that from the start they were determined to settle in America. The first Virginians had been employees of a company. They had come to Virginia to trade and had stayed to farm. The Pilgrims were religious refugees, escaping persecution in England. They had come to New England to establish a holy community. It was a great mission that they had set out on.

1. The Protestant Reformation and English Puritanism

MARTIN LUTHER'S QUESTIONS. To understand why the Pilgrims settled at Plymouth in 1620 involves going back a full century to a university town in Germany. There, in 1517 Martin Luther, a Catholic priest and professor, challenged another priest, Johann Tetzel (TET-zel), to debate 95 questions about the Roman Catholic faith. *Luther especially wanted to discuss the church's position on the forgiveness of sins and the link between one's faith in God and one's doing of good works in the world.*

Tetzel refused the challenge. But the questions were debated anyway. They were printed and circulated, provoking countless debates all over Germany and then throughout Europe. Rapidly, Europe began to split into two camps: those who sided with Luther and those who sided with the Roman Catholic Church.

The debate eventually grew into a great movement—the Protestant Reformation. Kings, queens, and nobles became involved. Before long Luther's questions were being debated on the battlefield rather than in the field of books and pamphlets. Europe was being engulfed in a series of religious wars, which would last for the better part of a century.

THE REFORMATION COMES TO ENGLAND. England, isolated by the sea, escaped the wars but not the Reformation. King Henry VIII, the ruler of England between 1509 and 1547, had been one of Luther's strongest opponents. *Yet it was through Henry that Protestantism took root on English soil.*

In 1533 Henry wanted to divorce his wife Catherine. After 20 years of marriage they had had only one child—a daughter, Mary. Henry's family, the Tudors, were new to the

Martin Luther's questions about the Roman Catholic faith provoked numerous debates all over Germany. How did his views affect the course of European history?

English throne. Henry felt he had to cement their position by passing the crown on to a son. Besides, he had already chosen the mother of this son and heir—Anne Boleyn (BUL-in), one of Queen Catherine's attendants.

The Roman Catholic Church, however, frowned on divorce. When the pope, as head of the church, denied Henry's request, Henry broke with the Roman Catholic Church. He declared himself head of the English Catholic Church and granted himself a divorce.

Divorce and remarriage, however, did not solve Henry's problem. Queen Anne gave birth to another girl—Elizabeth. This time Henry saved himself the trouble of divorce. He simply had Anne beheaded for treason and married again. Fortunately his third wife, Jane Seymour, produced a son, Edward. In his will Henry decreed that the crown should pass first to his son Edward, then to his daughter Mary, and finally to his daughter Elizabeth.

REFORMING THE CHURCH OF ENGLAND. Henry's break was with the pope, not with the church. In other words, he kept all the Roman Catholic ceremonies—including the Latin mass—while rejecting the pope's right to govern English Catholics. *Under Henry's son Edward, however, the situation changed. The Church of England became more Protestant and less Catholic.*

Edward was a child when he became king in 1547. Powerful advisers, called regents, ruled England in his name. They were Protestants influenced by the teachings of Luther and Luther's European followers. One of their aims was to remove traces of Roman Catholicism from the Church of England.

As a result, they eliminated the Latin mass, wrote a Book of Common Prayer so services could be held in English, limited the power of bishops, and got rid of bishops sympathetic to Rome.

Queen Elizabeth I ruled England for many years. How did the fact that she was Anne Boleyn's daughter influence her to firmly establish the Church of England?

MARY RESTORES CATHOLICISM. When Edward died at age 16, his half-sister Mary ascended the throne. Besides being devoutly Catholic herself, Mary was married to Philip II of Spain, a fierce opponent of Protestantism. *During her brief reign (1553–1558), Mary tried to bring Catholicism back to England.* Hundreds of Protestants fled to Europe, and some were even burned for their beliefs.

Upon her death in 1558, Mary was succeeded on the throne by her half-sister Elizabeth, a Protestant. *Under Elizabeth the Church of England was established by law.* It then became the official church of the nation.

PURIFYING THE CHURCH OF ENGLAND. Elizabeth's actions did not satisfy all English Protestants. There were some who felt the Church of England still had too many traces of Catholicism. They objected, for instance, to the special vestments worn by priests during mass and other ceremonies. They wanted sermons to focus directly on the Bible rather than on the teachings of the church, which were based only in part on the Bible. They felt that organ music, statues, stained-glass windows, and similar things were frills that had no place in a church. Because of their intense desire to purify the Church of England by removing traces of Catholicism, these Protestants became known as Puritans.

JOHN CALVIN AND PREDESTINATION. The Puritans also objected to the *theology* of the Church of England. They wanted to replace it with a theology based on the thought of John Calvin, the religious and political leader of Geneva, Switzerland.

Theology is a system of religious beliefs.

By the late 16th century, Calvin's ideas had attracted many followers in western Europe.

This English cartoon, done in 1641, comments on the religious turmoil of the period. The four figures "tossing" the Bible represent the major religious groups opposing the Church of England. How might a modern cartoonist have cast this scene?

Calvin believed that only God knew who would get to heaven. In other words, God alone knew who was truly virtuous and who only seemed to be virtuous. Calvin also maintained that those who go to heaven get there by the grace of God alone—by God's will—not by what they do during their lives on earth. Furthermore, Calvin concluded, God has known from the beginning of time who will be in heaven at the end of time, Judgment Day. To put it another way, certain persons are destined even before they are born to go to heaven after they die. This idea is called predestination. Those who were predestined for heaven were thought of as Saints while on earth.

THE SEPARATISTS. *Puritans who followed rigidly the Calvinist law thought the Church of England was too lax.* Everyone in England was allowed to join it. The strictest Puritans thought the Church should allow only Saints to be members. They even outwardly objected to attending church with sinners. But their objections were not taken seriously. Eventually, such Puritans concluded that the only solution to their problem was to separate from the Church of England. Thus, they were called Separatists.

PERSECUTION OF THE SEPARATISTS. *The Separatist Puritans wanted not only to separate themselves from sinners within the church, but also to separate church and state.* Although they were a minority, their radical views attracted much attention. Elizabeth's government tolerated the moderate Puritans—even when they were elected to Parliament (England's governing body) and tried to change the church by changing the country's laws. But the government considered the Separatists dangerous. It broke up their meetings and hanged their leaders for treason. As a result, the Separatists remained a tiny, fugitive sect, while middle-of-the-road Puritanism flourished.

When Elizabeth died in 1603, James I took over until his death in 1625. James continued Elizabeth's policies—including persecution of the Separatists. During his reign the Separatists began fleeing to the more tolerant atmosphere of Holland. But after some years they grew dissatisfied with life there as well. They decided they could preserve their holiness and their church only in a community built by themselves. So they decided to migrate to the wilderness of North America.

Section Review

1. Mapping: Refer to the map on pages xx-xxi. Then describe as fully as you can the location of the following places: England, Rome, the Netherlands (Holland), Spain.
2. Identify or explain: Protestant Reformation, Henry VIII, Elizabeth I, predestination, Separatists, King James I.
3. What reforms did the Puritans wish to make in the Church of England?
4. What two factors contributed to the Pilgrims' success in establishing a colony in the New World?

2. The Founding of New England

THE VOYAGE OF THE MAYFLOWER. *In 1619 the Separatists— already referring to themselves as Pilgrims because of their many travels— became a part of a joint stock company.* They got financial backing from friendly Puritans in London. Then, they obtained permission from the Virginia Company to settle in its colony. These arrangements enabled them to leave without arousing the suspicions of the king. In the fall of 1620, they sailed from Holland to Southampton, England, and then on to America.

Although their rented vessel, the *Mayflower*, was old and leaky, they managed to cross the Atlantic in it. *However, they landed not in Virginia but on the coast of New England.* Whether the landing was accidental or deliberate, no one knows. But the Pilgrims were certainly aware that religious freedom would have been impossible in Virginia, where the Church of England was established by law.

This painting shows the Pilgrims leaving England for America. What did they hope to find in America that they could not find in England?

THE MAYFLOWER COMPACT. After spending several weeks exploring Cape Cod Bay, the Pilgrims chose a town site, which they named Plymouth. Because they did not land in Virginia where laws existed, they decided to write their own laws. *As a result, before leaving the ship, they drafted the Mayflower Compact, an agreement that all would abide by the laws that they had made.* This Compact was a solemn recognition that people wanting a fresh start had to create their own laws and form their own government. Next, they elected a body of lawmakers headed by a governor. The first governor, William Bradford, was so popular that he was reelected annually for many years thereafter.

PLYMOUTH THRIVES. For a young, wilderness community, Plymouth enjoyed surprising prosperity. The Indians who came with Squanto brought beaver pelts to trade, and the Pilgrims found a ready market for them in England. Within a few years the Plymouth settlers had enough money to buy out their London shareholders. This they did in 1627. Although that act made them virtually independent of English authority, they never did succeed in obtaining legal ownership of their land. The king could still remove them at any time. For the moment, however, he was too preoccupied by his own difficulties with Parliament to concern himself with a community in far-off America.

ENGLAND'S TROUBLES. England in the 1620's was a troubled land. The economic changes that accompanied the Renaissance—a rise in prices, the availability of money for investment, the appearance of new industries—brought major social changes. The arrival of gold from the Americas raised prices all over Europe. Those who could adjust to *inflation* did well; others suffered. Landlords, finding wool more profitable than crops in the new, trade-based economy, threw their tenants off the land, converted their farmlands to pasture, and began raising sheep. The unemployed roamed the countryside in search of food.

Inflation is the economic condition that exists when prices rise rapidly but the purchasing power of money declines.

King James I was unable to deal with these problems. He refused to take advice from Parliament and even began jailing his critics—among them many Puritans—without the due process of a court trial. When James died in 1625, his son Charles I, who ruled until 1649, replaced him. Charles's solution to parliamentary criticism was to ignore it. *Eventually the conflict with Parliament led to civil war.*

Until 1628 the Puritans managed to cope with their difficulties by working for reform from within the Church of England. As a result, the government tolerated them, even though it hounded the Separatists. *But as economic, political, and religious conditions in England grew worse, the Puritans began looking for a religious refuge.* Naturally, their eyes turned toward the colony of their Calvinist cousins, the Pilgrims.

MASSACHUSETTS BAY COLONY. *By 1628 Plymouth Colony was becoming a commercial success.* Furs collected from the American Indians at trading posts, from Cape Ann to Narragansett (na-rah-GAN-set) Bay, were being sent through Plymouth to England. When a group of Puritans visited the post on Cape Ann (later to become Salem) in 1628, they were so impressed that they decided to start a Puritan colony there.

Returning to England, the Puritans obtained financial backing from some London merchants and formed the Massachusetts Bay Company. They even managed to win a charter for the company from the king and a grant of land in New England. They then rented a fleet of ships large enough to transport a thousand colonists with all their

The First Thanksgiving was painted many years after the event had actually taken place. What do you see in the painting that you think is accurate? What do you see that is inaccurate?

household goods, farm tools, and livestock. *The planning that went into Massachusetts Bay indicates how much the English had learned about the founding of a colony since the early disasters at Jamestown.*

THE CAMBRIDGE AGREEMENT.

Before departing, the *emigrants* met with other members of the company at Cambridge. This university town in eastern England was a Puritan stronghold.

An *emigrant* is a person who departs from a country to settle elsewhere. An *immigrant* is a person who comes to a country to take up permanent residence.

At Cambridge, with the consent of the whole company, the Puritans migrating to America agreed to take the company charter with them. *This Cambridge Agreement, as it became known, was made in order to free the new colony from royal supervision.*

The members of the joint stock company were the only ones with a role in government. They formed the governing body of the colony. The assembled Puritans then elected John Winthrop to be head of the Massachusetts Bay Company and the governor of the colony.

Because the tiny fort on Cape Ann could not accommodate all the arriving Puritans, some of them moved south to the Charles River (named after the king). There they founded Boston, Cambridge, and other settlements farther up the river. So large was their undertaking that Massachusetts Bay Colony overshadowed Plymouth almost from the beginning.

THE PURITAN COLONY.

With their arrival in the New World, the Puritans quickly separated themselves from the Church of England. They had no bishops and did not want any. They allowed each congregation to run its own affairs and to choose its own minister. Today this church is called the Congregational Church.

32

A RELIGIOUS COMMUNITY. *Because the Bay Colony was a religious community, the leaders made few distinctions between affairs of state and affairs of church.* Governor Winthrop ruled with the help of the General Court, the lawmaking body of Massachusetts Bay.

The General Court was elected, at least at first, by the company's stockholders. Then, in 1632 all adult men who were members of the church were given the vote. In 1644 each town won the right to send representatives to the General Court, thus establishing a representative form of government in Massachusetts.

Magistrates, or judges, administered the laws of the colony. They saw no important difference between civil and religious crimes. Sometimes they even consulted the Bible to find an appropriate punishment.

Because the Puritans went to Massachusetts with a plan for a model community, they saw no reason to tolerate anyone who disagreed with them. Those who wished to worship differently were banished from the colony. Religious freedom in Massachusetts meant the freedom to leave if you did not like the system.

THE VILLAGE FRONTIER. The Massachusetts town reinforced the alliance between government and church. For example, many of the early arrivals were groups led by ministers who had been deprived of their churches in England. On arrival to Boston, each group was granted a large tract of interior land by Governor Winthrop, with the approval of the government. Some of this land was reserved for use by the entire community. The rest of the tract was divided among the people. The size of each family's share depended on how much it had contributed to the cost of the ocean voyage. The ideal was for each family to live in the village and travel to its outlying lands to plant or harvest. But by 1650 most New Englanders lived on their own farms.

Sidenote to History
Cotton Mather Fights the Smallpox

In the spring of 1721, smallpox swept into Boston. The terrible disease had visited the city about every 10 years since its founding. And medical science in those days had no cure. The only treatment was bed rest and prayer.

This new epidemic, however, was destined to be different. Cotton Mather, the town's leading minister, had learned from a Black servant about how the disease was being prevented in Africa. The procedure used, called inoculation, involved giving a mild case of the disease to a healthy person. This was done by putting infected matter into a cut in the skin.

Boston's physicians were nearly all opposed to the idea because they feared inoculation would only spread the disease. But Mather persuaded a friend, Dr. Zabdiel Boylston, to give the procedure a try. Together they inoculated 240 people during the epidemic. But six of their patients died, which was 2½% of the total. Mather, however, discovered that of those not inoculated, 15% had died of the disease.

Realizing the significance of these figures, Mather published them. As a result, physicians in other colonies could read about his experiment. This proved especially significant a few years later when smallpox threatened Charleston, South Carolina. Doctors, having read about Mather, promptly inoculated the whole town. And no one died.

Cotton Mather thus helped to spread information about a new defense against epidemic diseases. And in so doing he pioneered the use of public health statistics. The end of the story was written 260 years later when, in the spring of 1980, the World Health Organization declared that smallpox no longer existed anywhere on earth.

This type of settlement had several advantages. For example, the Massachusetts community was compact and easily defended. Also, any town growth would also strengthen the church, for village and congregation were one. And all were under the watchful eye of the minister. So valuable was this system that the town became the basic unit of settlement for all New England.

PROBLEMS ARISE. In some respects the Massachusetts town was too tidy. *When all the lands were allotted, there were none left for the next generation.* Nor was there room for newcomers. What could be done, for instance, about someone like Thomas Morton, who came to Massachusetts seeking profit rather than salvation, and who simply squatted between towns? Settling right on the border between Bay Colony and Plymouth, Morton opened a tavern (it may have been America's first roadhouse), which attracted an assortment of American Indians and young Puritans. The place was so lively that authorities became worried about the morals of the youth. After

Shortly after arriving in Massachusetts, some families became very prosperous. This painting shows a Puritan woman and her daughter. What evidence can you see in this painting to support the suggestion that this family was prosperous?

numerous appeals, the two colonies sent a troop of soldiers to arrest Morton. He was shipped back to England in chains, but there were to be more adventurers like him.

THE SHADOWS OF DISSENT. People like Morton were an occasional problem to Massachusetts Bay. Of more immediate concern, however, were differences of opinion within the church. The magistrates had recognized from the beginning that allowing each congregation to run its own affairs might be dangerous. Inspired by new and forceful ideas, congregations might dash off into all sorts of theological directions. The whole system might come apart if the magistrates did not enforce some conformity.

Separatism seemed particularly dangerous to the magistrates because it questioned the connection between church and state. The idea that the church might be independent of the government and the community attacked the very foundations of Massachusetts Bay. *Indeed, it was the effort to root out Separatism that led to the founding of Rhode Island.*

ROGER WILLIAMS, TORCHBEARER OF RELIGIOUS FREEDOM. Roger Williams, a Puritan minister, arrived in New England in 1631 to become pastor of the church of Salem. Soon his preaching became a source of concern to Bay Colony authorities.

Williams felt strongly that the Indians should be paid for the lands taken by the colonists. In addition, he spoke of the need to keep his church free from evil influence— especially in its contact with the government. Unless the government itself was run by Saints, the church would find itself regulated by sinners. Called before a court in Boston, Williams boldly told the authorities that they had absolutely no power over his congregation.

The court banished him from the colony, and in the fall of 1635, Williams fled with a few friends south to the Narragansett country. There, on the shore of Narragansett Bay, he built a hut and called it Providence. The following spring his Salem congregation joined him, and Williams's hut became a village. Soon many other people came to join the settlement.

THE FOUNDING OF RHODE ISLAND. When king and Parliament began fighting each other in the 1640's, Williams obtained a charter for his colony from the Puritan-controlled Parliament. This charter provided for an elected governor and assembly. *But religion was left to Williams, who promptly decreed religious freedom for his colony.* There would be no laws on religion and no government interference in the churches.

This climate of freedom attracted new immigrants, among them Jews and Quakers. Both groups—prohibited from entering universities or public service—had been discriminated against in England. As a result, they often went into commerce. Thus, after settling in Newport, they soon turned that city into a thriving commercial center.

AMERICA'S FIRST WRITTEN CONSTITUTION. Good soil, hard to find in rocky, mountainous New England, was what attracted the first westward pioneers to Connecticut. Like Massachusetts, Connecticut was settled town by town, with ministers leading their congregations into the Connecticut River valley.

In 1638 three river towns—Hartford, Wethersfield, and Windsor—elected delegates to form a political union. The Fundamental Orders of Connecticut, which they drafted, was the first written constitution in America. It established a government much like that of Massachusetts, with an assembly elected by all church members and an elected governor.

THE PEQUOT WAR. Relations between the English settlers of New England and their Indian neighbors were generally

Sidenote to History

Anne Hutchinson

Governor John Winthrop sharpened his feather quill, dipped it, and wrote into his diary, under the date October 21, 1636: "One Mistress Hutchinson, a member of the church of Boston, a woman of ready wit and bold spirit, has brought over with her two dangerous errors." Thus began the tragedy of Anne Hutchinson.

She was 43 years old at the time, was married to a prosperous English merchant, and was the mother of 14 children. Unlike most women of her time, she had some formal education. The Holy Bible had been translated from Latin into English during her childhood and had been published for all to read. Intensely religious, Anne Hutchinson knew every chapter by heart.

It was religion that had brought her to Massachusetts, two years before her trial. Although she and her husband had lived comfortably in England, they had followed John Cotton, their minister, from England to Massachusetts. There, John Cotton soon became one of the most prominent ministers in the Bay Colony. And it was he who first began to wrestle with the ideas that brought Anne Hutchinson to ruin.

Calvinist theology held that a person became a Saint by God's grace alone. But what about those who led pious lives, but were not really Saints? In short, how do you tell Saints from hypocrites? Cotton and other ministers eventually concluded that you could not. They would be content if their followers merely led upright lives and attended church regularly.

This left Anne Hutchinson dissatisfied. Ministers who were willing to compromise might not be Saints themselves. If not, how could they minister to a real Saint? Furthermore, any Saint ought to be able to communicate directly with God. For that matter, a Saint does not need laws either. Laws are made for sinners, not Saints. A Saint, in fact, need not be responsible to anything but an inner conscience. That was a radical notion indeed!

It is easy to imagine what the church and the magistrates thought of Anne's ideas. If a few people who claimed to be Saints were allowed to do as they pleased, no one would bother to obey the law.

It is one thing to hold unpopular beliefs. It is quite another to express them openly. And that is where Anne Hutchinson got into trouble. A gifted teacher, she began holding meetings in her home, where she discussed the minister's sermon and offered her own views. The meetings became quite popular. Often the group numbered as many as 60, and soon nearly every home in Boston was in turmoil.

In 1638 she was brought to trial. The court heard testimony about her views and cross-examined her. John Cotton, who had started her chain of thought, refused to defend her. Even her husband fell silent. Alone before the court, she boldly defended her views and cast doubt on the holiness of her persecutors. The court ordered her banished, and the clergy threw her out of the church.

Roger Williams then invited her to Rhode Island. With her family, Anne Hutchinson left Massachusetts. She stayed in Rhode Island until her husband died. Then she moved into the wilderness of unsettled Long Island, where she hoped to work among the American Indians. In 1643 the Indians of southern New England and New York rose up in an effort to stop further European settlement on their lands. Anne Hutchinson was killed—a victim of the times and the society in which she lived.

peaceful during the decade following the Pilgrims' arrival. However, as English settlements spread rapidly from the seacoast to the interior, English-Indian relations began to deteriorate. *By 1635—14 years after Samoset's first visit to Plymouth—war had broken out between the Pequot and the English.*

The bitterness that resulted from the Pequot War made a second major conflict inevitable. It was just a matter of time before the Indians were strong enough to seek revenge. The time arrived in 1675, 40 years after the outbreak of the Pequot War.

METACOMET FIGHTS THE ENGLISH. In that year Metacomet, called King Philip by the English, gathered his people, the Wampanoag (wahm-pah-NOE-ag), and several allied tribes to make war on the English.

At first Metacomet and his forces were successful. They destroyed nearly 20 English villages. Ultimately, however, they were crushed by the English forces, who outnumbered them four to one. Metacomet was killed by a Christianized, or "praying," Indian. Other leaders of the war were executed, and many warriors were sent as slaves to the West Indies. The Indians who survived the war and managed to evade being captured by the English were more embittered than ever. Later, when conflicts erupted between English and French settlers, various Indian tribes allied themselves with the French and raided villages on the New England frontier.

Section Review

1. Mapping: On the map on page 44, locate Plymouth, Boston, Providence, and Salem. Judging by their locations, why do you think these sites were chosen for settlements?

2. Identify or explain: Mayflower Compact, Cambridge Agreement, John Winthrop, Fundamental Orders of Connecticut, Roger Williams, King Philip, Metacomet.

3. How did Plymouth Colony achieve its independence from the king?

4. Why were the government and the church united in Massachusetts Bay Colony?

5. How did the Puritans treat people who were religious dissenters?

3. The Proprietary Colonies

MARYLAND. In 1632, only two years after the founding of Massachusetts Bay Colony, King Charles I authorized another colony. This one was to be named Maryland, after his wife Henrietta Maria, who was a Roman Catholic. *The new colony was intended to serve as a refuge for English Catholics, who were as much the target of persecution as the Puritans.*

The Maryland charter was somewhat different from the other charters. Charles had given the Maryland charter to one man—Cecil Calvert, Lord Baltimore (Calvert was his family name, Lord Baltimore his title). He was a Roman Catholic and the king's personal friend. *Baltimore was to be the proprietor of Maryland, which meant that he would have complete control of the colony, including the appointment of its governor. But he would be responsible to the king, who retained final ownership and could take the colony back whenever he wanted.*

The first settlers arrived in Maryland in 1633 and established themselves on a small branch of the Potomac River. Able to purchase food and other supplies from their Virginia neighbors, the Maryland colonists had little difficulty getting started. Soon they were growing tobacco for the English market, like their neighbors to the south.

The first settlers were Roman Catholics, but they were soon outnumbered by others who had come to Maryland in search of opportunity. Lord Baltimore encouraged this sort of pioneer by offering 40 hectares (100 acres) to those people who would either transport themselves or finance the passage of others to Maryland. These hectares were not outright gifts, however; the colonists would have to pay Baltimore an annual fee, called a quit rent. Nevertheless, it was an attractive offer. Baltimore made the offer even better by *decreeing* religious toleration in 1634. It was the first such move in America. It not only offered security to Roman Catholics, but it was also a beacon to others. Maryland, like Rhode Island, offered a combination of freedom and opportunity. Settlers flocked to the lush shores of Chesapeake Bay, and the colony prospered.

Decrees are laws given out by a ruler. Since Baltimore, as proprietor, had complete authority, he issued all the laws.

CIVIL WAR IN ENGLAND. Even the king considered Maryland a success. When Charles I and Parliament declared open war on each other in the 1640's, Maryland and Virginia sided with the king. *Led by Oliver Cromwell, Parliament eventually won the civil war.* Charles I was executed in 1649 and his son (also named Charles) fled to Holland. For the next 11 years, Cromwell and Parliament ruled England.

England ended its experiment in republican government in 1660 and brought Charles II (1660–1685) out of exile to be king. Impressed with the success of the proprietary system in Maryland, Charles used that system for all later colonial grants.

CHARLES II AND THE DUTCH. Charles II eventually proved to be as stubborn and willful as his father. Nevertheless, he did confirm the charters given by Parliament to Connecticut and Rhode Island and allowed Massachusetts to extend its authority northward over New Hampshire and Maine. He even adopted Cromwell's policies toward Europe. Cromwell had fallen into war with the Dutch, and Charles II made plans to do the same.

The rivalry between England and Holland stemmed from trade competition. The English were particularly angered by the Dutch vessels trading in the English colonies. In 1651 under Cromwell, Parliament had passed a law prohibiting all foreigners from trading in the English Empire. The law was directed primarily at the Dutch, who retaliated by declaring war.

The biggest sore point was the Dutch colony of New Netherland, a trading post and smuggler's haven in the midst of the English settlements. The Dutch claim in North America, based on the voyages of Henry Hudson, extended from the Delaware River north to Connecticut. Established by the Dutch West India Company in 1624, New Netherland had yielded only moderate profits, under a succession of unpopular governors.

Although the Dutch stamped their architecture, customs, and language on the colony (giving to American English such words as "cookie," "boss," and "crib"), few ever came to America. Financially well off, united in their religion, and content with their government, the Dutch had no reason to leave home.

NEW NETHERLAND BECOMES NEW YORK. Despite its weakness, New Netherland irritated the English because it was a center for illegal trade. By shipping through New Netherland, American colonists could avoid English regulations and taxes. King Charles's solution was to offer the Dutch colony as a proprietary to his brother James, Duke of York. All James had to do was conquer it. Thus, when the king provided him

Margaret Brent arrived in the colonies in 1638. She was secretary to Governor Leonard Calvert. In 1649 she was forced out of a meeting of the colonial assembly when she demanded a vote for herself. After Calvert died, she was named his executor and, thus, became Acting Governor. She presided over the General Assembly, although she was still refused the vote since "it would set a bad example for ye wives of ye colony!"

with a fleet, James sailed in and took the colony, without firing a shot. (Apparently the residents saw little difference between Dutch rule and English rule.) James then renamed the colony New York, after himself. The year was 1664.

The new ruler generously assured the Dutch that they could keep their lands, an important gesture, since some of the wealthiest citizens had princely estates in the Hudson River valley. Eventually, James became as unpopular as the Dutch had been, but for the moment New York was calm.

THE CAROLINA GRANT. *If Maryland represented the proprietary system at its best, the Carolinas were examples of it at its worst.* Chartered at about the same time as New York, the Carolina proprietary went to eight men who expected to reap handsome profits from land sales. Of land, there

was plenty. The grant ran from Virginia to Spanish Florida and west to the Pacific.

Unfortunately, the Carolina proprietors were unwilling to risk their own funds in a settlement venture. They simply advertised the colony, offered headrights to those who would transport themselves, and sat back to watch cities blossom. It was years before anything but wildflowers blossomed on the sandy beaches.

ALBEMARLE SOUND AND CHARLESTON. By 1670 a few pioneers had drifted south from Virginia. They clustered around Albemarle Sound, where they planted some corn and tobacco. Farther to the south emigrants, who had left the overcrowded West Indies, began a settlement they called Charleston, named after the king. For some years they survived on deerskin trade with the Indians. About 1700 rice

This scene is a view of New York from the East River in 1673. To the left is the fort with the Dutch church in the background. The arch and wall at the far right occupy the site of the present Wall Street.

was introduced. This crop proved to be as important to the Carolinians as tobacco was to the Virginians.

Since the two Carolina settlements differed in interests and outlook, they soon developed in different ways. With the approval of the proprietors, each settlement chose its own assembly and governor. The Albemarle settlement was the germ of North Carolina; Charleston evolved into South Carolina. But neither colony was happy with its proprietors, and they petitioned the king to take them back. The king began to buy out the proprietors, and by 1744 both Carolinas were back into royal hands.

THE FOUNDING OF GEORGIA. By the mid-1700's the population of the colonies had swelled to more than a million. One new colony that contributed to this growth was Georgia. In 1732 James Oglethorpe and several of his friends received a charter from King George II to organize a colony south of the Carolinas. Oglethorpe and his associates planned to control the colony for 21 years, at which point it would automatically become a royal colony. They named the colony Georgia in honor of the king.

Oglethorpe and his friends had planned to make the colony a haven for the debtors and paupers who had filled the English jails in the 18th century. But from Oglethorpe's point of view, Georgia was a failure. He had advertised far and wide among the English poor, but few had ever become colonists. Instead, Georgia—like most of the other southern colonies—was settled by land-hungry men and women, people who quickly tired of Oglethorpe's well-meaning supervision.

The colony staggered along for 20 years. In 1752 Oglethorpe asked the king to take over. Under royal control the colony changed rapidly. Slaves were imported and cotton and rice plantations were established. And Georgia prospered.

THE QUAKERS SEEK REFUGE. Most of the early English colonies had some kind of religious motive behind them. *Only one, Virginia, was founded for trade and profit.* In 1660, after restoration of the monarchy, colonization resumed. Concern for material gain was usually the reason for setting up colonies. Proprietors expected to profit— either from trade, as in New York, or from land sales, as in the Carolinas. *Pennsylvania, the last of the colonies founded in this period, was the only one with a religious motive.* It was to be a refuge for members of the Society of Friends, or Quakers.

The government of Charles II was fairly relaxed about religious matters. It would have even tolerated the Quakers, just as it had the Roman Catholics, had the Quakers been a little less zealous. Instead, the government looked on the Quakers as a disloyal and rebellious group.

Excluded from the government, the military services, and the universities, there was little for Quakers to do but to enter trade. In this area they prospered. But they also grew more aware of the government's restrictions on them. Hence, before long the Quakers were looking for a refuge of their own in America.

SETTLEMENT OF NEW JERSEY. In the mid-1670's a group of wealthy Quakers purchased the western part of New Jersey from its proprietor. New Jersey had originally been part of the Dutch claim; it had thus gone to the Duke of York when he had conquered New Netherland. As in the Carolinas, the proprietor had the right to sell the land and to collect rents, but James had kept the power of government. When the Quakers bought western New Jersey, they were unhappy with this arrangement; they wanted to govern themselves. So they kept looking for new land.

The unfortunate Quaker being whipped in this picture is blindfolded and tied to a cart leading him out of town. Why do you think the Quakers were persecuted by Pilgrims and Puritans alike?

WILLIAM PENN, FOUNDER OF PENNSYLVANIA. William Penn, one of the Quaker leaders, saw the answer. His father had once lent the king a substantial sum of money. Instead of repaying the debt, Penn suggested, the king might grant him a new proprietary, somewhere west of New Jersey. King Charles II, ever in debt and often willing to ease his burdens by dispensing American real estate, agreed. *Under its charter of 1681, Pennsylvania ("Penn's woods") was sandwiched between New York and Maryland, and it extended west from the Delaware River.*

Although the charter gave Penn total authority over the colony, Penn believed in giving the people a voice. Thus, his "Frame of Government" (1682) established an elected council, which would furnish advice to the governor, and an assembly, which would pass laws. He also promised complete religious freedom (rather than mere toleration) in the colony. *In all, Pennsylvania had the freest, most democratic political system in the world at that time.*

Penn also insisted that Pennsylvania's American Indians be treated fairly. Land belonging to the Delaware and to other tribes of the area was to be paid for by the colonists. In addition, guidelines were set down by Penn himself to regulate the settlers' behavior toward the Indians. In his "Concessions of the Province of Pennsylvania," Penn wrote: "Whatever is sold to the Indians in exchange for their furs, shall be sold in the marketplace and will have to pass a test to make sure it is good merchandise. Furthermore, the Indians shall have the freedom to do anything to improve their land or provide for their families that the settlers are allowed to do."

This climate of freedom attracted many immigrants. Quakers were the first arrivals, establishing Philadelphia in 1682 and spreading into the rich farmlands of the Delaware Valley. German *Pietists* came next, followed by others who were attracted by a

Painted by Edward Hicks about 1840, "Penn's Treaty with the Indians" illustrates the goodwill that Penn wrote of when the purchase of Pennsylvania was arranged. Do you think the goods the English are offering are fair exchange for the land they are getting?

climate and landscape similar to that of western Germany. Then came the Scotch-Irish, Scotch Presbyterians who had established a colony in northern Ireland at the urging of King James I. Hard times there had inspired them to make another move—to America. Catholics and Jews from many European countries also came to Pennsylvania, and a small number of Africans were brought to the colony. ***Pennsylvania grew rapidly with these waves of immigrants, and before long Philadelphia was the gateway to the American West.***

Pietist is the name given a variety of religious sects, such as Mennonites, Moravians, and Amish, who carried their religious beliefs into their daily lives.

Section Review

1. Mapping: Using the map on page 44, locate the Delaware River, Albemarle Sound, Charleston, and Baltimore.
2. Identify or explain: Lord Baltimore, Cromwell, William Penn.
3. Give two reasons for Maryland's success as a colony.
4. How did New Netherland become New York?

4. Imperial Authority and Colonial Rebellion

THE KING'S AUTHORITY. The charter granted to Pennsylvania was almost the same as other proprietary charters, with one important difference. ***The king specifically retained the authority to enforce the laws and to collect taxes in Pennsylvania.*** This reservation suggests that King Charles II was becoming increasingly concerned about his authority over the empire. Although he felt that the proprietary system worked fairly well, he was concerned about the independent spirit in the colonies. By the time he created Pennsylvania, his last colony, Charles II was seriously considering some major changes.

42

THE NAVIGATION ACTS. From the beginning of his reign, Charles II and his advisors had thought it necessary to regulate colonial trade. Thus, to create economic unity within the empire, he reenacted a law that excluded foreign vessels from trading with the English colonies. This sort of regulation is called a navigation act. *It was designed to make the colonies and parent country free from foreign interference and dependent on each other.*

MERCANTILISM. The theory behind the Navigation Acts was called *mercantilism,* taken from the word "merchant." This theory maintained that profitable trade was of vital national interest. *It was important for a nation to sell more goods to its rivals than it bought from them.* Thus, trade was carefully regulated by the government.

Soon it became clear that one way a nation could avoid buying from rivals was by buying needed goods from its colonies. If England could obtain timber for its ships from New England and tar from North Carolina, it would be less dependent on Scandinavia for these articles. To the extent that England could get its tobacco from Virginia and rice from South Carolina, it would be free of Spain.

RESTRICTIONS ON "ENUMERATED" GOODS. In addition to creating a *monopoly* on shipping, the Navigation Acts were to make the empire self-sufficient. The empire could sell its products abroad, but it would not have to buy from anyone. Further, rivals would have to pay for English goods in gold, and gold meant power.

A *monopoly* means that one person, company, or country has complete control over a product or service. It is free from competition.

Under Charles II, Parliament passed a law declaring that certain listed, or "enumerated," colonial products—tobacco,

Sidenote to History
The Salem Witch Hunt

In the spring of 1692, the town of Salem, Massachusetts, was caught up in a hysterical panic. It is said that the panic started when some teen-age girls had violent fits and accused Tituba, a West Indian slave, of casting an evil spell on them. As the girls' stories became more and more extreme, other people became caught in the hysteria. More and more cases of apparently bewitched people turned up, and more and more people were accused of being witches.

A special court was set up to try all the accused. No one dared protest the trials, for fear of also being called a witch.

The madness finally ended in September, when the governor of Massachusetts dissolved the court. Only a few months had passed—but within that short time several hundred people had been arrested, many had been imprisoned, and 19 had been hanged. Eventually, most of the members of the court admitted that they had condemned innocent people as witches. Twenty years later the Massachusetts legislature canceled the convictions and made payments to the victims' heirs.

fish, lumber, rice—could be shipped only to England. England became the depot for the empire, and English merchants were given a monopoly on the sale of the main colonial products. But colonists were also given a monopoly on England (that is, English merchants could not buy tobacco or other enumerated articles elsewhere).

BACON'S REBELLION. King Charles II then turned his attention to the political reorganization of the empire. An uprising in Virginia in 1676 may have triggered the

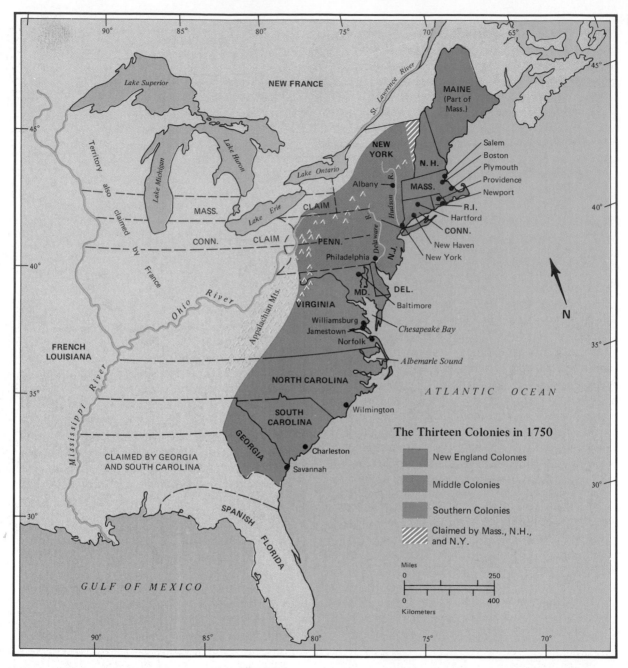

The Thirteen Colonies in 1750

New England Colonies

Middle Colonies

Southern Colonies

Claimed by Mass., N.H., and N.Y.

Miles
0   250
0   400
Kilometers

move. Virginia's governor, Sir William Berkeley, had little use for popular government. He did without the elected assembly whenever he could, relying for daily advice on a small circle of wealthy friends. When Indians began raiding the frontier, the governor refused to move against them. (The governor had a profitable fur-trading business with the Indians.)

Angry frontier people soon found a champion in a recent settler, Nathaniel Bacon. With a volunteer army, Bacon set out after the raiders. Finding none, he massacred a band of peaceful Indians.

THE AMERICAN COLONIES: A SUMMARY

Colony	Date	Leader	Type of Colony	Reasons Settled
New England Colonies Massachusetts Bay: Plymouth	1620	William Bradford	Corporate (1620–1691) Royal (1691–1776)	Pilgrims desired their own religious community.
Boston	1630	John Winthrop	Corporate (1630–1691) Royal (1691–1776)	Puritans desired their own religious community; trade.
Rhode Island: Providence	1636	Roger Williams	Corporate (1643–1776)	Williams founded his own settlement after being exiled from Massachusetts.
Connecticut: Hartford	1636	Thomas Hooker	Corporate (1643–1776)	Hooker and his congregation left Massachusetts, searching for more land for agriculture.
New Hampshire: Exeter	1638	John Wheelwright	Proprietary (1639–1679) Royal (1679–1776)	Expansion
Middle Colonies New York: (Originally New Netherland) New Amsterdam	1624	Peter Minuit (for Dutch) Duke of York (for English)	Proprietary (1663–1685) Royal (1685–1776)	Trade
New Jersey: scattered settlements	1664	John Lord Berkeley Sir George Carteret	Proprietary (1663–1702) Royal (1702–1776)	Trade and agriculture
Delaware: Wilmington (Taken by Dutch from Swedish in 1655; taken by English from Dutch in 1664)	1638	Peter Minuit (who left Dutch West India Company and went into Swedish service)	Proprietary (1682–1776)	Trade and agriculture
Pennsylvania: Philadelphia	1682	William Penn	Proprietary (1682–1776)	Religious refuge for Quakers; agriculture
Southern Colonies Virginia: Jamestown	1607	John Smith	Corporate (1607–1624) Royal (1624–1776)	Trade and agriculture
Maryland: St. Mary's	1633	George Calvert	Proprietary (1632–1776)	Religious refuge for Catholics; agriculture
North Carolina: Albemarle Colony	1653	Group of eight proprietors	Proprietary (1663–1744) Royal (1744–1776)	Agriculture
South Carolina: Charleston	1663	Group of eight proprietors	Proprietary (1663–1729) Royal (1729–1776)	Trade and agriculture
Georgia: Savannah	1732	James Oglethorpe	Proprietary (1732–1752) Royal (1752–1776)	Farming; place for the poor of England; buffer against Spanish Florida

To stop the growing discontent, the governor authorized the election of a new assembly. To his dismay, Bacon was elected and appeared in Jamestown, demanding a military commission that would allow him to fight more Indians. The frightened governor granted the commission, then declared Bacon a rebel. Bacon died a few weeks later of a fever. On Bacon's death, the governor hanged many of Bacon's followers.

Neither side found much glory in this first American rebellion. But the laws passed by the assembly during the uprising (known as Bacon's Laws) revealed a new spirit among Virginians. One act gave the vote to all adult men, regardless of wealth. Another listed the rights Virginians thought they possessed.

Bacon's death ended his laws, but the uprising did force the English to think more seriously about their empire. Their empire, after all, had come about without much planning. The English kings had given out grants and charters as such things suited their convenience. As a result, religious refugees and land-hungry adventurers had settled in America, and neither group was agreeable to royal supervision.

THE DOMINION OF NEW ENGLAND.
Massachusetts was the king's biggest problem. The Puritans had never taken kindly to imperial regulations or taxes. In addition, Massachusetts persisted in extending its boundary. By 1680, Bay Colony authorities were claiming both New Hampshire and Maine.

Charles's solution was to combine all the New England colonies into one unit. This would enable the colonies to pool their resources for defense. (King Philip's War had just been fought in 1675.) It would also give the government better control.

Charles began by persuading an English court to revoke the charter of Massachusetts Bay colony in 1684. But he died before he could put his scheme for a dominion of New England into effect.

THE DUKE OF YORK BECOMES KING. *James II (1685–1688), who succeeded his brother to the throne, carried out Charles's plan.* He even added his own colony of New York to the dominion. Then, he appointed Sir Edmund Andros governor.

Andros ruled Massachusetts with a heavy hand, abolishing the assembly and levying taxes without consent. In New York, Andros ruled through a military lieutenant, or lieutenant governor. The lieutenant governor ran the colony in close alliance with wealthy merchants. Under English rule or Dutch, the colony had never had the pleasure of a freely elected assembly. Both New York and Massachusetts were seething with discontent.

THE GLORIOUS REVOLUTION. The uprising started in England. James II had little use for Parliament and did without it whenever he could. In addition, he was a Roman Catholic—a fact that disturbed the Protestants. When James's wife gave birth to a son, the possibility of a new line of Catholic rulers brought matters to a head. A select committee made up of nobles and church leaders invited William of Orange—elected ruler of Holland and husband of James's daughter Mary—to come to England and rule with his wife. *On William's landing in November 1688, James fled to Paris, and the Glorious Revolution was complete.*

When news of the revolution reached America in early 1689, Massachusetts and New York both rose up, overthrowing both dominions' governors. In New York a radical leader, Jacob Leisler (LICE-lur), ushered in popular government. But he was too radical for the king, who hanged him in 1690. New York then became a scene of political unrest for several years.

Massachusetts, on the other hand, won a new charter in 1691, which combined the Bay and Plymouth colonies into the royal colony of Massachusetts. Under this charter the king would appoint the governor, but both council and assembly would be elected. The charter also took away the Puritans' political monopoly (land ownership, rather than religion, now qualified a person to vote and hold office). Even so, the Puritans were influential for more than a century.

THE IMPERIAL BALANCE. *By 1700, England and its colonies had reached an unspoken understanding.* The uprisings would be over for the moment. Still, each colony had achieved a certain degree of self-government. In most colonies, elected assemblies had won the right to levy taxes and spend money. And they well knew— from the experiences of Parliament in its battles with the king—that the power of the purse was the most important of all governmental powers.

In 1696 King William, who ruled until 1702, established the Board of Trade to oversee colonial affairs. It was to draft instructions for colonial governors and to advise the king on colonial laws (which the king still had the power either to approve or disapprove).

Thus, a balance was achieved. *The colonies had been reorganized by the king with the hope that the Navigation Acts would be enforced and the empire unified.* The colonists, on the other hand, retained a great deal of day-to-day power in decision-making. Their elected assemblies passed the laws that affected their daily lives.

The emerging conflict between imperial rule and colonial self-government was saved for a time in the future. It would come when the colonies had grown to maturity.

Section Review

1. Mapping: Look at the map on page 44. Which colonies had western claims in 1750? Which European nations claimed territory in America?
2. Identify or explain: Edmund Andros, William of Orange, Board of Trade, Nathaniel Bacon.
3. Briefly explain the theory of mercantilism.
4. What was the main purpose of the Navigation Acts? How was this purpose related to mercantilism?
5. How did Charles II attempt to solve his difficulties with the Massachusetts Bay Colony?

THE THREE TYPES OF COLONIES		
Corporate (Charter)	**Royal**	**Proprietary**
The king granted land to a company. The company governed this land. The charter companies were usually self-governed and the people retained their English rights.	The king and his ministers ruled the land.	The king granted land to a family, person, or group of people. These people (proprietors) had as much governing power as the king over their lands.
The governor was elected by those qualified to vote.	The king appointed a governor and a council of assistants. The governor had veto power.	The proprietor usually appointed a governor and a council of assistants.
Two-house legislature—the upper and lower houses were elected by the voters.	The governor and the council acted as upper house. The lower house was elected by voters.	The governor and the council were the upper house. The lower house was elected by voters.

Chapter 2 Review

Bird's-Eye View

During the early 1600's religious disputes troubled England. Persecuted minorities, including the Separatists and Puritans, escaped to the New World to establish communities of their own. First came Plymouth, then Massachusetts Bay, and then Connecticut and Rhode Island.

The English kings soon decided they had been too lax in issuing charters to companies that eventually ignored the crown's authority and its rules. Beginning with the Maryland charter of 1632, the kings experimented with a more personal sort of imperial relationship, the proprietary system. But even this proved inadequate, and by the end of the century, they were taking colonies back into royal hands.

Virginia was the first royal colony, and by the end of the century, kings were using it as a model for others. The dominion of New England was an attempt to join the New England colonies into a single royal colony. Although it failed, the king did unite the Bay and Plymouth colonies into the royal colony of Massachusetts. New York became a royal colony when its proprietor—James—became king. New Jersey followed soon thereafter. By the end of the century, the only proprietary colonies left were Pennsylvania, Delaware (also belonging to Penn), and Maryland.

With the establishment of the Board of Trade in 1696, the reorganization of the empire was complete. The Board advised the king on appointments and policies, drew up instructions for colonial governors, and reviewed colonial laws. After a period of turmoil and rebellion, the colonies accepted the system. A sort of unspoken compromise had been reached between imperial authority and colonial self-government. It was a delicate balance, but one that lasted for the next half-century.

Vocabulary

Define or identify each of the following:

Squanto	monopoly	colony
John Calvin	immigrant	Roger Williams
James Oglethorpe	Reformation	Quaker

Review Questions

1. Why did some religious groups want to purify the Church of England?
2. In what ways were the Mayflower Compact, the Cambridge Agreement, and the Fundamental Orders of Connecticut similar?
3. How is a royal colony different from a proprietary colony?
4. Contrast the settlement of New York with that of Georgia.
5. How did the Navigation Acts attempt to regulate trade between the colonies and England?
6. What was the importance of Bacon's Rebellion?

Reviewing Social Studies Skills

1. Using the map on page 44, answer the following questions:
   a. Which colonies made up the New England colonies? The middle colonies? The southern colonies?
   b. Estimate the distance from New York to Boston in both kilometers and miles.
   c. Name the major settlements in Virginia.
2. Using the chart on page 45, answer the following questions:
   a. Which colony was established first?
   b. Which colonies were settled for agricultural reasons?
   c. Which colony was originally founded by Swedes?
   d. In general, why were the New England colonies settled?
3. Using the chart on page 47, compare the king's power in each type of colony.

Reading for Meaning

1. Using a dictionary, define the following words: philanthropic, autonomy, covenant. Then, relate each of these words to a person or event in this chapter.
2. Using the evidence presented in this chapter, explain the importance of trade to the colonies.
3. One way to test reading comprehension is to take a heading in a book and use it to make a question. Then see if you can answer it. For example, "The Voyage of the *Mayflower*" is a heading in Section 2 and it can be changed into the question, "What was important about the voyage of the *Mayflower*?" Change each heading in Section 2 into a question. Answer the question you asked about "The Voyage of the *Mayflower*."

Bibliography

The Scarlet Letter and *The House of Seven Gables* are two novels by Nathaniel Hawthorne that give good examples of how Puritans lived in colonial America. They can be found in *Best-Known Works*, by Nathaniel Hawthorne (Books for Libraries).

Lois Lenski's *Puritan Adventure* (Lippincott) describes the life of a young woman in an early Puritan settlement.

Samuel E. Morrison's *The Story of the Old Colony of New Plymouth* (Knopf) is an exciting story, which makes you feel you are sharing in the adventures of the colonists.

Meet the Real Pilgrims: Everyday Life on Plimoth Plantation in 1627, by Robert H. Loeb, Jr. (Doubleday), contains photographs and line drawings of the pilgrims' homes, work, and surroundings.

Chapter 3

1700-1770

Shaping of America

What did America look like in the 1750's? To visitors it still seemed like mostly wilderness. The road from New York to Philadelphia was a dirt trail through a vast forest of oak and ash. The dark and forbidding woods were broken only by an occasional opening, where some pioneer or American Indian had labored half a lifetime to clear a patch for corn.

There were over one million Americans by then, but they were scattered along 4,800 kilometers (3,000 miles) of coastline. No settlement was more than 240 kilometers (150 miles) inland. Nearly everyone lived on farms or in small villages.

There were only a few cities, but these cities were very important and influential. They were the centers of trade and the sources for European goods. They published the newspapers and printed the books, they supported the doctors and the lawyers, and they were the centers of government.

By 1760 Philadelphia had about 20,000 inhabitants. It boasted of the first fire department, first library, and first public hospital in America. It had six newspapers—as many as London itself—and two were in German. Most of its streets and sidewalks were paved and lighted with lamps every night. A regular night watch patrolled the streets to keep order, to call out the time, and to give Philadelphians periodic weather reports.

Boston and New York each had about 16,000 people, although New York was rapidly surging ahead. By 1810 New York had surpassed Philadelphia to become the largest city in America. During the 1700's New York looked like the Dutch town it had once been. Most of the houses were brick, in the Dutch fashion, and many New Yorkers preserved Dutch customs. However, because New York was the headquarters of the British Army in America, it was also strongly influenced by England.

Although Boston had become an elegant city by the middle of the 18th century, traces of its Puritan origins were noticeable. To be licensed to run a tavern—the hub of a community's social life—a Bostonian had to be a person of outstanding moral character. And Bostonians looked on the theater with suspicion, thinking of it as a sinful pastime. In 1750 a riot nearly took place in Boston when people tried to put on a play.

By 1770, Charleston, South Carolina, and Newport, Rhode Island, each had about 10,000 inhabitants, and they were the smallest of the colonial cities. Yet, both had distinctive features. Charleston, for example, had America's oldest and best musical society and the most active theater on the continent. It also had the marks of a city strongly influenced by the French. This was because so many French Protestants had come to Charleston early in the 18th century. In Charleston wealthy young men and women were educated by French tutors and dancing masters. Newport, whose prosperity was based on the slave trade, claimed the best architect in America, Peter Harrison. His Redwood Library was among the most splendid buildings in the colonies.

Chapter Objectives

After you have finished reading this chapter, you should be able to:
1. Describe the status of Blacks in the colonies.
2. Explain how Benjamin Franklin was an example of the social mobility available in the colonies.
3. List the causes and results of the religious revival of the 1750's.

America in the 18th century was just beginning to develop. It was a society on the move, a society willing to consider ideas and contributions from many people. Although each free person had certain rights, that did not mean that people were equal in social standing. And the rights of some members of that society—women, Blacks, and Indians—were often not considered at all.

1. The Structure of American Society

THE EQUAL AND THE UNEQUAL. *Most Americans of the 1750's accepted the idea of social inequality.* They spoke of their society in terms of class. "The lower orders" was a common term for the poor. Although there was no *aristocracy* in America with inherited lands and titles, as in England, the wealthy Americans modeled themselves after the English upper class. They looked upon themselves as gentlemen or gentlewomen. Among this wealthy group of Americans—the gentry—it was better to inherit wealth than to make it oneself.

Aristocracy refers to the upper class or privileged class of a society.

Among this class, close attention was paid to dress, manners, polite speech, and education. The amount of lace people wore (regulated by law in Massachusetts), where they sat in church, and the places assigned to them at dinner parties were all marks of social status. "Esquire" was the closest thing Americans had to a title, and social rules carefully designated who could use it. George Washington often used this privilege whenever he signed his name.

INDENTURED SERVANTS. *At the other end of the social scale was the legally bound servant, either White or Black.* Temporary servitude was one of the means by which poor Europeans could come to America. In return for their ship passage, they would sign a contract, or indenture, agreeing to work without pay for a specified period of time, usually three to five years. There was no social stigma attached to this type of servitude. Moreover, indentured servants had specific legal rights that could be enforced in court.

When an indentured servant's time was up, he or she entered into American society with full legal rights. On becoming free, servants were entitled to freedom dues. These included a suit of clothes, farming tools, and in some colonies, 20 hectares (50 acres) of land. Nearly a third of the Europe-ans who came to America before the Revolution paid for their transport with temporary bondage.

BLACK SLAVES. Blacks, on the other hand, seldom won their freedom. The first Blacks came to America before the *Mayflower.* Pedro Alonso Niño, a pilot on one of Columbus's ships, was probably Black. Black *conquistadores* traveled through the

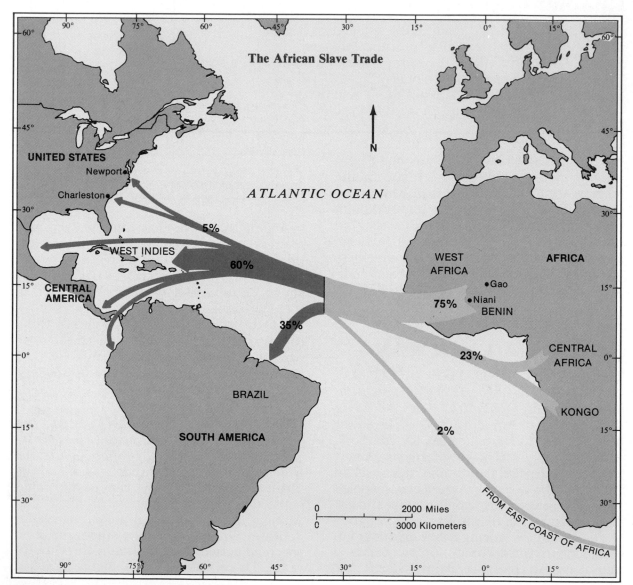

The African Slave Trade

Southwest with Coronado and Cabeza de Vaca and into Mexico with Cortés. Thirty Blacks worked with Balboa to clear the first road across the Isthmus of Panama in 1513.

In 1619 a Dutch warship sailed into Jamestown with a cargo of 20 Blacks it had taken from a Spanish slave ship. The Dutch evidently intended to profit from the sale of their captives. And the Virginians, ever short of labor, gladly bought them. The first Blacks were probably treated as indentured servants and then set free after a few years. Later arrivals were similarly treated. *It was not until about 1650 that Blacks were kept in permanent slavery.*

THE SLAVE TRADE. Throughout history many societies have accepted and even welcomed slavery. In fact, the institution is as old as civilization. Warring nations often enslaved their captives and sold them to the highest bidder. The Black kingdoms and empires of early West Africa—such as Mali, Ghana, and Songhai—practiced a form of slavery. (However, it was possible in most African societies for a slave to win his or her freedom.)

The slave trade was also an important feature of the early East African economy, with Black Africans and Arab traders cooperating in the capture and sale of other Africans. But the transatlantic slave trade was different. Its impact on African society was greater than that of the Arab or African trade. This was because the number of people sold into slavery was so much greater than before. *The demand for cheap labor in the Americas was limitless. The slave trade was geared to meet this demand.*

SLAVERY IN THE AMERICAS. Beginning in the late 1500's, the Spanish and Portuguese imported large numbers of Blacks to work on the sugar plantations in the West Indies and Brazil. The introduction of such slaves into Virginia and Maryland was only a question of time. The European colonists had first tried to enslave the Indians, but

they had disappeared too easily into the woods. Black Africans, uprooted from their own culture and thrown into a strange environment, whose geography and language were unfamiliar, were more easily controlled.

The first evidence of slavery in the Chesapeake colonies comes from the sales records of the 1640's. These records show that Blacks were nearly always sold for higher prices than White servants, apparently because they would be in permanent bondage. *The first legal recognition of slavery was a Virginia statute of 1662, which said that the status of a newborn child depended on the status of the mother.* If she was free, the child was free; if she was a slave, the child was a slave. Thus, slavery was inheritable.

Five years later the Virginia assembly decreed that conversion to Christianity did not

This engraving depicts the arrival in America in 1619 of the first 20 Africans. The Africans had been taken from a slave ship destined for the West Indies.

53

automatically free a slave. Such an action eliminated the remaining door to freedom for Blacks.

THE ROYAL AFRICAN COMPANY.
Until the last 30 years of the 17th century, there were only a few Blacks in Virginia. *The slave population only began to expand rapidly after 1670.* By that year the Royal African Company had been operating for seven years.

The company had been formed by Charles II in 1663. It had been given a monopoly on the slave trade, with some of the profits destined for the royal treasury. By 1698, when the monopoly expired, there were 6,000 Blacks in Virginia and twice as many in the other colonies. English mer-

chants dominated slave trading throughout the colonial period.

This ivory ornament is only a small example of the detailed carvings from the kingdom of Benin.

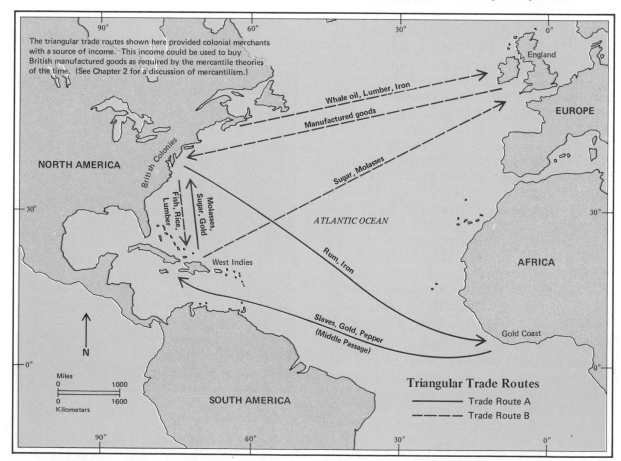

The triangular trade routes shown here provided colonial merchants with a source of income. This income could be used to buy British manufactured goods as required by the mercantile theories of the time. (See Chapter 2 for a discussion of mercantilism.)

Whale oil, Lumber, Iron

Manufactured goods

Sugar, Molasses

Fish, Rice, Lumber

Molasses, Sugar, Gold

ATLANTIC OCEAN

Rum, Iron

Slaves, Gold, Pepper (Middle Passage)

NORTH AMERICA

British Colonies

West Indies

SOUTH AMERICA

EUROPE

England

AFRICA

Gold Coast

N

Miles
0   1000
0   1600
Kilometers

Triangular Trade Routes

——————— Trade Route A

- - - - - - - Trade Route B

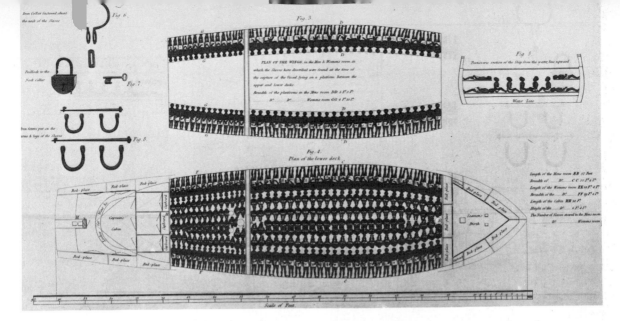

This sketch of a slave ship shows how hideously crowded conditions were on the infamous Middle Passage. Slave traders packed their ships with as many slaves as possible. Often, only one third of the slaves survived. Why do you think the slave traders packed so many slaves into one ship?

THE TRIANGULAR TRADE. *New England ship captains entered the slave trade after 1700, often combining the African trip with a stop in Europe or the West Indies.* The most common round-trip route for New Englanders was a sort of triangle. (See map, page 54.) A vessel would cross to Africa carrying colonial or European goods, which it would exchange for slaves. Then, it would embark on the terrible "middle passage" to either the West Indies or the mainland colonies. The slaves would be jammed between decks only 90 centimeters (3 feet) high and chained back to back in order to take up less space. The average space allotted to each one was 150 centimeters (5 feet) long and 40 centimeters (16 inches) wide. Many suffocated; others died of heat or disease. A slave ship that arrived with one half or two thirds of its cargo dead was not unusual.

The Blacks resisted as best they could. Many committed suicide; others jumped overboard whenever they were unchained. Occasionally a slave would get loose and free several comrades. More than 50 Black takeovers of slave ships were recorded. Hundreds more probably went unrecorded because either the vessels sank or they made their way back to Africa.

In the West Indies, English and New England slavers traded their human cargo for sugar and molasses (a by-product of sugar refining). These products were taken back to New England to be distilled into rum, a favorite colonial drink.

COLONIAL SLAVERY. *There were slaves in every colony, although in Pennsylvania and New Jersey, where Quakers frowned on the practice, there were fewer.* In New England slaves were used only as house servants by the wealthy. In New York, which had more slaves than any other northern colony, they were also used on farms. South Carolina had the harshest conditions and highest death rate. For example, rice, South Carolina's main staple crop, grew in marshes, along with mosquitoes, which carried deadly diseases, including

The Bethel African Methodist Episcopal Church was founded in Philadelphia in 1794 by Richard Allen, who became its first bishop. How do you think Blacks were received in the White churches of the city?

malaria and yellow fever. In the summer the South Carolina low country was so dangerous that the Whites left overseers in control of hundreds of slaves and fled to Charleston or to northern resorts.

THE SLAVE CODES. In 1705 the Virginia assembly *codified* its various regulations on slavery. Virginia's slave code became the pattern for most of the other southern colonies. *The purpose of the slave codes was to keep the Black population under control.* Slaves could not leave the plantation without written permission, and the Whites patrolled the roads, checking passes. Slaves could not gather in groups, except in authorized parties. And they could not own weapons or dogs.

To *codify* means to turn a group of laws on one subject, such as slavery, into a single system.

The slave codes also regulated the activities of free Blacks, who were targets of prejudice and objects of suspicion. All colonies permitted Whites to free their slaves if they wished. But in the South the planter had to get legislative permission. South Carolina required all freed Blacks to leave the colony. All colonies, North and South, prohibited marriage between Blacks and Whites.

BLACK REVOLT. *The slave codes were an expression of fear.* They were an admission that slavery was, if not wrong, at least dangerous. Although organized rebellions were not common in colonial America, there were at least enough to keep the White population tense. The first came as early as the 1640's in Virginia, when slaves banded together with White servants in an unsuccessful uprising. The most serious uprising took place in South Carolina in 1739. A band of nearly 100 slaves killed the Whites in their vicinity and marched off to Florida, only to be caught and slaughtered.

Running away was a more common form of resistance. However, it was seldom successful because there was no place to which slaves could flee.

DAWN OF ANTISLAVERY. *In colonial America slavery was almost totally accepted.* Before 1750 there was very little public criticism of it. In 1700 Samuel Sewall, a legislator and judge in Massachusetts Bay, published a small volume called *The Selling of Joseph.* The book spoke out against slavery. But it was not widely circulated within the colonies.

Quakers and Pietists were the first to insist publicly that bondage was inconsistent with religion—that one could not be both a slave owner and a good Christian. Moravians in Bethlehem, Pennsylvania, prohibited slavery in their community in the 1690's. A few years later Quaker leaders began discouraging members of their church from holding slaves and, eventually, prohibited it altogether. A Quaker, John Woolman, published an antislavery pamphlet in 1762. And a disciple of Woolman's, Anthony Benezet, founded the first society for the abolition of slavery in Philadelphia in 1775.

THE FREE BLACKS OF THE COLONIES. *Every colony had a free Black population.* It consisted mostly of slaves who had been set free and of the descendants of the first Black indentured servants. Also counted among the free Black population were the children of White mothers and Black fathers. In the colonies a child of a White mother was considered free, no matter what the background of the father.

RESTRICTIONS ON FREE BLACKS. *Although free Blacks were much better off then Black slaves, their lives were filled with many restrictions.* Blacks were often barred from testifying in court against Whites. But anyone could testify against a Black, whether the Black was slave or free. Free Blacks were generally taxed heavily and were often prohibited from owning real estate. Even when Blacks owned property—a qualification for voting—they were usually barred from the polls. In some colonies Blacks could not hold public office.

Blacks were routinely seated in a separate section of church. In many northern cities they were buried in separate parts of the graveyard. Even the Quakers, known for their antislavery position, marked off distinct burial plots for Blacks. Occasionally, one or two Black children attended school with White children. But most Blacks had little or no formal education.

Blacks were also pressured indirectly to remain in second-class social positions. They were often criticized for dressing too stylishly and for establishing social clubs that seemed to imitate various White organizations. In 1721 a Boston newspaper carried an article about a Black wedding at which an Englishman gave away the bride. The article suggested that the wedding had been arranged just to ridicule the government. In 1745 the colony of Massachusetts prohibited Blacks from taking part in a government lottery—perhaps to make sure that no Black would win.

Most free Blacks were forced to live in their own neighborhoods, far from the White sections of a town or city. Although White people would associate with Blacks in some public places, they rarely, if ever, invited Black people to visit their homes.

CONTRIBUTIONS OF COLONIAL BLACKS. *Despite these restrictions free Black men and women contributed significantly to the life of the colonies.* Benjamin Banneker—an astronomer, mathematician,

Benjamin Banneker, a free Black citizen of Baltimore, was a mathematician, astronomer, and surveyor. Pictured here is the title page of his almanac, widely sold in the 1790's.

surveyor, and mechanical genius— published an almanac that was almost as widely known as Benjamin Franklin's. Phillis Wheatley, a young Black woman educated by the people for whom she worked as a housemaid, became a well-known colonial poet. And Paul Cuffe, a young Black Quaker, used much of the wealth he had amassed from shipbuilding to educate Blacks less fortunate than he.

Section Review

1. **Mapping: a)** Using the map on page xiv, describe the geographic setting of one of the following cities: Philadelphia, Boston, New York, Charleston. **b)** Look at the map on page 54. How does the location of the West Indies give it particular advantages as a juncture in the triangular trade routes?
2. Identify or explain: indentured servants, slave codes, *The Selling of Joseph,* John Woolman, Benjamin Banneker.
3. Compare and contrast slavery and indentured servitude in the colonies. Why did the colonists prefer Black slaves to either Indian slaves or White servants?
4. Explain one way Black slaves tried to escape bondage.

2. A People on the Move

VALUES FOR SELF-MADE SOCIETY. Benjamin Franklin leaned over the side and watched his ship cut through the waters of the Gulf Stream. The year was 1757, and Franklin was journeying to England as the colonial agent for Pennsylvania. The Penn family had refused to allow their proprietary lands to be taxed, and Franklin had been appointed to express the grievances of the colony. Regular service between New York and England had been in-

troduced two years before. With a favorable wind, Franklin could look forward to a voyage of only four weeks.

Never one to be idle for long, Franklin soon turned away from the water and sat down to write a preface to a new edition of his yearly almanac. Perhaps bored by life on the ship, Franklin decided to include in the preface the best of his sayings over a lifetime of writing. His Boston publisher printed the preface as a pamphlet, called *Father Abraham's Speech.*

A man of many talents, Benjamin Franklin founded the Union Fire Company in 1736. He is shown here wearing his warden's hat.

58

This view of lower Manhattan was painted by Francis Guy in about 1800. The intersection is the corner of Wall and Water streets, and the building at left housed the first stock exchange. Compare this scene with an earlier scene of New York harbor on page 40.

In this essay Franklin captured the attitudes of a nation, composed of busy shopkeepers, artisans, and farmers. In short and clever sayings ("'Tis hard for an empty bag to stand upright," "Lost time is never found again"), he summarized the values and ethics of a people who would not only alter the spelling of "busyness" to "business," but who would give the word a new meaning. ***To the traditional virtues—faith, hope, and charity—Americans had added thrift, hard work, and perseverance.***

As an ethical system, America's principles were unbeatable. Success, even wealth, was the reward for being good. It had a set of values that seemed natural for a self-made society, for a people on the way up.

A SELF-MADE CITIZEN. Benjamin Franklin had already walked the trail of the self-made citizen. Climbing from the lower orders of society, he had made his own way to wealth and fame. Born in Boston in 1705, he was apprenticed to his older brother at the age of 14 to learn the art of printing. Finding his brother unnecessarily severe, he ran off, stowing away on a ship bound for Philadelphia. There he arrived with two pennies in his pocket, which he spent on a loaf of bread. It was the end of one life and the beginning of another.

He got a job in a printing shop and soon opened one of his own. In 1730 he founded a newspaper, the *Pennsylvania Gazette,* to keep his press busy. Three years later he

59

started an almanac, a yearly record of the phases of the moon, ocean tides, holidays, and other happenings and facts useful to a busy people. In addition to containing scientific and commercial information, his almanac was filled with his own wisdom. His easily remembered sayings ("A penny saved is a penny earned") were quoted throughout the colonies.

A COLONIAL LEADER.

Before long, Franklin owned a chain of printing shops from Boston to Charleston, each managed by a printer he had trained. Recognizing his position, the British government made Franklin Postmaster General of all the American colonies in 1750. He quickly put some order into the system, persuaded colonies to improve their roads, and established regular stagecoach routes between Boston, New York, and Philadelphia.

With such wealth and fame came an interest in politics. Again, Franklin rose quickly to the top, making himself leader of the anti-Penn party. It was in this role that he journeyed to England in 1757, the first of many trips across the Atlantic. He was to become, in time, the colonies' foremost diplomat.

SOCIAL MOBILITY.

Benjamin Franklin was not the average American. But in less dramatic ways, his success story was repeated over and over. American society was made up of distinct classes, or orders, just as European society was. But in America social mobility—movement from one class to another—was relatively easy. There were at least no legal barriers. *Most people were free to rise in the world as fast and as far as their abilities allowed.*

AMERICAN WOMEN IN THE 18TH CENTURY.

Even American women — limited as they were by laws and denied rights, such as voting—benefited from the

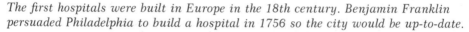

The first hospitals were built in Europe in the 18th century. Benjamin Franklin persuaded Philadelphia to build a hospital in 1756 so the city would be up-to-date.

Benson Lossing sketched historical scenes in the early 1800's. This sketch shows women packing medicines.

openness of American society. The flexibility of a society still being formed led to the lifting of many restrictions on women's work and made new opportunities available. Unlike British women, American women could own land in many areas. In early New England women who headed families were given their share of land for planting.

In 17th- and 18th-century America, most women's work was done in the home. But since every home was in reality a small factory, housework was far more demanding and varied than it is today. It was a form of highly skilled labor, since nearly everything a family needed had to be manufactured in the home. One of the most skilled and time-consuming activities was the manufacturing of cloth for clothing, bed coverings, sacks, and other household needs. Women were the major textile manufacturers of the colonies.

Because the shops of craftspeople and tradespeople occupied the same building as a family's living quarters, a woman often took part in her husband's trade or craft. And women often practiced such trades or crafts independently if they were widowed.

Various jobs were open to women outside the home as well. One of the oldest occupations was the keeping of taverns. Women raised garden seeds for sale; were shrewd traders; ran schools, mills, and distilleries; worked in sawmills, paper mills, and **gristmills;** and made and sold preserves, wines, and lace.

A **gristmill** is a mill used for grinding grain.

In the 18th century there were many women printers. Several colonial newspapers were published by women who also printed and published books and pamphlets. Some women were professional healers. Many others worked as midwives. It was taken for granted in colonial America that a woman knew how to prepare a wide range of medicines and how to tend to her family's illnesses.

In New England the kitchen was the hub of family life. Cooking was done over the open fire in large pots and kettles. What crafts were involved in making the furnishings shown here?

JEWS IN THE COLONIAL WORLD.

American society was more open and more mobile than European society because it was newer. It was also a nation of immigrants, of people bent on making a new life in a new world. On the eve of the American Revolution, there were more than 2,000 Jews among these immigrants. New York, Newport, Charleston, Philadelphia, and Savannah had the largest Jewish communities in the colonies. Jews went to these cities because their policies toward Jews were the most liberal.

Among these cities, Charleston and Newport were the most tolerant; New York the least tolerant. Roger Williams specifically invited Jews to settle in Rhode Island. There, Newport became the second largest Jewish community in America. Jews came there from Holland, Portugal, Spain, and Poland. One Jewish person, Jacob Rivera, a member of a leading family in Newport, invented a lamp that burned whale oil. This new invention created vast new markets for New England's whaling industry.

Charleston, South Carolina, equaled Newport's spirit of toleration. There, in 1703, Jews, for the first time in the western world, voted in a general election. Furthermore, they were allowed to enter any profession they wanted—a freedom denied both Jews and non-Jews in other colonies.

Although the Dutch West India Company that founded New Amsterdam—later to become New York—had several Jews among its officers, New Amsterdam was not as tolerant of Jews as Charleston, Newport, or Philadelphia. During Peter Stuyvesant's governorship, Jews were forced to live apart from other citizens, in an area known as Jews' Alley. They were not permitted to perform military service along with Christians, but were made to pay a tax instead. When the British took control of New Amsterdam in 1664, the condition of the city's Jewish inhabitants improved. By the mid-18th century, they had been permitted to build a synagogue (a house of worship for Jews) and had been given more freedom to worship as they pleased.

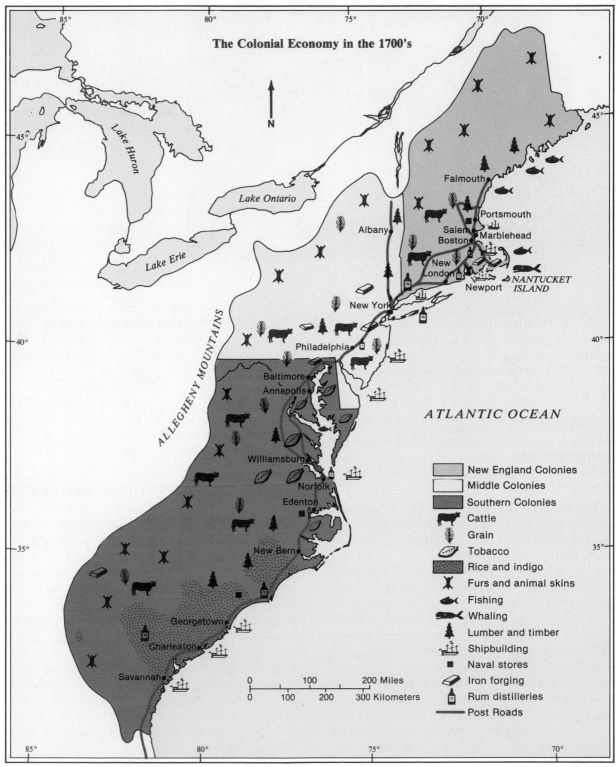

The Colonial Economy in the 1700's

N

Lake Huron

Lake Ontario

Lake Erie

Falmouth

Portsmouth

Albany

Salem
Boston Marblehead

New London

Newport NANTUCKET ISLAND

New York

ALLEGHENY MOUNTAINS

Philadelphia

Baltimore
Annapolis

ATLANTIC OCEAN

Williamsburg

Norfolk

Edenton

New Bern

Georgetown

Charleston

Savannah

	New England Colonies
	Middle Colonies
	Southern Colonies
Cattle
Grain
Tobacco
Rice and indigo
Furs and animal skins
Fishing
Whaling
Lumber and timber
Shipbuilding
Naval stores
Iron forging
Rum distilleries
Post Roads

0   100   200 Miles
0   100   200   300 Kilometers

Colonial architecture owed much to English models and handbooks. But the design of Peter Harrison's Redwood Library reveals a simplicity and restraint characteristic of early New England. The library, built of New England wood in 1750, is still standing in Newport, Rhode Island.

Puritan Massachusetts, **Anglican** Virginia, and Roman Catholic Maryland were so inhospitable to Jews that no Jewish communities of any size developed there. At Harvard University, Judah Monis, a Boston Jew, was awarded an honorary degree in 1720. But before he could teach at the university, he had to convert to Christianity.

Anglican refers either to the Church of England or to its members in other countries.

COLONIAL LAWYERS. *If American society was more open and fluid then European society, it was also more concerned with the practical side of life.* Both the openness and the practicality in colonial life were especially evident in the legal and medical professions.

In Britain the legal profession was elaborately organized. In America, however, the system was less established. The profession was open to anyone who could attract clients and sway juries. To be allowed to plead in court, the aspiring colonial lawyer merely studied a few law books. Those who desired more formal training could study in the office of a practicing attorney. If a course was

desired, the College of William and Mary in Virginia offered one in legal studies. Yet, despite that this course shaped some of the best legal minds of the Revolutionary generation, most lawyers were self-trained.

Law was also the shortest road to political power. Nearly every aspiring young politician began by studying the law. The Revolution, which resulted in the creation of state and national governments, presented many political opportunities to lawmakers.

PRACTICAL MEDICINE. The medical profession was almost as open to people and new ideas as the legal profession. Some American doctors were trained in Britain, but most learned their techniques and medicines in on-the-job training. As a result, *American doctors were inclined to be more practical in treating illness than European doctors.* For example, the European cure for a fever was to remove some blood. Although American doctors had no more knowledge of the causes of disease than Europeans did, some of their remedies—such as fresh air, sunshine, and bed rest—were more sensible than the standard European medical treatment. And at least such treatment did not harm the patients.

Sidenote to History

Crafts in Colonial America

The artisan was an important member of the community in colonial times. At first many crafts, such as baking and weaving, were carried on in each colonist's home. As the population grew, professional artisans established businesses in towns and villages. Setting up shop required little more than tools, materials, and a place to work. Often the place to work was the ground floor of the artisan's house. Usually, the artisan did the work by hand, perhaps with the help of family members and one or two apprentices.

In larger towns the artisan was a shopkeeper as well as a skilled worker. A sign over the door of the shop picturing the product made, along with a good reputation, were often the only advertisements needed. The artisans in a typical colonial town included cabinetmakers, weavers, dyers, bricklayers, shoemakers, and bakers. Other skilled workers included coopers, hatters, and shipbuilders.

The cooper was one of the most important workers in the southern colonies. Before such crops as wheat, flour, rice, and tobacco could leave the plantation, they had to be packed into casks, barrels, and boxes. And every household had to keep kegs for storing butter, salted fish, and meat. The manufacturing of these containers (coopering) required many skilled people. On the plantation most of the artisans were Black slaves.

Coopering involved several steps. Long pieces of wood were split into thin slats, called staves. These were trimmed to the proper width and shape and were stood upright within a circular frame. Metal hoops were placed around the ends of the staves to hold them tightly together. The wood was steamed to make it bend and take shape. Then the lids and bottoms were put into place.

Another important craft, especially in New York, was hatmaking. The hatter was skilled in turning fur into felt and in shaping the felt into top hats, called beaver hats. Creating a beaver hat took a great deal of work. First, a felt foundation was made by compacting small particles of rabbit fur onto pieces of wet linen cloth. Next came the dipping, drying, shrinking, and stiffening of the foundation, followed by the addition of beaver fur on the outside. Finally, the hat was blocked, dyed, and finished.

Hats were worn by both the rich and the poor, whether they were working, playing, walking, or riding. Hatmaking became such a successful trade in the colonies that England passed a law prohibiting the exporting of hats from the colonies.

Perhaps the most demanding of all the crafts was that of the New England shipbuilder. Building a ship took a year, and many artisans were involved. Among them were shipwrights, carvers, cabinetmakers, coopers, and blacksmiths. Before the vessel could be launched, the skills of the sailmaker and rigger were needed. Large canvas sheets were cut, stitched, and fitted. When they were ready, the sails were rigged, or attached to the mast.

New ships were always needed to carry on the growing trade between the colonies and the countries overseas. So shipbuilding and trade became a major part of the colonial economy. As a matter of fact, more than half the ships that plied the waters between the colonies and England were made in America.

In medicine, as in law, there were many people who were self-taught. In George Washington's library, side by side with law books, were practical handbooks on household medicine. Isolated planters had to be able to treat themselves, their families, and even their animals. Americans had to be handy and able to fend for themselves. Each of them had to be, in their own phrase, a "jack-of-all-trades."

THE JACK-OF-ALL-TRADES. Just as Benjamin Franklin was the model of the self-made American, he was also the model jack-of-all-trades. Diplomat, politician, business person, and printer—Franklin was also the colonies' leading scientist. He approached science with the same practicality as American doctors approached medicine.

Franklin knew little about European theories on electricity. But after hearing about European experiments, he purchased equipment that could produce sparks. Noticing that the sparks resembled lightning, he devised a test to determine if lightning was indeed electricity. He flew a kite in a thunderstorm. When a spark jumped off a key tied to the end of the kite string, he had his proof.

This experiment, followed by his invention of the lightning rod, won Franklin world fame. *Such resourcefulness reflected the society in which he lived, a society of people constantly on the move, a society always becoming, never finished.*

Section Review

1. Identify or explain: *Father Abraham's Speech,* ethics, almanac, Anglican.
2. What colonial values were expressed in Franklin's sayings?
3. What is social mobility? Why was it easier in the American colonies than in Europe?
4. Describe one restriction placed on Jews in the less tolerant colonies.

3. Rationalism and Revivalism

THE NEWTONIAN UNIVERSE. *People of the 18th century considered themselves enlightened and their times as an age of reason.* They felt that they understood the secrets of the universe, that humans had at last conquered superstition and ignorance. In France scientists began writing huge encyclopedias, summarizing human knowledge. They went on the assumption that there was nothing more to learn.

The major reason for this confident attitude was the discoveries of the English physicist, Isaac Newton. After conducting numerous experiments, Newton concluded that the entire universe was governed by scientific laws. These laws could be discovered by ordinary people and tested in various experiments.

Newton's conclusions started a revolution in human thought. Gone, suddenly, was the world of the Middle Ages, full of mysteries, wonders, and miracles. In its place was Newton's universe, a simple, uniform world, governed by law and capable of being understood by the human mind.

After Newton conducted his experiments, reason was seen as the key to the universe. Yet, the worship of reason, or rationalism, went far beyond the realm of physics. The political philosopher John Locke tried to arrive at the principles of government in the same way that Newton had arrived at laws of physics.

THE SOCIAL CONTRACT. Locke's *Treatises on Civil Government* were a defense of the English Revolution of 1688 against James II (see Chapter 2). Locke's argument went like this. Before there was government, people lived in some sort of primitive condition, or state of nature. *In this condition everyone enjoyed certain* *basic rights, particularly the rights to life, liberty, and ownership of property.* But as society became more complex, people felt the need to formalize law and order, or to create a government. Thus, they entered into a social contract, an agreement with a ruler that gives the ruler certain powers to govern. However, even under the contract, the people kept the basic rights they had earlier possessed. If the ruler violated those rights (by imprisoning someone without a court trial, for instance), the contract was broken and the people had the right to overthrow the ruler.

AMERICANS APPLY LOCKE'S IDEAS.
In John Locke's mind the contract was between the English ruler and the English aristocracy. But in the hands of Americans, the idea was easily broadened. Americans thought that they had the same rights as the English people, including the right to rebel. *Thus, when Thomas Jefferson wrote the Declaration of Independence, he incorporated Locke's point of view.* "We hold these truths to be self-evident," he wrote.

He then proceeded in Lockean fashion to state the rights of Americans (life, liberty, and the pursuit of happiness) and to show how the king had violated those rights. Governments, Jefferson concluded, must be formed to protect rights, not to violate them. And the only way governments can do this is by founding themselves on "the consent of the governed."

RELIGIOUS RATIONALISM.
Newtonian rationalism also affected 18th-century religion. If the universe was governed by laws of nature, people reasoned, those laws must have existed since the beginning of time. God, then, must have intended for the universe to be an orderly, rational place, in which certain principles worked always and everywhere.

This sort of religious thinking was called deism. Deists believed in God, but they thought of God only as the divine genius who had created the universe. God was

Electricity was used as a parlor game in the 18th century. These people were giving themselves electric shocks for fun! How do you think they were conducting the electricity?

viewed as a sort of watchmaker, one who had put the watch together, wound it up, set it to ticking, and then left it to work on its own.

Deism was not a religion or a church. It was a way of looking at the world. As such it was quite fashionable among the upper classes and the educated in both Europe and America. Thomas Jefferson was a deist; so were John Adams and Benjamin Franklin. It was part of the confident, rationalist attitude of the age.

A RELIGIOUS REVIVAL. Not surprisingly, deism offered little comfort to the common people, who wanted a less cold,

Sidenote to History

Tools for Frontier Living

The Conestoga wagon, the log cabin, and the rifle were three of the most important inventions of the colonial period. The wagon provided transportation, the log cabin gave shelter, and the rifle supplied food and protection. Without them, pioneer families would have found it difficult to have settled and survived in the wilderness.

The sturdy Conestoga wagon was named for the Pennsylvania town where it was invented by German settlers in the mid-1700's. Its broad-rimmed wheels kept the heavy wagon from sinking into the mud. Such wheels were removable—instantly transforming the wagon into a boat when rivers had to be crossed. Known as camels of the prairies, these wagons carried most of the westward-bound Americans and freight between the years 1770 and 1850. After 1850 the wagons were gradually replaced by the faster railroads.

The log cabin originated in Sweden—a heavily forested, northern land—and was first built in America by Swedish colonists. The log cabin was an ideal home for a pioneer family because it could be built with a minimum of tools and with the abundant materials of the forest—the trees.

After the settlers had cut their logs, they made notches in the ends. In this way the logs could be fitted together to form four cabin walls. Cracks between the logs were stuffed with moss, clay, or mud, and the roof was usually covered with bark or straw. Later, roofs often had wooden shingles. Window openings were covered with animal skins or greased paper; doors were made from split logs and hung on leather hinges. Most cabins had one story, perhaps with a loft for sleeping or storage. A fireplace and a chimney at one end of the cabin provided both light and heat and was used for cooking.

To provide food and protection, the frontier family had a third great tool for pioneer living: the rifle. This weapon was invented by Pennsylvania Germans. It took its name from the spiral grooves, or rifling, that were cut onto the inside of the barrel. The grooves gave a spin to the bullet, making it more accurate and enabling it to travel a greater distance. The length of the weapon, which was 210 centimeters (7 feet), added to this accuracy. Thus, the rifle was ideal for hunting, since it also used a small bullet. The user did not have to carry heavy lead shot on long walks through the forest. Such increased speed in loading and accuracy were also life-saving factors when the rifle was needed for defense.

more helpful religion. ***Thus, in the middle of the 18th century, a vast religious revival swept across both Britain and America.*** In Britain it was called the Methodist movement; in America, the Great Awakening.

THE GREAT AWAKENING. The revival sprang up in several places at about the same time. One focal point was Northampton, Massachusetts, where Jonathan Edwards, pastor of the Congregational Church, managed to recover some of the religious fervor of the first Puritans. ***By emphasizing emotion and personal commitment, Edwards sought converts, hoping that ultimately his entire town would become "Visible Saints."*** For a time in the late 1730's, converts multiplied to the point that his vision nearly came true.

In the Middle Colonies, Presbyterian minister William Tennent managed a "log college" for the training of ministers. "Graduates" of Tennent's school carried the torch of evangelism through Pennsylvania and New Jersey in the 1730's. Other evangelists blazed through Virginia and the Carolinas.

All of these preachers had a common enemy—indifference. The enthusiasm that had driven an Anne Hutchinson or a Roger Williams had withered with time. In its place was a chill formality. Congregations went through the motions of religious ritual without deep concern for salvation and the hereafter. The evangelists of the Great Awakening wanted to revive interest, to make people feel religion body and soul.

A NEW STYLE OF PREACHING. ***No one accomplished this religious aim better than George Whitefield (WIT-field), who landed in America in 1739.*** Whitefield was the chief disciple of John Wesley, the preacher who had sought to bring the English church closer to the common people. Whitefield toured the American continent from Georgia to New England. A brilliant orator, Whitefield was a new type of preacher. He relied on emotion. He demanded enthusiasm. He left behind him a new spirituality and a rise in church attendance.

THE FRUITS OF THE AWAKENING. ***The Awakening died out almost as swiftly as it had come.*** But currents of religious enthusiasm rippled American society periodically for the rest of the century. Those who benefited most from the crusade were the ***evangelical churches***—the Methodist and the Baptist. They sent preachers on horseback into the frontier settlements of the interior to spread the new spirituality.

The ***evangelical churches*** were those that stressed salvation through faith in Christ, personal conversion, and knowledge of the Holy Scriptures. Preaching was more important than ritual in evangelical religion.

The social and intellectual stir caused by the Awakening was further evidence of the openness of American society in the 1750's. Americans were a people quickly acquiring the ability to stand alone. With that maturity would come a desire for political independence.

Section Review

1. Identify or explain: Isaac Newton, John Locke, deism, the Great Awakening, George Whitefield, Jonathan Edwards.
2. What did Locke mean by a state of nature?
3. What is a social contract? How does a social contract end the state of nature?
4. Describe the Great Awakening. How, in your opinion, did the Great Awakening differ from the type of religious thinking called deism?

Chapter 3 Review

Bird's-Eye View

Eighteenth-century Americans assumed that people were born into certain stations in life. But they did not insist that people stay there. There were orders in society—high, middle, and low—but people could move from one to another. So vast was the American landscape, so rich were the resources, that there was opportunity for all. By the time of the Revolution, it was rapidly becoming a society, not of aristocrats and peasants, but of self-made men and women.

Black slaves were not permitted to enter American society, however. Although White servants would be free at the end of their terms of service, Blacks were forced to remain in permanent bondage. Blacks resisted slavery from time to time, and various religious groups protested it. But no solution to this problem was found in the colonial era.

In the decades before the American Revolution, this relatively open society experienced two intellectual currents. An intellectual minority of people believed that the universe had been created by a reasonable God and that it worked by rational laws. They thought that, because these laws were rational and could be grasped by the human mind, there was no limit to human knowledge.

The majority of Americans, however, held traditional beliefs. In the 1730's they experienced a religious renewal, known as the Great Awakening. They flocked to churches and revival meetings and sought intense religious experiences.

Vocabulary

Define or identify each of the following:

aristocracy	John Locke	gristmills
codify	Jonathan Edwards	Benjamin Banneker
slavery	Benjamin Franklin	indentured servant

Review Questions

1. What factors contributed to the development of slave trade in the colonies?
2. What restrictions were placed on free Blacks in the colonies?
3. How did women benefit from the openness of American society in the 18th century?
4. What were Benjamin Franklin's contributions to colonial America?
5. How were John Locke's ideas applied in the colonies?
6. What was the Great Awakening?

Reviewing Social Studies Skills

1. Using the map on page 54, answer the following questions:
   a. How did these trade routes reflect British economic policy?
   b. Why were the West Indies important to colonial America?
   c. What continents are shown on the map?
   d. What elements are in the map key?
2. Using the information presented in this chapter, prepare a chart, showing the similarities and differences between the New England, the southern, and the middle colonies.

3. Using the information in this chapter, make a time line, showing the history of Blacks in America between 1700 and 1790.

Reading for Meaning

1. In your own words explain each of the following sayings: "'Tis hard for an empty bag to stand upright;" "Lost time is never found again;" "A penny saved is a penny earned." How do these sayings reflect the colonial attitude toward life?
2. Facts and interpretations are two important parts of the writing of history. The dictionary defines a fact as something that has actually happened or been done; an interpretation is the explanation of what something means. Decide whether each of the following statements for this chapter is a fact or an interpretation:
   a. "Such resourcefulness reflected the society in which he [Franklin] lived, a society of people constantly on the move, a society always becoming, never finished."
   b. "In early New England women who headed families were given their share of land for planting."
   Explain your answers.
3. In this book, Bird's-Eye View is a summary of the chapter. A summary often leaves out evidence and facts. Select the first sentence of any paragraph in the summary. Then, using information in this chapter, write down three facts that provide evidence to support the sentence you selected.

Bibliography

William Byrd II, a Virginia planter, wrote *History of the Dividing Line* (Dover), which tells of a surveying trip he took in 1728. The book gives a good account of the life of a southern aristocrat.

Gerald W. Johnson's *America Is Born* (Morrow) is a general survey of early American history.

In John Neihardt's *Black Elk Speaks* (Pocket Books, Inc.), an American Indian vividly describes his memories of the old ways of his people.

Phillis Wheatley's poetry describes how it felt to be a slave in colonial times. Some of these poems can be found in her *Memories and Poems* (Black Heritage Library Collection).

Representative Americans: The Colonists, by Norman K. Risjord (Heath), provides biographical sketches of some of the most interesting people of this period.

Benjamin Banneker, by Silvio A. Bedini (Scribner), is a biography of the famous Black American.

Chapter 4

1608-1775

Empire and Revolution

The buckskin-clad figure slipped silently out of the forest and approached the young officer. The officer's uniform indicated the rank of major, though he could not have been more than 21 or 22. The officer's name was George Washington. He was a member of the Virginia militia. The man in buckskin was Washington's friend and wilderness guide, Christopher Gist. It was May 1754, and Gist had important information.

The French had beaten George Washington to the forks of the Ohio, the strategic river junction in western Pennsylvania. The French had already built a log fort there, which they had named Duquesne (doo-KAYNE), after the governor of French Canada. To make conditions worse, the French already knew that the Virginians had arrived. Even now a patrol was moving up the river toward them. What to do? A short distance to the south, Washington had built a log fort, aptly named Necessity. A more cautious officer might have returned there until reinforcements and further orders arrived. Washington, however, decided to attack.

His company, which numbered about 200, rode out of camp and down the river trail. At a rocky ravine they left the trail and slipped into the woods. When the unsuspecting French appeared, a storm of lead shot from the woods, and smoke covered the trail. The French detachment fled for the fort, leaving behind a dozen wounded and dying, including the young lieutenant who had led them.

It was the first shot in a new war. For 50 years France and Great Britain had engaged in periodic conflict. This particular contest was to be the climax. The prize would be the continent of North America.

Chapter Objectives

After you have finished reading this chapter, you should be able to:
1. Compare the French colonization of New France with the English colonization of New England.
2. Explain how the wars for an empire secured Britain's position as the major power in North America.
3. Recognize which events caused conflicts between the colonies and Britain between 1763 and 1770.
4. List the events that led to the outbreak of fighting at Concord.

How did the young Washington come to be in such a position? Did he have the authority to start a war? How could a small ambush in the Pennsylvania woods start a conflict that would involve all of Europe and half the world? To answer these questions, it is important to go back 150 years to the founding of the French Empire in America and to the beginning of imperial rivalry.

1. New France: A Colony Built on Fur

EARLY EXPLORATIONS. France became interested in the New World at about the same time that England did. ***Through the explorations of Jacques Cartier (kahr-TYAY) (1534–1543), France established its claim to the northern part of the continent, from New England to the Gulf of St. Lawrence.*** (See map, page 75.) There Cartier made friends with the Algonkian-speaking tribes and began trading with them.

In 1608, a year after the English had founded Jamestown, Samuel de Champlain sailed up the St. Lawrence River. His purpose in sailing out was to establish a fort at the point the American Indians called *kebec*, which meant a narrowing of the waters. Champlain, who had heard the Algonkian word, named his settlement Quebec.

The French were after furs, especially the rich brown pelts of beaver. The Indians, who were hunters and farmers, were happy to acquire European guns and goods in exchange. Nevertheless, Indian trade with the Europeans began undermining the Indian economy, and soon the various tribes began competing for the right to trade with the Europeans.

In the spring Champlain contacted the Indians of the river valley, the Algonkian-speaking Huron. To win their friendship, Champlain agreed to accompany them on

This engraving of a stockade in New France (1671) has numbers to identify the buildings. The windmill is number 1; number 3 is the church. Can you guess what some of the other numbered items are?

an expedition against their age-old enemies to the south—the Mohawk, an ***Iroquois-speaking*** tribe.

The ***Iroquois-speaking*** tribes who lived in what is now New York State were the Mohawk, Oneida (oe-NEI-dah), Onondaga (ah-nahn-DAW-gah), Cayuga (kee-YOO-gah), and Seneca. Together, they made up the Five Nations, or Iroquois League. After 1700 the Tuscarora of North Carolina joined the League.

The French and their Huron allies paddled up the rivers to a long inland lake that Champlain had named after himself. Halfway up the lake they met the Mohawk, who were no match for French arms and gunpowder. Such a bitter defeat was not to be quickly forgotten by the Iroquois nations. When the Dutch arrived in the Hudson River valley in the 1620's, the Iroquois tribes formed an alliance with them.

Partly because of Iroquois hostility, the colony of New France expanded very slowly. When Champlain died in 1635, the settlement at Quebec numbered only about 200 soldiers and fur traders. There were no women. The French were there to trade, not to raise children and corn.

THE *COUREURS DE BOIS*. Throughout New France certain merchants held a monopoly of the fur trade. As a result, an unlicensed trader was subject to fines and imprisonment. Nevertheless, a few of them did manage to penetrate the western Great Lakes.

The most daring of the *coureurs de bois* (koo-RUR duh BWAH) (traders of the woods) was Pierre Radisson (rah-dee-SAWN). After pushing through the rapids of the Sault Ste. Marie, Radisson spent a winter with the Indians of northern Wisconsin, before wandering through the spruce forests north of Lake Superior. On his return to Montreal (the fur capital at the mouth of the Ottawa River), Radisson had a boatload of furs and tales of a Northwest Passage. The Indians had told him of the Mississippi River in the west and of Hudson Bay to the north.

When the governor arrested him in Montreal for trading without a license and seized his furs, Radisson escaped to the English settlements in New England. There, with English financing, he explored Hudson Bay, helping to establish English trading posts on its shores. He even helped found Hudson's Bay Company, which would later dominate the Canadian fur trade.

LOUIS XIV AND THE EXPANSION OF NEW FRANCE. *During the reign of Louis XIV (1642–1714), France became the dominant power in Europe, while also improving its position in North America.* Louis's ministers encouraged agriculture, so the colony could feed itself. His ministers also sent over the first women, to give the French outpost the sense of a permanent settlement. Most importantly, the ministers sent energetic governors who encouraged territorial expansion.

Jesuit missionaries, hoping to convert the Indians to the Roman Catholic religion, were the advance guard of the French Empire. By 1670 they had established missions at the Sault Ste. Marie and at Green Bay on Lake Michigan. Such contact with the western tribes brought new tales of a mighty river to the west, which confirmed the earlier stories of Radisson. *In 1672 a Jesuit missionary, Father Jacques Marquette (mahr-KET), teamed up with the soldier and fur trader, Louis Joliet (zjoh-LYEH), to find this waterway, which would later open up the interior of the continent.*

MARQUETTE AND JOLIET. The explorers set out from the mission at Green Bay in May 1673. With their Indian guides they paddled up the gentle Fox River, across Lake Winnebago, and then upstream and over to the Wisconsin River. A month after they had started, they moved onto the broad Mississippi. For three weeks they paddled down this mighty river, watching the Missouri join it from the west and the Ohio join from the east, until they reached the mouth of the Arkansas. (See map, page 75.) At that point it was evident that the river flowed on to the Gulf of Mexico, and not wanting to fall into Spanish hands, they turned back.

Marquette and Joliet's return in 1673 coincided with the arrival of a new and able governor of Canada, Count Frontenac (FRAHN-t'nack), who quickly reached a truce with the Iroquois. *This peace ended the raids that had plagued the colony from the beginning and opened the way for further French expansion.*

LA SALLE CLAIMS THE HEART OF THE CONTINENT. With Frontenac's blessing, Robert de La Salle, the explorer, planned to establish a string of forts along the western rivers. These forts would serve as depots for the fur trade, while also extending French authority and control throughout the continental heartland.

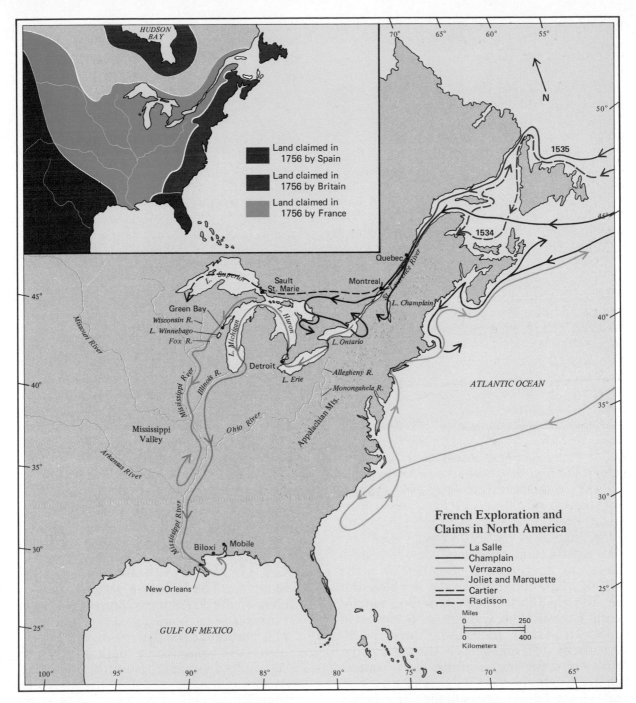

HUDSON BAY

Land claimed in 1756 by Spain

Land claimed in 1756 by Britain

Land claimed in 1756 by France

1535

1534

Quebec

Montreal

St. Lawrence River

Sault St. Marie

L. Champlain

L. Superior

Green Bay

Wisconsin R.

L. Winnebago

Fox R.

L. Huron

L. Michigan

L. Ontario

Detroit

L. Erie

Allegheny R.

Monongahela R.

Missouri River

Illinois R.

Mississippi River

Mississippi Valley

Ohio River

Arkansas River

Appalachian Mts.

ATLANTIC OCEAN

Mississippi River

Biloxi   Mobile

New Orleans

GULF OF MEXICO

French Exploration and Claims in North America

—— La Salle
—— Champlain
—— Verrazano
—— Joliet and Marquette
---- Cartier
- - - Radisson

Miles
0   250

0   400
Kilometers

Starting in the spring of 1682, La Salle followed the homeward route of Marquette and Joliet down the Mississippi. During his journey friendly Indian tribes provided him with food, shelter, and guides. When he reached the Gulf of Mexico, he claimed the entire valley for France and named it Louisiana, in honor of the king.

75

In the winter of 1681–1682, La Salle set off from Lake Michigan down the Mississippi. He is shown here with the Taensa Indians near present-day Natchez. The scene was painted by George Catlin, a century and a half later.

La Salle's claim embraced the whole interior of the continent. It stretched from the Appalachian Mountains to the Rockies. But the French title to this vast inland empire conflicted with the western land claims of American Indians and those of several British colonies. In addition, it threatened the interests of fur traders from New York to South Carolina.

Thus the French claim to the Great Lakes and the Mississippi valley set the stage for a gigantic imperial contest between Britain and France. The fighting broke out in 1689, only seven years after La Salle's journey.

Section Review

1. Mapping: The broad-ranging explorations of the French explorers gave France the basis for its early claim to a vast portion of the American wilderness. Give evidence to support this statement by mapping out the routes of two French explorers. Use the map on page 75.
2. How did La Salle's claim lead to conflict?
3. Name one way the French colonies differed from the English colonies.

2. The Wars for Empire, 1689-1763

LOUIS XIV TRIES TO EXTEND FRANCE'S BOUNDARIES. At the start most of the fighting between the European powers took place in Europe. *The first war stemmed from the ambitions of Louis XIV, who wanted to extend France's boundaries toward the Rhine River and the Alps.* Having little understanding of the causes of this war, American colonists simply called it King William's War, after King William of England, who ruled from 1689 to 1702. (See chart below.)

The first war saw little fighting in America, except for Indian raids. In 1690 French-Indian forces fell on Schenectady, New York, burning it and carrying its people back to Canada. There were similar raids in Maine and New Hampshire. Later that year a joint English-colonial force sailed up the St. Lawrence and attacked Quebec. But they failed to take it. The war in Europe resulted in a similar deadlock, and the peace settlement in 1697 was really only an armed truce.

THE WAR OF THE SPANISH SUCCESSION. Five years later war broke out again in Europe. In America fighting also broke out, and again it was confined to the frontier. In 1704 a French-Indian force burned the village of Deerfield, Massachusetts, and soon the whole New England frontier was ablaze. Even though the attempted British-colonial invasion of Canada had failed, a combined British-colonial force did capture the province of Nova Scotia.

The conflict in America was a draw, but France's losses in Europe forced it to buy peace. Thus, Britain (England and Scotland were joined in 1707 into the United Kingdom of Great Britain) got a good slice of the French Empire—Nova Scotia, Newfoundland, and the shoreline of Hudson Bay. From those bases Britain could cut into the heart of New France should war break out again.

NEW WORLD RIVALRIES. *Although the conflict in Europe was temporarily over, New World rivalries continued.* In 1728 New York erected the first British outpost on the Great Lakes, Fort Oswego. This enabled the western tribes of Indians to bring their furs to Albany rather than to traffic them through the French at Montreal. The French responded by building a fort at Crown Point, on Lake Champlain. (See map, page 80.)

THE WARS FOR EMPIRE	
European Event	**American Event**
War of the League of Augsburg (1689–1697)	King William's War (1689–1697)
War of the Spanish Succession (1702–1713)	Queen Anne's War (1702–1713)
War of the Austrian Succession (1740–1748)	King George's War (1744–1748)
Seven Years' War (1756–1763)	French and Indian War (1754–1763)

Sidenote to History

Blackbeard the Pirate

The wars for a New World empire were fought mainly on the sea. Since warships were expensive to build and maintain, kings and queens often supplemented their fleets with privateers. These were privately owned warships that fought for profit. They sailed the seas in search of richly loaded merchant vessels belonging to a rival nation. Some privateers did not bother to sort out the crown's enemies; they simply captured every vessel that came along. And that made them pirates.

The years from 1689 to 1713 were a time of almost constant warfare. When the wars ended temporarily in 1713, Britain's King George I offered to pardon any pirate who promised to reform himself. Many accepted the offer, but one who did not was Edward Teach, the notorious Blackbeard. He had just become a pirate. He didn't want to quit.

Blackbeard's crew numbered more than a hundred men. Rather than risk damaging his prey with cannon fire, he made captures by boarding and using hand-to-hand combat. So fierce was his reputation that most victims surrendered without a fight. To these victims Blackbeard offered a choice—either they join the pirates or they agree to be put ashore on a desert island. The captured vessels were either burned or added to Blackbeard's private flotilla, which eventually numbered five ships.

Blackbeard kept his men under control through fear. By draping half a dozen pistols and knives around himself, he gave the appearance of being a walking arsenal. The lighted wicks of gunpowder that protruded from under his hat, wreathing his head in smoke, gave his face a ghastly glow.

Greed, however, was his undoing. Not wanting to split the booty with his hundreds of followers, he tricked them into going ashore on a deserted island. Then, with only a dozen faithful men, he loaded the plunder onto his own ship, burned the other ships, and sailed off. A rich man, he settled in North Carolina, using its sandy capes as a refuge.

There, in 1718 on an autumn day, he was found by a British warship. Although hopelessly outnumbered in the ensuing battle, he went down fighting. Blackbeard's death ended piracy's golden age.

In the Southwest, Bienville, the French governor of Louisiana, became even more aggressive. In 1718 he founded New Orleans, near the mouth of the Mississippi, and made it the capital of his colony. He also set up an outpost at Mobile, Alabama, and encouraged the Indians to raid the Carolina frontier.

South Carolina, already menaced by the Spanish in Florida, begged for help. The British ministry's solution was to found a new colony, Georgia, that would serve as a buffer for the South Carolina plantations against both the Spanish and the American Indians. The move would also extend Britain's territorial claims south to the Florida border.

KING GEORGE'S WAR. *In 1744 Britain and France were again dragged into a general European conflict.* This time Britain paid more attention to the American battleground. In 1745 the British and an army of New Englanders captured the French fortress of Louisbourg. This left Quebec and the heart of French Canada exposed. However, French victories in Europe diverted British attention. In the peace settlement three years later, Louisbourg was returned to the French.

ENGLAND AND FRANCE LOOK TO NORTH AMERICA. *Both the British and the French emerged from the war more conscious of North America's importance.* Anticipating a renewal of their conflict in North America, both sides began building their strength. In 1749 King George II, who ruled England from 1727 to 1760, issued a charter to the Virginians who had formed the Ohio company. He gave them a huge tract of land on the Ohio River and permission to settle it. Since the lands were in territory claimed by France, the grant was certain to cause trouble. The Ohio Company employed Christopher Gist to lay out a road to the Monongahela River and to advertise for settlers.

At the same time, the French began moving south from the Great Lakes. The forks of the Ohio were their goal. But in the winter of 1753, the old problems started again. As a result, the Ohio company employed Christopher Gist and George Washington to spy on the French. Later, in the spring, the two were used still again, this time to build a fort at what is now Pittsburgh, Pennsylvania.

As you have seen at the beginning of this chapter, Washington and Gist managed to start a war. After successfully ambushing the French detachment, Washington withdrew to Fort Necessity. (See map, page 80.) French troops pursued him and forced his surrender in July 1754.

THE SIX NATIONS AND THE ALBANY PLAN. After the defeat at Fort Necessity, the British colonists felt increasingly insecure. The French had established outposts from the Allegheny Mountains to the Great Lakes. And France's Indian allies threatened British settlements in the North.

In 1754, seven British colonies and the Six Nations of the Iroquois Confederation

Washington and Gist crossed the Allegheny River on a raft to warn Virginia of the French threat. How would such a message be conveyed today?

sent delegates to Albany, New York. *The purpose of the meeting (called the Albany Congress) was to devise a plan for defeating the French.* The British were lucky to have as their allies the most powerful Indians in the eastern region—the Iroquois. And the Iroquois Confederation set an example to the colonists that influenced the plan drawn up by the congress—the Albany Plan.

Proposed by Benjamin Franklin, the Albany Plan called for a union of the British. If unified, Franklin reasoned, the colonies would be better able to defend themselves. The plan, however, was rejected because the colonies feared dependence on one another.

DISASTER ON THE MONONGAHELA. Following the defeat at Fort Necessity, the Virginians called for help. In 1755, only a few months after the Albany Congress, General Edward Braddock arrived from England with two regiments of Scottish soldiers. With Washington along as guide, Braddock marched across the mountains on the Ohio Company's road and proceeded down the Monongahela. At almost

13 kilometers (8 miles) south of Fort Duquesne (see map below), a French-Indian force intercepted him. Braddock was killed, and his second-in-command panicked. Ordered to retreat, the British abandoned their cannons and their wagons and fled to safety. Washington then led the Virginians in a rear-guard action. His bravery earned him command of all the Virginia forces. *For the next two years, Washington had his hands full protecting a frontier that extended from the Potomac River to the Tennessee.*

THE FRENCH AND INDIAN WAR.
War was formally declared in 1756. Braddock's defeat was the first in a string of British disasters in both Europe and America

that forced a change in the British government. In 1757 William Pitt became first minister of the British government. It was Pitt who recognized that Britain's true interests lay not in Europe but in America.

Pitt's strategy was simple: Let Prussia's Frederick the Great, supported by British gold, fight the European war. Britain would blockade the coast of France to cut France off from its empire.

By 1758 Pitt's strategy began to pay off. A new British army marched on Fort Duquesne, but by a different route. The army's commander, General John Forbes, preferred to build a new road, which became known as Forbes' Road, and to construct a chain of forts to protect his supply line. (See map,

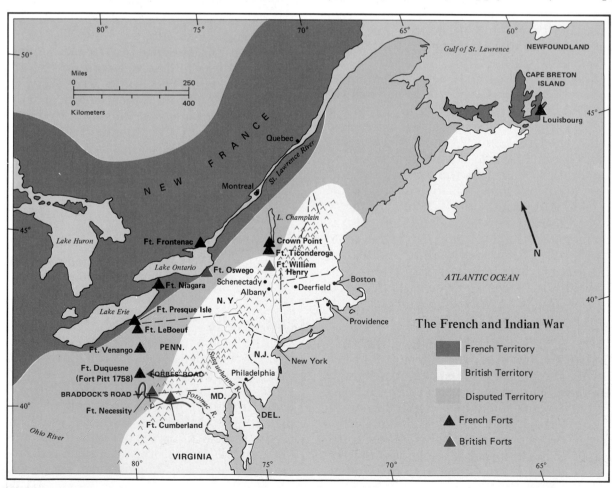

The French and Indian War

French Territory
British Territory
Disputed Territory
▲ French Forts
▲ British Forts

page 80.) When Forbes descended on Duquesne, the French blew up their own fort and paddled off down the Ohio. Forbes then took the fort, rebuilt the walls, and renamed it Fort Pitt.

To the north the British enjoyed similar success. A British and colonial force captured Louisbourg once again and stood ready to invade the St. Lawrence. The strategy for 1759 was clear. One army, led by General James Wolfe, would sail up the St. Lawrence to Quebec; another, under Lord Jeffrey Amherst, would move on Montreal by way of Lake Champlain.

Wolfe succeeded brilliantly. His army landed opposite Quebec, crossed the river, and scaled the cliffs onto the grassy meadow known as the Plains of Abraham. There they met the French forces, led by Montcalm, and the two armies shot it out in *Continental battle style.* Disciplined British firepower won the day. But both Wolfe and Montcalm lay dead on the field.

Continental battle style pitted two armies who were using muskets against each other at some 45 to 90 meters (50 to 100 yards) apart. To keep up a continuous stream of fire, the British arranged their soldiers in lines, each firing, kneeling, and reloading in turn.

THE TREATY OF PARIS, 1763. The following year, 1760, Amherst descended on Montreal. The governor-general of Canada soon surrendered all of New France. The war dragged on for three more years, until a world settlement was reached at Paris in 1763. But for the Americans the fighting was over, and they had shared in the glory.

In the final settlement Britain even managed to acquire Florida from Spain. Spain had entered the worldwide struggle on the side of France in 1762. In partial compensation, Spain received New Orleans and the part of French Louisiana west of the Mississippi River. Thus, New France was

"The Death of Wolfe" was painted by Benjamin West in 1771. Born in Philadelphia, West claimed that his first painting lessons had come from Indians. They had shown him how they made colors from clay to paint their faces. Later, West had gone to London to study art. Although West never returned to America, he could take pride in being the first painter of the American school.

no more. Disregarding the American Indians who inhabited the land, Britain and Spain claimed all of the land of North America. It was the climax of the first British Empire.

Section Review

1. Mapping: Using the key on the map on page 80, name three French forts and three British forts. Which forts were located in disputed territory?
2. Identify or explain: Bienville, Forbes' Road, Pitt, Wolfe, Montcalm.
3. What strategy did William Pitt suggest to the British Parliament? Was it successful?
4. How did France's defeat in the French and Indian War end its role as a colonial power in North America?

3. Coming of the Revolution: First Phase, 1763-1770

POSTWAR PROBLEMS. The great war for empire actually weakened the ties of the British Empire. With the French threat gone, the colonies had less need for protection. And with the war over, Britain no longer had to make any concessions to win colonial cooperation.

In addition, the great victory presented problems of its own. Britain now controlled half of a continent and was responsible for the interests of many people, including French Canadians and western Indians. The war also left Britain with a staggering debt. Britain thought the Americans should help pay for this cost of British expansion. *The attempt to solve the problems—by reorganizing the empire and taxing the colonists—triggered the events that led to revolution.* To further complicate matters, Britain was led at this time by George III, who ruled from 1760 to 1820.

PONTIAC'S CONSPIRACY. The first problem facing the British was an Indian uprising. With the construction of a road into the Ohio Valley, a flood of pioneers moved into western Pennsylvania. The Indians, some of whom had already been pushed out of their eastern homes and had often been cheated by fur traders, were dismayed at this new assault on their lands and decided it was time to take a stand. They wanted to make the Appalachian Mountains the barrier between the colonists' country and the Indians'.

Pontiac, an Ottawa leader, had a plan. His strategy, involving a number of tribes, was to strike every western outpost and to force the settlers to flee back over the mountains. (See map, page 83.) And he very nearly succeeded. In the spring of 1763, hundreds of settlers lost their lives. Every western fort fell to the Indians except Detroit and Fort Pitt. A British and colonial army finally relieved the forts and ended the war, but the echoes of conflict were heard for some time.

THE PROCLAMATION OF 1763. *The British government responded to the uprising by issuing a proclamation prohibiting colonies from making land grants west of the mountains.* The British believed that by keeping the Indians and the colonists apart, they could reduce the likelihood of war and the costs of defense. The British may also have thought that colonists confined to the seaboard would be easier to control. The proclamation also set aside some territory for the Indians, thus recognizing the Indians' limited rights to land.

The Indians accepted the proclamation, but many colonists were dismayed. There was still plenty of farmland available east of the mountains, but some people had western claims. Virginians especially had western holdings, stemming from the Ohio Company grant of 1749. Among these was George Washington. The proclamation was

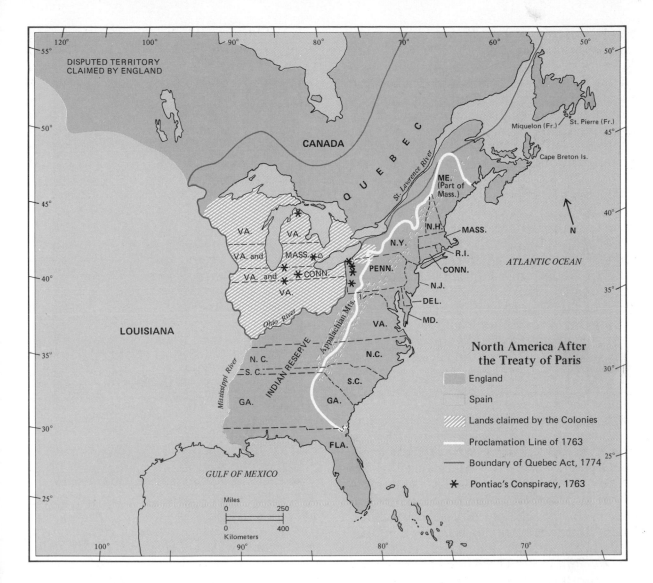

Map labels:

DISPUTED TERRITORY
CLAIMED BY ENGLAND

CANADA

QUEBEC

St. Lawrence River

Miquelon (Fr.) St. Pierre (Fr.)

Cape Breton Is.

ME.
(Part of
Mass.)

N.H.

MASS.

N.Y.

R.I.

CONN.

ATLANTIC OCEAN

VA.   VA.

VA. and   MASS.

VA. and   CONN.

VA.

PENN.

N.J.

DEL.

MD.

Ohio River

LOUISIANA

Appalachian Mts.

VA.

Mississippi River

INDIAN RESERVE

N. C.   N. C.

S. C.

S.C.

GA.   GA.

N

**North America After
the Treaty of Paris**

England

Spain

Lands claimed by the Colonies

Proclamation Line of 1763

Boundary of Quebec Act, 1774

✳ Pontiac's Conspiracy, 1763

FLA.

GULF OF MEXICO

Miles
0   250

0   400
Kilometers

no cause for open rebellion, but it was a sore point. One of many, it soon appeared.

THE WRITS OF ASSISTANCE. George Grenville, King George III's chief minister at the end of the war, recognized the need for reorganization. He began by focusing on the enforcement of trade regulations, particularly the collection of *customs duties.*

Customs duties are taxes levied (placed) on goods imported from abroad. Another name for them is a tariff. An excise is a tax levied on goods produced within the country.

Americans, it seemed, were some of the world's best smugglers. And their vast, uninhabited coastline enabled them to slip foreign goods into the colonies without detection. During the war British officials had tried to put a clamp on smuggling. *Customs officials were allowed to obtain written court orders, called writs of assistance, which enabled them to conduct general*

83

searches without stating in advance what they were looking for.

In 1760 a group of Massachusetts merchants hired James Otis, a lawyer, to defend them against this procedure. Otis came up with the theory that the writs violated the colonists' rights, among which was the right to privacy. Otis lost the case, but his brilliant argument would long be remembered.

THE REVENUE ACT OF 1764. Grenville's effort to make the empire more efficient came in the form of the Revenue Act of 1764, also called the Sugar Act because it reduced the duties on imported sugar and other products imported from places outside the British Empire. Previously the government had tried to prevent the colonists from buying French or Dutch sugar by placing high customs duties on the imported sugar. This would have forced the colonists to buy the more expensive sugar from the British West Indies. But smugglers had simply evaded the earlier duties.

Grenville's new law lowered the duties, encouraging the colonies to use foreign sugar, so the government could get revenue from the tax. To ensure that this tax would be collected and that smuggling would be wiped out, the act placed special courts in the major American seaports. These courts had no juries. Naval judges examined evidence, weighed guilt, and passed sentence. The system was simple and effective.

THE THREAT TO AMERICAN SELF-GOVERNMENT. British taxation brought on the American Revolution, but not because of the money involved. What concerned Americans was power. *They objected to being regulated, or taxed, by a foreign legislature in which they had no representation.* Since they were not allowed to elect members to the British Parliament, there was no one in that body to look out for their interests.

The stamps on these goods from abroad are proof that the required taxes had been paid. The protest against the hated Stamp Act marked the first really effective political cooperation among the colonies.

On the other hand, each colony had its own elected assembly, which had won some significant powers. The first of these was the power of the purse, the right to levy taxes and to spend the revenue. This was the key to every other power. In some colonies, such as Massachusetts, the assembly paid the governor's salary. This gave them substantial influence over that one official, who represented the king.

By 1763 each colonial assembly claimed the right to pass all laws necessary for the internal government of the colony. British officials and Parliament handled foreign affairs and external trade, but that was all. The colonies governed themselves until the issue of taxation arose. If Parliament could tax them without their consent, what could it *not* do? The hard-won right to internal self-government itself seemed at stake.

THE STAMP ACT. *In 1765 Grenville's search for revenue led him to propose a new imperial tax.* In addition to customs duties, he suggested an excise, a levy on various goods and services produced within the colonies. The tax would be paid for by the purchase of a stamp, which would be placed on the article. This proposed act would require stamps on newspapers, legal documents, playing cards, ship's papers, and the like. Parliament passed the act with little debate and less concern—an act that would help cost Britain an empire.

AMERICANS REACT TO THE STAMP ACT. Americans quickly saw the danger. They had tolerated customs duties because such duties were external concerns. But this new act provided internal taxation. If Parliament could force the sale

This warning appeared in the Pennsylvania Jour-nal in 1765. It says: "An emblem of the effects of the Stamp. O! the fatal Stamp."

Tax collectors were extended little mercy by the colonists. This engraving depicts the tarring and feathering of John Malcom.

of stamps, it could levy a tax on land and other property. Where then would the power of the purse lie?

The American reaction to the Stamp Act was swift and violent. In the Virginia assembly Patrick Henry pushed through some resolutions calling for open resistance. When the resolutions were printed in Boston, a mob broke into Governor Thomas Hutchinson's house and wrecked it. A few weeks later crowds tore up the house of the local stamp distributor and forced him to resign. Following the Boston example, rioters in every city prevented collection of the tax. By autumn the group was achieving some organization, calling itself the Sons of Liberty.

THE SONS OF LIBERTY. *The Sons of Liberty were ordinary people—ropemakers, dockworkers, butchers, bakers, and candlestickmakers.* Paul Revere, who became one of the leading Boston rebels and the chief messenger, was a pewter- and sil-

versmith. Merchants joined the group at first, but soon became dismayed at its violence.

In October 1765 colonial delegates met in a Stamp Act Congress in New York. The Congress professed loyalty to the king but vowed to resist all taxation levied without the consent of the colonial legislatures.

THE DECLARATORY ACT. In response to the American uproar, Parliament repealed the Stamp Act in the spring of 1766. ***But to save face, it passed the Declaratory Act, which declared that Parliament had full power to pass laws for or to levy taxes on America, "in all cases whatsoever."***

Therein lay the conflict. Did Parliament have the right to legislate for America or not? Was it possible to have both imperial authority and colonial self-government? The colonists would eventually conclude that Parliament had authority in *no* cases whatsoever.

THE TOWNSHEND TAXES, 1767. In the meantime Grenville resigned. The new finance minister, Charles Townshend, then suggested a new plan. *He asked Parliament to levy customs duties on various colonial imports—paint, tea, paper, lead, and glass.* Since the colonists had not objected to external taxes in the past, these duties seemed fairly harmless. But the Act said that part of the proceeds would be used to pay governors' salaries.

Once more the colonial assemblies were threatened! An independent salary would eliminate the only power they had against the governor. Moreover, the purpose of these new taxes was revenue. Previous customs duties had been levied to regulate trade patterns. *The colonists insisted that the power to collect revenue belonged to the colonial assemblies.*

NONIMPORTATION AGREEMENTS.

The colonial response this time was less violent and more organized. *Merchants refused to import British goods until the Townshend taxes were repealed.* This re-fusal was meant to hit British exporters in the pocketbook and make them put pressure on Parliament.

In Boston the officials charged with collecting the duties were openly threatened. The British reacted by sending a regiment to bring order to the city. The troops proved to be a new source of friction. The townspeople insulted and attacked them whenever possible.

THE BOSTON MASSACRE. Tension mounted into the spring of 1770, as the soldiers began meeting force with force. There were rumors of a military takeover. On March 5 some boys began hurling snowballs and stones at a small group of soldiers. Bells began ringing and a crowd gathered quickly. Someone gave the order to fire, and five citizens of Boston fell to the street, dead or mortally wounded. Among the dead was Crispus Attucks, a fugitive slave who had actively participated in previous encounters with the soldiers. Attucks was the first person to die in the Revolution.

The Boston Massacre began with a protest against the Townshend Acts and the quartering of British troops in Boston homes. The British troops opened fire and Crispus Attucks, a Black sailor, was the first person to die in the American Revolution.

Samuel Adams, one of the leaders of the Sons of Liberty, hoped the massacre would provoke the colonists into action. His newspaper ally, the *Boston Gazette*, shrieked for weeks about the incident. Otherwise, things had calmed down rather swiftly. Governor Hutchinson had used good judgment in handling the affair. He had arrested the soldiers and had ordered them brought to trial. As their defense counsel, the soldiers had hired John Adams, Samuel Adams's cousin. A skilled attorney, Adams got them off with a rather light sentence.

THE TOWNSHEND TAXES ARE REPEALED. *In 1770 Parliament repealed the Townshend Acts, but retained the tax on tea as a symbol of its authority.* For a brief period both sides seemed to back away from active confrontation. But unrest and discontent in the colonies continued to simmer.

Section Review

1. Mapping: Look at the map on page 83. Which colonies had territorial claims west of the Proclamation Line of 1763?
2. Identify or explain: Pontiac, customs duties, writs of assistance, Crispus Attucks.
3. Define "the power of the purse" and give at least one example of its use.
4. Give one reason why the Stamp Act made the colonists especially angry.
5. Give one reason why the colonists saw the Townshend taxes as a threat to their ability to govern themselves.

Sidenote to History

Samuel Adams: Pathmaker of Democracy

Politics was Adams's life, and the town meeting was his home. Town meetings were the central feature of local government in New England. They were the place where people met to discuss their problems and to find solutions. With the leadership of Samuel Adams, such meetings were turned into vehicles of popular protest, through shrewd organization and careful planning.

When Adams moved up to the assembly, he used his influence to secure the position of clerk, which enabled him to draft several petitions. Under Adams the Massachusetts assembly became the voice of popular colonial protest.

To add to the rising tensions within the colonies, Adams and his friends manufactured incidents, printed inflammatory handbills, and made up stories for newspapers. And he was an expert at recruiting people for his cause. For example, he persuaded his cousin, John Adams, to come to Boston to practice law. He also catered to the wealthy John Hancock, who had inherited a shipping business worth a fortune. To Samuel Adams, Hancock's purse belonged to the town. Thus, he persuaded the town to give Hancock a seat in the assembly.

Adams's goal, almost from the beginning, was political independence, and when it came, he felt his job was done. But he had done more than throw off the British yoke. He had opened up the path of democracy. Through Adams's methods many more people had become involved in politics. Sailors and dockworkers had participated in organized riots. Shopkeepers and cobblers had spoken up in town meetings. For people who were not wealthy or influential, it had been a political awakening.

This sweeping change in the concept of government within the colonies almost amounted to a second revolution. Popular interest in politics, popular participation in decision making—these are the essence of democracy. And the effects of that revolution never ended. Credit Samuel Adams with the beginning.

4. The Road to Concord Bridge, 1770-1775

THE COMMITTEES OF CORRESPONDENCE. *After the Boston Massacre the citizens of Boston, led by Samuel Adams, met in a special town meeting to create a Committee of Correspondence.* The idea for setting up Committees of Correspondence probably came from James Otis's brilliant sister, Mercy Warren, who lived in Plymouth. Warren was an eager rebel who often lent her pen to the cause, writing plays that poked fun at British officials. The purpose of the Committees of Correspondence was to help people in other colonies stay in contact with the Boston rebels. They could exchange ideas, coordinate plans, and reinforce one another. By the end of 1772, the network had extended throughout New England.

THE TEA PARTY. In 1773 a new British blunder caused more upheaval in the colonies. The British East India Company, which was experiencing financial problems, was being reorganized by Parliament. Parliament, to provide a financial boost, gave the company a monopoly on tea shipped to America. Parliament also allowed the com-

To protest the tax on tea, the Sons of Liberty sneaked onto a British merchant ship and dumped thousands of dollars worth of tea into Boston Harbor. Why did they dress as Indians?

pany to lower its prices in order to tempt colonists into buying the British tea. Even though the tea would be taxed under the Townshend duties, it would still undersell the tea of colonial merchants in America.

When the first tea ship, *Dartmouth,* sailed into Boston Harbor in November 1773, a delegation of the Committee of Correspondence met it at the dock. The ship could not unload, said the committee; it would have to return to Britain. The captain was agreeable, but Governor Hutchinson, who was unwilling to let the Sons of Liberty govern the harbor, refused to give it clearance to leave. The committee posted a guard at the dock—Stalemate.

But only for a time. On December 16 the vessel's permission to harbor would expire. It would have to either unload or sail. On the evening before the deadline, a huge public meeting gathered at Faneuil (FAN-yul) Hall. After a discussion and little agreement, Samuel Adams declared: "This meeting can do no more to save the country." It was apparently a signal, for the large crowd filed out of the hall and down the street to the docks. There a group of men dressed as Indians boarded the *Dartmouth* and dumped 342 chests of tea into the harbor. *Resistance to the Tea Act was general. New York and Philadelphia refused to let tea ships into their harbors and sent them back to Britain.* But nowhere was the destruction of property so great as in Boston.

THE INTOLERABLE ACTS.

Lord North, the king's new prime minister, was furious. So was Parliament, which quickly retaliated with four measures, all designed both to punish Massachusetts and to restore imperial authority. *The colonists called these measures the Intolerable Acts because they were sure they would be unable to endure them.* One of the acts closed the port of Boston until the city paid for the tea. Since the city depended on shipping for food and firewood, such an act would mean a cold, hungry winter for Boston.

A second act revoked the charter of Massachusetts, suspending the colony's civil government and placing it under military rule. A third measure, the Quartering Act, forced colonists to provide food and housing for the soldiers who ruled them. A fourth act permitted British officials who injured people while enforcing the law to return to Britain for their court hearings.

THE QUEBEC ACT.

A fifth act, the Quebec Act, was passed at the same time. Although it was not passed in response to the Tea Party, it was viewed by the colonists as one of the Intolerable Acts. It offered civil government to Canada, which had been under military rule, and granted religious tolerance to French Catholics. In addition, it extended Canada's border south to the Ohio River.

The Quebec Act was an enlightened piece of legislation for its time. It was probably responsible for keeping Canada in the empire during the Revolution. Nevertheless, the colonists viewed it with hostility. Giving the country south of the Great Lakes to Canada violated the western claims of several colonies, notably Virginia. And many people who lived in New England felt threatened by the offer of religious tolerance to Roman Catholics.

THE FIRST CONTINENTAL CONGRESS, 1774.

The Intolerable Acts were the final threat to colonial self-rule. If Parliament could destroy the government of Massachusetts, it could also impose military rule on Virginia. Boston was suffering, but the rights of all were at stake. The Virginians, who had long rivaled the Bostonians in revolutionary leadership, suggested an intercolonial meeting at Philadelphia to draft a united protest. All but Georgia agreed. The date was set for September 5, 1774.

The congress was not as united as its promoters had hoped. After much discussion the congress agreed on a resolution. This resolution asserted American rights and demanded withdrawal of the Intolerable

Acts. It prohibited the further import of British goods and authorized committees of safety in every colony to enforce the ban. If Parliament did not yield by the following January, the congress planned to halt colonial exports as well. It then adjourned until the following spring.

During the winter royal authority slowly dissolved. In many colonies governors closed local assemblies to silence their protests. But the assemblies simply reformed themselves into what they called conventions and governed as before. New England thus became an armed camp. *Minutemen* drilled on every village green; towns stockpiled arms and gunpowder. The British Army officially controlled Boston, but nothing else. Then, in the spring the army began moving out into the countryside, searching for the colonists' arms. That effort triggered a war.

Minutemen were a group of armed men who had agreed to take to the field at a minute's notice, both during and immediately before the American Revolution.

Section Review

1. Identify or explain: Mercy Warren, Samuel Adams, Committees of Correspondence.
2. Name two events that led to the Boston Tea Party.
3. Charting: Make a chart, listing the Intolerable Acts and giving a brief description of each one.

Viewpoints of History

Letters from English Soldiers

How did English subjects who lived in the colonies view events that led to the American Revolution? The following are pieces of historical evidence that express opposing points of view. The first selection is part of a letter written by an English officer who was stationed with his troops in Boston.

"According to my promise I am writing to you on my arrival here. The troops have just been put into their quarters. The workers at Boston were so stubborn and uncooperative that we had to send to Nova Scotia for carpenters and bricklayers to build a barracks for us. The country is very plentiful, and all sorts of provisions are cheaper here than in London. The people of this province, however, are at least a hundred years behind the people of England in every refinement. They lack every principle of common honesty and are the worst cheats and hypocrites on the whole continent of America. As to what you hear of their taking up arms to resist the force of England, it is more bullying. Believe me, any two British regiments here ought to be able to beat the whole force of the Massachusetts Province. Although they are numerous, the colonials are just a mob without order or discipline."

The second selection, which follows, is part of a letter received by a man in England from his son, a deserter from the British Army.

"Honored Father: The hospitable kindness I received from the country people on my way from Boston to Charleston is beyond my description. Every one that owned a horse offered it to me, and all brought me their best food. I find them the best-hearted, generous people in the world, ready to give everything to strangers.

"We hear of several British regiments that are coming down to Charleston. If that is true, they can do nothing in this country. There were not three men in my company who would fire on the people of this country. I am sure that there was not one Englishman that would do so. Last night a vessel arrived here from Salem. It was reported that a regiment there had mutinied and laid down their arms. If this is true, others will probably follow their example. To generous spirits, it must be altogether disgusting to have to destroy their friends."

Chapter 4 Review

Bird's-Eye View

For many years neither Britain nor France recognized the importance of its colonial claims in America. Even when fighting broke out between these European nations, nearly all of the early battles were fought in Europe, without much concern for the situation in America.

The British attitude changed, however, when William Pitt became prime minister of Britain. Pitt made the war a fight for the empire, a war in which adding new colonies was the chief aim. And he succeeded against France because New France was a hollow shell. Founded mainly as a trading outpost, it consisted of huge territorial claims of few people. With only the capture of two cities, Quebec and Montreal, New France collapsed. The British colonies, in contrast, had a hundred times as many people, a huge army of citizen-soldiers, and a stronger economic base. A French capture of one or two of their cities would make no difference at all.

The Treaty of Paris in 1763 was a great victory for the British. But, ironically, it also marked the beginning of the end of the empire. With the need for protection gone, British interference became more and more a source of resentment to the colonies. At first the colonists seemed willing to tolerate regulation of their trade. They even accepted import duties, so long as all internal taxation was left to the local assemblies. However, when Parliament passed the Townshend taxes, the colonists felt their only power—the power of the purse—had been threatened. If the British could soak up all the American revenue and independent colonial powers, there would be nothing of the powers of self-rule left to the colonial assemblies.

Tensions continued to mount. Violence broke out in Boston. And in response to this incident, known as the Boston Tea Party, Parliament passed the Intolerable Acts. The colonists considered these acts the final threat to colonial self-rule. Neither side would agree to a settlement, and war was the result.

Vocabulary

Define or identify each of the following:

Continental battle style	*coureurs de bois*	John Peter Zenger
excise tax	Pierre Radisson	Townshend taxes
minutemen	the Albany Plan	Samuel Adams

Review Questions

1. Who were the French explorers? Where did they explore?
2. Why were France and England at war almost continuously between 1689 and 1763?
3. What were the results of the French and Indian War?
4. In what ways were the Writs of Assistance and the Revenue Act of 1764 a threat to American colonial self-government?
5. What was the Stamp Act? Why did the colonists object to it? What actions did the colonists take against the Stamp Act?

6. "Taxation without representation" became a rallying cry of the American revolution. Why was taxation such an important issue to the colonists?

Reviewing Social Studies Skills

1. Using the map on page 75, list the waterways and bodies of water that the French explored.
2. Using the maps on pages 75 and 83, describe the land lost by the French. Which countries gained land?
3. Name the chart in this chapter. Explain what the chart shows.
4. George Catlin and Benjamin West were both famous painters. Select one of their paintings in this chapter and explain how it can be used as historical evidence.
5. Make a time line, listing important events in the French exploration and colonization in America.

Reading for Meaning

1. Historical fiction is a made-up story with a real setting. Imagine that you are a British citizen, living in the colonial period. Write a paragraph of historical fiction, explaining why you believe those "rebellious colonials" ought to be dealt with severely.
2. Summarize the evidence in this chapter that supports either of the following statements:
   a. Samuel Adams helped to bring common people into politics.
   b. Samuel Adams contributed to the success of the Revolution.
3. The word "Quebec" came from the Indian word *kebec,* which meant a narrowing of the waters. Look at the map of the United States, and name at least six other places that take their names from Indian tribes. You may want to use the map in Chapter 1, entitled "Major Indian Tribes in the United States in the 1500's."

Bibliography

A number of good historical novels deal with the French and Indian War. The one that is best known is Kenneth Roberts's *Northwest Passage* (Fawcett World Library), which opens with an exciting account of the raid on a village in Maine.

The Last of the Mohicans, by James F. Cooper (Franklin Watts, Inc.), gives a good fictional account of Indian life during the French and Indian War. The story takes place in the forests of upper New York State.

Scott O'Dell's *The King's Fifth* (Houghton Mifflin) tells a classic story of adventure in the colonial Southwest. Its heroine is a young Indian girl.

Edwin Tunis's *Colonial Living* (World Publisher) contains interesting descriptions of the everyday life of the colonists.

Unit 1 Review

Vocabulary

Define or identify each of the following:

estuary	Anglican	monopoly
emigrant	customs duty	decrees
aristocracy	gristmill	inflation

Recalling the Facts

1. Describe in general the culture of the Maya, the Aztec, the Mound Builders, and the Iroquois.
2. What inventions and discoveries aided the European explorers?
3. Why did the English settle in Jamestown?
4. How did the Reformation affect England?
5. What were the major differences between the Plymouth colony and the Rhode Island colony?
6. What was a proprietary colony? Give two examples of proprietary colonies.
7. How was an indentured servant different from a slave?
8. Describe three occupations available to people in the 1700's.
9. What was the Great Awakening?
10. What was the pattern of French colonization?
11. What were the results of the French and Indian War in North America?
12. List the British acts between 1763 and 1770 that Americans found objectionable. Explain why the colonists objected to these acts.
13. When and why was the First Continental Congress called?

History Lab

1. Assume that you have been asked to write a brief report on someone who played an important role in the colonization of the Americas. Choose that person, and then find out how much information about that person is available in your local library. List the materials you found. Then prepare a concise outline, one that you would use if you had actually been asked to write such a report.
2. The Indians, Spanish, French, Dutch, and English colonists left their traces in place names. Using an atlas and a dictionary, make a list of place names and words that reflect these origins.
3. Although the main events of world history during the colonial period took place in Europe, they also had a strong influence on the events in the colonies. Using your newspaper, collect four examples of how the major world powers today influence the destinies of smaller nations. Explain why you made your selections.
4. Pretend you are a lawyer during the colonial period. Plan an argument, one that you would use to defend one of the following: a) merchant who had refused to pay the Stamp Tax b) a colonist who had participated in the Boston Tea Party c) a British soldier who had participated in the Boston Massacre.

5. Choose one of the professions or occupations common in colonial times. Does this profession or occupation still exist? If so, how has it changed? If not, what has replaced it? Do some research. Then write a short summary, comparing a day's work in colonial times with one in modern times for the profession or occupation you chose.
6. As a member of the first colony on the moon, which of the problems that were troublesome to the early settlers of Jamestown would you expect to face? What form of government and social organization do you think would be best for your settlement?

Local History

As a class project, find out more about the early development of your town. Use sources in the library or interview town historians to find answers to these questions:
1. When was your town founded?
2. What group(s) of people settled your town? For what reasons?
3. Why was the site chosen?

Forming an Opinion

1. Today religion and government are separate. The Puritans believed that religion should have a strong effect on government. What is your opinion? Why?
2. What do you think could have been done in 1774 to prevent the Revolutionary War? Explain your answer.
3. During the 18th century people considered themselves enlightened. Do you agree or disagree? Why?

Time Line

Using the time line below, answer the following questions:
1. When did each of these events take place: the founding of Jamestown, the French and Indian War, the Boston Tea Party?
2. How many years after Jamestown was founded did the *Mayflower* arrive in Plymouth?
3. Using your textbook, find out when the other colonies were established. Then make a time line, showing when all the colonies were established.

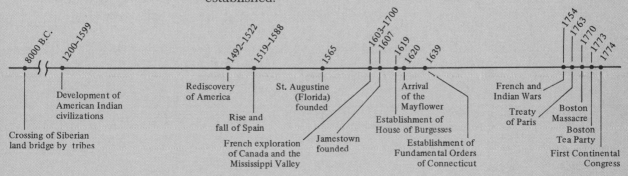

Building a Nation

The towns of early America were quite similar. The structures that first struck the eye were the village church and the courthouse, each set off from the bustling shops of the business district by a village green, or common. Often adorned with towering spires and imposing columns, the very appearance of the church and courthouse lent respect to the proceedings within. Each symbolized the community's values. The church stood for moral order and self-discipline. Without it, most Americans believed, society would dissolve into an anarchy of warring, self-interested individuals.

Those who violated the moral order had to face justice in the courthouse. And since law was as important as religion, the rituals of the courthouse were also as formal and elaborate as those of the church. The judge was addressed as "Your Honor;" motions and pleas followed special rules of procedure. The result of all this was a faith in the law, a certainty that human justice was just as unerring as divine justice.

These common values made for the strong sense of a village community. Individuals were expected to act for the good of the whole. Misfits and deviants were punished or driven from town. It was all right to get ahead in the world, but not at the expense of others. The community was a social ideal, a source of pride, and a psychological comfort. The sense of belonging spread far beyond the limits of the town. Even farmers in the most remote parts of the county shared this feeling and relied on the village for marketing, education, church services, and justice.

The village community and the values associated with it are still important in America. Our largest cities are divided into districts or boroughs and organized into neighborhood school districts. There is a longing for tradition and certainty, even amidst rapid change. Such things bind the nation together, and they bind the present to the past.

Courthouse, Newfane, Vermont

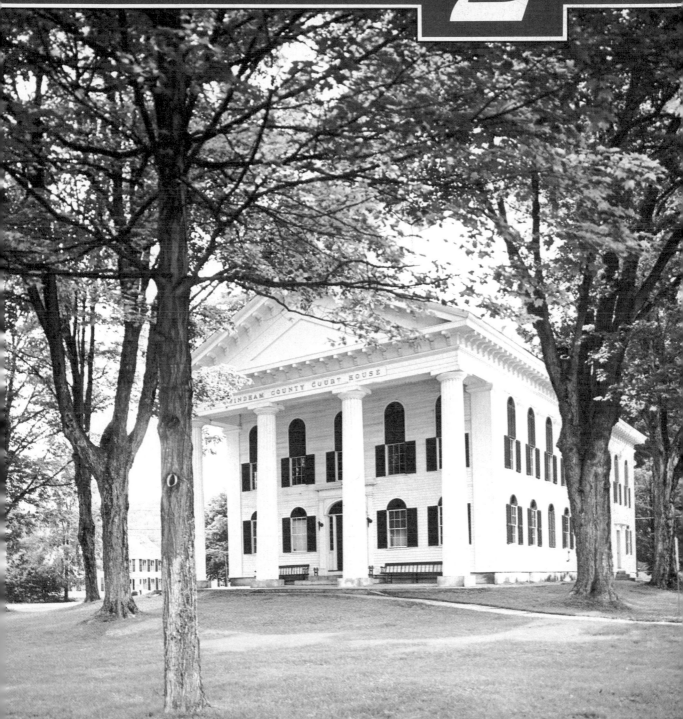

Chapter 5
1775-1783

The Triumph of Independence

The clock had just sounded midnight. The dusty rider leaped from his horse and pounded furiously on the parsonage door. The minister opened it and, with some irritation, asked the visitor his business. The breathless messenger quickly reported that a regiment of red-coated soldiers had landed on the west bank of the Charles River. Then the rider, Paul Revere, jumped back onto his horse and dashed off into the night. Upstairs, Samuel Adams, now fully awake, put on his clothes.

Adams and John Hancock—members of the Boston Committee of Correspondence—had fled Boston two weeks before. They had learned that General Gage, military governor of Massachusetts, had given orders for their arrest. The two were spending the night at the parsonage in the village of Lexington, outside Boston, after having spent a day-long meeting with rural patriots.

It was the 19th of April 1775, and the British were on their way to Lexington. Adams wondered why. To arrest him? Possibly. But more likely, it was to seize the arms and gunpowder stock hidden at Concord—a short distance from Lexington. The British had been searching for colonial arms all spring.

The village church bell tolled all night. By dawn 70-odd minutemen (farmers) had gathered on the village green at Lexington. John Hancock picked up his own sword and gun, but Adams stopped him. "That is not our business," he said, clapping Hancock on the shoulder. "We belong to the Cabinet." Their business was to create a government; others were charged with the fighting. So the two men crept to the edge of town and hid in a marsh.

The red-coated British column appeared in the gray light of dawn. Spotting the minutemen on the green, the soldiers wheeled into a line of battle. Somewhere, someone fired a shot. (Each side blamed the other for shooting first.) Then, the British line fired a volley. Eight Americans fell to the ground. The rest scattered, discharging their guns as they fled.

Chapter Objectives

After you have finished reading the chapter, you should be able to:
1. List in chronological order the events that led to the American Declaration of Independence.

98

2. Explain the basic American military strategy during the Revolutionary War in New England, in the Middle colonies, and in the South.
3. Describe the difficulties Franklin faced in negotiating the Treaty of Paris.

After this incident the British resumed their march to Concord. At the bridge north of the town, they encountered another group of armed farmers, or minutemen. An exchange of fire brought a few more losses on each side.

When the British arrived at Concord, they spent all morning searching for arms that were no longer there before starting back to Boston. Clanging church bells brought forth thousands of minutemen, who gathered behind trees and rock fences to shoot at the retreating column. Every step of the way back to Boston, the redcoats were harassed. They made the last stretch at a dead run.

So began the American Revolution.

1. Declaring Independence

BRITAIN VS. AMERICA: THE ODDS. It seemed at first that Americans had little chance against the mightiest empire in the world. The British Empire extended from Europe to India. The British outnumbered the Americans three to one. The empire had enormous financial resources, stockpiles of arms, and a mighty navy. Americans had few arms, little money, and no ships. *But they did have one very important factor on their side—distance.* A huge ocean separated them from Great Britain. This meant the British had to ship arms and armies over a wide stretch of water—a very expensive undertaking. In the end this distance, as much as anything else, defeated the British. *Distance was an important factor within the colonies, too.* American generals could

retreat over a vast, sparsely settled landscape without yielding control of anything important. Although British armies marched and conquered, they found themselves controlling nothing but the soil beneath their feet.

Americans were poorly trained in the military arts and quick to panic in the face of professional soldiers. *But in times of emergency, hundreds of citizen-soldiers could materialize from nowhere, tipping the military balance and upsetting British plans.* Moreover, the Americans were fighting for their political freedom on their territory. That gave them an enormous moral advantage over the British. As Thomas Paine, America's *propagandist* put it: "It is not a few acres of ground, but a cause that we are defending."

A *propagandist* is a person who spreads propaganda—statements that are used to win people over to a particular point of view.

THE BATTLE OF BREED'S HILL. In the weeks after the battles at Lexington and Concord (see map, page 101), armed militia headed for Boston from all over New England. By May there were nearly 10,000 at the crude headquarters in Cambridge, across the Charles River from Boston. By early June a British fleet with reinforcements had arrived in Boston, bringing a new commander, Sir William Howe. It appeared that the king meant business.

On the night of June 16, the Americans sent soldiers to occupy the hills north of Boston, across the Mystic River. With their

"The Battle of Bunker's Hill" was painted by Jonathan Trumbull during his period of study with Benjamin West in London in 1786. The battle was actually fought on Breed's Hill, which was similar in appearance to Bunker Hill. During the battle Peter Salem (the Black at right with the rifle) became a hero when he shot the British Major Pitcairn.

guns mounted on Breed's Hill, they could harass British shipping in the harbor. When June 17 dawned, the British spotted the new American fortifications, and General Howe decided to attack. He planned a frontal assault, with long red lines of soldiers marching up the hill. Howe thought the Americans would flee when confronted with British firepower, rather than stand their ground and fight.

He badly miscalculated. Three times the British marched up Breed's Hill that afternoon. And three times they were turned back by deadly American fire. The Americans fled only when they ran out of ammunition. Behind them lay nearly half of Howe's army. The British had won, but it was clear they could not afford many more such victories.

WASHINGTON TAKES CHARGE OF THE SIEGE. While American soldiers were defending Breed's Hill against a British assault, the Second Continental Congress, meeting in Philadelphia, was discussing candidates for Commander in Chief of the Continental Army. John Adams thought George Washington was the right choice—for several reasons. Since Washington was a Virginian, he would stop whispers about the war's being New England's fight. He was a gentleman of fortune, married to Martha Custis, the wealthiest woman in Virginia. Thus, he would satisfy conservatives from the middle colonies, who feared the American rabble more than the British king. He was a man of imposing height, of dignity, and of decisive bearing. He would inspire confidence in the largely amateur American army. Furthermore, he was available for the job. He had come to Philadelphia wearing the uniform of the Virginia militia, in which he was serving as an officer.

Congress agreed with Adams, and Washington became Commander in Chief of the Continental Army. Immediately, he departed for Cambridge, not to see his Virginia home for six long years.

SAGGING SPIRITS.
By the time Washington joined the army, its early mood of eager patriotism had given way to restlessness and boredom. Boston was under siege. The British who held it lacked the will to fight. The Americans lacked the gunpowder.

During the siege the number in Washington's army dwindled, as the New England militia, which had enlisted for only six months, went home. The departures did at least ease Washington's problems of supply, for he was short of food, clothing, and tents. Washington, it seems, fussed and shivered through his first winter as Commander in Chief.

THE QUEST FOR THE 14TH COLONY.
There was one operation that winter that was neither dull nor unromantic. It was a move to add Canada to the American cause. *The central figure in this operation was Benedict Arnold, a merchant from New Haven, Connecticut.*

When Arnold learned of the outbreak of fighting, he instantly thought of Fort Ticonderoga, on Lake Champlain. (See map below.) Unused in battle since the French and Indian War, Ticonderoga's walls were crumbling, and its garrison of soldiers was ill-prepared for a defense. It was an easy mark. And within the fort lay enough cannons and arms to equip an army. Beyond it lay the route to Canada.

Arnold got permission from Massachusetts authorities to lead a company of volunteers to Ticonderoga. Outside the fort in early May 1775, he encountered Ethan

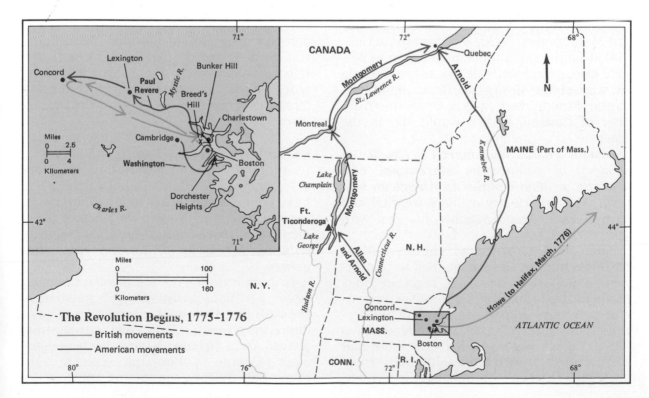

The Revolution Begins, 1775–1776

— — — British movements

——— American movements

Two women, wives of soldiers, accompanied Benedict Arnold's army on its trek through the wilderness to Quebec. The women worked as hard as any soldiers and were universally respected by the army.

Allen, a man with similar plans. Allen headed the Green Mountain Boys, a colonial group formed to protect Vermont from its neighbors. Joining forces, they captured the fort with ease.

The gateway to Canada lay open, but Arnold was not to have the honor of immediately marching through it. Instead, New York preferred to send its own army and to designate as its commander General Richard Montgomery. Next, Arnold went to General Washington and persuaded him to provide troops for a separate assault on Canada by way of the Kennebec River, in Maine. While Montgomery knocked at the front door of Canada, Arnold would slip in the back.

Arnold's wilderness march to Quebec is a story of exhaustion, starvation, and courage, seldom equaled in American history. Although a few soldiers wearied and turned back, Arnold reached his goal with over 600 left.

After Montgomery had captured Montreal, he hurried toward Quebec to join Arnold. On New Year's Eve, together, they stormed the fortress under cover of a snowstorm. They came within yards of the fortress' center, only to fail. Montgomery was killed, Arnold was wounded, and about half their troops were captured. Although Arnold besieged Quebec throughout the winter,

when British reinforcements arrived in the spring, he was forced to withdraw. Thus ended the American attempt to make Canada the 14th colony.

THE BRITISH EVACUATE BOSTON. *The colonial army was successful in its efforts to gain control of Boston Harbor.* During the winter the army, using both oxen and sleds, had dragged Fort Ticonderoga's cannons to Boston. Washington had then mounted the cannons onto the hills south of Boston, a move that forced the redcoats to evacuate. For the first time in eight years, Boston was free of British soldiers.

COMMON SENSE. During the long winter of 1776, Americans had time to reconsider their war aims. Initially, they had talked of defending their rights, but remaining in the empire. *Slowly they began to realize that those rights could be secured only by throwing off foreign rule altogether.*

In January 1776 the publication *Common Sense,* a pamphlet written by Thomas Paine, boosted the notion of complete independence even further. Paine had only recently arrived from Britain, having been encouraged to come by Benjamin Franklin. Yet Paine had quickly caught the spirit of the

Viewpoints of History

This view of Lexington is from a print done shortly after the battle. The British had instructions "on no account to fire . . . without orders." No one is really sure who fired the first shot, but when it was over eight Americans lay dead.

This view of the battle of Lexington was painted in 1855 by Hammat Billings, an artist and architect from Massachusetts. How does it compare with the earlier rendering above?

American struggle. In plain words that everyone could understand, Paine boldly advocated independence. He pointed out how silly it was for a continent to be ruled by an island. He showed how ridiculous it was for the leadership of a nation to be passed down within one family. Paine wanted a *republic* with an elected head.

A *republic* is a form of government in which the head of state is chosen by an elective process.

THE IMPACT OF PAINE'S PAMPHLET. Thousands of Americans read *Common Sense,* and their half-formed feelings were hardened into firm convictions. Soon demands for independence were heard in several legislatures. In April, North Carolina instructed its delegates in the Congress to vote for independence. Virginia did the same in May.

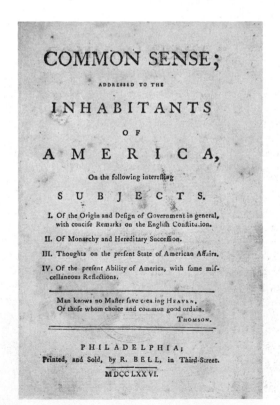

On June 7 Richard Henry Lee of Virginia presented Congress with a resolution, stating that the "united colonies are, and of right ought to be, free and independent states." He also suggested that they draft a plan of union and seek foreign allies.

The delegates from the middle colonies (New York, Pennsylvania, New Jersey, and Delaware) hesitated on independence. *But while they were stalling, the Congress appointed a committee to draft a declaration of the American position.* Although John Adams and Benjamin Franklin were on the committee, the key member was Thomas Jefferson. Jefferson was a Virginian whose political writings had revealed a gift for capturing common thoughts in unforgettable phrases. At the committee's request Jefferson went to work on the rough draft.

On July 2nd Richard Henry Lee's resolution passed Congress. On July 4th Jefferson's declaration was read to the assembled delegates. It passed with only minor changes by the committee and by the Congress. Now the nature of the war was changed. *It had become a struggle for total independence.*

THE DECLARATION OF INDEPENDENCE. Jefferson later confessed that he was not striving to say anything new in the Declaration. He sought only to summarize generally accepted ideas. He did indeed borrow heavily from other thinkers. His definition of human rights ("life, liberty, and the pursuit of happiness") was taken from John Locke. Other statements were taken from the Virginia Declaration of Rights, written only a few weeks earlier by George Mason. Yet, Jefferson—with help from Mason and other patriots—did make an important contribution. *The Declaration is a statement not only of the principles of human freedom but also those of popular government.*

The text of the Declaration of Independence is contained on pages 105–107. It is the finest statement anywhere of American ideals.

Benjamin Franklin is shown seated in the center of this painting of the signing of the Declaration of Independence, done in 1785 by Robert Edge Pine. Joked Franklin at the meeting, "We must indeed all hang together, or most assuredly we shall hang separately."

The Declaration of Independence

Preamble

When, in the course of human events, it becomes necessary for one people to dissolve the political bands which have connected them with another, and to assume, among the Powers of the earth, the separate and equal station to which the Laws of Nature and of Nature's God entitle them, a decent respect to the opinions of mankind requires that they should declare the causes which impel them to the separation.

New Principles of Government

We hold these truths to be self-evident: that all men are created equal, that they are endowed by their Creator with certain unalienable Rights, that among these are Life, Liberty, and the pursuit of Happiness.

That to secure these rights, Governments are instituted among Men, deriving their just powers from the consent of the governed. That whenever any Form of Government becomes destructive of these ends, it is the Right of the People to alter or to abolish it, and to institute new Government, laying its foundation on such principles, and organizing its powers in such form, as to them shall seem most likely to effect their Safety and Happiness. Prudence, indeed, will dictate that Governments long established should not be changed for light and transient causes; and accordingly all experience hath shown that mankind are more disposed to suffer while evils are sufferable, than to right themselves by abolishing the forms to which they are accustomed. But when a long train of abuses and usurpations, pursuing invariably the same Object, evinces a design to reduce them under absolute Despotism, it is their right, it is their duty, to throw off such Government, and to provide new Guards for their future security.—

Reasons for Separation

Such has been the patient sufferance of these Colonies; and such is now the necessity which constrains them to alter their former Systems of Government. The history of the present King of Great Britain is a history of repeated injuries and usurpations, all having in direct object the establishment of an absolute Tyranny over these States. To prove this, let facts be submitted to a candid world.

He has refused his Assent to Laws the most wholesome and necessary for the public good.

He has forbidden his Governors to pass Laws of immediate and pressing importance unless suspended in their operation till his Assent should be obtained; and when so suspended, he has utterly neglected to attend to them.

He has refused to pass other Laws for the accommodation of large districts of people, unless those people would relinquish the right of Representation in the Legislature, a right inestimable to them and formidable to tyrants only.

He has called together legislative bodies at places unusual, uncomfortable, and distant from the depository of their Public Records, for the sole purpose of fatiguing them into compliance with his measures.

He has dissolved Representative Houses repeatedly, for opposing with manly firmness, his invasions on the rights of the people.

He has refused for a long time after such dissolutions, to cause others to be elected; whereby the Legislative Powers, incapable of Annihilation, have returned to the people at large for their exercise; the State remaining, in the mean time exposed to all the dangers of invasion from without, and convulsions within.

He has endeavored to prevent the population of these states; for that purpose obstructing the Laws of Naturalization of Foreigners, refusing to pass others to encourage their migration hither, and raising the conditions of new Appropriations of Lands.

He has obstructed the Administration of Justice, by refusing his Assent to Laws for establishing Judiciary Powers.

He has made Judges dependent on his Will alone for the tenure of their offices, and the amount and payment of their salaries.

He has erected a multitude of New Offices, and sent hither swarms of Officers to harass our people and eat out their substance.

He has kept among us, in times of peace, Standing Armies. without the Consent of our legislature.

He has affected to render the Military independent of, and superior to, the Civil Power.

He has combined with others to subject us to a jurisdiction foreign to our constitution and unacknowledged by our laws; giving his Assent to their acts of pretended legislation:

For quartering large bodies of armed troops among us:

For protecting them, by a mock Trial, from Punishment for any Murders which they should commit on the Inhabitants of these States:

For cutting off our Trade with all parts of the World:

For imposing taxes on us without our Consent:

For depriving us, in many cases, of the benefits of Trial by Jury:

For transporting us beyond Seas, to be tried for pretended offenses:

For abolishing the free System of English Laws in a neighboring Province, establishing therein an Arbitrary government, and enlarging its Boundaries so as to render it at once an example and fit instrument for introducing the same absolute rule into these Colonies:

For taking away our Charters, abolishing our most valuable Laws, and altering fundamentally the forms of our governments:

For suspending our own Legislatures, and declaring themselves invested with Power to legislate for us in all cases whatsoever.

He has abdicated government here, by declaring us out of his Protection and waging War against us.

He has plundered our seas, ravaged our Coasts, burned our towns, and destroyed the lives of our people.

He is at this time transporting large armies of foreign mercenaries to complete the works of death, desolation, and tyranny already begun with circumstances of Cruelty & perfidy scarcely paralleled in the most barbarous ages, and totally unworthy the Head of a civilized nation.

He has constrained our fellow Citizens taken Captive on the high Seas to bear Arms against their Country, to become the executioners of their friends and Brethren, or to fall themselves by their Hands.

He has excited domestic insurrections among us, and has endeavored to bring on the inhabitants of our frontiers, the merciless Indian Savages, whose known rule of warfare is an undistinguished destruction of all ages, sexes, and conditions.

In every stage of these Oppressions We have Petitioned for Redress in the most humble terms. Our repeated Petitions have been answered only by repeated injury. A Prince whose character is thus marked by every act which may define a Tyrant, is unfit to be the ruler of a free People.

Nor have We been wanting in attention to our British brethren. We have warned them from time to time of attempts by their legislature to extend an unwarrantable jurisdiction over us. We have reminded them of the circumstances of our emigration and settlement here. We have appealed to their native justice and magnanimity, and we have conjured them by the ties of our common kindred, to disavow these usurpations, which, would inevitably interrupt our connections and correspondence. They, too have been deaf to the voice of justice and of consanguinity. We must, therefore, acquiesce in the necessity, which denounces our Separation, and hold them, as we hold the rest of mankind, Enemies in War, in Peace, Friends.

Formal Declaration of War

We, therefore, the Representatives of the united States of America, in General Congress Assembled, appealing to the Supreme Judge of the world for the rectitude of our intentions, do, in the Name, and by Authority of the good People of these colonies, solemnly publish and declare, That these United Colonies are, and of Right ought to be, Free and Independent States; that they are Absolved from all allegiance to the British Crown, and that all political connection between them and the State of Great Britain is, and ought to be, totally dissolved; and that, as Free and Independent States, they have full Power to levy War, conclude Peace, contract Alliances, establish Commerce, and to do all other Acts and Things which Independent States may

of a right do. And, for the support of this Declaration, with a firm reliance on the Protection of Divine Providence, we mutually pledge to each other our Lives, our Fortunes, and our sacred Honor.

Section Review

1. Mapping: Using the map and key on page 101, trace the British and American movements shown on the map. How far is Fort Ticonderoga from Boston? 79-100
2. Identify or explain: General Howe, the Green Mountain Boys, Thomas Paine, 99 Benedict Arnold.
3. Why did John Adams believe that George Washington was the best choice for Commander in Chief of the Continental Army?

2. The Fight for Independence

DOUBTS ABOUT INDEPENDENCE. Proclaiming independence was one thing. Winning it was quite another. It was to take seven years of bloody warfare.

The Declaration did force Americans to make an important decision—the decision of their loyalty. Many Americans viewed the independence movement with anger; some viewed it with fear. Public officeholders and members of the Church of England were often reluctant to sever ties with Britain. Many of the wealthy feared the breakdown of law and order and did not know what to expect from rule by the "lower orders." Their fears were sometimes confirmed by the heavy-handed actions taken by the Sons of Liberty in enforcing the restrictions demanded by Congress. "Which is better," grumbled a member of the New England clergy, "to endure a royal tyrant

3,000 miles away, or to suffer 3,000 tyrants not a mile away?"

Many of those who cooperated in the revolutionary movement—even those who served in the Continental Congress—feared that the Revolution might lead to the breakdown of social order. They argued that, before taking the final step of independence, Congress ought to create a national government. But the radicals had their way. Congress decided that a federal union would come after independence.

THE LOYALISTS. The Declaration forced the doubters to decide. It proclaimed the existence of a new nation. And in the resulting military emergency, opposition was treason. Wavering was no longer allowed.

Many of those who chose to remain loyal to Britain fled to Canada. Others kept silent until the approach of a British army enabled them to show their loyalty. In all, about one fourth of the White population sympathized openly or secretly with the British. A substantial number of these sympathizers enlisted in Loyalist regiments, which the British formed during the war.

WHO WERE THE LOYALISTS? It is hard to say who the Loyalists were. Some were wealthy men and women who feared the mob. Others were lawyers and physicians who disliked upheaval. In New England, members of the Church of England—a religious minority—were often Loyalists. In New Jersey and Pennsylvania, Quakers and Germans appeared to be neutral, if not hostile. In the South farmers in the back country were sometimes loyal to Britain. Apparently they disliked the wealthy planters who governed their colonies more than they disliked the British. In the Carolinas, Scottish Highlanders, recently arrived in America, fought for the British. The choice depended on the circumstances.

Even though some Loyalists joined the British Army, the American Revolution never became a civil war, a war of American against American. However, many families were split into Loyalist and Patriot sympathizers. Loyalist women had husbands who fought in the American Army, and Patriot women had husbands who fought with the British.

Throughout the war Loyalists were tolerated if they were outwardly peaceful. Those who fled to Canada or the West Indies during the war had their property seized. But they were allowed to return after the war. Although their property was never restored, they did receive, within a few years, full legal and political rights.

THE REVOLUTION AND BLACK FREEDOM. The revolutionary years were unsettling for Americans. However, the disruption of American society was not without its positive side. *Among those who benefited from it were Black slaves.* The Revolution offered many of them the first opportunity to change their status.

Sidenote to History
The 25,000 Runaway Slaves

Southern planters, unwilling to admit that their slaves had been discontented, claimed that the British had forcefully carried them away. But this seems unlikely. The British made no effort to keep them in slavery and actually found them an embarrassment. They carried the Blacks first to Halifax, Nova Scotia, where they nearly froze, and then to London, which they found equally uncomfortable. In 1787 the British government sent them back to Africa, establishing for them a new colony, Sierra Leone. It was the first effort to return Blacks to Africa, more than a quarter of a century before Americans founded the Black republic of Liberia for ex-slaves.

Running away had been a slave's common form of resistance to slavery. But it had rarely been successful because slaves had no place to go. With the Revolution, however, slaves had found a haven of freedom. When the British forces had landed in the southern colonies, thousands of slaves had fled to the British lines.

The contradictions posed by the fact of slavery and the principles of the Declaration of Independence also troubled many people. Vermont was the first to act. When it formed a constitution in 1777, it prohibited slavery by law. Other New England states had taken similar action during the war.

In Massachusetts, Quock Walker, a house servant, sued for and won his freedom on the grounds that the state constitution—a product of the revolutionary era—declared all persons to be free and equal. The court decision affected not only Quock Walker. The principle on which Walker won his freedom automatically freed other slaves in the state as well.

The colonies of New York, New Jersey, and Pennsylvania were more hesitant. They enacted laws after the Revolution that provided for the gradual freeing of slaves. Children born of slave parents were free when they reached a certain age. The problem with this system was that it was terribly slow. New York still had a few slaves in the 1820's.

The quickest road to freedom during the Revolution was enlistment in the army. All states except South Carolina and Georgia offered freedom to any slave who joined the army. And many did. About 5,000 Blacks

Hessians were mercenary soldiers who fought for the British during the Revolutionary War. Those pictured here were from the Drittes 3rd Regiment Guard. Many Hessians were surprised by America's fighting ability, since Hessians believed that soldiers had to be dressed properly to fight well.

fought with the colonists against the British.

Slavery was a difficult issue for many people. Thomas Jefferson objected to slavery in principle but could never bring himself to accept the idea of freedom. He feared that freeing the slaves would lead to bloodshed, since many Blacks would naturally want revenge.

Although the steps taken toward freeing slaves during the Revolution were limited, they were an important beginning. By 1785 the first *secular* antislavery society had been founded, in New York. Thereafter, the subject of *emancipation* was more frequently and openly discussed.

Secular means nonreligious, or not under church influence.

Emancipation is the act of freeing a person from slavery or strict rule.

THE FALL OF NEW YORK. In July 1776 a huge British force appeared suddenly in New York. The king clearly wanted a quick end to the war and had hired some 9,000 German soldiers to help do it. Pay and living conditions in the British Army were poor, and the British were always short of volunteers. So they employed professional soldiers—known as mercenaries—from the German states of Europe.

Americans strongly resented these foreign soldiers, who were fighting for pay instead of principle. And because many of them were from the German state of Hesse, all Germans serving with the British soon became known as Hessians. In all, about

This famous painting of Washington's Delaware crossing was done by Emanual Leutze, who had never been to America. There are a number of mistakes in the painting. The American flag did not yet exist, there are no mountains in the Trenton area, and there are too many people in the boat. Can you find another big mistake?

30,000 Germans served in America, and many stayed after the war.

Washington had anticipated the British arrival and had moved his army south from Boston during the spring. Placing his men on Brooklyn Heights, a series of low hills on the western end of Long Island, he worked throughout the summer to make it another Breed's Hill.

But Howe had learned his lesson. By carefully planning his strategy, he soundly defeated Washington, who escaped across the East River. Then, when Howe landed on Manhattan in mid-September, Washington was forced to retreat even further north.

Washington eventually crossed the Hudson River to defend a fort in New Jersey (see map at right), but Howe sent his best lieutenant, Lord Cornwallis, after him. With a deteriorating army, Washington was no match for Cornwallis, and he was forced to flee to the Delaware River. There, Washington grabbed the available boats and crossed the river to the security of Pennsylvania.

TRENTON AND PRINCETON. It was December 1776. The British were ready to call it quits for the winter. Washington was in desperate straits. His army had drifted

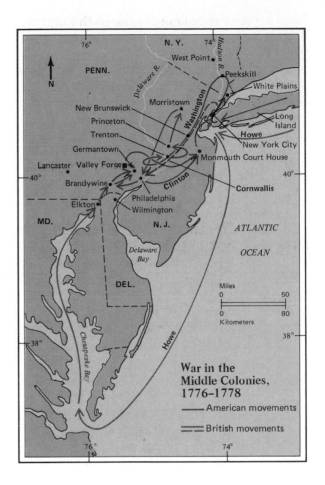

War in the
Middle Colonies,
1776–1778

—— American movements

==== British movements

Sidenote to History

The Valiant Death of Nathan Hale

After the British seized New York in September 1776, General Washington wanted information on the city's defenses. He sent out a request for a volunteer who would spy behind enemy lines. Captain Nathan Hale of Connecticut stepped forward.

Disguised as a school teacher, Captain Hale crossed from Connecticut, where his regiment was based, to Long Island. From there he took a ferryboat to New York. He wandered through the city, mapping the British defenses and noting the strength of the army. On the way out of the city, he got by all the guards—but the last. They stopped him, searched him, and found his notes, hidden in his shoe. Although Hale instantly identified himself as an officer in the American army, the British hanged him as a spy.

Nathan Hale's final words, as recorded by a British officer, were: "I only regret that I have but one life to lose for my country." That was truly the *Spirit of '76*.

away. It now numbered no more than 5,000. Many of those were due to go home at New Year's.

Then Washington saw his chance. The British garrison at Trenton, New Jersey, was isolated and small. A surprise attack might capture it. Thus, on Christmas night Washington crossed the Delaware River, hoping to catch the Hessians in the midst of holiday celebrations. The plan worked perfectly. With scarcely a shot he captured the entire garrison, though a few escaped to sound the alarm.

While Cornwallis hurried down from New York, adding to his forces as he went, Washington slipped around him and attacked Princeton, capturing that garrison and burning all its supplies.

For Washington it had been a brilliant campaign. In two short weeks he had restored American morale and had regained every advantage the British had won in six months. By January 1777 the British held New York City, and nothing more.

THE BRITISH STRATEGY. The British, however, were determined to make 1777 the year they would end the war and destroy the new nation. They planned to invade upper New York, by way of Lake Champlain, and proceed down the Hudson River to New York City. *This strategy was supposed to split the colonies into two and shatter American morale.*

BURGOYNE'S MARCH. Placed in charge of the invasion was General John Burgoyne (bur-GOYN), who had helped chase Benedict Arnold out of Canada the year before. The king supplied him with a fresh army of 6,000 soldiers. While Burgoyne marched on New York, Howe planned to attack Philadelphia and capture the headquarters of the American government.

Burgoyne's march would be a dramatic event, for there was much at stake. The Americans had to stop him, but there was no organized force to do it. Washington had to follow Howe south to Philadelphia.

Getting under way in June 1777, Burgoyne swept down Lake Champlain and captured the American force at Ticonderoga, with scarcely a shot fired. He then started over the mountain ridge to the Hudson River. This proved slow going, for Americans felled trees across the road every step of the way. The farther Burgoyne went into the New York woods, the more difficult it became to advance. The Green Mountain Boys were closing in behind him and threatening his supply lines. When Burgoyne sent several Hessians to Bennington, Vermont, to get food, they were surrounded and captured. Nevertheless, he pushed on in a desperate attempt to reach Albany. From there he hoped to make contact with the British army in New York City.

In Albany, General Horatio Gates was frantically building an army. Even though

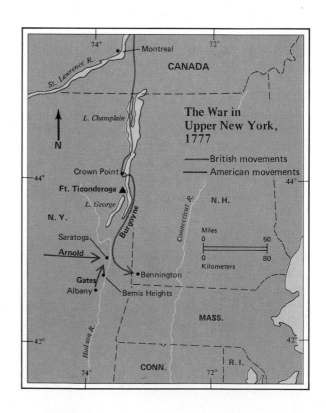

Washington had lent him a few regiments, he had to rely mainly on New England militia, who had flooded into his headquarters after Burgoyne's Indian allies attacked a few pioneer families.

During the war American Indian tribes sided with both the British and the Americans. The Oneida of New York, for instance, were allied with the Americans, as were the Tuscarora, Creek, and Cherokee of the southern states. The Mohawk, on the other hand, were strong supporters of the British. Thayendanegea, an important Mohawk leader—also known as Joseph Brant—led bands of British troops and Iroquois warriors on border raids.

Gates placed his army on Bemis Heights (see map, page 112), with the river on one side and the woods on the other. The fighting began on September 19th, when the colonial regiment of Virginia sharpshooters began sniping at the British troops from the woods. The fighting ended on October 7th, when an American detachment, led by Benedict Arnold, crushed the British force. *Ten days later, at the nearby town of Saratoga, Burgoyne surrendered his entire army.*

"PHILADELPHIA TAKES HOWE".

The campaign of General Howe fared somewhat better. He sailed from New York in July 1777, leaving Sir Henry Clinton in command of the city and with orders to aid Burgoyne.

Suspecting that Howe was bound for Philadelphia, Washington moved south and met Howe in September 1777 at Brandywine Creek, near the Pennsylvania-Delaware border. (See map, page 111.) *Despite Washington's efforts to hold the British back, Howe slipped past the American forces and took Philadelphia.* Washington retired to Valley Forge, Pennsylvania, and went into winter quarters.

When Benjamin Franklin, serving as American envoy to France, was told that Howe had taken the American capital, he

Joseph Brant, the Mohawk leader, allied with the British and raided colonial settlements throughout upper New York. Why do you think he formed an alliance with the British?

replied: "I beg your pardon, sir. Philadelphia has taken Howe." And so it seemed. It was a comfortable place to spend a winter, but there were no other military advantages. Howe controlled the city and that was all. In European warfare the capture of the capital city was enough to end a war. *In America the Continental Congress, chased out of Philadelphia, simply set up shop in Lancaster, Pennsylvania.*

THE FRENCH ALLIANCE. Benjamin Franklin was delighted by the news of Burgoyne's surrender at Saratoga. He had been sent to France a year earlier to persuade the French to enter the war on the American side. He had found the French minister, Vergennes (vair-ZHEN), willing to supply arms and money, but unwilling to enter into the war until he was more certain of America's staying power. The French were eager to embarrass their old enemies, the British, and Vergennes had arranged for secret arms shipments to America. The French had also agreed to lend Congress several million livres (LEE-vruh), a French coin equal to a portion of a dollar. For much of the war, it was the only respectable money Congress had.

When news of Saratoga arrived, Franklin pointed out that it was now time for a French alliance. Americans had proved they could win battles and carry their own weight. Vergennes agreed. *The treaty of alliance was signed in February 1778.* Three months later France entered the war, and in 1779 France's ally, Spain, joined as well. What had started as a spat between Britain and its colonies had become an international war.

EUROPEAN RECRUITS. *In addition to money and arms, Franklin recruited soldiers to go to America.* Knowing that Washington's army lacked experience, he offered military commissions to professional European soldiers willing to fight. Among the first to accept were the Polish cavalry officer Casimir Pulaski (pu-LAS-kee) and the great military engineer Thaddeus Kosciusko (kahs-ih-UHS-koh). Kosciusko played a major role in Burgoyne's defeat. He designed the fortifications at West Point and built Gates's defenses on Bemis Heights.

In the summer of 1777, the young French aristocrat Marquis de Lafayette sailed for America. There, Washington came to regard him as his best officer. *Other additions to Washington's army included women who had enlisted by pretending to be men.* Deborah Sampson Gannett, for instance, had joined the 11th Massachusetts Regiment under the name of Robert Shurtleff. Women had also taken over the military duties of their wounded or dead husbands. When her husband was killed, Margaret Corbin had taken over his position behind a cannon. After being injured in battle and

Deborah Sampson enlisted in the colonial army in 1782. She fought in several battles, was wounded, and then discharged. After the war she lectured on her experiences. In 1805 she began receiving a soldier's pension from the United States government.

losing the use of an arm, she was assigned to the Invalid Regiment at West Point.

THE BRITISH IN PHILADELPHIA. *Howe and his officers spent a very social winter in the American capital.* They waltzed through the season at a round of dances and dinners thrown by Philadelphia Loyalists.

At one point the British tried to attack American troops camped at Whitemarsh, north of Philadelphia. But their plans were foiled by Lydia Darragh, a determined Patriot. When she overheard British officers discussing plans for the attack, she formed a plan of her own to alert the Americans. First she asked General Howe, head of the occupying forces, for permission to go to the flour mill at Frankford, a town located outside Philadelphia. With permission granted,

Darragh walked through the snow to the mill—and kept walking—her destination, the American outpost at Whitemarsh. There she told an American officer of the British plans.

When the British arrived at Whitemarsh, the Americans were ready for them. The British, expecting to launch a surprise attack, discovered that they were less numerous than the Americans. So they turned around and went back to Philadelphia, without firing a shot.

WASHINGTON AT VALLEY FORGE. *While the British were enjoying Philadelphia's social life. Washington and his ill-equipped, poorly clothed, and untrained army were freezing at Valley Forge.* During that winter a German officer appeared in the American camp. He identified himself as Baron von Steuben (SHTOY-bun), a general in the armies of the European King,

Frederick the Great. Although he had exaggerated his rank (he was a captain) and his title (he had none), von Steuben made a good impression. Some of the other foreign arrivals had embarrassed Washington by demanding instant command. Von Steuben had merely offered to be helpful.

Washington made von Steuben the Inspector General and asked him to train the soldiers. Such a task was not easy, since Americans did not take kindly to military discipline. But von Steuben managed. He set up a system that worked. He taught the soldiers how to drill with muskets, how to march in step, and how to switch ranks from marching column to battle formation. He taught them how to fight in a professional manner.

FIGHTING SHIFTS TO THE SOUTH. In 1778 General Howe turned over his command to Sir Henry Clinton. Clinton, who

The battle of Monmouth, New Jersey, was fought on a scorchingly hot day in June 1778. Mary Hays' water bucket was a most welcome sight to the soldiers, who nicknamed her Molly Pitcher. When her husband was wounded, she assumed his place at the cannon.

115

had never approved of the Philadelphia venture, resolved to leave that city and return the army to New York. Washington then followed the strung-out British forces and pounced on them at Monmouth Court House, New Jersey. (See map, page 111.) In a day-long battle on an extremely hot 28th of June, the two armies fought to a draw. The next morning the British resumed their march to New York, leaving Washington with the field of battle and a technical victory.

After this the war in the North died down, and the scene of action shifted to the South. Except for an unsuccessful British attack on Charleston, South Carolina, at the beginning of the war, the South had so far escaped the fighting. This in itself was strange, for the southern colonies were the most valuable of all. The South grew such crops as tobacco, rice, and indigo—staples that Britain could not produce. The surplus from these crops brought a handsome profit on the continent. The southern colonies imported most of their manufactured goods and depended on Britain for banking services. Besides, rumor had it that there was a large number of Loyalists in the south just waiting to show their colors.

CORNWALLIS CONQUERS THE SOUTH. In December 1778 a British army landed at Savannah and overcame Georgia. As a result, Congress hastily organized a southern army and placed Benjamin Lincoln in command. Lincoln and the British maneuvered through the tidal swamps of South Carolina for a year, until Clinton bottled up Lincoln in Charleston and forced his surrender in May 1780. (See map below.) *The loss of Lincoln's army, of some 5,000 soldiers, was the biggest American defeat of the war.* Confident that South Carolina was under control, Clinton started toward New York, leaving Lord Cornwallis in command.

GATES'S DEFEAT. Congress designated the hero of Saratoga, Horatio Gates, as the new commander in the South. But when Gates encountered Cornwallis and the sight of British bayonets, at Camden, South Carolina, Gates's militia panicked and fled, sweeping their commander along with them. Congress then fired Gates and asked Washington to name a new commander in the South. Washington selected Nathanael Greene, who had been a Rhode Island bookseller before the war.

GREENE TAKES COMMAND. By the time Greene arrived in the South, the situation had changed considerably. Two victories had eliminated Cornwallis's western flank, and had enabled Greene to concentrate on the main army of the British.

Greene shrewdly let Cornwallis roam the woods of North Carolina without risking his

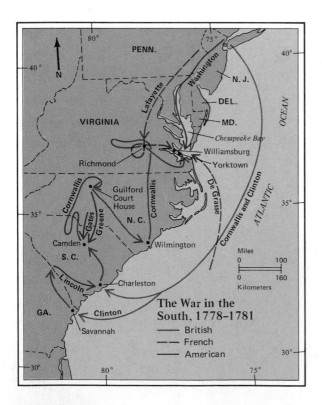

The War in the South, 1778–1781

— British
--- French
— American

own force in battle. As Cornwallis soon discovered, he could march triumphantly for hundreds of kilometers (miles) and find himself in possession of nothing but the soil under his feet. In March 1781, Greene at last gave battle at Guilford, North Carolina, and the two armies fought to a draw. Frantic for a victory, Cornwallis pursued Greene, but he had slipped nimbly into Virginia.

YORKTOWN: THE WORLD TURNED UPSIDE DOWN. Cornwallis was convinced that to hold the Carolinas, he would have to take Virginia. He decided to act. In April 1781, he started north, expecting Greene to follow. Instead, Greene slipped around the British forces and headed for South Carolina. While Cornwallis rampaged across Virginia, Greene captured, one by one, the British outposts holding South Carolina. Greene's action unfortunately left Virginia at Cornwallis's mercy.

Washington sent Lafayette south to keep an eye on Cornwallis, giving him command of a few regiments of Virginia and Maryland *Continentals.* After von Steuben and another officer, Anthony Wayne, joined forces with Lafayette, Cornwallis retired to Yorktown, near Chesapeake Bay, to await relief from New York. Lafayette then set up camp at Williamsburg and sent a letter to General Washington.

Continentals were soldiers in the service of the Congress, as opposed to those in the state militia. They served for three years, or less, depending on the duration of the war, and were generally better trained than the states' citizen-soldiers.

If Washington could bring the main army south before the relief ships arrived, wrote Lafayette, they might trap Cornwallis. Fortunately, Lafayette's letter arrived at Washington's New York headquarters along with word from French Admiral De Grasse that the French fleet would be in American waters that summer.

Washington then ordered De Grasse to Chesapeake Bay to blockade Cornwallis, while Washington headed south. De Grasse ferried him down Chesapeake Bay, and the combined French-American force joined Lafayette outside Yorktown. (See map, page 116.) When the British relief force arrived, the two fleets fought a battle that neither side won. But it was enough to send the British ships back to New York for repairs. Cornwallis was trapped.

On October 19, 1781, Cornwallis surrendered his army of about 7,000 soldiers. The British band piped a tune called "The World Turned Upside Down." The fighting had ended.

By then Greene was in possession of South Carolina, and the British were back to where they had started. They held only New York and Charleston. By the end of the year, they had evacuated Charleston, and in December 1782, after the first articles of peace were signed, New York was evacuated.

Section Review

1. Mapping: Using the map on page 116, notice the way British, French, and American troops met at Yorktown. Why do you think this city was so strategically important?
2. Identify or explain: Loyalists, Cornwallis, Corbin, Gates, Kosciusko, Pulaski, von Steuben, Quock Walker, Brant, Lafayette, Greene.
3. Why were the American victories at Trenton and Princeton especially important to the Revolutionary cause?
4. Why was Burgoyne's defeat at Saratoga a grave blow to British strategy?
5. Describe the strategy used by Washington and Lafayette to defeat Cornwallis at Yorktown. Why was the "world turned upside down" there?

3. A Victorious Peace

PEACE TERMS. Whenever anyone asked Benjamin Franklin about American peace terms, he had a standard answer. Peace was easy, he would reply; simply grant independence and remove all British armies. American friendship, however, was something else. The British had injured people and had damaged property. Americans would be much more willing to establish a better relationship with Britain if they were given Canada and Florida.

THE MONEY CRISIS. Franklin had no instructions on the terms of a peace settlement. In fact, even Congress did not begin thinking about the subject until 1779. And at that point the war was looking grim. The British were sweeping through Georgia and South Carolina. Congress was out of money and discouraged. Indeed, the nation was rapidly approaching a financial crisis.

Lacking gold and silver, Congress had financed the war by printing paper money.

People had accepted it at first. But when Congress kept printing more, they became suspicious. As farmers and merchants raised their prices, each shopper had to begin carrying a basket of money to the store to buy a small sackful of food. Thus, as the value of paper money declined, people stopped accepting the Continental paper altogether.

PEACE PROBLEMS. In the midst of this crisis, Congress was not very hopeful about a peace settlement. As a result, Congress told Franklin to follow the lead of France at the peace table. Franklin realized that this might not be the best approach. The French might help America fight for independence, but they would not help the new nation to win much territory. Vergennes might enjoy embarrassing the British, but he had no interest in creating a New World giant across the Atlantic.

So Franklin waited. A turn in the fortunes of war might give him the chance to negotiate a better settlement. He might even have to avoid the French altogether.

This painting of the Paris peace talks of 1783 was done by Benjamin West. West started with the American delegation (left to right): John Jay, John Adams, Benjamin Franklin, Henry Laurens, and William Temple Franklin. The picture was not finished because the British commissioners refused to pose. How might you explain their refusal?

THE PEACE OF PARIS, 1783. Then came news of Washington's victory at Yorktown and, shortly after that, of a change in British ministries. *Near bankruptcy and discouraged with the course of the war, Parliament had forced King George III to accept a new set of ministers, officials more inclined to make peace.* The new foreign secretary was a man who Franklin had known well in London before the war, and Franklin promptly contacted him. The secretary sent a secret agent to see Franklin in Paris, where they began peace talks in April 1782.

In the meantime Congress added John Adams and John Jay to its peace delegation. Adams and Jay arrived to find that Franklin and his British friend had taken some steps toward reaching a settlement. The two approved what Franklin had done and continued working on a settlement, before signing a preliminary agreement in November 1782. *The British agreed to American independence and promised to remove their armies. Boundaries of the new nation would extend north and west to the Great Lakes and the Mississippi and south to Florida.*

The Loyalists presented the stickiest problem. Britain demanded that the property taken from the Loyalists during the war be returned. Franklin informed them that this was impossible, since the states had already sold the property to finance the war. The resulting treaty was a compromise. It merely prevented the states from making future seizures.

DIFFICULTIES WITH FRANCE. Because these arrangements between the United States and Britain were made in secret, *they violated America's alliance with France. Each ally had pledged not to make peace without the other.*

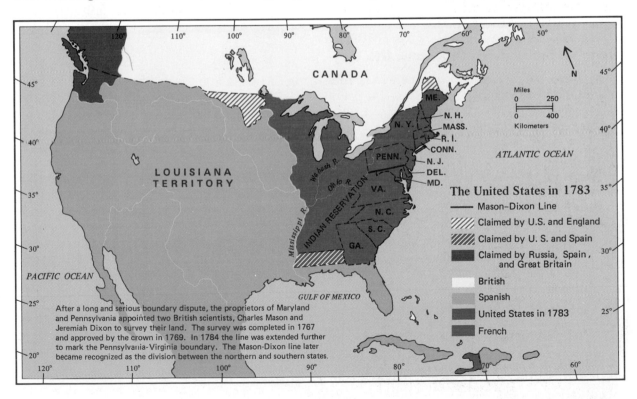

CANADA

LOUISIANA TERRITORY

ME.
N. H.
N. Y.
MASS.
R. I.
CONN.
PENN.
N. J.
DEL.
MD.
VA.
N. C.
S. C.
GA.

INDIAN RESERVATION

Wabash R.
Ohio R.
Mississippi R.

ATLANTIC OCEAN

PACIFIC OCEAN

GULF OF MEXICO

Miles
0   250
0   400
Kilometers

The United States in 1783
—— Mason–Dixon Line
Claimed by U.S. and England
Claimed by U. S. and Spain
Claimed by Russia, Spain, and Great Britain
British
Spanish
United States in 1783
French

After a long and serious boundary dispute, the proprietors of Maryland and Pennsylvania appointed two British scientists, Charles Mason and Jeremiah Dixon to survey their land. The survey was completed in 1767 and approved by the crown in 1769. In 1784 the line was extended further to mark the Pennsylvania-Virginia boundary. The Mason-Dixon line later became recognized as the division between the northern and southern states.

With the articles signed, the American commissioners sent Franklin to inform Vergennes, who was not surprised by what he heard. Further, there was little he could do about the situation. Franklin reminded him that a public split between the United States and France would only encourage the British.

Franklin then suggested that France give America another loan to demonstrate their continuing friendship. Vergennes agreed. Thus, *the vessel that Franklin had specially hired to speed the Anglo-American articles of peace to Philadelphia also carried another two million livres to restore the sagging pocketbook of the Continental Congress.* It was Benjamin Franklin's final triumph.

Sidenote to History

The Traitor and the Spy

The stranger rode at a trot down the road from the north. "Gentlemen," he greeted a patrol guarding the road to New York City, "I hope you belong to our party."

The soldiers stared, not understanding. "I am glad to see you," the stranger continued. "I am an officer in the British service, and I hope you will not detain me." Unimpressed, the soldiers rudely ordered him to dismount. The stranger then realized he had made a terrible mistake. These were not Loyalist troops at all.

The soldiers seemed confused. A British officer—yet, he wore the clothes of a farmer. What had he been doing in enemy territory? The stranger, trying to recover from his mistake, gave a laugh and showed a pass signed by the commander of the river fortifications. That was even more confusing. Why would General Arnold issue a pass to a British officer?

Suspicious, the soldiers had him undress. In one of his stockings, they found a packet of papers. One of the soldiers read the documents. Suddenly he cried out: "This is a spy!"

The soldiers quickly called their commanding officer, who took the documents to his headquarters for examination. The documents appeared to be descriptions of West Point and other forts along the Hudson. Concluding that they were forgeries intended to embarrass General Arnold, the colonel sent Arnold a note, asking what he should do with the spy. He sent the documents themselves to the Commander in Chief, George Washington.

The next morning Benedict Arnold sat down to breakfast at his headquarters across the river from West Point. His aides were about to join him when a messenger entered with a note. Arnold glanced at the message and excused himself. He then went upstairs into his wife's room. All was lost, he told her.

Through the door an aide announced that one of General Washington's servants had arrived, and the General himself was soon expected. Arnold shouted that he had to cross the river to West Point to prepare a reception for the commander in chief.

Minutes later General Washington arrived, accompanied by his young French friend, General Lafayette, and his aide, Alexander Hamilton. General Arnold, Washington was informed, had gone to prepare a reception for him at West Point.

Washington had come to inspect the forts along the river, which were an important part of the defenses that ringed New York City. When Arnold failed to appear, Washington inspected the forts himself, including the main stronghold, West Point. Mysteriously, there was no reception and no Arnold.

Washington felt vaguely uneasy. The forts were in a terrible state of disrepair. And there were not many soldiers around. In one place half the garrison had been sent off to look for firewood. With so much to be done, why had Arnold been so lax?

Suddenly Alexander Hamilton arrived with a packet of documents that had been taken that morning from a stranger on the road to New York City. Washington looked through the papers and found the answer to his question. The neglect was part of a plan. Arnold had tried to betray the forts to the British! Only the chance arrest of Arnold's messenger, Major John Andre, had thwarted the scheme. Alerted by the message sent by the colonel of the guards, Arnold had made his escape.

Such was the treason of Benedict Arnold—an attempt to turn over West Point and the related forts on the Hudson River to the British. Had he succeeded, it would have been a disaster. Once in control of the Hudson, the British could have used their naval strength to range deep into New York State.

Why did Arnold commit treason? No one knows. Arnold had lost his leg in the Saratoga campaign and was unfit for field command. In remembrance of his many contributions, Washington had placed him in charge of Philadelphia after the British had left the city. As a military hero, he was the social lion of Philadelphia. But his entertainment expenses soon exceeded his military pay. Before long he was deeply in debt and under suspicion for the mishandling of army supplies. Then, he met and married Peggy Shippen, whose friends were Loyalists.

Through Peggy, Arnold made contact with the British headquarters in New York. He resigned his Philadelphia post because of the investigation into the disappearance of military supplies. As a final favor he asked Washington to give him command of West Point.

What happened to Major John Andre, the messenger whose foolish blunder unmasked the betrayal? Washington ordered him tried by a military court as a spy. Andre was convicted and hanged, and his body was sent to New York. It lies today in the British hall of heroes, Westminster Abbey, London.

What of Peggy Shippen Arnold? While she was safely on board the *Vulture,* a British vessel that lay at anchor in the Hudson, Arnold wrote Washington, asking him to keep watch on Mrs. Arnold, who was innocent of wrongdoing. Seeing no reason to punish her, Washington let her return to her family in Philadelphia. She later joined her husband in England. They lived out their broken lives in a foreign land, never fully accepted or trusted by the people for whom they had sacrificed everything.

Section Review

1. Mapping: Using the map on page 119, trace the boundaries of the new nation. How did its territory compare in size with that of the 13 colonies?
2. Identify or explain: Benjamin Franklin, Vergennes, the Treaty of Paris, John Jay.
3. How did Franklin's diplomacy help to secure a better set of treaty terms for Americans?
4. What happened to Loyalists after the war?
5. What role did France play in the negotiations at the end of the war?

Chapter 5 Review

Bird's-Eye View

It is extremely difficult to suppress a guerrilla movement that has the support of the people. And the American Revolution had many of the characteristics of a guerrilla war. There were sudden raids on isolated outposts. There were generals who would run rather than risk defeat and who would fight only when they had the advantage. And there was the sudden massing of citizen-soldiers, who seemed to appear from nowhere.

It is hard to see how America could have lost the Revolution, no matter how grim things often looked. When the royal governors fled to British ships, there was no imperial authority anywhere. In addition, Britain had to conquer a vast amount of land.

Britain could never have stamped out the American movement for independence, but a string of British victories could have worn the Americans down. That was the importance of the French alliance. French arms and money enabled Washington to put a respectable fighting force in the field.

Yet, if the Americans had relied solely on France to have obtained their independence, they would have been unable to have made good their claim to the interior of the continent. Vergennes had planned to confine the young American republic to the seaboard, probably in the hope of some day recovering Louisiana for France. (France had ceded Louisiana to Spain in 1763.) It was the bold diplomacy of Benjamin Franklin that confirmed the final victory.

Vocabulary

Define or identify each of the following:

republic

propagandist

Deborah Sampson
  Gannett

Thomas Paine

Loyalists

mercenaries

General Horatio
  Gates

revolutionary

emancipation

Review Questions

1. Describe the Continental Army at the time that George Washington was named commander in chief.
2. The Declaration of Independence split the American colonists into different groups. One of these groups was the Loyalists. Who were the Loyalists?
3. What steps were taken during the revolution to end slavery?
4. Compare the British army in Philadelphia to the Continental Army at Valley Forge during the winter of 1777–1778.
5. What was the significance of the British surrender at Yorktown?
6. What were the provisions of the Treaty of Paris in 1783?

Reviewing Social Studies Skills

1. Using the map insert on page 101, answer the following:
   a. Where was the first battle of the Revolution?
   b. Where were the headquarters of the American forces?
   c. What is the name of the hill on which the Americans and British fought?
   d. What is the name of the site that Washington traveled to from Cambridge?
2. Using the map on page 111, list the cities that Washington's troops traveled through between 1776 and 1778.
3. Using the map on page 116, explain how the French helped the Americans win the war.
4. Using the map on page 119, locate the approximate longitude of the western border of the United States in 1783.

Reading for Meaning

1. Although the Declaration of Independence has no legal authority today, it serves as an inspirational basis for our government. What are the principles of human rights and of government set down in this document?
2. Benedict Arnold was a hero and a traitor. Describe both his contributions and his treachery during the Revolution.
3. Explain the meaning of the words or phrases underlined below, which are found in the Declaration of Independence:
   a. certain unalienable rights
   b. governments are instituted among men
   c. the consent of the governed
   d. repeated injuries and usurpations
   e. quartering large bodies of armed troops among us
   f. under absolute despotism
   g. by a mock trial
   h. the benefits of trial by jury
   i. absolved from all allegiance to the British crown
   j. we mutually pledge to each other

Bibliography

The American Heritage Book of the Revolution, by Bruce Lancaster and J. H. Plumb (Dell), is a good account of the Revolution.

Kenneth Roberts's novel *Rabble in Arms* (Doubleday) is a wonderful account of the Saratoga campaign.

The story of French aid during the Revolution is one of intrigue and espionage. Read about it in Carl Van Doren's *The Secret History of the Revolution* (Kelley).

Chapter 6
1776-1788

Forging a Republic

"The American war is over," wrote one signer of the Declaration of Independence, Dr. Benjamin Rush, shortly after the fighting stopped. "But this is far from being the case with the American Revolution. On the contrary, nothing but the first act of the great drama is closed."

Americans had done more than declare independence. Theirs was also a political revolution. They had ridded themselves of a monarchy and had created a republic. Americans wanted to select their rulers themselves, rather than have rulers chosen for them by an accident of birth. They had to answer many questions about how the republic would operate.

Chapter Objectives

After you have finished reading this chapter, you should be able to:
1. Recall why the states wrote constitutions.
2. List the social and political changes brought about by the Revolution.
3. Compare the advantages and disadvantages of the Articles of Confederation.
4. Describe not only how the Constitution provided for a strong central government but how it also protected the rights of the people.

A revolution to establish a republic was a bold step, for republics were not popular in the 18th century. In fact, Americans had to look back almost 2,000 years to ancient Rome to find a model for their government. They adopted the Roman eagle as their national emblem and named the upper houses of their state and federal legislatures senates, after the Roman model. Such symbols were comforting, but the new nation was still a very lonely republic in a world full of monarchies.

1. The Meaning of Independence

THIRTEEN REPUBLICS. After the Declaration of Independence, most of the new states began drafting *constitutions.* Some states elected delegates to conventions held for that purpose; in others, the legislatures undertook the task. Yet, in one way or another, all state constitutions were submitted to the people for their approval.

Americans took seriously Jefferson's phrase that government rested on the "consent of the governed."

A *constitution* contains the laws and principles set up to govern a nation or state.

The new state constitutions had several things in common. Most were similar to the charters under which the colonies had functioned. *There were many things Americans had liked about the British Empire and many things they had learned from the parent country.* Colonial assemblies, which were like miniature parliaments, had worked very well. So had the colonial court system. Therefore, these features were retained.

What Americans had objected to in the empire were the cords of royal and parliamentary authority. These were carefully weeded out. The colonial governor had been the main tie to imperial authority, and governors remained objects of suspicion even after independence. Thus, according to most state constitutions, governors were to

The Maryland State Capitol building served as the nation's capitol between 1783 and 1784

be mere figureheads; assemblies would have the real power. In some states the assembly would appoint both the governor and the state judges.

"A GOVERNMENT OF LAWS." Written constitutions were something new. Britain's constitution was unwritten. *By drafting written blueprints for a government, Americans were trying to make law the basis of society.* People might come and go, times might change, but the *fundamental law* would endure.

Fundamental law in the United States means a constitution. It was established in the United States by the people themselves and could be changed only by extraordinary means, such as another constitutional convention.

Despite the plans for written constitutions, states were still dissatisfied. Parliament had trampled on the states' rights, and so might a government of their own. Therefore, nearly every state added to its constitution a list of guarantees, rights of citizens that government could not violate. The rights listed were those that both the British and the Americans had long claimed—freedom of speech and press; right to trial by jury with legal advice, or due process; protection of homes from unauthorized government searches. *These bills of rights may have been the most important contribution of the American Revolution.* They said that government was strictly limited when it clashed with the rights of citizens.

THE BIRTH OF DEMOCRACY. What role did the people have in shaping these governments? How much say did the average person have in the new republic? Americans of the 18th century were suspicious of *democracy;* they equated it with mob rule. Voting, they felt, was not a right but a privilege, a privilege to be extended only to those

125

Sidenote to History

Abigail Adams Makes a Plea for Women's Rights

The British had finally departed from Boston, and talk of independence was in the air. Independence, which meant new governments and new laws, had set Abigail Adams to thinking.

"I long to hear that you have declared an independency," she wrote to her husband, John, in Philadelphia. "And by the way, in the new code of laws which I suppose it will be necessary for you to make, I desire you would remember the ladies and be more generous and favorable to them than your ancestors. Do not put such unlimited power into the hands of husbands. Remember, all men would be tyrants if they could. If particular care and attention is not paid to the ladies, we are determined to foment [incite] a rebellion, and will not hold ourselves bound by any laws in which we have no voice or representation."

Abigail's husband, John, knew that she was completely serious about women's rights. She was particularly concerned about the marriage laws that had made wives totally dependent on their husbands.

Wives were unable to enter into contracts of their own or even to sue in court. But John Adams also knew that in an assembly of males there was little chance that Abigail's thoughts would get a hearing. So he replied with a joke. He had heard rumors of trouble, he wrote—of children becoming disobedient and of colleges that had grown turbulent. "But your letter was the first intimation that another tribe, more numerous and powerful than all the rest, were grown discontented." He went on to assure her that men ruled only in theory, that women were in reality the dominant sex.

Abigail was not satisfied. "I cannot say," she replied, "that I think you are very generous to the ladies, for, while you are proclaiming peace and goodwill to men, emancipating all nations, you insist upon retaining an absolute power over wives. But you must remember that arbitrary power is . . . very liable to be broken; and, notwithstanding all your wise laws and maxims, we have it in our power, not only to free ourselves, but to subdue our masters, and, without violence, throw both your natural and legal authority at our feet."

---

who would use it properly. That meant people with landed property, for they could be expected to act responsibly. ***Thus, in all of the American colonies, the ownership of land or of a house and a lot in town was a condition for voting or holding office.***

Democracy is a way of governing in which the people participate in the decision-making process.

The political upheavals that had led to the Revolution, however, had given those without property a taste of power. They had taken part in political riots, had spoken up at town meetings, and had joined committees of safety. For them the Revolution had been a political awakening, and they had expected to have a voice in the new government.

In most states the wealthy yielded to this pressure. But it was only in Pennsylvania that property qualifications were abolished altogether, and the vote was given to all male taxpayers. Every state, however, reduced the amount of property necessary and, thus, extended **suffrage.** New York and New Jersey extended the vote to free Blacks, and New Jersey's constitution granted suffrage to women. (This right was taken away by the New Jersey legislature in 1807 because the men in power found that the women were not voting for them!)

Suffrage means the legal right to vote.

In several states the wealthy tried to maintain control by imposing stiff property qualifications for officeholders. For example, to serve as a governor in Maryland or South Carolina, a candidate had to be almost a millionaire. Expanding the role of the people in their government was an ongoing process. With the Revolution, this process had only begun.

Section Review

1. Mapping: Using the map on page 132, estimate the distance from Massachusetts to South Carolina and from New York to Georgia. Can you anticipate any problems in terms of travel and trade?
2. Identify or explain: fundamental law, suffrage, constitution.
3. List the features the new state constitutions borrowed from the British form

"The County Election" by George Caleb Bingham depicts the role of common people in government. In many states the voters made their choices orally. The candidates thanked each voter and sometimes treated their supporters to liquor. What are some of the advantages and disadvantages of this sort of system?

of government. What features were different?

4. Why did many Americans want to limit the right to vote to property owners?

2. The Revolution Within

SOCIAL CHANGES. A political democracy needs a strong social foundation if it is to survive. A democracy will always be shaky if there are great gaps between the rich and the poor or if there are conflicts between one's loyalties to the church and to the nation. It will also be shaky if the people are illiterate and uninformed. The Revolution brought changes in each of these areas, and these social changes were as important to American democracy as the changes in political structure.

LAND REDISTRIBUTION. By the end of the Revolution, the states had taken over the lands formerly owned by the king, proprietors, or Loyalists who had fled to Canada. Because the states needed money quickly to finance the war, they sold these estates to wealthy *speculators.* The speculators then broke up the estates and gradually resold the land. Eventually, rich landowners acquired at least as much new property from speculators as the landless poor. *Nevertheless, there was a huge redistribution of land during and after the Revolution and a great increase in property ownership by the middle and lower classes.* Colonial America had been a middle-class society with fair opportunities. By the end of the Revolution, it was even more so.

Speculators are people who engage in risky financial deals with the hope of making a large profit.

SEPARATING CHURCH AND STATE. *Freedom of thought and expression is another element vital to a working democracy.* Americans before the Revolution had a good deal of freedom, but there were some restrictions, particularly in the area of religion. In 9 of the 13 colonies, there were ties between church and state. In New York and the southern colonies, the Church of England was established by law. In New England, except for Rhode Island, the Congregational Church was the established church. Other churches were tolerated in these colonies, but the people had to pay taxes for the support of the established church.

Congregational New England retained the tie between church and state for some years after the Revolution. But New York and the southern states all disestablished the English Church. Virginia's Statute for Religious Freedom (1786), drafted by Thomas Jefferson, was the most explicit statement of all. Virginia declared that people had the right to worship as they pleased, including the freedom not to worship at all. The right of disbelief was as important as any other.

TOWARD AN EDUCATED CITIZENRY. *Separation of church and state had a profound effect on American colleges.* Of the nine colleges that existed before the Revolution, all but two were founded by religious denominations. They received support from the churches, and clergy served on the faculties. After the Revolution the clergy concentrated on the training of future ministers and people who were not members of the clergy began teaching the nonreligious subjects in the colleges.

The curriculum, or course of study, also changed. Universities, such as Harvard and Yale, still stressed Hebrew and the classical languages (Greek and Latin), along with theology—all aimed at producing cultured Congregational ministers. The College of Philadelphia, founded by Benjamin Franklin, introduced the study of science and astronomy, modern languages, and mathematics—all aimed at producing cultured

This view of the College of New Jersey at Princeton dates from 1807. The building at left is Nassau Hall, which at that time was the largest building in the nation. More than 100 students slept, dined, studied, and went to church in Nassau Hall.

young Philadelphia business people.

The steps toward popular participation in the government also helped change the purpose and direction of education. ***It was now important to produce an informed electorate.*** States that did not have colleges within their borders moved to establish state institutions. In 1789 North Carolina chartered a state university, which opened in 1795. Others soon followed. By 1800 the nine colonial colleges had tripled to 27.

Section Review

1. Mapping: Using the map on page 132 and the chart on page 45, locate the

lands formerly owned by the king or by proprietors.
2. Identify or explain: College of Philadelphia, Statute for Religious Freedom, Loyalists.
3. Describe the process of land redistribution after the Revolution. Do you think it affected a large or small number of people?

3. The Articles of Confederation

AN ORGANIZATION OF THE STATES. The resolution for independence, adopted on July 2, 1776, called for more than just independence and foreign aid. It also suggested an organization of 13 states. In fact, to people like John Dickinson, who served in the Continental Congress, a national union was the most important goal of all. Dickinson feared that declaring independence from the British Empire before creating a national union would result in mob rule and *anarchy.*

Anarchy refers to the political disorder and lawlessness that exists when there is no governmental authority.

But when Dickinson argued for his view, he lost, and the Congress moved ahead quickly with independence. Then, after approving Jefferson's Declaration, the Congress asked Dickinson to draft some Articles of *Confederation.* Although it took Dickinson just a few weeks to prepare the draft, the Continental Congress was so preoccupied with military affairs that the Articles were debated off and on for a year. By the time they were approved in the fall of 1777, the powers had been watered down.

The Congress had done this primarily to secure the support of the states, since all 13 would have to accept the document before it could go into effect. Even so, it took another four years before all the states gave their approval. The final holdout was Maryland, which insisted that its giant neighbor, Virginia, first give up its claims to vast amounts of western land. In 1781, Virginia surrendered to the Congress its claims to the Ohio Valley and the Great Lakes (see map, page 132). Maryland then ratified the Articles of Confederation.

Confederation means a loose union of states in which each member retains many powers of government.

A HESITANT UNION. *The Articles, as finally drawn, authorized the Continental*

Congress to continue functioning as it had always done. They added nothing to its powers, nor did they create other branches of government. Under the Articles there were no *executive* and *judiciary* branches, only a legislature. And that legislature, the Congress, had little authority. It could make war and treaties with foreign nations, and little else. The Congress held no power over trade, either among the states or with foreign nations. Congress did not even have the power to tax; instead it was expected to get along on the voluntary contributions of the states. All the day-to-day regulatory authority of government was left to the states.

The *executive* branch of government is headed by the President, who enforces the laws, commands the army and navy, and negotiates with foreign governments.
The *judiciary* branch is composed of court officials, who interpret the laws and resolve conflicts stemming from those laws.

Because of their weakness, the Articles of Confederation were criticized almost from the beginning. The critics (called Nationalists) wanted a stronger national government. They hoped for a government that would maintain law and order at home and win respect abroad. Military leaders, such as George Washington, believed that Congress was too weak to give adequate support on the battlefield. Merchants, especially those with international connections, wanted a government possessed of the power to regulate trade, so there would be a uniform set of rules under which to operate.

On the other hand, there were many who liked the Articles of Confederation. Farmers living in the interior preferred local authority. They were suspicious of remote *bureaucracies* in distant capitals. They also feared that they would be too easily controlled by the wealthy. A number of political leaders, such as Patrick Henry in Virginia and George Clinton of New York, spoke for these people. The states, they maintained, were quite capable of handling all problems.

Bureaucracy refers to a government that is run through a system of specialized departments.

DEVELOPING EXECUTIVE EXPERIENCE. *Despite its flaws, the Confederation could point to some notable accomplishments.* Although the Articles did not provide for a chief executive, the Congress did create some bureaus to manage its affairs. The Office of Foreign Affairs, for example, sent ministers abroad and handled treaty negotiations. This agency was the predecessor of the modern State Department.

The Congress also created the Office of Finance, naming Robert Morris of Philadelphia as its head. Morris, the richest man in America, was a good choice. He temporarily solved Congress' financial difficulties by issuing paper money backed by his own personal fortune. Since Morris's credit rating was better than that of the Congress, the bills eased the country through the last years of the war. When the *federal* government was established at the end of the 1780's, Morris's office became the Department of the Treasury.

A *federal* form of government divides power between the individual states and the central government. In the United States this term refers to the national government.

The confederation experiment, then, did provide Americans with some experience in governing. Granted, it was only a step toward "a more perfect union," but it was a step that made the next leap possible.

ORGANIZING THE WEST. *Besides the establishment of a primitive bureaucracy, the main achievement of the Confederation was an organizing of the West.* Virginia's surrender of the territory north of the

Ohio River influenced other states to follow suit. By 1785 Congress was in possession of an empire, which stretched from the Ohio River to the Great Lakes and west to the Mississippi. Over this territory Congress had complete powers of government.

But there were problems as well. Before settlers could move in, provisions had to be made for the survey and sale of the lands. And once they had moved in, they would need some sort of government. *The first problem Congress solved with the Land Ordinance of 1785; the second, with the Northwest Ordinance of 1787.*

THE LAND ORDINANCE OF 1785. Adopting the New England method of settlement by towns, Congress ordered the Northwest divided into squares, called *townships.* Each township would be 6 miles (9.6 kilometers) on a side and would contain 36 *sections.* Each section would consist of 640 acres (about 256 hectares). Section 16 in the middle of each township would be reserved for the maintenance of public schools, and the government would retain three other sections for its future use. The remainder would be sold for a minimum of a dollar per acre (.4 hectare). The minimum purchase was one section.

The Congress had hoped to profit handsomely from the sale of its western empire. But being desperate for money, it had turned to the quick sale of large tracts to speculators. These investors then divided the lands and sold them at their leisure— and at a profit—to farmers. Before long Congress was offering huge tracts for mere pennies an acre to land companies that had ready cash.

Although the Ordinance of 1785 benefited eastern speculators at the expense of western farmers, it did have some advantages. The system avoided confusion over land ownership. Each plot of land in the West was precisely defined in terms of section and township. So useful was the system that it was later applied throughout the American West.

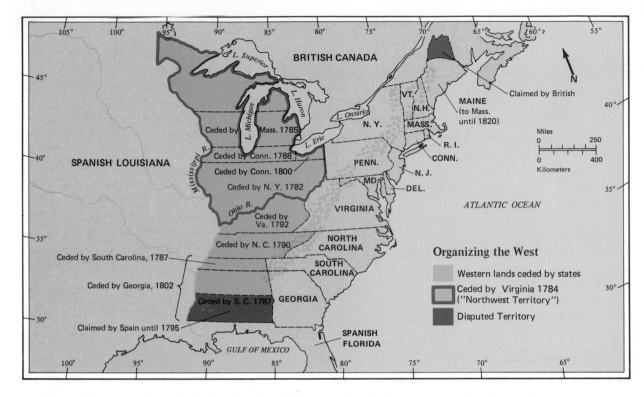

Map labels:
BRITISH CANADA
L. Superior
L. Michigan
L. Huron
L. Erie
L. Ontario
Ceded by Mass. 1785
Ceded by Conn. 1788
Ceded by Conn. 1800
Ceded by N. Y. 1782
Ceded by Va. 1792
Ceded by N. C. 1790
Ceded by South Carolina, 1787
Ceded by Georgia, 1802
Ceded by S. C. 1787
Claimed by Spain until 1795
SPANISH LOUISIANA
Mississippi R.
Ohio R.
VT.
N.H.
N. Y.
MASS.
R. I.
CONN.
PENN.
N. J.
MD.
DEL.
VIRGINIA
NORTH CAROLINA
SOUTH CAROLINA
GEORGIA
SPANISH FLORIDA
MAINE (to Mass. until 1820)
Claimed by British
ATLANTIC OCEAN
GULF OF MEXICO
N
Miles 0 — 250
0 — 400 Kilometers

Organizing the West
Western lands ceded by states
Ceded by Virginia 1784 ("Northwest Territory")
Disputed Territory

THE NORTHWEST ORDINANCE OF 1787. *This act provided a government for the Northwest.* Under it, Congress would appoint a governor and some judges to preside initially over the territory. Then, when the area had 5,000 free males of voting age, it would be entitled to its own legislature and would be allowed to send a nonvoting delegate to Congress. When any subdivision of the territory reached a population of 60,000 free inhabitants, the territory could be admitted to the Union as a state. The whole region between the Ohio River and the Great Lakes could eventually yield between three and five states (five was the final tally: Ohio, Indiana, Illinois, Michigan, and Wisconsin).

The Northwest Ordinance also included a bill of rights, which granted freedom of speech and of the press, freedom of worship, and protection of judicial due process. In addition, the ordinance set down a policy of "utmost good faith" with regard to the Indians. Their lands and property were not to be taken from them without their consent, and all precautions for "preventing wrongs being done to them, and for preserving peace and friendship with them" were to be taken. Unfortunately, this policy was ignored.

Finally, Congress added to the ordinance a clause prohibiting slavery north of the Ohio River. It was the nation's first attempt at limiting the spread of the South's "peculiar institution."

The Northwest Ordinance provided the means for newly settled areas to enter the Union on a basis equal with that of the older states. The steps for going from wilderness to statehood as outlined in the ordinance have been followed by every territory, except Texas, that has become a state since 1787. This is true even for the most recent admissions, Alaska and Hawaii, in 1959.

UPROAR OVER PAPER MONEY. Despite Congress' success in organizing its

western empire, it appeared weak and ineffective to many people. Part of its problem was a postwar *depression,* which began in 1784 and lasted into 1787. No government is popular in economic hard times. *The main symptom of this depression was a shortage of money, for the gold and silver were flowing to Europe to repay foreign debts.* Several states moved to relieve the shortage by printing money of their own. This alarmed the wealthy, who feared that money would lose its value, as it had during the war. The rich had made loans to people in good, hard coin; they did not want to be paid back in worthless paper.

A *depression* is a period marked by a decrease in trade, production, and employment.

A half-dozen states issued paper money during the 1780's. Where merchants were willing to accept it for goods, it circulated well. But in Rhode Island merchants refused to accept this money, and it lost its value. When the state legislature demanded that merchants take the money, many closed their shops and fled the state. This caused great concern among the wealthy everywhere. Perhaps, they argued, a stronger central authority could issue good currency of its own and put an end to such problems.

SHAYS' REBELLION. When the Massachusetts assembly refused to follow Rhode Island's example in issuing paper money, moneylenders began suing for payment. *To*

Sidenote to History

Noah Webster, Schoolmaster to a Nation

Noah Webster was destined for a public career, but not the kind that his family had imagined. He was sent first to Yale for culture, then to a law office for legal training. But Webster did not like courtrooms. So he became a teacher instead of a lawyer.

Webster soon recognized that the new nation needed schoolbooks of its own. Except for the *New England Primer* (the reading text used by generations of young Puritans), the books studied in American schools were printed in Britain. In reaction to this, in 1783, Webster declared that an independent America needed an independent literature. In that same year Webster produced his *American Spelling Book.* A few years later he followed it with a reader and a grammar book.

All of Webster's books had the same basic purpose—to produce an American language that would create a sense of national pride. Through uniform spelling and pronunciation, Webster hoped to eliminate regional variations. He believed a single tongue would bring about a united country.

Webster's speller incorporated American words that were unfamiliar to the English—words that described the American landscape, such as *prairie;* words of Indian origin, such as *tomato* and *squash.* He also changed some English styles of spelling to American styles, reversing the "re" in *theatre* and *centre* and dropping the unsounded "u" from *labour* and *favour.*

Webster's books filled a national need. By the time he died in 1843, the *Blue-Backed Speller* alone had sold some 15 million copies, and sales eventually reached nearly 100 million. Even at the tiny royalty of a halfpenny a copy, Webster's profits enabled him to live comfortably while working on the dictionary that bears his name. It appeared in 1828—the first major dictionary of American English.

Fort Harmar on the Ohio River in 1790 was the first settlement in the Northwest Territory. Across the river is Marietta, Ohio.

prevent debt collections, *a band of Massachusetts farmers, organized by Daniel Shays, interrupted court sessions in several counties during the autumn of 1786.* Although the angry farmers presented no real threat to state authority, the governor panicked and called up the militia. A large army marched into the villages and scattered the farmers to their homes.

Although hardly a rebellion, the Shays affair sent a wave of alarm the length of the Atlantic seaboard. *No other event of the time displayed so clearly the need for a strong national authority.*

Section Review

1. Mapping: Using the map on page 132, compare the area of the Northwest Territory with that of the 13 states. How many states were made from the Northwest Territory? What trend do you see in the size of states?
2. Identify or explain: John Dickinson, Robert Morris, Daniel Shays, Land Ordinance of 1785.
3. What powers did the Articles of Confederation give the government? In what way did the Articles of Confederation limit the powers of the government?
4. Name two provisions in the Northwest Ordinance of 1787.

4. Reforming the Federal Government

JAMES MADISON CALLS FOR CHANGE. James Madison was a man of modest wealth and background. Although he had inherited a tobacco plantation in Virginia, he had no interest in farming. Public service was his life, and he served his country from the time he entered the Virginia convention of 1776 until he retired from the Presidency in 1817.

Madison, aware of the weaknesses of the Articles of Confederation, was in favor of a stronger national authority. Alexander Hamilton, a young New York lawyer who had served as Washington's aide during the war, shared Madison's belief. Even Washington, who was in retirement, kept in contact with the Nationalists.

The Nationalists at first tried to amend the Articles of Confederation. When that failed, because they could not get the consent of all 13 states, they looked for ways to bypass the Articles. *Meeting at a conference on trade regulations in Annapolis in 1786, Madison and Hamilton persuaded the group to issue a call for a more general conference in Philadelphia.* Madison then persuaded Congress to endorse the Philadelphia gathering. In the winter, 12 states (all but Rhode Island) named delegates.

THE FEDERAL (CONSTITUTIONAL) CONVENTION MAY–SEPTEMBER 1787.

Nearly all the states sent their most influential people to the Philadelphia meeting. George Washington emerged from retirement. So did Benjamin Franklin and John Dickinson. James Madison actively participated and kept a journal, which described the meetings and the debates. (The journal was not published until after his death in 1836.)

The delegates to the convention believed that the country should not be plunged into argument and that they could work out their differences more easily in private. This was not surprising, for a majority of the delegates were Nationalists. Those who were content with the Articles of Confederation had not been inclined to attend a meeting to change them. For example, Patrick Henry had been nominated by the Virginia assembly, but had declined to be a delegate.

THE GREAT COMPROMISE.

Edmund Randolph, the governor of Virginia, came prepared with a plan. His scheme, called the Virginia Plan, outlined a government of three branches—executive, legislative, and judicial—each with sufficient powers to govern effectively by itself. The scheme was also a large-state plan because it provided for representation based on population.

Small states, preferring to keep the voting equal, objected to the plan. After weeks of wrangling, they reached a decision known as the Great Compromise. *The states agreed that their federal lawmaking body (Congress) would have two houses.* In the House of Representatives, the number of members from each state would depend on population; state representation in the other house, the Senate, would be equal.

THE THREE-FIFTHS COMPROMISE.

The Great Compromise did not end the convention's problems. Another debate soon developed—between the northern and southern states. The issue was slavery—not the institution itself, but the question of the representation of slaves in the government. Northerners believed that slaves should be counted when determining the share of federal taxes each state should pay, but not counted when determining each state's representatives in the House. Southerners, of course, wanted exactly the reverse.

The Constitutional Convention met in Independence Hall in Philadelphia, where the Declaration of Independence had been signed. This artist painted a sun mural behind George Washington to symbolize the dawning of a new age. Compare this picture with the one on page 105.

This disagreement was settled by what came to be known as the Three-Fifths Compromise. The original Constitution states that both representatives and taxes shall be apportioned according to "the whole number of free persons . . . and three-fifths of all other persons." This meant that, in effect, each slave was to be counted as three fifths of a person for both representation and taxation.

GEORGE MASON PROPOSES A BILL OF RIGHTS. With one question resolved, the delegates moved quickly through the other parts of the plan, and by mid-September the document was ready for signing. Then George Mason of Virginia pointed out that they had created a government with huge powers. He foresaw that the people would need protection against possible abuse of those powers, so he proposed a bill of rights. But the weary delegates, taken by surprise, rejected the bill. They would have done better to have taken Mason seriously, for the lack of a bill of rights became a rallying point for opponents of the Constitution.

THE FEDERALISTS DEFEND THEIR PLAN. Members of the Federal Convention knew they had to submit the Constitution to the people for approval, or ratification. So they asked each state to elect a special convention to consider the Constitution. They provided for the document to go into effect when nine of the states agreed.

As soon as the Constitution was published, essays and pamphlets were printed that examined, criticized, and explained every clause. From the outset New York was a critical battleground. Madison even went there after the convention, and during the winter of 1787–1788, he worked with Alexander Hamilton and John Jay on a series of newspaper essays. Later collected as *The Federalist Papers,* these essays explained and defended every feature of the Constitution. To this day they remain the best analysis of the American "experiment."

Alexander Hamilton, one of the authors of The Federalist Papers, *was also influential in establishing the Bank of the United States.*

Supporters of the Constitution called themselves Federalists; they wanted the country to have a strong federal government. Their opponents, the Anti-Federalists, objected to the Constitution; they thought the states were being asked to give too much of their power to the federal government. Many of the Anti-Federalists agreed that the Articles of Confederation needed amending, but they thought the Constitution went too far. On the other hand, they could not seem to agree on an alternative.

RATIFYING THE CONSTITUTION. Small states, which could not survive if the Union collapsed, were the first to ratify; these were Delaware, Connecticut, New Jersey, and Georgia. Although Georgia was potentially a large state in area and population, it was small at this time, and it was facing a conflict with its neighbors, the

Spanish and American Indians. Pennsylvania, a large state, also ratified early. By the spring of 1788, three more states—Massachusetts, South Carolina, and Maryland—had ratified. In June, New Hampshire followed suit, and the Constitution stood approved. (See map, page 137.) But two key states—New York and Virginia—had not given their approval.

THE BILL OF RIGHTS AND RATIFICATION.
In Virginia, George Mason sided with Patrick Henry against the Constitution. The Federalists could count on the support of George Washington. The state it seemed was evenly divided. *Then, at the state convention in the summer of 1788, James Madison made a surprise move by promising to work for a bill of rights.* He had decided that as long as the basic structure of the Constitution was unchanged, a few *amendments* protecting the rights of citizens would be acceptable. Virginia then rati-

fied the Constitution by a mere 10 votes. New York followed by an even slimmer margin of three votes. In both cases the promise of amendments was decisive.

An *amendment* is a formal change or addition to a major document.

Only two states remained opposed. North Carolina's convention voted to go home without taking action. Rhode Island ignored the whole thing. Eventually, both states joined the Union, after Congress threatened to treat them as foreigners.

A REMARKABLE DOCUMENT.
The Constitution is a remarkable document. Considered an experiment by those who wrote it, it has survived nearly two centuries. It has endured partly because its authors were realists who understood both the weaknesses and the strengths of humankind. It has endured also because Madison

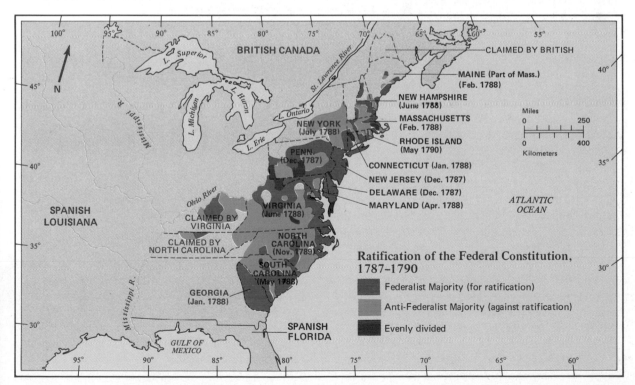

Ratification of the Federal Constitution, 1787–1790

- Federalist Majority (for ratification)
- Anti-Federalist Majority (against ratification)
- Evenly divided

and the other founders were concerned about the broad principles of power and authority rather than specific social goals. Thus, each generation has reinterpreted the Constitution to meet its own needs. In this way an 18th-century government blueprint continues to serve a space-age society. Pages 139–167 contain the Constitution and a discussion of what it means today.

Section Review

1. Mapping: Using the map on page 137, explain how the coastal areas voted on the issue of ratification. What other patterns of support and opposition to the Constitution do you find?
2. Identify or explain: James Madison, Alexander Hamilton, the Virginia Plan, *The Federalist Papers*, the Three-Fifths Compromise.
3. Describe two major provisions of the Virginia Plan and the compromise that made it possible for large states and small states to agree.
4. Describe two objections that some people had to the Constitution that made ratification a problem.

Sidenote to History

Dr. Benjamin Rush

Dr. Benjamin Rush was Philadelphia's most prominent physician. He thought about more than simply the illnesses of individuals. He was troubled by the ills of society, as well. Americans, he felt, had been corrupted by their colonial attachment to Great Britain. They had adopted European manners and a taste for luxury. He saw the Revolution as more than a war for political independence: it was an opportunity to sweep out social corruption and to establish a simple, humane community.

Rush wrote an essay against slavery in 1773. During the war he became the secretary of Philadelphia's abolition society. When the Federal Convention met to draft the Constitution, he presented a petition to prohibit slavery.

In 1782 he spoke to Congress about the need to pay the nation's debts. Also in 1782, he suggested the building of a navy to improve America's standing in the world. In an essay, he expounded on the evils of drinking. He even laid plans for a new college (Dickinson College) in western Pennsylvania.

Like Noah Webster, Rush thought the future of America depended on education. Public schools, he believed, would instill in America's youth a system of values, a sense of duty, and a proper patriotism. Further, Rush thought education should be free. He was the first American to advocate the idea of common schools, financed from public taxes. He was also one of the first supporters of education for females.

Rush was a pioneer in medicine, too. He spent his last years investigating the problems of mental illness. At that time the violently insane were put into jails or locked into attics. The nonviolent ones were simply allowed to roam the streets as "village idiots."

Rush's studies led him to the revolutionary notion that insanity was a disease, which could be cured by medical treatment. That notion, in turn, led to the idea of asylums, or hospitals, for the mentally ill.

By the time Rush died in 1813, he had sparked a widespread and growing concern for social reform. Practically every major reform movement of the next generation—the crusades against slavery, liquor, and war; the movements for women's rights, for public education, and for asylums for the mentally ill—could be traced to the fertile, compassionate, and deeply religious mind of Benjamin Rush.

5. The Constitution of the United States and What It Means Today

(Portions of the text within brackets have been changed by amendment or are no longer in effect. The text of the Constitution appears in black; annotations appear in red.)

Preamble

We, the people of the United States, in order to form a more perfect Union, establish justice, insure domestic tranquility, provide for the common defense, promote the general welfare, and secure the blessings of liberty to ourselves and our posterity, do ordain and establish this Constitution for the United States of America.

The Preamble. The opening is called the *Preamble*. It states the purpose of the Constitution. Note that it begins, "We, the people," not "We, the states. . . ."

Article 1. The Legislative Branch

Section 1. Congress
All legislative powers herein granted shall be vested in a Congress of the United States, which shall consist of a Senate and House of Representatives.

Section 1. This section states how Congress shall be organized and that it will have the power to make all federal laws. This clause has been modified in practice so that regulations made by certain federal agencies can function as federal laws.

Section 2. House of Representatives
1. Election and Term of Members. The House of Representatives shall be composed of members chosen every second year by the people of the several states, and the electors in each state shall have the qualifications requisite for electors of the most numerous branch of the state legislature.

Clause 1. Members of the House serve two-year terms. The term *electors* refers to voters.

2. Qualifications. No person shall be a Representative who shall not have attained to the age of twenty-five years, and been seven years a citizen of the United States, and who shall not, when elected, be an inhabitant of that state in which he shall be chosen.

Clause 2. A representative must be at least 25 years old, must have been a United States citizen for at least 7 years, and must be a resident of the state from which he or she is elected. The states are divided into congressional districts, each of which elects a representative.

3. Apportionment of Representatives. Representatives [and direct taxes] shall be apportioned among the several states which may be included within this Union, according to their

Clause 3. The number of members in the House of Representatives was to be determined by the number of "free persons" in each state, plus "three-fifths of all other persons." This meant that states could count only three-fifths of their

139

respective numbers [which shall be determined by adding to the whole number of free persons, including those bound to service for a term of years, and excluding Indians not taxed, three fifths of all other persons]. The actual enumeration shall be made within three years after the first meeting of the Congress of the United States, and within every subsequent term of ten years, in such manner as they shall by law direct. The number of Representatives shall not exceed 1 for every 30,000, but each state shall have at least 1 Representative; [and until such enumeration shall be made, the state of New Hampshire shall be entitled to choose 3; Massachusetts, 8; Rhode Island and Providence Plantations, 1; Connecticut, 5; New York, 6; New Jersey, 4; Pennsylvania, 8; Delaware, 1; Maryland, 6; Virginia, 10; North Carolina, 5; South Carolina, 5; and Georgia, 3].

4. Vacancies. When vacancies happen in the representation from any state, the executive authority thereof shall issue writs of election to fill such vacancies.

5. Impeachment. The House of Representatives shall choose their Speaker and other officers; and shall have the sole power of impeachment.

Section 3.   Senate
1. Number of Members and Terms of Office. The Senate of the United States shall be composed of two Senators from each state [chosen by the legislatures thereof], for six years, and each Senator shall have one vote.

2. Classification; Vacancies. [Immediately after they shall be assembled in consequence of the first election, they shall be divided as equally as may be into three classes. The seats of the Senators of the first class shall be vacated at the expiration of the second year, of the second class at the expiration of the fourth year, and of the third class at the expiration of the sixth year, so that one-third may be chosen every second year; and if vacancies happen by resignation, or otherwise, during the recess of the legislature of any state, the executive thereof may make temporary appointments until the next meeting of the legislature, which shall then fill such vacancies.]

Black slaves. This provision was overruled by the 13th Amendment (1865) and Section 2 of the 14th Amendment (1868).

Because representation is based on population, the Constitution provides for a national head count, or census, every ten years. The United States was the first nation to conduct a regular census. Every representative represents at least 30,000 people, but each state is entitled to at least one representative. In 1929, in order to prevent the House of Representatives from growing too large, Congress limited the membership of the House to 435.

Clause 4.   If a member of the House of Representatives dies or resigns, the governor of the state orders a special election to fill the vacant seat.

Clause 5.   By majority vote, the House can impeach, or accuse, officers of the executive branch or federal judges. The Senate tries all impeachment cases.

Clause 1.   Each state legislature was to elect two members to the Senate. Senators represent states, not people. This system was changed by the 17th Amendment in 1913. Senators are now elected directly by the voters of each state.

Clause 2.   Senators serve six-year terms. The paragraph defining "classes" of senators sets up a staggered system, whereby one third of the Senate comes up for reelection every two years. If a Senator resigns or dies, the 17th Amendment provides for the governor to call a special election to fill the vacancy or to appoint a temporary successor.

3. Qualifications. No person shall be a Senator who shall not have attained the age of thirty years, and been nine years a citizen of the United States, and who shall not, when elected, be an inhabitant of that state for which he shall be chosen.

4. The President of the Senate. The Vice-President of the United States shall be president of the Senate, but shall have no vote, unless they be equally divided.

5. Other Officers. The Senate shall choose their other officers, and also a president pro tempore, in the absence of the Vice-President, or when he shall exercise the office of the President of the United States.

Clauses 4 and 5. The Vice-President serves as the President of the Senate and votes only to break a tie. This is the only vice-presidential duty specified in the Constitution. If the Vice-President is absent or becomes President, the Senate elects a temporary president (pro tempore) to preside over its meetings.

6. Impeachments. The Senate shall have the sole power to try all impeachments. When sitting for that purpose, they shall be on oath or affirmation. When the President of the United States is tried, the Chief Justice shall preside; and no person shall be convicted without the concurrence of two-thirds of the members present.

Clauses 6 and 7. The trial of members of the executive or the judiciary accused by the House of Representatives is conducted by the Senate. A vote of two-thirds of the Senate is necessary for conviction. If convicted, the person is removed from office and is then subject to indictment and criminal proceedings according to the law. Andrew Johnson is the only President who was impeached (1868). He was not convicted. Conviction failed by one vote. Richard M. Nixon was the first President to resign from office. He did so in 1974, when the Judiciary Committee of the House of Representatives recommended that he be impeached. Following his resignation he was granted a presidential pardon, which spared him from possible prosecution.

7. Penalty for Conviction. Judgment in cases of impeachment shall not extend further than to removal from office, and disqualification to hold and enjoy any office of honor, trust, or profit under the United States; but the party convicted shall nevertheless be liable and subject to indictment, trial, judgment, and punishment, according to law.

Section 4. Elections and Meetings

1. Holding Elections. The times, places, and manner of holding elections for Senators and Representatives shall be prescribed in each state by the legislature thereof; but the Congress may at any time by law make or alter such regulations, except as to the places of choosing Senators.

Clause 1. The states set the conditions of congressional elections, determining who can vote. This was modified by the 15th Amendment (1870), which prevents the states from interfering with the right of Blacks to vote; the 19th Amendment (1920), which extends voting rights to women, the 24th Amendment (1964), which bans the poll tax as a condition for voting, and the 26th Amendment (1971), which lowers the voting age to 18.

2. Meetings. The Congress shall assemble at least once in every year, [and such meeting shall be on the first Monday in December,] unless they shall by law appoint a different day.

Clause 2. The date for Congress to assemble was changed by the 20th Amendment (1933). Congress now convenes on January 3.

141

Section 5. Procedure

1. Organization. Each house shall be the judge of the elections, returns, and qualifications of its own members, and a majority of each shall constitute a quorum to do business; but a smaller number may adjourn from day to day, and may be authorized to compel the attendance of absent members, in such manner, and under such penalties, as each house may provide.

2. Proceedings. Each house may determine the rules of its proceedings, punish its members for disorderly behavior, and with the concurrence of two-thirds, expel a member.

3. The Journal. Each house shall keep a journal of its proceedings, and from time to time publish the same, excepting such parts as may in their judgment require secrecy; and the yeas and nays of the members of either house on any question shall, at the desire of one-fifth of those present, be entered on the journal.

4. Adjournment. Neither house, during the session of Congress, shall, without the consent of the other, adjourn for more than three days, nor to any other place than that in which the two houses shall be sitting.

Section 6. Privileges and Restrictions

1. Pay and Privileges. The Senators and Representatives shall receive a compensation for their services, to be ascertained by law and paid out of the Treasury of the United States. They shall in all cases, except treason, felony, and breach of the peace, be privileged from arrest during their attendance at the session of their respective houses, and in going to and returning from the same; and for any speech or debate in either house, they shall not be questioned in any other place.

2. Restrictions. No Senator or Representative shall, during the time for which he was elected, be appointed to any civil office under the authority of the United States, which shall have been created, or the emoluments whereof shall have been increased, during such time; and no

Clause 1. Both houses have the right to refuse to seat members. A *quorum* is a majority of members of each house of Congress and is the minimum number required to be present to carry out business. In practice, however, business can be and often is transacted without a quorum as long as no member objects. Each house can compel the attendance of its members when their presence is needed.

Clause 3. The framers of the Constitution wanted the voters to be kept informed of the activities of Congress. Such a record would also enable the people to find out how their representatives had voted on particular issues. Such openness in government was unknown in Europe at the time the Constitution was written. The *House Journal* and the *Senate Journal* are published at the end of each session of Congress. The *Congressional Record* is published for every day Congress is in session. It records the action of both houses.

Clause 4. Once Congress is in session, the House and the Senate must remain at work until both agree on a time to adjourn. Because they work together, they must both work in the same place.

Clause 1. This clause permits members to speak freely by providing *congressional immunity* from prosecution or arrest for things they say in speeches and debates in Congress. Members of Congress set their own pay.

Clause 2. This clause underscores the principle of separation of powers. No member of Congress can hold any other government office. If Congress creates an office or raises the salary of an old one, no member of Congress may fill that office until his or her term expires. This provision was made to prevent the executive, or the President, from controlling Con-person holding any office under the United States shall be a member of either house during his continuance in office.

Section 7. Passing Laws

1. Revenue Bills. All bills for raising revenue shall originate in the House of Representatives; but the Senate may propose or concur with amendments as on other bills.

2. How a Bill Becomes a Law. Every bill which shall have passed the House of Representatives and the Senate shall, before it becomes a law, be presented to the President of the United States; if he approves, he shall sign it, but if not, he shall return it, with his objections, to that house in which it shall have originated, who shall enter the objections at large on their journal, and proceed to reconsider it. If after such reconsideration two-thirds of that house shall agree to pass the bill, it shall be sent, together with the objections, to the other house, by which it shall likewise be reconsidered and, if approved by two-thirds of that house, it shall become a law. But in all such cases the votes of both houses shall be determined by yeas and nays, and the names of the persons voting for and against the bill shall be entered on the journal of each house respectively. If any bill shall not be returned by the President within ten days (Sunday excepted) after it shall have been presented to him, the same bill shall be a law, in like manner as if he had signed it, unless the Congress by their adjournment prevent its return, in which case it shall not be a law.

3. Presidential Approval or Veto. Every order, resolution, or vote to which the concurrence of the Senate and House of Representatives may be necessary (except on a question of adjournment) shall be presented to the President of the United States; and before the same shall take effect, shall be approved by him, or being disapproved by him, shall be repassed by two-thirds of the Senate and House of Representatives, according to the rules and limitations prescribed in the case of a bill.

gress. In Britain in the 18th century, the king and his ministers controlled Parliament by promising offices as bribes.

Clause 1. Bills for raising money by taxes must be introduced in the House of Representatives. This was part of the compromise between the large states and the small states. The large states received proportional representation in one house, and that house was also given first authority over money and tax measures. This provision has little practical importance, however, because the Senate can amend such bills.

Clause 2. Every bill that passes both houses of Congress is sent to the President. If the President approves the bill and signs it, it becomes law. The refusal to sign is called a *veto*. A vetoed bill is sent back to Congress with a written statement of the President's objections. If both houses can pass the bill by two thirds majority (usually very difficult to obtain), Congress can *override* the President's veto and the bill becomes law. If not, the veto is *sustained* and the bill dies. If the President receives a bill and keeps it ten days without acting on it, it automatically becomes law. If Congress adjourns within those ten days, the bill must be introduced again in the next congressional session. This is called a *pocket veto*.

The Presidential veto is an important check of the executive branch of the government on the legislative branch. Congress checks the President when it overrides a veto.

143

Section 8.   Powers Delegated to Congress

The Congress shall have power

1. To lay and collect taxes, duties, imposts, and excises, to pay the debts and provide for the common defense and general welfare of the United States; but all duties, imposts, and excises shall be uniform through the United States;

2. To borrow money on the credit of the United States;

3. To regulate commerce with foreign nations, and among the several states, [and with the Indian tribes];

4. To establish a uniform rule of naturalization, and uniform laws on the subject of bankruptcies throughout the United States;

5. To coin money, regulate the value thereof, and of foreign coin, and fix the standard of weights and measures;

6. To provide for the punishment of counterfeiting the securities and current coin of the United States.

7. To establish post offices and post roads;

8. To promote the progress of science and useful arts by securing for limited times to authors and inventors the exclusive right to their respective writings and discoveries;

9. To constitute tribunals inferior to the Supreme Court;

10. To define and punish piracies and felonies committed on the high seas and offenses against the law of nations;

Section 8. This section lists the 18 *delegated* or *enumerated* powers granted to Congress. The first 17 specify areas in which Congress has authority and are called *expressed* powers. The 18th power is the elastic clause. The doctrine of *implied* powers developed from this clause.

Clause 1. Congress has the power to levy taxes to pay the nation's debts and to provide for national defense and for the general welfare of the people. All federal taxes must be the same throughout the country.

Clause 2. The Constitution sets no limit on the amount Congress can borrow—Congress itself sets the national debt.

Clause 3. Congress has the power to regulate trade with foreign nations. It also has direct control over interstate commerce. This phrase is so broad that it permits Congress to regulate transportation, the stock market, and the broadcasting industry.

Clause 4. Congress can decide how immigrants may become citizens. It can also make laws about procedures involved in business failures.

Clause 5. Congress can mint coins, print paper money, and set the value of both American money and foreign currency within this country. It can also set standard measurements for the nation.

Clause 6. Congress can make laws fixing the punishment for counterfeiting currency, bonds, or stamps.

Clause 7. Congress can designate which highways should be used to transport mail.

Clause 8. Congress can pass patent and copyright laws to give to inventors and artists sole rights to their works for a number of years. Anyone who uses patented inventions or copyrighted material without permission may be punished.

Clause 9. All federal courts except the Supreme Court are established by acts of Congress.

Clause 10. Congress can decide what acts committed on American ships are crimes and how such acts should be punished. It can also decide how American citizens who break international laws shall be punished.

144

11. To declare war, [grant letters of marque and reprisal,] and make rules concerning captures on land and water;

Clause 11. Only Congress may declare war. However, American forces have engaged in combat in some instances without congressional declarations of war—for example, in Korea and Vietnam. *Letters of marque and reprisal* refer to permission granted to American merchant ships to attack enemy ships, a practice common in early wars. This practice has been outlawed by international agreement.

12. To raise and support armies, but no appropriation of money to that use shall be for a longer term than two years;

Clause 12. All money for the army comes from Congress. However, Congress may not grant such money for longer than a two-year period. This is to make sure that civilians exercise financial control over the army.

13. To provide and maintain a navy;

Clause 13. There is no two-year limit on naval appropriations because the navy was not considered a threat to liberty.

14. To make rules for the government and regulation of the land and naval forces;

Clause 14. Because Congress can create the armed forces, it has power to make rules for the services. Such rules now include the air force.

15. To provide for calling forth the militia to execute the laws of the Union, suppress insurrections, and repel invasions;

Clause 15. Congress can call into federal service the state militia forces (citizen-soldiers now referred to as the National Guard) to enforce federal laws and defend life and property. Congress can empower the President to call out the militia, but only for the reasons named here.

16. To provide for organizing, arming, and disciplining the militia, and for governing such part of them as may be employed in the service of the United States, reserving to the states, respectively, the appointment of the officers, and the authority of training the militia according to the discipline prescribed by Congress;

Clause 16. The states may appoint officers for the militia, but Congress establishes rules for training the militia.

17. To exercise exclusive legislation in all cases whatsoever, over such district (not exceeding ten miles square) as may, by cession of particular states, and the acceptance of Congress, become the seat of government of the United States, and to exercise like authority over all places purchased by the consent of the legislature of the state in which the same shall be, for the erection of forts, magazines, arsenals, dockyards, and other needful buildings;—and

Clause 17. Congress has control over the District of Columbia as well as all forts, arsenals, dockyards, federal courthouses, and other places owned and operated by the federal government.

18. To make all laws which shall be necessary and proper for carrying into execution the foregoing powers, and all other powers vested by this Constitution in the government of the United States, or in any department or officer thereof.

Clause 18. The framers were very careful to ensure that Congress would be able to meet the needs of a changing society. Sometimes called the elastic clause of the Constitution, this clause enables Congress to frame laws that are related to specific powers listed in the Constitution. For instance, as part of its power "to raise and support armies,"

Congress can undertake the construction of roads. Such roads are "necessary and proper" for transporting, or maintaining, an army.

This elastic clause has enabled Congress to meet the changing needs of society over two centuries. The power that has become the most expandable is the power to regulate interstate trade and commerce. In the 20th century, Congress has used this power to pass Civil Rights Acts (protecting the free movement of people and trade) and labor legislation that guards the right of unions to organize (strikes interfere with interstate commerce).

Section 9.   Powers Denied to the Federal Government

1. [The migration or importation of such persons as any of the states now existing shall think proper to admit shall not be prohibited by the Congress prior to the year 1808; but a tax or duty may be imposed on such importation, not exceeding $10 for each person.]

Clause 1. "Such persons" refers to slaves. This clause was the result of a compromise between northern merchants and southern planters. The Constitutional Convention gave Congress powers to regulate commerce and to tax imports, while also providing that the importation of slaves would not be prohibited prior to 1808 and that there would not be an import tax of more than $10 per person. The importation of slaves was prohibited in 1808.

2. The privilege of the writ of *habeas corpus* shall not be suspended, unless when in cases of rebellion or invasion the public safety may require it.

Clause 2. A *writ of habeas corpus* protects citizens from arbitrary arrest. It is an order demanding that a person who has been arrested be brought before a court so that a judge can decide if he or she is being held lawfully.

3. No bill of attainder or *ex post facto* law shall be passed.

Clause 3. A *bill of attainder* is a law that declares an individual guilty of a crime without a court trial. An *ex post facto* law makes an act a crime after the act has been committed.

4. [No capitation or other direct tax shall be laid, unless in proportion to the census herein before directed to be taken.]

Clause 4. Congress must allocate direct taxes among the states according to their populations. This provision was included to keep Congress from abolishing slavery by taxing slaves. The 16th Amendment (1913) makes it possible for Congress to levy a tax on individual incomes without regard to state population.

5. No tax or duty shall be laid on articles exported from any state.

Clause 5. Southern delegates to the Constitutional Convention opposed a tax on exports because they exported goods, such as tobacco and cotton, to Europe. The Constitution permitted Congress to tax imports for revenue, but not exports.

6. No preference shall be given any regulation of commerce or revenue to the ports of one state over those of another; nor shall vessels bound to, or from, one state, be obliged to enter, clear, or pay duties in another.

Clause 6. No port in any state is to have preference over any other. Ships going from state to state may not be taxed by Congress.

146

7. No money shall be drawn from the Treasury, but in consequence of appropriations made by law; and a regular statement and account of the receipts and expenditures of all public money shall be published from time to time.

8. No title of nobility shall be granted by the United States; and no person holding any office of profit or trust under them, shall, without the consent of the Congress, accept of any present, emolument, office, or title, of any kind whatever, from any king, prince, or foreign state.

Section 10. Powers Denied to the States

1. No state shall enter into any treaty, alliance, or confederation; grant letters of marque and reprisal; coin money; emit bills of credit; make anything but gold and silver coin a tender in payment of debts; pass any bill of attainder, *ex post facto* law, or law impairing the obligation of contracts, or grant any title of nobility.

2. No state shall, without the consent of the Congress, lay any imposts or duties on imports or exports, except what may be absolutely necessary for executing its inspection laws; and the net produce of all duties and imposts, laid by any state on imports or exports, shall be for the use of the Treasury of the United States; and all such laws shall be subject to the revision and control of the Congress.

3. No states shall, without the consent of Congress, lay any duty of tonnage, keep troops, or ships of war in time of peace, enter into any agreement or compact with another state, or with a foreign power, or engage in war, unless actually invaded, or in such imminent danger as will not admit of delay.

Article 2. The Executive Branch

Section 1. President and Vice-President

1. Term of Office. The executive power shall be vested in a President of the United States of America. He shall hold his office during

Clause 7. Only Congress can grant permission for money to be spent from the Treasury. This provision permits Congress to limit the power of the President by controlling the amount of money to be spent to run the executive branch of government.

Clause 8. This clause prohibits the establishment of a noble class and discourages bribery of American officials by foreign governments.

Clause 1. The clauses in this section limit the powers of the states. Most of these limitations stemmed from complaints the nationalists had made against the states during the Confederation period. The prohibition of laws "impairing the obligations of contracts" was intended to prevent the kind of relief laws the states had passed during the hard times of the 1780's (the time of Shays' Rebellion). These laws protected debtors against lawsuits. A debt or other obligation was a contract, and a state could not interfere with it.

Clause 2. States cannot interfere with commerce by taxing goods, although they may charge fees for inspecting such goods. Any such inspection fee must be paid into the Treasury of the United States. Also, all tariff revenue goes to the national government and not to the states.

147

the term of four years, and together with the Vice-President, chosen for the same term, be elected as follows:

2. Electoral System. Each state shall appoint, in such manner as the legislature thereof may direct, a number of electors, equal to the whole number of Senators and Representatives to which the state may be entitled in the Congress; but no Senator or Representative, or person holding an office of trust or profit under the United States, shall be appointed an elector.

3. Former Method of the Electoral System. [The electors shall meet in their respective states, and vote by ballot for two persons, of whom one at least shall not be an inhabitant of the same state with themselves. And they shall make a list of all the persons voted for, and of the number of votes for each; which list they shall sign and certify, and transmit sealed to the seat of the government of the United States, directed to the president of the Senate. The president of the Senate shall, in the presence of the Senate and House of Representatives, open all the certificates, and the votes shall then be counted. The person having the greatest number of votes shall be the President, if such number be a majority of the whole number of electors appointed; and if there be more than one who have such majority, and have an equal number of votes, then the House of Representatives shall immediately choose by ballot one of them for President; and if no person have a majority, then from the five highest on the list the said House shall in like manner choose the President. But in choosing the President the votes shall be taken by states, the representation from each state having one vote. A quorum for this purpose shall consist of a member or members from two-thirds of the states, and a majority of all the states shall be necessary to a choice. In every case, after the choice of the President, the person having the greatest number of votes of the electors shall be the Vice-President. But if there should remain two or more who have equal votes, the Senate shall choose from them by ballot the Vice-President.]

4. Time of Elections. The Congress may determine the time of choosing the electors, and

Clauses 2 and 3. The framers of the Constitution did not want the President to be chosen directly by the people. They thought the voters would not become familiar with the qualifications of leaders living in distant states. Therefore they devised an electoral college. The electors, it was hoped, would be prominent individuals acquainted with leaders in other states. They would thus be able to make a wise choice for President. Originally, the state legislatures chose the electors, but since 1828 they have been nominated by the political parties and elected by the people. The electors from all the states make up the electoral college. Each state has as many electors as it has senators and representatives.

This system provided that each elector vote for two candidates, with the person receiving the largest number of votes (provided it was a majority) becoming President and the one who was runner-up becoming Vice-President. In 1800 the two top candidates tied, making it necessary for the House to choose the President. The 12th Amendment (1804) was passed to prevent a situation of this kind.

Clause 4. Elections for President are held on the first Tuesday after the first Monday in November. The electors cast

148

the day on which they shall give their votes; which day shall be the same throughout the United States.

5. Qualifications for President. No person except a natural-born citizen [or a citizen of the United States, at the time of the adoption of this Constitution], shall be eligible to the office of the President; neither shall any person be eligible to that office who shall not have attained to the age of thirty-five years, and been fourteen years a resident within the United States.

6. Filling Vacancies. In the case of the removal of the President from office, or of his death, resignation, or inability to discharge the powers and duties of the said office, the same shall devolve on the Vice-President, and the Congress may by law provide for the case of removal, death, resignation, or inability, both of the President and Vice-President, declaring what officer shall then act as President, and such officer shall act accordingly, until the disability be removed, or a President shall be elected.

7. Salary. The President shall, at stated times, receive for his services, a compensation, which shall neither be increased nor diminished during the period for which he shall have been elected, and he shall not receive within that period any other emolument from the United States, or any of them.

8. Oath of Office. Before he enter on the execution of his office, he shall take the following oath or affirmation:—"I do solemnly swear (or affirm) that I will faithfully execute the office of President of the United States, and will to the best of my ability, preserve, protect, and defend the Constitution of the United States."

Section 2. Powers of the President

1. Military Powers. The President shall be Commander in Chief of the Army and Navy of the United States, and of the militia of the several states, when called into the actual service of the United States; he may require the opinion in writing, of the principal officer in each of the executive departments, upon any subject relating to the duties of their respective offices, and

their votes on the first Monday after the second Wednesday in December.

Clause 6. If the presidency becomes vacant, then the Vice-President takes the office. Congress may decide by law who will become President when neither the President nor the Vice-President is able to serve. In the present succession law, the Speaker of the House is next in line, followed by the President pro tempore of the Senate. The 25th Amendment (1967) deals with the inability of Presidents to discharge their duties.

Clause 1. The President, who cannot be a member of the military, heads the armed forces. This clause places the armed forces under civilian control. The President can ask the heads of executive departments for written opinions about matters related to their departments. This clause provides the constitutional basis for the cabinet.

149

he shall have power to grant reprieves and pardons for offenses against the United States, except in cases of impeachment.

2. Treaties and Appointments. He shall have power, by and with the advice and consent of the Senate, to make treaties, provided two-thirds of the Senators present concur; and he shall nominate, and by and with the advice and consent of the Senate, shall appoint ambassadors, other public ministers and consuls, judges of the Supreme Court, and all other officers of the United States, whose appointments are not herein otherwise provided for, and which shall be established by law; but the Congress may by law vest the appointment of such inferior officers, as they think proper, in the President alone, in the courts of law, or in the heads of departments.

3. Filling Vacancies. The President shall have power to fill up all vacancies that may happen during the recess of the Senate, by granting commissions which shall expire at the end of their next session.

Section 3. Duties of the President
He shall from time to time give to the Congress information of the state of the Union, and recommend to their consideration such measures as he shall judge necessary and expedient; he may, on extraordinary occasions, convene both houses, or either of them, and in case of disagreement between them, with respect to the time of adjournment, he may adjourn them to such time as he shall think proper; he shall receive ambassadors and other public ministers; he shall take care that the laws be faithfully executed, and shall commission all the officers of the United States.

Section 4. Impeachment
The President, Vice-President, and all civil officers of the United States, shall be removed from office on impeachment for, and conviction of, treason, bribery, or other high crimes and misdemeanors.

150

Clause 2. The President can make treaties with foreign countries, but they must be approved by two thirds of those present at a session of the Senate. Note that this is a power given to the Senate but not to the House and is a part of the checks and balances system.

The Senate must also approve the appointment of American representatives abroad, judges of the Supreme Court, and any other government official not provided for in the Constitution. However, Congress may make laws allowing the President, the courts, or heads of departments to appoint minor government officials.

Clause 3. If vacancies occur in appointive federal offices when the Senate is not in session, the President may make temporary appointments.

Section 3. The President must give Congress information about the condition of the country. It has become customary for the President to deliver a "State of the Union" message to Congress every January. If the need arises, the President may call either or both houses of Congress into special session. The President has the power to end a session of Congress if the two houses cannot agree on an adjournment date. The President is to receive foreign representatives, see that the laws of the federal government are carried out, and commission all officers of the armed forces.

Section 4. (See annotation for Article 1, Section 2, Clause 5, and Section 3, Clauses 6 and 7.)

Article 3. The Judicial Branch

Section 1.   Federal Courts

The judicial power of the United States shall be vested in one Supreme Court, and in such inferior courts as the Congress may from time to time ordain and establish. The judges, both of the Supreme and inferior courts, shall hold their offices during good behavior, and shall, at stated times, receive for their services a compensation, which shall not be diminished during their continuance in office.

Section 2.   Jurisdiction of Federal Courts

1. General Jurisdiction. The judicial power shall extend to all cases, in law and equity, arising under this Constitution, the laws of the United States, and treaties made or which shall be made, under their authority; to all cases affecting ambassadors, other public ministers and consuls; to all cases of admiralty and maritime jurisdiction; to controversies to which the United States shall be a party; to controversies between two or more states; [between a state and citizens of another state;] between citizens of the same state claiming lands under grants of different states, and between a state or the citizens thereof, and foreign states, citizens, or subjects.

2. Supreme Court. In all cases affecting ambassadors, other public ministers and consuls, and those in which a state shall be a party, the Supreme Court shall have original jurisdiction. In all the other cases before mentioned, the Supreme Court shall have appellate jurisdiction, both as to law and fact, with such exceptions, and under such regulations as the Congress shall make.

3. Conduct of Trials. The trial of all crimes, except in cases of impeachment, shall be by jury; and such trial shall be held in the state where the said crimes shall have been committed; but when not committed within any state,

Section 1. The framers of the Constitution sought to control the power of the federal government with a system of checks and balances. Each branch of government—legislative, executive, and judicial—has certain checks against the other two. The President can veto acts of Congress, but Congress can override vetoes. In particular, the Senate must approve the President's appointments and consent to the President's treaties. The judiciary is an extremely important part of this system of balanced government.

Section 1 authorizes a Supreme Court and such lower courts as Congress shall establish. Both the President and Congress have checks on the courts. Congress determines the number of judges on the Supreme Court and creates by law all other courts. The President, with the consent of the Senate, appoints all federal judges. Federal judges hold office for life and may be removed only by impeachment.

Clause 1. Over the years the courts have defined their jurisdiction and established some checks of their own. In 1803 Supreme Court Chief Justice John Marshall asserted the power of the Court to determine the constitutionality of acts of Congress. If the Court finds a law unconstitutional, it is of no effect. Through Marshall's ruling, the Court made itself the interpreter of the Constitution. The Supreme Court has several times declared that the President is "under the law" as interpreted by the Court. Only once was there the threat of an open confrontation. In 1952 President Truman, acting in the emergency of the Korean War, seized the nation's steel mills. The Supreme Court, declaring that he had exceeded his constitutional powers, ordered him to return them to their owners. He did.

Clause 2. "Original jurisdiction" refers to the right to try a case before any other court hears it. Actually, very few cases come directly to the Supreme Court. Most federal court cases begin in the district courts. They can be appealed to the circuit courts and may finally be carried up to the Supreme Court. "Appellate jurisdiction" refers to the right to review cases appealed from lower courts. Most cases reaching the Supreme Court are taken to it on appeal. The Supreme Court has original jurisdiction in cases involving foreign representatives or in cases involving disputes between states. Congress determines appellate jurisdiction of the Supreme Court.

Clause 3. Except for impeachment cases, anyone accused of a federal crime has the right to a trial by jury. The trial must be held in the state where the crime was committed.

151

On July 23, 1788, a parade was held in lower Manhattan in celebration of the Constitution's ratification. The "federal ship," named in Hamilton's honor, was pulled along this New York street "with floating sheets and full sails."

the trial shall be at such place or places as the Congress may by law have directed.

Section 3. Treason

1. Definition. Treason against the United States shall consist only in levying war against them, or in adhering to their enemies, giving them aid and comfort. No person shall be convicted of treason unless on the testimony of two witnesses to the same overt act, or on confession in open court.

Clause 1. Treason is the only crime defined by the Constitution. Notice how strict the requirements are—there must be two witnesses to the same overt (open) act. The framers did not want anyone tried for treason merely for criticizing the government.

2. Punishment. The Congress shall have power to declare the punishment of treason, but no attainder of treason shall work corruption of blood or forfeiture except during the life of the person attained.

Clause 2. Congress has the power to fix the punishment for treason. But the families and descendants of a person found guilty of treason cannot be punished for his or her crime.

Article 4. Relations Among States

Section 1.   Official Acts
Full faith and credit shall be given in each state to the public acts, records, and judicial proceedings of every other state. And the Congress may by general laws prescribe the manner in which such acts, records, and proceedings shall be proved, and the effect thereof.

Section 1.   Each state must respect the laws, records, and court decisions of other states. If this were not the case, a person might move to another state to avoid legal punishment imposed by another state. The "full faith and credit" clause avoids much of the confusion arising from different state regulations.

Section 2.   Privileges of Citizens
1. Privileges. The citizens of each state shall be entitled to all privileges and immunities of citizens in the several states.

Clause 1.   This clause gives a person moving into a state the same rights the state gives to its own citizens. The state may still require a person to meet its own residency requirements for voting in elections and holding state office.

2. Extradition. A person charged in any state with treason, felony, or other crime, who shall flee from justice, and be found in another state, shall on demand of the executive authority of the state from which he fled, be delivered up, to be removed to the state having jurisdiction of the crime.

Clause 2.   If a person charged with a crime flees to another state, the governor of the state where the crime was committed may request that he or she be returned. Sending back such persons for trial is called *extradition*. In the vast majority of cases, the return is automatic, but in a very few cases state governors have refused to return the fugitives.

3. Fugitive Slaves. [No person held in service or labor in one state, under the laws thereof, escaping into another, shall in consequence of any law or regulation therein, be discharged from such service or labor, but shall be delivered up on claim of the party to whom such service or labor may be due.]

Clause 3.   This clause provided the constitutional basis for slave owners to have their escaped slaves returned to them. The 13th Amendment (1865) ended slavery, making this clause obsolete.

Section 3.   New States and Territories
1. Admission of New States. New states may be admitted by the Congress into this Union; but no new state shall be formed or erected within the jurisdiction of any other state; nor any state be formed by the junction of two or more states, or parts of states, without the consent of the legislatures of the states concerned as well as of the Congress.

Clause 1.   The Constitution specifically gave Congress power to govern the western territories. It can admit new states to the Union but cannot subdivide states without their consent. Subdivision has happened only three times. Kentucky was separated from Virginia in 1792. Maine was split off from Massachusetts in 1820. And during the Civil War (1863), West Virginia separated from Virginia and joined the northern Union.

2. Powers of Congress over Territories and Other Property. The Congress shall have power to dispose of and make all needful rules and regulations respecting the territory or other property belonging to the United States; and nothing in this Constitution shall be so construed as to prejudice any claims of the United States, or of any particular state.

Clause 2.   Congress may govern and make regulations for the territories and properties of the United States. "Territories" here refers to lands not under the control of any state.

Section 4. Guarantees to the States

The United States shall guarantee to every state in this Union a republican form of government, and shall protect each of them against invasion; and on application of the legislature or of the executive (when the legislature cannot be convened) against domestic violence.

Section 4. In practice, Congress determines whether a state has a republican form of government. The Constitution also requires the federal government to protect a state against invasion and, upon request of the proper state authorities, to protect it against rioting and violence. Sometimes Presidents have ordered federal intervention without request from states when federal laws were being violated.

Article 5. Methods of Amendment

The Congress, whenever two-thirds of both houses shall deem it necessary, shall propose amendments to this Constitution, or, on the application of the legislatures of two-thirds of the several states, shall call a convention for proposing amendments, which, in either case, shall be valid to all intents and purposes, as part of this Constitution, when ratified by the legislatures of three-fourths of the several states, or by conventions in three-fourths thereof, as the one or the other mode of ratification may be proposed by the Congress; provided that [no amendments which may be made prior to the year 1808 shall in any manner affect the first and fourth clauses in the Ninth Section of the First Article; and that] no state, without its consent, shall be deprived of its equal suffrage in the Senate.

Article 5. The framers of the Constitution recognized that later generations would need to make some changes in the Constitution. However, they wanted to make the process of change difficult so that the Constitution would not be battered by every popular trend. According to Article 5, Congress can propose an amendment by a two thirds vote of both houses. Or, if two thirds of the state legislatures request it, Congress calls a convention to propose an amendment. So far, all amendments have been proposed by Congress. An amendment must be approved by three fourths of the state legislatures or by conventions in three fourths of the states.

Considering the enormous changes in American society, there have been remarkably few amendments to the Constitution. The first ten (known as the Bill of Rights) were approved within two years, but there were only two more amendments before the Civil War. There has been a total of 26 amendments.

Article 6. General Provisions

1. Public Debts. All debts contracted and engagements entered into, before the adoption of this Constitution, shall be as valid against the United States under this Constitution, as under the Confederation.

Clause 1. All debts and treaties made under the Articles of Confederation were recognized by the United States. This action was favored by Alexander Hamilton and was one of several steps taken by Congress to establish the credit of the new government.

2. The Supreme Law. This Constitution, and the laws of the United States which shall be made in pursuance thereof, and all treaties made, or which shall be made, under the authority of the United States, shall be the supreme law of the land; and the judges in every state shall be bound thereby, anything in the constitution or laws of any state to the contrary notwithstanding.

Clause 2. This clause is the basic, constitutional statement of national authority. It makes the Constitution and federal laws, rather than state laws, supreme. Many years—even a Civil War—intervened before the precise relationship between the federal government and the states was worked out.

3. Oaths of Office. The Senators and Representatives before mentioned, and the members of the several state legislatures, and all executive

Clause 3. All the officials listed must pledge themselves to support the Constitution. But such a pledge, or oath, cannot include any religious test or requirement that a person be-

and judicial officers, both of the United States and of the several states, shall be bound by oath or affirmation, to support this Constitution; but no religious test shall ever be required as a qualification to any office or public trust under the United States.

long to a particular religious faith. This provision results from the principle of separation of church and state in the United States.

Article 7. Ratification

The ratification of the convention of nine states shall be sufficient for the establishment of the Constitution between the states so ratifying the same.

DONE in Convention by the unanimous consent of the States present the seventeenth day of September in the year of our Lord one thousand seven hundred and eight-seven and of the independence of the United States of America the twelfth. In witness whereof we have hereunto subscribed our names,
G. Washington—President and deputy from Virginia

Article 7. The final article sets up the process of ratification. The framers knew they had to submit their document for popular approval. But they wished to avoid the state legislatures, which might resent the powers of the federal government. As a result, they provided for specially elected ratifying conventions, one in each state. And when nine states approved, the Constitution would be considered in effect. Of the 55 people who attended the Constitutional Convention in the summer of 1787, 39 signed the Constitution.

NEW HAMPSHIRE
John Langdon
Nicholas Gilman

NEW YORK
Alexander Hamilton

DELAWARE
George Read
Gunning Bedford
John Dickinson
Richard Bassett
Jacob Broom

NORTH CAROLINA
William Blount
Richard Dobbs Spaight
Hugh Williamson

MASSACHUSETTS
Nathaniel Gorham
Rufus King

NEW JERSEY
William Livingston
David Brearley
William Paterson
Jonathan Dayton

MARYLAND
James McHenry
Daniel of St. Thomas Jenifer
Daniel Carroll

SOUTH CAROLINA
John Rutledge
Charles Cotesworth Pinckney
Charles Pinckney
Pierce Butler

CONNECTICUT
William Samuel Johnson
Roger Sherman

PENNSYLVANIA
Benjamin Franklin
Thomas Mifflin
Robert Morris
George Clymer
Thomas FitzSimons
Jared Ingersoll
James Wilson
Gouverneur Morris

VIRGINIA
John Blair
James Madison

GEORGIA
William Few
Abraham Baldwin

Amendments to the Constitution

(The first ten amendments constitute the Bill of Rights. They became an official part of the Constitution in 1791. They limit the powers of the federal government but not the powers of the states.)

Amendment 1. Freedom of Religion, Speech, Press, Assembly, and Petition (1791)

Congress shall make no law respecting an establishment of religion, or prohibiting the free exercise thereof; or abridging the freedom of speech, or of the press; or the right of the people peaceably to assemble, and to petition the government for a redress of grievances.

Amendment 1. This amendment guarantees to Americans the most essential freedoms. Freedom of religion guarantees the right to worship as one chooses without interference from Congress. The Supreme Court has interpreted this amendment as a guarantee of the separation of church and state. Freedoms of speech and press are limited only when they involve slander and libel (false and malicious statements) or statements that might be injurious to the general welfare of the nation. The First Amendment also entitles the people to hold meetings and to request the government to respond to their grievances.

Amendment 2. Right to Bear Arms (1791)

A well-regulated militia, being necessary to the security of a free state, the right of the people to keep and bear arms shall not be infringed.

Amendment 2. The states have the right to maintain armed militias for their protection. However, the rights of private citizens to own guns can be, and are, regulated by federal and state legislation.

Amendment 3. Housing of Troops (1791)

No soldier shall, in time of peace, be quartered in any house, without the consent of the owner; nor in time of war, but in a manner to be prescribed by law.

Amendment 3. One source of bitter complaint in the colonies had been the British practice of housing their troops in American homes. The Third Amendment guarantees that no soldier will be quartered in a private residence during peacetime or in wartime without specific congressional authorization.

Amendment 4. Searches and Seizures (1791)

The right of the people to be secure in their persons, houses, papers, and effects, against unreasonable searches and seizures, shall not be violated; and no warrants shall issue but upon probable cause, supported by oath or affirmation, and particularly describing the place to be searched, and the persons or things to be seized.

Amendment 4. This amendment was proposed and ratified in response to the British writs of assistance—blanket search warrants permitting officers to search any house at any time. For an American home to be searched, a warrant must be issued by a judge, and it must state precisely what the official expects fo find.

156

Amendment 5. Rights of Accused Persons (1791)

No person shall be held to answer for a capital, or otherwise infamous, crime, unless on a presentment or indictment of a grand jury, except in cases arising in the land or naval forces, or in the militia, when in actual service in time of war or public danger; nor shall any person be subject for the same offense to be twice put in jeopardy of life and limb; nor shall be compelled, in any criminal case, to be a witness against himself; nor be deprived of life, liberty, or property, without due process of law; nor shall private property be taken for public use, without just compensation.

Amendment 5. No person can be tried for a serious crime in a federal court unless indicted, or charged, by a grand jury. A grand jury is a group of 23 persons who hear in secret accusations against a person and then decide whether the person should be tried in court. "Twice put in jeopardy," or double jeopardy, means that no person can be tried twice in a federal court for the same crime.

People cannot be forced to give evidence against themselves that will help prove their guilt. This clause allows people on trial to refuse to answer questions, without paying penalties.

"Due process of law" has become quite complicated, but the framers wished to guarantee proper judicial procedures for a person accused of a crime (see Amendment 6). The taking of private property for public use is called the right of eminent domain. The government cannot take such property without giving owners fair prices for their property. The price is determined by a court.

Amendment 6. Right to a Speedy, Fair Trial (1791)

In all criminal prosecutions, the accused shall enjoy the right to a speedy and public trial, by an impartial jury of the state and district wherein the crime shall have been committed, which district shall have been previously ascertained by law, and to be informed of the nature and cause of the accusation; to be confronted with the witnesses against him; to have compulsory process for obtaining witnesses in his favor, and to have the assistance of counsel for his defense.

Amendment 6. This amendment defines the rights of the accused under due process of law. A person has the right to be informed of the charges against him or her and to a speedy and public trial by jury. Witnesses for and against the accused may be compelled to appear in court to give evidence. The accused is entitled to confront these witnesses and to be represented by a lawyer at all stages of the criminal proceedings.

Amendment 7. Civil Suits (1791)

In suits at common law, where the value in controversy shall exceed $20, the right of trial by jury shall be preserved, and no fact tried by a jury shall be otherwise reexamined in any court of the United States than according to the rules of the common law.

Amendment 7. If a sum of money larger than $20 is the object of dispute, the people involved may insist on a jury trial. However, in actual practice, cases do not reach federal courts unless much larger sums are involved.

Amendment 8. Bails, Fines, Punishments (1791)

Excessive bail shall not be required, nor excessive fines imposed, nor cruel and unusual punishments inflicted.

Amendment 8. The Eighth Amendment continues the enumeration of the rights of the accused. Before a criminal trial, the accused may remain free on payment to the court of a sum of money called bail. Bail is returned if the person appears for trial as ordered. Neither the amount of bail set nor the punishment inflicted should be excessive. The Supreme

Amendment 9. Powers Reserved to the People (1791)

The enumeration in the Constitution, of certain rights, shall not be construed to deny or disparage others retained by the people.

Amendment 9. This means that the rights listed in the Constitution are not necessarily the only rights that exist. Other rights shall not be denied to the people simply because they are not enumerated in the Constitution.

Amendment 10. Powers Reserved to the States (1791)

The powers not delegated to the United States by the Constitution, nor prohibited by it to the states, are reserved to the states respectively, or to the people.

Amendment 10. In the same vein as the previous amendment, the Tenth Amendment stipulates that those powers not given to the federal government are reserved to the states or to the people.

Amendment 11. Suits Against States (1798)

The judicial power of the United States shall not be construed to extend to any suit in law or equity, commenced or prosecuted against one of the United States, by citizens of another state, or by citizens or subjects of any foreign state.

Amendment 11. A state cannot be sued in any court other than the courts of the state. This amendment overruled a Supreme Court decision (*Chisholm* v. *Georgia*, 1793) that allowed two citizens of South Carolina to sue Georgia in a federal court.

Amendment 12. Electing the President and Vice-President (1804)

The electors shall meet in their respective states, and vote by ballot for President and Vice-President, one of whom, at least, shall not be an inhabitant of the same state with themselves; they shall name in their ballots the person voted for as President, and in distinct ballots the person voted for as Vice-President, and they shall make distinct lists of all persons voted for as President, and of all persons voted for as Vice-President, and of the number of votes for each, which lists they shall sign and certify, and transmit, sealed, to the seat of government of the United States, directed to the President of the Senate; the President of the Senate shall, in the

Amendment 12. This amendment nullifies Article 2, Section 1, Clause 3. At first the electors voted for President and Vice-President without specifying which person they wanted for each office. After the election of 1796, in which the people elected a Federalist President and a Republican Vice-President, and the election of 1800, which was a tie, the 12th Amendment was passed to require each elector to cast two ballots—one for President, one for Vice-President. Electors are nominated by the political parties and elected by the people. Each state has as many electors as it has senators and representatives in Congress. The electors of the party with the most *popular votes*—that is, votes cast by the people of the state—get to cast all the state's electoral votes for the party's candidates. The electoral votes are counted by the President of the Senate in the presence of both houses of Congress. Each candidate for President and Vice-President must receive a majority of electoral votes to be elected.

Political parties are not mentioned in the Constitution—the framers considered them unnecessary as well as harmful to national unity. The 12th Amendment recognized the fact that presence of the Senate and House of Representatives, open all the certificates and the votes shall then be counted; the person having the greatest number of votes for President shall be the President, if such number be a majority of the whole number of electors appointed; and if no person have such majority, then from the persons having the highest numbers not exceeding three on the list of those voted for as President, the House of Representatives shall choose immediately, by ballot, the President. But in choosing the President, the votes shall be taken by states, the representation from each state having one vote; a quorum for this purpose shall consist of a member or members from two-thirds of the states, and a majority of all the states shall be necessary to a choice. [And if the House of Representatives shall not choose a President whenever the right of choice shall devolve upon them, before the fourth day of March next following, then the Vice-President shall act as President, as in the case of the death or other constitutional disability of the President.] The person having the greatest number of votes as Vice-President, shall be the Vice-President, if such number be a majority of the whole number of electors appointed, and if no person have a majority, then, from the two highest numbers on the list, the Senate shall choose the Vice-President; a quorum for the purpose shall consist of two-thirds of the whole number of Senators, and a majority of the whole number shall be necessary to a choice. But no person constitutionally ineligible to the office of President shall be eligible to that of Vice-President of the United States.

political parties had developed since the Constitution was ratified.

Amendment 13. Abolition of Slavery (1865)

Section 1. Neither slavery nor involuntary servitude, except as a punishment for crime whereof the party shall have been duly convicted, shall exist within the United States, or any place subject to their jurisdiction.

Section 2. Congress shall have power to enforce this article by appropriate legislation.

Amendment 13. The 13th, 14th, and 15th Amendments were passed after the Civil War. The 13th Amendment abolished slavery and gave Congress the right to enforce the law.

Amendment 14. Citizenship (1868)

Section 1. Citizenship Defined. All persons born or naturalized in the United States and subject to the jurisdiction thereof, are citizens of the United States and of the state wherein they reside. No state shall make or enforce any law which shall abridge the privileges or immunities of citizens of the United States; nor shall any state deprive any person of life, liberty, or property, without due process of law; nor deny to any person within its jurisdiction the equal protection of the laws.

Section 1. The main purpose of this amendment was to give Blacks equal rights. The first sentence, by definition, gives Black Americans citizenship. The second sentence prohibits the states from interfering with any citizen's right to equal protection under the law or with the right of due process of law. In recent years the Supreme Court has interpreted the phrase "due process" to mean that the states must respect the judicial rights guaranteed by the Bill of Rights.

Section 2. Apportionment of Representatives. Representatives shall be apportioned among the several states according to their respective numbers, counting the whole number of persons in each state, [excluding Indians not taxed]. But when the right to vote at any election for the choice of electors for President and Vice-President of the United States, Representatives in Congress, the executive and judicial officers of a state, or the members of the legislature thereof, is denied to any of the [male] inhabitants of such state, [being twenty-one years of age] and citizens of the United States, or in any way abridged, except for participation in rebellion, or other crime, the basis of representation therein shall be reduced in the proportion which the number of such [male] citizens shall bear to the whole number of [male] citizens [twenty-one years of age] in such state.

Section 2. This section nullified the three fifths compromise and declared every man over the age of 21 to be entitled to one vote. Notice that Indians and women were still excluded. This section provides for a punishment against any state preventing its eligible citizens from voting. This penalty has never been imposed.

Section 3. Disability for Engaging in Insurrection. No person shall be a Senator or Representative in Congress, or elector of President and Vice-President, or hold any office, civil or military, under the United States, or under any state, who, having previously taken an oath, as a member of Congress, or as an officer of the United States, or as a member of any state legislature, or as an executive or judicial officer of any state, to support the Constitution of the United States, shall have engaged in insurrection or rebellion against the same, or given aid or comfort to the enemies thereof. But Congress may, by vote of two-thirds of each house, remove such disability.

Section 3. This section was designed to punish the leaders of the Confederacy for breaking their oaths to support the Constitution. Many southern leaders were excluded from public office by this amendment, but by 1872 most were permitted to return to public life. In 1898 all the Confederates were pardoned.

Section 4. Public Debt. The validity of the public debt of the United States, authorized by law, including debts incurred for payment of pensions and bounties for services in suppressing insurrection or rebellion, shall not be questioned. But neither the United States nor any state shall assume or pay any debt or obligation incurred in aid of insurrection or rebellion against the United States [or any claim for the loss or emancipation of any slave]; but all such debts, obligations, and claims shall be held illegal and void.

Section 5. Enforcement. The Congress shall have power to enforce, by appropriate legislation, the provisions of this article.

Amendment 15. Right to Vote (1870)

Section 1. The right of citizens of the United States to vote shall not be denied or abridged by the United States or any state on account of race, color, or previous condition of servitude.

Section 2. The Congress shall have power to enforce this article by appropriate legislation.

Amendment 16. Income Tax (1913)

The Congress shall have power to lay and collect taxes on incomes, from whatever source derived, without apportionment among the several states, and without regard to any census or enumeration.

Amendment 17. Electing Senators (1913)

Section 1. Method of Election. The Senate of the United States shall be composed of two Senators from each state, elected by the people thereof, for six years; and each Senator shall have one vote. The electors in each state shall

Section 4. This section dealt a harsh financial blow to the South. The war debt of the Union was declared valid; the war debt of the Confederacy was declared void. There would be no reimbursement on Confederate bonds and no payment for the loss of slaves.

Amendment 15. This amendment prohibits federal or state governments from preventing any citizen from voting because of "race, color, or previous condition of servitude." It was designed to guarantee voting rights to Black American men.

Amendment 16. This amendment permits Congress to tax individual incomes without basing the tax on state populations. The income tax is now the major source of revenue for the federal government.

Amendment 17. This amendment gave the people the right to elect senators directly. Before this, senators were elected by the state legislatures. If a senator dies or leaves office during his or her term of office, the governor of the state can either order an election for a successor or appoint a temporary successor.

have the qualifications requisite for electors of the most numerous branch of the state legislatures.

Section 2. Filling Vacancies. When vacancies happen in the representation of any state in the Senate, the executive authority of such state shall issue writs of election to fill such vacancies: *Provided* that the legislatures of any state may empower the executive thereof to make temporary appointments until the people fill the vacancies by election as the legislature may direct.

[**Section 3. Not Retroactive.** This amendment shall not be so construed as to affect the election or term of any Senator chosen before it becomes valid as part of the Constitution.]

Amendment 18. Prohibition (1919)

Amendment 18. This amendment forbade the manufacture, sale, and shipment of alcoholic beverages. It was repealed by the 21st Amendment.

[**Section 1.** After one year from the ratification of this article the manufacture, sale, or transportation of intoxicating liquors within, the importation thereof into, or the exportation thereof from, the United States and all territory subject to the jurisdiction thereof for beverage purposes is hereby prohibited.

Section 2. The Congress and the several states shall have concurrent power to enforce this article by appropriate legislation.

Section 3. This article shall be inoperative unless it shall have been ratified as an amendment to the Constitution by the legislatures of the several states, as provided in the Constitution, within seven years from the date of the submission hereof to the states by the Congress.]

Amendment 19. Women's Suffrage (1920)

Amendment 19. This amendment gave women the right to vote.

Section 1. The right of citizens of the United States to vote shall not be denied or abridged by the United States or by any state on account of sex.

Section 2. Congress shall have power to enforce this article by appropriate legislation.

Amendment 20. "Lame Duck" Amendment (1933)

Section 1. Beginning of Terms. The terms of the President and Vice-President shall end at noon on the 20th day of January, and the terms of Senators and Representatives at noon on the 3rd day of January, of the years in which such terms would have ended if this article had not been ratified; and the terms of their successors shall then begin.

Section 2. Beginning of Congressional Sessions. The Congress shall assemble at least once in every year, and such meeting shall begin at noon on the third day of January, unless they shall by law appoint a different day.

Section 3. Presidential succession. If at the time fixed for the beginning of the term of the President, the President-elect shall have died, the Vice-President-elect shall become President. If a President shall not have been chosen before the time fixed for the beginning of his term, or if the President-elect shall have failed to qualify, then the Vice-President-elect shall act as President until a President shall have qualified; and the Congress may by law provide for the case wherein neither a President-elect nor a Vice-President-elect shall have qualified, declaring who shall then act as President, or the manner in which one who is to act shall be selected, and such person shall act accordingly until a President or Vice-President shall have qualified.

Section 3. This section provides for succession to the Presidency when a President-elect dies or fails to qualify.

Section 4. Filling Presidential Vacancy. The Congress may by law provide for the case of the death of any of the persons from whom the House of Representatives may choose a President whenever the right of choice shall have devolved upon them, and for the case of the death of any of the persons from whom the Senate may choose a Vice-President whenever the right of choice shall have devolved upon them.

[**Section 5. Effective Date.** Sections 1 and 2 shall take effect on the 15th day of October following the ratification of this article.

Section 6. Time Limit for Ratification. This article shall be inoperative unless it shall

163

have been ratified as an amendment to the Constitution by the legislatures of three-fourths of the several states within the seven years from the date of its submission.]

Amendment 21. Repeal of Prohibition (1933)

Section 1. The eighteenth article of amendment of the Constitution of the United States is hereby repealed.

Section 2. The transportation or importation into any state, territory, or possession of the United States for delivery or use therein of intoxicating liquors, in violation of the laws thereof, is hereby prohibited.

[**Section 3.** This article shall be inoperative unless it shall have been ratified as an amendment to the Constitution by conventions in the several states, as provided in the Constitution, within seven years from the date of the submission hereof to the states by the Congress.]

Amendment 21. This repealed the 18th Amendment.

Amendment 22. Two-Term Limit for Presidents (1951)

Section 1. No person shall be elected to the office of the President more than twice, and no person who has held the office of President, or acted as President, for more than two years of a term to which some other person was elected President shall be elected to the office of the President more than once. [But this Article shall not apply to any person holding the office of President when this Article was proposed by the Congress, and shall not prevent any person who may be holding the office of President, or acting as President, during the term within which this Article becomes operative from holding the office of President or acting as President during the remainder of such term.]

Amendment 22. This amendment was passed because many feared that President Franklin D. Roosevelt's four terms had set a dangerous precedent. Prior to his election to a third term in 1940, Presidents had followed the tradition of serving no more than two terms.

[**Section 2.** This Article shall be inoperative unless it shall have been ratified as an amendment to the Constitution by the legislatures of three-fourths of the several states within seven years from the date of its submission to the states by the Congress.]

Amendment 23. Presidential Electors for District of Columbia (1961)

Section 1. The District constituting the seat of Government of the United States shall appoint in such manner as the Congress may direct:

A number of electors of President and Vice-President equal to the whole number of Senators and Representatives in Congress to which the District would be entitled if it were a state, but in no event more than the least populous state; they shall be in addition to those appointed by the states, but they shall be considered, for the purposes of the election of President and Vice-President, to be electors appointed by a state; and they shall meet in the District and perform such duties as provided by the twelfth article of amendment.

Section 2. The Congress shall have power to enforce this article by appropriate legislation.

Amendment 23. This amendment gave the residents of Washington, D.C., three members in the electoral college and hence the right to vote for President and Vice-President.

Amendment 24. Poll Taxes (1964)

Section 1. The right of citizens of the United States to vote in any primary or other election for President or Vice-President, for electors for President or Vice-President, or for Senator or Representative in Congress, shall not be denied or abridged by the United States or any state by reason of failure to pay any poll tax or other tax.

Section 2. The Congress shall have the power to enforce this article by appropriate legislation.

Amendment 24. When this amendment was passed, five southern states used the poll tax as a means of discouraging Blacks from voting. This amendment applies only to national elections.

Amendment 25. Presidential Disability and Succession (1967)

1. In case of the removal of the President from office or his death or resignation, the Vice-President shall become President.

2. Whenever there is a vacancy in the office of the Vice-President, the President shall nominate a Vice-President who shall take the office upon confirmation by a majority vote of both houses of Congress.

3. Whenever the President transmits to the President pro tempore of the Senate and the Speaker of the House of Representatives his written declaration that he is unable to discharge the powers and duties of his office, and until he transmits to them a written declaration to the contrary, such powers and duties shall be discharged by the Vice-President as Acting President.

4. Whenever the Vice-President and a majority of either the principal officers of the executive departments or of such other body as Congress may by law provide, transmit to the President pro tempore of the Senate and the Speaker of the House of Representatives their written declaration that the President is unable to discharge the powers and duties of his office, the Vice-President shall immediately assume the powers and duties of the office as Acting President.

Thereafter, when the President transmits to the President pro tempore of the Senate and the Speaker of the House of Representatives his written declaration that no inability exists, he shall resume the powers and duties of his office unless the Vice-President and a majority of either the principal officers of the executive department or of such other body as Congress may by law provide, transmit within four days to the President pro tempore of the Senate and the Speaker of the House of Representatives their written declaration that the President is unable to discharge the powers and duties of his office. Thereupon Congress shall decide the issue, assembling within 48 hours for that purpose if not in session. If the Congress, within 21 days after receipt of the latter written declaration, or, if Congress is not in session, within 21 days after

Amendment 25. This amendment clarifies Article 2, Section 1, Clause 6. The Vice-President becomes President when the President dies, resigns, or is removed from office. The new President then nominates a Vice-President, who must be approved by a majority of Congress. If a President is unable to perform the duties of the office, Congress must be informed of this fact in writing by the President or by the Vice-President and a majority of the cabinet. In this case, the Vice-President performs as acting President until the elected President is once again able to function.

This amendment was first used in a case in which Presidential disability was not a factor. In 1973 Vice-President Spiro T. Agnew resigned; President Richard M. Nixon filled the vacancy, according to Section 2 of this amendment, by naming Gerald R. Ford, a member of the House of Representatives, the Vice-President. Mr. Ford was approved by a majority of both houses of Congress. In 1974 Nixon became the first President to resign from office. Ford, in succeeding Nixon, became the first President not elected to that office or to the Vice-Presidency. To fill the Vice-Presidential vacancy, Ford appointed Nelson A. Rockefeller, who was then approved by a majority of both houses of Congress.

Congress is required to assemble, determines by two-thirds vote of both houses the President is unable to discharge the powers and duties of his office, the Vice-President shall continue to discharge the same as Acting President; otherwise, the President shall assume the powers and duties of his office.

Amendment 26. Voting Age Lowered to 18 (1971)

Section 1. The right of citizens of the United States, who are 18 years of age or older, to vote shall not be denied or abridged by the United States or any state on account of age.

Section 2. The Congress shall have the power to enforce this article by appropriate legislation.

Proposed Amendment 27. The Equal Rights Amendment

Section 1. Equality of rights under the law shall not be denied or abridged by the United States or by any state on account of sex.

Section 2. Congress shall have the power to enforce, by appropriate legislation, the provisions of this article.

Amendment 26. This amendment lowered the minimum voting age to 18.

Amendment 27. This amendment, submitted for ratification in 1972, would prohibit discrimination that is based on a person's sex. Thirty-eight states must ratify the amendment by June 30, 1982, for it to become law.

Section Review

1. Identify or explain: Preamble, impeach, veto, elastic clause.
2. In what way would keeping a journal of each house's proceedings benefit the voters?
3. Name and explain two limits on the powers of Congress that are contained in the Constitution.
4. Describe three powers that the Constitution gives to the President.

Chapter 6 Review

Bird's-Eye View

The American colonies became independent states because of their victory in the Revolutionary War. The next task for the people of these independent states was that of developing a government.

At first each state formed its own government and wrote its own constitution. Some of the features of these governments were borrowed from the British system. All the states adopted a republican form of government with an elected executive, but most were not democracies. The right to vote and to hold office was generally limited to free, male property owners.

Social as well as political changes were occurring at this time. Freedom of religion—even for nonbelievers—had been established by most states, and official churches had been disestablished. The separation of church and state was also being reflected in the educational programs of the major colleges, which had broadened their course offerings to include nonreligious subjects.

One of the major achievements of this period of American history was the establishment of rules for both the settlement and the governing of the frontier. The Ordinance of 1785 and the Northwest Ordinance of 1787 set a pattern that was used to develop the wilderness areas. Also important was the establishment of guidelines for the entrance of new states into the Union.

During this period many people recognized the need for government reorganization. Some people were satisfied with a loose confederation of states, but others were pressing for a strong central government. A constitutional convention, composed of delegates from the various states, met to consider the question. After lengthy debate they adopted a series of compromises and accepted a constitution that established a stronger federal government. Three branches of government were created, with an elaborate system of checks and balances between them. This Constitution is the basic framework for the American government of today.

Vocabulary

Define or identify each of the following:

constitution	suffrage	John Dickinson
Abigail Adams	Daniel Shays	bill of rights
Noah Webster	depression	amendment

Review Questions

1. After the Declaration of Independence, most of the new states drafted constitutions. How were these constitutions similar to one another?
2. Describe the social and political changes brought about by the Revolution.
3. Describe six successes of the nation under the Articles of Confederation.
4. What was James Madison's role in the creation of the new government?

5. Name and describe the two compromises made during the Constitutional Convention that helped shape the final document.
6. Why do historians consider the Constitution of the United States a "remarkable document"?

Reviewing Social Studies Skills

1. Examine the map on page 137. The charters of many of the original colonies gave the colonies control over large sections of land that are no longer a part of their territories. Use the map to answer the following:
   a. Explain the meaning of the term "cede."
   b. What colonies had land beyond their 1783 state borders?
   c. Use the directional indicator to describe the location of the ceded land.
   d. When did each state release their land to the central government?
2. Using the map on page 137:
   a. List the states in order of their ratifications of the Constitution.
   b. Generally, in which sections of the country did a majority of the population favor ratification?
   c. In which areas did a majority of the population oppose ratification?
3. Using the Constitution on page 139, answer the following questions:
   a. How many articles are there?
   b. How many amendments are there?
   c. Article 1 is on the Legislative Branch. How many sections are there in Article 1?
   d. What is Article 1, Section 3 about?
   e. Who signed the Constitution as a representative from New York?
   f. Which state had the most people signing the Constitution?

Reading for Meaning

1. Read the Preamble to the Constitution on page 139. What goals did it establish for the United States government?
2. Using the explanation printed in next to the text of the Constitution, define the following words or phrases:
   a. writ of habeas corpus
   b. bill of attainder
   c. impeach
   d. quorum
   e. congressional immunity
   f. patent laws
   g. militia
   h. double jeopardy
   i. due process of law

Bibliography

Carl Van Doren's *The Great Rehearsal* (Viking Press) is an interesting account of the writing and ratification of the Constitution.

Launching the Ship of State

New York was in a festive mood. Flags were draped from every building along the waterfront. This would be the city's finest hour. It was to host the inauguration of the nation's first President. No matter that it was already mid-April 1789 and that the first federal Congress had been in session for more than a month. A man of George Washington's stature was entitled to be late for his inauguration.

The new President, reluctant to leave retirement but ever responsive to the call of duty, had taken some time to put his estate at Mount Vernon in order. Celebrations in Baltimore and Trenton had delayed him still further. But at last Washington would ride into New York, and on April 30 he would take the oath of office.

Dressed patriotically in a suit of American-made cloth, Washington spoke at his inauguration of the great experiment the nation had launched. It had set up a very special form of government—a republic. No one knew whether it could last.

Chapter Objectives

After you have finished reading this chapter, you should be able to:
1. Explain why some people believed the first laws passed by the new federal government "completed the American Revolution."
2. Study Hamilton's plans to establish both a credit system and the bank and explain how they encouraged the development of two political parties.
3. Recognize what the challenges to American neutrality were and how the government responded to each of them.
4. List the factors that caused the Republicans to win the election of 1800.

Despite New York's playful atmosphere, the Federalists knew they faced real problems. Although they had successfully managed the first national election that winter, they still had to tackle several tasks. One of these was the organizing of the federal government. Further, the new administration needed to overcome any remaining fears of a strong central government. It also had to win the respect of foreign nations.

1. Organizing the Federal Government

THE NATION'S FIRST TARIFF. The first task for the new government was to obtain revenue. *James Madison introduced the nation's first tariff bill. If passed, it would levy a tax on certain goods imported from other countries.* Congress approved

On the way from Mount Vernon to his inauguration in New York, Washington was met by crowds of well-wishers. Of this journey he later wrote to a friend that he felt like "a culprit who is going to the place of his execution."

the tax with relatively little argument, so great was the need for money.

ORGANIZING THE EXECUTIVE BRANCH. The framers of the Constitution had been vague on the structure of the executive and judiciary branches. They had tried to avoid giving the Anti-Federalists too many details during the ratification process. The task now was to fill in the outline.

Congress began by authorizing three executive offices under the President. Carried over from the Confederation's government was the Department of War, together with its Secretary, Henry Knox. The old Department of Foreign Affairs became the State Department, headed by Thomas Jefferson. The third and largest department was the Treasury, containing over a thousand clerks and revenue agents. To head this department, Washington appointed his New York friend Alexander Hamilton.

The heads of these departments eventually came to be known as the President's cabinet. They met with him and advised him on decisions he had to make. When the office of Attorney General was created by the Judiciary Act of 1789, Washington named Edmund Randolph to that office. Randolph became the fourth member of Washington's cabinet, and he advised him on matters of law.

This engraving of the first cabinet was made from a painting by Alonzo Chappel. From left to right are Henry Knox, Thomas Jefferson, Edmund Randolph, Alexander Hamilton, and George Washington.

THE JUDICIARY ACT OF 1789. The next task was to organize the judiciary. The Anti-Federalists were afraid that federal courts would duplicate the work of the state courts and, being located in remote cities, would be of no use to the rural poor. *To help overcome these objections, the Judiciary Act of 1789 created a pyramid of federal courts.* At the top was the Supreme Court, with a Chief Justice and five associate justices. (The number of associate justices has since increased to eight.) John Jay was appointed the first Chief Justice. The Judiciary Act also established three circuit courts and 13 federal district courts under the Supreme Court.

This was the sort of structure that the Federalists had wanted—a uniform system of law administered by trained judges. But in a bow to Anti-Federalists, Congress had limited the *jurisdiction* of these federal courts to cases involving the Constitution, the interpretation of laws, or the treaties of the federal government. *Thus, all ordinary civil suits and criminal trials were left to the state courts.* And that, with certain exceptions, is the way it remains today.

Jurisdiction refers to the authority of a court—whether it has a right to hear a given case. Under the Constitution, Congress has the power to determine which cases the federal courts may hear.

THE BILL OF RIGHTS. Next, Congress turned to amending the document so recently written and ratified. *Madison wanted to keep his promise of drafting a bill of rights after the Constitution was approved.* Thus, he spent the summer of 1789 collecting the amendments suggested by the state conventions. Since there were many duplicates, Madison was able to condense them into 17, which he presented to the House of Representatives. Congress approved 12 of them and sent them to the states for ratification. Over the next two years, the states agreed to 10 of the 12. The Bill of Rights went into effect in 1791.

Taken together, the 10 amendments are a statement of the American belief that government must be limited in power and just in action. The Bill of Rights completed the American Revolution. It also ended the contest over the Constitution. With these amendments Madison deprived the Anti-Federalists of their chief complaint.

Section Review

1. Identify or explain: Madison, Knox, Jefferson, Judiciary Act of 1789.
2. List the rights protected by the first 10 amendments to the Constitution. (See pages 156–158.)

3. Why had the framers of the Constitution been so vague about the powers of the executive and judiciary branches?
4. How did the Judiciary Act of 1789 reflect the concerns of both the Federalists and the Anti-Federalists?

2. The Beginning of Political Parties

HAMILTON'S FINANCE. It had been a productive summer for the First Congress. By September 1789 the nation's legislators were ready to go home. One problem remained—the government was deeply in debt from the war and in need of new funding. This thorny problem the weary members of Congress handed to the Secretary of the Treasury. They asked him to prepare a report on the nation's financial state by the time Congress was to return in January 1790. But Hamilton did even more than that. *Over the next year he produced two reports on the nation's credit and one on a federal bank.* In 1792 he followed those reports with his *Report on Manufactures,* which sought to encourage American manufacturing. It was the first extensive survey of the nation's economy. A final report suggested a national mint to coin money.

PAYING THE NATION'S DEBT. The essence of Hamilton's system was this: the government could not run without money. Credit, Hamilton reasoned, was a matter of faith—money lent would be repaid. In order to establish the government's credit so it could borrow money in the future, the treasury would have to pay its past debts. In his first report Hamilton proposed the issuance of *government bonds,* bearing interest of six percent. *In addition, he proposed that the federal government assume the debts that had been incurred by the states in fighting the war.* The Revolution had been a common cause; it was only fair that the cost be borne by all.

Government bonds are contracts under which the government promises to pay back money lent to it, plus interest, by a certain date.

Hamilton's plans were not so simple as they seemed. The paper money and other certificates issued by the Congress and the states during the war had become practically worthless. Most of them had fallen into the hands of a few speculators, who had purchased them from the original holders at a fraction of their face value. To redeem them dollar for dollar would put a terrible burden on the government and give an enormous windfall to the speculators.

OPPOSITION TO HAMILTON'S PLAN. It was this feature to which James Madison objected. He thought the windfall was undeserved and too costly to taxpayers. *He also disliked the idea of a federal assumption of state debts, for it would increase federal authority at the expense of the states.* On this question Madison received enough support in Congress to force Hamilton into a compromise. In exchange for congressional approval of the assumption of state debts, Hamilton and his allies agreed to the removal of the nation's capital from New York. Thus, the capital was moved to Philadelphia for 10 years, while a permanent capital was being built on the banks of the Potomac. *Hamilton got his financial system and the Virginians won the nation's capital.*

THE BANK OF THE UNITED STATES. *A national system of banking was the crown jewel in Hamilton's design.* The system would be made up of a large central bank and branch banks in major cities. The bank would be chartered by Congress and would serve as an agent of the Treasury, which would hold funds on deposit and lend the government money when necessary. The bank would have the power

Sidenote to History

The Constitution in Brick and Marble

Americans were accustomed to creating cities out of the wilderness, but Washington, D.C., was something new. Never before, in America or in Europe, had a city been built for the sole purpose of housing a government. The designer, Pierre Charles L'Enfant, commissioned by President Washington, worked closely with the President and his cabinet. Thus, the city reflected the hopes and dreams of the nation's founders.

The most striking feature of the city was not the street plan (modeled on the French royal capital of Versailles) but the placement of buildings. The layout of the nation's capital represented the separation of powers within the government. The city was a brick and marble version of the Constitution.

Washington, D.C., also reflected republican ideas in other ways. The site was militarily indefensible and without commercial importance. The city, then, was dependent for support on the larger community that it governed. Kings and dictators would find it hard to survive. The government would have to interact with the people. And this was the essence of republicanism.

Thomas Jefferson was the first President inaugurated in Washington, D.C., and the most notable aspect of that occasion, noted one observer, was the absence of soldiers and weapons. The American government rested on popular respect, not on military force.

Washington, D.C., was far from finished when the government offices moved there in 1799. "A malarial hamlet," sneered one foreign diplomat, but like the republic for which it stood, Washington, D.C., was to have a magnificent future.

to issue money of its own, a "sound, uniform currency," backed by the bank's own reserves of gold and government bonds. The bank would also help the government with the national debt. The new six-percent bonds would hold their value because they could be exchanged for perfectly good bank notes.

Speculators, being the main holders of government paper, would become the major stockholders in the bank. The result would be a three-cornered pyramid—bank, government, and speculators. Out of this alliance would come firm government credit, a national currency, and political stability. The last, in some respects, was the most important. Hamilton's chief motive was that of strengthening the central government and ensuring the permanence of the Constitution. In Hamilton's view wealth meant power, and the speculators were wealthy merchants and landowners. By tying the wealthy and powerful to the government, he hoped the government would endure.

RISE OF THE REPUBLICANS. The alliance between the Treasury and the rich was what Madison basically disliked about the whole business. He approved of political stability and a strong national authority. But a government dominated by northern merchants was something else. And within the administration Jefferson took the same stand. But Jefferson failed to move the President, who approved the bill chartering the bank in the spring of 1791.

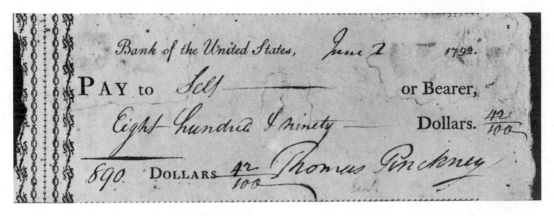

This check for $890.42 was drawn on the Bank of the United States by Thomas Pinckney, minister to Great Britain, in 1792.

Hamilton, who believed in government by the wealthy and powerful, split with Jefferson and Madison, two leaders who had more faith in the common people. The split was the first crack in the ranks of those who had drafted the Constitution. But it was more than a conflict of individual personalities. Hamilton's support was chiefly northern and mercantile. In order to promote American manufacturing and make the United States independent of European goods, Hamilton had suggested raising *tariffs* to protect American industries from foreign competition. Jefferson and Madison, who were basically southern and rural, had opposed Hamilton's plan. They feared that it would destroy foreign trade and foreign markets for American farm exports. Out of such regional and economic differences grew the first political parties.

When Congress places a low tariff on imported goods, it is not placed there to stop foreign goods from competing with American goods. Such a tariff is called a revenue tariff. The high rates of a **protective tariff** are meant to keep out foreign goods in order to protect American manufacturers from competition.

THE CONFLICT GROWS. In the autumn of 1791, Jefferson and Madison established a newspaper, the *National Gazette,* to acquaint the public with their views. As their editor they hired Philip Freneau (fray-NOE), a farmer-poet from New Jersey, whom Madison had known in college.

Freneau's daily blasts at Hamilton soon attracted public attention. By the end of that year, those holding Madison's and Jefferson's views even had a name—Republicans. That name was a shrewd choice, for it suggested that Jefferson and Madison were the true defenders of the republic and that their Hamiltonian opponents were monarchists in disguise. The Hamiltonians kept the name Federalists and hinted broadly that their opponents were Anti-Federalists in disguise.

THE ELECTION OF 1792. Although many Republicans thought Washington sided too often with Hamilton, Jefferson and Madison continued to respect him. *Washington won reelection in 1792 by the unanimous vote of the electoral college, and John Adams remained Vice-President.* Electors from Virginia and other Republican states, however, had cast their Vice-Presidential ballots for George Clinton of New York. This move signified the start of a New York-Virginia alliance and added another step to party development. *In the future each* *party would sponsor a ticket—with both a candidate for President and a candidate for Vice-President on it.*

Section Review

1. Identify or explain: Republicans, speculators, the election of 1792.
2. How did Hamilton propose to overcome the debts incurred by the United States during the Revolution?
3. How did Hamilton hope to improve the nation's financial condition by establishing a national bank?
4. Why did Jefferson and Madison's opposition to Hamilton's financial plans become the basis of a new political party?

3. The Politics of Neutrality

MONARCHY vs. REPUBLIC. *The French Revolution (1789–1799) and the outbreak of war in Europe created an even greater split between the Republicans and Federalists.* Beginning in 1789, the French had been busily drafting a constitution that would limit the power of their king. Then, in 1793 they executed Louis XVI (1774–1793) and declared France a republic. But soon the French found themselves at war with a coalition of European monarchies led by Great Britain.

Many Americans sympathized with the French cause. Here at last was another republic and an old friend who could be relied on in an hour of need. Jefferson, who witnessed in Paris the exciting events of 1789, cheered openly for France, and so did his Republican followers. Federalists, on the other hand, were leery of revolutions. In the European contest they leaned more toward the British side. Republicans naturally accused them of being monarchists at heart. Federalists replied that Republicans were agents of French radicalism. The accusations were rather emotional, but the division was clear. Voters began choosing sides.

THE MISSION OF EDMOND GENET. No political leader wanted to enter the European war; all agreed on American neutrality. The difficulty was that America was still tied to France by the Revolutionary alliance of 1778. That treaty did not oblige the United States to go to war, but it did require the nation to go to the aid of the French colonies

Pictured here are President George Washington and the American army. Washington sent the army to western Pennsylvania to put down the Whiskey Rebellion. Why do you think it was necessary for Washington to ensure that federal laws were enforced?

176

Sidenote to History

The Whiskey Rebellion

The Whiskey Rebellion started in 1794 when Congress, at the suggestion of Alexander Hamilton, placed internal (excise) taxes on such luxuries as liquor. It seemed a reasonable sort of tax to Congress, but to the people west of the Appalachian Mountains, it was an intolerable burden. Lacking roads, they could market their grain only by making it into whiskey, which could be easily transported. For farmers of western Pennsylvania, a summer harvest could be condensed into a couple of jugs and put onto the back of a horse bound for Baltimore or Philadelphia. There were 5,000 stills in western Pennsylvania, and many farmers counted their wealth in "Monongahela rye." The whiskey excise fell directly onto these people, and they refused to pay—especially when the proceeds ended in the pockets of eastern speculators.

When the government, in the summer of 1794, sent U.S. marshals into western Pennsylvania to enforce the law, armed farmers chased them away. President Washington, remembering the fear inspired by Daniel Shays, issued a proclamation, declaring that the West was in disorder, and marched an army across the mountains. The army, which Hamilton accompanied, scoured the countryside and captured a dozen farmers, who were then taken back to Philadelphia. Two of them were convicted, but the President, not wanting to create martyrs, pardoned them.

So ended the first challenge to federal authority under the Constitution. The Union had survived, but the administration had made enemies. Western Pennsylvania was Republican territory.

in the West Indies if attacked. The tension mounted when both the British and the French began seizing American cargo ships as they approached European waters.

In the spring of 1793, France sent a special envoy to America, Edmond Charles Genet (zheh-NAY). Genet hoped to enlist Americans to serve on French warships and to use American ports as French naval bases. When the American administration insisted on strict neutrality, Genet took his case to the newspapers. He hoped to play on the pro-French feelings of the American people. Instead, his bullying tone rallied support for the President, injured the French cause, and embarrassed the Republicans. Jefferson was relieved when the French government recalled its rather clumsy ambassador.

THE JAY TREATY. No sooner had the uproar over Genet subsided than the United States found itself at odds with Great Britain. Anglo-American relations had never been friendly. Britain had closed British colonies to American ships and had violated the peace treaty by keeping troops on American soil. (See map, page 180). Americans had behaved almost as badly, particularly in refusing to pay their prewar debts to British merchants. Southern planters owed most of these debts; the Virginian debt alone accounted for some two million dollars.

When war broke out in 1793, Britain declared a naval blockade of the French coast. American ships could trade through the blockade, provided they carried nonmilitary goods. France evaded the blockade by opening its West Indies colonies to American vessels. In the spring of 1794, Britain prohibited Americans from trading in the French Empire, and the Royal Navy seized several American ships in the West Indies.

Republicans wanted to retaliate, but Washington decided instead to negotiate. He sent Chief Justice John Jay to London to discuss the seizure of ships and other matters. Jay sailed in the summer of 1794, just as Britain seemed to be winning the war. Britain had smashed France's navy, and its allies were camped on French soil. With Britain in such a strong position, Jay had to take what terms he could get.

The treaty that Jay signed in November 1794 did contain some British concessions. The British agreed to remove their troops from the American Northwest by June 1, 1796, and to open their empire to a limited amount of American trade. Jay agreed to having a joint commission to work out the payment of prewar American debts. But Jay secured no guarantees on the critical question—the rights of American ships on the high seas.

PUBLIC PROTEST. Republicans had not expected much from Jay's mission, but they were outraged at the result. The failure to secure a definition of American trading rights seemed to leave the country at the mercy of Britain's navy. Moreover, the trade concessions Jay had been able to get would benefit only northern merchants. In exchange, southern planters would have to pay prewar debts. Injury was added to indignation.

The nation exploded in protest, and Republicans leaped to take advantage of the outcry. They staged mass rallies against Jay's treaty and filled the newspapers with resolutions. By the time it was all over, there were no political neutrals left. The first opposing political parties—Federalists versus Republicans—were formed.

PINCKNEY'S TREATY. Despite criticism, the Jay Treaty ushered in a period of improved relations between Britain and the United States. But it had quite a different effect on other nations of Europe. Spain and France had signed an agreement that had brought Spain into the war with the British. And both Spain and France were concerned that better relations between the United States and Britain might mean trouble for them. Spain especially feared for its New

World colonies. (The 1783 Treaty of Paris had given Spain control of Florida and the western part of the Louisiana Territory, including a portion of the Mississippi River and the port of New Orleans.) At the end of the Revolution, Spain had closed the Mississippi River to American traffic and had laid claim to lands south of the Tennessee River.

After Jay's treaty Spain reversed itself, fearing that Britain and the United States might open a joint assault on the Spanish Empire. In 1795 the Spanish premier summoned the American minister in Madrid,

After negotiating his treaty with Britain, John Jay sadly lamented that he could have found his way across the country on any night by the light of his burning effigies. Do you think Americans were justified in their anger with Jay?

Daniel Huntington painted this picture of a 1790 party held in Washington's New York residence. He entitled the painting "Lady Washington's Reception." Do you think Huntington was being critical of the ceremonies held during Washington's administration?

Thomas Pinckney, and offered an agreement. Spain gave up its territorial claims in the Southwest and agreed to the 31st parallel as the northern boundary of Florida. (See map, page 180.) For a period of three years, Spain would also allow Americans to use the Mississippi and the port facilities at New Orleans. This was particularly beneficial to western farmers, who needed this access to sell their goods to Europe. In all, Pinckney's treaty was an important victory for American diplomacy.

THE XYZ AFFAIR. *France, too, assumed that the Jay Treaty amounted to an Anglo-American alliance, but reacted in anger rather than fear.* The French government refused to receive the new American minister, Charles Coatsworth Pinckney (brother of Thomas), and ordered the seizure of American ships carrying British

goods. During the American Presidential election of 1796, the French minister to the United States announced that the election of another Federalist would worsen relations between the two countries.

Such heavy-handed meddling offended Americans. As a result the Federalist John Adams was elected as Washington's successor, and the Republican Thomas Jefferson, second in the electoral balloting, became Vice-President. By the time Adams entered office in the spring of 1797, French seizures of American ships in the West Indies had brought the two countries to the brink of war.

Following the practices of Washington, Adams sent a special commission—consisting of Charles Coatsworth Pinckney, John Marshall, and Elbridge Gerry—to discuss a settlement. The three envoys arrived in Paris in the fall of 1797, to be greeted by

179

stony silence. By then France was winning the war with Britain and saw no need to negotiate. The French foreign minister refused official contact with the Americans and sent three secret agents, whom President Adams later dubbed X, Y, and Z. The agents suggested that the wheels of French diplomacy needed to be greased. A bribe of $250,000 to the foreign minister would certainly be useful, but in addition the French government would need a substantial loan. The American agents were not offended at the request for a bribe; such things were normal in European diplomacy. *But the loan would have violated American neutrality and would have destroyed the recent understanding with Great Britain—which was precisely what the French wanted.* Refusing both requests, the commissioners returned home empty-handed.

UNDECLARED WAR WITH FRANCE. The American people were less

forgiving than their agents. The demand for a bribe was to them utter humiliation, beneath the dignity of a proud new nation. "Millions for defense, but not one cent for tribute," trumpeted the press.

Although Congress never formally declared war, for the next two years, American and French ships battled each other on the high seas. Some of the more extreme Federalists demanded an open declaration of war and a formal alliance with Great Britain, but Adams refused. Instead, he sent a new commission to Paris in 1799 to attempt a settlement.

This mission was well-timed—the French leader Napoleon had come to power in November of that year. *Bent on European conquests, Napoleon was anxious to repair relations with the United States.* In 1800 the two nations signed an agreement that ended the old alliance of 1778 and that restored commercial relations.

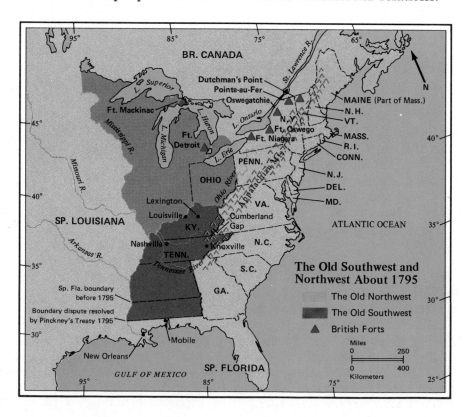

The Old Southwest and Northwest About 1795

☐ The Old Northwest
■ The Old Southwest
▲ British Forts

For the rest of his life, John Adams regarded the peace with France as his finest accomplishment. Perhaps it was, but that peace left his own party bitterly divided and his chances for reelection in 1800 exceedingly dim.

Section Review

1. Mapping: Using the map on page 180, describe how the lands claimed by Spain changed in terms of area, state borders, and latitude after the Pinckney Treaty.
2. Identify or explain: Edmond Genet, John Jay, Thomas Pinckney, Napoleon.
3. In what way did the French Revolution add to the growing political differences in the United States?
4. Outline the provisions of the Jay Treaty. Why was it so unpopular in the United States?

4. "The Revolution of 1800"

THE ALIEN AND SEDITION LAWS.
Till the end of his days, Thomas Jefferson referred to his election as "the Revolution of 1800." He felt it to be every bit as important as the Revolution of 1776. In his struggle with John Adams, Jefferson believed that the future of the republic was at stake.

The cause of Jefferson's alarm was some Federalist measures enacted during Adams's administration. Believing that the Republicans were agents of French radicalism, the Federalists took advantage of the French war-scare to move against their critics. During the summer of 1798, Congress passed a group of laws regulating *aliens*. Directed mainly at French immigrants (refugees from France and the West Indies), *the Alien Enemies Act gave the President power to deport any aliens he considered suspect.* Although John Adams never deported anyone, Republicans objected to the arbitrary power placed in the hands of the President.

Aliens are foreign immigrants who have not yet become American citizens.

Even more powerful was the Naturalization Act, which extended from 5 to 14 the number of years a foreigner needed to reside in the United States before becoming a citizen. Since most of the immigrants sympathized with the Republicans, this act effectively kept a large group of people from voting against the Federalists.

The **Sedition** Act, which followed in July 1798, struck directly at the Republicans. **This law made it a crime to criticize either the President or Congress.** In effect for two years (it expired in 1800), the law was intended to silence the Republican press during the Presidential election. Over the next two years, a dozen newspaper publishers—all Republicans—were convicted, fined, and imprisoned under the law. When he became President, Jefferson—who believed that the strength of a government depended on its popularity and not its use of force—released those still in jail.

Sedition is an action designed to generate opposition to or rebellion against a government.

VIRGINIA AND KENTUCKY RESOLUTIONS. The Republicans considered the Sedition Act a violation of the First Amendment's guarantee of freedom of speech and of the press. But what to do about it? Many Jeffersonians believed the Supreme Court had the power of judicial review—the power to determine the constitutionality of acts of Congress. This principle had been included in the Judiciary Act of 1789, but had never been used. The Court, however, consisted of Federalists, appointees of Washington and Adams.

Neither Jefferson nor Madison wanted to appeal to the Supreme Court. But during the autumn of 1798, Jefferson penned a series of resolutions, which were taken before the Kentucky legislature. Madison drafted similar resolutions for the Virginia assembly. **Together these resolutions stated the "compact," or "states' rights," theory of the Constitution.** The argument ran thus: The Constitution is a compact, or agreement, among the states that created the federal government and that gave that govern-

ment certain powers. But the states have final **sovereignty.** The federal government is merely their agent. Thus, when the federal government exceeds its powers by passing such laws as the Alien and Sedition acts, which the states think are unconstitutional, the states may protect their citizens by not enforcing these laws within the boundaries of their states.

Sovereignty means the legitimate authority to govern. The question of which was sovereign—the state or federal government—remained a major source of debate until the Civil War.

Opponents to the doctrine of states' rights feared that it threatened the Union. If the states were truly sovereign, they ought to be able to secede, or leave the Union, at any time. But Jefferson and Madison did not intend to carry the idea that far. They wanted only to expose the Federalists and to excite public debate. In that they succeeded. Although no other state besides Virginia and Kentucky approved the resolutions, nearly every assembly debated them. For the Republicans, the resolutions were a good starting point for the Presidential campaign of 1800.

THE FALL OF THE FEDERALISTS. Seldom has an American political party fallen from public favor so rapidly as the Federalist party. In 1798, in the wake of the XYZ affair, the Federalists were at the height of their popularity. But this popularity did not last for long. Two years later they were turned out of office forever.

The Alien and Sedition acts, which revealed the Federalists as heavy-handed rulers, were only partly responsible. **The larger issue in the Federalist downfall, it seems likely, was taxation.** As the Federalists discovered, Americans would tolerate much, but only until it began costing them money. Anticipating war before the XYZ blowup, Congress had greatly expanded the army,

This watercolor of the unfinished Capitol (now the Senate wing) was done by William Birch in 1800. In the background is the President's house.

installing George Washington as the commanding general. Congress had also created the Department of the Navy. This arms build-up proved expensive and forced Congress to raise taxes. Soon federal tax collectors met open resistance, and Federalist popularity fell.

INTERNAL DIVISIONS. Federalists were also troubled by internal divisions. When President Adams decided to send a new peace commission to France in 1799, he met opposition from his Secretary of State, Timothy Pickering. A strong Federalist from Massachusetts, Pickering wanted a declaration of war and flatly refused to dispatch the commission. So Adams fired him and sent the commissioners himself. Yet Pickering's dismissal angered Alexander Hamilton, who, though no longer a member of the government, kept in close contact with the President's cabinet. *As a result, Hamilton wrote a pamphlet, blasting Adams and exposing to public view the split in the Federalist party.* Federalist wrangling delighted the Republicans. "If one can believe what Mr. Hamilton has to say about Mr. Adams, and what Mr. Adams has to say about Mr. Hamilton," wrote one Republican editor who was commenting on the situation, "can anyone doubt that Thomas Jefferson ought to be President?"

THE ELECTION OF 1800. In 1796 each party had met in caucus (a secret, evening meeting of party members attending Congress) and chosen candidates for President and Vice-President. The same system was

183

used in 1800. The Federalists renominated John Adams, and with him ran the hero of the XYZ affair, Charles C. Pinckney. The Republicans went along with the same ticket they had run in 1796—Jefferson and Aaron Burr. Burr was a senator from New York with particularly strong support in New York City. The ticket represented a continuation of the traditional state alliance of New York and Virginia.

Despite Federalist error in policy and internal bickering, the election was quite close. *The party split was basically regional—North vs. South. Adams carried New England and New Jersey; Jefferson took the South and the West.* Pennsylvania split its electoral vote evenly. Thus, the election depended on New York.

In New York, as in several other states, the assembly chose Presidential electors. When the Republicans captured the assembly in the spring elections of 1800 (due largely to the shrewd political management of Burr), their victory was virtually assured. When the final tally came, the Republicans had 73 electoral votes to the Federalists' 65.

A TIE IN THE ELECTORAL COLLEGE. Then came trouble. When the electoral college met, each Republican cast one ballot for Jefferson and one for Burr. The result was a tie!

When one person failed to get a majority of the electoral votes, the President, under the Constitution, was to be chosen by the House of Representatives. After some maneuvering, in which the Federalists tried to promote Burr over Jefferson, the House declared Jefferson President and Burr Vice-President. To prevent such confusion from happening again, the 12th Amendment, passed in 1804, requires separate balloting for President and Vice-President.

"THE REVOLUTION OF 1800." Inauguration Day—March 4, 1801—dawned chilly and rainy on the half-built capital on the banks of the Potomac. John Adams, unable to bear his foe's triumph, slipped out of town at four o'clock in the morning. Jefferson, dressed in a plain dark suit, without badge or sword, walked from his boardinghouse to the Capitol, where he was given the oath of office.

It was a great moment for the young republic. One set of rulers had been turned out of office and another set installed. And, except for a salute by the Maryland militia, not a shot had been fired nor a soldier been seen. "I have this morning witnessed one of the most interesting scenes," wrote Margaret Bayard Smith, wife of a Republican newspaper editor. "The changes of administration, which in every government and in every age have most generally been epochs of confusion, villainy and bloodshed, in this our happy country take place without any disorder." *Such orderly transfer of power was a measure of the political maturity of the young republic.*

A CHANGE IN ATMOSPHERE. Jefferson's term of office was not quite the "revolution" that he later remembered. There had been no widespread dismissal of Federalist officeholders and no total removal of Federalist programs. Jefferson had even kept and used the Bank of the United States. Although Congress repealed the Naturalization Act in 1802, the Alien and Sedition laws had already expired. Jefferson had seen no need to do battle with ghosts.

Sidenote to History
Jefferson and Adams

Jefferson and Adams, who became good friends in old age, died on the same day, July 4, 1826—the 50th anniversary of the Declaration of Independence. John Adams's last words were: "Jefferson still lives."

Yet, there was a change in atmosphere with the new administration. John Adams had considered Federalists the party of the "rich and well-born," and he had stocked the government offices with people of family and fortune. Jefferson, on the other hand, announced that the government, including the office of President, ought to be open to all people of honesty, intelligence, and education. He sought constantly the advice of his cabinet, invited members of Congress (Federalists as well as Republicans) to dinner three times a week, and opened his door to all visitors.

"A WISE AND FRUGAL GOVERN-MENT." Jefferson was particularly concerned that government not be a burden. Together with his Secretary of the Treasury, Albert Gallatin, Jefferson eliminated all internal excise taxes. The government under Jefferson would live on the income from customs duties and the sale of western lands. To save money, the army was reduced to 3,000 soldiers (enough to take care of western forts) and most of the navy's vessels were sold. *Jefferson's aim, he had stated in his inaugural address, was "a wise and frugal government," which would leave citizens alone "to regulate their own pursuits of industry and profit."* In the four government departments—State, Treasury, War, and Navy—there were 97 clerks when Jefferson took office. When he departed eight years later, after nearly doubling the size and wealth of the nation, there were 94.

Open, responsive, concerned government—that was the essence of the "Revolution of 1800." It was also, as Jefferson had predicted, popular government. Voters turned out in increasing numbers. Republican strength spread even into New England. In the election of 1804, Jefferson swamped the Federalist opposition, and his party took control of Congress.

However, America was not yet a democracy. Most states still had property require-

Thomas Jefferson was the most versatile of all the American Presidents. He was an inventor and a designer.

ments for voting and officeholding. Women, Blacks, and American Indians were still denied the right to vote. Yet, inspired by Jefferson's concern of the common citizen, several states began modifying their property requirements. Further change would take another generation. But Thomas Jefferson, at least, had pointed the way.

Section Review

1. Mapping: From the description of the election of 1800, describe how political differences in the United States were also regional differences. Which regions identified with which parties? Use the map on page 180.
2. Identify or explain: Timothy Pickering, Jefferson, Aaron Burr.
3. Describe two provisions of the Alien and Sedition acts.
4. How did the election of 1800 indicate a problem in the electoral college as a mechanism for electing the President?

Chapter 7 Review

Bird's-Eye View

George Washington's inauguration had been a great occasion. But when the celebration ended, the new nation had to face the serious business of building a government. Many details had to be added to the structure of the Constitution. The financial problems of the republic had to be dealt with. And the remaining differences of opinion about the function of government had to be reconciled.

Executive departments and a federal court system were created and the jurisdiction of various courts defined. The Bill of Rights, an especially important item for the Anti-Federalists, was passed by Congress and the states. These first 10 amendments to the Constitution guaranteed certain individual liberties against the possible abuses of a powerful government.

The first Secretary of the Treasury, Alexander Hamilton, proposed the idea of a national bank and suggested that the federal government assume the debts incurred by the states during the Revolution. Although Madison and many others objected to this part of Hamilton's plan, a compromise involving the location of the nation's capital helped resolve the problem.

Foreign affairs were even more difficult to settle. Troubles in Europe threatened America's neutrality, and Europeans began seizing America's merchant vessels on the high seas. Still, despite the XYZ affair and the many protests from indignant Americans, President Adams managed to avoid war. Nevertheless, his foreign policy, the unpopular taxes enacted during his administration, and the controversy over the Alien and Sedition acts combined to hasten the downfall of the Federalist party. The election of 1800 ended in a victory for the Republicans, with Thomas Jefferson, the new President, announcing that the government should be open to all people of honesty, intelligence, and education.

Vocabulary

Define or identify each of the following:

jurisdiction	tariff	caucus
Henry Knox	Edmond Genet	sovereignty
cabinet	alien	sedition

Review Questions

1. Name the four executive departments first authorized by Congress and the individuals whom President Washington chose to head them.
2. What were the provisions of the Judiciary Act of 1789?

186

3. Alexander Hamilton made two proposals to establish a solid financial base for the new government. One involved the nation's credit, the other involved the national debt. Describe each of these proposals.
4. Why did the French Revolution cause internal conflict in the United States?
5. What were the Alien and Sedition acts? Why did the Republicans oppose these acts?
6. Why did the Federalists lose the election of 1800?
7. What changes did Jefferson bring to the Presidency in 1800?

Reviewing Social Studies Skills

1. Using the map on page 180, complete the following:
   a. List the natural geographic boundaries of the Old Northwest Territory.
   b. List the boundaries of the Old Southwest Territory.
   c. Locate and name the sites of the British forts.
2. Assume you are a Republican newspaper editor, opposed to the Alien and Sedition acts. Write an editorial expressing your displeasure with these measures.
3. Review the Bill of Rights on pages 156–158. What rights are guaranteed by these 10 amendments?
4. Construct a time line, listing the main events of the administrations of Washington and Adams.

Reading for Meaning

1. Using the material in Section 1, "Organizing the Federal Government," make a chronological list of the accomplishments of the new government.
2. Choose one of the following: Adams, Hamilton, Jefferson, or Madison. Go through the chapter and read all references to the person you have selected. What do you think is the author's opinion of that person? Write a paragraph, showing how the author conveys an opinion by a choice of words, tone, mood, etc.
3. List the financial issues that the government handled between 1789 and 1804. How did the issue of finance help to develop the two-party system?

Bibliography

James T. Flexner's *Washington, The Indispensable Man* (Little, Brown and Co.) is a good readable biography of the first President.

Adrienne Koch's *Jefferson and Madison, The Great Collaboration* (Peter Smith, Publisher, Inc.) tells the story of that great political friendship.

Chapter 8

1801-1823

Awakening of American Nationalism

During the summer of 1798, at the height of the uproar over the XYZ affair, Stephen Decatur sailed from Philadelphia in a ship that had been recently purchased and armed by the government. In Delaware Bay he encountered a French vessel that had been harassing American ships. Without warning, Decatur sailed up and opened fire. The French ship promptly surrendered. "Why have you fired upon the French flag?" the French captain cried when Decatur came on board. "I know of no war between our countries."

"The French have been making war on us for a long time," said Decatur. "Now we are defending ourselves."

The French captain watched the American flag run up the mast of his ship and said gloomily, "I wish it had been sunk."

Replied Decatur: "It would have been if you had stood on board and fought."

The exchange revealed a new American spirit, a new sense of national pride. It is called nationalism. It means loyalty and patriotism toward the whole nation, rather than just a state or locality.

Chapter Objectives

After you have finished reading this chapter, you should be able to:
1. Describe how the United States obtained Louisiana in 1804, and explain how it affected the Burr Conspiracy.
2. List in chronological order the causes of the War of 1812.
3. Recognize the major battles of the War of 1812.
4. Analyze the growth of nationalism and how the government contributed to it.
5. Define the Monroe Doctrine.

Jefferson disliked war, but he was concerned about the nation's honor and dignity. And his Presidency reflected the rising spirit of nationalism. Under Jefferson and his successors, James Madison and James Monroe, the nation made its weight felt in the world for the first time. When the Jeffersonians came into office, they were primarily concerned with domestic affairs, but it was in the field of diplomacy that they experienced their greatest triumphs.

1. National Honor and National Expansion

WAR WITH NORTH AFRICAN STATES. In May 1801, two months after Jefferson took office, the *pasha* in Tripoli cut down the flagpole at the American consulate. It was the *pasha's* way of declaring war.

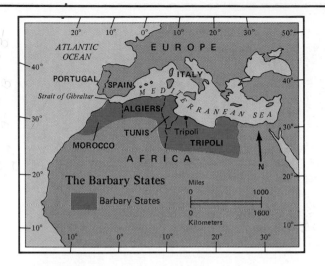

The Barbary States
Miles
0   1000
0   1600
Kilometers

The **Muslim states** of North Africa (see map above) often preyed on commercial vessels sailing the Mediterranean. **Many major seafaring nations, including the United States, bribed Muslims to leave their ships alone.** And an investigation revealed that the *pasha* of Tripoli did not really want war—just more money. At about the same time, the **dey** of Algiers had commandeered an American warship and had made it sail to Greece with one of his envoys.

The **Muslim states** of North Africa included Morocco, Algiers, Tunis, and Tripoli. A ruler of one of these states was called a **pasha** or **dey**. These rulers had both religious and civil authority.

Although no popular explosion resulted, as it had in 1798, Jefferson was determined to uphold American rights. He sent a squadron to patrol the Mediterranean, led by a 38-gun frigate, the *Philadelphia*. The squadron met disaster, however, when the *Philadelphia* ran aground and was captured. The North Africans then towed their new prize into the harbor of Tripoli, where fort and warship could be used to protect each other.

In 1803 Jefferson sent a stronger squadron to the Mediterranean, commanded by Edward Preble. Preble's first task was to deprive the North Africans of their prize. As commander, he assigned the job to Stephen Decatur. Decatur then sailed into the harbor in a captured North African gunboat under the cover of night. He boarded the *Philadelphia*, set it on fire, and sailed out—amid a storm of shots.

For the next two years, Preble blockaded the harbor and periodically bombarded the fort. At last, in 1805, the *pasha* agreed to a settlement. He released the crew of the *Philadelphia* for a ransom of $60,000. Nevertheless, trouble with the other Barbary States continued for the next 10 years. Finally, Stephen Decatur sailed to Tunis and Algiers, where he negotiated an end to the piracy and tributes—with the help of his loaded cannons.

It was America's second undeclared war in less than a decade. It provoked none of the popular outburst that the French crisis did. Yet, when it was over, in 1815, Americans took considerable satisfaction in knowing that they, alone, of all the seafaring powers, did not have to bribe their way through the Mediterranean Sea. Also, their young navy had gained a little more experience. It would need this. Its next foe would be imperial Britain.

A SECRET STRATEGY. While France and England were at war in Europe, Spain had switched sides and was now back with its old ally, France. *Fearing that Britain might seize Louisiana—its territory west of the Mississippi River—Spain secretly gave Louisiana to France for protection.* But it expected the territory back at the end of the war.

Knowing the United States would disapprove, the two countries kept the bargain a secret. For the moment Spain continued to govern the territory. But Jefferson learned of the deal and exploded in anger. He did not want a strong military power like France on his nation's western border. Yet, while Spanish officials remained in New Orleans, there was little he could do.

This mural is in the United States Capitol. It shows Monroe and Livingston negotiating with the French for Louisana.

In 1802 a truce ended the European war temporarily, and Napoleon took advantage of the peace by sending an army to America. Before going to America, however, the army was to go to Santo Domingo, in the West Indies, where Black slaves had revolted against the French plantation owners. (See map, page 209.) Led by the Black revolutionary Toussaint L'Ouverture (loo-vair-TYUR), the Blacks had declared their independence. Napoleon wanted his army to recapture the island. He then wanted them to go on and occupy Louisiana.

Anticipating the French arrival, Spanish authorities closed the port of New Orleans to American traffic in October 1802. The American reaction was violent. Cut off from its markets and threatened with economic strangulation, the West exploded in anger. The Kentucky militia threatened to seize the port.

THE LOUISIANA PURCHASE. To ease the situation, Jefferson sent a special envoy to Paris. His choice was James Monroe, a friend from Virginia. *Jefferson told*

Monroe either to buy New Orleans or to persuade Napoleon to open the port. If Napoleon refused to negotiate, Monroe was to sail to London and seek a military alliance with the British.

By the time Monroe arrived, the situation in Paris had changed dramatically. Napoleon's army had not been victorious in Santo Domingo, and many of his troops had been wiped out by yellow fever. He could no longer defend Louisiana. Expecting a renewal of the war with Britain, he was also in need of money. Since Louisiana was useless, why not sell it?

Napoleon summoned Robert R. Livingston, America's regular minister in Paris, and offered to sell not only New Orleans but also the entire inland empire that was drained by the Mississippi and Missouri rivers. At first Livingston balked at Napoleon's price—$15 million, which included war debts already owed to France—but then he agreed. The two had been coming to terms when Monroe arrived. At that point Monroe cooperated, and the treaty of purchase was signed in May 1803.

190

CONCERN OVER THE PURCHASE.

Monroe and Livingston had not followed their instructions. Told to buy a city, they had purchased an empire (see map, page 192) and had paid 50 percent more than authorized. But Jefferson was delighted. "An empire for liberty," he called it, room and freedom for generations to come.

Jefferson worried about whether he had the power to make the purchase. The Constitution did not specifically authorize a President to buy or conquer foreign territory. But the cabinet persuaded him to submit the treaty to the Senate.

In Congress, New England Federalists were bitterly opposed to the purchase. They saw that the new territory would further weaken their influence in the Union. They argued that the Constitution did not give the federal government the power to buy territory and that new territory could be added only with the consent of the original 13 states. Jefferson's use of executive power and Federalist opposition to it were a curious reversal of roles. It shows how ideas can change when people's situations and interests change. *The Senate, however, approved the treaty by a vote of 24 to 7. And the Congress quickly appropriated the money required to fulfill the treaty's terms.*

CONTROVERSY OVER WEST FLORIDA.

The Louisiana Purchase created new problems for Jefferson, both at home and abroad. It instantly provoked a crisis with Spain, which argued that Louisiana was its colony and that Napoleon had no right to sell it. The boundaries of Louisiana also posed another problem. How far west did it extend into Spanish Texas? How far east did it extend toward Spanish Florida? (See map, page 192.)

The eastern boundary was the more important one, both strategically and commercially. The Gulf Coast east of the Mississippi was an area known as West Florida. (See map, page 192.) Every major river system of what is now Alabama and Mississippi flowed into the Gulf through West Florida. The port of Mobile, in present-day Alabama, was nearly as important to the region as New Orleans.

Monroe and Livingston had been instructed to buy West Florida along with New Orleans. When the Louisiana sale was completed, they asked the French Foreign Minister, Talleyrand, whether West Florida was included in Louisiana. Talleyrand replied simply, "Gentlemen, you have made a good bargain for yourselves. I trust you will make the most of it."

As a result, Jefferson claimed that the United States owned West Florida. However, he did not attempt to occupy the area, for there were Spanish garrisons at Mobile and Baton Rouge. Later, he offered to buy the province from Spain. He even contemplated bribing Napoleon into getting it for him. Napoleon, who was always ready to deal in Spanish real estate, was interested, but he could not take time off from the war.

Finally, in 1810, the Americans who had moved into the territory seized the Spanish arsenal at Baton Rouge. They then proclaimed their independence and asked for admission to the Union. James Madison, who had succeeded Jefferson to the Presidency, ordered the army to occupy West Florida, on the grounds that the United States had owned it all along.

THE LEWIS AND CLARK EXPEDITION.

There was more mystery to Louisiana than its boundaries. What, after all, had the United States purchased? Mountains? Deserts? Trackless forests? What about the American Indians who lived there and regarded the land as theirs?

Jefferson was determined to explore Louisiana. *In early 1803, months before the purchase had been finalized, he had asked his friend and neighbor Meriwether Lewis to organize an expedition to explore the*

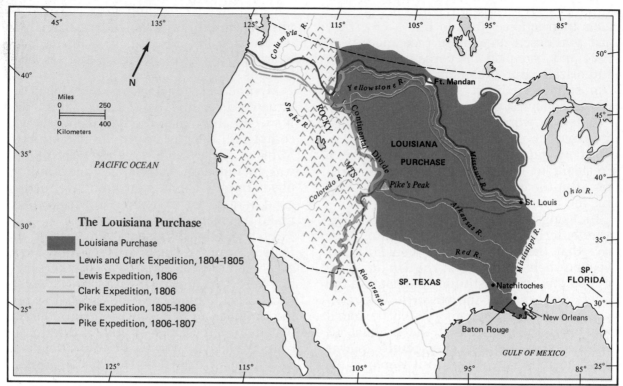

The Louisiana Purchase

- Louisiana Purchase
- —— Lewis and Clark Expedition, 1804–1805
- – – Lewis Expedition, 1806
- —— Clark Expedition, 1806
- —— Pike Expedition, 1805–1806
- – – Pike Expedition, 1806–1807

territory. Lewis, a captain in the army, had enlisted the help of another Virginian, William Clark. The two had recruited a force of 40 volunteers. The expedition left St. Louis in May 1804.

Throughout the long summer the people of this expedition rowed, waded, and poled their boats up the shallow Missouri River. Some rode horseback onto the plains and kept the expedition supplied with buffalo and deer meat. Their weapons and military discipline awed even the Sioux, who let them pass peacefully.

They spent the winter of 1804–1805 at the village of the friendly and generous Mandan Indians, near present-day Bismarck, North Dakota. There they met Sacajawea (sac-uh-juh-WEE-uh), or Bird Woman, a Shoshone who had been kidnapped by the Crow when she was about 12. When Lewis and Clark encountered her among the Mandan, she was married to a

French fur trader named Toussaint Charbonneau (sar-buh-NOE). During the visit the Mandan agreed to let Sacajawea and Charbonneau accompany the expedition as guides and interpreters. Sacajawea was eager to go because the journey west would return her to her own people.

The following spring the expedition set out again. First came the forks of the Missouri, then the forbidding ***Continental Divide.*** Sacajawea's relatives guided them through the mountains. At the village of the Nez Percé Indians, where the Snake River joins the Columbia, they borrowed canoes for the swift journey down the foaming Columbia River.

Continental Divide is the name used to describe the point in the Rocky Mountains that separates the rivers flowing east from those flowing west.

They spent their second winter at the mouth of the Columbia, and in the spring of 1806, they started for home. At the Continental Divide they split into two exploring parties in order to obtain further information. Lewis returned by the route they had followed coming out. Clark turned south toward the Yellowstone River, following that to the Missouri. Reunited at the Mandan village, Lewis and Clark swept down the Missouri, reaching St. Louis in September 1806. (See map, page 192.)

It was a marvelous feat. *They had brought back priceless information about the western landscape, together with samples of rocks, plants, and animal bones.* And in that strenuous trek across 4,800 kilometers (3,000 miles) of territory, only one person had died and only one had deserted.

Sacajawea's contribution to the expedition was publicly honored by the United States government. She was awarded the Jefferson Peace Medal. Today monuments to her stand in Oregon, Wyoming, and North Dakota.

PIKE'S TREK INTO THE WEST. While Lewis and Clark were crossing the Continental Divide, Lieutenant Zebulon Pike of the United States Army was exploring another part of the Louisiana Territory. *In 1805 Pike had been commanded to find the source of the Mississippi River.* Traveling north from St. Louis with a small party, Pike had searched unsuccessfully for the source of the great river. However, the records of his exploration provided much new and valuable information about the northern portion of the Louisiana Purchase.

A year later, in 1806, Pike was sent on a second expedition, this time to gather information about the southwestern part of the Louisiana Territory. *During this journey he and his party came upon a majestic mountain, which they named Pikes Peak, in what is now the state of Colorado.* (See map, page 192.) Pike then turned south toward the Rio Grande, crossing territory belonging to Spain. There he was intercepted, arrested as a spy, and brought to the Spanish governor of the territory. Soon, though, he was released and made his way back, carrying with him information about the Southwest.

THE CONSPIRACY OF AARON BURR. The Louisiana Purchase led to domestic squabbles. French and Spanish

This painting of the Lewis and Clark expedition shows York, a slave who was freed when the expedition was over, and Sacajawea, the Shoshone guide.

residents of New Orleans were not happy with the purchase. They were afraid the United States might not honor their laws, customs, and Roman Catholic faith. Such a situation made them ripe for intrigue. And in Washington, D.C., there was someone waiting for that type of opportunity—Aaron Burr.

Jefferson would have nothing to do with Burr after his behavior in the election of 1800. In fact, in the election of 1804, he dropped Burr as a running mate. Burr, however, ran for governor of New York that year and in his campaign made a bid for Federalist support. But his old enemy Hamilton prevented it. Angry and frustrated, Burr challenged Hamilton to a duel. When the smoke had cleared, Hamilton lay dying, and Burr stood a ruined man, wanted for murder— since dueling was illegal in the North.

BURR LOOKS TO THE WEST. *Burr's only hope lay in the West, a new land where the past was easily forgotten and the future belonged to the bold.* He found a willing conspirator in an old friend, General

Sidenote to History

The Hamilton-Burr Duel

During the United States Bicentennial celebrations, a group of historians became interested in the Hamilton-Burr duel. These historians wanted to make reproductions of the flintlock pistols used by Burr and Hamilton. (The duel had taken place on July 11, 1804, in Weehawken, New Jersey, just across the Hudson River from New York City.)

When gunsmiths took the original pair of pistols apart, they discovered a concealed hair trigger in the mechanism of each pistol. This type of trigger enables its shooter to fire a shot with only a slight squeeze. Such a trigger would have allowed the person using the pistol to have shot more quickly than an opponent if the opponent were unaware of the hidden mechanism.

Hamilton had borrowed these special weapons from his brother-in-law to use in the duel with Burr. It was the custom, when dueling, for one person's weapons to be used by both parties involved in the duel. Hamilton knew the guns were hair-triggered, but Burr probably did not.

Flintlock pistols contained only one bullet, and opponents in a duel had to be very deliberate in their actions. When Hamilton faced Burr on the morning of the duel, he may have held his pistol too tightly and have fired before aiming correctly. His bullet struck a tree some distance behind Burr. His only shot had been lost.

According to eyewitnesses, Burr took careful aim and fired at Hamilton. The bullet hit Hamilton in the stomach and lodged in his spine. Hamilton was carried away across the river to a friend's house, where he died 36 hours later.

The dying Hamilton gasped that he had never meant to kill Burr in the duel. Had he deliberately misfired? Perhaps he had intended merely to shoot his pistol into the air. But why had he borrowed his brother-in-law's hair-triggered weapons when he himself owned a fine pair of English dueling pistols?

Burr was already regarded by many as a scoundrel, so Hamilton's dying words were readily accepted at the time. People thought Burr had killed Hamilton even though Hamilton had avoided killing him. Whether or not this theory was true, Hamilton has been pictured until recently as the innocent victim of Burr's villainy. This view of the two men's personalities would have persisted if the discovery of the hair triggers had not cast new light on the events of the duel.

James Wilkinson, the ranking military leader in the West and the commander of the district of Louisiana. Unknown to his own government, Wilkinson had been in the pay of Spain for 20 years. He had been providing Spanish authorities with information and periodically advocating independence for the westerners he governed.

Exactly what the two plotted remains a mystery. Separation of the Southwest and establishment of a new nation is one possibility. An attack on Spanish Texas is yet another. The scheme was probably open-ended. They would have gone as far as they could have.

Burr made two visits to the West, one in the summer of 1805, the second in 1806. On the first visit he searched for support, particularly among the discontented citizens of New Orleans. On the second, he recruited an armed force and used an island in the Ohio River as his base. He had told the recruits that they were going to settle some lands in Texas that had been given to him by a merchant.

WILKINSON WRITES TO JEFFERSON. Then Wilkinson betrayed Burr. Deciding, apparently, that there was more profit in playing the role of the savior of the Union than in going along with Burr, Wilkinson wrote to President Jefferson about the plot. Of course, he carefully omitted mention of his own connection. Afterward he raced to New Orleans, where he arrested Burr's supporters.

Jefferson, on learning of the plot, issued a proclamation, ordering the arrest of the conspirators. Burr, coming down the Mississippi with his band of recruits, saw the proclamation in a newspaper and fled to Spanish Florida. The army intercepted him, put him on a gunboat, and shipped him to Richmond, Virginia, to stand trial for treason.

It was a curious trial. Burr charmed all who met him. Released on bail, he dined and danced with Richmond Federalists. Also, the *grand jury* came within two votes of *indicting* the government's star witness, General Wilkinson. Then, during the trial Justice John Marshall pointed out that the Constitution requires two witnesses to an open act of treason. Since Burr had only talked and recruited, the government's witnesses could not testify to any particular act. The government had to drop the case. But Burr was still wanted for murder in New Jersey, so he fled to Europe.

Indicting means accusing, or bringing to trial. A *grand jury* investigates to see if there is sufficient evidence to warrant an indictment.

This sketch of Aaron Burr was done during his trial for treason. Why was Burr acquitted?

Jefferson was frustrated, but the nation benefited from Marshall's definition of treason. **Treason is the only crime defined by the Constitution.** The framers of the Constitution deliberately required an open act, so as not to hamper criticism of the government.

Section Review

1. Mapping: Using the map on page 192, trace the route of the Lewis and Clark expedition.
2. Identify or explain: Stephen Decatur, the *pasha* of Tripoli, Sacajawea, Toussaint L'Ouverture, James Monroe, Meriwether Lewis and William Clark, Zebulon Pike.
3. Describe the terms of the Louisiana Purchase. Why was Napoleon willing to sell the Louisiana Territory?

2. The Second War for Independence

WAR RESUMES IN EUROPE. The war in Europe was resumed in 1803. *Having abandoned his dreams of a New World empire, Napoleon had set out to conquer Europe.* By 1807 he had dominated most of Western Europe and had forced Scandinavia and Russia into neutrality. Britain alone remained to oppose him.

ECONOMIC WARFARE. The result was a deadlock. Neither giant could reach the other. Napoleon dominated the Continent (mainland Europe); Britain controlled the seas. Each then resorted to economic warfare, trying to starve the other into submission. The British ministry declared a naval blockade of the western coast of Europe. Napoleon retaliated with decrees that barred British vessels from the Continent. He even ordered the seizure of neutral vessels that had stopped in Britain before going to continental ports. *The neutral United States was caught in the middle of this gigantic economic game.*

The profits from neutral trade were enormous. American beef and grain fed the armies of Europe. American cotton clothed them. When the British blockade had cut off France and Spain from their New World empires, American ships had moved in, carrying sugar from Cuba, coffee from Brazil, and silver from Mexico. Both sides were seizing American vessels and confiscating their cargoes. But the profits from the trade were so great that American merchants could afford the losses. Money was piling up in American banks. The economy was booming.

PAPER BLOCKADES. By 1812 Napoleon had seized nearly as many American ships as the British had. Nevertheless, American anger was directed mainly at the British. There were two reasons for this. The first was that British seizures had taken place on the high seas in violation, so Americans thought, of international law. Having no navy, Napoleon had seized American ships only when they had entered a French port, where they were under French law.

Under international law a blockade could interfere only with military cargoes. Britain was permitting American cotton and foodstuffs to pass into France. *But Britain's navy was seizing American vessels carrying cargoes belonging to French or Spanish merchants, even if the cargoes were as nonmilitary as tobacco or sugar.*

Defending the policy, Britain pointed out that the cargoes belonged to people with whom it was at war. France and Spain were evading the blockade by using American ships. The United States replied that the neutral American flag made the cargo neutral, regardless of who owned it. The American slogan was "Free ships make neutral goods."

Under international law a blockade also had to be genuine. Warships had to patrol every blockaded port. Sizable though it was, Britain's navy did not have nearly enough ships to patrol every port in western Europe. It was easier simply to station a frigate outside New York and search every ship that came out of the harbor. That added humiliation to injury. Secretary of State Madison denounced this practice as a "paper blockade" and a violation of American rights.

IMPRESSMENT. The other American grievance against the British involved their practice of *impressment. Britain had been kidnapping American sailors long before the Revolution.* But during the Napoleonic wars the numbers sharply increased.

Impressment occurred when the British stopped American ships to search for deserters from the British Navy. They often impressed, or kidnapped, American sailors and forced them to serve on British ships.

Living conditions in the British Navy were so bad that every time a British ship stopped at a port, a sizable portion of the crew deserted. Many of these sailors signed up for service on American merchant ships, where conditions and pay were better. The British regarded them as deserters. Americans considered them immigrants.

To recover their deserters, British ship captains stopped American vessels and "pressed" into British service any sailors who could not prove themselves to be Americans. As a result, many American citizens found themselves in Britain's navy, alongside British deserters. *By 1806, newspapers estimated that some 6,000 sailors had been impressed by the British.*

THE *CHESAPEAKE* AFFAIR. No one incident of impressment was enough to start a war. But one incident did trigger the chain of events that led to war.

In response to British seizures, Jefferson ordered the refitting of some of the ships that had been put away. Such ships had been put away when Jefferson took office. Among these was the *Chesapeake,* a 38-gun frigate. It was refitted at Norfolk, Virginia, in the spring of 1807.

Also lying in the harbor was a British frigate, the *Leopard,* which had put in for food and water. As usual, part of the British crew deserted. Four of the deserters joined the crew of the *Chesapeake.*

When the *Chesapeake* sailed from Norfolk in June 1807, the *Leopard* followed it out of the harbor. At sea the *Leopard* sent a broadside of cannon fire into the American vessel. The *Chesapeake* got off one shot and gave up. British officers boarded the American ship, caught the deserters, and hanged them. Then the *Leopard* sailed off into the blue, leaving the *Chesapeake* to limp back into Norfolk.

The American public was outraged by the *Chesapeake* incident. Cries for war echoed from New England to New Orleans. But the nation was unprepared for war.

THE EMBARGO. *Instead, Jefferson recommended another strategy—an embargo, or total cutoff, of American trade.* The stoppage would hurt both the British and the French, and it would give the United States time to prepare for war.

Congress passed the Embargo Act in December 1807, over howls of protest from New England Federalists. Northern merchants and their Federalist allies had little concern for impressed sailors. Even though they were losing ships, the profits of neutral trade more than made up for the losses.

Instead of getting the nation ready for war, Congress dawdled. The purpose of the embargo gradually changed. Jefferson came to regard it not as a first step toward war, but as an experiment in peace. He looked on it as an effort to pressure Britain into a settlement without having to fight. And it nearly succeeded. Within a year there were food shortages in parts of Britain, and textile mills were running out of raw cotton. In time Britain might have yielded.

Unfortunately, the United States did not have time. It suffered from the embargo more than the British. With the government's prohibition on even coastal trade, and with few roads and great distances to cover, commerce came to a standstill. Food rotted on wharves. Ships rotted at their moorings.

Amid general public outcry, Congress repealed the embargo. It came to an end on March 3, 1809, Jefferson's last day in office. The two departed together. It was hard to tell which was more unpopular.

In the election of 1808, Madison, a Republican, was chosen to succeed Jefferson. But the Federalists made sizable gains in Congress.

ANOTHER APPROACH TO THE PROBLEM.
After repealing the embargo, Congress experimented with several trade regulations. These regulations were designed to force either France or Britain to recognize American rights. In one measure, called Macon's Bill Number 2, Congress even tried to play off one nation against the other by reopening trade with both France and Britain. Under this bill when either nation formally agreed to respect America's neutral rights, Congress would cut off trade with the other.

Napoleon instantly accepted the terms and revoked measures that had offended the United States. Madison responded by cutting off trade with Britain. But the British refused to bend. They simply pointed out to Madison that he had been fooled by Napoleon. Despite promises, the French were still grabbing American ships.

THE WAR HAWKS.
The congressional elections of 1810 showed that America's patience was growing thin. A band of young politicians, eager for war, were voted into the House of Representatives. Among them were Henry Clay of Kentucky and John C. Calhoun of South Carolina. They formed the core of a group of legislators who came to be known as the War Hawks. Their purpose was to force recognition of American rights.

Clay was elected *Speaker of the House* on his first day in the House of Representatives. He used the power of this position to appoint fellow War Hawks to the important legislative committees. *Soon, Congress*

The snapping turtle in this cartoon represents the Embargo Act of 1807. Americans had fun playing with the letters of the word "embargo." The sugar smuggler might have referred to "mob rage" or "go bar' em." Where did he get the word "ograbme"?

began preparing the country for war. The administration cooperated, and on June 1, 1812, President Madison requested a formal declaration of war. The House approved the declaration by a vote of 79–49, the Senate by 16–14.

The **Speaker of the House** is the officer who presides over the House of Representatives.

The votes revealed the division that had existed in the nation since the embargo. The South and West were nearly all in favor of war. New England opposed it, and the middle states were divided. The division was along party lines as well as regional lines. Nearly all Republicans voted for war. Every Federalist in Congress voted against it.

The vote for war also indicated a rising spirit of pride in the new nation. **The War of 1812 stemmed from American nationalism.** In that sense it was, as people called it at the time, a "second war for independence."

Section Review

1. Identify or explain: impressment, embargo, the *Chesapeake* affair, War Hawks, John C. Calhoun, Macon's Bill Number 2.
2. Why were the Napoleonic wars in Europe profitable to Americans?
3. Define "blockade." What reasons did the British and French give for their blockades of American shipping?
4. Make a chart that shows the following: regions or groups in favor of the War of 1812, regions or groups against the War of 1812. Give the reasons for each side's position.

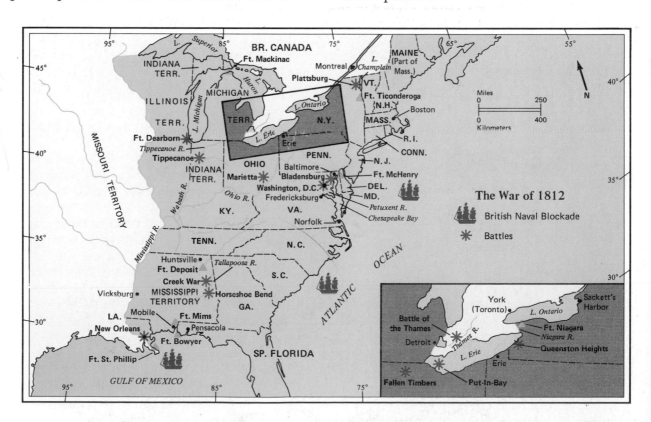

The War of 1812

🚢 British Naval Blockade

✳ Battles

3. Fighting the War of 1812

THE WAR BEGINS. *Divided against itself and unprepared for a fight, the United States fared badly at the outset of the war.* In the West, Tecumseh, a Shawnee leader, mustered an army of a thousand Indians and captured outposts at the Straits of Mackinac and at the foot of Lake Michigan. In Detroit an American general panicked and surrendered an army of 2,000 to a British-Canadian force of 200. On the New York frontier, an army crossed the Niagara River and won a quick victory at Queenston Heights. (See map, page 199.) But when reinforcements refused to cross the river, it surrendered.

The tiny American Navy gave a good account of itself. In a dozen ship-to-ship duels around the world, the Americans were victorious in all but one. The only loss was the unlucky *Chesapeake*. It had succumbed to a British frigate, *Shannon*, off Boston in early 1813. The encounter did, however, provide a motto for the American Navy. As the commander of the *Chesapeake*, James Lawrence, lay dying, he issued his last order: "Don't give up the ship. Fight her till she sinks!" From 1812 to 1813, a British blockade kept the American Navy at home.

THE CAMPAIGN OF 1813. By mid-1813 the situation was improving. In the West, Oliver Hazard Perry had built a fleet on Lake Erie and beaten the British at Put-in-Bay, off Sandusky, Ohio. Once in control of Lake Erie, Perry had ferried William Henry Harrison's army to Canada. Then, in October 1813, Harrison defeated a British-Indian force at the Thames River, some 80 kilometers (50 miles) east of Detroit. Tecumseh was slain, and the West was back in American hands. In the Southwest, Andrew Jackson led an army of Tennessee militia into the

Sidenote to History

Tecumseh: A Great Man

Tecumseh had reason to resent the intruders. When Tecumseh was very young, his father was murdered by two White hunters because he refused to carry a deer for them. In 1786, after Tecumseh had just turned 19, an army of Virginians senselessly burned his village in southern Ohio.

When the Whites crossed the Ohio River in 1788 and founded the village of Marietta, Tecumseh went to war. He realized he could not force the Whites to return to Europe, but he did think that the Ohio River was a reasonable boundary.

Although Tecumseh was not a chief, he had followers. Indian leaders were not chosen by birthright or election. They usually became leaders or chiefs through a combination of physical strength, boldness in battle, and speaking ability. The last was probably the most important. Among a people without a written language, speech was the most important means of persuasion. And Tecumseh was a brilliant orator. He also had a fabulous memory. He could recite the terms of every treaty signed between Whites and Indians—and the dates when the Whites broke them.

In 1790 President Washington sent an army into Ohio to overcome the Indians, but it failed to find them. The following year Arthur St. Clair, governor of the Northwest Territory, led an army into western Ohio and met total defeat. His losses—some 800 soldiers—were the largest suffered by the army in the history of the frontier.

Angered, Washington sent an army into the West, under General Anthony Wayne. In 1794 Wayne defeated the Indians at Fallen Timbers, near the present-day city of Toledo, Ohio. The following year he summoned delegates from all the tribes to his camp at Greenville. There, he forced them to sign a treaty, ceding almost all of Ohio to the United States. Tecumseh refused to sign the treaty, but he was alone in his defiance. The Indians were tired of war.

In 1800 the Indiana Territory was cut off from Ohio. William Henry Harrison became its governor. Encouraged by Jefferson, Harrison actively began seeking further Indian land cessions. He used every possible means—bribery, liquor, threats. Sometimes he would even persuade one tribe to sell him the lands of another. Such things were possible because the Indians were not concerned about precise boundaries and legal titles. Tecumseh, for example, thought that land was like air and water. It was there for all to use freely.

Tecumseh fought Harrison's policies, but could do little. Then, one day his brother had a religious conversion. Calling himself the Prophet, he began preaching the idea of Indian superiority and warning his followers to avoid the corruption of the White race.

The Prophet's fame spread across the West. To house their growing following, Tecumseh and the Prophet built a town in north central Indiana, where Tippecanoe Creek joins the Wabash. To all who came, Tecumseh talked of Indian unity. He wanted a confederation of all the tribes, so they could form a united front against the advancing Whites. He did not plan on war. Instead, he wanted a firm agreement among the Indians that there would be no more land sales.

Tecumseh was successful in getting pledges from the northwestern tribes. So in the summer of 1811, he decided to journey south, in the hope of bringing the powerful Creek and Cherokee into his alliance.

Tecumseh's departure was the opportunity Governor Harrison had wanted, and he hastily gathered an army. In the fall of 1811, he marched north through Indiana. By early November he was camped near the Prophet's town. The Prophet and his forces attacked at dawn on November 6. They penetrated Harrison's camp and nearly overran it, but despite their fierce fighting, they were driven back. Harrison eventually ventured into the Prophet's town, found it deserted, and burned it.

Harrison returned to his capital at Vincennes, claiming a great victory. It earned him the reputation as an Indian fighter that helped elect him to the White House in 1840. When Tecumseh returned from his trip, he was so angry that he banished his brother to the western plains.

Harrison's attack threw Tecumseh into the arms of the British. British authorities in upper Canada had encouraged Tecumseh's efforts for some time. They had even sent him guns, which Harrison had found, still unpacked, in the Prophet's town.

When war broke out in 1812, Tecumseh mustered up a thousand Indians and captured nearly every fort in the Northwest. But the British would not commit a major army to the area, and Tecumseh was eventually forced to the defensive. When William Henry Harrison invaded Canada in 1813, the British general retreated—until Tecumseh insisted on a stand.

Tecumseh was betrayed by the Whites even in death. While he and his warriors faced Harrison's furious attack, the British general was in his carriage, fleeing to the East.

Tecumseh's warriors carried his body from the field of battle and gave it a secret burial. His resting place has never been found.

Alabama Territory and defeated the Creek at Horseshoe Bend in March 1814. The two encounters crushed the Indians' efforts to resist the American takeover of lands east of the Mississippi River.

BRITISH STRATEGY IN 1814. Napoleon finally met his end. After his costly invasion of Russia in 1812, the nations of Europe allied against Napoleon and defeated him. He was sent into exile on an island in the Mediterranean. This left Britain free at last to swat the American wasp buzzing at its back. Three campaigns were planned, all reinforced by veterans from the war against France. The British would thrust south from Canada and west from the sea to the American capital, and through the Gulf of Mexico toward the territory of Louisiana.

Sidenote to History

Frigates

A frigate is a class of warship developed by the British. Frigates had three masts, had square sails, and usually mounted 38 guns. When the United States built its first frigates in 1798–1800, it installed 44 guns on them. It also built them of southern live oak to make them more resistant to saltwater worms. Live oak proved more resistant to cannonballs. Thus, the most famous of these American frigates, the *Constitution,* got the nickname *Old Ironsides.* Lesser vessels, used mostly for patrol and messenger duty, were brigs (two masts and 18–30 guns) and sloops (two masts with triangular sails and 10–20 guns). The *Philadelphia* was not so large as other American frigates, because it was donated by the merchants of Philadelphia—another indication of growing national pride.

In Chesapeake Bay a British fleet had spent the war harassing American ships and threatening Virginia's cities. *In August 1814, it landed a force on the coast of Maryland that marched into Washington, D.C.* After scattering a troop of Maryland militia, it set fire to the capital's public buildings and retired to its ships. Among those public buildings was the President's house. Previously called the Executive Mansion and colored a cream-yellow, it was painted white after the war to hide the burn scars. It has remained the White House ever since.

THE BATTLE OF NEW ORLEANS. After defeating the Creek Indians, Andrew Jackson established his defense in Baton Rouge. But when he learned of the British threat to New Orleans, he quickly led his troops to that strategic city on the Mississippi.

Jackson built his defense line slightly south of New Orleans, along a drainage canal that stretched from a swamp to the Mississippi River. He set up cannons there and manned them with pirates from the delta swamps. In the city he recruited two regiments of free Blacks and gave them rifles.

After some skirmishes with artillery, the British launched an infantry attack on January 8, 1815. But Jackson's sharpshooters cut them to pieces. By day's end more than 2,000 redcoats, including their commanding general, lay dead on the field. In the general's torn and bloody pocket was his commission to be governor of Louisiana. Jackson's losses were seven killed and six wounded.

THE PEACE OF CHRISTMAS EVE. Peace talks went on throughout the war, the commissioners meeting in the neutral city of Ghent, Belgium. The British at first demanded territory, especially land for their Indian allies. But by the autumn of 1814, it was clear that the fighting had ended in a draw. ***The peace treaty, signed on December 24, 1814, recognized the stalemate.*** Nothing was said of American neutrality rights or the impressment of sailors. Since the European war had ended, such things were no longer important. Neither side demanded territory. They both simply agreed to stop fighting.

News of the treaty agreement did not reach America for several weeks, however.

This painting depicts the British bombardment of Ft. McHenry during the War of 1812. The commander of the fort ordered a flag "so large that the British will have no difficulty seeing it at a distance." Francis Scott Key, a young poet, observed the bombardment. He was so inspired that he wrote the poem that became our national anthem.

Black riflemen helped to win the Battle of New Orleans. After the war, General Andrew Jackson thanked his Black troops: "I expected much from you, but you have surpassed my hopes."

As a result, the battle of New Orleans was fought after the war was technically over.

ANGLO-AMERICAN RELATIONS IMPROVE. *The Treaty of Ghent was a victory for common sense.* Neither side felt injured. In fact, after the war, relations between the two countries were friendlier than ever. In 1817 they agreed to limit the number of warships on the Great Lakes—the first arms limitation agreement in history. (This agreement is called the Rush-Bagot agreement.) In 1818 they agreed to administer the Pacific Northwest jointly. This gave the United States a claim to the Pacific Coast, far beyond the western boundary of the Louisiana Purchase. It was a satisfactory ending to a frustrating war.

Section Review

1. Mapping: Using the map on page 199, describe the location of the following battle sites: Chesapeake Bay, New Orleans. Choose one site and tell why you think it was important.

2. Identify or explain: Tecumseh, Oliver Hazard Perry, Andrew Jackson, James Lawrence.

3. How did events in Europe influence the war in the United States?

4. Describe the Treaty of Ghent. Why was it a treaty of common sense.?

5. Describe the British strategy of 1814.

4. Postwar Nationalism

NATIONAL NEEDS. The war revealed some flaws in the national fabric. And the nationalistic War Hawks, in full control of Congress, hastened to mend them when the war ended.

One of the problems was money. The Madison administration had allowed the Bank of the United States to go out of business when its charter expired in 1811. As a result, the government had to finance the War of 1812 in the way the Continental Congress had financed the Revolution— with paper money. *Problems of military supply had also revealed serious flaws in the nation's transportation system.* Furthermore, business people who had turned to manufacturing during the war were demanding help. The result was an outpouring of legislation after the war. It was active government responding to national needs.

Two of the new leaders in Congress at this time behind much of the legislation were War Hawks—Henry Clay and John C. Calhoun, Republicans from Kentucky and South Carolina. A third was Daniel Webster, a Federalist from Massachusetts, who had come to Congress in 1813. Webster was the one who spoke for the northeastern part of the country.

THE SECOND BANK OF THE UNITED STATES. *In 1816 Congress chartered the Second Bank of the United States.* Modeled on the first bank, it was also a partnership between business and government. It was to hold treasury deposits and issue notes, which would serve as a national currency.

THE TARIFF. *That same year Congress enacted a new tariff law, setting customs duties high enough to discourage imports.* The purpose was not to gain revenue but to protect the factories that had grown up in America during both the embargo and the war. American industry was still too young to withstand British competition. Until it came of age, it had to be protected by a wall of tariffs.

JUDICIAL NATIONALISM. There was much about the post-1815 nationalism that reminded one of Alexander Hamilton. Hamilton had advocated both a bank and a tariff. In fact, led by Clay and Calhoun, the Republican party in the years after the War of 1812 seemed to approve of all the programs of its old opponents, the Federalists. At this time John Marshall, a staunch old Federalist, sensed that his turn had come.

Marshall, a cousin of Thomas Jefferson and his lifelong foe, had been named Chief Justice of the Supreme Court at the end of John Adams's term. Jefferson had been concerned that Marshall might use his position to attack the Republican program. At first Jefferson's fears seemed justified.

In the case of **Marbury v. Madison (1803), Marshall had declared an act of Congress unconstitutional.** His decision established the principle of judicial review. This made the court the final authority in determining the constitutionality of laws. Republicans had worried that Marshall might use this new principle to wreck their entire program. But except for presiding over Burr's trial, Marshall had remained relatively quiet.

The nationalist mood of the country after the War of 1812 gave Marshall new opportunities to push his views. In *McCulloch v. Maryland* (1819), he ruled on the constitutionality of the Bank of the United States. *He declared that the federal government did have power to create a bank.* And, he added, since the bank was an arm of the federal government, the states could not interfere with it. Five years later, in *Gibbons v.*

Ogden (1824), he dealt another blow to states' powers by preventing New York from regulating traffic on the Hudson River. Only Congress, Marshall ruled, could regulate interstate commerce. Then, he defined "commerce" so broadly that he gave Congress considerable scope in that area.

These decisions are just a few of John Marshall's contributions to nationalism. He remained active on the Supreme Court for another decade. ***By the time of his death in 1835, he had adapted the Constitution to the needs of a rapidly changing society.***

Section Review

1. Identify or explain: John Marshall, judicial review, the Second Bank of the United States.
2. Name two major problems the nation faced at the end of the War of 1812.
3. List the important cases reviewed by John Marshall. Next to each case give a description of Marshall's decision and the legal principle that the decision established.

5. Guardian of the New World

REVOLUTIONS AROUND THE WORLD. The revolution that began in France in 1789 was not an isolated event. It was one of many revolutions against a monarchy and an empire. In 1791 Black slaves rose up on the West Indies island of Santo Domingo and formed the world's first Black republic (see page 209). Then came other revolutions in Latin America. Distracted by the war in Europe, Spain was unable to control its New World empire. By the time peace came to Europe in 1815, it was too late. Several Latin American republics had declared their independence, and more were moving along the same path.

JOHN QUINCY ADAMS. The United States rejoiced at the revolutionary movement in South America, but did not interfere. It did, however, want to clarify its own boundary with Spanish Mexico and, if possible, remove the Spanish from Florida. The man who accomplished both was John Quincy Adams, the son of the nation's second President.

Adams was born to public service. During the Revolution he had accompanied his father on a mission to Europe. His early education had been in the aristocratic schools of Paris. Then, his father had him sent home to learn American ways. After finishing Harvard College, he entered politics.

Adams began as a Federalist, like his father, but broke with his party over Jefferson's embargo. Adams felt the United States

This portrait of John Quincy Adams was done by the famous portrait painter John Singleton Copley. How does Adam's image differ from Jackson's on page 220?

should not humbly submit to British pressures. Instead, it had to retaliate. President Madison welcomed him to the Republican party by making him the minister to Russia. In 1814 Adams was part of the team that negotiated the Treaty of Ghent. When James Monroe became President in 1817, succeeding Madison, he named Adams Secretary of State.

ADAMS AND JACKSON. In family background, training, and every aspect of his life, John Quincy Adams was the opposite of Andrew Jackson. *But the two men, who came to cordially dislike each other, found their lives continually intertwined.* In 1815, for instance, Jackson secured on the New Orleans battlefield the peace that Adams had negotiated at the conference table.

Again, three years later, Jackson's fighting temperament aided Adams's diplomatic aims. As military commander in the South after the war, Jackson's chief duty was that of protecting the frontier against the Seminole, who lived in Florida. The Seminole frequently crossed into Georgia to take horses and slaves from Georgia plantations. Spain was obliged by treaty to prevent this but was too weak to do so.

In the spring of 1818, Jackson, pursuing a band of Indians, crossed the Florida border and captured the Spanish fort at Pensacola. When Spanish authorities protested, Secretary Adams suggested that the entire problem would be solved if Spain sold Florida.

THE PURCHASE OF FLORIDA. Spain agreed. Lacking mineral wealth, Florida had been nothing but an expensive burden. Mexico was far more important to Spain. However, Spain demanded a marked boundary between American and Spanish claims in the Far West. Adams quickly agreed, and drew a line across the map from Texas to the Pacific Ocean. *The Transcontinental Treaty, also called the Adams-Onís Treaty, was signed in February 1819.* (See map, page 208.) It was a feat of brilliant diplomacy. In it Spain sold Florida to the United States for $5 million. The transcontinental line through the West did not simply define American and Spanish claims. By extending the line all the way to the Pacific (it is the boundary today between California and Oregon), Adams staked an American claim to the Pacific Coast, without spending arms or money. He was one of the first to foresee a transcontinental republic, stretching from sea to sea.

A DIPLOMATIC CRISIS. Two years later, in 1821, Mexico won its independence from Spain. The line that Adams had drawn now bordered a friendly republic rather than imperial Spain. With Mexican independence the wave of Latin American revolutions was nearly complete. (See map, page 209.)

Monroe and Adams had delayed opening diplomatic relations with Latin America for fear of angering Spain during the delicate Florida negotiations. With the Transcontinental Treaty ratified, they promptly sent ministers to several Latin American republics.

Then, in 1823, a crisis developed. European monarchies seemed determined to stamp out republicanism wherever it appeared. There was even a possibility that France might help the Spanish monarchy recover its Latin American dominions. That notion alarmed both Britain and the United States.

Both trading powers were overjoyed at the breakup of the Spanish Empire. It had opened a vast new market that had been closed to the world since the time of Columbus. Spain had never been able to supply Latin America with the manufactured goods it needed. Britain and the United States could and would. But first they had to keep France from meddling.

THE MONROE DOCTRINE. Britain informed the French that, as an imperial

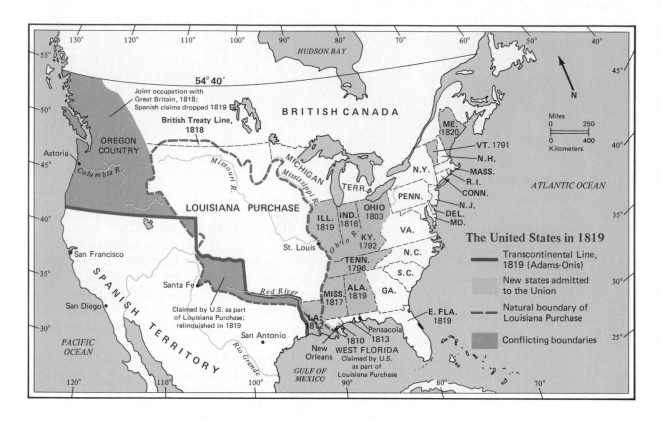

The map is titled "The United States in 1819" with the following legend:
- Transcontinental Line, 1819 (Adams-Onis)
- New states admitted to the Union
- Natural boundary of Louisiana Purchase
- Conflicting boundaries

Map labels include: HUDSON BAY, 54° 40', Joint occupation with Great Britain, 1818; Spanish claims dropped 1819, British Treaty Line, 1818, BRITISH CANADA, OREGON COUNTRY, Astoria, Columbia R., Missouri R., Mississippi R., MICHIGAN TERR., LOUISIANA PURCHASE, St. Louis, Ohio R., SPANISH TERRITORY, San Francisco, Santa Fe, San Diego, Claimed by U.S. as part of Louisiana Purchase; relinquished in 1819, Red River, San Antonio, Rio Grande, PACIFIC OCEAN, New Orleans, GULF OF MEXICO, WEST FLORIDA Claimed by U.S. as part of Louisiana Purchase, Pensacola 1813, 1810, E. FLA. 1819, ATLANTIC OCEAN, ME. 1820, VT. 1791, N.H., MASS., R.I., CONN., N.Y., PENN., N.J., DEL., MD., OHIO 1803, IND. 1816, ILL. 1819, KY. 1792, VA., N.C., S.C., TENN. 1796, MISS. 1817, ALA. 1819, GA., LA. 1812. Miles 0 250, Kilometers 0 400.

power itself, Britain could not object to Spain's desire to reclaim its empire. But if another nation, such as France, were to help Spain, "that would be a new question." It was Britain's hint to keep hands off the New World. Since Britain had a strong navy behind it, this hint was more effective than anything the United States could say or do.

Britain invited the United States to join in this policy, but Secretary of State Adams refused. The United States had factories of its own. It, too, wanted to sell goods in Latin America. Besides, Adams wanted to follow an independent policy of his own making. Thus, he drafted a reply, and President Monroe included it in his annual message to Congress on December 2, 1823. *The Monroe Doctrine, as the reply came to be called, involved three basic principles.*

1. Noncolonization.

Monroe stated that North and South America were no longer open to colonization by European powers. Since there was no room for new colonies in South America, this statement was directed not at Spain but at Britain and Russia. It was a warning to the British not to undertake a settlement in the Oregon country of the Northwest and a warning to the Russians not to expand beyond Alaska.

2. No Transfer.

Although not mentioned by Monroe, this principle had long been established American policy. It was repeated by Adams in private notes to Europe. It meant that the United States would not tolerate the transfer of New World colonies from one European power to another (such as Spain had done with Louisiana).

3. Nonintervention.

Monroe pledged that the United States would stay out of the affairs of Europe. Similarly, it would regard European intervention in the New World as "an unfriendly act."

Through the Monroe Doctrine the United States placed a diplomatic umbrella over the entire New World. It was some years, however, before the United States was strong enough to enforce the doctrine. At the time it was simply an announcement that the United States was reaching economic maturity and needed its own markets. At this point it could rival Europe in the production of manufactured goods.

The doctrine was thus a declaration of economic independence, as important in some ways as the 1776 declaration of political independence. It was also a triumph of American nationalism.

Section Review

1. Mapping: Using the map on page 208, trace the line of the Transcontinental Treaty. What was its significance to the growth of American nationalism?
2. Identify or explain: Santo Domingo, John Quincy Adams, Seminole Indians.
3. Describe the terms of the Transcontinental Treaty. Why was the treaty a triumph for the United States?
4. Name and explain the three important principles set forth in the Monroe Doctrine. How were these enforced?

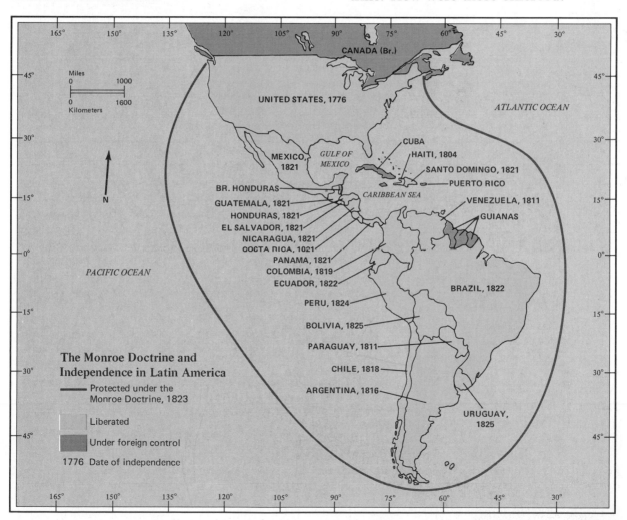

The Monroe Doctrine and Independence in Latin America
— Protected under the Monroe Doctrine, 1823
☐ Liberated
■ Under foreign control
1776 Date of independence

Chapter 8 Review

Bird's-Eye View

During the early 19th century, the United States began to see itself as a unified nation, rather than as a loosely federated group of states. This new feeling of nationalism expressed itself vigorously in United States dealings with other nations. It gave Americans the self-confidence, for example, to resist the demands of the North African states for tribute and to negotiate free access to the Mediterranean Sea.

The major international events of this period were the wars between France, Britain, and their European allies. The wars affected the United States in several ways. Both France and Britain interfered with American trade. American ports were blockaded. American ships were stopped in midocean, their cargoes searched, and members of their crews impressed. Ultimately, these and other insults led to the War of 1812, between the United States and Britain. The war was fought to a stalemate, with neither side achieving victory. It concluded with the Treaty of Ghent in 1814.

After the war American nationalism increased. Within the Congress a pronational majority emerged, especially in the House of Representatives. Within the judicial branch of government, the decisions of Chief Justice John Marshall reinforced the power of the government and contributed to this movement.

This early 19th-century surge of national feeling and assertion of national identity reached its peak in the Monroe Doctrine of 1823. It called on the nations of Europe to respect the independence of the Americas and expressed the determination of the United States to resist—if necessary, with force—any European encroachments on the Western Hemisphere.

Vocabulary

Define or identify each of the following:

Sacajawea	embargo	impressment
Speaker of the House	War Hawks	Transcontinental Treaty
Chesapeake	judicial review	economic warfare

Review Questions

1. Name the individuals involved in exploring the Louisiana Territory and cite the areas they explored.
2. List five problems that the United States faced because of the wars in Europe.
3. Why did the Embargo Act of 1807 hurt the United States more than it did the British?
4. Describe Andrew Jackson's military campaigns during the War of 1812.
5. Explain the decision in the case of *Marbury v. Madison*.
6. Explain the Monroe Doctrine's principles of noncolonization, no transfer, and nonintervention.

Reviewing Social Studies Skills

1. Using the maps on pages 208 and xv list the following:
   a. The states that were once part of the Louisiana Purchase.
   b. The states that were once part of the area that Lewis and Clark explored.
   c. The states that were once part of the area that Pike explored.
2. Find evidence in the text to support each of these statements:
   a. The United States was right in going to war with Great Britain.
   b. The United States should have gone to war with France.
   c. The United States should have remained neutral.
3. Historians attempt to draw cause and effect relationships between specific historical events. From the facts presented in this chapter, what effect did the following events have:
   a. Closing of New Orleans
   b. American settlement of West Florida
   c. Hamilton-Burr duel
   d. Election of the War Hawks
   e. Embargo Act of 1807
4. Study the cartoon on page 198. What is the artist's attitude toward the Embargo Act of 1807?

Reading for Meaning

1. Using a dictionary, write a clear definition for each of the following terms: domestic, commandeered, ransom, imperial, negotiate, expedition, discontented, violation, immigrants, broadside, encounters, neutral, and republic.
2. Alexander Hamilton has an honored role in American history, and Aaron Burr is seen as a rogue. How does the information in the Sidenote to History on page 194 cast doubt on Hamilton's character?
3. Both the United States and England claimed victory in the War of 1812. How was this possible?

Bibliography

The Age of the Fighting Sail, by C. S. Forester (Doubleday), is an interesting account of the naval battles of the War of 1812. Forester's *Captain from Connecticut* (Little, Brown) is also a novel about this war at sea.

Glenn Tucker's *Tecumseh: Vision of Glory* (Russell) is an interesting biography of this famous Indian leader.

Anthony Lewis's *The Supreme Court and How It Works* (Random House) explains the workings of this branch of government.

F. Van Wyck Mason's *The Battle of New Orleans* (Houghton Mifflin) gives a dramatic account of this campaign.

The March of Democracy

It was to be a new day, an "Era of Good Feelings," announced Boston's *Columbian Centinel* in its issue of July 12, 1817. Throughout the War of 1812, the *Centinel* had been the government's most violent critic. A Federalist newspaper, it had opposed the war and bitterly denounced President Madison as Napoleon's puppet. The prediction of an era of good feelings was a call for a political truce.

The newly elected President, James Monroe, toured the nation. Not since Washington had a President toured the country. And Monroe's visit to the New England states brought a steady outpouring of applause. He was a popular man, who had dedicated his life to public service. The last of the Revolutionary generation, he still wore the knee-length pantaloons, silk stockings, and buckled shoes of the 18th century. His successful tour marked a new spirit of national unity.

Chapter Objectives

After you have finished reading this chapter, you should be able to:
1. Explain the events that contributed to sectionalism.
2. Compare the way Adams and Jackson faced the challenges of sectionalism.
3. Define the term "Jacksonian Democracy."
4. Describe the appeal of the Whig party in 1840.

The tour also marked the end of party strife. The Federalist party was dead. Branded as unpatriotic for opposing the War of 1812, the Federalists had barely survived that conflict. Finally, they had simply collapsed. Rufus King, who had opposed Monroe in the election of 1816, had been the Federalists' Presidential candidate.

During Monroe's two terms in office, the nation was under the one-party rule of the Republicans. It might truly have been an "era of good feelings" had it not been for some new difficulties. Economic hard times

and a blowup over slavery in Missouri—both in the year 1819—had ushered in a decade of political turmoil. Out of this turmoil came two new political parties.

1. An Era of Good Feelings-and Bad

THE PANIC OF 1819. The postwar years were happy ones. The nation basked in prosperity. *The end of the British blockade had brought an increase in foreign trade.* War-torn Europe needed American goods.

By 1819, however, European agriculture had recovered, and American sales had declined. A bank panic that had begun in Britain and spread to America had sent the economy into a tailspin. Industry soon recovered, but the farm prices remained low for a decade. The South was particularly hard hit. In the prosperous times after the war, cotton growing had expanded into the rich soils of Alabama and Mississippi. *Throughout the 1820's the South simply produced more cotton than the world could use.*

Such distress caused a political reaction, as the South and West blamed their woes on the federal government. Reinforcing this ill feeling between sections of the country was the beginning of a controversy over slavery— a dispute that would simmer for the next 40 years, before finally boiling into civil war.

THE MISSOURI CONTROVERSY.

During the War of 1812, the Indians had tried to protect their lands from being taken over by the Whites. But their efforts were unsuccessful, and after the war many White settlers had flocked to the West. *In just four years, from 1816 to 1819, four new states had populations large enough to enter the Union—Indiana, Illinois, Alabama, and Mississippi.*

In February 1819 the House of Representatives took up a routine bill that would enable the Missouri Territory to form a state constitution. However, a congressman from New York, James Tallmadge, surprised the House with an amendment to that bill. The amendment would outlaw the introduction of new slaves into Missouri. It would also free the children of slaves already there, once those children reached the age of 25. Tallmadge did not intend to attack the institution of slavery itself. He merely wanted to limit its spread into the West. *Since Missouri was still a territory, Tallmadge and his supporters argued, Congress could limit slavery there, just as it had done in the Northwest by the Ordinance of 1787.*

Southerners instantly objected. Congress did not have power to limit slavery, they argued. Slaves were property, and the government could not deprive people of their property. Moreover, Missouri was about to become a state. As a state Missouri could have any social system it wanted, including slavery. By imposing restrictions on slavery at this point, Congress would make Missouri a second-class state.

Nevertheless, votes counted more than arguments. In the House of Representatives, the populous North had a majority. So the house attached the Tallmadge Amendment to the Missouri statehood bill and sent it to the Senate. In the Senate there happened to be an equal number of slave and free states. With the help of a few senators from the Ohio Valley, the South defeated the measure.

When Congress returned the following winter, Missouri again applied for statehood. Also asking for statehood was Maine, previously a part of Massachusetts. This situation raised the possibility of a bargain. *Speaker of the House Henry Clay, who came from the border state of Kentucky, mediated between the sides.* A compromise was worked out in the spring of 1820.

THE MISSOURI COMPROMISE.

Under the arrangement that became law in March 1820, Missouri entered the Union as a slave state, and Maine entered as a free state. In addition, the territory that remained from the Louisiana Purchase was divided along the line 36° 30′ north latitude. With the exception of Missouri, slavery was prohibited in states north of that line. (See map, page 214.)

The South had agreed to compromise in order to secure an additional slave state. But it had emerged from the controversy in a state of shock. For the first time on the floor

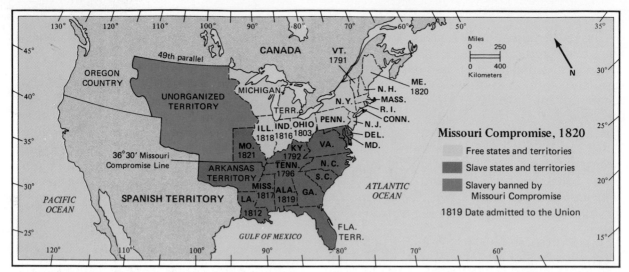

Map labels: 130°, 120°, 110°, 100°, 90°, 80°, 70°, 60°, 50°, 35°; CANADA; VT. 1791; 49th parallel; OREGON COUNTRY; UNORGANIZED TERRITORY; MICHIGAN TERR.; ME. 1820; N.H.; MASS.; N.Y.; R.I.; CONN.; N.J.; PENN.; DEL.; MD.; ILL. 1818; IND. 1816; OHIO 1803; MO. 1821; KY. 1792; VA.; 36°30′ Missouri Compromise Line; ARKANSAS TERRITORY; TENN. 1796; N.C.; S.C.; SPANISH TERRITORY; MISS. 1817; ALA. 1819; GA.; LA. 1812; FLA. TERR.; ATLANTIC OCEAN; PACIFIC OCEAN; GULF OF MEXICO

Legend:
Free states and territories
Slave states and territories
Slavery banned by Missouri Compromise
1819 Date admitted to the Union

of Congress, slavery had been denounced as a moral evil. Many southerners agreed with Thomas Jefferson that slavery was wrong. But they did not know what to do about it. If Blacks were freed, they believed, Blacks would naturally seek revenge for many past injustices.

Southerners drew back in fear and anger. "This momentous question," Jefferson wrote about Missouri, "like a fire-bell in the night, awakened and filled me with terror."

SOUTHERN SECTIONALISM. Ever since the federal ship had been launched, the South had been at the helm. With the exception of John Adams, every President had been a southerner—indeed, a Virginian. Southerners controlled the committee structure of Congress. A Virginian, John Marshall, presided over the Supreme Court.

This political dominance had masked the reality that after 1800 the South had fallen behind the North in population and wealth. The Missouri dispute had brought this new status home to the South. *Thus, faced with a hostile array of free states, the South became self-conscious and sectionalist.* Southerners began emphasizing things that pertained only to their section of the country—plantation agriculture, easygoing gentility, and above all, slavery. It did not matter

that fewer than a third of the planters in the South owned slaves. Southern poor Whites had nearly as much interest in retaining slavery as wealthy planters. Free Blacks would mean competition.

Feeling itself to be a minority in the nation, the South embraced states' rights. Federal power, said southerners, was limited to specific powers, as expressed by the exact words of the Constitution. The states kept all other powers, including the power to regulate slavery. *Hard times and low farm prices reinforced this feeling of southern sectionalism.* Southern planters blamed the federal government for their economic hardships. South Carolina, for instance, blamed its troubles on the tariff. Its planters had to sell their cotton in Britain. In return they bought British manufactured goods. The tariff on incoming goods, they felt, interfered with this trade. They saw it as a tax that they had to pay for but one that benefited only the northern manufacturers.

OPPOSITION TO THE BANKING SYSTEM. In the Southwest, Kentucky, and Tennessee, the institution of banking came under attack. *Westerners disliked all banks because rural ones were unreliable and often went broke.* Frontier settlers were suspicious of bank notes. Most of them

Sequoyah (si-KWAH-yuh) had a talent for creating things. Crippled for life by a hunting accident, he became a silversmith, making beautiful ornaments that sold readily in the market. Proud of his work, he asked a White trader to write Sequoyah in the English alphabet, so he could stamp his name on his creations. At this same time it occurred to him to create a special alphabet for his native Cherokee tongue. There was power in the Whites' "talking leaves," the written messages that communicated ideas. With a written language of their own, the Indians could translate the White people's treaties and read them to their own people. They could write down their tribal history, traditions, and religious beliefs.

The project took Sequoyah 12 years, and it was finally completed in 1821. He counted 85 basic syllables in spoken Cherokee.

For each he created a character, in the manner of modern Japanese or Chinese writing. Realizing the importance of what he was doing, the tribal council endorsed the project. A missionary board furnished money to make a printing press that could print both Cherokee characters and English letters. First a primer to be used in Cherokee schools was printed, then a Bible translation and a Cherokee newspaper.

Sequoyah's invention made him famous. Later, he was named a leader. The United States government gave him a pension. He devoted the rest of his life to Indian languages, traveling from tribe to tribe studying their speech. He hoped to find enough similarities among the languages to demonstrate the common heritage of all Indians. Before realizing his hope, he died in Mexico during a search for a lost band of Cherokee.

---

preferred hard money—gold and silver—for currency.

Disliking all banks, they naturally objected to the biggest one of all, the Bank of the United States, with its many branches around the country. During the panic of 1819, the bank had severely limited its moneylending activities in order to save itself. *In doing so it had ruined many other banks, especially those in the South and West.*

ANTI-INDIAN FEELING. *Georgia's problem was American Indians.* The Creek and Cherokee nations still held a substantial portion of the state. And Georgia's hard-pressed planters, caught between low prices and depleted soils, looked enviously at the Creek and Cherokee lands. The Creek and Cherokee were agricultural people. Some even had plantations and slaves. They had kept their lands not only because they had remained at peace, but also because they had refused to sign treaties with the Whites. In the 1820's the Cherokee had developed a written language and had started a newspaper, *The Cherokee Phoenix.* They had drafted a Cherokee constitution and had formed a government.

When the Monroe administration refused Georgia's demands for the removal of the Indians, Georgia resorted to using states' rights. It defied the federal government, which claimed an exclusive right to deal with Indian nations. It extended its own laws over the Cherokee. And since under Georgia's laws American Indians were not allowed to sue in court, the Cherokee

Oakland House was a racetrack in Louisville, Kentucky. What can you infer about the way of life of the patrons of Oakland House from this picture?

watched helplessly as Georgia's farmers moved into their lands and homes. The federal government objected, but seemed unable to help.

THE FRUITS OF SECTIONALISM. *Out of this tension between nationalism and sectionalism came a new political structure.* By the end of Monroe's second term in office (1821–1825), the old Republican party was breaking up. It was rapidly splitting into two wings—nationalist and sectionalist. This split produced a new two-party system.

Section Review

1. Mapping: Using the map on page 214, list the territories that are north of the 36° 30′ parallel and those that are south of it in the Louisiana Purchase. What geographic consideration was the basis for the Missouri Compromise?
2. Identify or explain: Era of Good Feelings, James Tallmadge, panic of 1819, *The Cherokee Phoenix*.

3. List and explain the differences between the North and South that led to the development of sectionalism.

2. The Birth of the Second-Party System

THE CANDIDATES. James Monroe was the last of the Virginia dynasty that had begun with Jefferson. When he retired from the Presidency, he had no clear successor. But there were many able politicians who wanted the job. Among them were Monroe's Secretary of State, John Quincy Adams, and Representative Henry Clay. *Both were nationalists with strong support in their regions—Adams in the Northeast and Clay in the West.* William H. Crawford of Georgia, Monroe's Secretary of the Treasury, was another candidate. He received the support of powerful southern politicians. But throughout the South and West, the most popular political figure was Andrew Jackson.

THE ELECTION OF 1824. Jackson proved to be not only the most popular candidate, but also the best vote getter in the entire election. He carried nearly every state. (See map below.) *Because there were so many candidates, however, Jackson failed to get a majority of the electoral votes.* For the second time in American history, the election was to be decided in the House of Representatives.

There, the most powerful figure was Speaker Henry Clay. Out of the running himself, Clay could play kingmaker. And he used his influence in the House to deliver the Presidency to John Quincy Adams, even though Adams had trailed Jackson in the popular election.

The new President promptly named Henry Clay Secretary of State. There had been no deal because none was necessary. Adams and Clay were both nationalists, who favored the bank and the tariff. One man was strong in the Northeast, the other in the West. It was a natural alliance. When Adams retired, it was assumed that Henry Clay would move directly into the White House.

BARGAIN AND CORRUPTION. Understandably, Andrew Jackson thought he had been robbed. He instantly accused the two "aristocrats" of a "corrupt bargain" to keep themselves in power. *With his accusation, Jackson became the champion of the people.*

The Jacksonian cry of bargain and corruption appealed to every interest. It fitted the westerner's picture of the conniving East, the farmer's suspicion of city slickers, and the worker's hostility to the silk-stockinged rich. It mattered little that Jackson had never before shown much interest in the common people. He was the new champion of democracy.

VOTING REFORM. Adams and Clay did seem to represent a bygone generation, a time of three-cornered hats and powdered wigs. They were accustomed to a political game practiced by the upper class, a game in which appeals to the people were few and modest. In the 1820's, however, they faced a new kind of voter.

After the War of 1812, many states revised their constitutions. These documents had originally been drawn up during the Revolutionary War. Many of their provisions had reflected the social conditions of that period. For example, nearly all state constitutions said that a citizen had to own property to be eligible to vote. *The revisions undertaken after 1812 removed this restriction on voting in most states.* As a result, there was a great increase in the number of people qualified to vote. This was because almost all White adult males were now eligible to vote. Women, Blacks, and certain White males were still disqualified.

At first these newly qualified voters did not appear at the polls in great numbers. Political affairs, as represented by the Clay-Adams generation, seemed far removed from their interests. But with the coming of Jackson, they began to appear.

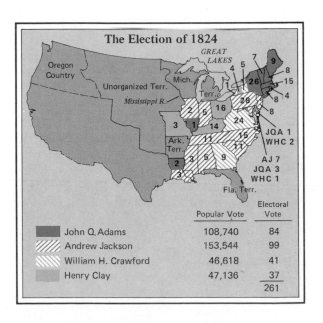

The Election of 1824

		Popular Vote	Electoral Vote
	John Q. Adams	108,740	84
	Andrew Jackson	153,544	99
	William H. Crawford	46,618	41
	Henry Clay	47,136	37
			261

JACKSON'S POPULARITY.

To many Americans Jackson was not simply a military hero. He had additional qualities that the new generation of American voters admired. A man of action, he seemed to care little for the diplomatic etiquette practiced by the older generation of politicians. *He appeared to be a man of iron, with the willful determination to get the job done.* He was a doer, not a thinker. In many ways he seemed to resemble the youthful republic he hoped to lead—rash, impulsive, belligerent, full of vitality and inventiveness, sometimes in error but never weak. He projected, in short, a public image with which a large segment of Americans wanted to identify their nation—and themselves.

ADAMS'S ADMINISTRATION: 1825–1829.

The Jacksonian cry of "corrupt bargain" was the first nail in John Quincy Adams's political coffin. Like his father, Adams was a brilliant man and a fine statesman. But he had the misfortune of being in the wrong place at the wrong time.

Adams had a grand vision of national greatness. He wanted the federal government to encourage the sciences and the arts and to establish a national university. His imagination was a century ahead of its time, but his political sense was a generation behind. He was stopped at every turn by the shrewdly led political opposition centered in Congress.

MARTIN VAN BUREN AND THE DEMOCRATIC PARTY.

With Jackson in angry retirement in Tennessee, a young senator from New York, Martin Van Buren, organized opposition to the Adams administration. *He formed an alliance between the southern sectionalists and northerners who disliked Adams and Clay.* It was a far-flung coalition, which included wealthy slave owners, northern workers, and western opponents of banks. Initially, it was held together only by a common regard for Andrew Jackson.

Van Buren's coalition called themselves Democratic Republicans. (After Jackson's election they shortened the name to Democrats.) Their opponents, the supporters of Adams and Clay, called themselves National Republicans.

THE TARIFF OF ABOMINATIONS.

Part of Van Buren's strategy involved turning Adams against himself. The Tariff of 1828 illustrates this strategy.

Adams and Clay favored high tariff duties to encourage American manufacturing. South Carolina and the rest of the South fumed when the subject was mentioned. New York and Pennsylvania favored the tariff.

To win the White House in 1828, the Jacksonians needed to win New York and Pennsylvania. So, in 1828 Van Buren came up with a plan. He had a friend introduce a bill in Congress to raise the tariff rates. The bill passed both houses, and President Adams signed it into law. It was the highest tariff enacted before the Civil War.

Van Buren then let New Yorkers know he had authored the bill. In the South, where the bill had been labeled "an abomination," he blamed it on Adams. Such antics earned Van Buren the nickname of The Little Magician. They also earned Andrew Jackson the White House in 1828.

THE ELECTION OF 1828.

Jackson swept into the Presidency in 1828 with ease. He carried every state in the South and West, plus New York and Pennsylvania. (See map, page 219.) For the first time a westerner would be in the White House. *Jackson would be the first President from a state that did not border the Atlantic.*

Feeling that the people's day had dawned, thousands had come to Washington to witness the inauguration. "A monstrous crowd of people is in this city," wrote Daniel Webster in awe. "I never saw anything like it before. Persons have come 500 miles to see General Jackson, and they really seem to think that the country is rescued from some dreadful danger."

Jackson delivered his inaugural address and then led the throng down Pennsylvania Avenue for a reception at the White House. There, they crowded into the mansion with their muddy boots, stood on the furniture to get a view of the President, and fought over the refreshments. Jackson, to avoid being crushed, was whisked out a back door. To relieve the congestion, punch and cake were served on the lawn—and the mob climbed through the windows to get to it. Democracy had come into its own—some called it King Mob.

THE RIVALRY OF VAN BUREN AND CALHOUN.

Jackson's first task was to mold into a political party the coalition that had brought him to office. His second task was to put down sectionalism and restore the national government's prestige. The two problems, as it turned out, were related.

The fragile coalition that had brought Jackson to office began falling apart soon after the election. Its strongest members were southerners, led by John C. Calhoun. Calhoun had made an agile leap from being

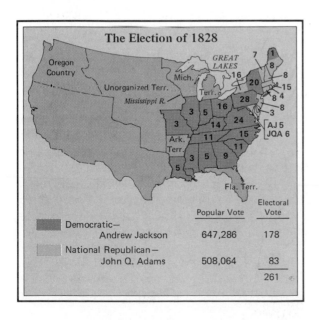

The Election of 1828

	Popular Vote	Electoral Vote
Democratic—Andrew Jackson	647,286	178
National Republican—John Q. Adams	508,064	83
		261

Vice-President under Adams to being Vice-President under Jackson. In fact, he and Van Buren, whom Jackson had named Secretary of State, both considered themselves heirs to the Presidency after Jackson retired. The resulting personal antagonism between the two reflected the North-South split within the party.

NULLIFICATION OF SOUTH CAROLINA.

Sectional hostility, which had been simmering since the Missouri controversy, began to boil during Jackson's first years in office. *The heat was coming from the Tariff of Abominations.*

In 1828 the South Carolina legislature published an essay entitled *South Carolina Exposition and Protest.* Although the legislature did not reveal the author's name, it was an open secret that the *Exposition* had been written by John C. Calhoun, the Vice-President of the United States. *In this document the tariff had been denounced as unconstitutional.* The argument used to support the essay's position had been based on the doctrine of states' rights.

Before the Constitution was ratified, argued the *Exposition*, the states had been independent units. They had not given up this independence by ratifying the Constitution. They had simply formed a compact, or contract, and created a federal government to execute the contract's terms.

According to those terms the government had only limited powers. And according to the *Exposition*, the states, not the Supreme Court, were the judges of what these powers were.

If the federal government were to go beyond its powers and enact an unconstitutional law, such as the tariff, a state could declare that law *null and void* within its boundaries. The law would then remain null and void until it was added to the Constitution as an amendment. Thus, the *Exposition* argued, a single state could block any controversial law until three fourths of the

On the way to his inauguration, Jackson was met by crowds of well-wishers at every town and station. Why was his inauguration different from those of other Presidents?

states approved it as a constitutional amendment.

The nullification arguments in the *Exposition* were an extension of the states' rights theory first put forth by Jefferson and Madison in 1798 in the Virginia and Kentucky Resolutions. ***The South, through this essay, hoped to protect its minority rights by claiming the power to veto federal laws.***

Null and void means having no legal force.

JACKSON'S REACTION TO NULLIFICATION.
Jackson was a southerner, a planter, and a slave owner, but he could not accept the thought of nullification. It threatened to bring the federal government to a standstill. No matter what the law, said Jackson, someone, somewhere, would want to nullify it, and ***ultimately the victim of***

nullification would be the federal government itself. So Jackson split with his Vice-President and, at Van Buren's urging, removed Calhoun's followers from the administration. In the following Presidential election, Jackson chose Van Buren as his running mate.

Jackson's opponent in 1832 was Henry Clay, who now had a firm grip on the National Republicans. In an effort to court the South, Clay supported a reduction in the tariff. But this reduction did not go far enough to suit South Carolina. Thus, in November 1832, a specially elected convention voted to nullify the tariff, and beginning in February 1833, federal customs duties could not be collected in the state of South Carolina.

CONFLICT AND COMPROMISE.
Jackson reacted in the expected fashion. He issued a proclamation denouncing the

220

nullifiers as rebels and threatening to march an army into South Carolina. Few doubted that he would carry out his threat. No other southern state had endorsed nullification. Nevertheless, it was also clear that if Jackson led an army into South Carolina, all the states in that section would leave the Union. Civil war loomed.

At the height of this crisis, Henry Clay worked out a compromise, meeting behind the scenes with Calhoun. They agreed on a new tariff act, which would reduce the tariff gradually over a period of 10 years. Calhoun also agreed to use his influence to secure a repeal of South Carolina's nullification ordinance. The administration cooperated, and Jackson signed the new tariff into law. On the same day he approved the Force Act, which gave him power to subdue South Carolina by military means.

The South Carolina convention met in March 1833. It repealed the ordinance that nullified the tariff and passed a new ordinance to nullify the Force Act. This last action was a face-saving gesture, and no one cared. The sectional crisis was ended. *By a judicious use of force and a willingness to compromise, Jackson had saved the Union.*

FORMATION OF THE WHIG PARTY.
Jackson's firm stand on nullification threw many southerners into Clay's camp. Calhoun, then completely alienated from the administration, formed a working alliance in Congress with Webster and Clay.

In 1834 the new coalition formally organized the Whig party. The name was a reference to the British Whig party whose members traditionally opposed royal authority. Hoping to rally popular support against Jackson's forceful actions as President, Henry Clay's Whigs dubbed Jackson King Andrew I.

With the formation of the Whigs, a second two-party system emerged. The political battle lines were clearly drawn once again—this time, Whigs versus Democrats.

Section Review

1. Mapping: Using the map on page 219, identify the states that voted for Jackson in the election of 1828. How did this vote indicate the strong role that regional thinking was beginning to play in American politics?
2. Identify or explain: John Quincy Adams, corrupt bargain, Martin Van Buren, John C. Calhoun.
3. Describe the doctrine of nullification. List the steps that Jackson took to oppose the doctrine of nullification. Use two columns, one labeled "threat" and the other one labeled "compromise."

Webster reacted to the nullification controversy with one of the greatest speeches ever given in the Senate. "Liberty and union," he thundered. "Now and forever, one and inseparable!"

3. The Meaning of Jacksonian Democracy

VOTER TURNOUT. By 1828 state laws permitted nearly all adult White men to vote. Jackson had nothing personally to do with this expansion of suffrage. It was largely completed by the time he took office. Jackson's contribution was to make those who could vote actually want to vote or to hold office.

Enlarging voter turnout is not a matter of changing laws. It is a matter of changing habits and attitudes. *In some way Jackson managed to persuade the common people that the political system worked for them and that it was responsive to their needs.*

THE SPOILS SYSTEM. In his first message to Congress, Jackson proclaimed that the duties of federal officers were so plain and simple that any honest person of intelligence could perform them. Here, indeed, was a new standard for federal service. Whereas John Adams had appointed only the rich and well-born and Jefferson had insisted on education and training, Jackson maintained that the government could be run by almost anyone.

Many believed that Jackson's election would mean a general housecleaning in the federal government. As a result, the people who had thronged to Washington, D.C., to witness his inauguration had included a large number of office seekers. Of course, Jackson did move to reward his supporters. But to do so he had to dismiss a number of followers of Adams and Clay from their positions.

Such dismissals disturbed many people. It was the first time that a substantial number of people had been dismissed from office for their political beliefs. When the opposition protested, a Jackson supporter defended the practice by saying, "To the victor belong the spoils of the enemy."

In that statement lay a new concept of party politics. To some Jacksonians, such as Van Buren, the political party was a war machine, and its sole purpose was that of gaining victory at the ballot box. Further, the purpose of victory was not to initiate new ideas or new policies but to reward faithful followers with political offices. This view of party politics came to be called the spoils system.

Although it ultimately led to political corruption and a decline in the quality of government officeholders, Jacksonians saw the spoils system as a positive move. *Jackson believed he was opening the federal government to the people.* He was also convinced that his system was giving more people more opportunities to serve. The new system seemed somehow more democratic than the old one.

THE KITCHEN CABINET. Jackson also opened the executive branch to new people. *Ignoring his official cabinet, which was splintered by the Van Buren-Calhoun rivalry, Jackson relied instead on a circle of informal advisers, whom his enemies dubbed "the kitchen cabinet."* Foremost among these was a Kentucky newspaper editor named Amos Kendall.

Kendall had been among the host of office seekers who had gone to Washington for Jackson's inauguration. He had also been among those who had won appointments. His was a minor post in the treasury. Soon, however, his writing ability came to Jackson's attention, and he was employed to write the President's public papers instead.

In 1830 Jackson, at Kendall's suggestion, invited another Kentucky newspaperman, Francis P. Blair, to Washington to start an administration paper, the *Washington Globe.* Blair had the common touch. He seemed to know exactly what average Americans thought, what they feared, and what they wanted. Under Blair's editorship, the *Globe* presented itself as the champion of the common people.

THE BANK'S ENEMIES. Jackson, Kendall, and Blair worked smoothly as a team. The best example of their teamwork and their ability to reach ordinary Americans is the episode known as the bank war. ***This battle between Jackson's administration and the Bank of the United States was the climax of Jacksonian Democracy.***

After a shaky start in the panic of 1819, the Bank of the United States became a useful and popular financial institution. Nicholas Biddle, its president from 1823 on, was a sound, responsible businessman, who kept the bank out of politics. Nevertheless, the bank had its enemies.

At this time the federal government minted coins, but it did not print paper money. As a result, bank notes were the nation's only currency. Since these were only as good as the reputation of the bank printing them, they varied greatly in value. Business people could keep track of their value, but the uninformed poor could not. Consequently, farmers and city workers distrusted bank notes and wanted to be paid in hard money—gold or silver coin. Thomas Hart Benton, the Jacksonian senator from Missouri, spoke for the hard-money view in

Political democracy worked in Jacksonian America because society was not divided into rigid social classes. On entering a country inn, such as the one portrayed above by John Lewis Krimmel, a French visitor to America—Alexis de Tocqueville—remarked, "We were introduced, as usual, into what is called the barroom . . . where the simplest as well as the richest . . . drink, and talk politics together, on the footing of the most perfect exterior equality." Does this painting portray any inequalities?

Congress. To Benton and his allies, the elimination of any bank would be quite a windfall. And eliminating the biggest one of them all, the Bank of the United States, would be considered a definite bonanza.

THE BANK VETO. Jackson criticized the bank in his early messages to Congress, but he made no move against it. The bank charter, issued by Congress in 1816, did not expire until 1836. Until then there was little Jackson could do about it.

In 1832, however, politics—in the person of Henry Clay—entered the scene. Running against Jackson in the election of 1832, Clay needed an issue, and the bank seemed perfect. This was especially true because the bank was popular in the North, especially in the key states of New York and Pennsylvania. If he could secure its recharter four years ahead of schedule, he might reap the political dividends. If Jackson vetoed the bank's recharter, the President would certainly reap nothing but disaster. Either Bid-

dle would get his bank or Clay would have his issue. It seemed foolproof, and Biddle agreed.

Clay's forces drafted a bill rechartering the Bank of the United States. It slipped easily through Congress. Even some Democrats voted for it. ***But when the bill reached Jackson's desk, he vetoed it without hesitation.*** "The bank is trying to kill me," he told Van Buren, "but I will kill it." Never in his life had Jackson turned down a challenge to duel.

Jackson's veto message, drafted by Amos Kendall, was a masterpiece. It pointed out that the bank was an arm of the rich that was useless to the poor. Among the bank's stockholders were a number of foreigners—in case of war, the message warned, there might be enemy influences in the nation's money system. The veto nevertheless hurt because the bank was popular in many places. Jackson was re-elected, but his margin of popular votes was no better than in 1828.

The first Bank of the United States was founded to control the nation's credit and currency. The early 19th century saw an American revival of Greek architectural style, and the bank's Philadelphia building is a good example of that movement. It was, for a time, referred to as the "Greek temple on Chestnut Street."

REMOVAL OF THE DEPOSITS.

Although Jackson's veto had left the bank mortally wounded, it still had four years before its original charter would expire in 1836. Thus, Jackson decided to finish it off. Removing the government money from the bank, Jackson reasoned, would eliminate its official position and reduce its operating funds. It would be indistinguishable from any other bank in Philadelphia.

The Secretary of Treasury, however, objected to taking the government's deposits out of the bank, since there was no other place to put them. So Jackson fired him. He fired the next Secretary, too, before finally finding the willing agent Roger B. Taney, his former Attorney General. In the fall of 1833, Taney (whom Jackson later named Chief Justice of the Supreme Court when John Marshall died in 1835) removed the government funds from the Bank of the United States and put them in selected state banks. These banks were called pet banks, because Jackson's opponents believed they were selected on the basis of their loyalty to the President.

Biddle retaliated by greatly limiting credit and by demanding that everyone owing the bank money pay up. Further, without government money Biddle had to restrict his operations somewhat. But he squeezed harder than necessary. In fact, it was soon clear that he was trying to cause a depression in order to build opposition to Jackson. Such actions proved only what the Jacksonians had been saying all along—the bank was a "monster" with too much power in irresponsible hands.

EFFECT OF THE BANK WAR.

Jackson and his friends regarded the destruction of the bank as a great victory for the common people against the rich. In reality it was a victory over the monopoly, since the states became more reluctant to allow business monopolies to exist. It also made the process of setting up a business easier.

BORN TO COMMAND.

OF VETO MEMORY.

HAD I BEEN CONSULTED.

KING ANDREW THE FIRST.

This represents a later, and decidedly different, view of Jackson, caricatured here as a king standing on the Constitution and the Bank of the United States. What is his source of power in the cartoon?

The demise of the bank was a step toward spreading the business enterprise among a large number of people. ***No longer would business be in the hands of a small group of merchants, as it had been during the time of the Federalists.*** To artisans, workers, farmers, and shopkeepers—all of whom aspired to getting ahead in the world—the government had brought new hope. That was the real meaning and significance of Jacksonian Democracy.

Section Review

1. Identify or explain: Amos Kendall, Thomas Hart Benton, Nicholas Biddle.
2. What was the spoils system? Was it a form of government corruption or an advance in democracy?
3. What was Jackson's kitchen cabinet?
4. Outline the steps Jackson took to destroy the Bank of the United States.

4. The Rise of the Whigs

BOOM AND BUST. Nicholas Biddle's economic squeeze was short-lived. *By 1835 the nation was filled with prosperity.* Southern cotton was again selling well in Europe. The nation had embarked on the construction of canals and railroads. State banks, no longer under the disapproving eye of the Bank of the United States, were lending money to anyone who asked for it. Soon, however, the banks found themselves swamped in a mass of paper currency and desperately short of gold.

The Jacksonians were worried. In the Senate, Thomas Hart Benton wailed that in place of one bank there were a thousand. Then, to curb the wild growth of paper currency, Jackson issued the *Specie Circular* in 1836. It directed federal land offices to accept only gold or silver currency in payment for public lands. Accordingly, people went to the banks for gold, but what they found were banks that had none.

When cotton prices collapsed in England, fear turned to panic and that panic led to a depression. The result was hard times, from 1837 to about 1843. The man who inherited the disaster was the President's hand-picked successor, Martin Van Buren.

THE ELECTION OF 1836. In 1835 the Democrats held a national Presidential nominating convention. The proceedings were dominated by the outgoing President, who had personally arranged Van Buren's nomination. Jackson had done this even though the New Yorker was not popular in the country. For the average voter there was not only too much mystery and intrigue surrounding Van Buren but also too much of the New Yorker about him to suit the South.

THE WHIG CANDIDATE. The Whigs thought they had a chance. What they needed was a candidate. First they thought of outdoing Jackson at his own game by finding someone even more rough-and-ready than he. Their eyes fell on David Crockett, a congressman from Tennessee. "Davy," as the Whigs nicknamed him, was an authentic frontiersman who hailed from the woods of west Tennessee.

Although uneducated and inexperienced, Crockett was a Whig, and Webster and Clay welcomed him with open arms. He toured New England at the Whigs' expense and was helped on his memoirs, *The Autobiography of Davy Crockett,* by a Whig newspaper reporter. As a Presidential candidate, though, Crockett never made it. He died in the Alamo in 1836 during the Texas revolution against Mexico.

In 1836 the Whigs ran a different candidate in every section of the country. They hoped that, by splitting the electoral vote, they would throw the election into the House of Representatives. The strategy failed and Van Buren won.

VAN BUREN AND THE DEPRESSION. *Van Buren's inability to do anything about the depression gave the Whigs new hope for 1840.* The hard times were the worst the nation had known. For the first time manufacturing was being hit by depression. There was also widespread unemployment. Finally, Whigs demanded government action. President Van Buren,

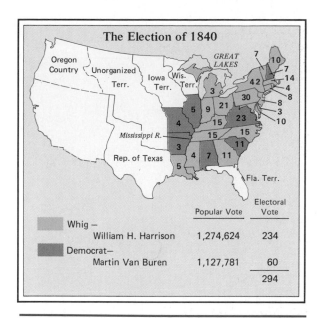

The Election of 1840

	Popular Vote	Electoral Vote
Whig — William H. Harrison	1,274,624	234
Democrat— Martin Van Buren	1,127,781	60
		294

however, rejected any sort of government interference in private business.

Such rejection allowed the Whigs to make a lot of Van Buren's remoteness from the people. Whig newspapers described him as living in princely splendor, eating from imported china with gold utensils. "Van, Van, is a used-up man," they chanted. And so it seemed.

THE LOG CABIN CAMPAIGN. In 1840 the Whigs at last found a candidate in the mold of Jackson—William Henry Harrison, or "Old Tip," a hero of the War of 1812. As Harrison's running mate they settled on John Tyler, an old Jeffersonian from Virginia. *The two candidates ran under the slogan "Tippecanoe and Tyler, too."*

The Whig convention closed without the drafting of a *platform. The convention decided instead to woo the voters with parades and picnics.* Then, when a Democratic newspaper sneered that Harrison would withdraw from the campaign if someone offered him a jug of hard cider, a pension, and a cabin to live in, the Whigs picked up the cue.

Although Harrison was born in a stately mansion, the Whigs portrayed him as a simple man of the frontier, aspiring to rise from log cabin to White House. They staged mass parades, led by people in coonskin caps and log cabin floats, and handed out jugs of cider.

A *platform* is a statement of the beliefs and policies of a political party, person, or group.

The strategy worked. Voters turned out in 1840 in record numbers—and they voted Whig. (See map, this page.) But the triumph was really Andrew Jackson's, for the Whigs had won only by imitating Jacksonian methods. Jackson had opened the government to the common people. His Presidency had been the symbol of promise and of opportunity—opportunity to get ahead in the world, to go from rags to riches, from log cabin to White House.

Section Review

1. **Mapping:** Using the map above, decide which state cast the most electoral votes for Harrison. Which state cast the most electoral votes for Van Buren?
2. Identify or explain: the *Specie Circular,* "Old Tip," Davy Crockett.
3. What strategy did the Whigs use in the election of 1836? Did it work?
4. List the causes of the economic depression between 1837 and 1840.

Chapter 9 Review

Bird's-Eye View

During the period immediately following the War of 1812, America's attention turned inward. Years of involvement in international affairs were followed by years in which many Americans were absorbed mainly with several national issues.

Much of the pressing business before the nation was related in one way or another to sectionalism. By the 1820's real sectional differences had surfaced within the United States. Citizens in different parts of the nation often had clashing political, social, and economic interests. These differences resulted in lively political controversies and disputes. Sometimes they even posed a very serious threat to national unity.

One of the most serious sectional disputes arose over the question of slavery. Should new states admitted to the Union be allowed to decide for themselves whether they were slave or free? This issue was resolved temporarily by the Missouri Compromise. In this agreement a line was drawn, dividing future slave states and free states at the 36th parallel. However, the challenge to slavery that had prompted the Compromise left a legacy of ill feeling between the North and South.

Southerners and westerners also differed from northerners in their opposition to high tariffs and to the policies of the Bank of the United States—both of which benefited the northern manufacturers.

The extension of suffrage—the right to vote—during this period contributed to the liveliness of the American political scene. The number of voters swelled as states made it possible for nearly all White adult males to vote.

In 1828 these new voters elected their candidate, Andrew Jackson, to the Presidency. As the acknowledged champion of the common people, Jackson acted to broaden participation in the federal government and to reduce the power of the Bank of the United States. He also initiated many important changes in the nature of American politics. Through the spoils system he began the practice of rewarding political supporters with government jobs. He was also the first President to have two cabinets—an official cabinet and an unofficial kitchen cabinet.

In addition, Jackson was largely responsible for the creation of two new political parties. Those who supported him in the election of 1824 started the Democratic party. Those who opposed his chosen successor, Martin Van Buren, in the election of 1836 formed the Whig party. In 1840 the Whig party elected its first President—William Henry Harrison.

Vocabulary

Define or identify each of the following:

null and void	Sequoyah	kitchen cabinet
platform	the spoils system	Davy Crockett
Specie Circular	Henry Clay	hard money

228

Review Questions

1. Explain the issues and provisions of the Missouri Compromise.
2. Compare the factors that led to the development of southern sectionalism with those that led to northern sectionalism.
3. John Quincy Adams did not receive a majority of either the popular or the electoral votes. How did he become President of the United States?
4. Describe the issues that led to the formation of the Whig party.
5. Explain the meaning of Jacksonian Democracy.

Reviewing Social Studies Skills

1. Using the map on page 214, answer the following:
   a. Explain the terms "free state" and "slave state."
   b. How many free states were there in 1819?
   c. How many slave states were there in 1819?
   d. Name the two states admitted to the Union as a result of the Missouri Compromise.
2. Compare the maps on pages 217 and 219, and answer the following questions:
   a. How many states voted for Adams in 1824? In 1828?
   b. How many states voted for Jackson in 1824? In 1828?
   c. Name the additional states that Jackson won in the election of 1828.
3. Make a chart entitled "Sectionalism in the United States, 1820–1840." List the basic positions taken by the North, the West, and the South on the issues of the tariff, slavery, the Bank of the United States, and states' rights.

Reading for Meaning

1. This chapter could probably be renamed "Jackson and the Advance of Democracy." Find five statements in the text that support the position taken by this new title.
2. This chapter could probably be renamed "Jackson and Power Politics." Find five statements in the text that support the position taken by this title. Which of the titles suggested in either question 1 or this question do you think is the more accurate description of Jackson's administration?
3. Consult your dictionary for a definition of the words "nullify" and "nullification." In your own words explain how these definitions apply to the events concerning nullification that are reported in the chapter.
4. Do you think the authors conveyed a positive, negative, or neutral opinion of Andrew Jackson? Cite at least two statements from the chapter to support your answer.

Bibliography

Stewart Holbrook's *Davy Crockett* (Random House) describes the wilderness adventures of this famous pioneer.

Esther Donty's *Forten the Sailmaker: Pioneer Champion of Negro Rights* (Rand-McNally) gives an interesting account of a Black businessperson in the early 1800's.

Unit 2 Review

Vocabulary

Define or identify each of the following:

constitution	confederation	tariff
democracy	federal	embargo
anarchy	secular	impressment
platform	emancipation	nationalism

Recalling the Facts

1. List the principal reasons for America's success in the Revolution.
2. Describe the difficulties of governing caused by the ineffectiveness of the Articles of Confederation.
3. What were the arguments used by the Federalists to win support for the Constitution?
4. Name the three branches of the United States government.
5. List several events that helped to develop and strengthen American nationalism.
6. The United States was deeply scarred by the War of 1812. Explain.
7. Name the obstacles that prevented national expansion.
8. How does sectionalism conflict with nationalism?
9. Explain the functions of the President, the Congress, and the Supreme Court.
10. Name the first Secretary of the Treasury.
11. List several powers denied to the federal government by the Constitution.
12. Name the two parties in the election of 1828.
13. What is meant by Jacksonian Democracy?
14. List the individual rights guaranteed by the Bill of Rights.
15. Who won the War of 1812?

History Lab

1. Using your local newspaper as a resource, clip and save five articles about the federal government. Then answer each of the questions below. In so doing, explain how each article relates to the Constitution.
   a. What officials are included?
   b. What branch of government is the article about?
   c. What article and section of the Constitution would your clipping apply to?
   d. What is the issue?
2. The Monroe Doctrine remains an important part of our national policy. Assume you are the Secretary of State and a South American nation has been threatened with invasion. What advice would you give to the President of the United States?
3. Assume you have been appointed to help a new nation write its constitution. Prepare an outline of the major elements you would include in such a document. Would you include a Bill of Rights?

Local History

1. Sectionalism still exists in the United States. People from one part of the nation are often easily distinguished by their speech patterns, food preferences, and clothing styles. Make a list of the unique characteristics or aspects of your area of the country.
2. The current two-party system of politics in the United States began in the period of history that you have just studied. In order to understand the workings of a party system, visit one of your local political party headquarters or contact the local committee chairperson. Offer your services in an upcoming election, and write a report on what you learned for your class.

Forming an Opinion

1. The Preamble to the Constitution established six goals for the people of the United States. List the six goals. Do you think these goals have been achieved? State the reasons for your answer.
2. The Equal Rights Amendment is intended to ensure that women have equality with men. Why is this an issue? Are you for or against the ERA? Explain why.
3. American Indian tribes are still suing the individual states and the federal government for violating treaties made during the 1800's. What is your opinion on this issue?

Time Line

Using the time line below, answer the following questions:
1. When did the Revolution begin and end?
2. How many years after the Declaration of Independence did the Constitution become the law of the land?
3. Who was President:
   a. When the Louisiana Territory was purchased?
   b. When the XYZ affair occurred?
   c. During the War of 1812?
   d. When Florida was purchased?
4. Make an expanded version of the time line below. It should contain the important events of the Revolutionary War. Begin it with the battles of Concord and Lexington, 1775, and end it with the Battle of Yorktown, 1781.

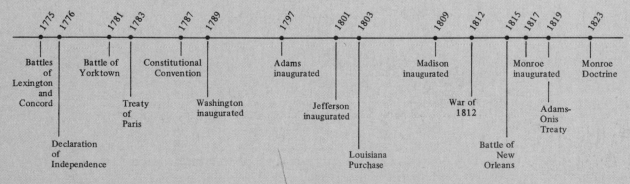

A House Dividing

American cities have always been built near water. Colonial cities were built on the shores of the bays and inlets along the Atlantic coast. Other cities were situated at river junctions or at points where rivers entered the Great Lakes. The only major city in the United States not located on a navigable waterway is Indianapolis, Indiana. This is because Indianapolis was founded after the invention of the railroad.

Cities were originally located near water because water was important to their livelihood. Commercial goods were moved by ship whenever possible, since overland travel was slow and expensive. Armies, too, were moved by water, whenever possible. Many inland cities began as forts, built to guard strategic river junctions. For example, St. Louis was a Spanish outpost near the mouth of the Missouri River. Pittsburgh (originally Fort Duquesne) began as a French sentinel post at the fork of the Ohio. Cincinnati (originally Fort Washington) was founded as an American army base during the Indian wars of the 1790's.

During the years covered in this unit, cities grew faster than at any other time in our history. Although the nation's population was increasing by about 30 percent every decade between 1820 and 1860, the cities were growing at about twice that rate. Setting the pace were the river towns of the Midwest.

The river-town success stories began in 1815, when the steamboat *Enterprise* puffed its way upriver from New Orleans to Pittsburgh. Previously, western traffic had been largely one way—downriver. On reaching their destinations, the rafts and flatboats had been broken up for lumber, and the boatmen had had to walk home overland. The steamboat, however, had changed all of this. It had turned the western rivers into two-way thoroughfares.

In the 1850's the steamboat gave way to railroads, and life in the river cities changed. A few of them adapted to this new form of steam locomotion. Pittsburgh, Cincinnati, and St. Louis became important rail centers. Other towns, which had never benefited much from their water location, blossomed under the magic of iron rails. Of these towns, Chicago and Cleveland are prime examples. But the age of the river cities was over. It had been a colorful chapter in the history of American communities.

John Casper Wild's "Cincinnati"

Chapter 10

1820-1850

People of Conscience

"In all the four quarters of the globe, who reads an American book?" sneered an English journalist in 1819. "Or goes to an American play? Or looks at an American picture or statue?"

The remark had hurt, but it was true. Although America had achieved its political independence nearly a half-century before, it was still intellectually dependent on Europe. Americans read British novelists and poets, and for artistic inspiration, they crossed the Atlantic to Europe. Culturally, America was still a colony.

Yet, there were signs of change. In that very year, 1819, Washington Irving produced *The Sketchbook,* the first piece of American writing to win international recognition. At the same time, James Fenimore Cooper began a series of novels, called *The Leatherstocking Tales,* based on life in the wilderness. Then, before the decade was out, both became international celebrities, making widely acclaimed tours of Britain and the Continent.

The pace of literary output was increasing with each passing decade. In one brief interval (1850–1855), the nation was treated to Nathaniel Hawthorne's *The Scarlet Letter* and *The House of the Seven Gables,* Herman Melville's *Moby Dick,* Harriet Beecher Stowe's *Uncle Tom's Cabin,* Henry David Thoreau's *Walden,* Henry Wadsworth Longfellow's *Song of Hiawatha,* Walt Whitman's *Leaves of Grass,* and four volumes of essays and poems by John Greenleaf Whittier. For such a short span of years, it had been a spurt of literary creativity unmatched in American history. Some have called it the American Renaissance.

Chapter Objectives

After you have finished reading this chapter, you should be able to:
1. Apply your knowledge about the writers and artists of the mid-19th century, and explain their contributions to the "burst of creative critical energy [that] . . . swept the nation. . . ."
2. List the reforms made in education, treatment of mental illness, temperance, and women's rights in the mid-19th century.
3. Describe the characteristics of slave life.
4. Define abolition, and trace the development of the abolitionist movement in the North.

Accompanying this burst of creativity was a self-conscious examination of American society. *Every aspect of society came under careful scrutiny, and where wrongs appeared, someone came forth to try setting them right.* This burst of social reform coincided with the political movement led by Andrew Jackson. It was another step in the march of democracy.

Most of these movements were centered in the parts of the country undergoing rapid social change. In New England the intellectual influence of church and clergy was lessening, the poorer farmers were moving west, the Irish and German immigrants were pouring off incoming ships, and the canals and railroads were under construction. New England was also a center of literary activity. Many of the nation's foremost writers lived within a few miles of Boston.

Western New York was a center of social reform. Indeed, so many heated crusades swept across that region that it became known as "the burnt-over district." A flood of farmers settled the lands formerly occupied by the Iroquois; the construction of the Erie Canal opened new markets. And for a time such easy access to the Erie Canal made wheat-growing New York the nation's breadbasket.

1. "The Stammering Century"

AN EXCITING TIME. "The stammering century"—that is what newspaper editor Horace Greeley called his own time. *He was referring to American society's search for improvement—to the chatter of ideas and suggestions, the cure-alls, and the crusades.* What makes a people examine itself and search for improvement? Why are some times and some places more exciting, more stimulating, than others? There are no absolute answers to these questions—only suggestions. But the suggestions are that at this

time there was a climate of freedom in America that encouraged inquiry and criticism. This was because the land was new and still developing. Since its habits of thinking were not set, the new, even the unusual, ideas were tolerated.

A FREE SPIRIT: HENRY DAVID THOREAU. The New England essayist Henry Thoreau (1817–1862) loved this atmosphere of freedom, and he struggled to preserve it. He disliked factories, machines, and cities because they stifled him. They made life too complicated. "Nature is sufficient," he declared, and to prove it he spent two years alone in a cabin on Walden Pond, near Concord, Massachusetts.

One aspect of social injustice that aroused Thoreau's anger was slavery. He rejected any government that would tolerate it. Believing that the war with Mexico in the 1840's was an effort to extend slave territory, he refused to pay his taxes and went to jail. *In an essay entitled "Civil Disobedience," Thoreau argued that the conscientious person is duty-bound to disobey unjust laws, and ought to resist a government concerned only with power and glory.* Thoreau's essay was not only sounded throughout 19th-century America, it was also sounded down through the generations and throughout the world.

THE SELF-RELIANT INDIVIDUAL: RALPH WALDO EMERSON. What made New England the center of both the literary and the social reform movements? Religious change was certainly one factor. From the time of the earliest colonial settlements, both the Congregational Church and Calvinist theology had had a strong hold on the people of New England. In Massachusetts the Congregational Church had even been the state-supported church until 1833. (Even before 1833 the church had been splitting into opposing factions.)

The most important break involved the **Unitarians.** These people objected to the belief in predestination, a Calvinist theory that the fate of every individual, whether saint or sinner, was determined before birth. Unitarians felt that such a belief eliminated moral responsibility. If all events were predestined, how could any individual be blamed for sinning?

Unitarians were so named because they believed in a single God, rather than the Trinity—Father, Son, and Holy Spirit. Christ, they felt, was great and good, but not divine.

Instead, the Unitarians emphasized the free individual, who was capable of choosing between good and evil. They encouraged each individual to study the Bible for its truths, and they welcomed sincere differences of opinion.

Ralph Waldo Emerson began his career as a Unitarian minister in Boston. But in 1832 he abandoned his pulpit to become "a preacher to the world." As a lecturer, essayist, and poet, Emerson achieved world fame. *Throughout Emerson's writings ran the Unitarian themes of self-reliance and tolerance.* He urged the people to stand on their own feet, to respect their fellow beings, and to improve their world. To his audiences Emerson's philosophy was a trumpet call to reform. Like 18th-century deism, Unitarianism was a religion of reason.

THE SECOND GREAT AWAKENING. The 1820's and 1830's also witnessed a revival of evangelism similar to the colonial Great Awakening. This movement spread far beyond the bounds of New England, however. The center of it, in fact, was western New York State. *There, Charles Grandison Finney, a spellbinding*

This painting, called "Taking the Census," is by Francis William Edwards. It shows a census taker in 1850. The census count for that year was 23,191,876. The Constitution requires a census every 10 years.

Sidenote to History

Democracy and the Machine

New inventions and new machines were transforming the American landscape in the 1830's and 1840's. The locomotive, the iron T-rail, and the airbrake revolutionized transportation. The sewing machine changed the home, and the typewriter altered the office. The telegraph offered instant communication across a continent, and the steamship narrowed the oceans. But no invention of the age had a greater social impact than the rotating cylinder press. Nor had one contributed more to democracy.

Invented in Germany in 1814, the cylinder press had changed dramatically the art of printing. Previously, words had been impressed on a sheet of paper by a block containing lead type, which had been smeared with ink. Printing had involved several operations and considerable time. This was because the printer had to place each sheet, one by one, under the press. Then, each time, in order to actually print something, the printer had to turn a screw to lower the block. The fastest printers could produce no more than a few hundred papers a day. As a result, newspapers in early America went only to the wealthy.

With the invention of the cylinder press, type could be imbedded onto a rotating cylinder, so that strips of paper could speed by it and rapid printing could take place. Powered by steam, the cylinder press could turn out thousands of copies a day. It reduced the cost of a newspaper to a penny and put one within reach of every person.

The *New York Sun,* begun in 1833 by a printer named Benjamin H. Day, was the first of the penny papers. It openly sought the readership of the poor and the less educated, and avoided politics and diplomacy. Instead, it concentrated on crime and human-interest stories. Circulation boomed, and it remained the nation's largest-selling paper until after the Civil War.

Day's paper also broke ground in the ways of selling news. Following the methods of London publishers, Day had hired people to sell his daily paper on the street corner, the idea being that no one could pass by a stack of papers without wanting to "read all about it." By the time Day retired from the newspaper business in the 1850's, the news vendor, the scoop, and the human-interest story had become important assets to newspaper selling throughout the country.

The person who made the penny press respectable was Horace Greeley, who founded the *New York Tribune* in 1841. An admirer of Henry Clay, Greeley was a solid Whig in politics. But he was also a born reformer, who endorsed every crusade that came along, from prohibition to women's rights.

The *Tribune* was a solid, informative paper, not given to sensational stories. At a penny a copy, nearly everyone could afford to buy it. And since it also sold widely outside New York City, it helped to convey, far and wide, the latest political theories and social ideas. As a result, the *Tribune* helped to produce a better informed, more responsible electorate.

The penny press was one step toward the advancement of popular education. It was a step made possible by the machine.

---

preacher, stormed from town to town, spreading the word of the Gospel.

Finney's message was a simple one—any sinner could be redeemed through Christ if he or she would repent, confess past errors, and start a new life. The new life was to be one of piety, upright behavior, and good works. The good works were to be the link between religion and society. The new convert, as God's servant, would be obliged to

Frontier families wanted a religion of exhilaration rather than contemplation. What is the mood of this group at the revival meeting?

serve God's will by bettering the world—specifically, by reforming his or her society.

Thoreau, Emerson, and Finney represented the forces behind this burst of creative critical energy that swept the nation in the mid-19th century. They stood for the revolutionary spirit, which viewed government with a critical eye. They also believed in the free, self-reliant individual, as well as an emphasis on good works and social reform.

Section Review

1. Identify or explain: Washington Irving, Henry David Thoreau, Ralph Waldo Emerson, Unitarian, Charles Grandison Finney.
2. List three important works of literature produced in the period spanning from 1850–1855.
3. List Emerson's most important ideas about the individual and society. How were these ideas related to the beliefs of the Unitarian religion?
4. Compare the ideas of Emerson with those of Thoreau. What basic theme do they have in common?

2. The Age of Reform

THE COMING OF PUBLIC EDUCATION. "In a republic, ignorance is a crime," declared Horace Mann, the great educational reformer of Jacksonian America. If the ordinary citizen was to be given the vote, thought Mann, then the ordinary citizen must be educated.

Since colonial times New England towns had been required by law to maintain public elementary schools. Elsewhere in the nation most schools were church-maintained or private. The step beyond the elementary schools was the academies, the forerunners of modern high schools. And these were privately operated, even in New England. In the South the sons and daughters of the well-to-do had private tutors. In the West, such schools, where they existed, were generally inadequate. By and large, education in early America was limited to the wealthy.

By the 1820's, however, the new democratic spirit had brought demands for expanded public education. The first public high school opened in Boston in 1821, and six years later Massachusetts required all towns of 500 or more families to maintain high schools at public expense. In the

1830's New York and Pennsylvania followed Massachusetts' example. They set up state systems of elementary education. By the 1860's free elementary education was available to nearly all children in the North. Outside New England, secondary education was still in the hands of the private academies.

HORACE MANN AND THE PROFESSIONAL TEACHER. Even in Massachusetts, elementary education was informal and uneven. Although the children learned a bit of reading and writing and were exposed to arithmetic, the quantity and quality varied from school to school. There was no standard curriculum. Teachers were often part-time employees who kept only a few pages ahead of the students.

Horace Mann, who became secretary of the Massachusetts Board of Education in 1837, set out to change that. He organized the local districts into a statewide system and introduced a uniform curriculum for teaching. On Mann's recommendation the legislature created normal schools, special colleges for the training of teachers. Imitated widely across the North, notably by Henry Bernard in Connecticut and Rhode Island, *Mann's reforms made education a profession.*

IMPROVEMENTS IN PRISONS. The nation's prisons also caught the attention of reformers. There were few prisons in early America. In general, criminals were punished by a public whipping, a branding with a hot iron, a public display, or a fine. Prisons were for those who could not pay their debts and for the insane, who were considered dangerous. *In the mid-18th century, the Italian reformer Beccaria (bake-uh-REE-uh) advanced the idea that the purpose of punishment was not revenge but the reform of the criminal.* Under this concept prisons were to be educational institutions, designed to make useful citizens of criminals.

New York adopted Beccaria's idea. In 1816 its legislature authorized the construction of a state penitentiary at Auburn, which was completed in 1824. In it each convict had a separate cell, but during the day all convicts worked in a common shop. The goods produced by their labor financed the entire cost of running the prison. To state legislatures this was the most attractive feature of all. By 1840 some 12 states had penitentiaries based on the Auburn plan.

DOROTHEA DIX'S CRUSADE FOR THE MENTALLY ILL. Not only the conditions, but also the populations in prisons needed careful examination. On a Sunday morning in March 1841, Dorothea Dix, a Massachusetts teacher, was asked to give religious instruction in the Cambridge, Massachusetts, city jail. Today it is difficult even to imagine what she saw there—drunkards, vagrants, debtors, orphans, hardened criminals, and the mentally ill crowded into unheated, filthy cells and cages. Men, women, and children were thrown together without regard for age, sex, or offense.

That day marked the beginning of a one-woman crusade for improving the plight of the mentally ill. It took Dorothea Dix through almost every state in the Union and through half the countries in Europe.

She began with a two-year survey of every jail, prison, and poorhouse in Massachusetts. She kept a careful record of what she saw, each day filling her notebook with new evidence of shocking cruelty and neglect. In 1843 she presented her findings to the state legislature. She called attention to the medical research indicating that insanity was an illness; victims needed to be in hospitals, not jails.

Supported by such prominent figures as Horace Mann, Dorothea Dix persuaded the assembly to finance a special hospital for the insane. She then undertook a nationwide campaign for publicly supported mental hospitals, using the tactics that had worked in Massachusetts.

Few people have had so direct an impact on an area of American life as Dorothea Dix. In 1843 there were 13 mental hospitals in the United States; by 1880 there were 123. Most states had stopped the whipping of prisoners, and men and women were being housed separately. And the laws requiring imprisonment for debt had been repealed. When she died in 1887, an English doctor called Dorothea Dix "the most useful and distinguished woman that America has ever produced."

WOMEN AND THE TEMPERANCE MOVEMENT. Dorothea Dix was not the only woman caught up in the reform movement. *Women were heavily involved in every reform of the day.* They were among the first to launch a crusade against alcoholic drink. But to their dismay, they were

Sidenote to History

Margaret Fuller

Margaret Fuller was an author, critic, teacher, feminist, and revolutionary. She was born at the beginning of the 19th century, and she helped to influence the intellectual growth of the United States. Europeans at this time looked down on Americans, but Margaret Fuller did much to change that.

Fuller had been born into a well-to-do Massachusetts family and was sent to the best schools for women. Soon she became friends with many learned people. By her early 20's she was recognized as an astounding intellect. But the career choices open to women during the early 1800's were limited. Most educated women became teachers. And that's the route Margaret Fuller followed.

While teaching, Fuller kept up her own studies and communicated with friends in the transcendentalist movement. Transcendentalism was a philosophy popular in New England in the 1830's and 1840's. Along with Margaret Fuller, Ralph Waldo Emerson and Henry David Thoreau were among its most famous advocates.

In 1840 Fuller joined Emerson in publishing a magazine of literary criticism, called the *Dial*. One of her feminist essays was later expanded into a book, *Women in the 19th Century*.

Published in 1845, this book soon became a leading work on American feminism.

In 1844 Horace Greeley, publisher of the *New York Tribune*, asked Margaret Fuller to join the newspaper. He wanted her to write on the current authors and leading questions of the day. After her acceptance Greeley sent her abroad as the *Tribune's* foreign correspondent, knowing that her reputation would gain her access to the great minds of Europe. While in Europe, Fuller met the English poet Wordsworth, the Italian patriot Mazzini (maht-TSEE-nee), the French author and feminist George Sand, and the Polish pianist and composer Frederic Chopin.

In 1847 Margaret Fuller met and married an Italian noble, and both became involved in Italy's fight for independence. When Rome was being attacked by French forces, Fuller was running an emergency hospital and carrying supplies to her husband's post in the city. When the revolutionary cause failed, she and her family fled to Florence.

Fuller, her husband, and their child soon left Italy, headed for the United States. They had taken passage on a ship bound for New York in 1850. But when the ship was destroyed in a storm just outside New York Harbor, the family was killed.

Margaret Fuller's talents and accomplishments were great. Her legacy is stated in her own words: "Very early, I knew that the only object in life was to grow."

This scene is of a temperance rally. Liquor is being burned in the center of town. Temperance laws were passed by towns, counties, and states in the 1800's. Why do you think there was support for the temperance movement? Who do you think opposed temperance?

not allowed a leading role in the ***temperance*** movement. Nor were the women delegates at national meetings allowed to speak or vote. These and similar experiences soon convinced women that they could do little to change the world until they secured their rights.

People who advocated ***temperance*** would tolerate temperate, or moderate, drinking. Advocates of total abstention (called teetotalers) wanted to prohibit the sale and use of all alcoholic beverages, even beer and wine.

THE PLIGHT OF WOMEN. *Women were certainly second-class citizens in the early republic.* In New England, girls attended the common elementary schools, and elsewhere the daughters of the rich often had tutors. But education for most young women ended at the eighth grade. In general, secondary schools were closed to girls. And there were no colleges for women at all.

The belief that women were intellectually inferior to men was the basis of the argument used to support this state of affairs.

241

Mrs. Miller was the first woman to wear this costume—considered outrageously masculine. However, Amelia Bloomer, who adopted and publicized the costume, got credit for it. The name "bloomers" also stuck because it was funnier than "millers." The trousers, worn under a shortened skirt, were gathered at the ankles, and they allowed women more freedom of movement. Why were people eager to ridicule this outfit?

Often, as the British reformer Mary Wollstonecraft noted, this belief and the limitations it caused forced the expected results to occur. When a dinner ended, for example, women had to leave the table so the men could freely discuss the topics of the day. It was believed that women were incapable of talking intelligently about such matters as current events and that certain subjects were fit to be discussed by men only.

Women also had no political rights. Legally, unmarried female minors were the dependents of male relatives. Adult women were not legally dependent on male relatives, although they might be economically dependent on them. A married woman's property belonged to her husband. A woman had little protection against cruel and violent treatment by her husband. Some states allowed divorce for cruelty. In other states women could sue for legal separation. However, both courses were often costly and difficult to pursue.

THE EDUCATION OF WOMEN. *One of the first objectives of the women's rights movement was the establishment of secondary schools and colleges for young women.* The Troy Female Seminary, begun in 1821 by Emma Willard, was one of the first secondary schools for women. Financed by the city of Troy, New York, the academy specialized in the training of elementary-school teachers. It performed this valuable service until women were admitted to state normal schools.

Originally, Emma Willard's goal had been to create a system of state-financed colleges for young women. This plan was abandoned, however, when she was ignored by the male politicians, whose help she needed to convince the state legislatures of her idea. Still, colleges for women were soon founded. But their support came not from state or federal governments, but from private citizens and private funds.

In 1836 Mary Lyon founded Mount Holyoke College at South Hadley, Massachusetts. She had envisioned a small enrollment. But even at the beginning of its second year, 400 applicants had to be turned away for lack of room. On November 1, 1848, the first medical school for women opened in Boston. Two years later the second one was organized in Philadelphia.

The first coeducational college in the

Sidenote to History

Amelia Bloomer and the Battle Over Dress Reform

The debate over women's dress reform began as something of a joke, but for women the problem was real. Women's fashions of the 1850's were impractical, unhealthy, and sometimes dangerous. Skirts flowed in a "Great Pyramid," from a tiny waist to a wide, floor-length hem. To achieve the effect women pinched their waists with corsets. This was sometimes done so tightly that women injured their organs. The skirt, which required more than 18 meters (20 yards) of material, was so massive that it was difficult to get through doorways and halls. An accidental brush against a fireplace, an oven, or a lighted candle was a constant danger. By hampering women's activities, the dress symbolized, perhaps even contributed to, their dependent role in society.

The debate began when a conservative newspaper editor in upstate New York jokingly suggested that those demanding equality for women ought to wear pantaloons in imitation of men. Amelia Jenks Bloomer, also in the publishing business, promptly took up the idea.

Amelia Bloomer had long sponsored a variety of reforms, including temperance and women's rights. Her home was Seneca Falls, New York, and both she and her husband had attended the Seneca Falls Convention of 1848. Her newspaper, *The Lily,* had been not only the first newspaper owned and edited by a woman, but also the first one devoted to the interests of women. When the rival editor made the sneer, she was ready to take up the cause of dress reform.

Another woman ready to participate in the cause was Elizabeth Smith Miller. On her honeymoon in Switzerland, Mrs. Miller had visited a hospital where women were recuperating from the damage wrought by the tight corsets. For their comfort these patients were wearing Turkish pantaloons. The pantaloons were gathered at the ankles and partially covered by knee-length skirts.

Elizabeth Miller brought the costume home to the Seneca Falls circle. Amelia Bloomer then adopted it and began broadcasting its advantages in *The Lily.* Soon, newspapers around the country picked up the story, and the Bloomer costume became a symbol of the women's rights movement (as well as a source of masculine mirth).

Although it was a useful idea, the costume was ahead of its time. The majority of women in the 1850's had neither the education nor the independence to make such a revolutionary change in their customs. The controversy over clothing had also obscured the more important issues, such as womens' legal rights. Amelia Bloomer herself recognized this and abandoned the costume after a short time, though it remained forever associated with her name. Instead, she devoted the rest of her long life to the temperance movement and to women's suffrage. She died in 1894, a quarter century before women got the vote. She would have applauded, we can be sure, the revolution in women's dress that began in the 1890's and that continued until after the suffrage amendment was passed.

Wesleyan College, in Macon, Georgia, which opened in 1836, was one of the first colleges for women in this country. It was originally called the Georgia Female College.

United States was Oberlin College in Ohio, founded in 1833 by an antislavery group. Oberlin was a pioneer in Black education, graduating some 250 Blacks by the time of the Civil War. Its first woman student was Lucy Stone, a New Englander who wanted to study for the ministry. Although the college omitted her from the class list when she graduated in 1850, she went on to become a nationally known feminist and opponent of slavery.

Antioch College, which opened in September 1835 under the leadership of Horace Mann, was the second college to welcome male and female students on an equal footing. Both Oberlin and Antioch were privately run colleges. The first public college to open its doors to women was the University of Iowa in 1856.

THE SENECA FALLS CONVENTION.
Elizabeth Cady Stanton, Lucretia Mott, and three other New York women called a meeting in 1848 at Seneca Falls, New York. There, over 100 people gathered to inaugurate officially the movement for women's rights in America. The participants included some men, among them leaders of the antislavery movement.

The Seneca Falls Convention issued the first formal declaration of the rights of women. Significantly, it was modeled on Thomas Jefferson's Declaration of Independence. In fact, its opening words echoed those of the 1776 declaration: "When, in the course of human events, it becomes necessary for one portion of the family of man to assume among the powers of the earth a position different from that which they have hitherto occupied, but one to which the laws of nature and of nature's God entitle them, a decent respect to the opinions of mankind requires that they should declare the cause which impel them to such a course."

The declaration went on to list the ways in which women were being denied their rightful place in American society. It reminded the public that women: could not vote, had no say in making the laws they were supposed to obey, were barred from all but the least desirable jobs, had limited educational opportunities, and were not allowed to own property or, in many cases, to dispose of the wages they had earned.

In their concluding statement the framers of the Seneca Falls declaration admitted that they anticipated "no small amount of misunderstanding, misrepresentation, and ridicule . . ." And ridiculed they were. Most men—and women—jeered at the convention, its members, and its goals.

THE MOVEMENT ACHIEVES SOME SUCCESS.
The leaders of the movement were determined. They made good their pledges in the declaration to "employ

agents, circulate tracts, petition the State and National legislatures, and try to enlist the pulpit and the press" on their behalf. And through their unrelenting efforts, they had some success. In the 1850's, for example, a number of states adopted laws that gave married women limited rights to control their own property. Unmarried women were granted the right to sue in court.

Accomplishment of the convention's prime objective—that of giving women the right to vote—took nearly 75 years. This was because state legislatures were in the hands of men—only a voter could run for public office and only men could vote. Furthermore, most politicians and legislators had little interest in sharing their power with anyone, least of all women.

WOMEN TAKE A LEADING ROLE IN THE ANTISLAVERY MOVEMENT. At least one prominent American took the Seneca Falls Convention and its declaration seriously—the Black reformer Frederick Douglass. He recognized in the proceedings at Seneca Falls a spirit of reform that could work not only for the rights of women but for the rights of all oppressed groups. *This crusading spirit led virtually all the leaders of the women's rights movement to take a leading role in the antislavery movement.* Recognition of their own plight had given these women a special sympathy for the plight of Black slaves.

Women were among the most effective speakers in the antislavery movement. They attracted much larger audiences than male *abolitionists.* Angelina Grimke (GRIM-key) was the daughter of a wealthy South Carolina planter. She was such a powerful orator that her husband, the noted preacher Theodore Weld, insisted that she share the platform with him wherever he spoke.

An *abolitionist* is one who strongly favors doing away with something that he or she thinks is wrong—in this case, slavery.

Angelina Grimke, her sister Sarah, and most other women's rights advocates had come to the women's rights movement via the abolitionist movement. It was the result of the discrimination encountered on their antislavery lecture tours. Such discrimination had made them determined feminists, as well as dedicated abolitionists.

Women's rights reformers were not the only ones to be attracted to the antislavery movement. Human bondage was the most serious problem in American society; it was the wrong that cried the loudest for redress. By the 1840's it had become the focal point of the entire reform impulse in America. But to understand this movement, it is necessary first to understand the American institution of slavery itself.

Section Review

1. Identify or explain: Horace Mann, Dorothea Dix, Emma Willard, Angelina Grimke, Lucy Stone, Oberlin College.

2. Draw a chart entitled "An Age of Reform." Divide the paper into three columns, marking them with the headings "Education," "Prisons," and "Facilities for the Mentally Ill." Next, divide the chart in half horizontally. Using the information in this chapter, list in the top half the conditions before reform. In the bottom half, list the changes made by the reformers.

3. Describe some of the advances made in the early movement for women's rights. Why was education so important to the leaders of the movement?

4. Many of the members of the different reform movements united in a crusade against slavery. In a brief paragraph, explain what these movements had in common.

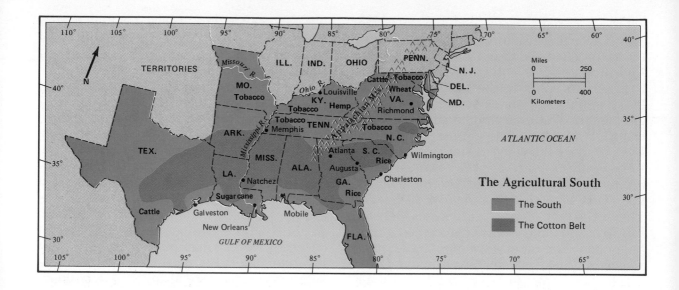

The Agricultural South
- The South
- The Cotton Belt

3. The Cotton Kingdom

THE CLIMATE. "Let us begin by discussing the weather." That is the way one historian began a book on the South, and his emphasis was certainly appropriate. *The southern climate—long, hot summers; rare frosts; and abundant rainfall— determined its history.* Climate and soil had combined to make it an ideal place for growing staples—tobacco, sugar, and cotton—which were in world demand. (See map above.) From 1815 until the Civil War (1861–1865), cotton had secured the nation's place in the world marketplace. "Cotton is king!" cried a southern member of Congress on the eve of the Civil War—and many thought it was true.

COTTON AND SLAVERY. Like northern industrialists, southern planters invested their profits in things that would increase production. *They invested in slavery because it was profitable to the cotton industry.* Slaveholders also earned good returns on their investments. This was because the price of slaves rose steadily. At the time of the Revolution a field worker sold for about $500. By the time of the Civil War the price had risen to about $1,500. Furthermore, slavery was a very flexible labor system. Slaves could be employed not only as field workers and house servants, but in a variety of other skilled and unskilled occupations as well. Slaves could work at the skilled crafts; on construction gangs; and in iron foundries, textile mills, and tobacco factories. Still, their labor and their skills were most profitable to the cotton industry.

Although cotton had been grown in colonial times, it had been grown only for home use. This was because the processing of the plant had been time-consuming—the seeds had had to be separated from the fiber by hand. *In 1793, however, the processing of cotton—and the economy of the South— was revolutionized by the invention of the cotton gin.* This machine could separate the seeds from the fiber by the turn of a handle.

The inventor, Eli Whitney, was a Yale graduate who had been working as tutor to the children of a Georgia planter. His invention tripled cotton production in 10 years. By 1860 cotton represented nearly two thirds of all American exports.

Cotton was also profitable for another reason: it was easy to grow. Planting, weeding, and picking were simple operations, and they could be performed by large groups of slaves with little supervision. Thus, planters were encouraged to clear more and more land for cotton growing and to increase their slaveholdings accordingly. In the fertile cotton belt of Alabama and Mississippi, plantations of 100 or more slaves became commonplace. It could be said, in fact, that cotton stamped slavery on the South. (See graph below.)

THE GROWING OF TOBACCO.

Tobacco, in contrast, was a difficult crop to raise. It required transplanting, worming, and regular removal of unwanted leaves. As a result, tobacco could be grown as efficiently on small farms as on large plantations. Thus, in the tobacco states, Virginia

and Maryland, there was often a slave surplus. Planters in those states could make additional profits by selling their extra slaves to people in the cotton-growing states.

SOUTHERN SOCIETY.

Actually, southern farmers raised more corn than cotton. *Cotton was the "cash crop," grown for export. It was also the crop of the wealthy.* Fewer than a third of the planters in the South owned slaves. In fact, in the mountains of western Virginia, Kentucky, and Tennessee, slavery was almost unknown. Farms there looked much the same as those in Ohio or Pennsylvania.

The farmers without slaves concentrated on corn and other grains, which they ate themselves and fed to their livestock. Occasionally, they would take a cow or pig to market. But they never knew anything of international trade. The mountains kept the people isolated—and comparatively poor.

FREE BLACKS.

There were about 250,000 free Blacks in the South, and the various legal regulations had placed them at the bottom of the social scale. Also, southern Whites regarded free Blacks with suspicion. Even when the Blacks kept to themselves, they were considered a threat. This was because their very freedom made other slaves envious, which in turn inspired uprisings. *Thus, the position of free Blacks deteriorated rapidly as slavery fastened itself to the South.* Free Blacks were eventually required to carry passes when traveling. They could not possess weapons or assemble in groups. Nor could they testify in court against Whites. And, although taxed, they could not vote. Furthermore, state laws made the freeing of slaves difficult. Newly freed persons were usually required to leave the state.

Such regulations clearly made free Black people second-class citizens. *Unwanted in the South, many might have moved to the North, except that conditions in the North were not much better.* When one wealthy

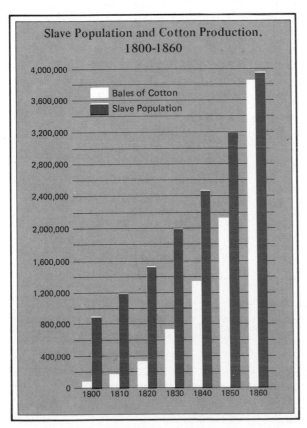

Slave Population and Cotton Production, 1800-1860

□ Bales of Cotton
■ Slave Population

Virginian freed his 300 slaves and financed their way to Ohio, Ohio would not let them in.

THE PLANTER GENTRY. *At the other end of the social scale were the gentlemen planters.* These were a tiny fraction of the population. The Census Bureau defined a planter as a farmer who owned 20 slaves or more. In 1860 there were 50,000 people in this category, or about two percent of the rural population. Yet, their wealth, social standing, and political power gave them an influence far out of proportion to their numbers.

Farmers with only a few slaves managed their slaves alone, often working in the fields with them. A family that owned only one or two slaves usually shared with their slaves their homes and dinner tables. The large planters, however, had overseers to manage their estates. Those with more than 100 slaves usually had several plantations, each under the supervision of the overseer. On the largest establishments the overseers placed "drivers" in charge of the slave groups. A driver was supposed to see that his group's assigned task was carried out. Most overseers were White. The drivers were slaves.

Growing crops for the world market was a highly competitive business, and a large plantation required skilled management. Overseers were a valuable help to planters, but they often needed careful supervision themselves. Nonetheless, the system allowed the planter time for public service, and experience in plantation management often made the planters leaders.

The southern political system relied on the planters' free time. For instance, the church *vestry,* which was made up of planters, did far more than supervise the church and name the minister. It also performed numerous social services, such as giving relief to the poor and caring for orphans. Justices of the peace, also planters, presided over the county courts—hearing civil suits and trying minor criminal offenses. In addition to its judicial functions, the county court collected taxes, authorized road and bridge construction, and made regulations regarding the conduct of inns and taverns. A planter experienced in the ways of local government might even move on to the state assembly, and then to Congress.

Vestry refers to a group of people who direct the affairs of their church's community.

WHO WERE THE SLAVES? Beginning with the European "discovery" of Africa in the 15th century and continuing until almost 1850, approximately 15 million men, women, and children were removed from the western region of the African continent. In 1526 an African king wrote to the king of Portugal: "Your agents and merchants seize upon our subjects and cause them to be sold; our country is being utterly depopulated." What was African civilization like when the Europeans arrived? And who were taken as slaves?

ANCIENT GHANA. *The five major African kingdoms—Ghana, Mali, Songhai (SONG-hie), Benin (buh-NIN), and Ashanti—had once been among the world's most advanced civilizations.* (See map, page 249.) Ghana had been a flourishing trade center and a rich source of gold and spices. For about 400 years, from 700–1100 A.D., its leaders had ruled an empire of almost a million people. But then late in the 11th century, Ghana came under attack by Berber warriors (Muslims of North Africa), and by about 1200, little was left of this prosperous kingdom.

MALI. When Ghana fell, its territory came under the control of the kingdom of Mali, which included Ghana and the surrounding conquered states. Mali, situated on the Niger River, was also a great trading center.

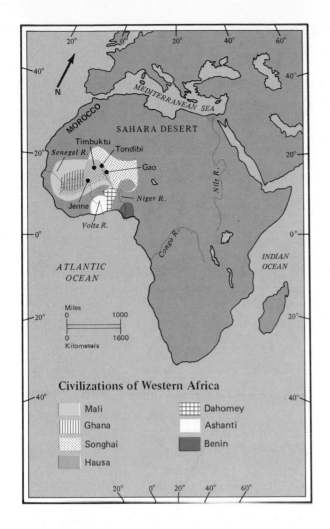

Civilizations of Western Africa

- Mali
- Ghana
- Songhai
- Hausa
- Dahomey
- Ashanti
- Benin

city. In the late 1400's under the leadership of Sunni Ali (SUN-ee AHL-ee), the empire had had a centralized government and a unified system of laws. Its army had conquered Timbuktu and Jenne (jeh-NAY), also a famous trading center, and had added even more strength to the empire.

Songhai reached its height under the rule of Askia Mohammed (ahs-KEE-uh moe-HAM-uhd), who had come to power in 1493. But when his three sons removed him from office in 1528, the kingdom of Songhai began its gradual decline. This decline was completed when Songhai was defeated by Moroccan armies in 1591.

BENIN. Benin, too, was a trade-oriented empire. The detailed ivory carvings, ironwork, and bronze sculpture of Benin have left an eloquent record of its civilization. European accounts of the splendor of Benin described streets as wide as those of Amsterdam and a palace as large as a whole European city.

ASHANTI. By far the most successful kingdom of precolonial Africa, Ashanti included after 1800 more than half of modern Ghana and parts of the neighboring states of the Ivory Coast and Togo. Europeans who saw Ashanti wrote of its clean, wide streets and houses and of its good sanitary facilities.

AFRICA AND THE SLAVE TRADE. Slavery was not a new concept to the Africans. Prisoners of war and convicted criminals had for centuries been taken as slaves, to be bought and sold as laborers. *Now, African rulers simply sold slaves to the Europeans, as they had always sold them to each other.* Eventually, the Ashanti developed such an efficient slave-trading operation that it supplanted even gold as their main source of wealth.

But the Africans who sold their own people into bondage viewed slavery differently from the Europeans and Americans. *In African society a rigid distinction did not*

Its people were merchants, farmers, weavers, metalworkers, and miners.

Timbuktu—one of Mali's most important cities—became world renowned as a center of Islamic scholarship, even after the internal power struggles had caused Mali to decline in the 15th century. And the influence of Mali's culture began spreading throughout North Africa.

SONGHAI. Songhai, a former state of Mali, became a powerful trading center during the 15th and 16th centuries. Gao (GOW), on the Niger River, was its capital

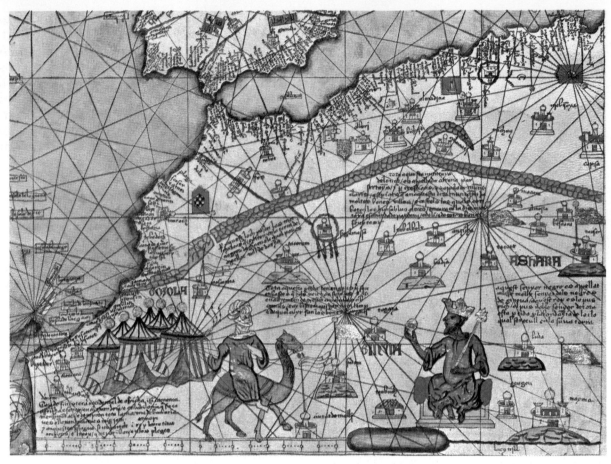

The greatest king of Mali, Mansa Musa, is shown seated on his throne in this old map of Africa. What does this picture tell you about the commerce and wealth of the African empires?

exist between the slave and the free. A slave could advance through good works or marriage and could buy freedom with the products of his or her labor or those inherited by wealth. Thus, the African people who were herded into foul and monstrously crowded ships to be sold as slaves in America were to have a very different way of life.

THE SLAVE COMMUNITY. What was it like to be a slave? Since slaves were often prohibited from reading and writing, few of them were able to record their own stories. White planters discussed them and White travelers described them, but that is hardly the same thing. As a result, the memoirs written by runaways who made it to the North are the best source of information. Their songs and folktales, handed down by word of mouth, tell some of what the slaves thought and felt.

Violence or the threat of it was ever-present in the life of a slave. Whipping was used as the common form of punishment, although other kinds of punishment, including starvation and overwork, were also used. Frederick Douglass recalled that when he resisted punishment, his master would send him to a special slavebreaker. Six months of daily whippings and unending work, he admitted, "succeeded in breaking me. I was broken in body, soul, and spirit." Not so broken, it might be added, that he was unable to escape and to eventually lead the antislavery movement.

The lash was ever present, but it was also used less often than might be supposed. Slaves were considered valuable property. A field hand in the prime of life in the 1850's cost about $1,500. The injury or death of a valuable slave through mistreatment could cause a serious financial loss to the owner. Moreover, many of the plantation owners were humane people who took care of their slaves, as well as their income and profit would allow.

Sidenote to History

Frederick Douglass

He was born a slave, but he was free in spirit. When his master tried to beat him, Frederick Douglass punched the man so hard with his bare fists that the master never laid a hand on him again. Not even a professional slavebreaker could completely crush his will to be free.

At his first opportunity, Douglass escaped to the North. He was aided along the way by friendly Quaker farmers in Delaware and Pennsylvania. Eventually, he settled in Newport, Rhode Island, hoping to pursue shipbuilding, the trade he had learned as a hired slave in Baltimore. But White carpenters objected to working side by side with a Black. So, the company allowed him to work only as a janitor.

Douglass soon found that many northerners, whatever they thought of slavery, cared little for Blacks. Northern states refused Blacks the vote, limited their right to testify in courts, and prohibited marriage with Whites. Northern cities maintained segregated schools and segregated streetcars. They even segregated their cemeteries.

Douglass' spirit, however, was no more crushed by northern prejudice than by southern slavery. Thus, he began a lifelong struggle for equality, in which his massive strength proved as useful as it had in slavery. On one occasion he deliberately took a seat in a railroad car marked "White Only." When the conductor told him to move, he refused. It finally took four men to move him—and in the struggle he pulled out two seats from their bolted moorings.

As a lecturer for the American Antislavery Society during the abolition movement, Douglass toured the country. When Garrison, the head of the American Slavery Society, became too bossy, Douglass resigned and went to Rochester, New York, where he founded a freedom paper, *The North Star*. When a public school in Rochester refused to admit his daughter, he published the fact in his newspaper. This so embarrassed the city that it desegregated its schools.

Douglass welcomed the Civil War and the changes it brought in the federal Constitution. But unlike other abolitionists, he did not quit the cause when the war was over. Until his death in 1895, Douglass continued his battle for equality and an end to the segregation laws in both the North and the South.

In 1793 Eli Whitney's cotton gin turned cotton into a profitable industry. The slaves in this picture are operating a gin while the White men haggle over a price.

LIVING CONDITIONS. *Many southerners claimed that the living conditions of slaves were no worse than those of factory workers in northern cities.* But only the worst of tenement slums equaled the majority of the slave's quarters. On most plantations the slave quarters were one-room log cabins with dirt floors. The cracks between the logs were just wide enough, complained one slave, that the wind and rain could come in but the smoke could not go out. Even on the wealthy plantations, where slave quarters were of wood-frame or brick construction, they were miserably crowded, with eight or 10 people jammed into a one- or two-room cabin.

Unlike the northern workers, the slaves did receive free medical attention and did have a certain amount of old-age security. Yet the surviving pictures of slaves suggest that their clothing was only as adequate as the poorest northerner's. The usual allotment was one new set of clothing per year.

The food of all lower-class southerners, slaves included, was monotonous and nutritionally inadequate. The staples of the southern diet were corn and pork. Slaves frequently complained that their alloted rations were not sufficient, but on most plantations slaves did have their own gardens. On Sundays (their one day off), many worked their own crops, went fishing, or trapped game.

Not all slaves lived on plantations. Some lived and worked in the cities. Those with some special skill or craft were often rented out. Such hired slaves had a limited amount of freedom of movement. A few were allowed to keep a portion of their wages as an inducement to work harder. In fact, there are some rare instances of hired slaves buying their freedom.

SLAVE FAMILIES AND RELIGION. *The heart of the slave community was the family.* Although formal marriages among slaves were not allowed, most slaves lived in family units. The separation of these families through the sale of slaves was probably the cruelest feature of the system.

Religion was the other pillar of the slave community, and the Blacks evolved one of their own. Slaves were permitted—sometimes required—to attend the regular churches. White ministers urged slaves to obey their masters, recalled one runaway. "But this was not what our people wanted to hear, so they would congregate after the White people retired."

The secret church was a mixture of music and Bible stories. Black spirituals stressed the hereafter. In many, such as "Steal Away" and "Follow the Drinkin' Gourd," there lay a double meaning, a longing for freedom—or a secret code for escape or rebellion.

DEFENSES AGAINST SLAVERY. Slaves, being under the constant threat of punishment, were unsure of the treatment they would receive beyond the plantation.

Thus, most resigned themselves to their lot, however grudgingly. But like all human beings in intolerable circumstances, slaves had to find ways to preserve their sanity and self-respect. Quick wit and remarks with double meanings helped; slaves could retaliate without earning a blow on the head. Their humble manner and happy-go-lucky smile could mask anger and bitterness, which, if shown, were likely to bring punishment. Others developed more aggressive ways of striking back, such as breaking tools and setting fire to plantation buildings. Some became deliberately unproductive.

ESCAPE AND REBELLION. *The slaves' most daring and dangerous methods of dealing with their conditions were*

"Old Kentucky Home" by Eastman Johnson was painted in 1859. How many scenes are depicted in this painting? How does the mood of the picture compare with your ideas about slave life?

escape and rebellion. By the 1850's southerners estimated that 1,000 slaves were escaping to the North each year. This accounted for only a fraction of those who had tried to escape. Many others had been caught or forced to hide out in the woods and swamps of the South.

THE UNDERGROUND RAILROAD.

The most highly organized means of escape was the Underground Railroad. It was not a railroad, but a network of houses and hideaways, stretching north to Canada, from such border slave states as Delaware, Maryland, and Kentucky. The male and female "conductors" guided the bands of fugitive slaves ("trains") by night from hideaway ("station") to hideaway. Each station was run by a "brakeman," often a free Black who was risking everything to help.

The Underground Railroad used any workable means to move slaves to freedom. For example, 28 slaves, pretending to be part of a funeral procession, once walked from Kentucky to Ohio.

Harriet Tubman, a former slave, was the most daring and successful conductor on the Railroad. Tubman made 19 trips into the South to bring 300 relatives, friends, and strangers to freedom. She was never captured and never lost a "passenger."

SLAVE REVOLTS. *Revolt was the most violent form of resistance to slavery.* There are dozens of rebellions and conspiracies on record. Most, however, were detected and stopped before the slaves could carry out their plans.

Between 1700 and 1860 there were at least 100 revolts, most of which took place between 1800 and 1860. One potentially major revolt was prevented in Charleston, South Carolina, in 1822. Denmark Vesey, a free Black, had organized slaves in order to capture the city. The revolt was betrayed by one of the participants. Thirty-seven Blacks were executed for their role in this plan.

Nat Turner was the leader of the first successful slave revolt. Why did his success frighten some southerners?

THE NAT TURNER REBELLION. *The bloodiest revolt, and perhaps the most famous, was that of Nat Turner.* It occurred in Southampton County, Virginia, in August 1831. Turner, a slave preacher, had been considered a model slave, obedient and respectful. Nevertheless, convinced that the he had been called by God to free the Blacks, Turner organized a band of slaves. They recruited more slaves as they terrorized the people of southern Virginia. Starting with the family who had owned the plantation on which he was a slave (whom he described as kindly people), Turner killed some 60 Whites, sparing no one, regardless of age or sex. During the hunt for Turner and his followers, nearly 100 Blacks were killed as well.

Turner's rebellion had been a war against the slave system itself. When, weeks after the beginning of the revolt, Turner had been caught and jailed, he had sat in his cell proud and defiant. He and about 20 of his followers were brought to trial and executed.

Given the brutality of the slave system, it is surprising not that revolts took place but that there were not more of them. It is difficult, however, to organize rebellions against established powers. Such rebellions require not only a depth of anger, a feeling of injustice, and a burning sense of purpose that ordinary people lack, but also more practical things—strong leaders, good organization and discipline, broadly based support, arms, and usually a certain amount of money. Without these, most rebellions fail or scarcely get off the ground.

A more tragic rebel than Nat Turner was the runaway who had been trapped at the Ohio River. Rather than let her children be taken back to slavery, she had stabbed them to death. She had been stabbing herself when she was caught and restrained. Her action was not an isolated one. According to antislavery publications, other slave mothers had also killed their children, so as not to see them destroyed by the hated slave system.

Section Review

1. Mapping: Using the map on page 246, list the states in which cotton was king. What geographic conditions led to the overwhelming dominance of the cotton culture in this region?
2. Identify or explain: Eli Whitney, Frederick Douglass, Nat Turner, Underground Railroad, Harriet Tubman.
3. Graphing: Look at the graph on page 247. What relationship do you see between the two sets of figures shown on this graph? What invention had a strong effect on the production of cotton?
4. Describe the life of slaves in the South. Use the following subtopics to organize your answer: working conditions, food and clothing, housing, family life, religion, methods of control and restraint.
5. List the five major African kingdoms, and briefly describe one feature of each kingdom.

4. The Antislavery Crusade

CRITICISM INCREASES. *The year of Nat Turner's revolt, 1831, was an important year for the antislavery movement.* Before then most of the criticism of slavery had been voiced by southerners. The biggest antislavery organization, the American Colonization Society, was chiefly southern in membership. In the winter of 1831, following Nat Turner's revolt, the Virginia assembly debated the wisdom of slavery. Although some Virginians denounced it as a burden that retarded southern economic development, they were outvoted by a small majority.

This was the last criticism of slavery heard in a southern legislature. Soon after these Virginia debates, stricter slave codes were introduced.

In January 1831, William Lloyd Garrison published in Boston the first issue of *The Liberator,* a newspaper devoted to the abolition of slavery. *With that move, criticism of slavery shifted to the North, and such criticism became much sharper in tone.*

THE COLONIZATION MOVEMENT. *Founded in 1817, the American Colonization Society hoped to solve the South's racial dilemma by sending the Blacks back to Africa.* The federal government cooperated in this effort by helping to establish the republic of Liberia on the west coast of Africa by giving $100,000 to the Society. The Society eventually developed numerous branches and began annual fund-raising drives. But it never commanded enough funds to purchase a significant number of slaves. Most of those it transported to Africa were free Blacks who had volunteered to go.

THE LIBERATOR. *William Lloyd Garrison was a deeply religious man who thought slavery was a terrible evil.* He made abolition his life's crusade.

Garrison announced his intentions in the first issue of *The Liberator:* immediate emancipation, with no compensation to slave owners. Since slavery was an evil, it had to be wiped out instantly. To compensate the slave owner for his financial loss would be to reward him for his sins. To Garrison it was a religious crusade. There was no room for moderation. "I am in earnest," he declared. "I will not excuse—I will not retreat a single inch—AND I WILL BE HEARD."

At first only a few listened. After a year Garrison had only 50 subscribers, nearly all free Blacks in Boston. Although many White northerners disliked slavery, they were not above discriminating against the free Blacks in their midst. Furthermore, the problem of slavery was remote. It was someone else's evil, of little immediate concern to them. To most northerners, moreover, Garrison seemed to be a fanatic. And his program for taking the southerners' property without paying them for it seemed both radical and farfetched.

Nevertheless, Garrison persisted. *In 1833 he organized the American Antislavery Society, with financial help from two devoutly religious New York merchants, Arthur and Lewis Tappan.* Within a few years the Society had claimed over 100 branches. By the mid-1830's it had organized a drive to petition Congress for the abolition of slavery in the one area Congress controlled, the District of Columbia.

THE GAG RULE. Most of the petitions were directed to John Quincy Adams, representative from Massachusetts. After serving as President from 1825 to 1829, Adams represented Massachusetts in the House from 1831 until his death in 1848.

Adams gladly used the petitions as an excuse to denounce slavery on the floor of the House. Even in 1837, when embarrassed southerners pushed through a House rule that such petitions were to be tabled automatically without debate, Adams refused to be silenced. When fellow representatives pushed Adams down into his seat, Adams shouted, "Am I to be gagged or not?"

For the next eight years, Adams conducted a one-man war against the Gag Rule and for the right of free petition. He finally won his case in 1844. And as the lonely fight went on, northerners began realizing that slavery affected more than the Black slaves. It was also affecting their own rights.

POLITICAL ABOLITIONISM. The abolitionists thrived on martyrdom. In 1835

Elijah Lovejoy, an outspoken critic of slavery, lost his press, his warehouse, and finally his life to an angry mob. Why do you think people reacted so violently to Lovejoy's politics?

256

Garrison was stoned and dragged through the streets of Boston by a howling mob. Two years later Elijah Lovejoy, an abolitionist editor in Alton, Illinois, was killed, defending his press against a mob. Yet, every defeat seemed to win more converts. *Many who had sympathized with the abolitionists' right to free speech came to sympathize with their cause as well.*

As the movement grew, it also divided. To many, Garrison's program seemed terribly impractical. Garrison, in fact, had no program at all. He relied on "moral suasion," as he called it—the assumption that planters would voluntarily free their slaves once they became aware of the evil they were doing. To him it was a moral question. And for that reason, he continued to shun politics.

Others realized that, because of the financial investment involved, slavery would have to be prohibited by law, perhaps even by force. Laws could be obtained only by political pressure. *Among the most prominent of the political abolitionists were Theodore Dwight Weld and Angelina Grimke Weld.* The Welds and their followers broke with Garrison in 1840, splitting the American Antislavery Society and virtually destroying its influence.

THE LIBERTY PARTY. Because 1840 was a Presidential election year, the Weld group formed a political party to field a candidate. The Liberty party nominated for President James G. Birney, an ex-slaveholder from Alabama who had come north to fight slavery. Birney's message was lost amid the Whig parade of log cabins that year, and he got only 6,000 votes. But four years later the party received 15,000 votes. Abolitionism was at last beginning to come into its own.

"FREE SOIL." But it was no longer Garrison's brand of abolitionism. With politics came compromise, as Garrison had predicted. *Thus, the Liberty party concentrated on stamping out slavery in the areas Congress controlled—the District of Columbia and the western territories.* In the southern states slavery was protected by state constitutions. The federal government had no power to prohibit it, even if it wanted to.

The program of the political abolitionists was at least more practical than Garrison's, but it did encourage further compromise. To some, slavery was becoming tolerable in the South, so long as it remained there. The antislavery forces, they thought, should concentrate on preventing the expansion of slavery into the West. *Their idea was called "free soil."* As a moderate program that would deprive no one of property without compensation, it had broad appeal.

The notion of free soil—preventing the expansion of slavery rather than abolishing it—was just coming into American thought when the war with Mexico exploded. And as a result of that war, America would conquer a vast empire in the Southwest. Would it be slave or free? That was the question facing the nation in 1848.

Section Review

1. Identify or explain: William Lloyd Garrison, Theodore Weld, the Gag Rule, *The Liberator,* the Liberty party.
2. Compare the goals of the American Colonization Society, the American Antislavery Society, the free-soil movement, and the 1840 Liberty party.
3. How did the debate about the issue of slavery in the House of Representatives lead to the Gag Rule? Why did this debate force people to view slavery as a national problem?
4. What were the basic differences in approach between the political abolitionists and Garrison? Can you infer the cause of or reason for these differences from the name "political abolitionists"?

Chapter 10 Review

Bird's-Eye View

Despite sectional differences, the American nation in the first half of the 19th century was characterized by a mood of intellectual growth and self-definition. In New England a rich and uniquely American literature was beginning to emerge. New England was also the center for a group of movements that aimed to correct some of the injustices in American society. In fact, it was because of such movements that some badly needed changes were made in the areas of education, prison conditions, and care for the mentally ill.

The South developed a rigid class system. Partly in response to northern hostility, the planter gentry cultivated a highly stylized, aristocratic life-style, and this class dominated the political and economic life of the region. The majority of the people were poor to middle-class White farmers, who made a sparse living by farming corn and by hunting. Free Blacks and slaves were at the bottom of the social ladder. Slaves were defined as property rather than as human beings.

Though there was some variation in how slaves were treated, all slaves were completely at the mercy of their owners. Slaves were almost always given at least enough food, clothing, and shelter to survive because of their value as property. But since the system was often maintained by terror and violence, punishment could also be given—and it could be extremely cruel. Slaves adjusted to the system as best they could by trying to maintain family ties and a strong religious life. Slave revolts were greatly feared, and those that occurred were forcefully suppressed.

In the North a small but determined group of abolitionists hoped to end slavery, or at least to keep it from spreading. This movement, based on the principle of the fundamental immorality of slavery, soon began to attract followers from other reform movements.

Vocabulary

Define or identify each of the following:

Dorothea Dix	abolitionist	Horace Mann
cotton gin	*The Liberator*	planter gentry
Timbuktu	Harriet Tubman	Denmark Vesey

Review Questions

1. Compare the beliefs of Henry David Thoreau with those of Ralph Waldo Emerson.
2. What did Horace Greeley mean when he called his own times "The Stammering Century"?
3. List four major reforms introduced during the first half of the 1800's.
4. Explain the economic importance of cotton to the South.
5. Compare the system of slavery in Africa with the one in the United States.
6. Describe the role of each of the following in the antislavery movement: Harriet Tubman, Nat Turner, Angelina Grimke Weld, John Quincy Adams, William Lloyd Garrison.

Reviewing Social Studies Skills

1. Study the map of the South on page 246, and then answer the following questions:
   a. Which states were major cotton producers?
   b. Which states were major tobacco producers?
   c. Which states were major cattle producers?
   d. What products other than cotton, tobacco, and cattle were grown in this area?
2. Examine the graph on page 247, and then answer the following questions.
   a. How much cotton was produced in 1810? In 1840? In 1860?
   b. How many slaves were there in 1810? In 1840? In 1860?
   c. What generalization can you make if you compare the amount of cotton produced to the amount of slaves involved in growing it?
3. Using the map on page 249, answer the following questions:
   a. In what part of Africa did the great African kingdoms exist?
   b. What were the four major cities in ancient West Africa?
   c. What two areas of African civilization are shown, but not described, in the text?

Reading for Meaning

1. Using the textbook, match the topic of each of the sentences below to a paragraph in the book whose topic is the same. To identify the paragraph, write the page number on which it appears and the first sentence of the paragraph. **a)** The philosopher had unusual ideas, which influenced the thinking of his own time and the ideas that people have today. **b)** The reforms of this educator had far-reaching consequences in American public education.
2. Read the selection about Frederick Douglass carefully. What can you infer about his character from the description of his life? Write a paragraph entitled "Frederick Douglass, the Person," based on your inferences.
3. Do you think the author approves or disapproves of Nat Turner's rebellion? What words give a clue to his opinion? Briefly rewrite the section about the Nat Turner rebellion, choosing words that reflect your opinion about the incident.

Bibliography

Olivia Coolidge's *Women's Rights: The Suffrage Movement in the United States, 1848–1920* (Dutton) describes the leaders in the crusades for women's rights.

Philip Sterling's and Rayford Logan's *Four Took Freedom* (Doubleday) describes the lives of four outstanding Black crusaders for freedom in the mid-1800's.

In Chains to Louisiana: Solomon Northup's Story, by Michael Knight (E. P. Dutton & Co., Inc.), is the true story of a free Black who was kidnapped and sold into slavery.

Chapter 11

Land of Promise

New England had always been a land of merchants. This was because the stony soil yielded only enough food for its people, never enough to export. When the pine forests had gone, lumber sales declined. Having nothing of their own to sell, the New Englanders began selling other people's goods. And the practice had sharpened their wits.

Yet, there was one commodity that New England had in abundance, at least in the winter—ice. "Why not sell New England's ice to the sweltering Caribbean?" someone joked at a Boston party in the summer of 1805. Frederic Tudor, 21 and searching for a career, decided to take up the dare.

Everyone had thought Tudor was crazy when he bought 117 tonnes (130 tons) of ice and had it shipped to the West Indies island of Martinique. And they had smiled knowingly when it melted and Tudor lost $4,000. Undaunted, Tudor ordered another shipment and went to Martinique himself. There he experimented with various designs for icehouses. Once he found the design that resisted heat best, he built it. Tudor experimented with the insulation—wood shavings, blankets, and straw—sitting for hours outside the icehouse, with watch in hand, timing the melt.

When the problem of preserving ice had been solved, Tudor turned to the task of showing West Indians what to do with it. He showed the man who ran a local amusement park how to make ice cream. The man objected at first, but later changed his mind, after selling $300 worth on the first night. Tudor then built an icehouse on every sizable island in the West Indies. Before long the demand outran the supply.

The usual method of sawing ice from New England ponds was time-consuming, and it produced irregular chunks. These chunks were difficult to store in ships and expensive to insulate. Together with a friend, Tudor developed an ice cutter, consisting of two sawtoothed runners drawn by a horse. By making repeated runs, a horse and a person could cut an entire pond into neat squares. Workers with iron bars could then pry off the cubes and float them to the icehouse. This device enabled Tudor to produce ice for ten cents a ton.

By 1825 Tudor was already known as the Ice King, and he was rapidly transforming the eating habits of Americans. People discovered the value of refrigeration in preserving food. And the icebox became a feature of every kitchen. Salted meat, half-spoiled fruit, and rancid milk gave way to a list of chilled drinks, fresh meat, and ice cream.

In 1833 Tudor capped his career by sending a shipload of ice to India. The voyage took four months and involved crossing the equator twice. By that date he had discovered the best and cheapest form of insulation—sawdust—and the ship's voyage was a resounding success. Tudor made such a nice profit that he sent another shipment. This time he sent along iceboxes and some well-preserved products of New England—apples, butter, and cheese. All were to be put up for sale.

Chapter Objectives

After you have finished reading this chapter, you should be able to:
1. Describe how the innovations in transportation affected expansion, industry, and immigration.
2. Explain the United States policy toward American Indians.
3. Compare the settlement of Texas with that of Oregon.
4. List in chronological order the events that led to the United States becoming involved in a war with Mexico.
5. Explain how California's rapid growth created a national crisis.

Tudor represented the kind of drive, imagination, and ingenuity that changed the face of the continent and ultimately the habits of the world. By the time of Frederic Tudor's death in 1856, the eastern wilderness had surrendered to tidy farms and bustling cities. The republic had spread west to the Pacific, and the plains and mountains in between were being populated.

1. Progress in Industry and Communications

CHANGES IN TRANSPORTATION. *One of the most striking changes of the era was in transportation.* In 1807 people moved in much the same way and at much the same pace as they had in ancient Greece and Rome. Horses and wagons filled the roads. Canoes and flatboats plied the rivers. Sailing ships moved across the seas.

TURNPIKES AND TRANSPORTATION. The revolution in transportation began with something very basic: roads. Without good roads, improved overland transportation would be useless. Even the waterways could not be exploited as fully as possible, for getting to a river easily was just as important as being able to travel on it.

The first major highway in the new nation—the Cumberland, or National, Road—was begun in 1811. By 1818 it stretched from Cumberland, Maryland, across the Appalachian Mountains to Wheeling, (West) Virginia. (See map, page 262.) It opened the West to settlers from the East and made it possible for western farmers to ship their products east.

The building of the Cumberland Road by the national government encouraged private interests to finance the construction of additional highways, called turnpikes. These highways, which charged tolls to those who used them, were built to connect

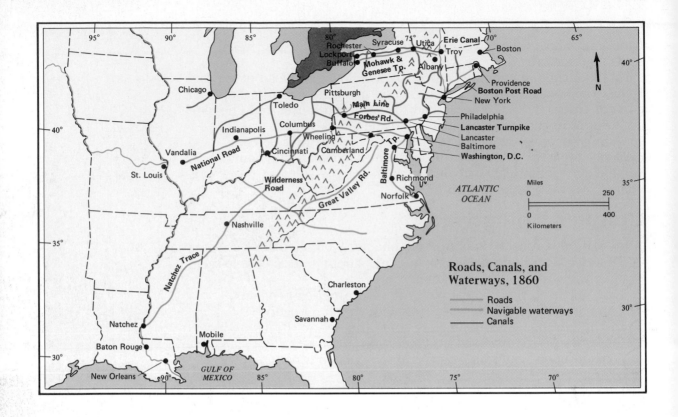

Roads, Canals, and Waterways, 1860

Roads
Navigable waterways
Canals

eastern cities. But a few also served the West. By the 1820's, westward-bound settlers could take the Baltimore Turnpike to Cumberland, Maryland; then the National Road to Wheeling, (West) Virginia. By 1852 they could follow it on to Vandalia, Illinois. The Lancaster Turnpike and Forbes' Road led to Pittsburgh, and the Mohawk and Genesee Turnpike to Lake Erie. (See map above.) Although the rivers were still the main arteries of transportation in the West, the system of turnpikes connected these rivers at crucial points, making the shipping of goods and the transporting of people easier than ever.

THE AGE OF STEAM. *Another development that revolutionized transportation was the invention of the steamboat.* The age of steam had dawned in 1807 when Robert Fulton drove his steamboat, the *Clermont,* up the Hudson River from New York to Albany. Four years later Fulton built another boat. It was to provide service on the Ohio River. By 1819 the first steamship had crossed the Atlantic.

Steamboats were of particular value on the western rivers where traffic previously had gone with the downstream currents. Then, the addition of paddle wheels to the sides of the steamboats had helped them to maneuver turns more easily. Engines placed on the deck had eliminated the need for a deep hull.

In the pre-Civil War years, river steamers had carried about four fifths of all the traffic in the Mississippi valley. After the Civil War they had yielded their role to another steam device, the railroad.

THE CANAL ERA. *Where there were no rivers, workers dug canals.* As a result, the eastern part of the country has several great canal systems.

It took eight years to build the Erie Canal, at a cost of over 7 million dollars. When it was completed, the cost of shipping freight across New York dropped 95 percent and traveling time was cut by two-thirds. So great was business on the canal that the canal paid for itself in 12 years.

The earliest canals were links between rivers. Before the War of 1812, canals were begun (though not always finished) to connect Chesapeake Bay, in Virginia, and Albemarle Sound, in North Carolina; the Chesapeake and Delaware bays; and the Hudson and the Delaware rivers. The canals were built by private companies, which got their money back by charging a toll for every boat that used the waterway.

THE ERIE CANAL. *After the war New York undertook one of its most ambitious enterprises—a canal connecting the Hudson River with Lake Erie, which would unite the waters of East and West.* Built mostly by immigrant Irish laborers, the Erie

Canal was completed in 1825. It was 1.2 meters (4 feet) deep and 12.6 meters (42 feet) wide, and it extended 581 kilometers (363 miles), from Troy, on the Hudson River, to Buffalo.

The Erie Canal was an instant success. On it, westbound barges carried German and Irish immigrants to the boom towns of the Middle West and returned laden with wheat and flour. Cities sprouted along the canal's route—Rochester, Syracuse, Utica, and Lockport. New York City, which was already the nation's largest city, doubled in size within a decade after the canal had opened.

Because a huge barge could be towed along the canal by a single horse or mule, freight rates dropped and farmers profited. The Erie Canal could even survive competition from the railroads. In fact, its peak traffic came in 1880, long after rail lines had spanned the route from New York to Chicago.

THE MAIN LINE CANAL. The success of the Erie Canal inspired imitation. Philadelphia merchants, jealous of New York's monopoly on midwestern trade, financed their own Main Line Canal across Pennsylvania to Pittsburgh. Although the Main Line

Sidenote to History

The Moonrakers

Americans had always been good at shipbuilding. During the War of 1812, Baltimore brigs had easily eluded the British warships blockading the American coast. Such ships had also plundered British commerce across the world. Narrow beamed, with masts raked (leaning back) for greater strength, and jammed with sails, these craft were the fastest on the sea, faster even than steamships. By 1830 they were making the run from New York to England in 14½ days, carrying passengers and mail. The final step in the development of the wooden sailing ship was the Yankee clipper.

No one person can be singled out as the inventor of the clipper ship. But there is no doubt that Donald McKay was the greatest designer of them all. McKay had come to America from Scotland in 1826 and had gotten a job in a shipyard. Interested in speed, he had begun working with model ships in a tank of water. Eventually, such experiments led to important changes in the shape of a sailing vessel. Discovering that width was a drag, he

had lengthened the ship until it was five times as long as it was wide. On steeply raked masts he had piled sail upon sail—mainsail, topsail, topgallant—and at the very tip, a tiny sail so high it was called a moonraker. And that became the nickname for the clipper.

McKay's first clipper, the *Staghound,* was launched in 1851. On its first voyage, around Cape Horn and on to San Francisco, it had netted its owner $80,000. Then, the California gold rush occurred. And it created a demand for speedy ocean transportation.

In response to this demand, in 1852, McKay produced his two masterpieces, the *Flying Cloud* and the *Sovereign of the Seas.*

The *Flying Cloud* made it from New York to San Francisco in 89 days, 8 hours—a record for a sailing ship that stands to this day. The *Sovereign of the Seas* was the greatest of the clippers. It was 79 meters (265 feet) long and 14 meters (44 feet) wide. The masts were 60 meters (200 feet) high, and each one carried over a third of a hectare (acre) of canvas.

The days of the clipper were short. Swift as they were, they could not keep pace with the latest steamships. Their best use had been in trade with the Pacific and the Far East, where the sources of coal for the steamships had been far apart. But the clippers were expensive to operate, and they had been easily worn out by captains crazy for speed. By the time of the Civil War, they had all but disappeared. But the moonrakers will always be remembered. No other human contrivance has ever been able to match their elegance, dramatic beauty, and grace.

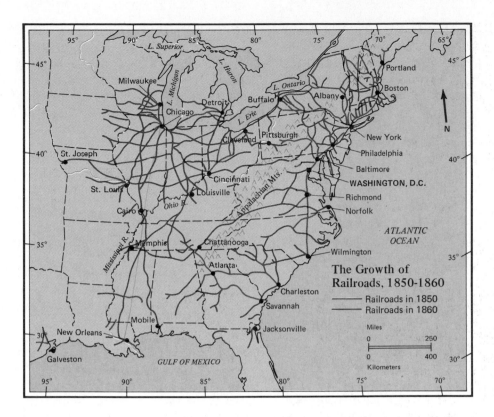

The Growth of
Railroads, 1850-1860

——— Railroads in 1850
——— Railroads in 1860

Miles
0 ————— 250
0 ————— 400
Kilometers

Canal was never able to compete with the Erie, its many tributary canals offered cheap transport to previously isolated parts of Pennsylvania.

A CANAL-BUILDING SPREE. *In the 1830's, state governments went on a canal-building spree.* Ohio and Indiana each built canals from Lake Erie to the Ohio River. By the time of the panic of 1837, which slowed construction, some 4,800 kilometers (3,000 miles) of canals had been built. (See map, page 262.) None was as profitable as the Erie, and most had gone bankrupt in a short time. But the value of these canals cannot be calculated in terms of their profit and loss. The amount by which they reduced transport costs was a hidden benefit for all involved.

THE RAILROADS. The steam locomotive was an English invention that had come to America in the 1820's. *The tracks for the nation's first railroad, the Baltimore and Ohio, were begun in 1828.* They were made of wood and capped along the top with strips of iron. The first locomotive, the *Tom Thumb,* was a noisy, hissing contraption, capable of doing only about 16 kilometers (10 miles) an hour.

The eastern cities, competing for a share of the midwestern grain trade, had financed routes into the interior. They had hoped that improvement would make the steam locomotive practical. By 1840 there were some 4,800 kilometers (3,000 miles) of track. By 1850 the amount had tripled, reaching 14,400 kilometers (9,000 miles). By 1860 approximately 48,000 kilometers (30,000 miles) of track crossed the country. (See map above).

America's faith in technology had also paid off by 1860. *Steel-reinforced engines; the iron T-rail, able to withstand grinding weights; flanged wheels that could hold the train on the track; and the Westing-house air brake—all of these combined to make the railroad the world's most efficient form of transportation.* Though never as cheap as water transport, the railroad's speed saved shippers money in another way.

The railroads contributed indirectly to the growing political sectionalism. The main railway trunk lines had been intended to connect eastern cities with the Middle West. As a result, most railroads ran east-west, rather than north-south. Thus, the region west of the mountains, long accustomed to trading downriver to New Orleans, would become dependent instead on New York and Philadelphia.

The northern states, moreover, had built tracks to the standard width. The southern states had used a narrower width. Thus, at the Mason-Dixon line—the dividing line between the North and the South—cars had to be lifted off one set of wheels and put onto another. In addition, no one bothered to build a bridge over the Ohio River until the very eve of the Civil War—another factor that limited the linking of railroads between the North and South.

The political effect of the shifts in trading partnerships is hard to measure. But it is interesting to note that Jefferson and Jackson each rode to victory on an alliance between the South and the West. In 1860 Abraham Lincoln fashioned his Presidential victory out of an alliance between the Northeast and the Northwest.

GROWTH OF POPULATION. The population grew rapidly in the decades before the Civil War. It was swelled by a stream of Irish and German immigrants. The Irish, driven from Ireland by famine and poverty, had congregated in eastern cities, where, like most newcomers, they were at the bottom of the social ladder. Irish labor built the sewage works and the waterworks for the rising metropolises, dug the canals, and laid out the railroads. The Germans, who had pushed on to the Middle West, were helping

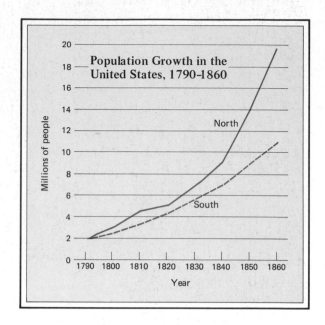

Population Growth in the United States, 1790–1860

to settle the prairies of Illinois and Wisconsin and to people the boom cities—Chicago, Cincinnati, and St. Louis.

In 1840 there were 26 states and 17 million people. Twenty years later the nation had 33 states and 31 million people. *This rapid increase in the population also indicated an unevenness between the development of the North and that of the South. (See graph above.)*

IMMIGRATION AND THE STEAMSHIP. *The invention of the steamship had an indirect effect on mid-19th century immigration.* When the steamships began crossing the Atlantic, they not only captured the business of wealthy travelers, but they also came to be used more and more to carry valuable cargoes. As a result, sailing ships had to scramble for passengers. They found them—by the thousands—in the immigrants. There were so many Europeans eager to migrate to the United States that the sailing ships began offering much lower fares than the steamships. In 1850 a person could take a sailing ship from England or Ireland to America for 10 dollars. This low fare made it possible for many people to

In 1846, just as the potatoes in Ireland were ready for harvest, a mysterious blight wiped out the entire crop. More than a million people died of starvation, typhus, and cholera during the potato famine. Nearly three million more left for Canada and America. This painting illustrates a group of Irish immigrants arriving in New York. Do you think this is the way they looked after the crossing?

come to America who, otherwise, would have been unable to afford the trip.

THE COMING OF MANUFACTUR-ING. *The nation had declared its political and cultural independence long before it was able to claim any commercial independence from Europe.* Fifty years after the Declaration of Independence—despite wars, embargoes, and tariffs—Americans were still dependent on Britain for many manufactured goods.

Around 1840, however, the situation began to change. The nation was experiencing a spurt of industrial growth. By 1860 this growth had made it the fourth largest producer of manufactured goods. Just 30 years later it would be in first place.

THE FACTORY CHANGES WORK PATTERNS. *In colonial and Revolutionary times, nearly all skilled laborers were independent artisans.* They owned their own shops and sold their own products.

The skilled artisan usually worked in his or her shop beside hired assistants, who were being trained, on the job, in a particular craft or trade. Such assistants looked forward to running their own shops one day. In fact, shop owners and their assistants shared a common outlook on life—by hard work and attention to business, both expected to get ahead in the world.

The factory system changed all that. Under this system owners and workers never labored alongside each other. The type of work done by a factory owner—what has come to be called paperwork—was far removed from that done by the factory hands at their machines. Moreover, factory owners rarely set foot in the factory itself. Many left the actual running of the factory to someone else—usually a hired manager.

The workers had almost no encouragement to improve their lot. In fact, after tending often dangerous machines for incredibly long hours, most workers had neither the time nor the energy even to think about the future.

THE RISE OF LABOR. *The problems faced by workers, both on and off the job, ultimately led some of them to search for ways to attack the problems.* It soon became clear that acting individually would get workers nowhere. Their only hope lay in working together.

This approach led to the formation of organizations called unions. The function of unions was to discuss and to try to remedy workers' problems with the factory owner or the owner's representative.

Sidenote to History

The Lowell Girls

What is the most distinctive feature of the modern world? Could it be the factory? In early times, manufacturing was done in the home. Even large-scale businesses gave raw cotton and wool to people to spin into thread or to weave into cloth in their homes. Cobblers and cabinetmakers worked in shops that doubled as houses. Those who lived in villages often did some farming on the side. People worked at their own pace and on their own time.

During the latter half of the 18th century, inventors developed ever larger and more complicated machines to speed up this work. Machines that were too big for the home required special buildings, or factories. The earliest of these machines was for spinning and weaving cloth. It was developed in England at about the time of the American Revolution.

For a long time England led the world in the Industrial Revolution. It also prohibited exports of its machines. But in 1791 Samuel Slater, a mechanic with a good memory, reproduced a textile machine in Rhode Island. Protected from English competition by Jefferson's trade embargo and the War of 1812, textile mills began spreading across New England. By 1815 the factories in Waltham and Lowell, Massachusetts, had steam-driven machines that could turn raw cotton into finished cloth.

Factories took manufacturing out of the home, but they also brought the home to the factory. Entire populations began regulating their lives by the factory whistle. Idle machines became wasted money, so factory hours came to include the hours from dawn to dusk.

The modern factories of Waltham and Lowell hired New England farm "girls" to work the machines. These "girls" were actually young women, who lived in the dormitories under close supervision. They were paid three dollars a week. From this amount the cost of room and board was deducted. Most did not plan to spend their lives tending the machines. They planned to stay only long enough to save money for a marriage dowry, to save the family farm, or to save enough to go to school for a couple of years. Proud of their abilities, they even published a magazine of essays and poems, called *The Lowell Offering*.

The Lowell girls were at the halfway stop between farm and factory, an interesting stage in the vast social process that ushered in the modern world. In the 1840's, factory owners replaced these girls with immigrants, who were willing to work for less money. These immigrants represented a new kind of worker, one tied for life to the factory and the machine.

Most unions formed before the Civil War were weak. This was because factory owners, when confronted with dissatisfied workers, could simply fire the workers and hire others. The most successful unions involved skilled workers. This was because skilled workers were more difficult to replace. Called trade unions, these more effective organizations were formed by shoemakers and printers as early as 1800.

In the late 1820's the Workingman's party entered the political scene. Its newspaper, *The Workingman's Advocate,* gave a voice to the workers' demands. Better pay and shorter hours—some factories had a 14- to 16-hour day—were their chief demands. They also wanted free public education and cheaper public lands in the West.

The panic of 1837, which brought serious unemployment, was a blow to the early labor movement. Many of the unions collapsed. The flood of immigrants in the 1840's and 1850's also slowed labor's organization. With labor in plentiful supply, a union had little bargaining power. The unions' only victory was President Martin Van Buren's order in 1840, which established a 10-hour day for government workers. Although it applied only to government offices, the order did set a standard that was gradually adopted in many northern factories. But it was only a beginning, and a rather faint one at that.

Section Review

1. Mapping: Using the map on page 262, trace the route of the Erie Canal. How did the canal help to encourage trade, industry, and immigration to the West?
2. Identify or explain: Robert Fulton, *Tom Thumb,* the Erie Canal.
3. How did the growth of railroads reinforce sectionalism?
4. Describe the growth of the population between 1840 and 1860. What role did immigrants play in this growth?
5. What were the main differences between the work habits of people in Colonial and Revolutionary America and those of workers in a 19th-century factory?

The Lowell mill owners regulated the activities of their workers inside the factory and out. They believed strict regulation of their female workers would increase productivity.

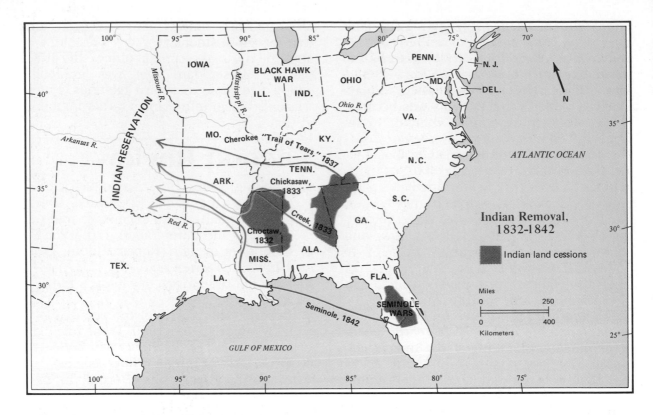

Indian Removal, 1832-1842

Indian land cessions

2. Indian Removal

AMERICAN INDIAN LANDS IN THE EAST. *The American Indians who held lands in the eastern half of the country had been squeezed, pushed, and surrounded by settlers as the frontier had moved westward.* In 1830, American Indians held large tracts of land in Illinois and Wisconsin. In the South they owned nearly a fourth of Georgia, Alabama, and Mississippi. Whites, who felt they could make better use of the land, wanted the government to move the Indians to land west of the Mississippi River.

President Jefferson and others of his time had wanted to break up the tribes and to absorb the Indians into American society. However, the American Indians rejected that solution. It would have meant a loss of their tribal identities and of their distinctive Indian culture. Because of the attitude of most of the Whites toward the American Indians, leaving them in possession of tracts of wilderness in the populous East was not politically feasible. Their removal to west of the Mississippi seemed the only solution.

CREATING AN INDIAN TERRITORY. *Everyone thought there was space enough for the Indians in the West.* In 1820 and 1821 Major Stephen Long had explored the northern plains. On his return he had proclaimed the area a "desert," unfit for farms and cities. Mapmakers, picking up on the notion, had filled in the empty space on their charts. Between the Missouri River and the Rocky Mountains they had written the words "Great American Desert." Once removed to this land, American Indians could have it forever, because no one else wanted it.

In 1824 the Monroe administration established a frontier line along the western boundaries of Minnesota, Iowa, Missouri, and Arkansas—sometimes called the middle border. West of that line would be a huge Indian reservation, from the Dakotas to Oklahoma. In the next few years, various Ohio valley tribes—Potawatomi (paht-uh-WAHT-uh-mee), Shawnee, Kickapoo, and Wyandots—would be persuaded to exchange their eastern lands for tracts west of the Missouri River. President John Quincy Adams would refuse to force anyone to move, however.

THE INDIAN REMOVAL ACT OF 1830. Andrew Jackson had no such qualms. With his full support Congress passed a new act, authorizing the government to exchange certain lands in the plains for the Indians' eastern holdings. Jackson moved quickly to carry out the act, using force where persuasion failed. *By the time he left*

office in 1837, most of the eastern Indians had been resettled in the West.

BLACK HAWK WAR. Defeated in war and demoralized by disease, the northern tribes put up little resistance to removal. The exception was Black Hawk, a young leader of the Sac and Fox. When aging Keokuk (KE-o-kuk), head of the tribe, agreed to move his people from their ancient tribal lands in Illinois to Iowa, Black Hawk objected. Still, he went with the tribe. In Iowa they experienced new difficulties. The Sioux harassed them, and the White settlers burned their crops.

In 1832 Black Hawk led a band, including women and children, back across the Mississippi, to Illinois. The band's intentions were apparently to recover their old lands. The Illinois settlers fled in panic, and

The Indian Removal Act required that tribes east of the Mississippi River exchange their homelands for territory in the West. Prodded along by United States soldiers, the Cherokee moved west, making a "trail of tears." They took with them what few belongings they could carry.

the governor called up the state militia. Black Hawk then fled north and next west, across Wisconsin to the Mississippi. At the place where the Bad Axe River joins the Mississippi, he and his band were trapped, caught on the river between the army and a gunboat. (See map, page 270.) Although his band was massacred, Black Hawk himself was saved from death. The person who had saved him was a young army lieutenant, Jefferson Davis. Later that lieutenant would become the president of the Confederate States of America.

THE "TRAIL OF TEARS." *The southern tribes, better organized and more closely tied to the land, put up more resistance to removal.* In the 1820's the Cherokee organized a government and hired lawyers. They even sued Georgia in the Supreme Court, asking Justice Marshall to stop Georgia's attempts to regulate them. Although Marshall sided with the Cherokee, Jackson ignored him. At Jackson's request a Cherokee delegation went to Oklahoma to inspect the land. They decided to stay in Georgia.

The Choctaw, weakest of the southern tribes, were the first to go. They moved to Oklahoma in 1832. As a reward the administration gave them a sizable portion of the territory. The Creek and Chickasaw followed a year later. Sent part of the way by steamboat, these Indians were subjected to overcrowding, cold, and hunger. A cholera epidemic killed hundreds.

The Cherokee held out until 1837, when Jackson lost his patience and sent the army. *The soldiers rousted the Cherokee from their homes and allowed them to take only what they could carry.* The journey then started, a long overland trek across Tennessee and Arkansas to Oklahoma. *The Cherokee called it the Trail of Tears.* Exhaustion, hunger, and cold took a heavy toll. Some 4,000 died along the way.

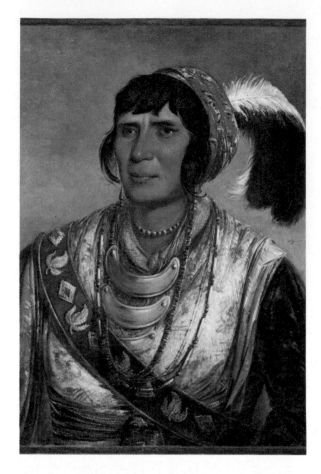

George Catlin painted this portrait of the Seminole leader, Osceola, in 1837.

OSCEOLA AND THE SEMINOLE WAR. *Bolstered by their fiery chief, Osceola (os-e-O-la), the Seminole of Florida, ancient foes of Jackson, refused to move.* An army sent to Florida in 1837 to round them up was defeated. However, the army did manage to capture Osceola, who died soon afterward in a South Carolina jail.

When new armies were sent to the territory, the Seminole hid in the swamps. For the next five years, they conducted a guerrilla war, ambushing patrols, raiding outposts, and eluding pursuers.

By 1842 some of the surviving Seminole, on the edge of starvation, agreed to removal.

The remainder slipped deeper into the Florida everglades, where their descendants remain today—proud, defiant, and undefeated. (During World War II the Seminole nation issued its own declaration of war against Germany and Japan.)

Section Review

1. Mapping: Using the map on page 270, determine how far the five Indian tribes were sent from their native lands.
2. Identify or explain: Major Stephen Long, Black Hawk, the Cherokee, Osceola.
3. List three ways in which Americans tried to deal with American Indians during the early 19th century.
4. Why did the Cherokee who were removed to the West describe their passage as a Trail of Tears?
5. Describe the Seminole resistance to removal. What geographic factors aided them in their long battle against removal?

3. Texas and Oregon

AN ADVANCING FRONTIER. *To the American Indians it seemed like a neverending tide. Immigrants poured across the ocean, filling both the populous eastern cities and the vast western plains.* By 1820 the advancing frontier had swept past the eastern Indians, crossed the Mississippi, and was creeping steadily up the Missouri and Arkansas rivers.

At the middle border it came to a halt. One obstacle was the Plains Indians, who had been put on guard by the experiences of the eastern tribes. Another obstacle was the land itself. No one was sure how to farm the ocean of grass that formed the Great Plains. There was no wood for fencing or houses. And the settlers' crude plows could not turn the tough prairie sod.

OPENING THE SOUTHWEST. In the Southwest the advancing frontier bumped up against Texas, territory belonging first to Spain and then to Mexico. Under Spanish rule Texas and the Southwest had been closed to American traffic. However, this policy began to weaken in 1820. *When Mexico obtained its independence in 1821, its new rulers welcomed contact with a neighboring republic.*

That same year William Becknell, a merchant of St. Louis, Missouri, blazed a trail from Westport Landing, on the Missouri River—now Kansas City—across the plains and the Cimarron Desert to Santa Fe. Santa Fe, New Mexico, was an old city. It had been founded by Spanish settlers in 1609, only two years after the English had arrived at Jamestown. Becknell's wagons, drawn by teams of mules, carried eastern manufactured goods, which he exchanged for furs and silver. Other settlers had followed, and the Santa Fe Trail was soon a trading artery. (See map, page 287.)

AMERICANS IN TEXAS. In 1820 Spanish authorities granted a tract of Texas land on the Colorado River to Moses Austin. It was granted on the condition that he settle it with 100 families who would become loyal subjects of Spain. But Moses Austin died before he could establish the colony.

In 1821, Mexico, now independent of Spain, gave Stephen F. Austin, the son of Moses, a renewal of the grant. *With this grant Stephen Austin began building an American colony in Texas in 1821.* The success of Austin's settlement attracted other *impresarios,* as the Mexicans called them. And by the end of the 1820's, there were several thousand Americans in Texas. After 1830 a wave of Texas fever spread across the South, and more than 30,000 settlers came to the province. By 1835, the Americans outnumbered the Mexicans in Texas by 10 to one.

CONFLICT BETWEEN TEXAS AND MEXICO. *Southerners—mostly planters—had been attracted by the rich soil of eastern Texas.* They had moved there, taking their slaves with them, to grow cotton. But before long they had grown unhappy with Mexican rule. The government in Mexico City had changed frequently. Then, in 1834 General Antonio López de Santa Anna made himself president. Changes such as this had particularly distressed Americans because they had tried to exercise more control over Texas. Periodic attempts by Mexico to abolish slavery in Texas also concerned them.

Mexico was also becoming alarmed—at the large number of Americans in Texas—and it began to restrict settlement. Some land grants were canceled. Many Texans, in turn, began to hold meetings to protest the situation. Occasionally, shooting broke out between the Mexican troops and the American cowboys.

REVOLUTION AND A NEW REPUBLIC. *In 1835 Santa Anna started north with an army to subdue his rebellious province.* In the meantime the Texans hastily organized themselves, drafted a constitution for the independent republic of Texas, and named Samuel Houston to command their army.

By the end of February 1836, Santa Anna was on the outskirts of San Antonio. (See map, page 275.) Houston, thinking the town was indefensible, retreated. But a band of 187 Texans resolved to stay and fight. They chose as their fortress the Alamo, an abandoned mission. Their aim was to "make victory worse to the enemy than a defeat." Among them were James Bowie and William B. Travis, commanders, and Davy Crockett, the Tennessee-born frontiersman and scout.

For 10 days Santa Anna assaulted the mission, finally overrunning it and killing the last of its garrison. But the victory cost him 1,544 soldiers.

Santa Anna then started after Houston. Houston, surrounded by a growing band of refugees, made his stand at San Jacinto (san jah-SIN-toe). (See map, page 275.) At noon

The members of this pioneer caravan have just spotted Santa Fe after a long trek from Missouri. Does the artist portray the group's excitement about the moment?

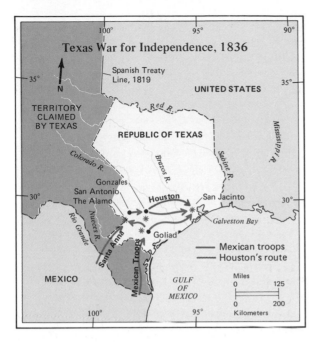

Texas War for Independence, 1836

Spanish Treaty Line, 1819

UNITED STATES

TERRITORY CLAIMED BY TEXAS

Red R.

REPUBLIC OF TEXAS

Mississippi R.

Colorado R.

Brazos R.

Sabine R.

Gonzales
San Antonio
The Alamo
Houston
San Jacinto

Galveston Bay

Nueces R.
Rio Grande
Santa Anna
Goliad

MEXICO

Mexican Troops

GULF OF MEXICO

—— Mexican troops
—— Houston's route

Miles
0   125
0   200
Kilometers

on April 21, Houston attacked, catching the Mexicans by surprise. Shouting "Remember the Alamo!" Houston's army killed 630 Mexicans and captured the rest, including General Santa Anna, who finally agreed to give Texas its independence.

As did most Texans, Houston, the president of the new republic, hoped Texas would join the United States. But President Andrew Jackson and his successors refused admittance, fearing that such approval would mean war with Mexico. Also, northerners objected, because Texas permitted slavery. Northerners believed that the admission of Texas to the Union would increase southern influence in Congress. Thus, for the next 10 years, Texas existed as an independent nation. It was called the Lone Star Republic.

THE MOUNTAIN MEN. North of Texas, the plains and central Rockies were Indian country. They remained so until after the Civil War. Before the Civil War the fur traders, operating from St. Louis, Missouri, had been the earliest outsiders to penetrate the area.

At first the trappers had made the long journey down the Missouri River every spring to sell the beaver and otter pelts they had gathered in the winter hunt. But in 1825 the St. Louis fur merchant William H. Ashley organized the rendezvous system. Under this system he would send upriver the tools, weapons, and ammunition for the trappers. The trappers and Ashley's agents would then meet at a prearranged spot, or

This painting shows the battle of the Alamo. Theodore Gentilz studied all the available information on the Alamo in order to paint a historically accurate picture.

Sidenote to History

Life in Spanish California

The migration of Americans to the West eventually resulted in an end to Spanish political and cultural dominance there. Slowly, the *rancho,* or ranch—one of the great California institutions established by the Spanish—began disappearing.

Along with the missions, established by Junípero Serra, the *ranchos* had been the center of Spanish culture in California. Located far from the interference of the Mexican government in Mexico City, the *rancheros,* or ranch owners, had lived an independent existence, raising cattle and horses and running huge landholdings with the help of their Indian workers. The following excerpt is taken from the writings of Guadalupe Vallejo, a *ranchero* who lived in northern California just as the Americans were making their appearance.

"In the old days everyone seemed to live outdoors. There was much gaiety and social life, even though people were widely scattered. We traveled as much as possible on horseback. Young men would ride from one ranch to another for parties, and whoever found his horse tired would let him go and catch another. The days of the rodeos—when cattle were driven in from the surrounding pastures and the herds of the different ranches were separated—were great events.

"Family life among the old Spanish pioneers was filled with dignity and ceremony, but it did not lack in affection. Children were brought up with great respect for their elders. Each one of the old families taught their children the history of the family and reverence toward religion.

"A number of American trappers and hunters came into southern California and settled down in various towns around 1828. The people were excited over their hunting clothes, their rifles, and their strange stories of the desert and things that no one in California had ever seen. After a long rest, the Americans made their way to Los Angeles, where they all married Spanish ladies, were given land, built houses, planted vineyards, and became important people. The most annoying feature of the arrival of the Americans was due to the mines, which drew away most of the servants. As a result, our cattle were left unguarded and were stolen by the thousands. Men who are now wealthy farmers and merchants were guilty of shooting and selling Spanish beef 'without looking at the brand,' as the saying goes."

---

rendezvous, where the goods would be exchanged for furs. After a wild spree lasting several weeks, the trappers would return to the woods. *As year-round residents of the wilderness, these trappers came to be called Mountain Men.*

JED SMITH AND JAMES BECKWOURTH EXPLORE THE WEST. Jedidiah Smith was a Mountain Man, but an unusual one. He avoided the annual party, saved his money, invested it in Ashley's business, and eventually formed a company of his own.

Blessed with extraordinary strength and great stamina, Jedidiah Smith explored the West. In 1824 he led a party across the Continental Divide, in southern Wyoming, and discovered the South Pass. (See map, page 287.) The South Pass was to become the main wagon route across the mountains. The following year he and his friend Jim Bridger became the first Whites to see the Great Salt Lake. Smith then walked overland to California—twice. In the process he explored the great Nevada basin and the Arizona desert. Then, in 1830, his career ended. At a barren water hole along the

Santa Fe Trail, he was killed by the Comanche. He was 33 years old.

Another outstanding Mountain Man was James P. Beckwourth. He had joined his first expedition at St. Louis in 1823. Beckwourth, who was Black, lived among the Crow Indians for six years. According to his autobiography, he also became their leader. In 1850 he discovered a mountain pass in California, which today bears his name.

By the 1830's the West had been trapped out, and the era of the Mountain Men was over. But in the few years of that era, the Mountain Men had managed to explore, at least to some degree, every river and every canyon of the West. Thus, because of their knowledge of the land, they came to be used as guides for army patrols and pioneer wagon trains. It was they who ended up blazing the main trails to the Pacific.

THE OREGON COUNTRY. *In 1818 the United States and Great Britain agreed to jointly occupy the Oregon country in the Pacific Northwest.* This agreement prevented diplomatic squabbles and left the final ownership to the nation that could settle the territory. Both American and British fur traders moved into the Northwest. And Britain's Hudson's Bay Company established an outpost near the mouth of the Columbia River.

In the 1830's American missionaries established churches in the fertile valley of the Willamette River, south of the Columbia. (See map, page 287.) This was done for the purpose of converting American Indians to Christianity. The missionaries had little success. But they soon discovered that the year-round mild temperatures (due to the warm Japanese current in the Pacific

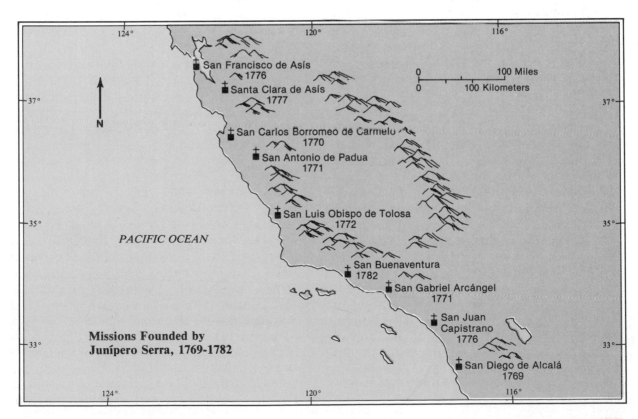

Missions Founded by Junípero Serra, 1769-1782

Ocean) and the abundant rainfall made Oregon ideal farm country.

In 1839 Marcus Whitman, a Presbyterian missionary, returned East to encourage people to go to Oregon. With the preacher's gift for vivid description, Whitman wrote and spoke of Oregon as a paradise on earth. Soon an Oregon fever was sweeping across the Middle West, and trains of covered wagons were winding their way westward.

THE OVERLAND TRAILS. The Oregon Trail started at the steamboat terminals of Westport and St. Joseph, on the Missouri River. It followed the Platte River across the plains and wound into the Continental Divide and through the South Pass. Then, it passed through southern Idaho and followed the winding Snake River to the Columbia.

For the fortunate ones the overland trek to the Willamette Valley took six months. The unlucky ones were buried along the trail. But the hardships of the journey failed to stem the tide. By 1845 there were over 5,000 Americans in the region south of the Columbia River.

Some of the overland migrants had split off at the Great Salt Lake and had headed for California. The California Trail followed the Humboldt River across the Nevada desert and climbed over the snowy Sierra Nevada Mountains. By 1845 there was a sizable American population in northern California.

The waves of settlers going to Texas, Oregon, and California alarmed the American Indians, who were living there. Their hunting grounds were being disrupted and their way of life was being threatened. Many were being pushed into Indian territory, into Mexico, or onto reservations. Reacting to these developments, American Indians began attacking wagon trains and raiding settlements. Friction and misunderstanding were part of the heritage of the movement west.

Sidenote to History
The Dark Horse and the Telegraph

The telegraph is a simple device. A piece of iron, surrounded by a coil of wire, acts as a magnet when electricity is sent through the wire. The magnet reacts to this electricity and taps against another piece of iron as the electrical circuit is opened and closed. A code of both long and short taps is used to send messages along the wire.

Many people recognized the message-sending potential of the telegraph. Samuel F. B. Morse, who eventually got credit for the invention, was only one of many who recognized it and who helped to develop it. Actually, Morse's main contribution was the dot-dash code that bears his name. His other contribution was that of persuading Congress to finance a telegraph line running from Washington, D.C., to Baltimore. Completed in the spring of 1844, the line ran to a coding key in the chambers of the Supreme Court. Surrounded by reporters, the daughter of the commissioner of patents chose a phrase from the Bible—"What hath God wrought?"—and sent the first telegraph message to Baltimore.

A few weeks later the Democratic National Convention met in Baltimore to pick a President. Amid much shouting of "Texas and Oregon" and "Fifty-four forty or fight," the delegates chose a relatively unknown man for their candidate, James K. Polk. The little-known contestant in a horse race is called a dark horse. And so was candidate Polk. Indeed, so "dark" was he that when the telegraph flashed news of the nomination in Washington, Congress refused to believe the newfangled contraption. They insisted on sending a delegation by horse to Baltimore to confirm the news.

The telegraph won the horse race and dark-horse Polk later won the Presidency.

278

A Shoshone Indian camp is featured in this painting, "Rocky Mountains," by Albert Bierstadt. Bierstadt went west in 1857 as a mapmaker, but soon began sketching and painting the vast, panoramic landscapes that are his principal contribution to American art. By 1870 his works were commanding the highest prices ever paid for American paintings. Why do you think his work was so well received?

DIPLOMATIC CRISES. *The immigrants to California found a warm climate and rich lands. But they soon became unhappy with Mexican rule, just as the immigrants to Texas had.* A few even began plotting a revolution. To the north the Oregon settlers organized a makeshift government and asked for admission to the Union. Such agitation created diplomatic crises with both Mexico and Great Britain.

MANIFEST DESTINY. The overland migration caught the fancy of Americans everywhere. Suddenly, there were colonies of Americans on the shores of the Pacific! *A New York newspaper spoke with excitement of the nation's "manifest destiny" — expansion to the Pacific.* Overnight the phrase caught the popular imagination. It brought visions of a continental republic, spreading from sea to sea.

"FIFTY-FOUR FORTY OR FIGHT!" The Democrats, who had been out of office since 1840 and were looking for a popular issue, seized "manifest destiny" and made it their own. In 1844 they nominated James K. Polk, a friend of Jackson's from Tennessee. To avoid sectional jealousies they demanded the annexation of both Texas and Oregon. Not just the part of Oregon south of the Columbia River, but the entire Northwest as far as Russian Alaska, 54° 40′ north latitude. It was a bold claim, and it risked war. But the Democrats did not care. "Fifty-four forty or fight!" they shouted.

The Whigs were less enthusiastic about expansion in 1844 and more interested in ridding themselves of John Tyler, who had vetoed key features of their system. (Tyler had become President in 1841, after the death of William Henry Harrison, who had served only one month as President.) The Whigs nominated the popular Henry Clay. But Clay lost the election to Polk. Banks and tariffs, the main elements of Clay's so-called American System, seemed dull in comparison to the heady and alluring promise of "manifest destiny."

Section Review

1. Mapping: Using the map on page 287, trace the route of the Oregon Trail. What geographic factors made the trip a hardship?
2. Identify or explain: William Becknell,

Santa Anna, Samuel Houston, Marcus Whitman, the *impresarios*.
3. How did the republic of Texas come into being? Trace the steps that led to its independence from Mexico.
4. What role did the Mountain Men play in opening up the West?
5. What did Americans mean when they spoke about "manifest destiny" in 1844?

4. War With Mexico, 1846-1848

TEXAS BECOMES A STATE. Although James K. Polk's election victory in 1844 was a close one, everyone assumed it meant popular support for expansion.

In its closing days the Tyler administration negotiated a treaty of annexation with Texas, which had been waiting for admission to the Union for 10 years. In submitting the treaty to the Senate for approval, Secretary of State John C. Calhoun admitted that his purpose in wanting the annexation of Texas was to enlarge the territory open to slavery. This aroused so much northern suspicion that the Senate rejected the treaty. *After Polk took office, however, Congress simply passed a resolution declaring Texas admitted to the Union, slaves and all.* In 1845 the Lone Star Republic became the Lone Star State.

THE TEXAS BOUNDARY. *By adding Texas, the nation inherited a long-standing boundary dispute between Texas and Mexico.* As part of Mexico, Texas' southern boundary had been the Nueces (noo-AY-ses) River. As an independent state, it claimed the Rio Grande. (See map, page 275.) The difference involved a large strip of land that extended far into the interior. Polk accepted the Texas claim and ordered an army, under General Zachary Taylor, to occupy the disputed area. It was a risky step. Much would depend on the mood of Mexico.

THE OREGON CRISIS. *When he opened the possibility of war with Mexico, Polk also moved against the British in Oregon.*

In the autumn of 1845, he announced the end of the joint occupation and told the British to evacuate Oregon within a year. Britain was not accustomed to such demands. In normal times such an order would have brought a British naval squadron to the President's doorstep.

Fortunately for Polk, who faced the possibility of a two-front war, these were not normal times. Britain was desperately trying to cope with a famine in Ireland. The prime minister was not willing to fight over a remote wilderness. *Thus, in the spring of 1846, Britain proposed a compromise at the 49th parallel of latitude, and Polk accepted it.* (See map at the right.) The crisis was resolved without a conflict.

MORE SETTLERS COME TO OREGON. *To stimulate migration into the new territory, the Oregon Donation Act of 1850 was passed. It promised land to anyone who would settle it by 1855.*

Women as well as men were allowed to take advantage of the Act and to claim their share of land. Single men or women got 128 hectares (320 acres) apiece, and a married couple got 256 hectares (640 acres)—128 hectares (320 acres) in each of their names.

Some settlers brought slaves with them to Oregon. However, by 1845 slavery was forbidden in Oregon. The same law required that the free Blacks leave Oregon within two years.

THE BEAR FLAG REVOLT. *In the fall of 1845, while Polk was pushing the British out of Oregon, a military expedition started overland to California.*

John C. Frémont, already famed as an explorer, commanded a force charged with surveying a railroad route across the mountains. Or at least that is what Frémont told the Mexican authorities when he appeared some weeks later in California. Mexican authorities suspected he was there to stir up trouble and ordered him to leave. Frémont lingered for awhile, but then moved slowly toward Oregon.

In the meantime President Polk and James Buchanan, the Secretary of State, sent messages to American residents in California, hinting that if they threw off Mexican rule they would be welcomed into the Union. With such encouragement the Americans became openly rebellious. Through the spring of 1846, there were armed clashes between Americans and Mexican soldiers. Then, in May another one of the President's agents appeared, a marine lieutenant who, in disguise, had come overland across Mexico. He carried secret dispatches for Frémont and news of an impending war with Mexico.

To this day we do not know what was in those secret messages. But after reading

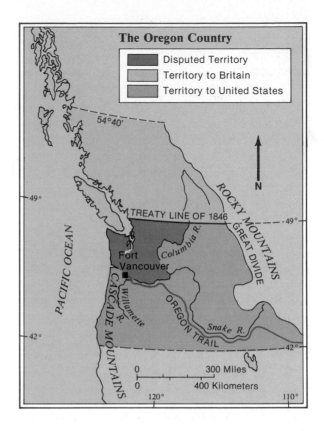

The Oregon Country

- Disputed Territory
- Territory to Britain
- Territory to United States

them, Frémont hurried back to California. There, in June 1846, his return triggered a revolution. And under a flag that pictured a grizzly bear, an American force defeated the Mexican army and sent it retreating south to Los Angeles. Frémont then occupied the capital of northern California, Monterey. But Mexico retained control of Southern California for several months. Finally, in January 1847 Frémont defeated a Mexican force led by Andrés Pico. This encounter marked the end of Mexico's resistance in California.

"WAR . . . BY THE ACT OF MEXICO HERSELF." *General Zachary Taylor's occupation of the disputed territory between Texas and Mexico was a challenge that Mexicans would not overlook.* Mexico had a large, well-trained army, and the Mexicans felt they were better soldiers than the Americans. In the last war that America had fought (1812–1815) its army could not even manage to mount a successful invasion of Canada.

Mexico accepted the challenge. In April 1846 a Mexican army crossed to the north side of the Rio Grande. After several clashes between the cavalry patrols, the two armies engaged in a general fight. But the Mexicans were short of gunpowder and were forced to underload their cannons. The cannonballs came bouncing harmlessly across the battlefield, while the American artillery fired effectively. The Mexicans retired back across the Rio Grande. General Taylor then sent word of the battle to the President and crossed in pursuit. (See map, page 283.)

Sidenote to History

"The Six-Shot Peacemaker"

As a child Samuel Colt had a way with guns and bombs. He could take apart a pistol and reassemble it before he was 10. He was also able to borrow chemicals from his father's factory and make bombs. At Amherst Academy he was sent home permanently when one of his bombs blew up part of the school.

At the age of 14, Samuel Colt took a trip to India. On it, as he was watching the turning of the ship's wheel, he got an idea for a new sort of pistol. Until the 1830's, rifles and pistols had been loaded from the front end and had fired one shot at a time. The process had been slow and laborious. Even later, when a bullet had been developed that combined the powder and the ball into one shell, shots could only be fired singly.

Colt's idea was to have a revolving cylinder with six chambers, with a bullet in each chamber. The cocking of the pistol would rotate the cylinder, bringing a new chamber into line with the barrel. The weapon could then be fired as rapidly as it could be cocked. By 1836 Colt had whittled a working model out of wood and obtained a patent on the invention.

It was a good year to go into the pistol-making business. The Texas revolution had created an instant demand for a weapon that could be fired rapidly from the back of a horse. In fact, the Texas Rangers had kept Colt in business before the Mexican War. After that, mass orders had come from the United States Army.

Colt was constantly improving his methods of production. He standardized the parts of the pistol so that each gun was identical. And he figured out a way to have the weapons put together on an assembly line.

His Colt .45, the "six-shot peacemaker," became the symbol of the American West. Inventor, businessman, and industrialist, Samuel Colt had come a long way. Even his former teachers at Amherst could be proud of him.

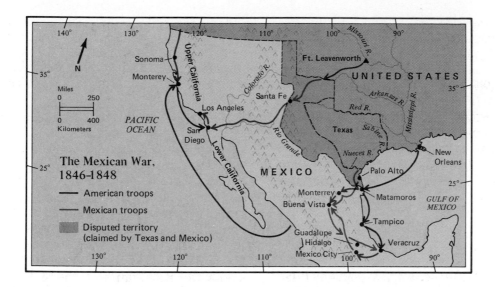

The Mexican War, 1846-1848

American troops
Mexican troops
Disputed territory (claimed by Texas and Mexico)

Taylor's report of the fighting reached Polk on Saturday, May 9. He then called together his cabinet, and they agreed on a declaration of war. By Monday morning President Polk appeared before Congress, asking for war. A Mexican army, he said, "has passed the boundary of the United States, has invaded our territory, and shed American blood upon the American soil." War, he then concluded, "notwithstanding all our efforts to avoid it, exists by the act of Mexico herself."

A NECESSARY OR UNNECESSARY WAR? *Since the soil where the fighting was taking place was in dispute between two countries, the President's description was not entirely accurate.* Northern representatives to Congress were troubled. In view of Calhoun's earlier admission that the South desired Texas as added slave territory, was it possible that this "slave power" also desired New Mexico and California? Even so, fighting had already started, and it was difficult to oppose a war already in progress. As it turned out, the declaration of war passed Congress by large majorities.

Yet, the conscience of one young congressman could not be stilled. At his first opportunity Abraham Lincoln, newly elected from Illinois, offered resolutions, daring the President to name the spot where American blood had been shed on American soil. Lincoln's "spot resolutions" showed that some people felt that President Polk had started an unnecessary war.

"OLD ROUGH-AND-READY." Still, the United States got what it wanted within three months after the war started. General Stephen Watts Kearney, with an army of Missouri volunteers, occupied Santa Fe, and with it fell all of New Mexico. The Bear Flag Revolt in California removed Mexican power from the Pacific Coast. The Southwest was in American hands. The only thing that remained was to convince Mexico of that.

General Zachary Taylor—"Old Rough-and-Ready" to his soldiers—pushed across the Rio Grande and occupied the Mexican state of Coahuila (koh-ah-WEE-lah). During the autumn of 1846, Mexico's aging hero Santa Anna, returned from exile, seized power in Mexico City, and started north with an army. He met Taylor at the village of Buena Vista (BWAY-nah VEES-tah) on February 22, 1847. For two days the Mexicans assaulted the American defenses, before retiring in defeat. Although Taylor emerged from this fight a national hero, he was still 1,280 kilometers (800 miles) from the Mexican capital.

"OLD FUSS-AND-FEATHERS." General Taylor's victories both pleased President Polk and worried him. Taylor was a Whig politically and a potential rival in the Presidential election of 1848. Besides, Taylor's strategy for conquering Mexico seemed impractical. Polk worried that as Taylor advanced through the mountains of northern Mexico, his supply line would come under attack from Mexican guerrillas. Taylor himself might even become trapped and surrounded.

It would be far easier, Polk decided, to send another army to conquer the capital. After landing on the coast near Veracruz, the army could make the comparatively short march inland to Mexico City. (See map, page 283.) To head this force, the President named General Winfield Scott. Scott, too, was a Whig, but he was too dull and colorless to be a political threat. "Old Fuss-and-Feathers," his soldiers called him.

Scott's army of 10,000 landed near Veracruz in March 1847. It then fought its way through the narrow canyons that led to the central plateau of Mexico. After several fierce battles, in which Santa Anna lost more than half his army, Scott stood at the gates of Mexico City. There, he stormed the fortified hill that guarded the causeway into the city, before fighting his way to the National Palace. Santa Anna surrendered on September 17, 1847.

THE TREATY OF GUADALUPE HIDALGO. Diplomats with the authority to negotiate a peace settlement had accompanied Scott's army. *Meeting at the village of Guadalupe Hidalgo (gwa-da-LOO-pay e-DAHL-go), just outside the capital, representatives of the two governments worked out a treaty in January 1848.* Mexico gave up all claims to Texas and sold the rest of the Southwest—from New Mex-

The Mexican port city of Veracruz, considered the key to Mexico City's capture, suffered a three-day bombardment before surrendering to the United States Army under General Winfield Scott. In this 1847 lithograph, the Mexicans are surrendering their arms to General Scott.

Theodore Gentilz came to San Antonio from France in 1843. He became fascinated with the Southwest. This scene is a market day in San Antonio. What Mexican influences can you see in the painting?

ico to California—for 15 million dollars. (See map, page 287.)

The Treaty of Guadalupe Hidalgo placed about 75,000 Spanish-speaking and American Indian people under United States rule. These people's culture was a mixture of Spanish, Mexican, and Indian ways of life—a culture that English-speaking Americans did not understand. As the area became settled, conflicts would arise and adjustments would be made.

Section Review

1. **Mapping:** In this chapter, you have read about how the measurements of latitude were involved in two border disputes—one in Oregon and one in Texas. Describe the state borders of the United States along one latitude line. In what ways are the borders of the North and the South different from those of the East and West?
2. **Identify or explain:** James K. Polk, Zachary Taylor, John C. Frémont, Winfield Scott.
3. Describe the events leading to the Mexican War. What was the underlying cause of the war?

5. The California Gold Rush

GOLD FEVER. The value of America's new empire in the Southwest was soon apparent. In the spring of 1848, Johann Sutter, a Swiss immigrant with a sizable ranch in northern California, decided to expand his operations. While digging a pond for Sutter's new mill, one of his employees discovered some flakes of yellow metal in the stream. Sutter instantly recognized it as gold and tried to keep it secret. But the secret leaked out, creating a rush to his valley.

By June, San Francisco was a ghost town. Its population of gold hunters had fanned out across the territory. Gold seemed everywhere—Clear Creek, the Feather River, the San Joachín (san wa-KEEN) valley. In some places nuggets could even be pried out of the soil with a penknife. In the riverbeds miners scooped up the soil with wash pans. They swirled the lighter sand away with water, leaving flakes of gold at the bottom.

News of the discoveries reached the East during the fall of 1848. President Polk confirmed them in his annual message to Congress in December, and the War Department put a pot of gold on display as proof. *By early 1849 gold fever had become a national disease, and the rush to California*

285

by thousands of forty-niners was under way.

THE ROUTE OF THE FORTY-NINERS.

The easiest routes to California were by sea. (See map, page 287.) Clipper ships offered a fairly comfortable passage around South America to the Pacific. But even these speedy vessels took months to round Cape Horn. Somewhat faster was steamship passage to the Isthmus of Panama, a short overland hop by mule, where one could transfer to another steamship bound for San Francisco. *But since sea travel was more expensive, most of the forty-niners went overland by way of the California Trail.*

In all, some 80,000 people were involved in the gold rush. Few found any gold. The surface gold soon disappeared, and as for the rest, most forty-niners knew little about mining. In the end the eastern mining companies took possession of the gold fields. Among the people who profited most from

This 1852 photograph shows a crew of gold prospectors in Auburn Ravine, California. Thousands of Chinese came to the West Coast during this period. They worked in the gold and silver mines and were instrumental in the building of railroads.

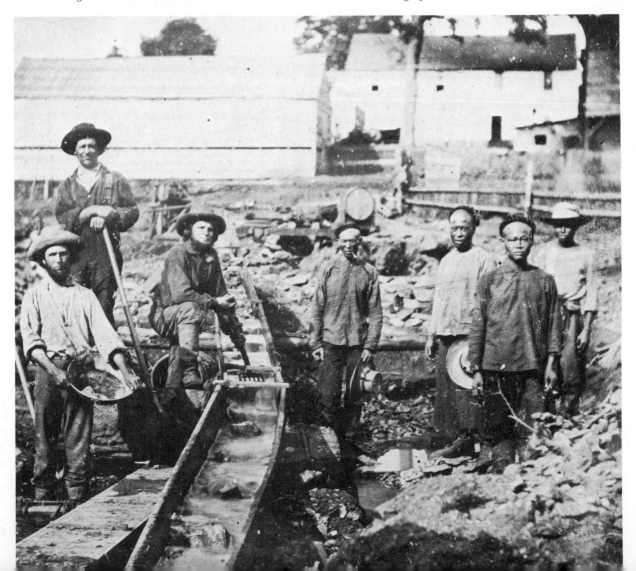

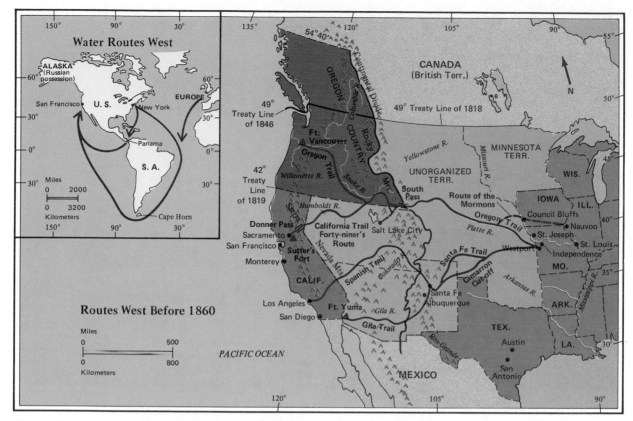

Water Routes West

ALASKA (Russian possession)

U.S.

EUROPE

San Francisco

New York

Panama

S. A.

Miles
0   2000
0   3200
Kilometers

Cape Horn

Routes West Before 1860

Miles
0   500
0   800
Kilometers

PACIFIC OCEAN

CANADA (British Terr.)

N

49° Treaty Line of 1818

OREGON COUNTRY

Rocky Mts.

Continental Divide

Columbia R.

49° Treaty Line of 1846

Ft. Vancouver

Oregon Trail

Willamette R.

42° Treaty Line of 1819

Snake R.

Yellowstone R.

Missouri R.

MINNESOTA TERR.

WIS.

Sierra Nevada

Humboldt R.

South Pass

UNORGANIZED TERR.

Route of the Mormons

Oregon Trail

IOWA

Council Bluffs

ILL.

Nauvoo

Donner Pass

Sacramento

San Francisco

California Trail Forty-niner's Route

Salt Lake City

Platte R.

St. Joseph

St. Louis

Sutter's Fort

Monterey

Nevada Mts.

Spanish Trail

Colorado R.

Santa Fe Trail

Westport

Independence

MO.

CALIF.

Los Angeles

Cimarron Cut-off

Arkansas R.

ARK.

San Diego

Ft. Yuma

Gila R.

Santa Fe Albuquerque

Gila Trail

Rio Grande

TEX.

Austin

LA.

MEXICO

San Antonio

the gold rush were the Californians who had stayed home to farm. For example, by the end of 1849, eggs in San Francisco were selling for a dollar apiece.

CALIFORNIA STATEHOOD. By 1849, there were 100,000 people in California, more than enough for statehood. Up to that point no government had been created in California. The miners had made their own law and had enforced it.

In the winter of 1849, a convention met and drafted a state constitution. This constitution outlawed slavery but discriminated against American Indians. The convention then presented its constitution to the federal government and asked it to make California a state. The request triggered a political crisis in Washington, D.C.

The question of slavery in the West had simmered during the Mexican War. Southerners had hoped to add to slave territory

with the war. The northerners had been determined that the Southwest remain free. California's knock at the Union door had brought matters to a head. It was another crisis that would lead finally to Civil War.

Section Review

1. Mapping: Using the map on page 287, trace the overland route to California by way of the California Trail. Trace the sea route around South America. Why did many people choose the longer sea route instead of the more direct land route?
2. Identify or explain: Johann Sutter, Cape Horn, the forty-niners.
3. What does gold fever refer to?
4. Why did the application for California statehood trigger a sectional crisis between the North and the South?

Chapter 11 Review

Bird's-Eye View

The first half of the 19th century in the United States was a period of growth, expansion, and enterprise. Innovations in transportation—such as steamboats, canals, and railroads—stimulated trade, travel, and a spirit of adventure. The political and economic crises in Europe stimulated immigration to the United States. These immigrants became the labor force for a growing American industry and the farmers for and expanding frontier. The beginnings of industrialism also stimulated the rise of a union movement.

As their numbers increased, the immigrants and settlers became jealous of the landholdings of the Indian tribes in the East. Soon, they began pressuring the federal government to make these lands available to them. Although they received no response from President Adams, President Jackson was willing to agree to their wishes. By social and economic pressure, persuasion, and ultimately armed force, virtually all the eastern tribes came to be pushed across the middle border into the Great Plains.

The territory of Texas was originally controlled by Spain but sparsely settled. When Mexico became a republic in 1821, it then controlled this territory and welcomed American settlers into it. But then Mexico became alarmed at the number of Americans living in Texas. And Americans soon found reasons to be unhappy under Mexican rule. Southerners, especially, feared Mexico's restriction on slavery. A series of battles between the Mexican army under General Santa Anna and the American settlers in Texas resulted in a victory for the settlers and independence for Texas.

North of Texas, Mountain Men, traders, and missionaries were blazing overland trails to the West, opening up the Oregon country and California for settlement. At first the United States and Britain jointly occupied Oregon. But then American settlers began insisting on exclusive rule. They believed it was the "manifest destiny" of the United States to become the ruler of a country that spanned the continent from ocean to ocean.

The boundary dispute with Britain was settled peacefully. But the one with Mexico led to war. The war ended when the American army occupied Mexico City. This resulted in the Treaty of Guadalupe Hidalgo, in which Mexico gave up all claims to the Southwest.

A settlers' revolt in California established the independence of that territory. Independence was confirmed in a treaty with Mexico. The discovery of gold in northern California led to the gold rush, with many thousands rushing west by sea and land routes. Few became wealthy. But California itself grew rapidly enough to apply for statehood. The issue of slavery in this new state provoked a sectional confrontation that foreshadowed the crisis of the future.

Vocabulary

Define or identify each of the following:

Cumberland Road	Stephen F. Austin	"manifest destiny"
Trail of Tears	Alamo	Colt .45
factory system	Mountain Men	forty-niners

Review Questions

1. List four important changes in transportation that occurred between 1810 and 1850.
2. How did the steamship affect immigration?
3. What changes occurred in manufacturing in the first half of the 1800's?
4. Describe the treatment of the American Indians by the state and federal governments.
5. What events led to the creation of the Lone Star Republic?
6. How did missionaries help in the settlement of the Oregon country?
7. Why did the United States fight a war with Mexico?
8. How did the discovery of gold at Sutter's Mill affect California?

Reviewing Social Studies Skills

1. Using the chart on page 266, list approximately how many people lived in the North in 1820, 1840, and 1860. How many people lived in the South in those years?
2. Using the map on page 270, answer the following questions.
   a. What tribes were resettled? Locate where they were forced to resettle.
   b. What were the original home sites of the resettled Indians?

Reading for Meaning

1. Using the text, give five examples of cultural conflicts. Choose one of the following to describe how each conflict was resolved: armed conflict, the threat of force, compromise, accommodation, assimilation.
2. The concept of "manifest destiny" gave Americans the feeling that they had a right to all land between the Atlantic and the Pacific. What do you think about this idea? How do you think an American Indian would feel about it? How would the Mexican government react to it?
3. Which do you think is the most appropriate title for the story of Frederic Tudor: a) "Yankee Ingenuity" b) "Growth of an Industry" or c) "Ice in America." Explain your choice.
4. Write a story about the Texas revolt against Mexico from the perspective of one of the following: a) a Mexican soldier b) an American Indian c) a Black slave.

Bibliography

Across the Wide Missouri, by Bernard De Voto (Houghton Mifflin), tells the story of the Mountain Men and the Rocky Mountain fur trade.

1846: Year of Decision, also by De Voto (Houghton Mifflin), tells, in fascinating detail, the story of President Polk's maneuvers and how they led to the Mexican War.

The Raven (Paperback Library), by Marquis James, is a good biography of Samuel Houston.

William Johnson's *The Birth of Texas* (Houghton Mifflin) tells the story of Austin, the Lone Star Republic, and the Alamo.

Chapter 12

A Fire Bell in the Night

It was a hot summer evening in August 1846. The war with Mexico was three months old, and Congress was discussing a bill to appropriate funds for the army. Santa Fe had fallen. Texas and California were in American hands. A vast empire in the southwest lay within reach.

Suddenly, the House stirred to life. A heavyset representative from western Pennsylvania, named David Wilmot, was on his feet with an amendment to the bill. Wilmot was proposing that any territory acquired from Mexico in the war remain, as it had been under Mexican rule, without slavery. In addition, he voiced a suspicion that the South had started the Mexican War in order to add slave territory.

Wilmot's amendment—called the Wilmot Proviso—spoke the language of free soil. For more than a decade, abolitionists had been denouncing slavery without much effect. The great majority in the North was simply not interested in the plight of the slave. And many felt that immediate emancipation would violate the property rights of slave owners. But that same northern majority could see the advantage of confining slavery, and Blacks as well, to the South. Free soil, then, would leave slavery where it was, but prevent its expansion into the West.

Chapter Objectives

After you have finished reading this chapter, you should be able to:
1. Recognize the causes and the results of the Compromise of 1850.
2. Explain how the Kansas-Nebraska Act increased the tension between the North and the South.
3. List the basic reasons for the split in the Democratic Party.
4. Describe the events that led to Lincoln's election and how that election caused the secession of the southern states.

The free soil movement had broad appeal. It appealed not only to prejudiced northerners who did not want Blacks in their midst, whether slave or free, but also to moderate reformers as a practical way to attack slavery. The first opportunity to test the idea was with the territory acquired from Mexico in the Southwest.

Free soil was one factor that helped to bring on the Civil War.

1. The Compromise of 1850

THE NEED FOR WESTERN GOVERNMENT. The South and its allies managed to defeat the Wilmot Proviso and to prevent it from ever becoming law. But the controversy surrounding it delayed the organization of the western territories. This

In 1846 Brigham Young and his followers began their movement westward toward "they knew not what." In the first year alone, over 15,000 Mormons had traveled west. When they reached the Great Salt Lake in Utah, Young announced simply, "This is the place."

delay became important when the Mormon trek into Utah and the gold rush to California added to the demands for a western government.

THE MORMONS AND UTAH. *The largest and most successful religious sect founded during the early 19th century was the Mormon Church, or the Church of Jesus Christ of Latter-Day Saints.* Its founder, Joseph Smith, was a religious enthusiast from Palmyra, New York. According to Smith he had received direct revelations from the angel Moroni. These revelations had enabled him to discover several golden tablets inscribed with symbols. He translated the symbols and published his translation in 1830 as the Book of Mormon.

Thousands joined Smith's church in the United States. Mormon missionaries converted thousands more in Great Britain and Denmark. But despite its popularity, the Mormons, like many other new religious sects, did not escape persecution. Feelings against the Mormons forced them to abandon settlements in western New York, Ohio, Missouri, and finally Illinois.

Many people disliked the Mormons because of their belief, as stated in the Book of Mormon, that they were the chosen people. Other people disliked them because of their closely knit organization and their thriving economic life. In 1839 the Mormons moved from Missouri to Nauvoo, Illinois. They thrived in Illinois where their numbers grew to 15,000. In 1843 Joseph Smith first disclosed a revelation which instructed the Mormons on the practice of *polygamy.* Under polygamy, some Mormon men could have more than one wife. Although this practice became an "open secret" in Nauvoo, the Mormons' power and success in Illinois led to problems with their non-Mormon neighbors, an outbreak of violence, and Smith's arrest and imprisonment. On June

27, 1844, an anti-Mormon mob murdered Joseph Smith. As a result, the Mormons were forced to abandon Illinois and to move farther west.

Polygamy is the practice of having more than one husband or wife at the same time.

Smith's successor, Brigham Young, led the Mormons across the Great Plains to the western deserts. There, they hoped to have no neighbors and, consequently, no enemies. In 1846 the Mormons trekked westward to Council Bluffs on the Missouri River. In the spring of 1847, they continued on to the Great Salt Lake, in Utah. There, they built Salt Lake City, which they called Zion. (See map, page 287.)

The Mormons were determined to succeed in their desert settlement, and they did. For one thing they mastered desert farming. This required a skill practiced by the Indian farmers of the western deserts, but one that most settlers from the East did not know. By channeling water from nearby mountains, they made the desert bloom. When the gold rush to California got under way, their thriving settlement was one of the most important stops.

The Mormons then declared their settlement the state of Deseret. But many easterners felt that a federal territory should be organized in the region. However, before either of these proposals could be acted on, California requested admission to the Union as a state. This request brought to a head the whole question of the governing of the West.

THE SECTIONAL CRISIS. President Polk refused to run again in 1848. The Democrats nominated Senator Lewis Cass of Michigan. A third party, the Free-Soil party, turned to former President Martin Van Buren, who had split the Democratic vote. The Whigs went for a military hero with little-known political views—General Zachary Taylor—and he won the election.

Although a southerner and a slave owner, President Taylor came under the influence of northern Whig leaders, notably William H. Seward of New York. Seward was an outspoken opponent of slavery. *Thus, when California asked for admission to the Union as a free state in December 1849, Taylor voiced his approval.*

The South felt betrayed by one of its own. Many southerners had voted for Taylor simply because he was a slave owner. Worse, the admission of California without the admission of a slave state would upset the sectional balance in the Senate, which had been maintained since the Missouri Compromise of 1820.

Reacting to Taylor's appeal for the admission of California, the southern representatives to Congress issued a call for a convention of southern states. The purpose of the convention, to be held in Nashville, Tennessee, would be the discussion of secession from the Union. As in the nullification crisis 20 years before, a dissolution of the Union and a possible civil war loomed on the horizon.

THE GREAT COMPROMISE. *At that critical moment, in February 1850, Henry Clay stepped in and suggested a compromise.* This became known as the Compromise of 1850. He presented to Congress a series of bills designed to solve all ongoing disputes between the North and South. Six of Clay's eight bills amounted to a package deal on the question of slavery. Under these six bills: ① California would be admitted as a free state; ② the rest of the land acquired from Mexico would be organized into two federal territories—Utah and New Mexico—and the decision on slavery would be left up to the settlers of the territory; ③ the use of the District of Columbia as a depot in interstate slave trade would be prohibited; ④ slavery in the District of Columbia would be abolished only with the consent of its residents and the state of Maryland; ⑤ a new and tougher fugitive slave act would be created so that southerners could more easily recover their slaves, if they ran away to the North; and 6 Congress would declare that it had no power to interfere with interstate slave trade.

The second of these six proposals—which was suggested by Senator Stephen A. Douglas of Illinois—was designed to remove the issue of slavery in the territories and to let the people most concerned decide for themselves. Known as the concept of popular sovereignty, it seemed a sensible solution to a thorny problem. Douglas believed that popular sovereignty was the solution to the nation's ills, and he spent the next 10 years advocating it for the western territories. Unfortunately, it did nothing to help those people already in slavery.

Congress debated Clay's package for seven months. Webster and Calhoun each delivered a major speech. Calhoun opposed the compromise. Webster favored it, though his stance was criticized in antislavery Massachusetts. President Taylor was another one opposed to the compromise, a major obstacle. But when Taylor died during the summer, the new President, Millard Fillmore, supported the compromise, and it passed in August 1850.

The sectional crisis had ended for the moment. The southern secession convention had met in Nashville and adjourned without taking action. The South would wait and see how things turned out.

In the end they turned out badly from the southern point of view, for not all northerners accepted Clay's fifth proposal, which concerned the return of fugitive slaves.

RESISTANCE TO THE FUGITIVE SLAVE LAW. In the background of each succeeding crisis were thousands of fugitive slaves. They were escaping to the North and attempting to make new lives there. But many northerners, even though they opposed slavery, were nevertheless anti-Black. In 1850 the Indiana constitution barred Blacks from entering or settling in the state. Even where they were seemingly accepted,

This painting of the great Senate debate of 1850 was done by Peter Frederick Rothermel. Henry Clay has the floor, and John C. Calhoun stands third from the right. Daniel Webster sits on the left, head in hand. From the facial expressions of the senators, can you detect their reactions to Clay's speech?

Sidenote to History

"Black Moses"

Harriet Ross was born a slave in 1819. At the age of six, she was hired out to a trapper, who made her wade into the swamps to recover his muskrats. When she caught pneumonia, she was forced to do housework. She cleaned house all day and took care of the children at night. She also ran away so often that she was sent into the forests to work with her father. Her father was a lumberjack who worked for a master in the woods along Maryland's eastern shore. In her 20's she married John Tubman, a free Black living in the neighborhood.

After her marriage she learned of the Underground Railroad. By 1849, at about the age of 30, she used it to escape. Once free, she took a job in Philadelphia, hoping to earn enough money to return to Maryland to help her family.

In 1850 she went back. But she found her aging parents unwilling to leave. Still, she managed to take out her sister and five other slaves who wanted to go. Then, after they were out, she got her idea for repeated trips. Instead of waiting until slaves fled to the North, why not extend the Underground Railroad into the South? So, for the next 10 years, she made 19 trips back to Maryland. As her tombstone says, "She never ran her train off the track and never lost a passenger."

Her appearance helped. Short, heavyset, and stooped, she would walk slowly down a country road singing to herself. The slave patrols considered her a half-wit who would eventually find her way home. But her songs were messages to her "train" of refugees who were hiding in the woods. When the patrol was gone, the slaves would resume their journey.

In the late 1850's the abolitionists learned of her adventures and made a hero of her. She then began giving talks to antislavery meetings, being introduced simply as Moses, after the Biblical hero who had led his people to the Promised Land. This false name was used because she was herself a fugitive slave. Under the federal law of 1850 she could be taken back into slavery at any time.

When the Civil War came, Harriet Tubman volunteered to work as a spy, but the army refused her services. Then, in 1861, her chance came. The navy had captured Port Royal, South Carolina, and the White planters had fled the Union army. The Blacks had remained, and after some time, they had been allowed to form a regiment.

The Port Royal Blacks conducted raids into the heart of South Carolina, burning plantations and freeing slaves. Harriet Tubman became a guerrilla leader. When the northern troops under General Sherman arrived in South Carolina, Harriet Tubman left. She spent the last months of the war as a nurse on the Virginia battlefields.

When the fighting ended she was given a railroad pass home. But the conductor—this time a real one—refused to honor it because she was Black. Despite her advancing years it took three men to wrench her out of her seat and to throw her into the baggage car.

She eventually settled in Auburn, New York. She made her house into a haven for unemployed Blacks who had come north looking for work. In her last years an Auburn neighbor, Susan B. Anthony, interested her in the women's suffrage movement. Though almost 90 years old, she brought to the movement all the strength and vigor of her years as an Underground Railroad conductor. She retained her strength to the very last. Having caught pneumonia, she summoned her circle of friends, conducted her own funeral service, led the group in singing "Swing Low, Sweet Chariot," and died. The year was 1913, seven years before women got the vote.

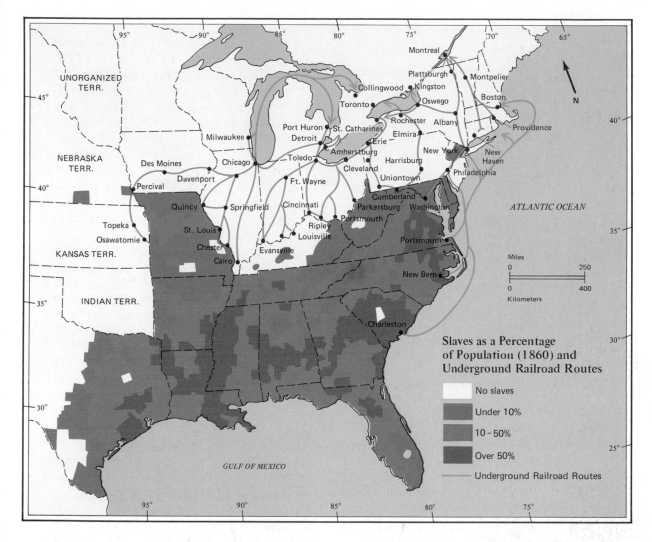

Slaves as a Percentage
of Population (1860) and
Underground Railroad Routes

No slaves

Under 10%

10 – 50%

Over 50%

Underground Railroad Routes

Blacks often lived in fear of being suddenly escorted to the town line by townspeople or back to slavery by the slave catcher.

The new federal law on fugitives permitted a slave catcher to recover a Black in the North simply by declaring before a court that the person was his slave. No hearing was required. The slave catcher's word was enough. The person who was pointed out as a slave had no defense. Under such conditions many free Blacks in the North—some of them successful runaways like Frederick Douglass—were in danger of being hauled into slavery.

Suddenly, slavery was no longer only the South's problem. It was a national problem. It began to dawn on the North that human bondage in one part of the country ultimately presented a threat to human rights everywhere.

Attempts to recover fugitive slaves met open resistance in northern cities. Mobs freed runaway slaves from jails in Boston, Massachusetts; in Troy, New York; and in Milwaukee, Wisconsin. The state of Wisconsin even tried to nullify the federal law by refusing to allow it to be enforced. The fugitive-slave problem had kept tempers

295

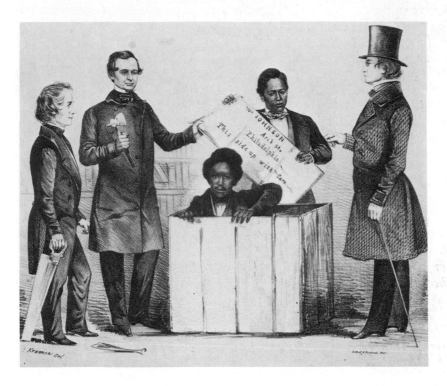

One of the famous escapes to freedom was Henry Brown's. He was packed into a crate with a canteen of water and some biscuits, then shipped from Richmond to Philadelphia. Once in Philadelphia, he made his home an Underground Railroad station.

from cooling after the Compromise of 1850. And before long a new crisis would further ignite them.

Section Review

1. Mapping: Using the map on page 295, identify the states with the most slaves.
2. Identify or explain: David Wilmot, Joseph Smith, Free Soil party, Zachary Taylor, Millard Fillmore, Brigham Young.
3. Make a chart on which you compare the Wilmot Proviso, the Compromise of 1850, and popular sovereignty as solutions to the problem of slavery in the West.
4. Describe the new fugitive slave law. How did it show northerners that slavery was a national problem?

2. The Kansas-Nebraska Act and "Bleeding Kansas"

THE BREAKUP OF THE WHIGS. The Whig party began to disintegrate after 1852. "Cotton" Whigs from the South found that they could not get along with the antislavery "conscience" Whigs of New England. Some southern Whigs even became Democrats. Others drifted into the anti-immigrant, anti-Black, Know-Nothing party. The Know-Nothings were an alliance of several anti-immigrant, anti-Black societies. Officially, they were the Order of the Star-Spangled Banner. But because members were sworn to secrecy and had refused to answer questions about their aims and activities, they came to be called the Know-Nothings.

A DOUGHFACE ADMINISTRATION.

The rising political tension resulted in much name-calling. People expressed their anger and their frustration through an array of ill-sounding nicknames. One of these was "doughface," meaning a northerner who sided with the South and slavery.

President Franklin Pierce, winner of the election of 1852, was a Jacksonian Democrat from New Hampshire. (Pierce defeated the Whig candidate, General Winfield Scott, a hero of the Mexican War.) Already a weak man, his strength was further undermined by the loss of his son as he was about to enter the White House. His son had been killed by a railroad train. *In office, Pierce fell under the influence of the most forceful personality in his cabinet, Secretary of War Jefferson Davis of Mississippi.* Davis was a militant southerner, prepared to leave the Union if the South's interests were not protected.

THE OSTEND MANIFESTO.

The bias of the Pierce administration soon became evident. Southerners were particularly anxious to add slave territory to the Union. The nearby island of Cuba seemed an attractive candidate. Spain had already refused an offer of $100 million for Cuba in 1848. *Then, in 1854 the American ministers to Great Britain, France, and Spain met at Ostend, Belgium. They issued a declaration on the right of the United States to seize Cuba by force.* Although the President denied responsibility for his ministers' statement, the abolitionists were convinced that

The "Know-Nothing" party grew out of a general movement in the Whig party against immigrants and Blacks. By 1850 the party was a secret society, whose members were pledged to answer "I know nothing" to all questions about their organization. This lithograph shows a riot in Philadelphia.

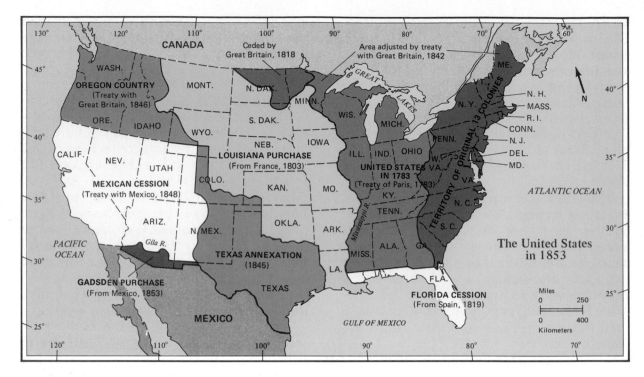

The United States in 1853

this administration was ready to go to war to add to the South's power base.

THE GADSDEN PURCHASE, 1853.
Complicating sectional tensions was the effort to build a transcontinental railroad to California. The choice of a route seemed crucial. A northern route, starting at Chicago or St. Louis, meant northern influence in California. A southern route, with a terminal at Memphis or New Orleans, meant that California would be tied to the South.

Actually, the rivalry delayed construction of the railroad until after the Civil War. But in 1853 the Pierce administration boosted the prospects for the southern route by purchasing additional territory from the Mexican government.

Pierce's emissary, James Gadsden, had persuaded Mexico to part with an area of land south of the Gila River, in Arizona, for 10 million dollars. (See map, page 298.)

It had seemed like an outrageous price at the time, for according to Kit Carson, a Mountain Man familiar with the territory, "not even a wolf" could survive in that barren land. But the acquisition did ease the problem of where to construct a railroad route. The route would run west from El Paso, Texas, to Los Angeles, California (the route ultimately followed by the Southern Pacific). Thus, it seemed that the President had given his blessing to the southern route.

THE KANSAS-NEBRASKA ACT. *The politics of the transcontinental railroad also brought on another sectional crisis.*
By 1854 territorial governments had been set up in every part of the West except the northern plains. Emigrants from Iowa and Missouri had begun to push into the region west of the Missouri River. They had naturally wanted a government that could preserve law and order. Railroad interests, which favored a northerly route to California, also wanted the territory organized.

These forces came to bear on Stephen A. Douglas, head of the Senate Committee on Territories. Thus, no one was surprised when, early in 1854, Douglas brought to the Senate floor a bill that would organize the Nebraska Territory. What was surprising was that he accepted two amendments to it from the floor. The first divided the region into two territories, Kansas and Nebraska. (See map, page 299.) The second repealed that portion of the Missouri Compromise of 1820 that prohibited slavery north of the 36° 30′ line between Missouri and the Rocky Mountains.

The repeal of the prohibition established by the Missouri Compromise meant that southerners could take their slaves into the new territories. And the creation of two territories had improved their chances for doing so. Nebraska, west of Iowa, would almost certainly remain free soil. But Kansas, west of Missouri, a slave state, might well be populated by southerners. In short, Douglas had not only violated an earlier agreement that had limited the spread of slavery, but he seemed to be offering the

South the free gift of a slave state. Although the North erupted in outrage, Congress paid no attention. It passed the Kansas-Nebraska Act, and President Pierce signed it into law.

DOUGLAS TESTS POPULAR SOVEREIGNTY. Why would Douglas, a senator from Illinois, do such a thing? It was part of his effort to test popular sovereignty. *He felt that if the decision on slavery were left to the people of the West, sectional tensions would subside and the nation would turn to other business.* Popular sovereignty would not get a fair test if southerners were prevented from moving into the area. Thus, he concluded that the Missouri Compromise had to be repealed.

By appearing to have favored the South, Douglas also hoped to get southerners to support his bid for the Democratic nomination. He wanted to be elected President in the 1856 election. At the same time, he felt the North would not lose anything. Since

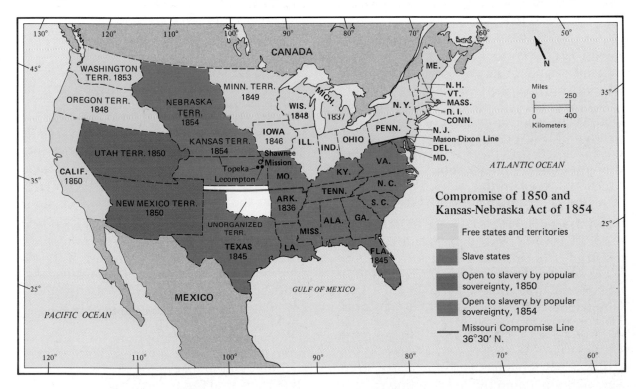

Compromise of 1850 and Kansas-Nebraska Act of 1854

Free states and territories

Slave states

Open to slavery by popular sovereignty, 1850

Open to slavery by popular sovereignty, 1854

Missouri Compromise Line 36°30′ N.

"Bleeding Kansas" was, in a way, a small-scale Civil War. Over 200 people lost their lives during direct confrontations between Free-Soilers and "border ruffians." Why was Kansas such a hotly disputed territory?

Kansas was not fit for cotton, it would not, in the long run, support slavery.

It all seemed very realistic. Unfortunately, Douglas missed the moral point. Many people thought slavery was evil. They were willing to tolerate it in the South as long as they thought they could prevent its expansion. But now it seemed that slavery could be extended as far as people wanted to extend it.

THE BIRTH OF THE REPUBLICAN PARTY. *Amid the popular uproar that followed the Kansas-Nebraska Act, the Whig party disappeared entirely and a new political party was born.* In June 1854 Horace Greeley demanded in his *New York Tribune* the formation of a new party. He even suggested a name for it—Republican. In popular meetings across the Middle West, local chapters of the party were quickly formed and the name approved. The

name was, after all, a natural choice, for it linked the new party to Jefferson and his well-known antislavery views.

In the fall elections the Republicans won a number of state offices and congressional seats, especially in New England. Absorbing both conscience Whigs and free-soil Democrats, the new party was well prepared to contest the Presidency in 1856.

"BLEEDING KANSAS." *If formation of the Republican party was the immediate result of the Kansas-Nebraska Act, the long-term effect of the act was bloodshed in Kansas.* Many in the North assumed that popular sovereignty meant a race to see who could populate the territory of Kansas first. The New England Emigrant Aid Society offered to help finance anyone willing to move to Kansas. Before long the Society was shipping rifles into the territory in boxes labeled

"Bibles." Soon towns, such as Lawrence and Topeka, had blossomed on the prairie.

Few slave owners went to Kansas. It was too risky to take slaves into a territory that might at any time vote to be free soil. Nevertheless, prosouthern Missourians did settle along the border. And at election time others crossed over into Kansas to vote illegally. The first territorial legislature, meeting at the Shawnee Mission, only a short distance from the Missouri line, was prosouthern. As a result, the Free Soilers organized their own government at Topeka, some 128 kilometers (80 miles) to the west. (See map, page 299.) *To Douglas's dismay, popular sovereignty in the territories had not only resolved nothing, but it was now threatening to create new conflicts.*

Violence was common on the American frontier. With the addition of sectional tensions, the bloodshed was inevitable. Gangs of border ruffians terrorized the countryside and "bushwhacked" travelers. One gang of southern supporters even seized the town of Lawrence and tried to burn it to the ground. In retaliation John Brown, an abolitionist from Ohio, descended, along with his sons, on several proslavery families living near Pottawatomie (paht-ah-WAHT-oe-mih), Kansas. There, John Brown and his sons massacred five men. So weak was the territorial government that these acts went unpunished.

There was violence on this same issue in Washington, D.C. When Senator Charles Sumner of Massachusetts denounced "the crime against Kansas" in a widely publicized speech, a member of Congress from South Carolina attacked him. This member, Preston Brooks, was so violent that he beat Sumner senseless with a cane—on the floor of the Senate. Sumner did not return to the Senate for several years. His seat in the Senate remained empty, a mute reminder of the scene.

THE ELECTION OF 1856. *Violence in Kansas and in the nation's capital formed the backdrop for the Presidential contest of 1856.* By then, representatives to Congress were carrying pistols for protection. Sometimes entire sessions were occupied in the wrangling over who would be Speaker of the House. The nation's legislative business ground slowly to a halt.

Stephen A. Douglas was the leading figure in the Democratic party. But his Kansas-Nebraska Act had made him unpopular in the North and had not won him friends in the South. The bloodshed in Kansas, moreover, had undermined his doctrine of popular sovereignty. As a result, the Democrats turned in 1856 to James Buchanan of Pennsylvania.

Buchanan, although a northerner, was acceptable to the South because he was an ardent expansionist. As Secretary of State under Polk, he had led the movement to grab all of Mexico. In 1854, while serving as minister to Great Britain, he had been one of the instigators of the Ostend Manifesto. *Although nothing had come of the threat to seize Cuba, it had shown that Buchanan was eager to add to slave territory.*

The Republicans also shunned their ablest leaders in 1856. Such men as Senator Sumner or Senator William H. Seward seemed too radical on the subject of slavery. They would not be acceptable to a national electorate. So Republicans followed the old Whig practice of choosing a military hero, hoping that his reputation would win popular support. Their nominee was John C. Frémont, hero of the Bear Flag Revolt in California.

The Republicans, under their platform, promised not to interfere with slavery where it existed, but they did demand a free West and a free Kansas. The party's slogan was "Free speech, free press, free soil, free men, Frémont, and victory!"

Buchanan won, but it was a close election. He carried the South and three northern states along the border—Pennsylvania, Indiana, and Illinois. Frémont carried the rest of the North, plus California. American politics was by now almost completely sectional. Four more years would complete the process.

Section Review

1. **Mapping:** Using the map on page 298, compare the latitude of Kansas with that of the southern states. How did the geographic position of Kansas make it vulnerable to pressure from both sides?
2. **Identify or explain:** Know-Nothings, Franklin Pierce, James Gadsden, Stephen Douglas, Horace Greeley, Ostend Manifesto.
3. List the provisions of the Kansas-Nebraska Act. How did Douglas hope to use the act to test popular sovereignty?

3. The Breakup of the Democratic Party

THE NATIONAL FABRIC WEAKENS. *Though scarcely any American institution could claim support in both the North and South, there was one exception—the Democratic party.* It could boast of such success because it had been able to find northern leaders willing to endorse southern programs. But that formula could not work forever.

The story of the next four years was largely the story of the breakup of the Democratic party. When it split apart in 1860 and lost to the Republicans—a northern-based, antislavery party—the preservation of the Union became even more difficult.

DRED SCOTT. In his inaugural address on March 4, 1857, President James Buchanan boldly predicted that the Supreme Court would soon solve the entire slavery controversy. The new President was referring to a case then before the Supreme Court. The case did indeed have an important political effect, but not in the way that either the President or the Chief Justice had anticipated.

The case involved Dred Scott, a slave who belonged to an army officer residing in Missouri. While on duty the officer had taken Scott to various army posts—one in Illinois, a free state, and one in the Wisconsin territory, which was free soil under the Missouri Compromise. Once the officer had died, his widow had given Scott to her brother, a Massachusetts abolitionist. The two had decided on a lawsuit in which Dred Scott would sue for his freedom on the grounds that he had once resided in free territory. *If the courts agreed, every runaway would be free the instant he or she touched free soil. The Fugitive Slave Law would then become meaningless.*

THE SUPREME COURT RULING. The case of *Scott v. Sanford* went through the state and federal courts in Missouri before reaching the Supreme Court in 1857. *There Chief Justice Roger Taney ruled that whatever Scott had been in Illinois or in the Wisconsin territory, he was a slave on his return with his master to Missouri, just like a recovered fugitive.* The Court also ruled that as a slave, Scott was not a citizen of the United States and therefore had no right to sue in any court, state or federal.

Had Chief Justice Taney stopped there the case might have been soon forgotten. But he went on to rule that, in any case, the Wisconsin territory was not free soil. *Invoking the Fifth Amendment clause prohibiting Congress from depriving a person of property without due process of law, Taney ruled the already repealed Missouri Compromise unconstitutional.* Restricting slavery north of 36° 30′ was in violation of the Fifth Amendment because it prevented

302

"Ride for Liberty—The Fugitive Slaves" was done by the same artist as "Old Kentucky Home," page 253. Does this painting give you a different idea about slave life? Are there similarities between the two works?

southerners from using their property as they wished.

With this decision Taney hoped to end the controversy over slavery by telling Congress that it had no power to legislate on the subject. This, however, was what the South had been saying for years. The southern position since the days of Calhoun had been that slaves were property and that Congress could not take them away. Taney, in short, gave the Supreme Court's blessing to slavery in the West.

Far from soothing the slavery controversy, as both Taney and Buchanan had hoped, the Dred Scott decision reopened it. It also confirmed northern suspicions about the influence of the South in national affairs. First, the South seemed to control the Presidency; now, it was reaching into the Supreme Court.

KANSAS AGAIN. Just before he left office, President Pierce officially recognized the pro-South government in Kansas and told it to draft a state constitution. The Shawnee Mission legislature accordingly announced that a constitutional convention would meet at Lecompton, Kansas. (See map, page 299.) Feeling themselves outmaneuvered, the free-soil people in Kansas refused to attend the convention. As a result, the Lecompton constitution permitted slavery in the new state. In Washington, President Buchanan, on succeeding Pierce, accepted the Kansas constitution and submitted it to Congress for approval.

When the Lecompton constitution came before the Senate in 1857, Stephen A. Douglas objected. Illegal voting by Missouri border ruffians, he felt, had prevented popular sovereignty from receiving a fair test. Thus, the constitution did not represent the feelings of the majority of Kansas residents. Douglas's opposition doomed the Lecompton constitution and delayed the admission of Kansas. *The state finally entered the Union in 1861, as a free state, after the South had seceded.*

303

THE EMERGENCE OF LINCOLN.

Douglas's opposition to the proslavery constitution of Kansas noticeably split the Democratic party. On one side were President Buchanan and his southern allies, supporting both the Dred Scott decision and slavery in Kansas. On the other side were Douglas and most northern Democrats, who claimed that Congress had the right to supervise Kansas until popular sovereignty got an honest test.

Among those ready to take advantage of this split was a rising political star in Douglas's home state of Illinois, Abraham Lincoln. A former Whig representative to Congress who had opposed the Mexican War because he felt it furthered slavery, Lincoln was an early convert to the Republican party and free soil. Although not an abolitionist, Lincoln did sense the immorality of slavery. And he understood the fears of the North.

When the Republicans nominated him for the United States Senate in 1858, Lincoln, in his acceptance speech, declared: *"A house divided against itself cannot stand. I believe this government cannot endure half slave and half free. I do not expect the Union to be dissolved—I do not expect the house to fall—but I do expect it will cease to be divided."*

Either the expansion of slavery had to be stopped, said Lincoln, or slavery would spread over the entire country, even into the North. Lincoln was telling poor working people in the North that their own positions would be threatened if the system were allowed to spread. It was the sort of argument that brought midwestern farmers and eastern laborers into the Republican party.

THE LINCOLN-DOUGLAS DEBATES

The Senate seat that Lincoln eyed was the one held by Douglas, who was up for reelection in 1858. *The two candidates had agreed to hold a series of debates across the state in order to acquaint the people with the issues facing the government.* Although Lincoln was not well-known outside of Illinois, Douglas was a figure of national prominence. Thus, because of the prominence of Douglas, newspapers all over the country reported the debates, which took place in seven Illinois towns.

The nationwide publicity enabled Lincoln to draw attention to the growing split in the Democratic party. At the village of Freeport, Lincoln raised the key question about Dred Scott and popular sovereignty. In the Dred Scott decision, the Supreme Court had ruled that the government had no power over slavery in the territories. Yet, Douglas had been arguing that under popular sovereignty the people could vote slavery out if they wanted. How was this possible, asked Lincoln, in light of the Dred Scott decision?

The question put Douglas on the spot, because President Buchanan and his southern friends had endorsed the Dred Scott decision. If Douglas stuck with popular sovereignty and stated that it was possible to limit slavery in the West, he would alienate an important segment of his party. Yet, if he abandoned popular sovereignty and went along with the Dred Scott decision, he would lose Illinois. It seemed that he had to choose between two possibilities—the Senate in 1858 and the Presidency in 1860.

THE FREEPORT DOCTRINE.

Douglas's reply, known as the Freeport Doctrine, was a clever attempt to escape the dilemma. Douglas agreed that under the Dred Scott decision a territory could not pass a law against slavery. But he added that the people could effectively prevent it merely by refusing to enact a slave code, the body of laws needed to support slavery.

The state legislature—still responsible at this time for electing senators—voted 54–41 for Douglas. However, the Freeport Doctrine drew national attention to the split between Douglas and Buchanan. And it worried the South. Could Douglas, as President, be trusted to care for southern interests? The answer was no. So southern leaders went to the Democratic convention in 1860 with two demands—the party candidate must be a southerner and the party platform must promise a federal slave code for the territories. It was the South's answer to the Freeport Doctrine. *Yet, the demands broke the Democratic party and helped Lincoln to win the Presidency.*

Section Review

1. Identify or explain: Dred Scott, Roger Taney, Lecompton constitution, Lincoln-Douglas debates.
2. What free territories would be affected by the Dred Scott decision?
3. What issue was raised in the case of *Scott v. Sanford*? On what principle of law did the Supreme Court base its decision?

4. Lincoln Elected: The South Secedes

TENSION MOUNTS. It had been a decade of rising tensions. First, there had been the protest against the Fugitive Slave Act, then the bloodshed in Kansas. People in both the North and the South had begun to feel like victims of the other side's aggressiveness. Northerners were worried that a great "slave power conspiracy" somehow manipulated the reins of government. Southerners felt trapped between an increasingly hostile northern majority and their own restless slaves. They worried that northern criticism might encourage their slaves to run away or rebel. *The worry turned to panic in October 1859, with John Brown's raid on Harpers Ferry, located in what is now West Virginia.*

JOHN BROWN'S RAID. Periods of social and political tension—such as that of the 1850's—often involve people in issues and crusades. And the crusades often attract extremists—people so convinced of the righteousness of their cause that they will use any means available to achieve their goals. Such means can even include violence.

John Brown was such an extremist. To Brown the goal of abolishing slavery was so right and just that he was willing to use even the most unlawful and inhumane means to achieve it. As his slaying of a family in Kansas showed, Brown considered human life secondary to antislavery.

Financed by abolitionists from New York and New England, John Brown's raid on Harpers Ferry had been carefully planned. *The idea was to seize the federal arsenal at Harpers Ferry. Brown would then distribute guns from the arsenal to the slaves who had joined him and lead a widespread rebellion to end slavery.*

With a party of 18, including five Blacks, Brown struck in the early-morning hours on October 16. He quickly captured the arsenal and issued his appeal for slave support. Unfortunately for Brown, he had picked a poor place to start an uprising. Communications were slow and slaves were few in that part of Virginia. Only a few Blacks made it to Brown's side.

Nevertheless, the telegraph and railroad had enabled the government of Virginia to respond quickly to the raid. Within a day a detachment of marines, commanded by Colonel Robert E. Lee, had invaded the arsenal and captured Brown. *The state gave Brown a fair trial and convicted and hanged him for "treason against the Commonwealth of Virginia."*

Although such abolitionists as Frederick Douglass and Lydia Maria Child applauded Brown's actions and spoke of him as a martyred hero, most northerners were shocked by the raid. But southern newspaper editors quickly publicized the abolitionist sentiments. They used them to support the theory that northerners had approved of Brown and his tactics. Soon sectional hostility had mounted still further.

THE ELECTION OF 1860. The South had extremists of its own. One group was known as the Fire-eaters. These men, which included Robert Barnwell Rhett of South Carolina and William Lowndes Yancey of Alabama, had been working for secession for years. An independent South, free of northern harassment, was their goal. And John Brown's raid, which had evoked the deepest fear of all—slave rebellion—had given them popular support. As a result, they had gone to the Democratic convention in 1860 prepared to rule or ruin.

THE DEMOCRATS MEET IN CHARLESTON. The Democratic convention met in Charleston, South Carolina, the heart of extremist feelings in the South. It was April; the weather was hot and tempers were easily flared. The southern delegates had come armed with an ***ultimatum:*** a southern-born candidate and a platform based on preserving slavery in the territories. But northern Democrats had suffered through two doughface administrations, Pierce's and Buchanan's. Now, they faced increasing competition from Republicans, and they felt that only Douglas had a chance of winning the election. Only popular sovereignty could satisfy the North on the slave issue.

An ***ultimatum*** is a demand that is final, and a rejection of that demand may result in punishment or the use of force.

After days of wrangling, Yancey of Alabama, taking offense at some remarks by a

Douglas supporter, led his delegation out of the hall. Delegates from other states of the Deep South followed. The southerners waited for an apology and an offer of compromise. None came. Instead the Douglas delegates voted to adjourn and to reassemble in Baltimore. The southerners decided that they would meet again later in Richmond, Virginia.

In the interval between the conventions, several southern states chose new delegates to go to Baltimore. They wanted to have a voice in selecting the President. But when the convention met in June, the Douglas supporters, who were in control of the key committees, refused to admit them. Shocked by this heavy-handed treatment,

After looking at this political poster, how would you describe Abraham Lincoln? What evidence can you find in the text to support your view?

the entire South walked out of this convention, along with some Buchanan Democrats from the North. The rest proceeded to nominate Douglas for President and to write popular sovereignty into the party platform.

The walkout delegates met at a market down the street. They nominated John C. Breckinridge of Kentucky and drew up a proslavery platform. The Richmond convention then endorsed Breckinridge as the nominee of southern Democrats. *The party split was complete.*

THE REPUBLICANS MEET IN CHICAGO. *The Republicans, meeting in Chicago that summer, had had little difficulty agreeing on Lincoln.* The other Republican leaders, such as Sumner and Seward, had been considered too extreme. The platform that the Republicans drew up was as moderate as their candidate. It said that there would be no interference with slavery in places where it existed; only its expansion into the West would be checked. In an open bid for support from the farmers and the laboring poor, the Republicans promised free grants of public land in the West to any head of family willing to make the land a homestead.

THE CONSTITUTIONAL UNION PARTY. As if three candidates were not enough, a fourth party entered the field in 1860. *Calling itself the Constitutional Union party, and being made up mostly of former Whigs, the new organization sought a middle ground.* The Constitutional Unionists called for adherence to the Constitution and the existing laws. This meant that they would not interfere with slavery, but they would also not promote it. John Bell of Tennessee was their candidate. In the election they carried several border states in the upper South.

RESULTS OF THE ELECTION. Bell, in fact, did better than Douglas, who fell between the pillars of sectionalism. Breckinridge carried the Deep South, from South

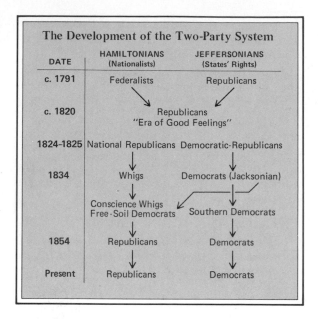

The Development of the Two-Party System

DATE	HAMILTONIANS (Nationalists)	JEFFERSONIANS (States' Rights)
c. 1791	Federalists	Republicans
c. 1820	Republicans "Era of Good Feelings"	
1824–1825	National Republicans	Democratic-Republicans
1834	Whigs	Democrats (Jacksonian)
	Conscience Whigs Free-Soil Democrats	Southern Democrats
1854	Republicans	Democrats
Present	Republicans	Democrats

Carolina to Texas. Lincoln carried nearly all the North—and with it enough electoral votes to win the election. (See map below.)

In terms of the popular vote, though, Lincoln was a minority President. He had received only 40 percent of the total popular vote; Douglas had received about 30 percent. Breckinridge and Bell had divided the remainder. Republicans were still a minority in the nation and in Congress. Whatever their plans were for slavery, they represented no immediate threat to the South.

THE SOUTH SECEDES. The South had spoken in moderate tones in the election of 1860. Douglas and Bell together had received more votes in the South than the southern-rights candidate, Breckinridge. A fair majority of southerners had favored compromise and the Union. And many people had pointed out that Lincoln promised no threat to slavery.

But most southern leaders now saw Lincoln as a symbol of northern hostility. Although Republicans might seem moderate, if they ever won control of Congress, there

was no telling what they might do. It was time to leave the Union.

South Carolina, the southern state that had been the most extreme since the nullification crisis, voted unanimously to secede from the Union. *Within a month the lower South, from Georgia to Texas, followed suit.* (See map, page 309.) Then, in February a convention in Montgomery, Alabama, drafted a constitution for the Confederate States of America. Although this new constitution was quite similar to the federal Constitution, its authors had been more cautious about preserving states' rights. Jefferson Davis of Mississippi, former senator and Secretary of War, became President of the Confederacy.

LINCOLN AND THE FIRST SHOT. "Go, erring sisters, depart in peace," said Horace Greeley. And many in the North agreed. They were glad to be rid of the South and its problems. But President Buchanan disagreed, and he announced that

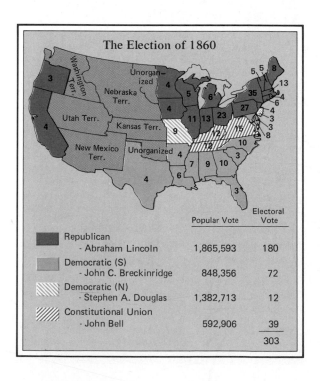

The Election of 1860

		Popular Vote	Electoral Vote
■	Republican - Abraham Lincoln	1,865,593	180
▨	Democratic (S) - John C. Breckinridge	848,356	72
▧	Democratic (N) - Stephen A. Douglas	1,382,713	12
▨	Constitutional Union - John Bell	592,906	39
			303

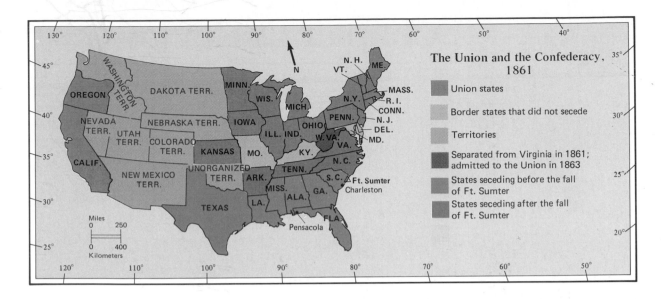

The Union and the Confederacy, 1861

- Union states
- Border states that did not secede
- Territories
- Separated from Virginia in 1861; admitted to the Union in 1863
- States seceding before the fall of Ft. Sumter
- States seceding after the fall of Ft. Sumter

no state had the right to secede. Nevertheless, he seemed powerless to actually do anything.

During the last days of his administration, Buchanan floundered in uncertainty, while one compromise proposal after another was shot down by the leaders in both the North and the South. The best that could be said for the outgoing President is that he did not take steps that would have tied the hands of his successor. Instead, he simply dumped the problem in Lincoln's lap and left for home.

At first Lincoln was equally cautious. He did realize, however, that some decisions would have to be made—and soon. One decision involved several federal army garrisons in the South, notably at Fort Sumter in Charleston Harbor and at Pensacola in Florida. To evacuate these would be to concede secession. To reinforce them would start a war. Lincoln could not afford to be too provocative. There were too many in the North who, like Horace Greeley, opposed a fight. Yet, Lincoln could not accept the dissolution of the Union.

So, he chose a middle course. *In early April 1861, he informed the governor of South Carolina that he planned to send supplies, but not reinforcements, to Fort Sumter. It was clear notice that he intended to maintain the garrison as a symbol of federal authority.*

Moderate though Lincoln's action was, it was more than the South Carolina extremists could bear. *On the morning of April 12, before the federal ships could arrive, they opened fire on Fort Sumter.* And it started a war that few wanted, but that nobody knew how to prevent.

Section Review

1. Mapping: Using the map on page 308, list the results of the election of 1860 by state. How did these results indicate the loss of national unity?
2. Identify or explain: John Brown, the Fire-eaters, John Breckinridge, Constitutional Unionists, Fort Sumter.
3. What positions were taken by southern and northern Democrats in the nominating convention of 1860?
4. How did the breakup of the Democratic party signal the end of national unity?
5. How did Lincoln try to avoid war? Why did this attempt fail?

Chapter 12 Review

Bird's-Eye View

Mounting sectional tensions between the North and the South continued to tear at the national fabric. Most northerners did not demand the abolition of slavery, but they did wish to confine it to the states in which it already existed. Free soil became the critical issue as settlers moved into Utah, California, and other western territories.

President Taylor infuriated the South by proposing to admit California to the Union as a free state without also admitting a slave state to balance the power in Congress. In fact, Southern secession seemed likely. But then Henry Clay suggested a compromise, which settled the crisis for the time being. His suggested compromise—the Compromise of 1850—gave the South a new Fugitive Slave Law in return for the admission of California. Two new territories, Utah and New Mexico, would then be created from the rest of the territory ceded by Mexico. Furthermore, these territories could decide the issue of slavery for themselves through popular sovereignty. The passage of the Fugitive Slave Law, however, angered many northerners. Eventually, these sectional feuds destroyed the national unity of the Whig party, and Franklin Pierce, a Democrat, became President.

In 1854 the Nebraska Territory was organized and divided into two parts, Kansas and Nebraska. Then, the Missouri Compromise of 1820 was repealed by the Kansas-Nebraska Act. Nebraska seemed likely to remain free, but under popular sovereignty Kansas could become a slave state. As a result, northerners rushed into Kansas to protect its free status, southerners settled near the border, and violence erupted in "bleeding Kansas."

In the election of 1856, Buchanan, the Democratic candidate, was opposed by John Frémont, the free-soil candidate of the newly formed Republican party. Buchanan won the election by carrying the South and the border states. Then, shortly after Buchanan took office, the decision of the Supreme Court on the Dred Scott case inflamed the slavery controversy. It did so by declaring that the property rights of slave holders were more important than the prohibition of slavery in the West. The Lincoln-Douglas debates that followed focused attention on the moral and legal elements of the conflict over slavery.

The Democratic party lost its national base when its southern members left the party and nominated independent candidates in the election of 1860. This move allowed Lincoln, as the Republican candidate, to be elected with only 40 percent of the popular vote. The election of Lincoln was the cue to the states of the Deep South to secede and form the Confederacy. Lincoln took a moderate stand on secession and hoped to avoid a confrontation. But his maintenance of the federal garrison at Fort Sumter brought the situation to a head—and the first shot of the Civil War was fired.

Vocabulary

Define or identify each of the following:

Mormons	expansionist	doughface
popular sovereignty	*Scott v. Sanford*	Ostend Manifesto
constituent	John Brown	ultimatum

Review Questions

1. List the provisions of Henry Clay's compromise.
2. What objections did Northerners have to the Fugitive Slave Law of 1850?
3. What were the issues that led to the Kansas-Nebraska Act?
4. How did the Lincoln-Douglas debates enhance Abraham Lincoln's political career?
5. What were the results of the election of 1860?
6. How did the Civil War begin?

Reviewing Social Studies Skills

1. Using the maps on pages 295 and 298, answer the following:
   a. What four southern cities were used as departure points by the Underground Railroad?
   b. Name the three states with the largest percentages of slaves.
   c. Which northern state had the most slaves?
2. Using the map on page 299, list the following:
   a. The free states
   b. The slave states
   c. The free territories
   d. The territories open to slavery
3. Translate the information from the map on page 298 into a chart. Your chart should show, in chronological order, the geographic additions to the United States. Give your chart a title.

Reading for Meaning

1. Read the Sidenote to History about Harriet Tubman on page 294. Why was she considered a hero? What do you think her two most important contributions were?
2. The following items are doctrines associated with the issue of slavery: a) free soil b) popular sovereignty c) abolition. Match the following beliefs with the appropriate doctrines:
   1) Slavery is morally wrong. 2) People should be able to make the policies that will affect them. 3) You cannot change some things, but you can control them.
3. Here are some possible approaches to problems: compromise, reason, legislation, force. Choose one of the policies toward slavery mentioned in the chapter, and show how it is an example of one of these approaches to problem solving.

Bibliography

Stephen Oates's *To Purge This Land With Blood* (Harper & Row) is a good account of John Brown's story.

Mercy Heidish's *A Woman Called Moses* (Bantam) is one of the best biographies of Harriet Tubman.

Chapter 13

Ordeal of Fire

Two days after the firing on Fort Sumter, Virginia voted to leave the Union. North Carolina, Tennessee, and Arkansas followed soon after. That made a total of 11 states in the Confederacy. Four other slave states—Delaware, Maryland, Kentucky, and Missouri—decided, after some hesitation, to remain in the Union. In addition, the mountain people in the territory of western Virginia sided with the Union cause. President Lincoln then appointed a temporary governor and helped them to organize a new state. West Virginia entered the Union in 1863.

Counting the border states and the Far West, the North numbered 23 states to the South's 11. It had a population of 22 million to the South's 9 million (3½ million of whom were slaves).

Most important of all was the North's overwhelming superiority in industry, transportation, and finance. The nation's manufacturing centers were all in the North. At the beginning of the war, the South did not have an arms factory. And its armies were continually hurt by shortages of guns, ammunition, and necessities.

The North had a similar edge in transportation facilities. Only one railroad crossed the entire South. When Union armies captured Chattanooga, Tennessee, the South was effectively cut in two. With northern gunboats patrolling the Mississippi River, Texas cattle and grain could not reach the starving army in Virginia.

The nation's financial centers were in the North. New York financiers dominated even the sale of southern cotton. The South, having no source of income, financed the war by issuing paper money, whose value fell rapidly. The Union government, by contrast, financed its effort through the widespread sale of government bonds. In four years of fighting, the federal government had borrowed the stupendous sum of 2½ billion dollars from its citizens—more than had been spent in all the years since the Revolution.

Chapter Objectives

After you have finished reading this chapter, you should be able to:
1. Compare the advantages and disadvantages of the North and the South at the beginning of the Civil War.
2. Explain why Lincoln hesitated to issue the Emancipation Proclamation.
3. Describe the cost to the North and the South of the Union victory.

No one expected a long war. On the day after the fall of Fort Sumter—April 15, 1861—President Lincoln called on the northern states to supply 75,000 soldiers. They were to be enlisted for only three months. A brief skirmish or two would surely convince the South of the error of its ways. One American fighting another American was unthinkable. But no one knew how to prevent it.

Had the war been a short one, the South might have achieved its goal of independence. It had a strong military tradition, and it had produced some of the nation's best soldiers. *In fact, at the outset of the war, many of the nation's ablest and most experienced commanders were southerners.* *And they had resigned to serve the Confederacy.*

The tactical abilities of the South were responsible for its early victories. Its only hope was that the North would become discouraged after these early losses and abandon the contest. In a long, drawn-out war, the South was certain to suffer under the weight of northern resources.

1. The South on the March, 1861-1862

TO BULL RUN AND BACK. *Since neither side was prepared for war, neither had given much thought to military strategy.* In early summer a southern army,

At the start of the war, feelings of patriotism were high, and young men in every state leaped at the chance to rally 'round their flags. New York's Seventh Regiment paraded down Broadway on April 19, 1861. That scene was sketched by Thomas Nast, the famous cartoonist. Seven years later Nast expanded his drawing into this oil painting.

War was an adventure for these Southern recruits. They are photographed here before the first Battle of Bull Run.

commanded by P. G. T. Beauregard, gathered near Manassas Junction. (See map, page 317.) In defense Lincoln hastily assembled an army to defend the capital. It consisted mostly of raw recruits. Prodded by public calls for action, the War Department ordered the army to cross the Potomac River and to confront the Virginians. Expecting a good show, members of Congress and their families journeyed out from the capital in carriages to watch the fight. Little were they prepared for the sad sight that followed.

Beauregard's army of 25,000 soldiers had gathered for battle along the waters of Bull Run Stream. The Union then attacked them on July 21, 1861. But the Union was badly organized. When General Irvin McDowell ordered a retreat, his untrained troops panicked and fled through the capital city, carrying the audience with them. Fortunately, the Confederate army was too exhausted to pursue.

Lincoln replaced McDowell with George B. McClellan, who spent the next nine months organizing and training soldiers in the Army of the Potomac.

BLOCKADING THE SOUTH. *Early in the war the Union Navy had set up a blockade. This blockade stretched from Virginia around Florida and went along the Gulf of Mexico to southern Texas.* Except for their contact with a small number of ships that had managed to slip through the blockade, the confederate ports had been effectively sealed off from trade with other countries.

Eventually, this blockade would handicap the South severely. This was because the manufactured goods southerners depended on from Europe would not be able to reach the Confederate ports. In the very beginning, however, the South had not been overly concerned about the blockade. They had believed Britain needed southern products badly enough that it would soon come into the war on the side of the South.

WAR IN THE WEST, 1861–1862. Early in the war the important military engagements took place in the West. Both the North and the South were courting Kentucky. If Kentucky joined the South, the lines of battle would be drawn at the Ohio River. If it sided with the North, Union armies would be able to penetrate the southern heartland.

In Kentucky the state legislature had voted against secession, but most of its people were sympathetic to the South.

Through the fall of 1861, the state was a battleground. And by the end of the year, Kentucky was in northern hands, in particular, those of General Ulysses S. Grant, the ablest of the Union commanders in the West. He was poised in the southwestern part of Kentucky, waiting for a chance to invade Tennessee.

To defend Tennessee, the Confederates had built forts on both the Tennessee and Cumberland rivers. (See map above.) But in early 1862, Grant had brought Union *gun-*

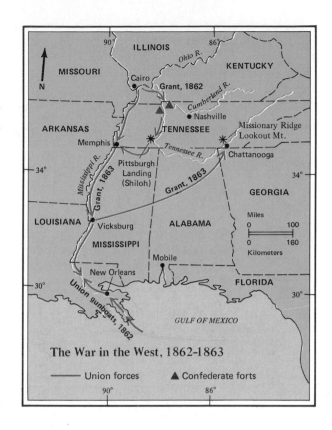

The War in the West, 1862-1863

——— Union forces   ▲ Confederate forts

boats up the rivers from the Ohio and had taken the forts. He had then pursued the Confederate army south across Tennessee. By early April he was at Pittsburgh Landing (Shiloh), just a short distance from the Mississippi border.

Gunboats were small warships that could navigate the shallow river waters.

Then, on the morning of April 6, 1862, the Confederates attacked Grant's flank at Shiloh and captured it. Although his army was badly disorganized, Grant counterattacked the next day. And in the bloodiest contest of the war in the West, he drove the enemy from the field. *In terms of losses the battle of Shiloh was a draw.* There were nearly 1,800 dead and 10,000 wounded on each side. But it halted Grant's advance.

315

THE PENINSULA CAMPAIGN. By the spring of 1862, the Army of the Potomac was an effective fighting force. During the winter the Confederates had moved their capital north from Montgomery, Alabama, to Richmond, Virginia. The new location was exposed to attack from the North. And McClellan had seen the opportunity. Taking advantage of northern naval superiority, McClellan landed his army on the James River, just 96 kilometers (60 miles) below Richmond. (See map, page 317.)

Robert E. Lee, the newly appointed commander of the army of northern Virginia, hastily organized a defense of the Confederate capital. For seven days McClellan assaulted Lee's defenses, but without success. The fight cost the North 15,000 soldiers and the South 20,000. *It had saved Richmond and it had caused a political uproar in the North.* Lincoln ordered McClellan home and named John Pope to serve as the supreme commander.

While McClellan was ferrying his army back up Chesapeake Bay, Lee and Thomas J. "Stonewall" Jackson were disposing of Pope. Just as Pope was venturing across the Potomac, Lee stationed himself at Bull Run. Jackson then moved up the Shenandoah Valley and descended on Pope's flank. When

Distressed by McClellan's reluctance to attack General Lee, President Lincoln arrived at Antietam on October 2, 1862. He wanted to have a personal talk with his commanding general. In this picture, McClellan stands facing Lincoln, sixth from left.

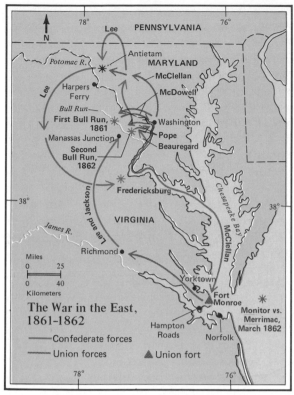

The War in the East, 1861–1862

— Confederate forces
— Union forces
▲ Union fort

Pope ordered a retreat, Lee pounced on his rear, turning a retreat into a rout. While Lincoln searched for a new general, the defense of Washington, D.C., fell on the shoulders of McClellan.

BLOODY ANTIETAM. The North was growing steadily in military might. Lee decided to take the war into Union territory, hoping to give the North a defeat on its own soil. On September 5, 1862, Lee crossed the Potomac. McClellan followed, and on September 17, the two armies met at Antietam Creek. (See map above.)

The battle of Antietam was the deadliest battle that had taken place so far. The losses were so heavy that it was described as a defeat for both sides. But because Lee had withdrawn back across the Potomac instead of pressing farther North, the Union army could at least claim a technical victory.

Although "bloody Antietam" had been a military draw, the halting of Lee's thrust

Sidenote to History

A Crisis of Conscience: Robert E. Lee

Many southerners accepted secession only after examining their consciences, and then with much pain and sorrow. One such southerner was Robert E. Lee, commander of the Army of Northern Virginia. Lee was a native of Virginia and a graduate from the top of his class at West Point. He had served with skill and bravery in the Mexican War.

In 1861 Lee wrote a letter to his son, parts of which are included here. In it Lee describes his feelings about secession before Virginia had seceded.

My dear Son,

The South in my opinion has been saddened by the acts of the North, as you say. As an American citizen I take great pride in my country, its prosperity, and institutions, and would defend any state if its rights were invaded. But I can see no greater calamity for the country than a breakup of the Union. It would be an accumulation of all the evils we complain of, and I am willing to sacrifice everything but honor for its preservation. I hope therefore that all constitutional means will be exhausted before there is a resort to force. Secession is nothing but revolution. The framers of our Constitution never [would have] spent so much labor and wisdom in its formation if it was intended to be broken by every member of the Confederacy at will.

Still, a Union that can only be maintained by swords and bayonets has no charm for me. I shall mourn for my country. If the Union is dissolved and the government disrupted, I shall return to my native state and share the miseries of my people, and, save in its defense, will draw my sword on none.

into the North had important political consequences. It had silenced, for the moment, northern criticism of how Lincoln was managing the war, and it had enabled the President to establish a new war aim—the freeing of the slaves.

Section Review

1. Mapping: On an outline map shade the Union states in one color and the Confederate states in another. Indicate the border states in a mixture of both colors. Use the map on page 309 to identify the border states. Why were the border states strategically important?
2. Identify or explain: "Stonewall" Jackson, P. G. T. Beauregard, Antietam, Irvin McDowell, Shiloh.
3. Make a chart, showing the relative advantages of both sides during the Civil War. Be sure to consider the advantages and disadvantages of each side in relation to the following categories: population, resources, industry, trade, morale, leadership, military training. What general patterns can you detect?
4. Why was the battle of Antietam politically important for Lincoln?

2. A War to Preserve the Union Becomes a War to Free the Slaves

LINCOLN'S POSITION. *From the first, Lincoln had made preservation of the Union his chief war aim.* "My paramount object in the struggle," he stated in 1862, "is to save the Union, and it is not either to save or to destroy slavery. If I could save the Union without freeing any slave, I would do it, and if I could save it by freeing all the slaves, I would do it. And if I could save it by freeing some and leaving others alone, I would do that. What I do about slavery . . . I do because I believe it helps to save this Union."

Lincoln took this position because it had the broadest appeal. Many northerners cared nothing for slaves. Indeed, there were still slaveholders in the Union. The border states—Delaware, Maryland, Kentucky, and Missouri—all had slaves. Lincoln could not afford to lose them. Moreover, he felt that he lacked the constitutional authority to free slaves. *Slavery existed by state laws and constitutions. Only an amendment to the federal Constitution could empower the President or Congress to do anything about it.*

THE COPPERHEADS. There were some in the North who opposed even a war to save the Union. *Made up mostly of northern Democrats, these Copperheads felt that preserving the Union was not worth the cost in lives and resources.*

Uncertain about how far such opposition extended, President Lincoln, early in the war, suspended the writ of *habeas corpus*. This suspension enabled the government to jail people without explaining why. Although only a few opponents of the war were actually put into jail, these violations of civil rights gave the Copperheads additional cause for complaint.

DRAFT RIOTS. Passage of a military conscription law in 1863 brought northern opposition to the war to a head. Many of those who were hostile or indifferent to the war had been willing to keep silent as long as they did not have to serve. *But the Conscription Act of 1863 made all able-bodied males between the ages of 20 and 45 liable for military service.* Draftees, however, were permitted to hire substitutes. Thus, by enabling the rich to avoid service, the act had angered many. It was, they said, "a rich man's war and a poor man's fight."

Passage of the Conscription Act caused riots to break out in several northern cities.

Riots broke out in July 1863 after the publication of the names drawn in the New York draft. The mob not only turned against all symbols of authority, it also attacked helpless Blacks, whom it blamed for its troubles.

The worst was in New York, where racial overtones had heightened the hostilities. Already in competition with Blacks for unskilled jobs, the newly arrived Irish immigrants did not want to fight a war that would increase the number of free Blacks in their midst. In New York the mob had turned against the houses and shops owned by Blacks. In four days of violence, 76 people were killed. Federal troops had to be summoned to restore order.

STILL A WAR FOR UNION. *Given this sort of opposition to the war, it is scarcely surprising that Lincoln made it a war for union, rather than a war against slavery.* He held to this policy for more than a year,

despite heavy pressure from abolitionists and Black leaders. When, in August 1861, General John C. Frémont, Union commander at St. Louis, Missouri, ordered the freeing of slaves belonging to rebels, Lincoln countermanded the order and replaced him. When someone suggested that freeing the slaves of planters who were warring against the United States would not hurt the border states and would possibly cause confusion in the South, Lincoln replied that he did not want to issue an order that would be ignored.

CONTRABANDS. *A change in the government's policy was gradually forced by Black slaves themselves.* Only a few weeks after the war opened, a small group of Blacks came knocking at the Union post of Fort Monroe, at the mouth of Virginia's James River. Having no authority to free slaves, the Union commander was uncertain of what to do. But then he discovered that the group had worked on Confederate fortifications across the river at Norfolk. *Since private property of military value was considered, under international law, contraband and liable to seizure, the Union general took the Blacks in as contraband.* They were then put to work on the general's fort.

Technically, the Blacks were not yet free, but at least they had not been sent back. As word spread, hundreds more Blacks crossed to Union lines. Although northern military policy did not permit them to fight as soldiers, they served as cooks, scouts, spies, nurses, and teamsters.

In November 1861 the Union navy seized Port Royal Island, South Carolina. They wanted to use it as a base for blockading the South. The White planters fled, but the Blacks remained. Although the navy did consider these Blacks to be contrabands, they were sent back to their plantations. With no White overseers present, the Blacks worked as free people, farming the land for food and profit.

Sidenote to History

Photography on the Battlefield

On February 14, 1849, a thin young man walked up to the White House and knocked on the front door. The special nature of his task had made him wear his best black suit. In appearance his most interesting aspect was the oblong wooden box that he carried in his arms. The box was a camera, and the young man's name was Mathew Brady. He had come to the White House to take the first picture of a President in office.

Even at the youthful age of 26, Brady was well-known as a portrait photographer. But his real fame would come during the Civil War, when he and his assistants would dodge cannon shells and bullets to take photos of the fighting. By the end of the war, Brady had ruined himself financially, having spent $100,000 of his own money to follow Union troops from battle to battle. But the pictures he and others took exist today as important historical evidence of a sad period in the nation's history.

They contain many details that otherwise would have been lost. The following is a description of picture-taking during the Civil War.

The Confederates had begun shelling Union lines when Roche (a photographer, and one of Mathew Brady's assistants) appeared with his camera. Disregarding the warnings, Roche took his camera out beyond the protection of the trenches and began taking pictures in the middle of the bombardment. He had taken several views before folding his tripod and running toward a more exposed position. But before he could reach that position, shells started falling. Earth, mud, and stones were being thrown skyward. Roche was stunned. But within a moment he had shaken the dirt from his clothes and had wiped the lens of his camera. He was getting ready to move the camera to the smoking shell hole and to spread the tripod over it.

Then, he exposed his next plate, folded his tripod, and casually walked back to the Union trenches. There, an army officer, who had watched him with his heart in his mouth, asked Roche if he had been scared when the shells had started falling. Roche arched his eyebrows. "Scared?" he said with a grin. "Two shots never fell in the same place, Cap'n."

BLACKS ARE RECRUITED TO SERVE AS SOLDIERS. *In the summer of 1862, the demand for soldiers finally forced a change in northern military policy concerning the use of Blacks as soldiers.* The War Department sent a general to Port Royal with authority to recruit five regiments of Blacks. At the same time Massachusetts and other northern states began organizing regiments of Blacks. The most famous of these regiments, the 54th Massachusetts, went to Port Royal in 1863. Joining with local regiments, it led raids far into the interior of South Carolina. In July 1863 the 54th was the spearhead for an attack on Fort Wagner, which was guarding the entrance to Charleston Harbor. (See map, page 331.) Advancing through a rain of artillery and rifle fire, the regiment penetrated the fort's defenses, but then fell back, leaving more than half of the 54th dead.

By 1864 the Union army was openly recruiting Blacks in both the North and the South. By the end of the war, Black soldiers accounted for almost half of the Union soldiers fighting in Tennessee. A total of almost 200,000 Blacks were serving in the Union army and navy and were fighting in nearly every battle of the Civil War.

Black and White soldiers did not receive equal treatment in the service. The Black soldiers were frequently assigned to

This recruiting poster urged Blacks to fight for their freedom. By the end of the war, over 200,000 Blacks had served the North. "Better even die free than to live slaves," said Frederick Douglass.

menial chores around camp, and until Congress required equal pay for them in 1864, they were paid less than White soldiers. They were often treated badly, not only by White soldiers but by northern White civilians as well.

Despite being treated badly and being underpaid, they fought gallantly. One colonel remarked that they had "demonstrated the highest order of courage which America demands." For outstanding heroism in the course of the war, 21 Blacks received the Congressional Medal of Honor.

THE CONFISCATION ACTS. The flight of the Blacks from slavery encouraged Congress to take some action to help them. A number of Republican representatives in Congress were more radical than President Lincoln on the subject of slavery. They joined the abolitionists in crying for a war against slavery. In early 1862 Congress abolished slavery in the District of Columbia and the western territories. *Then, in July 1862, it passed an act that allowed the government to confiscate the property, including the slaves, of all persons in rebellion against the United States.*

This measure put additional pressure on Lincoln to do something. By then, also, the border states were secure, and there was less to fear about the opinions of slave owners in that quarter. Lincoln summoned a cabinet meeting to consider an antislavery proclamation, but Secretary of State Seward urged a delay. He wanted to wait for a northern victory on the battlefield, lest an order freeing the slaves sound like "our last shriek on the retreat."

THE EMANCIPATION PROCLAMATION. The battle of Antietam, which had stopped Lee's invasion of the North, had presented an opportunity to Lincoln to issue his Emancipation Proclamation. *Beginning January 1, 1863, he declared, the slaves* belonging to persons in rebellion against the United States were free. But the Proclamation did not free slaves in the border states or even those in parts of the South, such as Tennessee, that were under Union control. Lincoln still felt he did not have constitutional authority to free slaves belonging to loyal planters. The Proclamation was a war measure, designed to embarrass the enemy.

Since it could not be enforced in the South, Lincoln's Proclamation did not actually free any slaves. *But it did give a moral tone to the war.* The conflict became a crusade to rid the nation of slavery.

THE DIPLOMATIC SCENE. *The Emancipation Proclamation also ended* *any possibility that Great Britain might intervene on the side of the South.* Ruling circles in Britain had sympathized with the South at the beginning of the war. British industry was largely dependent on southern cotton, and British aristocrats liked the gentility of the southern planters. To them, the Yankees were upstarts, who had betrayed their background with their rude manners and rough speech.

But the British did learn to respect Lincoln's minister to London, Charles Francis Adams (son of ex-President John Quincy Adams). And Adams had constantly reminded the British ministry of the dangers of intervention.

Early in the war the Confederacy had sent two commissioners—James M. Mason and

The first Black soldiers recruited for the Union army served in the 54th Massachusetts Regiment. In the storming of Fort Wagner, South Carolina, 247 Blacks lost their lives fighting for freedom.

In this representation of the drafting of the Emancipation Proclamation, Lincoln is surrounded by symbols of democracy and religious ethics. They include the Presidential oath; the Holy Bible; the works of Webster, Calhoun, and Douglas; and the scales of justice. What other symbols can you identify?

John Slidell—to London in an effort to secure diplomatic recognition. The two diplomats had taken passage on a British steamer, the *Trent*. When a Union warship had intercepted the *Trent* and arrested the two Confederates, Britain had reacted angrily. Lincoln had avoided trouble by releasing the Confederates, although Secretary Seward had argued that it was a simple case of impressment, with which the British ought to have been familiar. When the Confederate diplomats finally arrived in London, Charles F. Adams had persuaded the ministry not to give them any formal recognition.

Adams, however, had also worked closely with antislavery reformers in Britain. Thus, when Lincoln made the freeing of slaves a Union war aim, the British sympathy for the South had died away.

CONFEDERATE RAIDERS. At first Adams was not very successful in preventing the Confederates from purchasing ships in Britain. The British argued that they had the right to sell unarmed vessels to anyone. *However, by using secret agents, the Confederacy was purchasing ships in Britain and having them armed in France.* Raiders, such as the *Alabama* and the *Florida*, were then prowling the seas, destroying northern merchant ships.

The ensuing battle between two ironclad ships, the Union's *Monitor* and the Confederacy's *Virginia*, introduced a new element into the war at sea. So successful had the *Virginia* been in ramming the wooden warships blockading Chesapeake Bay that the North feared that any more such vessels in the hands of the Confederacy might prove fatal. *So, when Confederate agents in Britain ordered the construction of two more ironclad rams, Adams decided to intervene again.* This time the British confiscated the rams, and the crisis was eased.

THE CONFEDERACY IS SEALED OFF. *By the end of 1863, the Union blockade of the South was taking its toll.* The South had to export its products—such as tobacco, cotton, and sugar—in order to obtain money to buy military equipment and manufactured goods in Europe. But the blockade prevented this. As the blockade

323

continued, European goods were no longer available in the South and southern manufacturers could not provide what was

needed. Soon the army and the people of the South began to suffer from a lack of these goods, despite the effort by many to make up

Sidenote to History

Women During the War

One of the most important results of the Civil War was the greater freedom and opportunities granted to women. In both the North and South, many women developed their own jobs and decided how they would be carried out.

Women were most active in organizing and providing relief for the wounded during the Civil War. People, such as Dorothea Dix, had organized a volunteer army nursing corps. After convincing the Union military leaders of the value of such nurses, Dix had received a commission from the United States War Department to head the volunteer nurses. As part of her job, Dix was responsible for setting up military hospitals, supplying nurses, and administering the flow of supplies from individuals and associations to the hospitals.

Clara Barton, a clerk in a Washington, D.C., patent office at the outbreak of the war, organized a soldiers' aid society. Barton carried supplies from one Union hospital to another in a caravan of wagons, often narrowly escaping death from exploding cannon shells. Reporting the missing in action to Union families was another one of Clara Barton's jobs, which she initiated and carried out at her own expense. Congress reimbursed her for her efforts after the war.

One of the most outstanding hospital organizers in the South was Phoebe Levy Pember. In Richmond, Virginia, Pember operated one division of the largest military hospital in the world.

Women on both sides made bandages and clothes. The output of handmade clothing in the Confederacy was remarkable, considering the lack of materials and the 14 hours of work it took one woman to produce a soldier's shirt.

Economic pressures in both the North and the South and the lack of a full labor force resulted in many women working either in factories, making rifle cartridges, or in government offices. Women worked for longer hours and for less pay in wartime than their male counterparts would have worked for in the same jobs in peacetime. In the South many women were left in charge of farms and plantations.

At the conclusion of the war, women sought a greater voice, especially in the political sphere. Sojourner Truth, a former slave freed in New York in 1827, spent most of her life before and during the war years supporting abolition, women's rights, temperance, and prison reform. Until her death in 1883, Sojourner Truth made numerous tours of the North, speaking on behalf of equal rights for freed Blacks and women.

Mary Livermore, one of the prime fund raisers of medical relief for the Union Army, turned to the struggle for women's rights in the post-Civil War years. As a married woman, she had no legal right to make contracts, despite having handled thousands of dollars as part of her job. Livermore resolved to change this situation by speaking about and publishing journals on women's rights. From the 1870's to the early 20th century, women would organize for their own benefit, demanding the vote and a place as active, equal members of society.

Belle Boyd, pictured on the left, was a spy for the Confederacy. She secretly relayed information from Union officers in Virginia to the Confederates. She was imprisoned twice and released both times. Harriet Tubman, pictured on the right, worked as a guerilla leader for the Union army in South Carolina. (See Sidenote to History, page 294.)

the deficiencies. For example, many people, mostly women, were making fabrics for clothes and uniforms.

Also, by the end of 1863, the Confederate raiders had been either destroyed or confined to port. The port cities of Norfolk, Virginia; St Augustine, Florida; and New Orleans, Louisiana, were in Union hands. Then, in August 1864 Admiral David Farragut led a squadron of ships through a watery *mine-field* in Mobile Bay and captured a key port. As a result, the Confederacy was sealed off from the world. Without arms or medicines, it was being slowly strangled to death.

By the time of the Civil War, fixed mines, called torpedoes, were commonly used to protect harbors. The area in which they were placed is called a ***minefield***.

Viewpoints of History

A Family Divided

During the Civil War many families found their loyalties divided between the Union and the Confederacy. It was not unusual for one brother to fight on one side and another brother to fight on the other.

Such a conflict of loyalties is expressed in the following letters written by two brothers, James and John Welsh, at the beginning of the war. John Welsh lived in Virginia and supported the Confederacy. His brother James lived in Illinois and supported the Union.

Letter by John Welsh in Virginia. About 700 men in all have gone to join the army, and they are drilling men all over the country. So far as I can learn, the North expects to crush the South at once, but they are mistaken. We look upon the war as a just cause, and we are united men and women. A people united and determined, as the South is, won't be conquered in a day.

I have always opposed secession, but I shall vote for it today because I don't intend to submit to Republican rule any longer. The Republicans say, "You must submit, we have the government in our own hands, we have the army and the navy, we will have no compromise, we will make you submit." We don't intend to trouble the North, but they must let us alone. Write and say what you please, it will make no difference to me. You are as dear to me as ever, farewell.

Letter by James Welsh in Illinois. I sometimes ask myself, can it be that I have a brother that would raise a hand to tear down the glorious Stars and Stripes, a flag that we have been taught from our cradle to look on with pride? My country has been attacked, and my country's flag has been insulted, and it matters not to me whether it is by foes from within or from outside. I would strike down my own brother if he raised a hand to destroy that flag.

There has been a President elected [Lincoln] who you are dissatisfied with, and you appeal to arms. Suppose you get a separation of the Union, what next? If some portion of your country becomes dissatisfied with another, it may secede and refuse to pay its taxes. What has the Republican party done that is so bad, pray tell me?

Section Review

1. Identify or explain: Conscription Act of 1863, the Copperheads, 54th Massachusetts Regiment, Charles Francis Adams, Admiral Farragut, the *Virginia*.
2. Describe the reasons for and results of the following policies toward slaves: **a)** contraband; **b)** the Confiscation Act; and **c)** the Emancipation Proclamation. Why was Lincoln slow to abolish slavery?
3. Why was the war opposed by the Copperheads, draft rioters, and new immigrants? How did the Union government respond to their opposition?
4. Why were relations with Britain so important to both sides? What caused a change in British sympathy?

3. Union Triumph, 1863-1865

FREDERICKSBURG. Although General McClellan had been victorious at Antietam, he had nonetheless been criticized in the press for letting Lee escape back across the Potomac. After Antietam, Lincoln had replaced McClellan with Ambrose Burnside, an unfortunate choice. For example, Burnside had marched into Virginia in the winter of 1862 and had found Lee securely entrenched on a hill overlooking the city of Fredericksburg. But instead of seeking another approach, Burnside had ordered the federal forces to charge across the broad, open plain through a steady rain of Lee's artillery fire. When he finally retired from the battle, Burnside had left almost 12,000 killed or wounded lying on the field.

CHANCELLORSVILLE, MAY 2–4, 1863.

As spring turned the Virginia woods green, the Union army resumed its advance. "Fighting Joe" Hooker, Burnside's replacement, moved across the Rappahannock River to Chancellorsville. (See map on the right.) The battle opened when Lee divided his army, sending Stonewall Jackson on a wide flanking march. Jackson marched all night, finally hitting the Union army from the rear at dawn. Two days later Hooker retreated back across the river. It was Lee's finest victory, but also his costliest. Among the dead was Stonewall Jackson, shot accidentally by his own soldiers.

GETTYSBURG, JULY 1–3, 1863.

After the Chancellorsville victory Lee confessed: "We had really accomplished nothing. We had not gained a foot of ground, and I knew the enemy could easily replace the men they had lost."

The Virginia campaign was a frustrating one for both sides. Lee won victory after victory, yet the blue-clad soldiers kept coming. Despite its losses, the Army of the Potomac still outnumbered the Confederate army by more than two to one. Lee needed a political victory. So he decided to invade the North a second time.

Gettysburg, July 1863
— Confederate forces
— Union forces

Swinging to the west to avoid the Union army, Lee marched northward along the edge of the mountains, across Maryland, and into southern Pennsylvania. Hooker followed, and the scouts from the two armies made contact near the village of Gettysburg on July 1.

On the eve of the battle, Lincoln juggled his generals once more, replacing Hooker with George G. Meade. Meade selected a low ridge, protected by hills on each side, and waited for Lee to attack. On the third of July, Lee ordered General George Pickett's brigade to charge up the center of the ridge, where Meade was waiting for them. Pickett's charge reached the center of the ridge and then fell back. It was the beginning of the end for the Confederacy. The next day Lee retired back across the Potomac. On that same day Grant took Vicksburg, Mississippi.

General Lee, at the left, and Stonewall Jackson, at the right, met for the last time at dawn on May 2, 1863. At 9:00 that night, Jackson and his staff were returning from a scouting mission when a nervous Confederate regiment mistakenly opened fire. Jackson was mortally wounded.

THE WAR IN THE WEST. *The fighting in Virginia had attracted a great deal of attention, but the war was really won in the West.* Possession of Tennessee had given the Union armies access to the southern heartland. They had cut the South in two by controlling the Mississippi River.

Then, they had cut it again by marching across Georgia to the sea. These were the morale-crushing campaigns that had broken the Confederacy.

In May 1863 Grant moved south along the Mississippi and surrounded the city of Vicksburg. New Orleans was already in

Sidenote to History

The Gettysburg Address

In November 1863, some five months after the battle of Gettysburg, a group of northern dignitaries gathered at the battle site to dedicate the Soldiers' National Cemetery. President Lincoln presided at the dedication, but Edward Everett, the nation's foremost orator, was the main speaker. Everett delivered a long speech, praising the dead and denouncing secession.

Lincoln's dedication took two minutes to deliver. Using a few simple words, he expressed the main idea of the event. Lincoln's address was almost immediately recognized as a masterpiece. The entire Gettysburg Address, as it was preserved for the future, follows.

Fourscore and seven years ago our fathers brought forth on this continent a new nation, conceived in liberty and dedicated to the proposition that all men [people] are created equal.

Now we are engaged in a great civil war, testing whether that nation or any nation so conceived and so dedicated can long endure. We are met [meeting] on a great battlefield of that war. We have come to dedicate a portion of that field as a final resting place for those who here gave their lives that that nation might live. It is altogether fitting and proper that we should do this.

But, in a larger sense, we cannot dedicate—we cannot consecrate—we cannot hallow—this ground. The brave men, living and dead, who struggled here, have consecrated it far above our poor power to add or detract. The world will little note, nor long remember, what we say here, but it can never forget what they did here. It is for us the living, rather, to be dedicated here to the unfinished work which they who fought here have thus far so nobly advanced. It is rather for us to be here dedicated to the great task remaining before us—that from these honored dead we take increased devotion to that cause for which they gave the last full measure of devotion—that we here highly resolve that these dead shall not have died in vain—that this nation, under God, shall have a new birth of freedom—and that government of the people, by the people, for the people, shall not perish from the earth.

Union hands. Vicksburg was the last Confederate post on the river. And Grant took it after a month-long seige. Grant then started east to aid the Union army that was attacking Chattanooga, the railroad hub of the South. The Union captured Chattanooga in September, and during the autumn it drove the Confederate army from the heights—Lookout Mountain and Missionary Ridge—overlooking the town.

THE WILDERNESS, MAY–JUNE, 1864. The brilliant Tennessee campaign had brought General Grant to Lincoln's attention. Thus, the President had ordered him east in March 1864 and had made him commander of the Army of the Potomac.

Grant had brought with him a new idea of warfare. Instead of marching and maneuvers, he planned to wear down the enemy by repeated attacks, replacing the soldiers he lost with new recruits. It would be costly, but effective.

Grant opened his campaign in May 1864, in the dense forests west of Fredericksburg, Virginia. (See map, page 330.) His army of 118,000 was twice the size of Lee's. But in the tangled mass of honeysuckle vines, such numbers meant little. Combat was hand-to-hand.

By May 12 Grant had lost 26,000 soldiers, but he had also pushed Lee back toward Richmond. At Cold Harbor on June 3, Grant ordered a frontal attack on an entrenched Confederate position and lost 12,000 soldiers in eight minutes.

News of the blood bath encouraged the peace movement in the North and increased criticism of Lincoln. *But the President had to stick with Grant, his most successful general thus far.*

SIEGE OF PETERSBURG.
After Cold Harbor, Grant crossed the James River, hoping to come on Richmond from the south. First, however, he had to take the city of Petersburg. (See map on the right.) So, for four days Grant threw his troops at Petersburg's hastily prepared defenses. But on June 18 Lee arrived with reinforcements, and Grant began a long siege. Petersburg held out until April 2, 1865.

SHERMAN'S MARCH TO THE SEA.
While Grant's campaign was bogged down in trench warfare, William Tecumseh Sherman was preparing for his dramatic thrust into the heart of the Confederacy. Leaving Chattanooga in May 1864, he was

The War in Virginia, 1864–1865

in sight of Atlanta, Georgia, by mid-July. Then, instead of defending Atlanta, the Confederate commander, J. B. Hood, slipped around Sherman and headed for Tennessee, hoping the Union army would follow in pursuit. (See map, page 331.) Sherman ignored this threat to his supply

"Prisoners from the Front" by Winslow Homer sums up much of the heartbreak and bitterness of the Civil War. Harper's *magazine sent Homer to the front, where he produced some of the finest pictorial representations of the war. Can you describe some of the feelings that the Union officer might have had as he received his Confederate prisoners?*

line, lightened his baggage, and prepared to live off the country.

On November 4, 1864, Sherman began his march from Atlanta to the sea. His army of 60,000 advanced along four parallel roads, 24 kilometers (15 miles) a day, destroying everything in its way. Sherman reached Savannah in mid-December, rested his troops for a month, and then cut a new path of destruction northward across the Carolinas. *This was a new kind of war, designed not to defeat enemy armies but to break civilian morale and destroy the South's will to fight.*

THE ROAD TO APPOMATTOX. Lee's army, defending Richmond and Petersburg, starved through the winter. Short of clothing and shoes, its lines thinned by desertion. Grant opened his spring offensive on April 1, 1865, and the Confederate lines buckled. Lee retreated west, hoping to join the Confederate army that was facing Sherman in North Carolina. Grant moved rapidly to cut him off. Unwilling to press his tired and hungry troops further, Lee asked for surrender terms.

The two commanders met at Appomattox Court House. (See map, page 330.) Grant allowed the Confederate soldiers to return home, surrendering only their arms and artillery. Lee did not offer his sword in defeat; Grant did not ask for it. The agreement was signed on April 9. Five days later President Lincoln was shot while attending a play at Ford's Theater—a tragic ending to a tragic war.

Section Review

1. Mapping: Trace Lee's invasion of the North to Gettysburg. If he had won at Gettysburg, what geographical obstacles would he have had to have overcome?
2. Identify or explain: Ambrose Burnside, Joe Hooker, William Sherman, Appomattox.
3. Make a chart of late Civil War battles, including Chancellorsville, Gettysburg, Vicksburg, Fredericksburg. Use the following headings: location, date, generals, results.
4. Give at least five reasons for the northern victory. Why was the South defeated even though its military strategies were often superior to those of the North?

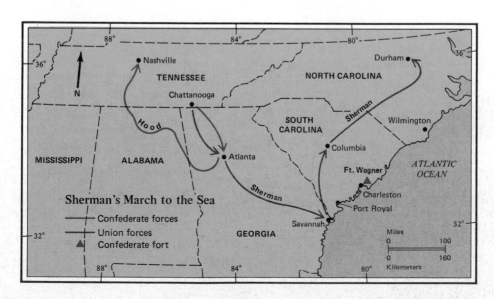

Sherman's March to the Sea
— Confederate forces
— Union forces
▲ Confederate fort

Chapter 13 Review

Bird's-Eye View

The war that no one wanted turned into a long, bloody, and bitter struggle. Although the South had the advantage of skilled military leadership, the North's industrial output, transportation networks, natural and financial resources, and superiority in sheer numbers eventually prevailed.

The South had hoped to end the war quickly by an aggressive attack on Washington, D.C., but was unable to capture the capital.

Disagreements on policy threatened to undermine the northern war effort. As a result, the government was forced to take rather stern measures to silence Copperhead dissent. Conscription was bitterly opposed by many. The poor, and particularly the immigrants, felt that the burden of fighting had fallen most heavily on them. This resentment led to draft riots in several northern cities.

Slaves who sought refuge with the Union armies were at first accepted only as contrabands of war. But the prospect of at least the semblance of freedom had encouraged many slaves to flee to Union lines. Initially, they were used only in supportive capacities, but soon they began to be recruited into the regular army.

The Confiscation Act of 1862 put pressure on Lincoln to take some action concerning slavery. In 1863 he issued the Emancipation Proclamation, declaring all slaves in the rebellious states freed.

The Emancipation Proclamation strengthened the moral position of the North and ended the threat of British intervention on the side of the Confederacy.

Southern victories gained no new territory; they only slowed the advance of the northern armies. In 1863 General Lee tried once again to invade the North, but was defeated at Gettysburg. On that same day Grant was victorious at Vicksburg, and the Union army's mission of controlling all Mississippi River ports was complete. As the new commander of the Army of the Potomac, Grant attempted to push Lee back toward the Confederate capital, Richmond. At the same time Sherman was executing his devastating march through Georgia and the Carolinas. Lee surrendered formally at Appomattox. The war was over, but the bitterness would be evident for years to come.

Vocabulary

Define or identify each of the following:

Bull Run	Copperheads	George Pickett
gunboats	contraband	Sherman's march
conscription	Phoebe Levy Pember	Appomattox

Review Questions

1. Why was the South's strategy one of trying to win the Civil War quickly?
2. Explain the Union's strategy in the first stage of the war.
3. Trace the course of Lincoln's thinking and his actions about slavery and emancipation.
4. What role did Blacks play in the Union army?

5. Robert E. Lee, thought by many to be the greatest general of the war, won battle after battle. Yet, he was finally forced to surrender. Why?
6. What was the cost of the war in materials, soldiers, and morale to the South?

Reviewing Social Studies Skills

1. Make a chart of the battles noted in the text. Indicate the state in which they were fought, the date of the battle, and the winning side. If given, list the number of casualties on both sides.
2. Reread the Gettysburg Address on page 329. The Gettysburg Address is a primary source. *People and Our Country* is a secondary source. What are the differences between the Gettysburg Address and your textbook?
3. Draw a time line of the Civil War years. Show the battles on one side of the line and the nonmilitary events on the other.

Reading for Meaning

1. Find evidence in the chapter to support or refute the following hypothesis: A northern victory was inevitable. Draw a conclusion about this hypothesis, based on the evidence you found most convincing.
2. Many words relating to the war are used in this chapter. Here is a brief list of terms: siege, strategy, blockade, emancipation, and contraband. First, see if you can infer their meanings from their use in the text; then, check the meanings in a dictionary.
3. Reread the information in this chapter on northern generals. Then, choose an appropriate title from this list to head a section describing northern generals. Explain your choice. **a)** Brilliant Strategists Win Easy Victory **b)** Superior Military Skill Makes the Difference **c)** Lincoln Seeks a Winner.
4. The Civil War forced the United States to redefine the role and status of Black Americans. Find a sentence in the chapter that describes each of the following situations: **a)** slaves as property **b)** slaves as contraband **c)** Blacks serving in supportive capacities to the military **d)** Blacks as soldiers.

Bibliography

Bruce Catton has written a number of books on the Civil War, and they are all good. Among them are *A Stillness at Appomattox* (Doubleday) and *Never Call Retreat* (Paperback Library).

A good survey of the Civil War is Carl Sandburg's *Storm Over the Land* (Harcourt Brace Jovanovich). He also wrote *Abe Lincoln Grows Up* (Harcourt Brace Jovanovich), the famous biography of Lincoln.

Ben Ames Williams's *A House Divided* (Houghton Mifflin) is an interesting novel about the Civil War, with a splendid description of the Battle of Gettysburg.

Peter Burchard's *North by Night* (Coward) describes the escape of a young Yankee from a Confederate prison.

Chapter 14

1865-1877

Restoring the Union

On September 4, 1865, Sidney Andrews, a reporter for the *Chicago Tribune* and the *Boston Advertiser,* sent north this description of Charleston, South Carolina—one of the leading cities of the Confederacy: "A city of ruins, of desolation, of vacant houses, of widowed women, of rotting wharves, of deserted warehouses, of weed-wild gardens, of grass-grown streets, of pitiful barrenness— that is Charleston, wherein Rebellion loftily reared its head five years ago."

The name of many another southern city and town could have been substituted for that of Charleston. By 1865 the South had been shattered, the proud and defiant Confederacy ruined. Andrews and other reporters had been appalled at what they had seen after the smoke of battle had cleared. Columbia, another South Carolina city, which had been thought by many to have been the most beautiful city in North America, had been left, according to one traveler, "a wilderness of ruins. . . . Its heart . . . but a mass of blackened chimneys and crumbling walls. Two thirds of the buildings in the place were burned. . . . Not a store, office, or shop escaped; and for a distance of three fourths of a mile on each of 12 streets there was not a building left."

The rural areas looked just as devastated. Fields had been stripped of their fences. Bridges had collapsed and had not been replaced. Roads, neglected for so long, had become virtually impassable. Farm tools and machinery had rusted and rotted. Dams and levees had been destroyed. And as a result, much farm land had been washed out by floods.

Because more than 250,000 men and boys had been killed in the war, a crushing burden had been placed on the shoulders of southern women. They had been left, in many cases, to cope with destroyed farms and plantations by themselves. In fact, so many farm animals had died, had strayed off, or had been taken by the Union and Confederate soldiers that women often yoked themselves to the plow to turn over fields for planting.

Southern society had been left just as devastated as the southern farms and towns. The school system was at a standstill. So many churches had been destroyed that religious services had been suspended in many areas. Local governments had vanished in some parts of the South, and had left people subject to bitter, violent bands of ex-soldiers.

Many freed Blacks were sent to contraband camps for lack of other facilities to house them. These camps were so filthy and crowded that nearly 25 percent of the inmates had died from epidemics, crime, and lack of proper food, clothing, or shelter.

Economically the South was in ruins, too. Its 2.5 billion dollar investment in slaves had evaporated overnight. Land values had dropped 50 percent. Confederate war bonds and currency were worthless, and those who had invested in them had suffered irrecoverable losses. The billions that had been spent by the Confederacy and the individual southern states in fighting the war had drained the South of capital. The banks were wiped out. And southern industry had been ground to a halt.

The North had also suffered grave losses, but in many ways it had benefited from the war. Although some industries had been hard hit, northern industry as a whole had profited. The North had been given a great boost by the 4 billion dollars the federal government had spent on the war, money that had been pumped into northern industries and businesses. In fact, the war, for the North, had been the beginning of a period of rapid economic expansion. As John Sherman wrote to his brother, General William T. Sherman, in 1865, "The war leaves us with our resources unimpaired and gives an elevation, a scope, to the ideas of leading capitalists, far higher than anything ever undertaken in this country before. They talk of millions as confidently as formerly of thousands."

Chapter Objectives

After you have finished reading this chapter, you should be able to:
1. Compare the differences between Lincoln's plan for reconstruction and the Radical Republicans' plan.
2. Identify the causes of Radical opposition to Andrew Johnson.
3. Explain why Congress did the following: established military reconstruction in the South, introduced the 15th Amendment, impeached President Johnson.
4. List the positive and negative results of reconstruction in the South.
5. Trace the progress that has been made in the area of Black civil rights, from reconstruction to 1900.

It was in this postwar atmosphere—of expansion and optimism on one hand and ruin and desolation on the other—that the work of reconstruction took place. And hard work it was. The immediate problems were staggering and numerous. Among the most important were the rebuilding of the South and the restoration of its economic life on the basis of free labor. Another problem was finding a way to restore the seceded states to their places in the Union. And then there was the question of the newly freed Blacks. There was no doubt that legally the Blacks were free. But there were many questions to be resolved about the status of free Blacks in the South, where they had so recently been slaves.

1. Lincoln and the Radicals

CONCERNS OF RECONSTRUCTION. *Reconstruction involved two things: the return of the South to the Union, with representation in Congress, and the restoration of civilian governments in the southern states occupied by federal troops.* Underlying both was another question—the status of the newly freed Blacks. No one knew what guarantees the freed Blacks might need. Should they, for instance, be given the right to vote? Without that, could they preserve any other rights?

THE RADICALS. The Republican party had never been united in its attitude toward slavery and secession. The more outspoken opponents of slavery—called Radicals—had not been happy with Lincoln's election in 1860 and had objected to the President's delay in dealing with the question.

Led by Thaddeus Stevens of Pennsylvania, Benjamin F. Wade of Ohio, and Charles Sumner of Massachusetts, the Radicals had drawn up the wartime Confiscation Acts. Now they talked of punishing the South for having started the conflict. They argued that the southern states had "committed suicide" by seceding. And, having been defeated, they were "conquered provinces" at the mercy of Congress. The anger and bitterness that had resulted from the war had lent the Radicals some public support. However, they remained a minority within the Republican party.

THE MODERATES. President Lincoln himself reflected the views of the Moderate wing of the Republican party. *"With charity for all, and malice toward none,"* Lincoln hoped to heal wartime bitterness and restore the South to the Union as quickly *and painlessly as possible.* Furthermore, he expected to do it himself, through Presidential orders under his wartime powers.

Virginia presented him with the first opportunity. At the beginning of the war, Virginia's western counties had decided to remain in the Union. Lincoln had named a temporary governor for them, and the governor had called a convention to draft a state constitution. These counties became West Virginia and entered the Union in 1863.

In that same year federal troops had gained control of the northern and eastern parts of Virginia. Lincoln's governor of West Virginia then moved to Alexandria to govern there. When parts of Tennessee, Arkansas, and Louisiana came under Union control, Lincoln appointed other provisional governors for these states as well.

LINCOLN'S BRAND OF RECONSTRUCTION. On December 8, 1863, Lincoln issued his Proclamation of *Amnesty* and Reconstruction. This proclamation outlined Lincoln's program for reconstruction. *First, he offered to pardon any southerner who would take an oath of loyalty to the Union and who would agree to accept all Presidential decrees and congressional acts relating to slavery.* Excluded from the amnesty, however, were Confederate government officials, high-ranking army officers, and former United States representatives to Congress. These people would not be allowed to take part in the political life of the reconstructed South. *Second, in any Confederate state when 10 percent of the people who had been eligible to vote in 1860 took the oath of loyalty, they could organize a government, elect representatives to Congress, and consider themselves restored to the Union.*

Amnesty is a general release from prosecution that a government issues for an offense. It is often granted before a trial or conviction and frequently applies to a large group of people.

Because the war was fought on southern soil, many parts of the South were devastated. Southern cities were often reduced to piles of rubble. This photograph of Charleston, South Carolina, was taken in 1865 by Mathew Brady, the famous photographer of the period.

Lincoln's program was hardly revolutionary. The voters in 1863 were the same as those in 1860. Thus, it was probable that the same leaders would be chosen. The freed Blacks would have only those rights that those leaders were willing to give them.

Two states, Arkansas and Louisiana, quickly complied with the President's terms. However, when they sent representatives to Congress, the House and the Senate refused to seat them. The Radicals in Congress had other plans for reconstructing the South.

THE WADE-DAVIS BILL. Radicals were a minority in the Republican party. But many members of Congress agreed with the Radical argument that reconstruction had to be accomplished by congressional legislation, not simply by Presidential order. The President's move offended much of the Congress and temporarily gave Radicals the upper hand.

In July 1864 Congress passed the Wade-Davis Bill, drafted by Benjamin F. Wade, Henry Winter Davis, and other Radicals.

This miniature painting of Lincoln and his son Tad was done by Frances Bicknell Carpenter, who lived in the White House with the Presidential family for six months during 1864. Compare this view of Lincoln with those you have seen in previous chapters. What dimensions do you see in his personality?

The bill declared that Congress, not the President, was entitled to determine the conditions under which the Confederate states would be readmitted to the Union. It proposed placing the southern states under military rule, with northern generals serving as governors. The governor would enroll all White males and administer a loyalty oath. When a majority of the men in any state had taken the oath, the state could set up a civil government. The Wade-Davis Bill also provided for the immediate abolition of slavery.

DIFFERENCES BETWEEN THE TWO PLANS. *The congressional plan differed from Lincoln's in three important respects:*

1. It involved all White males, not just the few who had been able to vote under the prewar southern constitution.

2. The oath involved past loyalty, thereby excluding from the new governments all who had aided the Confederacy. Only southern Unionists (scalawags) and northerners who had drifted into the South (carpetbaggers) could in good conscience take such an oath.

3. A majority of White men had to take the oath, rather than Lincoln's 10 percent. Since most White men in the South had aided the Confederacy, military rule could be prolonged indefinitely.

What the radicals had in mind was nothing less than a social revolution. They wanted to remake southern society. They hoped that when the South finally did reenter the Union, it would look like the North and would vote Republican.

The Radicals' aims, though not fully formed, were too extreme for Lincoln. He believed that slavery could be legally abolished only by a constitutional amendment, not by Congress. In addition, Lincoln declared that he was not willing to commit himself to any one plan of reconstruction. He did agree, however, that if any southern state preferred the congressional plan to his own, he would take immediate steps to implement it. *So, he refused to sign the Wade-Davis Bill, and it never became law.* But if the Radicals ever got the upper hand, they had a bill that could be used as a blueprint for reconstruction.

THE ELECTION OF 1864. While Congress discussed the Wade-Davis Bill, both parties held conventions to choose Presidential candidates. Despite the Radical opposition, Lincoln won renomination on the first ballot. He then left the choice of his running mate to the convention. The Moderate majority selected Andrew Johnson, a pro-Union Democrat from Tennessee.

Lincoln's nomination was an open bid for a united party front in the war emergency,

This engraving for Harper's Weekly *shows John Wilkes Booth shooting President Lincoln as he sits watching the comedy* Our American Cousin. *After the shooting, Booth reportedly leaped to the stage, shouting "Thus always to tyrants."*

and many Democrats supported the Lincoln-Johnson ticket. But a remnant of the Peace Democrats also held a convention, and they nominated General George B. McClellan. In the election Lincoln carried all but three Union states—New Jersey, Delaware, and Kentucky.

THE 13TH AMENDMENT. Throughout his career Lincoln stood opposed to the institution of slavery. However, he was convinced that it could not be abolished either by Presidential order or by a congressional bill. Only an amendment to the Constitution, duly ratified by the people of each state, could, in his opinion, legally abolish slavery. It was fitting, therefore, that Lincoln's final triumph as President—barely three months before his death—was the fashioning of such an amendment.

In January 1865 Congress took up a constitutional amendment to abolish slavery everywhere in the United States and its territories. Even at that late date, however, there was substantial opposition to so modest a change. But Lincoln put the full weight of his office behind the 13th Amendment, persuading, pleading, and bargaining.

Without the President's tireless support, the amendment might not have passed. In the House of Representatives, it barely obtained the necessary two-thirds majority. Lincoln's support for this amendment, alone, justly earned him the title of "the Great Emancipator," which history had given him.

LINCOLN IS ASSASSINATED. On April 14, 1865, only five days after General Lee's surrender at Appomattox, President Lincoln attended an English play—*Our American Cousin*—at Ford's Theater in Washington, D.C. Lincoln watched the play from a box, overlooking the stage. In the middle of the drama, John Wilkes Booth—an actor and the son of one of the most famous 19th-century actors, Edwin Booth—entered the box. Locking the door behind him, Booth aimed his pistol at Lincoln's head and fired. He then slashed with a dagger at the President's guest for the evening, Major Rathbone; leaped to the stage (breaking his leg in the process); and fled.

Lincoln was carried across the street to a house, where he died the next morning. Booth was found hiding in a barn in Virginia. When he refused to surrender, shots were fired, and he died. However, it is not known whether he shot himself or whether he was killed by a soldier. Booth's fellow conspirators were subsequently rounded up, tried, and hanged.

Horror, mixed with outrage, swept the country. Lincoln had hoped to restore the Union, "with charity for all and malice toward none," as he had said in his second inaugural address only a month before. That fond hope died with him.

Had he lived, Lincoln would have had difficulty maintaining his program of moderate, Presidential reconstruction. But he might have tempered the Radicals' harsh treatment of the South, while yielding, as he

had during the war, to the demand for Black rights. Andrew Johnson, Lincoln's successor, had no such chance.

Section Review

1. Identify or explain: Thaddeus Stevens, Radical Republicans, Andrew Johnson, John Wilkes Booth, the Wade-Davis Bill.
2. Make a chart, comparing Radical and Moderate proposals for reconstruction. What are the major differences between the two?
3. List the goals of the Wade-Davis Bill. How were the policies in it designed to implement those goals?

2. Johnson and the Radicals

PRESIDENT ANDREW JOHNSON. The new President, Andrew Johnson, had many admirable qualities. He had started life as a tailor and had been taught to read and write by his wife. Like Andrew Jackson, the man he most admired, he had pulled himself to the top by his own efforts. Coming from a poor background, he had no more liking for aristocratic planters than the Radical Republicans. But his background also hindered his understanding of the needs of freed Blacks.

By the time he took office, the Radicals were moving well beyond mere abolition of slavery. *They had come to realize that freedom for Blacks meant little without certain legal guarantees—access to courts, for instance; perhaps even access to the ballot box.* Balancing the many passions tearing at the nation—party politics, prejudice, idealism—required the utmost tact and political skill. The new President, unfortunately, possessed neither.

JOHNSON'S AMNESTY PROCLAMATION. In May 1865 President Johnson issued his own Amnesty Proclamation. It resembled Lincoln's in its lenient attitude toward the South. The only additional condition he imposed on the southern states was that they ratify the 13th Amendment. The South moved to comply. *And those states that had not already set up civil governments under Lincoln's plan did so under Johnson's.* They ratified the 13th Amendment and elected representatives to Congress.

Both Lincoln and Johnson had worked with the southern Whites who had had the vote before and during the war. Lincoln and Johnson asked only that these voters be loyal to the Union in the future. Not surprisingly, the southern Whites returned to office many of the leaders they had elected before. Among those elected to Congress by the reconstructed South were a number of Confederate officials and army officers, including the Confederacy's vice-president, Alexander Stephens.

Johnson had made another gesture to the South that southerners had interpreted as a sign of his goodwill. He had appointed M. F. Pleasants, a former Confederate colonel, to the position of clerk of pardons. Pleasants's job was to process the many requests for clemency addressed to the President by southerners.

THE JOINT COMMITTEE ON RECONSTRUCTION.
Johnson's plans for the South, like Lincoln's, bypassed Congress, irritating Radicals and Moderates alike. When southern representatives and senators appeared in Washington at the opening of Congress in December 1865, Congress refused to let them take their seats. *Instead, it appointed a congressional committee to investigate conditions in the South.* Heading the Joint Committee on Reconstruction was a Moderate Republican, Senator William Pitt Fessenden of Maine. The committee also contained Radicals, including Thaddeus Stevens. Radicals and Moderates were dismayed by the testimony about what had happened in the South.

BLACK CODES.
The southern legislatures established under the Presidential scheme had passed a number of laws concerning the freed Blacks. Called Black Codes, these laws were similar to the old slave codes. They did, however, contain certain improvements in the civil rights granted to former slaves. For example, the Black Codes permitted former slaves to own personal property, to sue and be sued in court, and to legally marry members of their own race. But the codes also denied Blacks their basic civil rights. They prohibited Blacks from voting or performing jury duty or from loitering or assembling in public places. The codes also regulated Black labor and Black travel from job to job, while forcing segregation of the races in all public places. In one state unless a Black could pay 100 dollars for a license—an enormous sum in those days—he or she could not work except as an agricultural laborer. Blacks who could not prove that they were gainfully

Vinnie Ream was 19-years-old when she sculpted the statue of Lincoln that stands in the Capitol.

employed could be arrested for vagrancy and their labor then auctioned off to employers.

To southerners the Black Codes seemed a reasonable way to manage a whole class of people who had been kept in poverty and ignorance. Some southerners believed that to set former slaves free without restraints would result in chaos.

Northerners surveyed the South and found ex-Confederates in key offices, with Blacks under a regimented system that seemed to be slavery in all but name. What, they wondered, had four years of bloodshed accomplished? Soon, Radicals found new ammunition in the revelations of the Joint Committee on Reconstruction. They peppered the newspapers with stories of the treatment of Blacks. And northern opinion began to turn against the President.

THE FREEDMEN'S BUREAU. *Prodded by the exposures of the Joint Committee, Congress in February 1866 passed a law expanding the authority of the Freedmen's Bureau.* (Note that at that time the term "freedmen" referred to all former slaves—women, children, and men.)

The Bureau was an army agency whose official name was the Bureau of Refugees, Freedmen, and Abandoned Lands. Created by Congress just before the end of the war, its purpose was to aid refugees and freed Blacks by furnishing supplies and medical services, by establishing schools, and by supervising contracts between freed Blacks and their employers. The Bureau was also empowered to manage confiscated or abandoned lands. The Commissioner of the Freedmen's Bureau, General Oliver O. Howard, was authorized to set aside such lands and to assign to every male citizen, whether refugee or freed Black, not more than 16 hectares (40 acres) of these lands.

The new law passed by Congress in 1866 extended the Bureau's power to help south-

Sidenote to History

Thaddeus Stevens

"Old Thad Stevens," they called him. But it was not a friendly greeting. He had been 75 at the end of the war. He had been in the House of Representatives for nearly 15 years. Stevens, who had been crippled since his youth, had had a passion for reform and for justice. Strongly opposed to slavery, he had defended fugitive slaves and charged nothing. His speeches in the House had been eloquent, but he had a sour disposition, few admirers, and fewer friends. And he had never liked the South.

Stevens was not simply antisouthern. He was an idealist who had devoted much of his life to the cause of reform. As a member of the Pennsylvania assembly in the 1830's, he had led the movement for a statewide public school system. He had been an early convert to the cause of antislavery. But he had also seen that the freeing of slaves was not enough. The freed people had to be given legal and political rights. More important, they had to be given enough property to survive. "Forty acres and a hut," he felt, was the most important right of all. If that meant breaking up the great plantations, then broken up they must be.

Southern Whites listened to Stevens's pronouncements with horror. If he had his way, he would change their way of life forever. Blacks looked at him as a hero, one of the few politicians who understood their needs. Most northerners considered him a sour, old man, whose harsh attitude toward the South was likely to leave lasting wounds. But everyone was right. The many faces of Thaddeus Stevens were the many faces of reconstruction.

ern Blacks whenever their rights or working conditions were threatened. Furthermore, the law authorized the Bureau to use military courts to try all cases of discrimination against freed Blacks.

Within four years of its founding, the Freedmen's Bureau had issued millions of food rations to White refugees and had freed Blacks. It had also built more than 40 hospitals and had spent over two million dollars treating close to 500,000 cases of illness. The Bureau had helped to settle about 30,000 people who had been displaced by the war.

Most of the abandoned lands in the South were returned to pardoned Confederates. Freed Blacks received only a small portion of the lands confiscated by the Union during the war. For the most part they received the poor and unattractive parcels. Although the Bureau provided free transportation to these lands and funds to support the settlers for one month, most Blacks could not take advantage of the opportunity. During the many months that it would take to develop the land and to grow and harvest a crop, they would have no means of support.

THE FREEDMEN'S BUREAU AND EDUCATION. *The Freedmen's Bureau was very successful in the area of education.* It established countless schools— elementary and secondary schools, technical schools, colleges, and universities. It also cooperated with other groups, such as the American Missionary Society, in supporting many educational institutions. Howard University, Hampton Institute, Atlanta University, Scotia Seminary, Fisk University, and other schools received support from the Freedmen's Bureau.

By 1870 there were nearly 250,000 Blacks in over 4,000 schools, and the Bureau had spent more than five million dollars on education. *By 1877—the end of reconstruction—more than 600,000 Blacks were enrolled in southern schools.*

The Freedmen's Bureau was set up under Lincoln's reconstruction program to provide aid for former slaves. It distributed food, clothing, and medical aid; organized schools; and helped people find jobs. Here, in a Freedmen's school in Richmond, Virginia, women are sewing clothing for former slaves.

The teachers who worked in these schools were mostly White women from the North and Black women from the South. Isabella Gibbins, a teacher in Virginia, had been a slave until the end of the war. After teaching all day in the school for freed Blacks in Charlottesville, she continued her own studies at night with the director of the school, Anna Gardner.

CIVIL RIGHTS. *In March 1866 Congress passed the Civil Rights Act, designed to undo the Black Codes.* It guaranteed the federal protection of certain legal rights, including the right to travel and to assemble freely.

Never before had Congress passed a law concerning rights. That had always been a matter for the states. For this reason President Johnson vetoed both the Civil Rights

During the congressional election of 1866, President Andrew Johnson went on a speaking tour to encourage support for members of his party. His efforts were unsuccessful, however. Wherever he went, he was shouted down and abused. The Radical opposition triumphed in the election.

Act and the Freedmen's Bureau Act. However, Congress mustered the two thirds majority necessary to override the President's veto.

The President's interpretation of the Constitution was technically correct, but his vetoes were a sad political error. The evidence turned up by the Joint Committee showed that the freed Blacks needed federal protection, at least for a time. On this question, at least, Moderates agreed with Radicals.

THE 14TH AMENDMENT. *To settle the constitutional question raised by the President, Congress in June 1866 proposed a new amendment to the Constitution.* A compromise between Moderate and Radical Republicans, this Amendment accomplished the following:

1. It formally made the freed Blacks citizens of the United States.

2. It required the states to extend to each citizen "equal protection of the laws" and prevented the states from taking away a citizen's rights or property without "due process of law."

3. It prohibited officials of the Confederate government and ranking officers in the Confederate army from holding federal or state office.

The 14th Amendment seemed moderate enough. It was intended only to ensure that the Blacks got equal treatment. Yet, the President opposed this law, too, largely because of its restriction on ex-Confederates. But, with the Moderates and Radicals joining forces, Congress passed it over the President's opposition. Now it was the President who was beginning to seem extreme.

THE ELECTION OF 1866. When Congress departed for home that summer, attention was turned to the off-year congressional election. This election would determine where public feeling lay—with the congressional view of reconstruction or with the Presidential view.

Realizing the stakes, the President made a national speaking tour that summer. It was a total failure. He was not a good public speaker, and exhaustion and tension had made him worse. He had harassed rather than persuaded and had sometimes made no sense at all. *As the President's prestige slipped, that of Congress rose.* The Republicans swept the election, and within the Republican ranks, the Radicals seemed to have gained the upper hand.

LAME DUCK LAWS. The new Congress would not be sworn in until March 4, 1867, but the old Congress, meeting in its *lame duck* session (December to March 3), had paved the way. First, Congress had provided for the new Congress to begin its session as soon as it was sworn in. The Radicals wanted no gap between congressional sessions, since the President had used one such gap in 1865 to reconstruct the South in his own way.

A *lame duck* session of Congress was one that met after an election but before the new President and Congress were sworn into office. It was called lame duck because in this period between administrations its effectiveness was crippled. It contained many members who had not been reelected and who often voted irresponsibly. The 20th Amendment (1933) eliminated the possibility of a lame duck Congress by changing Inauguration Day from March 4 to January 20.

Congress then passed the Command of the Army Act (March 2, 1867), which forced the President to go through the office of the General of the Army if he wanted to issue an order for the army. Ulysses S. Grant, who was thought to be a Radical, held that office. The Act had further provided that General Grant could not be removed from office without the Senate's consent.

The *Tenure of Office* Act, passed the same day as the Command of Army Act, prohibited the President from dismissing members of his own cabinet without the consent of the Senate. The purpose of this law was to protect the lone Radical in the Cabinet, Secretary of War Edwin Stanton. As the civilian head of the army, he was a crucial figure. *Congressional reconstruction, following the path marked by the Wade-Davis Bill, was to be a military operation.* Control of the army was essential. By these laws Congress ensured that the army would be in the hands of the Radical Republicans.

Tenure of office refers to the period in which a person has the right to remain in office.

PRESIDENTIAL VETO. *President Johnson considered both laws unconstitutional and vetoed them.* Again, he was probably right. Certainly, the legislation was far more restrictive than the Civil Rights Act of the previous year. Once again Congress passed the laws over the President's veto. Congress' action was a measure of the extent to which the President's inflexibility had driven the Moderates into the Radical camp.

Congress sat back to wait for new members to be sworn in on the fourth of March. That done, it would proceed to reconstruct the South in its own way.

Section Review

1. Identify or explain: Andrew Johnson, Black Codes, Freedmen's Bureau, Thaddeus Stevens, lame duck.
2. What were the Black Codes? How was the Civil Rights Act designed to counteract the rules of the Black Codes?
3. What were the provisions of the 14th Amendment? Why was it considered necessary to supplement the 13th Amendment?

3. Congressional-Military Reconstruction

THE RECONSTRUCTION ACTS. *Between March 1867 and March 1868, Congress passed four Reconstruction Acts.* They had the following impact on the South:

1. The existing governments in the South, created under the plans of Lincoln and Johnson, were removed.

2. The South was divided into five military districts, each commanded by a Union general who ruled by military law.

3. The requirement for readmission to the Union was the same as that originally proposed by the Wade-Davis Bill—there must be a majority of White males able to take an oath of past loyalty. Thus, the new southern governments would be dominated by Unionists and Yankees.

4. The new governments had to give the vote to Blacks and had to ratify the 14th Amendment.

When Congress passed the 15th Amendment in 1870, providing for Black suffrage across the entire nation, southern states had to approve that amendment, as well, before they could rejoin the Union. (How a state that was not a member of the Union could ratify an amendment to the Constitution as a means of joining the Union remains a mystery. When Secretary of State Seward announced in December 1865 that three fourths of the states had ratified the 13th Amendment, he counted the approval of eight Confederate states, which were so far out of the Union that their representatives were not seated in Congress. Such unusual times prompted unusual solutions.)

RADICAL RECONSTRUCTION. The destroying of established governments and the imposing of military rule on the South two years after the war ended seems harsh indeed. It caused bitterness among southern Whites that lingered for generations.

And it must be said that many in the North, including Thaddeus Stevens, wished to punish the South.

At the same time the Radical program was not so harsh as it might have been. No civil war in modern times has ended with so few reprisals. Only one Confederate was executed after the war—Henry Wirz, the commander of the prisoner-of-war camp at Andersonville, Georgia, where many northern soldiers had died of starvation. Jefferson Davis, the president of the Confederacy, spent only two years in jail. Robert E. Lee was quickly pardoned and spent his last years as the honored president of Washington College in Virginia. Northern military rule was mild (only 20,000 troops spread across the entire South) and relatively brief. Six states were readmitted in 1868. The

The 15th Amendment guarantees Blacks the right to vote. This sketch was done by Alfred Waud. His depictions of the Civil War and its aftermath are among the most valued works of the era.

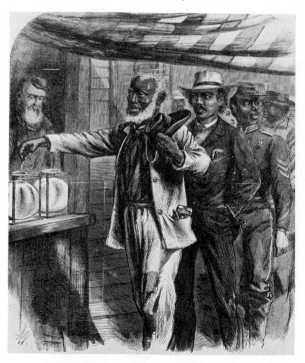

other four voluntarily remained under army rule for another two years rather than give the vote to Blacks.

CONGRESS ASSERTS ITS POWER.
While Congress was asserting the power of the federal government over the southern states, it was also enlarging its own position in the government.

Congress restricted the President's powers, notably in the removal of cabinet officers. It even moved against the Supreme Court. To prevent the President from appointing a Moderate Republican or a Democrat to the Court, Congress in 1866 passed an act stating that no new Supreme Court justices could be appointed until the number on the court was reduced, through death or retirement, to six. It was a clear warning that the Court was not to meddle with the Radicals' reconstruction program.

IMPEACHMENT OF PRESIDENT JOHNSON.
The climax of this effort to make Congress supreme was the *impeachment* of President Johnson. Removal of the President, had it succeeded, would have been the ultimate expression of congressional supremacy.

Impeachment is a charge of misconduct brought against a public official. An impeachment is only an accusation, and the person continues in office until he or she is tried and found guilty of the charges.

The President and Congress had been on a collision course since Johnson had taken office. Johnson's vetoes had angered Congress, and his public criticism had led to whispered talk of impeachment. Congress had needed only a good excuse, and the President had provided that by his dismissal of Secretary of War Stanton in August 1867. Johnson had replaced Stanton with General Grant, who, he had hoped, was on his side. But when the Senate objected to the appointment, Grant resigned.

Encouraged by the Radicals, Stanton returned to the War Department and barricaded himself in, claiming that, under the Tenure of Office Act, the President could not remove him. The President considered the act unconstitutional, and to test it he appointed another general, Lorenzo Thomas, Secretary of War. With Stanton occupying the office day and night, however, there was little for Thomas to do but to attend Washington social functions.

In the midst of the stalemate, the House of Representatives voted for 11 articles of impeachment against the President. Under the Constitution the House of Representatives draws up the list of accusations. The impeached official is then tried before the Senate, with members of the House serving as prosecutors. A guilty vote by two thirds of the senators present is necessary for conviction and removal from office.

THE ACCUSATIONS.
Most of the House's accusations dealt with the President's violation of a law, the Tenure of Office Act. (Johnson had violated this law by removing his Secretary of War without the consent of the Senate.) But the House also accused him of having subjected Congress to "disgrace, ridicule, contempt, and reproach." It was hardly an impressive list of charges. The Tenure of Office Act itself was of doubtful constitutionality, and Johnson's criticizing of Congress was nothing unusual. But the charges did reveal the political bitterness that had come to poison the atmosphere of national government.

After a two-month trial, the Senate at last came to a vote on May 10, 1868. *It voted in favor of convicting the President by 35 to 19, missing by just one vote the necessary two-thirds majority.* Helping to save President Johnson were Democrats and seven Moderate Republicans. They thought that removal of the President was too serious a matter to be done out of party spite alone.

THE ELECTION OF 1868. In June 1868, a month after the President's impeachment trial, Secretary of State Seward announced that six southern states had qualified under the Reconstruction Acts for readmission to the Union. (See chart, page 349.) All six had new constitutions that provided for Black suffrage; all had Republican governments; and all had ratified the 14th Amendment.

The mass admission was a bit hasty, but the Secretary had good reason to hurry. A Presidential election was approaching. And the electoral votes of the reconstructed South would be a big boost to the Republican cause.

It hardly seemed as if the Republicans needed a boost. They had a popular candidate in Ulysses S. Grant, and their campaign oratory took advantage of wartime hatreds. With a technique known as "waving the bloody shirt," the Republicans denounced their opponents as traitors, who had sympathized with the South and who had prolonged the war. (The term "bloody shirt" had been used after a Republican had actually brought back a bloody shirt that had been taken from a Union soldier killed in

Compare this campaign poster for Ulysses S. Grant with other posters you have seen in this book. How does Grant's image compare with Lincoln's? With Jackson's?

battle. The shirt had been used to make a point.) The Democrats, moreover, were disorganized and without popular leaders. Their candidate was the wartime governor of New York, Horatio Seymour. Grant swamped Seymour in the election—214 electoral votes to 80. (See map at the left.)

Four southern states (Virginia, Georgia, Texas, and Mississippi) remained out of the Union. They had refused to comply with the Reconstruction Acts, preferring military rule to Black suffrage. It did them little good. *After the election the Radicals in Congress introduced the 15th Amendment to the Constitution. It prohibited the states from denying the vote to anyone "on account of race, color, or previous condition of servitude."* Black suffrage would become part of the federal Constitution,

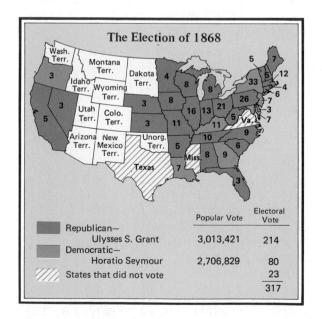

The Election of 1868

	Popular Vote	Electoral Vote
Republican— Ulysses S. Grant	3,013,421	214
Democratic— Horatio Seymour	2,706,829	80
States that did not vote		23
		317

THE CONFEDERATE STATES' READMISSION TO THE UNION

	Readmission
Tennessee	1866
Alabama	1868
Arkansas	1868
Florida	1868
Louisiana	1868
North Carolina	1868
South Carolina	1868
Georgia	1870*
Mississippi	1870
Texas	1870
Virginia	1870

*Georgia had been readmitted to the Union in 1868, but after failing to comply with the terms of the Reconstruction Acts it was returned to military rule until 1870.

applicable to the North as well as the South.

Grant's election and the passage of the 15th Amendment were the high-water marks of Radical reconstruction. But they were also the beginning of the end. By the time the last four southern states had reentered the Union in 1870 and the 15th Amendment had gone into effect, the crusade for Black rights had largely spent itself.

Section Review

1. Mapping: Using the chart on this page and the map on page 309, list the states that were readmitted to the Union in 1868 and those that chose to remain under military occupation.
2. Identify or explain: impeachment, 15th Amendment, Ulysses Grant, "waving the bloody shirt."
3. List the provisions of the Reconstruction Acts of 1867 and 1868. What additional qualifications for returning to the Union were imposed on the southern states?
4. Why did the South believe that the terms of reconstruction were harsh? Why did the North believe that they were relatively mild?
5. What were the main charges brought at the impeachment of Andrew Johnson?

4. The South—Reconstructed and Redeemed

SEPARATING FACT FROM FICTION. The days of reconstruction lingered in southern memories and in southern folklore for many years. Carpetbaggers and scalawags were often considered the worst of villains. The idea of Black rule haunted White southerners. And White Democrats, who eventually regained control of the southern governments, were thought to be redeemers, saving society from evil. But although there were many abuses and extensive corruption under Radical Republican rule, it is necessary to sift fact from fancy.

CARPETBAGGERS AND SCALAWAGS. The scalawags, or southern Unionists, who cooperated with reconstruction were not all renegades, serving their selfish interests. Many of them were deeply religious mountain people who had never approved of either slavery or the Confederacy. Tennessee mountaineers had elected a Republican government even before passage of the Reconstruction Acts. Scalawags also included business people who wanted to revitalize the South by reducing its dependence on cotton. Some were ex-Confederates, among them, General James Longstreet, whose brigade had fought so well at Gettysburg.

Carpetbaggers were also a mixed group of people. The nickname suggested that they were mere adventurers, with their worldly possessions packed in suitcases made of carpet, seeking to take advantage of the war-torn South. Many carpetbaggers were seeking a profit, but others were genuine idealists, who had gone south to promote the cause of the freed Blacks.

Northerners, whether profit seekers or not, did dominate the reconstruction governments, at least in their early stages. This was partly because they had the support of the new Black voters and partly because many White southerners had been denied the right to vote. Their influence was most evident in the new state constitutions, drawn up under the Reconstruction Acts.

THE RECONSTRUCTION CONSTITUTIONS. *Under the Reconstruction Acts every state had to draft a new constitution that included a provision for Black suffrage.* The carpetbaggers had added several other features to these new constitutions. For one, they had expanded the White electorate by abolishing the property qualification for voter eligibility in those states that still had it. They had also practiced reapportionment in those states where representation had been out of balance. They had embraced such social reforms as free public education, expanded rights for women, and liberalized criminal codes. *Next to the 13th, 14th, and 15th amendments to the federal Constitution, these constitutions were the most lasting achievements of the reconstruction era.*

Reapportionment involves redefining the boundaries of election districts or revising representation within an area. Two common reasons for reapportionment are population increases and decreases and redivisions of political units such as cities and townships.

RECONSTRUCTION GOVERNMENTS. All the conventions to create new state constitutions for the South had Black members. *But Black reconstruction did not mean Black rule.* The Radical governments were run mostly by Whites. In Louisiana the Blacks and the Whites were equally represented. But only in one state—South Carolina—did Blacks even have a majority in the legislature. And everywhere the top executive and judicial posts were held by Whites.

The main reason for this state of affairs was that few freed Blacks were educated enough to seek office. Those who did and were elected performed with credit, and they talked little of revenge against their former owners. Several Black leaders even favored giving ex-Confederates the vote.

The Charleston, South Carolina, *Daily News,* in fact, maintained that "the best men in the convention are the colored members. . . . They have assembled neither to pull wires, like some, nor to make money, like others; but to legislate for the welfare of the race to which they belong."

BLACKS IN PUBLIC OFFICE. *During reconstruction, Blacks did hold public offices on the local, state, and national levels of government.* Many sat in the state legislatures. Alonso Ransier, Richard Gleaves, Oscar Dunn, P. B. S. Pinchback, and C. C. Antoine were lieutenant-governors. Pinchback was also an acting governor of Louisiana for 43 days in 1873 when the governor, Henry C. Warmouth, was removed from office. Samuel J. Lee and Robert B. Elliott each served as Speaker of the House of Representatives in South Carolina. Francis L. Cardozo, who had been educated at British universities, was South Carolina's Secretary of State from 1868 to 1872 and its treasurer from 1872 to 1876.

Many Blacks were also elected to Congress. Two—Hiram Revels and Blanche K. Bruce—served in the Senate, representing Mississippi. Revels was a free Black from North Carolina who had migrated to Indiana, Illinois, and Ohio. Educated for the ministry in Ohio, he had taught school, recruited Blacks for the Union army, served as chaplain to a Black regiment in Mississippi, and founded a school for freed Blacks in St. Louis. In 1870 he had been elected to the Senate to fill the seat previously occupied by Jefferson Davis.

Blanche K. Bruce had been born a slave in Virginia. During the war he had escaped to Hannibal, Missouri, where he had set up a school for Blacks. After the war he had gone to Mississippi. Later, he had entered politics and had held several public offices, ranging from tax collector to superintendant of schools. When P. B. S. Pinchback was denied the Senate seat to which he had been elected from Louisiana, Bruce had spoken for him. But his effort had been in vain. Pinchback was never allowed to take the seat.

Twenty Blacks served in the House of Representatives. Most had had some experience in public service before going to Washington. They had been delegates to constitutional conventions, state legislators, and local officials. Their main concerns in Congress were education and civil rights, but they also worked in other areas as well. For example, Representative Hyman of North Carolina developed a program to provide relief for the American Indians.

THE ABUSES. *Along with the positive accomplishments of reconstruction, there was plenty of wrongdoing.* The Radical regimes were sometimes corrupt and often

Sidenote to History

P. B. S. Pinchback

Among the numerous Black political leaders who rose to prominence during the early reconstruction period, P. B. S. Pinchback was one of the most outstanding. During his career Pinchback held more political offices than any other Black in American history.

Pinckney Benton Stewart Pinchback was born in Macon, Georgia, in 1837. He was one of 10 children born to a Mississippi planter and a Black woman, a former slave. The family had moved north so the children could be raised as free men and women and receive an education. Young Pinchback was tutored at home and at schools in Cincinnati, Ohio.

After his father's death, Pinchback became a cabin boy on a Mississippi riverboat. When the Civil War broke out, Pinchback organized a company of Black volunteers for the Union army and became the captain.

When the war ended, Pinch, as he was called, turned to politics, thinking it a suitable outlet for his ambition and intelligence. A Republican, he became lieutenant-governor of Louisiana in 1871. Then, in 1872 Pinchback became acting governor of Louisiana, the only Black to have ever served as governor of a state. In the fall of the same year, he was elected to the House of Representatives, and in 1873 he was elected to the Senate.

Pinchback went to Washington as both congressman-elect and senator-elect, an unusual circumstance. Pinchback's opponents, however, claimed that certain laws had been violated in both elections, and the House and Senate refused to allow him to take his seat. White Louisiana officials chosen by the same methods were declared to be legally elected.

Despite the reversal of his political fortunes, the nation had not heard the end of P. B. S. Pinchback. In 1870 Pinchback began publishing a weekly newspaper, *The New Orleans Louisianian,* and he continued to publish it until around 1880. Of the many Black political leaders of the reconstruction era, P. B. S. Pinchback was one of the most successful.

extravagant in expenditures. The governor of South Carolina pocketed $100,000 in his first year in office, though his salary was only $8,000. And the legislature of that state maintained a free restaurant for its own use. The Radical governments freely issued bonds for railroads and other public works with little concern about the future. The public debt of Florida increased tenfold under its Radical regime, while that of South Carolina tripled.

Such corruption was not limited to the South. Northern cities were sewers of political corruption. By 1872 the mayor of New York was bilking the city treasury at the rate of a million dollars a month. The United States Senate was filled with party bosses who had kept themselves in power by graft and by the sale of offices. *Corruption, therefore, was not strictly the result of reconstruction.* And it was not exclusively Republican. When the Radical Republican governor of Mississippi fled the state in 1875, he left $300,000 in the treasury, which the incoming Democrat promptly embezzled.

THE KU KLUX KLAN. Most White southerners resented the reconstruction

This cartoon appeared in Puck *in 1880. It depicts President Grant in a large carpetbag, riding on the back of the burdened South. What do you think was the political point of view of the magazine?*

Sidenote to History

Rebuilding the South

In the 1870's the South slowly began to revive itself economically. After the Civil War many of the large plantations had been broken into small landholdings. Many people, who had been able to save some money, had bought these parcels from impoverished planters.

The cotton yields rose throughout the 1870's, and they increased with every growing season. With the profits from this increased output, farmers could get out of debt and reinvest the money left over. Consequently, the number of small farms also rose steadily in the 1870's. Crops other than cotton were also being grown in abundance. Tobacco, rice, sugarcane, corn, and fruit were some of the staples that helped to boost the economy of the South.

Many people, however, could not afford to buy their own farms. As a result, tenant farming and sharecropping became firmly established in the agricultural South. A tenant farmer rented a piece of land from a planter. A tenant farmer usually supplied his or her own tools, animals, and other farm items. Some tenant farmers were eventually able to save enough money to buy their plots of land from the owners. But most remained tenants.

The sharecropper worked the land owner's farm in return for lodging, tools, and a piece of land. In return for work actually done on the land, the sharecroppers received a portion of the crops. Because sharecroppers did not get paid until the harvest was in, they had to buy food and other items on credit. And in order to get credit, they had to mortgage future crops. If they couldn't pay all their debts in one year, the remainder was added to the next year's bill. Many sharecroppers remained in debt to the landowner for their entire lives.

In addition to these changes in the agricultural system, the South experienced rapid industrial progress in the 1870's. Railroads, destroyed by Union forces during the war, were rebuilt, and new ones were pushed into areas of great mineral wealth. The Missouri Pacific and the Iron Mountain lines made their way into the pinewoods of Arkansas. Sawmills sprang up, and lumber was transported from the South to other parts of the nation.

In Alabama and Tennessee the railroads gained access to rich coal and iron deposits. The city of Birmingham, a cotton field in 1870, was a recognized iron center by 1878. By the early 1900's Birmingham was the leading industrial city of the South.

Manufacturing, which had started in the South before the war, regained its momentum in the postwar years. This increase in manufacturing, combined with other forms of industrial growth, helped to change the traditional roles of the southern population. Some women who had exerted their independence during the war years had managed to maintain their independence to a great extent after the war. Many of these women became workers in the new factories and textile mills that developed in the late 1800's and early 1900's.

Children, not yet prohibited from working by child-labor laws, were also a source of cheap factory labor—both in the North and in the South. However, most Blacks could not find jobs in industries. They would not become a part of the urban industrial working force in the South until well into the first half of the 20th century. Although they were free men and women, Blacks in the post-Civil War years still found themselves tied to the soil by the forces of tradition or other circumstances beyond their control.

governments and were opposed to the Blacks voting and holding public office. In addition, many former plantation owners, faced with the loss of slave labor and their destroyed lands, were experiencing severe economic problems. Therefore, the higher taxes, which were imposed on southerners to pay for the schools and other programs initiated by the reconstruction governments, created even further dissatisfaction with Republican rule.

As their resentment increased, the Whites began forming secret organizations. The best known were the Knights of the White Camelia and the Ku Klux Klan. Members of these organizations dressed in ghostly costumes and rode the countryside at night, terrorizing both Blacks and Whites who did not approve of their policies. They also prevented Blacks from exercising their rights.

Congress reacted to such tactics with force of its own. *In a series of Force Acts in 1870–1871, Congress made it illegal to prevent people from voting.* And it authorized the President to suspend the writ of *habeas corpus* so the government could make arrests even when it lacked the normal amount of evidence to do so. President Grant ordered federal troops into the parts of the South where violence was most widespread. Hundreds of Klan members were arrested and convicted and the organization broken. By the end of 1871, the Klan's activity had greatly declined.

THE RETURN OF THE DEMOCRATS. Although the secret societies had declined, White intimidation of Blacks continued. By 1873 Blacks were afraid to vote in most parts of the South. And White Democrats were gaining control of the assemblies. In some states Democrats were able to take advantage of the split among Republicans, and by cooperating with the Moderates, they managed to oust the Radicals. In other states they simply forced the carpetbaggers to flee for their lives.

When Democrats won control of the Mississippi legislature in 1876, they threatened to impeach the Republican governor. The governor saved them the trouble by resigning. By that date the White "redeemers" had captured all but three of the southern states. In South Carolina, Louisiana, and Florida, federal troops had propped up Radical Republican regimes. *When President Rutherford B. Hayes removed the federal troops in 1877, the reconstruction period came to an end.*

Section Review

1. Identify or explain: carpetbaggers, scalawags, reapportionment, Blanche K. Bruce, Hiram Revels.
2. List the reforms in the reconstruction constitution. Which groups in society benefited from these reforms?
3. What were some of the abuses of the reconstruction period?
4. How did southern Whites try to prevent Blacks from voting?

5. The Collapse of Reform

THE END OF RECONSTRUCTION. *The end of reconstruction also marked the end of the nationwide crusade for Black rights.* This crusade was not to reassert itself vigorously for many years. The humanitarian ideals that had aroused people in the decades before the Civil War had found their expression in the constitutional amendments that had freed the Blacks and had sought to secure their rights. But thereafter the spirit of reform began to evaporate. The aging reformers either lost interest or gave up. William Lloyd Garrison folded up *The Liberator* when the 13th Amendment went into effect, feeling that his job had been done. The great Henry Ward Beecher, the nation's antislavery conscience in the 1850's, retired into obscurity, pursued by unpleasant rumors of a scandal.

Many people in the North had never cared much about the fate of the freed Blacks. Although Republicans had often attacked slavery, their stress on individual rights had not included massive government aid to the Black people. In 1869 the Freedmen's Bureau, the only government agency devoted to Black welfare, quietly went out of business. Blacks, it seemed, would have to fend for themselves.

SEGREGATION. *The Whites who regained control of the South in the 1870's restored the segregation of the races in schools, railroads, and other public facilities.* Blacks, afraid to vote, found themselves helpless.

Black Congressman Robert Brown Elliott of South Carolina was a lonely voice of protest. But he did help to prod Congress into a final act of reform. The Civil Rights Act of 1875 prohibited discrimination by state governments or by businesses that served the public. Even this effort failed when the Supreme Court ruled in 1883 that civil rights was a question for state regulators. The 14th Amendment, declared the Court, did not grant Congress power to regulate social relationships among American citizens.

PLESSY V. FERGUSON. In 1896 segregation became the law of the land. The Supreme Court ruled in the case of *Plessy v. Ferguson* that "separate but equal" accommodations on railroad cars did not deprive Blacks of their right to equal protection under the law. The concept of separate-but-equal was quickly applied to all public facilities, from schools to amusement parks.

By 1900 most southern states had effectively *disfranchised* the Blacks through the use of complicated literacy tests, poll taxes, and grandfather clauses. (Those who failed the literacy test could vote only if their grandfathers had been or were now eligible to vote. This was a device that allowed illiterate Whites to vote, but not illiterate Blacks.)

Disfranchise means to deny or to prevent a person or persons from exercising the right to vote.

Such legislation effectively dismantled reconstruction and left the Blacks with a very limited kind of freedom. *The restoration of Black civil and political rights would have to wait for the "second reconstruction" of the 1950's and 1960's.*

Section Review

1. Identify or explain: the Civil Rights Act of 1875, *Plessy v. Ferguson*, grandfather clauses.
2. Cite two reasons given in this section that might explain why the spirit of reform evaporated after reconstruction.
3. In 1883 the Supreme Court ruled on the meaning of the 14th Amendment. Explain this ruling and its significance.
4. How were grandfather clauses used to prevent many Blacks from voting?

Robert B. Elliot served two terms as a congressional representative from South Carolina. He was also a lawyer and a scholar.

Chapter 14 Review

Bird's-Eye View

The period of reconstruction was filled with the bitter feelings that had been generated by the war. Andrew Johnson, Lincoln's successor as President, tried to carry out Lincoln's policies, but he was unable to deal with an angry Congress. This led to a struggle for supremacy between the President and Congress. The Moderates wished to restore citizenship to southerners and civil government to the southern states as rapidly as possible. The Radicals insisted on a more definite demonstration of loyalty to the Union and a broadening of suffrage in the southern states.

After Lincoln's death Johnson declared an amnesty, which allowed the southern states to form new governments. Congress responded by forming a committee to investigate the process of reconstruction. They found many abuses, including the passage of laws, called Black Codes, which were used to restrict the rights of Blacks. Congress then established the Freedmen's Bureau to provide assistance and services to freed Blacks and to help them secure their rights. The Civil Rights Act and the 14th Amendment also strengthened the position of Blacks. The 14th Amendment made all Blacks citizens and guaranteed equal protection of the law to all citizens.

The results of the congressional election of 1866 strengthened the position of the Radicals even more. Thus, Congress passed several laws restricting the actions of the President. Then, it set up a congressional plan of reconstruction, which made many former Confederates ineligible to participate in public life. This plan also required states to ratify the 13th, 14th, and 15th Amendments in order to be readmitted to the Union.

Despite their strong position in Congress, many Radical Republicans grew increasingly angry at the constant opposition of President Johnson. Impeachment charges were brought against him, and the Senate came within one vote of the two-thirds majority needed to remove Johnson from office. Then, in the election of 1868, the Radicals ran their own candidate, Ulysses S. Grant. Grant won the election by a tremendous margin, mainly because of his reputation as a war hero.

Although the South remembers the reconstruction period with bitterness, that period was not severe in comparison to other postwar military occupations. Though abuses and corruption did exist in many situations, some major accomplishments were achieved in the areas of political and social reform. However, by the end of the reconstruction period, many Blacks were being denied their civil rights, and the crusade for reform was on the decline.

Vocabulary

Define or identify each of the following:

amnesty	Freedmen's Bureau	impeachment
13th Amendment	14th Amendment	reapportionment
Black Codes	lame duck	disfranchise

Review Questions

1. What were the major political and economic problems facing the nation after the Civil War?
2. Explain President Lincoln's attitude toward reconstruction.
3. Explain the attitude of Congress toward reconstruction.
4. What actions did Congress take to complete reconstruction of the South?
5. Identify four positive and three negative results of reconstruction of the South.
6. What was the social, political, and economic position of Blacks at the close of the reconstruction period?

Reviewing Social Studies Skills

1. Make a chart, comparing the economic situation of the North with that of the South at the conclusion of the Civil War.
2. Make two lists to show the evidence in the Johnson impeachment trial. The first list should include items that show why Johnson was innocent. The second list should include evidence of his guilt.
3. Compare the provisions of the Black Codes and those of the Civil Rights Act. Which point of view was dominant during reconstruction? Which one was dominant after the election of Hayes? What point of view is expressed in the *Plessy v. Ferguson* case?

Reading for Meaning

1. What does Abraham Lincoln's attitude, "With charity for all, and malice toward none," reveal about his character? Remember, he was referring to persons who had engaged in armed rebellion against the nation.
2. Find evidence in the text to support both of these statements: **a)** Reconstruction was harsh and punishing. **b)** Reconstruction was relatively mild, and it led to important reforms in the South.
3. Using the evidence gathered in question 2, write a paragraph about the reconstruction period and how it came to be one of the great controversies in American history.
4. A specific propaganda technique—"waving the bloody shirt"—is mentioned in the text. Can you explain why this is a propaganda technique? Find examples of other propaganda techniques cited in the text.

Bibliography

Claude Bowers's *The Tragic Era: The Revolution After Lincoln* (Houghton Mifflin) tells the story from the President's point of view, portraying him as the victim of a self-interested Congress.

Eric McKitrick's *Andrew Johnson and Reconstruction* (University of Chicago Press) sympathizes with the Republican Moderates and blames the President's errors for the triumph of radicalism.

Ernest Gaines's *The Autobiography of Miss Jane Pittman* (Bantam) is a fictional account of the life of a Black woman from the end of slavery to the 1900's.

Unit 3 Review

Vocabulary

Define or identify each of the following:

Emma Willard   impeachment   Thaddeus Stevens
reapportionment   abolitionist   constituents
temperance   tenure of office   amnesty
Nat Turner   reconstruction   Trail of Tears

Recalling the Facts

1. Name six authors of American literature mentioned in this unit. For each one list at least one of their works.
2. What changes occurred in the United States during the Age of Reform?
3. Explain the economic factors that split the North from the South politically before the Civil War.
4. Describe both the early Black and the northern intellectual resistance to slavery.
5. How did new modes of transportation change the nation?
6. How did the country handle the Whites' desire for American Indian land before the Civil War?
7. Explain the ways in which the independence movements in Texas and California were similar.
8. What were the results of the Mexican-American War?
9. What congressional action resulted from the slavery controversy in the territories?
10. Describe how the country reacted to the election of Abraham Lincoln as President.
11. Explain why the South was successful during the first year of the Civil War.
12. What factors during the Civil War led to a northern victory?
13. Explain the Moderate attitude toward reconstruction of the South.
14. Explain the Radical attitude toward reconstruction of the South.
15. The Civil War brought an end to slavery, but it did not provide economic, social, or political equality for former slaves. Explain.

History Lab

1. During the early 19th century in America, reforms were made in prisons and mental-care institutions. A similar reform movement occurred during the 1960's and 1970's. Prepare a report for your class on current reform movements in prisons.
2. Assume that the South had won the war and had continued to have a viable government. What do you think the political geography of the North American continent would be today? Draw an outline map, depicting your ideas.
3. Write a diary entry from the point of view of: a) a Union soldier, b) a Confederate soldier, or c) a former slave fighting in the Union army. Compare your entry with those of your classmates. How do the points of view differ?
4. Prepare a campaign poster that might have been used to promote one of the candidates in the Presidential election of 1856, 1860, 1864, 1868, or 1872.

Local History

1. What was the status of your state during the Civil War? Did it remain in the Union; did it secede; or was it still part of a territory?
2. Did soldiers from your state and community serve in the armies? Research town and city records from the time of the Civil War and report the findings to your class. Libraries often have microfilms of newspapers from that period. If your local library does, read an account of one of the battles and report on it.

Forming an Opinion

1. The nation's first military conscription (draft) law was passed in 1863. What is your opinion of the draft? Should all persons be required to serve in the military or, as an alternative, to spend a period of time in service to the country?
2. Henry David Thoreau, believing that the Mexican-American War was an unjust war, refused to pay taxes to the government because he did not want to support the effort. He was jailed and remained there until his friend, Ralph Waldo Emerson, paid the tax for him. What is your opinion about this form of protest? Was Thoreau justified in refusing to support what he felt was an unjust war?
3. The Civil War had many tragic consequences. Among these was an immense loss of life and great suffering, particularly in the South. Nevertheless, the war did help the South to break away from its past and to become part of the modern world.
   Do you agree or disagree with this last statement?

Time Line

Using the time line below, answer the following questions:
1. When did the Civil War end?
2. When did the war with Mexico begin?
3. Which of the events on the time line were a Black uprising against slavery?
4. What act canceled the Missouri Compromise? When was this new law passed?
5. Which event on the time line brought an official end to slavery in those states rebelling against the Union?
6. What year was Lincoln elected President?
7. How many years was it from Nat Turner's Rebellion to the Emancipation Proclamation?

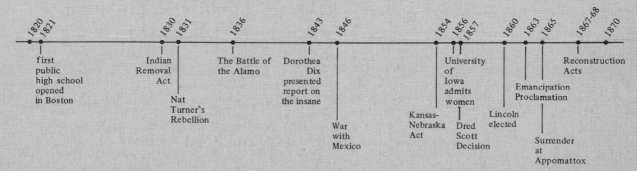

An Expanding Nation

America is a land of opportunity, and Americans have always been opportunists. Never were they more opportunistic than in the middle decades of the 19th century, when a rich and untouched continent lay at their feet. Lumber, coal, iron, gold, and silver were there for the taking. Promotion, development, and growth were the watchwords of the day. Growth was good for business, for the country, and for its own sake. A "booster" spirit was infused into Americans.

The westward movement spawned a new kind of booster—the urban promoter. This peculiar breed of American combined the civic pride of a Benjamin Franklin with the acquisitiveness of a railroad tycoon. He began with a patch of prairie and a dream. He laid out lots, gave names to nonexistent streets, and advertised for settlers. If they came, he had a city. If not, he moved to a new location, leaving behind a shack or two on a dusty road. Upstart cities and ghost towns dotted the American landscape.

The career of one promoter tells the tale of all such adventurers. William Larimer (1809–1875) grew up in Pennsylvania. When a depression ruined his business, he went west to start anew. A gold strike in the Pike's Peak area drew him to Colorado in the fall of 1858. On Cherry Creek, a branch of the South Platte River, he found a small miner's settlement. He formed a partnership with the miners to build a city and began construction of a hotel. They called the place Denver.

As "donating agent" for the partnership, Larimer had authority to give a city lot to anyone who promised to build a cabin or set up a store. To add a touch of culture, Larimer offered a prize to anyone who established a newspaper. A race ensued, and citizens took bets. The winner was the founder of the *Rocky Mountain News*, which came out on April 23, 1859, at 10:30 P.M., 20 minutes ahead of its rival.

People drifted into town, attracted by the hubbub. Denver flourished. When Colorado entered the Union in 1876, the year after Larimer died, Denver was its capital.

The Denver story was reenacted all across the American West—Salt Lake, Phoenix, Dallas, and Seattle among them. Each place was a monument to the American faith in the future.

Cripple Creek, Colorado

The Gilded Age

"The Gilded Age" was Mark Twain's description of the post-Civil War era. The great American novelist used the phrase as a title for one of his books. And he meant gilded, not golden. The post-Civil War era was shiny on the surface. The economy boomed through much of the period, despite financial panics. People flowed onto the western prairies. American wheat fed many Europeans. Art and literature flourished. Newspapers attained a literary quality seldom seen before or since.

Yet, beneath the glittering surface was a seamy side. Corruption was rampant. Political machines dominated the cities. Bosses ruled the states, often in alliance with business people looking for favors. Heads of railroads and utilities bribed government officials for special treatment. Public office was so profitable that aspiring politicians sometimes had to pay the party bosses several thousand dollars for the privilege of sitting in the legislature. The corruption extended to the doorstep of the White House during the Grant administration.

There were some critics of the Gilded Age, reformers who wanted to regulate the worst business practices and clean up the government. But their voices were few, and their achievements were fewer. Not until the end of the century did the reform protest gain sufficient strength to make some lasting changes.

Chapter Objectives

After you have finished reading this chapter, you should be able to:
1. List the economic and social legislation that was passed by northern Republicans during the Civil War.
2. Compare the ways Rockefeller, Gould, Vanderbilt, and Fisk increased their wealth during this period.
3. Name three kinds of corruption in government.
4. Organize into a chart the reforms the Mugwumps wanted to introduce.
5. Define the term Social Darwinism and explain how it was applied to the post-Civil War period.

A moral letdown after a war is perhaps to be expected. It has happened several times in the nation's history. People are tired of restraints, eager for fun. War dislocates society. People are wrenched from routine lives; many are thrown into the horror of the battlefield. When the war is over, they are told to drop their swords and pick up their plowshares. Some who survive the battlefield cannot survive the peace. Unemployment increases after a war, and so does the crime rate. A civil war is more upsetting than any other.

1. The Triumph of Business and Industry

A MECHANICAL REVOLUTION. Like all major wars, the Civil War brought vast social changes. Before the war, America appeared to be a nation of farms and villages, with vast spaces of unconquered wilderness. *After the war, tourists saw cities and factories, railroads, and large steamships.*

Actually, this transformation had been going on for some time before the war began. The pace of change merely quickened during the conflict. Pressed by the demands of the army, the clothing industry moved from the tailor's shop to the factory. The sewing machine, first patented in 1846 by Elias Howe, revolutionized the making of both clothing and shoes. The need for guns and cannons put enormous pressure on the steel industry. Before the war the nation had been largely dependent on British steel. Under wartime demand, British methods of steelmaking were adopted and improved on. This enabled American steel production to mushroom.

The mechanical revolution also touched the farm. Cyrus McCormick's reaper (for cutting grain) and John Deere's steel plow opened up the rich prairies of Indiana, Illinois, and Iowa. Although both devices had been invented in the 1830's, the wartime demand brought them into general use. At his harvester plant in Chicago, McCormick was able to mass-produce reapers on an assembly line. Then, through such selling techniques as traveling demonstrators and installment buying, harvesters were placed on nearly every midwestern farm. The mechanization of the farm enabled the North to feed not only its own vast armies but part of Europe as well. Great Britain, increasingly dependent on American grain, could not have aided the South even if it had wanted to. *In the end it was not cotton that was king but wheat.*

THE GHOST OF HENRY CLAY. The Republican party was happy to encourage these economic advances. It had absorbed much of the old Whig party and the programs once associated with Henry Clay. Ever since the Presidency of Andrew Jackson, Clay's American System—bank, tariff, and internal improvements—had been blocked by southern opposition. When the South seceded from the Union, the legislative dam seemed to burst. Republicans proceeded to enact the American System, tailoring it to fit a new generation.

THE MORRILL TARIFF. *The first item on the Republican agenda was a tariff to encourage manufacturing.* Under the Democratic administrations of the 1840's and 1850's, customs duties had been reduced to almost nothing. Then, in March 1861, a few days after the southern congressional representatives departed for home, Representative Justin Morrill of Vermont introduced a bill to restore the rates that had existed in the early 1840's.

Passage of the Morrill Tariff increased the appetite of manufacturers for protection. Congress raised customs rates several times during the war. By the end of the war, duties on some items amounted to 100 percent of their value. The average level of rates was 47 percent. For nearly a century thereafter, the United States remained a high-tariff nation.

THE NATIONAL BANK SYSTEM. *The difficulties of wartime finance also revived the idea of a national bank.* The federal

"WESTWARD THE COURSE OF EMPIRE TAKES ITS WAY" WITH McCORMICK REAPERS IN THE VAN.

McCormick's reaper and Deere's steel plow turned the American Midwest into the largest grain-producing area in the world. In this somewhat romantic advertisement, a group of pioneers have suddenly come upon vast expanses of land being harvested. Do you think such an advertisement might have influenced people to go west?

government entered the war laboring under the hard-money system left by the Jacksonians. A bewildering variety of bank notes circulated in the nation's markets, while the government kept most of its accounts in gold and silver. Because it did not possess enough gold to finance the war, the government printed notes, called greenbacks. The value of the greenbacks lessened with every Union military defeat.

In 1863 Congress moved to solve both the banking and the money problem in one stroke. *It authorized a system of national banks, each privately owned but under the general supervision of the United States Treasury.* Each bank that joined the system was required to invest at least one third of its capital, or working money, in government bonds (in effect, lending the government that amount of money for the war effort). The remainder of its capital was gold, obtained through the sale of shares of stock.

The national banks could issue notes intended to be the nation's main form of money. So that the notes would keep their value, they were backed by government bonds and gold in the banks' vaults. One could exchange bank notes for bonds or for gold.

In 1865 Congress levied a 10 percent tax on notes issued by state banks, thus driving them out of circulation. Until the Federal Reserve System was created 50 years later, the national banks and the money they issued were the heart of the nation's monetary system.

THE TRANSCONTINENTAL RAILROAD. In Henry Clay's day "internal improvements" meant roads and canals. Later the burning question was the transcontinental railroad. Many companies were eager to lay tracks across the West, but all agreed that government help was necessary. The amount of money required to span the plains, mountains, and deserts of the West was more than any private corporation could muster. Nor were there enough people in the West to support a railroad. Some time would have to pass before such a venture became a paying proposition. No one thought of having the government build the railroad. It did not have the facilities. Besides, it had its hands full with the Confederacy.

In 1862 Congress authorized the Union Pacific and Central Pacific railroads to build a railway across the West. The railroads planned to follow a central route from Nebraska to northern California. To finance construction, the railroads were given millions of dollars in government bonds and a grant of public lands extending 32 kilometers (20 miles) on each side of the track. *By 1869 iron rails bound the nation.*

THE HOMESTEAD ACT. Banks, tariffs, and railroads benefited business people, but the Republican Congress during the Civil War was also concerned about farmers and working people. For years cheap, easily accessible public lands had been demanded by both western farmers and eastern laborers.

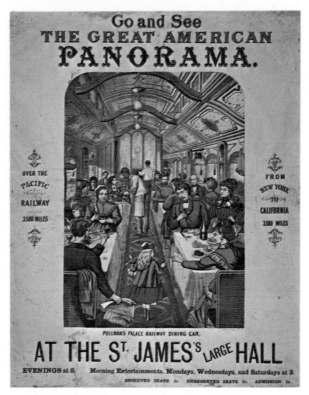

Go and See
THE GREAT AMERICAN PANORAMA.

OVER THE PACIFIC RAILWAY 3500 MILES

FROM NEW YORK TO CALIFORNIA 3500 MILES

PULLMAN'S PALACE RAILWAY DINING CAR.

AT THE ST. JAMES'S LARGE HALL
EVENINGS at 8.   Morning Entertainments, Mondays, Wednesdays, and Saturdays at 3.
RESERVED SEATS 3s.   UNRESERVED SEATS 2s.   ADMISSION 1s.

The Union Pacific met the Central Pacific to form the first transcontinental railway. This railway spanned 5,600 kilometers (3,500 miles), from New York to California. This advertisement shows a lavish dining car on one of the trains.

The Republicans had promised free ***homesteads*** in 1856, and Congress had approved the idea, only to see it vetoed by President Buchanan.

A ***homestead*** is a piece of land and the buildings on such land occupied as a home.

The Homestead Act of 1862 granted 64 hectares (160 acres) of government land to any head of family on condition that he or she live on it for five years. By the end of the war 1 million hectares (2.5 million acres) had been occupied under the act. The postwar decades witnessed a rush of homesteaders into the West. Between 15 and 20

365

percent of the land was acquired through homesteads. Other land was bought through government cash sales or purchased from the railroads. Lumber and mining companies took advantage of loopholes in the act to gobble up huge tracts of land. But on the whole, it served the interests of the farming poor.

AMERICAN INDIANS AND THE RUSH OF SETTLERS. The rush of people into the West during and after the Civil War settled on land occupied by and held sacred by the American Indians. The newly arrived railroads helped to scare away the buffalo and brought even more settlers. Many Indian leaders felt that force was the only way to protect their lands and way of life. *During the early 1860's, while the Union and Confederate forces fought each other, American Indians met White settlers and railroaders in a series of bloody conflicts.* Attacks upon the Minnesota and Colorado frontiers resulted in loss of life and property on both sides. In retaliation the Colorado militia in 1864 attacked and killed about 500 Cheyenne and Arapaho Indians. This attack worsened relations between the White settlers and American Indians throughout the West.

The government hoped to solve the problem by moving American Indians away from land being settled. *To accomplish this a council of 4,000 Indians was called in 1867 at Medicine Lodge, Kansas.* Among the tribes represented were the Arapaho, Cheyenne, Kiowa (KIE-oe-way), and Comanche. The leaders of these tribes agreed to move to reservations south of the Arkansas River.

However, many members of the Cheyenne and Arapaho tribes, bitter because their leaders had given away their land, attacked the Texas and Kansas frontiers in 1868. The army was called in to put down the uprising. After six years of fighting, the American Indians were defeated and forced back to the reservations. *Their defeat, however, was only a temporary pause in the long series of conflicts that characterized the onrush of homesteaders into the West after the Civil War.*

LAND GRANT COLLEGES. With the rush of settlers to the West, the Republican Congress also decided to do something about higher education. The Morrill Land Grant Act of 1862 offered a state 12,000 hectares (30,000 acres) of public lands for each of its members in Congress, based on the 1860 census. The land was to be used to endow colleges.

Because the East had numerous colleges, the main effect of the law was to stimulate interest in education in the West. *Public universities financed by land grants became state enterprises in the West.* Specializing in practical fields, such as farming and mechanical arts, they appealed to a busy people concerned with getting ahead in the world.

And such people dominated post-Civil War America. A new age developed after the war, an age of coal and iron.

Section Review

1. Identify or explain: Elias Howe, Cyrus McCormick, Justin Morrill, greenbacks.
2. How did the Civil War act as a spur to business and industry and the increased mechanization of farming?
3. List the changes in policy on the tariff and the national bank made by the Republican administration during the war. How did these measures encourage the growth of industry?
4. How did the following serve as incentives to the development of the country: the Homestead Act, land grant colleges, and the building of a transcontinental railroad. How did American Indians living in the West judge these developments?

This is a picture of the home of Cornelius Vanderbilt at 59th Street and Fifth Avenue in New York City. In what way does this residence reflect the extravagance of the Gilded Age?

2. Wild Times in the World of Business

THE PURSUIT OF WEALTH. America in the last half of the 1800's was a nation of go-getters, people pursuing success. And success often meant great wealth. A continent lay at their feet, its riches waiting to be exploited. On the eve of the war, fabulous silver deposits were discovered in Nevada, and the first oil wells were drilled in Pennsylvania.

TITANS OF THE BUSINESS WORLD. *The war brought forth a new generation of business people.* J. P. Morgan, who dominated the nation's banking system for the next half century, got his start in wartime finance. John D. Rockefeller, learning of the oil strikes in Pennsylvania, opened a refinery in Cleveland. By the end of the war, his

was the largest refining operation in the country. Cornelius Vanderbilt, the "Commodore" who made a fortune carrying gold seekers to California, sold his ships to the government during the war and began investing in railroads. Two other promoters, Collis P. Huntington and Leland Stanford, stood ready to take advantage of Congress' generosity in the building of a transcontinental railroad.

These were some of the titans who dominated the postwar world of business. Most were people of great personal honesty. John D. Rockefeller was an intensely religious man, a leader in the Baptist Church, and a philanthropist who gave away millions to worthy causes. Yet, he was a ruthless competitor. American business was like a wrestling match with no holds barred. The government did not serve as referee. Government remained what it was before the war, small and weak, seemingly content to let the people care for themselves. However, the ruthlessness of business practices in the Gilded Age revealed the need for some kind of government regulation.

VANDERBILT GAINS CONTROL OF THE ERIE. Commodore Vanderbilt turned from shipping to railroads during the Civil War. He began consolidating local lines into the New York Central system. By 1873 he achieved his goal of a rail line from New York to Chicago, following the "water level route" along the Hudson River, the Erie Canal, and the Great Lakes. *When the railroad was completed, Vanderbilt controlled the profitable traffic between midwestern farms and seaboard cities.*

To finance construction of the railroad, Vanderbilt sold shares of stock to the public. That in itself was a new idea. Business corporations were owned by only a few investors, sometimes by a single family. *Vanderbilt pioneered the notion of a public corporation, owned by hundreds, even thousands, of stockholders.* The realization of the idea transformed American business.

Vanderbilt foresaw competition in the race for Chicago. To avoid this he tried to gain control of the Erie Railroad, a broken-down line that straggled through southern New York and into Ohio. After several bankruptcies, the Erie was controlled by a stock manipulator, Daniel Drew. Vanderbilt purchased a majority of the Erie's shares of stock. But Drew, determined to retain control, printed more. Angered, Vanderbilt bribed the company's directors to oust Drew. The two men reached a compromise. Drew would manage the Erie, Vanderbilt would own it, and they would split the profits.

THE ERIE WAR. In 1867 Drew found two allies, Jay Gould and Jim Fisk, who had helped him gain control of the Erie. Gould and Fisk had both made huge fortunes dur-

ing the Civil War, speculating in gold and government paper. The Erie Ring—Drew, Gould, and Fisk—got Vanderbilt's permission to issue more stock and then dumped 10 million dollars worth on ·the market at one time. When the price plummeted to a few cents a share, the Erie Ring bought control of the railroad and ousted Vanderbilt from the board of directors. When Vanderbilt countered the move by buying shares, the Erie ring printed more.

Vanderbilt obtained a court order prohibiting the Erie from issuing more stock. The ring issued another 100,000 shares anyway, causing havoc on the *Exchange.* They fled with the railroad's books across the Hudson River to New Jersey, where they barricaded themselves in a Jersey City hotel named Taylor's Castle. Vanderbilt, enraged, sent an army of hirelings across the river. But the

After the Erie Ring defied Vanderbilt's court order, Gould and Fisk fled to New Jersey with the railroad's books and $6 million in cash. Here, Gould is shown escaping from his office barely one step ahead of the law. In what way did an event like the Erie War affect the railroad?

ring, with the aid of a fleet of tugboats owned by Jim Fisk, repulsed the attack.

An *exchange* is a place where shares of stock, bonds, and other securities are traded. The exchange referred to is the New York Stock Exchange.

Amid the confusion Jay Gould slipped out of the hotel with a suitcase full of cash. He headed for Albany, the capital of New York State. His object was to bribe the New York legislature into passing a law that would enable the Erie to issue more stock. Vanderbilt learned of the move and sent his own delegation. The price of a vote reached a new height.

When both sides were nearly broke, Vanderbilt and the ring compromised. Vanderbilt withdrew his court action against the railroad, enabling it to return to New York City. In return the Erie Ring gave him part ownership of the line. The war ended, but the real victim was the railroad. The Erie was left with a staggering burden of debt. It is little wonder that when reformers began to talk of government regulation, attention centered on the railroads.

THE "GOLD CORNER" OF 1869. Fresh from their victory over Commodore Vanderbilt, Gould and Fisk looked for new worlds to conquer. The "gold corner" was their most imaginative scheme. Gold, after all, was the basis of the nation's currency. Controlling most of the available supply would be the ultimate monopoly: a monopoly on money itself. Although it seems incredible, it was possible to corner the gold market.

Gold was money, but there was relatively little of it in circulation. Government paper dollars, or greenbacks, issued during the war, circulated for some time in the postwar period. But greenbacks were not considered as good as gold. Given a choice, people spent greenbacks and hoarded gold. Only about 15 million dollars in gold was in circulation.

For wealthy people like Gould and Fisk, cornering a good portion of this 15 million dollars was within the realm of possibility.

What would it accomplish? A corner, or control of the market, would drive up the price of gold, for gold was a *commodity,* traded openly like bushels of wheat. Bars of gold had a price in paper dollars, like any other salable product. Unlike wheat, gold was a commodity that some people, such as merchants involved in foreign trade, could not do without. Thus a corner, which forced buyers to pay inflated prices, could yield a handsome (if unethical) profit.

A *commodity* is something of economic value. It is generally a product of mining, farming, or manufacturing.

First, Fisk and Gould had to prevent the government from breaking their gold monopoly by dumping its stocks of gold on the market. They sought to accomplish this by selling some of their shares of gold to the assistant treasurer in New York. This official would thus profit from any increase in price.

Fisk and Gould then contracted for the delivery in September 1869 of about 20 million dollars in gold. Competition among speculators who had to make good on their contracts to Fisk and Gould caused the price to rise. By September 23, 1869, "Black Friday," the price of gold reached 144½: an amount of gold that could be minted into 100 dollars in coin cost 144.50 dollars in paper dollars.

That night President Ulysses S. Grant learned of the corner and ordered the New York treasurer to sell government gold. The next morning, when the price was 162, Gould and Fisk sold every speck of gold they owned. At noon the government dumped its gold on the market. In 15 minutes the price plummeted to 135. A mob of angry speculators formed on *Wall Street,* but Gould and Fisk escaped. Their profit from the escapade was 11 million dollars.

Lydia E. Pinkham made her fortune in home remedies. Her Vegetable Compound was called the "Greatest Remedy in the World." Her honest face disarmed those who read the words below her picture—"Contains 18% Alcohol."

Wall Street is a street in lower Manhattan in New York City. The major banking and brokerage houses as well as the exchanges are located on or around the street, making it the principal financial center of the nation. The New York Stock Exchange was established there in 1792. Wall Street was so named because of a wall built there 300 years ago by the Dutch to protect themselves from the Indians.

Gould and Fisk were not typical of business people, even in the Gilded Age. But their antics caught the public eye and revealed the need for greater government supervision. Such change was delayed, however, for the government seemed incapable of supervising even its own affairs.

Section Review

1. What was the Erie War? What roles did Cornelius Vanderbilt, Jay Gould, and Jim Fisk play in it?
2. Identify or explain: J. P. Morgan,

John D. Rockefeller, the Erie Ring, Jay Gould, Jim Fisk, Wall Street.

3. Describe Vanderbilt's plan for the New York Central system. What role did the sale of stock play? How did Drew use the sale of stock as a competitive technique?
4. What was meant by the gold corner? How did Gould and Fisk achieve control of the gold market?
5. Find a definition in your dictionary for the word "speculator." Find two examples in this section that fit your definition.

3. The Spoils of Public Office

THE SPOILS SYSTEM AND CORRUPTION. "To the victor belong the spoils of the enemy," said the Jacksonians. To them it seemed only natural that a turnover of officeholders ought to follow a party victory at the polls. *Forty years later the Jacksonian ideal had become a system riddled with corruption.* Many people sought public office not to promote some principle or policy but simply to reward their followers. People involved in the spoils system governed cities and states, selling offices and favors to special interests. The system began well before the war, but it was not exposed until a series of scandals in the 1870's.

POLITICAL BALANCE. Although tainted by wartime cries of treason, the Democratic party recovered after the war with surprising speed. But it did so by imitating its Republican opponent. *The Democrats who governed the "new South" after the war promoted banks and railroads and manufacturing.* Northern Democrats looked for advice and financial aid to such conservative business people as the New York dry-goods merchant August Belmont. Many business people were not concerned with Blacks and poor Whites.

The Democrats' political strength was concentrated in the eastern cities and among immigrants. The Republicans drew their strength from established nationalities and midwestern farmers and villagers. The parties disagreed on tariffs and the silver policy, but, in fact, there were few differences between the two political parties.

Elections throughout the Gilded Age were close, and party turnovers were frequent. Ulysses S. Grant was the last President in the century to serve two consecutive terms in office. The rest were turned out after four years. Congress was equally divided. No President between 1865 and 1897 had a friendly majority in both houses of Congress throughout his term in office.

Partly because they were evenly balanced, the parties avoided controversial issues. There were plenty of problems to be solved—taxes, money and banking, railroad regulation, labor strife, and low farm prices, to name a few—but neither party dared take a stand on any of them. At election time Republicans campaigned for the high tariff to encourage manufacturing and "waved the bloody shirt" to keep alive Civil War hatreds. Democrats talked vaguely of clean government and a modest reduction in the tariff. Their strongest stand on an issue was probably their devotion to laissez-faire (LEH-say-FAIR), a government policy of noninterference with business and industry.

Most of the electorate sided with one party or the other out of sheer habit. But voter turnout at election time was extraordinarily high. Voters thronged to political rallies. They were interested in politics as a contest, a game, a spectacle.

CORRUPTION IN GOVERNMENT. Congressional machinery was so creaky and outdated that the oil of corruption was almost the only thing that would make it work. In the House of Representatives, the Speaker was all-powerful. Thomas B. Reed, who ruled with an iron fist through much of the 1880's and 1890's, was called the czar. He named all committee chairpersons.

Committees were of the utmost importance because of the vast increase in legislative business. The first Civil War Congress (1861–1863) handled some 613 pieces of legislation. By the 1880's each Congress struggled with over 11,000 bills. Under such an avalanche of proposals, only the pet projects of committee chairpersons stood a chance of passage.

Many senators owed their office to the spoils system. Party machines in nearly all states controlled the legislatures. (State legislatures were responsible for electing U.S. senators until 1913.) The machines kept themselves in power through graft and the sale of offices. Heading each machine was a boss. The boss' followers in the state legislature often elected him to the U.S. Senate. Both parties boasted of senators who owed their positions to this system.

JAMES G. BLAINE.
The most important figure in the Republican party was James G. Blaine, the "white-plumed knight" from Maine. Blaine was speaker of the House through Reconstruction (1869–1875). He was the leading contender for the Republican Presidential nomination in every convention until his death in 1892. Although Blaine secured the nomination only once, in 1884, he helped dictate the choice in every other convention. He cut a dashing figure and was universally admired. But in a political career that spanned more than 40 years, Blaine was not responsible for laws of any importance. The high tariff and the "bloody shirt" were his creed.

HALF-BREEDS AND STALWARTS.
The Republican party remained divided in the 1870's, as it had been during the war, but the names of its factions changed. *Blaine's followers were called the Half-Breeds. The opposing faction called itself the Stalwarts.* It was led by Roscoe Conkling, a senator from New York and head of a party organization that controlled the federal customs house in New York City. The New York customs house offered numerous opportunities for graft and patronage.

The conflict between Half-Breeds and Stalwarts was a contest for control of the Republican party. No important principle or policy separated them.

THE HERO PRESIDENT.
President Ulysses S. Grant (1869–1877) was personally honest and very naive. He staffed the White House with his old military friends and flatly refused to believe that any of them could be corrupt. He did not realize that his private secretary, Colonel Orville Babcock, was up to his elbows in graft.

Grant was a political innocent. When he went outside the White House to smoke his after-dinner cigar, he would stand at the gate on Pennsylvania Avenue and chat with passersby, amiably revealing government plans and policies. At the height of the gold corner, he went riding with Jim Fisk in New York's Central Park, thus contributing to the impression that the government was involved in the scheme and was helping raise the price of gold.

President Grant cannot be held responsible for all the corruption of the age. Much of it began before he took office. And no scandal ever involved him directly.

THE CRÉDIT MOBILIER.
The first scandal to hit the press involved Congress. The Crédit Mobilier (kray-DEE moe-bee-LYAY) was a construction corporation hired to build the Union Pacific Railroad. It charged the railroad several times what the job actually cost. When Congress investigated the affair in 1872 and 1873, it discovered that the owners of the Crédit Mobilier were also directors of the railroad. They had created a dummy corporation to loot the railroad and enrich themselves. Hoping to avoid inquiry and make political friends, they had

even given shares of stock to several representatives in Congress.

THE "SALARY GRAB." Along with illegal misuse of power came some legal abuses. Amid the confusion of the Crédit Mobilier scandal, members of Congress decided in 1872 to vote themselves a 50 percent raise, increasing their salaries from 5,000 dollars to 7,500 dollars per year. As if this were not enough, the increase was made retroactive for two years. This meant that each representative and senator would get 5,000 dollars in back pay at the next distribution of salary. The voters were so incensed by this salary grab that the act was repealed at the beginning of the next congressional session. The profiteering of congressional representatives was another symptom of the greed characteristic of the age.

THE WHISKEY RING. *During President Grant's last years in office, one scandal after another rocked the government.* Bribes, kickbacks, and outright theft were uncovered in the Treasury Department, the Post Office, and the Bureau of Indian Affairs. But the biggest fraud of all was the Whiskey Ring. This was a conspiracy among distillers and treasury officials to defraud the government of the taxes on distilled liquor. Some of the proceeds were even diverted to the treasuries of party organizations in the Midwest.

Apparently, the conspiracy had begun during the war. It expanded its operations when President Grant appointed General John A. McDonald supervisor of Internal Revenue at St. Louis, Missouri. St. Louis was the center of the conspiracy, and McDonald was one of the ringleaders. Suspicious treasury officials in Washington were bribed to keep silent. The President's secretary, Orville Babcock, prevented any prying from the White House.

In 1874, as a result of other scandals, President Grant appointed a new Secretary of the Treasury and gave him orders to clean house. The secretary discovered the Whiskey Ring and sent agents to raid its headquarters in St. Louis. The result was the indictment of some 238 government officials and distillers, the largest single episode of corruption in the nation's history. Among those brought to trial was Orville Babcock. But when the President testified to his secretary's good character, Babcock was acquitted. It was a sign of the times.

THE TWEED RING. Not all of the corruption was in the federal government. States and cities were infected as well, but their problems simply attracted less attention. The exception was New York City, a place already regarded by many in rural America as a den of sin. William M. Tweed was a senator in the New York legislature and leader of Tammany Hall, the local Democratic party organization. Tweed was a champion of the poor, and as state senator he obtained a number of laws that benefited New York and provided jobs for its people.

Such projects were expensive, however. The New York City courthouse, originally estimated to cost 250,000 dollars, ultimately cost 8 million dollars. Between 1860 and 1870 the city's debt tripled. By 1871 newspapers were filled with rumors of corruption. Tweed and his fellow politicians probably received some kickbacks, but so did numerous building contractors. The root of the problem was that New York was fast becoming a modern metropolis. It had an urgent need for police and fire services (it had a volunteer fire department until 1865) and for parks and mass transportation. The demand for services was beyond the city's means. It is a problem not fully solved by cities today.

Samuel J. Tilden, an ambitious young Democrat, led an investigation of New York's corruption. Tweed was indicted and brought to trial. The exposure made Tilden nationally famous. He went on to become

WHO STOLE THE PEOPLE'S MONEY? — DO TELL. N.Y.TIMES.   'TWAS HIM.

In 1869 "Boss" Tweed ordered all contractors to add 100 percent to their bills and to give the overcharge to the Tammany Ring. Under this system, New York City managed to pay $170,730 for 40 tables and chairs! This cartoon from Harper's Weekly was done by Thomas Nast in 1871.

the Democratic Presidential nominee in 1876. Tweed, convicted of failing to keep proper city accounts, spent the rest of his life in jail. He died in 1876.

Section Review

1. Identify or explain: salary grab, James G. Blaine, Orville Babcock, Samuel J. Tilden, Stalwarts.
2. What offices did people involved in the spoils system hold? What was their main reason for holding public office? Why were they not interested in political principles?
3. Why did the committee system become so important in Congress during this period?

4. Explain the kind of government corruption that was practiced in each of the following: Crédit Mobilier, the Tweed Ring, the Whiskey Ring.

4. Mugwump Reform

A FACTION FOR HONEST AND EFFICIENT GOVERNMENT. By the 1880's the Republican party had another faction called the Mugwumps. It was a derisive name, suggesting that its members were fence straddlers, halfway between Republicans and Democrats. (A mugwump was supposed to be a bird that sat on a fence with its "mug" on one side and its "wump" on the other.) *The Mugwumps wanted clean government and a professional civil service.* They were middle-class reformers, business people, and journalists who had little sympathy for the laboring poor or the problems of farmers. They approved of free enterprise and had no desire to change the system. They wanted to make government more honest and efficient. Some wanted to reduce the tariff, believing that high duties protected monopolies from foreign competition.

Civil service refers to filling government jobs on the basis of merit. Many people wanted civil service reform in order to reduce the number of people appointed to office as a result of the spoils system.

CIVIL SERVICE REFORM. The demand for clean government was made early in the Grant era, even before the major scandals became public. As early as 1869, Carl Schurz, a German-born senator from Missouri, introduced a bill in Congress calling for the appointment and promotion of federal officeholders by merit rather than through patronage. The bill failed because of the opposition of people involved in the spoils system. But the demand for a professional civil service rose with each exposé of corruption.

THE LIBERAL REPUBLICAN MOVEMENT. By the end of Grant's first term in office (1873), the rising level of corruption led Republican reformers to demand a more vigilant candidate. When the party regulars renominated Grant in 1872, the reformers held a convention of Liberal Republicans. They nominated Horace Greeley, famed publisher of the *New York Tribune. Greeley's platform advocated civil-service reform and a reduction in the protective tariff.* Democrats, still hampered by war hatreds and short of leadership, endorsed Greeley.

THE ELECTION OF 1872. It was a curious campaign. President Grant hardly opened his mouth, letting Republican professionals, such as Roscoe Conkling, do the speechmaking. Greeley, on the other hand, continued to talk—and write—too much. In a lifetime of reform causes, he had advocated everything from vegetarianism to socialism. Republican orators had a grand time quoting Greeley against himself. When they were finished, Greeley admitted that no one could tell what he was running for. Grant won handily, 286 electoral votes to 66.

A WOMEN'S RIGHTS CANDIDATE. There was a third party in the field, the National Radical Reformers, who had nominated the nation's first woman candidate for the presidency, Victoria Woodhull. Her running mate was her sister, Tennie C. Claflin. Woodhull and Claflin ran on a program of women's rights and women's suffrage. Their party platform summoned the poor to rise against the rich. The campaign provoked the usual male derision, fed, unfortunately, by Mrs. Woodhull herself. Mrs. Woodhull's comments wrecked her campaign and dealt a serious blow to the women's rights movement of that time.

THE HAYES-TILDEN ELECTION, 1876. With Greeley's defeat the Liberal Republican movement collapsed, although it was reborn in the Mugwump faction of the 1880's. In the meantime reform leadership passed to the Democrats. Samuel J. Tilden, a hero to reformers for exposing the Tweed Ring, set about reorganizing the Democratic party after 1872. He soon had a strong organization in New York and other eastern states and benefited from the "redemption" of the South by Democrats. Tilden was the party's obvious choice for President in 1876. Popular sentiment against such scandals as the Whiskey Ring helped him win strong support.

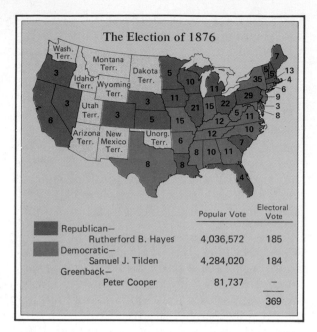

The Election of 1876

	Popular Vote	Electoral Vote
Republican—		
Rutherford B. Hayes	4,036,572	185
Democratic—		
Samuel J. Tilden	4,284,020	184
Greenback—		
Peter Cooper	81,737	—
		369

Republicans remained divided in 1876 between Stalwarts and Half-Breeds. When Conkling and Blaine vetoed each other, the party turned to the little-known governor of Ohio, Rutherford B. Hayes.

The election was the closest in history. Tilden won some 250,000 popular votes more than Hayes and at first had the edge in the electoral votes of four states where the returns were in dispute—Oregon, South Carolina, Louisiana, and Florida. Oregon had only one disputed vote, and that was quickly settled in favor of Hayes. The three remaining states were all in the South and were still under Republican carpetbag rule. The three states together had 19 electoral votes. If Hayes got all of them, he would win by one vote, 185–184. The carpetbag regimes were quite willing to turn their votes over to Hayes, but Democrats everywhere raised an outcry.

A COMPROMISE. Congress set up a joint committee to examine the returns. It was composed of eight Republicans and seven Democrats. By strict party vote, the committee awarded all three states and the

election to Hayes. (See map at the left.) At the same time some backstairs bargains silenced the Democrats. *The new President agreed to remove the federal troops from South Carolina, Florida, and Louisiana, thereby allowing the last southern states to be "redeemed" by Democrats. Republican leaders also agreed that southern railroad projects, such as the Texas Pacific, would get the same kind of government aid given the Union Pacific.*

The chain of bargains ended the crisis, and Hayes was sworn into office without incident. It also ended an era—an era that had begun with secession, an era in which Americans resorted to military arms to resolve their differences. The bargain of 1877, shoddy though it was, at least restored the spirit of compromise.

HAYES VS. THE SPOILS SYSTEM. Hayes was not known as a reformer, although as President he introduced several reforms. He did not dismiss thousands of officeholders and replace them with his political favorites. He made Carl Schurz Secretary of the Interior. Schurz promptly placed his department on the merit system, eliminating patronage and influence peddling. To head the treasury, a department riddled with corruption under Grant, Hayes chose John Sherman, younger brother of the Civil War general. Sherman began an investigation of the customs houses, especially the one in New York City. He quickly ran afoul of Roscoe Conkling, whose state machine depended on the customs house for patronage. Sherman managed to remove Chester A. Arthur, Conkling's chief lieutenant, from the customs house, but Conkling prevented any replacement. The result was a stalemate. Hayes failed to dramatize his cause or appeal to the public for support. The government drifted for the remainder of his term.

ELECTION OF 1880. President Hayes took office announcing that he would be a

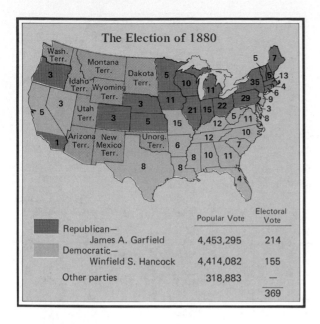

The Election of 1880

	Popular Vote	Electoral Vote
Republican—		
James A. Garfield	4,453,295	214
Democratic—		
Winfield S. Hancock	4,414,082	155
Other parties	318,883	—
		369

one-term President. It was just as well. He so alienated Senator Conkling and the Stalwart wing of the party that he would not have won renomination anyway. The Stalwarts in 1880 wanted to return to the good old days and reelect Grant, but the Blaine forces blocked his nomination. Again the Republican convention turned to a relative unknown, James A. Garfield, a general in the Civil War and a representative in Congress. To appease the Stalwarts the convention nominated Chester A. Arthur for Vice-President.

In 1880 the Democrats sought to escape the "bloody shirt" by nominating a Civil War general of their own, Winfield S. Hancock. The tactic nearly worked. The Democrats controlled the South and parts of the West. *But Conkling's machine, managing to deliver New York to the Republicans, won the election.*

PRESIDENT GARFIELD IS ASSASSINATED.
On July 2, 1881, four months after he took office, President Garfield was shot to death by Charles Guiteau (gi-TOE), an office seeker who had failed to get a job. One good thing came of the insane deed. A shocked public concluded that if office seekers would go to that length, it was time to put federal appointments on a more systematic and impersonal basis.

THE PENDLETON CIVIL SERVICE ACT.
The new President, Chester Arthur, although a product of the spoils system, lent his support to the cause of reform. In 1883 Congress passed the Pendleton Act, which created a *bipartisan* commission to administer competitive examinations for persons seeking government employment. The "classified" positions—those for which examinations had to be taken—were only about 12 percent of all federal jobs, but the act did authorize the President to extend the list. It also prohibited the party in power from seeking campaign contributions from government officials.

A *bipartisan* commission is one that includes representatives of both political parties.

The Pendleton Act was a milestone in civil-service reform. Although limited in scope, it benefited from party turnover. The next 20 years witnessed a succession of one-term Presidents, each of whom increased the number of positions that were placed on the classified list. Therefore, by the end of the 19th century, virtually the entire government was under the civil service system.

"RUM, ROMANISM, AND REBELLION."
Although Arthur spent the rest of his term courting party support for reelection, he did not succeed. Roscoe Conkling fell from power in 1881, when the New York legislature refused to return him to the Senate. James G. Blaine was left in control of the party. Blaine demanded and got the Republican nomination in 1884. Reformers were dismayed, for Blaine was the boss of bosses.

The Democrats quickly picked up the fallen torch of reform by nominating Grover

Cleveland, a former governor of New York. Cleveland had a reputation for honesty and independence. Republican Mugwumps bolted their party and supported Cleveland.

The election was expected to be close, as usual. Much depended on New York. Blaine's chances in that state received a fatal blow when a Protestant minister at a public rally denounced the Democrats as the party of "rum, Romanism, and rebellion." The "rebellion" slander was merely a new version of the "bloody shirt," but "rum" and "Romanism" were jabs at the Catholic Irish, most of whom were Democrats. The offensive remark certainly eliminated any chance Blaine might have had in New York. Cleveland won, 219 electoral votes to 182. (See map at the right.)

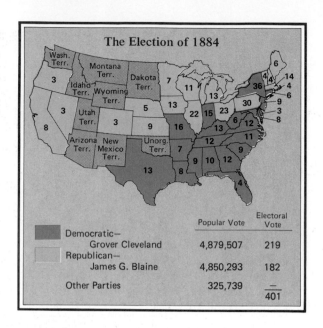

The Election of 1884

	Popular Vote	Electoral Vote
Democratic— Grover Cleveland	4,879,507	219
Republican— James G. Blaine	4,850,293	182
Other Parties	325,739	—
		401

President Garfield was shot in Union Station, Washington, D.C., four months after taking office, on July 2, 1881. Secretary of State Blaine is shown at the right, looking on in amazement. Garfield died of blood poisoning caused by a bullet lodged in his spine. The assassin was hanged on June 30 of the following year.

378

In 1884 Belva Lockwood, a prominent lawyer, became the second woman to run for President on an Equal Rights ticket. Her platform encompassed all her interests— women's suffrage, equal rights for all, uniform marriage laws, and world peace. Her campaign caused considerable ridicule. In one incident the men of Rahway, New Jersey, dressed in costumes to protest her position against alcohol. Do you think their form of protest was respected?

CLEVELAND'S FIRST TERM, 1885–1889. *Grover Cleveland's presidency was both the climax and the end of the movement for liberal reform.* True to his reputation, the new President waged war on spoils and corruption. He doubled the number of federal offices on the classified list, and he halted the giveaway of excessive pensions to Civil War veterans. He also tried to recover millions of hectares of public land illegally occupied by railroads, cattle barons, and lumber companies. Toward the end of his term, he made reduction of the tariff his special crusade. When Congress refused, he went to the voters with the issue in the election of 1888. He lost to the Republican Benjamin Harrison.

The Mugwumps achieved their main goal of cleaner government, but the goal itself was limited. By the 1880's the nation faced serious social problems—labor unrest, low agriculture prices and the prospect of farm revolt in the South and the western prairies, periodic banking crises, and money shortages. Such problems were beyond President Cleveland's ability to recognize or

379

to solve. His shortcomings were also the shortcomings of the liberal reformers of the Gilded Age. By the time Cleveland left office in 1889, a more radical reform movement was on the horizon.

Section Review

1. Mapping: Using the three election maps in this section, compare the voting patterns of states in the elections of 1876, 1880, and 1884. In which election year did the voting pattern in the south differ in these three elections? How did it differ?
2. Identify or explain: Mugwumps, Horace Greeley, Pendleton Act, Victoria Woodhull, Roscoe Conkling, Rutherford B. Hayes.
3. Briefly describe the elections of 1872 and 1876. How did the closeness of the election of 1876 help the South to resume its role in national politics?
4. List and explain the reforms put into effect during the terms of Presidents Hayes, Arthur, and Cleveland.
5. How did the idea of the merit system in civil service grow out of the reforms of this period?

5. The Gilded Age: A Climate of Conservatism

THE GILDED AGE AND REFORM. *Pre-Civil War America bubbled with intellectual ferment.* Women's rights, temperance, peace, abolition of slavery—all competed for public attention. But after the war, concern seemed to fade away. The only change that reformers of the Gilded Age proposed was a more professional civil service.

Why the change? A postwar letdown seems to be part of the answer. People tired of agitation and social criticism. Of equal importance was the intellectual climate of the Gilded Age. The prevailing ideas of that time did not encourage reform. Historians have given the name Social Darwinism to the set of ideas that swept America after the Civil War.

SOCIAL DARWINISM. In 1859 an English scientist, Charles Darwin, suggested in his book known as the *Origin of Species* that the various species of plants and animals in nature had evolved and adapted over time. Through a process of natural selection, certain species had survived, whereas others, such as dinosaurs and saber-toothed tigers, had died out. Darwin's theory was by no

Sidenote to History

Work and Win: Horatio Alger

The success stories of Carnegie, Rockefeller, and Vanderbilt suggested that a hard worker could get ahead and even build up a sizable fortune. The individual most responsible for presenting the philosophy of hard work to young Americans was Horatio Alger. In the last half of the 19th century, Alger spun this message for his youthful audience: Always be on the alert, never fail to catch the attention of your boss or perform some heroic act to gain praise, and fame and fortune will be yours.

In one of Alger's best-known stories, "Fame and Fortune," written in 1868, the main character is Richard Hunter, an orphan and a former bootblack. Hunter goes to work in a small business that is owned by one man. He eventually becomes a partner in the business. Readers of Alger's books believed that his stories of success provided the keys to success in business.

means new. Other scientists had been groping in the same direction. Indeed, 10 years before Darwin published his work, an English philosopher, Herbert Spencer, had applied the theory of evolution to human society.

HERBERT SPENCER. In a short book entitled *Social Statics* (1850), Herbert Spencer outlined his idea that human society evolves through competition. In the race to get ahead in the world, certain people come out on top because they are stronger, or smarter, or more hardworking. Spencer called this process the "survival of the fittest." He argued that civilization benefits from it. Because each generation is fitter than the last, society continuously improves itself. *Human progress is natural and inevitable—inevitable because progress stems from competition itself.*

Spencer's theory did not sit well with the English, but it caught the fancy of Americans. Between 1850 and 1900, *Social Statics* sold 500,000 copies in the United States. *It appealed to Americans because it justified precisely what they were doing.* The United States was a nation of ambitious individuals struggling competitively to get ahead. Americans believed that free, open competition promoted development. They were delighted when Spencer told them it promoted civilization itself.

ANDREW CARNEGIE. *One of the most spectacular success stories of the age was that of Andrew Carnegie, a Scot who came to America at the age of 12.* His first job was working in a textile mill for 1.20 dollars a week. Determined to get ahead, he invested in the young oil business, made a little money, and turned to steel. He knew nothing of steelmaking, but he was a shrewd judge of people and drove himself and his associates relentlessly. When one of the plant managers telegraphed him, "We broke all records for making steel last week," Carnegie wired back, "Congratulations! Why not do it every week?" When he retired in 1901, he sold his steel company for 480 million dollars.

"THE GOSPEL OF WEALTH." Spencer's ideas appealed to Carnegie, who wrote magazine articles that helped popularize the notion of Social Darwinism. In an article entitled "The Gospel of Wealth" (1889), Carnegie made Social Darwinism the basis of a moral code. Poverty, said Carnegie, resulted from some character flaw, such as laziness or a lack of thrift. *In a free, open society, those who worked hard and saved their money were bound to get ahead. They*

This is the billiard room in the Vanderbilts's summer "cottage," which cost $3 million to build in 1895.

Sidenote to History

The Master Showman

Americans of the 1800's regarded amusement as sinful and the theater as disreputable.

Phineas Taylor Barnum helped change that image. He helped make culture popular by popularizing culture. Barnum's home was the American Museum on lower Broadway in New York City. The museum was filled with scientific specimens, fossils, bones, and stuffed animals. Barnum soon discovered that special attractions brought larger crowds, although he was careful to ensure that amusement was tied to science.

Barnum was a master of publicity. Deciding that the nation lacked culture, he contacted Jenny Lind, called the Swedish nightingale, and the greatest singer in Europe. To induce her to come to America, he guaranteed her 1,000 dollars for each appearance. Because few Americans had ever heard of Jenny Lind, Barnum had to advertise. He sent short biographies to newspapers and notices of her European acclaim. Her tour in 1850 was a tremendous success, netting Barnum 500,000 dollars.

Barnum took advantage of news events that gave him free publicity. When the famed explorer John C. Frémont was lost in 1844, the nation mourned. When he was found, it rejoiced. Shortly thereafter Barnum exhibited a new find, a woolly horse, supposedly discovered by Frémont deep in the mountains. The animal was covered with thick, curly hair. Barnum described it as a combination of deer, buffalo, horse, and sheep. He claimed that it solved all the problems of the West because it could be ridden, shorn, and eaten.

The Gilded Age was Barnum's own. When his museum burned down in 1867, he built a bigger one and made even more money. At Bridgeport, Connecticut, he built an oriental villa, with onion-shaped domes. He installed an elephant to plow the garden. His success story, *The Life of P. T. Barnum Written by Himself,* was on the bookshelves of most business people.

When his museum burned down again in 1871, Barnum bought a circus and began touring the country. The circus was far from new—Europeans had watched traveling acts and exhibits for centuries. But Barnum introduced the big top, an enormous tent that held thousands of people for a single show. He also conceived the idea of separating the tent floor into rings so two acts could go on at once.

In 1881 Barnum merged with his main competitor, James A. Bailey. From the merger came "The Greatest Show on Earth." It opened in Madison Square Garden in New York City, and for the occasion the number of rings was extended to three. The three-ring circus was the triumph of popular culture: something for everyone, so much going on that the eye could not follow it all.

The circus appealed to the American love of bigness. Barnum's final triumph was Jumbo, the world's largest elephant, owned by the London Zoological Gardens. His daily intake of hay was enormous. He also ate 15 loaves of bread and drank 5 pails of water every day. Barnum bought him from the London Zoo in 1882 for the princely sum of 10,000 dollars. The sale caused an uproar in Britain. (The British were still smarting from Barnum's attempt to purchase Shakespeare's home and transport it to New York.)

deserved their riches. Success was the reward of virtue.

Government, Carnegie believed, must not interfere with this competitive struggle. Government aid to the needy merely benefited the "unfit." *The only role of government, he said, was to maintain order and protect property.* But he also believed that the rich were obliged to use their wealth for the benefit of society. By endowing museums, libraries, and universities, the wealthy would contribute to the progress of humanity. Thus, Carnegie spent his last years on these kinds of philanthropic projects. "I started life as a poor man," he declared, "and I wish to end it that way." Libraries, universities, and foundations bearing his name testify to his philanthropy.

HENRY GEORGE. "The Gospel of Wealth" discouraged government regulation. It thus blended well with the prevailing conservatism of the Gilded Age. It appealed to those who were benefiting from the nation's spectacular economic growth, but it offered little comfort to those who were not doing well—to southern Blacks and poor Whites, to farmers on the *sod-house frontier,* to immigrants who worked Carnegie's steel mills for a dollar a day.

The *sod-house frontier* was so named because most settlers who moved west built houses of sod—the upper part of the soil filled with the roots of grass or other herbs. Sod walls provided warmth in the winter and coolness in the summer.

There were critics of Social Darwinism in its own day. Among these was Henry George, who wrote *Progress and Poverty* in 1879. George was distressed by the prevalence of poverty amid great wealth. He wondered if "The Gospel of Wealth" really explained the great inequalities in American society. Did the rich really have higher moral character, or were they the lucky few who happened to grab the best land and the richest resources? George decided it was the latter. He proposed a system of land taxation designed to reduce great fortunes and provide benefits for everyone. Such notions, however, were far too radical for the Gilded Age.

Section Review

1. Identify or explain: Charles Darwin, Herbert Spencer, "The Gospel of Wealth," Henry George.
2. How did Spencer's idea of survival of the fittest coincide with Darwin's theory of natural selection? Why were Americans interested in Spencer's ideas?
3. What did Carnegie mean by the term *gospel of wealth*? How did his life reflect this concept?
4. What, in Carnegie's opinion, should government's role be?
5. Did Carnegie think that the wealthy had any obligations to society? If so, what were these obligations?
6. How did Henry George attempt to refute "The Gospel of Wealth" and Social Darwinism? How were his ideas received?

Chapter 15 Review

Bird's-Eye View

During the so-called Gilded Age, Americans abandoned for a time the moral passions and crusading spirit of the early 19th century. Instead they turned to industrial and economic development. Spurred by the needs of the armed forces for supplies and materials, much of this development started during the Civil War. Individuals such as Cornelius Vanderbilt, John D. Rockefeller, and J. P. Morgan accumulated vast fortunes as they built railroads, oil refineries, and banking empires. Ingenuity, daring, and a cheap labor force became the foundation of a new economic order. On the seamier side of the foundation rested stock manipulation, speculation, and out-and-out fraud.

Fortunes were made in government as well as industry and business. People who believed in the spoils system viewed both elective and appointed offices as economic opportunities. President Grant, although not personally corrupt, was blind to the corruption of others in his administration. Rutherford B. Hayes won a narrow victory over Samuel J. Tilden, a reform candidate, by covertly promising the withdrawal of the last remaining federal troops from the South. Then, early in his Presidency, Hayes surprised many by refusing to replace government officeholders with his political favorites and by appointing several people committed to government reforms. Chester Arthur also lent his support to reform by approving the Pendleton Act, which set up a system of competitive examinations for a number of civil service jobs. In 1884 Grover Cleveland was elected President on a reform platform, but his campaign for lower tariffs cost him the election of 1888. By the time he left office, a more radical reform movement was on the horizon.

Social Darwinism, or the concept of the survival of the fittest, captured the American imagination with its glorification of individual competition. Steel baron Andrew Carnegie, in his "Gospel of Wealth," further popularized the philosophy of equating financial wealth with moral virtue. A few reformers such as Henry George spoke out against the existence of poverty amid so much wealth. But his ideas found their forum in another place, at another time.

Vocabulary

Define or identify each of the following:

homestead	commodity	civil service
land grant colleges	laissez-faire	bipartisan
Jay Gould	Wall Street	Social Darwinism

Review Questions

1. Name three inventors and an invention of each. Then, describe how the invention helped to mechanize American industry or agriculture.
2. Describe the measures passed by the Republican party during the Civil War that aided the expansion of manufacturing and transportation.

3. How did Fisk, Gould, Rockefeller, and Vanderbilt each make a fortune?
4. What was the spoils system? Who introduced it to government? After 40 years what problems did the system have?
5. Briefly tell how the Crédit Mobilier, the Whiskey Ring, and the Tweed Ring were examples of corruption in government.
6. How did the Pendleton Act bring about reform in the federal government?
7. In what ways was Andrew Carnegie influenced by the ideas of Social Darwinism?

Reviewing Social Studies Skills

1. Make a time line, showing the term of office for each President mentioned in this chapter. Then, list the major events that took place during the administration of those Presidents.
2. Using the maps on pages 376–378, answer the following questions:
   a. In what section of the country did the Democrats maintain strength in all three elections?
   b. Name the seven states that had the greatest number of electoral votes.
   c. Name the seven states that had the fewest number of electoral votes.
3. Write a paragraph about the Erie War. In the first sentence state your opinion about the war. Then, using the textbook, find at least three pieces of evidence to support your opinion. Put that evidence into three sentences.

Reading for Meaning

1. Explain how the chapter title "The Gilded Age" describes American society after the Civil War.
2. Look at the cartoon on page 374 and describe what you see. What does the cartoon suggest about who was responsible for the stolen money mentioned in the caption?
3. Using material from your textbook and from reference books in your library, write a brief biography of J. P. Morgan, Andrew Carnegie, or John D. Rockefeller. How did each of these individuals reflect the values of the period in which they lived?

Bibliography

Those interested in P. T. Barnum might read *The Fabulous Showman: The Life and Times of P. T. Barnum* by Irving Wallace (Alfred A. Knopf, Inc.).

Matthew Josephson records in colorful detail the schemes of Vanderbilt, Gould, Fisk, Stanford, and other business people of the Gilded Age in *The Robber Barons* (Harcourt Brace Jovanovich).

May McNeer's *America's Mark Twain* (Houghton Mifflin) is an interesting biography of this famous author.

Chapter 16

The Industrial Frontier

December 31, 1879, was an exciting day—a day that the people of the village of Menlo Park, New Jersey, would never forget. The *New York Herald* broke the extraordinary news. EDISON'S LIGHT THE GREAT INVENTOR'S TRIUMPH, it headlined. "It makes a Light without Gas or Flame, Cheaper than Oil, Success in a Cotton Thread," the news story continued.

Menlo Park's most prominent citizen had made good on his boast. A year earlier he had announced that he would invent an electric light. And here it was! He planned to light up the entire village as a demonstration.

Alerted by the press stories, people crowded into Menlo Park to see Thomas Edison's "light of the future." To carry out his feat, Edison had to develop a special generator and then string copper wires throughout the village. At the appointed hour on New Year's Eve, 1879, he turned on 40 light bulbs, producing a breathtaking sight.

Thomas Edison was a new kind of inventor. Gone was the day of the lonely scientist, tinkering in a workshop, hoping to discover something important. Edison did not wait for such a chance discovery. Invention, he thought, required organization and purpose. He believed that teams of people working on a coordinated plan could turn out inventions as regularly as a factory produced goods.

Edison got his first job as a telegraph operator at the age of 15. From that day his life was associated with electricity. He obtained his first patent before he was 21—for a telegraphic vote-recording machine. Observing how tedious it was to count congressional votes, he devised a wire system that would enable members of Congress to register their votes by pushing buttons. To Edison's dismay, Congress rejected the invention. Congress preferred slower procedures. Speed meant more bills and more work. It was a lesson Edison never forgot. Thereafter he made sure that there was a commercial demand for an idea. He invented for the marketplace.

By the time he was in his mid-20's, Edison had several patents—most involved improvements in the telegraph—and was able to attract financial support. In 1876 he opened a laboratory for invention in Menlo Park, New Jersey. There he brought teams of mathematicians, electronics experts, and toolmakers and gave them the best possible equipment. By coordinating their efforts on a single project, he planned to turn out inventions on an assembly-line basis. They would produce "a minor invention every ten days," he boasted, "and a big thing every six months or so."

Electric lighting attracted his attention and in 1878 he formed the Edison Electric Light Company. He set his experts to the task of inventing a special kind of bulb. The principles of electric lighting had been known for some years. But such lighting seemed to require enormous amounts of electricity and was far too bright for households and offices.

Edison's solution involved the use of a carbon filament of cotton thread in a light bulb, which required much less power to produce much more light. Edison patented the device in October 1879. He was not content with one invention. He also developed a wiring system of extremely thin copper so that entire cities could be wired at manageable cost.

The electric light was only the beginning of his achievements. The Menlo Park invention factory was as good as Edison's boast. Over the next 20 years his teams developed the modern storage battery, the dictaphone for secretarial dictation, the phonograph (with records made of hard wax), motion pictures, and the electric locomotive. By the time he died in 1931, Edison had taken out patents on 1,033 inventions.

Chapter Objectives

After you have finished reading this chapter, you should be able to:
1. Explain the changes the Industrial Revolution brought to American life in the mid-19th century.
2. List and describe the inventions and ideas used to develop and expand big business after the Civil War.
3. Compare the National Labor Union, the Knights of Labor, and the American Federation of Labor.

Edison's story was the story of American business in the years following the Civil War. Business had achieved rapid advances in technology and enormous leaps in production and had developed advertising and merchandising techniques to appeal to an army of consumers. The United States doubled and tripled in a few years the level of technology and output that had taken the world centuries to attain. In 1860 the United States was ranked fourth in the world in volume and value of manufactured goods. By 1890 it was in first place. And by 1894 it produced more than the total number of goods manufactured by the second- and third-place nations (Great Britain and Germany).

1. Industry Comes of Age

WHAT AND WHEN WAS THE INDUSTRIAL REVOLUTION? *As an epoch in world history, an industrial revolution*

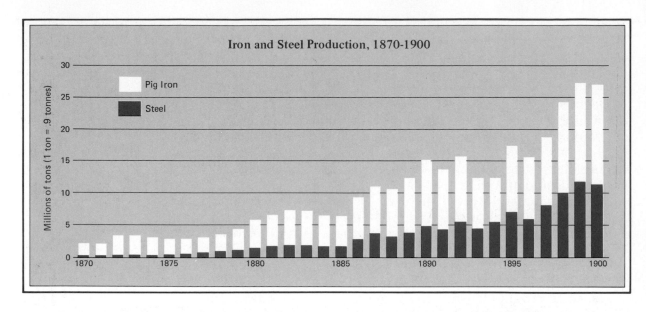

Iron and Steel Production, 1870-1900

Millions of tons (1 ton = .9 tonnes)

Pig Iron
Steel

means the time when a nation develops its simple rural economy into a complex technology requiring large investments in factories and machines. Great Britain started this process about the time of the Revolutionary War in America, and the rest of western Europe followed a similar course soon after. The United States began the process of industrializing later than Europe, partly because American energies were devoted to settling the continent.

Factories had appeared in New England around 1800, but it was not until about 1840 that the process began in earnest. Civil War demand boosted it along, and by 1900 the nation reached its industrial maturity.

INVENTIONS, POWER, PROCESSES. *These were the things that made an industrial revolution—inventions that improved technology, new sources of power to run the machines, and new processes that expanded output.* In Great Britain the Industrial Revolution began in the latter part of the 18th century, when inventions revolutionized the techniques of spinning and weaving cloth.

James Watt's steam engine provided a new source of power. Coal came into use

instead of wood. Attaching a steam engine to the new spinning and weaving machine required a separate building for the machinery. Thus, the factory was born. Workers who used to do spinning and weaving by hand moved from farm to factory. Houses and shops sprang up in its vicinity. The factory changed people's lives and their environment.

RAILROADS AND STEEL. Railroads, rather than textile mills, paced America's Industrial Revolution. During the 1840's and 1850's the spurt of railroad building climaxed in the transcontinental Union Pacific line.

Railroads increased the demand for steel because iron was not strong enough for powerful engines or hard enough for lasting rails. Steel is an exceptionally hard form of iron. It had been used for centuries in making knives and swords, but it was too expensive for such massive projects as railroads.

In 1859 an Englishman named Henry Bessemer discovered a way of rapidly turning iron into steel. Bessemer's steelmaking process was readily adopted by American steel mills. But for use in railroads even Bessemer steel was not good enough. The Bessemer process left tiny bubbles in the steel, a source of structural weakness. The open-hearth method, another English invention, solved this problem and produced a higher grade of steel. By 1900 the open-hearth process had become the mode of production. It enabled American steelmakers to produce 9.9 million tonnes (11 million tons) of steel annually. (See graph, page 388.)

THE BIRTH OF MASS PRODUCTION.

Higher quality steel permitted the development of fine-grade tools—lathes, drills, presses—in short, machines to make machines. *Development of a machine-tool industry permitted standardization of parts.* If each part of a complicated machine is fashioned by a precision tool so that similar parts are interchangeable, the machine can be put together rapidly on an assembly line. Eli Whitney discovered this principle in 1800 and used it for the mass production of army muskets. Others applied it to more complicated mechanisms. Isaac Merit Singer mass-produced sewing machines by the 1860's, and Cyrus McCormick used interchangeable parts in his harvesting machines.

The ultimate development of the process came in 1908, when Henry Ford introduced the moving assembly line into the manufacture of automobiles. Each worker

This painting of the Bessemer converter in a Bethlehem Steel plant was done in 1895 by S. B. Shiley. Bessemer in 1859 had patented a process for burning out impurities in molten iron that revolutionized the steel industry and facilitated the building of the transcontinental railroad. Can you name two tycoons who, in part, owe their fortunes to the Bessemer process?

YEAR	INVENTOR	CONTRIBUTION
1851	Henry Bessemer (Eng.) William Kelly	Bessemer process of making molten steel
1852	Elisha Otis	Passenger elevator
1859	Edwin Drake	Successful oil drilling at Titusville, Pennsylvania
1864	George Pullman	Railroad sleeping car
1866	Cyrus Field	Transatlantic cable
1867	Christopher Sholes	Typewriter
1868	George Westinghouse	Air brake for railroad trains
1869	I. W. McGaffey	Suction-type vacuum cleaner
1871	Andrew Hallidie	Cable streetcar
1872	Amanda Jones	Vacuum process of preserving food
1876	Alexander G. Bell	Telephone
1878	Thomas Edison	Phonograph
1879	Thomas Edison	Incandescent lamp
1882	Jan Matzeliger	Shoe-lasting machine
1882	Thomas Edison	First large central power plant in the United States
1884	Otimar Mergenthaler	Linotype printing machine
1889	Singer Manufacturing Company	Electric sewing machine
1895	George B. Selden	First patented automobile
1896	C. Francis Jenkins Thomas Armat	Motion picture projector
1903	Wilbur and Orville Wright	Successful flight in a motor-powered plane

was assigned a task that could be performed in a very short time as the automobile under construction passed by. The division of labor made each worker an expert at one task. The work was paced by the speed of the moving line.

ASSEMBLY-LINE FOOD. Actually, Henry Ford was not the first to conceive of the moving line. That honor belongs to the meat-processing pioneers, Gustavus Swift and Phillip Armour. Both men went to Chi-cago in 1875, when the city was becoming the rail center of the Midwest.

Because beef spoiled so easily, cattle had to be shipped alive from the West to the East. The process was expensive. The animals had to be fed on the way, and the shipper had to pay for the 35 percent of the animal that could not be sold as meat. The principle of refrigeration was known, but refrigerated cars were not effective. To make matters worse, the handling of dressed beef

"The Bowery at Night, 1895," painted by Louis Sonntag, is a good example of realistic American art of the period. How many features of this scene would not have existed 20 years earlier?

was so slow that the meat sometimes spoiled between railroad car and butcher shop.

The solution to the problem was not so much technology as organization. Swift and Armour developed both. ***By 1881 Swift found an effective refrigerator car.*** He then devised a moving assembly line that almost extended from Chicago slaughterhouses to New York butcher shops. With the cooperation of the railroads, refrigerator cars sped the beef from Chicago to the East Coast without interruption. In the rail yards of eastern cities, the cars pulled to a stop opposite the doors of cold-storage buildings. Other moving lines unloaded the cars.

The trip was a model of efficiency—from pasture to butcher shop, across great distances, in a few days. It was so efficient that the price paid for beef was cut nearly in half.

THE DEPARTMENT STORE. Attention to the consumer was the most distinctive feature of America's Industrial Revolution. ***American production was geared to the mass market.*** Such techniques as the assembly line brought goods that had been previously considered luxuries within the reach of many more people.

John C. Wanamaker opened one of the nation's first department stores in Philadelphia in 1876. R. H. Macy in New York and Marshall Field in Chicago were not far behind. The department store was a brand-new world. Goods had always been sold in specialty shops catering to neighborhood customers. Each shop specialized in one item—leather goods, fabrics, hats, cutlery, and so on. The department store, on the other hand, offered a little of everything. Its "departments" were miniature specialty shops within an enormous store. Crowds wandered among its displays, trying on ready-made clothing and examining luxuries. Arranged in attractive displays, goods sold themselves. "Goods suitable for the millionaire," R. H. Macy advertised in 1887, "at prices in the reach of millions."

Macy can also be credited with recognizing the value of women employees. Margaret Getchell LaForge started her career at Macy's as a cashier and worked her way to superintendent of the large store. Her administrative and marketing talents enabled her to influence every area of policymaking, from initiating lines of merchandise to managing personnel.

"THE FIVE AND TEN CENT STORE."
The fixed price was an important feature of the department store. Indeed, it brought into being entire classes of goods that were bought not because of their quality or function but because of their price. F. W. Woolworth discovered that price itself, if low enough and in convenient coin, could sell goods.

Finding that handkerchiefs sold well at five cents apiece, he set up a special table of five-cent items—thimbles, soap, harmonicas, safety pins, and crocheting needles. They sold out in one day. Why not an entire store devoted to such items? Woolworth opened the first "Five and Ten Cent Store" in Utica, New York, in 1877. The first store failed. He tried again in 1879 in Pennsylvania. The second store was so successful that

Sidenote to History

Merchants to the Millions

Another business development of late 19th- and early 20th-century America was the mail-order house. Mail-order businesses such as Montgomery Ward and Sears, Roebuck provided thousands of Americans—especially farmers—with a wide variety of reasonably priced merchandise. Armed with either a Ward's or a Sears' catalog, an Iowa farm family "shopping at home" could order anything from a centrifugal cream separator for $24.00 to a 48-bone corset for $25.

Among the mail-order houses, Sears, Roebuck was the most successful. Sears, Roebuck got its start in 1886, about 10 years after the first success of Montgomery Ward. Established by an enterprising railroad-station agent named Richard Sears, the company began by selling watches. Joining forces with Alvah Roebuck, a watchmaker, Sears increased sales by selling a wide variety of goods. In 1896 the first Sears, Roebuck general catalog was published.

It advertised everything the members of a household might require. Through the use of catalog copy, testimonials from satisfied customers, and money-back guarantees, the mail-order business continued to grow.

The success of mail-order businesses would not have been possible without railroads, post offices, and rural free delivery. The system of rural free delivery seems to have made the most impact. Rural mail carriers traveled along the roads of rural America. They carried newspapers, magazines, and merchandise to be delivered to farm families. They put the mail in silver-painted mailboxes placed alongside the road. Each mailbox had a little red flag on its side, which the mail carrier lifted to let the farmer know the mail had been delivered. By 1917 rural free delivery—or RFD, as it came to be known—extended to most rural areas. This system eventually led to parcel-post service and the development of more mail-order firms.

Inventors during the 1880's and 1890's brought forth numerous contraptions that enjoyed short-lived popularity. The Pedespeed seemed to have obvious advantages at first, but faded quickly into obscurity. Can you give one reason why its appeal did not last?

he opened similar stores in other cities, helping to pioneer the chain store. By purchasing items in enormous quantities and selling them through numerous outlets, Woolworth offered quality items at prices everyone could afford.

STREETCAR CITIES. The department store came into being largely because of the streetcar. Retail merchants had operated on a small scale because they were confined to neighborhoods. Their customers lived within walking distance of the stores. *The streetcar not only spread out the city and encouraged suburbs but also created the "downtown" marketing center.* People could come from great distances to shop.

The first form of public transportation was a horse-drawn carriage. Similar to a stagecoach, it lumbered slowly down city streets. Putting the coach on rails made the ride faster and more comfortable. A standard five-cent fare and free transfers attracted customers who might otherwise have walked. Some people moved to the outskirts of the city for a more wholesome and spacious rural environment. They depended on the streetcar for transportation to work.

In 1850 urban Boston extended a little over three kilometers (2 miles) from the city center; by 1880, with only a modest increase in population, its physical dimension doubled. After 1890, when the electric streetcar was introduced, the city tripled its geographical sprawl.

Section Review

1. Mapping: Using the map on page 395, locate Chicago. Describe its position in terms of longitude and latitude and in relation to the rest of the country. Why do you think it became a great railroad center?
2. Identify or explain: Henry Bessemer, Isaac Merit Singer, Industrial Revolution, F. W. Woolworth, R. H. Macy, Gustavus Swift.
3. Define assembly-line production. Explain how Henry Ford improved this process.
4. How were department stores different from previous kinds of retail stores?

2. The Rise of Big Business

CORPORATIONS. America was founded by business corporations. Joint stock companies established and governed the earliest colonies in Virginia and New England. After the Revolution, the American states chartered hundreds of companies that operated roads, canals, bridges, and banks. The corporation seemed to be the ideal way of doing business. By selling shares of stock to the public, it collected huge amounts of *capital. If the corporation made money, its investors received profits in the form of dividends and increased stock value.* If the corporation went broke, however, its owners were not personally liable for its debts. Limited liability meant that corporations could undertake risky ventures—its owners stood to lose only the value of their stock.

> *Capital* is wealth and property invested in business for the purpose of making a profit.

Originally, each corporation was chartered or licensed by an act of the legislature. But as the nation matured, this process proved cumbersome. Even before the Civil War, the states began adopting general incorporation laws, setting up an administrative process through which anyone who followed certain steps and paid a registration fee could become a corporation. As a result, business was revolutionized. Corporations were mass-produced under standardized procedures.

RAILROAD COMBINATIONS. Besides expanding in number after the Civil War, corporations increased dramatically in size. Before the war, only a few investors—sometimes a single family—owned each corporation. The railroads, which required vast amounts of capital for construction and equipment, were among the first businesses to go public, that is, to sell their shares of stock on the open market. The railroads were also among the first businesses to understand the value of consolidation. Grand trunk lines, connecting major cities and seaports, were far more profitable than small feeder lines running from farm to city. *Commodore Vanderbilt's New York Central system, a combination of dozens of local railroads connecting New York City and the Great Lakes, showed the way.*

Railroads found combination rewarding in other ways. A steam engine could pull 20 cars almost as easily as 15. And it used very little more fuel in hauling loaded cars than it used in moving empty ones. Thus, the railroads made larger profits with longer, more heavily loaded trains.

To attract customers shipping bulky goods, they cut prices or offered secret *rebates.* When two railroads served the same cities, they sometimes got into disastrous price wars, each trying to undersell the other. To avoid this kind of warfare they often made secret deals under which they both set shipping rates and pooled the profits. *For better and for worse, the railroads became the model for big business.*

A *rebate* was a refund of part of the rate charged for transportation. It was generally

The Kodak camera—developed by George Eastman of Rochester, New York—revolutionized the fields of medicine, astronomy, journalism, and education. These cartoons on the perils of photography appeared in Scribner's Monthly in 1889. Can you identify the problem in the donkey-cart picture?

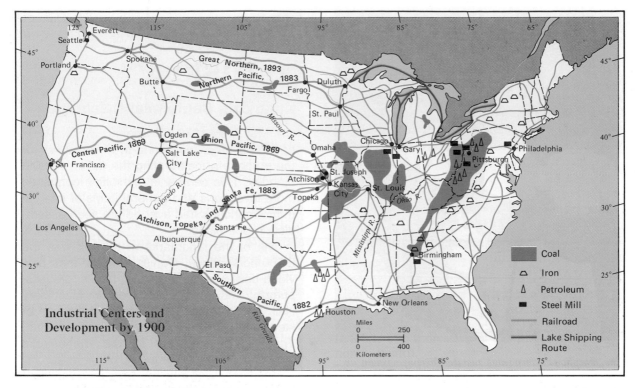

Industrial Centers and Development by 1900

Coal
Iron
Petroleum
Steel Mill
Railroad
Lake Shipping Route

granted to favored customers in order to maintain business without resorting to general rate reductions. Customers who paid the published rate bitterly resented the granting of rebates. Rebates were eventually declared illegal.

BUSINESS ON A NATIONAL SCALE.
Big business meant corporations operating on a national scale. Corporations drew their raw materials from substantial distances and marketed their products across the country. The emergence of national business firms was perhaps the most important development of the post-Civil War period.

Not only did railroads show the way but they made big business possible. *To develop a national market, business had to have a fast, cheap transportation network.* Canals were cheap but slow. Highways—before the development of the modern automobile— were slow and expensive. By 1860 railroads connected the major eastern cities. A decade later they spanned the continent.

Between 1870 and 1900, railroads improved in speed and safety. Single track was replaced by double sets of tracks, permitting traffic to flow in two directions at one time. Coal, a more efficient fuel, replaced wood as the source of energy for locomotives. The railroad cut shipping time between New York and Chicago and New York and New Orleans from months to days, even hours. Passenger travel on railroads also improved. George Pullman and others developed sleeping cars, dining cars, and parlor cars.

FROM TELEGRAPH TO TELEPHONE. *Of equal importance was the communications revolution brought about by the telegraph.* Western Union completed its telegraph line across the continent on the eve of the Civil War. The telegraph reduced the time required to send a message from New York to San Francisco from months to seconds. In 1866 Cyrus W. Field succeeded in laying a telegraph cable across the Atlantic Ocean.

"The Trust Giant's Point of View" was the caption on this cartoon by Horace Taylor. By 1882 the Standard Oil Trust included 14 companies and controlled 26 more. Rockefeller is depicted here as having the government in the palm of his hand.

when the nation's first oil well was drilled at Titusville, Pennsylvania, Rockefeller instantly saw the possibilities—for the city nearest the oil field, which happened to be his home, Cleveland, Ohio. He invested in an oil refinery, and soon bought out his partners. By 1865 he had the largest oil-refining operation in Cleveland.

Rockefeller entered into a close association with the railroads. The size of his refinery enabled him to guarantee the railroads a certain number of oil shipments each year. Railroads kept their trains full, profited handsomely, and slipped Rockefeller rebates. Rebates enabled Rockefeller to undercut his competitors in selling oil. Some competitors

went broke. Others sold out. By 1872 Rockefeller's Standard Oil Company was refining 10,000 barrels of kerosene a day, and it was the largest in the nation.

A CORPORATION OF CORPORATIONS. Rockefeller was not satisfied. The price of oil fluctuated wildly because of competition and rate wars. He experimented for a time with a cartel, a secret agreement among refiners to limit production and fix prices. But he gave up such schemes. Cartels were considered conspiracies under the law, and they didn't work. In hard times a weak refiner bolted the cartel and lowered prices to increase sales.

In 1879 Rockefeller hit upon another device, the trust. He persuaded the stockholders of the Standard Oil Company to transfer their shares to nine trustees. ***The stockholders received trust certificates on which the company would pay dividends.*** Rockefeller and the other trustees had full power to run the company. The stockholders would receive the profits. Interested more in profits than in power, stockholders in rival companies also swapped their shares for trust certificates, enabling Rockefeller to absorb his competitors.

The Standard Oil Trust, organized formally in 1882, was thus a "corporation of corporations." The main job of the trust was not refining oil but owning oil refineries. It eventually controlled 90 percent of the refining business in the country. Rockefeller combined vertically as well as horizontally by obtaining oil fields, pipelines, and retail outlets. So efficient was his operation that he was able to reduce the price of oil. Nonetheless, it is likely that the price would have fallen even further had he permitted competition.

THE SHERMAN ANTITRUST ACT.
The Standard Oil Company inspired imitation. During the 1880's trusts appeared in numerous industries, from sugar refining to the manufacture of matches. Small producers who were pushed out cried for help. And the public became alarmed about the decline of competition. Stories of Rockefeller's ruthless methods contributed to the outcry. His competitors complained of intimidation and spying.

In 1890 Congress passed the Sherman Antitrust Act, which outlawed "every

Joseph Keppler drew this cartoon in the magazine Puck *in 1889, shortly before Congress was about to debate the Sherman Antitrust Bill. What does the closed door at the People's Entrance symbolize?*

organizations intact. In 1877 the Baltimore and Ohio Railroad announced a 10 percent wage cut as a result of the depression. The railroad workers went on strike. When other railroads tried wage cuts, nonunion workers joined, and the strike spread throughout the East and into the Middle West. About two thirds of the nation's rail mileage was eventually shut down.

Then violence broke out. Mobs burned trains and clashed with police. In Chicago armed business people patrolled suburban

Sidenote to History

Catherine Beecher and Scientific Housekeeping

She came from quite a distinguished family. Her father, Lyman Beecher, was one of the country's best-known ministers in Andrew Jackson's day. Her brother, Henry Ward Beecher, was an equally famous clergyman in the Civil War era. Her sister, Harriet Beecher Stowe, was renowned as the author of *Uncle Tom's Cabin.* Refusing to be overshadowed, Catherine Beecher carved a career and earned a reputation of her own.

Catherine Beecher's specialty was educating women. She opened a girls' school in Hartford, Connecticut, in 1823, when she was only 23. She founded institutes in Cincinnati and Milwaukee and provided funds and advice for dozens of others. Like Margaret Fuller and others of her generation, Catherine Beecher viewed education as a means of liberating women from the social and legal restraints that bound them. She wanted to train women and to make them professionals in their work. Because the vast majority of women worked in their homes, she believed that she could do the most good by making housekeeping a science. In 1841 she published her theories in *A Treatise on Domestic Economy.*

No theory of scientific management could help a homemaker who lacked mechanical appliances. And the home described by Catherine Beecher in 1841 was a very primitive one. Heating was by fireplace, lighting by candle, toilets were outdoors, and bathing was done in a portable tub. The kitchen was the center of a food complex that included icehouse, spring, root cellar, washhouse, and wood pile. Meat was preserved by smoking or salting, and root vegetables were kept in the cellar. Canned fruits and vegetables could be purchased at the store, but home canning was unknown until the Mason jar was invented in 1858. Under such conditions housework was hard labor.

The technology associated with the industrial revolution had a profound effect on the American home in the middle decades of the 19th century. The development of labor-saving devices, in turn, made possible the domestic science that Catherine Beecher had sought. In 1869 Catherine collaborated with her sister Harriet in producing *The American Woman's Home,* a work on the profession of housekeeping. The household described in this work revealed the impact of industrialization. A coal-burning Franklin stove replaced the fireplaces; gas lights replaced candles and kerosene lamps. There was a laundry in the basement, a complete bathroom on the second floor. Water pipes, connected to a municipal water system, replaced pump and well. The kitchen was equipped with cabinets, drawers, and counters.

Much was lacking in the ideal home of 1869. A gas stove, central heating, electrical appliances, and home refrigeration were unknown. But by encouraging the use of technology in the home, Catherine Beecher laid the foundation for a science of management, the art of housekeeping.

The world's first great modern suspension bridge took 13 years, $15 million, and 20 lives to build. John Roebling, the designer of the Brooklyn Bridge, was killed during its construction, and his son was crippled working on it. President Arthur attended the gala celebration of the opening of the bridge on May 24, 1883. The East River was jammed with boats, the air was filled with fireworks, and crowds of people lined both sides of the river. Many bridges have opened since then, but the Brooklyn Bridge remains to many "The Eighth Wonder of the World."

streets and talked of revolution. At the request of several state governors, President Hayes sent federal troops to the trouble spots, and the strike collapsed. Although there was no real danger of revolution, the violence of the strike revealed a new militancy in American labor.

THE KNIGHTS OF LABOR. The quest for a national labor organization led to the formation of the Knights of Labor. Founded in 1869, the Knights struggled through the depression as a secret organization, more social club than labor union. The return of prosperity in 1879 brought an increase in membership, and in that same year the Knights obtained a dynamic leader, Terence V. Powderly.

The Knights were a new kind of labor organization. *Members believed that trade unions divided labor by craft and ignored the unskilled.* The Knights sought a universal union of labor, skilled and unskilled, Blacks and immigrants, women and men.

Women workers were recruited by the Knights of Labor. In 1886 the union established a department of women's work, headed by Leonora Barry, a hosiery worker from Amsterdam, New York. Barry traveled around the country, establishing a total of 113 "separate but equal" women's locals of the Knights. Among the members, both Black and White, were rubber workers, farmers, weavers, pencilmakers, factory workers, and housekeepers.

The Knights reflected Powderly's interest in broad social reform. They endorsed political candidates and lent support to various crusades, from paper money to temperance.

403

KINDS OF JOBS IN THE LATE 19TH CENTURY

Occupation	Male	Female	Occupation	Male	Female
Agricultural pursuits			**Trade and transportation**		
Dairymen, dairywomen	16,161	1,734	Bankers, brokers	35,458	510
Farm owners, overseers	5,055,130	226,427	Boat operators, sailors	76,823	51
Hired hands (farm)	2,556,958	447,104	Bookkeepers, accountants	131,602	27,772
Lumberjacks	65,838	28	Company executives	39,683	217
Gardeners, florists	70,186	2,415	Drivers, teamsters	368,265	234
Wood choppers	33,665	32	Hostlers, stable hands	54,014	22
			Hucksters, peddlers	56,824	2,259
Professional service			Livery stable owners	26,710	47
Actors	23,200	4,583	Messengers, office helper	48,446	2,909
Architects, designers, drafters	17,134	327	Salesmen, saleswomen	205,943	58,451
Artists, art teachers	11,681	10,815	Railroad employees	460,771	1,442
Clergy	87,060	1,143	Stenographers, typewriters	12,148	21,270
Dentists	17,161	337	Telegraph, telephone operators	43,740	8,474
Engineers, surveyors	43,115	124			
Journalists	20,961	888	**Manufacturing and mechanical pursuits**		
Lawyers	89,422	208	Bakers	57,910	2,287
Musicians, music teachers	27,636	34,519	Blacksmiths	209,521	60
Literary, scientific persons	8,453	2,764	Bookbinders	12,298	11,560
Officials (government)	77,715	4,875	Brewers, maltsters	20,294	68
Physicians, surgeons	100,248	4,557	Broom and brush makers	8,949	1,166
Teachers, college professors	101,278	246,066	Cabinet makers	35,891	24
			Carpenters, joiners	618,044	198
Domestic and personal service			Confectioners	17,577	5,674
Barbers, hairdressers	82,157	2,825	Coopers	47,438	48
Bartenders (hired)	55,660	146	Dressmakers	836	292,668
Lodginghouse keepers	11,756	32,593	Fishers, oysterers	59,899	263
Hotel keepers	38,800	5,276	Harness and saddlemakers	42,647	833
Janitors, sextons	23,730	2,808	Millers	52,747	94
Laundry workers	31,831	216,631	Miners, quarry workers	386,872	376
Nurses, midwives	6,190	41,396	Paperhangers	12,315	54
Restaurant keepers	16,867	2,416	Photographers	17,839	2,201
Saloon keepers	69,110	2,275	Tailors	123,516	64,509
Servants, waiters	238,152	1,216,639	Wheelwrights	12,855	1
Guards, police officers, detectives	74,350	279			

The Knights gained strength in the early 1880's by supporting a series of successful strikes against western railroads. In 1885 they took on the Wabash Railroad, owned by the hated Jay Gould, and won. Membership soared from 100,000 to 700,000. Then a series of poorly planned strikes failed, and Powderly began to show his weaknesses as a union leader. The Haymarket affair was the beginning of the end for the Knights of Labor.

THE HAYMARKET RIOT. The idea of an eight-hour work day for all workers became popular in the 1880's, and the Knights were in the forefront of the movement. Prosperity gave labor more bargaining power, and strikes spread rapidly. By the spring of 1886, several hundred thousand workers were on strike in various parts of the country.

In Chicago in May 1886, the Knights helped organize a strike against the McCormick Harvester Company. *Anarchists* moved in to take advantage of the ill feeling. When a striker died in a clash with company police, the anarchists called a protest meeting in Chicago's Haymarket Square. City police appeared at the meeting to maintain order. Someone threw a bomb at the police, killing seven officers.

Anarchists are extreme radicals who oppose all forms of government.

Eight radicals were convicted of the crime on rather flimsy evidence, but the real losers were the Knights. Although the Knights had nothing to do with the bombing, the public associated them with violence and radicalism. Membership declined. By the time of Powderly's death in 1892, the organization was virtually dead.

THE AMERICAN FEDERATION OF LABOR. In the same year as the Haymarket affair, 1886, an organization was formed to replace the Knights of Labor. *The American Federation of Labor was the brainchild of Samuel Gompers, an official in the National Cigarmakers Union.* True to his background, Gompers wanted organizations of national craft unions. Each union would represent skilled workers in a separate trade or craft, such as plumbing, printing, and carpentry; Gompers argued that only skilled workers had sufficient bargaining power to form strong unions. The unskilled could too easily be replaced. That, he believed, was the fatal weakness of the Knights.

Because each trade union was zealous in protecting its powers and independence, Gompers proposed a loose federation. Each trade would run its own affairs. *By confining itself to trade unions, the A. F. of L. embraced only a small minority of American workers.* It ignored the unskilled, a group that included many immigrants and Blacks.

IMMIGRANTS AND THE A. F. OF L. Because many immigrants were unskilled workers, they were ignored by the A. F. of L. Many skilled immigrant workers who could have joined unions were opposed to union membership. *These immigrants objected to the restrictions imposed by unions, such as union rules, dues, and wage controls.* They had left Europe to be as free as possible. Also, many believed that however bad working conditions were in the United States, they were worse in Europe. Nevertheless, many union leaders, including Gompers, were of foreign birth, and several labor organizations depended on immigrants for their membership.

Immigrant workers also met widespread prejudice among native-born American workers. From 1870 to 1900, around 11 million men, women, and children came to America. A large percentage of these people entered the work force, competing with native-born workers for jobs. They often worked for lower wages and were used by

In 1874 the owners of the Pennsylvania coal mines cut wages to below minimum without reducing the prices for rent or for services in their company town. When the workers struck, the owners imported labor from Europe. By 1876 the miners had been starved into submission. Here, miners' wives, facing eviction, attack a sheriff's posse in front of their company-owned homes.

employers to break strikes. Prejudice on the part of native-born Americans deepened.

BLACKS AND THE A. F. OF L. *Most A. F. of L. unions excluded Black workers.* Prejudice and the fact that the majority of Blacks were unskilled workers explained why most Blacks were kept out of unions. Union constitutions did not exclude Black members, but practice did. As they did with immigrants, employers in the North used Blacks as strike-breakers, intensifying feelings of racial prejudice.

WOMEN AND THE A. F. OF L. *The A. F. of L. did not pursue women members,*

although its leaders at one time expressed interest in organizing them. One of the member unions of the A. F. of L. was the International Ladies' Garment Workers Union. However, many unions did not admit women to membership. On the other hand, the United Mine Workers employed Mary "Mother" Jones to organize local unions and to educate and aid workers.

GOMPERS AND THE A. F. OF L. Although the A. F. of L. fragmented the labor movement, Gompers might have been correct in believing that federation meant strength. The public was generally hostile to all forms of labor organization, and without public sympathy, the unskilled could do little. Gompers planned to organize the strong, thus creating a nucleus on which a national labor movement could build. By 1900 the A. F. of L. had about half a million members. It was hardly "big labor," but it was a start.

Gompers stamped his personality on the A. F. of L., and it was decidedly conservative. He believed that Powderly's interest in broad social reforms had spread his energies and divided the Knights. **_Under Gompers, the A. F. of L. stayed clear of politics and concentrated on the issues most important to labor._** The A. F. of L. called for an eight-hour day and a six-day work week, higher wages and better working conditions, and legislation to protect workers on dangerous jobs and to compensate them and their families in case of injury or death.

Until Gompers' death in 1924, the A. F. of L. never endorsed a political candidate. Although the C. I. O. (Congress of Industrial Organizations), which was formed in the 1930's, was more politically minded, the American labor movement has generally adhered to Gompers' strategy of focusing on "bread and butter" demands.

Section Review

1. Identify or explain: National Labor Union, Terence Powderly, Samuel Gompers, Knights of Labor, the Haymarket affair.
2. List the changing conditions of industrial workers that led to the rise of a union movement.
3. Compare the aims and the methods of the three trade union movements discussed in the section.
4. What important advantages did the A. F. of L. have? What were its weaknesses as a national trade union movement?

Sidenote to History

Mother Jones: Labor Organizer

Among the most colorful and hard-working individuals in the early history of the American labor movement was an Irish immigrant named Mary Harris Jones. From 1870 to around 1920, Mother Jones, as she was called, traveled throughout the United States, attracting attention to the injustices suffered by many workers.

Mary Jones was born in Ireland in 1830. She came to the United States via Toronto, Canada. She settled in Memphis, Tennessee, and worked as a dressmaker and teacher. In the early 1860's she married and began a family. Her personal happiness was short-lived, however, because in 1867 her husband and four children died in a yellow-fever epidemic.

During the 1870's, as she traveled to different parts of the country as an organizer of the United Mine Workers, Mother Jones observed many of the horrible working and living conditions under which miners and their families suffered. She was primarily responsible for unionizing the coal miners who worked in West Virginia.

Later in her life, the abuse of children in the Pennsylvania textile factories again brought Mother Jones into the forefront to protest. She organized a band of boys and girls, many of whom had been maimed while working near machinery, to march to President Theodore Roosevelt's summer home to voice their grievances. Although the President did not see the group, the public was aroused and influenced the Pennsylvania legislature to pass child labor laws. Mother Jones died in 1930 at the age of 100. She had spent her long life trying to gain justice and dignity for America's working men, women, and children.

Chapter 16 Review

Bird's-Eye View

Perhaps the most important development of the late 19th century in the United States was the coming of the Industrial Revolution and the changes it brought to American life. A new class of industrial engineers organized the land, labor, mineral resources, and capital of the nation to maximize production and profit.

This period saw the emergence of the corporation. Inventions, improved transportation and communication, and the use of assembly-line techniques made possible the growth of huge, nationally based industries with enormous financial and political influence.

Post-Civil War America experienced a revolution in the work and life patterns of its people. A nation of small independent farmers, craft workers, and merchants became one of big business and factory workers. Immigrants and farmers alike poured into the large industrial centers to compete for jobs. The streetcar introduced the possibility of urban sprawl, and so the cities grew. Even the mode of shopping was transformed, as the department store brought to consumers a wide variety of products at standardized prices.

As business grew, complex forms of business organization came into being—horizontal and vertical combinations, trusts, and holding companies. By controlling an industry from raw materials to retailing, corporations could eliminate competition. The Sherman Antitrust Act was the first attempt to outlaw "combinations in restraint of trade."

Another response to the growth of industrial power was the birth of a national labor movement. From the Knights of Labor and the American Federation of Labor, American workers learned the advantages of organizing for their own protection.

Vocabulary

Define or identify each of the following:

steel	capital	trust
mass production	rebate	wholesale price index
Industrial Revolution	cartel	anarchist

Review Questions

1. Name the three factors that were the basis of the Industrial Revolution in the United States.
2. Explain the term "mass production." How did each of the following help the development of mass production: standard parts, the assembly line, division of labor?
3. What is meant by a national business firm? What part did railroads play in the development of a national market?
4. Contrast vertical combination to horizontal combination as forms of business growth.
5. Why did Congress pass the Sherman Antitrust Act?
6. Describe the working conditions of the average industrial worker in the late 1800's.
7. Name the three early labor unions. Identify who each one appealed to and the cause (if any) of each one's decline.

Reviewing Social Studies Skills

1. Use a dictionary to define "pig iron." Then, using the graph on page 388, answer the following questions:
   a. What was the combined production of pig iron and steel in 1870? In 1890? In 1900?
   b. Did pig iron or steel production increase the most by 1900?
2. Read two accounts of the Haymarket affair other than the one in your textbook. Use textbooks or other sources in your library. What differences do you notice in the way facts are presented in different sources? How do you explain the differences?
3. Assume you are a reporter about to interview John D. Rockefeller. Develop at least four questions to ask him. Then, write what you think his responses would be to each question.
4. Using the chart on page 404, answer the following questions:
   a. In which occupation are there the most women? The most men?
   b. In which occupation are there the fewest women? The fewest men?
   c. In general, what types of jobs are most available to women?

Reading for Meaning

1. Using the heading "Ways of Organizing a Business," list, and then define, the new ways in which businesses were organized after the Civil War. What words do the authors use to convey whether they consider these means of organizing ethical or unethical?
2. Write a paragraph entitled "The Worker and the Machine." Explain how machines have both helped and harmed workers.
3. Cooperation and competition are fundamental processes in American industry. Find three examples of each in the chapter. Why are some forms of cooperation considered harmful to society?
4. Look at the chart on page 404. You will notice that the total number of male jobs listed is much higher than the total number of female jobs. Why do you suppose this is true? Why are the jobs that some females hold not included on a list like this? What do you think the status of women was in the late 19th century?

Bibliography

The best general study of the rise of industry in America is Thomas C. Cochran's and William Miller's *The Age of Enterprise: A Social History of Industrial America* (Harper & Row).

Two good biographies are Frederick Lewis Allen's *The Great Pierpont Morgan* (Harper & Row) and Matthew Josephson's *Edison* (McGraw-Hill).

Katherine Shippen's *This Union Cause* (Harper & Row) describes the growth of America's labor unions.

Mary Wade's *The Master Builders* (Little, Brown) tells of Hill, Bell, Carnegie, and Ford.

Chapter 17

1859-1900

The Last Frontier

Henry P. Comstock came from a Connecticut family that could trace its lineage to the Puritans. Comstock had come west with the forty-niners and had drifted around the gold fields for a decade. He had a reputation as the laziest man in the "diggings." Friends had nicknamed him Old Pancake because he was too lazy to bake bread. By the spring of 1859, Comstock and other prospectors had moved into the Washoe country on the eastern slope of the Sierra Nevada Mountains. The miners lived and built as they pleased.

The date was June 10, 1859. Henry P. Comstock was jogging along the trail on a mule so tiny Comstock's legs dangled in the sagebrush. He was climbing a mountain that had been hopefully named Gold Hill when he came upon two old friends, Peter O'Reilly and Pat McLaughlin. They were working through some strange blue earth to build a reservoir for spring water. Water was scarce in the mountains. Miners needed it to wash gold from the earth. Seeing specks of gold in the blue earth, Comstock decided to lay claim to the place. He persuaded the two Irishmen that he had purchased the land the winter before, and so they brought him into the partnership.

While Comstock sat idly by, talking of "my mine" to anyone who would listen, his partners resumed their digging. Soon they came upon a heavy blue rock. Suspecting that it might be valuable, they sent a sample across the mountains to California to be tested. The "blue stuff" turned out to be three fourths silver ore and one fourth pure gold, worth 3,876 dollars a ton! It was the richest find in mining history. When the Comstock Lode—as it came to be called—was finally exhausted some 20 years later, it had yielded ore worth 306 million dollars.

Chapter Objectives

After you have finished reading this chapter, you should be able to:
1. Describe the characteristics of the mining frontier.
2. Describe, in chronological order, the events that led to the loss of American Indian territory.
3. Explain how the government helped finance railroad construction.
4. Trace the history of the American cowboy from the time of the Spanish Americans to the introduction of barbed wire.
5. List the problems that farmers on the Great Plains had to overcome before they could farm successfully.

The mine brought fame to Henry P. Comstock, but it brought little else. He and his partners sold out for a few thousand dollars to the first investors who came along. News of the discovery brought a rush of prospectors into the Washoe country, where they founded Virginia City. (See map, page 412.) But few came away rich. The *mother lode* came near the surface at only two points, and then it ran deep into the heart of the mountain. Mining companies with the capital to dig tunnels and shore them with wooden beams were the beneficiaries of the bonanza.

A *lode* is a large mineral deposit in the earth. A *mother lode* is slang for the largest part of a huge mineral deposit.

Nevertheless, the gold rush populated western Nevada. Within a few years Virginia City boasted a population of 15,000. Soon, its citizens demanded statehood. The prospect of three more electoral votes in 1864 appealed to the Lincoln administration, and Nevada was admitted to the Union. The story of Henry Comstock, Virginia City, and the state of Nevada is only one of the many marvels of the last frontier.

1. The Mining Frontier

THE LAST FRONTIER. *The California gold rush of 1849 brought America's westward movement to the shores of the Pacific Ocean, but it skipped over a vast part of the continent.* Going west from the Missouri River, the overland traveler crossed in succession the Great Plains, the Rocky Mountains, and the Utah-Nevada basin. Each seemed more uninviting than the last. Dry and treeless in some parts, impossibly rugged in others, this last frontier could not be tamed in the usual way. It was too dry for

With the discovery of gold in the West, dozens of new towns sprang up all through the Rocky Mountains. This is the main street of Last Chance Gulch, which later became Helena, Montana.

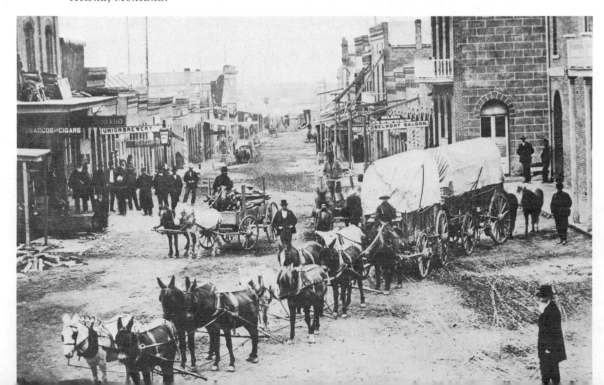

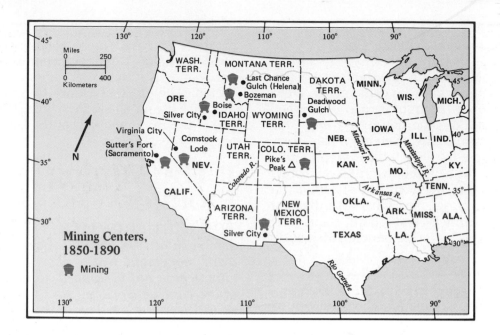

Mining Centers, 1850–1890

Map labels: WASH. TERR.; MONTANA TERR.; Last Chance Gulch (Helena); Bozeman; DAKOTA TERR.; MINN.; WIS.; MICH.; ORE.; Boise; Silver City; IDAHO TERR.; WYOMING TERR.; Deadwood Gulch; IOWA; ILL.; IND.; Virginia City; Comstock Lode; UTAH TERR.; NEB.; Missouri R.; Mississippi R.; Sutter's Fort (Sacramento); NEV.; COLO. TERR.; Pike's Peak; KAN.; MO.; KY.; Colorado R.; CALIF.; ARIZONA TERR.; NEW MEXICO TERR.; Silver City; OKLA.; Arkansas R.; TENN.; ARK.; MISS.; ALA.; TEXAS; LA.; Rio Grande; Miles 0 250; Kilometers 0 400; N; Mining

normal agriculture. And the lack of trees meant there would be no wood for houses, fencing, or fuel.

With good reason, pre-Civil War Americans passed over this area and swept into the more inviting environments of California and Oregon. After the war, pioneers moved into the Great Plains and the Rockies, but they were a different breed. Farmers, who had once been the leaders of settlement, lagged behind. In the forefront were miners and cattle ranchers.

"PIKE'S PEAK OR BUST." In 1859, the year of the Washoe rush in Nevada, another stream of wagons crossed Kansas. The rush started when a prospector turned up in Kansas City with a sackful of gold dust that he had washed out in the South Platte River, near Pike's Peak. (See map above.)

With "Pike's Peak or Bust" scribbled on their wagons, farmers and city dwellers— many of whom had never seen a nugget— started for Colorado. Unfamiliar with mining methods, many returned east, "busted" after a few weeks. But enough gold

was found to attract more experienced prospectors, and soon there were gold **strikes** all over Colorado. Denver mushroomed like Virginia City, Nevada, and before long people were demanding a government. ***When Kansas entered the Union in 1861, Congress created the territory of Colorado.***

Strike is used here to mean "discovery."

THE MONTANA GOLD RUSH. *From Colorado prospectors fanned north into Wyoming and Montana.* In 1862 promising discoveries were made at Bannack, Montana, and nearby Alder Gulch, where another Virginia City exploded onto the map. Two years later Last Chance Gulch revealed a rich vein of gold, and in a matter of weeks, the city of Helena became the largest in the territory. (See map above.)

Chunks of gold, or nuggets, were the most dazzling feature of Montana mining. Every valley seemed to hold a few. Over the next 20 years, some 500 mines dug into Montana's gulches yielded 175 million dollars in precious metals.

THE BLACK HILLS. *From Montana the mining frontier spread west into Idaho and east into the Dakotas.* In 1874 gold was discovered in the Black Hills of South Dakota by an army force constructing a road to Fort Laramie.

The discovery brought the mining frontier into direct conflict with the Indians. *With the development of mining communities and the movement of more people into the West, pressure had been mounting between the settlers and the American Indians.* For a decade the American Indians had watched the invasion of their territory with growing dismay. In the mid-1860's the Sioux, under their leader, Red Cloud, had gone to war to prevent the army from building forts and a road across their hunting grounds. The war ended in 1868 with an agreement guaranteeing the Black Hills to the Sioux as a permanent reservation. With the discovery of gold, the government tried to persuade the Sioux to alter the agreement, but it failed. Prospectors rushed into the Black Hills anyway, and the city of Deadwood sprang up to serve them. The Sioux took up arms once again. Other tribes joined, and before long the whole West was in an uproar.

Section Review

1. Mapping: Using the map on page 412, locate the mining frontier. Using the physical map on page xiv, identify the kind of land found here, and what it can be used for. How does this explain the fact that this area was also the last frontier?
2. Identify or explain: Henry Comstock, Red Cloud, mother lode, Pike's Peak, Black Hills.
3. Who were the first settlers of the last frontier? Why was this area inviting to this group and not to others?
4. Why did the gold rush in the Black

Hills bring prospectors into conflict with American Indians? How did American Indians react to this conflict?

2. "I Will Fight No More Forever"

THE END OF THE BUFFALO. *By 1870 the American Indians of the plains and mountains had been forced to accept sizable reservations, such as the Sioux home in the Black Hills.* They surrendered the rest of the West to the government. The American Indians might have remained there—despite the trespass of gold miners—had it not been for the destruction of the *buffalo.* The Plains Indians had built their entire culture around the buffalo herds. *The killing of the buffalo doomed the Plains Indians as well.*

The true name of the animal that Americans call *buffalo* is bison. The buffalo is actually a Southeast Asian animal.

The buffalo had adapted well to the harsh environment of the plains. They could withstand the frigid winters, go for long periods without water, and thrive on the rough prairie grasses. The buffalo were so numerous that the first explorers compared them to fish in the sea. General Philip Sheridan, commanding officer in the southern plains, placed their number at 100 million. The Plains Indians relied on them for all the necessities of life—food, clothing, and shelter. And because the buffalo were nomadic, the Indians were, too. They followed the herds as the herds followed the seasons.

In 1870 someone discovered that buffalo hides were commercially usable. Sent a few samples, a New York tannery found they could be made into machine belts. The following year a thousand hunters fanned out onto the plains, killing everything in sight.

In this painting by George Catlin, Catlin himself is the figure at the right. Both he and his Indian companion dressed in wolfskins in order to get as close as possible to the buffalo herd. Having shed the skins, the Indian is getting ready to hunt.

In addition to the commercial value of buffalo, some army officers and government agents encouraged the killing of buffalo as a means of keeping the American Indians on reservations. They believed that if they destroyed the main source of food, clothing, and shelter for the Plains Indians, the Indians would have to stay on the reservations.

Armed with a fast horse and a repeating rifle, a good hunter could kill up to 300 animals a day, while a small army of skinners trailed behind, ready to begin their work. The skins sold for a dollar apiece, and the carcasses were left to rot in the sun. The waste was shocking. Soon the stench of rotting flesh fouled the air of the plains.

THE LAST INDIAN WARS. By 1874 there were not enough buffalo left to justify the expense of hunting. It was then that the Plains Indians realized what had happened to their livelihood. They went to war in the summer of 1874.

From Kansas to Arizona, war parties attacked settlers, stagecoaches, and wagon trains; they ambushed army patrols. Hundreds of people died. Brutality was evident on both sides. The army struck back quickly. Expeditions rode into Indian country, burning villages, arresting women and children, and shooting all who resisted. *By the end of 1875, the fighting on the southern plains was ended.* The tribes were back on reservations. Without the buffalo they would be increasingly dependent on the federal government for food, clothing, and housing.

WARFARE IN THE BLACK HILLS. Then the Black Hills erupted in warfare. Having been guaranteed the Black Hills as a permanent reservation in 1868, the Sioux were angered by White invasions of their lands. (See map, page 416.) Bands of Sioux, led by Sitting Bull and Crazy Horse, left the reservation and roamed the northern plains, living off the land as they always had.

In the summer of 1876, three armies went after the Sioux to drive them back to the Black Hills reservation. One wing of the Seventh Cavalry regiment under George A. Custer was surrounded by Indians near Sitting Bull's camp and this force was annihilated in what became known as Custer's Last Stand. The Seventh Cavalry losses totaled 276.

Despite such victories, the American Indians could not survive for long without the buffalo. They straggled back to the reservation in groups. Sitting Bull and a band of followers fled to Canada. But even he surrendered in 1881.

CHIEF JOSEPH AND THE NEZ PERCÉ. Some smaller mountain tribes were unable to resist their confinement on reservations. One memorable exception were the Nez Percé. *The Nez Percé Indians were a seminomadic tribe, long held in high esteem for their intelligence and independence.* They gave Lewis and Clark a friendly reception in 1804 and offered no resistance to the stream of wagons that passed through their Snake River paradise to Oregon. But when the mining frontier infringed on their country in the 1860's and the federal government demanded land cessions, they resisted.

Led by Chief Joseph, the Nez Percé rejected the government's gifts and promises year after year. Tension increased between the Nez Percé and the miners. In 1877 younger members of the tribe attacked White settlements without Chief Joseph's permission. When the army arrived to punish the attackers, the reluctant leader was forced to fight.

Organizing his tribe into a disciplined fighting unit, as he tried to make his way to Canada, Chief Joseph fought a running battle with the army. Taking women and children with him, the Nez Percé leader slipped through mountain passes and eluded pursuit. In one canyon, he was caught by surprise, but marshaled his force and defeated the surrounding army. Later he got revenge by stampeding the army's horses through its camp.

With four armies in pursuit, he was cornered at last at Bear Paw Mountain in Montana. In a dramatic moment of surrender, he

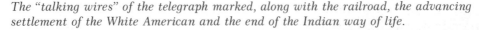

The "talking wires" of the telegraph marked, along with the railroad, the advancing settlement of the White American and the end of the Indian way of life.

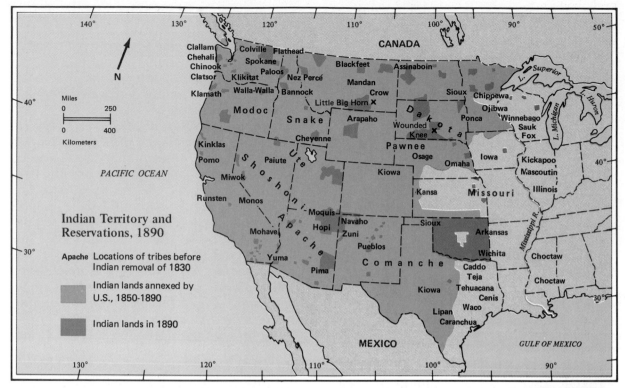

Indian Territory and
Reservations, 1890

Apache Locations of tribes before
Indian removal of 1830

Indian lands annexed by
U.S., 1850-1890

Indian lands in 1890

---

informed his pursuers that his people were cold, hungry, and wounded and could go no farther. He called the roll of warriors who had fallen and then said simply, "My heart is sick and sad. From where the sun now stands, I will fight no more forever." In 75 days of fighting on the run, he had led the United States Cavalry across 2,114 kilometers (1,321 miles) of the most rugged mountains on the continent. It was an outstanding feat in the annals of warfare.

MORE BLOODSHED. Chief Joseph's fight was the last Indian war, but not, unfortunately, the end of the bloodshed. *Isolated bands fled the reservations, causing minor crises throughout the 1880's.* The most famous of these bands were led by the Apache leaders Geronimo, Mangas Coloradas (Red Sleeves), Cochise, and Victorio. The final episode was, in many ways, the saddest of all—the army's massacre of Sioux Ghost Dancers at Wounded Knee in 1890.

THE GHOST DANCE RELIGION. When their lands were taken from them and the buffalo, their source of livelihood, were gone, the Sioux turned to religion. The religion they embraced had originated among the Paiutes of the Nevada mountains. It was a mixture of Indian and Christian beliefs. It envisioned an end to time, a day of judgment, and a heaven on earth. But heaven resembled the Indians' past life: The Whites would depart, the buffalo would return, and the dead warriors would rise from their graves. Worship centered on a dance ritual that was supposed to hasten the day of judgment and bring back the dead. Whites called it the Ghost Dance.

Many of the western tribes practiced the Ghost Dance religion, but no one seized on it more eagerly than the Sioux. A proud tribe, once rulers of the plains, the Sioux were jammed onto five barren reservations at the edge of the Black Hills. With the buffalo gone, the Sioux were dependent on federal food rations. In a misguided economy move, in 1889 Congress cut in half the beef rations for the Sioux reservations. To their other miseries was added hunger.

THE ARMY ARRIVES. *Sensing that the Ghost Dance religion meant resistance, the agents in charge of the reservations tried to stop the chants and dancing.*

When the Sioux ignored them, the agents sent frantic reports to Washington that the situation was getting out of control. In the spring of 1890, the army was given control of the Sioux reservations, and the Seventh Cavalry entered the situation.

The Seventh and the Sioux had a history of hatred, going back to Custer's fall at the Little Bighorn River in 1876. Sitting Bull,

Sidenote to History

The Adventures of Annie Oakley

The day of the cowhand was a short one, but the Wild West lived on in legend and in theater. No one did more to blend the romance of the West and the glamour of "show biz" than William F. Cody. He earned the nickname Buffalo Bill when he was a professional hunter. When the buffalo slaughter ended, he formed a Wild West show and began touring the country. In 1887 Queen Victoria invited him to give a performance at her Golden Jubilee.

The heart of "Buffalo Bill's Wild West Show" was sharpshooting. Using a rifle, a sharpshooter smashed rows of glass balls from the back of a running horse or put a hole through a coin thrown into the air. For many years the star of the show was W. F. "Doc" Carver, who had spent his boyhood as a captive among the Sioux. Carver's greatest feat was smashing 59,350 out of 60,000 glass balls over a period of six days. He was driven to such a heroic effort by competition from a newcomer to the Wild West Show, a short, young woman from Ohio named Annie Oakley.

Annie Oakley was born in 1860, the fifth of seven children in a poverty-stricken farm family. Too frail to do the usual farm chores, she was sent into the woods to shoot game for the family dinner table. By the time she was 10, she was shooting more game than the family could eat and was selling it in the market. A few years later, she began entering shooting contests at county fairs. In 1875 she outdueled a touring-exhibition shooter named Frank Butler. Butler brought her into his act, and they were married a year later. Their romance was immortalized many years later in the Broadway musical comedy *Annie Get Your Gun.*

Butler taught her how to put on a show, and before long Annie had a spectacular act that included breaking glass balls from horseback, shooting cigars from the mouths of volunteer spectators, and making designs with bullet holes. She handled firearms like a gunfighter.

The Butlers joined Cody's Wild West Show in 1885 and accompanied him on his tour of Europe two years later. Annie Oakley was a sensation in Europe, where women had never been permitted to handle guns. Queen Victoria gave her a medal. The Grand Duke of Russia, a famous sharpshooter, challenged her to a contest and lost. The Crown Prince of Germany let her shoot a cigarette out of his mouth. She was one of the most famous women in the world when she returned to the United States. Long after the "Wild West" faded from public memory, the legend of Annie Oakley remained bright.

the victor, was still alive and was nursing his hatred of the Whites. He was reputed to be a leader of the Ghost Dancers. His followers gave a menacing turn to the ritual by donning white shirts, which, when given a special blessing, were considered bulletproof.

When the army arrived, thousands of Sioux fled the reservations and hid in the neighboring Bad Lands, an area of South Dakota where wind and water erosion had created a maze of hills and hidden canyons. Ghost Dancing died down during the fall of 1890. Only Sitting Bull's camp continued the ritual. The army sent Indian police (employed by the Indian Agency) to arrest Sitting Bull. When his followers objected, the police shot the aging leader in the head. The army then moved against the American Indians in the Bad Lands. The Sioux did not resist. On December 27 they returned to the reservations.

THE FIGHT AT WOUNDED KNEE. The next day, December 28, 1890, four troops of the Seventh Cavalry—about 200 soldiers, commanded by Major S. M. Whiteside—encountered a band of Sioux who had fled the army and were camped on the edge of the Bad Lands. The group numbered 340. Less than a third were warriors. The rest were women and children. The band's leader, Big Foot, was ill with pneumonia and too sick to ride a horse. He surrendered peacefully. The cavalry troop conducted his band to the village of Wounded Knee. There Big Foot made camp, and the soldiers set up their tents nearby. General Nelson Miles, commanding the entire Seventh Cavalry, sent in two more regiments.

The next morning the soldiers surrounded the Sioux camp. On a nearby hill they placed four Hotchkiss guns—rapid-fire cannons that shot two-inch explosive shells. The cavalry then demanded that the Sioux surrender their guns. What happened next has always been shrouded in confusion. Accounts differ. But when the smoke cleared, some 130 Sioux lay dead. Perhaps

another hundred had crawled off into the brush to die of their wounds. Twenty four soldiers were dead and 33 wounded. *Wounded Knee was a sad ending to many years of mistreatment.*

THE RESERVATION SYSTEM. Even when the wars between the American Indians and the Whites were over, the problem was far from solved. *The reservation system never worked well, and the American Indians detested it.* Most of the later Indian wars began when tribes escaped from the barren and dreary reservations and tried to return to their familiar hunting grounds. The federal agents who supervised the reservations were often incompetent and sometimes corrupt. Even the best of them had little respect for the American Indian culture and made deliberate efforts to nationalize the tribes. They prohibited traditional dress and dances. Some even forced the men to wear their hair short. A few reformers argued that the American Indian traditions and culture ought to be preserved, but they were a tiny minority.

THE DAWES ACT. In 1881 Helen Hunt Jackson recorded in *A Century of Dishonor* the dismal history of White–American Indian relations—the unnecessary wars, broken treaties, briberies, and betrayals. *This was the first widely read criticism of Indian policy, and the book provided ammunition for the reformers.* Because the reservation system seemed a failure, reformers took up the idea—first suggested by Thomas Jefferson—of giving American Indians individual parcels of land and absorbing them into White society as if they were immigrants.

Although well intentioned, the allotment scheme played into the hands of miners and cattle ranchers who looked greedily at the remaining American Indian lands. Breaking up the reservations was precisely what they wanted. They joined forces with the reformers. President Grover Cleveland lent his sup-

Viewpoints of History

Three Views of Wounded Knee

Historians put together the past by using documentary records. There are many such records of the battle of Wounded Knee, and they vary greatly. Three are included here. The first is given by Black Elk, a holy man of the Oglala Sioux, who arrived on the scene shortly after the fighting ended. The second is the report of the editor of the Chadron, Nebraska, *Democrat*. The third is an excerpt from a telegram that was sent to the War Department by General Nelson A. Miles, commander of the army units operating in the Sioux reservations.

Black Elk. "After the soldiers marched away, I heard from my friend Dog Chief how the trouble started. He was right there by Yellow Bird. This is the way it was:

"In the morning the soldiers began to take all the guns away from the Big Foots, who were camped in the flat below the little hill. The people had stacked most of their guns, and even their knives, by the tepee where Big Foot was lying sick.

"Some of the people had not yet given up their guns, and so the soldiers were searching all the tepees. There was a man called Yellow Bird, and he and another man were standing in front of the tepee where Big Foot was lying sick. They had white sheets over them, and they had guns under these. An officer came to search them. He took

the other man's gun and then started to take Yellow Bird's. But Yellow Bird would not let go. He wrestled with the officer, and while they were wrestling, the gun went off and killed the officer. As soon as the gun went off, an officer shot and killed Big Foot, who was lying sick inside the tepee.

"Then, suddenly, nobody knew what was happening, except that the soldiers were all shooting and the wagon guns began going off right in among the people. The women and children ran into the gulch, and the soldiers shot them as they ran. The warriors rushed to where they had piled their guns and knives. They fought soldiers only with their hands until they got their guns."

C. W. Allen, editor of the Chadron, Nebraska, *Democrat*. "After all the guns in the village had been secured, the soldiers began to search the Indian men, who were held in a circle. They disarmed eight or ten of the men when a brave jumped up and said something and fired at the soldier who was standing guard over the arms. The first gun had no sooner been fired than it was followed by hundreds of others, and the battle was on. The fighting continued for about a half hour and then was continued in skirmish. . . ."

General Nelson A. Miles. "These Indians under Big Foot were among the most desperate. Before leaving their camps on the Cheyenne River, they broke their wagons and started south for the Bad Lands. They evidently meant to go to war. Troops were placed between them and the Bad Lands, and they never succeeded in joining the hostiles there. All their movements were anticipated, and their severe loss at the hands of the Seventh Cavalry may be a wholesome lesson to the other Sioux."

---

port to the cause, and in 1887 Congress passed the Dawes Allotment Act.

Working on the same principle as the Homestead Act, the Dawes Act offered 64 hectares (160 acres) of public land to every American Indian head of family, with *lesser amounts for orphaned children.* To prevent the Indians from immediately selling the property to speculators, the government retained legal ownership for 25 years. The American Indians were not forced to leave the reservations. But to encourage the

In this humorous painting, John Steuart Curry depicts the race to settle the Oklahoma Territory in 1889. What aspects of the pioneer spirit do you think the artist is satirizing?

Indians to do so, the states in which they were to settle agreed to give them full legal rights, including the right to vote.

AMERICAN INDIAN HOLDINGS DECREASE. As had happened so often before, the American Indians were the losers. The government, committed to the principle of individual ownership, was less able to resist the demands of land-hungry Whites. It steadily sliced away at the reservations. *By 1900 American Indian holdings in the West were half what they had been in 1887.* The biggest slice came in Oklahoma, which had been regarded as Indian Territory since the time of Andrew Jackson.

The Dawes Act did not apply to the Five Civilized Tribes, who had been moved to Oklahoma in the 1830's. President Cleveland purchased from them the unsettled western part of Oklahoma. On his last day in office, Cleveland signed a law opening the Oklahoma Territory to homesteaders. Each settler would be given 64 hectares (160 acres) of land as quickly as he or she could

claim them. Cleveland's successor, Benjamin Harrison, proclaimed that entry time would be noon on April 22, 1889. He sent the army to patrol the borders to make sure that no one got there sooner to stake an illegal claim.

"HARRISON'S HOSS RACE." By 1889 the public lands were nearly gone. Oklahoma was the last territory of any size where the poor settler could get a free farm. As the appointed day drew near, people by the thousands lined up on the border for "Harrison's hoss race." The noon signal brought a wild rush. Wagons turned over, crashed into one another, and sank in the sandy stream beds. Stagecoach drivers whipped their teams, special trains chugged across the landscape, and farmers fought over windswept parcels.

As usual, a few profited. Many were disappointed. Clever "sooners" entered the territory ahead of time and hid themselves until the official entry time. Some were busy plowing their fields when the legal homesteaders arrived. *Towns like Oklahoma City and Guthrie sprouted overnight, even faster than the western mining towns.* Speculators who dealt in town lots became territorial millionaires.

The American search for a western paradise came to an end in Oklahoma. In the following year, 1890, the U.S. Census Bureau announced that all land within the country contained at least two people per square mile. The frontier was gone.

THE FAILURE OF THE DAWES ACT. The American Indians who accepted the government's offer of a homestead fared no better than those remaining on the reservation. To be successful, farming requires knowledge and experience. Many of the men and women who went west to take up homesteads failed. Not surprisingly, many Indians, who knew only hunting and fishing, also failed. *More would probably have succeeded had they possessed decent land, but, by the late 1880's, the best lands were in private hands.*

Although the government recognized that most American Indians lacked the technical knowledge for farming, Congress failed to appropriate funds for education and training. The "century of dishonor" became a century and a half before the government attended to the problem.

In 1924 Congress granted full citizenship and voting rights to all American Indians, partly as a reward for those who served in the armed forces during World War I. Except for the fortunate few whose Oklahoma lands contained oil, most Indians continued to live in poverty, however. *In 1934 Congress belatedly acknowledged the failure of the Dawes Act by authorizing the restoration of tribal organizations and local control of reservations for those groups who still clung together.* Difficulties remained, of course. But the government at last gave the American Indians a choice in their own destiny.

Section Review

1. Mapping: Study the map of Indian Territory and reservations on page 416. Then compare it with the other two maps in this chapter. Does your comparison confirm what you have read in Section 2? If so, how?
2. Identify or explain: Sitting Bull, General Custer, Wounded Knee, Chief Joseph, Geronimo, Helen Hunt Jackson, "Harrison's hoss race."
3. How did the loss of the buffalo change the American Indians' way of life?
4. List the provisions of the Dawes Act. Compare the goals of those who supported the act with the results of the act.
5. Write a brief paragraph describing the Oklahoma land rush.

3. Building the Transcontinental Railroads

THE NEED FOR RAILROADS. One more change was necessary before the West could be settled and farmed—the building of railroads. The West was utterly dependent on railroads. In the East large amounts of goods moved by water—along the seacoast, on rivers, or by canal. In the West the rivers were too shallow for steamboats, and the distances were too vast for canals. The stagecoach and the covered wagon served the first pioneers. *But only the railroad could carry the bounty of the West—cattle, wheat, lumber, and metals—to the marketplaces of the world.*

THE RACE TO UTAH. *When Congress decided to undertake construction of a transcontinental railroad during the Civil War, it gave the job to two companies.* The Union Pacific was to build west from

Omaha, Nebraska, and the Central Pacific was to extend east from Sacramento, California. To help finance the enormous project, Congress gave the railroads government bonds and tracts of land. Because the size of the land grant depended on the amount of track laid, Congress, in effect, created competition between the two companies.

Both companies started slowly. The Central Pacific had to begin by crossing the Sierra Nevada Mountains. Some 9,000 laborers, most of whom were Chinese, carved the roadbed out of rock with blasting powder, hammer, and pickaxe. Accidents cost hundreds of lives. It took them two years to break through to the Nevada plateau. The Union Pacific had an easier roadbed until it reached the Rockies. But Indian raids slowed construction.

As the terrain became easier and the methods of building more systematic, both sides picked up speed. By 1867 the Central Pacific was laying a little more than a kilometer and a half a day, completing 579 kilometers (362 miles) in a year. In the spring of 1869, both crews were working furiously in Utah. Neither wanted its tracks to meet those of the other. They were actually passing each other by when Congress intervened and declared Promontory the meeting place. (See map, page 424.) There, on May 10, 1869, a golden spike was driven into the last tie, while telegraphs flashed the news across the nation.

The Chinese, Irish, Mexicans, and American Indians worked side by side to lay the tracks of the transcontinental railroad. Twelve workers carried a rail, and when the boss signaled, the crew dropped the rail into place. Spike drivers locked 10 spikes to each rail with three blows to each spike. In one minute, a crew could set four rails.

RAILS WEST. Congress gave bonds and land grants to three other railroad corporations during the Civil War and to a fourth—the Texas Pacific—when the South returned to the Union. Mismanagement and construction difficulties delayed all of them, however, for some years.

In 1883 the Northern Pacific completed the second transcontinental link, running from St. Paul, Minnesota, to Portland, Oregon. The Atchison, Topeka, and Santa Fe linked up with the Atlantic and Pacific about the same time, connecting Chicago with Los Angeles. The Southern Pacific (owned by the same men who built the Central Pacific, Leland Stanford and Collis P. Huntington) completed tracks from California to New Orleans in 1882. This gave the South the connection with California it had sought ever since the Gadsden Purchase. A fourth transcontinental line, the Great Northern, from St. Paul, Minnesota, to Everett, Washington, was finished in 1893. Both it and the Southern Pacific were built without federal loans or land grants. (See map, page 424.)

Construction of the western railroads was an almost superhuman feat, marred by corruption, waste, and warfare. The real heroes were thousands of laborers, Chinese and Irish *gandy dancers* who placed the ties and rails. But the rails opened the West—even before they were completed.

Gandy dancers was the slang term for railroad construction workers because the sledgehammers that they swung, or "danced with," were made by the Gandy Manufacturing Company of Chicago.

Section Review

1. Mapping: Use the map on page 424 to answer these questions: **a)** How did the railroad routes help determine the location of cities? **b)** How are the railroad routes related to the old cattle trails?
2. Identify or explain: the Central Pacific, Leland Stanford, gandy dancers, Promontory.
3. How did the government help the companies that were building the railroads?
4. Why did the northern and southern parts of the nation require their own railroads?
5. List some of the difficulties that delayed railroad construction.

4. The Day of the Cowboy

CATTLE RANCHERS MOVE WEST. *While the mining frontier was moving eastward from California, cattle ranchers were moving onto the Great Plains.* Like the miners and the railroads, the cattle ranchers appeared before the American Indians were conquered. With six-shooter and railroad they completed the destruction of the Plains community. And they heralded the advance of the farming frontier.

THE SHEEPHERDERS OF THE PLAINS. *Cattle ranchers came into conflict not only with the Plains Indians but also with sheep ranchers and herders.* Before the day of the cowboy dawned, sheepherders ranged over the western plains from the Rio Grande valley in Texas to the mountainous country of Montana. Many sheep flocks were enormous. The C. de Baca family of New Mexico owned one of the largest flocks—slightly more than one million sheep.

The sheep industry, like the earliest stages of the cattle business, was dominated by Spanish Americans. Flocks were owned by very wealthy families called *ricos*, from the Spanish word meaning rich. The head of such a family was known as the *patrón*. If the owner had a very large flock, he or she employed a *mayordomo* (mie-yor-DOH-moh), or manager, and several overseers, called *caporales* (kap-oe-RAH-lays). The *caporal* supervised the herders. He was also responsible for seeing that the sheep were taken to the right grazing grounds in different seasons and that they had enough water.

One herder usually had charge of a thousand sheep. He traveled with the flock each day—often great distances—while they grazed on the plains. The herder's life was lonely. He traveled alone with the flock.

Often weeks passed before he met another human.

THE TEXAS LONGHORN. The early Spanish explorers introduced cattle as well as horses to America. Some cattle escaped and evolved into a tough, wild breed called longhorns. *In the grasslands of southern Texas, the longhorns became as numerous and as well adapted to the environment as had the buffalo.* They could withstand the intense heat of the Texas summer, go for long periods with little water, and they thrived on the harsh prairie grasses.

For centuries Mexicans had raised and herded these cattle. As early as 1714 some of the *ricos* branded their cattle to mark the animals as the private property of individual ranchers. When Americans began to move into Texas in the 1820's, many of them adopted the techniques used by the Mexicans and set themselves up as cattle ranchers.

As early as the 1840's, Texans drove some of these cattle north to see if they had any commercial value. The demand for meat

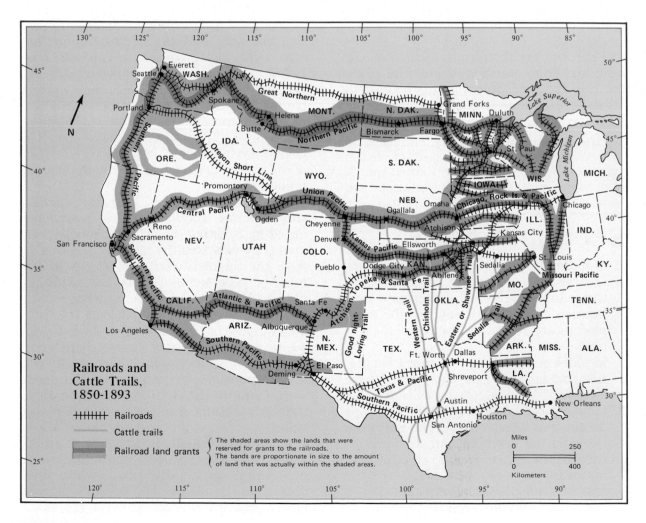

Railroads and Cattle Trails, 1850-1893

|||||| Railroads

Cattle trails

Railroad land grants

{ The shaded areas show the lands that were reserved for grants to the railroads. The bands are proportionate in size to the amount of land that was actually within the shaded areas.

Sidenote to History

The Pony Express

The march of the frontier eastward created a demand for improvements in transport and communication. Settlers in such isolated areas as Denver, Salt Lake, and Virginia City pressured Congress to subsidize overland routes for carrying freight and mail. In Washington politicians worried that the rising American empire might collapse without communication links binding West and East.

A transcontinental railroad was the obvious solution, but it was hopelessly bogged down in the politics of sectionalism. Even the overland freight companies became involved in the rivalry between the central route to California favored by the North and the southern route desired by the South.

The firm of Russell, Majors, and Waddell established the first western freight service in 1854, using the central route from Kansas City to Salt Lake. Using thousands of wagons and oxen, the company established a string of freight stations across the plains, each one a day's march from the other. The company soon planned a stagecoach line that would carry passengers and mail all the way to California. To make that possible it had to secure the very profitable government mail contract. That's where Russell, Majors, and Waddell ran into sectional conflict. Out of the conflict came the pony express.

John Butterfield established the first transcontinental passenger and mail service in 1858. The Butterfield Overland Mail Company used the southern route, from St. Louis to Los Angeles. Its stagecoaches left St. Louis and Los Angeles twice a week, on Mondays and Thursdays, and made the journey in 23 days. Butterfield won a government contract of 600,000 dollars to carry the mail.

To win the mail contract, Russell, Majors, and Waddell believed they had to demonstrate the superiority of the central route in order to show that their carriers could reach California in record time. Pondering the problem, William Russell hit upon the idea of a pony express. Relays of carriers, riding at top speed and changing mounts frequently, would carry mail from Missouri to California.

The plan was simple. But putting it into operation was not simple at all. Five hundred horses had to be purchased and distributed along the route. The company built "home stations" for riders every 48 kilometers (30 miles) and "swing stations" for changing horses every 16 kilometers (10 miles). Riders had to weigh less than 61 kilograms (135 pounds) and carried only a knife and a revolver.

On April 3, 1860, the first rider left St. Joseph, Missouri. The mail arrived in San Francisco, welcomed by a band and booming cannons, on the morning of April 14—a little more than 10 days later. The pony express caught the fancy of the nation, but it was not a success. Russell, Majors, and Waddell lost money on it and never won the government contract.

Perhaps fortunately for its founders, the pony express became obsolete within 16 months after it began. On July 4, 1861, Western Union started building a telegraph line westward across the plains. Another crew worked eastward from California. The pony express operated in the ever-narrowing gap between construction crews. Its day was over when the telegraph line was completed on October 24, 1861. Russell, Majors, and Waddell returned to the wagon business. That business, too, fell victim to technology—to the railroad.

"Laugh Kills Lonesome," by Charles Russell, captures the spirit of life around the campfire. What does the title of this painting tell you about the life of the cowboy?

during the Civil War increased the possibilities, and, at the end of the war, several herds were driven into southern Missouri. However, farmers in Arkansas and Missouri objected to the trespass across their lands, and a new way had to be found.

THE CATTLE TRAILS. The Kansas Pacific was laying tracks across the prairie and was eager for business. The Chisholm Trail led from central Texas northward through American Indian country, avoiding settlements and homesteads. *Joseph McCoy had the idea of linking cattle trails to railroad routes.* All he needed was a rendezvous. He persuaded the leaders of Abilene, Kansas, which consisted in 1867 of a dozen log huts with dirt roofs, to let this location serve as a cattle-shipping point.

Within 60 days McCoy transformed Abilene into the West's first cow town. He built a stockyard capable of holding 3,000 head of cattle and installed weighing scales, a barn, an office, and "a good three-story hotel." Then he sent agents across Oklahoma and Texas, instructing them to direct every wandering cattle drive to Abilene. Within a year the Chisholm Trail was a highway. As the railroad moved west, other shipping centers appeared (Wichita, Dodge City) and the trails multiplied. (See map, page 424.) *By the time the drives ended in the 1880's, some 4 million Texas steers had been shipped to Chicago and eastern markets.*

THE COWBOY. *The first cowboys were Mexican vaqueros* (vah-KAIR-oes). They

426

originated the costume, equipment, and life style that were eventually taken over by American cowpunchers and ranchers. The language of the range was Spanish. *Rancho, bronco, corral,* and *palomino,* for example, are Spanish words.

The cowboy's style of riding, the art of roping, and the **roundup,** or *rodeo,* were all learned from Spanish Americans. And the costume that helped them adapt to the harsh plains environment had been worn for generations by Mexicans. *Vaqueros* had learned that a deep-crowned, wide-brimmed hat not only protected their eyes from glare and served as an umbrella in sun and rain, it also substituted for a bucket at a water hole. A bandanna tied around the neck shielded nose and mouth from the dust kicked up by the herds. Leather *chaparreras* (shah-pah-RAY-rahs), or chaps, protected legs from cactus and sagebrush. And high-heeled boots with pointed toes held the cowboy's feet in the stirrups and still permitted easy mounting and dismounting.

In the early days of the cattle kingdom, the animals were grazed on public lands without fences. Ownership was determined by brands seared into each animal's hide with a hot iron. The employees of several ranchers cooperated with one another to round up the cattle twice a year. In the spring **roundup,** calves were captured and branded. Each was given the same brand as the cow that it followed. Autumn brought a beef roundup, in which the best animals were selected for the drive to the railroad.

The costume was colorful, and the life was romantic. But the job was also hard, dirty, and at times dull. The cowboy was often a poorly paid migrant worker, usually without home or family. Between flurries of hard labor, such as the spring and the fall roundups, life was one of dull routine. On the trail drives cowboys worked incessantly, keeping the cattle together by day and guarding them at night. In a chance stampede they had to risk life and limb to preserve the herd.

Many cowboys were freed slaves who had moved west seeking a new and freer life. Freed slaves made up about a quarter of those involved in cattle raising. A trail crew that drove cattle to places like Abilene typically consisted of eight cowboys. Generally, two or three cowboys were Black.

THE END OF THE OPEN RANGE. *The day of the cowboy was also a brief one.* By the 1880's the cattle drives had ended. The wild cow towns became respectable. Those that continued to excite the imagination of easterners, like Deadwood in South Dakota (where Wild Bill Hickock met his end) or Tombstone in Arizona (home, for a time, of Wyatt Earp), were mining towns, not cow towns. The cowboy survived—in myth and movie, if in nothing else—but after the 1880's, the cowboy was just another farmhand. The romance was gone. The expansion of the railroads brought an end to the cattle drives. Barbed wire ended the open range.

BARBED WIRE. Fencing was a great problem throughout the Great Plains. East of the Mississippi fences were made of split rails or rocks, but there was neither timber nor stone on the Plains. Wire was useless because cattle walked right through it. Some farmers tied barbs or spurs on the wire, but the process was time-consuming and expensive.

In 1873 Joseph Glidden of DeKalb, Illinois, invented a way to mass-produce barbed wire by weaving strands together. Cheap fencing meant the end of the open range. It changed the cattle business. It enabled ranchers to improve their stock by selective breeding and to introduce European strains (like the English Hereford, or "whiteface") that offered better meat than the rangy longhorn. Barbed wire made ranching a farm enterprise. It also opened the Great Plains to farmers and the plow.

Section Review

1. Identify or explain: Joseph McCoy, Abilene, *vaqueros,* roundup, Joseph Glidden.
2. How did Abilene become the first cow town?
3. Describe the Spanish and Mexican contributions to the cowboys' way of life.
4. What developments transformed the cowboy into just another farmhand?

5. The Sod-House Frontier

A DIFFICULT ENVIRONMENT. The Great Plains were a new and forbidding environment for the American farmer. *The lack of wood for housing, fuel, and fencing was only part of the problem. A shortage of rainfall was serious, too.* It meant that the farmer could not grow familiar crops in familiar ways.

The soil, moreover, was quite porous, having been formed originally by the erosion of the Rocky Mountains. Thus, what little rainfall there was filtered quickly through the soil to the *water table.* Because the water table itself was far below the surface, wells had to be drilled quite deep, and windmills had to be used to pump water. Strange soils and severe winters added to the problems of the plains farmer. As a result, nearly half the homesteaders failed.

The *water table* is the upper limit of the portion of the ground that is completely saturated with water. It is usually deep below the surface of the ground.

THE SOD HOUSE. *Immigrants from Scandinavia, Great Britain, Germany, and Russia led the way onto the plains frontier.* As late as 1910 more than a fourth of the population of North Dakota was foreign born. Their children made up another 40 percent.

The new arrivals adapted to the land, as immigrants had done since Jamestown. *The shortage of wood for housing was solved by building houses of prairie sod.* Cut from the earth in bricklike chunks, the sod was piled to form walls. Trees cut from a river bank framed the roof, which was covered with another layer of sod. Although it sounds dirty and dingy, the sod house was often spacious and comfortable. The sod made it well insulated, and so it was cool in summer and warm in winter. Sometimes it was even finished off on the inside with plaster board and wallpaper. Stoves using oil brought by railroad provided heat. In remote *hamlets,* where there was no railroad, buffalo chips (dried manure) were burned instead.

A *hamlet* is a small, rural village.

DROUGHT AND GRASSHOPPERS. On the other hand, the plains farmers were never able to overcome the problem of water. Drilling methods developed by oil companies helped in digging wells on the plains. But a well could serve no more than the needs of a family and its livestock. It could not store enough water for crops, and few parts of the West could be irrigated. The effort to farm the West was delayed until strains of drought-resistant wheat and hybrid corn were developed in the 20th century.

It took time to recognize the climatic problems of the area, however. By chance, the movement onto the plains frontier in the 1870's and early 1880's occurred during a period of abnormally high rainfall. Railroads encouraged people by advertising the West

The Shores family, homesteaders in Custer County, Nebraska, posed for this portrait in 1887. Notice their sod house in the background.

as a lush new paradise. James J. Hill, owner of the Great Northern Railroad, almost single-handedly populated the Red River valley of the Dakotas and Minnesota by blanketing Europe with propaganda posters offering free transportation to immigrants.

Then, beginning in 1886, came successive years of drought, followed by dust storms and a grasshopper plague. Clouds of grasshoppers, so thick that the sky was dark at midday, ravaged the land and ate everything in sight. Between 1886 and 1889, tens of thousands of people from Kansas gave up and went back east. Those who remained formed the core of the farm revolt of the 1890's.

Section Review

1. Identify or explain: James J. Hill, the sod house, the Great Plains.
2. Why were 64 hectares (160 acres) of land not enough land for a farm in the Great Plains?
3. What special problems did settlers on the Great Plains have to face?

Chapter 17 Review

Bird's-Eye View

Developments occurred as enterprising individuals in the western part of the United States discovered resources and found ways to use them. The discovery of gold in the Rocky Mountains and the Black Hills attracted prospectors to these unsettled regions of the country. These discoveries opened the area to settlement. Gold also brought prospectors into direct conflict with the Plains Indians, who held many of these lands by treaty.

American Indians were so outraged at this invasion of their lands and at the destruction of the buffalo, their main livelihood, that they waged war one last time. But they were defeated by the superior numbers and firepower of the United States Army. American Indians were pushed back once again, and more and more lands were taken away from them. The Dawes Act, drafted to help the American Indians, also contributed to their destruction.

The penetration of railroads into the western lands helped transform a wilderness into a land of opportunity. Great stretches of railroad track were linked. They formed vast rail networks that spanned the continent from east to west.

The open plains also attracted cattle ranchers, who grazed their herds on the open range. Then they drove them to the cow towns, where they were picked up by the railroads to be shipped to Chicago and then to the East.

Farmers also went to the Great Plains to claim the last free western lands. Many settlers were recent emigrants from Europe. They built sod houses because there was little timber. They dug deep wells and coped as best they could with drought and grasshoppers. Some gave up and returned east, but a surprising number remained.

Vocabulary

Define or identify each of the following:

lode	Ghost Dance	longhorns
strike	sooners	barbed wire
buffalo	gandy dancers	water table

Review Questions

1. What was the Last Frontier? What were its riches?
2. Describe the effect of the following on the life of the Plains Indians: a) The discovery of precious metals in western lands. b) The discovery that buffalo hides were commercially valuable. c) The construction of the transcontinental railroads. d) The settlement of the sod-house frontier. e) The expansion of the cattle industry.
3. Why was the Dawes Act ineffective in solving the problems of the American Indians?
4. Explain the significance to the nation of the golden spike at Promontory Point.
5. Describe the job of the American cowboy. How did the cowboy's job change when barbed wire enclosed the range?

Reviewing Social Studies Skills

1. Using the map on page 416, answer the following:
   a. What is the title of the map?
   b. List the tribes that lived near the Mississippi River.
   c. What does the pink area on the map show?
   d. What is the purpose of this map?
2. Using the map on page 424, answer the following:
   a. Starting in North Dakota, name the states that are on the route of the Northern Pacific.
   b. All of the cattle trails start in Texas. What was common about their destinations?
3. Using the map on page 416, locate the Nez Percé, the Sioux, and the Apache lands. Then, using the physical map on page xiv, list the geographic features of the areas these tribes inhabited.

Reading for Meaning

1. Reread the Viewpoints of History on page 419. Then, identify the attitude of each of the writers. Select one sentence or phrase that could be used to support your analysis of the writer's attitude. How does attitude influence the work of a writer?
2. When historians use colorful or vivid expressions, they often make history come alive for the reader. Tell how one of the following expressions, which was used in this chapter, brought history to life for you: mother lode, gandy dancers, cattle kingdom, cow town. If you don't think it enlivened history, tell why, and suggest expressions that you would have liked to have seen in its place.
3. The headings that introduce the chapter, the sections, and the subsections of this chapter have a practical function. They alert you to what will be covered. In what other ways do these headings make your reading easier? What do you think the characteristics of a good heading arc? If you had to change the titles of the chapter and four of the sections, what titles would you give to them?

Bibliography

Alvin Josephy's *The Patriot Chiefs: A Chronicle of American Indian Resistance* (Viking Press) contains short biographical sketches of American Indian leaders, including Crazy Horse and Chief Joseph.

The novels of Mari Sandoz are all good reading. Perhaps the best one is *Cheyenne Autumn* (Avon), the fantastic story of the Cheyenne's resistance to the reservation system.

O. E. Rolvaag's novel *Giants in the Earth* (Harper & Row) gives a superb picture of the sod-house frontier.

Dee Brown's *Bury My Heart at Wounded Knee* (Holt, Rinehart and Winston) is an Indian history of the American West.

Paul Wellman's *Race to the Golden Spike* (Houghton Mifflin) gives an exciting account of the race to build the transcontinental railroad.

Chapter 18

Populists and Gold Bugs

Farming is the world's oldest occupation. It goes back to about 6000 B.C., when women discovered that they could grow their own crops in gardens instead of gathering wild plants. But for almost 80 centuries, farming methods changed very little. The average farmer in 1850 was working with the same implements— plow, hoe, and rake—that farmers had used a thousand years before.

The farmer's life was hard. A typical farm family awoke before dawn to milk cows, feed chickens, gather firewood, and pump water from the well. The farm woman cooked on a wood-burning stove, baked her own bread, and made most or all of her family's clothing. In the winter months children often walked several miles to a one-room elementary school, where they were taught basic reading, writing, and arithmetic. During the rest of the year, however, children were needed on the farm to help with planting and harvesting. Farmers depended mostly on such hand tools as axes, pitchforks, sickles, and scythes and on their own labor and the work of horses, oxen, or mules to plow their fields and pump their wells. For most, farm life was a hard, isolated, lonely existence.

Chapter Objectives

After you have finished reading this chapter, you should be able to:
1. List the ways farming changed after it became mechanized and the problems mechanization brought to the farm.
2. Recall how and why farmers organized.
3. Identify the causes of the rise and the decline of the Populists.
4. Explain what happened in 1896 to the cause of Populism.

By 1850 vast changes in farming were under way. John Deere's steel plow and Cyrus Hall McCormick's reaper were on the market, and more inventions were on the way. Civil War demands encouraged farmers to invest in machinery. The process quickened after the war. The result was a revolution in agriculture that was as important as the Industrial Revolution. By enabling a small portion of the population to feed the rest, it made possible the Industrial Revolution.

1. The Agricultural Revolution

INCREASED CULTIVATION AND SPECIALIZATION. *The movement into the Great Plains after the Civil War brought great increases in the amount of land under cultivation.* The flood of immigrants from Europe and the use of barbed wire for fencing hastened the conquest of the frontier. Between the founding of

This photograph illustrates a barn-raising scene—an important event in the history of rural America. In this picture the neighbors have helped one of the farmers raise the framework and are preparing to celebrate with a special dinner. Why were such activities important to farm communities?

Jamestown in 1607 and the year 1870, American farmers put to the plow some 163.2 million hectares (408 million acres) of land. That figure was more than doubled in the next 30 years.

Specialization further increased the efficiency of the farmer. Certain climates and soils, it was found, were better suited to some crops than others. The Great Plains farmers quickly concentrated on wheat. Cotton remained the specialty of the South. Dairying became important in Wisconsin. Raising corn and hogs became the main economic activity in Illinois and Iowa.

FARM MECHANIZATION. Labor-saving machines did for the farm what they did for the factory and the city. McCormick's harvester was only the beginning. It was followed by the tie-binder that mechanically baled and tied hay and the combine that cut, threshed, and cleaned grain in one operation. The use of steam engines instead of horses permitted larger machines and plows with multiple blades.

The savings in time and labor were enormous. A government commission estimated that it took a farmer working by hand almost three hours to harvest and thresh a bushel of wheat. With a combine the operation took four minutes. To cut and shell a bushel of corn by hand required an hour and a half. A steam-operated corn sheller did it in a minute and a half.

PRODUCING FOR THE WORLD. With such enormous leaps in productivity, it is not surprising that Americans could not eat all the food farmers were growing. Large amounts were shipped abroad, mostly to Britain and western Europe. At the start of the Civil War, America exported about 35 million bushels of wheat annually. By 1900 it was selling almost six times as much abroad. Exports of cotton, beef, and pork tripled over the same period. *American farmers fed not only their own country's rising urban population but the factory workers of Europe as well.*

Indeed, America was producing more foodstuffs than even Europe could consume. By the 1880's there was a surplus of agricultural staples in the world market, and prices were falling. Wheat, which averaged

a dollar a bushel in the 1870's, went for 63 cents in the 1890's. A bushel of corn sold for 50 cents in 1880 and fell to 25 cents in 1890. Cotton prices dropped by two thirds between 1870 and 1890. At such prices, farmers grimly observed, it was cheaper to use grain for fuel than to buy coal.

A WORLDWIDE DEPRESSION. From the mid-1870's to the mid-1890's there was worldwide depression in farm prices. Except for moments of financial panic in 1873, 1883, and 1893, American industry boomed, and profits soared. But farmers found themselves in a corner. *If they worked harder and grew more crops, they added to the world surplus, caused prices to fall, and ended up earning less.*

A symptom of the depression was the rise in farm tenancy. Americans had always prided themselves on owning their own farms. With the government giving land away, there seemed no reason for anyone to rent farmland. Yet some farmers had bought their land on credit from speculators and

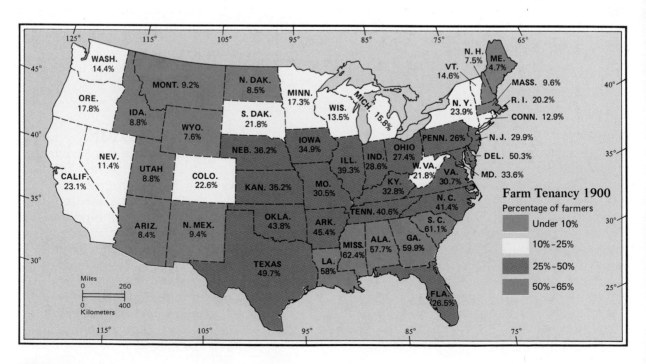

Farm Tenancy 1900
Percentage of farmers

Under 10%
10%–25%
25%–50%
50%–65%

railroads. And in the depression they found themselves unable to make payments. As a result, in 1880 the government discovered that one fourth of the nation's farmers were renting the land they cultivated. The situation began to improve toward the end of the 1890's. But many farmers remained caught in an economic squeeze. *By 1900 one third of all American farmers were tenants, cultivating land owned by someone else.*

A SPECIAL ENEMY: THE RAILROADS. Farmers had other grievances, too. Prime among them was the railroads. Because water transportation was not available, western farmers were dependent on the railroads. But because they shipped individually, they could not bargain for special rates. John D. Rockefeller could negotiate special rates because he could guarantee the railroads a large volume of oil shipments. But the ordinary farmer had to pay what the railroads demanded.

TAXES AND BANKING CREDIT. The nation's financial system worked to the disadvantage of the farmer. Local government was supported by property taxes, and these kinds of taxes hit landowners hardest. The federal government was financed by customs duties. These tariffs protected industry from foreign competition. At the same time they increased the price of the machinery that farmers had to buy. Farmers also found it difficult to obtain loans. The national banks could not legally permit land to be used as *security* for loans. Yet land was the one *asset* that most farmers possessed. In addition the national banks—and thus the nation's money supply—were concentrated in the cities of the Northeast. The rural South and West were chronically short of capital to be used for investment.

When something is used as *security,* it is being pledged to guarantee payment of a loan. If the borrower cannot repay the loan, the lender can take the security as payment.

An *asset* is an item of value that is owned.

THE CROP-LIEN SYSTEM IN THE SOUTH. *In the South the problem of credit led to a lending system that virtually enslaved the poorest farmers, White as well as Black.* Since banks were few in the South, farmers turned to village merchants, buying the food, clothing, seed, and tools they needed on credit. Because many were tenant farmers, they had nothing but their crops to pledge as security. The merchant thus took a *lien* on the farmer's crop as security for the loan. When the crop, usually cotton, was harvested, the farmer took it to the local merchant, who sold it for the farmer and deducted from the proceeds the amount of the farmer's debt.

A *lien* (LEEN) exists on someone's property when the property is used to guarantee a debt. If the debt is not repaid, the person holding the lien can take the property as repayment.

Merchants cared little what price they got for the cotton, as long as they recovered their money. Thus, the proceeds were often barely enough to cover the debt. As a result, the farmer had to go back to the merchant the following spring for new credit, and the cycle started all over again.

One solution to these difficulties was organization. By uniting, farmers could gain some leverage against railroads, and cooperative markets (co-ops) would permit farmers to escape the tyranny of town merchants.

Section Review

1. Using the map on page 434, identify the states that had the highest percentage of farm tenancy. Why do you think this was so?
2. Identify or explain: farm mechanization, specialization, farm tenancy, crop-lien system.

3. List the problems of farmers during the last quarter of the 19th century.
4. How did the tax and banking systems work against the farmers?
5. How were farmers kept in debt by the crop-lien system?

2. The Farmers Organize for Protest

THE GRANGE. During the latter part of the 19th century, business organized itself into large corporations, and labor formed unions. Faced with mounting problems, the farmers did the same. They organized, and for much the same reason: In unity there was strength.

The first farm organization was the National Grange of the Patrons of Husbandry. At first the Grange was a secret group. It was founded in 1867 by Oliver Hudson Kelley, a clerk in the Department of Agriculture. When it began, the Grange concentrated on educating farmers in methods of plowing and cultivating and on organizing cooperative associations. A farm cooperative was owned and managed by the farmers. They sold the produce of a group of farmers directly to customers. The cooperative bypassed distributors such as *grain elevator* operators and stockyard owners, who had to be paid for their services. Cooperatives also bought farm goods and machinery in large quantities at wholesale prices. Some cooperatives succeeded, but most failed because farmers lacked business experience and the necessary capital to compete with the owners and operators of established businesses.

A *grain elevator* is a building used to elevate, store, discharge, and sometimes process grain.

It soon became apparent to the Grange that most of the farmers' problems re-quired political solutions. By the early 1870's the Grange boasted over a million members. Its locals in midwestern states had developed the power and the machinery to demand political action. Investigations of unfair business practices of railroad companies led to state laws fixing maximum freight and storage rates and making rebates to major clients illegal.

The new laws provoked heavy opposition from the railroads and led to a series of Supreme Court cases known as the Granger cases. The most famous of these was the case of *Munn* v. *Illinois* in 1876. Munn, the owner of a grain elevator, complained that an Illinois law regulated his profit and thus deprived him of his property without due process of law. The Court ruled, however, that Munn's business, although private and for profit, was "affected with a public interest" and therefore could be regulated by the public.

THE FARMERS' ALLIANCES. During the 1880's farm organizations grew rapidly. Great Plains farmers formed the Northwest Alliance, headquartered in Omaha. The most powerful farm organization was the Southern Alliance, begun in Texas in 1875. By 1890 it claimed a million members across the South. The Southern Alliance undertook an ambitious co-op program to help its members escape the crop-lien system. The Alliance Cooperative in Dallas, Texas, was one of the largest farm markets in the world. The Southern Alliance, unfortunately, excluded Blacks. But the National Colored Farmers' Alliance claimed a million members spread over 30 states.

THE INTERSTATE COMMERCE ACT. The alliances were more politically minded than the Grange. *In the 1880's—under pressure from the alliances—more states set up railroad commissions and regulated rates.* Efforts at state regulation received a severe blow, however, when the

This Granger poster sums up the type of rural life the Grange hoped to accomplish. Although the Grange did not achieve all of its purposes, it did bring rural Americans together and lessen some of the loneliness of their lives. Compare this picture with the one on page 433. Would you agree that the barn-raising photograph is a more realistic representation of rural life? Why or why not?

Supreme Court ruled in *Wabash Railroad* v. *Illinois* (1886) that the states could not regulate interstate railroads. Only Congress could prescribe rules relating to interstate commerce.

Disappointing as the Wabash decision was to farmers, it did lend urgency to the call for federal action. Small shippers, who paid higher rates than the giant trusts, had long demanded railroad regulation. Congress responded in 1887 with the Interstate Commerce Act. The act prohibited unjust and unreasonable rates, rebates, and other railroad abuses. And it created the Interstate Commerce Commission (ICC), composed of five members appointed by the President and confirmed by the Senate. The ICC could accept and hear complaints against the railroads and could issue orders.

The act was a landmark in American development, for it marked the first break in laissez-faire. It was the federal government's first attempt to regulate the prices and practices of privately owned business corporations.

The Interstate Commerce Act was of little immediate help to farmers and other shippers, however. Whenever the Interstate Commerce Commission issued an order, the railroad took it to court, claiming the decision was unfair. And the courts usually sided with the railroads. In 1896 the Supreme Court deprived the ICC of rate-setting authority.

By the time the Interstate Commerce Act was passed, the farm protest had broadened to other issues. The depression in prices renewed interest in the supply of money in circulation. The failure of railroad regulation also left farmers disenchanted with the political system. By 1890 they were giving some thought to a political party of their own.

THE MONEY QUESTION. The fall in world prices stimulated the farmers' interest in money. When the price of wheat fell by 50 percent, the farmers had to raise twice as much in order to pay their debts. The farmers blamed their problems on the scarcity of money in circulation rather than on changes in the supply of and the demand for crops. A plentiful supply of *cheap money,* they reasoned, would raise prices and ease debt payments.

Cheap money is currency whose exchange value is not as great as its face value. For example, a dollar would be cheap money if it could be exchanged for only 65 cents in gold.

In theory, paper money rested on gold. National bank notes were like gold certificates. Each certificate represented gold on deposit in the banks. People could exchange certificates for gold at any time. They did not do so because paper money was more convenient to handle. But by being as "good as gold," the national bank notes were not cheap money.

Greenbacks were a different matter. These were bills issued by the federal government during the Civil War. They were a form of government debt to be redeemed for gold in the future. Their value thus depended on the government's credit, and that varied with the fortunes of war. By the end of the war, a greenback dollar was worth about 67 cents in gold. That made the greenback cheap money. The debtor's ideal was to borrow in gold and pay back in greenbacks.

THE GREENBACK PARTY. For a decade after the war, the government did not have enough gold on hand to retire the greenbacks. When farm prices began skidding in the mid-1870's, *inflationists* formed the National Greenback party. Its object was the printing of more paper money. The party attracted a variety of reformers. In 1876 and 1880 the Greenback party ran candidates for President.

Inflationists are those who favor an economic situation in which the supply of money and credit is so much greater than the supply of goods that prices rise substantially and continuously.

The government, however, wanted to retire the greenbacks and so began hoarding gold to redeem them. On January 2, 1879, Secretary of the Treasury John Sherman offered to buy greenbacks, dollar for dollar, with gold. Some greenbacks continued in circulation thereafter, but, like the national bank notes, they had become as "good as gold."

FREE SILVER. As interest in greenbacks was dying out, silver became an issue. Until 1873 both gold and silver were the bases of the nation's money. *As the rest of the world went on the gold standard, so did the United States.* The government stopped coining silver dollars in 1873. By chance, western silver mines were at that moment reaching a peak of production. With the government cutting its coinage, there was less of a market for the metal. The price plummeted. Where previously 448 grams (16 ounces) of silver had equaled the value of 28 grams (one ounce) of gold, it now took 560 grams (20 ounces) of silver to buy 28 grams (one ounce) of gold. It soon occurred to inflationists that if the government began coining silver at the old ratio of 16 to 1, a silver dollar would be worth only 80 percent of a gold dollar, or 80 cents: cheap money.

Richard Bland, representative from Missouri, helped draft a bill passed in 1878 (the Bland-Allison Act). It provided for the purchase and coinage of between 56 to 112 million grams (two to four million ounces) of silver per month. In January 1879, Secretary Sherman offered to exchange the silver dollars for gold ones, as he did with the greenbacks. The farmers failed again to get cheap money.

THE SHERMAN SILVER PURCHASE ACT. *During the 1880's, as farm prices dropped further, the search for cheap money became frantic.* If the government's coinage of silver were free and unlimited, some reasoned, the mint would have to accept all the silver brought to it. When silver coins became numerous enough, the government would not be able to back every one of them with gold. Eventually the treasury would have to accept cheap money or a silver standard. Either way, it would mean more money in circulation.

As the market price for silver fell, the mountain states joined the farmers in the demand for unlimited coinage of silver. The alliance was not strong enough to sway Congress. In 1890 representatives in Congress who favored silver made a bargain with eastern members. They agreed to vote for a revision in the tariff rates if the East would support free silver. The result was the passage of the McKinley Tariff and the Sherman Silver Purchase Act. The new duty imposed the highest rates of the century, averaging almost 50 percent on the price of goods.

The Silver Purchase Act authorized the treasury to purchase 126 million grams (four and a half million ounces) of silver a month, paying for it with paper notes. That amount was the estimated output of all the silver mines in the country. With the treasury buying all their output, miners expected the price of silver to rise, and farmers anticipated a flood of paper money into the economy. Both were disappointed. The mines produced far more than expected, and the price of silver did not rise. There was more silver, as well as more paper money, but the increase was not enough to affect the economy.

Frustrated by the government's policies, the farm organizations began to talk more openly of direct political action. Neither of the national parties, Republican or Democratic, responded to their demands. Perhaps it was time to form a new party, one devoted to the interests of the common people—a People's party!

The general store played an important role in the rural community. People often gathered there not only to shop but also to pick up their mail and engage in conversation. Are any of the items shown in this picture available in your local supermarket?

Section Review

1. Identify or explain: *Munn* v. *Illinois,* the Grange, Interstate Commerce Commission, Richard Bland, Greenback party, McKinley Tariff, Bland-Allison Act.
2. Why did farmers favor federal regulation of the railroads?
3. What is meant by cheap money, and why did farmers want it?
4. How did farmers hope the Sherman Silver Purchase Act would help them?

3. The Rise and Fall of the People's Party

A PEOPLE'S PRESIDENT. The farmers' protest movement had experienced nothing but failure. Efforts to regulate the railroads were overturned in the courts. The attempt to relieve the depression by expanding the money supply was resisted by the President and the treasury. The election of legislators friendly to the farmers' movement was not enough. It was becoming clear that the system itself had to be changed. Perhaps a people's President— someone who could shake up both the courts and the government bureaucracy— was the answer.

UPROAR IN THE WEST AND SOUTH. *By 1890 the demands for change echoed from the humid swamps of South Carolina to the arid flats of the Dakotas.* Orators with colorful names and radical ideas harangued crowds from every stump. In South Carolina Benjamin Tillman— known as Pitchfork Ben after he promised to "tickle old Grover Cleveland's fat ribs" with

In this picture a farmer and his children sell vegetables to townspeople. What does this picture tell you about the interdependence and interaction of the farm and town people?

his pitchfork—was made governor. Minnesota's contribution was Ignatius Donnelly, who wrote newspaper essays and pamphlets with a pen that seemed to have been dipped in acid. From Kansas came "Sockless Jerry" Simpson, "the sockless *Socrates* of the prairies"; Annie Diggs, editor of the *Alliance Advocate* and powerful political lobbyist; and Mary Elizabeth Lease, who made over 100 fiery speeches during the 1890 election campaign. Lease was most troubled by the glib explanation that farmers caused their own problems by overproducing. How can there be overproduction, she cried, "when 10,000 little children starve to death every year in the United States?"

Socrates was a famous ancient Greek philosopher and teacher.

In 1890 the Southern Alliance nearly succeeded in its effort to gain control of the South. In the elections Alliance candidates won majorities in some state legislatures. "Pitchfork Ben" Tillman won reelection as governor of South Carolina. A few Alliance members even won election to Congress.

But the newly elected representatives simply voted with the Democrats. In the White House, Republican President Benjamin Harrison ignored the rural outcry. "There has never been a time in our history," President Harrison reported to the nation, "when work was so abundant or when wages were so high."

Nonetheless, the near success of the Southern Alliance encouraged further moves into politics. The year 1891 witnessed new efforts to unite the various farm organizations and further talk of a People's party.

BIRTH OF THE PEOPLE'S PARTY.
The Presidential election of 1892 brought matters to a head. Neither party seemed responsive to the cries for change. The Republicans renominated Benjamin Harrison. The Democrats returned to Grover Cleveland, whom Harrison had defeated in 1888. Cleveland was no better than Harrison, in the view of farmers. While President, he had vetoed a small appropriation for drought-stricken Texas farmers on the grounds that "though the people should support the government, the government should not support the people."

The People's (or Populist) party was launched in Omaha, Nebraska, on July 4, 1892. Reformers flocked to the Omaha convention—*socialists, suffragists,* temperance advocates, Knights of Labor. At the core of the new party were the farm alliances. Their Presidential nominee was an old Greenbacker, James B. Weaver.

Socialists advocated government ownership and control of the means of production.

Suffragists advocated giving women the right to vote.

THE POPULIST PLATFORM. The platform was drawn up at Omaha. It was the most radical statement to emerge from a major political party. It proclaimed that "the interests of rural and civic [urban] labor are the same; their enemies are identical." *The Populists wanted to unite all working people, from the factory as well as from the farm.* But they did not want government ownership of business corporations. They wanted to narrow the gap between rich and poor by proposing such devices as a graduated income tax.

The Populists did, however, want the government to own utilities that served the public. Declaring that "either the people must own the railroads or the railroads will own the people," the platform advocated government ownership of railroads and telegraph and telephone facilities. Populists also believed that issuing money was a function of government, not of private business. Permitting bankers to print money, they believed, gave bankers an undeserved windfall. Thus, the Omaha platform demanded that the government issue paper money and resume the coinage of silver. The platform also proposed that the government meet the farmers' need for credit by making loans on the security of stored crops. And it proposed an eight-hour day for workers.

Radical though it seemed in its day, the Populist platform was a comprehensive response to the problems created by the growth of industry and the mechanization of farming. Marking an end to the sterile politics of the Gilded Age, the Populists proposed a genuine effort to bring the nation's political thought in tune with its economic might. *Moreover, nearly every Populist proposal—except for free silver and government ownership of rails and utilities—was enacted over the next 25 years.*

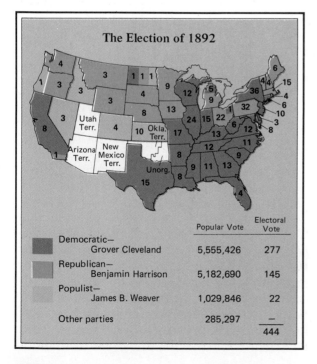

The Election of 1892

	Popular Vote	Electoral Vote
Democratic— Grover Cleveland	5,555,426	277
Republican— Benjamin Harrison	5,182,690	145
Populist— James B. Weaver	1,029,846	22
Other parties	285,297	—
		444

THE ELECTION OF 1892. For a brand-new party the Populists did remarkably well in the election. They won the electoral votes of Kansas, Colorado, Idaho, and Nevada. (See map below.) They elected 10 members of Congress and three state governors. But the Democrats did even better. Cleveland defeated Harrison by a margin of 370,000, an overwhelming victory in comparison with the close elections of the 1880's. (In 1888 Harrison had won by a slim margin in the electoral college, while trailing in the popular balloting.)

The results suggested that the Populist platform had only limited appeal. In the South wealthy planters were angered by the Populist attempt to unite poor farmers, Black and White. Poor White farmers were suspicious of being grouped with the Blacks. And because the Populists did not support federal supervision of elections, Blacks found it difficult to vote at all. Thus, the Populists fared poorly in the South.

Most of the million votes the Populists polled were in the mining states of the West. There silver miners echoed the cry for free silver. But they had little interest in other Populist reforms.

Elsewhere the Populists did best where they joined forces with *Silver Democrats.* This alliance forced the Populists to drop some of their more radical proposals, but it held out some promise for future success. In 1892 the Democrats were riding high and in no need of allies. *Then, a depression—the worst of the century—and the troubles of President Cleveland changed their outlook.* By 1896 Populists and Democrats were ready for marriage.

Silver Democrats favored free and unlimited coinage of silver.

THE PANIC OF 1893. It started as a financial panic similar to those the nation had experienced about every 10 years since the

In 1893 a spectacular World's Fair was held in Chicago. The fair combined entertainment and a display of many of the newest inventions. What would farm people find appealing about such a fair? What appeal would such a fair have for people who live in the city?

Civil War. But it quickly spread throughout the country. The great boom in railroad construction had created the prosperity of the 1880's. When the boom came to an end, there was less demand for steel and machine tools. Factories shut down, and people lost their jobs.

The American promise that anyone with energy and ability could get ahead in the world was broken. The American on the move was now a "tramp," riding the railroads from town to town, looking for work.

REPEAL OF THE SHERMAN SILVER PURCHASE ACT. President Cleveland summoned Congress into special session, but the only remedy he could think of was repeal of the Sherman Silver Purchase Act. In the depression people hoarded gold, exchanging their silver coins and paper dollars for gold coins. And the government's gold reserves were alarmingly low.

Congress complied with the President's request. *Nevertheless, repeal of the Sherman Silver Purchase Act did nothing to relieve the depression.* It merely made enemies for the President in the silver wing of his party.

THE CLEVELAND LOANS. As the depression deepened, nervous holders of government notes continued to exchange them for gold. By mid-1894 the government's gold reserves had fallen to 60 million dollars. The treasury claimed it needed 100 million dollars to support the currency, or it would have to turn to silver.

In desperation President Cleveland turned to the New York banks. *J. P. Morgan formed a group of bankers who bought gold in Europe with government bonds and turned it over to the treasury—after taking a tidy profit for themselves.* That relieved the treasury for the moment, but when gold hoarding continued, the President had to turn to the bankers again. He managed to save the gold standard at enormous cost to the government. Outraged Silver Democrats began laying plans to capture the party in 1896.

COXEY'S ARMY. The President's relationship with New York bankers stood in contrast to his harsh attitude toward the unemployed. Unemployment was a new experience for Americans. Labor had always been in short supply. The prevailing view had been that those who were out of work were simply lazy. But in the hard times of the 1890's, there were thousands able and willing to work and no jobs available. Many left homes and families to tramp the highways in the hope that things would be better in other parts of the country. In December 1893 Populist Governor Lorenzo Lewelling of Kansas issued a "Tramp Circular" explaining that tramps and vagabonds were not persons to be feared and punished. They were Americans looking for work.

Jacob S. Coxey was a self-made Ohio businessman and a Populist. He decided that the government ought to relieve unemployment by putting people to work. When told that such a radical notion would be ignored in Washington, he decided to petition Congress in person. With a band of 100 supporters, he left his home in Massil-lon, Ohio, in the spring of 1894 and started on foot for Washington. "Coxey's army" sparked a good deal of sympathy as it wound its way across the Allegheny Mountains. When it reached Washington, it numbered 500. At the Capitol the army was met by a detachment of nervous police who panicked and charged the crowd, injuring some 50 people with their clubs. Coxey and two other leaders were arrested—for walking on the grass.

Coxey won a great deal of public sympathy. In fact, his was the first of several "armies" organized to march on Washington in 1894 and 1895. The rest caused less disturbance, but the President's reputation continued to suffer. Many viewed Cleveland as a weakling coddled by bankers. His gov-

In 1894 Jacob S. Coxey, a Populist, led an army of unemployed workers on a march to Washington. Why do you think this particular protest movement aroused a great deal of public sympathy?

ernment seemed so frightened that it sent armed police galloping into groups of peaceful protesters. Others were fearful that the system was crumbling and that the nation was on the verge of revolution. A labor blow-up in Chicago in the summer of 1894 reinforced that impression.

THE PULLMAN STRIKE. *In addition to unemployment, a number of strikes erupted during this depression.* Strikes are usually associated with prosperity. When labor is in high demand, it seeks higher rewards. But the strikes of 1894 were strikes of desperation. In that year alone there were 1,400 strikes against wage cuts and layoffs. One of them—at Pullman, Illinois—was the bloodiest since the great railroad strike of 1877.

Pullman, Illinois, was a company town, built for the employees of the Pullman Palace Car Company. Houses and shops were owned by the company. The town was well planned, but rents were higher and services poorer than in neighboring communities. In the summer of 1894, the company announced a cut in wages, which, it claimed, would avoid laying off workers. At the same time, it refused to cut rents in the company town. As a result, Pullman employees went on strike.

The Pullman strike attracted the notice of the American Railway Union (ARU), headed by Eugene V. Debs. Debs was short of funds and not eager to enter the Pullman strike. But union members began showing sympathy for the strikers by refusing to hook up Pullman cars in the Chicago railroad yards. When the railroads fired ARU workers for participating in the boycott, the ARU struck back against the railroads. Before long, train service was interrupted in 27 western states.

THE GOVERNMENT INTERVENES.
President Cleveland's Attorney General, Richard Olney, had no patience with strikes.

He wanted to intervene in the Pullman affair. Federal intervention in such matters usually proceeded only upon the request of a governor. Governor John P. Altgeld of Illinois sympathized with the strikers. And because there had been no violence, he saw no need for federal troops. Olney, however, claimed that the federal government had an obligation to protect the mails. When he learned that a train halted by the ARU contained a mail car, he sent in the army.

On July 4, 1894, 2,000 soldiers arrived in Chicago. Their appearance created an outburst of violence. Angry workers derailed trains and battled soldiers. Twenty people died, and 2,000 railroad cars were destroyed before order was restored.

UNITED STATES V. DEBS. Before sending in troops, Attorney General Olney secured a court *injunction* against the strike. Olney secured the injunction because he anticipated violence. It was the first time an injunction had been used in a labor dispute. When Debs ignored the court order, he was arrested and jailed. *Debs appealed to the Supreme Court of the United States, arguing that courts cannot prohibit peaceful strikes merely because they might lead to violence.* In 1895 the Court rejected Debs' argument and upheld the use of the injunction. For the next 35 years, the injunction was a powerful weapon that employers and courts used to prevent strikes.

An *injunction* is a court order designed to prevent injury before it occurs.

THE CONGRESSIONAL ELECTION OF 1894. The violence of the Pullman strike was also the undoing of labor. Sympathy for the worker evaporated. There was still a depression, and voters needed a scapegoat. The Democrats were in power, so they were the natural target. In the off-year election of 1894, the Republicans swept both

houses of Congress. In the House of Representatives, the transfer of seats from one party to another was the largest in history. Republicans emerged with a firm majority of 132.

The election was a major turning point for the Republicans. For the next 35 years, until another depression caused another reaction in 1932, only one Democratic President was elected—Woodrow Wilson. And he succeeded in 1912 only because the Republicans split their vote.

The election of 1894 also revealed the public fear of radicalism and the Populists. Even the Great Plains, hotbed of Populist oratory, elected 44 Republicans and only two Populists to Congress. Weakened by defeat, both Democrats and Populists were ready to cement an alliance. The glue was colored silver.

Section Review

1. Mapping: Using the map on page 442, locate the states won by Weaver, the Populist candidate, and by Cleveland, the Democratic candidate. Compare the states won by Cleveland with the states he won in the election of 1884. (See map, page 378.) What states did he gain in the election of 1892? In 1884, who carried the states won by the Populists in 1892?
2. Identify or explain: Benjamin Tillman, Ignatius Donnelly, Mary Elizabeth Lease, Jacob Coxey, Eugene V. Debs.
3. List the demands of the Populist platform. Why do you think the platform was considered so radical?
4. How did the panic of 1893 affect the labor movement? How was the congressional election of 1894 affected by both?
5. How did Coxey's army and the Pullman strike help to create a fear of Populists?

4. 1896: The Battle of the Standards

WILLIAM JENNINGS BRYAN. For two years an obscure young lawyer had been stumping the country seeking the Presidency. In his mid-30's, with four years of experience as a Democrat in the House of Representatives, William Jennings Bryan had a gift for public speaking and the ability to attract enormous crowds. *He had listened closely to the Populists of the plains and designed his views around those issues he believed had the broadest appeal—in particular, free silver.*

THE CROSS OF GOLD. Before long Bryan came to the attention of the Silver Democrats, who were determined to rid the party of Grover Cleveland. When the Democratic convention met at Chicago in the summer of 1896, it was obvious that the silver wing had done its homework. Silver Democrats demanded and won an open debate on the silver question. Bryan was scheduled to speak last.

His speech was electric. He appeared to speak for the ordinary people so long ignored by the politicians. He declared war against established interests everywhere. "We do not come as aggressors," he assured them. "Our war is not a war of conquest; we are fighting in defense of our homes, our families, and prosperity. We have petitioned, and our petitions have been scorned; . . . we have begged, and they have mocked when our calamity came. We beg no longer; we petition no more. We defy them!"

Here was the authentic voice of the prairie, convinced that agricultural production was the only true source of wealth. Turning to the Gold Democrats, he cried: "You come to us and tell us that the great cities are in favor of the gold standard; we reply that the great cities rest upon our broad and fertile prairies. Burn down your cities and leave our farms, and your cities will spring up again as if by magic; but destroy our farms and the grass will grow in the streets of every city. . . .

"Having behind us the producing masses of this nation and the world, supported by the commercial interests, the laboring interests, and the toilers everywhere, we will answer their demand for a gold standard by saying to them: 'You shall not press down upon the brow of labor this crown of thorns; you shall not crucify mankind upon a cross of gold!' "

The climactic ending of Bryan's Cross of Gold speech created an uproar in the convention, but the delegates were not to be stampeded. The silverites had a clear majority, but they cast several ballots for Richard Bland of Missouri. Bryan finally won the nomination on the fourth ballot. And to appease the gold wing, he chose as Vice-Presidential candidate a New England banker, Arthur Sewall.

THE POPULISTS IN 1896. Free silver was the only part of the Populist program that Bryan and the Democrats endorsed. But free silver was a symbol of change, and Populists could reasonably expect Bryan to undertake others. Besides, they had no practical alternative to Bryan. The Populists did not have enough strength to run a candidate of their own, and an independent campaign would divide the forces of reform. Thus, their convention also nominated Bryan for President, although they maintained some independence by choosing as Vice-Presidential candidate Tom Watson of Georgia. *Even so, many Populists believed that the grand vision of the Omaha platform had been sold out for silver.*

REPUBLICANS NOMINATE McKINLEY. While reformers were capturing the Democratic party, a revolution of another kind was occurring among the Republicans. The architect was an Ohio industrialist,

William Jennings Bryan, the Democratic candidate for President in 1896 and 1900, favored free silver and opposed the gold standard. How did the fact that the Populists also endorsed Bryan contribute to his downfall?

Marcus Alonzo Hanna. *Mark Hanna was a new kind of political boss, a man who ran the Republican party with the tight efficiency of a business corporation.* As a result of his careful planning, the Republican nomination in 1896 was a foregone conclusion. Hanna's man, Representative William McKinley of Ohio, won on the first ballot.

Mark Hanna also lined up the nation's business interests, tapping them for a campaign war chest of 3.5 million dollars.

Alarmed by western radicalism, business people had been joining the Republican party for some years. Railroad baron James J. Hill and department-store pioneer John Wanamaker managed Benjamin Harrison's campaigns in 1888 and 1892. They were able to solicit sizable sums from business. Mark Hanna completed the alliance between Republicans and business and made the fund-raising operation more efficient. The Standard Oil Company alone gave the Republicans 250,000 dollars, a sum equal to the Democrats' entire campaign chest. And J. P. Morgan gave a quarter of a million.

THE BATTLE OF THE STANDARDS.
There was more to the election of 1896 than the question of a gold standard or a silver standard, but the money issue swallowed up all the others. In large part this was Bryan's fault. He failed to capitalize on the many grievances of working people and small business people, ranging from tariffs and taxes to trusts. Eastern factory workers had no use for cheap money. A silver dollar with a silver content worth only 53 cents seemed to them no better than paper. They wanted their wages paid in gold. One of the most effective weapons the Republicans had was a campaign button that looked like a silver dollar, with the eagle emblem and the phrase "In God We Trust—for the other 47¢."

Bryan campaigned extensively, traveling through 27 states by rail, making over 600 speeches to an estimated five million people. He undoubtedly brought to the polls people who had never voted before, but he made little impact on the urban East. McKinley won by 600,000 votes, the biggest margin any candidate had achieved since reconstruction.

As in 1894, the Republicans appealed successfully to the immigrants who flooded into the country in the 1880's. The immigrants blamed the Democrats for the

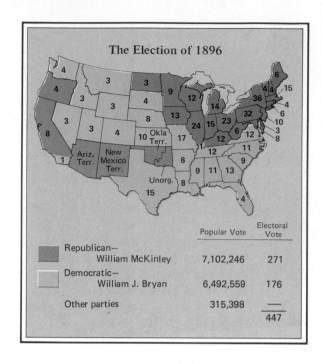

depression, and they responded to the Republicans' promise of "a full dinner pail." Western states with heavy immigrant populations—Wisconsin, Illinois, Iowa, Minnesota, and North Dakota—voted for McKinley, and so did the boom cities of the West—Chicago, St. Paul, Omaha, and Kansas City. (See map above.) All remained Republican for many years.

THE COLLAPSE OF POPULISM. One of the biggest factors in Bryan's defeat was the Populist endorsement. *Populists were never able to overcome the eastern suspicion that they were a combination of ignorant "hayseeds" and wild-eyed fanatics.* Nor were they ever able to convince factory workers that Populist interests were identical to their own. The party struggled on, holding conventions annually until after 1900. It continued to lose strength even in the plains and the South. The return of prosperity in the late 1890's—stimulated, ironically, by an increase in the world money supply caused by gold discoveries in Alaska and Australia—relieved much of the rural distress.

POPULISTS AND BLACKS. In the South, Populists ran headlong into the wall of prejudice. Black farmers had traditionally voted Republican. They were natural allies for southern Populists, who were fighting the conservative Democratic establishment. The union of all working classes, without regard to race, was also part of the Populist ideology. Addressing poor Whites and Blacks, the Populist Congressman Tom Watson declared: "You are kept apart that you may be separately fleeced of your earnings. . . . You are deceived and blinded that you may not see how this race antagonism perpetuates a monetary system which beggars both."

Southern White Democrats countered the Populists' argument by appealing to racial hostility. To many poor Whites, Blacks represented competition. Whites could preserve their standing only by keeping Blacks on a lower rung of the social ladder.

The appeal nearly destroyed the Populists and created a movement to eliminate Blacks from southern politics. *Beginning with Mississippi in 1890, the southern states passed a number of laws designed to bypass the 15th Amendment (which prohibited them from restricting voting on the basis of race).*

Until it was declared unconstitutional in 1915, the most common device was the grandfather clause. This permitted any male to register if his father or grandfather had been a voter in 1868—a condition that only Whites could meet because no Blacks had been permitted to vote in 1868. The literacy test was widespread and lasted longer. Prospective voters were required to read a portion of the state constitution. The requirement was so vaguely worded that White registrars could exclude Blacks but admit illiterate Whites by claiming that they "understood" the constitution, even if they could not read it. Many states also adopted a poll tax—a set tax imposed on everybody as a requirement for voting—to keep Blacks from voting.

By 1900 Blacks were effectively disfranchised in the South. They remained so until the civil rights acts of the 1950's and 1960's. Toward the end of the 1890's, Populists, burned by their experiment in Black-White union, joined in the crusade to remove Blacks from politics.

THE LEGACY OF POPULISM. *The irony of the agricultural revolution is that it made the United States an urban nation by enabling a very few to feed the many.* And in a nation of smoke-belching factories and slum-ridden cities, Bryan and free silver seemed oddly out of place. Nevertheless, Bryan and the Populists awakened people to the numerous injustices in the economic system. There were many who admitted that reform was necessary. This feeling lingered even in states that voted for McKinley in 1896. *By 1900 a new reform movement, called Progressivism, was under way. And it had support in both political parties.*

Section Review

1. Mapping: Using the map on page 448, locate the states won by the Democrats and by the Republicans. Compare the results state by state with the map on page 442 showing the election of 1892. What do your comparisons indicate?
2. Identify or explain: William Jennings Bryan, "cross of gold," Mark Hanna, grandfather clause, William McKinley.
3. Describe the role of the Silver Democrats in the convention of 1896.
4. What role did business play in the Republican campaign of 1896?
5. How was the racial issue used by southern Democrats to fight Populism?

Chapter 18 Review

Bird's-Eye View

The revolution in agriculture created problems for American farmers. The more they produced, the lower prices fell, and the less money they made. Local merchants, banks, and especially the railroads, set up systems that cost farmers more of their earnings.

As their situation deteriorated, the farmers organized. The Grange was founded in 1867, and farmers entered into various alliances in the 1880's. Through these organizations farmers formed cooperatives and applied political pressure. The government responded by setting up the Interstate Commerce Commission to regulate the railroads. The political strength of the railroads, however, led to a series of Supreme Court decisions that made the ICC ineffective. By 1890 the farmers were looking for a political solution of their own.

The cause they rallied to was cheap money. The Greenback party of the 1870's had organized around the same principle, but the Treasury Department had rendered it powerless by backing every greenback with a dollar in gold. The cheap-money issue was renewed with the discovery of silver in the West. Nevertheless, the farmers were disappointed again.

With the nominations of the unsympathetic Grover Cleveland and Benjamin Harrison in 1892, the farmers realized that neither established party was serving their needs. The Populist party was born in Omaha on July 4, 1892.

Conditions worsened when the panic of 1893 led to an economic depression. President Cleveland acted to save the gold standard but did nothing to relieve the economic distress of the workers. There were widespread strikes. Labor lost public support because people feared that strikes would lead to greater economic disruptions. The result was a Republican victory in Congress.

The defeated Democrats sought an alliance with the Populists. In 1896 both parties nominated William Jennings Bryan. Concentrating on the issue of free silver, Bryan lost the election. Populism died, but the nation was awakened to numerous economic injustices.

Vocabulary

Define or identify each of the following:

combine	cooperatives	Populists
asset	Greenbacks	suffragist
crop-lien	inflationist	injunction

Review Questions

1. Why was there a food surplus in the 1880's?
2. Name the two major farm organizations and explain why they were formed.
3. Why did farmers want to reform the transportation regulations?

4. How did the gold standard hurt farmers?
5. Why was the Populist party platform considered radical?
6. What was the main issue of the 1896 Presidential election? Who won, and why?
7. How did each of the following disfranchise Black voters in the South: **a)** The grandfather clause? **b)** The poll tax? **c)** The literacy test?

Reviewing Social Studies Skills

1. Draw a time line, showing the political activity of farmers between 1870 and 1900.
2. What can you learn about the success or failure of Populism by studying the election maps of 1892 and 1896?
3. Using the map on page 434, complete the following:
   a. Which states had less than 10 percent farm tenancy?
   b. Which states had over 50 percent farm tenancy?
   c. Why do you think there was such a high rate of farm tenancy in the South in 1900?
4. Make two lists, comparing the advantages and disadvantages of cheap money.

Reading for Meaning

1. Farmers believed that, in comparison with the rest of the country, they had special economic disadvantages. List the evidence in this chapter that supports such an assertion.
2. The main concept of the free silver platform was:
   a. Workers preferred to be paid in silver, rather than paper money, since they were sure of its value.
   b. Silver money keeps its value, but paper money fluctuates.
   c. Silver money is cheap money, unlike the money backed by gold.
   Explain your choice.
3. A demagogue is an individual who is able to move and lead people by appealing to their emotions. Reread the quotes from William J. Bryan's famous Cross of Gold speech. What words or phrases in his speech have emotional appeal? Was Bryan a demagogue, or did he merely reflect the feelings of the people?

Bibliography

Main-Travelled Roads, by Hamlin Garland (Holt, Rinehart and Winston), is a collection of short stories about life in the Midwest.

My Antonia, by Willa Cather (Houghton Mifflin), is a novel of frontier life in Nebraska.

Samuel P. Hays's *Response to Industrialism, 1885–1914* (University of Chicago Press) is an interesting book, and it covers some of the important issues of this area.

Chapter 19

The New Colossus

By 1890 the West, but not the American wanderlust, had been tamed. The pioneers had merely changed directions. They were moving from the farm to the city, from the South to the North, from the Midwest to the Far West. Social scientists who have examined city directories at the turn of the century have found that 10 percent of the people listed one year were gone the next. That means that the entire population of the country averaged a move every 10 years. Even the urban ghetto—long a symbol of human despair—experienced enormous turnover. The ghetto remained, but the people came and went.

Chapter Objectives

After you have finished reading this chapter, you should be able to:

1. Compare the pattern of European and Chinese immigration in the 1880's.
2. Describe the problems faced by the poor in the cities.
3. Explain how changes in education supported the growth of newspapers and magazines.
4. Recall the way realism expressed itself in the arts.
5. Identify the changes that took place in American religious tolerance.

Movement had become the national pastime. It was commented on by every foreign visitor. Why? Social mobility was the original promise of American life—the promise of opportunity. Americans were guided by the hope that a new place and a fresh start would bring success. The hope was not always realized, the opportunity did not always materialize, but the promise remained.

1. The Flood Tide of Immigration

IMMIGRANTS SEEK A NEW START.
The promise of American life was symbolized by a statue in New York Harbor. It was a gift from the French people on the occasion of the nation's centennial in 1876. On a tablet inside the main entrance to the Statue of Liberty is a poem by Emma Lazarus, entitled "The New Colossus." It reads, in part:

"Give me your tired, your poor,
Your huddled masses yearning to breathe
* free,*
The wretched refuse of your teeming shore.
Send these, the homeless, tempest-tost, to
* me,*
I lift my lamp beside the golden door!"

In the quarter century after the statue was placed on New York's Liberty Island, some 10 million immigrants passed through that "golden door," seeking a new start. By 1900 they were arriving at the rate of a million a year. *Germans and Irish continued to make up a substantial portion of the immigrant population, but by 1900 the majority were coming from southern and eastern Europe—Italians, Greeks, Poles, Russians, Austro-Hungarians, and Jews.*

MOVING ON. Immigrants had always tended to cluster in the cities, filtering from there into the countryside. Before the Civil War, the Irish moved into New York and Boston, while the Germans helped populate Chicago, St. Louis, and Cincinnati. The new immigration was not much different, although it was attracted more to the boom cities of the West. By 1900 Chicago had more Bohemians than any other city in the world except Prague, the capital of Bohemia (now Czechoslovakia). Italians, Poles, Bohemians, Croats, and Serbs worked in the steel mills of Pittsburgh, Pennsylvania, and Gary, Indiana. Other nationalities moved straight to the farm. The Dakotas were populated to a large extent by Russians and Norwegians.

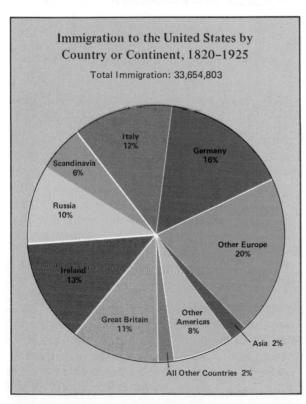

Immigration to the United States by Country or Continent, 1820–1925

Total Immigration: 33,654,803

Germany 16%
Italy 12%
Scandinavia 6%
Russia 10%
Ireland 13%
Great Britain 11%
Other Europe 20%
Other Americas 8%
Asia 2%
All Other Countries 2%

Minnesota's Red River valley attracted a mixture of Scandinavians and Germans.

MOVING UP. For some, the "golden door" fulfilled its promise. Consider the case of a young German boy, the son of poor peasants, who was brought to America at the age of three months. He was raised in poverty but attended public schools. After working for a time on a railroad construction gang, he decided to study law. In 1875 he moved to Chicago and opened a law office. For two years he slept in his office until he earned enough to rent a room. In 1879 he made his first investment in city real estate. Within a decade he was worth half a million dollars. In 1892 John Peter Altgeld was elected governor of Illinois. Had he not been born abroad (the Constitution permits only a native-born American to become President), he might have been the Democratic nominee in 1896.

Altgeld's case was unusual. Few immigrants could expect to rise that far or that fast. A study of the top business executives in the nation in 1900 shows that more than 80 percent were children of native-born parents.

Even so, it was a rare immigrant who regretted coming. The Polish youth living in a crowded tenement and working in a *sweatshop* was able to own, perhaps for the first time, a white shirt and a pair of shoes. Freedom from religious and political persecution also compensated for much of the dreariness of the immigrant's life. And for some, life was not worse than it had been at home. A young woman who had migrated from Poland to work in a New York clothing factory told a legislative committee that while she made only 4.50 dollars a week, she and her roommate each spent only 2.00 dollars a week. "Of course," she added, "we could have lived cheaper, but we are both fond of good things and felt that we could afford them."

453

A ticket for passage to America on the German liner S.S. Patricia *cost $30 from Hamburg, Germany. This photograph of immigrants on deck was taken by Edwin Levick in 1906. What does it tell you about the journey?*

Sweatshop is a word that originated in the New York garment industry, where entire families stitched clothing by hand in hot, stuffy attics. It gradually came to mean any small factory in which conditions were poor and hours long.

MOVING FORWARD. *The immigrants made a tremendous contribution to America's industrial development.* They were about 15 percent of the population in 1900, but they made up nearly 30 percent of the total work force. The reason was that most immigrants were men, in the prime of life, between the ages of 14 and 45. Thus, they went to work immediately, often learning skills on the job.

PREJUDICE TOWARD IMMIGRANTS. Many immigrant workers encountered prejudice on the part of native-born American workers. As the labor force swelled, competition for jobs was keen and wages went down. Moreover, as the cities became more crowded, housing costs went up. *Many native-born American workers resented the newcomers as competitors for a better way of life.* Chinese workers, particularly in California, were the first victims of anti-immigrant feeling.

THE CHINESE. The "golden door" was not the only entrance to the United States. *The Chinese who entered the country through the San Francisco customs house perhaps experienced more hostility from Americans than any other immigrant*

454

group. The first wave of immigrants from China arrived between 1848 and 1850, during the California gold rush. From the start, their attitude about migration differed from that of European immigrants. The Chinese came to make their fortunes. But they hoped to return to China to improve the lives of the families they had left behind. Many took jobs that other workers would not do.

Then, in the 1860's, a second wave of Chinese arrived. *Chinese laborers made an outstanding contribution to the construction of the transcontinental railroad line.* More than 1,200 of them died building the railroads. Their often ingenious solutions to the physical barriers of the Pacific coast led one historian to say that they "salvaged for the West millions of acres of the richest farmland and urban real estate. They could not have given more."

By 1870 there were over 100,000 Chinese in the country, most still hoping to return to China. Because they were forced to live in Chinatowns, they made little or no adjustment to western ways, retaining the language, clothing, and customs of their homeland. When the first wave of hostility against them broke out, these customs became the object of suspicion, criticism, and ridicule.

THE CHINESE EXCLUSION ACT. The hostility against Chinese was first written into law when California workers influenced the revision of their state constitution in 1879 to prevent Chinese people from owning property and working at preferred jobs. In the same year Congress passed an exclusion bill, limiting the number of Chinese immigrants. President Hayes vetoed the bill, however, because it violated a treaty with China. *Finally, in 1882 the Chinese Exclusion Act was passed and continued in effect until World War II. In addition to setting immigration quotas, it denied American citizenship to Chinese born in China.*

This Chinese grocery in San Francisco displayed many of the popular ingredients of Chinese cuisine, including bok choy, ginger root, and Chinese yams. Can you use this picture to make a statement about the Chinese adjustment to western society?

OTHER RESTRICTIONS. The Chinese Exclusion Act was the first restriction on immigration passed primarily because of pressure from worker groups. In 1885 the Contract Labor Law, which permitted employers to recruit workers in Europe, was repealed. Over the next 30 years, workers pressured Congress to pass a bill forbidding entry to immigrants who could not read and write. A literacy bill was finally enacted in 1917 over the President's veto. Needless to say, the immigrants' long-range contribution to American industrialization offered scant comfort to those who resented the newcomers as competitors.

Section Review

1. Identify or explain: Emma Lazarus, John Peter Altgeld, sweatshop, Chinese Exclusion Act.
2. During the late 1800's, how was the growth of industry, cities, and immigration related?
3. What important contribution did the immigrants make to the United States?
4. What was the aim of the Chinese immigrants who came to the United States? Why was hostility toward them so intense?

2. The Coming of Metropolis

CITIES AND DIVERSITY. *The rise of great cities was perhaps the most important development in America between the end of the Civil War and the turn of the century.* The cities were populated by immigrants, but not all of them came from abroad. Indeed, probably about half the migrants to cities came from American farms. The revolution in farm technology created a surplus rural population that drifted into the newly risen factories of the cities.

Then, as now, the cities presented wide contrasts. Opulent mansions, museums, and opera houses coexisted with warehouses, factories, and slums. The wealthy sailed on yachts and cruise ships from the ports to which the immigrants flocked. Broad avenues and orderly squares gave way to narrow streets and dark alleyways. Cities were as diverse as the people living in them.

THE PACE OF URBAN GROWTH. During the decade of the 1880's, when industrial growth reached its peak, urban growth increased markedly. (See graph below.) Even the already sizable eastern cities increased in population by about a fourth over the decade. New York went from just under two million to two and a half million, and Philadelphia grew from 800,000 to one million. The most spectacular gains were made in the Midwest. Chicago, which had been doubling in size every decade since 1840, continued the pace and reached a million. Kansas City tripled in size, and Minneapolis

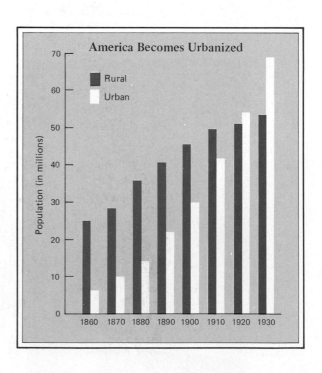

America Becomes Urbanized

■ Rural
□ Urban

Population (in millions)

1860 1870 1880 1890 1900 1910 1920 1930

and St. Paul quadrupled their populations over the decade. Denver increased its size by five times.

STANDING ROOM ONLY. Such astounding growth, not surprisingly, created housing problems. Speculators met the sudden demand by purchasing tracts of land and erecting rows of identical multifamily dwellings called tenements (meaning a dwelling for tenants, or renters). The typical tenement was a wooden structure four or five stories high with small, often windowless rooms for living and sleeping. Sometimes entire families were crowded into a single room. *Because of the crowded conditions and high turnover and because landlords were reluctant to make repairs, the buildings deteriorated quickly into ramshackle, leaky, unpainted slums.* In 1900 some 2.4 million people were packed into tenements on New York City's Manhattan Island.

Under such conditions crime flourished. The urban crime rate rose sharply after 1880, and gangs ruled city streets. In one small section of Chicago in 1893, one fourth of the population was arrested at least once in the course of the year.

CORRUPTION AND BOSS RULE. Slums and crime were signs of social disorganization, and urban governments were ill equipped to handle it. City government was a mirror of state government, with an executive, or mayor, and a legislature, or council,

"Hester Street," in lower New York, was painted by George Luks in 1905. One of the foremost realists of the period, Luks used as his subjects dockworkers, slum children, and various city scenes. What does this painting tell you about life on Hester Street?

all elected by the people. Because the people of early America distrusted power, city charters distributed authority widely, giving a bit to the mayor, a bit to the council, and some to independent boards and commissions. Under such conditions decisive leadership was rare, buck-passing the norm, and chaos the result.

To make things worse, the people who went to the cities in the 1880's and 1890's, whether peasants from eastern Europe or farmhands from rural America, were not used to urban life and had little concept of democracy. When someone with a talent for organization came along, they were ready to follow.

As a result, political organizations, or machines, sprang up in most large cities. They existed side by side with the elected government. At the head of the machine was a boss, who usually held no office and was content to wield power without publicity. ("Boss" Tweed of New York was a notable exception to this rule during the late 1860's.) The boss led the machine in somewhat the same way a general commanded an army, issuing orders to lieutenants, who transmitted them to the elected authorities. Each lieutenant, or ward heeler, was in charge of a section of the city and often held a public office. Below these ward leaders were precinct captains, who patrolled the neighborhoods.

The machine kept itself in power by serving the needs of its clients, both rich and poor. It filled its treasury with kickbacks from corporations desiring to do construction work for the city. Building inspectors who failed to enforce building regulations or fire laws got secret payments from merchants. The poor, and especially immigrants, got help of a different kind. Precinct captains helped them find jobs, often on public projects, and intervened when they got into trouble with the law. At election time precinct captains herded their grateful followers to the polls. It was neither honest nor democratic, but the system worked in its own way.

SETTLEMENT HOUSES. In 1889 another kind of institution that helped to make life more bearable for the city's newcomers appeared. *Jane Addams, a humanitarian reformer and dedicated crusader for peace, purchased a building called Hull House in the slums of Chicago and opened it to the public.* Hull House offered a variety of services for Chicago's slum dwellers. It had an adult education program that ranged from college-level literature to cooking and home management. It sponsored concerts and lectures, provided recreation programs and day-care centers for children, and offered child-care education.

Addams also waged an extensive campaign for city regulation of sweatshops and was considered a powerful figure in the crusade against corruption in city politics. She lobbied for collection of garbage, public parks and child-labor laws, and in 1931 she received the Nobel Prize for her contribution to the cause of world peace.

In New York, Lillian Wald's Henry Street Settlement specialized in medical services for the poor and the training of nurses. In addition, it offered a wide variety of recreational and educational services. Other cities had similar operations.

THE URBAN WOMAN. Professional women, like Jane Addams, who headed large and complex organizations, were part of the urban experience. *The cities vastly increased opportunities for women.* Living quarters in the city were smaller and required less care. The development of cheap, ready-made clothing and the appearance of commercial laundries eased or eliminated two of the tasks that had occupied women for centuries. Other chores for which women had been responsible on the farm—milking, butter churning, raising chickens, and canning—were handled in the city by a quick trip to the grocery store.

The Henry Street Settlement, founded by Lillian Wald in 1893, provided various forms of recreation for urban children. On hot summer days a sprinkler was set up in the schoolyard for children who were far away from country beaches and swimming holes.

Women went to work in the factories and also found some opportunities in business. With the advent of the typewriter, women worked as typists and stenographers. However, because of traditional roles and prejudices, most women in business were excluded from management positions.

WORKING FOR WOMEN'S SUFFRAGE. Along with increasing opportunities for women came a renewed demand for women's rights, especially the right to vote. *Disappointed that the 14th and 15th Amendments did not give women the right to vote, Elizabeth Cady Stanton and Susan B. Anthony had organized the National Woman Suffrage Association in 1869.* Their goal was a women's suffrage amendment to the Constitution.

People like Lucy Stone and Julia Ward Howe had favored a more conservative approach. They founded the American Woman Suffrage Association, whose goal was to secure voting rights for women by amending state constitutions. In 1890 the two groups merged to form the National American Woman Suffrage Association.

These leaders, along with others, made progress in gaining acceptance for women's participation in public affairs. However, by 1900 only four western states had given women the right to vote. Twenty years elapsed before women gained this right on a national scale.

Section Review

1. Identify or explain: tenement, ward heeler, Elizabeth Cady Stanton, settlement house, National American Woman Suffrage Association, Jane Addams.
2. Using the bar graph on page 456, identify the period in the 19th century in

459

which the greatest movement of people to urban areas occurred.

3. Why did tenements tend to become slums so quickly?
4. What problems in city government led to the rise of the political machine? How did the nature of the population contribute to the machine's growth?
5. How did city life alter the role of women?

3. Mind and Matter in an Industrial Society

THE IMPACT OF INDUSTRIALIZATION. Industrialization did more than change the American economy; it transformed American life. By altering living patterns, it forced Americans to reexamine their social attitudes, their educational structure, and even their religious beliefs.

EDUCATION FOR AN URBAN ENVIRONMENT. Education underwent more change between 1890 and 1910 than it had in the previous 100 years. The advent of public, tax-supported, education before the Civil War had done little to change the curriculum or teaching methods. Elementary school pupils everywhere received a dash of spelling and arithmetic, imprinted upon faulty memories by sheer repetition. They learned to read from one of McGuffey's readers, which incorporated lessons on proper social conduct. Those who went on to high school or private academies spent time learning Latin, Greek, and mathematics, which were considered good exercise for the mind. The system might have served a rural society well enough, but it was insufficient for a complex urban society.

JOHN DEWEY. In 1896 John Dewey opened a different kind of school in Chicago. *Impressed by the methods of modern science, Dewey believed that education ought to be a process of discovery.* Children should "learn by doing," he said, by experimenting in the same way scientists did. Facts discovered by this means would be held much longer than those gained by memorization. And the learning experience itself would relate to everyday life. Dewey's ideas helped to inspire a fresh look at the whole concept of education.

EDUCATION FOR LIFE. By 1900 many cities were broadening their curricula to include natural sciences, history, and geography. Dewey's idea that schools were part of life was easily translated into practical courses that prepared people for jobs (although that is not what Dewey had in mind). Elementary accounting, typing, shop, stenography, and home economics became part of the high school curriculum.

THE MODERN COLLEGE. Higher education needed similar changes. Post-Civil War colleges were still wedded to ancient languages and "moral philosophy" and did not respond to the needs of an industrial age. The founding of schools that specialized in science and technology, such as the Massachusetts Institute of Technology (M.I.T.) and the Case Institute of Technology, began to offer a practical solution. With the Morrill Land Grant Act adopted by Congress during the Civil War, the federal government offered public lands to the states for the support of colleges that would specialize in agricultural and mechanical arts. Most of the state universities of the West received aid under the law.

In 1869 Harvard University named as its president Charles W. Eliot, a professor of chemistry from nearby M.I.T. An innovative leader, Eliot instituted the elective system, by which students chose their own subjects of study. In 1876 Johns Hopkins University of Baltimore pioneered the notion of a graduate school devoted to advanced training in science and the arts. Eliot quickly adopted the idea at Harvard. Alert universities in the

Midwest—Chicago, Michigan, Wisconsin— soon followed the examples of Johns Hopkins and Harvard.

The graduate school furthered the idea of specialization—the breakdown of "moral philosophy," for instance, into history, economics, geography, and philosophy. Consequently, by 1900 the educational jack-of-all-trades was no more. Rapid advances in technology demanded highly trained professionals. *The modern college, a complex of disciplines and professors, was education's response to industrialism.*

HIGHER EDUCATION FOR WOMEN.
Beginning with Oberlin in the 1830's, a few colleges opened their doors to women before the Civil War. The University of Iowa admitted women from the time it was founded in 1856. But opportunities for women were limited. After the war, pressure on colleges increased as women graduated from high school in ever-increasing numbers. By 1900 their number exceeded the number of male graduates from high school.

When Vassar College opened in 1861, it had 350 women students and more applications than it could handle. Nearly all state universities began admitting women after the Civil War, although women teachers at the college level remained a rarity for many years. Smith College, started in 1875, was the first to be endowed by a woman; and Wellesley, founded in the same year, was the first college to appoint an all-woman faculty and a woman president. *By 1901 there were 128 women's colleges, and women made up 25 percent of the total undergraduate enrollment.* Although their numbers increased steadily in the schools and professions, most women found limited opportunities for success.

BLACKS IN WHITE AMERICA.
Thirty years after the Civil War, southern Blacks seemed to be little better off than they had been in 1865. Most were tenants, farming someone else's land in return for a share of

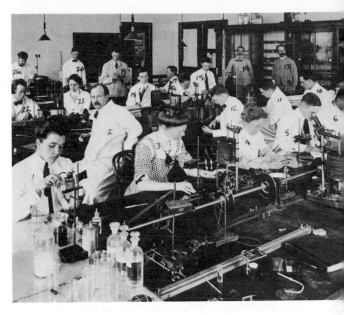

By 1872 Cornell University was entirely coeducational. This physics lab at Cornell was photographed in 1900.

the crop. *By law the southern states and some northern ones segregated the races in public places.* Jim Crow laws required the separation of races in schools, streetcars, railroads, railroad stations, parks, and other public facilities. The accommodations for Blacks were always inferior. The ballot, used by Blacks so effectively during reconstruction, was taken away by grandfather clauses, poll taxes, and literacy tests.

HIGHER EDUCATION FOR BLACKS.
Blacks were excluded from most White colleges and had few schools of higher learning of their own. Furthermore, the pioneers of Black education favored vocational rather than academic training. They considered academic training too theoretical to be of practical value to such an oppressed people. General Samuel C. Armstrong, the founder of the Hampton Institute in Virginia, taught his students respect for labor, vocational skills, and good character. Hampton Institute's most distinguished pupil was Booker T. Washington.

461

BOOKER T. WASHINGTON. *In 1881 Washington founded the Tuskegee Institute in Alabama, where he spread the doctrine that equality must be earned.* To get ahead and be recognized as equals, Blacks must first become skilled workers.

Washington was as popular among Whites as he was among Blacks. Few Whites wanted Blacks to obtain political power and receive academic educations. But most did not object to Blacks being educated for trades. Money poured into Tuskegee from all over the country, and Washington found himself the spokesperson for his race. Whenever a Black was to receive a political appointment, Washington's advice was sought. When money was to be allocated for Black schools, Washington made sure the institutions conformed to his philosophy. He even controlled the editorial policies of various Black newspapers. His influence in Black affairs was considerable.

In 1895 the political leaders of Georgia invited Washington to an exposition in Atlanta celebrating the South's progress since the Civil War. No Black in the South had ever shared a platform with Whites on an occasion of such importance. Washington's address drew national attention. Often called the Atlanta Compromise by both friends and critics, it summarized Washington's philosophy.

To many Blacks, especially the young, Washington's philosophy was out of date in 1895. The spread of segregation and Jim Crow laws and the disfranchisement of Blacks in the South had left them bitter and suspicious of Washington's idea of earned equality through patience and vocational training.

W. E. B. DU BOIS. Around the turn of the century, a group of progressive Blacks began to make their opposition felt. The most outspoken of these critics was a young man from Massachusetts, the first Black to receive a Ph.D. degree from Harvard,

W. E. B. Du Bois. In his book *The Souls of Black Folk* (1903) Du Bois sharply criticized Washington's approach. He demanded equal rights. *Washington's error, Du Bois pointed out, was ignoring the systematic discrimination by which Blacks were prevented from getting ahead.*

THE NIAGARA MOVEMENT. Aided by William Monroe Trotter, the founder of the *Boston Guardian*, and 28 leading Black intellectuals, Du Bois proposed in 1905 a national conference on civil rights to oppose Washington's power. The delegates met on the Canadian side of Niagara Falls because hotels on the American side refused to admit Blacks. The following year they met at Harpers Ferry, in honor of John Brown, and drew up a resolution demanding full equality and the guaranteed right to vote.

In 1908, in the aftermath of a race riot and two lynchings in Springfield, Illinois, a group of Progressives, led by Mary White Ovington and Oswald Garrison Villard, proposed the founding of the National Association for the Advancement of Colored People (NAACP). The letter calling for the formation of the group was written by Villard, grandson of William Lloyd Garrison, and signed by 60 leading citizens, including Du Bois and Jane Addams.

In 1911 the Niagara Movement was absorbed into the NAACP, and the organization went to work to implement its demands. The program, considered radical for its time, was based on obtaining equality through legislation, the courts, and education. Hardly a radical organization, the NAACP has worked through the existing political order to achieve change, winning, among other things, a decision declaring the grandfather clause unconstitutional. The need to train Blacks to participate in industrial society led to the formation of organizations demanding full equality for Blacks.

THE CHANGING NEWSPAPER. The "penny press," or mass-circulation daily,

Above is the editorial office of Crisis, *the magazine of the NAACP devoted to news about Blacks and the NAACP. As editor of* Crisis *from 1910 to 1932, W. E. B. Du Bois (shown standing at right) contributed editorials criticizing racial attitudes in America.*

began in Andrew Jackson's day, but most newspapers after the Civil War catered to the educated few. In 1870 there were only 600 daily newspapers in the United States. With the advent of industrialization, that number increased rapidly to over 2,000, including numerous foreign-language papers and at least 150 catering to various Black communities. The invention of the type-writer and the linotype certainly contributed to the growth. The linotype, invented in 1885, mechanically set type and speeded up the whole printing process. *Perhaps of more significance was the rapid expansion of the market for newspapers: The American public could now read.*

JOSEPH PULITZER. Joseph Pulitzer, who came to America from Austria-Hungary in 1864, was the first to exploit the potential of linotype. After serving in the Union Army, he went into newspaper publishing in St.

Louis and made the *Post-Dispatch* one of the outstanding papers in the Midwest. In 1883 he purchased the *New York World* and turned it into a popular sheet devoted to scandals, tragedies, and crime. He introduced the comics page, the sports section, and a features section for columnists. Pulitzer's brand of sensational, or yellow, journalism was sometimes denounced as unfair competition, but Pulitzer was more than a scandalmonger. *His paper was successful because it presented stories of genuine interest written in a punchy style designed to appeal to the widest possible readership.*

Pulitzer defied convention again when he hired the first woman reporter, Elizabeth Seaman. Writing under the name Nelly Bly, Seaman pioneered the field of investigative journalism. To find out about conditions in a factory, she posed as a day laborer and then wrote a biting exposé. She managed to get arrested and then wrote a shocking series of articles on prison conditions. While investigating an insane asylum, she pretended to be insane and was hospitalized.

WILLIAM RANDOLPH HEARST. With such imaginative methods, Pulitzer dominated the field of big-city journalism until William Randolph Hearst purchased the *New York Journal* in 1895. San Francisco born and Harvard educated, Hearst inherited the fortune his father had made from Henry Comstock's silver mine and began building a newspaper empire. He started with the *San Francisco Examiner* and then moved into New York with the purchase of the floundering *Journal*. He raided Pulitzer's staff of writers, including the inventor of the colored comic strip, and soon made the *Journal* a financial success. On the day after the election of 1896, the

Sidenote to History

The Ragtime Music of Scott Joplin

It swept the world as the waltz had done a century before. And, like the waltz, it was both a new musical beat and a new dance step. It was called ragtime. It might have been the first truly American musical form. It was surely the first attempt to combine Afro-American and European-American musical elements. Ragtime evolved among a group of mostly Black composers during the 1890's. It came to world attention in 1899 when Scott Joplin published "The Maple Leaf Rag."

Scott Joplin was born in 1868 in Texarkana. Whether his birthplace was on the Texas or the Arkansas side of the line is subject to argument. His father was an ex-slave from North Carolina. His mother was a free Black from Kentucky. Joplin's talent for music was so obvious that the village piano teacher gave him free lessons. The teacher, a German immigrant, introduced him to the European classics of Bach and Beethoven. Their blend of elegant form and joyous rhythm made a lasting impression on him.

Ragtime sprang from two popular dances of the 1890's, the cakewalk and the two-step. Joplin disciplined their bouncy rhythm by imposing a symphonic form, often referred to as A–B–A (*i.e.*, introducing melody-theme, enlarging on it, and then restating it). The resulting music was elegant, sprightly, and melodic.

"The Maple Leaf Rag" was a world hit, the first song to top the million mark in sales of sheet music. "Paris Has Gone Rag Time Wild" an American newspaper headlined in the summer of 1900. The fine print contained a story about thousands of people doing the cakewalk in the streets of the French capital.

Ragtime remained the standard musical form until World War I, when it yielded to the looser, brassier chord progressions of Dixieland jazz. During the heyday of ragtime, Scott Joplin produced more than thirty popular ragtime pieces. But he was not satisfied. He wanted to lift Afro-American music to the level of the European classics. He wrote two ragtime operas, and he was reportedly working on an Afro-American symphony when he died at the age of 48 in 1916.

The shift in musical tastes shortly thereafter buried his rhythms and his memory. Only in recent years, after one of his ragtime hits, "The Entertainer," formed the theme for the hugely successful motion picture, *The Sting,* have we come to recognize Joplin's true genius.

Journal printed 1.5 million copies of several editions. Few newspapers can boast a run that large today.

The success of the *Journal* led Hearst to establish similar papers in Chicago, Boston, and other cities. ***An assortment of newspapers under single ownership became known as a chain.*** And, like the trusts that Hearst never tired of denouncing, a chain of newspapers had numerous marketing efficiencies. It shared correspondents, especially in foreign countries, pooled special features and comics, and bargained for special rates from such news syndicates as Associated Press (begun in 1847 as a telegraph-sharing pool).

MASS-CIRCULATION MAGAZINES. In 1905 Hearst added *Cosmopolitan*, a monthly magazine, to his growing empire—a move that spread yellow journalism to the field of magazines. Early magazines, like newspapers, were directed at the educated few. Some were literary digests. Others discussed current events in sober prose. But, even before the Civil War, magazines aiming at a wider circulation began to respond to the needs of a changing society. ***The first mass-circulation magazines were directed at women.*** The *Ladies' Home Journal,* founded in 1883 and priced at a dime, was the magazine version of the penny press. Edited by a Dutch immigrant, the *Journal* set the tone for a number of periodicals. *Cosmopolitan, Redbook,* and *McClure's,* to name a few, all followed the Pulitzer-Hearst formula of Progressive politics, investigative reporting, and sensational exposés. ***After 1900 mass-circulation magazines also played an important role in awakening people to the need for reform in state and municipal government.***

Section Review

1. Identify or explain: Joseph Pulitzer, John Dewey, W. E. B. Du Bois, Tuskegee Institute, Elizabeth Seaman, William Randolph Hearst, Atlanta Compromise.
2. What were the effects of John Dewey's ideas on American education?
3. Describe Booker T. Washington's plan for achieving equality for Blacks. Do you think his plan could have worked? Why or why not?
4. What was W. E. B. Du Bois's basic objection to Washington's ideas? How did he and his followers implement their own plan?

4. The Arts in America

REALISM. *During the last decades of the 19th century and the first decade of the 20th, American art reflected the new urban, industrial age—its preoccupations, problems, conflicts, hopes, successes, and failures.* Many refer to this period as the age of realism in the arts—the period during which the public demanded and artists produced works that dealt with life as it was, not as people wished it to be.

In literature William Dean Howells was one of the most influential realists. As editor of the *Atlantic Monthly* in the 1870's and *Harper's Monthly* in the 1890's, Howells wielded considerable power in the literary world. The test of a good novel, Howells once observed, was whether it was "true to the motives, the impulses, the principles that shape the lives of actual men and women." Howells' most famous novel is *The Rise of Silas Lapham* (1885). It tells the story of an honest, somewhat uncultivated man who wins success by sheer hard work. The story is true to life, full of sorrow and triumph.

Writers like Stephen Crane and Hamlin Garland also considered themselves realists. Crane's *Maggie: A Girl of the Streets* (1893) describes the plight of a young slum girl.

"Central Park," Maurice Prendergast, 1900–1902

The late 19th century saw a revolution in American art—from romanticism to realism. Many of the artists studied or lived in Paris during their careers. Whistler, for example, left for France in 1855 and never returned. His works clearly show the influence of French impressionism, and his influence is evident in the works of other Americans of his time. Of the paintings in this group, which would you say is the most typically "American"?

"Sunday, Women Drying Their Hair," John Sloan, 1912

466

"The Artist in His Studio," James McNeill Whistler, 1864

"Hammerstein's Roof Garden," William Glackens, 1901

"Young Women Picking Fruit," Mary Cassatt, 1891

"The Puritan," Augustus Saint-Gaudens, 1887

Crane's masterpiece, *The Red Badge of Courage* (1895), portrays with chilling accuracy the fears of a young Civil War soldier under fire. Garland, a native of the Midwest, exposed the hardships and isolation of farm life in *Main-Travelled Roads* (1891).

Henry James and Edith Wharton towered above the other realists in their artistic skill and vision. But they differed from them in an important respect. Although their works dealt with uniquely American themes and their main characters were usually Americans, both James and Wharton lived and worked in Europe as mature writers. Many of their works were set in America, but both novelists were interested in exploring the American character in a European setting as well.

THE LOCAL-COLOR SCHOOL.

Another major literary form to appear in this period was the local-color novel or story. Local-color writers tried to create a regional literature. ***Their aim was to describe as precisely and faithfully as possible the life of their particular localities.*** In fact, the local colorists thought of themselves as realists. They insisted on making their stories conform as closely as possible to real life.

Although their stories were concerned with life in America's regions—the South, the Midwest, New England, the West—the local colorists attracted a national audience. They were read by Americans eager for information about distant parts of the country and about ways of life rapidly vanishing with the spread of modern industrial life.

The leading local colorists of the South were George Washington Cable, Kate Chopin, and Grace King of Louisiana; Thomas Nelson Page of Virginia; Charles W. Chesnutt, a Black novelist from North Carolina; and Joel Chandler Harris, the Georgian whose "Uncle Remus" stories won widespread and lasting fame.

The most widely read local colorist was Mark Twain (born Samuel Langhorne Clemens). American life springs from every page of his novels—its half-formed thoughts, regional speech, daily routines, and social values. *The Adventures of Huckleberry Finn* (1885) and *The Adventures of Tom Sawyer* (1876) are classics of our national literature.

Twain was also an acute and penetrating critic of society. In *The Gilded Age* (1873), which he wrote in collaboration with Charles Dudley Warner, Twain satirized the values and life style of industrial America.

THE DIME NOVEL.

While writers like Helen Hunt Jackson were giving Americans a realistic—and not always pleasant—view of the West, the dime novels were creating another West—romantic and adventure-filled. ***The West of the dime novels was pure fiction. Nonetheless, it shaped most Americans' view of the West.*** Typical of the dime novel's cowboy heroes was gun-toting Buck Taylor, the creation of Prentiss Ingraham, a press agent for Buffalo Bill's Wild West Show. Kate Sharp, a fearless young woman of the West, was one of the heroes of Frank Starr's popular *American Novels*—some of which sold as many as 500,000 copies.

AMERICAN ART.

At the end of the Civil War, there was no outstanding museum in America. ***But by the turn of the century, every American city had at least one good gallery or museum.*** This surge of interest in the arts was primarily the result of lavish spending by men and women who had made and were making their fortunes in business and industry. Determined to be cultured, they bought countless art treasures, regardless of the price. At first they displayed them in their palatial homes. When their homes were filled to overflowing, they founded public galleries and museums.

Most of the art treasures were from Europe. Even when a painting or sculpture

Sidenote to History

The Inside-Out Building

Cities flourished because they were centers of trade and business. Because they flourished, cities attracted more people. Increasing population put a premium on land, resulting in ever-higher buildings for both housing and offices.

Increased height demanded some kind of mechanical lifting device, for climbing multiple flights of stairs several times a day was more than most people would tolerate. A cage lifted by ropes and pulleys was the obvious solution, but it seemed dangerous until Elisha Graves Otis invented a device that held the cage in place even if a rope broke. His safety elevator was put in use after the Civil War.

The elevator permitted the construction of buildings as high as 10 stories, but that was not enough. Masonry buildings, made of stone or brick, were built like pyramids. As their height increased, the walls at the lower stories became thicker, and the buildings occupied more land.

The tallest masonry building ever constructed—put up in Chicago in 1891—required walls that were almost two meters (six feet) thick at the base. In 1884 William L. Jenney boldly introduced a steel frame into the core of a building for the Home Insurance Company of Chicago. In doing so he turned the building inside out.

Instead of being sustained by outside walls, Jenney's building was a steel skeleton. Walls were only the outer skin. Steel was strong and workable. When long beams were formed into triangles and other geometric patterns, they provided enormous strength. They required relatively little space and weighed comparatively little. Steel buildings could tower skyward.

Another Chicago architect, Louis Sullivan, gave the steel-frame building a design. His plan for the Wainwright Building (St. Louis, 1891) emphasized the height of the building with upward-flowing lines of identical windows. With this and other buildings, Sullivan established the contour of the modern skyscraper.

---

was the creation of an American artist, it reflected European rather than American influences. This was because most American painters and sculptors of the post-Civil War years received their training in Europe. Some remained in Europe. Among such artists were James McNeill Whistler, a painter whom some regard as the genius of American art, and John Singer Sargent, a portraitist of international reputation.

Another group of equally gifted artists consciously resisted European influence. They worked vigorously to achieve a distinctly American style of painting. The most outstanding of these artists were Winslow Homer and Thomas Eakins.

Homer began his career as an illustrator for *Harper's Weekly* magazine and won fame for his paintings and sketches of Civil War scenes. Then he became fascinated with the sea, painting stark and forceful scenes of life on the rugged New England coast. Eakins was interested in tools, technology, and science. Several of his most famous paintings focused on surgeons performing operations. The pictures were so graphically detailed that they offended the sensibilities of the age. Eakins was one of the first painters to make sports a subject of his pictures.

AMERICAN SCULPTURE. The work of American sculptors as well as painters was influenced by European art. Italy exerted the greatest influence at mid-century. American sculptors turned out statues of prominent leaders that looked more like ancient Roman senators than 19th-century Americans.

Gradually American sculptors broke away from European models and like painters, began to work for a unique and distinctive American style. John Quincy Adams Ward was one of the first sculptors to create statues of American Indians and Blacks. Daniel Chester French produced realistic statues of notable Americans, including the famous statue of Abraham Lincoln in Washington, D.C.'s Lincoln Memorial. The most renowned American sculptor of the period was Augustus Saint-Gaudens, an Irish immigrant. Among his well-known works are statues of Generals Grant and Sherman, Admiral Farragut, and the statue of Lincoln in Lincoln Park, Chicago.

Section Review

1. Identify or explain: William Dean Howells, Stephen Crane, Thomas Eakins, Edith Wharton, Mark Twain, the local-color school.
2. How did the literature of the late 19th and early 20th centuries reflect the life-style of industrial America?
3. Describe the ways in which Europe influenced American art. How did some American artists react to this influence?

5. Religion and Reform

PROTESTANTISM. Although there are a great many religious groups in America today, most Americans belong to one of three religions: Protestantism, Catholicism, or Judaism. All three religions have been practiced on American soil for hundreds of years. During the 1600's America was settled by European Protestants, Catholics, and Jews.

Although all three groups arrived at more or less the same time, one group—the Protestants—was more numerous and more powerful than the other two. During the early days of the nation, Protestantism often dominated at the expense of the other religious groups. Both Catholics and Jews suffered discrimination in varying degrees. By 1900 America was still a Protestant country, with Protestants holding nearly all offices of political, social, and intellectual power. But the situation was beginning to change. *The number of American Catholics and Jews increased rapidly, as hundreds of thousands of Europeans poured into the United States during the great surge of immigration between 1880 and 1920.*

AMERICAN JEWS. Although Jews had lived in America since the earliest colonial days, they, like Roman Catholics, were considered a minority group. On the eve of the Civil War in 1861, there were about 150,000 Jews in the United States. The majority were German Jews who had come to America around the middle of the 19th century. Some were skilled in various crafts. Others were very well educated.

Many succeeded in American society. Solomon Kuhn was a founder of Kuhn, Loeb and Company, one of the nation's most prestigious investment banking houses. An immigrant peddler, Levi Strauss, invented what has probably become the most famous and distinctively American article of clothing—denim pants called *Levi's.* Meyer Guggenheim and his sons founded a huge mining and smelting company, which provided the funds for the Guggenheim Foundation—an organization that gives fellowships to hundreds of scholars and artists each year.

Sidenote to History

Culture Under Canvas

Where, in turn-of-the-century America, could you hear an inspirational speech, discuss the teachings of Socrates, attend an opera, and generally improve your mind, all in one spot? The answer is: at the Chautauqua (shah-TAWK-wah). The Chautauqua was a system of popular adult education that started in 1874 at Lake Chautauqua, New York. Putting forth a program of religion, education, and recreation, the Chatauqua attracted millions of Americans thirsting for culture.

The Chautauqua Institution was founded by John Vincent, a Methodist preacher, and Lewis Miller, an Akron, Ohio, merchant. They hoped to get Sunday school teachers together for a two-week training program in pleasant summertime surroundings. Thus, the first summer school in the United States was opened. It was an almost immediate success. The idea of continuing one's education during the summer appealed to many Americans. The first book club in America was established through the Chautauqua, and willing Chautauquans read and discussed great literature of the world. For those who could not attend the upstate summer school, correspondence courses were established. They were heavily subscribed. Reading groups sprang up from Schenectady to Dubuque as men and women read and discussed "great ideas."

By 1900 the series of lectures and cultural entertainment that made people want to take the trip to Lake Chautauqua was sent around the country. The so-called Chautauqua Circuit was born. The traveling Chautauquas reached their peak in the early 1920's. In 1921 it was estimated that around 35 million Americans had attended the traveling Chautauquas. The Chautauqua's huge canvas tent was a common sight throughout the United States. Cooking lessons, diction classes, and physical training sessions were held under one roof.

Once motion pictures and radio made their way into American life, the influence of the traveling Chautauqua began to fade. However, the Chautauqua Institution still holds its series of summer schools in the New York town after which it was named.

MIXING IN. Jews scattered widely across the continent. Several western towns were named after Jews and bear witness to their presence on the frontier. Included among these cities were: Mayer and Solomonsville, Arizona; Levy, New Mexico; Newman, California; Altman, Colorado; Roseburg, Oregon; Rose Canyon, California; Weiss Bluff, Texas; and Mount Davidson, Nevada.

The process by which immigrants become part of their new society is usually a slow one. But the Jews who arrived in America during the crisis-ridden decades just before the Civil War assimilated rapidly. Jews were on both sides of the slavery question, as were other Americans. Ten thousand Jews served in the armies of the North and the South, although most were in the Union forces. Judah P. Benjamin, a Jewish senator from Louisiana, became Attorney General of the Confederacy, acting Secretary of War, and Secretary of State.

DISCRIMINATION. For the most part, however, Jews were the objects of discrimination whether they were new arrivals or Americans of long standing, successful or unsuccessful, rich or poor. *Anti-Semitism,* like anti-Catholic feeling, was related in the late 19th and early 20th centuries to anti-immigrant sentiment. Between 1881 and 1924, it is estimated that more than two million eastern European Jews arrived in America. The Jews from eastern Europe were

The 1913 garment workers' strike united Italian and Jewish immigrant laborers in their efforts to achieve a shorter work week. How many languages are represented on the picket signs?

poorer and far less educated than their predecessors, the German, Spanish, and Portuguese Jews. They tended to cluster in the large industrial cities, where unskilled or semiskilled work was available.

Anti-Semitism refers to hostility toward Jews. It is often accompanied by social, economic, and political discrimination.

WORK AND LABOR UNIONS. Most eastern European Jewish immigrants were employed in the garment industry. It was a trade in which many had worked in Europe, and many factory owners were German Jews who were willing to hire them. Working conditions in the garment industry were terrible, and wages were scarcely enough to live on—even in poverty. Such conditions led Jews to join the labor movement. *The International Ladies' Garment Workers, led by David Dubinsky, and the Amalgamated Clothing Workers of America, led by Sidney Hillman, exposed conditions to* *the public and forced factory owners to make improvements.*

CULTURAL LIFE. The first generation of eastern European Jews created a much broader Jewish-American cultural life than had the German Jews. They organized Jewish community centers, theaters, clubs, and literary societies, founded schools, and started newspapers and magazines. They also participated actively in American civic life, supporting education for their children, going to night school, and becoming involved in politics.

The fact that Jewish immigrants developed a distinctly Jewish culture in America aroused some suspicion and hostility among their non-Jewish neighbors. They were accustomed to immigrants who were eager to blend into the great American melting pot. They could not understand a group of people who wanted both to be Americans and to preserve their own distinct culture and traditions. Consequently, Jews, like Catholics, suffered—and to some extent still suffer—from prejudice.

THE GROWTH OF AMERICAN CATHOLICISM. Roman Catholics were among the earliest settlers of America. The colony of Maryland, in fact, was founded as a refuge for English Catholics. Some Catholics achieved prominence. Charles Carroll, a signer of the Declaration of Independence, was reputed to be the wealthiest man in 18th-century America. In 1809 Elizabeth Seton of Baltimore founded a religious order for women, and in 1976 she became the first native-born American to be made a saint by the Catholic Church. But the number of Catholics remained small until the 1840's, when thousands of Irish Catholics migrated to the United States.

Between 1850 and 1900 the number of American Catholics increased rapidly. In 1850 there were about 1.5 million Catholics in the nation—about 6 percent of the population. By 1909 they numbered nearly 12 million, or 16 percent of all Americans. The vast majority of these 12 million Catholics lived in large cities. Many were recent immigrants to the United States from the countries of southern and eastern Europe.

WORK WITH THE POOR. The Roman Catholic Church had involved itself in caring for the needs of the poor and the destitute for centuries. This tradition was carried on by the Catholic Church in the United States.

Isaac T. Hecker, a convert to Catholicism, founded the Paulist Fathers in 1858 to work with the impoverished New York Irish. Mother Frances Xavier Cabrini established hospitals, orphanages, and schools for the Italian-American communities of New York, Chicago, and other large cities. In 1900 she became the first naturalized American citizen to be made a saint by the Roman Catholic Church. The Catholic Church also undertook an ambitious and wide-ranging program to Americanize Roman Catholic immigrants. This process of transformation was primarily accomplished through the parochial school system.

ANTI-CATHOLICISM. For many years there had been a strain of anti-Catholicism among the Protestant majority. It was stimulated in part by the feeling that Catholics and their clergy had a deeper allegiance to Rome—the headquarters of their church—than they did to the United States. *Anti-Catholic feeling intensified during the last decades of the 19th century for several reasons.* Because so many of the new immigrants were Catholic, anti-immigrant and anti-Catholic feeling often went hand in hand. When the Catholic Church achieved success in working with the great masses of urban poor, some Protestants began to suspect that priests were planning to take over the nation.

The American Protective Association (APA), formed in 1887, tried to capitalize on these and other fears. They warned Protestants that a hidden force of 700,000 papal soldiers was ready to seize the government. The majority of Protestants refused to have anything to do with the APA, however.

URBAN REVIVALISM. By the end of the century, American Protestants were divided among a bewildering variety of churches and sects, some brought from Europe, and others native-born. The Methodists formed the largest church. They numbered nearly one third of all Protestants in 1890. Next in size came the Baptists and the Presbyterians, both products of the frontier revivals that swept the country periodically in the 18th and 19th centuries. Fourth were the Lutherans, strongest in the Midwest and the Great Plains. Lutherans were mostly of German and Scandinavian origin.

One of the most important events in American Protestantism after the Civil War was the migration of the revival from the frontier to the city. The shift was an expression of the movement of population from rural to urban places. It also reflected the emotional and religious needs of the new city dwellers.

Dwight L. Moody, a former shoe salesperson from Boston, was probably the most effective of the modern revivalists. Teaming up with a singer, Ira D. Sankey, Moody launched his crusade for souls in Chicago in the 1870's and soon carried the crusade to every major city in the country. Moody reached millions by preaching a faith that was as simple to understand as it was democratic and comforting to practice. Salvation and heaven were open to all, Moody assured his audiences.

Sidenote to History

Seventh-Day Adventist Ellen Harmon White

Ellen Harmon grew up in a family of devout Methodists in Portland, Maine. In 1840 she experienced her own religious awakening at age 13, during a Methodist revival meeting. Shortly thereafter, William Miller, the traveling evangelist, visited Portland. He predicted that Jesus Christ would return by "about 1843." The Harmons then became "Millerites" and were expelled from the Methodist Church. After Miller's prediction failed to come true, most of his followers drifted back to their original churches.

At a women's prayer group in December 1844, Ellen Harmon fell into a trance. On recovering, she described a vision she had of the Advent people who had traveled to the City of God. It was the first of some 2,000 visions she would have in her lifetime.

Thereafter, she became a traveling evangelist, preaching that Christ would come soon. She also advocated the keeping of Saturday as the Sabbath, since the Bible specified that God rested on the seventh day, after creating the world. In 1846 she married James White, another Advent preacher. They had four children and continued their preaching activities. In 1855 the family moved to Battle Creek, Michigan, and shortly thereafter, they formed the Seventh-Day Adventist Church.

Ellen Harmon White maintained an active role in the church until her death in 1915. Following her lead, the church was strongly opposed to the use of alcohol, tea, coffee, tobacco, and drugs. Ellen White placed great importance on exercise, fresh air, and pure water. She believed that education ought to include practical skills as well as culture. Under her guidance the Seventh-Day Adventists founded numerous schools and colleges. It is a church that has affected many lives.

England was the source of three influential American organizations dedicated to this religious spirit—the Young Men's Christian Association, founded in 1851 as the offshoot of an English society; the Young Women's Christian Association, founded in 1858; and the Salvation Army, organized by "General" William Booth, an English Methodist, and introduced to America in 1880. All three organizations grew rapidly. By 1897 the YMCA and YWCA had over 300,000 members, and the Salvation Army boasted a corps of 3,000 officers and nearly 25,000 privates.

CHRISTIAN SCIENCE. The most important church to be founded during this period—the Church of Christ, Scientist—was also urban in origin. It was started by Mary Baker Eddy, a New England woman who had been cured of a mysterious ailment. After her cure, Eddy began instructing others in the art of healing by faith. She developed a following in the factory towns of Massachusetts. In 1875 she published her interpretation of Christianity in *Science and Health*. According to Mary Baker Eddy, disease "is caused by the mind alone" and therefore the mind can overcome it through faith.

Because it assured its followers that Christianity was a science, or a means of healing, Christian Science characterized the technological age. Although it met hostility because of its rejection of standard medical practices, it grew quickly. By 1900 the church counted 35,000 members, most of whom were city dwellers. It also spread to the cities of Europe, becoming, with Mormonism, one of the two native American religions to achieve worldwide importance.

THE SOCIAL GOSPEL. By 1890 a number of Protestant ministers were arguing that the churches ought to adapt to the new world of the city. Washington Gladden, an Ohio minister familiar with the struggle of workers to organize unions, believed that the church was losing influence among working people. To regain influence, he advised ministers to adapt the teaching of religion to the problems of slums, political corruption, and factory working conditions.

In 1907 Walter Rauschenbusch, minister of a Baptist church in New York City, published a book, *Christianity and the Social Crisis*. Rauschenbusch argued that religion ought to concern itself with this world rather than the next. He believed that Christian principles of justice, humanity, and brotherhood ought to be applied to such problems as the sale of spoiled meat.

The Social Gospel—the effort to make Christianity a force for reform—was one of several social currents that revived the reform impulse at the turn of the century. It represented a new concern for the evils of this world and a new determination to correct them. By 1900 this political revival, often called the Progressive movement, was well under way. The Progressives shared many of the concerns of the Populists of the 1890's—monopolies, railroad regulation, reducing tariffs—but they also concerned themselves with some of the problems created by industrial and urban growth. The Progressive movement showed that America was attempting to bring its social and political system into line with its economic might.

Section Review

1. Identify or explain: Levi Strauss, Isaac Hecker, Frances Xavier Cabrini, Judah P. Benjamin, the American Protective Association, Walter Rauschenbusch, Mary Baker Eddy.
2. Summarize the reasons some Protestant Americans were prejudiced against Roman Catholic Americans.
3. Describe the distinct cultural life developed by Jewish immigrants in the late 19th and early 20th centuries.
4. What was the Social Gospel movement, and what were its concerns?

Chapter 19 Review

Bird's-Eye View

The economic and social life of the United States changed a great deal during the late 19th century. Industry continued to expand, and many people moved into cities to work at new industrial jobs. People came to the cities both from other countries and from American rural areas. Many of the immigrants from other countries encountered prejudice on the part of native-born Americans. Major industrial cities experienced huge increases in population. Tenements built to house the newcomers often provided poor living conditions. City governments were frequently too weak to deal with rapid growth. As a result, political machines held power in most major cities.

Other areas of life reflected the urbanization of society. In education, practical approaches to learning were advanced and competed with the ideas of classical learning. New and more practical courses of study were introduced into schools and colleges. Blacks began to demand equality in education and politics. The works of Booker T. Washington and W. E. B. Du Bois and the founding of the NAACP helped begin the implementation of those demands.

Newspapers and magazines designed to appeal to a mass audience became influential. Literature began to focus on the everyday issues of life. A new realism also surfaced in art. Some Protestant sects came into being during this period. Christian Science tried to combine the principles of religion and science. Revivalism spread to the cities. Some people believed in a set of ideas called the Social Gospel. They tried to apply Christian concepts to bring about social reform. Their theories helped prepare the way for the ideas of Progressivism.

Vocabulary

Define or identify each of the following:

sweatshop	Hull House	Niagara Movement
Chinese Exclusion Act	Social Gospel	realism
tenements	Booker T. Washington	Levi Strauss

Review Questions

1. What were the experiences of the Chinese in the West? Compare their experiences with those of other immigrant groups.
2. By 1900, what was the composition of the European immigrant population?
3. List five problems created by the rapid growth of cities that existed by the turn of the century.
4. Compare the goals and the methods of Booker T. Washington and Du Bois.
5. Describe the changes in education that occurred during the period of history described in the chapter.
6. How did the invention of the linotype change the printing process?
7. Explain the term realism. How did it apply to the arts and literature?

8. What changes were taking place among religious groups around the turn of the century?

Reviewing Social Studies Skills

1. Using the graph on page 456, answer the following:
  a. Where did most people live in 1860? In 1900? In 1930?
  b. What general trend is depicted in the graph?
2. Using the pie graph on page 453, answer the following:
  a. What years are covered?
  b. What is the total number of immigrants?
  c. Which country accounted for the most immigrants?
  d. What percentage of immigrants came from Italy? Asia? Russia?
  e. Translate the information to a bar graph.
3. Write a paragraph describing the literature of this period. Show how it reflected both the traditional values of American society and the concerns of a changing society.

Reading for Meaning

1. Which statement best expresses the philosophy of the American people in the late 1800's? **a)** You can become wealthy if you work hard. **b)** Even the most needy people have a chance for a good life. **c)** Only skilled immigrants are welcome. Explain your answer.
2. Support one side of this question: Is the political boss a benefactor who helps people unfamiliar with the political system, or is the boss a corrupt individual who takes advantage of the ignorance of people? Defend your position using evidence from the chapter.
3. Reread the story of John Peter Altgeld, who became governor of Illinois. What point do you think the authors were trying to make by including this story?

Bibliography

Allon Schoener's *Portal to America: The Lower East Side, 1870–1895* (Holt, Rinehart and Winston) is a good account of the Jews of New York's Lower East Side.

If you have not read Mark Twain's *Huckleberry Finn* (Franklin Watts), try it.

A Bintel Brief, edited by Issac Metzer (Doubleday), contains a cross section of letters written to the *Jewish Daily Forward.* It gives a good impression of how Jews felt during the period.

John Hope Franklin's *Three Negro Classics* (Avon) includes books by Washington, Du Bois, and Johnson.

Herbert G. Gutman's *The Black Family in Slavery and Freedom, 1750–1925* (Random House), is a recent study that emphasizes the importance of family relationships within the Black community in America.

Unit 4 Review

Vocabulary

Define or identify each of the following:

civil service	anarchist	Socialists
commodity	homestead	suffragist
wholesale price index	trust	Populists
bipartisan	Wounded Knee	transcontinental railroad

Recalling the Facts

1. Why did the homesteaders' interests conflict with those of the American Indians?
2. How did the exposure of the Tweed Ring and the Whiskey Ring demonstrate the need for government reform?
3. Explain how Andrew Carnegie's life, the Gospel of Wealth, and the Horatio Alger stories all epitomized the mood of America during the Gilded Age.
4. List four industries that developed in the period following the Civil War.
5. What new inventions helped to bring about the American Industrial Revolution?
6. How were the railroads important to the growth of the nation's agriculture and industry?
7. What business practices prompted the need for the Sherman Anti-Trust Act?
8. What conditions made the opening of the mining frontier possible?
9. How did the settling of the Rocky Mountain area create problems for the American Indians?
10. What was the attitude of the nation's farmers toward the gold standard?
11. How did the Populist party influence reform movements in this country?
12. How did the nation's population change between the Civil War and the turn of the century?
13. List the factors that changed the nation from a rural to an urban country.
14. Cite three examples of either religious or ethnic prejudice in America around the end of the century.
15. Why were labor unions formed? Identify the first labor unions.

History Lab

1. Reread the section on Thomas A. Edison, and list his inventions. Then, write a short essay, describing what life would be like if Edison had never lived.
2. Political cartoons were an important form of expression during the late 1800's. Draw a cartoon that illustrates an abuse in economic or political life during this period.

478

3. The federal government's monetary policies either work to encourage or to discourage inflation. Look in the economic sections of the weekly periodicals in your library and find out what the government's present economic policy is. Do you believe the policy is in the best interests of this country? If not, what should the policy be?

Forming an Opinion

1. In the late 19th century, immigrants made several contributions to American life. Today, immigration is restricted by quotas, which have fixed the number of people who may come here. Do you agree with this policy? Why or why not?
2. The Civil Service system was developed to cure the evils of the spoils system. Today, some critics say that the government bureaucracy has grown too large and too powerful and that it is a burden on the nation's economy. They also question the effectiveness of the people who work in government jobs. Do you think the Civil Service system is in need of another reform? Why or why not?
3. Newspaper technology progressed from manual typesetting to the linotype machine to present-day electronic typesetters. Visit your local newspaper, and investigate its process for setting type. Report your findings to the class.

Local History

1. Every state has one or more state universities. Research the origin of the state university closest to you. What relationship does it have to the Homestead Act of 1862?

Time Line

Using the time line below, answer the following:
1. What time period does this time line cover?
2. List the events directly related to the American Indians.
3. How many years were there between the A. F. of L.'s founding and the Pullman strike?
4. How many years were there between the assassination of Garfield and the Pendleton Civil Service Act?
5. If you were going to divide this time line into two sections, where would you divide it? Why?
6. What title would you give to the time line?

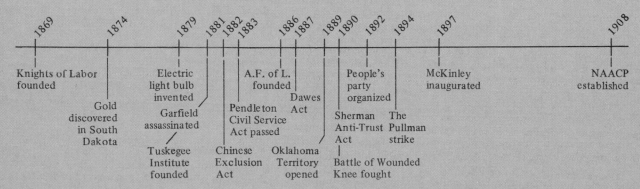

An Age of Reform

The year 1893 was the 400th anniversary of Columbus's return to Spain to announce news of a glorious New World. It seemed a good occasion for an exposition celebrating the civilization he had helped found. Congress chose Chicago as the site because of the city's remarkable recovery from its devastating fire of 1871. Chicago obligingly set aside a tract of land along the lake shore and employed a team of planners to create a model city. They were to demonstrate that a city need not be crowded, dirty, smelly, and noisy. Instead, it could be open, healthful, and inspiring.

Daniel Burnham, the nation's most prominent city planner, headed the project. He assembled a team of architects that included the founder of landscape design, Frederick Law Olmstead. Olmstead's design of Central Park in New York some twenty years earlier had initiated a nationwide effort to beautify American cities by using greenery. "The City Beautiful" was the slogan of the day. City planners hoped that tenement life would be more bearable if the poor could walk in the lush openness of a park. Planners believed that people would behave better if they were surrounded by beauty. People would take pride in their city. Crime would cease. "The City Beautiful" was a reformer's dream.

The "White City" erected by Burnham and his associates in Chicago's Jackson Park was a huge success. Buildings, streets, sewers, the water system, and parks fit into a gigantic master plan. The architectural theme was classical, a style that mingled grandeur with beauty.

After 1900, new voices were heard among city planners. Pretty parks and monumental buildings were very nice, some said, but the poor were still living in tenements. John Nolan, a Massachusetts architect, wanted city development to be planned so that transportation and utilities accompanied housing construction. This plan required city regulations. Nolan's concept was called "The City Useful."

Nolan won a major victory in 1916, when New York adopted the first citywide zoning code. New York legislators did not reject Burnham's ideas, however. The code provided for zones of greenery and recreation. City master plans from that day to this have usually blended these two ideas—The City Beautiful and The City Useful.

Site of World's Columbian Exposition, Chicago, 1893

unit 5

Chapter 20

1900-1912

Curing the Ills of Democracy

America is a land of many faiths, but there is one faith its people have always shared—a faith in progress. From the first settlements, the land became a miracle of progress and development. Americans generally assumed that their physical and intellectual betterment would continue indefinitely. Why, then, are the years from 1900 to 1917 called the Progressive era? What made people of that time more progressive than those of any other? The answer is that a new spirit swept the country around the turn of the century—new ways of thinking, new ways of looking at the world. From this intellectual revolution came a reexamination of American society, an urge to change and improve social conditions, a spirit of reform like the zeal of reformers before the Civil War.

Chapter Objectives

After you have finished reading this chapter, you should be able to:
1. Explain why the middle class accepted Progressive ideas.
2. List the Progressive reforms introduced at the state and local levels and the reasons for their introduction.
3. Describe the Progressive reforms Theodore Roosevelt brought to the national government.
4. Compare Taft's policies with Theodore Roosevelt's in order to cxplain why Roosevelt decided to run for President in 1912.

Americans of the Gilded Age believed that progress was the inevitable result of competition. In the struggle to get ahead, the weak failed and the strong prospered—and society was the winner. The role of government was to pass rules to ensure that the struggle was fair. Otherwise, it should do nothing to interfere. Any tampering only encouraged the weak and hampered progress. Progress not only encouraged political conservatism; it depended on it.

The Progressives turned that logic around. They believed in free individuals and their ability to better themselves. They rejected the notion that the individual was subject to such forces as the laws of supply and demand. They believed that free individuals could promote progress by their own efforts. Through "creative intelligence," said the educator John Dewey, individuals could improve their surroundings, which would better their lives and those of others. Progress was not a game that required winners and losers. By changing social conditions—eliminating slums or business monopolies—everyone could move ahead.

482

1. The Progressive Mind

A MIDDLE-CLASS MOVEMENT. In the 1890's a Kansas newspaper editor and publisher, William Allen White, became famous after he published an editorial in the Emporia *Gazette*. The title of the editorial was "What's the Matter with Kansas?" White's forthright answer was "the Populists." As a result of Populism, White charged bitterly, "we have become poorer and ornerier than a distempered mule. We, the people of Kansas, propose to kick. We don't care to build up, we wish to tear down." A few years later, White, the staunch opponent of Populist reform, became the ardent champion of Progressive reform. His conversion reveals a great deal about the nature of the Progressive movement.

The Progressive movement appealed to White and others like him because it was essentially a middle-class movement. The Progressives never believed in such ideas as government ownership of business, nor did they focus on class conflicts in American society. Indeed, they had little interest in poor farmers and less in workers. Like the Mugwump reformers of the 1870's and 1880's, the Progressives had no complaints about the American system. They wanted to make it work better. "Th' noise ye hear is not the first gun iv a revolution," said Mr. Dooley, a creation of Irish humorist Finley Peter Dunne. "It's only th' people iv th' United States batin' a carpet."

PROGRESSIVE CONCERNS. *Progressivism was concerned with the things that bothered these middle-class Americans. They were concerned with political corruption, monopolies that squeezed out small businesses, tariff duties that raised the prices of goods, and food and drink that were diluted or spoiled.* Much Progressive legislation actually benefited American business. The regulatory agencies created by the Progressives became referees in the competitive marketplace. They enabled businesses to make their operations more scientific and, incidentally, more profitable.

Some of the Progressive reforms were based on goals that conflicted with one another. Others, such as the prohibition of alcoholic beverages, failed to work. But in their piecemeal, experimental approach to social change, the Progressives laid the foundation for 20th-century political thought.

AN INTELLECTUAL REVOLUTION. Progressivism began as an intellectual revolution. In the universities and colleges, teachers and students revitalized ideas and developed challenging notions of what America should be. *Most important, they tried to bring the world of ideas—economics, sociology, literature, history, and philosophy—to bear on national life, especially on the activities of government.*

In *Sin and Society,* University of Wisconsin sociologist E. A. Ross showed that crimes were committed every day for which no one felt responsible. The modern corporation had become so big and impersonal that no one felt responsible for the acts of the institution. Thus, a big meat-packing company could package and sell spoiled meat that could kill people, but no one would feel guilty. The solution, suggested Ross, was government regulation of industry in the interest of the consumer. *Ross' remedy for social ills expressed the essence of the Progressive mind—the belief that government must take action when the free, competitive marketplace does not produce the maximum public good.*

Economists, such as Richard T. Ely and Thorstein Veblen, questioned the theory of free enterprise. Free competition, they

Like muckraking journalists, cartoonists could also sway public opinion toward reform. This cartoon, showing public enthusiasm for food inspection, was drawn by Frederick Opper. How have Americans recently shown concern about their food and other consumer items?

pointed out, does not always lead to greater production and social benefit. Excess wealth, argued Veblen in *Theory of the Leisure Class*, leads not to greater investment but to conspicuous consumption. An example of such spending was J. P. Morgan's yacht. It was frequently said about the yacht, "If you have to ask the price, you can't afford it." Like E. A. Ross, the new economists called for government action in certain cases, breaking up monopolies, for instance.

THE MUCKRAKERS. Popular magazines spread the reform spirit by exposing the ills of society and by making people aware of the need for change. ***Copying the techniques of the "yellow press," journalists published accounts of their investigations of business fraud and political corruption.*** They believed that Americans would not fight for reforms unless their indignation had been aroused by exposures of the evil that was disintegrating the fabric of American life.

President Theodore Roosevelt derisively called these writers muckrakers. He condemned them because he believed that their exposures would cause unrest. But in the new atmosphere of reform, the nickname became a badge of honor.

The muckrakers were given a forum by magazines such as *Everybody's, Cosmopolitan, Collier's* the *American Magazine,* and *McClure's.* S. S. McClure made the pages of his journal available to such able investigative reporters as Ray Stannard Baker, Ida M. Tarbell, and Lincoln Steffens. He also gave them generous subsidies for research. Ida Tarbell's research revealed the underhanded methods by which John D. Rockefeller had risen to the top. Each article cost around 4,000 dollars, a huge sum in 1904.

Every aspect of American society came under the critical eye of the muckrakers. David Graham Phillips exposed *The Treason of the Senate,* as he called it, by revealing the extent to which senators represented the interests of banks and corporations rather than those of the people. The article encouraged the demand, voiced earlier by the Populists, that senators be elected directly by the voters, instead of being chosen by state legislatures. The reform became law in 1913, when the 17th Amendment to the Constitution was ratified.

MUCKRAKING BOOKS. The muckrakers published books as well as magazine articles. Perhaps the most famous and widely read was *The Jungle* by Upton Sinclair. It was a vivid and nauseating description of the meat-packing industry. John Spargo's *The Bitter Cry of the Children* described the horrible conditions of child labor. Ray Stannard Baker discussed the plight of Black Americans in *Following the Color Line.* And Gustavus Myers' *History of the Great American Fortunes* showed the extent to which American fortunes had been built on corruption and exploitation.

In some ways, the greatest of the muckrakers was Lincoln Steffens. He specialized in exposing urban corruption. A collection of his articles—*The Shame of the Cities*—revealed that urban corruption was not exclusively eastern and not the fault of immigrants, as many had long assumed. Old,

Sidenote to History

Ida Tarbell, Reporter-Detective

The magazine rack in almost every middle-class American home contained a copy of *McClure's.* Although it published an occasional exposé of corruption or governmental incompetence, *McClure's* was considered a respectable journal. Thus, its readers were surprised when they opened the November 1902 issue and found a blistering attack on one of the nation's largest businesses, the Standard Oil Company. The author was Ida M. Tarbell, one of the few women journalists. She had spent four years investigating John D. Rockefeller and the Standard Oil Company. For eighteen months she wrote electrifying installment after installment on the company's operations and misdeeds. John D. Rockefeller, the deeply religious millionaire, slipped from his position as household idol.

Ida Tarbell admired Rockefeller's organizational genius. She was tolerant of his domination of an industry. What she exposed were his ruthless methods, his use of force to get his way, and his acceptance of kickbacks from railroads in order to undersell his competitors. Americans admired success. Tarbell thought they ought to discover how it was won. "A thing won by breaking the rules of the game," she wrote, "is not worth the winning."

Her argument was as appealing as her courage. She and other investigative reporters helped create a healthy national mood, a climate of reform.

485

upright midwestern cities such as Milwaukee, Minneapolis, and St. Louis were run by political bosses, too. They filled city offices with loyal followers and financed their operations with bribes from utilities and other businesses and companies.

Muckraking books and articles posed a challenge to their readers. Confronted with clear-cut documentary evidence of nationwide corruption, what would the average citizen do—ignore the evidence or demand reform? Overwhelmingly, Americans chose the latter alternative. *The muckrakers' exposures sparked reform crusades throughout the country.*

Section Review

1. Identify or explain: William Allen White, S. S. McClure, 17th Amendment.
2. List three muckrakers, the industries or institutions they wrote about, and the abuses they exposed.
3. How did the ideas of muckraker Upton Sinclair and sociologist E. A. Ross combine to show the need for federal regulation of the meat-packing industry?
4. Compare Progressivism and Populism. Why did Progressive reform appeal to middle-class Americans who had become unsympathetic to Populist reform?

2. The Reform of Cities and States

REFORM AT THE MUNICIPAL LEVEL. *The reform crusade began on the local level. Later it spread to the states and the federal government.* During the 1890's many reform organizations were established in American cities. New York's Tammany Hall was overthrown by reformers in 1894. In the same year, Carter Harrison, a reform candidate, was elected mayor of Chicago.

Reform successes in Cleveland and Toledo made them model cities for years. Tom Johnson, a colorful business leader turned politician, made Cleveland one of the nation's best-governed cities. He began important tax reforms, introduced city planning, and invented the streetcar fare box. Samuel "Golden Rule" Jones did the same for Toledo. Their examples inspired other municipalities to rid their governments of corruption.

In general, reform at the municipal level was a failure. Most cities were controlled by state legislatures that granted the cities operating charters. Thus, although a city might want to reform itself, powerful interests at the state level could block reforms. There was little a mayor could do when the trail of corruption led to the state legislature. In most cities, the governmental machinery remained the same. Bosses were able to creep back in after the first burst of reform energy had waned.

NEW FORMS OF GOVERNMENT. *More was accomplished when the Progressives began to insist on developing more efficient forms of government.* The first of these new forms—the replacement of the mayor and the city council by a commission—originated in Galveston, Texas. In 1900 Galveston suffered a disastrous hurricane that killed a sixth of its people and wrecked its economy. Because the Galveston city council was unable to cope with the emergency, the Texas legislature created a five-member commission with complete power to govern the city. The city commission worked well in Galveston. By 1914 over 400 cities across the country were run by commissions. But by that time the commissioners were elected rather than appointed.

In 1913 another disaster, the flooding of Dayton, Ohio, resulted in the introduction of another form of government. It was a modification of the commission idea. Under the Dayton plan, the elected commissioners appointed a professionally trained city manager to run the various city departments. Thus, expertise in management was combined with democratic government. More than 300 cities were following the Dayton plan by 1923.

Both forms of city government used experts who had broad knowledge of the unique problems of the city. The professionals were responsible to the elected officials, the mayor, and the council. But their appointment was a step away from the popular democracy of Jackson, Lincoln, and Bryan. The use of experts illustrated the Progressives' concern with efficiency. They believed government should be honest and effective as well as democratic.

"THE CURE FOR THE ILLS OF DEMOCRACY . . ." *Muckrakers who examined state governments found that they, too, were frequently ruled by bosses.* They were not, however, the familiar bosses of the Gilded Age. Gone were the flamboyant days of Roscoe Conkling. The bosses of 1900 were seldom seen. They pulled the strings of government with silent efficiency. Those who benefited from the machine considered it smooth and effective. But Progressives found it undemocratic.

Against this invisible government the Progressives mounted a campaign to return control to the people. "The cure for the ills of democracy is more democracy," argued the Progressives. The problem was that the people no longer ruled, as they had in the days of Jackson and Lincoln. To correct this situation the Progressives developed a variety of devices to ensure direct popular participation in government.

POLITICAL REFORM: THE DIRECT PRIMARY. Most important of these devices was the direct primary. It was instituted in Wisconsin in 1903. By 1915 it had been adopted by every state. Since Andrew Jackson's time, political conventions nominated candidates for office. The party organization did the choosing. Voters were left with a choice between the two party tickets. Besides limiting the voter's role, the nominating system was easily controlled by bosses. *The primary, or nominating election, gave the voters of each party the opportunity to choose their party's nominee for the regular election.*

INITIATIVE, REFERENDUM, AND RECALL. Other reforms designed to give citizens a greater role in the political process were the initiative, referendum, and recall. All three reforms were proposed in the Populist platform of 1892 and were instituted by Populists in South Dakota in 1898.

The initiative was a means of overcoming one of the chief tactics of legislative conservatives—the refusal to consider measures they opposed. *Under the initiative, a group of citizens could draft a bill and send it to the legislature with a petition signed by a certain percentage of the voters in the state.* (Usually from 5 to 15 percent was required, depending on the state.) The legislature was obliged to consider the bill but did not have to pass it.

The referendum was the other side of the initiative coin. *It permitted the legislature to submit a measure directly to the voters for approval.* The initiative and referendum have been adopted by some 20 states and many localities. It is used chiefly to deal with touchy financial matters affecting the pocketbooks of voters.

The recall was designed to give voters greater control over long-term elected officials, such as judges. *If enough voters— usually about 25 percent of the electorate— signed a petition, a special election would be held to determine whether the voters wanted to keep the official in office.*

THE AUSTRALIAN BALLOT. *Another device recommended by the Populists and adopted widely after 1900 was the secret ballot.* The states used long written ballots

This photograph shows Robert La Follette making a speech in Cumberland, Wisconsin, in 1897. La Follette began supporting Populist reforms while still a congressman. Later he was elected the governor of Wisconsin on a Reform ticket. La Follette and his sons dominated Wisconsin politics for almost 40 years. How would you compare the campaign styles of candidates during the 1890's with those of the 1980's?

for voters, but they left the printing to political parties. Thus, each party ticket, or list of candidates, was printed on a distinctive ballot, which the voter was expected to deposit into a box on election day. Ticket splitting—voting for members of each party for different offices—was virtually impossible with such ballots. And voters were subject to intimidation because party workers, watching the boxes, could tell how people had voted. The secret ballot, developed in Australia, listed the names of all the candidates on a single sheet printed by the government. Voters marked, folded, and deposited their ballots privately.

THE WISCONSIN IDEA. During the governorship of Robert M. La Follette, the state of Wisconsin adopted virtually all these reforms. Other states soon adopted the "Wisconsin Idea."

"Fighting Bob" La Follette was a Republican who had little use for Populism or William Jennings Bryan. As he worked his way through the Republican party ranks in the 1890's, he recognized that the Populists had a number of good ideas. He battled the Republican machine that controlled Wisconsin. In 1900, he appealed to farmers and workers and won the governorship.

Governor La Follette established close relations with Charles R. Van Hise, president of the University of Wisconsin. Van Hise was pioneering a broad concept of the state university. His notion was that the boundaries of the university were the boundaries of the state. The university should not be an isolated tower of learning. Instead, it ought to serve the people. Contact between the governor and the university brought the new philosophy of reform into the mainstream of politics.

Among the university professors, or the brain trust, that La Follette used were two economists, John R. Commons and Richard T. Ely. Commons and Ely thought that economics need not be a dismal science governed by iron laws. They believed economists should practice an experimental science and be willing to try new techniques. Government policies ought to be judged by what worked, not by abstract principles. Above all, they believed, economics ought to be humanitarian, that is, concerned with the welfare of human beings.

Guided by the "new economics," La Follette pushed through laws creating commissions to regulate railroads and public utilities. He levied heavier taxes on business corporations and the inheritances of the wealthy. Wisconsin also pioneered a workers' compensation law. The law provided automatic compensation for workers injured on the job, regardless of who was at fault. The state government also began a conservation program to preserve Wisconsin's forests and lakes from further exploitation.

IMPROVING THE MACHINERY OF DEMOCRACY. The many devices adopted by the Progressives did not cure all the ills of democracy. The reformers managed to turn many of their reforms into law. But the laws had to be respected and enforced to be effective. Party machines found ways to get around the reformed political process and make it work for them. Recall was rarely used. Money was still used to influence government. In many cases the Supreme Court was unsympathetic to Progressive legislation. However, the hard work of reforming was not done in vain. *Although machines and corruption continued to mar American politics, they soon became the exception rather than the rule.* Whatever their failures, the Progressives made substantial improvements in the machinery of democracy.

Section Review

1. Identify or explain: Tom Johnson, Samuel "Golden Rule" Jones, the Wisconsin Idea, Charles R. Van Hise, Richard T. Ely.
2. Define each of the following terms and explain why each was an important political reform: direct primary, initiative, referendum, recall.
3. Explain the city commission and the city manager forms of government. Why are these forms of government considered reforms?
4. What is the meaning of invisible government? How did the Progressives attack it?

3. Progressivism in the National Government

THE ERA OF THEODORE ROOSEVELT BEGINS. The beginning of Progressivism in the cities and states is hard to pinpoint. Much of it began in the 1890's, partly as a spillover from Populism. Progressivism at the national level can be dated. It began in the year 1901, with the Presidency of Theodore Roosevelt.

When an anarchist shot President William McKinley on September 6, 1901, it was not clear that an era of reform was about to begin. McKinley's Vice-President, Theodore Roosevelt, was a man of independent wealth. Born in New York to an old Dutch family, Roosevelt was heir to an upper-class, traditional way of life. Most people of Roosevelt's social class looked on politics as a disreputable profession. They considered it the business of robber barons and political bosses.

Roosevelt was dismayed by the corruption of American politics. But he believed that it was better to work to change the situation than remain on the sidelines and bemoan it.

THE RISE OF THEODORE ROOSEVELT. Roosevelt's first experiences as a member of the governing class were in minor political offices. He served in the New York State legislature. He ran unsuccessfully for mayor of New York in 1886 against the radical reformer Henry George. From 1889 to 1895 he served as a member of the Civil Service Commission under Presidents Harrison and Cleveland. In 1895 he became president of the New York Board of Police Commissioners—a post in which he tried energetically to reform the corrupt police force.

McKinley appointed Roosevelt Assistant Secretary of the Navy in 1897. He served in that post briefly, leaving to fight in the Spanish-American War. During the war he vaulted to national fame by recruiting a cavalry regiment, the Rough Riders, for service in Cuba. Wearing his uniform to the New York State Republican convention in 1898, he was chosen Republican candidate for governor—an election he won. After a flamboyant term in which he alienated all the party regulars, he was placed on the Presidential ticket with McKinley in 1900. Tom

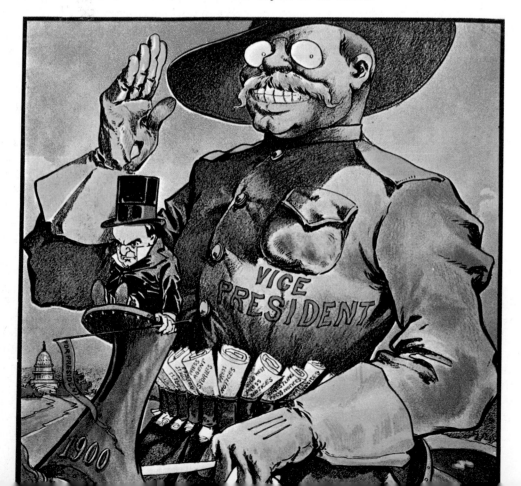

William McKinley was reelected President in 1900. His running mate, Theodore Roosevelt, became the nation's youngest Vice-President. What does this cartoon say about Roosevelt's wartime activities and their impact on the voters?

Platt, the New York State Republican boss, was glad to have Roosevelt out of New York. But the party's national head, Mark Hanna, was dismayed to see him arrive on the national scene—even though the Vice-Presidency was considered a political graveyard. "Don't any of you realize that there's only one life between that madman and the White House?" the exasperated Hanna complained to party leaders. But no one listened. In September 1901, after McKinley died, "that madman" lived in the White House.

ROOSEVELT AS A PROGRESSIVE. *Mark Hanna objected to Roosevelt's boisterous temperament, not his political views.* Before Roosevelt took office, his attitudes were quite conventional. In 1896 he denounced Bryan and the Populists with all the fervor of any eastern "gold bug." He felt Blacks were inferior and fretted that the birth rate of immigrants was outpacing that of "native" Anglo-Saxons. He favored making the economic system more equitable and humane but opposed any interference with free competition.

Roosevelt's contribution to Progressivism was less in what he did than in what he said. He was able to grasp the concerns of ordinary people—small business people, prosperous farmers, and skilled workers. And he voiced them with a flair that no President had shown since Lincoln. Considering the Presidency a "bully pulpit," he preached from it the new politics of reform. He drew national attention to the need for change and made change seem natural and a matter of common sense. He was Progressivism's publicity agent, giving the movement a respectability Populism never gained.

Roosevelt's personality, style, and dash revitalized the office of the President, which had been filled with lackluster men since the death of Lincoln. Roosevelt understood Presidential powers, and he flexed Presidential muscle when necessary.

Sidenote to History
Life in the White House

Everything about Theodore Roosevelt seemed to bubble over with excitement. He dedicated himself to living an active life from the time he was a very young man and pursued this goal all his life. With his stocky build, walrus mustache, spectacles, and "bully" air, T. R. immediately captured the imagination of the American public and held it throughout his tenure as President from 1901 to 1909. During his years in office, the public watched and waited for the President to do something exciting. When he did, they were generally satisfied.

The President's children took after their famous father in practically every detail. Theodore and Edith Roosevelt's six children were youngsters while living in the White House. Newspaper photographers took great pleasure in recording their activities for the public. Alice, the oldest child, made her society debut in the White House and was later married there. Both events were front-page news items of the year. A color, "Alice Blue," was named after her. The other children, Ted, Jr., Kermit, Ethel, Archie, and Quentin, were active in their own ways. They were fond of animals. They were said to ride their ponies in the White House elevators. During the Roosevelts' stay in the presidential mansion, there were baseball games on the front lawn, tag in the hallways, and a group of pets, including dogs, birds, rabbits, a badger, and a small black bear.

Rather than try to control his high-spirited family, Roosevelt usually let them have their way. He often joined in their games. Roosevelt's family life during the post-White House years was saddened by the death of his youngest son, Quentin, killed in a World War I airplane battle. Six months after Quentin's death, T. R. died at the age of 61.

Roosevelt was the most popular politician of his day, and he knew how to use his popularity to exert leadership. The first President of the 20th century, he firmly established the role of the 20th-century Presidency.

SETTLING A COAL STRIKE. Shortly after he took office, Roosevelt had an opportunity to flex his muscles. In the spring of 1902, a strike broke out in the Pennsylvania coal fields. The miners wanted the companies to recognize the United Mine Workers as their agent in collective bargaining. They also sought a nine-hour day and a 20 percent wage increase.

As the strike dragged on into the autumn, it looked as though there would be a serious coal shortage. With factories closing and the forecast of a chilly winter, Roosevelt intervened. He summoned representatives of both sides to the White House in October. John Mitchell, head of the United Mine Workers, agreed to arbitrate the dispute. But the mine owners declared they would never negotiate with the union. However, when Roosevelt threatened to send federal troops to take over the mines, the owners yielded. They granted the wage-and-hour demands but refused to allow union officials on the arbitration commission. Roosevelt got around this problem in a characteristically ingenious way. He appointed to the commission a former president of one of the railroad unions, calling him an eminent sociologist.

The miners won only part of their demands. But the settlement was significant in one respect. It was the first time in the history of the United States that a President had intervened in a labor dispute without suppressing the strike. *Roosevelt seemed genuinely concerned for the rights of all—management, labor, and the public.*

ROOSEVELT AND MINORITIES. Except for the coal strike, Roosevelt showed little interest in organized labor. He also showed little sympathy for minorities, except when they were politically useful. With much fanfare he invited Booker T. Washington to lunch at the White House. Southerners criticized the affair and he did not renew the invitation.

He was the first President to place a Jew in his cabinet. He named the head of Macy's department store, Oscar Straus, Secretary of Commerce and Labor. The appointment was announced during the New York gubernatorial election of 1906. And there was a strong suspicion that the President's motive was purely political.

THE TRUST BUSTER. *Roosevelt's constituency was urban middle-class America.* What concerned these people was the growth of business monopoly. Monopolies squeezed out little businesses. Monopolies raised prices for consumers. One of the chief sources of Roosevelt's popularity was his reputation as a "trust buster." Ironically, this reputation rested to a large extent on the federal government's prosecution of the Northern Securities Corporation. It was a juicy political plum because the man behind Northern Securities was the mysterious, widely feared banker, J. P. Morgan.

Northern Securities was a holding company that had been organized in 1902 to hold controlling interests in the three great railroads of the Northwest—the Great Northern, the Northern Pacific, and the Burlington. The company was formed by the nation's two largest financial empires, the Rockefeller group and the house of Morgan. The two financial giants realized that cooperating with each other would be more profitable than competing.

Northern Securities had a monopoly over all the railroad traffic between Chicago and the Pacific Northwest. Hardly anyone doubted that the company would use its position to charge customers what the traffic would bear. Amid public uproar against the company, Roosevelt ordered Attorney General Knox to file suit to break up the monopoly under the Sherman Antitrust Act.

The announcement of the suit convinced Wall Street that Roosevelt was about to attack other financial giants. Outraged, J. P. Morgan rushed to Washington to see the President. He suggested that Roosevelt "send your man to my man, and they can fix it up." That was the way the government had worked for years. Roosevelt refused to "fix" anything. "Mr. Morgan," Roosevelt recalled, "could not help regarding me as a big rival operator, who either intended to ruin all his interests or else could be induced to come to an agreement to ruin none."

The suit was in court for two years. In 1904 the Supreme Court declared Northern Securities to be a conspiracy in restraint of trade and ordered it dissolved. Roosevelt called the decision "one of the greatest achievements of my administration. . . . The most powerful men in this country were held to accountability before the law."

The victory encouraged him to order the Attorney General to undertake a few other prosecutions. He moved against the beef trust, whose methods had turned the President's stomach. But Roosevelt's general approach to the trusts was one of caution. *He initiated fewer antitrust suits than either of his successors, William Howard Taft or Woodrow Wilson.*

ELECTION OF 1904. The Northern Securities case was a public-relations victory for Roosevelt. In the Presidential election

This is a detail of a 1902 membership certificate in the United Mine Workers union. Founded in 1890, the UMW fought to improve working conditions, shorten hours, and increase wages for the nation's coal miners.

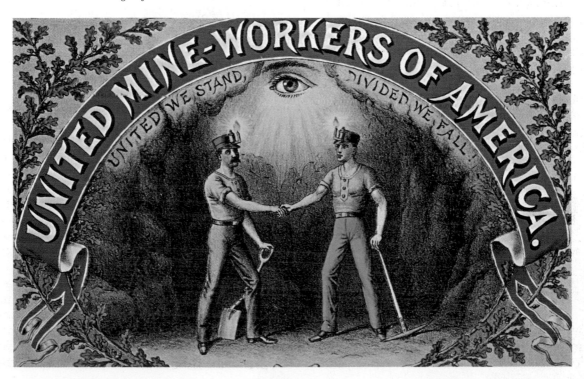

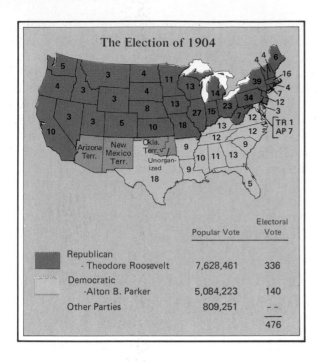

The Election of 1904

	Popular Vote	Electoral Vote
Republican - Theodore Roosevelt	7,628,461	336
Democratic -Alton B. Parker	5,084,223	140
Other Parties	809,251	--
		476

later that year, Roosevelt was returned to office by an unprecedented margin. He defeated a lackluster Democratic candidate, Alton B. Parker of New York, by 2.5 million votes and carried every state outside the South. (See map above.) Parker, said a humorist of the time, "was defeated by acclamation." Republicans retained their majority in Congress that year as well, with two-to-one margins in both houses.

The election seemed, at first glance, to give Roosevelt a majority that would enable him to accomplish whatever he wanted. But the Republicans were becoming increasingly divided over the issues of Progressive reform. A band of conservatives had formed around Senator Nelson Aldrich of Rhode Island and Speaker of the House Joseph Cannon of Illinois. Aldrich, whose daughter had married into the Rockefeller family, spoke for the banking interests. Cannon was a dictatorial leader who frequently used his office to block legislation. Appointments to committees and de-

bates on legislation were so firmly in his control that the Progressives in the House were forced either to cooperate with him or sit by in silence.

The Progressive Republicans rallied around George W. Norris of Nebraska, who entered the House of Representatives in 1902, and Wisconsin's Bob La Follette, who moved from the governorship to the United States Senate in 1906. Progressives were a minority among Republicans, and so Roosevelt was forced to deal with the conservatives. Nowhere was conservative power more evident than on the question of railroad regulation.

RAILROAD REGULATION: THE HEPBURN ACT. Roosevelt and the voters were as eager to put limits on railroads as they were to break up trusts. After the election, Roosevelt put railroad regulation at the top of his agenda. He informed the railroads that the only alternative was government ownership.

The Hepburn Act of 1906 restored the Interstate Commerce Commission's authority to set maximum railroad rates and to order the railroads to comply with the new rates within 30 days. Its decisions, however, were subject to review by the courts. The judicial provision was inserted by conservatives. Roosevelt accepted it in the spirit of compromise. It was better, he said cheerfully, to "accept half a loaf" than none at all.

More important, after 1906, the courts began accepting the decisions of the ICC, instead of overruling them. *The Hepburn Act thus laid the foundation for modern railroad regulation.* The regulatory system was completed in 1913 with the Physical Evaluations Act. It enabled the ICC to determine the value of a railroad as a basis for fixing its rates.

REGULATING FOOD AND DRUGS. *In 1905 Roosevelt recommended that Con-*

gress pass legislation to regulate the production of food and drugs. He had been persuaded to do this by Dr. Harvey W. Wiley, a chemist in the Department of Agriculture, and other scientists. During the course of their research, they had found that dangerous substances were being used in the preparation of drugs and processed foods. The food and drug industry reacted to Roosevelt's proposal with anger. They were used to preparing their products as they saw fit and were ready to resist any interference by government.

A year later Roosevelt's proposal received a boost with the publication of Upton Sinclair's novel *The Jungle.* Sinclair's description of the disgusting practices of the Chicago meat-processing industry swung over public opinion to Roosevelt's side. And in July 1906 a federal meat-inspection law was passed. The exposures of another muckraker, Samuel Hopkins Adams, persuaded the President and Congress to regulate the drug industry. The Pure Food and Drug Act was enacted, also in 1906, to control the distribution of medicines and food. The law did not give full protection to the public, but it did attack the worst abuses.

CONSERVATION OF NATURAL RESOURCES. Roosevelt had worked in the West and written a history of the frontier. He brought to the White House a deep interest in conservation. It was the source of one

Sidenote to History

The Fight to Save the Wilderness

It was summer when 30-year-old explorer, mountaineer, and naturalist John Muir walked into Yosemite Valley in the Sierra Nevada Mountains of California. Muir stayed in Yosemite from 1868 to 1873. During that time and until his death in 1914, Muir was a devoted crusader for forest conservation in the United States. He struggled to get the federal government to take an active role in conservation. In 1890 Congress passed the Yosemite National Park Bill establishing Yosemite and Sequoia national parks in eastern California. Muir became friendly with President Theodore Roosevelt, a determined naturalist, and did much to persuade him to set aside 60 million hectares (150 million acres) of forest wilderness, a move that led to the national parks system.

John Muir was born in Scotland in 1838. He moved to Wisconsin when he was 11. After studying at the University of Wisconsin, he travelled to Europe, Asia, Africa, and the Arctic and finally back to the United States. Muir's interest in nature was not always appreciated by others, as in his book, *Yosemite:* "Arriving in California by the Panama steamer, I stopped one day in San Francisco and then inquired for the nearest way out of town. 'But where do you want to go?' asked the man to whom I had applied for this important information. 'To any place that is wild,' I said. This reply startled him. He seemed to fear I might be crazy and therefore the sooner I was out of town the better, so he directed me to the Oakland ferry."

Muir kept a record of his exploration of Yosemite Valley. One can use it to follow his trip through the sequoia groves, river canyons, and granite mountains of the high Sierras. When the park was open to the public, Muir guided visitors on wilderness outings as a means of educating them on the importance of conservation. The outings continue to this day under the supervision of the park's personnel and by the Sierra Club. Muir founded the Sierra Club in 1892. Today it is one of the leading conservation organizations in the nation.

of his most important achievements.

As early as 1891 Congress had authorized the President to set aside forest preserves. But the Presidents of the 1890's did little to implement the act. ***Roosevelt marked some 60 million hectares (150 million acres) for public use. It was the beginning of the national parks system.***

As in so many other areas, Roosevelt's main contribution to conservation involved stimulating public interest. In 1908 he invited the state governors to a conference at the White House. They set up a National Conservation Commission, with a branch in each state. After centuries of ruthless exploitation of the continent's resources, Americans were becoming aware of the need to conserve, even to preserve. Theodore Roosevelt deserves much of the credit.

Section Review

1. Identify or explain: "bully pulpit," Oscar Straus, Northern Securities, Nelson Aldrich, the Hepburn Act.

2. What actions earned Theodore Roosevelt the reputation of being a "trust buster"?
3. What steps did Roosevelt take to improve the quality of life for the average American?
4. What was the source of Representative Joseph Cannon's power in the House of Representatives? How did his power affect the Progressives' ability to pass reform legislation?

4. The Taft Years

PRESIDENT WILLIAM HOWARD TAFT. *When Roosevelt retired after the customary two terms in office, he designated William Howard Taft his successor.* It was a curious choice. Taft did not want the job. He was a competent administrator, having served well as governor of the Philippines and as Roosevelt's Secretary of War. He had no taste for the rough and tumble of politics. His early career had been spent in

Theodore Roosevelt and John Muir at Yosemite, California, where the two men camped together for four days in 1903. What does Roosevelt's visit with Muir indicate about his personal feelings toward conservation?

the law. His real ambition was a seat on the Supreme Court—a dream that was realized in 1921 when he became Chief Justice. Taft often seemed indecisive and excessively cautious. These traits were the result of his judicial training. A careful, methodical, and distinguished legal thinker, Taft was used to pondering every issue in great detail.

Roosevelt was a hard act to follow, and Taft never had a chance. The voters were noticeably unenthusiastic. Taft was successful because of the Democrats' mistake in nominating the twice-rejected William Jennings Bryan.

THE PAYNE-ALDRICH TARIFF, 1909.
Taft began by fumbling the tariff, an issue that Roosevelt had refused to handle. Roosevelt avoided the tariff, not only because there seemed little mileage in it, but also because it promised to widen the rift in his party. Steadily rising prices, however, brought the tariff under Progressive attack. The Dingley Tariff of 1897 had set average tariff rates at an all-time high of 57 percent. The National Consumers League argued that the wall of protection enabled American manufacturers to maintain artificially high prices. During the election of 1908, Taft, to demonstrate his sympathy for reform, promised a reduction in the tariff. As soon as he was installed in office, he summoned Congress into special session. *In less than a month, the House passed the Payne bill. It provided for substantial reductions in the tariffs on a number of items. In the Senate, Nelson Aldrich attached some 800 amendments that restored the rates to their previous levels.* When special-interest lobbyists descended on the House, it yielded to the pressure, and the Payne-Aldrich Tariff became law. It was signed by President Taft, who considered it better than nothing.

The humorous Mr. Dooley congratulated the poor senators, "steamin' away under the majestic tin dome of the capitol," trying to reduce the tariff to a size where it could stand on the same platform with the President, who was over 135 kilograms (300 pounds), without collapsing the structure. Mr. Dooley said that life would be easier for Americans because Senator Aldrich had thoughtfully removed the duties on a number of items. "Practically ivrything necessary to existence comes in free," he chortled. "Curling stones, teeth, sea moss, newspapers, canary bird seed, hog bristles, marshmallows, silkworm eggs, stilts, skeletons, an' leeches. Th' new tariff bill puts these familyar commodyties within th' reach iv all."

Progressives felt betrayed. And Taft made matters worse by calling the Payne-Aldrich Tariff "the best tariff bill that the Republican party has ever passed, and therefore the best that has been passed at all."

THE BALLINGER-PINCHOT AFFAIR.
Taft then tripped over the U.S. Forest Service. While he was on a speaking tour defending the new tariff act, Gifford Pinchot, head of the U.S. Forest Service, leveled accusations against the Secretary of the Interior, Richard A. Ballinger. Pinchot, the nation's leading conservationist during Roosevelt's Presidency, accused Ballinger of turning water-reservoir sites over to private land developers.

The accusation was misleading. Ballinger was a preservationist, a nature lover, as Pinchot scornfully called him, who believed in preserving natural sites that were unique and beautiful. Ballinger believed that what was not worth preserving ought to be developed by private capital.

Pinchot was a "scientific" conservationist, who believed that resources such as water and timber should be managed by the government. His notion of conservation was to dam the rivers of the West to provide water for irrigating desert lands (and, incidentally, adding to the nation's existing farm surpluses).

Compare this campaign poster for William Howard Taft with pictures of Theodore Roosevelt you have seen. How would you describe the personalities of the two men, based on this information?

It was a dispute between two kinds of conservationists (a dispute that remains very much alive today). The issues were not clearly understood then. When Taft backed Secretary Ballinger, Progressives accused him of deserting the conservation movement. Pinchot was dismissed and went off to join Roosevelt in Africa, where the ex-President was shooting everything in sight (nine lions, five elephants, thirteen rhinoceroses, and seven hippopotamuses).

RISING PROGRESSIVISM IN CONGRESS. President Taft set out to clip the wings of Speaker Joe Cannon. The Speaker of the House had enormous powers. He appointed all the House committees and named members to chair them. Because congressional status depended on committee assignments, every member of the House was at his mercy. Cannon, in addition, had named himself head of the Rules Committee, the body that determines which bills reach the floor. He was in a position to paralyze the entire legislative process if he so desired.

President Taft disliked Cannon. He considered him "dirty and vulgar" and resented being photographed with him. But he controlled his dislike of Cannon under pressure from Senator Aldrich and other conservatives. Republican Progressives, headed by George Norris, then picked up the cue. *In alliance with House Democrats, the Republican rebels in early 1910 forced a change in the House rules.* They made election the method for determining the membership of the all-important Rules Committee. They excluded the Speaker from membership. Cannon was finished. The President, who had played both sides of the fence, was criticized by the conservatives and the Progressives. The Democrats were the winners.

When the Republicans mangled the tariff, the Democrats picked up the pieces. In the off-year congressional elections of 1910, they blamed the tariff for rising prices. They campaigned as the champions of the consumer. It worked. The Democrats won control of Congress for the first time in 16 years, a development that showed promise of a Democratic victory in the presidential contest of 1912. To extend their support among the urban middle class, the Democrats opened an investigation of business monopoly as soon as the new Congress convened.

THE TRUST ISSUE. Having handpicked his successor, Roosevelt gave Taft advice and loyal support. But he was increasingly dismayed by Taft's political bungling. What finally split them apart, ironically, was Taft's trust busting. *In his first two years in office, Taft initiated more antitrust suits against business corporations than Roosevelt had in eight years.* Roosevelt was dismayed because he was beginning to change his mind on the subject of "big business."

Even before he left office, Roosevelt had concluded that the problem of trusts was not simply one of size. A trust should not be prosecuted, he believed, unless it had done something wrong. By 1910 he had given the matter further thought. It made no sense to break up big business, Roosevelt and other Progressives concluded. It was not possible to return to an economy of small shopkeepers. Industrialism was here to stay and so was big business. Besides, there were advantages to bigness. Mass production reduced prices to consumers. Big corporations could standardize goods and finance research. Only if they monopolized the market should they be broken up. Only if they became power hungry and abused their size should they be punished.

THE NEW NATIONALISM. In a speech at Osawatomie, Kansas, in August 1910, Roosevelt outlined his developing creed, which he called the New Nationalism. *It was a plea for stronger national authority, a government that would put national need above personal advantage.* "I stand for the square deal," he declared. "But when I say that I am for the square deal, I mean not merely that I stand for fair play under the present rules of the game, but that I stand for having those rules changed so as to work for a more substantial equality of opportunity." As a start, Roosevelt called for the establishment of a government office to regulate business, a watchdog agency to ensure that big corporations conducted their operations in the public interest.

THE "RULE OF REASON." Within a year the Supreme Court helped clarify Roosevelt's stand. The case before it involved the Standard Oil Company, one of the "bad trusts," in Roosevelt's view. Before he left office, he initiated proceedings to break up Standard Oil under the Sherman Antitrust Act. The case finally reached the Supreme Court in 1911. *The Court agreed with the government and ordered Standard Oil to be broken up into smaller companies on the ground that it was an "unreasonable restraint of trade."*

Did "unreasonable" mean that it was possible to be a "reasonable" trust? Yes, said the Court. Mere bigness is not an offense. A corporation must be guilty of abusing its power by interfering with commerce in some substantial way. This "rule of reason," as it was called, was developed by the Court to bring the law into line with the economic revolution that had taken place since the Civil War.

APPROACH OF THE ELECTION OF 1912. With his New Nationalism speech, Roosevelt threw down the gauntlet to President Taft. The speech was an open bid for the Republican nomination in 1912. But it was also a challenge to Progressives, especially Democrats, who thought that the best way to ensure the public interest was to restore free competition. That meant breaking up the trusts, regardless of how "good" they were. *The election of 1912 thus became a three-way struggle for power and ideology. It was the climax of Progressivism.*

Section Review

1. Identify or explain: the Payne-Aldrich Tariff, Gifford Pinchot, Joe Cannon, unreasonable restraint of trade.
2. Reread Mr. Dooley's comments on the Payne-Aldrich Tariff of 1909. What is the meaning of these remarks? How did the Progressives react to this tariff? Why did President Taft give it his support?
3. What was the key issue in the dispute known as the Ballinger-Pinchot Affair? Why do you think this issue remains very much alive today?
4. What were Roosevelt's new ideas on big business? Why did he call for a stronger national authority?

Chapter 20 Review

Bird's-Eye View

The Progressive era was a period of reform. The goals of the Progressives were to make the system fair and reasonable, not to make basic changes in the system. Some of these changes were stimulated by the work of a group of journalists, called muckrakers, and by social and political scientists.

Reforms were attempted at different levels of government. At the municipal level, the city-commission and city-manager systems became popular. Wisconsin Progressives promoted such reforms as the direct primary, the referendum, and the secret ballot at the state level.

The ascendance of Roosevelt to the Presidency marked the beginning of Progressivism at the national level. Roosevelt helped popularize many Progressive reforms. He arbitrated a miners' strike and considered the interests of all the parties. He earned a reputation as a trust buster. He easily won a second term of office. During that term, he dealt with the regulation of the railroads as well as the food and drug industries. He helped introduce the American people to the idea of conserving resources and wilderness areas.

Roosevelt's successor, William H. Taft, was a competent administrator but was neither as colorful nor as politically adept as Roosevelt. Progressives felt betrayed by his handling of the tariff issue. Taft's attempt to settle a dispute between two officials who represented different views on conservation led to the accusation that he was not in favor of the conservation movement. Taft did go after some of the larger trusts, however. But in doing this he alienated Roosevelt, who had changed his view of trust busting. Roosevelt then challenged Taft by proclaiming a new political platform, which he called the Square Deal and the New Nationalism.

Vocabulary

Define or identify each of the following:

muckraker	referendum	recall
Ida Tarbell	*The Jungle*	Pure Food and
direct primary	city manager	Drug Act
		Payne-Aldrich Tariff

Review Questions

1. What were the concerns of the Progressives?
2. List five Progressive reforms introduced between 1900 and 1917.
3. How was Roosevelt's style as President different from that of other Presidents?
4. What was the impact of Upton Sinclair's novel, *The Jungle*?

5. What was Roosevelt's contribution to the conservation movement?
6. Explain Roosevelt's plan for a New Nationalism.

Reviewing Social Studies Skills

1. Using the map on page 494, complete the following:
   a. Where was Parker's political strength?
   b. Which section of the country had the most electoral votes?
   c. How many electoral votes did Roosevelt receive?
   d. How many votes did Parker receive?
2. Organize the following data into a chart: the reforms introduced by the Progressives and the dates and places where they were introduced.
3. Using issues that are of current interest on a local, state, or national basis, write two proposals that might be subjects for a referendum.

Reading for Meaning

1. Write a paragraph entitled "Theodore Roosevelt, an Activist President." Write and underline the topic sentence. Find evidence in the chapter to support this idea, and include this supporting material in the paragraph.
2. Roosevelt was known as much for his personality as for his actions in office. Make a list of the words used in the text to describe the personal characteristics of Roosevelt and Taft. How do these words tell you what the authors thought of these two men?
3. Read the section entitled "The Ballinger-Pinchot Affair." Both of these individuals were conservationists, yet they differed on issues. Make a list comparing their differences. What similarities do you believe they probably had that are not mentioned in the text?

Bibliography

William O'Neill's *The Progressive Years* (Dodd, Mead & Company) is a good, recent survey of this period.

Lincoln Steffens's *Autobiography* (Harcourt Brace Jovanovich) is very long, but it is an interesting story of one man's war against city bosses.

Eve Merriam's *Growing Up Female in America: Ten Lives* (Doubleday & Co) contains biographical sketches of women. Some are well-known, some are not—but they are all interesting.

Finley Peter Dunne's *Mr. Dooley on Ivrything and Ivrybody* (Dover) is a collection of Mr. Dooley's best.

Chapter 21
1910-1919

Wilson and the New Freedom

Woodrow Wilson was born in the Shenandoah Valley of Virginia. Influenced by his father, a Presbyterian minister, the fires of Calvinism burned within him. From his youth, he carried the religious person's urge to serve the world. He never aspired to be a Presbyterian minister. His ambition was to minister to the needs of the world through politics.

Public service was his goal. He first went to law school because law was the traditional path to politics. But, after a year of practice, he returned to graduate school to study politics and economics. He graduated from Johns Hopkins University in 1886 with a Ph.D. After several teaching jobs, he became a professor at Princeton. In 1902 the Board of Regents made him president of the university. No one had ever used the presidency of a university as a steppingstone to the White House. But Wilson did.

In 1910 the Democratic party bosses of New Jersey asked Wilson to run for governor. The professionals saw in him an ideal party figurehead—clean, popular, and meek enough to take orders. Wilson fooled them all. Once elected governor, he broke with the bosses and pushed through the legislature the basic Progressive reforms of the Wisconsin Idea—a direct primary, a clean elections act, compensation laws for workers, regulation of utilities, and a law permitting cities to adopt the commission form of government.

Then Wilson cast his eyes on the White House. In the spring of 1911, he went on a national speaking tour to make himself better known to the Democratic party and to the people.

Chapter Objectives

After you have finished reading this chapter, you should be able to:
1. Explain why Wilson, a Democrat, was elected in 1912.
2. List the reforms Wilson introduced in his first term in office.
3. Describe the conditions that led to the passage of Prohibition and Women's Suffrage.

Like Roosevelt, Wilson was shocked at the ruthlessness of the trusts. Unlike Roosevelt, he was not sure regulation was the answer. Perhaps business was too big to be controlled. A handful of great financiers had the entire nation in their grip. Wilson's solution was to break that grip and restore open, free, honest competition.

502

To break the trusts or to regulate them, that was the question. The people were asked to provide the answer—in the Presidential election of 1912.

1. 1912: The Climax of Progressivism

THEODORE ROOSEVELT RETURNS. Theodore Roosevelt had also begun to work his way back to the White House. He retired from public office in 1909, respecting the tradition that a President serve only two terms. But at 51, he was not ready to abandon public life. Returning to America in June 1910 after a big-game hunt in Africa, Roosevelt became editor of the Progressive *Outlook* magazine. He made no public statements on Republican politics. But he was distressed by Taft's handling of Progressive issues. He concluded that Taft had "completely twisted around the policies I advocated and acted upon."

Then, Roosevelt introduced his idea of New Nationalism. *He insisted that the nation needed a strong federal government that would focus on social justice, human welfare, and the rights of the whole community, rather than on the privileges of a small group of wealthy men and women.*

He also demanded that Americans be given a Square Deal by their government. This program included compensation to workers for injuries suffered on the job, regulation of child labor, protection for women workers, lowering of the tariff, and firm regulation of big business. Roosevelt also asked for a graduated income tax—that is, a tax system in which the incomes of the rich would be taxed more than the incomes of the poor. Progressives hailed the program, and conservatives shuddered.

Although Roosevelt had made a stunning impression with his program, he stated that he was not seeking the Republican nomination for President. When Progressives formed the National Progressive Republican League in January 1911, they intended to work for the nomination of Robert La Follette.

A year later, Roosevelt changed his mind. On a speaking tour in 1912, La Follette became ill and withdrew temporarily from the campaign. When Roosevelt made it known that he was willing to step into La Follette's shoes, many of La Follette's supporters switched sides. Roosevelt thus acquired an instant constituency of Republicans.

THE REPUBLICAN CONVENTION OF 1912. Roosevelt won the battle, but the most important battles of the war lay ahead of him. He still had to wrest control of the Republican party from Taft. The President had firm control of the party machinery. With a mere 19 delegates pledged to him, Roosevelt lost the Republican nomination before the convention opened. Taft won handily on the first ballot. *Roosevelt, who had already announced that he would not be bound by the convention's decision, bolted the party.* His supporters flocked after him. And the conservatives were left in complete command of the party.

THE BULL MOOSE PARTY. Roosevelt and his followers met in Chicago in August 1912. At the meeting, a third party formed— the Progressive party. The convention nominated Roosevelt as its Presidential candidate. Accepting the nomination, Roosevelt roared that he felt strong as a bull moose. The phrase became the party's nickname.

The Bull Moose platform of 1912 was the most forward-looking set of principles since the Populist platform of 1892. It embodied most aspects of Roosevelt's New Nationalism and Square Deal. The platform endorsed the principles of democracy that were part of the Wisconsin Idea—initiative,

In this picture, Roosevelt, as the Progressive party candidate, speaks to a crowd in Morrisville, Vermont. Note the moose head propped on the podium. Why do you think it is there?

referendum, recall, direct primaries, and direct election of senators. It also endorsed women's suffrage, becoming the first major party to do so. In the realm of social needs, the platform approved workers' compensation laws, prohibition of child labor, and regulation of the working conditions of women. These ideas implied a commitment to the use of government as an instrument for social change. The platform also approved Roosevelt's solution to the trust problem— the creation of a Federal Trade Commission to watch over business practices.

THE DEMOCRATS NOMINATE WILSON. *Woodrow Wilson had to wage an uphill battle against party regulars to get his party's nomination.* They did not know what to make of a man with the manner of a professor and the tone of a minister. William Jennings Bryan harbored some Presidential ambitions, as always, although many party leaders believed that the voters had grown tired of him as the Democratic candidate. Wilson was finally nominated on the 46th ballot, after Bryan abandoned the chase and threw his support to him. Wilson later made Bryan his Secretary of State.

THE GREAT TRUST DEBATE. *For his campaign adviser Wilson chose Louis D.*

Brandeis, the leading Progressive lawyer in the country. Brandeis had come to national attention some years earlier when he submitted to the Supreme Court what came to be known as a *Brandeis brief.* In *Muller v. Oregon* (1908), Brandeis persuaded the Supreme Court to accept sociological statistics as evidence in upholding an Oregon law that regulated the working conditions of women.

Law courts had never before considered the statistical data gathered by social scientists to be reliable enough to qualify as legal evidence. A legal precedent was established by the *Brandeis brief,* which showed the ill effects of long hours on women's health.

Brandeis was a fervent believer in freedom of business enterprise. He believed that the great enemy of freedom was monopoly and the special privileges, such as tariff protection, that permitted monopoly to exist.

Brandeis helped clarify Wilson's thinking and sharpen the differences between Wilson and Roosevelt. Wilson's aim was to break the trusts. Roosevelt's was to regulate them. On most other social issues of Progressivism, the two were in agreement. And both candidates attacked Taft as a symbol of the status quo.

THE ELECTION OF 1912. Wilson took as the theme of his campaign the idea of "a new freedom." It was a subtle play on Roosevelt's brand of Progressivism—New Nationalism—but struck a very different note. *Wilson claimed that his goal was to restore the freedom of the nation's early days, to create a climate in which small businesses could operate freely.* Roosevelt's program, Wilson charged, would provide real opportunities only for big business. Wilson also promised freedom to labor—especially freedom from the Sherman Antitrust Act—so that unions could make use of collective bargaining.

Wilson's ideas about traditional freedoms and the importance of small business won him a large following in rural areas. The people who used to come out for Bryan now flocked to Wilson's side.

Because the Republican vote was split between Taft and Roosevelt, Wilson carried the electoral college. The electors gave Wilson 435 votes, 88 to Roosevelt, and 8 to Taft. (Eugene V. Debs, the Socialist party candidate, won no electoral votes, although he polled one million popular votes.)

In the popular balloting, however, Wilson polled only 42 percent. (See map, above.) Although Wilson entered the White House without an overwhelming mandate, his Presidency was strengthened by the fact that the Democrats kept control of Congress.

Section Review

1. Using the map on this page, list the states that voted for Taft. Why was this election a triumph for Progressivism?
2. Identify or explain: Woodrow Wilson, Square Deal, Bull Moose party, Louis D. Brandeis, New Freedom.
3. Why did Roosevelt and his followers form the Bull Moose party?

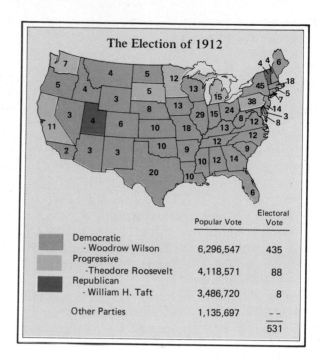

The Election of 1912

	Popular Vote	Electoral Vote
Democratic - Woodrow Wilson	6,296,547	435
Progressive -Theodore Roosevelt	4,118,571	88
Republican - William H. Taft	3,486,720	8
Other Parties	1,135,697	--
		531

2. The New Freedom

A SHREWD PARTY LEADER. Roosevelt strengthened the Presidency through his forceful personality. Wilson strengthened it through shrewd party leadership. Although he had little experience in party politics, Wilson worked well with Congress. He conferred with its leaders, accepted suggestions, and used patronage when necessary. When his proposals ran into a roadblock of special interests, Wilson appealed to the public and rallied support to his side. Not since Thomas Jefferson had a President been so successful in pushing a comprehensive program through Congress.

TARIFF REFORM. The tariff was the first item on Wilson's agenda. His aim was to bring to a speedy end the era of high tariffs. Calling Congress into special session, Wilson presented his program in person.

The House cooperated by passing the Underwood Tariff. *The tariff—which was the first overall reduction since the Civil War—cut the rates in half.* It also removed all duties from important consumer items, such as sugar.

The Underwood Tariff contained another Progressive feature—an income tax, made possible by the ratification of the 16th Amendment to the Constitution.

Reformers had long argued that an income tax would help reduce the gap between rich and poor. Congress, however, was more interested in recovering revenue lost through tariff reduction than in redistributing wealth. All incomes above 4,000 dollars a year were taxed at only 1 percent, although additional rates of taxation were levied on the very wealthy. For example, an income of 500,000 dollars a year was taxed at the rate of 6 percent.

When the tariff reached the Senate, it ran into trouble. Protariff lobbyists put pressure on senators to vote against the Underwood bill. Wilson responded by publicly denouncing the lobbyists for seeking "to overcome the interests of the people for their private profits." The Underwood Tariff finally passed when Senator La Follette and other Progressives forced certain senators to reveal the personal financial interests they had in keeping tariffs high.

ATTACKING THE MONEY TRUST. In 1911 Wilson claimed that the "great monopoly in this country is the money monopoly. So long as that exists, our old variety and freedom and individual energy of development are out of the question." In 1913 a congressional committee under the direction of Representative Arsene Pujo published a report that astounded the nation. The Pujo committee had amassed data showing that Rockefeller and Morgan interests controlled virtually all the nation's finances. They held a total of 341 directorships in 112 corporations whose combined wealth was well over 22 billion dollars. This was more than three times the assessed value of all the property in the 13 southern states and more than the value of all the property in the 22 states west of the Mississippi. *In other*

In 1913 Congress passed a bill, giving the control of reserve banks to the federal government. This cartoon shows President Wilson announcing the death of big-money trusts.

words, the "money trust" had a stranglehold on the nation's economy. Because they controlled the nation's money and credit, they could control corporations by rejecting or granting the loans they needed to stay in business.

Wilson was convinced that the money trust should be broken. When the public heard the news—through a series of articles by Brandeis called "Other People's Money"—it rallied to the President's position. The result was that banking reform got top priority on the congressional agenda.

A WEAK BANKING SYSTEM. Financiers were able to wield their enormous power because the nation's banking system was weak. Only if the system were strengthened could the stranglehold of the powerful money trust be broken.

In 1903 and again in 1907, panics had caused banks to close their doors in order to preserve their funds. A system of reserves was needed so that banks could draw additional money in times of trouble. National bank notes, founded on gold, were not sufficient to meet the needs of an expanding economy. The problem no longer centered on a question of "cheap" money, such as the Populists had wanted. It involved circulating greater quantities of "good" money. National bank notes did not meet the demand.

THE FEDERAL RESERVE SYSTEM.

Democrats and Republicans agreed on the need for banking reform. But no one could agree on how the reform should be carried out. Republican Senator Aldrich proposed creating a central bank, modeled on the Bank of England. Democrats wanted a decentralized banking system that would be privately owned but free from Wall Street control. Progressives on both sides wanted the banking system to be controlled by the government.

In 1913 Democratic Representative Carter Glass of Virginia suggested an imaginative compromise. His plan left banking in private hands at the local level but provided government control and supervision at the national level. *He proposed not one central bank but a federation of 12, distributed around the country.* The banks created by the Federal Reserve Act of 1913 were not ordinary banks. They were "banker's banks," from which private banks could secure temporary funds when they ran into trouble. The existence of reserves would prevent panic and stabilize the entire banking system. All national banks were required to join the system. State banks meeting certain requirements could join if they wished.

The new banks were also empowered to issue money, Federal Reserve notes, that would be based in part on gold and in part on commercial paper—forms of paper that substituted for money. Because the amount of commercial paper in circulation reflected the amount of business being carried on, the paper—and hence the bank notes—expanded with the needs of the economy. The volume of notes could be controlled as the economy demanded.

The Federal Reserve banks were to be private corporations doing business for profit. But the law placed them under the supervision of a Federal Reserve Board appointed by the President. The board had power to set the rate of interest that the Reserves would be required to charge private banks for money. By setting interest rates, the board could influence the flow of money and thus exert some control over the economy. Experience later showed that the board did not have enough power. *With some revisions— mainly in the 1930's—the Federal Reserve is the basis of the American banking and currency system today.*

COMPROMISING THE TRUST ISSUE.

During the election of 1912, the chief difference between Roosevelt and Wilson centered on their approaches to the trusts. But the gap between the two was not so wide. Wilson favored competition over monopoly, but he was not prepared to "bust" every big corporation. "I am for big business, and I am against the trusts," he declared during the election. It was a stand akin to Roosevelt's distinction between good and bad trusts.

Louis Brandeis helped shape Wilson's attitudes toward the trusts. After the election, Brandeis recommended a solution. In addition to breaking up trusts, he concluded, it was necessary to establish rules of fair competition. And rules required an umpire, a government agency, to enforce them. He advised the President to propose a pair of acts, approved by Congress in the fall of 1914, that reflected Wilson's New Freedom and Roosevelt's New Nationalism.

THE FEDERAL TRADE COMMISSION.

The first act—the Stevens Act— created a government watchdog agency to monitor business practices. Appointed by the President, the Federal Trade Commission had authority to investigate unfair business practices. When it found evidence of such practices, it could order the company to "cease and desist" and enlist the aid of the courts in enforcing its orders.

The act did not define unfair business practices. That was left to the second act, the Clayton Antitrust Act. *The Clayton Act outlawed certain activities that impaired free and fair competition.* Among these unfair practices were: **1)** price discrimination—charging one price to one customer and a different price to another; **2)** exclusive selling or leasing of contracts—such as an agreement under which General Motors used only DuPont paint on its cars; **3)** interlocking directorates—the same people serving as directors of competing corporations; **4)** the purchase of another company's stock in order to reduce competition—such as DuPont's purchase of General Motors stock so that it could force GM to buy its paint.

LABOR AND THE ANTITRUST LAWS. *The Clayton Act included some provisions that organized labor considered of vital importance.* One provision exempted labor unions from the antitrust laws. When the Sherman Antitrust Act was drafted, no one thought that it applied to labor unions. But, in 1908, the Supreme Court said precisely that in the case of the Danbury hatters.

The hatmakers' union had gone on strike against a hat company in Danbury, Connecticut. To increase pressure the union organized a nationwide boycott of the company's hats. The company went to court, arguing that the boycott was a conspiracy in restraint of trade, illegal under the Sherman Act. The Supreme Court agreed and fined the union triple damages, as the act prescribed.

The decision was considered a threat to the entire labor movement. Labor leaders feared that any work stoppage might be considered a conspiracy in restraint of trade. The American Federation of Labor started an intensive campaign to exempt unions from the antitrust law. The provision in the Clayton Act was the result of that campaign.

The Clayton Act also attacked another problem that had weakened the labor movement since the Pullman strike and the jailing of Eugene Debs. *It prohibited the use of court injunctions against labor strikes unless they were deemed necessary to prevent irreparable damage to property.* The measure did little to halt the use of injunctions because the courts almost always expected strikes to be destructive. Never-

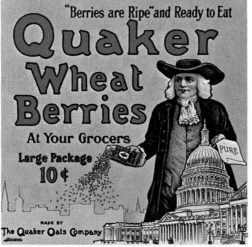

The passage of the Pure Food and Drug Act in 1906 influenced advertising content. These ads show products still in existence. Which one reflects the influence of the 1906 legislation? How?

508

theless, the provisions were important. They represented the first efforts undertaken by the federal government to aid labor unions.

WILSON AND SOCIAL JUSTICE. The antitrust compromise showed that Wilson was flexible in his attitudes. He became more flexible on other matters as well. Before he became President, Wilson showed little interest in the welfare of farmers and workers. A southern Jeffersonian at heart, Wilson felt that welfare legislation was the responsibility of the states. He changed his mind in office.

Although the Democrats retained control of Congress in the election of 1914, they had lost their big majority. The country seemed to be returning to its customary Republicanism. Wilson became convinced that he had to broaden his appeal in order to secure reelection in 1916.

Wilson's change was not purely political. It was, in some respects, a progression from a narrow preoccupation with bankers and tariffs to a broader concept of social justice. *The change also marked Wilson's shift from being a 19th-century liberal who considered government the enemy of freedom, to becoming a 20th-century liberal who hoped to use the power of government to improve the quality of life.*

ACTS FOR FARMERS AND WORKERS. With the President's encouragement, Congress approved a number of measures to benefit groups the Progressives had ignored. The Federal Farm Loan Act (1916) answered the farmers' long-standing demand for easier credit. It established special federal banks to make loans to farmers. The La Follette Seamen's Act (1915) regulated the working conditions of merchant sailors. And the Adamson Act (1916) established an eight-hour day for railroad workers. Congress was prevented from helping other segments of the working population because its power extended over only those workers involved in interstate commerce.

THE SUPREME COURT AND SOCIAL LEGISLATION. The Supreme Court had consistently ruled that workers in ordinary factories were not engaged in interstate commerce. Thus, factories could be regulated only by the states. The Court had ruled (in *Lochner* v. *New York,* 1905) that state laws regulating working conditions violated the "due process" clause of the 14th Amendment. As a result, neither the federal government nor the states could regulate factories and their workers. By judicial decision, laissez faire had become part of the Constitution.

President Wilson tried to break out of the judicial straitjacket in two ways. *With his active support, Congress passed the Keating-Owen Child Labor Act in 1916.* This legislation prohibited the interstate shipment of goods made by child labor. It was hoped that the act would at least prevent companies doing interstate business from employing children.

In that year President Wilson appointed Louis Brandeis to the Supreme Court. Brandeis was an advocate of social welfare legislation. Brandeis and Justice Oliver Wendell Holmes, Jr., a Roosevelt appointee, brought a fresh breath of Progressivism to the nation's highest tribunal. Brandeis' appointment was important for another reason. He was the first Jew to sit on the Court—a victory for religious equality.

Holmes and Brandeis were not able to overcome the Court's basic conservatism. In 1918 the Court declared the Child Labor Act unconstitutional (*Hammer* v. *Dagenhart*). The purpose of the act, said a majority of the Court, was to regulate labor conditions. And such regulation was beyond the constitutional powers of Congress. The decision was a setback for Wilson's goals of social justice. Federal legislation providing for the welfare of citizens had to wait some 20 years, until the Court changed its mind.

THE END OF PROGRESSIVISM. By 1918 President Wilson had lost interest in

Progressives tried hard to control child labor practices in the early 1900's. This photograph, taken by Lewis Hine, a photographer for the National Child Labor Commission, shows children working in a cannery.

reform. ***Since 1914, when war broke out in Europe, Wilson had become increasingly preoccupied with foreign affairs.*** The problems of neutrality and the need to arm the nation also engaged public attention. The election of 1916 was less a judgment of Wilson's Progressivism than a test of his foreign policy. The death knell of Progressivism sounded in 1917 with America's entry into World War I.

Section Review

1. Identify or explain: Pujo committee, Underwood Tariff, Oliver Wendell Holmes, Jr., 16th Amendment, Federal Trade Commission, Keating-Owen Child Labor Act.
2. List and briefly explain the provisions of the Clayton Antitrust Act.

3. Why was antitrust legislation a problem for labor? How did Congress try to solve this problem?

3. Prohibition and Women's Suffrage

WORLD WAR I AIDS TWO PROGRESSIVE MEASURES. *Although World War I ended most Progressive crusades, it furthered two of them—temperance and women's suffrage.* The two were closely related, for women were the most militant leaders in the war against alcoholic drink. Women's suffrage and temperance sprang from the grass roots, and both dated to the age of Andrew Jackson. Neither movement, even though associated with Progressivism, got more than lukewarm support from

Progressive leaders such as Roosevelt and Wilson.

THE TEMPERANCE CRUSADE. The crusade against "the demon rum" began with the humanitarian awakening of the 1840's and 1850's. By the time of the Civil War, most northern states had enacted restrictions on the sale of alcoholic beverages. After the war, the movement withered. Most states repealed their laws. And it was assumed that the experiment had failed.

During the Gilded Age, drinking became a national problem. Saloons multiplied. "Whiskey rings" helped finance political corruption. Families were the chief victims of alcoholism and Protestant churches its main enemies. Rural Protestants blamed the nation's drinking habits on city life and immigrants. They associated drinking with crime and poverty. *The Women's Christian Temperance Union, headed by Frances Willard in 1879, united families and Protestantism in the crusade against alcohol.*

The temperance movement made little headway until the 1890's, when science began to demonstrate that alcohol was a dangerous substance. Laboratory studies proved that alcohol was not a stimulant, as had been supposed, but a depressant, which also did varying amounts of damage to the brain, heart, and liver.

The temperance crusade began in earnest with the formation of the Anti-Saloon League in 1895. Methodist, Baptist, Presbyterian, and Congregational churches gave the ASL financial backing and provided local bases of operation. The Anti-Saloon League focused on taverns, which were widely regarded as centers of vice. At first, the league concentrated on local regulations. Not until 1913, when half the counties in the nation were "dry," did it start a national prohibition campaign.

MAKING PROHIBITION NATIONAL. Nationwide prohibition required an amendment to the Constitution granting Congress

This painting by Ben Shahn shows women marching in support of temperance. For what reasons did women want to prohibit the use of alcohol?

power to pass such a law. By 1917, when the United States entered World War I, 27 states were dry. Only nine more had to be won over to secure ratification of such an amendment. The war provided the final boost. Prohibitionists argued that the grain used to make alcoholic drinks was needed to feed American armies and the starving refugees of Europe. *Congress approved the 18th Amendment in 1918. It was ratified within a year.*

The Volstead Act (1919), passed under authority of the amendment, prohibited the manufacture or sale of beverages containing more than one half of one percent alcohol—a level that made beer and wine illegal. The extremity of the act contributed to its downfall. Many Americans were not prepared to go that far. Without substantial popular support, the act proved virtually unenforceable.

THE WOMEN'S MOVEMENT. Not surprisingly, women played an important role in the prohibition movement. But they were involved in other Progressive crusades as well. *As women became better educated, they found themselves searching for meaningful outlets for their intellectual energies.* Many of the most highly regarded professions—law, medicine, engineering—were closed to them. Many women found themselves trapped in what Jane Addams called "a snare of preparation." They had been educated but not trained for work.

Social work, such as Jane Addams pursued, was one possible outlet. Although the great majority of women married and assumed responsibility for homemaking, many accepted Jane Addams's rule that pure homes required a pure environment. Thus, said Jane Addams, it was a woman's duty to reform whatever threatened the home, whether it was the corner saloon, child labor, or adulterated food.

An alumnus of Addams's Hull House who put this philosophy into practice was Florence Kelley. She was responsible for much of the labor legislation that benefited women

Frances Willard devoted much of her life to the temperance movement.

and children during this period. For 32 years Kelley served as executive secretary of the National Consumers League, an organization of men and women interested primarily in labor problems. It was she who gathered the sociological evidence that persuaded Oregon legislators to enact the Ten-Hour Law for women. And it was she who hired Louis Brandeis to defend that law before the Supreme Court.

WOMEN'S CLUBS. *One popular device that enabled the American woman to affect society was the women's club.* In the decades after 1890 a tremendous expansion of these organizations occurred. Many began as self-improvement societies. But before long they became involved in political causes. Their interest in such causes as urban reform, pure food and drug laws, conservation, and child labor was aroused in part by women's magazines. These periodicals published the exposés of the muckrakers.

WOMEN'S SUFFRAGE. Organizations of middle-class women also provided a natural constituency for the suffrage movement. Like other reforms, the issue of women's suffrage weakened after the Civil War, but it did not die out. Susan B. Anthony and Elizabeth Cady Stanton carried on into the 1890's. *Progressivism breathed new life into the suffrage movement.* And various women's organizations gave it grass roots strength.

By 1900 four western states—Wyoming, Colorado, Utah, and Idaho—had given women the right to vote in all elections. Other states had granted them limited voting rights—for example, the right to vote for school board members and other local officials. When the state of Washington passed a women's suffrage amendment in 1910, several other states considered it.

Big victories for the movement came in 1912, when California extended the franchise to women and the Progressive party endorsed the idea in its platform. By 1914 a total of 11 states had granted women the right to vote. The pace then began to slow, as liquor interests financed a campaign against suffrage. They feared that giving women the vote would ensure the success of the movement to prohibit alcoholic beverages. It soon became clear that the extension of suffrage through state legislation would take a very long time.

ALICE PAUL AND THE SUFFRAGE AMENDMENT. Alice Paul was a young Quaker who earned a doctorate at the University of Pennsylvania. She went to England to continue her graduate studies in sociology. She became impressed with the

Women supported reform causes in the early 1900's even though they did not have the right to vote. This photograph shows women campaigning for female suffrage. How do the methods of women seeking equality in that era compare with those used by women today?

methods of English feminists. They resorted to violence to bring public attention to their cause. They even fired rifles at railroad trains and set fire to the prime minister's house. Alice Paul joined the English feminists in their protests. She was arrested seven times and jailed three times.

Returning to the United States in 1913, Alice Paul organized a march of 5,000 women to demonstrate at Wilson's inauguration. A mob of men attacked the march, causing the police to intervene. A number of marchers were injured, and women around the country rallied to the cause. Feminists, once numbering in the thousands, soon numbered in the millions. Alice Paul organized the Women's party to agitate for a constitutional amendment giving the vote to women. The party soon had over 50,000 members.

The amendment idea brought to life Susan B. Anthony's National Woman Suffrage Association, which had been laboring under conservative leadership. In 1915 the association elected a dynamic president, Carrie Chapman Catt, who promptly announced a six-year timetable for the suffrage movement—two years for Congress to approve it, four years for the states to ratify it. Catt was a superb organizer. She financed her operation with the contributions of millions of sympathetic women. When New York yielded women the right to vote in 1917, it was clear that Congress could not hold out much longer.

THE 19TH AMENDMENT. At that point Alice Paul's Women's party became an obstacle to success. Wearing long white dresses and carrying purple, white, and gold banners, party members became "silent sentinels" outside the White House. They compared "Kaiser Wilson" to the unpopular emperor of Germany, declaring that "An Autocrat at Home is a Poor Champion of Democracy Abroad." Wilson, whose political antennae were ever alert to new voters, was prepared to endorse women's suffrage. But

he could not afford to give way publicly to such an outspoken pressure group.

World War I resolved the situation. Women volunteered in large numbers, selling government bonds, working for the Red Cross, and moving into factories when men were drafted. *In January 1918 President Wilson announced that women had demonstrated they were as fit as men and had earned the right to equal citizenship.* Congress passed the 19th Amendment later that year. And with intensive lobbying, it was ratified in time for women to participate in the election of 1920. A majority of those who did participate voted for the Republican candidate, Warren G. Harding.

Having secured passage of the voting amendment, leaders of the women's suffrage movement continued their work to upgrade the status of American women.

Carrie Chapman Catt's years of work in organizing state suffrage campaigns were instrumental in the passage of the 19th Amendment.

On July 4, 1916, 22-year-old Adeline Van Buren (on the left) and her 24-year-old sister Augusta (on the right) completed the first transcontinental motorcycle trip by a woman. The Van Burens wanted to prove that women, as well as men, could be depended on if the country went to war. However, when Adeline volunteered for the army a year later, she was rejected. What does that indicate about the attitude toward the role of women in society at that time? In what ways has that attitude changed?

Alice Paul began working on an equal rights amendment and, with Alva Belmont, revived the Women's party. In 1923, on the 75th anniversary of the first women's rights convention, the party voted to work for the E.R.A.

Carrie Chapman Catt returned to her Wisconsin home to form the League of Women Voters, an organization that would both educate women about the issues and mobilize them to vote. The league proved to be an organization of great value. But feminist leaders were distressed that women's votes seemed to make no obvious difference in American politics. Jane Addams sorrowfully observed that women in Congress were united only by their enthusiasm for larger armies and navies. She did not live long enough to observe that the only member of Congress to vote against American entry into both World War I and World War II was Jeannette Rankin of Montana.

Section Review

1. Identify or explain: Frances Willard, Anti-Saloon League, Jane Addams, Volstead Act, Alice Paul, Carrie Chapman Catt.
2. Why do you think that the first states to give women the right to vote were in the West?
3. Describe the basic platform of the temperance crusaders. List the provisions of the Volstead Act. Why did some people believe that this law was too extreme?
4. How was Jane Addams' idea of a pure home in a pure environment used to extend women's concern for their homes into a general concern about social welfare? How did involvement of this kind pave the way for the political participation of women?

Chapter 21 Review

Bird's-Eye View

The election of 1912 was the zenith of Progressivism. Two of the three candidates—Roosevelt and Wilson—ran on Progressive platforms. Together they outpolled the conservatives' candidate, Taft. Thus, Wilson took office with a mandate to realize the Progressive program that he called the New Freedom.

Wilson's reforms touched many areas of national life—from big business to social welfare. One of his first proposals was the lowering of the tariff. His administration initiated an income tax, restructured the nation's banking system, and created the Federal Trade Commission to curb "unfair business practices." It also helped strengthen labor by proposing the Clayton Act, which exempted unions from prosecution under antitrust laws. Wilson's social welfare laws helped farmers and workers.

Although many of Wilson's programs were successful, some were declared unconstitutional by the Supreme Court. The Court took the position that such laws as the Keating-Owen Child Labor Act were unconstitutional because Congress had no power to regulate labor conditions.

Two other reform movements occurred during Wilson's administration, although they were not part of the President's program for reform. These were the temperance movement and the movement to give women the vote. After long campaigning and many local victories, the Anti-Saloon League and the Women's Christian Temperance Union succeeded in winning a constitutional amendment that prohibited the sale and the use of alcoholic beverages throughout the nation.

The women's suffrage movement, which began in the mid-19th century, mobilized American women to fight for the vote. Like the temperance crusaders, the suffragists had to fight long and sometimes hard battles. They had to win many local victories before they convinced Congress to propose a constitutional amendment giving women the right to vote in all elections. By 1920 the amendment had been ratified by three fourths of the states.

Vocabulary

Define or identify each of the following:

Square Deal	Money Trust	Alice Paul
Bull Moose Party	Clayton Antitrust Act	Susan B. Anthony
Brandeis brief	Federal Reserve System	Women's Christian Temperance Union

Review Questions

1. Why did Roosevelt leave the Republican party to run for President?
2. Why was Wilson able to win the election of 1912?
3. How did Wilson strengthen the Presidency?

4. List three acts Congress passed that conformed with Wilson's idea of social justice. What reform was brought about by each act?
5. Describe the sequence of events that led to the passage of Prohibition.
6. How did the general spirit of reform lead to a reawakening of the suffrage movement?
7. How did Alice Paul and Carrie Chapman Catt organize women to work for the passage of women's suffrage?

Reviewing Social Studies Skills

1. Make a time line, showing the reforms passed during 1890–1917.
2. The substitution of income tax for tariffs as a source of revenue was considered a democratic reform at the time. Can you infer from the text why people considered the income tax more democratic than tariffs?
3. The electoral college assigns each state a certain number of votes, based on population. To win the election, a President must win a majority of the votes in the electoral college. Using the map on page 505, answer the following questions:
   a. What was the total number of electoral votes available in 1912?
   b. How many electoral votes did each candidate receive?
   c. Approximately how many people voted?
   d. The Republican vote was split between Taft and Roosevelt. How did this enable Wilson to get so many electoral votes?

Reading for Meaning

1. Louis D. Brandeis is cited several times in the chapter. He not only helped Wilson in the shaping of policy, but he also helped to shape social legislation. Using the evidence in the text, write a short report on Brandeis's contributions.
2. The Clayton Act gives the government the right to regulate big business but not to control it. Do you agree or disagree with this statement? Cite three pieces of evidence from the text to support your conclusion.
3. The authors' remarks on the Volstead Act imply that a law will be unsuccessful if it does not have the support of the majority. Can you think of any examples of laws that are generally ignored?

Bibliography

J. A. Garraty's *Woodrow Wilson* (Harper & Row) is a close look at the good and bad aspects of Woodrow Wilson.

Arthur S. Link's *Woodrow Wilson and the Progressive Era* (Harper & Row) is another interesting study of Wilson.

William L. O'Neill's *Everyone Was Brave* (Times Books) is a study of the Women's suffrage movement.

Making Headway in the World

Commodore George Dewey peered through the morning mists and aimed his spyglass at the Spanish ships anchored in a line off a naval station in the Philippines. It was May 1, 1898, and the United States had declared war on Spain 10 days before. Dewey had learned of the outbreak of war at Hong Kong and had sailed with his squadron of light cruisers to the Philippines. He had slipped into Manila Bay during the night of April 30. The Spanish vessels that loomed in the morning mists were equal in number to his own, but they were hopelessly antiquated.

"You may fire when ready, Gridley," Dewey said to his gunnery officer. The cannons barked, and black smoke enveloped the bay. By noon it was all over. The Spanish ships lay sunk or burning. Dewey suffered only one casualty, a sailor who died of heat exhaustion.

Chapter Objectives

After you have finished reading this chapter, you should be able to:
1. Describe the changes in United States foreign relations that took place in the 1890's.
2. Explain why the United States declared war on Spain.
3. Explain the new American foreign policy that resulted from the Spanish-American War and the Open Door policy.
4. List in chronological order the causes and the results of American intervention in Central America, the Caribbean, Mexico, and Venezuela from 1901 to 1917.

The battle of Manila Bay brought the Philippines into American hands and the United States into the Far East. Its outcome affected the course of events throughout the 20th century. The battle was the opening shot in a war between the United States and Spain. The cause of the war was halfway around the world—the island of Cuba in the West Indies. How had it all happened?

1. The Awakening of American Imperialism

INTEREST IN THE FAR EAST. American interest in the Far East began nearly a half century before the Spanish-American War. The object was trade, not colonies. *In*

1853 Commodore Matthew Perry sailed boldly into Japan's Yedo Bay and demanded that the emperor open his island to American ships. Impressed more by Perry's cannons than his arguments, the emperor yielded. A treaty opening Japan to trade was signed the following year.

Further efforts in the Far East were interrupted by the Civil War. Shortly after the war ended, Secretary of State Seward persuaded Russia to part with Alaska for 7 million dollars. Although Alaska was part of North America, the long chain of Aleutian Islands that came with it pointed straight to the heart of the Far East. (See map, page 527.) In that same year, 1867, the United States Navy occupied Midway Island in the central Pacific.

The acquisition of Alaska aroused little public enthusiasm. "Seward's folly," some called it; "Seward's icebox," jeered others. Not until gold was discovered in 1898 did Americans begin to realize that Seward had made one of the best buys in history.

THE SEARCH FOR TRADING PARTNERS. In the 1870's President Grant resumed the search for Pacific trading partners by dispatching naval officers to various island kingdoms. *In 1875 one of Grant's agents signed the Reciprocity Treaty with the kingdom of Hawaii.* It provided for the mutual exchange of goods. The effect was to make Hawaiian sugar cheaper in the United States than West Indian sugar. American planters moved in. With its economy tied to

Commodore Perry's second trip to Japan in 1854 resulted in a treaty with the Japanese government. Here, American gifts to the emperor—including an iron stove and two telegraph sets—are being unloaded at Yokohama. Is there any evidence in this painting to indicate that it was done by an American artist?

the American sugar market, Hawaii became a virtual colony. Annexation was merely a matter of time.

In 1878 Grant's envoy negotiated a similar arrangement with the island kingdom of Samoa. In addition to mutual trade, this treaty provided for American protection of the islands. Both Britain and Germany had designs on the islands. In 1881, to avoid competing with one another, the three powers divided Samoa into *spheres of influence.* Then, in 1899, the British withdrew, leaving the islands to Germany and the United States. The American sphere included the splendid harbor at Pago Pago (PANG-o PANG-o), which the navy had wanted to use for some years. As with Hawaii, outright annexation was simply a matter of time.

A *sphere of influence* is an area in which another nation exercises strong political and economic influence.

THE NEW IMPERIALISM. *These activities in the South Pacific reflected the bare awakening of American interest in foreign affairs.* Up to 1890 the nation had been preoccupied with domestic problems—sectional conflict, industrialism, the conquest of the West. But by 1890 the frontier had come to an end, Civil War wounds had healed, and industry had come of age. From that point on, the nation became increasingly interested in the rest of the world. The result was a burst of expansionism that climaxed in the Spanish-American War.

America had never thought of itself as an *imperial* power. It had battled the imperial pretensions of Britain, France, and Spain in the New World. Americans had identified with colonized peoples, not colonial powers, and had sympathized with revolutions in other countries. What caused the change?

An *imperial* power is one that follows a policy of establishing colonies and building an empire.

PROBLEMS OF INDUSTRIAL MATURITY. Some old problems had been solved by 1890, but new ones arose to replace them. The United States had become the foremost industrial nation in the world. But it was soon apparent that American factories were producing more than the American population could afford to buy. The realization sunk in with particular force in the depression of 1893. *American businesses intensified their efforts to find markets abroad for their products.* Labor leaders agreed, for the interests of the workers could only be achieved by keeping factories operating. Farmers, burdened by surplus, shared the concern.

WORLD IMPERIALISM. *The American awakening to the outside world corresponded with a global revival of imperialism.* The great imperial powers, Britain and France, had been quiet for some years. They seemed content to sit back and administer the vast empires they had acquired overseas, rather than scramble for additional territory. This complacent mood was shattered in the 1890's, when a new and aggressive spirit of imperialism—in the form of Germany and Japan—swept the world. Britain and France found themselves challenged on their own colonial doorsteps. In a matter of years, Africa was carved up into colonies, and China was divided into spheres of influence.

AN EXPANSIONIST LITERATURE. Empire building became romantic—technology against jungle, firearms against spears. It suggested all the color and drama of an adventure novel. Fiction writers made the most of it. The English poet Rudyard Kipling wrote of the duty of Europeans to spread their cultures and styles of government to supposedly less fortunate races—"The White Man's Burden," he called it.

Many Americans shared this attitude. In *Our Country* (1885) Congregational minister Josiah Strong predicted that the American branch of the "Anglo-Saxon race" would extend its culture, technology, and governmental expertise over Latin America, Africa, and Asia. There was little scholarly merit in the thesis, but it served the interests of national pride.

An even more stirring call to glory was a book, *The Influence of Sea Power Upon History, 1660–1783,* written in 1890 by a naval captain, Alfred Thayer Mahan. Mahan sought to demonstrate that the influential countries of modern times—the Netherlands, France, and Britain—had risen to greatness through sea power. If the United States wanted to follow in their footsteps, argued Mahan, it had to have a powerful navy. It would also have to have a strong merchant marine as a training ground for sailors. But to have a healthy merchant marine, it was argued, a nation needed colonies to supply raw materials and consume the products of its industry. *From sea power to empire was thus considered a short, logical step.*

THE GREAT WHITE FLEET. Among those stepping toward empire with Mahan was an influential senator from Massachusetts, Henry Cabot Lodge. From the floor of Congress, Lodge called for a fleet of modern steel-plated battleships and a world network of naval bases and coaling stations where ships could refuel. Lodge called his plan the Large Policy. And scarcely a segment of American society failed to see some benefit in it. By the middle of the decade, four modern battleships, painted a gleaming white, were ready to slide into the water. And the world wondered what the United States would do with this "great white fleet."

Sidenote to History

Queen Lil and the Hawaiian Revolution

Sugar was Hawaii's main export. Most of it was grown by American planters. To work their great plantations, the Americans imported Japanese workers. By 1890 foreigners in Hawaii outnumbered the native population. In 1890 American business interests staged a bloodless revolution and forced King Kalakaua (kah-LAH-KAW-oo-ah) to accept a constitution that gave White foreigners the vote. Because property qualifications prevented most native Hawaiians from voting, Americans ran the country. The following year Kalakaua died. His sister, Liliuokalani (le-LEE-woe-kah-LAH-nee), ascended the throne.

Queen Lil, as Americans called her, was a firm opponent of foreign rule. She rallied Hawaiian nationalists and tried to do away with the "bayonet constitution" that had been forced on her brother.

In 1893, with the help of troops from an American cruiser conveniently anchored offshore, an uprising took place. The rebels asked for annexation, and Secretary of State Foster agreed.

The treaty of annexation was before the Senate when President Harrison left office. Suspecting that the uprising was the result of a plot involving the State Department, the new President, Grover Cleveland, withdrew the treaty and ordered an investigation. It was discovered that the American minister in Hawaii had been in league with the rebels. By then there was little the President could do about the rebellion. He recognized the new republic of Hawaii, but he refused to annex the islands. In 1898 Congress passed a joint resolution annexing Hawaii to the United States.

Section Review

1. Identify or explain: Pago Pago, "Seward's folly," Commodore Matthew Perry, great white fleet, coaling stations, Henry Cabot Lodge.
2. Explain the concept of "The White Man's Burden." How was this concept expressed in the United States?
3. Explain the argument advanced by Alfred Thayer Mahan in his book *The Influence of Sea Power Upon History, 1660–1783.*

2. War with Spain

JINGOISM. The 1890's was a decade of international tension. Britain and Germany entered into a naval shipbuilding race. Russia and Japan locked horns in the Pacific. French and British armies came close to blows in one part of Africa. French and German armies were at swords' points in another. In South Africa, British and **Boers** fought open warfare.

Boers are South Africans who are of Dutch descent.

The United States felt the rising spirit of belligerence. Jingoism, Americans called it—foreign policy with a chip on the shoulder. In 1892 some American sailors got into a barroom brawl in Valparaiso, Chile. Two were killed and 17 injured. Secretary of State James G. Blaine demanded that Chile compensate the widows and the injured men. The possibility of war loomed behind Blaine's demand. But the crisis passed when he died.

Blaine's successor, John Foster, was no better, however. In early 1893 an uprising in Hawaii, led by Americans, gave him an opportunity to demand formal annexation of the islands. A treaty was signed, but the new President, Grover Cleveland, shelved it.

Cleveland followed his own brand of jingoism. In 1895 Venezuela and British Guiana got into a border dispute. Because Guiana was a British colony, Cleveland claimed that the dispute was an instance of European interference in the Western Hemisphere. Invoking the Monroe Doctrine, he told Britain to yield on the boundary question. It was a curious use of the doctrine. Britain ignored it. Cleveland then publicized the affair in a special message to Congress. The Monroe Doctrine, he said, involved more than diplomatic protection of Latin America. It involved commercial matters as well. A monopoly of trade with Latin America, he declared, was of "vital interest" to the United States. From Cleveland's point of view, the Monroe Doctrine excluded European nations from Latin American trade. How Latin Americans felt about that can be guessed.

REVOLUTION IN CUBA. The United States had become militant in its diplomacy. But had there been no uprising in Cuba, it probably would not have plunged into war.

Cuba, "the pearl of the Antilles," was one of the last relics of the once mighty Spanish Empire in America. It was within the commercial orbit of the United States. Sugar was the island's main cash crop and export. So, like Hawaii, Cuba was tied to the large American sugar market. Although the market was lucrative, most plantation workers—the majority of workers in Cuba—made barely enough to stay alive. The depression and the high American tariffs caused even greater hardships. Plantations closed down, and thousands were out of work. Spanish rule—a mixture of ineptitude and broken promises—was unable to cope with the situation. In 1895 revolution broke out.

Determined to hold onto Cuba, Spain reinforced its military garrison there. The Spanish commander on the island, Valeriano Weyler, set up "zones of concentration" in which to isolate the revolutionaries. Reports reached the United States of camps full of displaced persons, miles of barbed-wire fences, and horrible tortures. Joseph Pulitzer's *New York World* and William Randolph Hearst's *New York Journal* roused public opinion against Spain with lurid headlines and stories of unbelievable atrocities. Americans were bombarded with headlines like "200,000 People Are Starving" and "General Weyler Trying to Kill Off the Breed." Beneath the headlines they read articles about "General Weyler's policy of killing women and children by slow starvation under the guns of Spain's forts. . . ." "Butcher" Weyler became the greatest villain of the day.

In the election of 1896, the Republicans and Democrats pronounced themselves in favor of an independent Cuba. But no responsible person in the United States wanted active intervention. It was Spain's affair. And so it would have remained except for an extraordinary chain of errors.

"REMEMBER THE *MAINE*." President McKinley took office in 1897 without having made a public commitment concerning Cuba. His attitude was one of moderation. Spain seemed equally flexible. After its hard-line prime minister was assassinated, a new, liberal cabinet recalled General Weyler and promised Cuba a limited amount of self-government. The rebels were not satisfied, but intelligent diplomacy might have achieved a settlement.

Then, in January 1898, riots broke out in Havana, and President McKinley sent the battleship *Maine* on a "courtesy call" to the port. What he expected to accomplish is not clear. It was a risky move. Tension was so high that some kind of incident seemed inevitable.

On February 15 the incident occurred. The **Maine** *exploded at its anchorage and sank, carrying with it some 260 American sailors.* With the cooperation of Spanish authorities, a board of American naval officers sent deep-sea divers to examine the wreck. They concluded that a submarine mine had exploded under the ship, setting off its powder magazine.

Who was responsible? We will never know. There was no reason to suspect the Spanish authorities, for they had much to lose by American intervention. The Cuban rebels stood to gain the most if America's anger were stirred. In all likelihood, it was an accident. Probably, a mine broke loose from its moorings and exploded.

Congress remained calm until the naval investigating board issued its report on March 28. The President maintained a discreet silence. But the yellow press screamed for blood. A continuous barrage of atrocities in words and pictures greeted Americans at every newsstand. "The readers of the *Journal*," boasted Hearst's paper, "knew immediately after the destruction of the *Maine* that it had been blown up by a Spanish mine." The *Journal* clearly blamed the Spanish. Soon even conservative papers and religious journals declared that the United States had a moral responsibility to intervene in Cuba. The war cry "Remember the *Maine!*" echoed from coast to coast.

PRESSURE FOR WAR. *During March 1898 Congress became more critical of Spanish policies in Cuba. Pressure on the President increased.* In the Navy Department, Assistant Secretary Theodore Roosevelt expected war from the moment the *Maine* sank. He had cabled instructions to Commodore Dewey in Hong Kong to move into the Spanish-held Philippines when war was declared. When the President showed no signs of moving, Roosevelt fumed that McKinley had "no more backbone than a chocolate eclair."

Yielding to pressure from Congress and the press, McKinley sent an ultimatum to Spain late in March. He demanded that Spain disband the concentration camps, halt the fighting, and begin negotiations with the rebels leading to a grant of independence. On April 9 the Spanish cabinet declared an armistice in Cuba and offered to negotiate. The American minister in Madrid cabled home that he hoped nothing further would be done to humiliate Spain.

DECLARATION OF WAR. The President, having joined the war hawks, refused to swerve from his course. *Ignoring the Spanish concessions, he sent a message to Congress on April 11, requesting authority to use the military forces of the United States to stop the war in Cuba.* Congress debated for a week before approving the request. The margin in the Senate was close (42–35). In the House it was substantial (311–6). When the government learned of the congressional action, Spain severed diplomatic relations and declared war on the United States. Congress replied with its own declaration of war.

It was an avoidable war. Those who wanted peace could well agree with Theodore Roosevelt that the President lacked backbone. He failed to stand up to jingoist pressure from Congress and the press. The war was not McKinley's alone. It was one of the most popular wars the nation had ever fought. Americans believed they were going to the aid of a suffering people, fighting to remove one more corrupt monarchy from the Western Hemisphere.

This idealism found expression in the congressional resolutions authorizing intervention. According to one resolution, prepared by Senator Henry M. Teller of Colorado, the United States had no intention of exercising control over Cuba. It would leave government of the island to its people. Senator Teller wanted the world to know that the United States had no designs on Cuba, "whatever we may do as to some other islands."

"A SPLENDID LITTLE WAR." *Within 10 weeks the fighting was over. And the*

Black soldiers, segregated into all-Black regiments, fought valiantly in the Spanish-American War. Here, members of the all-Black Tenth Cavalry support an attack by Teddy Roosevelt's Rough Riders.

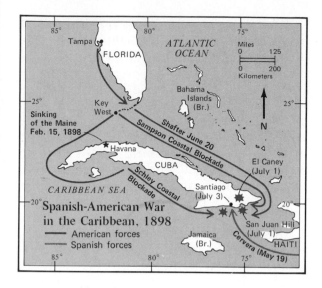

Spanish-American War
in the Caribbean, 1898
— American forces
— Spanish forces

United States possessed the nucleus of an overseas empire. After Commodore Dewey broke Spanish power in the Philippines, an army of occupation was hastily formed in San Francisco and sent across the Pacific. (See map below.) On the way it stopped to lay claim to uninhabited Wake Island, in the central Pacific, and to Spanish Guam, chief island of the Marianas. (See map, page 527.) Having no telegraphic communication, the Spanish authorities in Guam were unaware of the war until the cruiser *Charleston* sailed into its harbor and lobbed a few shells into its deserted fort. The Spanish at first thought it was a salute. But when the shells exploded, they surrendered.

Across the world in Cuba, attention quickly centered on the main Spanish fleet—four armored cruisers and three destroyers commanded by Admiral Cervera. The location of the squadron was not known, causing some invasion jitters along the Atlantic seaboard. But when the Spanish turned up in Santiago, on the south coast of Cuba, the American fleet closed in. (See map above.)

On June 15 a hastily equipped and ill-organized American army of 16,000 landed on the coast near Santiago. The army fought its way inland. After a sharp fight, in which

Theodore Roosevelt and his Rough Riders distinguished themselves, the American forces seized San Juan Hill overlooking the city.

Trapped between America's army and navy, Admiral Cervera slipped out of Santiago Harbor on July 3. He fled along the coast toward a more secure haven. Commodore William T. Sampson and the Atlantic Fleet gave chase. Every Spanish vessel was sunk or run aground. The battle of Santiago ended any Spanish hope of defending Cuba. On July 16, the Spanish surrendered. Two days later Spain asked for peace. But before the conflict ended, an American force seized the island of Puerto Rico. So feeble was Spanish resistance on the island that the humorist Mr. Dooley characterized the landing as "a moonlight excursion."

An armistice was agreed upon on August 12. American battle casualties numbered 345. *The American flag flew around the world, from Puerto Rico to the Philippines.* The Secretary of State summed it up. It was, said John Hay, "a splendid little war."

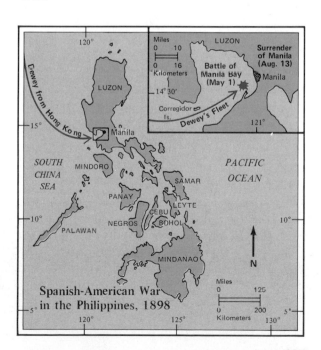

Spanish-American War
in the Philippines, 1898

Section Review

1. Mapping: Using the maps in this chapter, describe the location of each of the following in terms of its latitude and longitude: the Marianas, Guam, Wake Island, the Philippines, Puerto Rico, Cuba.
2. Identify or explain: jingoism, James G. Blaine, the pearl of the Antilles, "Butcher" Weyler, Commodore George Dewey, the Rough Riders.
3. How did Grover Cleveland extend the meaning of the Monroe Doctrine?

3. Consequences of the Spanish-American War

WHAT TO DO? After the war came the headaches. Did the United States really want all those islands? What would be done with them? Would they be incorporated into the Union as territories and states? Or would the United States follow the path of European imperialism and keep them as colonies? Suppose these islands wanted their independence?

KEEPING THE PHILIPPINES. The Philippines were on the doorstep of China. And China was a vast potential consumer market of 400 million people. Hawaii, Guam, and Samoa were natural stepping-stones across the Pacific. The islands offered opportunities too good to turn down. To give up the islands now "would be an act of inconceivable folly," declared the New York *Journal of Commerce*. Other reasons occurred to the State Department. The destruction of Spanish authority in the western Pacific had left a power vacuum. If the United States did not establish its authority over the Philippines, some other power, such as Germany or Japan, might do so.

Missionary organizations lent their support to annexation. Providence, they believed, had presented the United States with a unique opportunity to spread its civilizing influence. Their influence helped persuade President McKinley, who was a deeply religious man, to keep the territories. McKinley told a delegation at the White House that he realized "there was nothing left for us to do but to take them all, and to educate the Filipinos, and uplift and civilize and Christianize them. . . ." Because the Philippines had been Roman Catholic for centuries under Spanish rule, the President's missionary zeal was, at best, misdirected. But the reasoning seemed sufficient to the victor to demand the islands in the peace settlement.

THE PEACE SETTLEMENT. Peace negotiators met in Paris in the autumn of 1898, and the treaty was signed on December 10. Cuba was granted independence from Spain. Spain ceded the Philippines (for which the United States paid 20 million dollars), Puerto Rico, and Guam. The United States negotiated separate treaties of annexation with Hawaii and American Samoa.

The United States promised religious freedom to the inhabitants of the former Spanish colonies. But the treaty stipulated that their civil and political rights would be "determined by the Congress." *For the first time in a treaty ratifying the acquisition of territory, the United States did not promise American citizenship to the people it had begun to govern. The islands were to be dependencies, part of an American empire.*

THE FILIPINOS FIGHT FOR INDEPENDENCE. *The Filipinos were not at all happy with the outcome of the conference.* They had played an important part in the American capture of Manila, believing that they would be given independence at the end of the war. They soon realized that the American commitment to freedom for

Cuba did not include freedom for the Philippines.

Just before the Senate was to vote on the treaty, the Filipinos, under the leadership of Emilio Aguinaldo, declared their independence. They formed a government near Manila and resolved to rid their island nation of its latest foreign invader. The United States was just as resolved to hold onto the Philippines. The result was war.

Between 1899 and 1901, Aguinaldo and his army of Filipino patriots valiantly fought off the United States Army of Occupation. They maneuvered skillfully from island to island. But in the end, they were beaten. The United States spent 600 million dollars, used 70,000 troops, and lost 4,300 lives in subduing the Philippines. *The war that had begun to end Spanish tyranny in Cuba ended, ironically, in the crushing of the Filipino effort to win independence.*

THE LONG ROAD TO INDEPENDENCE. After the suppression of Aguinaldo's uprising, an American civilian

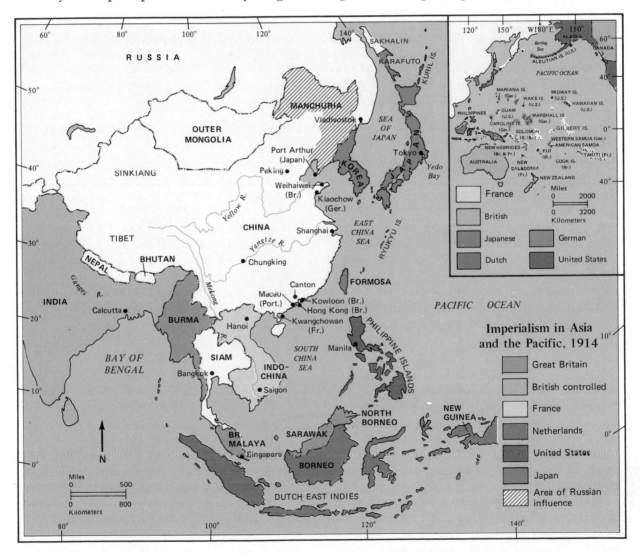

Imperialism in Asia and the Pacific, 1914

government took control of the islands. William Howard Taft was appointed governor. American culture—including a public school system—was introduced. And the standard of living was improved. But to the Filipinos, these practical benefits were no substitute for independence. Year after year they repeated their demands for freedom.

In 1934, as part of Franklin D. Roosevelt's Good Neighbor Policy, Congress passed the Tydings-McDuffie Act. It stated the intention of the United States government to "recognize the independence of the Philippine Islands as a separate and self-governing nation. . . ." It promised independence after a new Philippine government had been operating for 10 years. *The government was established in 1936, and in 1946 the Philippines finally achieved the independence they had fought for nearly 50 years before:*

PUERTO RICO: CARIBBEAN COMMONWEALTH.
The island nation of Puerto Rico was also acquired by the United States in the treaty settling the Spanish-American War. As early as the mid-19th century, Puerto Ricans tried unsuccessfully to win their independence from Spain. Thus, they, like the Filipinos, were less than happy when they traded one group of foreign rulers for another.

After the treaty settlement, many Puerto Ricans continued their work for independence. In 1952 the United States government granted the island the status of a self-governing commonwealth. From that time on, the island's association with the United States continued on a voluntary basis. As a result of its commonwealth status, Puerto Rico has kept close ties with the United States. For example, there are no restrictions on Puerto Rican immigration to the United States.

Today some Puerto Ricans would like to see their island become the 51st state. However, just as many want to retain the special relationship they have with the United States. Only a very small percentage favors complete independence.

A LINGERING HOLD ON CUBA. *Cuba also forced the United States to compromise some of its principles.* The Teller Amendment, promising the independence of Cuba, expressed the idealism of the war.

Sidenote to History
Miguel Antonio Otero

In 1912, New Mexico entered the union as a state. Miguel Antonio Otero, New Mexico's territorial governor, was one of the people most responsible for its admission. Otero was a Spanish American born in St. Louis, Missouri, in 1859. On graduating from college, he entered politics at the local level. He worked his way through the ranks of the territorial judicial system. In 1897 Otero was appointed governor of New Mexico by President William McKinley. He held this position until 1908.

At the outbreak of the Spanish-American War, Theodore Roosevelt recruited his Rough Riders from the cowboys of the Southwest. Otero volunteered to serve as an officer in the regiment. He wired Roosevelt: "Can raise a battalion of riflemen in about a week."

As a descendant of a respected Spanish-American family, Otero was in a unique position as the territory's governor. He was able to communicate with both the Spanish-speaking members of the region and the English-speaking settlers. When a proposal was made to admit Arizona and New Mexico as one state, Otero spoke out against it. He maintained that New Mexico's cultural makeup was so different from Arizona's that any union of the two territories into one state was out of the question. Otero's argument was successful, and New Mexico was admitted as a separate state.

But the longer the United States remained in Cuba, the more reluctant it was to leave.

The army occupying Cuba did do some good. After being nearly wiped out by yellow fever, the army started an islandwide sanitation program. It also helped the Cubans establish a republican government and a system of public education.

The United States wanted to make sure that Cuba would be able to survive after its troops left. This feeling surfaced in an amendment to a 1901 army bill. It was drafted by Senator Orville Platt of Connecticut. The Platt Amendment was incorporated into the Cuban constitution of 1902 and became part of a treaty between the United States and Cuba in 1903. *The amendment granted the United States the right to send military forces into Cuba to protect the lives and property of Cuban citizens whenever they were threatened by their own government.* It also gave the United States a long-term lease on the naval base at Guantánamo Bay on the southern coast of Cuba.

Under the Platt Amendment, the United States intervened repeatedly in Cuba, landing marines whenever there was turmoil. A treaty in 1934 abolished the Platt Amendment. But it renewed the lease on Guantánamo Bay, which is still in American hands.

THE OPEN DOOR: A FOREIGN POLICY FOR THE 20TH CENTURY.

The imperial awakening of the 1890's had been sparked by an interest in world trade and markets. It was fitting that the Spanish-American War closed with a general statement of market diplomacy. *The statement, known as the Open Door Policy, became a cardinal feature of American diplomacy in the 20th century.*

For some years American business people had been interested in the China market. By the end of the 1890's, Americans faced stiff competition in China from business groups representing other nations with similar interests. Americans did not fear competition. They feared the lack of it. Russia, Japan, and the countries of western Europe were doing in China what had earlier been done in Africa—carving out spheres of influence and winning trade monopolies within those spheres. In 1898 France, having occupied Indochina, extended its influence into southern China. Britain rented the port of Kowloon, and its warships patrolled the mighty Yangtze River. Germany obtained a lease on the port of Kiaochow. Russia menaced Manchuria.

OPENING THE DOOR. The United States came late to the imperial game and feared it might be left out. The United States had no territorial ambitions in China. But it did want to keep the commercial door to China open as wide as possible. In September 1899 Secretary of State John Hay sent letters to the various powers interested in China. He asked that they keep open all "treaty ports" and guarantee equal trading rights and tariff rates in China. He urged that special privileges be given to no one. The replies Hay got were grudging at best. Each country's agreement was based on the agreement of all the countries involved. Putting the best face on it, Hay announced that everyone had complied with America's demands and declared the Open Door Policy in effect.

Then, in early 1900, came the *Boxer* Rebellion, an uprising by Chinese nationalists against foreign influence. Foreign envoys and missionaries fled to Peking, where the student-led rebels besieged them until an international army, composed of American, Japanese, and European troops, came to the rescue.

Boxers was the name given by westerners to a Chinese secret society. The Chinese name meant "righteous, harmonious band" but had been mistranslated to mean "righteous, harmonious fists."

Fearing that the European powers might use the incident as an excuse to partition China into colonies, Hay restated American policy in a circular letter in July 1900. *In addition to free trade, said Hay, it was American policy to "preserve the territorial and administrative entity" of China.* The letter seemed to work. The international army disbanded after lifting its siege, and China remained independent. Two years later, when Japan seized Korea, the United States repeated its statement of support for the territorial integrity of China, warning Japan to go no further.

THE RUSSO-JAPANESE WAR. *In 1903 President Theodore Roosevelt used the Open Door Policy to express his anger over Russia's expansion into Manchuria.* However, instead of involving the United States in a war with Russia, Roosevelt encouraged Japan's efforts to halt Russia's moves. Japan attacked the Russian fleet in 1904 at Port Arthur, Manchuria, and started the Russo-Japanese War.

The Japanese won several important victories. But as a result of their military efforts, they soon faced great financial difficulties. Fearing that their financial problems would cause them to lose the war, they asked Roosevelt to mediate. Roosevelt responded by calling a peace conference at Portsmouth, New Hampshire, in the summer of 1905. For his role in settling the Russo-Japanese War, President Roosevelt was awarded the Nobel Peace Prize. His intervention helped preserve peace in Asia by maintaining the balance of power between the two nations.

EXTENDING THE OPEN DOOR. *The concept of the open door originated in America's policy toward China, but the principles it embodied—free trade and the territorial integrity of independent nations—were as old as the United States.* They were capable of extension far beyond China. In the 20th century, American Presidents applied them around the world.

1. Mapping: In the language of geography, the Philippines are known as an *archipelago*. Using the dictionary, write a one-sentence definition of the term. Then, using a map of the world, locate at least two other archipelagoes.
2. Identify or explain: Emilio Aguinaldo, the Platt Amendment, John Hay, the Boxer Rebellion, sphere of influence.
3. Why do the authors maintain that United States involvement in Cuba and the Philippine Islands led to compromises of American principles?

4. The Panama Canal and Dollar Diplomacy

INTEREST IN LATIN AMERICA. In Latin America, as in the Far East, echoes of the Spanish-American War were heard for years after the shooting stopped. The United States had always taken a special interest in Latin America. After 1900 United States policy toward Latin America became more aggressively domineering. The government actively encouraged businesses to invest in Latin American properties and then moved to protect investments with its military might. Its guardianship of Cuba (which was called a protectorate) made that country a colony in all but name. Latin Americans resented such meddling.

THE ISTHMIAN CANAL. The trip around South America took a long time. By the time the ships in the Caribbean joined the ships in the Pacific, the Spanish-American War was over. After the war the United States had imperial interests on both sides of the continent. It seemed that the United States would have to maintain two navies, one in the Atlantic and the Caribbean, the other in the Pacific. *Hence, the first order* *of business when the war ended was the construction of a canal across Central America.* A canal would make it possible for one fleet to pass quickly from one ocean to the other. (See map below.)

There were two possible routes. One was across the Republic of Nicaragua. This route made use of a chain of lakes. The other, shorter route was through the Isthmus of Panama. It offered a further advantage: a ditch had already been dug. A French canal company had begun a canal in the 1880's. The French had abandoned the project, however, because of a lack of funds. They were willing to sell their lease on the property and their machinery.

In 1901, President Theodore Roosevelt gave a top-priority rating to construction of the canal. The following year he negotiated the Hay-Herrán Treaty with Colombia, which owned the Isthmus of Panama. The

treaty granted the United States a 99-year lease to a strip of land across Panama for a 10-million dollar down payment and a 250,000-dollar annual rental. The Colombian Senate refused to approve the treaty. The lease was due to expire soon. On that date the equipment would belong to Columbia. Colombian officials would then be able to negotiate even better terms with the United States.

REVOLUTION IN PANAMA. Roosevelt was infuriated by Colombia's action. He began to talk about Colombia's despotic government and the possibility of Panamanian independence. Others might also benefit from Panamanian independence, among them Philippe Bunau-Varilla (boo-NOE-vah-REE-yah), a French citizen who exercised political influence in Panama and a shareholder in the French company.

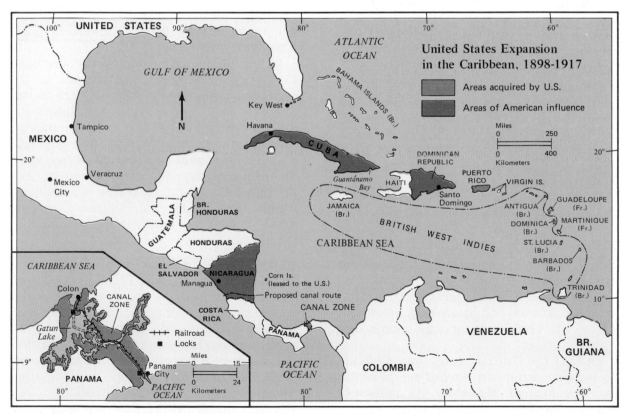

United States Expansion in the Caribbean, 1898-1917

Areas acquired by U.S.

Areas of American influence

Bunau-Varilla secretly visited the United States and requested the aid of the State Department. Although he was refused overt military support, Bunau-Varilla came away with the idea that an American warship would visit Panama in November 1903.

The gunboat *Nashville* arrived on the second of November. Revolution broke out two days later. Colombia, anticipating trouble, had landed a military force in Panama. But American marines prevented it from acting. When asked by what authority they interfered, the Americans pointed to an 1846 treaty that gave the United States the right to protect free passage across the isthmus.

THE PANAMA TREATY.

With the Colombian Army checked, the Panamanian revolutionaries quickly gained control of the country. On November 6 the United States recognized the independent republic of Panama. Two weeks later Bunau-Varilla, Panama's ambassador to the United States, signed a treaty establishing the Canal Zone. The financial arrangements were the same as those negotiated earlier with Colombia— a 99-year lease for 10 million dollars down and 250,000 dollars in annual rental. The treaty also gave the United States the right to intervene in Panama if the canal was threatened. In return the United States promised that the canal would be forever open in peacetime to the commerce of all nations.

Sentiment in favor of a Nicaraguan canal remained strong in Congress. During the debate on the Panama treaty, Bunau-Varilla placed on every senator's desk a Nicaraguan postage stamp depicting an active volcano in the middle of Lake Nicaragua. A few days later the volcano obligingly blew up and buried a city. The Senate hastily approved the Panama treaty.

In 1921 the United States gave Colombia 25 million dollars in partial compensation for the loss of Panama. As conscience money, however, it was scarcely enough to blot out the growing image of the strong-arm Yankee. Nor did it help when Roosevelt boasted in 1911, "I took the Canal Zone and let Congress debate." That was not quite the way it happened. But as far as Latin America was concerned, it might as well have been.

BUILDING THE PANAMA CANAL.

Construction of the canal was a triumph of American ingenuity and engineering. The first requirement was to make the jungles safe for work crews. Central America had been a graveyard for Europeans because of yellow fever, a highly contagious, often fatal disease. In Cuba an American medical team headed by Dr. Walter Reed discovered that yellow fever was transmitted by mosquitoes. One of Reed's associates, Dr. William C. Gorgas, eliminated the mosquitoes by spraying oil on their breeding places. In 1904 he was placed in charge of the sanitation program in Panama and made the new republic one of the healthiest nations in Latin America.

Under the supervision of the engineer George W. Goethals, construction of the canal was completed in August 1914. It had taken 10 years to build. It cost almost 400 million dollars. The first ships were moving through the canal as World War I began in Europe. *The canal's contribution to United States naval strength was enormous.* And its value as a commercial route was immeasurable. To this day the Panama Canal remains one of the most vital sea arteries in the world.

ROOSEVELT'S COROLLARY TO THE MONROE DOCTRINE.

President Roosevelt considered the Panama Canal a vital part of the American defense system. By making Cuba and Panama into American protectorates, he hoped to prevent any foreign military intervention in the area. European business investments were another matter. America had no jurisdiction over European trade with Latin Americans. But

THE WORLD'S CONSTABLE.

Teddy Roosevelt, whose famous motto was "Speak softly and carry a big stick," is criticized here for such diplomacy. This cartoon dates from early 1904. What incidents in Latin America might have influenced the cartoonist?

business practices sometimes led to political difficulties. Rulers in Latin America over-borrowed and their governments went bankrupt. When revolutions occurred, the new regimes often refused to honor debts.

One crisis loomed in 1902, when Venezuela reneged on its debts to Britain, Germany, and Italy. In retaliation the European powers blockaded the Venezuelan coast and seized several gunboats. ***Roosevelt, concerned that the move could lead to a serious violation of the Monroe Doctrine, persuaded the parties to submit the dispute to arbitration.*** The incident convinced him that a formula was needed to prevent similar crises in the future.

The opportunity came a year later, when the Dominican Republic declared bankruptcy. It owed money to several European countries, which threatened to take over its customs houses in order to recover their funds. ***To prevent this, Roosevelt announced his famous corollary, or extension, to the Monroe Doctrine.*** If the doctrine prevented Europe from intervening in the Americas, Roosevelt reasoned, then ". . . in the Western Hemisphere the adherence of the United States to the Monroe Doctrine may force the United States, however reluctantly, in flagrant cases of . . . wrongdoing or impotence, to the exercise of an international police power."

As protector of the New World, Roosevelt argued, the United States had to be its police officer to prevent any nation in Latin America from taking advantage of its political immunity to evade financial obligations. So saying, he negotiated an arrangement through which American officials would control Dominican customs houses, supporting the Dominican government with half the proceeds and using the rest to discharge European debts. When the Senate rejected the agreement, Roosevelt put it into effect anyway by executive order.

TAFT AND DOLLAR DIPLOMACY.
When a private corporation declares bankruptcy, it is put into receivership. An outside agency, usually a bank, moves in to manage the company's finances and bargain with its creditors. Until the company is sound, it remains in the hands of the receivers. Roosevelt followed this example in part by sending receivers to collect taxes in the bankrupt Dominican Republic. His successor, William Howard Taft, carried out the rest of the plan.

The occasion for Taft's policy arose in 1909. There was a revolution in Nicaragua in which the dictator, an opponent of foreign influence in his country, was overthrown. The new president, Adolfo Diaz, was friendly to American interests. He worked out an agreement with President Taft for refunding his nation's debts. Under the agreement, United States bankers refinanced the Nicaraguan debt with loans and recovered their money by collecting Nicaragua's customs duties. In addition, the Americans received control of the National Bank of Nicaragua and the government-owned railroad.

When Nicaraguan reaction to this agreement touched off another revolt, Diaz asked for American intervention. The United States sent in 2,000 marines to protect its interests and suppress the revolution. When the marines departed, they left a military "guard" that remained in the capital, Managua, for the next 13 years. Nicaragua was in receivership, and it was an American protectorate. Like Roosevelt, President Taft justified the move as necessary to keep Europeans out of the Caribbean.

Using diplomacy to aid and protect American business interests abroad was not a new political tactic. American Presidents had done it long before Taft, and they have done it since. ***Taft turned the relationship around—he used bankers and private funds to promote the strategic aims of American diplomacy.*** Taft used money to enforce the Monroe Doctrine. Critics called Taft's contribution "dollar diplomacy."

THE REPUBLIC OF HAITI.
Woodrow Wilson loudly denounced dollar diplomacy during the election of 1912. But in 1914, when the republic of Haiti teetered on the edge of collapse, Wilson sent in the marines. Secretary of State William Jennings Bryan demanded the right to appoint a customs receiver, the right to supervise Haitian elections, and control of the Haitian police force. A treaty signed in 1915 created a dictatorship managed by American officials with the support of the United States navy and marines. If not democratic, American rule was at least efficient. It lasted until 1934.

Unlike Taft, Wilson resorted to such methods with great reluctance. "I am going to teach the South American republics to elect good men," he remarked to a British visitor at the beginning of his administration. Whether the image of Uncle Sam the schoolteacher was any better than Uncle Sam the banker was an open question. In any case, the shortcomings in Wilson's teaching methods were soon evident in Mexico.

AMERICAN INTERVENTION IN MEXICO.
In 1911 the Mexican people overthrew Porfirio Diaz, a dictator under whom they had suffered for many years. Their new president, Francisco Madero,

tried to reform the economy for the benefit of small farmers and landless workers. But he soon ran afoul of foreign business interests, which helped finance a revolution in 1913. Madero was shot by one of his generals, and a new president, Victoriano Huerta (WAIR-tah), took over the government. President Taft was shocked by the assassination. He refused to give diplomatic recognition to the new regime. *With this expression of disapproval, Taft evidently hoped to teach the Latin Americans democracy.*

When Wilson became President, he advocated a policy of "watchful waiting." He asserted that the United States "will never again seek one additional foot of territory by conquest." But there were many Americans in Mexico whose lives and property were under attack. Hundreds of small revolutionary bands roamed Mexico inflicting injury and damage at will. The Americans in Mexico demanded action.

A crisis arose in 1914, when some American soldiers were mistakenly arrested in Tampico. Although they quickly released the soldiers, Mexican officials offered no apology. To make matters worse, a shipment of German supplies and guns was rumored to be heading toward Veracruz, the main Mexican seaport.

THE ABC CONFERENCE. The situation grew worse. On April 21 the American Navy bombarded Veracruz Harbor and occupied the city. Wilson allowed arms to be shipped to rebels fighting the Mexican government. The United States was very close to war with Mexico. *Argentina, Brazil, and Chile—the "ABC powers"—offered to mediate the dispute.* At a conference at Niagara Falls, Ontario, a proposal to remove Huerta and establish a provisional government was rejected by Mexico. The pressure on Huerta to resign proved too strong, however. On July 15, 1914, he left office, and American forces were withdrawn from Veracruz.

ENTER PANCHO VILLA. Despite the establishment of a more democratic regime, the rebels Wilson had helped to arm continued their activities. The revolutionary leader Pancho Villa (VEE-yah), who had been chased into northern Mexico, raided an American border town. He murdered American citizens in a deliberate effort to provoke a fight between the United States and Mexico. A war would topple his enemy and perhaps enable him to seize power. To capture Villa—dead or alive—Wilson sent an expedition, commanded by General John J. Pershing, into northern Mexico. The American Army occupied northern Mexico for nearly a year, departing in February 1917. Villa was not caught.

Wilson, to his credit, did avoid war. He helped bring to power a regime committed to the social progress of the Mexican people. *But his heavy-handed meddling (some called it gunboat diplomacy) left a legacy of suspicion that took years to dispel.*

Section Review

1. Mapping: Using the maps on pages 527 and 531, locate the places that came under American control or influence. Of what advantage and/or disadvantage were these acquisitions to the United States?

2. Identify or explain: protectorate, Philippe Bunau-Varilla, the *Nashville,* Dr. Walter Reed, yellow fever, receivership, Victoriano Huerta, Pancho Villa.

3. Describe the chain of events leading to the construction of a canal across the Isthmus of Panama. How did these developments affect United States relations with Latin America?

4. Explain Roosevelt's corollary to the Monroe Doctrine.

5. Why was Taft's Latin American policy called dollar diplomacy? Illustrate your answer with examples.

Chapter 22 Review

Bird's-Eye View

By 1890 the American frontier had come to an end, and industry had come of age. Because American factories could produce more than the American people could consume, the country looked outside the United States for new markets. The search for trade outlets coincided with a worldwide burst of imperialism, and soon the United States was busy amassing an empire. A belligerent foreign policy, jingoism, was fueled by the yellow press at home, and Americans felt morally compelled to bring their civilization to underdeveloped areas. As a result, the United States went to war with Spain over Cuba. After a "splendid little war" of 10 weeks, America found itself in possession of Cuba, Puerto Rico, the Philippines, and Guam.

The Spanish-American War closed with the issuance of a general statement of market diplomacy. Known as the Open Door Policy, it was a demand that imperialist nations maintain free trade and respect the territory of independent nations. The policy was directed toward China, which was being carved into spheres of influence.

Negotiations with Colombia for rights to build a canal across the Isthmus of Panama floundered until an American-supported Panamanian revolution took place. Construction of the canal was a triumph of engineering, and American medical personnel succeeded in wiping out yellow fever in Panama.

Events in Venezuela and the Dominican Republic convinced President Roosevelt of the need for a clear policy statement. Roosevelt's corollary to the Monroe Doctrine announced the right of the United States to police Latin American financial activities while it provided military protection. President Taft's extension of this policy—dollar diplomacy—was used to gain temporary control of Nicaragua.

In 1914 the United States came dangerously close to war with Mexico, where a revolution had established a military dictatorship. Mediation by the ABC powers avoided war, but United States troops occupied Mexico until 1917, leaving a legacy of suspicion that took years to dispel.

Vocabulary

Define or identify each of the following:

sphere of influence	*Maine*	ABC Conference
imperial	Emilio Aguinaldo	Dollar Diplomacy
Alfred Thayer Mahan	Platt Amendment	receivership

Review Questions

1. What was the major change in the United States foreign policy between 1890 and 1917?
2. How did the construction of the Panama Canal help the United States to put into practice the ideas advanced by Mahan in his book on sea power?
3. What role did the press play in drawing the United States into war with Spain?

4. What were the results of the peace settlement with Spain? How did this settlement affect the citizens of the new territories?
5. Explain the problems created by the United States takeover of the Philippine Islands.
6. What are the two basic principles of the Open Door policy?
7. By what means did the United States gain economic control over several Latin American nations?

Reviewing Social Studies Skills

1. Using the map on page 527, indicate the nation that controlled each of the following areas:
   a. Borneo
   b. Indo-China
   c. Burma
   d. India
   e. Korea
   f. Philippine Islands
   g. Manchuria
   h. Formosa
   i. Hong Kong
2. Using the map on page 531, answer the following:
   a. Which two countries border Panama?
   b. Approximately how wide is the Panama Canal (in both kilometers and miles)?
   c. List the countries under American influence.

Reading for Meaning

1. Slogans, quotes, and memorable phrases appeal to the emotions. Often they verge on jingoism. Explain the historical significance of each of the following. Also decide whether the following are examples of jingoism.
   a. A splendid little war
   b. White Man's Burden
   c. Remember the Maine!
   d. Seward's folly
   e. Open Door Policy
   f. righteous harmonious band
   g. Speak softly and carry a big stick.
2. Historians can communicate their opinions of someone either directly or indirectly. When authors use the direct method, you can tell right away what they think of someone. For example, the adjectives in the following sentence immediately convey the author's opinion: "Elizabeth Jones was a brilliant and imaginative politician." When an author uses the indirect method, it takes more time to determine the opinion of the author. On pages 531–532, the authors use the indirect method to convey an opinion of Philippe Bunau-Varilla. What is that opinion? How do you know?
3. Examine the pictures in this chapter. Do they enhance the information you have read? If so, how?

Bibliography

Panama Canal (Random House), by R. B. Considine, is an easy-to-read story of the task of building a canal.

The Splendid Little War (Little, Brown), by F. Freidel, is a dramatically written and well-illustrated version of the Spanish-American War.

Chapter 23

1914-1920

Call of World Leadership

The guns of war sounded across Europe in August 1914. For years the continent had been an armed camp, a collection of fortress nations tied into two opposing alliance systems. Each alliance was based on the willingness of all members to come to the aid of one warring member. A conflict between two nations belonging to opposing alliances could soon involve the entire continent.

That is exactly what happened. On June 28, 1914, Archduke Franz Ferdinand, heir to the throne of Austria-Hungary, and his wife, Countess Sophia, were assassinated by a young Serbian. The assassinations set off a chain reaction. Franz Joseph, the emperor of Austria-Hungary, chose to use the assassination as an excuse to destroy Serbian power. He blamed Serbia for the incident and threatened war. Russia moved to aid Serbia. Germany rushed to Austria's side. Britain and France were drawn in through their alliance with Russia. Long-formed battle plans went into effect. No one expected a long war. Once war began, no one knew how to stop it. Before it was over, the battle involved 30 nations and ended the lives of eight million men and women.

Chapter Objectives

After you have finished reading this chapter, you should be able to:
1. List the events that led to the American entrance into World War I.
2. Explain how the United States was able to mobilize the economy and the military in order to fight the war.
3. Compare the peace treaty Wilson hoped to achieve with the actual Treaty of Versailles.
4. Explain why the United States signed a separate peace treaty with Germany in 1920.

Six weeks after the assassinations, most of Europe was at war. The incident had ignited embers that had been smoldering for some time. Among these embers were intense feelings of nationalism expressed throughout Europe and the overseas colonies. This desire of a people to throw off foreign rule was one of the underlying causes of tension.

The assassination of the heir to the Austro-Hungarian throne had been planned by Serbian nationalists pledged to free all *Slavs* living under Austro-Hungarian rule. Austria-Hungary declared war on Serbia in order to crush Serbian nationalism. And Russia, a Slavic country, came to the aid of Serbia.

In addition to nationalism, there were intense rivalries between the major powers to extend their influence, territory, and colonial holdings. Germany had a small colonial empire and wanted to expand it. France wanted to recover Alsace-Lorraine, an area the Germans had taken in the Franco-Prussian War of 1870. Russia was looking for an ice-free harbor in the Baltic Sea and for an outlet to the Mediterranean Sea.

As the tensions mounted, each nation searched for security by building up its military forces and by forming alliances with other countries. The system of alliances formed as a result of this search had been completed by 1907. Thus, when Austria-Hungary declared war on Serbia on July 28, 1914, the whole system of alliances was set off. The countries that sided with Austria-Hungary and Germany were known as the Central Powers. Those supporting Russia, France, and Great Britain were the Allied Powers, or Allies. (See map, page 543.)

1. Wilson's Quest for Neutrality with Honor

THE WAR BEGINS. The German battle plan called for a surprise move through neutral Belgium. This approach would enable German forces to strike at the French from behind the French defenses. To the surprise of the Germans, the Belgians held up the German armies for more than two weeks. The delay gave Britain and France time to mobilize.

In September 1914, the Allies stopped the Germans at the Marne River, a mere 96 kilometers (60 miles) from Paris. The Germans fell back, and both sides dug in. ***By the end of the year, lines of trenches stretched 960 kilometers (600 miles) from the English Channel to the Swiss border.*** (See map, page 543.) Despite heroic efforts to break out of the trenches—France alone lost a million soldiers in 1915–1916—the lines remained substantially unchanged until the Americans arrived in the spring of 1918.

There were other fronts as well. The Central Powers fought to a bloody standoff with the Russians in the east. Austria and Italy battled each other in the Mediterranean. The Ottoman Empire (Turkey), allied with the Central Powers, fought a desert war

In this painting, the Serbian nationalist Gavrilo Princip is firing at Archduke Franz Ferdinand of Austria-Hungary and his wife Sofia as they drive through Sarajevo. The assassination of the archduke created a crisis that sparked World War I.

with the British, French, and Arabs. Japan, an Allied Power, swept up the German colonies in the Pacific.

A TRIAL FOR BRITISH-AMERICAN RELATIONS. In some respects, the most fateful tie was an informal one. *An understanding between Britain and the United States, based on mutual language, literature, and law, proved to be the most important factor.*

The relationship had not always been friendly. Throughout the 19th century there were lingering memories of the wars the two countries had fought. And periodic disputes over the Canadian and Alaskan boundaries kept the bitterness alive.

By the late 1890's the two nations had resolved all their outstanding disputes. President Theodore Roosevelt thought that the British connection ought to be the foundation of American foreign policy. He was particularly pleased when the British, who had expressed interest in an Isthmian canal, readily agreed to let the United States build and manage it. President Wilson was equally friendly toward Britain, and so were his most intimate advisers.

The common language and similarities in government disposed many people in America to sympathize with the British and the Allied cause. Stories of German misdeeds in Belgium and Turkish atrocities in the East gained many supporters for the Allies. Yet there were many in America who remained suspicious of the British. The millions of Americans who were of German and Irish extraction either favored the Central Powers or remained firmly neutral. *Whatever their sympathies, however, most Americans wanted to remain out of the war.* They generally approved when President Wilson declared neutrality and asked American citizens to be "impartial in thought as well as in action."

The war quickly put Anglo-American friendship to the test. The British Navy blockaded the German coast. The Admiralty turned the North Sea into a gigantic minefield in an effort to keep the German fleet confined to the Baltic. To the dismay of Americans, the British even interrupted trade with neutral countries, such as the Netherlands, Norway, Sweden, and Denmark. British ships seized as contraband (war goods) products that had previously been considered innocent, such as food and clothing. To enforce their rules, the British forced all neutral vessels to stop at British ports and submit to inspection. Such highhanded measures had brought Britain and the United States to war a century before. Wilson vigorously protested the British regulations. But in the end he submitted to them.

AN ARSENAL FOR THE ALLIES. By accepting the British regulations, Wilson, in effect, turned the United States into an industrial reservoir for the Allied war machine. The British prevented munitions shipments to the Central Powers. But there was nothing to prevent American arms manufacturers from selling their hardware to the Allies. *Between 1914 and 1916 American arms sales to Europe increased from 40 million dollars to 1.3 billion dollars.* By 1916 munitions accounted for nearly one fourth of all American exports. Foodstuffs made up a good portion of the remainder. Fed by war profits, the American economy boomed, and all segments of the population benefited—industrialists, workers, and farmers.

THE MORGAN LOANS. In the beginning the Allies shopped for American arms on a cash-and-carry basis. *But by early 1915 both Britain and France were out of funds. They asked the President for permission to borrow money from American banks in order to continue munitions purchases.*

Secretary of State William Jennings Bryan objected, stating that such loans would seriously compromise American neutrality. Nevertheless, Wilson granted the

Sidenote to History

Rosika Schwimmer and The Peace Movement

To supporters of the peace movement, American involvement in World War I was a blow to plans for further international cooperation. At the outset of the 20th century, peace groups in the United States and Europe tried to promote understanding between nations through a variety of peace conferences. For example, 26 nations sent delegates to the first Hague Conference, held in the Netherlands in 1899. The delegates urged the settling of international disagreements through mediation or arbitration. The Permanent Court of Arbitration was established at the Hague to fulfill this goal. A second Hague Conference was called by the tsar of Russia and President Theodore Roosevelt in 1907. With 44 nations sending delegates, the conference drafted more rules for the conduct of war. A third Hague Conference was being planned when war broke out in Europe.

Among the Americans trying to keep America from joining the fight were social reformers Jane Addams and Lillian Wald. Among the Europeans urging American leadership to help end the war was the Hungarian feminist and pacifist, Rosika Schwimmer.

Schwimmer's pacifist activities were well known in Europe before she came to America in 1914. With tremendous energy and confidence in her cause, she launched a speaking tour of the United States aimed at convincing the American people to end the war through mediation. In 1915 she and Jane Addams won the backing of the Hague Congress of Women to pressure the remaining neutrals to join in offering mediation to the warring nations. It was arranged that Addams would visit the warring nations and Schwimmer the neutrals.

On her return from visits to the neutral governments of Europe, Rosika Schwimmer met Henry Ford, who was reported to be opposed to the war. With Ford's financial backing, Schwimmer developed the idea of forming an unofficial neutral conference for mediation of the war. A peace ship would be used to bring interested Americans to Europe to take part in the conference. The ship, the *Oscar II,* set sail from Hoboken, New Jersey, on December 4, 1915, with 168 Americans aboard. Despite the criticism and ridicule the expedition received from the American press, the first meeting of the conference was held in Stockholm, Sweden. It was the first peace conference of the war and succeeded in keeping small nations neutral. The long-range goal of the peace conference—mediating a settlement of the conflict—was never achieved, however.

In 1929 Rosika Schwimmer attempted to become a citizen of the United States. She did not gain her wish, however, mainly because of the hostile political environment of the 1920's. Anti-Schwimmer agitators brought up her pacifist background as cause for denying her citizenship. Others accused her of having been a German spy. When her request for citizenship was rejected by the Supreme Court on the grounds that she refused to bear arms in defense of the country, Justice Oliver Wendell Holmes stated in the dissenting opinion that Rosika Schwimmer was "a woman of superior character and intelligence, obviously more than ordinarily desirable as a citizen. . . ." A woman without a country, she lived in New York City as an alien resident until her death in 1948.

Allies' request. He also permitted banks to lend money to the Central Powers. But this evenhandedness meant little. The British blockade prevented any substantial trade with Germany and Austria. The loans, arranged by the international financier, J. P. Morgan, played an important role in the Allies' military survival. *By the time the United States entered the war in April 1917, loans to the Allies totaled over 2.2 billion dollars.*

The Morgan loans permitted the continuation of the flow of supplies across the Atlantic. To win the war Germany had to interrupt that flow. Without a surface navy to match that of the British, Germany tried to stop the munitions traffic with the only naval weapon it had—the submarine.

SUBMARINE WARFARE. Germany had only 21 usable *unterwasser* craft, or U-boats, when the war began. No one took them very seriously. They were flimsy vessels with limited range. They were also of doubtful legality because international law required bringing a neutral, unarmed merchant vessel into port and allowing the crew to disembark before sinking the ship. Submarines could not do this because they were not armed to defend themselves while on the surface.

The German Navy persuaded the Kaiser that a submarine blockade could force Britain to ask for peace in six weeks. Accordingly, on February 4, 1915, Germany announced a blockade of the British Isles, to bc enforced by U-boats. Only British and French ships were to be sunk, and the Germans advised neutrals not to send passengers or goods on such ships. President Wilson protested the German move as contrary to international law. He warned Germany it would be held accountable for any American lives lost.

SINKING OF THE *LUSITANIA*. The inevitable incident happened on May 7, 1915, when the German captain of a submarine fired the only torpedo he had left and struck the *Lusitania,* a British ocean liner. The great liner exploded and sank in 18 minutes, carrying with it 1,198 people, including 128 Americans. As on other liners, hundreds of cases of ammunition were carried in the hold. The explosion of the munitions caused the liner to sink so rapidly.

Americans were outraged at such "barbaric" warfare, and President Wilson promptly protested. When the German government gave a noncommittal reply, Wilson sent a second, stronger note. Further sinkings of unresisting passenger liners, he implied, would be considered an unfriendly act leading, perhaps, to war. Secretary Bryan, who preferred a stricter neutrality, resigned in protest.

GERMAN "PLEDGES." *Impressed by Wilson's stance, the German government issued orders to its U-boat captains not to sink passenger liners.* When the British liner *Arabic* went down in August 1915, with the loss of two American lives, Germany made the orders public. In what came to be known as the *Arabic* pledge, Germany promised not to attack unarmed passenger liners unless the vessels resisted or tried to escape. A submarine torpedoed the French freighter *Sussex* in March 1916, and Germany extended the principle to merchant vessels as well. The *Sussex* pledge in effect meant the end of submarine warfare. Because almost all merchant vessels carried hidden guns, submarines could not afford to come to the surface to give warning. Germany kept its promise for nine months.

PREPAREDNESS AND PRESIDENTIAL POLITICS. At President Wilson's request, Congress appropriated funds for huge increases in the army and navy in the spring of 1916. The reasoning was that the United States ought to be prepared for any eventuality. The President also believed that this move would strengthen his hand in diplomacy. There had been a strong peace

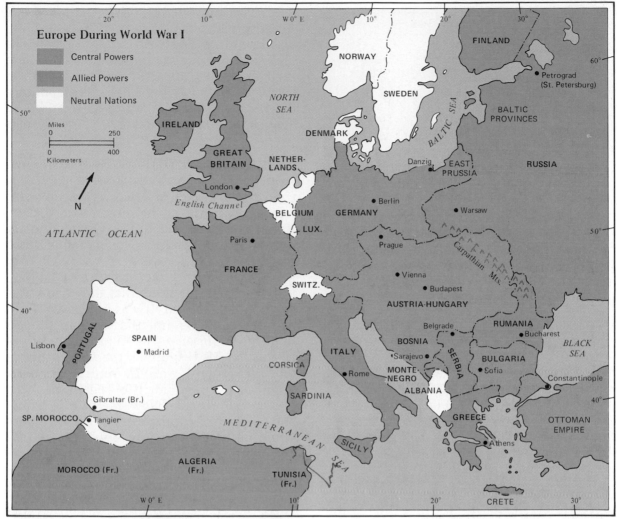

Europe During World War I

- Central Powers
- Allied Powers
- Neutral Nations

Miles 0 — 250
Kilometers 0 — 400

N

NORWAY
SWEDEN
FINLAND
Petrograd (St. Petersburg)
BALTIC PROVINCES
RUSSIA
NORTH SEA
BALTIC SEA
IRELAND
GREAT BRITAIN
London
English Channel
NETHER-LANDS
DENMARK
Danzig
EAST PRUSSIA
Warsaw
BELGIUM
LUX.
GERMANY
Berlin
Prague
Carpathian Mts.
ATLANTIC OCEAN
FRANCE
Paris
SWITZ.
Vienna
Budapest
AUSTRIA-HUNGARY
RUMANIA
Bucharest
PORTUGAL
Lisbon
SPAIN
Madrid
Gibraltar (Br.)
CORSICA
ITALY
Rome
Belgrade
BOSNIA
Sarajevo
SERBIA
MONTE-NEGRO
ALBANIA
BULGARIA
Sofia
Constantinople
BLACK SEA
SARDINIA
SP. MOROCCO
Tangier
MEDITERRANEAN SEA
SICILY
GREECE
Athens
OTTOMAN EMPIRE
MOROCCO (Fr.)
ALGERIA (Fr.)
TUNISIA (Fr.)
CRETE

movement until 1915. But the sinking of the *Lusitania* jolted public opinion. Strategies for maintaining neutrality were urgently sought. One possible strategy was to warn American citizens not to travel on the vessels of nations at war. In the spring of 1916, the Gore-McLemore resolution proposed precisely that, and it got strong support in Congress. Wilson objected, however, on the ground that to relinquish one American right would lead to other "humiliations." He persuaded the Democratic majority to vote against the proposed resolution.

That autumn the peace issue became tangled in presidential politics. The Republi-

cans nominated Supreme Court Justice Charles Evans Hughes, a Progressive who had made no statements on foreign policy. Wilson, having talked of preparedness for months, accepted the Democratic slogan "He kept us out of war" and succeeded in pleasing almost everybody.

Hughes, equally inconsistent, pledged to maintain peace while defending "the rights of American citizens on land and sea." The electorate sensed little difference between the two. On election night Americans went to bed thinking Hughes the winner. On awakening they learned that California had gone Democratic and that Hughes had lost.

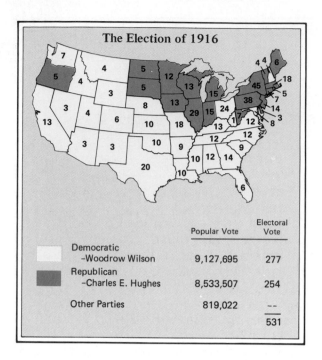

The Election of 1916

	Popular Vote	Electoral Vote
Democratic –Woodrow Wilson	9,127,695	277
Republican –Charles E. Hughes	8,533,507	254
Other Parties	819,022	--
		531

Wilson's margin of victory, 277 electoral votes to 254, was the closest since 1876. (See map above.) However, the President got three million more popular votes than he had received in 1912. He took this as an endorsement of his policies.

"PEACE WITHOUT VICTORY." Assured of another term, Wilson made a determined effort to end the war. He offered his services as a mediator to both sides. To reassure the Germans that he would be fair, he made public his view of a reasonable settlement.

Appearing before the Senate on January 22, 1917, Wilson asked for "peace without victory." *A stable world could be achieved, he declared, only if there were no victors and no vanquished.* "Only a peace between equals can last." Among the important principles that he wished to see in the peace settlement were government by consent of the governed, freedom of peoples from alien rule, freedom of the seas, and limitation of armaments.

The speech was a stirring summons to American idealism, but in Europe no one was listening. The German high command had already come to the conclusion that it had to resume submarine warfare in order to "bring England to her knees." On January 31, 1917, the German ambassador informed Wilson that unrestricted submarine warfare would resume the next day.

MOVING TOWARD WAR. *Wilson's response to Germany's resumption of submarine warfare was to break off diplomatic relations.* However, he announced that he would not go to war unless Germany committed "actual overt acts" against the United States.

On February 24 the British handed Wilson a German telegram that they had intercepted and decoded. It was a message from Arthur Zimmermann, the German foreign minister, to his envoy in Mexico City. It proposed that Mexico attack the United States in the event of war. In return Germany promised to help Mexico regain its "lost provinces," Texas, New Mexico, Arizona, and California. *Publication of the Zimmermann note outraged the American people and convinced Wilson that Germany desired war.* Still, Germany had not committed an overt hostile act.

AMERICAN ENTRY INTO THE WAR. On March 12, 1917, a revolution in Russia overthrew the autocratic rule of the tsar. Trouble had been brewing in Russia for years, but the revolutionary explosion was set off by the war and a series of Russian defeats at the hands of the Germans. Wilson had been reluctant to become involved in an alliance with the tsarist *autocracy.* But now that Russia seemed on the way to democracy, his qualms disappeared. If the United States were to enter the war, it would be entering a clear contest between the democratic powers of Europe, represented by the Allies, and the autocratic powers, Germany, Austria, and their allies.

Autocracy is government without popular consent or concern for popular rights. Germany and Austria were ruled by emperors, who obtained advice from a narrow circle of aristocrats.

On March 18, 1917, news came that German U-boats had sunk three American merchant vessels. Now there seemed no choice. The nation had to go to war. *On March 20 Wilson's Cabinet advised him unanimously to ask Congress to declare war on Germany.*

When Wilson appeared before a joint session of Congress on April 2, he requested a resolution recognizing that a state of war existed between Germany and the United States. He reminded Congress of the many times Germany had violated American rights, acts that forced him to conclude that "armed neutrality, it now appears, is unworkable. . . ." Then he expanded on the idealistic principles of his "peace without victory" speech. "The world must be made safe for democracy," he declared. "Its peace must be planted on the tested foundations of political liberty. We have no selfish ends to serve. We desire no conquest, no dominion." America's only goal in entering the war was to champion the rights of people. "We shall be satisfied when those rights have been made as secure as faith and the freedom of nations can make them."

Wilson believed that permanent peace could be attained only by reforming the entire system of international relations. But he also realized that if he wanted to influence the peace settlement, he had to enter the war. The war became, in his mind, a war to end all wars. Congress was ready to declare such a war. The Senate approved the declaration of war by 82 to 6, the House of Representatives by 373 to 50.

Opposition to the war came mostly from two sources. One was the Midwest, where people of German ancestry were concen-

trated. The second was the Progressives, such as Nebraska's Norris and Wisconsin's La Follette. They recognized that foreign war would bring an end to domestic reform.

Section Review

1. Mapping: Using the key to the map on page 543, list the countries known as the Allied Powers and the Central Powers during World War I. List the neutral countries also.
2. Identify or explain: the Central Powers, contraband, William Jennings Bryan, *unterwasser* craft, *Lusitania*, autocracy, *Sussex* pledge, Charles Evans Hughes.
3. What were the Morgan loans, and why were they important to the Allied war effort?
4. Why did Woodrow Wilson object to the Gore-McLemore resolution?

2. The Great Crusade at Home and Abroad

RAISING AN ARMY. America entered the European conflict almost totally unprepared for war. Since 1916 the navy had been building and buying ships, but little had been done to prepare the army. An army of several million had to be created quickly. Speaker Champ Clark opposed conscription, declaring that "there is precious little difference between a conscript and a convict." But in the last analysis, conscription, not used since the Civil War, seemed the only way. *At the President's request, Congress imposed a military draft.* Furthermore, it rejected the use of substitutes, the means by which many wealthy men had evaded military service during the Civil War.

Training an army of citizen-soldiers took time. The first contingent of American troops, under General John J. "Blackjack" Pershing, arrived in France in the summer of 1917. Another year passed before there were enough Americans in Europe to influence the course of battle.

MOBILIZING THE ECONOMY. *American industry was even more unprepared for war than the military.* Factories that had been producing automobiles and ice-boxes had to shift to making trucks and tanks within a matter of months. In fact, the entire economy had to be redirected.

At first the mobilization effort lagged behind government expectations. Congress charged the military with inefficiency and accused the Secretary of War, Newton D. Baker, of dragging his heels. Under fire from Senate Republicans, Wilson acted quickly and decisively. *He asked Congress to approve a bill that would give him virtually unlimited powers to mobilize the economy.* Congress complied and passed the bill in April 1918.

Wilson immediately overhauled the War Industries Board, which had been created in July 1917. Its new director, Bernard Baruch, was given broad powers to intervene in the economy and establish production priorities. Baruch did such an outstanding job that his methods were used years later in coping with the emergency of depression.

PRODUCING AND CONSERVING FOOD. *Organizing the nation's food supply was the task of the Food Administration, under the direction of Herbert Hoover.* Hoover came to public attention in 1916, when he directed a successful food-relief program for war-torn Belgium. He would prove to be one of the great administrators of the century—and one of the outstanding civilian heroes of the war.

Hoover's job as head of the Food Administration was to increase the production of food, to reduce the hoarding and waste of food, and to urge Americans to consume plentiful foods rather than scarce foods. By appealing to patriotism Hoover was able to convince Americans to comply voluntarily with his program. Reminded by posters that

In this poster, women are asked to participate in the war effort by raising food. What is the effectiveness of that appeal? Are there any scarcities today that might require a similar appeal? Which ones?

"Food will win the war," people planted "victory gardens" and observed "meatless" and "wheatless" days. Farmers were encouraged to increase production through the use of a variety of incentives. Hoover guaranteed that the government would buy the entire 1917 wheat crop, for example. As a result of Hoover's imaginative and resourceful administration, American farmers were able to feed much of Europe and keep the United States from having to ration food.

SOCIAL AND ECONOMIC CHANGE. Preparing for war resulted in other social and economic changes. Before the war there had always been more than enough workers in the labor force. Industry had often used this situation as a way of controlling workers' demands for improved conditions, higher pay, and shorter hours. If some workers went out on strike, there were always others who were waiting to take their places.

The war changed the situation. Now there was more work to be done than workers to do it. A strike or work stoppage posed a very serious threat to the war effort. Workers

Sidenote to History

The Lincoln Highway

Americans' love affair with the automobile began in the early years of the 20th century. The first automobiles were handmade and expensive. They were considered the playthings of the rich. In 1908 Henry Ford introduced the "people's car." It was a mass-produced vehicle called the Model T. Five years later, Ford made his production methods even more efficient by using a moving-assembly line. By 1913 there were half a million cars on the highway.

"Highway" is hardly the proper term, for most roads were dirt trails. An improved road was a trail over which gravel had been scattered. Nor was there any coherent network of roads. Each one went from farm to town and from town to city. With the automobile came the vision of transcontinental motoring.

The first to undertake the feat was a Vermont physician, Dr. Horatio Nelson Jackson, who drove from San Francisco to New York in 1903 in a two-cylinder Winton. Accompanying him were a mechanic and a stray bulldog he found in the middle of Idaho. In parts of the West he had to cut across grassland and sage, guided only by a compass. Other motorists followed. In the summer of 1909, four women made the jaunt from New York to San Francisco in a Maxwell-Briscoe touring car.

In 1912 Carl Fisher, who inaugurated automobile racing on the Indianapolis Speedway, started a campaign for a national road. He wanted to name it after his hero, Abraham Lincoln. When both the Ford Motor Company and Congress refused to give him funds, he organized the Lincoln Highway Association to gather private donations. In 1913 Fisher led a 17-car caravan, accompanied by two trucks carrying spare tires and parts, from Indianapolis to San Francisco. The tour, which took 34 days, stirred excitement in the West. Boosters considered a national highway a means of promoting tourism and business. Townspeople throughout Nevada and Utah turned out to build roads and bridges so that Fisher would have something to drive on when he passed through.

Despite the publicity, states were slow to appropriate funds, and Congress showed no interest. In 1919 the U.S. Army decided to test its ability to get across the country. It sent a convoy of 79 heavy trucks from Washington to San Francisco, following Fisher's route. The parade rekindled public interest. The army's discouraging report on the condition of the nation's roads spurred Congress to action. In 1923 the federal government took over the job of finishing the Lincoln Highway. By then the notion of a national highway network had given birth to a numbering system. The Lincoln Highway was designated U.S. 30. Today, in many areas of the country, it is known as Interstate 80.

By 1923 Carl Fisher had taken on other projects, notably the construction of a winter playground at Miami Beach, Florida. To open the beach, he built a causeway across Biscayne Bay from the city of Miami. He named it Lincoln Road.

sensed this change immediately. At first many strikes took place. Then Samuel Gompers, head of the American Federation of Labor, struck a bargain with industry and the government. *The A. F. of L. agreed not to strike if industry met two of its demands: an eight-hour day and the right of workers to organize into unions.* The government not only met these demands, it set up the National War Labor Board to mediate labor-management disputes. As a result of this agreement, there were few strikes during the course of the war. Workers' wages improved. And the membership of the A. F. of L. increased.

The war also had an impact on the lives of Black Americans. Drawn by the promise of jobs and improved opportunities, thousands of Blacks moved north. Although most found higher paying jobs in northern cities, they had trouble adjusting to city life. They found discrimination and inequality there, too. Nonetheless, the North continued to attract Black southerners, and the migration that began during the war lasted for the next half-century.

Women also found more opportunities during the war years. For one thing, many women had to take the jobs of men who had gone off to war. *Women worked in a wide range of occupations, most of which had been closed to them before the war.* The entry of large numbers of women into the labor force increased women's political clout, which contributed to the passage of the 19th Amendment.

WHIPPING UP SUPPORT FOR THE WAR. Morale is ever-important in war. It was especially important in World War I. Never before had the nation made such an enormous investment in a war.

To whip up support for the war effort, Wilson created the Committee on Public Information, headed by George Creel, a newspaper reporter. Well over 100,000 writers, artists, and speakers contributed their services to "selling" the war. Millions of pieces of prowar literature were distributed throughout the nation and the world. And thousands of volunteers traveled across the country, making brief, stirring appeals to patriotism.

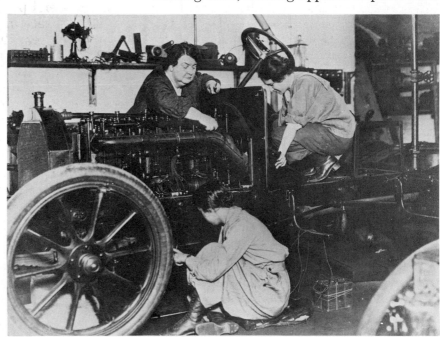

While the men were off in Europe fighting World War I, the women were being trained at home to do other jobs. Women became telegraph messengers, elevator operators, streetcar conductors, traffic cops, and automobile mechanics. Do you think this change in roles affected passage of the 19th Amendment?

CONTROLLING OPPOSITION AND DISSENT.

Creel's committee was so successful that the nation moved swiftly, but sometimes violently and unjustly, to stamp out all opposition to the war. *Congress moved to silence critics of the war with the Espionage Act and the Trading with the Enemy Act in 1917 and the Sedition Act in 1918.* The three acts made it a crime to hamper the war effort by word or action.

The Espionage Act provided for heavy fines and long prison terms not only for sabotage and spying but for obstructing the draft and speaking out against the issuance of bonds to finance the war. The act also gave the United States Post Office the right to ban from the mails anything considered antiwar. The Trading with the Enemy Act censored international communications, newspapers, and magazines in foreign languages.

The Sedition Act of 1918 was the most important restriction on free speech in American history. (The Federalists had tried briefly and unsuccessfully to limit criticism of the government in the years 1798–1800; see page 181.) People could be arrested under the act not only for making formal speeches against the war but for making casual remarks that could be interpreted as antiwar. Over 1,500 people were arrested for making "seditious" remarks. In Illinois a German-American man was taken from jail and lynched by a mob.

Anti-German, prowar furor was expressed in other ways. Sauerkraut was renamed liberty cabbage, and hamburgers became liberty sausage. German music was banned. German books were hauled out of libraries and burned. And the teaching of the German language was forbidden in many schools.

The fear of foreign people and things whipped up during the war was to have an effect well beyond the war years. It stimulated a revival of antiforeign prejudice that marked the postwar decade.

"CLEAR AND PRESENT DANGER."

The Espionage Act of 1917 was historic for reasons its framers had not foreseen. The act gave the Supreme Court its first chance to interpret the 1st Amendment's guarantee of free speech—the case of *United States* v *Schenck,* 1919.

The case involved the arrest of a war opponent while he was distributing antidraft leaflets outside a military installation. Writing the decision for the Court, Justice Oliver Wendell Holmes pointed out that the right of free speech was not absolute. For instance, one does not have the right to shout "Fire!" in a crowded theater. There were times and places at which certain things could not be said. Among these times, said Holmes, was when the nation was in "a clear and present danger." *When the nation's security was at stake, declared Holmes, Congress had the right to limit activity that might hamper the war effort.* The Espionage Act was constitutional, said the Court. Until changed substantially by Court decisions in the 1950's and 1960's, Holmes' interpretation gave important powers to federal police agencies.

How great was the danger? There was never any real threat of German invasion. The combined British and American navies saw to that. By the end of 1917, they had largely eliminated the U-boat threat to Atlantic shipping. Nevertheless, no one knew how long the war would last. And in a long conflict, public morale was an important factor. It was believed that a divided nation would have been ineffectual in war and ignored at the peace table.

THE AEF IN FRANCE.

Bogged down for three years in sodden trenches, the war in Europe turned into a race after America's entry. The German command knew that resumption of submarine attacks would bring the United States into the conflict. But with the aid of submarines, they hoped to knock out the Allies before America could

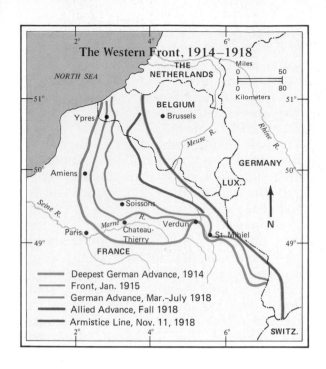

The Western Front, 1914–1918

Legend:
- Deepest German Advance, 1914
- Front, Jan. 1915
- German Advance, Mar.–July 1918
- Allied Advance, Fall 1918
- Armistice Line, Nov. 11, 1918

send effective aid. *While the United States worked to build an army, the Germans searched in desperation for victory.*

American troops did not arrive in significant numbers until the spring of 1918. Britain and France held on, bolstered by American money and munitions. In May 1918 the Germans launched a final effort to break through to Paris. The American Expeditionary Force (AEF), having merged with British and French units, helped stop the attack. In midsummer the Allies opened a counteroffensive that pushed the Germans back toward the borders of Belgium and Luxembourg. (See map at the left.) In September, the American First Army, numbering 500,000, opened an offensive of its own at St. Mihiel (SAN mee-YEL), in eastern France. Within a few weeks the American force penetrated the German frontier.

The life of an aviator was one of the most romanticized aspects of warfare during World War I. Flyers were often trained in a few weeks and sent off to battle soon afterward. In this picture, painted by French artist Henry Farre, a ground crew waits for a squadron to return from a mission.

These Black soldiers were part of the 369th Regiment. The 369th was the first of the Allied forces to reach the Rhine River. In the trenches for 191 days, these men never lost any ground, any trench, or any soldier through capture.

BLACK AMERICANS IN WORLD WAR I. Among the first American forces to break through the German lines was the 369th Regiment, made up of Black Americans. (The armed forces were segregated in World War I.) The regiment was under fire for 191 days and never lost any ground, any trench, or any soldier through capture.

Blacks contributed about 370,000 soldiers and 1,400 commissioned officers during World War I. A little more than half did duty in France. The first two soldiers to be cited for valor by the French were Blacks, Henry Johnson and Needham Roberts. Nevertheless, for most Black Americans the war experience was often a humiliating one. Trained for combat, many Blacks were forced into labor battalions or assigned to duties as orderlies.

THE WAR ENDS. In early November a revolution toppled the German government. The kaiser fled to the Netherlands, and a republic was proclaimed. A truce agreement that halted the fighting was signed on November 11, 1918. American losses in the war totaled 116,000, high for the short time in combat but low when compared to the 1,700,000 Russians, 1,357,000 French, and 900,000 British who died. ***The Allies might have survived without American aid, but they could not have won.*** American intervention converted a military stalemate into an Allied victory.

Section Review

1. Mapping: Using only the phrases *north of, south of, west of,* and *east of* and a map of the world, describe the location of St. Mihiel in relation to Germany, Belgium, Luxembourg, and Italy.
2. Identify or explain: Blackjack Pershing, Bernard Baruch, Sedition Act, Herbert Hoover, liberty cabbage, the AEF, Committee on Public Information, Needham Roberts, and Henry Johnson.

3. What was conscription? How did conscription during World War I differ from conscription during the Civil War?
4. How did the idea of "clear and present danger" affect an American's right to free speech during World War I?

3. Wilson and the Peace

SECRET TREATIES. The Communist revolution in Russia, November 8, 1917, had a profound impact both on the war and the peace settlement. Leon Trotsky, the *Bolshevik* commissar for foreign affairs, published the various secret agreements that the tsarist government had signed with the Allies. *The secret treaties, drafted in 1915 and 1916, demonstrated that Britain, France, and their allies had intended to profit from the war.* Britain and France had planned to take over large parts of the German and Turkish empires, leaving some morsels for Russia and Japan in the East. Italy was offered chunks of Austrian territory as a bribe to join the war. With considerable justice, Americans felt hoodwinked. While President Wilson had been talking of "peace without victory," the Allies were dividing up the world.

Following the March revolution in Russia, a second revolution occurred in November during which the **Bolsheviks,** a party of radical Communists, seized power and executed the tsar.

WILSON'S FOURTEEN POINTS. President Wilson did not know the extent of the secret dealing among the Allies, but he was aware that their war aims were more selfish than his. As a result, he refused to join the British and French in a formal alliance. The United States was considered only an "associated power." And Wilson expected to play an independent role in the peace settlement.

Wilson was also aware of the Communist menace in Europe. Lenin, head of the new Bolshevik state, called for a worldwide socialist revolution that would end war and the selfish interests that caused it. *Between the excesses of communism in Russia and the militant imperialism that raged in France and Germany, Wilson felt there had to be a middle ground.* There was need for a new world order, one government devoted to justice and ruling by law. He envisioned a new freedom for the world.

On January 8, 1918, Wilson appeared before Congress to define the liberal principles that he hoped would form a lasting peace. *His address contained 14 points. The first five were statements of principle for which the United States had long contended: open treaties and an end to secret diplomacy, freedom of the seas, free trade, reduction in armaments, and the elimination of wars for empire. Points 6 to 13 called for national self-determination in Europe. Political boundaries would be set by cultural and language ties.*

THE LEAGUE OF NATIONS. Wilson's 14th point was a call for "a general association of nations" that would guarantee "political independence and territorial integrity to great and small states alike." The idea had gained wide support in the United States during the war. Wilson endorsed the idea in 1916 and became one of its leading advocates. *A peacekeeping organization that would protect the weak and resolve disputes among the strong had become the foundation of his new world order.*

INTERVENTION IN RUSSIA. The Fourteen Points helped restore some moral authority to the tarnished Allied cause, but they were not enough to keep the Russians in the war. On March 3, 1918, Soviet representatives signed a treaty with Germany. In the process they renounced Russian claims to huge chunks of territory in the Baltic, Poland, and the Ukraine.

The Armistice was a joyous occasion, as shown by this painting of the victory parade in New York. Painted by American artist George Luks, the returning troops were greeted by crowds, Allied flags, and confetti.

Four days later a British force occupied the Russian Arctic port of Murmansk. The Allies were eager to keep the Russian front active in order to tie up the German armies. And they hoped to encourage anti-Communist elements in Russia. Wilson resisted Allied appeals for intervention. In June 1918, however, he sent a small force to the Arctic port of Archangel to guard British supplies.

In the East, China took advantage of Russia's distraction and recovered Manchuria. And Japan landed an army to patrol the Trans-Siberian Railroad. Wilson sent a force of 14,000 to the Siberian port of Vladivostok to aid an army of Czechs who were stranded in Siberia. The Americans withdrew in April 1920 with little to show for their efforts. *American force did not prevent the Bolsheviks from gaining control of all Russia. But the intervention left a legacy of suspicion that proved difficult to overcome.*

WILSON AT VERSAILLES. The conference to arrange a general peace settlement was originally scheduled at Geneva, Switzerland. At the insistence of the French, it was moved to the former royal palace of Versailles (vur-SI), near Paris. The shift had much symbolic meaning. It was at Versailles that the victorious Germans had imposed a humiliating settlement on the French in 1871. French desire for revenge boded ill for the conference.

Wilson departed for France in December 1918, the first American President to visit Europe while in office. He was greeted by an enthusiastic crowd of some two million. They showered flowers on his coach as his caravan passed a banner reading "Honour to Wilson the Just." Wilson had made himself the moral conscience of the world.

The Germans had agreed to the armistice on the understanding that the peace settlement would be based on Wilson's Fourteen Points. German leaders did not feel they had lost the war. German soil had not even been invaded. They expected a generous peace; Wilson had virtually promised it.

This painting by Sir William Orpen recreates the meeting at Versailles. In the center sits Clemenceau of France; to his right, President Wilson. The German delegate, with his back to the artist, is signing the peace treaty.

The Allies had misgivings about the Fourteen Points. Britain specifically rejected the notion of freedom of the seas because that would restrict its powers of blockade. The French wanted both reparations (reimbursement for war damages) and a slice of German territory. All the Allies looked greedily at the German colonies in Africa, Asia, and the South Pacific.

THE BIG FOUR. Every government involved in the peace conference had a sizable staff of experts and advisers. The American delegation alone filled an entire hotel. Geographers, political scientists, historians, and economists hoped to solve problems that had baffled Europeans for centuries. Unofficial and uninvited observers went to Ver-

sailles to defend the interests of colonial peoples. Among them were W. E. B. Du Bois who spoke for Africa and the man who would call himself Ho Chi Minh when he became president of North Vietnam. Four national leaders made the key decisions: President Wilson, British Prime Minister David Lloyd George, French Premier Georges Clemenceau (klay-mahn-SOE), and Vittorio Orlando, Premier of Italy.

DRAFTING A CHARTER FOR THE LEAGUE. *At Wilson's insistence, the first weeks of the conference were devoted to the drafting of a charter for the League of Nations.* The League's covenant (constitution) was made the first article of the peace treaty. The world organization was to

Viewpoints of History

The Treaty of Versailles

From the moment it was made public, the Treaty of Versailles was the center of controversy. People argued not only about the terms of the treaty, but also about the principles on which the treaty was based. The Germans and many liberals protested that the treaty was too harsh. The French and their supporters believed that it was too soft. Some charged that the principles on which the treaty was based had little to do with the realities of international politics. Others claimed that the treaty signaled the defeat of idealism and the triumph of the old order in foreign affairs. Historians soon joined the debate. And they have been arguing about the treaty to this day.

John Maynard Keynes, the English economist-historian who advised the British delegation, represented the views of disillusioned liberals in his book *The Economic Consequences of the Peace.* "In the first place," said Keynes, "this treaty ignores the economic solidarity of Europe, and by aiming at the destruction of the economic life of Germany, it threatens the health and prosperity of the Allies themselves. In the second place," Keynes continued, "by making demands the execution of which is . . . impossible, it leaves Europe more unsettled than it found it. The treaty," he concluded, "by overstepping the limits of the possible, has in practice settled nothing. The true settlement still remains to be made out of the ashes of the future. . . ."

Twenty years later, historian Paul Birdsall analyzed the treaty in a seminar at Williams College. The results of his analysis were published in *Versailles, Twenty Years After.* Birdsall considered the treaty the result of a "struggle between Wilsonian principles of a new world order and the principles of reactionary nationalism." In his opinion, the document was neither all good nor all bad. It was a mixture of each. And this mixture, he believed, was the inevitable result of the compromises necessitated by the need to bring peace quickly to a "turbulent and disintegrating Europe."

In 1948, Richard Hofstadter published another view of the treaty in *The American Political Tradition and the Men Who Made It.* Hofstadter maintained that, as idealistic about world order and world peace as Wilson and others at the conference might have been, they were forced by the realities of the moment to forge a compromise based on political realities rather than philosophical ideals. Thus, although the "program Wilson took to Paris envisioned a world order based upon free trade, national self-determination, and a League of Nations to keep the peace," what resulted was "a political peace in which the fundamental arrangements of 19th-century Europe were taken for granted."

In his *Between the Wars: America, 1919–1941,* published in 1979, David Shannon wrote: "Given the complexity of the League issue in American politics, that the treaty fell short of the principles enunciated in the Fourteen Points, that a vast majority of the Senate had favored ratification with reservations but had failed to ratify because of Wilson's unbending refusal to compromise, and the complex and diverse motives of those who opposed the treaty, it is clear that the view of the treaty fight which sees Wilsonian international idealism defeated by Republican isolationism is too oversimplified and partisan to be respected. But it is not clear that American failure to join the League of Nations led ineluctably to World War II. It is impossible to say what would have happened if the United States had been a member of the League. Whether or not the way the treaty fight ended made any great difference for the next generation we shall never know."

consist of a general assembly, in which each nation had a single vote, and an executive council made up of five permanent members (Great Britain, France, Italy, Japan, and the United States) and four rotating members. Germany and the Soviet Union were excluded from League membership.

The League was not given military forces of its own, but it could ask member nations to lend troops for peacekeeping. Article 10, called by Wilson the heart of the League, bound members to joint action against any aggressor nation. It made the League a mutual security alliance.

THE VERSAILLES TREATY.
In mid-February 1919 Wilson returned home for a month-long visit to sign bills from Congress and explain the League covenant to the American people. In his absence the European powers framed the rest of the treaty. Wilson was able to modify its worst features when he returned to Paris. But in general the treaty was a harsh document.

Germany and Austria lost sizable chunks of territory and faced staggering charges for war damages. (See map, page 557.) Both countries' armies and navies were severely restricted. And the Rhineland, in western Germany facing France, was to be a demilitarized buffer zone. In addition, Germany had to accept full responsibility for starting the war.

The Germans pointed out that the treaty went far beyond the armistice agreement and violated the Fourteen Points. But it was too late to resume the war. They had to sign.

WILSON'S ACHIEVEMENTS AT PARIS.
So harsh was the Versailles settlement that it set the stage for another war. From the bitter ashes of defeat would come the fires of a new German nationalism. *In the 1930's Adolph Hitler rose to power on his promise to unravel the Versailles Treaty.*

It would be unfair to blame Wilson for the treaty's shortcomings. Had he not attended the Paris conference, the treaty would probably have been more severe. Wilson's most important imprints on the Versailles peace settlement were the principle of national self-determination, the mandate system, and moderated reparations payments.

THE PRINCIPLE OF NATIONAL SELF-DETERMINATION.
In his Fourteen Points speech, Wilson had stressed that the peoples of central and eastern Europe ought to have governments of their own choosing, with political boundaries following ethnic and linguistic boundaries. The result was a host of new republics in Europe: Poland, Czechoslovakia, Hungary, Rumania, and Yugoslavia. (See map, page 557.)

THE MANDATE SYSTEM.
In place of the wartime agreements awarding German and Turkish colonies to Britain and France, the Versailles Treaty turned them over to the League until they were ready for independence. European powers were given a mandate to administer them for the League. France had a mandate to govern Syria, and Britain had a mandate to rule Lebanon and Palestine. South Africa obtained a mandate over German Southwest Africa. In the Pacific, Japan undertook to govern the Gilbert and Caroline islands. The system worked with varying success. It was a reasonable compromise between the imperial demands of the Allies and the hopes and ideals of Wilson's Fourteen Points.

MODERATED REPARATIONS PAYMENTS.
Hoping to keep Germany economically weak for years to come, the Allies demanded huge sums in payment for war damages. Realizing that this would wreck the German economy and cause new problems, Wilson worked to modify their demands. He achieved only partial success. A reparations commission finally settled on a figure of 33 billion dollars. Even that

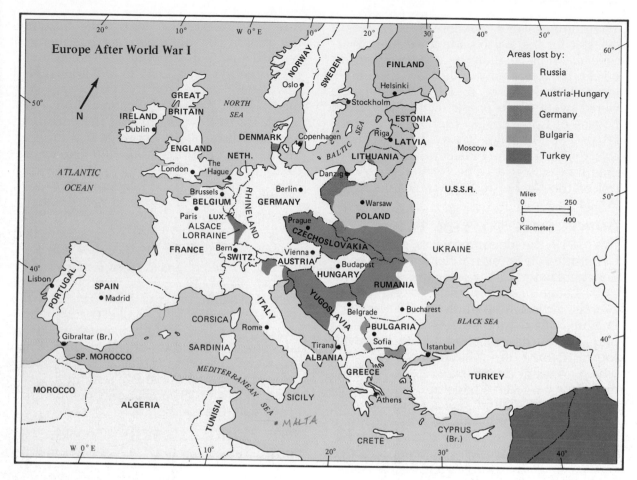

Europe After World War I

Areas lost by:
Russia
Austria-Hungary
Germany
Bulgaria
Turkey

amount caused severe stress, runaway inflation, and political turmoil in Germany.

On the whole, Wilson's mission to Paris
must be counted a success. His tragedy was
that he had raised too high the expectations
of most Americans. They reacted to the provisions of the treaty with bitter disillusionment. The public mood turned from one of
crusading to sad withdrawal. The change in
the nation's spirit foreshadowed trouble for
both President Wilson and the League of
Nations.

Section Review

1. Mapping: Compare the maps on pages
543 and 557. What countries were created after the war? What countries no
longer appeared on the map of Europe
after the war?

2. Identify or explain: Leon Trotsky, the
Fourteen Points, Honour to Wilson the
Just, Versailles, reparations.

3. Why did Woodrow Wilson refuse to
join the British and the French in a
formal alliance? Do you think he was
right to take this stand?

4. The Battle over the League of Nations

**THE CONGRESSIONAL ELECTION
OF 1918.** *The change in the popular mood
was evident even before the war ended.*

The congressional election of 1918 was a disaster for the Wilson administration. Wartime elections usually benefit the party in power, for voters rally to the side of the President. It was not so in 1918. Republicans were swept into power controlling both houses of Congress for the first time since 1910. The Versailles Treaty, like any other treaty signed by the President, had to be ratified by the Senate. The election gave control of the Senate to a party hostile to the President.

OPPOSITION TO THE TREATY. In July 1919 the document was sent to the Committee on Foreign Relations, chaired by Senator Henry Cabot Lodge of Massachusetts. Lodge had little faith in world organizations, although he might have accepted a League with diluted powers. He was also a bitter foe of the President and thus unwilling to approve any international order for which Wilson might take credit. Wilson, moreover, angered Lodge and many of his colleagues by failing to take any senator, Democrat or Republican, to Versailles with him. The treaty, in the view of many senators, was a Democratic document. Lodge was too clever to make ratification a *partisan issue.* If the treaty was to be defeated, he was determined that the President and the Democrats would bear some responsibility.

A *partisan issue* is one that becomes associated with a particular political party.

Even before the peace conference ended, Lodge took aim at the most controversial feature of the treaty, the League of Nations. A round robin letter, critical of the League, was signed by a third of the Senate, enough to defeat the treaty.

THE PRESIDENT FALLS ILL. The President put up a bold front. In sending the treaty to the Senate, he asked the upper house to do its "great duty" by giving it prompt approval. "The Senate is going to ratify the treaty," he confidently informed the press. His optimism at that moment seemed justified. The public seemed to approve the idea of a League of Nations. Had the Senate acted quickly, public pressure might have forced ratification. Lodge delayed. He took weeks to read the document and then held public hearings that dragged on into the autumn. Public support for the treaty eroded.

In September the President went on a nationwide speaking tour to revive support and put pressure on the Senate. In three weeks he traveled 12,800 kilometers (8,000 miles) and delivered 32 speeches. On September 25 he collapsed from exhaustion in Pueblo, Colorado. His train whisked him back to Washington. But a few days after his return, he suffered a stroke that left him partially paralyzed. He remained incapacitated for six months, shielded from Congress and the press by his wife, becoming even more uncompromising in his views. And it was soon clear that only compromise could save the treaty.

THE LODGE RESERVATIONS. The Senate voiced a range of opinions on the League of Nations. At one extreme was a band of "irreconcilables" who would not accept a League under any conditions. At the other end were the Wilsonian Democrats who insisted on all or nothing. In between were many senators from both parties who would accept a League with some modifications. They were particularly concerned with Article 10, the nonaggression pact. Some senators believed that it automatically committed the United States to war against aggression anywhere in the world.

During the President's western tour, Lodge's Committee on Foreign Relations reported on the treaty to the Senate. Attached to the report were 14 amendments, or reservations. Lodge's *stipulations* were moderate enough. Most were designed to protect American national interests. The most important one modified Article 10 by

Edith Wilson's important role in government during President Wilson's illness caused a lot of controversy.

stating that only Congress could authorize the use of armed forces in the defense of another country.

Stipulations are express demands or conditions of agreement.

Wilson, nevertheless, announced that none of the Lodge reservations was acceptable. He asked the Democrats to vote against them. The President refused to yield even when leaders in Britain and France announced that they could accept the reservations as the price of American membership in the League of Nations.

DEFEAT OF THE TREATY. *On November 19, 1919, the Senate refused to accept the treaty, with reservations or without.* Most Democrats followed the President's orders and voted against the reservations. During the winter, efforts were made at compromise. The list of amendments was shortened. Party leaders felt confident of obtaining the needed two-thirds majority. But the President remained adamant. When one Democratic leader visited the bedridden President and begged him to compromise,

he rose up on his one usable elbow and growled, "Let Lodge compromise!"

The final vote came on March 19, 1920. The Senate voted in favor of the treaty 49 to 35, seven votes short of the needed two thirds. Voting to kill the treaty were 14 "irreconcilables" and 21 Wilson Democrats. Seldom has there been a more tragic mixture of pride, vanity, and hatred. *The United States concluded its own peace agreement with Germany, but it never did join the League of Nations.*

Not only President Wilson and Senator Lodge can be blamed. The American people lost interest in the League of Nations. Wilson hoped to make the election of 1920 a "great and solemn referendum" on the League, but it was nothing of the kind. The Democratic nominee, James Cox, was a champion of the League. But the Republican, Warren G. Harding, ignored the issue, and so did the voters. Harding's margin of victory, a thundering 60 percent, was an expression not of public opposition to the League but of public weariness. Americans had been summoned to one crusade too many. They had answered the call for reform of their cities and states. They had gone "over there" to make the world safe for democracy. Now they were tired. Candidate Harding's call for "a return to normalcy" was strange grammar, but it fitted the popular mood. Progressivism, at home and abroad, was dead.

Section Review

1. Identify or explain: irreconcilables, Article 10, James Cox, Henry Cabot Lodge, Warren G. Harding.
2. Why were some members of Congress worried about Article 10 of the League of Nations Treaty? How did the Lodge reservations modify Article 10?
3. What was the significance of Harding's 60-percent margin of victory in the Presidential election of 1920?

Chapter 23 Review

Bird's-Eye View

When World War I broke out in Europe, the United States was determined to stay out of the conflict. Between 1914 and 1917, the United States helped the Allies indirectly. Americans sold them arms and food and, through the banker J. P. Morgan, lent them over $2 billion. Germany broke its pledges not to attack unarmed American ships. When the Zimmermann note was made public, and Germany sank three merchant vessels, the United States was forced into the war.

The nation entered the conflict almost totally unprepared for war. However, it mobilized with amazing speed. A military draft was quickly imposed on all eligible males. Under the guidance of Bernard Baruch's War Industries Board, factories switched from peacetime to wartime production. Herbert Hoover's Food Administration saw to it that the nation produced enough to feed itself and its soldiers and allies abroad.

The disruption of daily life during the war caused hardships to many but held benefits for others. Women, Blacks, and labor found opportunities and experienced a greater sense of freedom. Those who opposed the war found their freedoms severely restricted, however.

With American aid and troops, the war came to an end in November 1918. Wilson wished for a "peace without victory," but the Allies had misgivings about his Fourteen Points. They felt that Germany should be severely punished. As a result, the Treaty of Versailles was a harsh document.

Upon returning to the United States from the peace conference, Wilson sought to convince the nation to ratify the Treaty of Versailles. Among other things, the treaty provided for a League of Nations. Opposition to the League developed in Congress. A compromise might have been possible. But both Wilson and Senator Henry Cabot Lodge, leader of the anti-League forces, refused to yield. As a result, Congress failed to ratify the treaty, the nation concluded a separate peace agreement with Germany, and Americans did not participate in the League of Nations. As Wilson's successor, Warren G. Harding, put it, Americans wanted to settle down to "normalcy." For the time being, they had had enough of crusades and wars.

Vocabulary

Define or identify each of the following:

Slavs	national self-	mandate
autocracy	determination	partisan issue
U-boat	reparations	stipulation
	Fourteen Points	

Review Questions

1. How did the United States help the Allies before actually taking part in the fighting in Europe?
2. What led the United States to declare war on Germany?

3. How did the United States government mobilize the nation's economy for participation in World War I?
4. What social and economic changes occurred in the United States because of the war?
5. What were the main principles of Wilson's Fourteen Point program for peace?
6. Why didn't the United States join the League of Nations?

Reviewing Social Studies Skills

1. Using the maps on pages 543 and 557, answer the following questions:
   a. Which countries ceased to exist after the war?
   b. Which nations were created as a result of World War I?
   c. Which countries lost territory in Europe as a result of the war?
2. Make a chart, illustrating America's involvement in European affairs between 1914 and 1920. Your chart should have three vertical columns—Politics at Home, Foreign Affairs, and National Economy—and four horizontal columns—Names, Dates, Places, and Events. After you have finished your chart, answer these questions:
   a) Which two columns have the most entries? b) What conclusions can you draw from this chart about America's involvement in European affairs between 1914 and 1920?

Reading for Meaning

1. Read the Sidenote to History on page 541. List the activities Rosika Schwimmer was involved in between 1914 and 1929. Write a paragraph supporting or opposing her attempt to become a United States citizen.
2. On page 556 the authors describe "Wilson's most important imprints on the peace settlement." Outline these three imprints in such a way that someone reading your outline would be able to tell a) the general areas in which Wilson had an impact; b) what this meant in practical terms; and c) how important you think each general area was.
3. Examine the sentences in Bird's-Eye View. Then, select three sentences that are fact and three that are interpretation. Compare your sentences with those of the other members of your class. Why are there differences?

Bibliography

Some of the most interesting accounts of the war are in fiction. Ernest Hemingway's *A Farewell to Arms* (Scribners) and Erich Remarque's *All Quiet on the Western Front* (Fawcett-World) are sharply critical of war. They reflect the disillusionment of the 1920's.

John Dos Passos's *Mr. Wilson's War* (Doubleday) is a splendidly written history of the conflict.

Barbara Tuchman's *The Guns of August* (Macmillan), *The Zimmermann Telegram* (Macmillan), and *The Proud Tower* (Macmillan) are three excellent histories of the World War I period.

Chapter 424

When Life Was Fun

The single-engine craft dipped out of the clouds and flew low over the mass of people waiting at the airport. The date was May 21, 1927. The place: Le Bourget (luh bohr-ZHAY) Field, near Paris. The pilot, a young American, Charles A. Lindbergh, had just completed the first nonstop solo flight across the Atlantic from New York to Paris. Newspapers had cabled the news of Lindbergh's departure from Roosevelt Field, outside New York City, some 33 hours before. Parisians, eager to embrace this new international hero, flocked to Le Bourget. The saga of a lone flier braving the elements had caught the imagination of the world.

Chapter Objectives

After you have finished reading this chapter, you should be able to:
1. Describe the postwar conditions that created an atmosphere of national tensions.
2. List the evidence that demonstrates that the 1920's marked the end of the Progressive reform period.
3. Compare the increase in freedom concerning social attitudes to the increase in social tensions and conflicts.
4. Contrast the positive and the negative effects of the "Second Industrial Revolution."

The year of Lindbergh's flight—1927—was a vintage year in many ways. That was the year of the first talking movie, *The Jazz Singer,* featuring Al Jolson. Babe Ruth hit 60 home runs, establishing a season record. Major-league baseball attracted 10 million fans, and college football drew 30 million. On September 22 almost 105,000 people jammed into Chicago's Soldier Field to see heavyweight champion Gene Tunney defeat challenger Jack Dempsey.

It was a remarkable year in many other ways. In 1927 world records for both flag-pole sitting and marathon dancing were set. The 15-millionth Ford Model T was produced, and a member of the President's cabinet was brought to trial for accepting bribes while he served in office. Two Italian immigrants, Sacco and Vanzetti, were executed for a crime without substantial evidence to prove their guilt. Like the decade of which it was part, 1927 offered a taste of glory and of despair.

1. Postwar Tensions

THE EARLY YEARS OF THE DE-CADE. Discussions of the 1920's often mix history with nostalgia. A generation that experienced a terrifying depression, World War II, and then a tense Cold War looked back on the twenties as a time of peace, prosperity, and pleasure. Actually, the golden moments of the twenties were rather brief. The early years of the decade were troubled by the tensions of *demobilization,* labor strife, fear of revolution, rising racial tensions, and wild fluctuations in the economy. At the end of the decade, the country had slipped into the worst depression in its history.

Demobilization refers to a return to a peacetime condition—to the disbanding of wartime forces.

DISMANTLING THE WAR MACHINE. *The first task facing the country at the end of the war was demobilization.*
Returning the country to peacetime conditions was a massive undertaking. It was as strenuous an effort as preparing for war. Demobilization required strong direction. But no one gave much thought to the possibility of government action to ease the transition.

The armed forces, which had grown to four million during the war, were disbanded almost overnight. Each soldier was given 60 dollars and a railroad ticket home. The thousands of men and women who returned were soured by heroes' welcomes that did not include jobs.

The prosperity farmers had enjoyed during the war came to an end when European agriculture recovered and American exports dwindled. The prices of farm products remained low for the entire decade. Thousands of farmers lost their farms because they could not pay their debts.

The transition from wartime production to peacetime production in the factories caused unemployment. Factories often shut down or operated with reduced staff while new equipment was installed.

The cost of living, which had begun to climb during the war, continued to rise. By 1920 it was double the prewar level. Demand for consumer goods that had been in limited supply during the war also stimulated inflation. Unemployment, low farm prices, low wages, and a rising cost of living led to an increasing swell of discontent.

LABOR STRIKES. Prices rose steadily throughout the war. Wages had risen more slowly, however, and when the war emergency ended, so did the enforced truce between labor and management. During 1919 more than four million workers were on strike at one time or another. Three of the strikes that occurred during 1919 were especially significant.

THE BOSTON POLICE STRIKE. A strike by Boston's police force began in September 1919, when the police commissioner refused to let his officers form a union. Overnight, Boston was without police protection. When Massachusetts governor Calvin Coolidge sent state troops to patrol the streets and prevent looting, the police realized they had lost. They offered to go back to work, but the commissioner refused to reinstate them. When A. F. of L. president Samuel Gompers sent a wire to the governor offering to mediate the dispute, Coolidge replied: "There is no right to strike against the public safety by anybody, anywhere, anytime." So perfectly did the statement fit the public mood that it made Coolidge a national hero overnight. In 1920 he appeared as the Vice-Presidential candidate on the Republican ticket headed by Warren G. Harding.

THE STEEL STRIKE. As Boston returned to normal, the steel-producing cities of northern Indiana erupted in violence. Steelworkers had long been dissatisfied with their working conditions. They also believed that they should be able to form a union. In September 1919 the steelworkers, under the direction of William Z. Foster, organizing secretary of the A. F. of L., went on strike.

Despite the fun-loving image of the 1920's, it was an era of strong industrial growth in the United States. The glory of labor is shown in this painting by Thomas Hart Benton. His work is an outstanding example of American regionalist style.

Their chief demand was employers' recognition of the union as the workers' bargaining agent.

Foster was a skilled and persistent organizer. But his effectiveness was lessened by his political beliefs. Foster's avowed radicalism seemed to confirm the average American's worst fears of a revolutionary labor movement. The steelworkers, whose grievances were substantial, were viewed by many people as anti-American.

The 1919 steel strike also heightened racial tensions. Steelworkers who went out on strike were often replaced by Blacks who were willing strikebreakers. Their previous experience with the A. F. of L. had been as members of segregated locals, which gave them access to only the lowest-level jobs. The strike was an opportunity for Blacks to find a place in an industry from which they had been barred.

Public support of the steel companies allowed the managers to use state and federal troops to prevent the strikers from meeting and picketing. In January 1920 the strike collapsed. Three years later the steel industry established an eight-hour day. However,

15 years passed before the steel industry was unionized.

THE COAL STRIKE. *In November 1919 the United Mine Workers (U.M.W.) went on strike.* The coal industry had been operating under a wartime agreement that controlled wages. John L. Lewis, newly elected head of the U.M.W., claimed that the signing of the armistice made the agreement invalid. With President Wilson's support, Attorney General A. Mitchell Palmer secured an injunction against the union and sent the miners back to work. Lewis' moderation and political views were reflected in his action. He called off the strike, stating, "I will not fight my government." The miners received some pay adjustments but did not get a reduction in their work week.

THE COUNTRY'S MOOD. *The economic conditions that led to the strikes of 1919 started to change by 1920.* The techniques used to break strikes were discouraging: injunction, strikebreaking, and Supreme Court rulings that restricted labor organizing. Added to these techniques was the mood of the country. Scare headlines, fear and hatred of immigrants, congressional investigations of communism, and big industry's campaign to portray labor as Socialist or Communist supported the mood.

THE RED SCARE. The edginess of the country turned to hysteria in the spring and summer of 1919. More than 30 bombs were mailed to prominent citizens. Although the bombings were the work of a few fanatic radicals, they were considered part of a Communist strategy.

Attorney General Palmer began a strenuous campaign against aliens and radicals. He was convinced that there was a revolutionary conspiracy in the country. (The bomb that exploded in front of Palmer's home, severely wounding his would-be assassin, might have stimulated the Attorney General's zeal.) The bombings frightened Americans, who feared that radicals would follow the Bolshevik example of violent and destructive revolution.

Revolutionaries, in short, were a tiny fraction of American society. The Red Scare was the product of fear. It was a symptom of tension in a society unsettled by war and demobilization. It set the stage for a major reversal of immigration policy, condoned the new Ku Klux Klan, supported rising racial tensions, and made victims of people like Sacco and Vanzetti.

Sidenote to History

Will Rogers

Will Rogers was born in the Indian Territory before it became Oklahoma. He was part Cherokee and proud of his Indian ancestry. "My ancestors didn't come over on the *Mayflower*," he liked to tell audiences. "They met the boat."

He was a cowboy for a time and then worked as a rope artist in a Wild West show. He soon found that his Oklahoma accent and homely humor were more popular with his audiences than his act. His wit and his rope got him to Broadway. He played in a number of musical shows, including the *Ziegfeld Follies* (1916–1918). The *Follies* gave him the line for which he is best known: "The only thing I know is what I read in the papers."

A humorist in the style of Mark Twain and Mr. Dooley, he was immensely popular. He appeared onstage in a crumpled suit that looked as if he had slept in it. His face was rough and weatherbeaten, but crinkled with a winning grin. He played his "natchell self."

He was a friend to senators and Presidents (except for Harding, who did not like being kidded about his golf game). He spared none of them. After observing Wilson's frustrated efforts at European diplomacy in 1919, Rogers commented: "The United States never lost a war or won a conference." After a tour of Europe as the President's goodwill messenger in the mid-1920's, he told an audience that he was the only American who had visited Egypt and never bothered to see the Sphinx. "I didn't need to," he explained. "I've already met Calvin Coolidge." His wry humor provided a perfect antidote to the tensions of the times.

He made numerous movies in the 1930's and was at the height of his career when he decided to take a 'round-the-world trip with his friend and fellow Oklahoman, Wiley Post. Off Point Barrow, Alaska, their plane developed engine trouble and dropped into the Arctic Sea.

SACCO AND VANZETTI. In April 1920 a robbery resulted in the death of a paymaster and a guard at a factory in South Braintree, Massachusetts. Two weeks later state police arrested, in another part of the town, Nicola Sacco and Bartolemeo Vanzetti. They were Italian immigrants who had led an outspoken public protest against the Palmer raids. Although there was no direct evidence linking them to the crime, they were convicted and sentenced to death. Outraged liberals helped finance court appeals, but their efforts were to no avail. Nicola Sacco and Bartolomeo Vanzetti were executed in 1927.

On January 2, 1920, government agents raided Communist party headquarters across the country. Palmer's agents arrested some 2,700 people, including those who had visited friends in jail.

The Espionage Act, passed during the war to punish traitors, was still in effect. It was used to arrest and fine suspected revolutionaries. Among those arrested were 556 aliens, who were deported under the law. In addition, many states passed laws to punish advocates of revolutionary change.

How real was the danger? There were some radical organizations in the country. The Industrial Workers of the World (Wobblies) had made some revolutionary pronouncements. But their membership was largely confined to migratory farm workers on the West Coast. Eugene Debs, running on the Socialist ticket, polled about 900,000 votes in the election of 1920. Party membership was not over 40,000. And Debs never threatened revolution.

HEIGHTENED RACIAL TENSIONS. During the war years rapid industrial growth in the North had lured many Blacks who hoped to escape the cycle of poverty and discrimination of the South. But Blacks did not find the equal opportunity they sought. They had great difficulty in finding adequate housing, and they got the lowest paid jobs. Black soldiers resented the restrictions they found upon returning to the United States.

In 1917 a silent parade of 15,000 Blacks, organized by the NAACP, marched in New York City to protest discrimination and har-

The artist Ben Shahn first attracted attention with his social protest paintings. This one is of the Sacco-Vanzetti case. Shahn portrayed, from left to right, a protest demonstration, Sacco and Vanzetti, and the two men in their coffins. What was Shahn's attitude toward the trial?

assment against them. By 1919 there had been race riots in more than 20 cities. The riots, in which Whites attacked Blacks, solved nothing. But they led many Black Americans to become far more militant. Brilliant young men like the magazine editor Asa Philip Randolph and the poet and novelist Claude McKay became more and more outspoken in their views.

An early leader in the struggle for Black identity was Marcus Moziah Garvey. He founded the Universal Negro Improvement Association in 1914. Garvey saw no hope of justice for Blacks in America and preached for them to return to Africa. Garvey created a Black expression, "soul," giving many Blacks a new sense of racial pride. He was arrested in 1925 on charges of using the mails to defraud and was eventually deported to his native Jamaica. Garvey's movement collapsed without his leadership.

The ranks of Spanish-speaking Americans in the United States were swelled by half a million Mexican immigrants who arrived during the 1920's. Most of the newcomers were forced to work as migrant laborers. They found discrimination in all aspects of their lives. They were resented by labor groups because they accepted almost any rate of pay. They were also resented by other Americans because they had the option of returning to Mexico when economic conditions improved.

Section Review

1. Identify or explain: Calvin Coolidge, A. Mitchell Palmer, Eugene Debs, the Wobblies, Sacco and Vanzetti.
2. What was demobilization? What problems did it cause?
3. Describe the conditions that produced the Red Scare of the 1920's.
4. Why is September 1919 an important date in the history of the organized American labor movement?

2. Republicans in Command

THE ELECTION OF 1920. Warren G. Harding's landslide victory in 1920 forecast a decade of Republican rule in the nation's capital. Not until 1930 did the Democrats win control of Congress. Not until 1933 did they regain the White House.

Harding ran on a platform that promised low taxes, higher tariffs, restriction of immigration, and aid to farmers. He called for a return to "normalcy," something that most Americans were eager to experience again.

The election of 1920 was the first in which all eligible women could vote. However, there seemed to be no change in voting patterns with the addition of women voters. (See map below.) Harding looked like an ideal picture of an American President. And he was immensely popular.

HARDING'S APPOINTMENTS. Harding had not wanted the Presidency. He did

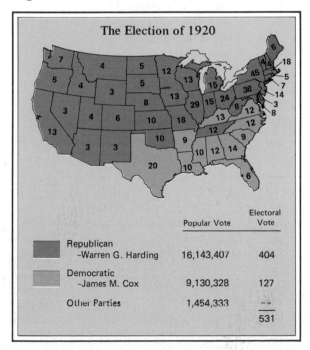

The Election of 1920

	Popular Vote	Electoral Vote
Republican —Warren G. Harding	16,143,407	404
Democratic —James M. Cox	9,130,328	127
Other Parties	1,454,333	--
		531

not feel adequate to do the job. In that judgment he was probably right. Some of his appointees were able people. He named Charles Evans Hughes Secretary of State and Herbert Hoover, the rising star in the Republican party, to take command of the new Department of Commerce.

One of Harding's most influential advisers was Secretary of the Treasury Andrew Mellon, a self-made multimillionaire from Pittsburgh. Mellon believed that taxing the wealthy would inhibit their investments and therefore slow down economic growth. He also stopped the expansion of social services for the poor. Under his guidance and that of Charles G. Dawes, the first Director of the Budget, the government began to reduce the national debt.

Harding's awareness of his own limitations led him to prefer the company of people less qualified than Hughes, Hoover, and Mellon. He appointed many politicians from his home state who came to be known as the Ohio Gang.

Senate investigations after Harding's sudden death in 1923 revealed that the Ohio Gang had engaged in a mad scramble for loot. Harding was not involved, but he certainly was aware that all was not well. He admitted to a journalist shortly before departing on his last western trip that his friends had betrayed his trust.

THE TEAPOT DOME. *A number of government offices suffered mismanagement and fund shortages under Harding.* Charles Forbes, head of the Veterans' Bureau, pocketed a substantial part of the 250 million dollars spent by the agency. And Thomas W. Miller, the alien-property custodian, defrauded the government in the sale of foreign-owned properties seized during World War I.

The most spectacular scandal involved government oil lands. These were public properties located at Elk Hills, California, and Teapot Dome, Wyoming. The lands contained oil deposits, which the government

held in reserve for the future needs of the navy. In 1921 Albert Fall, Harding's Secretary of the Interior, persuaded the President to transfer control of the lands from the Navy Department to the Interior Department. Fall then leased the lands to oil companies that began drilling.

When reporters published accounts revealing that Secretary Fall's New Mexico ranch had become unusually prosperous, the suspicions of the Senate were aroused. The Senate began an investigation in the fall of 1923. It turned out that oil speculators had secretly given Fall 100,000 dollars and stocked his ranch with thoroughbred cattle. All were tried for conspiracy to defraud the government, but the oil speculators were acquitted. Fall was eventually convicted of accepting a bribe and spent a year in jail. *He was the first official of cabinet rank to be convicted of a crime while in office.*

KEEPING COOL WITH COOLIDGE. Harding's death in September 1923 brought Calvin Coolidge to the Presidency. *The new President, a model of New England honesty and integrity, unconnected with any of the scandals, was the right man for the time.* He promptly appointed a new Attorney General, Harland Fisk Stone (later a justice of the Supreme Court), and gave him orders to weed out the Ohio Gang.

The government came to mirror the President—smooth, silent, and efficient. And that was exactly what Americans wanted—an absence of problems.

Coolidge was impressed by wealth and those who had it. His attitude helped create faith in business. Production, profits, and consumption rose throughout the 1920's. With them rose the idea that business was the ethical and social force that would make the United States great. Articles written on business and business people were full of admiration. This was the era when the large universities began to establish graduate schools of business and when the advertising industry came of age.

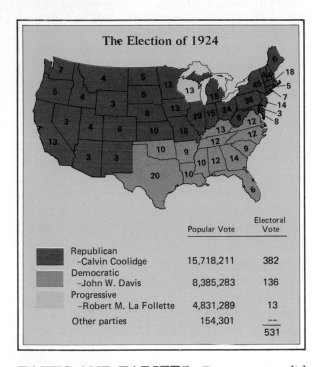

The Election of 1924

	Popular Vote	Electoral Vote
Republican —Calvin Coolidge	15,718,211	382
Democratic —John W. Davis	8,385,283	136
Progressive —Robert M. La Follette	4,831,289	13
Other parties	154,301	--
		531

TAXES AND TARIFFS. Government did not do much in the 1920's, but what it did chiefly benefited business and the wealthy. "The business of America is business," declared President Coolidge. *And in 1922, with the Fordney-McCumber Tariff, the Republicans rewarded manufacturers by restoring tariff duties to the level at which they had been before the Wilson administration.* The higher duties, together with a booming economy, meant substantial revenue for the government. The Treasury accumulated a surplus in every year of the decade, and it managed to pay off nearly half the war debt. Secretary of the Treasury Andrew Mellon proposed to reduce taxes on the wealthy. Instead, Congress passed a general tax reduction in 1926.

THE TRIUMPH OF LAISSEZ FAIRE. What happened to Progressivism? Americans in the 1920's seldom saw or felt the workings of their government. The machinery the Progressives had created to regulate business and ensure fair competition was available but unused. The government ignored the antitrust laws. Business corporations combined to achieve production economies and stabilize prices. In the course of the decade, 25 percent of American industry fell under the control of holding companies. In some industries, such as electric power, vast empires were built by creating holding companies to own other holding companies. Samuel Insull, president of Chicago's Commonwealth Edison, pyramided holding companies until he controlled nearly all the electric output from Chicago to Florida.

The machinery created by the Progressives fell under the control of the interests it was supposed to regulate. Railroads dominated the Interstate Commerce Commission. Utilities ran the Federal Power Commission. In 1925 the head of the Federal Trade Commission announced that there was no need for his agency. Business was thought capable of self-regulation.

By 1924 the country had come to identify prosperity with the silent man in Washington. The Republicans nominated Coolidge for a term as President in his own right. He won the election easily, but the five million votes that La Follette polled as the Progressive party candidate suggested that a sizable minority was interested in reform. (See map above.)

WHERE WERE THE PROGRESSIVES? Some Progressives were gone. Senator Robert La Follette died in 1925. Others carried on lonely crusades. Nebraska's George Norris fought to prevent the government from leasing to private industry the Wilson Dam on the Tennessee River at Muscle Shoals, Alabama. Norris wanted the government to experiment with public production of electric power. Norris' idea was the beginning of the Tennessee Valley Authority (TVA), created in the following decade.

THE CONSERVATIVE MOOD. Contrary to President Coolidge's notion, not every

American was in business, and not everyone benefited from silent government. Labor organizations remained weak. Wages and prices rose only slightly over the decade. Farmers, after a flurry of wartime prosperity, returned to the more familiar conditions of overproduction and low prices. Farm interests in Congress pushed through the McNary-Haugen Bill, authorizing the government to buy farm surpluses for sale abroad. But President Coolidge vetoed it on the grounds that it was legislation for the benefit of a special-interest group. That was curious reasoning. The administration's tariff policies admittedly benefited manufacturers, and the Department of Commerce collected statistics for business corporations. But the veto was in keeping with the mood of the day.

H. L. MENCKEN, SOCIAL CRITIC. No one symbolized the end of Progressivism better than H. L. Mencken, editor of the *American Mercury* magazine. The *Mercury* was the major channel for reformist thought in the 1920's. And Mencken was one of the few critics of the day. He disliked what he saw in American society, but he offered no solutions. He had little use for democracy and less for the common person. Mencken's cynical criticism marked the grave of Progressivism.

HERBERT HOOVER, PROPHET OF PROSPERITY. *More representative of the 1920's was Herbert Hoover.* Self-made and successful, Hoover was a living example of the American myth. He worked his way through Stanford (where he served as equipment manager for the football team that upset the mighty University of California) and earned his first million before he was 40.

As civil engineer, food administrator during the war, and Secretary of Commerce under Harding and Coolidge, Hoover made his mark wherever he worked. The phrase "rugged individualism" expressed his phi-losophy. He meant not a free-for-all, a jungle of cutthroat competition, but a footrace. He believed that through free public education the government provides contestants with an equal start and provides agencies to judge the results and ensure fairness. Hoover restated the old promise of American life, and in the flush of the 1920's that promise seemed close to reality for many people. Hoover became the prophet of prosperity.

Hoover also personified the Republican party of the 1920's. Republican strength lay in small-town America, the midwestern heartland, and among people of Yankee or early immigrant stock, White and Protestant.

THE ELECTION OF 1928. Late in 1927 President Coolidge summoned reporters to his office and announced: "I do not choose to run for President in 1928." That opened the door for Hoover, and the Republican convention nominated him on the first ballot.

The Democrats, weak and divided, had more difficulty selecting a candidate. For

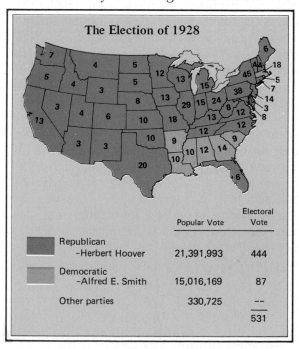

The Election of 1928

		Popular Vote	Electoral Vote
	Republican —Herbert Hoover	21,391,993	444
	Democratic —Alfred E. Smith	15,016,169	87
	Other parties	330,725	--
			531

many years the Democrats had relied on the Solid South for electoral strength. But the Bryan wing of the western and southern Democrats had apparently forgotten the Populism they once expressed. Democrats from the immigrant-dominated, industrial cities saw little difference between their conservative southern colleagues and the Republicans. They wanted a more forceful government that would be oriented toward the working people.

In 1928 the urban wing won. The Democratic party nominated Alfred E. Smith of New York. Al Smith had begun his political career by declaring war on New York City's sweatshops. As governor of New York, he had reorganized finances and administration and promoted public health, workers' compensation, and civil liberties. His record was firmly Progressive.

The campaign of 1928 was the first to be conducted by radio, and the new communications medium had a profound impact. Listeners in the South and West found Al Smith's New York accent harsh and abrasive. Furthermore, with his brown derby hat and inevitable cigar, Smith looked every inch the "city slicker." Hoover's flat, midwestern voice conveyed integrity and candor. His professional appearance suggested an appropriate degree of intelligence and efficiency.

Smith was also a Roman Catholic (the first of that faith to run for President) and an advocate of repeal of the prohibition amendment. His candidacy was a challenge to the small-town values that dominated the United States.

Religion was a significant factor in some parts of the country. But ultimately it was the prosperity of 1928 that defeated Smith. That was the year of the great leap in the stock market. Everyone was buying a chunk of big business. Many struck it rich as stock prices rose steadily. For the first time economic growth seemed to be benefiting the common people as well as the rich. In accepting the Republican nomination Hoover declared: "We in America today are nearer to the final triumph over poverty than ever before in the history of any land." *Hoover won the election with ease, 444 electoral votes to Smith's 87.* (See map, page 570.) Smith did not even carry New York. And several southern states went Republican for the first time. Smith carried the 12 largest cities and cut into the traditional Republican agricultural vote in the West. Once again, a minority vote indicated a future trend. Another indicator was the election of Oscar De Priest of Chicago to Congress. De Priest was the first northern Black to be sent to Congress. Urban Blacks were becoming a political force.

Six months after Hoover affirmed the oath of office, the stock market collapsed, setting off the worst depression in American history. The prophet of prosperity spent his Presidency grappling with unemployment, hunger, and want. It was the saddest irony of the times.

Section Review

1. Mapping: Using the maps on pages 569 and 570, compare the results of the elections of 1924 and 1928. How can you account for the increase in the Democratic popular vote in 1928, when the Democrats carried fewer states than they won in 1924?
2. Identify or explain: the Ohio Gang, Andrew Mellon, George Norris, H. L. Mencken, Alfred E. Smith, Albert B. Fall.
3. List, in chronological order, the events that led to the bribery conviction of Secretary of the Interior Albert Fall.
4. What information in this section could be used to support Coolidge's remark that "the business of America is business"?
5. Why did radio have "a profound impact" on the election of 1928?

3. Social Tension in the Golden Years

POSTWAR LETDOWN. The political backlash against Progressivism in the 1920's was part of a broader postwar letdown. Tired of summonses to reform and crusades for democracy, Americans turned to pleasure and material comfort. *Prosperity and new machines, such as the automobile, enabled them to seek enjoyment on a greater scale than ever before.* The breakdown of *Victorian* moral codes, a process that had begun before the war, encouraged more freedom of expression.

Victorian refers to the latter half of the 19th century, when Queen Victoria sat on the British throne. Moral codes were strict in the United States and Britain, and prudery—such as placing pants on piano legs—was common.

Because young people led the revolution in attitudes and behavior, the tensions that resulted were partly generational. A symbol for the 1920's might be the rumble seat—the open seat at the back of an automobile that carried two people. The rumble seat became a byword for pleasure, romance, and social freedom.

GAINS FOR WOMEN. Women, expressing new-found political rights, shed their petticoats, bustles, and ankle-length skirts in favor of a simpler, lighter, more practical garb. Some smoked cigarettes in public and accompanied friends to illegal taverns (called speakeasies because of their secretive atmosphere). Many women of the 1920's showed their new independence by wearing short skirts, bobbing their hair, and applying lipstick. They were modern women, or flappers.

As a result of industrialization, homemakers' burdens were eased by new equipment—washing machines, refrigerators, stoves, and inexpensive sewing machines. Packaged foods and canned goods made meal preparation easier. The leisure created by these new products gave middle-class women time to follow other interests. Magazines like *Reader's Digest* (1922) and *Time* (1923) appeared. There was more time for women to become volunteers in civic affairs, schools, and hospitals. Many women who achieved national prominence often excelled in volunteer jobs.

Less-privileged women were able to find work in the rapidly increasing mills, factories, and plants. In addition, women found job opportunities as sales clerks and office workers. *As women participated more and more in activities outside their homes, changes in female roles were made.*

THE FAILURE OF PROHIBITION. *Prohibition began in an effort to bolster morality and ended by aggravating geographical and religious tensions.* It pitted the city against the country, the South and the West against the Northeast, Protestant against Catholic, native American against immigrant. So great was the opposition that the law proved impossible to enforce. People who objected to it evaded it.

Since distilling liquor was a crime, only criminals operated the distilleries. Gangsters such as Chicago's Al Capone made fortunes in "bootleg" liquor and diverted the profits to other rackets. Bootlegging became a big business controlled by criminals.

In 1933 the 21st Amendment was ratified, ending the prohibition era. This amendment repealed the 18th Amendment and returned the control of alcoholic drinks to the states.

NATIVISM. The 1920's underscored the intolerance in American society. *Prejudice is ever-present in America, but in the 1920's it seemed more rampant than usual.* The Red Scare was an example. It stemmed not only from the fear of communism; it was also a reaction against those who warned that the world was complex.

Who was the flapper? Was she the jazz-loving woman with cropped hair and rolled-down stockings, as shown in John Held's cover for McClure's Magazine? *Or was she one of the women shown in Kenneth Hayes Miller's painting, "Finishing Touches"? Which picture do you think comes closer to portraying what women were like during the 1920's? Using information from the two pictures, how would you describe the status of women during that era?*

The revival of **nativist** feelings was nowhere more evident than in the reappearance of the Ku Klux Klan. The original Klan, the White terrorist organization of the 1870's, had died away with the end of Reconstruction. A new organization with the same name appeared in 1915 under the direction of Edward Clarke.

Nativism is an attitude or a policy that favors the native-born inhabitants of a country over immigrants. American Indians—who were ignored by most Americans—did not receive favored treatment, however.

By the middle of the decade, the Klan had between four and five million members who were devoted to attacking Blacks, Jews, Catholics, and foreigners in general. The Klan became a political force in several states, including some in the North. In 1924 the urban wing of the Democratic party won a platform statement denouncing the Klan, but the dispute nearly tore the party apart.

IMMIGRATION RESTRICTIONS. *Nativists, with help from labor leaders who feared cheap competition, closed the door on immigrants.* There had long been

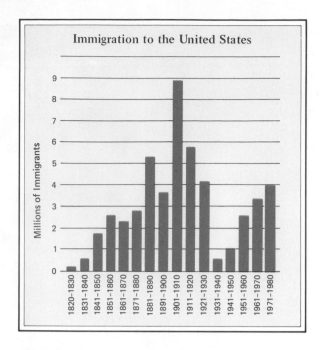

Immigration to the United States

Millions of Immigrants

1820–1830	
1831–1840	
1841–1850	
1851–1860	
1861–1870	
1871–1880	
1881–1890	
1891–1900	
1901–1910	
1911–1920	
1921–1930	
1931–1940	
1941–1950	
1951–1960	
1961–1970	
1971–1980	

restrictions on immigration, and they had always been racially motivated. In 1882 Chinese were excluded by law. And in 1907 President Theodore Roosevelt arranged a Gentlemen's Agreement with Japan, under which the Japanese government limited emigration to the United States.

The influx of immigrants from southern and eastern Europe after 1900 provoked hostilities. (See graph, page 453.) Coming from different cultural backgrounds, people from these areas were slow to blend into the "melting pot." In 1917 President Wilson vetoed a bill that would have imposed a literacy test on immigrants as a condition of entry. But Congress passed it over his veto.

The Red Scare increased suspicion of foreigners. *In 1921 Congress passed an Emergency Quota Act, which imposed an annual immigration quota on each foreign nationality.* The limit was three percent of the number of persons of that nationality who resided in the United States in 1910. An even more restrictive law was passed in 1924. It reduced the quota to two percent of the number of persons of each nationality

and set the base year at 1890. This law discriminated against Italians, Russians, and Slavic peoples of eastern Europe, who did not start coming to the United States in significant numbers until after 1890.

In 1929 the National Origins Act lessened the discriminatory feature of the quota by making 1920 the base year for calculating national quotas, but it limited the number of immigrants who could be admitted in any one year to a mere 150,000.

WRITERS AND SOCIETY IN CONFLICT. Out of the anger and frustration

NATIONAL ORIGINS ACT, 1929	
Country of Origin	**Immigrants Allowed Per Year**
Austria	1,413
Belgium	1,304
Bulgaria	100
Czechoslovakia	2,874
Denmark	1,181
Finland	569
France	3,084
Germany	25,721
Great Britain	65,721
Greece	307
Hungary	869
Iceland	100
Ireland	17,853
Italy	5,802
Netherlands	3,153
Norway	2,377
Poland	6,524
Portugal	440
Rumania	295
Spain	252
Sweden	3,314
Switzerland	1,707
Turkey	226
U.S.S.R.	2,784
Yugoslavia	845
Other European	1,538
European total	150,591
*Asian total	1,323

*Areas included are China, Japan, India, the Philippines, and Hong Kong.

This painting, entitled "White Trumpet Flower," is one of many paintings by the American artist Georgia O'Keeffe. O'Keeffe was born in 1887 in Wisconsin and started doing close-ups of flowers in 1926. Why do you think she painted a flower close-up? Is her style realistic?

that American writers felt toward society came works that endure to this day. Some of the writers looked to traditional American values. Among them were Willa Cather, Edith Wharton, and Ellen Glasgow. These women wrote novels in which they examined society and its contrasting values.

Other writers were caught between the old and the new. In *Main Street* and *Babbitt,* Sinclair Lewis wrote sharp satire in which he captured the hypocrisy and materialism he found in the middle class. Sherwood Anderson and Theodore Dreiser wrote about small-town, middle-class people and aspects of modern life.

Ernest Hemingway and F. Scott Fitzgerald, two other novelists of the 1920's, wrote of people totally changed by the postwar world. Hemingway created characters who became models for the young rebels. Fitzgerald's characters searched for happiness at party after party. In *The Great Gatsby* (1925) the hero's search ends in death.

The poets of the 1920's were interested in breaking with tradition. They found support in Harriet Monroe, who established the magazine *Poetry* in 1912. Within a few years, *Poetry* had published the work of all those who became the major American poets of the first half of the 20th century. The works of poets like Vachel Lindsay, Edgar Lee Masters, Carl Sandburg, e. e. cummings, Ezra Pound, T. S. Eliot, and Robert Frost varied in style, form, and content, but they recorded the present.

THE HARLEM RENAISSANCE. Most Black leaders in the 1920's rejected Garvey's separatism. But they shared his pride of race. Alain Locke's book *The New Negro* stressed the importance of Black culture and achievements. The new Negro, he argued, ought to stop being defensive. Only through their own initiative could Blacks open the gates to full equality.

The idea of a new Negro swept the Black community in the 1920's and helped inspire a flowering of literature, painting, and music. ***The Black renaissance throbbed in many cities, from New York to New Orleans. But its center was Harlem, in New York City.***

She was called The Empress of the Blues. Bessie Smith sold millions of records, but few Whites in the 1920's even knew her name.

The leaders of the Harlem renaissance were not separatists. They wrote for Whites as well as Blacks. Countee Cullen worked to become a great poet, and he succeeded. In poems such as "Shroud of Color" he explored the condition of Blacks. Novelist Claude McKay set his stories in Black communities (for example, *Home to Harlem,* 1928) and filled them with heroes and heroines who were the victims of injustice and discrimination. Never before had such ideas been the subject of novels.

The music of the Harlem renaissance owed more to African traditions than to American or European influences. Jazz was born in New Orleans about the turn of the century, a mixture of African and West Indian rhythms and religious spirituals. Black bands played it, usually with wind and brass instruments. Their music experimented with chords and introduced "blue"

notes. (Musical notes flatted in a special way are called blue notes.) Black musicians such as Louis Armstrong carried jazz up the Mississippi to St. Louis and then on to Chicago before the war. And the Harlem renaissance brought it to national attention. *Shuffle Along* (1921) was the first jazz musical comedy and marked the beginning of the Jazz Age. *Running Wild* (1924) gave the world the "Charleston" in song and dance.

The Harlem renaissance developed a pool of Black talent. It laid a solid foundation of pride and self-confidence on which later generations of Blacks could build.

Section Review

1. Identify or explain: 21st Amendment, Countee Cullen, Gentlemen's Agreement, Edward Clarke, Edith Wharton, Louis Armstrong, nativism, Emergency Quota Act, Sinclair Lewis.
2. What developments signaled a change in the social attitudes of Americans during the 1920's?
3. What was the Harlem renaissance?
4. What is the significance of the revival of the Ku Klux Klan in the 1920's?
5. What effect did prohibition have on the United States?

4. The Second Industrial Revolution

TRANSFORMING AMERICAN SOCIETY. What makes an industrial revolution? New sources of power, new techniques of manufacturing, new materials, and new inventions—these are at least some of the elements. In the mid-19th century, coal, steam, steel, and railroads helped transform American society. In the 1920's electricity, the moving assembly line, new materials, and new inventions once more transformed American society.

THE MOVING ASSEMBLY LINE. The
Bessemer process of manufacturing steel
was one of the new techniques that sparked
the 19th-century Industrial Revolution. In
the 1920's it was the moving assembly line.
The idea was Henry Ford's. And it was first
put into practice by Ford in the manufacturing of his Model T in 1913. Standardization
and interchangeability were not new. Eli
Whitney and Isaac Merit Singer had experimented with mass-production techniques.
But the moving assembly line was different.
*Each worker had an assigned task, which
he or she repeated over and over. The moving line determined the pace of work.* The
automobile took form as it moved through
the factory.

The moving assembly line, adopted
widely in the automobile industry and other
industries during the 1920's, permitted
enormous savings. The price of a Model T
was 1,500 dollars in 1913. By 1929 it sold for
600 dollars. By that date there was one car
for every six Americans. Statistically, the
entire nation could be on the highway at one
time.

NEW MATERIALS. The growing auto-
mobile industry also provided a new market
for the steel industry. Steel production had
sagged after completion of the railroads.
*During the 1920's new materials came on
the market to compete with steel. Among
them were aluminum, plastics, and certain artificial fibers.* Prior to the war the
United States had been largely dependent
on Germany for chemicals. The war stimulated the domestic chemical industry. And
one result was the spread of inventions.
Nylon and fiber glass came along in the
1930's.

ELECTRIC POWER. Coal and steam
were the symbols of 19th-century industrialization. Electric power was the hallmark of
the 1920's. Despite Thomas Edison's pro-
motional efforts, only 10 percent of American homes had electricity in 1920. By the

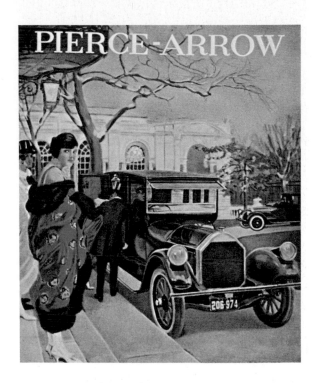

*American advertising came of age in the 1920's.
Businesses throughout the country tried to lure the
public into buying items by appealing to their desire for sophistication, or "class." In this ad, a
well-dressed woman is about to get into her Pierce-
Arrow car. Have you ever bought something because of an advertisement? Explain.*

end of the decade, the proportion had increased to two thirds. In 1929 only rural
areas—where consumers were too spread
out to permit profitable lines—remained
without electricity.

*Electric power permitted the develop-
ment of industries that had enormous social impact.* Among these were the radio
and movie industries. The radio was invented in Europe shortly before the war, but
it was Americans who turned it into a medium for mass entertainment. The first commercial station, KDKA of Pittsburgh, began
broadcasting the election returns in 1920.
By the end of the decade there were ten mil-

lion sets. And listening to the radio was the standard evening entertainment.

Motion pictures also began before the war, but the industry did not blossom until it moved to Hollywood in the 1920's. The star system, fostered by the popular magazines, stimulated public interest. Greta Garbo, Rudolph Valentino, and Mary Pickford were the folk heroes of the time.

THE CONSUMER SOCIETY.
The industrial developments of the 1920's differed in one important way from the earlier Industrial Revolution. The 19th century focused on so-called heavy industry—on steel production, machine tools, and other productive machines such as locomotives. *The 1920's changed the focus to consumer items, such as automobiles, radios, and iceboxes.* The increase in consumer buying was aided by the introduction of the installment plan as a way of paying for goods. Future business growth would depend to a large extent on national consumption.

The supermarket was a natural product of the age. The first supermarket, named Piggly Wiggly, opened in Memphis, Tennessee, in 1916. The theory behind it was that goods would sell themselves—often to consumers who did not know that they wanted an item until they saw it on the shelf. Marketing enterprise, mass production, and the search for satisfaction were all reflected in the supermarket shopping cart.

SCIENTIFIC MANAGEMENT.
Accompanying the advances in technology was a revolution in business methods. This revolution began before the war with the work of Frederick W. Taylor, who did time and motion studies in order to increase the efficiency of each worker. The idea that business could be a profession, that management could be a science, was new. Herbert Hoover, as Secretary of Commerce, encouraged the idea, and a number of universities developed special business programs and established schools of business to teach a separate academic discipline.

THE GREAT BULL MARKET.
All these changes brought tremendous leaps in production and a general feeling of optimism. *Nothing reflected the optimism of the 1920's as much as the steady rise in the stock market.* In an effort to finance its expansion, American business went public in the 1920's, attracting the funds of millions of small investors. Playing the market was often a profitable game because the entrance of new players lifted prices. The great bull market of 1927–1929 became the symbol of prosperity and hope.

THUNDERCLOUDS ON THE HORIZON.
The prosperity was soft. The economy had weaknesses. *Millions of people knew only unrelieved misery and insecurity during the so-called good times.* Racial minorities knew little of prosperity. Industry had vastly increased its productive potential but had not made similar efforts to increase its markets. Prices were not lowered, nor were wages raised. Despite spectacular reductions in the price of automobiles, prices in general remained unchanged throughout the 1920's partly because of business combinations. By the end of the decade, a few corporations controlled each industry and managed prices. Scientific businesses wanted to avoid price wars. They competed instead through cost controls and advertising. But as a result, prices and profits remained artificially high.

Wages also remained stable. Because of the new technology, the hourly output of each worker increased by a third over the decade. But wages rose only 8 percent. The rest was profit, poured back into a business to buy more machines or to be distributed through stock dividends. Stockholders benefited, and stock prices jumped, stimulating the great bull market.

Trouble loomed. *Because of low wages, wealth was poorly distributed.* Only 5 percent of the people received one third of the nation's income. There was thus a small pool of consumers who could afford such durable goods as houses, furniture, and automobiles. Thus, one of the prime causes of the depression was underconsumption—most people could not afford to buy everything business could produce.

By the spring of 1929, there were danger signs on the horizon. Yet the stock market continued to rise through the summer, buoyed by the entrance of amateur speculators. The market crash in October 1929 did not cause the depression—that was already under way. But because the market reflected the hopes of millions, its crash brought millions to despair. It turned a temporary economic readjustment into a national calamity. And with it came an end to the good times of the twenties.

Section Review

1. Identify or explain: KDKA, Piggly Wiggly, time and motion studies, great bull market.
2. How did the moving assembly line revolutionize American industry?
3. Which of the following developments do you think had the most far-reaching effect on American life: electric power, the switch from heavy industry to consumer goods, scientific management. Why?
4. What economic weaknesses contributed to the stock market crash of October 1929?

Chapter 24 Review

Bird's-Eye View

The early years of the 1920's were troubled by the problems of demobilization, labor strife, fear of revolution, and rising racial tensions. The period was marked by strikes, a Red Scare, and a search for Black identity.

These were not the only symptoms of the social tensions that plagued the nation. With the breakdown of the Victorian moral code and the resulting freedom of expression came fear that the nation's moral fiber was being weakened. Women found new freedom and began defining new roles. But fear led to intolerance. There was a revival of nativist, or antiforeign, sentiment, and with it a resurgence of the Ku Klux Klan, the imposition of severe restrictions on immigration to the United States, and new problems and tensions created by prohibition.

Out of the anger and frustration of the period also came some of the country's most enduring works of literature. The search for Black identity inspired a flowering of Black literature, painting, and music.

The landslide victory of Warren G. Harding in 1920 installed Republicans in the White House for over a decade. Although Harding was personally honest, his administration was marred by scandal. Harding's death in September 1923 brought Calvin Coolidge to the White House. Acting on Coolidge's dictum that "the business of America is business," the federal government functioned chiefly for the benefit of big corporations and the wealthy.

Prosperity was still within the reach of many Americans, however, and no one symbolized the promise of American life better than Herbert Hoover. In the Presidential election of 1928, Hoover, the midwesterner, easily defeated New York's Governor Alfred E. Smith. Yet six months after Hoover's inauguration, the American economy collapsed and the "prophet of prosperity" spent his term in office fighting unemployment, hunger, and want.

What caused the collapse? During the 1920's the American economy expanded rapidly. New manufacturing methods, new materials, and new sources of power brought leaps in production and a general mood of optimism. The stock market rose steadily. Most people could not afford to buy everything that business could produce. In October 1929 the stock market crashed, ruining the lives of millions.

Vocabulary

Define or identify each of the following:

The Jazz Singer	flapper	bootlegging
demobilization	Alfred E. Smith	nativist
Marcus Garvey	Victorian morals	Harlem renaissance

Review Questions

1. What were the three major strikes in 1919? What were the causes of the three strikes?
2. What was the Red Scare?
3. What was Warren G. Harding's platform?

4. What was the philosophy of government during the 1920's?

5. How did the prosperity of the 1920's affect American society?

6. Describe the social tensions that American society experienced during the 1920's.

7. What developments created a second industrial revolution?

8. Describe the state of the stock market between 1927 and 1929.

Reviewing Social Studies Skills

1. Using the graph on page 574, answer the following questions:
   a. During which 10-year period was there a peak in immigration into the United States?
   b. In which 10-year period did the fewest immigrants enter the country?
   c. During which period in the 20th century was the immigration rate at its lowest?

2. Using the chart on page 574, answer the following questions:
   a. What is the name of the chart? What does it show?
   b. Which three nations were able to send the most immigrants to the United States each year?
   c. Which three nations were allowed to send the least number of immigrants to the United States each year?
   d. How many individuals were allowed to enter the United States from Asia?

3. Using the maps on pages 567, 569, and 570, describe the voting pattern of the people in the United States during the 1920's.

Reading for Meaning

1. Make an outline of Section 4, The Second Industrial Revolution. Use the textbook's eight subheads as the major headings in your outline. Then, identify specific details from the text that support these major points.

2. One way to find the meaning of a word or phrase is to look it up in the dictionary. Another way is to figure out the meaning from the context—that is, by gathering clues about the word or phrase from the words surrounding it. Choose three of the following words and phrases, and find their meaning by using a dictionary. For the remaining three words, figure out their meaning from the context: **a)** consumer goods **b)** flapper **c)** melting pot **d)** holding company **e)** soul **f)** rugged individualism.
   Which method provided you with the most accurate meanings? Why?

Bibliography

Frederick Lewis Allen's *Only Yesterday: An Informal History of the 1920's* (Harper & Row) was written shortly after the '20's had ended.

Another contemporary piece, Sinclair Lewis's novel *Babbitt* (Harcourt Brace Jovanovich), is a lively, satirical account of the 1920's.

August Meier and Elliott Rudwick's *From Plantation to Ghetto: An Interpretive History of American Negroes* (Hill & Wang) is a good account of the adjustment of Blacks to freedom after the Civil War.

Unit 5 Review

Vocabulary

Define or identify each of the following:

incumbent	Boxers	stipulations
Brandeis brief	autocracy	demobilization
sphere of influence	Bolsheviks	Victorian morals
imperial power	partisan issue	nativism

Recalling the Facts

1. What social, political, and economic conditions did the Progressives seek to reform in the early 1900's?
2. What was the role of the muckrakers in the reform movement?
3. List the reforms made under the administrations of Roosevelt, Taft, and Wilson.
4. What caused the decline of the Progressive movement after the end of World War I?
5. Explain the concept of Dollar Diplomacy? How did it work?
6. Explain how the United States secured the right to build the Panama Canal.
7. What was the national attitude toward prohibition?
8. What rights does the 19th Amendment cover?
9. Cite six examples of American imperialism.
10. How did the Spanish-American War establish the United States as a world power?
11. What evidence presented in this unit supports the contention that the national immigration policy was anti-Asian?
12. List the nations that made up the Central Powers and those that made up the Allied Powers. Use the map on page 543 to help you answer this question.
13. What immediate problems did the United States have to overcome as it entered World War I?
14. How did Woodrow Wilson hope to achieve a lasting peace after the end of World War I?
15. Describe American society during the 1920's.

History Lab

1. Read Upton Sinclair's novel *The Jungle*. Report to your classmates about the conditions that existed in the meat-processing industry, as described by Sinclair.
2. On an outline map of the world, locate, label, and color-shade United States possessions, both past and present. Indicate the ethnic background of the inhabitants and the principal language of each area.
3. World War I was the first war in which extensive submarine warfare played a major role. Do research in the periodical collection of your school library. Look for information on the United States and the Soviet nuclear submarine fleets. Use the *Reader's Guide to Periodic Literature* to find several articles on the topic. Write a report on the size, purpose, and missions of the fleets. Give a report to your class.

4. Draw a poster encouraging Americans to eat less so that more food can be sent to Europeans who are nearing starvation as a result of World War I. In making your appeal, try to strike a balance between words and pictures.

Local History

1. Interview a senior citizen in your community. Ask about her or his recollections of prohibition, World War I, or the 1920's. Either write down your interview questions and the answers you get or tape record the interview and play it for the class.
2. Many United States cities at one point established the city-manager form of government, which originated during the Progressive era. Most, however, reverted to their older systems. Research your city or the one closest to you. What is the structure of its government? Make a chart, illustrating the city's present structure.

Forming an Opinion

1. Both the impeachment process, established by the Constitution, and the recall process, instituted during the reform movements of the early 20th century, have the same purpose—the removal of a government official. Do you believe these two processes have made our system more democratic? Have they been effective in promoting honest leadership?
2. In 1978 the United States signed a treaty that will eventually transfer control and ownership of the Panama Canal to the country of Panama. There has been opposition to this treaty. Do you think the signing of this treaty was a good idea? What would Alfred Thayer Mahan have said about the transfer? Does a country that wants to be a world leader need to maintain a strong naval force?

Time Line

Using the time line below, answer the following:
1. When did the United States enter the war?
2. How many years after the sinking of the *Lusitania* did the United States enter the war?
3. When did the Spanish-American War begin?
4. What event was part of the Red Scare?
5. Using the material in this unit, identify five other events that you think should be added to the time line. Give a reason for selecting each.

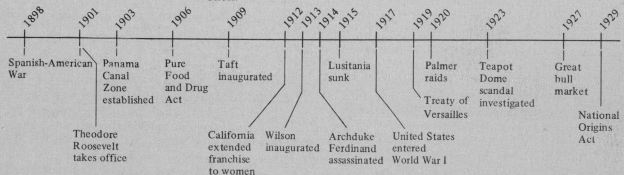

A Time to Rebuild

"Rome was not built in a day." Nor was any city. Few cities can point to the date of their founding—most just grew up haphazardly. As a result, many of them are disorderly collections of streets and buildings. Even planned cities, such as William Penn's Philadelphia or Latrobe's Washington, D.C., did not follow the dreams of their designers. Unregulated growth altered the plans. Efforts to control development through zoning ordinances had some cosmetic effects. Parks and greenery can make cities more beautiful. But some urban planners wanted to do more.

In the early part of this century, a new concept caught the fancy of city planners. Why not, they wondered, plan a community from the beginning? Start with a vacant patch of land and design the complete community. Build a place where people can live, work, and play without ever having to leave the neighborhood.

The first of these new towns was Sunnyside Gardens, New York, begun in 1924. Located on Long Island, within easy commuting distance of Manhattan, Sunnyside was planned to house 1,200 families on a tract of 22.4 hectares (56 acres). Its special features were its low-cost housing in an attractive environment. Sunnyside, however, was not a self-contained community. Rather, it was a well-planned suburb, dependent on New York City.

After World War II there was a need for inexpensive housing, since veterans and their families were flooding the market. Abraham Levitt, a New York developer, attempted to answer this need. His answer was a community of mass-produced houses. The community, called Levittown, was located on Long Island. It contained shopping facilities and light industry. It was so successful that in the 1950's Abraham Levitt and his sons, William and Alfred, established two more Levittowns, one not far from Philadelphia and one in New Jersey.

In the early 1960's, developer Robert E. Simon carried the Levittown idea to Virginia. There he established the new town of Reston near Washington, D.C. Simon put up various kinds of housing to appeal to people at all levels of income. He also included structures and opportunities for leisure activities. The 25,000 inhabitants of Reston can, if they choose, work and play and live and learn without ever leaving their community.

Levittown, Long Island, in New York State

Chapter 25

1929-1939

When Times Were Tough

THURSDAY, OCTOBER 24, 1929—"BLACK THURSDAY"—For ten days the Stock Exchange on New York's Wall Street had been gripped by fear. Stock prices had been falling every day. No one knew why. Perhaps it was inevitable. Speculators had driven stock prices too high. Then, when prices fell, the speculators sold out. Prices fell five or six dollars a share daily for a week. On Monday, October 21, six million shares were dumped onto the market, the highest number of shares traded in six months. The exchange staggered through until Thursday. Then, panic struck. Amid wild confusion 12,894,650 shares were sold, and the steepest one-day drop in prices recorded. At one o'clock that afternoon the ticker, a telegraphic device that recorded sales, was an hour and a half late, adding to the panic. No one knew the current price of any stock. Outside on Wall Street mounted police struggled to keep crowds moving.

A few hours later, a group of bankers met in the offices of J. P. Morgan & Co. and decided to support the market. The following day, in a further effort to restore public confidence, President Hoover declared: "The fundamental business of the country—that is, the production and distribution of goods and services—is on a sound and prosperous basis." In a sense, Hoover was right. There had been no business failures, no bankruptcies of the kind that had triggered all previous financial panics. Most of the trading, moreover, involved highly speculative stocks in risky corporations. It was "a gambler's panic," said the *New York World*.

That is how things stood on Friday, the 25th. By buying huge blocks of shares, the bankers halted the panic and stabilized the market—but only for the next few days. On Black Tuesday, October 29, panic again seized the market. This time 16 million shares were sold. The catastrophic fall in prices affected some of the country's strongest corporations—General Electric, U.S. Steel, American Telephone and Telegraph. For the next few months, stock prices wavered, but then they slid downward. By the time the stock market hit bottom, the nation was sliding into a long and deep depression.

Chapter Objectives

After you have finished reading this chapter, you should be able to:
1. List the causes of the depression and the measures President Hoover took to encourage recovery.

How had the country sunk into such a severe depression? For one thing, the economy was not in as "sound and prosperous" condition as the President maintained. Income was distributed unevenly, and many people could not afford to buy the goods on which the economy depended. In addition, the government's high tariff policies had provoked European retaliation. There was no sizable market for American manufactured goods outside the country. Thus, when surpluses developed, prices fell. In an attempt to curb surpluses and raise prices, manufacturers cut production and laid off workers. The unemployed workers could not purchase goods, and this led to more surpluses, further cutbacks, and additional unemployment. There seemed to be no end to the downward spiral.

1. President Hoover and the Depression, 1929-1932

THE FRAGILE STOCK MARKET. The cutbacks in production began in the spring of 1929, several months before the market crashed. People do not buy durable goods, such as automobiles and home furnishings, every day. Thus, the supply of such goods occasionally becomes too large. And manufacturers cut production. Such temporary slumps are called recessions. The recession of 1929 might not have become a depression had the stock market not crashed.

The "great bull market" of 1927–1929 had been a symbol of prosperity. It reflected the hopes and the ambitions of millions of people. The crash was a devastating blow to morale. It produced a mood of pessimism that lingered for years. Business people were fearful of the future. They declined to invest their money or expand business production. Unemployment remained high. People did not buy many goods and production was cut even more. Pessimism fed on itself. The prophecy of doom brought doom.

Why had the stock market been so fragile? The great bull market had begun soundly. In the mid-1920's optimistic business people planned to expand their operations and sold stock to obtain funds. Many average Americans entered the stock market for the first time. They bought slices of big corporations, believing that they were pursuing the road to wealth.

BUYING ON MARGIN. Large numbers of people without ready funds were attracted by the rising market. These people put down whatever money they had and borrowed the rest from a broker. The broker, who charged a customer interest on a margin account, would borrow money from a bank, using the customer's stock as collateral. This is called buying on margin. The broker usually required a down payment of 25 percent of the price of the stock. If the stock happened to go up in a few weeks or months by, say, 25 percent, the speculator could sell it, pay off the bank, and realize a profit on the original investment. Or the speculator could hold on to the stock, expecting the price to rise further, and simply count the "paper" profits. Dreams were made of such paper profits.

The system had a built-in panic button. If the shares of stock bought on margin declined, the value of the 25-percent down payment to the broker also declined in value. The speculator then had to give the broker an additional sum to cover the loan. If the speculator had no other funds, she or he had to sell stock instantly in order to cover the loan. Thus, at the first drop in stock prices, marginal speculators rushed to sell in order to cut their losses. And the selling rush drove prices down further. If the marginal speculator failed to realize enough from the sale of stock to pay back the loan, he or she had to sell a car, furniture, even a home. When the Stock Market crashed, there were stories of many people committing suicide. These stories might have been exaggerated, but thousands faced ruin.

The panic weakened the banks. Many banks experienced difficulty in recovering loans. ***Foreclosures*** brought the banks stocks and real estate for which they had no use. The banking system staggered through the Hoover years until it gave in to panic in the winter of 1933.

Foreclosures came about when banks took the property of people who had used it as security for loans that they could not repay.

HOOVER AND THE DEPRESSION.

President Hoover believed that each individual should be responsible for his or her own welfare. But he realized that this was not possible when the country faced such a serious emergency. He decided that the government would have to support business and agriculture. ***In the winter of 1929, Hoover asked Congress to help create jobs by increasing funds for public works.*** The money was spent to finish Boulder Dam

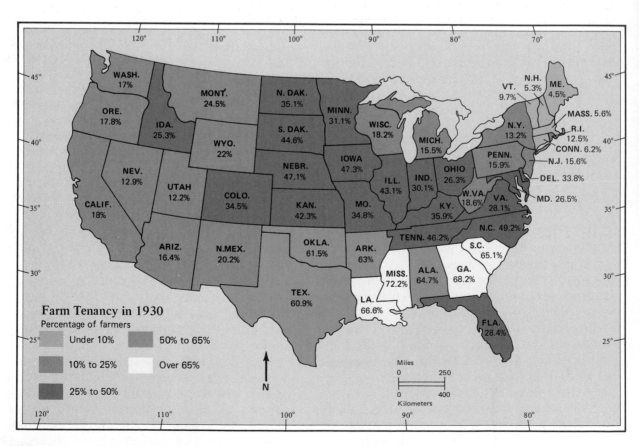

Farm Tenancy in 1930
Percentage of farmers
- Under 10%
- 10% to 25%
- 25% to 50%
- 50% to 65%
- Over 65%

(now Hoover Dam), which had been started under Coolidge. In an effort to shore up farm prices, Hoover instructed the Federal Farm Board to buy up agricultural surpluses. He asked for a tax cut. Congress obliged, but the cut made little difference, for federal income taxes were already low—three percent on the average taxpayer, five percent on millionaires.

THE HAWLEY-SMOOT TARIFF.
Hoover signed a bill, authorizing the Hawley-Smoot Tariff in 1930. He did this to protect American businesses and to keep American workers employed. He believed that the new, high tariff would benefit American industry by making foreign goods very expensive in the United States. By 1930 the European countries were also suffering from the depression, and each nation was trying to protect its economic interests. The tariff created hard feelings toward the United States.

HOME LOAN BANK ACT.
In 1932, at the urging of Hoover, Congress passed the Home Loan Bank Act. *It authorized lending federal funds to businesses that specialized in home mortgages, such as savings and loan associations and insurance companies.* By providing these businesses with funds, Congress hoped to reduce foreclosures on home mortgages and to stimulate the building of houses.

THE RECONSTRUCTION FINANCE CORPORATION. *Hoover's main weapon against the depression was the Reconstruction Finance Corporation (RFC), created by Congress in 1932.* Its function was to lend money to financially troubled businesses—railroads, manufacturing companies, banks—to prevent them from failing. Although the RFC did not reverse the depression, it did enable many companies to hold their own. The RFC was taken over and expanded by Hoover's successor, Franklin D. Roosevelt.

NORRIS-LA GUARDIA ANTI-INJUNCTION ACT.
A measure of President Hoover's flexibility was his willingness to accept the nation's first federal labor legislation. This anti-injunction law was proposed by Congress. It was sponsored by two Progressive Republicans, Senator George Norris of Nebraska and Representative Fiorello La Guardia of New York. The act outlawed yellow-dog contracts, which required a worker to promise never to join a union, and it prohibited the use of court injunctions to stop strikes. *In this law the federal government for the first time recognized that unions and strikes were legitimate ways for working people to protect their rights.*

RELIEF FOR THE UNEMPLOYED.
The RFC and the Norris-La Guardia Act show how different Hoover's ideas had become by the end of his term in office. He had taken several steps to cope with the depression, but he held firm on one issue: no relief for the unemployed. Because prices were low, an employed worker managed to escape poverty. But the standard of living was greatly reduced. Many jobs were cut back to only two or three days a week, and workers' salaries were cut accordingly.

The worst part of the depression seemed to be that it went on year after year, with little hope of recovery. Unemployment rose steadily. By 1932 one fifth of the nation's labor force was idle. This meant that 20 percent of American families suffered. (See graph, page 607.) Most families had only one breadwinner. When that person was out of work, the whole family went without proper food, clothing, and medical care. Many lost their land and their homes and wandered about the country in search of a livelihood.

Churches and other charitable organizations did what they could. They set up soup kitchens and bakeries for the hungry. The bread line—with its hundreds of people waiting for handouts—became a common

The breadline was a familiar sight during the 1930's. Despite charitable handouts and, later, federal food distribution, millions of people had inadequate diets. The only consolation for many poor families was that others had similar problems.

sight in American towns and cities. Private charities were soon overwhelmed, and the cities did not have enough resources to handle such tremendous numbers of needy people.

RELIEF AGENCIES. *If unemployment was the chief symptom of the depression, relief was its biggest headache.* Care of the poor and needy had always been the responsibility of private charities and local governments. Counties maintained poorhouses for needy citizens. Organizations such as the Red Cross coped with emergencies. The resources of local government and private agencies were limited. Many laws to aid the poor were so outdated that they could not be applied to 20th-century problems. Furthermore, most Americans felt it was degrading to ask for relief.

As time passed and the situation grew desperate, it became clear that the problem could never be solved by local agencies and the Red Cross. ***Still, Hoover resisted setting up a government-sponsored relief program.*** The press backed him, publishing editorials and articles, stating that a federal program would bankrupt the nation and weaken the moral fiber of Americans.

THE BONUS MARCH. In 1930 the Democrats were swept into power. They took control of both houses of Congress. And they demanded more aid for the unemployed. Among other things, liberal Democrats proposed giving a cash bonus to World War I veterans. Veterans had been issued bonus certificates some years before, but they were not supposed to be cashed until 1945. While Congress debated whether the certificates should be cashed immediately, thousands of veterans flooded into the nation's capital in the spring of 1932 to demand immediate cash payments. Many brought their families with them. They vowed they would stay until their demands were met.

By June there were about 11,000 people living in hastily built shacks on the marshy banks of the Potomac. The Senate refused the veterans' demands. But Congress did provide enough money to send them home. All but about 2,000 veterans left. Afraid that they might cause a dangerous situation in the nation's capital, the President ordered the army to remove the remaining veterans. With the use of infantry, cavalry, and tanks, federal troops pushed out the veterans and burned their shacks. Many considered this incident an illustration of the hardhearted indifference of the Hoover administration to the plight of the unemployed.

HOOVER RUNS FOR REELECTION. The Republicans renominated Hoover in 1932, largely for lack of an alternative. The

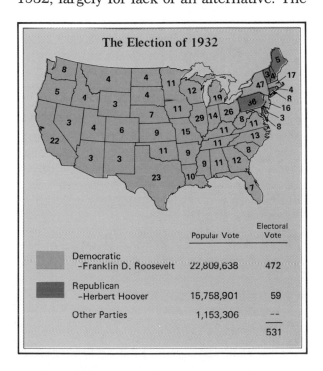

The Election of 1932

	Popular Vote	Electoral Vote
Democratic —Franklin D. Roosevelt	22,809,638	472
Republican —Herbert Hoover	15,758,901	59
Other Parties	1,153,306	--
		531

President defended his record. The depression, he argued, was the result of world economic forces over which he had no control. He was at least partially correct, but the voters had to blame someone. Hoover pointed to his efforts to combat the depression, such as the Reconstruction Finance Corporation. *Voters, however, could not understand why it was all right to give relief to banks and railroads but not to the unemployed.* People expressed their anger and resentment in bitter terms. The shantytowns, where victims of the depression lived, were named Hoovervilles, and the newspapers they used to cover themselves were dubbed Hoover blankets.

FRANKLIN DELANO ROOSEVELT. Hoover's opponent in 1932 was no stranger to politics. Franklin Roosevelt was a distant cousin of Theodore Roosevelt. He came from a wealthy, old New York family. Franklin's early career mirrored that of his cousin Theodore. He served as Assistant Secretary of the Navy under Wilson and was the Democrats' candidate for Vice-President in 1920. When still a young man, he was struck down by infantile paralysis, which left him partially paralyzed, unable to walk alone.

The illness interrupted Roosevelt's political career. But in 1928 he was persuaded to run for governor of New York, and he won the election. *In 1930 Roosevelt was the first state governor to call for massive public-relief measures.* New York's program became a model for those of other states. The Democratic party emphasized Hoover's failures on the issue of unemployment relief by making Roosevelt its nominee in 1932. In accepting the nomination, Roosevelt promised "a new deal for the American people."

Even usually Republican newspapers, such as the *Chicago Tribune,* supported Roosevelt. Roosevelt received 23 million popular votes to Hoover's 16 million. He carried 42 states and won 472 electoral votes to Hoover's 59. (See map at left.) Never had the Democrats won such a victory.

THE 20TH AND 21ST AMEND-MENTS. In 1933, as the nation wondered what the new President would do, the states ratified the 20th Amendment to the Constitution. *The 20th, or Lame Duck, Amendment moved the opening day of Congress and the President's inauguration day to January in order to retire lame duck Presidents and sessions of Congress.* Because certain members of Congress had been rejected by the voters—in other words, their wings had been clipped—they were called lame ducks.

Before 1933, sessions of Congress began in December, but new members did not take office until 13 months after their election. The newly elected President was not inaugurated until four months after his election, in March. Thus, if a person running for reelection had been defeated in November, he or she would continue to serve in an entire session of Congress before being replaced by the newly elected member. And the defeated President would serve for several months after having failed to be reelected.

In 1933 Congress proposed the 21st Amendment. It repealed the 18th Amendment, thereby abandoning the experiment at nationwide prohibition. One of the reasons that states ratified the amendment so quickly was that they hoped the manufacture of alcohol would help eliminate the grain surplus.

Section Review

1. Identify or explain: the Hawley-Smoot Tariff, Fiorello La Guardia, yellow-dog contract, the Bonus March, the 20th Amendment, the 21st Amendment, lame duck.
2. Describe the practices that weakened the stock market during the 1920's.
3. What measures did Hoover take to solve various problems associated with the depression?

2. The First New Deal, 1933-1934

ROOSEVELT TAKES OFFICE. It was a dark, gloomy day—March 4, 1933—when Franklin Delano Roosevelt took the oath of office. A banking crisis at the beginning of the year, resulting from panicky withdrawals of deposits, had caused many banks to close. And business could not function without the banks. The nation's economic machine seemed to be grinding to a halt. Fifteen million were unemployed. Some Americans feared that the hungry masses would revolt.

All the elements of the American creed—self-help, rugged individualism, and free enterprise—seemed to have failed. People were frightened. They looked to Washington for some word of hope. In his inaugural address the new President attempted to restore confidence. "This great nation will endure as it has endured," he said. "It will revive and will prosper. So, first of all, let me assert my firm belief that the only thing we have to fear is fear itself."

A FLEXIBLE, OPEN-MINDED EXECUTIVE. President Roosevelt had two great strengths—he was a superb public speaker, and he had a flexible mind. He was the first President to make use of radio as a means of communicating directly with the people. He established a series of informal evening broadcasts, which he called Fireside Chats, to explain government policies. He created the impression that the government cared and that it was doing something to combat the depression. He succeeded in gaining the confidence of the people.

Roosevelt had no ready-made cure for the depression. In fact, he entered office without a comprehensive program. But this in itself had certain advantages. A certain amount of experimentation was inevitable, and flexibility was Roosevelt's strong point. He was open-minded and willing to try new measures. "It is common sense," he told his associates, "to take a method and try it. If it fails, admit it frankly, and try another. But, above all, try something."

The New Deal was a period of experimentation. Some of Roosevelt's plans were unsuccessful, but many brought long-lasting benefits. Although modified, many of Roosevelt's programs endure today.

THE HUNDRED DAYS. The first New Deal was concerned mainly with recovery. A special session of Congress met from March to June 1933 to consider legislation that would pull the country out of its crisis. This three-month period is called the Hundred Days. During that short time, 15 bills were enacted by Congress.

THE BANKING CRISIS. *President Roosevelt's first task was to reopen the banks.* Two days after his inauguration, he closed every bank in the country by declaring a nationwide "bank holiday." He then authorized the Treasury to supervise the reopening of only those banks that were financially sound.

In a Fireside Chat he explained the government's moves and appealed for support. The plan was a success. Within days many of the banks reopened, and depositors returned. By April confidence was restored, and the crisis ended.

To prevent a recurrence of the panic, Congress created the Federal Deposit Insurance Corporation (FDIC).

The FDIC insured individual deposits up to 2,500 dollars. (In later years the amount was increased. Today it is 100,000 dollars.) People no longer needed to fear bank failures, for the government guaranteed that they could recover their funds.

EMERGENCY RELIEF. *Roosevelt's next important task was to find some way to provide relief for the millions of unemployed throughout the nation.* He suggested that the federal government make

FDR's fireside chats, which were informal explanations of policy, brought the President into the homes of America. They helped make Roosevelt a beloved father figure to many in the nation.

grants of money to the states. The grants were made through the Federal Emergency Relief Administration (FERA), which was established by Congress in 1933.

Under the direction of Roosevelt's friend Harry Hopkins, the FERA began work with a budget of 500 million dollars. In return for grants of money, Hopkins and his assistants demanded that the states establish high professional standards in their relief administrations. Hopkins set the standard by appointing to the FERA people with high qualifications without regard for the political party they belonged to.

ATTACKING THE DEPRESSION. In 1933 Congress established the Civil Works Administration (CWA). Roosevelt named Harry Hopkins to manage its programs. A former social worker, Hopkins believed that his primary task was to reduce hunger and distress. The CWA put four million jobless people directly on the federal payroll before it was ended by Congress early in 1934. *The President's frontal attack on the depression came in June 1933 with passage of the National Industrial Recovery Act (NIRA).* This act created two key agencies, the National Recovery Administration (NRA) and the Public Works Administration (PWA).

THE NATIONAL RECOVERY ACT.
The NRA was designed to enable industries to cooperate in finding jobs for the unemployed and to raise wages. It allowed the various companies in each industry to form agreements on prices and production. The purpose was to prevent cutthroat competition and to bring production in line with consumer demand. Such practices were forbidden by the antitrust laws. In order to permit such cooperation, the NIRA suspended the antitrust laws.

Companies entering into such agreements were required to permit their employees to form labor unions. Workers were guaranteed the right to bargain with their employers. They could not be forced by their employers to join specific unions.

The NRA never worked very well. When companies succeeded in restricting production and raising prices, consumers suffered. Small businesses objected to the NRA because they said it favored large corporations. And businesses, both large and small, disliked the regulations and paper work imposed by the NRA. Called by many the National Runaround, the NRA had lost its usefulness by the time the Supreme Court declared it unconstitutional in 1935. The agreements among business people, ruled the Court, were in effect laws. And Congress could not turn over its lawmaking authority to private enterprise.

THE PUBLIC WORKS ADMINISTRA-
TION. The other agency created by the Industrial Recovery Act was the Public Works Administration. *The PWA was given funds to undertake large-scale projects, such as public buildings, dams, and bridges.* By stimulating the construction industry, it helped reduce unemployment. The idea was a good one, but such projects took time to plan and did not give the economy the immediate boost it needed.

THE CIVILIAN CONSERVATION CORPS.
The longest lived, and one of the most useful of the New Deal's relief projects, was the Civilian Conservation Corps. This project was directed at one of the chief victims of the depression, the young. Unable to continue in school because their families could not afford the expense, many young people searched for jobs, swelling the ranks of the unemployed. Because they lacked experience, they were often the last hired and the first fired.

The Civilian Conservation Corps (CCC), created in March 1933, combined relief with conservation. It set up work camps in rural areas for young men between the ages of 18 and 25. There they labored on such projects as reforestation and improving wildlife habitats. They received 30 dollars a month plus clothing and food and the chance to learn technical skills. By 1940 the CCC employed about 2.25 million young men.

THE FARM PROBLEM.
The Agricultural Adjustment Act (AAA) of May 1933 authorized the Secretary of Agriculture to enter into agreements with farmers to limit production. It was hoped that this would raise prices. *The government reimbursed farmers for the lowered output. But it recovered this money by levying a tax on food processors such as canneries.*

By the time the act was passed, farmers had completed their planting. The Agriculture Department had to destroy the crops or wait a year until its restrictions could take effect. It chose to destroy crops immediately

THE FIRST NEW DEAL			
Name of Act or Agency	Some Provisions	Name of Act or Agency	Some Provisions
Emergency Banking Relief Act, 1933	Regulated banking transactions and the foreign exchange.	National Recovery Administration (NRA), 1933	Helped industry set up fair codes of cooperation; gave labor the right of collective bargaining.
Civilian Conservation Corps (CCC), 1933	Set up work camps for conservation.	Civil Works Administration (CWA), 1933	"Made" work for the unemployed.
Federal Emergency Relief Act (FERA), 1933	Federal money was given to states for direct relief.	Public Works Administration (PWA), 1933	Established public works projects to provide employment and increase business activity.
Agricultural Adjustment Act (AAA), 1933	Limited farm surplus by limiting production; set up banks to lend money at low interest rates.	Gold Reserve Act, 1934	Gave federal government control over devaluing the dollar.
Federal Deposit Insurance Corporation (FDIC), 1933	Insured bank deposits.	Securities and Exchange Commission (SEC), 1934	Set up commission to supervise stock exchanges.
Tennessee Valley Authority (TVA), 1933	Set up a publicly owned corporation to develop the resources of the area.	Reciprocal Trade Agreements Act, 1934	Gave President the power to bargain with other countries for mutual tariff reductions.
Federal Securities Act (Truth-in-Securities Act), 1933	Investors were able to get complete information about new securities.	Federal Housing Administration (FHA), 1934	Assured bank loans for construction and repair of houses.
Home Owners Loan Corporation (HOLC), 1933	Provided mortgage loans at low interest to non-farm homes.	Public Utilities Holding Company Act, 1935	Allowed only one level of holding companies in utilities.

in order to prevent more farm surpluses. Southern farmers were persuaded to plow under about four million hectares (10 million acres) of cotton. And in the Midwest, about six million pigs were slaughtered.

In 1936 the Supreme Court found some parts of the AAA unconstitutional. The altered act remained the government's basic farm policy.

CURRENCY DEPRECIATION. Despite all the administration's programs, the economy seemed as sick in the fall of 1933 as it had in 1930. *Roosevelt thus undertook an experiment—dollar depreciation.* In October he went on the air and explained this new policy in a Fireside Chat. Because of the decline in prices, he explained, the dollar had nearly doubled in purchasing power.

A small team of photographers took hundreds of thousands of photographs of rural America during the depression of the 1930's. This one of a migrant mother was taken by Dorothea Lange. Lange described her subject this way: "She sits under a shelter on the edge of the pea fields, with no work because the crop froze. On this morning the family sold the tires from their automobile for food."

If the dollar were reduced in value—by reducing the gold content, for instance—the dollar would buy less. In other words, prices would rise.

The Gold Reserve Act of January 1934 gave Roosevelt the authority he requested. To prevent people from hoarding gold or hiding it in foreign banks, American citizens were prohibited from possessing the metal. The government would keep gold on deposit at Fort Knox, Kentucky. But it would no longer exchange paper notes for gold. In 1900 Congress had fixed the value of the dollar at 25 grains of gold. Roosevelt reduced it to 15 grains, lowering the value of the dollar to 59.6 cents.

Of all the New Deal's experiments, currency manipulation is one of the most diffi- *cult to assess.* The economy improved to some extent over the next three years. But improvement probably resulted from the great number of things the government was doing. It cannot be said that devaluing the dollar increased prices. There is no way of knowing whether higher prices would have brought more production and employment. *The main thing the currency experiment proved was that the gold standard was not sacred.* The economy worked without it. The ghost of William Jennings Bryan could be laid to rest.

THE TENNESSEE VALLEY AUTHORITY. The Tennessee Valley Authority, or TVA, was an undeniable success. After the election of 1932, Roosevelt visited the Tennessee River valley. He was accompanied by George Norris, a long-time advocate of public power. Norris wanted the government to produce electric power to see if its costs were lower than the rates of private utilities. Roosevelt combined the idea of public power with the idea of rehabilitating an entire region of the country that had long been depressed by floods, erosion, and exhausted soil.

The Tennessee Valley Authority, created in May 1933, was a public corporation. It combined government resources with the flexibility of private industry. By damming the Tennessee River and its tributaries, the TVA furnished enough cheap power to an area covering about 64,000 kilometers (40,000 miles) in seven states. Investors and industry were attracted by cheap power. In addition, the TVA project provided flood control and other conservation projects. The production of inexpensive fertilizers restored worn-out farmland to production. In this way, one of the country's most poverty-stricken areas was aided.

By 1950 the TVA had invested a billion dollars of federal money. But the government had recovered at least that much from increased tax receipts in the region. *The TVA was one of the New Deal's most successful projects.*

REVIVAL OF PROGRESSIVISM. The first New Deal did not focus on reform. It was preoccupied with combating the depression. However, Congress did enact a few measures reminiscent of the Progressive administrations of Theodore Roosevelt

In 1934 a severe drought combined with unusually high winds. This produced the tragedy of the Dust Bowl, which affected huge sections of land in Kansas, Oklahoma, Texas, New Mexico, and Colorado. This Oklahoma farm was photographed by Arthur Rothstein in 1936.

and Woodrow Wilson. Among these was the regulation of the stock exchanges—institutions that had been under suspicion since the crash of 1929. In 1934 the Securities and Exchange Commission (SEC) was set up to oversee the stock exchanges and prevent dishonest practices.

In 1935, Congress passed the Public Utilities Holding Company Act. This act was a form of antitrust legislation. It prevented holding companies from acquiring other holding companies in the utilities field. The purpose was to forestall the creation of great holding company empires.

The most important of these "Wilsonian" reforms was tariff reduction. It was achieved in an imaginative way through the Trade Agreements Act of 1934. This act authorized the Secretary of State to enter into agreements with other countries for the mutual reduction of duties on selected items. Through international treaties the United States abolished protective barriers against specific American exports and foreign imports. The act remains the cornerstone of the nation's tariffs and trade policy.

Section Review

1. Identify or explain: the Hundred Days, Harry Hopkins, Fireside Chats, the Tennessee Valley Authority, the Gold Reserve Act.
2. Give full names and brief descriptions of the following: FDIC, FERA, CWA, NIRA, NRA, PWA, CCC, AAA.
3. Which two programs of the first New Deal were declared unconstitutional by the Supreme Court?

3. The Second New Deal, 1935-1938

CRITICS OF THE NEW DEAL. Americans were desperate when Franklin Roosevelt took office in March 1933. They were prepared to accept almost any remedy he proposed. The speed with which Congress moved and the volume of legislation enacted during the Hundred Days indicated general agreement that something had to be done.

By the end of 1933, however, criticism was beginning to mount. Right-wing critics accused Roosevelt of destroying free enterprise and undermining individualism. Business people grumbled about the fussy regulations of the NRA. Republicans worried about the massive powers the government was assuming. Even a number of Democrats became alarmed when Roosevelt devalued the dollar.

In 1934 these critics formed the Liberty League, an organization to help finance the election of anti-New Deal congressional candidates from both parties. Prominent among the League's members were the Democratic Presidential candidates of the 1920's, Alfred E. Smith and John W. Lewis.

ROOSEVELT'S TRANSFORMATION. The criticism surprised Roosevelt. Most of his programs were aimed at helping business. He had saved the banking system and, through the NRA, had given business virtual immunity from the antitrust laws.

Roosevelt had more or less ignored labor. But the attack from the right forced him to seek support elsewhere. And the labor movement was an obvious ally. At the same time, he thought it necessary to undercut the criticism of the radical left. Much of the reaction from the left came from those who believed the New Deal had not done enough for them. They wanted a larger piece of the economic pie.

Louisiana Senator Huey Long started a campaign to "share the wealth and make every man a king." Communists and Socialists claimed that capitalism had collapsed and called for a revolution to be waged with guns or ballots. By moving a bit to the left, Roosevelt hoped to take some of the steam out of these radical movements. *The result*

Not everyone loved FDR. As this cartoon illustrates, his name was virtually a dirty word in many homes.

"Mama, Wilfred wrote a bad word!"

was the development of a set of ideas that amounted to a second New Deal. As outlined in his State of the Union message to Congress in January 1935, Roosevelt's new program had three basic features—a massive, semipermanent relief program, social security, and labor legislation.

PRIMING THE PUMP. Most of the relief measures of the first New Deal were stopgaps. They were based on the assumption that the depression would soon end. In 1935 Roosevelt announced that temporary measures were not sufficient, that the nation could not expect an early end to the depression. A massive, semipermanent relief program was necessary, he declared. And it would be based on a new economic concept—the depression remedy proposed by the British economist John Maynard Keynes.

Depressions, argued Keynes, come about through a lack of confidence. People stop spending, and investors stop investing. The result is a downward spiral of falling prices, lowered production, and unemployment. *Keynes believed that the spiral could be reversed by government investment. Through deficit spending—deliberately unbalancing the budget—the government would "prime the pump."* By putting people to work on public projects, the government would put money in the hands of consumers, who would buy more goods. Prices would improve, businesses would invest in machines and factories, and unemployment would drop. The downward spiral would be reversed. That, at least, was the theory.

THE WORKS PROGRESS ADMINIS-TRATION. *Congress appropriated five billion dollars and created the Works Progress Administration (WPA) to administer the program.* Roosevelt placed Harry Hopkins in charge. Over the next six years, the WPA spent 11 billion dollars and put over three million men and women to work.

The WPA was accused of "make-work" projects, but much of what it did was immensely useful. It built or surfaced a good part of the nation's highway network, dredged rivers and harbors, and engaged in soil and water conservation. Eventually the WPA hired authors, teachers, actors, and painters. Its public records project—the collection and cataloging of early state records—has proved of lasting value to historians. One of its agencies, the National Youth Administration, provided part-time jobs that enabled young women and men to stay in school. To millions the WPA offered jobs, self-respect, and a stake in society.

On the other hand, deficit spending failed to cure the depression. In 1939, after four years of overspending, there were still nine million people out of work. The depression ended only with the coming of World War II. The employment of many people in the military services and the enormous production of goods necessary for the war effort restored prosperity.

SOCIAL SECURITY. *The Social Security Act of 1935 gave expression to ideas that reformers had recommended for years.* But it was a departure for Roosevelt, who had refused to support a social security scheme in 1934. The act created two programs. One was a form of direct relief, which provided payments to the unemployed for a certain number of days. The other was an insurance program for the aged. It set up a special fund independent of the government budget. Individual workers contributed to the fund through payroll taxes, and their contributions were matched by their employers. When the employee retired, he or she was entitled to monthly payments for life.

The old-age insurance program was something new in American life. Americans had always assumed that each individual was responsible for his or her own future, that each would provide for retirement with lifetime savings. With the Social Security Act, the government took over this responsibility. It obliged individuals to save and obliged employers to contribute to a retirement fund. It was the New Deal's most radical legislation. At first it applied only to workers on factory payrolls. But in later years it was expanded by both political parties to include all workers in the private sector, such as farmers, teachers, and the self-employed. Both of these programs are in effect today. They have helped thousands gain some financial security.

LABOR LEGISLATION. The Social Security Act helped further the political alliance between the New Deal and organized labor. Another act that favored labor was Roosevelt's approval of Senator Robert Wagner's bill to give government protection to the labor movement. After lying on the shelf for two years, the National Labor Relations Act, or Wagner-Connery Act, became law in 1935. *It created the National Labor Relations Board (NLRB) to protect the right of workers to organize.* The NLRB had power to supervise elections held to determine whether a union had won the right to serve as the collective bargaining agent for a company's employees. Management had to accept the results of the election. The NLRB prohibited unfair labor practices, such as dismissing an employee for joining a union.

ELECTION OF 1936. The liberal legislation of the second New Deal was designed to build a base of popular support among working people, the aged, the unemployed, and the rural poor. And it succeeded. Roosevelt was reelected in 1936 by the biggest margin in modern times. He defeated the Republican candidate, Alfred M. Landon, compiling 28 million votes to Landon's 17 million. Roosevelt carried every state except Maine and Vermont. He won 523 electoral votes to Landon's 8.

ROOSEVELT AND THE SUPREME COURT. *Strengthened by this popular endorsement, Roosevelt decided to combat his chief critic, the Supreme Court.* The Court had struck down both the NRA and the farm program. And it continued to obstruct state laws regulating labor conditions.

Roosevelt and his supporters objected to the Court's narrow view of the Constitution. The powers granted to Congress, they believed, were broad enough to cover the needs of modern times. By their rigid legalism the justices were thought to be in conflict with the elected representatives of the people. Part of the problem was that all the justices had been appointed by Republican Presidents.

In early 1937 Roosevelt asked Congress for authority to appoint an additional justice for each justice who remained on the Court past the age of 70 (six of the nine judges were over 70). The President argued that justices who remained on the bench beyond the normal retirement age in the private sector needed help in managing the Court's heavy load of cases. Critics quickly saw the

THE SECOND NEW DEAL	
Name of Act or Agency	**Some Provisions**
Works Progress Administration (WPA), 1935	Provided for large-scale national work programs.
Rural Electrification Administration (REA), 1935	Provided isolated rural areas with low-cost electricity.
National Youth Administration (NYA), 1935	Provided part-time work for needy students.
National Labor Relations Act (Wagner-Connery Act), 1935	Set up National Labor Relations Board (NLRB) to settle employer-employee differences.
Social Security Act, 1935	Provided unemployment compensation and set up a system of old-age insurance.
United States Housing Authority (USHA),1937	Federal loans to local agencies for slum clearance and housing projects.
Agricultural Adjustment Act (second AAA), 1938	Provided for government purchase and storage of farm surpluses to help maintain farmers' income.
Food, Drug, and Cosmetic Act, 1938	Required manufacturers of foods, drugs, and cosmetics to list products' ingredients.
Fair Labor Standards Act, 1938.	Set up minimum wages and hours for workers in interstate trade. Prohibited child labor under age 16.

President's move as an attempt to pack the Court with New Dealers. The public considered the proposal an attempt to tamper with one of the nation's most sacred institutions. Congress rejected the request.

THE JONES AND LAUGHLIN DECISION. The Supreme Court, however, got the message. Later that spring Chief Justice Charles Evans Hughes wrote the majority decision that reversed the position of the Court. The Court's decision in *Jones and Laughlin Steel* v. *NLRB* approved an important piece of legislation, the Wagner Act. The case involved the steel company's dismissal of a union organizer in violation of the National Labor Relations Act. The company claimed that the act was unconstitutional because manufacturing was not interstate commerce. And for that reason Congress could not regulate factories or their employees. But Chief Justice Hughes pointed to another aspect of Congress' power to regulate commerce. Since the Pullman strike of 1894, the government had repeatedly broken up strikes because they interfered with the flow of trade. The Wagner Act, said Hughes, was preventative. By outlawing unfair labor practices, the act tended to reduce labor strife and prevent obstructions of commerce. Under the commerce power Congress had the right to prevent obstructions. The act was constitutional.

The *Jones and Laughlin* decision forecast a shift in the Court's attitude toward the New Deal. More important was the death or retirement of several justices during the next few years. By 1941 Roosevelt replaced all but two of the original justices. *Appointees Hugo Black and Felix Frankfurter gave the Court a more liberal cast.*

FAIR LABOR STANDARDS. With the Supreme Court taking a more moderate stance, the administration rounded out its labor legislation. *The Fair Labor Standards Act of 1938 set minimum standards for all workers in interstate commerce.* The maximum work week was set at 44 hours, to be decreased to 40 by 1940. The minimum wage was set at 25 cents an hour, with an increase to 40 cents in 1945. The act also restricted child labor by excluding child-made goods from interstate shipment.

THE SECOND AGRICULTURAL ADJUSTMENT ACT. After the Supreme Court declared the AAA unconstitutional in 1935, the New Deal had to go back to work on its farm program. *The second Agricultural Adjustment Act of 1938 was more carefully drawn.* It contained a number of measures designed to cut back farm production without hurting small or tenant farmers. With the approval of two thirds of the farmers in an area, the Agriculture Department could set crop production quotas. That is, it could tell a farmer how much of a certain crop to grow for market.

The new law also provided for the storage of surplus crops. Thus, crops would not have to be destroyed as they had been in 1933. The farmer could then place the crop in storage until the price seemed right. In the meantime, the government would lend the farmer money for living expenses.

When was the price right? That was determined by a system known as parity, which means equality. *Parity was an attempt to give farmers the same purchasing power they had in the years 1909 to 1914, the last period of farm prosperity.* The average of farm prices in those years was used as the base. When current prices came close to the parity base, the farmer sold the stored crop and repaid the government loan. When the market price remained below parity, the farmer kept the loan and the government kept the crops.

The second farm program was better than the first, but some time passed before it was tested. Wartime demand raised food prices and brought unparalleled prosperity to farmers. Then bumper harvests in the postwar period created a huge surplus.

THE END OF REFORM. After a brief flirtation with recovery, the economy collapsed again in 1937. The stock market experienced another panic. Unemployment climbed once more. Congress appropriated funds to "prime the pump," but it was unwilling to undertake any experiments or approve new programs.

With the off-year congressional elections of 1938 approaching, Roosevelt decided to *purge* his party. His targets were conservative Democrats, many of them southerners. Singling out several by name, he asked the voters to defeat them in the primaries and elect representatives more friendly to the New Deal. This scheme backfired as badly as his "Court-packing" plan. All but one of Roosevelt's enemies were reelected. To add to his troubles, the Republicans made substantial gains.

A *purge* is designed to rid a party of its disloyal members.

Sensing the mood of the country, Roosevelt announced the end of reform in his annual message of early 1939. Existing programs would continue but nothing new would be started. Instead, he was much more concerned about the deteriorating world situation. China and Japan were at war. Germany had taken over Austria and was demanding portions of Czechoslovakia. The President thought it was time to arm the nation once again.

The arms buildup and the war, which began in Europe later that year, ended the depression. The general structure of the New Deal remained—labor legislation, the farm program, banking and securities reform, and old-age insurance established the political base for the next generation.

Section Review

1. Identify or explain: the Liberty League, Senator Robert Wagner, John Maynard Keynes, the Works Progress Administration, Alfred M. Landon, Charles Evans Hughes, parity.

2. List the three basic features of Roosevelt's second New Deal. Choose one feature and describe it in detail.
3. Explain the economic theory known as pump priming. How did the New Deal put this theory into practice?

4. The New Deal and People

THE FIRST LADY OF THE PEOPLE. President Roosevelt spoke often of his concern for the American people. Through his many programs of relief and regulation, he did his best to help them. But to many his administration was a confusing maze of alphabet agencies and officious bureaucrats.

More than anyone else, Eleanor Roosevelt, the President's wife, helped humanize the New Deal. Born a Roosevelt (she was the niece of ex-President Theodore), Eleanor Roosevelt devoted her energy, education, and talents to the welfare of "the ill-housed, ill-clad, and ill-nourished." In her travels around the nation, Eleanor Roosevelt gathered information about people's attitudes and emotions, information that the President could not obtain himself.

WOMEN AND THE NEW DEAL. Eleanor Roosevelt's active role encouraged other women to seek professional and government service. *Partly through her prodding, the President named Frances Perkins his Secretary of Labor in 1933.* She was the first woman to serve in a President's cabinet. Organized labor objected at first but soon grew to respect Perkins' abilities. She served longer than any other member of the administration.

ROOSEVELT AND BLACKS. Eleanor Roosevelt also helped persuade her husband to name Blacks to important positions in the government. *Mary McLeod Bethune was the first Black in history to become head of a government agency.* An educator who had helped found Bethune-Cookman College at Daytona Beach, Florida, Mary Bethune was named director of the Division of Negro Affairs of the National Youth Administration in 1936. The establishment of the agency was testimony to the new concern for the welfare of Blacks.

Blacks responded in kind. Ever since they won the vote after the Civil War, Blacks had voted for the party of Abraham Lincoln. Even in 1932, in the depths of the depression, most Blacks voted Republican. However, with the promise of the New Deal, they allied themselves with the Democratic party. This was largely due to Roosevelt's commitment to welfare programs and to the principles of equality. The Black vote has remained strongly Democratic since 1936.

BLACKS WORK FOR CIVIL RIGHTS. The atmosphere of official concern encouraged Blacks to renew their old struggle for social and political rights. They attempted to pool their talents and political power by forming organizations that would work for full citizenship. Some of these organizations remain active today. They have made possible major gains for Black Americans.

One of these organizations was the National Negro Congress. It was founded in 1935 to help promote the interests of Blacks within the many New Deal agencies. Another important organization, and one of the oldest dedicated to furthering the rights of Blacks, is the National Association for the Advancement of Colored People (NAACP), established in 1909. One of the main activities of the NAACP is to lobby for legislation that will "protect civil rights and bar racial discrimination."

In 1940 Blacks who thought that the NAACP had become too conservative founded the Congress of Racial Equality (CORE) to wage a more active assault on the barriers of discrimination. CORE was designed to carry out nonviolent direct action to end discrimination against Blacks. It conducted many such protests, including the Freedom Rides of 1961 that helped desegregate public places such as waiting rooms and restaurants.

Believing that Roosevelt was a friend, *many Blacks shifted allegiance from the Republican to the Democratic party.* The first Black Democrat to enter Congress was Reverend Adam Clayton Powell of New

Viewpoints of History

The New Deal

The stock market crash of 1929 brought great economic woes to the United States. In his acceptance speech before the 1932 Democratic convention, Franklin Delano Roosevelt pledged himself to "a new deal for the American people." He said that the main issue of the campaign would be the nation's economic depression, against which his administration would take direct and vigorous action.

Although the New Deal and its reforms won much support for Roosevelt, it evoked strong opposition. Some argued that the New Deal was moving the country toward socialism, whereas others said that it was far too conservative.

Robert L. Lund, writing in *Truth About the New Deal,* expressed the extreme view that the New Deal followed the communistic philosophy of Karl Marx.

"The present administration has in the so-called New Deal adopted the policies of the Socialist party. These policies follow very closely the communistic philosophy of Karl Marx. Shocking as this realization is to the American people, the fact remains that the New Deal is a dangerous and tragic error on the part of the administration—not because it is socialistic, but because it has failed and will continue to fail to bring both recovery and reemployment."

Taking the opposite view in his book *The Coming of the New Deal,* Arthur M. Schlesinger, Jr., stated that the New Deal restored faith in American democracy.

"It was hard to understate the need for action. It was now not just a matter of staving off hunger. It was a matter of seeing whether a representative democracy could conquer economic collapse. At the beginning of March, as Walter Lippmann summed up, the country was in such a state of confused desperation that it would have followed almost any leader anywhere he chose to go. In one week the nation, which had lost confidence in everything and everybody, had regained confidence in the government and in itself."

Frank Friedel viewed the New Deal sympathetically, but he maintained that it was a conservative reform movement.

"The fact was that Roosevelt and most of his contemporaries unquestioningly believed in the American free enterprise system. On the whole, they were suspicious of strong government and would indulge in it only as a last resort to try and save the system. On the other hand, part of their Progressive legacy was also a humanitarian belief in social justice. There were but few areas, such as old-age security, in which they believed that government must intervene to protect the individual."

In his book *Out of Our Past,* author Carl N. Degler stated that although Roosevelt was a conservative, the New Deal was a revolutionary movement, completely unlike anything America had ever seen before.

"Above all, Franklin Roosevelt understood the temper of his people. He did not shy away from new means and approaches to problems when circumstances demanded it.

"The conclusion seems inescapable that, traditional as the words may have been in which the New Deal expressed itself, in actuality it was a revolutionary situation. The searing ordeal of the Great Depression purged the American people of their belief in the limited powers of the federal government and convinced them of the necessity of the guarantor state."

In 1927, FDR founded the Warm Springs Foundation in Georgia to help victims of infantile paralysis. Here, President and Mrs. Roosevelt meet with children at Warm Springs.

York's Harlem district. Despite the administration's concern for Blacks, there were limitations to the New Deal's racial liberalism. One of the chief demands of Blacks in the 1930's was a federal antilynching law. Lynching—the killing of a suspect by a mob before he or she could be brought to trial—was illegal everywhere. But in some sections of the country, mobs sometimes got out of control. The number of lynchings had declined since the 1890's (when as many as 100 a year took place). But a dozen or so occurred every year during the 1930's.

By making lynching a federal crime, Blacks hoped to bring an end to it altogether. Liberal northerners introduced such a bill in 1938, but southerners staunchly opposed it. Roosevelt backed the idea at first. Then he dropped his support in order to get southern votes for his naval construction program. ***The bargain was one of the ways in which the coming war held back domestic reform.***

INDIANS AND THE NEW DEAL. A change in the laws concerning American Indians had been considered for some time. In 1928 an official investigation revealed serious flaws in the Dawes Act. The attempt to "Americanize" Indians was a failure. Those who took up farming often did not succeed, partly because they had no training and partly because the land given to them was poor. The reservations were little more than rural slums. And the schools provided by the government destroyed the tribal identity of Indian children without training them for White society.

605

To resolve some of these problems, Congress in 1934 passed the Indian Reorganization Act (also called the Howard-Wheeler Act). This law stopped the practice of breaking up reservations by giving land to individual Indians. It also permitted tribes to choose whether they would reestablish tribal governments, laws, and customs. Special schools were established for both adults and children. The schools emphasized vocational and agricultural training for those who wanted to work and live independently. They also taught cultural heritage and crafts. The act provided for increased medical care, training programs for farm practices, and conservation. It did not cure the poverty of the American Indian. But by restoring local control rather than control from Washington, it gave American Indians a voice in their own destiny.

THE RISE OF BIG LABOR. *Of all the segments of American society, none benefited more from the policies of the New Deal than organized labor.* Even before Roosevelt entered office, labor began to prosper.

The Norris-La Guardia Act of 1932 eliminated the legal restrictions on union activities. Through the NRA codes the government gave its blessing to unions, and with the Wagner Act of 1935 it set up a means to protect their rights. As a result, union membership shot up. Union leaders began to focus attention on the unorganized mass-production industries, such as steel and autos.

The American Federation of Labor (A. F. of L.), long dominated by trade unions of skilled workers, was critical of the mass unions, which were organized by factory rather than by occupation. In mass-production industries it was not possible to distinguish workers by craft. Organization of the industry as a whole was the only practical way. Yet A. F. of L. president William Green, successor to Samuel Gompers, re-

mained hostile to mass unions. He thought they were weak because unskilled workers lacked bargaining power. Despite his view, there were a few mass unions in the A. F. of L. Among the strongest was John L. Lewis' United Mine Workers.

THE BIRTH OF THE CIO. In November 1935 John L. Lewis and Sidney Hillman, president of the Amalgamated Clothing Workers, held a conference of industrial unions at Atlantic City, New Jersey. The purpose of the conference was to encourage further organization of the mass-production industries. Green of the A. F. of L. ordered the group to cease their activities. When they refused, he expelled them from the A. F. of L. *The mavericks then organized the Congress of Industrial Organizations (CIO) as a rival union.*

Even before the CIO was formed, mass-production unions decided to force the unions and the steel and auto industries to recognize their right to represent the workers. A majority of workers in both industries were union members. But they could not get company recognition. If the workers went on strike, the companies replaced them.

To overcome their weakness the auto workers came up with a strategy—the *sit-down strike.* It began at the Fisher Body plant in Cleveland in December 1936 and quickly spread to the General Motors assembly plant in Flint, Michigan. By occupying the plants instead of walking out, the union members prevented the company from hiring strikebreakers. If the company tried to throw them out, it risked destruction of the plant. When the governor of Michigan refused to interfere, General Motors surrendered.

Sit-down strikes are strikes in which workers sit by their machines, sometimes for days, refusing to work and preventing others from taking over their jobs.

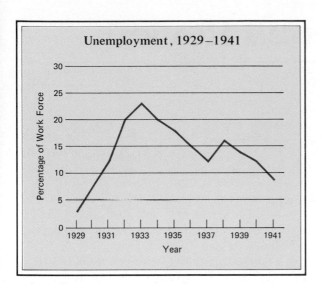

Unemployment, 1929–1941

Percentage of Work Force

30
25
20
15
10
5
0

1929 1931 1933 1935 1937 1939 1941

Year

In 1937 the steelworkers went on strike for union recognition. When the governor of Pennsylvania offered the services of the state relief agencies to the striking workers, U.S. Steel gave up. By 1941, when Henry Ford finally gave in, both the steel and auto industries were organized.

LABOR STRIFE. The stands taken by the governors of Michigan and Pennsylvania reflected the shift in public attitudes toward unions that had taken place since the 1920's. *Backed by a sympathetic public, organized labor made enormous gains during the 1930's.* By the end of the decade, the CIO had five million members and the A. F. of L. claimed four million. Big labor had emerged on the national scene.

And with it emerged problems. The CIO was a more militant organization than the A. F. of L. It was quicker to strike and more tolerant of violence. It also abandoned the A. F. of L.'s tradition of political neutrality. For instance, the CIO's Political Action Committee raised sizable campaign funds for the Democratic party. The rise of the CIO also created conflict within the labor movement. Rival unions fought for workers' loyalties. One unfortunate result of this ri-

valry was the jurisdictional strike. When a shop or a plant held an election, there might be two unions claiming to represent the employees. One might be affiliated with the A. F. of L., the other with the CIO. The losing union would then walk off the job, defending its claim that it had the right to enlist workers. The union strike was not against the employer but against the other union.

RISING PUBLIC CRITICISM. Such actions cost the labor movement much public support. By the end of the 1930's, the public was becoming increasingly critical of the New Deal in general. Government powers had been vastly expanded—some thought dangerously so—and government bureaucrats had a hand in almost every aspect of American life. By 1939 Congress was cutting drastically the budgets of such agencies as the WPA and the CCC. Public reaction was actually delayed by the war. But when it came in 1946, it went in two predictable directions—toward a reorganization of the government, with emphasis on economy and efficiency, and toward a restriction of the sometimes abused powers of big labor.

Section Review

1. Identify or explain: alphabet agencies, Frances Perkins, Mary McLeod Bethune, Adam Clayton Powell, lynching, the Indian Reorganization Act, John L. Lewis, big labor, sit-down strike, William Green, National Negro Congress.
2. What role did Eleanor Roosevelt play in the New Deal?
3. How did Roosevelt's administration show concern for Black Americans? For American Indians?
4. List three ways in which the American labor movement changed during the New Deal period.

Chapter 25 Review

Bird's-Eye View

On Thursday, October 24, 1929, the nation's stock market began the long downward slide that plunged the country into a deep and lasting depression. President Hoover took various measures to cope with the economic collapse. But because he could not accept the idea of massive government spending to alleviate the disastrous situation in which Americans found themselves, he was unable to rescue the nation. In 1932 voters expressed their dissatisfaction with Hoover and their eagerness for change by electing Franklin D. Roosevelt to the Presidency by an overwhelming margin.

Promising the American people "a new deal," Roosevelt initiated several government-sponsored experiments designed to put the nation back on its feet. Roosevelt's program had two phases—the first New Deal (1933–1934), which was concerned mainly with recovery, and the second New Deal (1935–1938), which involved more experimentation and the development of unusual methods to combat the depression. Some of the New Deal programs were unsuccessful, and some brought long-lasting benefits. In the long run, they had a profound impact on national life, for they redefined the responsibilities of government toward the individual and expanded the role of government in American life.

The New Deal ceased in 1938, when Roosevelt announced the end of domestic reform. Existing New Deal programs were carried on, but no experiments were begun. The nation turned its attention to the world scene, where deteriorating international relations threatened war.

During the New Deal period, the situation of four groups improved—women, Blacks, American Indians, and labor. For the first time in American history, a woman—Frances Perkins—was named to serve in a President's cabinet. Blacks were named to important positions in government, giving a boost to their fight for equal political and social rights. American Indians benefited when the Dawes Act was replaced by the Indian Reorganization Act of 1934. Labor unions increased their membership and expanded the scope of their activities.

By the end of the 1930's, the public was becoming increasingly critical of the New Deal. After World War II, criticism was turned into action as the government was reorganized, with an emphasis not on experimentation but on economy and efficiency.

Vocabulary

Define or identify each of the following:

foreclosure	yellow-dog contract	Frances Perkins
buying on margin	20th Amendment	deficit spending
Reconstruction Finance Corporation	the Hundred Days	sit-down strike

Review Questions

1. Summarize the economic conditions that led to the depression.
2. What did Hoover do to try to help people recover from the depression?
3. What was Franklin D. Roosevelt's attitude toward the depression?

4. What was the Tennessee Valley Authority experiment?
5. What was John Maynard Keynes's theory on ending a depression? How did Roosevelt use the basic Keynesian idea in the United States?
6. What was Roosevelt's political base of support in the 1936 election?
7. Why did Black voters support Roosevelt and shift to the Democratic party?
8. Why was the CIO established?

Reviewing Social Studies Skills

1. Using the maps on pages 434 and 588, complete the following:
   a. Did the number of states with fewer than 10 percent of tenant farmers increase or decrease between 1900 and 1930?
   b. Did the number of states with more than 50 percent of tenant farmers increase or decrease between 1900 and 1930?
   c. Name the five states that had the highest percentages of tenant farmers in 1900. In 1930.
   d. What was the percentage of tenant farmers in your state in 1900? In 1930?
   e. What general statement can be made about farm tenancy between 1900 and 1930?
2. Using the graph on page 607, complete the following:
   a. In what year did the highest rate of unemployment occur?
   b. What percentage of the work force was unemployed during the worst year of the depression?
   c. What was the percentage of unemployed at the start of the depression?
   d. What general conclusion can be drawn from the employment rate during the 1930's?
3. When historians analyze an event, they often present studies of cause and effect; that is, they conclude that factors, or causes, led to results, or effects. Using the information in Chapter 25, write a brief essay that analyzes the depression in cause-and-effect terms.

Reading for Meaning

1. The main character in Chapter 25 is Franklin D. Roosevelt. You have been given much information about Roosevelt, but nowhere have you been told what he valued. Using the information in the chapter, prepare a list of the values Franklin D. Roosevelt probably held. Cite evidence to support each value you list.
2. The New Deal established programs that expanded the role of the federal government in the lives of its citizens. Since that time the federal government has grown even larger. What areas of everyday life did the New Deal enter?

Bibliography

Studs Terkel, a newspaper reporter, recorded on tape the people's memories of the Great Depression, and he published their stories in *Hard Times* (Avon).

John Steinbeck's novel *The Grapes of Wrath* (Viking Press) is a fascinating fictional account of the "Okies" who moved from the "dust bowl" to California during the depression.

Chapter 26

1919-1941

"No, Sir! This is Pearl!"

The three men sat grimly in the office of the Secretary of the Navy. It was Sunday afternoon, December 7, 1941. The streets of Washington were quiet. Government offices were closed, except for the War and Navy Departments. Recent dispatches from Japan had brought the military heads back to work that Sunday.

The Navy Secretary was Frank Knox, a Republican who had been brought into President Roosevelt's cabinet in an effort to counter the opposition in the developing emergency. Across from him sat the Chief of Naval Operations, Admiral Harold E. Stark, and next to him his chief aide, Rear Admiral Richmond Kelly Turner. Earlier that day a decoding team, known as Magic, had intercepted a coded Japanese telegram. The Japanese government had instructed its ambassador in Washington to hand a highly important message to Secretary of State Cordell Hull at 1:00 P.M. Washington time.

Why on a Sunday? And why at that particular hour? A glance at the world time zone showed that 1:00 P.M. Washington time was midmorning on the West Coast, dawn in Hawaii, and midnight in the Philippines. Earlier messages intercepted and decoded by Magic indicated that the Japanese were preparing for war. A naval squadron, with transports carrying 25,000 men, was heading south from Japan. But where was it going? Japan already had a foothold in Indochina. Was it going to extend its reach into Malaya or the Dutch East Indies? Was it possible that the Japanese planned to start a war with the United States by striking at the Philippines?

Secretary Knox thought that Ambassador Nomura's message might contain clues to the answer. At 1:00 the Secretary received a phone call from the Japanese embassy: the ambassador was not ready. Could the meeting be postponed to 1:45? The three men sat back to wait. At 1:45—no ambassador. Secretary Knox decided to have lunch. Then at 1:50 a navy radio operator rushed in with a message from the Pacific:

From: Commander in Chief, Pacific Fleet
Action: Chief of Naval Operations, Washington
AIR RAID ON PEARL HARBOR. THIS IS NOT A DRILL.

Admiral Stark read the message and handed it to the Secretary. "This can't be true!" Knox exclaimed. "This must mean the Philippines!"

"No sir," said Stark. "This is Pearl!"

It was 1:50 P.M. in Washington and dawn in Hawaii. Japan had done an incredible thing. It had sent a squadron of aircraft carriers undetected across 6,400 kilometers (4,000 miles) of ocean to make a surprise attack on Pearl Harbor, the American naval base in the Hawaiian Islands and the headquarters of the Pacific Fleet. The act triggered a world war.

Chapter Objectives

After you have finished reading this chapter, you should be able to:
1. Describe the United States policy toward Japan, Europe, and Latin America in the 1920's and 1930's.
2. Explain Hitler's rise to power in Germany and Hitler's actions that led to war.
3. List the ways in which the United States helped the Allies before entering the war.
4. Analyze the reasons Japan decided to attack Pearl Harbor.

At the Versailles peace conference President Wilson had sought a "peace without victory" because he had believed that only such a peace—one among equals—could last. To achieve it Wilson worked tirelessly to fashion a treaty that would be fair and just rather than harsh and vengeful. Britain and France looked at the situation from different perspectives. They were bent on revenge. They thought that Germany should be punished for its role in World War I. Thus, the decisions made at Versailles to settle "the war to end all wars" created conditions that precipitated another war—one that would be fought not only on the battlefields of Europe but around the world.

1. A Policy of Limited Goals, 1919-1933

WAR DEBTS AND REPARATIONS. *The wartime years of 1914 to 1919 ushered in the United States' rise to economic dominance.* Foreign trade, industrial and agricultural production, and a high national income enabled the United States to achieve greater self-sufficiency than any other country.

The critical economic issue after the war involved the payment of the war debts owed by the Allies. The United States Treasury had loaned seven billion dollars to the Allies during the war and another three billion dollars afterward for the rebuilding of Europe.

Britain and France hoped that the United States would forgive their debts because of the Allies' joint war effort on the battlefields of Europe. But President Coolidge ignored their argument, noting, "They hired the money, didn't they?" Throughout the 1920's America insisted on the payment of war debts while maintaining tariff policies that made payment impossible.

Europe could meet its obligations if it could sell its goods to the United States. The American tariff barriers of the 1920's, the highest in the nation's history, kept European products out.

In 1921 an international commission set the fantastic amount of reparations Germany was to pay the Allies for war damages. The next year Britain announced that it could repay the United States only what it received from Germany as reparations. Germany had managed a few payments after the war. But the effort strained its economy and contributed to runaway inflation. Payments ceased by 1923.

It became clear that debts and the issue of German reparations were not separate. With the government's approval, American bankers helped the European countries reduce the reparations and establish schedules for payments. The final plan was drawn up by Owen D. Young and J. P. Morgan in 1929. The Germans were to pay approximately eight billion dollars over a period of 58½ years at 5½ percent interest. By 1986 the Germans would pay off their debt.

Despite the compromise and loans from American and European banks, the worldwide depression forced Germany to cease payments by 1930. Thus, the Allies could not meet payments on their war debts. In 1931 President Hoover proposed a one-year moratorium, or suspension, on the payment of both reparations and war debts. By that time Germany had ceased paying. After some token payments, so did the Allies. Of the 20 countries that had borrowed money from the United States during or after the war, only Finland paid its debt in full.

THE SEARCH FOR WORLD PEACE. The United States remained concerned about world peace, although it never joined the League of Nations. The Harding administration worried about Japan's military build-up and its expanding navy.

Under the leadership of Secretary of State Charles Evans Hughes, the Washington Naval Conference of 1922 drew up a treaty based on his proposal for an international agreement to prevent a naval armaments race. Five nations signed the treaty. They agreed to limit construction of battleships and aircraft carriers. The American and British fleets would be equal in size, and Japan's fleet would be three fifths as large as theirs. (The navies of France and Italy would be one third the size of the fleets of the two major powers.)

The idea of naval arms limitations had vast potential, but the reality proved disappointing. *Even though Japan's navy was so tiny that the agreement permitted it to build many ships, the Asian nation felt insulted by its inferior status.* When Japan reached the treaty's limits in 1934, it renounced the agreement and kept on building. At the outbreak of World War II, Japan had the world's most powerful navy.

THE KELLOGG-BRIAND PACT. *The search for peace also led to an effort to outlaw war.* In 1927 French Foreign Minister Aristide Briand (bree-AHN) proposed an agreement to the United States under which the two countries would pledge never to wage war. Frank B. Kellogg, Coolidge's Secretary of State, suggested that all countries be invited to participate. Eventually 62 nations, including Japan, Germany, and Italy, signed the Kellogg-Briand Pact of 1928, renouncing war as "an instrument of national policy."

Because there was no way to enforce this extraordinary pledge, it had no binding power on the nations that signed it. It became a symbol of the shallow optimism of the 1920's. In 1931, three years after the signing of the pact, the Japanese invaded Manchuria. And the world did nothing but reprimand the Japanese.

JAPAN'S RISING POWER. During the 1920's Japanese interests and investments focused on Manchuria, China's most economically advanced province. In 1911 a revolution overthrew the Manchu Dynasty and established the Chinese republic. The rebels soon fell to quarreling among themselves. In 1927 a revolution overthrew the republic which Sun Yat-sen (SOON yaht-SEN), the founder of modern China, had established in 1911. China dissolved into civil war between the Nationalists under Chiang Kai-shek (chee-AHNG kie-SHEHK) and the

The 1936 Olympics were held in Berlin. Hitler, anticipating easy victories for the German athletes, was eager to display his team. But Americans swept the track and field events. The worst blow was the success of the American Blacks, particularly that of Jesse Owens, who broke Olympic records in the 100- and 200-meter dashes and in the broad jump.

Communists led by Mao Tse-tung (MAH-oe dzuh-DOONG). Weakened by internal conflict, China could not resist Japanese advances. ***In 1931 the Japanese occupied Manchuria, declaring it to be an independent state.*** But the ruler of Manchukuo, as Manchuria was renamed in 1932, was nothing more than a puppet of the Japanese government.

America's position in Asia was threatened by the Manchurian crisis. Japan had violated the Open Door Policy by intruding on the territorial integrity of China. It had also broken the Covenant of the League of Nations and many of the nonaggression treaties signed after the war.

Hoover's Secretary of State, Henry L. Stimson, announced that the United States would not condone any actions that threatened the independence of any part of China. ***The Hoover-Stimson Doctrine of 1932 was an attempt to exert moral rather than economic or military pressure on Japan.***

The League of Nations, echoing Stimson's nonrecognition doctrine, failed to insure China's security or punish Japan's aggression. Japan realized that even with America taking the lead, the world powers would not band together to stop Japanese advances in Asia. Within a few years Japan renounced the disarmament treaties and withdrew from the League of Nations. The chain of events that would precipitate World War II had already begun.

RECOGNITION OF THE SOVIET UNION. When Roosevelt entered office in 1933, he immediately began a policy of world neighborliness. One of his first acts was to end the 16-year diplomatic boycott of the Soviet Union. Recognizing the government of the Soviet Union created a storm of

613

political controversy. Critics said Roosevelt should have consulted Congress. The Soviet Communist party, they pointed out, was committed to international revolution. Roosevelt met these arguments by getting the Soviets to promise that they would cease *propaganda* activities in the United States. The promise was not kept, however. And American-Soviet trading never flourished, as Roosevelt had hoped it would. Nevertheless, the United States was finally dealing with, rather than ignoring, a regime that had been in power for 16 years.

Propaganda is the spreading of ideas, information, or rumors to further a cause or to damage an opposing cause.

THE GOOD NEIGHBOR POLICY.

Unlike Roosevelt's foreign policy toward the Soviet Union, his approach toward Latin America was enormously popular and a great success. *His Good Neighbor Policy, built on the foundations laid by Coolidge and Hoover, was based on the concept that "the neighbor who resolutely respects himself . . . respects the rights of others."* This policy was the high point in relations between the United States and Latin America.

During the early 1900's, Presidents Theodore Roosevelt, Taft, and Wilson had used the Monroe Doctrine to justify United States intervention in Latin America. The United States claimed it had to protect its citizens and property, watch over the Panama Canal, and stop European influence in the Caribbean. A shift in attitude toward Latin America began in the 1920's. Coolidge quickly withdrew all but a small detachment of marines sent to Nicaragua in 1926 to protect American investments. In 1933 Hoover removed the remaining troops.

Between 1913 and 1916 Wilson twice sent troops into Mexico in unwelcome and unsuccessful attempts to help that nation achieve reform without revolution. In 1917 the new Mexican constitution required foreign investors to abide by Mexican laws. At the urging of Coolidge's ambassador to Mexico, Dwight L. Morrow, Mexico revised its laws on foreign investments and adjusted the claims of American business interests.

Morrow's victory in Mexico benefited both Coolidge and Hoover, who made great efforts to improve relations between the United States and its southern neighbors. *In 1930 the State Department announced that the Roosevelt Corollary to the Monroe Doctrine would no longer be used to justify American intervention in Latin American domestic affairs.*

Roosevelt's Good Neighbor Policy was the climax of the friendly policy toward Latin America that had been begun by his predecessors. At a 1933 conference in Montevideo (mahn-tuh-vuh-DAY-oe), Uruguay (YOO-ruh-gwie), the United States and the other American nations of the Western Hemisphere pledged that they would not intervene in the internal or external affairs of another state. The United States soon carried out the pledge by removing its troops from Haiti. In 1934 the United States and Cuba agreed to a revision of the Platt Amendment. The United States abandoned its 33-year-old right to intervene in Cuban affairs. In 1936 the United States reached a similar agreement with Panama.

The Montevideo pledge was a major turning point in American diplomacy. "The definite policy of the United States from now on," said Roosevelt, "is one opposed to armed intervention." He was as good as his word. In 1938 the Mexican government confiscated the properties of all foreign oil companies. Roosevelt refused to intervene and suggested that American companies negotiate with the Mexican government. They did, and they won compensation for their losses. Cooperation rather than coercion guided the Good Neighbor Policy.

Section Review

1. **Mapping:** Using a map of the world, identify the peninsula closest to each of the following: **a)** the European nation that paid off its war debt to the United States; **b)** the Latin American nation to which Coolidge sent marines in 1926; **c)** the part of China that was invaded by Japan in 1931.
2. **Identify or explain:** reparations, Owen D. Young, Frank B. Kellogg, Chiang Kai-shek, Mao Tse-tung, Hoover-Stimson Doctrine.
3. What agreements were reached at the Washington Naval Conference of 1922? How did Japan respond to the treaty?
4. Why do the authors call the Montevideo pledge "a major turning point in American diplomacy"?

2. Dictators Menace World Peace, 1933-1939

HITLER COMES TO POWER. A few weeks before President Roosevelt took office, the last free election in Germany led to the appointment of Adolf Hitler as chancellor. Hitler's National Socialist (Nazi) party promised to tear up the Versailles Treaty—a "dictated peace," in his opinion—and restore Germany to its former position of leadership in Europe.

Hitler gained support by exploiting the disorder and political turmoil that had disrupted Germany during the Great Depression. Furthermore, he fed on people's fears and frustrations, singling out Jews and minorities as scapegoats. On the other hand, Hitler's Nazism rekindled the Germans' sense of historical pride and military tradition. It also reminded them of Germany's vast economic potential. The magnetic appeal of the Austrian-born *dictator,* coupled with his ruthless *fanaticism,* enabled him

to consolidate his power within a year. He jailed and executed opponents as he began rearming Germany.

A *dictator* is a ruler who governs with absolute power, often brutally and oppressively. *Fanaticism* is excessively enthusiastic and intense behavior.

THE AXIS POWERS. With the exception of Italy, the other countries of Europe were preoccupied with their own economic troubles and were indifferent to the rise of Hitler. Only Italy, under the dictatorship of Benito Mussolini (1922–1943), did not

This poster for Hitler's National Student Organization glorifies the Nordic qualities of the German people. The caption reads, "The German student fights for leader and land."

underestimate the fanaticism and determination of the führer (leader) to conquer all of Europe. Mussolini had seized power in 1922, promising to restore the ancient glory of Italy with his Fascist party rule.

Given Italy's weak economic position, Mussolini knew that the future he had pledged lay in allying himself with Hitler. Mussolini predicted that Europe would some day be dominated by the "Rome–Berlin axis" upon which the world would turn thereafter. The glorified military state was the basis of the dictatorships of Hitler and Mussolini. German and Italian *fascism* worked on the assumption that the state could grant or deny rights to individuals, whose only purpose was to serve the state. A formal military alliance between the two dictators was only a matter of time.

Fascism is a political philosophy, movement, or government that exalts nation and race. It is based on a system of centralized dictatorial rule that imposes severe economic and social standards and suppresses opposition.

Mussolini moved first. In October 1935 his armies attacked the defenseless kingdom of Ethiopia on the northeast coast of Africa in the hope of amassing a great African empire. (See map, page 622.) As in the case of Manchuria, the League of Nations protested but had no political power to intervene. Also in October, Germany and Italy signed a formal alliance, calling themselves the *Axis powers.*

The *Axis powers* got their name from Mussolini's statement about the "Rome–Berlin" axis. Eventually Japan became a member of the Axis powers. The nations that opposed the Axis powers were known as the Allies.

In March 1936 Hitler sent German troops into the Rhineland, the part of western Germany that had been declared a neutral

buffer zone under the Versailles Treaty. (See map, page 622.) In July of that year, the Fascist leader General Francisco Franco started a revolution against the republican government in Spain. The Axis powers immediately shipped arms to Franco.

AMERICAN ISOLATIONISM. *Despite this mounting threat to peace, American opinion remained firmly isolationist.* The public wanted the government to tackle only the nation's problems, not those of the world. Disillusionment with the outcome of World War I remained strong. People believed that the war had not brought peace, disarmament, or democracy. In 1934 *Fortune* magazine gave the isolationists plenty of ammunition. An article entitled "Merchants of Death" sought to demonstrate that bankers' loans to the Allies and arms manufacturers had increased production and pulled the United States into World War I. A Senate committee, headed by Gerald P. Nye of North Dakota, investigated those claims and found that the Morgan loans had given the United States a strong stake in an Allied victory. Many people concluded that the country had gone to war to protect its investment.

THE NEUTRALITY ACTS, 1935–1937. Between 1935 and 1937, Congress passed several neutrality acts to prevent the United States from becoming involved in foreign wars. *These acts gave the President power to impose an arms embargo "whenever he shall find that there exists a war."* Thus, if the President chose not to "find" a war, arms shipments would not be restricted. Nations at war had to pay cash for any goods bought in the United States and carry them abroad in their own ships. The acts also prohibited American citizens from traveling on the vessels of warring nations.

The isolationists' position was strengthened by those who thought that the battle against the Great Depression should be America's only war in the 1930's and by pacifists, who opposed war on any grounds. Interventionists, however, argued that fascism was denying people the rights for which World War I had been fought. They believed that it was a moral duty of Americans to aid the victims of *totalitarian*

Sidenote to History

Amelia Earhart: First Woman of the Air

Amelia Earhart was 19 when America entered World War I. The romantic exploits of the Royal Flying Corps and the Eagle Squadron caught her imagination. Airplanes were still a novelty in the 1920's. Barnstorming, or traveling, air shows featured stunts and acts of daring, attracting crowds to dusty runways across the land. Commercial air service was in its infancy. People loved to watch the shows but were afraid to fly.

Earhart's opportunity to become the first woman to fly the Atlantic came as a result of another woman flier's ambition. Inspired by Lindbergh's transatlantic flight, Amy Phipps Guest had purchased a three-seater plane and chosen two pilots when her family rejected the daring plan. Amelia Earhart was asked to take her place. The threesome took off from Newfoundland on June 17, 1928, landing in Britain 20 hours and 40 minutes later.

Although Earhart's only role was to keep the log of the journey—a point she never failed to stress—the voyage brought her international fame. Young women, searching for more active roles in the 1920's, made her a hero. The older generation was attracted to her conservative dress, unaffected manners, and wholesome way of life. Unassuming and attractive, her tall frame was topped by a shock of blond hair.

Amelia Earhart reminded everyone of Charles Lindbergh, who had made the first transatlantic flight.

She described her flight in *20 Hrs., 40 Min.* Other books followed. She had never really been satisfied with her limited role in that first flight. In 1932, Earhart crossed the Atlantic again—the first woman to fly the Atlantic alone.

In 1937 she decided to take a trip around the world, working in collaboration with Purdue University, which furnished the airplane. The purpose was not to set a speed record but to study the performance of both aircraft and humans at high altitudes and over long distances. On June 1 she and her copilot flew east from Miami, Florida, to the coast of Africa. For a month they flew over jungles, deserts, and oceans. On July 2 they were ready for the last and most difficult leg of the journey. Between Lae, New Guinea, and Hawaii there was only one stopping place—tiny Howland Island in the mid-Pacific. Only under perfect weather conditions would her Lockheed Electra have enough gasoline to fly the 4,090 kilometers (2,556 miles). Amelia Earhart was never seen again. A coast guard cutter stationed off Howland received some garbled radio messages that fuel was running low and no land was in sight. Then there was silence.

Unwilling to believe that she had perished, many Americans thought she probably had landed on a Japanese-held island in the Pacific. Rumors that the Japanese were holding her prisoner, possibly for ransom, were circulated throughout World War II. But at the end of the war it was learned that the Japanese knew nothing of her.

Here, Adolf Hitler and Benito Mussolini meet in Munich in 1938. Two years before, they had formed the Axis alliance. By 1939 they had changed the name to the Pact of Steel. What does this new name tell you about the ambitions of the two leaders?

aggression. Such aid, they pointed out, was being held back by the isolationist Neutrality Acts.

Totalitarian is a system of government in which the individual serves the state that controls all aspects of life.

CHINA IS ATTACKED. The new laws were tested almost immediately. ***In July 1937 Japan opened a full-scale war against China, bombing cities and occupying the coastal provinces.*** Nationalists and Communists in China called a truce in their civil war so that they could fight the common enemy. But they were no match for the airborne Japanese. President Roosevelt, failing to "find" this war, did not have to impose an embargo. The United States supplied China with arms shipments as well as volunteers for the Chinese Army.

QUARANTINE FOR THE DICTATORS. In October 1937 Roosevelt first alerted the American people to the growing danger. Noting that "an epidemic of world lawlessness" was spreading, he suggested that the aggressor nations ought to be isolated in the same way a community quarantines persons with infectious diseases. Should aggression triumph in Europe and Asia, Roosevelt warned the isolationists, "let no one imagine that America will escape." The public listened and applauded and went back to work. Congress narrowly approved his request for funds to begin a shipbuilding program.

Two months later Japanese planes attacked a United States gunboat, the *Panay,* and three American oil tankers on the Yangtze River, in China. (See map, page 527.) But even the *Panay* incident did not deter the advocates of American isolationism.

THE MASTER RACE. As Hitler consolidated his power, he demonstrated that he was more than a German nationalist trying to unravel the Versailles Treaty. Prison camps housed thousands of his political opponents. *Near the end of 1938, Nazi storm troopers began systematically identifying German Jews. They were prohibited from working, and forced to close their businesses.* Many Jews became prisoners in their own homes.

Hitler's Germany was not the only western nation to breed religious and racial bigotry in the period between the wars. In the Soviet Union and in parts of Eastern Europe there were periodic massacres ("pogroms") of Jewish communities. Germany, however, was the only country to make racism part of the philosophy of government. The Nazis believed that they belonged to a "master race" that was destined to rule others. Among the "biologically inferior" whom the Nazis disdained were Jews, gypsies, and the Slavic nationalities of Eastern Europe.

THE MUNICH SETTLEMENT. In March 1938 Hitler forced the resignation of the Austrian government, placing that country under the control of the Nazis. (See map, page 622.) About 76,000 Austrians were arrested by Hitler's secret police, the Gestapo.

After his Austrian victory, Hitler demanded the Sudetenland (soo-DAY-t'n-land), a strip of western Czechoslovakia inhabited by German-speaking people. Neither Britain nor France was prepared to fight a war for Czechoslovakia. The French and British heads of government flew to Munich, Germany, in September 1938 to talk to Hitler and Mussolini. Hitler assured them that he was only trying to recover land that had once been German and that he had no designs on the rest of Czechoslovakia. The British and French leaders accepted his explanation, thinking that this last morsel of territory might appease Hitler's appetite. British Prime Minister Neville Chamberlain flew back to London announcing that he had brought the world "peace in our time."

By allowing Hitler to seize the Sudetenland, Britain and France had demonstrated to Hitler that they had little interest in Czechoslovakia. Hitler waited six months. His armies swallowed up the rest of Czechoslovakia in March 1939. A month later Mussolini took over Albania. Appeasement failed. Another world war was inevitable.

THE NAZI-SOVIET PACT. The fall of Czechoslovakia triggered diplomatic activity. *Fearful that Hitler would soon devour Poland, Britain and France quietly signed a treaty guaranteeing the integrity of Poland.* Meanwhile, Nazi Germany entered into a nonaggression pact with the Soviet Union. Each country agreed not to attack the other. In addition, a secret clause gave the Soviet Union the right to occupy the Baltic States of Estonia, Latvia, and Lithuania, as well as a slice of Poland. (See map, page 622.) *The Nazi-Soviet pact was signed on August 23, 1939.* No longer fearing a two-front war, Hitler sent his armies across the Polish frontier on September 1. Two days later, on September 3, Britain and France honored their pledge to Poland and declared war on Germany. World War II had begun. Americans watched anxiously, but few were willing to go "over there" again.

Section Review

1. Mapping: Using the maps on pages 543 and 557, compare Germany before and after World War I. Why do you think Germany seized the Sudetenland?

2. Identify or explain: the Axis powers, General Francisco Franco, Gerald P. Nye, the *Panay* incident, "peace in our time," the Munich settlement, the Nazi-Soviet pact.
3. Why did the United States take a neutral, even isolationist, position in foreign affairs during the 1930's? What steps did Congress take to legislate neutrality between 1935 and 1937?
4. How do the authors explain Hitler's rise to power in Germany during the 1930's? Can a similar explanation be given for Mussolini's rise to power in Italy?

3. America-Arsenal of Democracy

PREPARATION FOR WAR. As Hitler had predicted correctly, Britain and France could do little to help Poland. Ill-equipped Polish armies put up a spirited defense, but by midwinter Poland had disappeared once again from the map of Europe. It was divided between Nazi Germany and Communist Russia.

Britain landed an army in France, and the two allies prepared to fight the trench stalemate of World War I. They reinforced France's Maginot (MAZH-uh-NOH) Line, a chain of concrete forts along the German frontier, and waited for Hitler to attack.

BLITZKRIEG. German generals had developed an effective method of attack—lightning warfare, or, in German, *blitzkrieg* (BLITZ-kreeg). Dive bombers in the air, combined with tanks and mounted artillery on the ground, concentrated intense fire on one section of the enemy line. The German infantry then rolled through the break in the enemy line and conquered the territory. *Europe fell to the German blitzkrieg within two months.* (See map, page 622.) The spring of 1940 brought good weather

for air and ground operations and for Hitler's armies.

In April 1940 German paratroops descended on Denmark and Norway, seizing governments that had hoped to remain neutral. German panzer (armored) divisions swept through the Low Countries around the Maginot Line and into northern France. Mussolini, hoping to gain a seat at the peace table, declared war and attacked France from the rear. France yielded in June. Hitler got the northern half of the country and the promise that the French military ruler in the southern half would remain neutral.

Trapped at the Channel port of Dunkirk (DUN-kerk), the British Army carried out a desperate and daring evacuation of personnel and war equipment by motor launch and fishing craft. In the next few months, German and Italian armies swept across southern Europe as far as Greece, on the eastern Mediterranean.

THE BATTLE OF BRITAIN. Britain's position in western Europe was grim. It stood alone, surrounded by Axis-controlled countries or countries that remained neutral—Sweden, Finland, Switzerland, and Spain. Britain had no land defenses, and Hitler's bombers controlled the English Channel.

Nothing stood in Hitler's way but the Royal Air Force (RAF), which was hopelessly outnumbered. Through the summer and fall of 1940, Hitler's air force, the *Luftwaffe* (LOOFT-vah-fuh), pounded Britain, blasting both civilian and military targets. The new prime minister, Winston Churchill, was a dynamic leader who declared that Britain would not surrender. "Hitler knows that he will have to break us in this island," Churchill announced, "or lose the war." In tests of courage and skill reminiscent of the wooden ship duels of centuries ago, the RAF fought back. The British held on. "Never in the field of human conflict," Churchill said, in his tribute to the

RAF, "was so much owed by so many to so few."

In October Hitler was informed by his military advisers that an invasion of Britain would fail, so he postponed his plans till spring.

AMERICANS CHOOSE SIDES. *Americans sided with the Allies from the beginning of the war.* A *Gallup* Poll in early 1940 showed 84 percent favoring the Allies and a mere two percent supporting the Axis powers. But 64 percent preferred peace to intervention.

The Gallup Poll was started in 1935 by George Harris *Gallup.* He used market research methods to study public opinion on social and political issues.

President Roosevelt had been in advance of public opinion for some time. Even if the Axis powers did not attack the Western Hemisphere, he feared they would close down world markets and strangle the American economy. Therefore, Roosevelt thought that the nation had to send aid to Britain and rearm itself.

At the end of 1939, the President persuaded Congress to alter the neutrality laws to enable munitions makers to sell arms to the Allies. The cash-and-carry feature of earlier laws was continued. Germany's blitzkrieg increased Roosevelt's sense of urgency. He agreed to Churchill's request of August 1940 for the loan of 50 American *destroyers.*

Destroyers were comparatively small warships used for patrols and in convoys to protect larger ships from submarine attacks. Larger attack vessels were called cruisers; the biggest warships were battleships and aircraft carriers.

In return, America got long-term leases on British bases, from Newfoundland to the

During the Battle of Britain, the Germans bombed the civilian population of London. St. Paul's cathedral is in the background.

Caribbean. Although he considered the agreement a good bargain for the United States, Roosevelt made it without consulting Congress. *In effect, he had ended the policy of neutrality, committing the country to the British cause.*

DEFENSE OF THE WESTERN HEMISPHERE. While Roosevelt was trying to work out a way to help the Allies in Europe, he was devoting time to the problem of

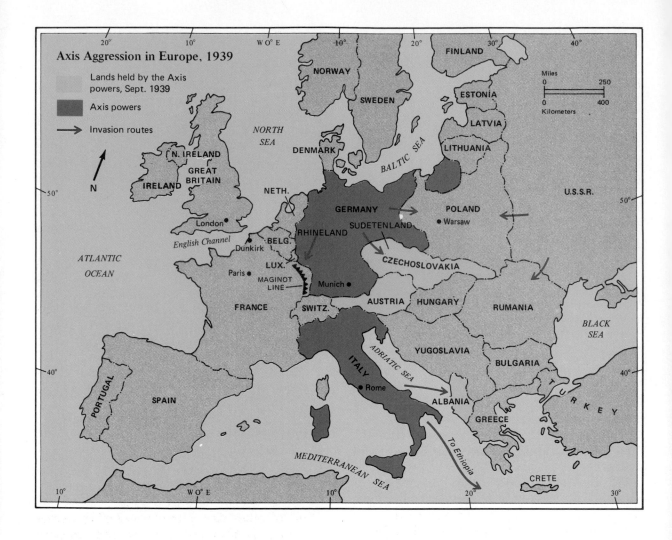

Axis Aggression in Europe, 1939

Lands held by the Axis
powers, Sept. 1939

Axis powers

Invasion routes

hemispheric defense. ***In October 1939 the
United States joined with other nations of
the hemisphere to proclaim the Declaration of Panama.*** The declaration, drawn up
by delegates at a meeting of the Pan-
American Union in Panama City, established a safety zone around the Americas
from which other warring nations were
barred. Germany, Great Britain, and France
questioned the validity of the declaration,
maintaining that no nation had the right to
cut off access to any part of the ocean. Despite this technical objection, the declaration was important as a forceful statement of
inter-American cooperation.

In July 1940 the Pan-American Union
served a second notice on non-American
nations of its intention to defend the Western Hemisphere. The Act of Havana and the
Convention of Havana were the results of
the meeting of Secretary of State Cordell
Hull with the foreign ministers of Latin
America. They stated that an attack on one
American state by a non-American power
would be considered an attack on all the nations of the Americas.

The value of these proclamations of cooperation and solidarity was not immediately
apparent. However, it became very clear
after December 1941, when the United

States found itself fighting a two-front war in Asia and Europe. The nations of the Western Hemisphere joined the Allied camp.

THE ELECTION OF 1940. *The question of neutrality dominated the Presidential election of 1940.* The America First Committee, formed by midwesterners opposed to intervention, had strong support among Republicans. They believed that intervention conflicted with the national interest. Among the committee's most effective speakers was the aviation hero, Charles A. Lindbergh. The Republicans agreed with the Democrats that it was necessary to build up the American military. The Republicans finally nominated Wendell Willkie of Indiana. Although he was a very able leader, Willkie offered no real alternative to Roosevelt.

The chief criticism of Roosevelt's candidacy was that it broke the tradition that Presidents served only two terms. For years Republicans had accused Roosevelt of using high-handed, dictatorial methods. His effort to continue in power seemed to support their claim. Even labor leader John L. Lewis broke with Roosevelt and supported Willkie.

When criticized for giving aid to the Allies, Roosevelt agreed with his opponent that active intervention in the war was unthinkable. "Your boys are not going to be sent into any foreign wars," he told a Boston audience. The public agreed with him that the United States ought to be able to defend itself against attack.

During the election campaign, Congress established a selective service system at the request of the President. *Although it was the first peacetime draft in American history,* there was scarcely a murmur of protest. Roosevelt had won the people's trust, even though he never took them into his confidence by informing them about the world situation. He was reelected by a large electoral majority, becoming the only President to serve a third term. (See map at left.)

LEND-LEASE. In the wake of the election, a Gallup poll reported that 50 percent of Americans favored all-out aid to the Allies, short of open war. *Hitler's growing persecution of Jews and his unceasing appetite for conquest made neutrality seem increasingly immoral.* As always, Roosevelt was in the forefront of this shift in public opinion. In December 1940, in a Fireside Chat, he explained the need to lend Britain war materials without demanding payment. Britain could no longer afford a cash-and-carry deal. The President promised to make the United States "the arsenal of democracy."

Some people argued that Roosevelt's lend-lease proposal would enable America to avoid full-fledged participation in the war. Others said that it was the next step toward involving the United States in a war. *In*

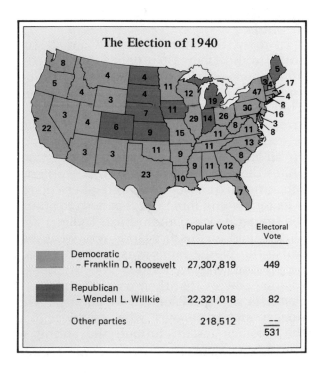

The Election of 1940

	Popular Vote	Electoral Vote
Democratic – Franklin D. Roosevelt	27,307,819	449
Republican – Wendell L. Willkie	22,321,018	82
Other parties	218,512	--
		531

spite of all objections, Congress passed the Lend-Lease Act in March 1941. It authorized the President to lend American military equipment to Britain and the other Allies. These included the Free French forces under General Charles de Gaulle, who had fled to Britain after the fall of France. Within 15 months approximately 30 billion dollars worth of supplies were shipped abroad, more than the New Deal had spent on all its relief programs.

ABANDONING NEUTRALITY. Once the Lend-Lease Act had been passed, America was involved in the war except for the commitment of troops. By the summer of 1941, American naval vessels were helping *convoy* supply ships across the Atlantic, while American troops occupied the Danish colonies of Greenland and Iceland to keep them out of German hands.

To *convoy* means to form a protective escort for ships, persons, or goods.

When Hitler attacked the Soviet Union in June 1941, violating their nonaggression agreement, the United States extended lend-lease to the Russians. Germany tolerated these actions in order to avoid all-out war with the United States. Hitler issued orders to his submarine commanders not to sink American vessels. This situation might have been prolonged indefinitely as long as Britain and the Soviet Union held out. But United States policy toward Asia turned the tide, bringing America into a full-scale world war.

Section Review

1. Mapping: Using a map of the world, explain, in terms of geography, why the German occupation of northern France, the Low Countries, Norway, and Denmark posed such a threat to Great Britain.

2. Identify or explain: blitzkrieg, Dunkirk, the *Luftwaffe*, the America First Committee, the Maginot Line, Winston Churchill, Wendell Willkie, lend-lease.
3. Why was the election of 1940 different from any other Presidential election?
4. Briefly describe America's plans for defense of the Western Hemisphere.

4. The Road to Pearl Harbor

THE OPEN DOOR IN CHINA. In 1938 Japanese prime minister Prince Konoye announced the formation of the Greater East Asia Coprosperity Sphere. It was a trading cooperative that included China, Manchukuo, and the Japanese possessions in the Pacific. Japan claimed that its position in Asia was like the United States position in the Western Hemisphere. Japan argued that it had as much right to dominate Asia as the United States had to dominate the Western Hemisphere. Japan added that such a move would help check the spread of communism in China.

In reply, Secretary of State Cordell Hull stuck to the Open Door policy. *The United States opposed the dismembering of China and could not tolerate armed aggression.* The Roosevelt administration gave what arms it could to Chiang Kai-shek, who had retreated into the interior. Meanwhile, it cut off all military sales to Japan. The United States did not stop exporting the two items Japan needed most—steel and oil. To do so, it feared, would force the Japanese to attack the mineral-rich Dutch East Indies. The Dutch hold on these islands was weak because the Netherlands was under German occupation. Japan warned the European colonial powers that their empires in Southeast Asia and the Pacific were doomed. The uneasy stalemate over who would control the colonies lasted through the spring of 1941.

Sidenote to History

First in Peace: Representative Jeannette Rankin

Montana granted women the vote in 1914, six years before the women's suffrage amendment went into effect. In 1916 Jeannette Rankin was elected to the House of Representatives. She was the first woman to serve in Congress. On April 6, 1917, four days after she had been sworn into office, the House voted on President Woodrow Wilson's request for a declaration of war on Germany. "I want to stand by my country," she told the House, "but I cannot vote for war."

Not only was Rankin personally opposed to the war, but she also believed that the people in Montana were overwhelmingly against the war. Voting with her were fifty-six other members of Congress, most of them from the Mid-west. Whatever they had thought about the war before it had started, Montanans came to support it—and Rankin was not reelected.

During the 1920's and 1930's, Rankin worked with women's rights groups and a pacifist organization, the National Council for the Prevention of War. In 1940 when war with Germany again loomed, Rankin again won a seat in Congress. She fought the Roosevelt administration's efforts to arm the country, and on December 8, 1941, the day after the Japanese attack on Pearl Harbor, she again voted against a declaration of war. This time she was the only member of the House to oppose the war. She was the only member of Congress to have voted against American entry into both world wars.

In the 1950's Rankin spoke as a private citizen against the Cold War, and in the 1960's she was prominent in her opposition to the Vietnam War. Only failing health prevented her from running for a third antiwar term in Congress in 1968. Even those who disagreed with her admired her consistent pursuit of peace.

INDOCHINA IS INVADED. Then in June Japanese troops landed in the French colony of Indochina. (See map, page 635.) Although the pro-German Vichy (VEE-shee) government in unoccupied southern France approved the invasion, the United States considered it a threat to peace. Indochina's main product was rubber, an item crucial to the military. Moreover, possession of the peninsula would enable Japan to menace the East Indies to the south or Burma and India to the west. *President Roosevelt promptly stopped oil and steel shipments to Japan and froze all Japanese funds in the United States.* In August he extended lend-lease to China.

These actions posed a dilemma. Japanese military experts estimated that Japan had only a two-year supply of steel and oil. *Either the Japanese had to yield to American demands that they withdraw from China and Indochina, or they had to go to war before their supplies ran out.* In September 1941 Prince Konoye, sensing that his control over the military was slipping, made an offer to negotiate. His terms did not seem satisfactory, and Roosevelt refused to talk. In October the militarists took over the Japanese government, and General Hideki Tojo replaced Konoye as prime minister. The Japanese military began making plans for a massive offensive throughout Asia. Their plans included a surprise attack on Pearl Harbor, the site of the American naval base in the Hawaiian Islands.

A LAST-MINUTE EFFORT AT PEACE. *On November 20, the Japanese ambassador to Washington, Kichisaburo*

Nomura (NO-mu-ra), made a peace proposal. Secretary of State Cordell Hull knew it was Japan's final offer because American experts had cracked the Japanese diplomatic code and obtained all secret communications. Japan proposed to withdraw from Indochina on two conditions—the United States had to agree to Japan's occupation of parts of China, and it had to restore shipments of steel and oil.

In the old politics of power diplomacy, Japan's proposal was not unreasonable. Such an arrangement was the kind of settlement the European nations had been imposing on one another for centuries. But Roosevelt and Hull, like Woodrow Wilson, were not content to pursue power politics. They believed that America, as a world power, had to carry the burden of responsibility, the burden of ensuring a moral order in the world. The United States might have to tolerate aggression in a far-off corner of the world, but it could never approve of it. Thus, Hull and Roosevelt rejected the Japanese offer. The Japanese attack force had already been dispatched, although it could have been recalled by radio if the peace mission had succeeded.

THE ATTACK ON PEARL HARBOR.

The Japanese began their attack on Pearl Harbor at 7:55 A.M. on Sunday, December 7, 1941. Planes from their aircraft carriers swept in low over the Hawaiian Islands, dropping bombs amid the mass of warships in the harbor and blasting American planes on the ground. In just under two hours, eight battleships—the core of the Pacific Fleet—as well as several destroyers and cruisers were sunk or heavily damaged, and more than 150 United States planes were destroyed; 2,403 Americans were killed, and 1,178 were wounded.

President Roosevelt, describing December 7 as "a date which will live in infamy," asked Congress to declare war against

Japan. On December 8, the Senate passed the declaration unanimously. Only one dissenting vote was cast in the House. Three days later, when Germany and Italy honored their commitment to Japan by declaring war on the United States, Congress in turn declared war on the other Axis powers. The world was engulfed in battle.

WHY WAS PEARL HARBOR CAUGHT BY SURPRISE? Having broken the Japanese code, the United States knew that an attack was coming. But American leaders apparently never dreamed that the Japanese would hit a naval base 6,400 kilometers (4,000 miles) from their homeland. An attack on the East Indies or possibly on the Philippines seemed more likely. Even so, knowing that war was going to break out somewhere in the Pacific, the military commanders in Hawaii ought to have been more alert.

Pearl Harbor was caught in a condition of Sunday morning sleepiness. The attack was a bigger blunder for the Japanese. Their strategy rested on the assumption that Hitler's imminent conquest of the Soviet Union would occupy Britain and the United States for some time. By destroying the American Navy in a surprise attack, the Japanese hoped to win time to conquer the East Indies and develop the mineral resources necessary for a long-term war. They thought that the United States and Britain would not be able to fight a two-front war—in Asia and Europe—and would therefore sign a peace agreement in the Pacific.

The Japanese failed to reckon on America's abundant resources or gift for mobilization. The crippling of the Pacific Fleet at Pearl Harbor delayed the American war effort by only six months. And the sneak attack on Pearl Harbor united the nation. "Remember Pearl Harbor!" echoed across the land as Americans rolled up their sleeves for the job ahead.

During the attack on Pearl Harbor, over 2,000 American soldiers, sailors, and civilians lost their lives. Nineteen ships were destroyed or damaged. Among them was the battleship West Virginia.

Section Review

1. **Mapping:** Place names change often throughout history. A map made in one era shows place names that differ from those on a map made years earlier or later. Using a current map of the world, determine the names now given to Manchukuo, the Dutch East Indies, and Indochina.

2. **Identify or explain:** General Hideki Tojo, Cordell Hull, the Greater East Asia Coprosperity Sphere.

3. What sequence of events led the Japanese to attack the naval base at Pearl Harbor, Hawaii? Why didn't the United States anticipate the attack on Pearl Harbor?

4. Using sections 3 and 4 of this chapter, list in chronological order the steps that culminated in the United States' declarations of war on Japan, Germany, and Italy.

627

Chapter 26 Review

Bird's-Eye View

In the years between the close of World War I and the mid-1930's, the United States pursued isolationism in foreign affairs. The nation remained intensely concerned about world peace. And to help ensure peace, the government participated in various international efforts to limit armaments and outlaw war. Efforts were also made to improve relations between the United States and its neighbors in Latin America.

When Franklin D. Roosevelt took office in 1933, he undertook to lead a nation of Americans whose main concern involved recovery from the Great Depression. The United States had become a major world power. But its people preferred to concentrate their energies on problems at home rather than abroad.

While the nation looked to its domestic affairs, bitterness over the settlement of World War I and the effects of the global depression brought to power Hitler's Nazi party in Germany, Mussolini's Fascists in Italy, and a militaristic government in Japan. By the late 1930's, those powers had begun to threaten world security. The American public had to be persuaded that in such a climate, isolationism and neutrality might threaten the security of the United States.

By the time war broke out in Europe between the Axis powers and the Allies in 1939, the United States had modified its position. It was prepared to give aid of various kinds to the Allies, but it was determined to remain out of the actual fighting. It was able to maintain this position until December 1941. On December 7 Japan's devastating surprise attack on the American naval base at Pearl Harbor, Hawaii, forced the United States into the war. On December 8th Congress declared war on Japan. Three days later, when Japan's Axis allies declared war on the United States, Congress responded by declaring war on them as well. The second global war had begun.

Vocabulary

Define or identify each of the following:

propaganda	fascism	Nazi-Soviet pact
dictator	isolationism	blitzkrieg
Good Neighbor Policy	totalitarian	destroyers

Review Questions

1. What steps toward the goal of world peace were taken by the nations of the world during the 1920's?
2. Cite three examples of changing American foreign policy attitudes in the Western Hemisphere.
3. What was the Munich settlement? What were the implications of this settlement?
4. What military advantage did Germany hope to gain from the Nazi-Soviet nonaggression pact?
5. How was the United States involved in World War II before Congress declared war on the Axis powers?

6. What military actions did the Japanese take in the 1930's?
7. Why did Japan attack Pearl Harbor?

Reviewing Social Studies Skills

1. Using the map on page 622, complete the following:
   a. List the Axis powers and the countries they controlled in September 1939.
   b. Name the two countries Italy invaded.
   c. List the countries that were conquered by the Axis powers. Describe the geographic relationship of each country to Germany by using such terms as north, southeast, and so on.
2. The rise of militarism around the world was one of the developments of the 1920's and 1930's. Formulate a definition of militarism. Then develop a hypothesis that explains the role of the military in causing World War II.
3. Chapter 26 contains a number of references to treaties that were signed and then broken. Make a four-column chart of these treaties. Head the columns Treaty, Nations Signing, Provisions, Violations.

Reading for Meaning

1. How did Hitler's concept of the master race affect European Jews? What does this information tell you about the values of Hitler and those of his associates?
2. The extermination of European Jews by the Nazis is often referred to as the Holocaust. Look up the meaning of this word in a dictionary. Then write a paragraph expressing your views on this statement: The word *holocaust* should be used only to describe the extermination of six million Jews by the Nazis because the event was so unusual in human history.
3. Throughout this chapter the authors use examples of cause and effect to explain historical events and developments. (Remember— a cause can produce more than one effect, and more than one cause can often produce the same effect.) Choose three of the following causes, and find the effects of each in the chapter: a. the Versailles Treaty; b. the Great Depression; c. the Washington Naval Conference; d. civil war in China; e. the last free election in Germany; f. the Nye Committee investigations; g. the Munich Conference of 1938; h. Roosevelt's halting of oil and steel shipments to Japan.

Bibliography

Robert A. Divine's *Illusion of Neutrality* (University of Chicago Press) is a well-written summary of the nation's efforts to maintain neutrality.

Walter Lord's *Day of Infamy* (Holt, Rinehart and Winston) is a fascinating account of the attack on Pearl Harbor.

Anne Frank's *Diary of a Young Girl* (Pocket Books) tells the story of a European Jewish family that was persecuted by the Nazis.

Chapter 27

The Last World War

1941-1945

The American cruiser *Augusta* floated on the chill waters of Argentia Bay, Newfoundland. On board the cruiser was the President of the United States, Franklin Roosevelt. A wreath of smoke at the entrance to the bay announced the arrival of the British battleship carrying Prime Minister Winston Churchill. The two leaders of the western Allies were holding their first meeting. It was August 9, 1941. The United States was not yet in the war. But President Roosevelt wanted to reach an agreement on Allied war aims before giving the Allies any further aid.

The Atlantic Charter was signed by the two leaders on August 12. It was a statement of war aims and hopes. In it were many echoes of Woodrow Wilson's proposals for "peace without victory." The Allies renounced territorial ambitions for their countries. They promised to restore self-government to the conquered peoples. When the war ended, they promised, there would be a new world order—freedom of the seas, an opening of trade through the reduction of tariff barriers, general disarmament, and a postwar system of international security. Like Wilson's Fourteen Points, the Atlantic Charter gave the conflict a moral purpose.

Chapter Objectives

After you have finished reading this chapter, you should be able to:
1. Describe how American production was critical to war efforts of the Allies.
2. Explain the strategy of the Allies in Asia, North Africa, and the Soviet Union.
3. Design a chart, showing the year, the location, and the results of the major battles in Europe.
4. Explain the strategy used to defeat the Japanese.
5. List and explain the factors that led to tensions among the Allies in 1945.

Neither Germany nor Japan expected to defeat the United States in war. Germany expected to conquer the Soviet Union before the United States could mobilize. Then the Axis powers would be in control of half the world's population and Britain and the United States would have to agree to a truce.

Hitler invaded the Soviet Union in the summer of 1941. By early fall, Germany occupied White Russia together with most of the Ukraine and the Crimean peninsula. (See map, page 641.) By mid-November, the German Army was poised on the outskirts of Moscow. But, like Napoleon in the previous century, Hitler had not anticipated the severity of the Russian winter. The Russians launched a counteroffensive in December and saved their capital city. The harsh winter was not the only Soviet advantage—American war supplies were being shipped to the Soviet Union (through the lend-lease program) from the first week of the Nazi attack. This war was to be won on the assembly line.

1. Winning the Battle of Production

MOBILIZING THE ECONOMY. Since 1938 Roosevelt had been pressuring the nation to prepare for war. As a result, the United States was better equipped for war than it had been in 1917. *Agencies the New Deal had created to fight the Great Depression were mobilized to help fight the war.* The Reconstruction Finance Corporation lent money for the construction of defense plants. The TVA's electrical energy was used to make munitions. Members of the CCC became army drill sergeants.

The depression left a surplus of both workers and machines. Thus, at first it was possible to arm without cutting the production of consumer goods. By the fall of 1941, however, there were shortages of certain materials, and it was clear that the economy needed more direction. The President hired Donald Nelson of Sears, Roebuck & Company to head the new War Production Board. In January 1942 Nelson was given complete charge of the nation's economy.

Nelson's first task was to convert the automobile industry to military production. Because the industry was geared to assembly-line methods, converting from autos to tanks, trucks, and even aircraft was not difficult. By February 1942 the last passenger cars rolled off the assembly line, and military production was under way.

America's productive capacity astounded the world. By 1943 General Motors alone was producing more war materials than Germany and Japan combined.

Another production miracle of World War II occurred in shipbuilding. Henry J. Kaiser, who had never built a ship in his life, revolutionized the industry. Borrowing assembly-line techniques from the auto industry, he reduced the time it took to build a standard vessel, or Liberty ship, from six months to 17 days.

Equally impressive was the output of the nation's farms. Although their numbers were greatly reduced by the draft, American farmers managed to produce record-breaking quantities of crops. Throughout the war they raised enough food for the American civilian population, the American military, and the Allies.

FINANCING THE WAR. In order to finance this immense effort, the government raised personal income taxes higher than they had ever been. Corporations making excess profits from war production had to pay a special tax. *Because the war effort needed more money, the government sold war bonds.*

The national debt rose by 210 billion dollars between 1941 and 1945. The total cost of the war—400 billion dollars—was more than the United States government had spent since the birth of the nation in 1776.

A PEOPLE AT WAR. Although America's industrial might was the chief factor in the war, it still took people to win it. The Selective Service Act of 1940 required that all men between 21 and 35 register for military service. By the time war was declared, there were 1.6 million men in service, almost as many as had enlisted in all of World War I. By 1945 there were more than 12 million men and women in military uniform.

Don't miss your great opportunity..

THE NAVY NEEDS YOU IN THE WAVES

Women were actively recruited by all branches of the armed services during World War II. This poster encourages women to join the navy.

Women played a greater role in the armed services than ever before. Previously serving as nurses, women served for the first time as WACS (army), WAVES (navy), and SPARS (coast guard). Women were barred from combat. They worked as typists, machinists, ambulance drivers, record keepers, and radio operators, freeing men for combat duty.

Civilian workers were mobilized for the war effort. After war was declared, all men between the ages of 18 and 44 were liable for the draft unless they were in essential occupations such as farming or working in war plants. As a result, about 30 million workers were in occupations directly related to war production.

The figure included some two million women. Never before had the nation made such full use of its human resources. Women entered war plants and worked in shipyards. "Rosie the Riveter," a hit song of 1943, reflected the nation's admiration. **When the war ended few people seriously doubted the ability of a woman to perform any job in the American work place.**

FEELING THE PINCH. Even those who were not directly related to the war effort felt the pinch of wartime scarcities. Rubber, previously imported from Southeast Asia, was in short supply. To conserve rubber and oil, the government rationed gasoline. Motorists were given a number of coupons depending on their needs and occupations. Meat, sugar, and shoes were also rationed for a time.

To prevent inflation, the Office of Price Administration (OPA) set ceiling prices on every important consumer product. Merchants were required to post prices in their stores. It was against the law to charge more than the OPA ceiling price. Prices rose anyway partly because prewar prices were at depression levels. But the overall wartime price rise of 33 percent was less than the inflation caused by any war the country has fought since 1945.

RACIAL PROBLEMS. The war effort strained every human resource. About 25,000 American Indians volunteered for military service, and many thousands more went to work in war plants. A million Blacks entered the military services. But despite the protests of Black leaders, they were kept in segregated units. The navy and the marines had few Blacks in their ranks. Black army regiments fought with valor. Some received unit citations—a medal awarded to every man in the regiment. (After the war, all the armed services were desegregated by Presidential order.)

The most tragic story of the home front involved Japanese Americans. Fear com-

These Japanese American soldiers saw action in Africa, Italy, and southern France. Many received the Purple Heart and Presidential Citations. This photograph was taken in June 1945, as the soldiers awaited 30-day furloughs and subsequent discharges.

bined with racial bias produced one of the sorriest spectacles of the times. An epidemic of invasion jitters swept the West Coast after the attack on Pearl Harbor. Military officers feared that Japanese living in the area might try to sabotage coastal defenses. Together with certain West Coast congressional representatives they put pressure on the President to do something about the situation.

Early in 1942 Roosevelt ordered the removal from the West Coast of most persons who were of Japanese ancestry. The army rounded up about 112,000 people, 71,000 of whom were American citizens. They were put into detention camps in the Rocky Mountains. There they lived like jailed convicts until the end of the war. Although the government held their property and businesses in trust, most internees found it difficult to resume their previous positions after the war. Japanese Americans, nevertheless, remained loyal American citizens. They formed a unit to fight in Europe where they served heroically.

Section Review

1. Identify or explain: Donald Nelson, Henry J. Kaiser, SPARS, "Rosie the Riveter."
2. Describe the various ways in which the nation mobilized for World War II. Which two industries were the "production miracles" of the war?

3. What significant change did World War II make in the place women occupied in American life?
4. How were the lives of Japanese Americans on the West Coast affected by fears aroused by the war?

2. The "Hinge of Fate"

THE JAPANESE BLITZKRIEG. Japan struck with dazzling speed in the weeks after Pearl Harbor. Within days the Japanese Navy captured Guam (GWAHM) and Wake Island and landed an army on the main Philippine island of Luzon (loo-ZAHN). General MacArthur, commander in the Philippines, put up a hard fight. Throughout the spring his outnumbered troops were pushed inch by inch down the Bataan peninsula to the fortress island of Corregidor (kuh-REHG-ih-dawr). In March General MacArthur slipped out by PT (patrol torpedo) boat and submarine to Australia, where he assumed overall command of the war in the Pacific. Those left on Bataan were captured in April. Corregidor surrendered in May. The loss of 15,000 soldiers on Bataan was the biggest defeat in the history of the American armed forces.

By the time Corregidor surrendered, the Japanese had seized the Dutch East Indies, the British colonies of Burma, Malaya, and most of New Guinea, and the French Solomon Islands. (See map, page 635.) The Japanese controlled most of the important islands and coastal areas in the South Pacific. They were ready to attack Australia and India. Even the American West Coast was within their reach. These were frightening times for the Allies in the Pacific.

THE CORAL SEA. Japan might have been wise to halt at that point. Its outer defenses were thousands of kilometers from Japan. Every island in the South Pacific was a fortress. It would be years before the United States could retake all that territory. Japan's best strategy would have been to go on the defensive and concentrate on developing the mineral and rubber resources in the land it occupied. But it is difficult to halt a victorious army.

In May 1942 Japanese military commanders had one more goal—Port Moresby, on the southern coast of New Guinea. Occupied by Australian forces, the base was a gap in the Japanese chain of defenses and could be used by Americans to launch a counterattack. A Japanese attack force, accompanied by aircraft carriers, was sent to seize the base. On May 7 and 8, a small group of American aircraft carriers intercepted them in the Coral Sea, southeast of New Guinea. It was a battle of carrier-based airplanes. The two fleets never came within sight of each other. Because each side lost a carrier, the battle was a draw. But it frustrated the Japanese invasion.

PACIFIC TURNING POINT: THE BATTLE OF MIDWAY. The Japanese fleet that had attacked Pearl Harbor was still operating in the Central Pacific. Its new target was American-owned Midway Island, the most important naval and air station between Hawaii and Japan.

At Pearl Harbor, Admiral Chester Nimitz learned of the Japanese plan from the *intelligence* people who had broken the Japanese code. He massed airplanes on Midway Island and sent a carrier force to help. *The Battle of Midway (June 3–6, 1942) was a major American victory.* It eliminated the threat to Hawaii and the West Coast and restored the balance of naval power in the Pacific. The Japanese lost all four of their aircraft carriers and about 275 planes. Japan could ill afford the losses, for it lacked the steel to build more. In American shipyards, by contrast, a dozen more carriers were nearing completion.

Intelligence (operation): an agency involved in obtaining information about an enemy.

GUADALCANAL, THE FIRST MAJOR OFFENSIVE. In August 1942 American marines landed on Guadalcanal (GWAHD'L-cah-NAL) in the Solomon Islands and captured the airport. Japanese forces had reached the islands only weeks before and had not had time to fortify them. The Japanese rushed in reinforcements, and a six-month battle followed on land, sea, and in the air. During the autumn seven major naval battles werc fought in the straits between the Solomons and New Guinea. The American Navy was trying to stop the flow of Japanese troopships, or the Tokyo Express, as some called it. Both sides suffered heavy losses, and before long the straits were cluttered with sunken vessels.

The decisive naval battle came in November. Thereafter the Japanese were prevented from landing reinforcements on the island. American armies reinforced the marines, and by February 1943 the Japanese had evacuated Guadalcanal. In Winston Churchill's phrase, the "hinge of fate" had swung the other way.

THE TURNING POINT IN NORTH AFRICA. By the spring of 1942, Germany and Italy were in control of the Mediterranean Sea, blocking the Suez Canal. Passage

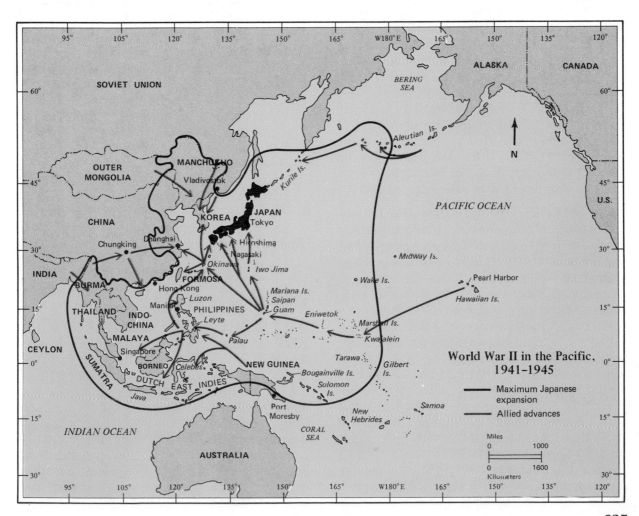

World War II in the Pacific, 1941–1945

—— Maximum Japanese expansion
—— Allied advances

through the canal was vital to Britain's effort against Japan in India. Without it, British ships had to go around Africa to reach the Indian Ocean. (See map, pages xx–xxi.) American lend-lease supplies going to the Soviet Union through the Persian Gulf had to pass through the canal. In June 1942 a German army under General Erwin Rommel reached the border of Egypt. The army was ready to take control of the canal. It was time for the Allies to go on the offensive.

On October 23 General Bernard Montgomery and the British Eighth Army stopped Rommel at El Alamein (el AL-uh-MAIN), only 112 kilometers (70 miles) west of Alexandria. On November 8 a huge force of Americans, British, and Canadians under America's General Dwight D. Eisenhower poured onto the beaches of Morocco and Algeria. Eisenhower raced across North Africa, pushing aside the dispirited Italian armies in his drive to trap Rommel. The Desert Fox, as Rommel was called, escaped the trap. But at the beginning of April, the Allied forces succeeded in encircling their enemy in Tunisia. *With the surrender of 250,000 troops on May 13, 1943, the North African campaign was officially ended.*

THE SIEGE OF STALINGRAD. *As important as the North African victory was, the most critical turning point that winter was on the Russian front.* The Russian armies had melted under the first German thrust. They yielded thousands of kilometers of territory and most of the country's industrial cities. However, the Germans failed to capture either Moscow or Leningrad in 1941. And neither the Soviet economy nor its government had been struck in a vital spot.

In August 1942, the Germans launched an all-out assault on Stalingrad, the key to the Volga River and the Caspian Sea. Stalin ordered his namesake city held at all costs. *After weeks of fighting, Soviet forces under General Zhukov (ZHOO-kawf) saved the city and then launched a new offensive to regain the territory they had lost.* The German commander surrendered on February 2, 1943. The Soviets captured 22 German divisions. Some 330,000 German soldiers were lost. Paralyzed by the cold and short of supplies, the Germans retreated all along the Russian front. The "hinge of fate" had turned in Europe, as well as in the Pacific.

Section Review

1. Mapping: Using the map on page 635, identify and list the Pacific islands that played a strategic role in World War II. Then, using the directional symbol, classify the islands into two groups: islands southwest of Japan and islands southeast of Japan.
2. Identify or explain: General MacArthur, Admiral Nimitz, intelligence people, General Montgomery, the Desert Fox.
3. What strategic error did the Japanese make in May 1942? How did this error help the Allied cause?
4. Why do the authors state that by February 1943 "the 'hinge of fate' . . . had swung the other way"?
5. Why was the battle of Stalingrad a critical turning point in the war in Europe?

3. Eliminating the Nazi Menace

DIFFERENCES IN ALLIED STRATEGY. It was generally agreed that the defeat of Hitler's Germany had top priority. Hitler's insatiable appetite for conquest and his evil treatment of the conquered peoples of Europe made Germany a bigger menace than Japan or Italy. By 1940 Hitler's armies were occupying France, Belgium, Holland, Luxembourg, Norway, Denmark, and most of eastern Europe. And the mass execution of Jews, which began midway through the war, made Nazi occupation a reign of terror.

On New Year's Day 1942, three weeks after the attack on Pearl Harbor, the representatives of 26 nations met in Washington to sign the Declaration of the United Nations and declare war on the Axis powers. Signers of the Declaration committed themselves to the principles of the Atlantic Charter and promised not to conclude a separate peace. This made the conflict truly a world war. In practice, Roosevelt and Churchill made the key decisions. Stalin refused to leave Moscow until late in the war. He communicated his desires from a distance.

THE CASABLANCA CONFERENCE.
In January 1943, Roosevelt, Churchill, and a Soviet delegate met at the African coastal resort of Casablanca, in French Morocco. *Churchill persuaded the Americans to continue the Mediterranean thrust by invading Sicily and Italy.* He hoped that the action would bring Turkey into the war and lead to an Allied invasion of the Balkans. Roosevelt and Eisenhower agreed. But they realized that the commitment of troops and landing craft in the Mediterranean would postpone an invasion of Europe across the

The abbreviation G.I., taken from the Government Issue stamp on American supplies, came to stand for everything in the war, including the men who fought it. G.I. Joe was many things to many people. The war correspondent Ernie Pyle described him this way: "G.I.'s lived like men of prehistoric times, and a club would have become them more than a machine gun." But no one captured the G.I. better than Bill Mauldin, cartoonist for Stars and Stripes. *How does Mauldin's view differ from that of Pyle? In what ways was the American Army an extension of American society?*

Fresh, spirited American troops, flushed with victory, are bringing in thousands of hungry, ragged, battle-weary prisoners. (News item)

"Awright, awright—it's a gen'ral! Ya wanna pass in review?"

English Channel until 1944. Stalin, when he learned of the decision, protested loudly. The western Allies replied that an invasion of Italy would tie down the German armies. The Soviet leader felt that he had been betrayed because the decision meant that no major offensive would be launched to get the Germans away from the Russian front.

At the conclusion of the Casablanca meeting, Roosevelt told a press conference that the Allies would insist on the unconditional surrender of the Axis. However, both he and Churchill stressed that unconditional surrender did not mean harsh revenge on Germany and the German people.

SICILY AND ITALY. *In July of 1943 British, Canadian, and American troops landed in Sicily and swiftly overran the island.* The campaign was notable for the emergence of an American war hero, General George S. Patton. A born fighter who sported a pair of ivory-handled pistols at his belt, Patton was a master of fast-moving, mechanized war. If the Germans pioneered the blitzkrieg, Patton brought it to perfection.

Discouraged by the Allied victory, the Italian people threw out Mussolini, replacing him with the pro-Allied Marshal Pietro Badoglio (ba-DO-lyo). When the Allies landed on September 3, 1943, Italy surrendered.

German armies quickly occupied Italy, and a grueling campaign for the Italian peninsula began. The mountainous terrain slowed the Allied advance. Before long, everything bogged down in snow and mud. Battling the elements as well as the Germans, the Allies finally fought their way into Rome, the Italian capital, on June 4, 1944. Two days later General Eisenhower launched the long-awaited cross-channel invasion of France.

THE BATTLE OF THE ATLANTIC. The buildup in Britain for the cross-channel invasion took two years. One reason for the delay was the German submarine warfare in the Atlantic Ocean. American entry into the war meant a huge increase in the number of ships in the Atlantic, and thus, new targets for submarines. The German admiralty moved its U-boats close to the American coast, where they found rich picking among unescorted merchant vessels and tankers. During the first six months of 1942, almost 400 ships were sunk in the Atlantic, the Caribbean, and the Gulf of Mexico. Realizing the importance of the convoy to the war, the Germans doubled their production of submarines in 1943. But during that year the American and British navies, with the help of radar and sonar, learned to detect the underwater ships. By mid-1943 the output of American shipyards exceeded losses in battle, and by the end of that year, the battle for control of the Atlantic was won.

THE AIR WAR OVER GERMANY. By the time the United States entered the war, the British were beginning to retaliate for the German bombardment of British cities, such as London, which had suffered devastation from the *Luftwaffe's* nightly raids. Bombing at first was limited to military installations along the European coast because Britain lacked fighter protection for its bombers. British fighter planes, such as the famous Spitfire, had been designed for home defense. The American development of long-range fighters, such as the P-47 Thunderbolt and the P-51 Mustang, enabled bombers to strike at the heart of Germany.

The initial targets of the Allied air forces were aircraft production plants, ball bearing plants, and oil depots. By the end of 1944, the *Luftwaffe* was grounded, and the Allies were in charge of the air. Thousand-plane raids, causing enormous destruction to Germany, were almost a nightly occurrence.

D-DAY, JUNE 6, 1944. General Eisenhower picked French Normandy as the site for the invasion of Europe. That part of the French coast had good beaches for landing

This panorama of the Normandy invasion was taken by a coast-guard combat photographer. Troops and supplies are arriving on ships and heading inland by truck, while balloon barrages float overhead, guarding against enemy aircraft.

craft, and the nearby port of Cherbourg (sher-BOORG) could accommodate supply facilities. In anticipation of an invasion, the Germans had lined the channel coast with every fortification their military scientists could devise. But the Allies had planned their arrival to the last detail. Ten thousand planes provided aerial protection. To provide a haven for ships until Cherbourg was cap-

tured, army engineers built concrete breakwaters and towed them across the channel.

Delayed twice by bad weather, the landing came at last in the predawn hours of June 6, 1944 (D-Day). The largest armada ever assembled, totaling 4,000 transports, landing craft, and warships, ferried more than 130,000 American, British, and Canadian troops across the channel. In a week the Allies landed 326,000 soldiers, 50,000 vehicles, and 100,000 tons of supplies on the coast of France. Under the command of General Eisenhower, the Allies set up a **beachhead** and maintained a front in Normandy.

A **beachhead** is an area on a hostile shore that is occupied to secure further landing of troops and supplies.

Sidenote to History

Dr. Charles Drew and the Blood Bank

Dr. Charles Drew was a Black surgeon and inventor. He developed a way to preserve and store blood for use in transfusions. This discovery helped save the lives of thousands of soldiers.

Drew was born in Washington, D.C., in 1904. He worked as a medical researcher at the Presbyterian Hospital in New York City, where he developed a method of preserving red blood cells and a fluid called plasma, the two components of human blood. This was a major breakthrough in medical science because it enabled hospitals to freeze and store blood components for several years.

Dr. Drew's invention led to the first blood bank. It became possible for blood to be shipped wherever it was needed.

In 1940 Dr. Drew was asked by the British government to direct its blood plasma program. In 1941 he became the director of a new project to collect blood plasma for the American armed services. (It was ironic that the Red Cross segregated the blood of Black and White donors in the banks established for wounded soldiers.) Three months after he took up the post, Dr. Drew resigned from the army blood project and became head of surgery at Howard University School of Medicine. He held that position until his death in 1950.

CLOSING THE RING. Breaking out of the beachhead at the end of June, the American armies dashed for Paris, while the British and the Canadians pushed into Belgium. Paris fell on the 25th of August. General Patton's highly mechanized Third Army swept across the Marne, through Chateau Thierry (shah-TOE tyeh-REE) and Verdun (vair-DUHN), scenes of the gory trench warfare of World War I.

Stalin opened a major offensive in June 1944 along a 1,280-kilometer (800-mile) front from the Baltic Sea to the Ukraine. In five weeks the Russians swept across Poland to the gates of Warsaw. Rumania, which had sided with Germany, sued for peace when Soviet armies appeared at its border. By October 1944 the Russians had linked up with Marshal Tito's guerrilla forces in the mountains of Yugoslavia.

THE BATTLE OF THE BULGE. Germany was strong enough to force the Allies to fight through another winter. In December 1944 Patton's army bogged down near the French city of Metz. The British struggled through the Low Countries. The Germans counterattacked in the densely wooded country on the border of Belgium and Luxembourg. Slipping between Allied armies, the Germans penetrated 80 kilometers (50 miles), creating a "bulge" in the Allied line. The bulge did not last long. Patton's army drove swiftly north. And with the help of some unusually good weather, which permitted close air support, he drove the Germans into retreat.

The Battle of the Bulge delayed the Allied entry into Germany. Eisenhower's

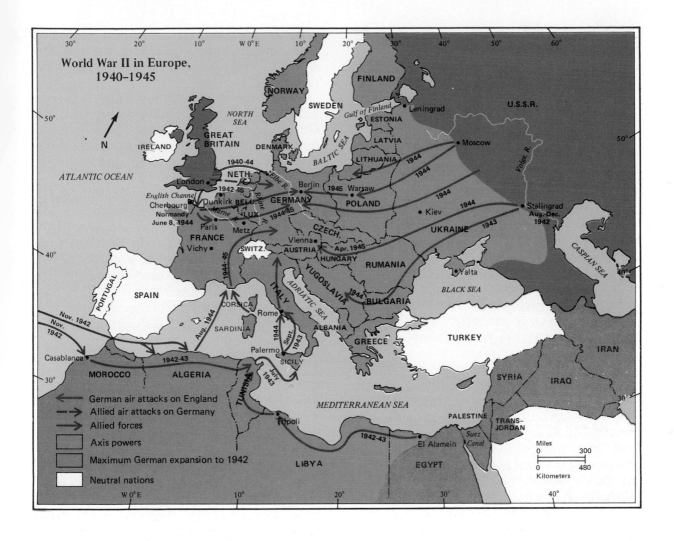

World War II in Europe, 1940–1945

Legend:
- ← German air attacks on England
- ⇢ Allied air attacks on Germany
- → Allied forces
- Axis powers
- Maximum German expansion to 1942
- Neutral nations

Miles 0 — 300
Kilometers 0 — 480

forces did not cross the Rhine River until the seventh of March. By that time the Russians were not far from Berlin. When the British-American armies reached the next river barrier, the Elbe, in early April, the Russians had surrounded Berlin and were pouring artillery fire into the city.

How far the Allies should penetrate and whether they should head for Berlin or pursue the retreating enemy into southern Germany were questions to be answered by Allied policy makers. Unfortunately for Eisenhower, the politicians and diplomats had no answers. President Roosevelt had

fallen seriously ill. He died before Germany surrendered.

Section Review

1. **Mapping:** Using the map above, describe the areas into which the Germans had expanded by 1942.
2. **Identify or explain:** the Declaration of the United Nations, George S. Patton, D-Day, beachhead, Marshal Tito, June 6, 1944.
3. At the Casablanca Conference of 1943, what strategy did Churchill persuade

Roosevelt and Eisenhower to adopt? Why did Stalin feel betrayed by this move?

4. What effect did the Battle of the Bulge have on the British and the American strategy toward Germany?

4. Victory in the Pacific

JAPAN'S DEFENSE SYSTEM. Anyone who looked at a map of the Pacific early in the war could tell that defeating Japan would be difficult. Japan had a defense line stretching thousands of kilometers into the ocean, and within this area were hundreds of heavily fortified islands. Every island was like an unsinkable aircraft carrier. To capture them all would cause enormous bloodshed and might take years.

A second glance at the map, however, revealed that the Japanese defense system was vulnerable. Japan's fortified islands might be unsinkable, but they were also immovable. It was not necessary to capture all or even most of the islands. If one island in every chain could be captured, it could be used as a staging base for the next island. Each island would bring the American forces closer to Japan. The other islands could be left to die on the vine. Japanese soldiers, left stranded on these islands, would be just as harmless as if they were in prison camps.

ISLAND-HOPPING TO JAPAN. In 1943, MacArthur battled his way along the northern coast of New Guinea. At the same time the navy and the marines penetrated the outer rim of the Japanese islands. From Bougainville (BOO-gen-vil) on the northern end of the Solomon chain, the navy moved into the Marshall and Gilbert islands. Tarawa (ta-RA-wa), the first objective, was a small coral reef, but capturing it cost the lives of a thousand marines. By 1944, Amer-

icans had learned the art of amphibious attack, and Kwajalein (KWAJ-a-lin) and Eniwetok (e-NE-we-tok) were taken more easily.

The Marianas—islands with musical names like Saipan, Tinian (tin-e-AN), and Guam—were next. These islands were within bombing distance of Japan. The Japanese Navy understood the importance of the Marianas and threw its entire carrier force against the American landing force. On June 19, 1944, American carriers met the Japanese squadron in the waters off the island of Saipan. *Called the Battle of the Philippine Sea, it was the greatest naval-air battle of the war. American pilots, better trained and flying more heavily armed planes, won a major victory.* By the end of the day, Japan had lost 405 airplanes, three carriers, and dozens of other ships.

THE RETURN TO BATAAN. The navy wanted to move to the next island chain. But MacArthur demanded a landing in the Philippines. The islands had no great military value, but there were important political considerations. They were, after all, America's chief colonial possession in the South Pacific, and MacArthur felt a special responsibility for them. Moreover, in 1934 Congress had promised the Philippines independence in 10 years. The United States wanted to carry out its promise. Relieving the islands of the Japanese occupation would create goodwill, some believed, and would ensure friendly relations in the future. MacArthur landed in October 1944 and quickly swept the Japanese out of the main islands of Leyte (LAY-teh) and Luzon. "People of the Philippines," he announced, on splashing ashore at Leyte Island, "I have returned."

The Philippine landing brought the Japanese Navy out for its last effort. Most of its carriers had been sunk. But it still had some of the finest battleships in the world. Admiral Nimitz sent every available ship to meet the Japanese. The Battle of Leyte Gulf was actually three separate actions in different parts of the Philippines, and the Americans won them all. In terms of people and ships involved, it was the largest sea fight in history. When it was over, the Japanese Navy was completely destroyed.

IWO JIMA AND OKINAWA. By the fall of 1944, America's new airplanes, the long-range B-29 Superfortresses, were able to reach Japan from Tinian in the Marianas. But to save time, fuel, and planes, the air force asked for closer bases. That meant landings in the innermost circle of Japanese

The flag raising atop Mt. Suribachi on Iwo Jima was photographed by Joe Rosenthal and was widely circulated throughout the world. Shown here is a statue near Washington, D.C., which commemorates the American victory.

defense, islands that had been part of the Japanese Empire for centuries.

Iwo Jima (EE-woe JEE-muh) is an island of volcanic rock jutting out of the ocean. In February 1945 the United States Marines hit the ashen beaches of Iwo Jima. The Japanese waged a fanatical defense of the island. They had to be rooted out of every nook and cranny on Iwo Jima. It was one of the nastiest, costliest fights of the war.

Next came Okinawa (oe-kih-NAH-wah), an island on the doorstep of Japan. The landing on April 1 brought the Japanese Air Force out for its final effort. Realizing that the war was lost, the Japanese resolved to make victory as expensive for the United States as possible. Suicide pilots called kamikaze (KAH-mih-KAH-zee) filled their planes with dynamite and tried to crash them into American ships. The planes were huge, piloted bombs, and they wreaked havoc. The kamikaze sank 27 American ships, including four carriers. Sixty-one other ships were damaged so badly that they were never returned to action. When the battle was over, the Japanese Air Force was destroyed.

THE BOMBING OF JAPAN. With the destruction of the Japanese Air Force, the home islands were at the mercy of American bombers. By the spring of 1945, massive raids struck Japanese cities in an effort to destroy civilian morale. Firebombs were particularly effective because Japanese houses and office buildings were made of wood (wooden buildings withstood earthquakes better). In a single raid, on March 9, 1945, one fourth of Tokyo, then the world's largest city, was turned into a raging inferno.

The fanatical defense of Iwo Jima and Okinawa worried American military authorities. If the Japanese defended their homeland with the same tenacity, a landing would be costly. Some estimated that the conquest of mountainous, heavily populated Japan might result in the loss of a million lives. Should the Japanese be bombed into submission instead? Should the Russians be asked to help? These were political questions. By the spring of 1945, the situation in both Asia and Europe required difficult diplomatic decisions. President Roosevelt's illness delayed the search for answers. His death on April 12, 1945, brought a new leader to the Presidency.

Section Review

1. Mapping: Using the map on page 635, identify the Pacific archipelagoes on which major battles were fought in the years 1943–1944 as part of the Allied island-hopping strategy.
2. Identify or explain: "People of the Philippines, I have returned," kamikaze, Superfortresses, Iwo Jima.
3. Why was the Japanese defense line of Pacific islands vulnerable to the battle strategy of the Allies?
4. What questions did Japan's "fanatical defense" of Iwo Jima and Okinawa raise in the minds of American military authorities? What event delayed the search for answers to these questions?

5. The End of the War

HARRY S TRUMAN. There was little in Harry S Truman's background to indicate future greatness. He was born on a farm in Missouri. He served a stint in the army in World War I, opened a clothing shop after the war, went bankrupt, and entered politics. He was a county judge for a time and with the help of Kansas City's political machine was elected to the Senate in 1934. Truman was an honest and efficient administrator and an able, if colorless, senator. Early in World War II, he headed a Senate committee that exposed a great deal of waste, inefficiency, and even fraud in mobilizing for the war. The investigation brought him to the public's attention.

THE ELECTION OF 1944. Midway through the war the American government had to consult its constituents, the American people. President Roosevelt, who might otherwise have retired after three terms, decided to see the war through to the end. The Democratic party accepted the logic of his decision, adopting the election slogan "Don't change horses in the middle of the stream!" *However, Roosevelt had difficulty selecting a running mate.* Southern Democrats vetoed Henry Wallace, who had been Roosevelt's Vice-President since 1940. Labor, speaking chiefly through the CIO's Political Action Committee, vetoed the South's candidate, James F. Byrnes. Truman, a moderate from the border state of Missouri, was the compromise choice.

The Republicans chose a real vote-getter— Thomas E. Dewey, the governor of New York. Like Willkie, Dewey was both liberal in politics and international-minded. He defeated his conservative opponent, John Bricker of Ohio, in the Republican primaries and then put him on the ticket as the Vice-Presidential nominee.

Dewey did better against Roosevelt than the three previous Republicans. But he was defeated because of the general feeling that the President, having led the nation into war, ought to have the chance to lead it into peace. Roosevelt carried 36 states with 432 electoral votes. Dewey won 12 states with 99 electoral votes.

SHAPING THE POSTWAR WORLD. The first face-to-face meeting among Allied leaders took place in November 1943 at Tehran (teh-HRAHN), capital of Persia (Iran). It was a neutral location, accessible to Roosevelt and Churchill and close enough to the Soviet Union for Stalin to keep his eye on the home front. Goodwill pervaded the meeting largely because Roosevelt refused to press Stalin on the subject

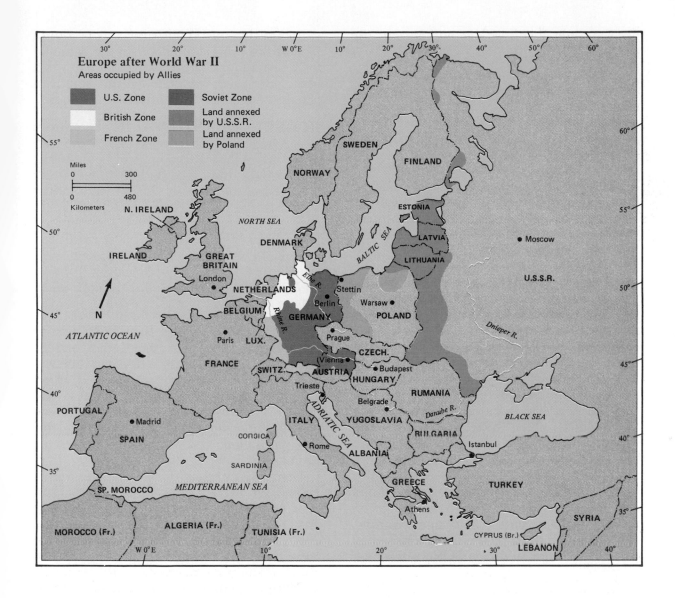

Europe after World War II
Areas occupied by Allies

U.S. Zone
British Zone
French Zone
Soviet Zone
Land annexed by U.S.S.R.
Land annexed by Poland

of eastern Europe. ***Roosevelt agreed to let the Soviet Union hold the Baltic States and the part of Poland it had seized in 1939. In return Stalin promised free elections in eastern Europe and agreed to join a postwar organization.***

Stalin's private attitude toward eastern Europe was different, however. He believed that he had the right to set up governments friendly to the Soviet Union on his European frontier. He intended to establish a buffer zone between the Soviet Union and Western Europe.

THE YALTA CONFERENCE. The Allied leaders did not meet again until February 1945, 15 months later. By then the collapse of Germany was near, and the defeat of Japan was not far off. The conference was held at the Black Sea resort of Yalta in the Crimean region of Russia. ***The Yalta Conference was the most important meeting of***

the war, for it shaped the contours of the postwar world:

1. *Japan:* The Soviet Union agreed to enter the war against Japan after Germany surrendered. In return the Soviets would recover territory that had been lost to the Japanese early in the century during the Russo-Japanese War.

2. *Germany:* The Allies would divide Germany into four zones of occupation until an overall peace settlement could be reached. Berlin, which fell geographically within the Soviet zone, would be divided into four sectors of occupation. The United States, Britain, and France would retain the right of free access to the city.

3. *Eastern Europe:* Stalin promised "free and unfettered elections" in Poland. The fate of the rest of eastern Europe, rapidly being occupied by Soviet armies, was left uncertain.

4. *The United Nations:* Stalin agreed to the general outline of the world organization and dropped his demand that each of the 16 republics of the Soviet Union be represented.

President Roosevelt was in failing health at the time of the Yalta Conference. He died six weeks after it ended. Critics of the Yalta agreement thought it was a sellout that left the Soviets in control of eastern Europe. They accused Roosevelt of being a sick man under the influence of pro-Communist advisers.

Stalin won nothing at the conference table that Soviet armies could not have taken anyway. Short of going to war with the Russians, there was no way the United States could save eastern Europe from Soviet domination.

As for the promised Soviet declaration of war against Japan, American military authorities thought Soviet help was needed. The atomic bomb, which finally brought the defeat of Japan, was still on the drawing boards. It had not been tested at the time of the Yalta Conference.

Roosevelt's mistake, if any, was in failing to alert the American people to the potential for international conflict after the war. As a result, the Cold War shocked the American people who wanted to return to normalcy.

ROOSEVELT AND STALIN. The Soviet Union had been badly weakened by the war. About 21 million Russians had been killed; 1,700 towns and cities had been destroyed. Twenty-five percent of the nation's industrial machinery had been wrecked. Stalin thought his country needed a generation to recover. Perhaps Roosevelt sympathized with Stalin's plight. Unable to protect eastern Europe, he might have thought he had a chance of influencing Stalin through goodwill.

TRUMAN AND THE SOVIETS. President Truman, on the other hand, had no such thought. He was a lifelong believer in Woodrow Wilson's principles of international order and self-determination. *He made it clear that he would defend eastern Europe by diplomacy, if not by force.* He was particularly distressed by Soviet action in Poland.

The Soviet armies were sweeping across Poland. In August 1944, Polish patriots had tried to bust the Nazis. The rebellion was put down and the Polish leaders were executed. The Soviet armies had stopped their advance across Poland long enough to enable the Germans to suppress the uprising. After the Germans were pushed out of Poland, the Soviets set up a Communist government there.

Before he died, Roosevelt expressed to Stalin his "bitter resentment" over Soviet actions in Poland. A few weeks later, Soviet Foreign Minister Vyacheslav Molotov (MAW-loe-tohv) stopped in Washington to confer with Roosevelt's successor. Truman lashed out at the Soviet minister for his country's refusal to allow the Poles free elections. "I have never been talked to like that in my life," Molotov complained.

"Carry out your agreements, and you won't get talked to like that!" Truman shot back. As soon as the war with Germany ended, Truman terminated lend-lease shipments to the Soviet Union, even though the Russians were committed to the war against Japan.

FORMATION OF THE UNITED NATIONS. A postwar world organization was discussed at all the wartime conferences. By early 1945 there was general agreement on its framework. Invitations to a conference that would draft the organization's charter went out before Roosevelt's death. *One of Truman's first actions was to confirm the meeting. The conference assembled in San Francisco in May 1945.* It took two months to draft a charter. Although there were a number of disagreements, the final document was signed by all 50 nations attending the conference.

The charter provided for a General Assembly in which each nation would have one vote. Its primary function was to discuss problems. The Security Council, consisting of five permanent members (the United States, Britain, France, the Soviet Union, and China) and six elected nonpermanent members, was given power to resolve international disputes. At the insistence of the United States, each of the major powers was given a right to veto Council actions. The veto would permit the great powers to protect their vital interests. In the United States, the veto silenced the critics of internationalism.

The Secretariat, or the office of the Secretary-General of the United Nations, was given the power to bring important matters to the Security Council. The Secretariat was to conduct the daily affairs of the UN. The fourth major division, the Economic and Social Council, consisted of 18 members chosen by the General Assembly. Members were given the power to make recommendations on worldwide social, economic, health, educational, and cultural matters.

The Senate ratified the United Nations Charter with only two dissenting votes. It was a measure of how far the country had moved away from isolationism.

THE DEFEAT OF GERMANY. In the early days of May 1945, Soviet troops forced their way into Berlin, Hitler committed suicide in his blast-proof bunker, and the German armies surrendered. Nazi leaders were arrested so that they could be tried for war crimes.

As the Allied armies advanced into Germany, they gradually discovered the awful truth of the *Holocaust.* Hitler had ordered the extermination of all Jews in Germany and, ultimately, in Europe. *Of the six million Jewish men, women, and children killed by the Germans, four million of them were systematically and diabolically killed in specially built extermination camps.* When the Allied armies arrived at the concentration camps, they found hundreds of starving people.

Holocaust: a great destruction of life. It is the word used by Jews to refer to Hitler's extermination of about six million Jews in concentration camps during World War II.

The trial of Nazi leaders at Nuremburg, Germany, for these and other war crimes, was one of the central events of the postwar years.

THE POTSDAM CONFERENCE. Toward the end of June, 1945, the Allied leaders held their final wartime conference at Potsdam, a suburb of Berlin. High-level negotiations were a new experience for President Truman. But he took it in stride. "Churchill talks all the time," he confided to his mother, "and Stalin just grunts, but you know what he means." The conference worked out the details for the division of Germany and Austria into Soviet, British, French, and American zones. Stalin promised to declare war on Japan on August 8, a

These paintings are two of many found in the diary of Alfred Kantor, a survivor of three Nazi concentration camps. Kantor spent a total of three-and-a-half years in the concentration camps of Terezin, Auschwitz, and Schwarzheide. During his years of imprisonment, Kantor endured hard physical labor with little food and a lot of harsh treatment. He admits that without food packages from his sister, he surely would have died.

Ten weeks after being liberated in July 1945, Kantor recorded the things he had witnessed in the camps. For some of the paintings, he used as guides the pencil sketches he had drawn in the camps. But most he had been forced to destroy to avoid being caught and punished. Those Kantor committed to memory. Later he painted the impressions with remarkable detail and accuracy. The captions were written by Kantor in English, rather than in his native Czech. Otherwise, he realized few people would understand them in America, where he would soon be living.

The painting on the left shows the roundup of prisoners en route to Auschwitz. People were ordered to throw away all their belongings. They were then herded onto open trucks, which would take them to the camp. The painting on the right is evidence of the hundreds of thousands of families whose lives were shattered by the Holocaust.

Throw away all your baggage and hurry to the trucks!
food, cloth, money and valuables in the dust-...

31

40.000 Hungarian women kept in a small camp. Their children and parents were killed, their men sent to another camp.

May 1944

date that would give him time to move his armies to the east.

THE ATOMIC BOMB. During the Potsdam Conference, President Truman received a telegram from General Leslie R. Groves at White Sands, New Mexico. It informed him that the atomic bomb on which Groves and other physicists had been working was ready. It had been tested in the New Mexico desert, and it worked.

Truman immediately informed Churchill and Stalin of the new weapon. They decided to close the conference by issuing an ultimatum to Japan: "The alternative to surrender is prompt and utter destruction." Japan rejected the ultimatum. President Truman then had to decide whether to use the terrible weapon he had at his disposal.

DEBATE OVER THE ATOMIC BOMB. The scientists who developed the atomic bomb had expected it to be used against the hated Nazis. *Many of them objected to its use against Japan, where the morality of the war was less clear.* Why not a demonstration? they asked. The United States could blow up a desert island in the Pacific in the presence of Japanese observers. At the very least, they argued, Japan should be informed of the bomb's terribly destructive potential.

President Truman rejected all such arguments. United States scientists had been able to make only three bombs, one of which had already been exploded in New Mexico. If one of the others fizzled or if the Japanese were unimpressed by a demonstration on a desert island, the United States would be out of bombs.

The invasion of Japan was certain to be a bloodbath. *If dropping a bomb would end the war quickly, Truman believed that the saving of American lives required it.* There were other considerations. Truman hoped to end the Pacific war before the Russians could enter it. He wanted to prevent the kinds of complications that were developing in Europe. He might even have hoped that the bomb would give him additional leverage against the Russians in Europe.

HIROSHIMA. On August 6, 1945, a single B-29, the *Enola Gay,* flew over the Japanese industrial city of Hiroshima (hee-roe-SHEE-mah). Not a siren sounded. Then there arose a blaze of light many times brighter than the sun, a ball of fire, and a mushroom-shaped cloud. The whole center of the city was gone. About 100,000 men, women, and children died instantly. Hundreds of thousands were injured. On August 8, as promised, the Soviet Union declared war. The next day America's last atomic bomb leveled the city of Nagasaki.

On August 10 Japan sued for peace. A cease-fire was arranged on August 15. General MacArthur, aboard the battleship *Missouri,* sailed into Tokyo Bay and accepted Japan's formal surrender on September 2, 1945. The war was over. But a true peace was yet to come.

Section Review

1. Identify or explain: Thomas E. Dewey, Vyacheslav Molotov, Potsdam Conference, the *Enola Gay,* the *Missouri,* atomic bomb.
2. Charting: Using the information given on page 647, make a chart showing the organization of the United Nations.
3. Why was the Democratic party's slogan "Don't change horses in the middle of the stream" a logical choice for the election of 1944?
4. List the four basic agreements of the Yalta Conference. What was the major criticism leveled against the United States position at the conference?
5. What reasons did President Truman have for authorizing the atomic bombing of Hiroshima and Nagasaki in August 1945?

Chapter 27 Review

Bird's-Eye View

The first battle of World War II was fought on the home front—the battle of production—in which the United States mobilized its economy for war. As a result of Roosevelt's foresight, the nation mobilized much more rapidly than it had in 1917. Consumer industries were converted rapidly and efficiently to wartime production. Defense plants were constructed.

Twelve million men and women served in the armed forces. And about 30 million worked in civilian jobs directly related to war production. The home front also helped by cutting back consumption of such scarce items as rubber and gasoline.

Japan struck quickly after its attack on Pearl Harbor and won the first series of battles in the Pacific. With the Battle of Midway the tide turned in the Allies' favor, for Japanese suffered crushing losses. At the same time, there was a dramatic reversal in the war in Europe. Allied armies defeated the Germans in North Africa and on the Russian front, Soviet armies beat German forces at Stalingrad. The Germans struck back with intensified submarine warfare, sinking about 400 American ships. Because the production of American ships far exceeded their destruction, the submarine threat was soon eliminated.

After the Allied forces landed on the beaches of Normandy, France, the war in Europe was virtually won. Victory in the Pacific resulted from the Allies' island-hopping strategy.

President Roosevelt died six weeks after the important Yalta Conference. Despite the fact that Britain, America, and the Soviet Union were united against the Axis powers, they were in conflict with one another over the issue of who would control eastern Europe. The formation of the United Nations promised to ease some of the tensions. But it was clear to Truman, as it had not been to Roosevelt, that trouble loomed ahead.

Truman's most pressing problem in 1945 was not how to deal with these tensions but how to bring the war in Asia to a close. Military authorities believed that very drastic measures would have to be taken to force the surrender of Japan. Drastic measures were taken on August 6 and 9, 1945, when atomic bombs were dropped on the cities of Hiroshima and Nagasaki. In two devastating blows, Japanese power was crushed and the war ended.

Vocabulary

Define or identify each of the following:

war bonds	the Desert Fox	kamikaze
Battle of Midway	D-Day	Yalta Conference
intelligence operation	beachhead	Security Council

Review Questions

1. How did the war aims and hopes expressed in the Atlantic Charter echo those of Woodrow Wilson?
2. How was the economy mobilized to prepare for World War II?
3. Describe the American strategy in the Pacific.

4. What strategy did the Allies use to defeat the Axis Powers in Europe?

5. In what important respect did Roosevelt and Truman differ in their relations with the Soviet Union?

Reviewing Social Studies Skills

1. Using the map on page 635, answer the following:

    a. What territory was in the area of maximum Japanese expansion?

    b. What was the approximate distance from the Aleutian Islands to Sumatra? From Manchukuo to New Guinea? From Wake Island to northern Burma?

2. Using the map on page 641 and the material in the chapter, locate and explain the importance of the following:

    a. El Alamein   **e.** Sicily

    b. Casablanca   **f.** Dunkirk

    c. Stalingrad   **g.** Normandy

    d. Moscow   **h.** Yalta

3. Make a chart, listing the major meetings of the Allied leaders. Include the following items on the chart: **a)** the name of the meeting, **b)** the date, **c)** the location, **d)** the participants, and **e)** the outcome.

Reading for Meaning

1. What was Truman's argument for dropping the atomic bomb on Japan? Who objected to dropping the bomb?

2. Characterization is the art of making someone come alive on the printed page. A writer will characterize someone by describing his or her appearance, by talking about the person's career and accomplishments, or by quoting things he or she has said. The authors of this book use several means to characterize Harry S Truman. Identify four characterizations, giving page references to prove your point. Then, in a brief paragraph, tell which method brought Truman most vividly to life for you.

3. A historian's writing style influences the way we see the history that she or he is writing about. Each of the sentences below is an example of the author's style. If the phrase in italics were changed, in each case, to the phrase in parentheses, how would your view of history change?

    a. "Japan struck *with dazzling speed* (quickly) in the weeks after Pearl Harbor."

    b. "*The Desert Fox* (Rommel) escaped the trap."

Bibliography

Cornelius Ryan's *The Longest Day: June 6, 1944* (Simon and Schuster) gives an exciting account of the D-Day landing.

Bob Considine and Ted Lawson's *Thirty Seconds Over Tokyo* (Little, Brown, and Company) gives a first-hand account of the bombing of Tokyo during World War II.

Night, by Elie Wiesel (Avon), is a fictional account of a boy in a concentration camp.

Chapter 28

From Hot War to Cold

1945-1949

Winston Churchill had aged. The strain of war had taken its toll on his health. There was a lonely sadness about him, too. The British people, in the first postwar election, had swept him and his party out of office.

But some of the old fire was there. And it had never burned brighter than when Churchill stepped onto the stage at Westminster College in Fulton, Missouri, on March 5, 1946. Having been invited to the college to speak, Churchill decided to use the opportunity to make a plea to all Americans. President Truman was in the audience. He knew what the former British prime minister was going to say. And he approved it.

"From Stettin in the Baltic to Trieste (tree-EST) in the Adriatic," intoned Churchill gravely, "an iron curtain has descended across the continent of Europe. . . ." Police governments controlled the people of Eastern Europe, he continued. And unless Soviet communism were stopped, it would sweep into the Near East and the Balkans. Italy and France might fall victim to their own Communist parties. The entire western world would then be endangered.

Churchill's words were fighting words. They reflected the tense mood of the postwar era. World War II had ended, but the ending had not brought peace. Germany and Austria were divided by treaty among the victorious Allies. And the division symbolized the growing division of the world into two armed, hostile camps.

Two giant powers—the United States and the Soviet Union—dominated the world. Soviet armies occupied central Europe, where Soviet diplomats were setting up pro-Soviet governments. In Asia, the United States occupied Japan; and Korea, Japan's former colony, was divided into American and Soviet occupation zones. In China the old civil war between Chiang Kai-shek's Nationalists and Mao Tse-tung's Communists had resumed.

Chapter Objectives

After you have finished reading this chapter, you should be able to:
1. List the economic issues that faced the country after World War II.
2. Describe the conflicts Truman had with Congress between 1946 and 1948.
3. Explain the social and civil rights reforms of the Fair Deal that Congress enacted.

The rivalry between the United States and the Soviet Union was the most important fact of the postwar decade. More than power and influence were involved. It was a contest between two rival political systems—democracy and dictatorship—and between two rival economic systems—capitalism and socialism.

The contest had begun well before the war ended. Friction between the Allies during the war was one sign. The spirited disputes that took place in the conferences near the close of the war were others.

In February 1946 Josef Stalin told the Soviet people that they must expect the world to remain tense and uneasy for some time. Therefore, the Soviet Union had to remain under arms. He demanded more sacrifices from the Russian people.

Churchill's Iron Curtain speech embodied the western democracies' response to the crisis. Both announcements amounted to a declaration of war—not a hot war of weapons and bloodshed, but a war of talk and maneuver—a cold war.

1. Americans Search Again for Normalcy

WINDING DOWN THE WAR MACHINE, 1945–1946. Americans were slow to respond to Churchill's warning. About 300,000 American young people had died in a long, trying conflict. They were tired of wartime shortages and restraints and were eager to return to the "pursuit of happiness." Even as Churchill spoke, the army was discharging 25,000 men and women a day.

EASING DEMOBILIZATION. Remembering the mistakes of World War I demobilization, the army tried to spread out discharges so that the economy could absorb returning veterans. But the public insisted on speedy discharges. Thus, by July 1946, the armed services had been cut from 12.5 million to two million members.

Rapid discharges caused fears of massive unemployment. But with careful government planning, these fears did not materialize. The War Assets Administration helped by selling surplus materials to veterans who wished to start small businesses. The Servicemen's Readjustment Act (popularly called the G.I. Bill of Rights) provided special unemployment benefits for veterans who could not find jobs. It also offered low-interest loans to those who wanted to start businesses.

The G.I. Bill had a great impact on education. It offered monthly income payments to all former G.I.'s who enrolled in vocational schools or colleges. Some eight million vets

Norman Rockwell was one of America's most popular illustrators. In this painting Rockwell depicted a G.I.'s homecoming. Who are the characters in the illustration? What values are expressed by the artist?

received training under the program, the largest and probably the most successful public education project in history. Most important, the program offered a college education to millions who might otherwise never have had the opportunity.

THE FAIR DEAL. President Truman wasted no time in formulating and announcing his postwar program. *On September 6, 1945—four days after the Japanese surrender—he presented Congress with a 21-point domestic plan that he called the Fair Deal.* Among its provisions were: **1)** expansion of social security; **2)** raising of the minimum wage from 40 to 65 cents an hour; **3)** a full employment act; **4)** a permanent Fair Employment Practices Act; **5)** public housing and slum clearance; **6)** protection of natural resources; **7)** public work projects like the TVA; **8)** government support of scientific research; **9)** federal aid to education; **10)** health insurance and prepaid medical care; and **11)** nationalization of atomic energy. Truman declared that his program "symbolizes for me my assumption of the office of President in my own right." Unfortunately for Truman, Congress faced more pressing problems. The Fair Deal would have to wait.

INFLATION PLAGUES THE NATION. *Although demobilization and conversion to a peacetime economy went more smoothly than they had in 1919, the end of the war brought problems, too. Among the most serious was rapidly spiraling inflation.*

After the war people expected the market to be flooded with all kinds of surplus goods. But their expectations were frustrated. Instead, there were serious shortages. Goods in short supply ranged from appliances to clothes, from nylon stockings to beef.

By working overtime in wartime jobs, many people had earned more money than ever before. With nothing to spend it on, they had stashed excess funds in savings accounts. At war's end, they had roughly 140 billion dollars in savings, which they

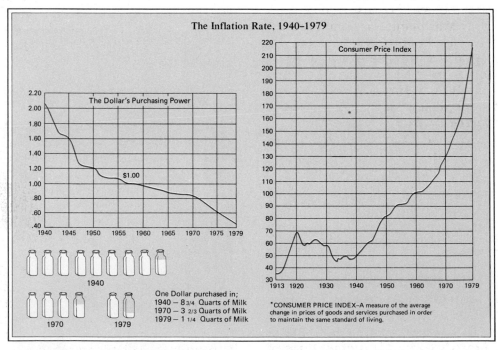

The Inflation Rate, 1940–1979

The Dollar's Purchasing Power

$1.00

1940

1970   1979

One Dollar purchased in:
1940 — 8 3/4 Quarts of Milk
1970 — 3 2/3 Quarts of Milk
1979 — 1 1/4 Quarts of Milk

Consumer Price Index

*CONSUMER PRICE INDEX–A measure of the average change in prices of goods and services purchased in order to maintain the same standard of living.

were eager to spend. Businesses wanted to purchase new equipment. Farmers wanted the latest machinery. And consumers were ready to purchase all the things they had been forced to do without during the war. To make matters worse, the demand for goods and food was not only domestic, it was also foreign. The rest of the war-torn world desperately needed American products to survive.

The shortage of goods and increased demand put intense pressure on prices. Although the Office of Price Administration tried, it could not hold prices in line as it had during the war. By the end of 1945, inflation threatened to overwhelm the economic system.

LABOR STRIFE. The spiraling cost of living made workers restless. *Although prices were rising, wages were not.* In some cases workers were making less than they had during the war years because of reduced overtime work.

Organized labor had made substantial gains during the war because the government required war plants to unionize. Also, labor had promised not to strike in wartime. And in general the promise was kept, even though it often meant that workers' hourly pay rose very little during the war.

In 1945 high prices, less work, and huge profits reported by industry persuaded labor leaders that a different strategy was called for. In January 1946 workers went on strike in many vital industries—first the auto industry, then oil refining, electrical products, and steel. In a short time two million people were on strike.

President Truman's policy was to appoint fact-finding commissions to help settle the disputes. With government mediation, labor emerged with hefty wage increases.

THE COAL MINERS' STRIKE. In April 1946 John L. Lewis led 400,000 miners out on strike. *Lewis's demands included wage increases, improvement in mine safety rules, and management contributions to a special miners' health and retirement fund.*

Within a matter of weeks, coal supplies dwindled to nothing, and many industries had to cut back on production. *When a railroad strike threatened, Truman had the government take over the coal mines.* With the mines under government control, Lewis was granted most of his demands, and the miners went back to work.

The following November, when the government was still running the mines, Lewis called another walkout. This time the government secured a court injunction against the strike. Lewis ignored the court order, pointing out that the law prohibited the use of injunctions. The court replied that the law did not apply to strikes against the government. It fined Lewis 10,000 dollars and the United Mine Workers 3,500,000 dollars. The fines, later upheld by the Supreme Court, marked the end of the close relationship between government and labor that had existed under the New Deal. Public approval of the huge fines also indicated the extent to which labor's actions had angered many people.

DEMANDING AN END TO PRICE CONTROLS. *While unions were striking for higher wages, business and agriculture were pressuring the government to end price controls.* They argued that continuing wartime controls were hampering productivity, depriving people of a fair profit, and creating a black market. *Fortune* magazine bolstered the argument by reporting in June 1946 the willingness of people to pay wildly inflated black market prices for certain goods. Nylon stockings sold for $7.50 a pair and a pound of butter for $1.50. Carpenters' nails were going for $15 a barrel. And manufacturers of alcoholic beverages were willing to pay astronomical illegal prices for sugar to be used in the distilling process.

Several members of Truman's administration urged him to end price controls. However, Congress resisted. On June 28, 1946, just before the act that had created the Office of Price Administration was to expire, Congress passed a law extending the life of the agency. *But Truman vetoed the bill, and ended price controls.*

By July prices jumped 25 percent. By October earnings dropped 12 percent. Consumers were furious with the Democrats and with the President. Truman's popularity, high at the end of the war, sank dramatically, as people joked, "To err is Truman."

"HAD ENOUGH?" *High prices, labor strife, shortages of consumer goods, and falling wages spelled trouble for the Democrats in the congressional elections of 1946.* To make matters worse, there was ill feeling within Truman's administration. Secretary of the Interior Harold Ickes resigned in protest over Truman's appointment of a wealthy oil magnate as Undersecretary of the Navy. Secretary of Commerce Henry Wallace was fired by Truman in a dispute over foreign policy. Several officials then left the administration in protest over the firing. And people in government complained that Truman never intervened in a crisis until it was about to explode.

The Republicans quickly capitalized on Truman's troubles. "Had enough?" they asked. "Vote Republican." And people did. *For the first (and so far, the only) time since 1928, the Republicans captured control of both houses of Congress.* When the new 80th Congress assembled in January 1947, the Republicans at last had a chance to shape an alternative to the policies they had so long opposed.

Section Review

1. Identify or explain: the G.I. Bill of Rights, the Office of Price Administration.

2. What steps did the government take during World War II to prepare for demobilization?
3. What was the Fair Deal? Outline its provisions, and explain why it was important to President Truman.
4. What arguments did business and agriculture use to bolster their demand for ending price controls?
5. Explain why there was serious postwar inflation.
6. Describe the ways in which labor strife affected the nation in 1946.

2. The Government Gets a Trimming, 1947-1949

REPUBLICANS CONTROL CONGRESS. The Republican victory in the 1946 elections was reminiscent of Warren Harding's landslide election after the First World War. Americans longed for peace and normality and wished to be left alone. In each election they voted against progressive demands and wartime restraints.

Republicans won the White House in 1920. They were able to have a decade of conservatism and to dismantle Progressivism. In 1947, however, Republicans did not control the White House, and so there were limits to what they could do. Rather than trying to dismantle the New Deal, they contented themselves with trimming some of its more ragged edges.

THE HOOVER COMMISSION. At the end of the war, it was generally agreed that the government needed trimming. Hundreds of alphabet agencies had been created to meet the emergencies of depression and war. Many of their powers overlapped. Some had outlived their usefulness.

In 1947 Congress created a commission to reorganize the federal bureaucracy. To head it President Truman appointed former

President Herbert Hoover. The commission studied the government for two years. In 1949 it submitted its findings in 18 extensive reports. About 350 changes were recommended. These changes primarily involved the combining of agencies and the eliminating of overlapping powers. Thus, while the commission suggested a much-needed streamlining, it did not recommend that the government be greatly reduced in size.

Congress reviewed and approved the suggestions of the Hoover Commission. The Reorganization Act of 1949 gave President Truman the power to develop practical plans for reorganizing the government. Over the next two years, 35 plans were submitted and approved.

THE NATIONAL SECURITY ACT. *Congress undertook to reorganize national defense.* Investigation of the Pearl Harbor disaster revealed serious flaws in the nation's intelligence system. It also uncovered rivalry among the various military services, which actually impaired smooth operation.

The National Security Act of 1947 separated the air force from the army and placed all three services under a single Department of Defense. It also created the Central Intelligence Agency (CIA) to coordinate the nation's intelligence gathering and to analyze the information. Finally, the act created the National Security Council. It was to be made up of the President, key members of the cabinet, and the head of the Joint Chiefs of Staff. The function of this group was to advise the President about international relations and defense strategy.

THE TAFT-HARTLEY ACT. Truman cooperated with Congress in reorganizing the federal bureaucracy, but the alliance fell apart when the Republicans moved to clip the wings of big labor. The strikes of 1946 and the actions of John L. Lewis had convinced many that it was as important to protect the rights of employers and consumers

as it was to safeguard the rights of labor. *As a solution to the labor problem, the newly elected 80th Congress drafted the Taft-Hartley Labor-Management Relations Act.*

Drafted in part by Senator Robert A. Taft of Ohio, grandson of former President William Howard Taft, the act prohibited various labor practices. Among them were *closed shop* agreements and excessive union contributions to political campaigns. It established a means for settling strikes in key industries on which the public depended. When bargaining between labor and management broke down and a strike threatened to tie up some important part of the economy, the President could delay it with an 80-day, cooling-off period.

A *closed shop* was the result of an agreement between unions and management to hire only union members for particular jobs.

During the cooling-off period, the President would appoint a board of inquiry to help management work out a final offer. If the union rejected this offer, the problem would be turned over to Congress. Union leaders and employers were also required to sign oaths stating that they were not members of the Communist party.

President Truman vetoed the Taft-Hartley Act on June 20, 1947, calling it "a slave labor law." On the same day a coalition of Republicans and conservative Democrats passed it over his veto by the huge margin of 331 to 83. Organized labor criticized the act bitterly. But most people considered it a reasonable compromise. And it has stood the test of time. Revised in minor ways, it remains the basis of our national labor legislation.

TRUMAN'S "DO-NOTHING" CONGRESS. The heated battle over the Taft-Hartley Act was only part of the friction between Truman and the Republican 80th

Congress. Congress repeatedly slashed his requests for money and rejected most of his proposals for legislation. His Fair Deal programs got nowhere with Congress.

By mid-1948 Truman was denouncing the 80th Congress for its "do-nothing" attitude. And he hoped to make that an issue in the approaching Presidential election. Having served out Roosevelt's fourth term, Truman wanted a term of his own.

THE ELECTION OF 1948. The Democratic party nominated Truman for President on the first ballot. But it did so with little or no enthusiasm. He had made little mark of his own and was chiefly known for quarreling with Congress.

The party was also badly divided. Liberal Democrats succeeded in placing a strong civil rights plank in the party's platform, triggering a southern walkout from the convention. In July 1948 delegates from 13 southern states formed a States' Rights party and nominated Governor J. Strom Thurmond of South Carolina for President. Formation of the party threatened the Democrats' traditional hold on the South.

Pollsters and political analysts had predicted a Dewey victory over Truman in the 1948 Presidential election. Here, a victorious Truman shows a headline written from those predictions. What does this picture indicate about the forecasting of such events as political elections?

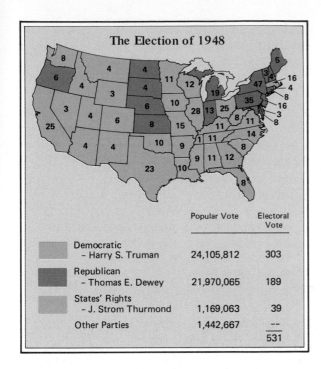

The Election of 1948

	Popular Vote	Electoral Vote
Democratic – Harry S. Truman	24,105,812	303
Republican – Thomas E. Dewey	21,970,065	189
States' Rights – J. Strom Thurmond	1,169,063	39
Other Parties	1,442,667	--
		531

Truman also faced rebellion among liberal Democrats. Henry Wallace had been one of Roosevelt's Vice-Presidents and a former member of the cabinet. He thought Truman's foreign policy was unnecessarily belligerent. In Wallace's opinion, the Soviet Union had real security needs in Eastern Europe. If the United States recognized this fact, Cold War tensions would be lessened. Wallace also maintained that the United States had been as responsible for the breakup of the wartime alliance as the Soviet Union. Finally, the liberals backing Wallace thought that Truman was weak in the domestic reform area.

Liberals who agreed with Wallace formed the Progressive Citizens of America. Then they nominated Wallace for President. With the Democratic party splintered left and right, many wondered what support Truman had left.

Republicans were jubilant about the disintegration of the Democrats. The congressional elections of 1946 had shown a shift in public mood. They were sure it would bring them the White House in 1948. *With confident enthusiasm the Republicans renominated their popular candidate of 1944, Thomas E. Dewey.* His running mate was the personable Governor Earl Warren of California.

TRUMAN'S WHISTLE-STOP CAMPAIGN. *Republicans failed to reckon with the resourcefulness of Harry Truman.* Using a "whistle-stop" technique, Truman traveled across the country by rail. He gave eight to 10 speeches a day in his blunt, off-the-cuff style. Wisely avoiding an attack on Dewey, whose policies were like his own, Truman concentrated on the Republican Congress. In virtually every speech, he denounced the do-nothing legislators who ignored the little guy, the average American.

In mid-campaign Truman paused to prove his point. He called Congress back into session on July 26 to enact some of the measures in the Republican platform. These measures, Truman well knew, were in direct conflict with the policies the Republicans had been pursuing in the 80th Congress. During the special two-week session, Congress did virtually nothing. With the nation watching, Truman made his point.

Despite such strategies and his efforts to rebuild the New Deal coalition of minorities, farmers, and labor, Truman seemed to lag behind Dewey. Newspapers scoffed at his energetic campaign, and opinion polls gave Dewey a substantial lead. But on Election Day, it was a different story. Truman outpolled Dewey by over two million votes. And he captured the electoral college by 303 to 189. On the liberal left, Henry Wallace received a million votes but failed to carry a single state. Strom Thurmond's states' rights "Dixiecrat" ticket received over a million popular votes and 39 electoral votes.

The Democrats regained control of Congress in the election of 1948, thereby ensuring greater cooperation between the two

Sidenote to History

Perle Sturgis Mesta

Perle Sturgis was born in 1890. After graduating from the University of Kansas, she married George Mesta, a Pittsburgh industrialist. In the election of 1924, George Mesta contributed heavily to Calvin Coolidge's campaign, and the Mestas became prominent in Washington social circles. In 1935 Perle became active in politics by joining the National Woman's Party. Then, after George Mesta's death, Perle settled in Washington and became involved in both Republican politics and the women's rights movement. In 1940 she left the Republican party in protest over the failure of the conservatives to support Wendell Willkie.

Two years later, while lobbying for the Equal Rights Amendment, she met Harry Truman, then a Senator from Missouri. She became close friends of the Trumans, while simultaneously earning a reputation as a Washington hostess. Her parties were large, well planned, and entertaining. Because Bess Truman disliked giving parties, Perle Mesta became the unofficial hostess for the administration after Truman became President.

In 1949 President Truman appointed Mesta Minister to the Grand Duchy of Luxembourg. She was one of the first women to be appointed to a diplomatic post. Mesta accepted, in the hope that "it would clear the way for the appointment of other women to diplomatic and other government posts."

Perle Mesta proved to be a highly successful ambassador. She knew a good deal about steel production, Luxembourg's leading industry, and she traveled widely on behalf of both commerce and educational exchange. She retired in 1953.

branches of government. The election also brought some fresh faces to the political scene, among them Senators Hubert H. Humphrey of Minnesota, Paul Douglas of Illinois, and Estes Kefauver of Tennessee. The way seemed clear for Truman's Fair Deal.

Section Review

1. **Mapping:** Using the map on page 659, answer these questions: **a)** In which regions of the country were Truman and Dewey strongest? Weakest? **b)** Where did most of Thurmond's support come from?
2. Identify or explain: The Hoover Commission, the National Security Act, "do-nothing" Congress, J. Strom Thurmond, the Progressive Citizens of America, Earl Warren.
3. What conditions prompted Congress to pass the Taft-Hartley Act? Explain the provisions of the act.
4. Explain the campaign tactics that helped Harry S Truman win the Presidential election of 1948.
5. Why did the election of 1948 seem to pave the way for the enactment of Truman's Fair Deal?

3. The Fair Deal at Work

LIBERALS AND CONSERVATIVES REACT. President Truman's stunning election victory revived the spirits of liberals and reformers across the country. They were convinced that the nation had rejected a postwar Harding-style reaction and had embraced instead the cause of social progress and human betterment. Truman's Fair Deal, they believed, would improve and extend the essential features of the New Deal.

Conservatives, however, viewed Truman's reelection with dismay. They feared that Fair Deal programs would increase the role of government and ultimately lead to a socialistic system.

As it happened, both the liberals and the conservatives were wrong. *The Fair Deal achieved a number of important reforms.* But it was neither radical nor long-lived. Truman got several proposals through Congress. But a conservative coalition of Republicans and southern Democrats blocked the rest. And before long the President was distracted from the Fair Deal to other problems—those created by communism at home and abroad. A Red Scare and another war weakened the Fair Deal.

There were, nonetheless, some solid reforms in the Fair Deal legislation that did get through Congress.

LEGISLATION FOR SOCIAL PROGRESS.
Under Truman's prodding, Congress increased the federal minimum wage to 75 cents an hour. It voted amendments to the Social Security Act that increased benefits for retired workers by 75 percent and extended coverage to an additional 10 million persons. The National Housing Act of 1949 provided federal funds for the construction of about 810,000 housing units for low-income families. And Congress made additional grants for slum clearance and the construction of rural housing. It increased appropriations for the development of electric power, for the reclamation of lands in the West, and for the TVA.

Immigration laws were changed by the Displaced Persons Act of 1950. Truman insisted that pre–1950 legislation discriminated against people from southern and eastern Europe—people who were mostly Catholic and Jewish. The act doubled the number of people who could immigrate to the United States from that part of the world.

"You Folks Hear Any Talk About A Housing Shortage?"

The severe housing shortage after World War II was one of the problems faced by the Truman administration. Here, the cartoonist comments on the role of a congressional investigation in solving the shortage. What is the point of the cartoon?

Other progressive social programs were blocked in Congress, including a national health insurance plan with prepaid medical and dental services financed by a payroll tax. The American Medical Association called the plan socialized medicine. They raised 3 million dollars to campaign against it.

Congress defeated proposed federal aid to education because no one could decide whether aid should go to parochial schools. It also blocked the proposed reform of farm subsidies.

661

CIVIL RIGHTS. *The Fair Deal's principal departure from the New Deal was in the realm of civil rights.* Roosevelt seemed primarily concerned with the material well-being of Americans. Truman's concerns included their social improvement. Truman made progress in bettering the position of America's racial and ethnic minorities. His housing and urban renewal programs were aimed at improving the living conditions of the disadvantaged.

During the war President Roosevelt created the Fair Employment Practices Commission to eliminate racial discrimination in

Sidenote to History

The Frenzied Forties

Movies, plays, show business personalities, and fads in the 1940's managed to lessen the concerns of the nation, even if only for a few hours. Almost every American home had a radio. Listeners tuned in to their favorite programs. Shows such as *The Lone Ranger* held the attention of children during the war years. In the postwar era the show was translated into a television series. Comedian Bob Hope began a longtime partnership with singer Bing Crosby in the early 1940's, blending comedy and songs. Cowboy stars, comics, crooners, and radio detectives—now mostly forgotten—had avid fans.

In the world of show business, the biggest single attention getter in the 1940's was a skinny, blue-eyed singer from Hoboken, New Jersey. When Frank Sinatra appeared at the Paramount Theater in New York in 1944, police had a hard time controlling 30,000 screaming fans who packed the theater to hear him sing songs.

When not attending their idol's concerts, teenagers listened to his recordings on the jukebox, a record-playing contraption found in almost every soda shop during the 1940's and early 1950's. Teenagers spent Saturday nights dancing to the latest jukebox hits.

Dances like the jitterbug required some acrobatic skill and good coordination, as young men and women jumped, hopped, and threw each other around.

In an attempt to look different from their elders, the younger generation tried to acquire an appearance of studied sloppiness. A favorite outfit for young women was their fathers' or brothers' shirts worn over rolled-up jeans. The look was accented by loafers or saddle shoes worn with the inevitable bobby socks. For a while some of the civilian adult male population found the zoot suit appealing. But the broad and baggy suit with its wide stripes, loud colors, and floor-length key chain proved to be too extreme for most tastes, and the fad soon died out.

Many people regularly paid 30 cents to see the latest double feature at the local movie house. Hollywood contributed a romanticized version of the war, and total escape could be found in the "all-singing, all-dancing" musicals that movie audiences realized were harmless fantasy.

Fans of the Broadway stage had reason to rejoice during the 1940's. Three great musicals—*Oklahoma, Carousel,* and *South Pacific*—made entertainment history. The musical dramatists responsible for this string of successes were Richard Rodgers and Oscar Hammerstein II. Together they turned out one unforgettable song after another.

war-related industries. In 1949 Truman asked Congress to make the commission permanent and to enact legislation that would prohibit job discrimination. The proposed legislation, however, fell victim to a *filibuster.*

A *filibuster* is an extended speech lasting hours, even days, in the Senate (which has no rule limiting the length of time a senator can speak). The speaker's aim is to "talk a bill to death." The senator talks so long that other members finally agree to abandon the measure so that other public business can be transacted.

Truman salvaged what he could through administrative action. He resurrected the Fair Employment Practices Committee to supervise defense contracts. He prohibited federal housing money from being used to fund racially segregated projects. He appointed Blacks to prominent positions in the government. And he ordered the armed forces desegregated. The air force and the navy, which had few Blacks, complied quickly. The army was slower in complying with the President's order to desegregate. But by 1952 it was racially integrated, both in Europe and in the United States.

THE SUPREME COURT AND CIVIL RIGHTS. *The Supreme Court, with a solid majority of Roosevelt and Truman appointees, became a more active partner in the search for civil equality.* In 1944 it ruled that a political party was not a private club. Thus, it could not exclude Blacks from voting in primary elections. In 1947 the Court declared that segregation on interstate buses and railroads was unconstitutional. In the following year it stated that discriminatory real estate contracts could not be enforced in federal courts.

In the case of *Sweatt* v. *Painter* (1950) the Court held that the "separate but equal" concept, under which many states maintained segregated school systems, did not apply to graduate schools. A separate Black law school, said the Court, could never be equal to the University of Texas Law School in reputation, library resources, and faculty. Separation itself suggested inequality. Four years later the Court extended this line of reasoning to all forms of public education.

THE DEATH OF THE FAIR DEAL. In 1950, for the first time since reconstruction, there were three Blacks in the House of Representatives. Gwendolyn Brooks was the first Black poet to be awarded a Pulitzer Prize. UN mediator Ralph Bunche, a Black diplomat, was awarded the Nobel Peace Prize. By that date, too, the Fair Deal was dead. In June American troops were sent to Korea. The rising concern over communism at home and abroad left the Fair Deal forlorn and forgotten as the United States moved into the fifties.

Section Review

1. Identify or explain: National Housing Act, the Displaced Persons Act of 1950, filibuster, separate but equal, *Sweatt* v. *Painter.*

2. How did Fair Deal programs aid the following groups: retired workers, low-income families, slum dwellers, immigrants?

3. Which Fair Deal programs were not enacted? Why?

4. How did the Fair Deal improve the civil rights of Black Americans? What role did the Supreme Court play in this important development?

5. What developments at home and abroad left the Fair Deal "forlorn and forgotten" at the beginning of the 1950's?

Chapter 28 Review

Bird's-Eye View

World War II solved some problems and created others. One of the most serious postwar problems was the growing division of the world into two hostile camps—the Soviet bloc and the western democracies. The conflict represented a new kind of war—a war not of weapons and bloodshed but of talk and maneuver—a cold war. In 1946 Winston Churchill warned the United States of the threat this conflict posed to world peace. But Americans had had enough of war and wanted to return to normalcy.

Remembering the mistakes of World War I demobilization, the nation demobilized much more smoothly and efficiently after World War II. Careful government planning helped men and women discharged from the military services readjust as rapidly as possible to civilian life. Reconverting from a wartime to a peacetime economy brought some problems. One of the most serious was inflation, which led to labor unrest and a series of nationwide strikes. Unions demanded higher wages to help workers meet the rising cost of living. Higher wages led to higher prices. Inflation spiraled upward, threatening to overwhelm the economic system.

Republicans captured both houses of Congress in the 1946 elections. Believing that the government had become too complex, the Republicans worked to trim some of its more ragged edges. Agencies were combined, overlapping powers were eliminated, and the bureaucracy was streamlined. One of the most important actions of the 80th Congress was the passage of the Taft-Hartley Act, prohibiting various labor practices that many believed had led to the disruptive strikes of 1946. Although President Truman vetoed the act, it was passed over his veto by a huge margin.

Congress repeatedly cut Truman's requests for funds and rejected most of his proposals for legislation. The President, in turn, denounced Congress as a "do-nothing" body, making this the main issue of his 1948 campaign. Truman won by a landslide. His victory was due largely to a vigorous whistle-stop campaign and the public's agreement that the 80th Congress was doing nothing.

The Democrats won the White House and recaptured Congress in 1948, paving the way for the enactment of Truman's domestic program, which he called the Fair Deal. Its accomplishments, though significant in such areas as civil rights, immigration, and housing, were not as far-reaching as Truman had hoped. Many Fair Deal programs were blocked by a conservative coalition in Congress. And in the end, the program was forgotten as the nation turned to the problem of communism both at home and abroad.

Vocabulary

Define or identify each of the following:

iron curtain	States' Rights party	Hoover Commission
Cold War	price controls	CIA
G.I. Bill	filibuster	Ralph Bunche

Review Questions

1. What led to the situation known as the Cold War?
2. What economic problems did the United States face after World War II?
3. What domestic conditions did the Republicans use against the Democrats in the congressional election of 1946?
4. How did Harry Truman win the 1948 Presidential election?
5. What effect did the studies of the Hoover Commission have on the government?
6. List three Fair Deal acts aimed at reform.

Reviewing Social Studies Skills

1. In his March 5, 1946, speech, Winston Churchill declared that "from Stettin in the Baltic to Trieste in the Adriatic, an iron curtain has descended across the continent of Europe." Use the map on page 645 to answer the following questions:
   a. What countries were behind the iron curtain?
   b. How long was the iron curtain in kilometers and miles?
2. Review the material in this chapter on the Fair Deal programs, on Truman's criticism of the 80th Congress, and on his reaction to the Taft-Hartley Act. Make a list of the values you think Truman held. Then rank these values in the order of importance you think they had for Truman and in the order of importance they have for you. Do your values differ from Truman's? How?

Reading for Meaning

1. The first section of this chapter is titled "Americans Search Again for Normalcy." Write a paragraph explaining in what ways this heading implies a connection between the moods of Americans after World Wars I and II.
2. On page 653, the authors state that after World War II Americans were "eager to return to the pursuit of happiness." The phrase "pursuit of happiness" was taken from the Declaration of Independence. Write a paragraph explaining why you think the authors used this phrase in writing about the attitudes of Americans in the years immediately following the war.
3. Write two paragraphs on the progress made in civil rights during Truman's administration. The first paragraph should identify the specific changes made through the use of executive order, court decision, and legislation. The second paragraph should explain which means of securing civil rights you think is the most effective.

Bibliography

Lloyd Gardner's *Architects of Illusion* (Quadrangle) sketches the people who were responsible for American foreign policy in the 1940's.

Paul Y. Hammond's *The Cold War Years: American Foreign Policy Since 1945* (Harcourt Brace Jovanovich) is a good survey of American diplomacy from Truman to Lyndon Johnson.

Margaret Truman's *Harry S Truman* (Morrow) is a lively biography of the President by his daughter.

Chapter 29

1946-1955

Truman, McCarthy, and Korea

In 1946, a Canadian royal commission announced that it had uncovered an extensive Soviet spy ring. The ring, it claimed, had been feeding to the Soviet Union information needed for the development of radar.

The Canadian announcement filled many people in the United States with fear. Prodded by Congress, President Truman tightened government security. First, he appointed a committee to investigate the loyalty of government employees. On the basis of the committee's report, Truman issued an executive order establishing a loyalty program for the federal government. The grounds on which employees could be judged disloyal were vague. And the program's legality was questioned by many liberals.

Not content with these measures, the government attacked the American Communist party, a legal political party at the time. Eleven members of the party were charged with teaching and advocating the overthrow of the government. When they appealed to the Supreme Court, that tribunal upheld their conviction. This resulted in a reinterpretation of the "clear and present danger" concept developed by Justice Holmes in 1919.

In February 1950 the British government discovered that a spy ring, headed by physicist Klaus Fuchs, had been giving atomic secrets to the Soviet Union. The strict security measures imposed by the Truman administration seemed justified. And when information provided by Fuchs implicated two Americans, Ethel and Julius Rosenberg, in the spy ring, the nation was more convinced than ever that the United States was the focus of a Communist plot whose aim was to subvert democracy from within.

Chapter Objectives

After you have finished reading this chapter, you should be able to:
1. Describe the shift in the balance of power after World War II and the United States' policy of containment.
2. Explain why McCarthy was able to become so powerful in the early 1950's.
3. List in chronological order the events that led to United Nations intervention in Korea, and then list the events that took place during the conflict.
4. Describe Eisenhower's election in 1952 and identify the issues he had to face on taking office.

The arrest of Fuchs and the Rosenbergs seemed to answer one riddle—how the Russians had been able to develop an atomic bomb in such a short time. In fact, the information passed to the Soviets probably did them little good. Russian technology, as the United States learned later, was capable of developing a bomb. But the conviction and execution of the Rosenbergs answered another question. It showed how deeply the fear of an international Communist conspiracy had infected American life.

1. The Formation of Cold War Policy

AMERICAN ATTITUDES CHANGE. President Truman usually had to battle Congress tooth and nail on domestic questions. There was remarkably little disagreement about foreign policy. The lack of controversy is the more remarkable because American attitudes toward the world were undergoing a complete about-face during this period.

Prior to World War II the prevailing spirit was isolationist. Only rarely and in time of crisis were Americans dragged onto the world stage. Then they retired as soon as they thought their job was done. That mood prevailed for a fleeting moment at the close of World War II. *But by the end of 1947, a popular majority was prepared to endorse far-flung American commitments.*

FROM ISOLATIONISM TO INTERNATIONALISM. Isolationism was not the policy of one political party or one economic interest. In the 1930's business leaders were isolationist because they saw no need to spend the nation's treasure in solving other people's problems. Liberal reformers were isolationist because they thought the improvement of American society and institutions, not those of foreign nations, was the first order of business.

The shift to internationalism was *bipartisan.* President Franklin D. Roosevelt and his Democratic followers led the way by their opposition to Axis aggression in the late 1930's. In 1941, on the eve of World War II, the case for internationalism was summarized in an editorial in *Life* magazine entitled "The American Century." The author was none other than Henry Luce, head of the publishing empire of *Time-Life-Fortune* and a long-time critic of Roosevelt and the New Deal.

Bipartisan means "supported by two parties"—in this case, the Republicans and the Democrats.

In the editorial Luce criticized Roosevelt for not entering the war quickly enough. Axis aggression knew no bounds, said Luce. Once the Axis powers had gobbled the rest of the world, they would be ready to swallow up the United States. Americans, Luce insisted, had to make war to protect themselves in advance. Luce also expressed the hope that the United States would not retreat into isolation at the end of the war. He concluded by calling for an "American century" in which the nation would lead the world, not through force and brutality but through example. America's sense of justice, its morality, and its concern for human rights, he believed, would inspire imitation.

Another Republican convert to internationalism was Wendell Willkie, the Republican Presidential candidate of 1940. In 1942 President Roosevelt sent him on a goodwill tour of the Middle East, the Soviet Union, and China. Willkie's book *One World* (1943), based on the trip, was a plea for postwar international cooperation. It was read widely during the war.

As a result of these and other writings, Americans became more international in outlook by the time the war finally ended. Then came the jolt of Soviet aggression in

Eastern Europe, brought to public attention by Winston Churchill's iron curtain speech. Once again the reaction was bipartisan. *Liberals, hoping to breathe life into the United Nations, pleaded for a more active American role in foreign affairs. Conservatives, worried about the expansion of communism and the threat to American world trade, agreed.*

COLD WAR ATTITUDES. Accompanying this shift to internationalism was the formulation of a set of ideas and attitudes that shaped American foreign policy throughout the Cold War. The most important were:

1. There was a need to learn from the mistakes of the past. The isolationism of the 1930's was sentimental escapism, an effort to avoid world problems by burying our heads in the sand. Because isolationism was unrealistic, so ran the argument, it led to *appeasement,* or the attempt to get along with dictators by yielding to their demands. The Munich Conference and the subsequent fall of Czechoslovakia proved that appeasement only whetted dictators' appetites. Thus, the conclusion was drawn that because of its power the United States had world responsibilities. Among them was the obligation to help resist aggression.

Appeasement means to satisfy or concede to the demands of a nation.

---

2. Communism was not another passing fancy. It was an economic system alien to the American system of *free enterprise.* It could exist only in a dictatorship. Because it promised power and success to the lower classes of society, it was attractive to the down-and-out people of the world. Communism was expansive by nature. And all Communist leaders had tried to foment world revolution. Because it was alien, dictatorial, and expansive, communism was a threat to the United States.

Free enterprise is an economic system that permits private ownership of the means of production. It is characterized by large amounts of capital used in production, relatively great freedom of economic activity, and the great importance of the corporate form of business.

Soviet foreign policy was dictated by Communist ideology and the need to spread Communist revolution. Thus Soviet movements into Eastern Europe were not the result of the age-old Russian search for security. They were the first steps in global conquest. They were Munich-style aggression under another name. They would therefore have to be resisted.

3. The main hope of resisting international communism was through the revival of realistic balance-of-power diplomacy. That meant rebuilding Europe and restoring the strength of the Atlantic community. Specifically that meant rebuilding Germany. Germany would first have to be reconstructed economically. Then, if necessary, it should be rearmed. America's foreign policy, at least for the time being, ought to concentrate on Europe.

The policy that evolved from these assumptions was known as containment. It meant holding the line against Soviet advances in Europe through economic aid and military alliances.

THE TRUMAN DOCTRINE. These assumptions and conclusions were not reached instantly. They evolved slowly over a period of years. To some extent they were reactions to events. Each crisis gradually shaped the American response.

Throughout 1946 attention centered on the eastern Mediterranean. Stalin was determined to win control of the straits that led from the Black Sea—his only warm water port—to the Mediterranean. To achieve this goal he threatened Turkey with military intervention. At the same time, he installed Communist regimes in Rumania and Bul-

In 1948 Congress approved a 17-billion-dollar program to help Europe recover from the devastation of World War II. This bill, known as the Marshall Plan, was named after the Secretary of State who proposed it. Here, American soldiers are working to rebuild war-torn France.

garia and financed the Communist rebels in Greece.

For a century the British had been the dominant influence in the eastern Mediterranean. British gold shored up both the Greek and Turkish governments. Churchill had sent British troops into Greece at the end of the war to keep the Soviets out.

Great Britain, unfortunately, was in financial difficulties at the end of the war. In early 1947 the British government informed the United States that it could no longer afford aid to Greece and Turkey. The United States could not step in and lend money, as it had after World War I, because Greece and Turkey could not pay it back. The United States would have to give whatever it sent. To do that meant assuming the British role in the region.

Isolation yielded to internationalism in March 1947, when President Truman asked Congress for 400 million dollars in aid to Greece and Turkey. Henceforth, he said, America would consider itself obligated "to support free peoples who are resisting attempted subjugation by armed minorities or by outside pressures."

Truman was proposing that the United States place a diplomatic umbrella over free peoples—like the Monroe Doctrine's umbrella over Latin America. He was determined to resist both outside pressures (such as Soviet threats against Turkey) and revolution by armed minorities (as in Greece). *Newspapers called this policy the Truman Doctrine. It amounted to a pledge by America to resist communism around the globe.*

Senator Arthur Vandenberg of Michigan, Republican head of the Foreign Relations Committee, agreed. "The fall of Greece," he said, "followed by the fall of Turkey, would establish a chain reaction around the world which could easily leave us isolated in a Communist-dominated earth." American postwar foreign policy was gradually taking shape.

THE MARSHALL PLAN. Meanwhile, the State Department was becoming increasingly worried about the economic health of Western Europe. Postwar loans to Britain and France had failed to do much good. *In June 1947 Secretary of State George Marshall called for a massive sum of money to rebuild Europe.* Avoiding the narrow anti-Communist focus of the Truman Doctrine, Marshall declared that his plan was directed "not against any country or doctrine but against hunger, poverty, desperation, and chaos." He even intended to offer funds to the Soviet Union.

Later that summer a European conference met to plan ways of using the money. Soviet foreign minister Molotov attended the conference. But when the Western European countries decided on a cooperative plan of reconstruction, he walked out. The departure of the Soviets at least made it easier to secure the appropriation from Congress. Even so, a handful of isolationists, led by Senator Robert Taft, objected to the Marshall Plan, calling it "an international WPA."

Early in 1948, while Congress debated the Marshall Plan, the Soviets helped Czech Communists overthrow the democratically elected government of Czechoslovakia. This action struck many people as further evidence that the Soviets were embarked on a world conquest as menacing as Hitler's. Their techniques of *subversion* were more subtle, but their goal was the same—global control.

Subversion means the undermining of a government, or its overthrow from within.

The message of Czechoslovakia was not lost on Congress. *By large margins, it approved 17 billion dollars in Marshall Plan aid to Western Europe—including Germany.* The aid was distributed over the following three years with spectacular results. European countries combined American funds with hard work and investments of their own to rebuild their economies. By 1951, when the plan came to an end, Western Europe was strong, stable, and self-confident.

THE BERLIN BLOCKADE. After Congress approved the Marshall Plan in the spring of 1948, the nations of Western Europe (Britain, France, Belgium, the Netherlands, and Luxembourg) formed an alliance to administer the funds. The United States, which had never signed a formal alliance in peacetime, considered joining. And there was talk of combining the American, British, and French occupation zones in Germany.

All this activity alarmed Stalin, who was having difficulties of his own. Josip Broz, or Tito, as the Communist ruler of Yugoslavia was called, rejected Soviet direction. A wartime guerrilla leader, Tito had expelled the Germans from his country without Soviet help. Since there were no Russian armies in Yugoslavia, he pursued an independent course. In June 1948 Stalin threw Tito out of the world Communist movement. And in a massive purge, Stalin removed from office every non-Communist politician in Eastern Europe.

Then, on June 24, 1948, Stalin ordered a blockade of all road and canal routes into Berlin, the former German capital located 160 kilometers (100 miles) inside the Soviet zone. The move violated the Yalta agreement, which had provided free access to Berlin for the American, British, and French authorities governing the city.

Why did Stalin make such a dangerous move? The best guess is that he wanted to force a solution to the German problem.

The United States and Great Britain airlifted huge quantities of supplies into West Berlin during the blockade of 1948–1949. What mood is conveyed by this photograph, which was taken near the Berlin airport?

Fearful that the western powers might unite their occupation zones into a new Germany, Stalin hoped to use Berlin as a bargaining lever. He might also have hoped to regain some of the prestige lost through Tito's defection by forcing the western powers out of Berlin.

THE BERLIN AIRLIFT. Caught by surprise, the Truman administration reviewed its alternatives. To send an armed convoy through the blockade would risk war. Truman rejected that proposal. But he also rejected the idea of withdrawing from an indefensible position. That would have amounted to appeasement. "We are going to stay, period," he declared. But how?

The method finally worked out was a massive airlift to feed and supply the two million people who lived in the western sectors of Berlin. From airfields in western Germany, American planes transported coal, oil, flour, fruits and vegetables, clothing, and even automobiles into Berlin. Once a minute, 24 hours a day, transports zoomed into Berlin's Templehof Airport, unloading 11,700 tonnes (13,000 tons) of supplies a day. It was one of the most impressive displays of technology, timing, and organization in modern times. It went on for 324 days, ending only when Stalin lifted the blockade in May 1949.

THE BIRTH OF NATO. The Berlin crisis and the threat of war forced the Truman administration to review its defense posture in Europe. As a warning to Stalin, Truman ordered three squadrons of B-29's, equipped with atomic bombs, to certain bases in England. Truman had no intention of starting an atomic war over Berlin. He hoped to avoid war by strengthening the Atlantic alliance.

Soviet tactics presented a real problem for

the western democracies. No single move by the Russians—in Poland, Czechoslovakia, and Berlin—seemed to warrant a declaration of war. Yet the total number of governments taken over by the Soviets was worrisome. One American official likened it to the slicing of a salami—soon there would be nothing left.

Dean Acheson, who became Secretary of State when General Marshall retired, had a solution. *One of the chief architects of containment, Acheson wanted to carry the policy to its logical conclusion—a formal alliance among nations of Western Europe, together with the United States and Canada.* He believed that collective security, based on the principle that an attack on one was an attack on all, would contain Soviet expansionism—and end the salami slicing.

In April 1949 12 nations signed the pact creating the North Atlantic Treaty Organization (NATO). The treaty established a line of containment opposite the iron curtain, from Norway in the Arctic to Italy in the Mediterranean. With the later addition of Greece and Turkey, the line was extended to the shores of the Black Sea.

In April 1949, 10 European nations and the United States and Canada signed a pact that created the North Atlantic Treaty Organization (NATO). Here, Dean Acheson signs for the United States, while President Truman and Vice-President Barkley look on.

This poster commemorates the victory of Mao Tse-tung in the Chinese revolution. What other messages are conveyed by the poster?

The Chinese civil war, interrupted by World War II, resumed after the war. Truman asked General George C. Marshall to mediate. Marshall spent two months in China. He arranged truces, only to see them broken by one side or the other. He finally concluded that Chiang Kai-shek's Nationalist government was too unpopular and too corrupt to withstand the disciplined Communists. In 1947 he returned home to become Truman's Secretary of State.

Chiang held his own against the Communists for a while. But then his government folded. His forces outnumbered the Communists, but he lost every battle. In December 1948 he fled to the island of Formosa (Taiwan).

The fall of China forced the American government to review the concept of containment. Then, in September 1949, President Truman announced that the Soviet Union had tested an atomic bomb years before anyone expected them to develop the weapon. That ended the American monopoly on atomic weapons and changed the character of the Cold War. From that point on, every Cold War conflict raised the threat of world destruction.

THE FORMATION OF TWO GERMANIES. Later, in the summer of 1949, the American, British, and French zones of occupation were combined into the Federal Republic of Germany. Shortly after, Soviet authorities set up the German Democratic Republic in their zone. This area was controlled by German Communists. Each part of Germany reflected the social and economic system of its occupier.

THE FALL OF THE NATIONALISTS. Until 1949 the Cold War had centered on Europe. The policy of containment was designed to preserve the territorial and political integrity of Western Europe. In 1949 the situation changed when China was taken over by the Communists.

Section Review

1. Identify or explain: Senator Arthur Vandenberg, Dean Acheson, "The American Century," the Marshall Plan, Tito, the fall of China.
2. Describe the steps through which the United States moved from a position of isolationism to a position of internationalism. Why do the authors state that the shift to internationalism was bipartisan?
3. Explain the three most important ideas that shaped American foreign policy throughout the Cold War.
4. What was the Truman Doctrine? How was it similar to the Monroe Doctrine?

5. What development in Eastern Europe convinced Congress to approve the Marshall Plan?
6. How did the Berlin Blockade violate the Yalta agreement?

2. The Second Red Scare

A GLOBAL COMMUNIST CONSPIRACY. Because their attention was riveted on Europe, the American people were unprepared for the fall of the Nationalists in China. It came as a terrible shock. Since 1900 the defense of China had been the cornerstone of America's Far Eastern policy.

Long before the Communist success in China, however, the United States government was talking openly of a global Communist conspiracy. In 1947 Truman asked Congress for aid to Greece and Turkey. Congress was cutting military appropriations and slashing the President's budget in every way it could. It was a bad time for President Truman to be requesting money for a far-off corner of the world.

INFLUENCING PUBLIC OPINION. When Dean Acheson went to Arthur Vandenberg, chairperson of the Senate Foreign Relations Committee, to explain the problem, he found the Michigan Republican sympathetic. But, said Vandenberg, to convince Congress to approve such a drastic departure would require public pressure. *Therefore, the next year government officials talked openly of a global Communist conspiracy and the need for both rearmament and foreign aid.* Foreign events seemed to bear them out as the small countries of Eastern Europe tumbled one after another into the Soviet orbit. By the time Czechoslovakia suffered a Communist coup in February 1948, the American people were thoroughly scared.

WHITTAKER CHAMBERS AND ALGER HISS. In July 1948 the Soviet blockade of Berlin had American nerves drawn tight. *The House of Representatives' Un-American Activities Committee began an investigation to determine if the American government was in danger of subversion.* Elizabeth Bentley and Whittaker Chambers, two former Communists, gave the committee the names of 50 people allegedly involved in secret Communist activities. Many were government employees. Alger Hiss, one of those named, appeared before the committee to deny the charge. A movielike tale of espionage and intrigue followed. It climaxed in a trip to Chambers' Maryland farm where microfilm of State Department documents lay hidden in a hollowed-out pumpkin.

These documents, as well as other evidence, indicate that Hiss probably had given information to the Soviet Union. Hiss was convicted of perjury (lying under oath) and sentenced to prison.

TRUMAN HUNTS COMMUNISTS. The President, too, was busy hunting Communists. Attorney General J. Howard McGrath toured the country in 1949. He addressed patriotic groups, hinting that there were Communists in the nation's universities. He urged the publication of anti-Communist books. "There are today many Communists in America," he explained to one audience. "They are everywhere—in factories, offices, butcher stores, on street corners, in private business. And each carries in himself the death of our society."

Later that year the administration secured the conviction and imprisonment of 11 members of the Communist party for advocating the violent overthrow of the government. The Communist party is a legal political party in the United States. These party leaders were convicted under the Smith Act of 1940, which makes it a crime to advocate the overthrow of the government by force. The Supreme Court upheld their convictions. But in a later case (1957) it ruled that the First Amendment's guarantee of free speech protected revolutionary talk. To be convicted of such a crime a person had to attempt to overthrow the government by some overt act.

ENTER JOSEPH McCARTHY. On February 9, 1950, several months after the fall of China and six days after Britain uncovered the atomic spy ring led by Klaus Fuchs, Wisconsin's Senator Joseph McCarthy addressed a meeting of Republican women in Wheeling, West Virginia. In the course of

Sidenote to History

Dr. Ralph Bunche Citizen of the World

Palestine, a small colony on the eastern coast of the Mediterranean Sea, had been governed since World War I by Great Britain under a League of Nations mandate. At the end of World War II, it sprang suddenly into the news when many European, Jewish refugees migrated to Palestine.

Jews and Arabs had lived in Palestine in peace. But the desire of the Jews to form a Jewish state in the territory provoked trouble. Britain tried to stop the flood of Jews from Europe until a settlement could be reached with the neighboring Arab countries. But the Jewish immigrants kept coming. In 1948 the British mandate came to an end. The Jews proclaimed the state of Israel, and the Arabs declared war.

An American citizen, Dr. Ralph Bunche, helped arrange an end to the Middle East war. His work won him the Nobel Peace Prize in 1950—the first time a Black was awarded the prize.

As a boy, Ralph Bunche had shined shoes and had sold newspapers to get money for his family. He had paid his college tuition by work-

ing as a building custodian. His job, however, did not keep him from excelling in studies and sports. From college he went to graduate school, earning a doctorate in political science from Harvard University. Then, he taught at Howard University in Washington, D.C.

During the war Dr. Bunche served with American intelligence agencies, becoming an expert on Africa, especially the French colonies. Bunche joined the United Nations in 1945 and was appointed director of the division concerned with colonial mandates. When war broke out in the Middle East, he and Count Folke Bernadotte, the official UN mediator, worked tirelessly to achieve a settlement. When Bernadotte was assassinated in September 1948, Bunche became the official mediator.

Initially, Bunche had suggested that Palestine be divided into Arab and Jewish states, each with its own government. The Arabs rejected the solution. They wanted to eliminate Israel on the battlefield. The Jews, however, fought ferociously for what they considered their homeland. By early 1949 the Arabs were ready for peace.

Bunche helped both sides negotiate ceasefires, which left the borders of Israel approximately where the Israeli armies had set them. It was not a permanent settlement. (Indeed, the Arab states refused to recognize Israel's right to exist.)

Ralph Bunche was called on once again when civil war broke out in the Congo in 1960. Before his death in 1971, the Nobel Prize winner was given honorary doctorates by more than 40 colleges and universities.

his rambling remarks, he declared that Communists in the State Department were responsible for American setbacks around the world. Waving a piece of paper, he continued: "I have here in my hand a list of 205." A wild week followed. In a speech at Reno the next night, he mentioned 57 Communists. At Salt Lake City a week later, it was 81. Recognizing Senator McCarthy's accusations as sensational, the press broadcast the story.

McCarthy's charges seemed to unravel a lot of mysteries. Many believed him. The extent of the publicity probably surprised even McCarthy. But he welcomed it. Elected to the Senate in the 1946 Republican landslide, he was up for reelection in 1952. In progressive Wisconsin (he defeated Robert La Follette, Jr.) McCarthy's reelection chances were uncertain. An anti-Communist crusade was bound to win votes.

TYDINGS CHALLENGES McCARTHY. *During the spring of 1950 the Senate Foreign Relations Committee was headed by Democrat Millard Tydings. The committee investigated McCarthy's charges.* The Wisconsin senator proved impossible to pin down. He answered every demand for evidence with new accusations. Challenged at last to come up with a single name, McCarthy pinpointed Owen Lattimore, a professor at Johns Hopkins University and an occasional consultant to the State Department. The Tydings committee investigated and cleared Lattimore. It embarrassed McCarthy further by pointing out that the professor played no role in State Department decisions.

Senator Tydings was up for reelection in the fall of 1950. *During the election campaign McCarthy went to Maryland to level accusations against Tydings. He used falsified photographs as part of his evidence.* When Tydings was defeated McCarthy's position was secure. No senator dared face him openly lest he or she became the focus

On evidence that many felt was not only shaky but also illegal, Julius and Ethel Rosenberg became the first Americans convicted of treason in a time of peace. They were executed in 1953.

of accusations. For the next five years, Joseph McCarthy was the most important political figure in Washington.

THE PHENOMENON OF McCARTHYISM. In five years of investigating, with the full force of a Senate committee and its staff behind him, Joseph McCarthy failed to identify a single Communist spy. Furthermore, he never uncovered a subversive in the government. What, then, explains his extraordinary influence?

Part of it was timing. The string of Communist victories from Czechoslovakia to China created an atmosphere of tension and fear. McCarthy's claim that American Communists had sold out Chiang Kai-shek and had given the Russians the atomic bomb offered a simple, understandable explanation

676

for a complex and bewildering world situation. The sensational spy cases—Hiss, Fuchs, the Rosenbergs—made it believable.

Republicans, out of power for 20 years and frustrated by the 1948 defeat, rallied to McCarthy's side. His charges enabled them to embarrass the administration. And these charges gave the Republicans a popular issue on which to go to the country in 1952.

Truman, it must be said, handled the whole matter badly. At first he dismissed the affair as a red herring raised to sidetrack his domestic program. But that charge was unconvincing because the Truman administration had been hunting Communists. As early as 1947, he had demanded a loyalty check of government officials and dismissed those who refused to cooperate. (That in itself might have been the source of McCarthy's initial "lists.") Truman then shifted ground and began denouncing McCarthy as "the Kremlin's biggest asset."

AMERICA'S FEARS AND PREJUDICES. There was more to McCarthyism than politics. *The Wisconsin senator's criticism of Secretary of State Dean Acheson, a polished New York lawyer, appealed to many people who disliked the eastern establishment.* When McCarthy blocked Truman's nomination of foreign service officers with aristocratic-sounding names, like John Patton Davies and John Stuart Service, he appealed to the age-old American suspicion of the professional, the Harvard-trained egghead.

Finally, McCarthy exploited the press with masterful ingenuity. Knowing that reporters hungered for sensational stories that would make headlines, he timed his announcements to give them what they wanted. The news media cooperated. Although, in an apparent effort to be objective, they labeled McCarthy's victims controversial, they rarely investigated his charges. The result was that the victims never got rid of the label. Before long, to be called controversial was to be purged from American society. By December 1952, more than six million people had been checked out as security risks. And 25,000 had been singled out for full FBI investigations.

Senator McCarthy came on the scene at just the right moment. And he managed to appeal to American fears and prejudices. His Red hunt might have been short-lived but for another crisis abroad—the outbreak of war in Korea.

Section Review

1. Identify or explain: Whittaker Chambers, Elizabeth Bentley, Alger Hiss, Owen Lattimore, Senator Millard Tydings, Joseph McCarthy.
2. What led the Truman administration to suggest to the nation that Communists were conspiring to take over the world? What effect did this suggestion have?
3. Describe the Smith Act of 1940. How did the Supreme Court clarify its various provisions?
4. Describe the activities of Senator Joseph McCarthy. What tactics did he use to intimidate the Senate?

3. A Police Action in Korea

AMERICANS AND SOVIETS IN KOREA. After World War II, Korea was a poor and overpopulated country. It is located on a peninsula jutting out from China into the Sea of Japan. Korea suffered centuries of occupation. The Japanese occupied Korea in the early part of the century. After World War II Soviet and American forces occupied the country, arbitrarily dividing it at the 38th parallel. (See map, page 679.)

As the Cold War developed, the two superpowers created governments in Korea—the Soviets in the north, the

Americans in the south. Neither government was democratic. North Korea was a Communistic dictatorship. The pro-American ruler in the South, Syngman Rhee, kept himself in power with strong-arm police. Originally intended as a temporary border, the 38th parallel became the dividing line between two Koreas.

In 1949 the American and Soviet armies departed. Border clashes began to occur with increasing frequency. Each Korean regime tried to unite the country under its own rule. On June 25, 1950, North Korean armies rolled across the 38th parallel.

STALIN'S ROLE. How did it happen? It is believed that Stalin authorized the attack. He resented the fact that China's new leader, Mao Tse-tung, was challenging his role as world Communist leader by backing revolutions throughout Asia. *In Stalin's view, a unified Korea under Soviet domination would deflate Mao's prestige.* It would also serve as a warning to Japan.

In 1949 the United States signed a peace treaty with Japan, receiving the right to maintain military bases in the Japanese islands. Stalin probably hoped that a strong, armed Korea would blunt any threat from those islands. When the Soviets withdrew from Korea, they left behind a well-equipped North Korean Army, which they had trained in the use of sophisticated Soviet weapons. Stalin could not lose by urging the North Koreans to attack the South Koreans. If they won, he stood to gain. If they lost, it would be their problem, not his.

TRUMAN WORKS THROUGH THE UNITED NATIONS. When he learned of the attack, President Truman asked for a special meeting of the UN Security Council. The council met with the Soviet delegate absent (he was protesting the UN's refusal to admit Communist China). It called on the North Koreans to withdraw from South Korea. When the North Koreans ignored the order and pressed their attack, Truman then authorized General MacArthur to begin air strikes against the invaders south of the 38th parallel.

On June 27, 1950, the Security Council adopted a resolution branding the North Koreans aggressors and asking all UN members to assist South Korea. The Soviet delegate's absence prevented a Russian veto of the resolution. American policy had the backing of the UN. Three days later, with the South Korean Army in retreat, Truman ordered American ground troops into battle. Truman never asked Congress for a formal declaration of war. When a reporter asked him to describe the conflict, he called it a police action.

The term police action was significant. It showed the direction of the President's thinking. North Korea's aggression, he thought, was similar to Hitler's takeovers in the 1930's. To ignore or appease the North Koreans would encourage further aggression. The United States had to police the world, stopping aggression wherever it appeared.

A UNITED NATIONS WAR. This was familiar reasoning. Truman and Acheson had used it in the Berlin crisis. In fact, they probably would have sent American forces into Korea without the UN. *The resolution made it a United Nations war.* And it gave the American action an enormous advantage in world opinion. The Soviet Union's failure to vote against the resolution condemning North Korea was one of its biggest blunders of the Cold War.

Sixteen nations contributed troops to the UN command in Korea. Fairly sizable units were sent by Australia and New Zealand. Nevertheless, it remained an American war. The United States furnished the bulk of the ground forces and nearly all the air and naval units. Americans maintained command throughout the war. And the Joint Chiefs of Staff made all the key decisions.

The world organization rubber-stamped their orders.

DEFEAT AND RECOVERY. Despite all the Cold War tension, the United States was unprepared for a hot war. There were only 592,000 troops in service in 1950, less than half the army's strength at the beginning of World War II. General MacArthur's soldiers in Japan were inexperienced draftees, untested in combat. Unable to halt the North Korean advance, MacArthur concentrated on building a strong defense line around the port of Pusan (POO-SAHN) on the southern tip of the peninsula. There the North Korean assault was finally stopped toward the end of August.

Rather than battle his way back up the Korean peninsula, MacArthur made use of American naval and air power to make a surprise landing at Inchon (IHN-CHON) on the west coast near the South Korean capital of Seoul. (See map at the right.) In just two weeks, his tactics succeeded in cutting off supply lines and tearing apart the North Korean Army.

TRUMAN SHIFTS OBJECTIVES. *MacArthur's sudden victory led Truman and Acheson to raise their hopes.* The initial American objective had been to turn back aggression and restore the boundary of the 38th parallel. On September 11 the President authorized MacArthur to pursue the enemy into North Korea, providing there was no sign that the Chinese might intervene.

The possibility of Chinese intervention was real. Communist China and North Korea share a border along the Yalu River. China could be expected to react to an American army on the Yalu as the United States would react to a Chinese army on the Rio Grande. Even so, because of the strength of American air and sea power, the administration did not think Chinese intervention was likely. Secretary Acheson told a news conference that it would be "sheer

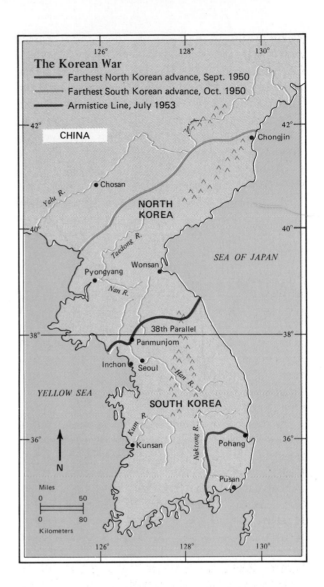

The Korean War

Farthest North Korean advance, Sept. 1950
Farthest South Korean advance, Oct. 1950
Armistice Line, July 1953

madness" for the Communist Chinese to intervene.

On October 7, 1950, the UN adopted an American resolution recommending the reunification of Korea after free elections. *What had started as an action to deter aggression had become a crusade to establish a united democratic Korea on the doorstep of China.*

REESTABLISHING THE 38TH PARALLEL. During that month, MacArthur's forces pushed into North Korea. MacArthur announced that he planned to proceed all the way to the Yalu River. Still worried about Chinese intervention, President Truman flew to Wake Island to confer with his Far Eastern commander. MacArthur assured him if the Chinese moved in without air support, there would be the "greatest slaughter." The President returned, satisfied that China would not aid North Korea.

Unknown to MacArthur, 300,000 Chinese soldiers had crossed the Yalu River. On November 26 they struck, sending the American Army reeling back across the 38th parallel with heavy losses. Winter storms made American air power almost completely ineffective.

By mid-January, the Chinese advance was halted. The Americans began a slow counterattack that took them back across the dividing line in April 1951. There, strung along a range of hills just north of the 38th parallel, the front remained for the next two years.

THE GREAT DEBATE ON COLD WAR STRATEGY. The advent of Communist China and the Korean War gave congressional Republicans a good deal of ammunition to use against Truman and the Democrats. Republicans charged that Truman and Acheson, by focusing their attention on Europe, had let Asia go down the drain and that the nation was battling an infectious ideology. It had to fight communism in

President Truman traveled to Wake Island in October 1950 to discuss Korean policy with General MacArthur. In a surprise ceremony, Truman gave the general a Distinguished Service Medal. Six months later, President Truman fired MacArthur.

every quarter of the globe—in Europe, in Asia, even at home.

Thus, the debate over military strategy abroad mingled with the Red Scare at home. And that hampered the discussion of possible alternatives. "It seems that the only argument some persons can present," complained Texas Senator Tom Connally, "is to holler about Alger Hiss and then refer to Yalta. Every time something comes up, they get out a Communist and chase him around."

Instead of questioning the policy of containment, the Republicans wanted to extend it. That was a prescription for trouble because it would force the United States to maintain a global line of defense, not knowing where the foe might attack. The Communist side, given the initiative, could probe the line at its weakest points, from the icy mountains of Korea to the jungles of Indochina.

TRUMAN REMOVES MacARTHUR.
In the midst of the congressional debate, President Truman set off an even louder controversy by dismissing his commander in Korea. The cause was MacArthur's refusal to follow Truman's orders.

MacArthur fretted about the limited American commitment in Korea. He saw no point in any war aim short of total victory. To achieve that, he advocated bombing China to cut off the flow of supplies into North Korea. He also wanted Chiang Kai-shek to distract the Chinese with raids on the mainland. Truman had little confidence in Chiang Kai-shek. Truman realized that bombing China would risk Soviet intervention and nuclear war. The Chinese assault had prevented him from obtaining the democratic Korea he wanted. He believed it was time to cut losses and get out.

As commander in chief, Truman ordered his general to limit the war. Instead, MacArthur appealed to Congress for support. In April 1951, Truman relieved him of command. At stake, said Truman, was the authority of the President over the military.

REACTION AT HOME. *MacArthur, who had not been in the United States since 1937, returned to a hero's welcome.* In New York City, millions turned out to express appreciation for his services in both World War II and Korea.

Republicans were outraged at Truman's action. Representative Richard Nixon accused the President of appeasement for removing his best general. And McCarthy called for Truman's impeachment. The Senate Foreign Relations Committee opened hearings on the question. And for a change, the Truman administration functioned with smooth efficiency.

General George Marshall, who had been called out of retirement to head the Joint Chiefs of Staff in the Korean emergency, pointed out that the kind of victory MacArthur demanded would require a total commitment of American arms. That would leave Western Europe defenseless and at the mercy of the Soviets. General Omar Bradley, who had helped lead the final assault on Germany, said that MacArthur would "involve us in the wrong war, at the wrong place, at the wrong time, and with the wrong enemy."

For a time MacArthur enjoyed public support. He gave a stirring speech before a joint session of Congress and said his farewell by quoting the lines of a West Point song, "Old soldiers never die, they just fade away."

To his utter surprise, MacArthur did just that. He let it be known that he was available for the Republican Presidential nomination in 1952. But he won only a spot on the convention stage. Hungry for victory, the Republicans wanted a more moderate candidate. And they had one who could match MacArthur's hero credentials—General Dwight D. Eisenhower, commander of the Allied Forces in Europe during World War II.

Section Review

1. Identify or explain: Syngman Rhee, General Omar Bradley, Mao Tse-tung, a United Nations War.
2. What reasons did Stalin have for encouraging the attack by North Korea on South Korea?
3. Why did President Truman describe the conflict in Korea as a police action?
4. Why did President Truman relieve General MacArthur of command in Korea?

4. Republicans Take Command

EISENHOWER BECOMES A CANDIDATE. Dwight Eisenhower served as president of Columbia University after the war. At Truman's request, he returned to the army in December 1950. To stress the importance of NATO in the administration's defense strategy, Truman asked Eisenhower to become Supreme Commander of the Allied Powers in Europe.

Eisenhower's military capabilities were well known. But no one was sure of his politics. In 1948 members of both parties explored the possibility of making him a candidate. He resisted the offers, explaining that he was not a politician.

By 1952, however, General Eisenhower was having second thoughts. The Asia-first feeling, expressed by Republican conservatives, disturbed him. Eisenhower agreed with Truman and Acheson that Europe could not be written off and that the war in Korea must be limited. However, he disagreed with Truman's Fair Deal. He considered himself a Republican.

In early 1952, when Senator Taft, leader of the conservatives, declared he would seek the Republican nomination, Eisenhower decided to oppose him. Without returning from Europe to campaign, he won every primary that he entered. Eisenhower won the nomination on the first ballot. Many Republicans who preferred Taft agreed that the general was their best chance to win.

THE ELECTION OF 1952. The Democrats were in deep trouble in 1952. *One scandal after another rocked the Truman administration in its last years.* None of them was very serious, but they left a troublesome aroma of corruption. The biggest scandal involved the "five-percenters," people who claimed to know the right people in the federal bureaucracy. They secured favors for their clients in return for a fee amounting to five percent of the value of the favor. Then it was discovered that General Harry Vaughn, the President's military aide and card-playing pal, had used his position to aid some of the five-percenters. In return he received a freezer as a gift. Instead of cleaning house, Truman grumbled and made excuses. The freezer became a campaign issue.

Vaughn's indiscretion did not amount to much, but it came on top of some sensational revelations by a Senate Committee investigating organized crime. *Headed by Senator Estes Kefauver, a crusading Tennessean, the committee exposed on nationwide television the relationship between the bosses of organized crime and the big-city Democratic machines.*

Making use of his television exposure, Kefauver campaigned for the Democratic nomination, winning victories in a number of primaries. When the Democratic convention opened, Adlai Stevenson, governor of Illinois, agreed to be a candidate in order to head off the overly colorful Kefauver. Stevenson was nominated on the third ballot and then named Kefauver his running mate.

THE REPUBLICAN SCANDAL. The Republicans suffered a corruption crisis of their own when it was discovered that Richard Nixon, who had been put on the ticket as Eisenhower's running mate to appease

The Republican party united behind Dwight D. Eisenhower at the nominating convention of 1952. Judging from this picture, how much support do you think Taft had at the convention?

the conservatives, had used a secret fund to meet some of his expenses as a senator. Nixon worked his way back to public favor with an emotional speech on television. It was highlighted by a reference to his dog, Checkers.

Although he was a military officer by profession, Eisenhower proved an expert political campaigner. A friendly grin and modest manner endeared him to voters. Eisenhower swept to victory with 55 percent of the popular vote. It was a personal victory rather than a party one. Republicans gained enough seats to win marginal control of the House. But they had to settle for a tie in the Senate.

THE END OF THE KOREAN WAR. Ike had not won over the conservative wing, however. McCarthy and other Republican conservatives were unhappy with the way the Korean War ended. Truman had opened negotiations with the Chinese and North Koreans shortly after he dismissed MacArthur. A boundary line between North and South Korea was agreed on. But the negotiators then ran into the question of prisoners of war.

A mutual return of prisoners was the normal aftermath of war. But it turned out that tens of thousands of North Koreans did not want to return to their Communist homeland. The Communists, unable to believe

Army Counsel Joseph Welch (seated left) won the nation's respect because of the dignity with which he faced McCarthy's attacks during the 1954 hearings. McCarthy stands at the right.

that anyone could pass up life in a "perfect" society, insisted on their return. Truman did not think it fair to force them. The negotiations broke down. And fighting resumed.

On the eve of the election, Eisenhower made the dramatic announcement that if elected, he would fly to Korea to review the situation. Perhaps more than anything else, the promise won him the victory. Less than a month after the election, he fulfilled the promise. The Chinese and North Koreans remained unimpressed.

Then, in March 1953, Stalin died, leaving a vacuum in Soviet leadership and uncertainty about future Soviet policy. The Chinese apparently decided to mend their fences in Korea. They agreed to resume negotiations. An armistice was finally signed on July 27. Some 21,809 Chinese and North Korean prisoners were allowed to stay in South Korea. And 359 members of the UN forces, including 23 Americans, chose to live in China.

The police action that had taken over 33,000 lives was over at last. Americans breathed a sigh of relief. Republican conservatives were disappointed with the politi-

cal stalemate. California's William Knowland, who succeeded to the Republican Senate leadership when Taft was stricken with cancer, called it "peace without honor."

McCARTHY IN THE SADDLE. The change in administration meant little to Joseph McCarthy. Eisenhower's appointees, he believed, were cut from the same cloth as Truman's. McCarthy declared that Charles E. Bohlen, whom Eisenhower appointed ambassador to Moscow, was a security risk. His suspicions apparently were aroused by Bohlen's long and distinguished career in the State Department. Any connection with Dean Acheson's State Department was enough to provoke McCarthy's ire. As a result, Bohlen was confirmed with difficulty.

Republicans had made use of McCarthy while they were the opposition. But now that they were in power, he was considered an embarrassment. To curtail his activities, the Senate leadership shifted him from the newsworthy Internal Security Subcommittee to a position on the relatively obscure Government Operations Committee.

Undeterred, McCarthy turned his new committee and its staff into an investigative bureau. The State Department became its special target.

McCARTHY VS. THE U.S. ARMY.
President Eisenhower regretted McCarthy's activities. "It's a sorry mess," he told a friend. "At times one feels almost like hanging his head in shame." But he did little to stop McCarthy, preferring to see the senator hang himself.

At the end of 1953, the Gallup Poll showed that McCarthy had broad public support. Fifty percent of those polled favored the Wisconsin senator—his best showing in the polls—and only 29 percent were critical. (The rest had no opinion.) Encouraged by this strong showing, McCarthy launched an attack on the army. It proved to be a fatal move. No one believed that the U.S. Army was a hotbed of communism.

McCarthy discovered that the army had promoted and honorably discharged a dentist of allegedly leftist views who had refused to give information to McCarthy's committee. Army officials, summoned before McCarthy's committee, were hounded ruthlessly. Then, in March 1954, the army counterattacked. It revealed that the senator had sought special treatment for his young aide, David Schine, who had been drafted in 1953. McCarthy charged that the army was trying to blackmail him and demanded public hearings. Television cameras were wheeled into the room.

McCARTHY'S FINAL MOMENTS.
Everything seemed to come to a halt. It was as if the entire country had paused in mid-step. For 36 incredible days Americans were glued to their television sets, watching the most powerful and feared man of the day destroy himself.

McCarthy's sarcasm, his disdain for legal procedure, his interruption of testimony with "Mr. Chairman, point of order!" violated Americans' sense of fair play. By contrast, the army's attorney, Jo-

seph Welch, calmly and quietly responded to McCarthy's charges. In desperation McCarthy leveled accusations against one of Welch's aides. Welch wheeled around to face the senator and asked, "Have you no sense of decency, sir, at long last? Have you no sense of decency?"

News reporters in the room stood and applauded. And as the room slowly emptied, McCarthy was left alone, asking, "What did I do wrong?" Millions watching on TV realized that he would probably never know. That autumn the Senate voted 66 to 21 to censure McCarthy, breaking his power. After that he slowly faded from the scene. He died in 1957.

President Eisenhower's strategy of giving McCarthy enough rope to hang himself paid off, but at a considerable price. In the interim McCarthy had held the country in an intellectual stranglehold. Because criticism was so easily branded subversive, it was virtually impossible to question America's policies or suggest alternatives. As a result, the untested assumptions that framed Truman's Cold War policies became dogma under Eisenhower.

McCarthy's fall ended the first phase of the Cold War, one characterized by tension and overreaction both at home and abroad. A second and considerably less tense phase began in 1955. The failure to rethink America's role in the world spelled trouble for the future.

Section Review

1. Identify or explain: the five-percenters, Estes Kefauver, Adlai Stevenson, Charles E. Bohlen, Joseph Welch.
2. How were Eisenhower's ideas like Truman's? How were they different?
3. Describe the scandals that marred the Democratic and Republican campaigns in 1952.
4. What was the fatal move that led to Senator Joseph McCarthy's undoing?

Bird's-Eye View

Although President Truman and the Republican-controlled Congress disagreed on domestic issues, they generally agreed on the course the nation should pursue in foreign affairs. This policy of internationalism was shaped by three main ideas: **1)** the need to learn from the mistakes of the past; **2)** the belief that communism was a direct threat to the United States, a threat that had to be dealt with; and **3)** the belief that the first step in resisting communism was the rebuilding of Europe.

The United States became more anxious about communism when it was revealed that a British scientist had fed atomic secrets to the Soviet Union. This climate of fear set the stage for the emergence of Joseph McCarthy.

Although McCarthy's accusations were not supported with evidence, his willingness to "name names" intimidated Congress. Skillfully manipulating the press and appealing to American fears and prejudices, McCarthy built a nationwide power base.

The Korean War, lasting from 1950 to 1953, kept "McCarthyism" alive by providing a real instance of Communist aggression. Truman called the war a police action. Although it was a United Nations conflict, Americans commanded throughout the war.

The war cost the nation 33,000 lives. And Truman's peace negotiations, which the Republicans and others considered an appeasement of the Communists, probably cost the Democrats the election of 1952.

Dwight D. Eisenhower, the World War II hero, was elected President on the Republican ticket. Shortly after his administration took office, the Korean War came to an end.

Eisenhower's Presidency brought an end to the era of McCarthyism. In the spring of 1954, during televised hearings, McCarthy lost control of himself. He made a mockery of the hearings and finally leveled accusations against a lawyer representing the army. That autumn McCarthy was censured by the Senate, and his power was broken. McCarthyism made it impossible to criticize America's policies. Alternatives to the Cold War could not be developed—a failure that haunted the nation in the future.

Vocabulary

Define or identify each of the following:

bipartisan	Marshall Plan	Alger Hiss
appeasement	subversion	38th parallel
containment	NATO	limited war

Review Questions

1. What was the Truman Doctrine?
2. How did the Truman Doctrine support developing attitudes about the Cold War?

3. How did the United States help rebuild the economies of the Western European countries after the war?
4. Describe Senator Joseph McCarthy's rise to power in the 1950's.
5. How did the United Nations become involved in the Korean War?
6. Summarize the dispute between Truman and MacArthur over war strategy in Korea. How was the dispute resolved?
7. What factors led to the election of Dwight D. Eisenhower as President of the United States in 1952?
8. Explain Senator McCarthy's fall from power. What role did the media play?

Reviewing Social Studies Skills

1. Using the map on page 679, complete the following:
   a. What river marks the northern border of Korea?
   b. What country is north of Korea?
   c. Using directional terms, describe the area of South Korea not occupied by North Korean troops.
   d. What is the dividing line between North and South Korea?
   e. Describe the approximate location of Inchon in terms of its latitude and longitude.
2. Write a brief editorial either defending or criticizing President Truman's dismissal of General MacArthur.

Reading for Meaning

1. Make a chart that lists across the top attitudes toward the Cold War. Down the side, list the following: the Marshall Plan; the Berlin Blockade; NATO; the fall of the Nationalists. Then fill in the chart by inserting specific information that shows how Cold War attitudes were affected by each event.
2. Define McCarthyism. Then write a paragraph explaining how McCarthyism was able to take hold of the country. Write another paragraph explaining your thinking on the question: Could something like McCarthyism happen again?
3. Make a list of at least 10 words that are critical to understanding the content of this chapter. Then use a dictionary to define each word.

Bibliography

Eric F. Goldman's *The Crucial Decade and After: America, 1945–1960* (Random House) is a good short account of the Truman administration and the Korean War.

Richard Rovere's *Senator Joe McCarthy* (World Publishers) is a biography of the senator from Wisconsin.

John Gunther and Bernard Quint's *Days to Remember: America, 1945 to 1955* (Harper and Row) is a fascinating pictorial history of one decade.

Secretary of State Dean Acheson tells his story in *Present at the Creation: My Years in the State Department* (Norton).

Unit 6 Review

Vocabulary

Identify or define each of the following:

foreclosure	dictator	closed shop
purge	totalitarian	filibuster
sit-down strike	intelligence operation	appeasement
propaganda	beachhead	subversion

Recalling the Facts

1. Describe the economic condition of the United States between 1929 and 1932.
2. Compare the first New Deal to the second New Deal.
3. Why was the CIO formed?
4. What was Hitler's racial theory?
5. What role did the United States play in the war between 1939 and 1941?
6. Why did the Japanese attack Pearl Harbor? What was the result of the attack?
7. How did America mobilize its production forces for World War II?
8. Explain the significance of the battles of Guadalcanal, El Alamein, and Stalingrad.
9. Briefly describe how Germany was defeated in Europe and how Japan was defeated in Asia.
10. What steps were taken by the federal government to return to peacetime conditions after World War II?
11. What reforms were carried out under Truman's Fair Deal?
12. What policies of the Soviet Union led to the Cold War?
13. Explain the Marshall Plan and its achievements.
14. What events contributed to the rise and fall of McCarthyism?

History Lab

1. Using the map on page 645, complete the following:
   a. List the areas in Europe annexed by the Soviet Union.
   b. What other countries annexed German territory?
   c. Describe the status of Germany.
2. Make a chart of the four Presidents discussed in this unit. List the major problems each President faced.
3. Look at the photograph of Truman on page 658. Why is the President smiling?

Local History

1. Interview someone who was in the armed services during World War II or the Korean War. Ask that person to tell you about the experience. Write a report based on the information you obtained. Describe your impression of what the war was like.
2. During the early stages of America's participation in World War II, living conditions on the home front were altered. Ask people who lived through those years the meanings of the following: victory stamps, victory bonds, victory gardens, ration books, scrap drive, blackout shades, air raid warden, the USO. Write down the answers they give you.

Forming an Opinion

1. Franklin D. Roosevelt was frustrated by the conservative Supreme Court. He attempted to change the structure of the Court. Although he received little support and was accused of trying to "pack" the Court, he was faced with a Court that contained many Justices over 70. Many people think that Supreme Court Justices should be required to retire at age 70. What do you think about this issue?

2. Adam Smith, an English economist who wrote *Wealth of Nations*, believed that government should not interfere in a nation's economy. John Maynard Keynes, another English economist, proposed that governments combat depressions by deliberately unbalancing the budgets to create work. The United States government has operated at a deficit nearly every year since Franklin D. Roosevelt became President. Attempts have been made to draft an amendment to the Constitution that would prohibit deficit spending. Would you support such an amendment, or do you favor Keynesian views?

3. The Kellogg-Briand pact of 1928 was an attempt to outlaw warfare as an instrument of national policy among the countries of the world. It did little if anything to prevent war in the 20th century. Is war inevitable? Can you foresee a time when nations will no longer use military means to settle problems?

4. Although he disapproved of Senator Joseph McCarthy, President Eisenhower did not move to stop the senator. He preferred to let McCarthy undermine himself. What do you think of Eisenhower's decision?

Time Line

Using the time line below, answer the following questions:

1. What were the dates and places of Axis aggression?
2. When did North Korea invade South Korea?
3. When was D-Day?
4. What events relate directly to Japan?
5. Create a detailed time line of one of the following: the war in the Pacific, the war in Europe, Hitler's rise to power, the two New Deals, Roosevelt and minorities.
6. If you were asked to divide the time line into two or three sections, where would you make the division(s)? What title would you give to each section?

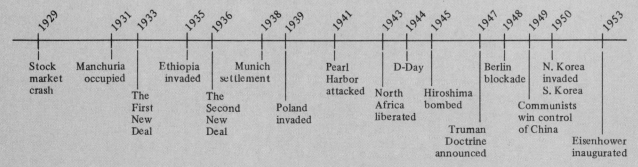

689

Years of Trial and Hope

The United States census has recorded two major population shifts in the 20th century. In 1920 the census revealed that more people were living in cities than on farms. The United States had become an urban nation. Fifty years later the census reported that Americans had left the cities to live in nearby communities.

The 1980 census revealed no such dramatic change. Its findings were significant nonetheless. The suburbs continued to grow during the 1970's but at a slower pace. People moved not to the country but across the country, from the aging metropolises of the North and the East to the Sunbelt communities of the South and the West.

By 1980 many suburbs were showing familiar signs of age—rising crime rates, drug abuse, and racial friction. The skyrocketing price of gasoline also made the suburbs less attractive. The suburbs and the automobile developed together. Improved forms of mass transit will preserve some suburbs, but the station wagon loaded with children and pets is no longer a symbol of the American way of life. The inner city may be the community of the late 20th century.

City officials have encouraged this trend by making urban areas more habitable. They have brought the suburb downtown. The downtown shopping center contains enclosed malls and parking facilities. Close to the shopping center are housing complexes, usually in the form of condominiums. A condominium combines the convenience of apartment living with the tax advantages of home ownership.

Atlanta's Peachtree Center, the first of these projects, became the model for the rest. The heart of Peachtree Center is the futuristic Hyatt Regency Hotel, with its roof-high atrium, glass spaceship elevators, and revolving dome. Department stores, restaurants, theaters, and an ice-skating rink complete the center. Begun in the early 1970's, Peachtree Center has been widely imitated. Peachtree's architect, John Portman, also designed the Embarcadero Center in San Francisco and the Renaissance Center in Detroit. Kansas City has its Crown Center, Minneapolis its Nicollet Mall, New York its Roosevelt Island. These may be the bases for the development of urban communities in the future.

Peachtree Center in Atlanta, Georgia

Chapter 30

1950-1960

A Time of Hope

The fall of Senator Joseph McCarthy brought a change in President Eisenhower. For five years McCarthy had dominated the news, winning headlines with his sensational charges of espionage and treason. President Eisenhower took little action during his first year in office. He spent his time acquainting himself with the job and waiting for the McCarthy phenomenon to fade away. When the Senate condemned McCarthy, Eisenhower took command. He quickly stamped his personality on the administration.

A career military officer, "Ike" had superb qualities of leadership. Early in World War II, General George Marshall, Chief of Staff, had reached beyond a number of generals with greater seniority to tap Eisenhower as commander of the European theater. Ike had borne out the wisdom of Marshall's judgment. He had organized, equipped, and trained an invasion army that had finally numbered two million. He had dealt with temperamental Allied leaders with tact and skill. He had carried his war record with modesty, and his broad grin had caught the public's fancy.

After McCarthy fell, the nation seemed to relax. Ike's politics fitted the national mood. He was practical enough to realize that most Americans approved of the changes introduced by Roosevelt and Truman, and conservative enough to want to make those changes more efficient and less costly.

Reporters kidded him for butchering the language. He spoke sentences that had neither beginnings nor endings. Much of his strange sentence structure was purposeful. Like the celebrated New York Yankee manager Casey Stengel, Ike made statements that kept his opponents off balance, but kept his options open. During one particularly heated foreign policy crisis, his press secretary wanted a policy statement to issue to waiting reporters. "Don't worry," Ike replied, "I'll just go out there and confuse 'em."

Chapter Objectives

After you have finished reading this chapter, you should be able to:
1. Explain why the United States experienced a period of economic growth after the war.
2. Identify the components of Eisenhower's modern republicanism.
3. List the major events in the civil rights movement during the Eisenhower administration.
4. Define and give several examples of mass-produced culture.

The nation paused for breath in 1955. Americans had witnessed a generation of strife and bitterness—depression, New Deal, world war, Cold War, and Red Scare. Tensions relaxed. The changes of the past were accepted. It was time to enjoy life.

1. The Post-War Economy

ECONOMIC GROWTH. World War II ended the depression of the 1930's. *The postwar years were years of unparalleled prosperity.* Wartime scarcities and a population explosion created a huge backlog of consumer demand. Factories labored to fill orders. Jobs were plentiful. The cycle of consumption - production - labor - wages - consumption spiraled upward. The *Gross National Product* (GNP) more than doubled between 1945 and 1960, climbing from 214 billion dollars to approximately 500 billion dollars. (See graph on the right.) This was an enormous increase in the rate of economic growth. Moreover, the increase was fairly steady. There were minor recessions in 1949 and 1958, when production exceeded consumer demand. But they did not last long.

The *gross national product* is the dollar value of all goods and services produced in the nation.

The unemployment rate averaged 4.6 percent throughout the 1950's. During the Korean War, there was a shortage of workers in some industries.

SUSTAINING PROSPERITY. *Consumer habits were changed by prosperity.* The use of credit cards became extensive, and improved advertising techniques encouraged people to buy goods and services. By

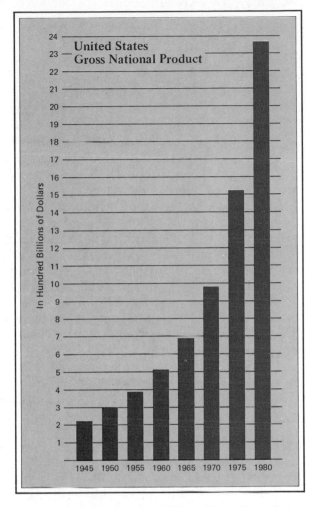

the end of the decade, three fourths of the nation's households had at least one car. Five out of six households had television sets, washing machines, and refrigerators.

Helping sustain prosperity was a boom in the housing industry. Wartime savings permitted families to invest in homes. Automobiles encouraged them to move to the suburbs. Cities sprawled into the countryside as developers put up standardized houses with assembly-line efficiency and speed.

At the height of the boom in the mid-1950's, a million dwellings were put up each year. In 1960 one fourth of the houses in the country were less than 10 years old. The building boom created demands for construction workers, building materials, and home appliances.

FOREIGN TRADE. A relatively large amount of foreign trade also helped sustain prosperity. Tariff reduction—begun by the 1934 General Agreement on Tariffs and Trade and made into a world system that by 1951 included 53 nations—encouraged international exchange. *The United States became the world's workshop.* The country imported raw materials from rubber to uranium and flooded the world's markets with the latest gadgets.

Between 1950 and 1960 the value of America's exports doubled, reaching 20 billion dollars a year. Imports climbed to 14 billion dollars. Those figures did not represent the total of America's overseas commerce. *During the 1950's the biggest American corporations began producing and selling goods abroad. The profits returned to the United States.* All the major car manufacturers, for instance, opened plants and offices in Europe to manufacture and sell American-designed cars.

GOVERNMENT INVESTMENT. Housing construction and foreign trade were features of the boom that made it different from other periods of prosperity, such as the 1920's. *Another distinctive feature was the level of government spending.* Cold War tensions led the government to spend billions annually on military weapons and scientific research. By 1960 the jobs of 7.5 million Americans (about one tenth of the entire work force) depended on the government's annual military appropriation.

In a curious way, these government expenditures helped demonstrate the theories of the British economist John Maynard Keynes. Lord Keynes advocated government expenditures as a way out of the depression. President Roosevelt embraced Keynes's theory but failed to make it work.

President Eisenhower rejected the theory, while proving that it worked. *Thus, in the 1950's government spending, justified in the name of national security, helped sustain prosperity.*

THE AUTOMATION REVOLUTION. Automation was the most important economic development of the postwar decade. Automation refers to operations that are automatically controlled. The best-known form of automation is the computer.

The first modern computers came into use shortly after World War II. By 1956 almost 1,000 were being used, and by 1968 15,000 were in use in almost every kind of business. Computers were an asset because they could produce volumes of calculations in split seconds.

Other automated equipment was used for tasks that usually required many people and hours. Many jobs were eliminated. But other jobs were created because human energy was needed to service, adjust, start, and stop these machines. Highly trained experts and professionals became essential for the efficient operation of the equipment.

LABOR PRODUCTIVITY. *Automation greatly increased the output of each worker.* Between the end of World War II and 1960, the hourly production of factory workers increased by a tremendous rate. It was higher than the enormous production increase achieved during the first wave of industrialization in the 1880's. By 1960 a miner using machines could dig twice as much coal in an hour as a miner in 1945. At the end of the war, it took 310 work hours to make an automobile. In 1960 it took half that many—155. With this enormous increase in productivity, business could increase wages without raising prices. And that meant an improved standard of living for all.

AN INCREASE IN SERVICE EMPLOYMENT. *The number of people in service jobs was proof of the nation's*

694

increasing economic maturity. A young economy first develops industries related to survival—farming, mining, manufacturing—industries that provide people with food, shelter, and basic necessities. The more efficient an economy becomes in providing basic needs, the more it can afford services such as education, advertising, the arts, and entertainment. In 1940 about one third of the labor force was engaged in the performance of services rather than the production of goods. By 1960 the figure was more than one half. Clerks, salespeople, and laboratory assistants are all considered service employees.

Many service occupations—those of doctors, dentists, teachers, bankers, lawyers—required some degree of professional training and technical skill. The desire to secure these jobs spurred an increase in college and graduate school enrollment.

WORKING WOMEN. The war helped remove some job barriers against women. They worked in defense plants, shipyards, and the armed forces. ***Between 1940 and 1960 women entered the labor force in greater numbers than ever before.*** About 9.4 million women were employed during this period, holding a much wider range of jobs. By 1960 two of every five adult women were employed outside the home. Women were about a third of the working population.

The war was only one of the factors that increased the employment of women. Many women worked in order to give their families a higher standard of living. Others joined the work force because they had to work. Some worked because they were ambitious or because jobs outside the home provided challenging, satisfying, and enriching experiences.

Many professions—law, medicine, education, science, and engineering—slowly began to open their doors to women. However, some discrimination was still evident. Women were not given the same salaries or the same chances for advancement as men.

TIME FOR LEISURE. The huge jump in labor productivity meant more than higher pay. It also meant fewer hours in the work week. The average factory work week was 44 hours in 1940. By 1960 most people worked 40 hours per week. In some skilled crafts, weekly hours were down to 35. The average vacation was one week in 1940, two weeks by 1960. Before the war, paid vacations were virtually unknown. If a worker

Women in the Labor Force, 1890–1980

Television was introduced into American homes during the late 1940's and the early 1950's. Watching television became a favorite evening pastime for many American families. How do you think television has affected family life in America?

did not punch a time clock, he or she did not get paid. By 1960 paid holidays, vacations, and sick leave were common.

The effects of leisure were evident everywhere. Highways became jammed in the summertime with people on vacation. Motel operation became a major industry. Visits to national parks and historic sites boomed. Expenditures on power tools for home workshops tripled between 1945 and 1950 and then tripled again in the next decade. Power boats and launches, toys of the rich before the war, became commonplace on lakes, rivers, and along the coast. People enjoyed fine food and drink and dined out often. Trips to the beauty parlor, the race track, and the golf course became frequent.

Americans had learned to mass-produce leisure in the same way they mass-produced everything else.

Section Review

1. Identify or explain: Dwight Eisenhower, the General Agreement on Tariffs and Trade, GNP.
2. How did the role of women in the work force change between 1940 and 1960?
3. Explain how each of the following affected the economy during the 1950's: *a)* labor productivity; *b)* the increase in service employment; *c)* the spread of leisure time; and *d)* automation.

2. Eisenhower's Modern Republicanism

A VAGUE BUT EFFECTIVE PHILOSOPHY. Politics reflected the nation's mood in the mid-1950's. Recognizing that it was time to ease tensions, President Eisenhower sought to bring his party to an understanding and acceptance of the changes that had taken place since the 1920's. He called his philosophy modern republicanism. When reporters asked him to define the term, Ike said it meant "Progressive moderation and moderate Progressivism." He was liberal about individuals and their rights and conservative about the taxpayers' pocketbooks.

President Eisenhower might have had trouble defining his philosophy, but its vagueness was one of its virtues. A piece-meal approach to national problems, without grandiose pronouncements, is sometimes effective. It was in the 1950's, when ideology was out of fashion. Rather than attack the New Deal, Eisenhower accepted it. He even expanded the social security system to include farmers and professional people.

THE INTERSTATE HIGHWAY SYSTEM. On the President's recommendation, Congress undertook the most massive construction project in the nation's history, the interstate highway system. It began in November 1956, with the opening of a stretch of highway near Topeka, Kansas. By September 1980, 64,098 kilometers (40,061 miles) of its projected 68,000 kilometers (42,500 miles) had been completed. (See map below.)

The impact of the interstate highway system can be compared to the impact of

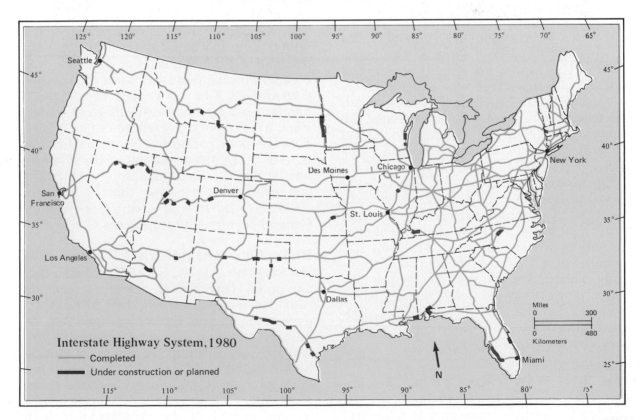

Interstate Highway System, 1980
— Completed
■ Under construction or planned

the railroads in the 19th century. The highways brought prosperity to some towns and ruined others. With the highways came suburbs, shopping centers, and restaurant and motel chains. Patterns of commerce, work, and recreation were changed. People could live farther from work and reach vacation spots that had been out of reach before.

The interstate highway system was an imaginative response to one of the problems of prosperity—roads choked with traffic. Some people have suggested that a similar investment in mass transit is necessary.

THE FARM SURPLUS HEADACHE.
The farm problem was a tougher nut to crack. Farm surpluses mounted after the war. When Eisenhower took office in 1953, he discovered that the government owned 10 billion dollars worth of stored crops. Storage costs alone were almost one billion dollars a year.

Pesticides and weed killers made American farms more productive. But increased productivity threatened farmers with bankruptcy. The capital investment required to run an efficient farm was staggering, so even one-family operations incorporated. Thousands of failing farmers abandoned the land. By 1960 four million farm families fed the entire nation—and there was still a surplus.

Eisenhower's Secretary of Agriculture, Ezra Taft Benson, wanted to get the government out of agriculture by cutting the level of price supports. Without government storing, prices would find their own levels and farmers would adjust production accordingly. This meant that only the biggest corporate farmers would survive. Family farms would be doomed. And that would bring political uproar. So the supports were continued, and the surpluses mounted.

THE SOIL BANK SOLUTION. *The government's answer to the dilemma was a soil bank.* Farmers were paid to take land out of production and "bank" it for the future. About 4,800,000 hectares (12 million acres) were put in the soil bank, but it had little effect on surpluses. The solution to America's farm problem was the growth in world population. Increased exports to hungry people in other nations almost eliminated American stockpiles by the end of the 1960's.

There was another side to the farm problem. While the farmer suffered from low prices, everyone else benefited. The cost of food for city dwellers was lower in America than anywhere else in the world. In Western Europe workers typically spent about a third of their income for food. In the Soviet Union they spent more than half. In the United States the grocery bill was about one fifth of an average family's total budget.

GOVERNMENT ON A BUSINESS-LIKE FOOTING. There were limits, of course, to modern republicanism. The President was conservative by nature. He had the military person's capacity for delegating authority. His cabinet members were nearly all business people borrowed from the nation's corporations. They governed their departments with little supervision from above. Each tried to put the government on a businesslike footing. Defense Secretary Charles E. Wilson, former president of General Motors, summarized the philosophy. He told a congressional committee that he thought "what is good for our country is good for General Motors, and vice versa."

BUDGET BALANCING. Eisenhower also subscribed to the Republican belief that too much government spending leads to ruin. He conscientiously tried to hold expenses down, and he kept a tight rein on military spending. His efforts met with limited success. Eisenhower began by cutting back on credit and reducing spending, but during his term the country suffered three recessions. These cut the government's income and upset the President's budget.

Eisenhower did balance the budget three times during his eight years in office.

A CONSERVATIVE PRESIDENT. The President's conservatism was evident in other ways. The development of atomic energy, originally a government enterprise, was turned over to private corporations. A 1954 tax reduction helped encourage private investment, even though it did little for the individual taxpayer. Eisenhower was opposed to the distribution of the Salk antipolio vaccine. The administration feared it might encourage socialized medicine.

Eisenhower Republicans did continue and did extend some of the welfare measures of other administrations. In 1953 the Department of Health, Education, and Welfare was established. This department consolidated several agencies under one administrative head.

Section Review

1. Mapping: Using the map on page 697, figure out the distance in kilometers or miles from your town to the nearest city labeled on the map. How many hours would it take you to drive there?
2. Identify or explain: Ezra Taft Benson, modern republicanism, interstate highway system, Charles E. Wilson.
3. How did increased farm productivity create a farm problem? List one of the Eisenhower administration's responses to the problems.
4. How did Eisenhower's cabinet reflect his conservative philosophy?

3. Beginnings of the Civil Rights Revolution

LIBERTY AND JUSTICE FOR ALL. One of America's biggest postwar problems was making America a land of liberty and justice for all. Black veterans suffered the same kinds of injustices at home as those they had fought against abroad. *Vast changes were needed to improve the status and living standards of Blacks in the United States.*

Racism and discrimination were evident in the North as well as in the South. And Blacks were taking new forms of action by the 1950's.

NEW GAINS AND NEW DISAPPOINTMENTS. For some Blacks the postwar era offered significant gains in employment and education and greater opportunities in sports, the military, and the entertainment industry. *By 1950 Black enrollment in colleges had increased 2,500 percent over the previous decade.* In Hollywood actor Sidney Poitier became an Academy Award winner. Gwendolyn Brooks won a Pulitzer Prize for poetry. Hulan Jack was elected president of the borough of Manhattan in New York City. Benjamin Davis, Jr., became the air force's first Black general.

But these people were a small part of the Black population. *The vast majority experienced poverty, chronic unemployment, discrimination in jobs, and inferior housing and schooling.* (See graph, page 709.) These conditions were even more visible than they had been before, because mass-media advertising was constantly reminding Blacks of the affluence of others.

DISCRIMINATION IN PUBLIC SCHOOLS. Official discrimination—established by law and enforced by public officials—was the least excusable and the easiest to attack. *Of all the forms of official discrimination in America, the segregation of races in the public schools was the most obvious.* Black schools lagged miserably behind those of Whites in equipment and facilities.

The 14th Amendment to the Constitution, adopted shortly after the Civil War, guarantees that the states would give to all citizens the "equal protection of the laws." In the 1890's, however, in the case of *Plessy* v.

Sidenote to History

Breaking the Color Line

Who was the greatest baseball pitcher of all time? There are some students of the game who would name Leroy "Satchel" Paige. Tall, gangly, and ageless, his feet so large that they reminded people of suitcases (or satchels), Paige had an arm like a buggy whip. He called his fast ball Little Tom. His *fast* fast ball he called Long Tom. But Satchel Paige was not even in the major leagues. Paige was Black. And American baseball was White.

Satchel Paige earned his living by forming Black exhibition teams that toured the country. He challenged and bested some of the greatest hitters of the day. When 21-year-old Joe DiMaggio got a single off Paige in four trips to the plate, the Yankees knew that "Dimagg" was ready for the big leagues. But not Paige. He didn't make it until the end of his career, after "Long Tom" was long gone. How old was he? No one knew. He was 45, maybe 60, when the Cleveland Indians finally gave him his chance. Pitching infrequently, he won six and lost one that season and saved a game in relief during the World Series. That was in 1948, one year after Jackie Robinson finally broke the color line.

It took two men to break baseball's ban against Blacks. The other was Branch Rickey, a White. Rickey detested America's habit of racial discrimination. When he became general manager of the Brooklyn Dodgers toward the end of World War II, Branch Rickey had his opportunity to end segregation in baseball.

By the mid-1940's pressures were mounting on baseball and other professional sports to drop their color barriers. Rickey sent his scouts into the field. The name most frequently mentioned was Jackie Robinson, a shortstop for the Kansas City Monarchs, an all-Black team that included Satchel Paige on its roster.

The scouts said Robinson was good. What worried Branch Rickey: Did the man have the guts? Robinson would have to listen to racial slurs from the opponents' dugouts, from coaches on the sidelines, and from the stands. And he would have to answer not with his fists but with his bat and glove.

Rickey signed Robinson in 1946 and sent him to the Dodger's Montreal farm club. The following year Robinson was called up to Brooklyn. A couple of Dodgers refused to play with Robinson. Rickey traded them to other teams. Some members of the St. Louis Cardinals tried to organize a league boycott against the Dodgers. The commissioner of the National League was able to stop the move by threatening to throw the Cardinals out of baseball.

Robinson started slowly because of the pressure, but gradually his play picked up. By midsummer Robinson was in full stride, and the Dodgers were leading the League. They went on to win the pennant that year. Robinson hit .297 and won baseball's Rookie of the Year title.

Robinson had broken the color barrier. The next year there were three Blacks in the major leagues, including Satchel Paige. Then, team owners scrambled to tap the enormous pool of Black talent. In 15 of the next 20 seasons, Blacks won the Most Valuable Player award.

Unfortunately, it was too late for the "ageless" Satchel Paige, who had finally slowed down. His greatness had gone into the barnstorming circuit, not into the record books. That was one of the costs of the nation's prejudice.

Ferguson, the Supreme Court ruled that separate facilities for different races, as long as they were of equal quality, did not violate the 14th Amendment. The separate but equal doctrine referred to railroad accommodations. But the nation assumed that it applied to other facilities as well, including public schools. As a result, many states maintained segregated school systems.

BROWN V. BOARD OF EDUCATION.
The Supreme Court helped knock down some of the nation's racial barriers in its ruling in the case of *Brown* v. *Board of Education* (1954). The suit actually involved a number of school systems, from Topeka, Kansas, to Washington, D.C.

Speaking for a unanimous Court, Chief Justice Earl Warren declared that separation is inherently unequal. The only reason for segregation was that one race considered the other inferior. Segregation hurt and humiliated Black children and thus reduced their chances for educational development. The following year the Court ordered 17 states to develop plans for eliminating segregation "with all deliberate speed."

REACTION TO DESEGREGATION.
Some states complied. But other states defied the Court. White citizens' councils sprang up. In many parts of the South, no judge could be found who was willing to issue orders. One local government, Prince Edward County, Virginia, closed its public schools when ordered to desegregate.

In Congress 100 southern members issued a manifesto approving all legal resistance to school desegregation.

CRISIS IN LITTLE ROCK.
President Eisenhower tried to steer clear of the question. Publicly he said it was his duty to enforce the Constitution. Privately, he confessed that he thought the Court's decision was wrong.

Blacks asked him to exert his leadership by summoning a conference of southern moderates or by making a public appeal for tolerance. He refused. Eventually, however, White militancy forced his hand.

In September 1957 a federal court ordered Central High School in Little Rock, Arkansas, to admit nine Black students. To prevent the school from carrying out the order, Governor Orval Faubus summoned the national guard and ordered it to surround the school. President Eisenhower, then vacationing in Newport, Rhode Island, summoned Faubus to a conference. After his visit with the President, the governor did not withdraw the troops until a federal court issued an injunction barring him from obstructing the students' entry. It was not until September 1958 that the situation was finally resolved. The schools reopened, integrated.

THE MONTGOMERY BUS BOYCOTT.
In the absence of Presidential leadership and congressional legislation, desegregation was painfully slow. It proceeded city by city, district by district, school by school. *In the six years after the Supreme Court's decision, Blacks, acting by themselves, accomplished more than the government did.*

On December 1, 1955, Rosa Parks, a 40-year-old Black seamstress living in Montgomery, Alabama, boarded a bus and sat near the front. By southern custom, Blacks were supposed to sit at the rear. But she had worked hard that day, and she was tired. After a couple of stops, the bus became crowded. The driver ordered Mrs. Parks to stand in the rear so a White could have her seat. She refused and was arrested. This act started the civil rights revolution.

The next day the city's 50,000 Blacks boycotted the buses. Martin Luther King, Jr., a 26-year-old minister, took charge of the operation, terming it "an act of massive noncooperation." King's influence was crucial, for he kept the action peaceful. The city's Blacks refused to board buses. Some walked to work; others organized car pools. The city bus system, heavily dependent on Black riders, drifted into bankruptcy. After 80 days, King and other leaders were arrested. But the boycott continued.

The government held on until the Supreme Court, 11 months after Rosa Parks' arrest, declared the Alabama segregation laws unconstitutional. Fresh from victory, Reverend King called a meeting of Black leaders from the South. In January 1957, they formed the Southern Christian Leadership Conference (SCLC). ***The purpose of the organization was to encourage Blacks to break down the nation's racial barriers by peaceful means.***

Rosa Parks's refusal to relinquish a seat on a crowded bus in Montgomery, Alabama, in 1955 sparked the civil rights revolt. This movement dominated much of the 1960's. Why did Mrs. Parks's action have such a widespread effect?

THE RIGHT TO VOTE IS DENIED.

President Eisenhower tried to ignore the growing Black protest. But there was one right he could not ignore—the right to vote. Since the turn of the century, southern states had discouraged Blacks from voting. The grandfather clause had been declared unconstitutional. The poll tax, however, was still in common use. This was a tax on each poll (meaning head, or individual) in the state. A receipt showing that the poll tax had been paid was required in order to vote. Many times registrars came up with reasons for making receipts held by Blacks invalid. In addition, voter registration requirements were so complicated that poorly educated Blacks became confused and discouraged. As with the poll tax, the system allowed White registrars leeway in choosing who would pass into the polling booth.

As a result, only a few Blacks were registered to vote in the South, even in those counties in which they constituted a majority of the population. Without political power they had no way of protecting their other rights.

CIVIL RIGHTS LEGISLATION.

In 1957 the President sent to Congress a bill empowering federal judges to supervise voting registrars. Civil rights measures had come to Congress before, but they had all fallen victim to congressional maneuvering. Some ended up in the dusty pigeonholes of congressional committees. Others died during filibusters. *The President's measure would have suffered the same fate except that the Democratic leader of the Senate, Lyndon B. Johnson, a Texan with Presidential aspirations, intervened.* Johnson avoided a Senate filibuster by eliminating from the bill some features to which the South most objected. The act that finally emerged was considerably watered down. *The Voting Rights Act of 1957 was the first civil rights legislation since the reconstruction era.*

In 1960 Congress passed a second voting rights law after overcoming a southern filibuster that lasted nine days. This act authorized the Justice Department to search through county voting records. If investigators found a pattern of discrimination, Justice officials could appoint referees to register voters.

The act was an important step, but even with federal referees, it was some years before Blacks registered in significant numbers. White politicians fought the movement. And Blacks were still harassed to such a degree that they did not bother to register.

1960: YEAR OF THE SIT-INS.

Official discrimination was contrary to the 14th Amendment. *But many forms of discrimination stemmed from social custom, not laws.* Hotels and restaurants in both North and South often refused to admit non-Whites. "Whites only" signs blocked access to swimming pools, rest rooms, waiting rooms, and cemeteries.

In February 1960 four Black college students in Greensboro, North Carolina, sat down at a "Whites only" lunch counter. When they were refused service, they did not get up, eventually forcing the lunch counter to close. Like the Montgomery bus boycott, the Greensboro sit-in was a spontaneous act, a product of growing Black pride. And like the bus boycott, it was peaceful.

Other Black students followed the example, and soon there were "wade-ins" and "swim-ins." All forms of discrimination came under attack. Local authorities arrested as many as 1,500 Blacks for trespass, but the protesters won. By the end of the year, northern hotels and restaurants were quietly abandoning their discriminatory practices. And several national chain stores desegregated their lunch counters in southern towns and cities. Another barrier had been cracked, although not quite broken.

"The Family,"
Charles Alston, 1955

"Christina's World," Andrew Wyeth, 1948

The art of the post-World War II era often depicted the mixed emotions of the times. In the above pictures the Black artist, Charles Alston, expresses a sense of despair and desolation, a theme also reflected in the work of Andrew Wyeth. What other feelings do you get from these two pictures?

RESIDENTIAL SEGREGATION IN THE NORTH. Throughout the 1950's the news media focused on the racial tensions of the South. *Virtually unnoticed was a developing pattern of segregation in the North that meant trouble in the future.* Whites were fleeing the northern cities and moving to the suburbs. For the first time the nation's largest cities (except Los Angeles) declined in population. Nevertheless, the movement from farm to city continued, as it had for a century. Indeed, by 1960 almost 70 percent of Americans lived in an urban setting. The flight to the suburbs exceeded the number of new arrivals in the central city.

Suburbia ranged from plush dwellings for the rich to large housing developments for working people. Most suburbs grew quickly, without any planning. As more and more people came, so did some of the problems that had caused the exodus to the suburbs. Crime rates and taxes rose. Schools became overcrowded, and some public services deteriorated. However, most suburbanites chose to remain in the suburbs rather than return to the inner cities.

Blacks who could afford to move to the suburbs were usually steered to certain communities. *Those who moved to "restricted" areas often met open resistance*

Sidenote to History

The Warren Court

Chief Justice Earl Warren retired from the Supreme Court in 1969. Nearly everyone agreed it was the end of an era. He was a Republican and had been appointed to the Court by Eisenhower. But he had come to symbolize a liberal, activist Court. The Court's desegregation decisions in the 1950's alienated much of the South. Its concern for the rights of criminals in the 1960's angered many others.

Much of the Court's difficulty stemmed from the fact that it was misunderstood. In a time of rising crime rates, ghetto riots, and student demonstrations, people were concerned with order and stability. Police had their hands full, and the Court's concern for individual rights at the expense of authority seemed untimely at best. Yet, the concern for civil rights and civil liberties in a time of stress showed the basic health of the American political system.

The Court's most unpopular decision was also its most misunderstood. In 1962, in the case of *Engel* v. *Vitale,* the Court ruled that compulsory prayers in the public schools were

unconstitutional. The uproar was deafening. Congress fumed for many days and held hearings and discussions on the question. Gigantic petitions carrying thousands of signatures asked Congress to restore God to the classroom. The Court had not removed God from the classroom. The Court had said that a public board had no right to compose an official prayer and then force everyone to say it. That violated the separation of church and state.

The Court's decisions on criminal rights were similarly misunderstood. *Escobedo* v. *Illinois* and *Miranda* v. *Arizona* caused the most controversy. The Court held that suspects were entitled to legal counsel and to be informed of their rights before police could interrogate them. In one case, the police had tried for hours to get a suspect to confess without letting him see a lawyer. The Court applied restrictions listed in the Bill of Rights. In succeeding years, lower courts interpreted the decisions so broadly that police claimed they were unable to do their jobs. The rising crime rate gave them political ammunition. In the mid-1970's the Supreme Court, more conservative because it contained Nixon appointees, defined more narrowly the rights of the accused. The conflict between individual freedom and society's need for order is one of the continuing themes of American history.

Suburban communities, such as this one, prompted millions to leave the nation's cities in the 1950's. Suburbia's attractions were many—clean air, open space, new schools. Can you think of any disadvantages to suburban living?

and hostility from Whites who felt that Blacks would lower property values. In many instances the homes of Blacks were damaged, and families were intimidated, forcing them to leave White neighborhoods. On many occasions the movement of a few Black families into an all-White area caused for sale signs to appear all over the neighborhood. Many Whites felt they had to go before more Blacks came. When the San Francisco Giants' star center fielder Willie Mays bought a house in an all-White section of town, he was told: "Thank the people of San Francisco for letting you buy this house!" "What do I have to thank anybody for?"

Mays shot back. "For letting me spend 40,000 dollars?"

The flight to the suburbs and the concentration of Blacks in certain neighborhoods resulted in what came to be known as de facto segregation in the North. De facto segregation is segregation that exists because of neighborhood residency patterns. It does not exist by law. As a result of de facto segregation, neighborhood schools in the North were segregated. Many were ordered to integrate.

SEGREGATION IN CITIES. Within the cities, poverty contributed to racial segregation. New arrivals—Blacks from the South,

706

Cubans, and Puerto Ricans—began at the bottom of the employment ladder. Many found it impossible to find jobs of any kind. As a result, they jammed into the poorest of the old tenements. Sometimes a dozen or more people shared the same apartment. *New York's Harlem, symbol of the Black renaissance in the 1920's, became in the 1950's a symbol of hopeless squalor.* By 1960 Washington, D.C., was 50 percent Black, and New York City had more Puerto Ricans than Puerto Rico's capital, San Juan. American cities were becoming seething cauldrons—and during the next few years, they boiled over.

Section Review

1. Identify or explain: Sidney Poitier, Earl Warren, Orval Faubus, Rosa Parks, Martin Luther King, Jr., Benjamin Davis, Jr., the Voting Rights Act of 1957.
2. Explain the idea of "separate but equal." On what grounds did the Supreme Court reject this idea in the case of *Brown* v. *Board of Education?*
3. Describe de facto segregation in the North.

4. Mass-Produced Culture

AN EXPLOSION OF CULTURE. What was the most important development of the 1950's? *It might very well have been the mass production of culture.* At no other time in the nation's history had there been such an explosion of culture as during the postwar years. Literature and art came within the reach of millions. And huge sums of money were spent on comic books, records, novels, and paperbacks. Television was introduced into a major portion of the homes in the United States. New marketing techniques made it possible to release the same books, films, and records all over the country at the same time. All the entertainment arts were affected.

THE ARRIVAL OF TELEVISION. There were 8,000 television sets in the entire country at the end of the war and 46 million by 1960. Earlier forms of entertainment, such as plays and concerts, were individual efforts, catering to a few hundred people at a time. Even the movies were like traveling stage companies. Hundreds of different films were circulated in thousands of theaters for months or even years. *With television, millions of Americans shared the same cultural experience at the same moment.* A lumberjack from Michigan could meet a lawyer from the South in a New York hotel and find common ground by discussing a television program each had seen the night before. The result was a growing homogeneity, or sameness. Differences in dress, speech, and manners that had characterized parts of the country began to disappear.

Television became a superb news medium, too. Millions of people watched events unfold before their eyes instead of waiting to read about them in newspapers. As years passed, television also served educational purposes.

THE FILM INDUSTRY. With television on the scene, the film industry had to make a tremendous effort to keep business booming. Half the nation's theaters closed because people stayed at home to watch television.

In a frantic effort to recapture its dwindling audience, Hollywood began to spend lavish sums on such spectacular films as *Cleopatra* (which cost an estimated 42 million dollars) and *The Ten Commandments*. The industry finally came to uneasy terms with television by selling its films for rerun on television and turning over its old movie lots to television producers.

In 1956 Elvis Presley became one of the greatest pop phenomena of all time. Why do you think he became an instant idol to millions of teenagers?

THE RECORD INDUSTRY. Mass-production technology soon invaded other aspects of American culture. The introduction of unbreakable, slow-speed phonograph records in place of the brittle "78's" greatly reduced the price of each recording. *Record sales, previously counted in the thousands, were tallied in the millions.* Recordings were a big business.

Musical figures became folk heroes. Frank Sinatra, who set bobby-soxers screaming and swooning in the mid-1940's, was perhaps the first of these youth heroes. A decade later Elvis Presley and Chuck Berry aroused similar feelings, although the style changed from crooned ballad to amplified rock-and-roll. Dizzy Gillespie, Duke Ellington, and Charlie Parker were among the musicians who developed new sounds in jazz, and artists like Ray Charles gave rhythm-and-blues a national audience.

THE REVOLUTION IN LITERATURE. The paperback book, unknown before the war, ushered in a similar revolution in the publishing world. *By 1960 there were about 35,000 titles in paperback.* The most popular paperbacks were selling more than a million copies apiece. Drugstores and supermarkets sold more books than bookstores.

Mass production permitted substantial price reductions. Serious literary works became more readily available. But most of the new productions were works of sensationalism, geared to the public's taste.

A few serious writers were concerned that American society was becoming as homogenized as the milk it drank. People dressed alike—gray flannel suits became almost a uniform among business and professional people in the early 1950's. They lived in identical houses (Cape Cod bungalows for some, ranch-style homes for others), watched the same TV programs, and read the same magazines. In such a world, how could one find identity or individuality? In such a world, how could one avoid becoming a mere number—a social security number in order to work, a medical statistic in order to die? The quest for identity was a theme of the literature of the 1950's.

J. D. Salinger's *Catcher in the Rye* recounts the rebellion of an adolescent youth in his own language. The plight of Blacks in a world of prejudice was explored by Ralph Ellison in *The Invisible Man*. The most discouraging aspect, thought Ellison, was that people did not even see their prejudice. How can one establish individuality when others do not even know they have deprived individuals of personality? "I am an invisible man," declared Ellison. "I am invisible, understand, simply because people refuse to see me." James Baldwin and Saul Bellow were leading novelists of the era who focused on the theme of identity.

World War II was another topic for many writers of the 1950's. Norman Mailer and James Jones were especially effective in portraying elements of military life.

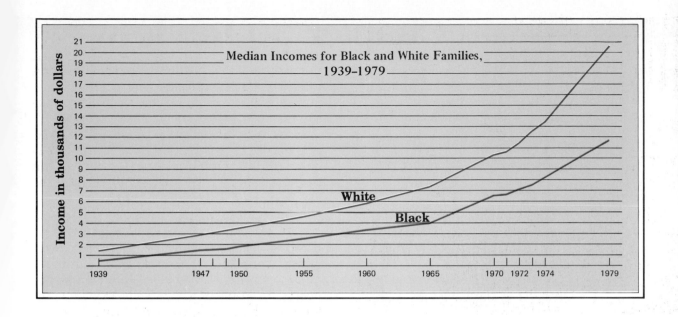

Median Incomes for Black and White Families, 1939–1979

Income in thousands of dollars

White

Black

1939   1947   1950   1955   1960   1965   1970   1972   1974   1979

AFFLUENCE? The affluence of the 1950's changed the lives of many Americans, rich and poor, Black and White, young and old, contented and restless. It tore down class distinctions and brought the good life to millions who had been economically insecure. *Traditional life-styles in families and communities were reshaped, and new ways of thinking began to surface.*

Affluent America neglected millions of its people, denying them the bare necessities of life. While millions were able to enjoy the new affluence, others were left feeling worse because they had less than ever before. The economic differences that had become more pronounced in the 1950's caused turmoil in the next decade.

AN END TO IDEOLOGY. The Red Scare produced intellectual caution. Those who had dissented had risked being branded security risks. Not only government employees, but actors, scriptwriters, and teachers had found their careers ended by ill-founded suspicions. "What is the new loyalty?" asked one scholar, as the Red Scare came to a close. "It is, above all, a conformity. It is the uncritical and unquestioning acceptance of America as it is."

In the 1950's a well-known sociologist declared "an end to ideology"—and an end to the social tensions that created conflicting ideologies. Americans were not concerned with the fine points of ideology. They were practical people seeking practical solutions to practical problems. Dwight D. Eisenhower—pleasant of personality, modest of achievement, and conservative in outlook—fitted this mood. And he was the most popular President the nation had ever known.

Section Review

1. Identify or explain: Frank Sinatra, Elvis Presley, *Cleopatra*, Ralph Ellison.
2. How did the growth of television help encourage the growth of mass culture?
3. What changes in American culture occurred as a result of the increase in popular records and paperback books?
4. Why did individuality become a problem in the 1950's?

709

Chapter 30 Review

The 1950's were a time of great prosperity for the United States. The housing industry boomed. People spent their wartime savings on all kinds of consumer goods. Foreign trade increased. Some results of this period of prosperity were increased productivity, an increase in the number of service jobs, a work force that included more women, and more leisure time for the average person.

Dwight D. Eisenhower, President during this period, symbolized the national mood. He defined the Republican party's stance as one of "modern republicanism." Eisenhower attempted to deal with problems in a practical way, avoiding ideology as much as possible.

Although the nation was prosperous, many abuses remained. Among the most flagrant was discrimination against Blacks. Despite the changes brought about by World War II, discrimination and segregation remained the rule in many parts of the nation. In 1954 the Supreme Court struck down the doctrine of "separate but equal" and ordered the public schools to desegregate. There were abuses in the area of voting rights. Therefore the federal government passed civil rights laws aimed at securing for Black people the right to cast their ballots in all elections.

Although the government acted on behalf of civil rights, much more was accomplished by the actions of Black people. Under the leadership of the Reverend Martin Luther King, Jr., and others, Blacks began a long campaign of peaceful resistance that eventually led to the desegregation of public places.

Social and cultural as well as political changes took place during the 1950's. Mass-production techniques and the influence of television created a mass culture that tended to "homogenize" the nation. Books, records, movies, and magazines that reached a nationwide audience wiped out many regional differences. Tensions—loss of identity, persistence of prejudice, and poverty—cast a shadow over the 1950's and boded ill for the future.

Vocabulary

Define or identify each of the following:

Gross National Product	*Brown* v. *Board of Education*	poll tax
computer		de facto segregation
soil bank	Little Rock Central High School desegregation	affluence

Review Questions

1. What contributed to the rising prosperity of the 1950's?
2. How did the interstate highway system change life for Americans?

3. What was the effect of farm overproduction?
4. How did northern segregation differ from southern segregation?
5. What steps did the federal government take to end segregation?
6. How were Blacks denied the right to vote, and what federal law tried to ensure Black voting rights?
7. How did the growth of the television industry change the nation?
8. What are three examples of mass-produced culture?

Reviewing Social Studies Skills

1. Using the bar graph on page 693, translate the information into a line graph.
2. Using the map on page 697, estimate the distance between the following cities in kilometers or miles.
   a. San Francisco and Los Angeles
   b. Seattle and Dallas
   c. New York and Miami
3. Television played an important role in the creation of mass culture. Why do the authors believe that it tends to eliminate regional differences and promote similarities? Do you agree? Defend your opinion.

Reading for Meaning

1. What do the authors mean when they say that Eisenhower didn't believe in the ideas of John Maynard Keynes but used them anyway?
2. What evidence is given to support the idea that the Eisenhower years were a time of prosperity? Is any evidence cited in the text to show that prosperity was not shared by everyone? If so, what groups were excluded?
3. Define the terms boycott and sit-in. How did the civil rights movement use these techniques? To what extent were these techniques effective?
4. List some of the examples that the authors give of popular culture in the 1950's. Can you add to this list?

Bibliography

Lorraine Hansberry's *Raisin in the Sun* (Random House) dramatizes what happens to a poor Black family in Chicago when they collect on an insurance policy.

Frank Bonham's *Durango Street* (Dutton) gives a good account of the life people faced in inner-city ghettos.

Isidore Stone's *Haunted Fifties* (Random House) is an interesting account of the period.

Eisenhower and the Cold War

"Forces of good and evil are massed and armed and opposed as rarely before in history. Freedom is pitted against slavery, lightness against dark." These were the words of Dwight D. Eisenhower in his first inaugural address, January 20, 1953. To the new President the Cold War was not a contest for power, territory, or trade. It was a conflict of ideas and ideals. Not since the religious wars of the 17th century had the rivalry among nations been expressed in such stark, moralistic terms. President Eisenhower's view gave a new dimension to the Cold War.

To conduct a diplomatic policy of morality, President Eisenhower could not have made a more apt choice for Secretary of State than John Foster Dulles. He was the grandson of one Secretary of State and the nephew of another. Dulles had spent his life in the foreign service. He had served on the American delegation at Versailles in 1919 and helped draw up the United Nations Charter in 1945. Although he was a Republican, he had helped form President Truman's Cold War policies. And in 1951 he negotiated the final peace agreement with Japan.

Despite his involvement with the Truman administration, Dulles was critical of the policy of containment. He believed it was too passive. It gave the Communists the initiative. And, in a world divided between good and evil, it was important that good take the offensive. By expressing moral indignation at tyranny, suggested Dulles, America could "change the mood of the captive peoples" of the world and put the Communists on the defensive.

Chapter Objectives

After you have finished reading this chapter, you should be able to:
1. Identify where and how the United States implemented the policy of containment between 1953 and 1955.
2. Explain what led to the relaxation of global tensions between 1955 and 1958.
3. List the events that led to the collapse of the 1960 summit conference.

Fortunately for a world threatened by nuclear destruction, neither President Eisenhower nor Secretary Dulles was as militant in manner as in speech. Their rigid morality cloaked a foreign policy that was limited in aim and flexible in practice. They talked often of war and occasionally risked it. But throughout their eight years in power, Eisenhower and Dulles kept the nation at peace. Given the dangers of the 20th-century world, that was a considerable achievement.

1. Holding the Line of Containment, 1953-1955

THE IDEOLOGICAL WAR. The great debate that accompanied the Korean War produced some changes in American attitudes. At the outset of the war, Republicans had accused Truman and Acheson of letting Asia fall to the Communists by concentrating too much on Europe. Eisenhower and Dulles believed that Europe was of central importance. They resisted the Asia-first wing of the Republican party. But they did agree that communism was a world menace. The line of containment in Truman's administration had gone only as far as Europe. Under Eisenhower it was extended around the world.

During the Korean War and the Red Scare, Republicans had also accused Truman of underestimating the force of Communist ideology, both at home and abroad. Because it was assumed that communism itself was an evil, all Communists had to be contained. It did not matter whether they were allied to the Soviet Union or not. Thus, even domestic uprisings in far corners of the earth were a threat to world peace if Communists were involved. *Carried to its logical conclusion, this line of reasoning meant that the United States would have to police the world, cleaning up pockets of Communists wherever they were found.*

THE "NEW LOOK." Republicans had also accused Truman of excessive spending. Many feared national bankruptcy more than the threat of aggression from abroad. President Eisenhower seemed to agree. *To cut defense spending, the military services adopted a "new look," deemphasizing ground forces and relying on air power.* This approach meant a greater reliance on technology than on infantry troops.

MASSIVE RETALIATION. How could cuts in defense spending be consistent with America's role as the world police officer? Dulles had grappled with this problem and persuaded the President to accept his view. In January 1954, Eisenhower stated that the United States did not have the troops to defend a containment line around the world. It could not even afford a ground war against Asian Communists.

Instead, America would develop and train local forces. Behind these local forces, such as the powerful ROK (Republic of Korea) Army in South Korea, would stand American air power, with its "great capacity to retaliate, instantly, by means and at places of our choosing." It was believed that the threat of massive retaliation with nuclear bombs would deter aggression everywhere in the world.

The policy of massive retaliation implied that any dispute, however remote, could become an occasion for nuclear annihilation. It was a chilling prospect indeed—even more so because the Soviet Union had built up an arsenal of nuclear weapons.

Six months earlier, in the summer of 1953, the Soviet Union had exploded a hydrogen bomb—a weapon 1,000 times more powerful than the atomic bomb dropped on Hiroshima. The United States had detonated its first thermonuclear device less than a year earlier. Soviet technology was rapidly closing the gap. Before long, each nation would have the power to annihilate the other, regardless of who struck first. The two countries, said physicist Robert Oppenheimer, were like "two scorpions in a bottle, each capable of killing the other but only at the risk of his own life." *Massive retaliation made the threat of a confrontation the keystone of American foreign policy.*

Sidenote to History

The Oppenheimer Case

Julius Robert Oppenheimer was born in New York City in 1904. He took courses in philosophy and physics at Harvard and graduated in three years. After studying for his doctorate in Europe, he returned to the United States and became professor of physics at the University of California at Berkeley and at the California Institute of Technology. Before the war, he founded the first major school of theoretical physics in this country.

At the age of 39, he became head of the government's atomic bomb project at Los Alamos, New Mexico. Even before the bomb was exploded, Oppenheimer and other scientists on the project were aware of the destructive power of their creation. They began a drive to educate citizens about the dangers and assets of atomic energy. Funding used for developing weapons, they believed, would be better used in atomic energy research for medicine and industry.

Oppenheimer was chief adviser to the Atomic Energy Commission from 1947 to 1953. He staunchly opposed the government's building of the hydrogen bomb. He thought that the development of a superbomb would motivate other nations to build similar bombs, thus causing an arms race. The possible outcome of an arms race, in Oppenheimer's view, would be the destruction of the world. It was immoral, he said, for any nation to take such a risk.

Oppenheimer's stand attracted wide public and government attention and led the government to withdraw his security clearance in 1954.

He was labeled a security risk and was no longer trusted to work on secret government projects relating to nuclear energy. Critics of Oppenheimer claimed that he had no right to voice his doubts about a weapon viewed as crucial to the postwar balance of power. They saw his prewar friendships with people of left-wing causes as good reason for denying him security clearance. Friends and supporters argued that government officials knew about his associations when they hired him to head the atomic bomb project. The government was withdrawing its trust in someone who had been proved trustworthy.

Despite the storm brewing around him, Oppenheimer continued to influence American scientists. As head of the Institute for Advanced Study in Princeton, New Jersey, from 1947 to his death in 1967, Oppenheimer taught theoretical physics to advanced students. He was a brilliant thinker and organizer. His reputation as an internationally respected physicist and teacher continued to grow.

Oppenheimer's loyalty was never questioned, but his honest and unpopular opinions sparked a debate over the role of scientists in determining government policies. At a time when the United States was locked into a race with the Soviets for nuclear superiority, dissenting voices, especially those of respected scientists, were not appreciated. The arms race that Oppenheimer predicted occurred exactly as he said it would.

THE FIRST VIETNAM WAR, 1946–1954. The flaws in massive retaliation were soon made clear by a crisis in French Indochina, called Vietnam by its inhabitants. Japan occupied the French colony at the beginning of World War II. Vietnamese *guerrillas* resisted the Japanese throughout the war. The guerrillas were a mixture of nationalists, who sought independence, and Communists, called Vietminh (VYET-min), who fought for independence from French rule and a Communist regime.

Guerrilla warfare is fought by small bands engaged in irregular methods of warfare, such as "hit-and-run" sabotage.

Ho Chi Minh, the Vietminh leader, proclaimed an independent republic at the end of World War II. The French were willing to concede a large measure of self-rule to the Vietnamese but not total independence. When negotiations failed, the French pre-

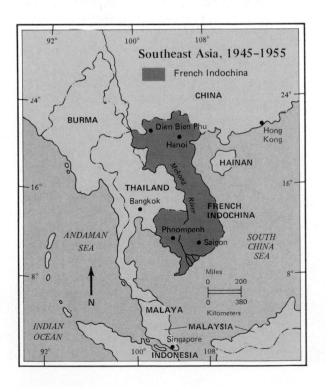

cipitated active fighting by shelling the Vietminh capital, Hanoi, in December 1946. (See map below.) The French claimed that because the Vietminh had seized control of the independence movement, France was not trying to preserve 19th-century colonial privileges. Instead, it was halting the spread of world communism. Jungle warfare spread over the Indochina and Malay peninsulas.

When the United States reassessed its Asian policy at the outbreak of the Korean War, it also considered the war in Indochina. The Truman administration sent money and supplies to the French forces. Meanwhile, Ho Chi Minh began to get aid from China and the Soviet Union. The jungle war continued.

Suddenly, in May 1954, the Vietminh guerrillas massed their forces around the French outpost of Dien Bien Phu in the remote northwestern corner of the country. (See map below.) The French garrison of 10,000 was trapped. The only way to evacuate the troops was by air. The French government appealed to the United States for help.

Did the Vietminh guerrillas represent a world Communist threat? Was the line of containment to be drawn through the jungles of Indochina? Eisenhower and Dulles answered yes to both questions. They based their reasoning, Eisenhower explained, on "what you would call the 'falling domino' principle. You have a row of dominoes set up, you knock over the first one, and what will happen to the last one is the certainty that it will go over very quickly." The President did not say what dominoes he had in mind. But a glance at a map and knowledge of Communist movements suggested Indochina's neighbors—Burma, Thailand, Malaya, and Indonesia—each of which faced internal Communist unrest. *The domino principle, then, was an attempt to profit from the mistakes of the past, notably the bargain with Hitler at Munich in 1938.* At

715

that time diplomats had learned the hard way that appeasement encourages more aggression.

THE DOMINO THEORY. The United States was convinced that it could not act alone. To move in suddenly might precipitate a reaction from the Soviets or the Chinese. America had to act in concert with its European allies, Great Britain and France.

Some members of the Eisenhower cabinet considered using American arms against the Vietminh Army around Dien Bien Phu, but the British would not support such a plan. The French asked for nonnuclear air strikes, but American military officials were skeptical. It appeared impossible to limit involvement. As in Korea, air units would be followed by ground forces. Illuminating the problem, one Pentagon official said, "One cannot go over Niagara Falls in a barrel only slightly." Handcuffed by the doctrine of massive retaliation, the administration decided to do nothing.

THE PARTITION OF INDOCHINA. Unable to obtain military aid from the United States, the French garrison at Dien Bien Phu surrendered to the Vietminh on May 7, 1954. Two months later representatives of Britain, France, the Soviet Union, and Communist China met in Geneva, Switzerland, to determine the fate of Indochina. Secretary of State Dulles went to the conference to observe but not to participate. The administration would not place itself in the

In this photograph a Vietnamese rice farmer is guiding his water buffalo and plow. A French task force is also stopping along the road. The task force is on its way to the front line. The photograph was taken by Robert Capa in 1954.

716

position of negotiating concessions to Communists.

Two agreements were made at the Geneva Conference: 1) Three nations were created from Indochina—Laos, Cambodia, and Vietnam. The area of Vietnam north of the 17th parallel became the Communist territory of North Vietnam. Vietnam south of that line became the pro-French South Vietnam. (See map, page 718.) *2) Within two years free elections would be held to bring about the reunification of Vietnam.* Once established, the unified government would be forbidden to join military alliances, and foreign troops would be banned from the country. A unified Vietnam, it was hoped, would be neutral in the Cold War.

Given the hopelessness of the French cause, the Geneva agreements were a reasonable settlement. Although the United States refrained from signing them, President Eisenhower endorsed them in a separate statement.

The proposed free elections were never held. Eisenhower acknowledged that had the elections been held as scheduled, "possibly 80 percent of the population" would have chosen Ho Chi Minh as leader of all Vietnam. *Instead, America began a military and economic buildup to maintain a pro-Western regime in South Vietnam.*

Eisenhower had avoided intervention and had helped establish a neutral zone in the world confrontation. In addition, the first Vietnam War showed Americans and Communists alike that the policy of massive retaliation was too hideous to be enforced. The world was achieving what Winston Churchill called "a balance of terror."

EXTENSION OF ALLIANCES.
Although the doctrine of massive retaliation proved ineffective, John Foster Dulles implemented the other feature of his Cold War policy—arming local units. In the wake of the Vietnam crisis, he moved to shore up the containment line in Southeast Asia. In September 1954, representatives of the United States, Britain, France, Australia, New Zealand, Pakistan, Thailand, and the Philippines formed the Southeast Asia Treaty Organization (SEATO). Dulles hoped that SEATO would be another NATO, but the pact never had the strength of the Atlantic alliance. In the first place, Southeast Asia needed economic development and social modernization, not a military pact. And the treaty nations were committed not to defend but merely to consult one another in case of attack. Nor was the organization as homogeneous as the Atlantic alliance. The eight participants constituted a global hodgepodge, of which only the Philippines and Thailand were actually part of Southeast Asia.

The most important powers in the region, India and Indonesia, refused to have anything to do with SEATO. Indeed, they resented the American presence in Asia. In 1955 Indonesia organized a conference of 29 Asian and African *Third World* nations at Bandung, Indonesia. Participants pledged themselves to neutrality in the Cold War.

The *Third World* consists of the developing areas of the world that do not have adequate resources to provide food, shelter, or energy for their citizens.

Undaunted, Secretary Dulles moved his line of local defense into the Middle East. In February 1955 the countries along the southern frontier of the Soviet Union— Turkey, Iran, Pakistan, and Iraq—joined with Great Britain to form the Baghdad Pact. (See map, page 721.) Although Dulles created the agreement, at the last minute he decided that the United States should not join. Instead, it would "cooperate with" the organization. A formal alliance with Arab nations might compromise America's support for Israel.

The Baghdad Pact was even weaker than SEATO. Its members detested one another almost as much as they feared the Soviet Union. Before long, Iraq withdrew. And the alliance's name was changed to the Central Treaty Organization (CENTO).

In addition to multilateral alliances, the United States had agreements with Japan, South Korea, Nationalist China (Taiwan), and, by 1955, South Vietnam. The line of containment encircled the Soviet Union and Communist China, from Norway to the Mediterranean and from the Pacific to Alaska. By 1956 the United States had defense agreements with 42 nations. As the Democratic party leader Adlai Stevenson observed dryly, "The sun never sets on an American commitment."

QUEMOY AND MATSU. How much probing at this global line would the United States tolerate? There were remote, tiny islands that fell right on the dividing line. Were they also to be defended? Events in Asia in early 1955 raised such questions.

In the Formosa Straits, a short distance off the coast of mainland China, lay two islands, Quemoy and Matsu. (See map below.) The islands were occupied by Chiang Kai-shek's Nationalist forces. They are hundreds of kilometers from Taiwan and within artillery range of the mainland. In the fall of 1954, the Chinese Communists began shelling Quemoy and Matsu. Invasion seemed the next step. An American fleet patrolled the straits to protect the Nationalists on Taiwan. Was the United States obliged to protect the two rocky islets? Earlier Eisenhower had persuaded Chiang Kai-shek to abandon islands that were closer to the Chinese mainland. Chiang was unwilling to retreat farther without at least a show of resistance.

In January 1955 President Eisenhower asked Congress for authority to use armed force to defend Taiwan and "related localities." Senate Democrats tried to confine the authorization to Taiwan, but the effort died when Wisconsin Senator Alexander Wiley declared: "Either we can defend the United States in the Formosa Straits now, or we can defend it later in San Francisco Bay." The resolution passed in each house.

The President's authority under the resolution was stated in broad and vague terms. And Eisenhower used it with considerable skill to keep the Chinese off balance. He refused to say whether he would go to the defense of the offshore islands if they were invaded, leaving the Chinese to guess at his intentions. During the height of the crisis in March 1955, both Eisenhower and Dulles indicated that they would not hesitate to use atomic weapons if the United States became involved. The Chinese Communists refused to test this resolve. Instead, their shelling gradually slackened. By May 1955 the crisis ended.

THE POLICY OF BRINKMANSHIP. Secretary Dulles later boasted to a *Life* magazine reporter about his handling of the

John Foster Dulles (on the right) enjoyed the complete confidence of his boss, President Eisenhower (on the left). This relationship allowed Dulles to become one of the most influential Secretaries of State in our nation's history. Dulles once said to an aide, "The State Department can only keep control of foreign policy as long as we have ideas." How did Dulles's role in the foreign policy of the 1950's reflect his view?

Formosa Straits crisis. "The ability to get to the verge without getting into the war," he explained, "is the necessary art. If you cannot master it, you inevitably get into war. If you try to run away from it, if you are scared to go to the brink, you are lost." Referring to the Formosa crisis, he added, "We walked to the brink and we looked it in the face. We took strong action."

Thereafter Dulles's foreign policy was referred to as "brinkmanship." Brinkmanship was not a foreign policy—it was the absence of policy. What Dulles failed to note, however, was that President Eisenhower kept the crisis under control. He kept American bombers under wraps and the Chinese off balance without committing the nation to defend two barren islands off the coast of China.

The Formosa Straits crisis revealed how difficult it was to define containment and showed the fragility of world peace.

Section Review

1. Mapping: Using the map on pages xx–xxi, locate the member nations of SEATO. Where are the majority of them located?
2. Identify or explain: John Foster Dulles, Dien Bien Phu, Chiang Kai-shek, Quemoy and Matsu, Ho Chi Minh, the Baghdad Pact.
3. In your own words, define the policy of massive retaliation.
4. What is meant by the term brinkmanship? Who developed the idea?

2. The Relaxation of Tensions, 1955-1958

NIKITA KHRUSHCHEV AND THE SOVIET UNION. Although it was some time before the United States realized it, the first break in Cold War tensions came with the death of Soviet leader Josef Stalin on March 5, 1953. Stalin's adventurist moves in Eastern Europe and Berlin had created much international tension. In his last years, the Soviet leader was so secretive and so suspicious of everyone around him, that he appeared to verge on insanity. No one—not even other Soviet leaders—knew what he might do next. The realization that such a person possessed nuclear weapons fueled anxiety about atomic warfare and annihilation.

After Stalin's death, the Communist party experimented with collective leadership, but eventually Nikita Khrushchev assumed power. The new government was clearly more sociable. It encouraged an end to the Korean War, reopened diplomatic relations with Yugoslavia, Greece, and Israel, and renounced claims to Turkish territory. In a tour of Europe—the first by a Soviet leader—Khrushchev sailed through a round of parties and press conferences, proclaiming the need for peaceful coexistence.

A MEETING OF WORLD LEADERS.

After staring at the brink of destruction in the Formosa Straits crisis, the leaders of the United States and the Soviet Union realized that it was time for face-to-face discussions. But first President Eisenhower wanted some clear sign that the Soviets were ready to do something for peace. As early as 1953 he had suggested that a peace treaty, ending the postwar occupation zones in Austria, would be such a sign.

In May 1955 the Soviet occupation ended. Austria recovered its sovereignty in return for a pledge to remain neutral in the Cold War. Secretary Dulles was skeptical of talks with the Soviets, but after the Austrian treaty was signed, he resigned himself to a *summit* conference of leaders. However, he cautioned Eisenhower not to smile when photographed with Soviet leaders.

In diplomatic terms, *summit* refers to the highest level of officials, in particular, heads of government.

THE GENEVA SUMMIT CONFERENCE, JULY 1955.

The leaders of the Big Four—the United States, the Soviet Union, Britain, and France—met at Geneva, Switzerland, in July 1955. The future of Germany headed the two-item agenda. The United States had begun rearming West Germany during the Korean War. And in 1954 the German Federal Republic was given full sovereignty and allowed to join NATO. The Soviets had countered this move by rearming East Germany and integrating it into the East European alliance system known as the Warsaw Pact. *At Geneva American leaders proposed the reunification of Germany based on free elections and the withdrawal of foreign armies.* The Soviets agreed, but they demanded that the new Germany be declared a neutral nation like Austria.

Two years before, in June 1953, the East Germans rebelled against Soviet occupation. They battled Soviet tanks with bricks torn from the streets of East Berlin. The uprising was suppressed, but the flood of refugees escaping daily from East Germany indicated the unpopularity of the Soviet regime.

If proposals for uniting Germany had been accepted, free elections and the departure of occupation armies almost certainly would have resulted in a pro-Western Germany. The Soviet occupation of Eastern Europe might have been rolled back. For such an outcome a neutral Germany was a small price to pay. Dulles, nevertheless, rejected the idea, insisting that Germany had to remain in NATO. A rare opportunity was lost.

NUCLEAR DISARMAMENT.

The other subject discussed at Geneva was nuclear disarmament. Since 1947, when the United States first proposed limitations on atomic weapons, discussions had bogged down on the subject of inspection. The United States was understandably reluctant to give up its nuclear stockpiles without ironclad guarantees to prevent cheating. The Soviets refused to open their closed society to foreign inspectors.

When the Soviets adhered to their stand at Geneva, Eisenhower decided it was time to try something new. Some of his advisers, among them Nelson Rockefeller, had suggested aerial inspection. Without alerting British and French leaders, the President made his "open skies" proposal. Periodic mutual inspection of war-making facilities from the air, he declared, would at least prevent surprise attacks and relax tensions. As trust built up, the United States and the Soviet Union could proceed to more substantial forms of disarmament. Khrushchev responded with a plan for immediate nuclear disarmament. But he flatly rejected open skies, claiming that such an arrangement would give America's air force a target map of Soviet military installations. This time it was Khrushchev who missed a good opportunity for peace.

THE SPIRIT OF GENEVA. The open skies proposal never got off the ground. But it promoted President Eisenhower's reputation as a peacemaker. The conference accomplished little else. But the fact that leaders of East and West met to engage in polite discussion suggested that the Cold War had entered a new phase. Newspapers called the softened relations between East and West the spirit of Geneva. Americans were overjoyed. Eisenhower's popularity in the Gallup Poll reached a record 79 percent. The spirit of Geneva coincided with the Senate's condemnation of Senator McCarthy, indicating that the hostility of the early days of the Cold War had lessened.

FOCUS ON THE MIDDLE EAST. In the fall of 1955, Khrushchev embarked on a tour of Third World countries. The trip signaled a more open and flexible policy on the part of the Soviet Union. It was designed to win friends and extend Soviet influence. Dulles worried that some African and Asian countries might find communism attractive.

The United States focused its concern on the Middle East. In the 1950's the area had a series of successful nationalistic uprisings. Although the Anglo-French political hold had been broken, Arab nationalists were a long way from attaining their goal of uniting all the Arab people.

Aside from the importance of its immensely rich oil fields, the Middle East

seemed to Dulles to be a battleground in the ideological Cold War. Newspaper columnists predicted a Soviet thrust into the region, not with military force, but with money, armaments, and secret agents. Gamal Abdel Nasser, a military officer who had driven out the Egyptian monarch, set up a military-dominated regime in 1952. With Nasser at its head, Egypt emerged as a leader among Arab states.

THE SUEZ CRISIS. *Nasser was a master at taking advantage of Cold War rivalries.* Although vehemently anti-Communist, he sought and obtained arms and economic aid from the Soviet Union as well as from the United States. Early in 1954 America, in a gesture of friendship, agreed to help finance one of Nasser's pet projects, a gigantic dam on the Nile River at Aswan. (See map below.) The Aswan Dam would tame the Nile River, whose floods had tormented Egypt for centuries, and would provide hydroelectric power for new industries.

In retaliation for Nasser's friendship with the Soviets, the United States backed out of its commitment to finance the building of the Aswan Dam. On July 19, 1956, Dulles brusquely informed the Egyptian ambassador of America's intention, explaining that

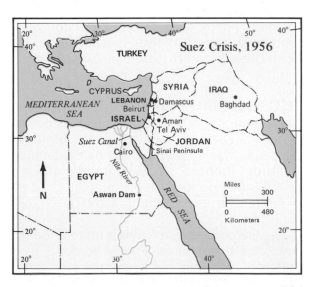

Suez Crisis, 1956

he doubted the ability of the Egyptian economy to undertake such a project. A week later Nasser responded by seizing the Suez Canal.

Although the canal was on Egyptian territory, it had been owned and operated by an international company, which had allowed passage from the Mediterranean to the Red Sea to ships of all nations on equal terms. Profits from the canal, Nasser told the world, would be used to build the Aswan Dam—without America's help.

Since 1882 British troops had been stationed at the Canal Zone to safeguard it and protect British interests in Egypt. Egypt had wanted the British to leave after World War II, and Britain complied in 1954. One month before Nasser took the canal, the last British troops were withdrawn. Britain was furious, but there was little it could do. Suez was Egyptian territory. The British had been mere tenants.

The neighboring state of Israel stood by, cautious and alert. With Nasser's encouragement, Arab terrorists had stepped up their raids on Israel, hoping to regain the land from which almost a million Arabs had fled after the creation of the Jewish state in 1948.

The Eisenhower administration faced a Presidential election. It limited itself to following a policy of wait-and-see. The crisis continued, as one White House aide put it, "with the soft and rhythmic ticking of a time bomb."

THE ELECTION OF 1956. Eisenhower's renomination by the Republicans was never in doubt. The only excitement in Republican ranks was a clumsy effort by moderates to dump Richard Nixon from the ticket. Eisenhower seemed agreeable, but failed to support the movement actively. Nixon stayed on.

The Democrats had a much more difficult time. Adlai Stevenson finally bested Estes Kefauver in a long and hectic primary campaign, but his prospects were dim. Stevenson was beloved by intellectuals for his introspection and wit. But these were qualities that irritated many voters. Stevenson had difficulty in finding a good election issue. He created a brief stir by suggesting an international treaty banning atomic tests to stop the hazards of nuclear fallout and ease Cold War tensions. Ironically, Stevenson lost popularity as soon as the Soviets indicated they liked the idea.

Eisenhower had brought the nation peace and prosperity—an unbeatable combination. No wonder many people still "liked Ike."

THE POLISH AND HUNGARIAN UPRISINGS. As the election neared, crises erupted all over the world. In October 1956 riots in major Polish cities forced the resignation of the hard-line Communist government and brought Wladyslaw Gomulka (go-MOOL-kuh) to power. After a tense confrontation with Khrushchev, Poland was

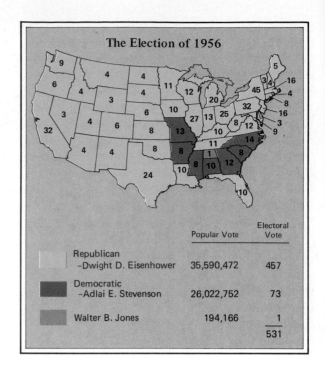

The Election of 1956

	Popular Vote	Electoral Vote
Republican —Dwight D. Eisenhower	35,590,472	457
Democratic —Adlai E. Stevenson	26,022,752	73
Walter B. Jones	194,166	1
		531

During the Budapest riots, a large monument to Stalin was removed from Stalin Square and taken to the center of town by a tractor. The uprising started as a peaceful demonstration by college students, but quickly developed into a bitter, armed revolt.

allowed to steer a more independent course on the condition that it remain within the Soviet alliance system.

Then Hungary erupted into anti-Soviet rioting. Khrushchev agreed to a change in Hungary's leadership. When the new leaders announced their intention of withdrawing from the Warsaw Pact and pursuing a neutral policy, Khrushchev drew the line. On November 4, two days before the American election, Soviet troops swept into Hungary with overwhelming force. The action ended any illusion that the peoples of Eastern Europe supported Communist regimes.

The Hungarian freedom fighters put up a gallant fight, battling Soviet tanks through the streets of Budapest. But their radio cries for help soon faded. A shocked world listened and watched, unwilling to move. *President Eisenhower believed that any strong American action would lead to a Third World War.*

THE MIDDLE EAST ERUPTS. On October 29, 1956, the Suez time bomb, ticking since July, exploded. The Soviets had their hands full with the Hungarians, and the Americans were preoccupied with the Presidential election. The Israelis decided it was a good time to thwart the invasion of Israel that Nasser had been threatening. *They launched a devastating attack on the Egyptian forces in the Sinai Peninsula.* (See map, page 721.) Two days later French and British paratroops seized the Suez Canal and began marching on Cairo, claiming that they were safeguarding the canal from Israeli attack. In fact, Britain and France had planned the operation with the Israelis because they feared that Egyptian control of the canal would threaten their oil supplies in the Near East.

The Anglo-French rationale for intervention seemed to Eisenhower a case of 19th-century imperialism. They wanted the Suez

723

Canal, and they grabbed it. "I've just never seen great powers make such a complete mess and botch of things," he exclaimed. "There can be no peace without law."

Britain and France put the United States into an embarrassing diplomatic position by forcing America to turn against its NATO allies. Eisenhower believed that an attack on Nasser would drive the Arabs into Moscow's camp. Therefore, he announced that he would work through the United Nations to end the aggression in the Middle East.

Khrushchev denounced the Suez seizure and threatened to send rockets over British and French cities. In response, Eisenhower put American forces on a worldwide alert. *But in the United Nations, the United States joined with the Soviet Union to pass a resolution condemning the attack on Egypt and calling for a cease-fire.* A General Assembly resolution condemned the Soviet assault on Hungary.

ELECTION DAY, 1956. When Americans trooped to the polls on November 6, Cold War tensions were greater than at any time since the Berlin blockade. Soviet tanks in Hungary patrolled the streets of Budapest. Khrushchev was threatening to send "volunteers" to Egypt. "If those fellows start something," Eisenhower told one of his aides, "we may have to hit 'em—and, if necessary, with everything in the bucket." That morning, Great Britain, suffering a financial crisis because of the war, gave in and agreed to a cease-fire. France and Israel had no choice but to do the same.

That evening, early election returns showed a strong trend toward Eisenhower. The trend turned into a landslide during the night. In an atmosphere of crisis, Americans rallied to the President. He won by an even bigger margin than in 1952. Eisenhower carried all but seven states, making important inroads into the Democratic South. He won 58 percent of the popular vote. (See map, page 722.)

The Democrats were bitter. They claimed that the Eisenhower administration's treatment of Nasser had precipitated the crisis in the first place. Complained one of Stevenson's aides, "Apparently all you have to do to win elections is make fatal mistakes in foreign policy."

THE EISENHOWER DOCTRINE. The administration's Middle Eastern policy had not been fatal, and had momentarily raised American prestige in the Third World. But it could hardly be counted a success. Britain and France were humiliated. France concluded that the Atlantic alliance meant nothing, and decided to build a French atomic arsenal. The Soviets, by their firm support for Egypt, increased their influence among the Arabs.

Meanwhile, Nasser was left in control of the canal. He continued to bar Israeli shipping. He had stood up to the European powers and, with the aid of the UN, had forced all three invading nations to withdraw. Although Nasser's forces were defeated by the Israelis on the battlefield, he emerged the political winner in the Suez crisis.

With Britain's prestige damaged and the Soviets gaining in the Middle East, Eisenhower and Dulles decided it was time to exert more American influence. In January 1957 the President asked Congress for authority to aid any Middle Eastern nation that asked for help against an aggressor "controlled by international communism." Labeled the Eisenhower Doctrine, the request was approved by Congress later that spring.

Eisenhower gained broad but vague powers. What did "controlled by international communism" mean? Did that include Syria, whose military rulers were importing Soviet arms and technicians? In February 1958 Egypt and Syria joined to form the United Arab Republic. Was that an advance for international communism or a step toward

Arab unity? Nasser denounced the Eisenhower Doctrine as an excuse for the United States to meddle in Middle Eastern affairs.

INTERVENTION IN LEBANON. *The administration's first chance to invoke the Eisenhower Doctrine came in the summer of 1958, in Lebanon.* The country's two political parties—one Christian, the other Islamic—had taken turns governing since the country won its independence in 1945. In the spring of 1958, the incumbent Christian President, Camille Chamoun (SHAH-mun), violated the understanding by seeking reelection. The Islamics objected and threatened revolution. Chamoun asked the United States for help, claiming there were Communists among his enemies. Eisenhower was reluctant to intervene in what was clearly an internal squabble.

Then, in July 1958, pro-Nasser Arab nationalists seized control of Iraq in a bloody coup. They renounced membership in the Baghdad Pact. Fearing that pro-Nasser forces were gaining control of the Middle East, Eisenhower decided to act. On July 15 approximately 1,700 marines landed on the beaches of Lebanon. They were greeted by bathers, soda vendors, and camera-laden tourists. Within a few weeks there were 14,000 marines patrolling Beirut, the capital. The marines left three months later, President Chamoun permitted an election, and an Islamic won. No one knew what it all had had to do with international communism, but Middle East tensions were eased.

Section Review

1. Mapping: Using the map on page 721, locate the Suez Canal. Can you tell from its location why it is important to so many countries?
2. Identify or explain: Nikita Khrushchev, Gamal Abdel Nasser, Adlai Stevenson, open skies.
3. What was the spirit of Geneva? Why did it give people hope, even though it achieved few concrete results?
4. What was the main idea of the Eisenhower Doctrine?

3. Anxious Years, 1958-1960

HAPPY DAYS YIELD TO GLOOM. On November 25, 1957, President Eisenhower suffered a mild stroke that left his speech impaired for a time. Coming two years after a heart attack, the stroke caused many Americans to wonder whether he would survive his second term.

The President recovered fairly quickly from the stroke, but aides felt he was a changed man. He seemed much older and more easily tired. His chief White House aide, Sherman Adams, undertook to shield him from some of the burdens of office. For the next few months, Adams became assistant President, making day-to-day decisions on minor matters and screening the President's visitors. Politicians and reporters complained that the President was becoming remote and out of touch. The public wondered why he seemed to spend so much time on the golf course.

The happy mood of the mid-1950's vanished. An economic recession ended the good times. Soviet scientific triumphs raised questions about the superiority of American technology. Revelations of corruption raised questions about America's moral fiber. The administration blundered through a succession of diplomatic crises. Gloom descended on Eisenhower's last years in office.

SPUTNIK. President Eisenhower's troubles began six weeks before his stroke on October 4, 1957. On that day the Soviet Union launched *Sputnik* (Russian for "tiny moon"). They orbited the first artificial satellite around the earth. The American government had already announced plans to

The New York Times.

VOL. CVII..No. 36,414.

© 1957, by The New York Times Company, Times Square, New York N. Y.

NEW YORK, SATURDAY, OCTOBER 5, 1957.

LATE CITY EDITION
U. S. Weather Bureau Report (Page 39) forecasts:
Cloudy and cool today and tonight.
Mostly fair tomorrow.
Temp. range: 65—53. Yesterday: 62.4—49.2.

10c beyond 100-mile zone from New York City

FIVE CENTS

SOVIET FIRES EARTH SATELLITE INTO SPACE; IT IS CIRCLING THE GLOBE AT 18,000 M. P. H.; SPHERE TRACKED IN 4 CROSSINGS OVER U. S.

HOFFA IS ELECTED TEAMSTERS' HEAD; WARNS OF BATTLE

Defeats Two Foes 3 to 1 —Says Union Will Fight 'With Every Ounce'

Text of the Hoffa address is printed on Page 6.

By A. H. RASKIN
Special to The New York Times

MIAMI BEACH, Oct. 4—The scandal-scarred International Brotherhood of Teamsters elected James R. Hoffa as its president today.

He won by a margin of nearly 3 to 1 over the combined vote of two rivals who campaigned on pledges to clean up the nation's biggest union.

Senate rackets investigators and Hoffa critics in the union rank-and-file immediately opened actions to strip the 44-year-old former warehouseman from Detroit of his election victory.

A jubilant Hoffa exhibited, however, greater concern over the possibility that his union might be ousted from the American Federation of Labor and Congress of Industrial Or-

IN TOKEN OF VICTORY: Dave Beck, retiring head of the Teamsters Union, raises hand of James R. Hoffa upon his election as union's president. At right is Mrs. Hoffa.

Associated Press Wirephoto

FAUBUS COMPARES HIS STAND TO LEE'S

Flu Widens in City; 10% Rate Predicted; 200,000 Pupils Out

ARGENTINA TAKES EMERGENCY STEPS

COURSE RECORDED

Navy Picks Up Radio Signals—4 Report Sighting Device

By WALTER SULLIVAN
Special to The New York Times

WASHINGTON, Saturday, Oct. 5—The Naval Research Laboratory announced early today that it had recorded four crossings of the Soviet earth satellite over the United States.

It said that one had passed near Washington. Two crossings were farther to the west. The location of the fourth was not made available immediately.

It added that tracking would be continued in an attempt to pin down the orbit sufficiently to obtain scientific information of the type sought in the International Geophysical Year.

[Four visual sightings, one of which was in conjunction with a radio contact, were reported by early Saturday morning. Two sightings were made at Columbus, Ohio, and one each from Terre Haute, Ind., and Whittier, Calif.]

Press Reports Noted

Soviet newspapers reported several weeks ago that the Soviet satellites would broadcast on frequencies in the neighborhood of twenty and forty mega-cycles. More exact frequencies

The New York Times   Oct. 5, 1957

The approximate orbit of the Russian earth satellite is shown by black line. The rotation of the earth will bring the United States under the orbit of Soviet-made moon.

Device Is 8 Times Heavier Than One Planned by U.S.

Special to The New York Times

WASHINGTON, Oct. 4—Leaders of the United States earth satellite program were astonished tonight to learn that the Soviet Union had launched a satellite eight times heavier than that contemplated by this country.

560 MILES HIGH

Visible With Simple Binoculars, Moscow Statement Says

Text of Tass announcement appears on Page 3.

By WILLIAM J. JORDEN
Special to The New York Times

MOSCOW, Saturday, Oct. 5—The Soviet Union announced this morning that it successfully launched a man-made earth satellite into space yesterday.

The Russians calculated the satellite's orbit at a maximum of 560 miles above the earth and its speed at 18,000 miles an hour.

The official Soviet news agency Tass said the artificial moon, with a diameter of twenty-two inches and a weight of 184 pounds, was circling the earth once every hour and thirty-five minutes. This means more than fifteen times a day.

Two radio transmitters, Tass said, are sending signals continuously on frequencies of 20.005 and 40.002 megacycles. These signals were said to be strong enough to be picked up by amateur radio operators. The trajectory of the satellite is being tracked by numerous scientific stations.

This headline from The New York Times announces the launching of Sputnik, the first artificial satellite to orbit the world. How did Americans react to the news?

---

launch a satellite that year. No one had expected the Russians to launch one first.

Technological supremacy was an article of faith among Americans. The Soviet success came as a rude shock. For years Americans had mistakenly but hopefully believed that the Soviet Union was a backward land, suffocating under an oppressive, unworkable political system. Shock turned to despondency two months later, when the first American satellite exploded on the launching pad. On January 31, 1958, the army finally put up a grapefruit-sized satellite, *Explorer*. But shortly thereafter Soviet scientists outdid America again by launching a satellite large enough to carry one passenger —a dog.

THE MISSILE GAP. *The Soviets' ability to throw that much weight into orbit suggested that they were well ahead in missile development.* By 1957 both Cold War rivals were trying to perfect an intercontinental ballistic missile (ICBM) capable of carrying an atomic warhead 8,000 kilometers (5,000 miles). The owner of this weapon would have an enormous military advantage. The American Atlas **missile,** fueled by a liquid petroleum mixture, was less powerful than the Soviet missile. Soviet tests also suggested a superiority of numbers.

A **missile** is a self-propelled, self-guided aerial weapon.

Americans were suddenly faced with the possibility that in a surprise attack the Soviet Union might have the power to wipe out American defenses. Leaked government reports indicated that by 1959 the Soviets might have enough missile superiority to strike. *Senate Democratic Majority Leader Lyndon Johnson began talking of a "missile gap."* He demanded a crash program to catch up.

President Eisenhower refused to panic. Liquid-fueled missiles such as the Atlas were inaccurate and vulnerable to attack. President Eisenhower preferred to wait for the development of a second generation of solid-fueled missiles that could be carried aboard submarines or buried in concrete silos. Reports from American spy planes indicated that the Soviet missile program was not as advanced as America feared. The President could not convey his knowledge to the public without revealing the source of his intelligence information. He expected people to trust his judgment. But the public was no longer in a trusting mood. Many Americans saw only failure, confusion, and drift.

BACK TO THE FORMOSA STRAITS. The administration's handling of another crisis off China was not reassuring. In August 1958 the Chinese Communists resumed their shelling of the offshore islands of Quemoy and Matsu. Many Americans wondered why the President had not quietly abandoned such militarily useless islands after weathering the 1955 crisis in the Formosa Straits. Instead, he had permitted

Sidenote to History

The Bomb Shelter Boom

During the early 1950's a vision of the mushroom-shaped cloud loomed in the minds of Americans. Reports of the atomic bomb's effect on Hiroshima and Nagasaki convinced most Americans that horror would result from a nuclear war. Cold War tensions and the Soviets' development of nuclear bombs and space rockets prompted the United States government to take various precautions against nuclear attack. An attempt was made as part of the country's civil defense program to help Americans build bomb shelters.

Any underground space, such as a subway tunnel or a deep cellar, could provide shelter. Such areas had proved useful during World War II, when the people of London took shelter from German bombs in the stations of their subway system. But the important thing to remember in building shelters against nuclear attack, civil defense experts pointed out, was making them airtight. After a nuclear attack, the atmosphere would be contaminated by radioactive particles that would be deadly to anyone who breathed the air.

The national civil defense organization worked through local chapters to train volunteer air-raid wardens to direct citizens in case of attack. Detailed instructions for building bomb shelters were distributed. Schools and other public institutions drilled their students and personnel in techniques to protect themselves and others should an air raid occur. In an era when nuclear attack seemed likely, many people bought commercially produced shelters, and others designed and built their own. Shelters were built all over the United States during the early 1950's. When Cold War tensions were reduced slightly, so was bomb shelter construction. Before the close of the decade, shelters were being turned into storage space or playrooms for children. They serve to remind people of an era when fear of the bomb was prevalent.

Chiang Kai-shek to place 100,000 troops on Quemoy and Matsu for possible raids against the mainland. This was one third of Chiang's army. The force could not be removed under Communist fire, and surrendering them was unthinkable.

Eisenhower believed that he had no choice but to go to the brink of war. *Informing the public that there would be no appeasement, he ordered the United States Navy to help protect and supply the islands.* After a month of acute tension, the Chinese bombardment subsided. The President avoided war once more. But many wondered if a little foresight might not have prevented the entire affair.

UNEMPLOYMENT AND UNION PROBLEMS. *By mid-1958 every aspect of American life seemed to be coming apart.* The economy skidded into a recession, the worst since the end of World War II. By summer seven percent of the nation's work force was unemployed. Although the economy improved by the end of the year, unemployment persisted. The slowdown reduced government tax revenues, forcing the President to accept a budget deficit of 12 billion dollars, the largest peacetime deficit up to that time. Adding to the feeling of unease was a succession of scandals that ranged from labor unions to the White House.

Jacob Lawrence, one of America's foremost Black artists, painted the people and places where he lived. This painting, entitled "Street Shadows," shows the streets of Harlem, in New York City, on a summer night.

Once the voice of the down-and-out of American workers, big labor had settled into a self-satisfied conservatism after the war. Wages were high, unemployment minimal, and strikes rare. Most unions found it better to reach compromise settlements with management rather than risk their treasuries. Gone was the militant, anti-business attitude of the early years. Union leaders received handsome salaries and enjoyed the same life-style as business executives.

In 1955 the A.F. of L. and CIO settled their differences and merged into a single organization of about 15 million members. George Meany, the first president of the AFL-CIO, exemplified the second generation of labor leaders.

"American labor never had it so good," Meany boasted in 1955. But, in reality, the labor movement was in trouble. About 35 percent of the labor force was unionized. But that percentage was declining. The number of *blue-collar* workers in industry decreased. Efforts to unionize the factories that were springing up in the South failed, and most unions ignored the growing number of *white-collar* service workers.

Blue-collar workers are the wage-earning group whose jobs require manual labor.
White-collar workers are salaried employees who perform office work.

CORRUPTION IN LABOR UNIONS.
The labor movement was even less effective in cleaning out corruption than in recruiting members. Early in the 1950's the New York Crime Commission discovered that the International Longshoremen's Union, an organization of dock workers, was governed by *racketeers.* These racketeers threatened shipping lines with crippling strikes and slowdowns unless they were paid tribute on demand. The A.F. of L. expelled the ILU, but the dock workers continued to stick by their organization, resisting a cleanup.

A *racketeer* is one who obtains money or advantages by threats of violence, blackmail, or unlawful interference with business.

The ILU controversy was dying down when a Senate committee uncovered illegal activities in the Teamsters' Union, a huge and powerful organization of truck and taxi drivers. The committee learned that the union owned a string of taverns and gambling houses in Portland, Oregon, and that the organization's president, Dave Beck, was using union funds to lead a princely life in Seattle, Washington.

Under pressure Beck resigned and subsequently went to jail for income tax evasion. Unshaken, union members elected as their president James Hoffa, notorious for his associations with gangsters. (Hoffa's gangster connections eventually caught up with him. He was kidnapped in 1975 and has not been found.)

The AFL-CIO expelled the Teamsters, with no more effect than the expulsion of the longshoremen. In fact, the Teamsters gained by signing up white-collar workers previously ignored by other unions—police officers, firefighters, and schoolteachers. It was a sad commentary on the condition of organized labor.

THE FALL OF SHERMAN ADAMS.
Americans were beginning to wonder if the illegal activities of the labor unions were not also a commentary on society. Their concern deepened when corruption turned up in the White House. In June 1958 a congressional investigating committee discovered that Sherman Adams, the President's closest aide, had accepted gifts amounting to several thousand dollars from a New England textile manufacturer. In return Adams had used his influence on behalf of the manufacturer with several federal agencies, causing investigations into the manufacturer's business to be dropped.

Khrushchev was so impressed with the farm technology in Iowa in 1959 that he tried to induce Russian farmers to grow corn in Siberia.

Adams claimed he had done nothing wrong, but reporters had a field day. Since Eisenhower's heart attack, Adams had been protecting the President from overwork. As part of his duties, he controlled appointments to the President. Reporters were invariably turned away. When Adams got into trouble, journalists had their revenge. They labeled him the abominable no-man who did all the President's dirty work. Congressional Republicans, facing an election that fall, demanded his removal. In September Adams resigned.

Even with Sherman Adams out of the way, Republicans faced disaster in the congressional election of 1958. Consistently high unemployment rates and the exposés of corruption gave the Democrats handy campaign issues. People were in the mood for change. The Democrats gained seats in the House and in the Senate, giving them commanding majorities in both houses of Congress. Senate Majority Leader Lyndon Johnson made no secret of his White House ambitions. When Eisenhower gave his annual State of the Union address, Johnson issued one of his own.

WAGING PEACE, 1958–1959. Sensing unease in the popular mood, President Eisenhower embarked on a search for a Cold War settlement that would restore public faith—and his reputation—before he left office. Direct negotiations with the Soviet Union, long stymied by John Foster Dulles, became possible when Dulles, ill with cancer, resigned early in 1959.

In midsummer the President announced that Premier Khrushchev would visit the United States in September. The Soviet leader arrived in an amiable mood. After meeting with Eisenhower, Khrushchev embarked on a 12-day tour, which was marred by an angry outburst when he was barred from California's Disneyland on security grounds.

He conferred with the President for three days at the Presidential mountain retreat, Camp David. They agreed only to continue negotiating. In December 1959 the President capped his experiment in personal diplomacy with an around-the-world trip that took him to 11 nations. At his urging, European leaders agreed to another summit conference scheduled for Paris in May 1960.

THE U-2 AND THE SUMMIT. In January 1960 the Gallup Poll reported the President's popularity had risen to 70 percent, the highest rating in three years. The economy was showing signs of vigor, and the national mood was brightening. The approaching summit conference offered the President a chance to leave office with a personal triumph—an end to the Cold War.

Then disaster struck. On May 1, days before the summit conference was to open, the Soviets shot down an American U-2 spy plane and captured its pilot, Francis Gary Powers. Since 1956 spy planes had been flying over Soviet territory at altitudes beyond the range of Soviet antiaircraft rockets. A public protest by the Soviets would have amounted to confessing the limitations of their defense system. By 1960, however, their improved rocketry made protests unnecessary—they brought down an American spy plane.

At first the American government claimed that the aircraft was a weather ship that had strayed off course. The Soviets responded by putting pilot Powers on television. American officials were caught in a series of lies. President Eisenhower finally admitted the truth and took full responsibility for the affair. He justified the flights on the grounds that the Soviet Union's policy of extreme secrecy

made such flights necessary in order to prevent a surprise attack. He also announced that the flights would continue.

On the eve of the summit conference, suspending such flights might have been a diplomatic course of action. Khrushchev regarded the continuance of flights over the Soviet Union as an intolerable insult. And in Paris, he refused to attend the opening session of the conference. Instead, he demanded that President Eisenhower suspend the flights as the price of continuing the conference. When Eisenhower refused, Khrushchev withdrew an invitation that had been extended to the President to visit the Soviet Union.

Khrushchev abruptly terminated the meeting. He expressed the hope that the United States government to be elected the following year might be able to approach such a conference with an understanding of "the futility of pursuing aggressive policies."

Bad luck and diplomatic blunders doomed the Paris summit conference. It also seemed to symbolize President Eisenhower's second term. Many Americans thought it was time for a change. Waiting in the wings was a vibrant young Democrat who promised to "get the country moving again." The young Democrat's name was John Fitzgerald Kennedy.

Section Review

1. Mapping: Using the map on page 718, locate Quemoy and Matsu in terms of their latitudes and longitudes, distance from China, and distance from each other.
2. Identify or explain: Sherman Adams, *Sputnik*, George Meany, Francis Gary Powers, missile gap.
3. List and briefly explain the causes of American self-doubt about the country's position as a leader in science and technology.

Bird's-Eye View

Relations between the United States and the Communist nations were a central concern of the Eisenhower administration. John Foster Dulles, the Secretary of State, wished to see the United States take a more aggressive and global approach to the spread of communism throughout the world.

In Vietnam, French occupying forces, at war with Vietnamese guerrillas, were driven out. At a postwar peace conference, it was decided to divide Vietnam into two zones on a temporary basis. The United States was not certain of what its position in Asia should be. The American commitment in the area was soon tested by Chinese action in the Formosa Straits.

The death of Stalin, the subsequent ascent to power of Khrushchev, and the Geneva Conference led to lessened tensions between the United States and the Soviet Union. But rivalries continued in various parts of the world.

Eisenhower was nominated for a second term, as crises erupted in Hungary, Poland, and the Suez. Eisenhower announced the Eisenhower Doctrine, which suggested that the United States had the right to go to the aid of any nation facing invasion by "international communism."

Eisenhower's second term was plagued by many problems, including his ill health. The Soviet launching of *Sputnik* troubled many Americans. On the domestic front, union corruption lowered morale. Sherman Adams, Presidential assistant, was accused of using his position for private gain. Eisenhower hoped a new round of summit talks would overshadow these problems. But the conference was doomed by the shooting down of an American plane over Soviet territory.

Vocabulary

Define or identify each of the following:

guerrilla warfare	SEATO	summit conference
domino principle	Quemoy and Matsu	*Sputnik*
Third World	brinkmanship	U-2

Review Questions

1. What strategies did the Eisenhower administration pursue to contain communism?
2. What formal commitments did the United States make in its policy of containment?
3. What led to the easing of tensions between the United States and the Soviet Union?

4. What role did France and Britain play during the Suez crisis?
5. What did the participants at the summit conferences hope to accomplish? Were they successful?
6. Why did Lyndon Johnson express concern over the "missile gap"?

Reviewing Social Studies Skills

1. Make a time line of the Eisenhower years. Include at least 10 important events that occurred during his administration.
2. Using the map on page 721, locate the Suez Canal in terms of bodies of water to which it has access. How does this help account for its position in world trade?
3. Locate Vietnam on the map on page 718, and answer the following:
   a. What countries border Vietnam?
   b. In what three places did the United States make a commitment to stop communism?
   c. Using approximate latitudes and longitudes, describe the locations of Hanoi and Saigon.

Reading for Meaning

1. List evidence in the chapter that shows progress made toward lessening tensions between the United States and the Soviet Union. Use that evidence to write a paragraph describing relations between the United States and the Soviet Union in the 1950's.
2. The authors state that the Hungarian crisis proved that Eastern Europeans were not willing Communists. How does the Hungarian crisis support the authors' contention?
3. Compare the Eisenhower Doctrine, the Monroe Doctrine, and the Truman Doctrine. What are the similarities and the differences among the Presidential pronouncements?
4. What evidence do the authors cite to support the view that serious problems were developing within the American labor movement?
5. Imperialism, one nation controlling another nation, was a direct or an indirect cause of several incidents during the Eisenhower administration. Name those events, and explain why they were a result of imperialism.
6. Develop a glossary of at least five Cold War terms used in this chapter.

Bibliography

Townsend Hoopes's *The Devil and John Foster Dulles: The Diplomacy of the Eisenhower Era* (Little, Brown) is a biography of one of the chief figures in the decade.

Cold Warriors, by John C. Donovan (Heath), tells about policymakers during the Cold War.

Chapter 32

1960-1964

New Frontier to Great Society

Americans had been through troubles before. They had endured war and depression. They had gone to the brink of nuclear disaster. But seldom had things looked as bad as they did in the summer of 1960.

Shocked by the apparent Soviet lead in space technology, Americans began to doubt themselves and their system. Critics attacked the American educational system, pointing out that the Soviet Union was training more scientists and engineers. Economists thought the fault lay with American society, which annually spent more on cosmetics than it did on education. Others bemoaned the sluggish growth rate of the American economy, comparing it with the rapid advances claimed by the Soviet Union. If the growth rates were maintained, they predicted, the Soviet Union would be outproducing the United States in a few years.

Soviet leader Nikita Khrushchev made the most of the situation. "We will bury you!" he boasted. And no one knew whether he meant by economic competition or military force. American nerves drew tighter when he predicted that the grandchildren of Americans would someday be Communists.

Everything seemed wrong with the world that summer. In June the Japanese government informed President Eisenhower that it could not guarantee his safety during a scheduled visit to the country. It was a humiliating moment for Eisenhower.

A few weeks later, the African nation of Congo dissolved into civil war when Belgian colonial authorities departed. Taking advantage of the confusion, Khrushchev sent Soviet arms and technicians into the country. A United Nations peacekeeping force eventually restored order, but concern over growing Communist influence in Africa lingered.

Even more alarming were the developments in Cuba. The new head of the Cuban government, Fidel Castro, openly declared that he was a Communist and asked the Soviets for aid. Castro had won control of Cuba by ousting an unpopular dictator. And many Americans had sympathized with his revolution. Learning that he was a Communist shocked some Americans. Because of Cuba's nearness to the United States, the appeal for Soviet help was worrisome.

In July Khrushchev announced that he would unleash his atomic missiles if the United States interfered with Cuba. When the United Nations General Assembly opened in September, both Castro and Khrushchev attended to deliver anti-American tirades. To accentuate his points, the Soviet leader even took off his shoe and pounded it on the rostrum.

Chapter Objectives

After you have finished reading this chapter, you should be able to:
1. Describe the Cuban and Berlin crises.
2. List and describe the major New Frontier programs.
3. List in chronological order the events that occurred during the civil rights movement and the war in Vietnam.
4. Explain how President Johnson was able to get social legislation passed.

All in all, 1960 was a year Americans preferred to forget. Except for one thing. It was also a Presidential election year, one of the most important elections of recent times.

1. Getting the Country Moving Again

THE ELECTION OF 1960. Because of Eisenhower's troubles the Democrats had the best chance of winning an election since Roosevelt's death. Not surprisingly, they had a multitude of aspiring candidates. Senate Majority Leader Lyndon Johnson had made himself a shadow President, telling the administration what it would receive from Congress and what it would not. His main rival for the Democratic nomination was Massachusetts Senator John F. Kennedy. Rich, handsome, and talented, Kennedy had a superb campaign organization and a youthful image that projected well on television. His promise to "get the country moving again" was exactly what a gloomy nation wanted to hear.

Kennedy's main political drawback was his Roman Catholic religion. No Catholic had ever served as President. But his pri-

mary victories over Senator Hubert Humphrey in Wisconsin and West Virginia proved that voters no longer considered religion a barrier to the White House. Kennedy won the Democratic nomination and, in a gesture of party unity, asked Lyndon Johnson to be his running mate.

The Republican candidate, Vice-President Richard Nixon, faced a difficult task in

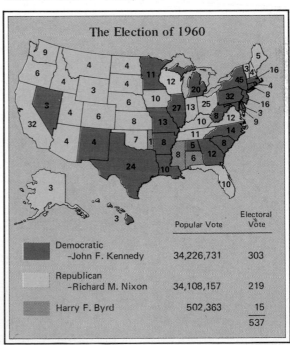

The Election of 1960

	Popular Vote	Electoral Vote
Democratic — John F. Kennedy	34,226,731	303
Republican — Richard M. Nixon	34,108,157	219
Harry F. Byrd	502,363	15
		537

1960. He had to identify himself with Eisenhower's prestige and popularity, while divorcing himself from the disasters that had beset the nation in recent years.

In a series of nationally televised debates—the first in an American election—Kennedy's charm won him a slight edge. But the contest was one of the closest in history. A shift of a few thousand votes in Illinois and Texas would have given the election to Nixon. (See map, page 735.)

THE KENNEDY LEGEND. Kennedy's style, energy, and grace were the stuff legends were made of. Kennedy surrounded himself with some of the ablest people in the country and gave each a problem to solve—unemployment, Cold War tensions, the missile gap, a sluggish economy, foreign aid. Nothing seemed beyond reach. ***Kennedy's experts set out to overcome the nation's troubles.***

Under Kennedy and his wife, Jacqueline, the White House came to life. Washington took on a festive mood. Dinner parties and formal dances were in vogue. Cabinet members were photographed playing squash and tennis. The President exercised, not on the golf course but by playing touch football. He spent his vacations not in the solemn confines of Camp David but sailing off the Massachusetts coast. A legend was born.

CLOSING THE MISSILE GAP—AND THEN SOME. ***The people surrounding Kennedy were brilliant, but they had little that was new to offer the country.*** Secretary of State Dean Rusk viewed the Cold War in the same terms as John Foster Dulles but without Dulles' moralism. Secretary of Defense Robert McNamara, former president of the Ford Motor Company, brought great managerial skill to the Pentagon but little change in policy. His principal

This photograph was taken at a dinner party held by the Kennedys on May 22, 1962. President Kennedy (on the right) is escorting Felix Houphouet-Boigny, President of the Ivory Coast. Mrs. Kennedy and the Secretary of State, Dean Rusk, are close behind.

objection to Eisenhower's defense policy was its excessive reliance on aircraft and missiles. McNamara, with Kennedy's blessing, proposed to build up American ground forces so they could fight minor "brushfire" wars anywhere in the world. Only in that way, he believed, could Communist probes in the far corners of the containment line be controlled.

At the same time, McNamara had no intention of abandoning the doctrine of massive retaliation. He soon discovered what Eisenhower had known all along—that there was no missile gap. By mid-1961 the Pentagon acknowledged that the United States had approximately the same number of ICBM's as the Soviet Union. It achieved a substantial lead when McNamara strategically positioned the missiles already built. And he ordered a 100 percent increase in the production of second-generation missiles.

Even with the savings that McNamara introduced with computers and efficiency experts, Kennedy's defense budgets were 50 percent higher than Eisenhower's. The United States was in a position to annihilate the Soviet Union over and over again. Far from bringing security, the American effort merely induced the Soviets to redouble their own spending. By the end of the decade, the two countries were again roughly equal in missile forces.

THE BAY OF PIGS. Kennedy's promise to get the country moving again led to one early disaster. His chief complaint about Eisenhower's management of foreign policy was that it was too passive. Khrushchev always seemed to take the initiative. Eisenhower was always on the defensive, reacting to situations created by others. Kennedy wanted to take some quick, bold, decisive action that would help Americans regain their self-confidence. Cuba seemed to present an opportunity.

Throughout 1960 Fidel Castro drifted closer to the Soviet Union. Toward the end

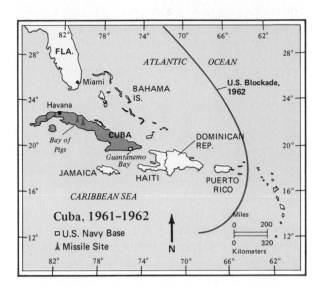

Cuba, 1961–1962
□ U.S. Navy Base
▲ Missile Site

of the year, Eisenhower lost patience and cut off diplomatic relations with Cuba. After the election Kennedy was informed that the CIA was training an army of Cuban exiles in Guatemala for a landing in Cuba. The CIA expected the invasion to trigger an anti-Communist uprising in Cuba. Kennedy gave the plan the go-ahead. ***On April 17, 1961, a force of 1,500 landed at the Bay of Pigs, on the south coast of Cuba.*** (See map above.)

It was a fiasco. The landing site was too far from the mountains to afford protection. The popular uprising never came. And Castro's army quickly pinned down the landing force and wiped it out in two days, taking 1,000 prisoners. Kennedy refused to risk war by landing American troops or providing air cover.

In a TV address he took full responsibility for the disaster, and his popularity leaped in the polls. Americans thought he had given the invasion the old college try. Unfortunately, both the President and the public missed the main point—that there were limits to American power.

THE BERLIN CRISIS. Berlin was the biggest threat to world peace when Kennedy took office. For several years Khrushchev had been threatening to sign a treaty with

Communist East Germany that would formally end World War II and grant independence to the country. Such a move would have given the East Germans control of the access routes to Berlin, allowing them to harass or block traffic at will. To keep the highways open, the western powers occupying Berlin—the United States, Britain, and France—would have to negotiate with the East Germans. This would amount to recognizing the legitimacy of its Communist government.

The 1960 summit conference was supposed to focus on the Berlin issue. When the conference collapsed, tensions were heightened. In the spring of 1961, Khrushchev hinted that he would sign a treaty with the East Germans by fall.

Fidel Castro and Nikita Khrushchev had never met before September 20, 1960. Yet they greeted each other with the elation of long-lost friends. Both were in New York for a meeting at the United Nations.

In July 1961 Kennedy and Khrushchev met in Vienna, Austria, to discuss the problem. Khrushchev had been dominating world news for more than a year. He felt tough and self-confident. Refusing to bend on any point, the Soviet leader insisted on a settlement by the end of the year. When Kennedy stated that the United States would stay in West Berlin, Khrushchev replied: "I want peace, but if you want war, that is your problem."

Shaken by Khrushchev's crude belligerence, Kennedy decided that the Soviet leader would be influenced only by a show of force. He summoned army reservists to active duty and ordered the mobilization of two army divisions and 54 air squadrons.

Instead of backing down, the Soviets moved in an unexpected direction in August 1961. ***They began construction of a wall between East and West Berlin.*** The purpose was to stop the flow of refugees that was a constant source of embarrassment to the Communist regime.

The refugees, numbering up to 1,000 a day in the 1950's, drained East Germany of skilled workers. (The West sent back refugees who could not qualify for jobs in West Germany.) The exodus was a continuing rebuke to communism. Unable to express themselves under communism, joked westerners, the refugees were "voting with their feet."

Building the Berlin Wall was a confession of weakness. But Communist authorities apparently believed it was better than the depopulation of East Germany. In October Khrushchev dropped his threat to negotiate a treaty with the East Germans.

THE CUBAN MISSILE CRISIS. Kennedy's use of brinkmanship in the Berlin crisis alarmed some people even though he regained the diplomatic initiative. With a wall around people in his own backyard, Khrushchev could scarcely undertake jaunty Third World tours talking of the blessings of communism. Through substantial increases in foreign aid spending, Kennedy restored some of the prestige and influence in Africa and Latin America that the United States had lost in the 1950's. In Europe Kennedy was becoming a folk hero.

In fact, it might have been Kennedy's success in wooing the world that forced Khrushchev into the desperate gamble that produced the Cold War's tensest moment. For Americans the story began October 14, 1962. A U-2 spy plane, taking routine photographs of Cuba, discovered signs of missile launching pads under construction. The missiles themselves were probably en route from the Soviet Union. And no one doubted that they would be pointed at the United States.

Kennedy summoned his inner circle of advisers. The military wanted to invade Cuba. But it was decided to try less drastic measures first. In a television address on October 22, Kennedy explained the problem and outlined his policy. *He had ordered the navy to intercept any Soviet vessels carrying missiles to the island.* Cuba would be placed under quarantine but not total blockade.

Kennedy then followed the tough line that he had used in the Berlin crisis a year before. The United States, he said, would consider the launching of missiles from Cuba against any country in the Western Hemisphere an attack by the Soviet Union, requiring full American retaliation. He then called on Khrushchev to end his threat and remove the missiles.

Over the next few days, the tension was almost unbearable. Work continued day and night on the Cuban launching pads. In Florida an immense invasion force slowly built up. The navy sighted 20 Soviet merchant vessels heading toward Cuba.

On the morning of the 24th, the Soviet ships stopped in the water. They turned around and headed for home. Khrushchev was going to respect the American quarantine. "We're eyeball to eyeball," said Secretary of State Dean Rusk, "and I think the other fellow just blinked." The world sighed with relief.

But the crisis was not over. Unless the bases in Cuba were dismantled, Kennedy might have to order an invasion. On October 26 Khrushchev sent a long message to Kennedy, expressing his fear of nuclear war. *He offered to remove Soviet missiles if the United States would promise not to attack Cuba.* The next day a second, more warlike, Soviet note arrived. Obviously drafted by hardliners in the Soviet government, it offered to remove the missiles from Cuba if the United States dismantled its missile sites in Turkey.

Kennedy ignored the second offer and accepted the first. He promised not to attack Cuba and demanded removal of the missiles. He added a threat that if the missiles were not removed, he would attack. On October 28 Khrushchev agreed, and the crisis was over.

RESULTS OF THE CUBAN CRISIS.

Once again the world stepped back from the brink. A few months later the United States removed its obsolete missiles from Turkey.

Kennedy's threats can hardly be called diplomacy, but his cool handling of the crisis won universal admiration. *His ability to call Khrushchev's bluff twice in two years boosted American morale.*

For Khrushchev, the Cuban crisis was the beginning of the end. Soviet leaders were unhappy with his international buffoonery. His recklessness in starting the Cuban crisis and his retreat from it brought opposition into the open. He was removed from office the following year.

Section Review

1. Mapping: Using the map on page 737, describe the geographic relationship of Cuba to the United States in terms of

distance and direction. Why do you think the United States considered Cuban missiles a threat?

2. Identify or explain: Fidel Castro, Nikita Khrushchev, John F. Kennedy, Richard Nixon, Dean Rusk, Robert McNamara.
3. How did the election of Kennedy to the Presidency help boost American morale?
4. Describe the Bay of Pigs invasion. Why did it fail?

2. The New Frontier

THE ROAD TO PROGRESS AND PROSPERITY. In his acceptance speech at the Democratic convention, Kennedy called for a new frontier, an outburst of American energy and sacrifice that would match the conquest of the West. Inevitably, the newspapers tagged his program the New Frontier. But the phrase soon had little meaning.

DIFFICULTIES WITH CONGRESS. Prospects for the New Frontier seemed bright. Democrats controlled the House of Representatives and the Senate. But their majorities were deceptive. In the House, 101 Democrats were conservative southerners who frequently voted with Republicans. As a result, on social welfare issues the House was almost evenly divided. To compound Kennedy's troubles, conservative southerners controlled many key congressional committees.

During the spring of 1961, Kennedy's program for national health insurance for the aged (a revival of Truman's proposal) was pigeonholed by the House Ways and Means Committee. A bill for federal aid to education went down to defeat on the issue of aid to *parochial schools.* The administration's one achievement that spring was a modest increase in the federal minimum wage.

Parochial schools are affiliated with churches and synagogues. Most in this country are Roman Catholic. Financial aid to such schools, some assert, would violate the 1st Amendment which guarantees the separation of church and state.

THE MOON PROGRAM. On April 12, 1961, Soviet cosmonaut Yuri Gagarin (gah-GAH-rin) became the first human to orbit the earth. The Soviets had achieved another space spectacular. Five days later, April 17, came the Bay of Pigs fiasco.

With his legislative program buried in Congress, President Kennedy looked for some means of keeping his promise to get the country moving again. He asked Vice-President Johnson, a long-time space enthusiast, what could be done in the space program to achieve a dramatic result. Johnson recommended placing a person on the moon ahead of the Soviet Union.

Scientists indicated that it could be done within the decade. But some wondered if it was worth the money. Space probes or space laboratories, without human pilots or passengers, would, they argued, bring in more scientific data for less money. Kennedy overruled them.

On May 25, 1961, he went on nationwide television to announce the moon program. He declared that it was time the nation took the lead in space achievements. Most Americans, delighted with the President's ambition, applauded the announcement. President Eisenhower, in retirement on his Pennsylvania farm, spoke for the dissenters: "Anybody who would spend 40 billion dollars in a race to the moon for national prestige is nuts."

ESTABLISHING THE PEACE CORPS. Congress not only agreed to fund the moon program, it also appropriated money for the Peace Corps. *This was one of the most imaginative and one of the most popular of the New Frontier programs.* The idea originated with Hubert Humphrey during the election campaign.

John Glenn, the first American to orbit the Earth, is shown in the capsule of the Friendship 7, a liquid-fueled, Mercury Atlas-D rocket. His five-hour journey on February 20, 1962, took him around the Earth three times. This photograph was taken with a fish-eye lens.

The plan was to send men and women overseas to do volunteer work in developing countries that requested American aid. Using skills they had learned in high school, college, and on the job, members of the Peace Corps would serve as teachers, agricultural advisers, technicians, mechanics, and in many other roles. Through thousands of these goodwill ambassadors, the nation hoped to repair its image abroad. And the world would benefit from American know-how. Within a few years, 10,000 volunteers were serving overseas.

LATIN AMERICA: ALLIANCE FOR PROGRESS. The Peace Corps showed that President Kennedy was interested in new approaches to diplomacy and not simply in shipping arms to any country that asked for them. ***The Alliance for Progress, also launched in 1961, marked a major shift in the attitude of the United States toward Latin America.***

The United States had worried about Communist influence in Latin America from the outset of the Cold War. In 1947 delegates from the Western Hemisphere met in

The Peace Corps, created by President Kennedy's executive order in 1961, sent thousands of young volunteers—teachers, doctors, farming experts—into underdeveloped nations. Such volunteers taught people to read and write and helped people to improve their living standards. In this photograph a teacher from Pennsylvania is teaching arithmetic to a small Bolivian boy.

Rio de Janeiro to form an alliance against aggression. The Rio Pact, as it was called, was the beginning of the United States' global alliance system.

Aggression from abroad was never a serious threat. More dangerous were the poverty and discontent of the Latin American people. Few nations in Latin America were democracies. Most were under the control of military or business interests often in league with American corporations. Because of its history of intervention, the United States was a traditional target of resentment in Latin America. And because United States investors were often linked to the ruling classes of Latin American countries, demands for social and political reform often turned into anti-Americanism. Communists tried to exploit unrest by promising equita-

ble distribution of wealth. ***Thus, it was not easy to distinguish between a Latin American reformer who was against the United States, and one who was pro-Communist.***

Kennedy's Alliance for Progress was intended to reverse priorities. Instead of sending arms and money to Latin America to bolster existing regimes, the United States and Latin American nations would provide funds to promote social progress and democratic institutions. It was a grand idea.

That the program was not fully realized was not entirely Kennedy's fault. Some improvements were made in education and health care. But such things as housing construction lagged behind the explosive birthrate. Ruling classes in Latin America resisted any substantial change in landholding or tax systems. Much of the money ended up in the hands of big businesses. Many times American arms aided in military takeovers. In what Kennedy had hoped would be a "historic decade of democratic progress," 16 military coups took place in Latin America.

BAN ON NUCLEAR TESTING. *It is very likely that John F. Kennedy's most enduring achievement was the Nuclear Test Ban Treaty he signed with the Soviet Union in 1963.* Both nations suspended atmospheric testing in 1958, amid a worldwide outcry over nuclear fallout. But underground testing continued. In August 1961, at the height of the Berlin crisis, the Soviets resumed testing, and the United States followed suit.

By then both countries were using the tests to gain diplomatic leverage. All scientific requirements could be met by underground tests that did not poison the air. As radiation levels built up, world protest resumed. The two superpowers began to realize that they had a mutual interest in limiting the spread of nuclear weapons. Britain had already entered the "nuclear club." France and China were knocking on the door. A world treaty limiting tests might discourage others.

For years the question of inspection had prevented agreement. In the summer of 1963, Kennedy proposed that they ban atmospheric testing. Through fallout-detection devices, such tests could be monitored without onsite inspection. That would also remove the radiation hazards. The more complicated problem of underground tests could be resolved later.

Khrushchev agreed, and a "hot line," consisting of direct teletype communication, was installed between Moscow and Washington to guard against the accidental outbreak of nuclear war. Representatives of the United States, Britain, and the Soviet Union signed the treaty in July 1963. Over the next few years, many countries signed the treaty.

THE NEW FRONTIER: AN APPRAISAL. President Kennedy's program was only a partial success. At the time of his death in November 1963, his most important proposals—Medicare, aid to education, a new civil rights act—lay buried in Congress. Billions of dollars had been spent building up the nation's nuclear might and its conventional military forces. The main effect of the buildup was to make it possible—and thus more tempting—for Presidents to intervene in distant conflicts.

On the other hand, the space program was in full gear. The first American in space, Commander Alan B. Shepard, made a *suborbital* flight in May 1961. In February 1962 Colonel John Glenn circled the earth three times. Before the year was over, two more flights were made. And an unpiloted mission was on its way toward Venus.

Suborbital means not being in orbit.

By the time of Kennedy's death, the nation had taken the lead in space technology, and the moon program kept it there. Prosperity had returned, and the public mood was considerably brighter than in 1960. Americans looked to the future with self-assurance.

There were some clouds on the horizon—a nagging war in Vietnam and a civil rights revolution at home. Kennedy had not been able to deal with either effectively. They would have continued to cause difficulties had he lived. And they ultimately spelled doom for his successor, Lyndon Johnson.

Section Review

1. Identify or explain: Yuri Gagarin, Peace Corps, John Glenn, Alliance for Progress.
2. List some of the programs of the New Frontier. Why was it difficult to get these programs through Congress?

3. What was the goal of the Alliance for Progress? How well did it succeed in achieving this goal? Why?
4. List the terms of the Nuclear Test Ban Treaty.

3. Lengthening Shadows: Vietnam and Civil Rights

SOVIET AND AMERICAN FOREIGN POLICY. At the close of the 1950's, the Cold War had spread to the Third World. The United States and the Soviet Union both sought support among the peoples of Asia and Africa. The desire for self-government had spread rapidly among these peoples after World War II. And the European powers were forced to dismantle their empires. Some did so gracefully. Others yielded only after long and bloody guerrilla wars.

In the mid-1950's Premier Khrushchev injected the Cold War into these troubled areas. He announced Soviet support for all antiimperial movements, or what he termed wars of national liberation. Some guerrillas welcomed Soviet support. Others tolerated Communists in their ranks. Either way, Soviet intervention posed a cruel dilemma for the United States.

To attempt to control or counteract this influence placed the United States in a position of opposing freedom and self-government. A Communist victory anywhere might trigger what President Eisenhower had described as the domino effect.

AFTER THE FIRST VIETNAMESE WAR. *Vietnam provided the critical test for both Soviet and American policies.* The first Vietnamese War, which ended in 1954, left the country divided between Communist North Vietnam, under Ho Chi Minh, and a weak neutral government in South Vietnam. (See map, page 718.) The collapse of French authority in the area left a vacuum that the United States tried to fill. In 1955 Secretary of State Dulles persuaded President Eisenhower to send financial aid and military advisers to South Vietnam to help build a defense force similar to South Korea's. With American backing, Ngo Dinh Diem (noe din ZEE-em), who was living in the United States, returned to South Vietnam to become prime minister.

The Geneva agreement that ended the first Vietnamese War called for free elections to unify the country. Anticipating that the Communists would win the elections, Diem chose to cancel them and Eisenhower approved.

THE SECOND VIETNAMESE WAR. The second Vietnamese War began early in 1956. The rebels, or Vietcong, were a mixture of Communists and anti-Diem nationalists. At first they apparently got little aid from North Vietnam. But the situation in South Vietnam deteriorated steadily. *The Communist National Liberation Front (NLF) was organized in 1960. It vowed to unseat the South Vietnamese government.* By then the Vietcong controlled most of the countryside. The Diem government was confined to the cities. When it sent patrols into the countryside, they were ambushed.

WAR SPREADS TO LAOS. By 1960 the conflict had spread into neighboring Laos. (See map, page 718.) Rival factions, one backed by the United States and the other by North Vietnam, struggled for control. The Communists seemed to be getting the upper hand.

In early 1961 Kennedy took a close look at the situation in Laos. When the Joint Chiefs of Staff informed him that intervention in Laos would require 250,000 soldiers, Kennedy rejected that course of action. Instead, he sent veteran diplomat Averell Harriman to arrange a settlement. After more than a year of negotiations, Harriman signed an agreement creating a coalition government in Laos pledged to neutrality.

INCREASING INVOLVEMENT IN VIETNAM.
President Kennedy took a firmer line on South Vietnam. He did not subscribe to Eisenhower's domino theory. But he did consider South Vietnam a test of Communist intentions. If South Vietnam fell, the Soviets and Communist Chinese could sponsor other liberation wars in Southeast Asia.

Kennedy sent Green Berets to train the South Vietnamese in guerrilla warfare. He also sent helicopter teams to give them greater mobility.

American aid enabled the South Vietnamese to hold their own through 1962. But by early 1963 things began to go badly again. The Vietcong emerged from the jungles and engaged in open battle. They chewed up the inept South Vietnamese Army. It became clear that American training had failed to help. *Without massive American intervention the war would be lost.*

DETERIORATION IN SOUTH VIETNAM.
President Diem became increasingly unpopular. He not only failed to carry out promised political reforms, he jailed all political critics. Buddhists, whose religion forbade fighting, tried to stay neutral in the conflict. But Diem, a Roman Catholic, treated them as enemies and arrested their leaders. In June 1963 a Buddhist monk shocked the world by dousing himself with gasoline and setting himself on fire in protest against Diem's policies. Other burnings followed. It became clear that Diem could not govern. *With American approval, South Vietnamese military leaders took over the government on November 1.* The United States tried to ensure Diem's personal safety. But he was caught trying to escape and was executed.

Thus, when President Kennedy was assassinated a few weeks later, President Johnson was faced with a dangerous and deteriorating situation in Vietnam. It was beginning to look as if General de Gaulle had been right. "I predict to you," he had said to Kennedy in 1961, "that you will, step by step, be sucked into a bottomless military and political quagmire."

THE CIVIL RIGHTS REVOLUTION.
Civil rights proved equally troublesome to the President. Kennedy entered office with no commitment to and little interest in the question. His early battles with Congress, moreover, showed that his legislative program depended on southern support. To win that, he steered clear of the Black civil rights revolution as long as he could.

While the President occupied himself with foreign policy and national defense, his brother, Attorney General Robert Kennedy, developed a civil rights policy. He drafted no legislation. Instead, he sought to enforce acts already on the books. The Civil Rights Acts of 1957 and 1960 gave the federal government authority to supervise the registration of Black voters. The Eisenhower administration filed six lawsuits on behalf of Blacks who were denied the right to register. Under Robert Kennedy, the Justice Department eventually filed 37 suits.

Unwilling to wait for the slow wheels of federal justice, Blacks stepped up efforts on their own behalf. In the spring of 1961, the Congress of Racial Equality (CORE), under the vigorous leadership of James Farmer, sent "freedom riders" into the South to test segregated facilities. The resulting publicity forced the government to act. In September 1961 the Interstate Commerce Commission prohibited segregation on interstate rail and bus facilities.

JAMES MEREDITH'S CRUSADE.
Although school desegregation continued at a slow pace, most southern colleges had opened their doors to Blacks by 1962. One exception was the University of Mississippi. When James Meredith, a Black air force veteran, was denied admission, he secured a court order in his favor.

When the university opened for the fall term in September 1962, Governor Ross

Sidenote to History

"I Have a Dream"

As head of the Southern Christian Leadership Conference, the Reverend Dr. Martin Luther King, Jr., became the outstanding civil rights leader of the 1960's. In August 1963 he was the main speaker at the march on Washington. The 250,000 people who gathered at the Lincoln Memorial in support of civil rights heard King deliver the most famous speech of his career. Parts of it are included here. In eloquent terms, he expressed his vision of America. In 1964 Dr. King was awarded the Nobel Peace Prize, the youngest person ever to receive the honor.

". . . I say to you today, my friends, so even though we face the difficulties of today and tomorrow, I still have a dream.

"It is a dream deeply rooted in the American dream. I have a dream that one day this nation will rise up and live out the true meaning of its creed: 'We hold these truths to be self-evident, that all men are created equal.'

"I have a dream that one day on the red hills of Georgia the sons of former slaves and the sons of former slave owners will be able to sit down together at the table of brotherhood. . . . I have a dream that one day even the state of Mississippi, a state sweltering with the heat of injustice, sweltering with the heat of oppression, will be transformed into an oasis of freedom and justice.

"I have a dream that my four little children will one day live in a nation where they will not be judged by the color of their skin but by the content of their character. . . .

"I have a dream that one day every valley shall be exalted, every hill and mountain shall be made low, the rough places will be made plain and the crooked places will be made straight and the glory of the Lord shall be revealed and all shall see it together. This is our hope. This is our faith that I go back to the South with. With this faith, we will be able to hew out of the mountain of despair a stone of hope. With this faith we will be able to transform the jangling discords of our nation into a beautiful symphony of brotherhood. With this faith we will be able to work together, to pray together, to struggle together, to go to jail together, to stand up for freedom together, knowing that we will be free one day. . . .

"And if America is to be a great nation, this must become true. So let freedom ring. From the prodigious hilltops of New Hampshire, let freedom ring. From the mighty mountains of New York, let freedom ring.

"From the heightening Alleghenies of Pennsylvania, let freedom ring. From the snow-capped Rockies of Colorado, let freedom ring. From the curvaceous slopes of California.

"But not only that; let freedom ring from Stone Mountain of Georgia. Let freedom ring from Lookout Mountain of Tennessee. Let freedom ring from every hill and molehill of Mississippi. From every mountainside, let freedom ring.

"And when this happens, and when we allow freedom to ring, when we let it ring from every village and every hamlet, from every state and every city, we will be able to speed up that day when all of God's children, Black men and White men, Jews and Gentiles, Protestants and Catholics, will be able to join hands and sing, in the words of the old Negro spiritual:

Free at last, free at last,
Thank God Almighty, we're free at last."

Barnett vowed to keep Meredith out of the university. To avoid a showdown, the Kennedys extracted a promise from the governor that he would not interfere with the court order. However, a mob formed to protest Meredith's admission. When rioting broke out on the university campus, the governor's state police did nothing to stop it. Furious, the President ordered in federal troops, who quickly restored peace. With a bodyguard of federal marshals and the protection of 23,000 soldiers, Meredith registered and began attending classes.

CONFRONTATION IN BIRMINGHAM. In April 1963 Martin Luther King, Jr., helped organize the Black community in Birmingham, Alabama, to protest the city's segregated hotels and restaurants. Arrested for trespassing, the protesters went peacefully to jail. Before long, city police were arresting 500 Blacks a day.

Blacks returned in larger and larger groups. Finally the Birmingham police commissioner, Eugene "Bull" Connor, overreacted. He ordered the protesters sprayed with fire hoses and set trained police dogs to chase them. *President Kennedy, who had previously urged King to tone down the demonstrations, felt obliged to intervene.* With federal mediation, Birmingham business leaders agreed to desegregate their facilities and hire a number of Black employees.

A FEDERAL CIVIL RIGHTS LAW. Birmingham demonstrated the need for federal legislation. On June 11, 1963, Kennedy made an eloquent appeal to the nation's conscience. "The time has come," he said, "for this nation to fulfill its promise of full equality. Those who do nothing are inviting shame as well as violence." A few hours later Medgar Evers, head of the Mississippi branch of the NAACP, was assassinated. It was time for the government to act.

A week later Kennedy sent to Congress a comprehensive civil rights bill, requiring the desegregation of all facilities—hotels, restaurants, theaters—that did interstate business of any kind. Constitutionally, the measure would rest on the power of Congress to regulate interstate commerce.

To support the measure, Black leaders arranged a huge march in Washington on August 28, 1963. It was an enormous success. About 250,000 Americans assembled peacefully in front of the Lincoln Memorial for a day-long celebration of song and prayer, climaxing in a moving address by Martin Luther King, Jr.

Like Vietnam, civil rights was unfinished business when Kennedy died in November 1963. The bill, a belated recognition of the civil rights movement, was mired in congressional committees with little chance for passage. Even if it passed, it was uncertain whether it would satisfy Black leaders. "For years now I have heard the word 'Wait,'" complained Martin Luther King. "It rings in the ear of every Negro with piercing familiarity. This 'Wait' has always meant 'Never.'" Even King's doctrine of nonviolent resistance was coming under attack as Black patience grew thinner and thinner.

Section Review

1. Mapping: Using the map on page 718, describe the relative location of South Vietnam and Laos in terms of the boundaries and latitude of each country.
2. Identify or explain: Vietcong, Averell Harriman, Robert Kennedy, James Meredith, Martin Luther King, Jr., Medgar Evers, freedom riders, CORE.
3. How much and what kind of aid did the United States send to South Vietnam in the early 1960's? Why did President Diem turn out to be an unpopular leader?
4. How did President Kennedy hope to end segregation?

On November 25, 1963, a stunned and bereaved nation mourned the death of a dynamic young President who had been shot by an assassin. Why should a Presidential candidate consider such an event before selecting a running mate?

4. Lyndon Johnson and the Great Society

KENNEDY IS ASSASSINATED. In November 1963 President Kennedy journeyed to Texas to help repair the Democratic party in the Lone Star State. On November 22, as his motor caravan wound slowly through downtown Dallas, shots rang out from a warehouse for school textbooks. The President was struck in the back of the head and died within an hour. Texas Gover-nor John B. Connally, riding in the car with President Kennedy, was wounded but later recovered.

Shortly afterward Lee Harvey Oswald was arrested for shooting a Dallas police officer, who had been chasing him. For two days Dallas police questioned Oswald, but he admitted nothing. Then, while Dallas police were transferring him to another prison, Oswald was killed—in front of television cameras—by Jack Ruby, a nightclub operator and police buff. *An investigation by a special commission, headed by Chief Justice Earl Warren, concluded that Oswald was the person who assassinated Kennedy and that he had acted alone, and from his own motives.*

Few events in history have so deeply shocked a society—a youthful leader, full of zest and humor, suddenly struck down for no apparent reason. Television coverage involved every household in the land with the deed and its incredible aftermath—the shooting of Oswald in front of the TV cameras. Not since 1901 had an American President been assassinated. Nor for many years had a public official been seriously threatened. Grief was not enough. It was time for people to examine their consciences, to search for lost ideals, a lost identity. The search went on for the rest of the decade.

LYNDON JOHNSON TAKES COMMAND.
Vice-President Johnson, who accompanied Kennedy to Texas, had ridden in a separate car. The new President took the oath of office aboard the Presidential plane. Appearing on television on November 27, Johnson pledged to continue Kennedy's programs and asked Congress for support. The public rallied to his side, feeling fortunate to have a man of such experience and ability to take charge.

Congress, too, was prepared to cooperate. In the spring of 1964, the Senate unlocked a tax cut bill that Kennedy had asked for a year before. Kennedy had reasoned that permitting consumers to keep a larger share of their incomes would stimulate the economy. Senate conservatives, fearing a budget deficit, held it in committee. Johnson appeased them by cutting several billions from the budget. And the tax cut slipped through Congress.

The new President showed similar skill in securing passage of Kennedy's civil rights bill. Two days before Kennedy's death, the House approved the bill barring segregation in public accommodations. But a filibuster loomed in the Senate. Liberals feared that Johnson might agree to compromises, as he had in 1957 and 1960, in order

to avoid a filibuster. Instead, he held firm even when some of his other measures were stalled because of the debate. The expected filibuster came in the spring of 1964 and lasted for two months. But in the end, the Senate voted to cut off debate and passed the bill.

THE OTHER AMERICA.
The tax cut and the civil rights act were Kennedy's measures. With a Presidential election approaching, Johnson was eager to put his stamp on the administration. One way to do so was to respond to the mounting public concern over poverty in America. In 1962, a book titled *The Other America* by Michael Harrington called attention to persistent poverty in the midst of the country's great wealth. About 35 million Americans, he estimated, lived under wretched conditions. They were poorly housed, ill-clothed, and often hungry.

MIGRANT WORKERS.
The poorest of the poor were migrant workers, who tended the citrus groves and truck gardens of the South and Southwest. Most of these workers were of Hispanic origin—Mexican Americans and Spanish Americans in Texas and California and Cubans in Florida.

Two million migrant workers lived under conditions that can only be described as brutal. Their work was seasonal, varying with the planting and harvest seasons. During long periods of unemployment, they retreated to shanty communities built of stray lumber, sheets of tin, and cardboard. When work was available, the hours were long and the labor backbreaking. Federal laws regulating wages and hours did not apply to them. A few growers paid their workers as little as 16 cents an hour for a 60-hour week. President Johnson understood their plight. He had taught their children as a young Texas schoolteacher. And he remembered their rags and hunger.

THE "WAR ON POVERTY."
In his State of the Union message on January 8, 1964,

The working conditions faced by these Mexican-Americans in 1968 had not changed much from those of the 1930's. What programs did President Johnson propose to help migrant workers?

President Johnson declared an "unconditional war on poverty in America." ***During the spring, with a combination of charm and arm-twisting that was soon to become famous, he pushed through Congress a 10-point program.***

Special funds were voted to retrain workers displaced by machines. Job Corps camps, modeled on the CCC camps of the 1930's, offered city youth training in mechanical skills. VISTA was a kind of domestic Peace Corps, sending young men and women into urban ghettos and rural shantytowns to work as teachers, medical aides, and service workers. The community action program offered grants to local organizations aiming at self-improvement in the

hope of involving the poor in the war on poverty. Johnson appointed Sargent Shriver, Kennedy's brother-in-law and director of the Peace Corps, to organize this diverse effort. He became head of the Office of Economic Opportunity.

THE ELECTION OF 1964. Johnson's broad social concern, together with his ability to get Congress to act, made him the natural choice for the Democratic nomination that summer. ***So broad was his support that he probably would have defeated any candidate the Republicans offered.*** (Even conservatives were impressed with his money-saving efforts, which included turning off the White House lights at night.)

The Republicans turned to one of their most conservative members, Senator Barry Goldwater of Arizona. Goldwater's candidacy reflected the growing fear among Republicans that their party had become nothing but an echo of the Democrats. Goldwater spoke out against big government, civil rights legislation, and arms control negotiations. At times he seemed too extreme, as when he advocated selling the TVA, dismantling the social security system, and providing nuclear weapons to local commanders in Vietnam. Goldwater's stands enabled Johnson to occupy the political center. There he appeared the man of reason, the healer who had brought the country together.

INCIDENT IN THE TONKIN GULF. As the Presidential campaign was getting under way in August 1964, the Far East flared up once again. On August 2 the American destroyer *Maddox*, which was loaded with electronic eavesdropping equipment, was attacked by Communist patrol boats in the Tonkin Gulf, off the coast of North Vietnam. Two nights later, the commanders of the *Maddox* and another ship, the *C. Turner Joy,* claimed to have been attacked. However, neither ship saw an enemy vessel on that occasion. Although neither ship was damaged, President Johnson ordered reprisal air raids against torpedo boat bases and oil storage tanks in North Vietnam.

Johnson asked Congress for authority to "take all necessary measures to repel any armed attack against forces of the United States and to prevent further aggression." In effect, the President asked for authority to do anything he wanted in Southeast Asia. *Amid the general excitement of the raids and reprisals, Congress passed the Tonkin Gulf Resolution—unanimously in the House of Representatives and with only two dissenting votes in the Senate.*

JOHNSON'S ELECTORAL LANDSLIDE. Johnson's swift and forceful action in Vietnam deprived Goldwater of the one election issue he had. The Republicans had criticized the way the Vietnamese War was being conducted. They demanded a greater use of American air power. Having displayed his muscle, the President talked of peace and limited involvement. He won an overwhelming 61 percent of the votes, a bigger margin than Roosevelt achieved in 1936. Goldwater carried only five Deep South states and Arizona.

LAUNCHING THE GREAT SOCIETY. Johnson spoke of his dream for a Great Society as early as May 1964. It meant, he explained, an end to poverty and an end to racial injustice. The election gave him a huge Democratic majority in Congress—the largest since New Deal days—and the way seemed clear for his ambitious program.

Medicare, federal aid to education, and civil rights legislation quickly passed Congress. The President predicted an end to want and misery. Then everything came apart. The cities erupted in violence as Black patience wore out. And the war on poverty surrendered to rising defense costs. Vietnam became a frustrating succession of defeats and official untruths. The Great Society became the shattered society.

Section Review

1. Identify or explain: John B. Connally, Lee Harvey Oswald, Barry Goldwater, the Great Society, *The Other America.*
2. List the names and the goals of the Kennedy bills that Johnson was able to get through Congress.
3. List and briefly explain the provisions of the "war on poverty."
4. Describe the events leading to the Tonkin Gulf Resolution. Explain the major points of the resolution.

Chapter 32 Review

Bird's-Eye View

During the early 1960's the problems of American society seemed to rise to the surface more rapidly than they had before. Thus, it was not surprising that the election of 1960 was won by John F. Kennedy, a candidate who promised not only change but a New Frontier.

One of the first challenges Kennedy faced as President involved United States relations with Cuba. Fidel Castro's revolutionary regime had declared itself Communist and had formed an alliance with the Soviet Union. As a result, two crises developed. First, an American-backed counterrevolutionary force invaded Cuba at the Bay of Pigs. Next, a confrontation occurred over the installation of Soviet missile sites on the island. Kennedy's administration had a showdown with the Soviet Union in another area—the city of Berlin.

On the domestic front Kennedy developed proposals for sweeping changes in the areas of unemployment, taxation, education, and health care. However, his proposals bogged down in the committees of a conservative Congress. Facing frustration in these areas, Kennedy established a space program, the Peace Corps, and the Alliance for Progress.

One of the most significant failures of Kennedy's administration was its inability to solve the problems of Vietnam. Another problem was the growing Black movement for civil rights, a problem on which Kennedy's administration was slow to move. When it did, civil rights legislation was blocked in Congress.

The Kennedy era ended abruptly with the President's assassination in Dallas, Texas, in November 1963. Vice-President Lyndon Johnson became President. An experienced legislator, Johnson was more effective than Kennedy in getting bills through Congress, including a wide-ranging civil rights bill. He declared a "war on poverty" in the nation and aggressively pursued the conflict in Vietnam, receiving broad powers with the passage of the Gulf of Tonkin Resolution. However, it soon became apparent that American society was being torn apart by the problems and conflicts of the past.

Vocabulary

Define or identify each of the following:

Bay of Pigs	Nuclear Test Ban	VISTA
Berlin Wall	Treaty	Tonkin Gulf
Alliance for Progress	Yuri Gagarin	Resolution
	James Meredith	Great Society

Review Questions

1. Why did Kennedy send troops to the Bay of Pigs, Cuba? What happened to the troops?
2. How did the Soviet Union respond to the American quarantine of Cuba during the Cuban missile crisis?
3. Why did the Soviets build the Berlin Wall?

4. What programs were established under the New Frontier?
5. Why did Kennedy have trouble getting his programs through Congress?
6. How did the United States become involved in the Vietnam War?
7. How did the Civil Rights movement gain momentum in the early 1960's?
8. What factors allowed President Johnson to succeed in convincing Congress to pass legislation that had been stalled in committees?

Reviewing Social Studies Skills

1. Describe the geographic position of Cuba in terms of its relationship to the United States and the rest of the hemisphere. What is its strategic importance in modern warfare?
2. Using the map on page 735, complete the following:
   a. In what areas of the nation did Kennedy receive his greatest support?
   b. In what areas of the nation did Nixon receive his greatest support?
   c. Where did Byrd receive support?
   d. If Nixon had won Byrd's electoral votes, would he have been elected President?
   e. How did your state vote in the 1960 election?
3. Draw up a list of New Frontier and Great Society programs. Compare their goals.

Reading for Meaning

1. Reread in the Sidenote to History on page 746 the excerpt from Dr. Martin Luther King's Lincoln Memorial speech. What was his vision of America? Compare it to the ideas expressed in the Declaration of Independence.
2. What was meant by nonviolence in the civil rights movement? Under what conditions did violence occur?
3. Kennedy visited Berlin to declare to its residents that the United States supported their rights. He said, "Ich bin ein Berliner" (I am a Berliner). What do you think he meant?
4. The conclusion of the Warren Commission, which investigated the Kennedy assassination, is that Oswald acted alone. What do you think? Cite evidence from the chapter to support your opinion.

Bibliography

William L. O'Neill's *Coming Apart: An Informal History of the 1960's* (Quadrangle) is a judicious and entertaining account of a wild decade.

Philip Caputo's *A Rumor of War* (Holt, Rinehart and Winston) is a fascinating account of one marine's experiences in Vietnam.

James T. Dekay's *Meet Martin Luther King, Jr.* (Random House) is a good biography.

Black Women in White America (Knopf), edited by Gerda Lerner, is a documentary history of Black women in American society from the early 19th century to the present.

In this picture President Lyndon B. Johnson is shown signing a piece of his Great Society legislation. Johnson hoped the new legislation would improve the life of all Americans, especially that of the poor. The war in Vietnam soon took precedence over domestic needs.

the summer ended Congress eliminated the discriminatory features of the immigration laws, established a cabinet-level Department of Housing and Urban Development (HUD), voted 2.4 billion dollars for higher education, placed restrictions on billboard advertising on the interstate highway system, and enacted the first water and air pollution laws. It was the most productive congressional session since the early days of the New Deal.

For President Johnson the 1965 session of Congress was more than a personal triumph. *It was a victory for his politics of consensus, his strategy of enlisting broad public support for piecemeal reform.*

However, there were signs of trouble. Echoing the violence of Selma and Watts were military moves in the Caribbean and Vietnam. Johnson's foreign policy led to his downfall.

THE DOMINICAN INTERVENTION. Trouble appeared first in the Dominican Republic, a small Caribbean country long ruled by right-wing dictators. After the overthrow of Rafael Trujillo Molina (troo-HEE-yoe moe-LEE-nah) in 1961, the country experienced a succession of *coups d'état*. It ended up under the control of a committee of generals. In April 1965 a reform party, in league with junior military officers, seized power.

A *coup d'état* is a sudden overthrow of a government.

President Johnson worried that the reformers might include Communists, and that the country might become "another Cuba." The American ambassador in Santo Domingo, the capital, reported disorder and expressed fears for the safety of the thousand Americans who were in the city.

On April 28, 1965, President Johnson sent in the marines, who restored order. On television he informed the public that the action had been taken to protect American lives in Santo Domingo. The soldiers restored the military to power.

The President offered another explanation for the intervention. The rebel movement had been full of Communists, he said. The American ambassador provided the press with a list of 77. Most turned out to be anti-American nationalists with no known Communist connections. *The President was guilty of the kind of reasoning that plagued Latin American relations throughout the Cold War—the tendency to assume that anyone who is anti-American must be a Communist.* The intervention increased anti-Americanism.

THE SITUATION IN VIETNAM WORSENS. President Johnson shared the Cold War assumption that Communist uprisings ultimately threaten American security. The threat drew his attention to Vietnam, where the situation reached crisis proportions by the spring of 1965. The South Vietnamese regime had lost control of the countryside. Its army remained in the cities, afraid to venture out. After a visit to Saigon, South Vietnam's capital, McGeorge Bundy, a Presidential adviser on national security, and Defense Secretary Robert McNamara reported to the President that without American intervention the South Vietnamese government would collapse. Abandoning the country as a lost cause was one possibility. But Johnson rejected it. The surrender of South Vietnam would not bring peace, Johnson informed the public by television, "because we learned from Hitler at Munich that success only feeds the appetite of aggression."

ESCALATING THE WAR. On February 7, 1965, the Vietcong raided a camp of American military advisers, killing eight and wounding 100. Johnson immediately ordered air strikes against North Vietnam in retaliation. The bombing continued for the rest of the year. When the air bases in South Vietnam came under Vietcong mortar fire, Johnson sent in ground forces to protect them.

In April 1965 there were 33,500 American troops in Vietnam. By June the number doubled. Within two years the United States had 500,000 troops in Vietnam. American deaths had risen to 20,000. North Vietnam sent troops to aid the Vietcong.

It became a war of numbers against technology. American air cavalry units in helicopters crisscrossed the jungle, seeking the elusive guerrillas. Communist-held areas were declared "free fire zones," where every moving thing was a legitimate target. Rocket-carrying helicopters turned miles of jungle into cratered wasteland.

In this guerrilla war, where every village was a potential battleground, the devastation of civilian life was enormous. About 150,000 civilians died annually, and thousands were injured and maimed. More than five million people were forced to flee to refugee camps. Secretary of State Dean Rusk argued that the United States was obliged to enter the war because of its treaty with South Vietnam. Considering the devastation, some people began to wonder about the price of the commitment.

THE COST OF THE WAR MOUNTS. At first President Johnson tried to finance the war out of regular tax receipts. The nation could afford both guns and butter, he said. But the massive escalation of the war brought a rapid rise in costs. The war cost eight billion dollars in 1966, 27 billion dollars by 1968.

Faced with a monumental 28 billion dollar budget deficit in that year, Johnson finally asked Congress for additional taxes. To win approval he had to lop six billion dollars off domestic expenditures. It marked the end of the Great Society. The President chose guns over butter.

Section Review

1. Identify or explain: Medicare, the Department of Housing and Urban Development, Selma, Alabama, McGeorge Bundy.
2. Explain the Voting Rights Act of 1965.
3. How did President Johnson justify sending the marines into the Dominican Republic?
4. How did the increase in expenditures for the war in Vietnam affect the programs of the Great Society?

2. Voices of Protest

TEACH-INS AND MARCHES. Vocal opposition to the war began with the bombing of North Vietnam and escalated as the bombing increased. In March 1965 a group of University of Michigan faculty and students stopped classes for a day to hold a "teach-in." Its purpose was to stimulate discussion of the war. The idea spread to other college campuses.

The Dominican intervention a month later brought a wave of protest meetings. At the University of California at Berkeley, 12,000 students spent two days listening to a variety of people denounce the war. *The teach-ins represented the first widespread political dissent since the McCarthy era.* Critics claimed teach-ins were Communist inspired, but others said they were educated Americans expressing opposition to official policies.

By 1967 the antiwar demonstrators equaled a small army. In April an estimated 125,000 surged through the streets of New York City to the United Nations to ask for UN intervention to end the war. In October 75,000 descended on the Pentagon, the headquarters of the Department of Defense in Washington, D.C. The demonstrators

blocked the building in a massive act of civil disobedience. By the end of the year, opinion polls reported that only 29 percent of the people thought the President was doing a good job. It was the lowest popularity rating given to a President since the Korean War.

THE IMPACT OF TELEVISION. How had it happened? What had caused a limited military action in a far-off corner of the earth to become the most unpopular war in United States history? Television is one explanation. *This was the most widely photographed war in history.* The horror of war and its grisly weapons came into American homes.

The movies were the closest contact many Americans had had with earlier wars. The image of World War II in the movies was Errol Flynn making wisecracks over the intercom of his Flying Fortress. The image of the Vietnam War, on the other hand, was that of a child running down a street of thatch-covered houses, her clothes aflame.

THE CREDIBILITY GAP. *Government falsehoods—what the press called the credibility gap—added to the disillusionment.* The administration's statements frequently contradicted one another. This gave people the feeling that the country's leaders were fooling themselves as well as the people.

Statistics issued on enemy casualties provide one example of the credibility gap. The American effort rested on the assumption that the Communists did not represent a majority of the Vietnamese people. Therefore, Vietcong guerrillas were either recruiting members by fear or their ranks were being reinforced by substantial numbers of infiltrators from North Vietnam.

The Pentagon's figures belied these assumptions. On January 1, 1965, the army estimated that there were 103,000 Vietcong guerrillas in South Vietnam. In the course of the year, the army reported that the enemy had suffered 79,000 casualties and that an estimated 40,000 new guerrillas had infiltrated from the North. At year's end the total enemy force should have been 64,000. But on January 1, 1966, the army estimated the number of Vietcong at 237,000. Where did the recruits come from? If they were not volunteers, they must have been frightened into enlisting and then prevented from deserting. That meant each Vietcong guerrilla had to terrorize continuously 2½ recruits. The official statistics made no sense.

THE COST OF THE WAR. The cost of the war made no sense either. The ratio between the enemy casualty statistics released by the army and the cost of the war suggests that every dead Communist cost the United States dollars. Had the American and South Vietnamese forces been able to occupy and pacify visible amounts of territory, such costs might have been bearable. But they were not. In 1969, when the American withdrawal began, the Saigon government controlled no more territory or people than it had in 1965.

Most Americans did not blame President Johnson for entering the war. They faulted him for failing to win it. The President certainly tried. He supplied his generals in Vietnam with nearly everything they asked for, short of total war. He ordered more bombs dropped on Vietnam than the United States dropped on Germany in World War II. It did not seem to make much difference.

THE NEW LEFT. The antiwar movement had broad support, but extremists gave the movement a bad name. The phrase New

In this picture a helicopter has deposited troops and medical supplies on an airfield at Khe Sanh, an American stronghold in Vietnam. In what way does this picture reinforce the importance of Charles Drew's contribution to medical science (see page 640)?

Sidenote to History

César Chávez and La Causa

Many causes gained support during the 1960's. None was in more urgent need of attention than *La Causa* of the Mexican Americans in California. The grape pickers in California's vineyards were the poorest and the most exploited laborers in the nation. They worked at most six months a year, and pay was low. Their annual income was about 2,000 dollars, a third of what the government estimated was necessary for adequate living. In most industries labor costs amount from a third to a half the cost of finished products. In the California vineyards, wages accounted for only about five cents of every dollar spent by growers.

César Chávez was 41 when the strike *(La Huelga)* began. He spent his youth as a migratory farm worker. Determined to help his people, he went to work for a labor organization. Chávez spent 10 years learning the art of organizing. Then he moved to Delano, California. He went back to work in the vineyards, picking grapes and winning recruits. His Mexican-American National Farm Workers Association had about 300 members (out of 5,000 in the area) when the strike broke out. *La Huelga* started among Filipino workers organized by the AFL-CIO. They were no stronger than Chávez's group, but he joined them. In December 1965, the AFL-CIO merged the two groups into a single union.

Such movements had appeared before in the California vineyards. They had always been defeated by intimidation and dismissals. Grape growers had a nearly unlimited source of strikebreakers in Mexican nationals, who were given temporary permission to enter the United States at harvest time. Chávez's chief assistant complained, "The growers are using the poorest of the poor of another country to defeat the poorest of the poor in this country. That's about as low as you can get." But the strike was not crushed by strikebreakers. Students, aroused to social action by the civil rights and antiwar movements, came to the aid of Chávez. So did a number of churches. In addition, the AFL-CIO provided Chávez with funds.

As the struggle wore on, advocates of violence appeared, as they had with the civil rights and feminist movements. Firmly committed to nonviolence, Chávez protested their intervention by launching a 25-day hunger strike. The publicity enabled him to keep control of the movement. He organized a nationwide boycott of table grapes. Mayors of eastern cities, such as New York, helped by canceling government orders. As the growers began to weaken, President Nixon gave them support by eating grapes at a political rally and ordering the Pentagon to order grapes for the army. That kind of support enabled the growers to hold out another year. They began to buckle in 1969. By 1970 they gave in.

In a decade marked by raucous voices, César Chávez stands out as a calm and consistent leader. When the rest of the country seemed to have gone mad, he proved the power of nonviolence. Through him the AFL-CIO regained some of its interest in the poor. Most important, he inspired pride in his people. What began as a labor dispute ended as a broad-based movement to achieve equal rights for Mexican Americans: *La Causa.*

Left, which first appeared in a 1960 essay by Berkeley Professor C. Wright Mills, suggested a new type of American radicalism.

The "old left," whether Socialist or Communist, had failed to make much headway in America, largely because it looked to the Soviet Union for guidance. The Soviets' crude repression of revolts in East Germany (1953), Hungary (1956), and Czechoslovakia (1968) ended any pretense that communism was a liberal creed. Thus the New Left avoided the word Communist, preferring to style itself radical instead. And it aimed not at working people, as the old left had, but at college students and intellectuals.

Beginning with the free-speech movement at the University of California at Berkeley in 1964 and spreading with the antiwar teach-ins, many American universities experienced a chaotic period. Harried administrators were presented with nonnegotiable demands. Classes were disrupted with everything from screams to snowballs.

The radicals got support from draft-age students who objected to being forced to serve in the army to fight a war they opposed. Public burning of draft cards, which every man of draft age was required to carry, became one of the gestures of opposition.

In the end the New Left defeated itself. Their violent methods antagonized virtually everyone in the country. In the meantime, the violence made the 1960's a difficult decade.

Section Review

1. Identify or explain: C. Wright Mills, teach-ins, the credibility gap.
2. What significance did the teach-ins have?
3. List and explain three factors that caused the Vietnam War to become the most unpopular war in United States history.
4. What tactics did the New Left use to protest the Vietnam War?

3. New Rights for Blacks and Women

A DECADE OF CRITICISM. The 1960's were also a decade of social criticism and struggles for human welfare. Not since the depression had Americans examined themselves and their society so closely and so critically. Not all the criticism was a result of the war in Vietnam. The civil rights movement and the women's movement began before the President's Asian venture.

FROM CIVIL RIGHTS TO BLACK POWER. The civil rights movement turned a corner in the spring of 1966, when Stokely Carmichael took command of the Student Nonviolent Coordinating Committee. SNCC ("Snick") had been in the forefront of the voting rights drive in the South. It coordinated the work of thousands of vacationing college students who helped Blacks register. SNCC was led by Whites and followed Martin Luther King's doctrine of nonviolence.

Stokely Carmichael was Black, educated, articulate, and disillusioned with nonviolence. Like many other Blacks, he resented the way White liberals dominated the civil rights movement, using their money and education to occupy positions of leadership. Coining the slogan "Black Power," he told Blacks they would never be free until they cut themselves off from White leadership, formed their own organizations, banks, businesses, and political parties, and wrote their own history.

The idea was appealing. Pride and self-respect are essential to every people. But in the atmosphere of militancy of the late 1960's, Black Power led to some problems. In 1967 Carmichael was forced to yield leadership of SNCC to the more belligerent

H. Rapp Brown, who talked of war and revolution. Organizations such as the Black Panthers threatened war between the races.

GHETTO RIOTS. *Urban riots added to the growing feeling that the nation was under siege.* The uprisings in Watts (Los Angeles) and other areas in 1965 were only the start.

In 1966 disturbances broke out in Chicago, Cleveland, and San Francisco. In 1967 Newark, New Jersey, where 200,000 Blacks were jammed into an inner-city ghetto, erupted in flames. As Newark was dying down, the worst riot broke out in Detroit. About 14,000 paratroops, tanks, and machine guns were used to suppress the Detroit riot. Thirty-eight people died. Property damage was estimated at about 500 million dollars. In April 1968, when Martin Luther King, Jr., was assassinated, the violence reached a climax. Outraged Blacks rioted in more than 100 cities. Entire blocks of the nation's capital were flattened by fire and explosions.

CIVIL RIGHTS MOVES NORTH. *Urban violence signaled that the civil rights revolution was shifting from the South to the North.* The 1950's flight to the suburbs had left the central cities to the Blacks and other recent immigrants. People lived in old, run-down apartment houses, whose White owners collected rents but seldom made repairs. Most employed inner-city residents worked in menial positions at wages below national averages. Many residents could find no work at all. The national unemployment rate hovered around five percent. In the urban ghettoes, it was 30 percent or more.

Black outrage at White prejudice and indifference caused the riots. The riots were not a race war, nor were they caused by the speeches of Black extremists. Whites who happened to get caught up in the uprisings were jostled and cursed but seldom hurt. Nearly all the casualties were Blacks, injured or killed by police and soldiers. The buildings that went up in flames were the dwellings and stores of ghetto residents. Blacks struck out at their environment and the hopelessness of their situation.

THE CIVIL RIGHTS ACT OF 1968. The violence helped persuade Congress to make a further move in the field of civil rights. *The act of 1968 prohibited discrimination in the renting and selling of houses and apartments.* It did not, of course, end residential segregation. Only higher wages, better education, and time could accomplish that. The riots ceased almost as suddenly as they had begun. The election of Black mayors in Detroit and Cleveland helped, as did better police training and the hiring of Black police officers. Most important, Blacks realized that they were the chief victims of violence.

THE FEMININE MYSTIQUE. The 1960's produced many thought-provoking books. One of the most influential was Betty Friedan's *The Feminine Mystique* (1963). Friedan illustrated the difference between society's conception of women and their real status.

Although large numbers of women had entered the work force, especially since World War II, the view prevailed that woman's place was in the home. Employed women seldom attained positions of responsibility, and their pay—for equal work—was lower than what men received. White women earned less, on the average, than Black men, and Black women earned least of all.

Women accepted inferior status, said Friedan, because they were trained to accept it by parents, by educational authorities, by popular magazines, by every aspect of their culture. The virtues society demanded of women were domesticity, obedience, weakness, and dependence.

A NEW WOMEN'S MOVEMENT. Millions of people were influenced by *The Feminine Mystique*. It ushered in a new

Sidenote to History

Ralph Nader: Public Defender

One of the results of the 1960's student protest movement was a big jump in the number of applicants for law schools. Students realized that the police and the national guard were agents of the courts and the executive branch of government. Because the government stood for order and stability, political leaders used law to resist change. Some of those who wanted to change the system realized that they would have to become lawyers.

A lawyer whose career was defending the public interest was new. Fresh out of Harvard Law School and determined to make a career of defending the public interest, Ralph Nader began investigating a new car put out by General Motors. A compact, with its engine mounted in the rear (both new features for General Motors), the car had more than the usual share of new-car "bugs." Nader pub-

lished his findings in a muckraking exposé, *Unsafe at Any Speed* (1964).

The book probably would have been confined in libraries and soon forgotten had General Motors ignored its author. Learning of Nader's investigation, the president of General Motors hired private detectives to dig up something that the company could use against Nader. Nader found out and informed Congress. A Senate committee investigating the automobile industry summoned the president of General Motors and persuaded him to apologize. In 1966, Congress passed the Highway Safety Act, which set up the first safety standards for automobile manufacture.

Nader sued General Motors and collected 500,000 dollars in damages. He used this award and royalties from his book to establish a public-interest law firm. Student volunteers flocked to the firm, and soon "Nader's Raiders" were a familiar sight in factories and government offices. Nader lived simply and poured his resources into the firm. There were nine Nader's Raiders in 1968. A year later there were 100. By then thousands of idealistic students were applying to law school, planning to defend the public interest.

phase in the women's movement. To distinguish the struggle for equality from the suffrage movement of the early part of the century, feminists called the movement women's liberation.

In 1966 Friedan formed the National Organization of Women (NOW) to promote legislation that would guarantee equality to women. It became the largest of the women's organizations. However, the movement spawned dozens of other organizations. Like the civil rights movement, the women's movement contained extremists. They expressed the fury of their long suppression by using such tactics as disrupting Senate hearings on birth control pills and picketing Miss America contests.

Much of the feminist anger was due to frustration. Most reform movements in America have been taken seriously. But women's movements have always been greeted by laughter. The suffrage crusade of World War I, which eventually involved millions of women, battled ridicule until the 19th Amendment was ratified.

The liberation movement of the 1960's encountered scorn from the outset. Some liberals who openly sided with the Black protest scoffed at the demands of women. The 1964 Civil Rights Act prohibited discrimination in hiring. By the early 1970's, the courts had begun to uphold equal pay and retirement benefits for women. In 1972, a constitutional amendment guaranteeing

The pictures on this page show outstanding examples of art from the 1960's. Frank Stella used fluorescent acrylic paints for his "Darabjerd III," done in 1967. Andy Warhol's "Campbell's Soup Can, 1965" is the period's prime example of pop art. Alexander Calder's engineering background is reflected in his 1965 outdoor steel-plate sculpture "Two Discs."

equal rights for women passed both houses of Congress and was sent to the states. By the end of the decade the laughter, scorn, and ridicule had almost disappeared.

Ideologies came and went in the 1960's. So did celebrities. Radicals with a cause—fiery orators demanding equality—blazed into newspaper headlines and used television to win instant fame. Many were quickly forgotten. But the struggle for equality made a deep and lasting impression. It had come to stay.

Section Review

1. Identify or explain: the Student Nonviolent Coordinating Committee, Stokely Carmichael, the Civil Rights Act of 1968, Betty Friedan, the National Organization of Women.
2. Explain the concept of Black Power. What were its roots?
3. What was the significance of the urban riots of the 1960's for the civil rights movement?
4. Explain the argument put forth by Betty Friedan in *The Feminine Mystique*. How did this argument help change the direction of the women's movement?

4. 1968: An Ugly Year

AN ANTIWAR CANDIDATE EMERGES. Few Americans were acquainted with Minnesota's Senator Eugene McCarthy. Nor was he thought to be powerful in the Senate. Among Senate leaders he was considered too liberal by some, too much a maverick by others. Yet he declared himself a candidate for the Democratic presidential nomination. "There comes a time," he said, "when an honorable man simply has to raise the flag."

It was November 30, 1967, almost a year before the election. The antiwar movement had its first political candidate. The Minnesota senator was going to contest an incumbent President of his party for the sole purpose of bringing an end to the war.

JOHNSON STANDS FIRM. By the end of the year, President Johnson was almost a prisoner in the White House. The Secret Service would not let him travel around the country because they could not guarantee his safety. The President continued the bombing of North Vietnam. He blamed the antiwar activists for the Communists' failure to negotiate. Their demonstrations, he believed, encouraged the North Vietnamese to hold on, expecting an American pullout. If the nation showed unity and purpose, the President was certain, the Communists would yield under the fury of the American bombing. Many Americans agreed with him. Opinion polls at the end of 1967 indicated that a majority still supported the President's war effort.

THE TET OFFENSIVE. Then in January 1968, the Vietcong made a surprising move. Tet is the Vietnamese New Year, a time of celebration and relaxing. The Vietcong guerrillas took advantage of the national lull to swoop down on every city of substantial size in South Vietnam and dozens of American bases.

Several thousand guerrillas penetrated into the heart of Saigon. They laid siege to the American embassy for six hours. A section of the capital city was demolished before the attackers were beaten back. Ben Tre, a city of 35,000, was occupied by three battalions of Vietcong, who were driven out only after American bombers leveled the city. "It became necessary to destroy the town to save it," an American officer explained. Many began to wonder if the military was applying that rationale to the entire country.

The Tet offensive demonstrated that despite three years of war, the Vietcong was still a military power. It also demonstrated that the Vietnamese people had turned against their government. The Vietcong had managed to infiltrate combat units into the heart of Saigon. It had moved forces that thousands of peasants must have known about. Yet the government knew nothing until the assault began.

General William Westmoreland, commander of the American Army in South Vietnam, claimed a great victory in repelling the attacks. Then he asked the President for another 250,000 soldiers. Reporters on the scene saw Tet as the beginning of the end.

McCARTHY MAKES HEADWAY. The guns of Tet were still booming when the nation held its first Presidential primary in New Hampshire. President Johnson's advisers had scoffed at McCarthy's candidacy and predicted that the senator would get a measly five percent of the vote in New Hampshire.

McCarthy's candidacy offered an outlet for people who opposed the war and disliked violence and confrontation. From all over the nation, college students flocked to New Hampshire to help in the campaign. Reporters call it "McCarthy's children's crusade." Young campaign workers passed out literature and rang nearly every doorbell in the state.

On primary day, McCarthy polled a stunning 42 percent of the Democratic vote to the President's 49 percent. And New Hampshire was a solid, conservative state. What might happen in a state with a more liberal tradition was anybody's guess.

BOBBY KENNEDY ENTERS THE RACE. The Tet offensive and McCarthy's near victory in New Hampshire brought Robert Kennedy into the race. After his brother's assassination, Robert resigned as Attorney General and won election to the Senate from New York. By 1968 he was an outspoken critic of the war. He pointed repeatedly to the way it starved the President's

Robert F. Kennedy was assassinated during the 1968 Democratic Presidential primary campaign. He is shown in this picture with his wife Ethel and with aides just minutes before he was shot. What kinds of precautions should be taken to protect the lives of political leaders?

domestic programs. The Kennedy magic was still apparent. The young senator garnered the support of the discontented—Blacks, women, students. Suddenly the President's reelection seemed in doubt.

JOHNSON QUITS. The President probably could have been renominated anyway. He might even have been reelected. But to do so would have torn his party apart. *On March 31, 1968, Johnson went on television to announce that he was suspending the bombing of North Vietnam to open the way for negotiations. Then he stunned the country by declaring that he would neither seek nor accept nomination for President.* In order to devote all his efforts to peace, he was going to sacrifice his political life. It might well have been his noblest act.

ESCALATING VIOLENCE. It was almost the only noble act in that ugly year. *Five days after the President's announcement, April 5, 1968, Martin Luther King, Jr., was gunned down as he stood with friends on a motel balcony in Memphis, Tennessee.*

In every city in the country, Blacks took to the streets to vent their rage. The upheaval lasted a week and eventually took 55,000 troops to quell. It was the largest military operation in a civil emergency in the country's history. And that was only the beginning. A national student organization counted 221 major demonstrations at American colleges and universities that spring. The demonstrators were becoming increasingly destructive.

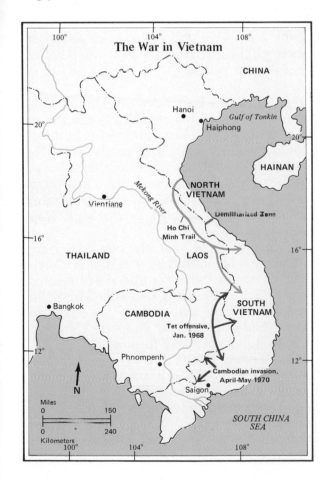

On June 5 Bobby Kennedy defeated Eugene McCarthy in the crucial California primary. That night, in his Los Angeles hotel headquarters, he was shot to death by an Arab fanatic.

Kennedy's death seemed to open the way for McCarthy. The senator won the New York primary. Then Vice-President Hubert Humphrey stepped into the fray. Although he had not entered a single primary, he had the President's support and much of the party organization.

CHAOS IN CHICAGO. *The Democratic convention, which met in Chicago in August 1968, was the wildest in history.* Antiwar protesters by the thousands descended on the city. Some hoped to get the Democratic party to pledge formal opposition to the war. Others were there, as one said, "to start a revolution for the heck of it."

When Mayor Richard Daley ordered the police to remove protestors camping in Lincoln Park, the police ran amuck, battering students, passers-by, and even people sitting peacefully in restaurants. An investigative commission later termed it flatly a police riot.

The convention hall was bedlam. McCarthy delegations from California and New York disrupted the proceedings by standing on their seats and singing "We Shall Overcome." On the night Humphrey was nominated there was a full-scale riot in the streets outside the hall.

Television cameras recorded it all. Millions of viewers watched aghast as the screen shifted back and forth from the riot in the streets to the bedlam in the hall.

NIXON'S COMEBACK. After the Democrats tore themselves to pieces in Chicago, the stage was set for one of the most astonishing political comebacks in memory. After he lost his bid for the Presidency in 1960, Richard Nixon spent his spare time on the campaign circuit, helping candidates for governor, Congress, and state offices.

By 1968 many party professionals were in Nixon's debt. And he was ready to cash the IOU's. His only important rival for the nomination was California Governor Ronald Reagan, a conservative with southern support. Nixon eliminated the Reagan threat by promising he would appoint conservatives to the Supreme Court. After winning nomination on the first ballot, he placed a southerner, Governor Spiro Agnew of Maryland, on the ticket as Vice-President.

REPUBLICAN VICTORY.

Curiously enough, the war was not an issue in the election campaign. Nixon announced that he had a plan to end the war but refused to disclose it. Humphrey, as Johnson's Vice-President, could hardly denounce the war. It helped him some when Johnson, on the eve of the election, ended all bombing in Vietnam. (The air force had been bombing the demilitarized zone between North and South Vietnam to cut down infiltration.)

Nixon made law and order the chief issue in the campaign. Law and order meant many things. To people who were alarmed by the Black riots and the student demonstrations, it meant restoring tranquillity to the streets. To people worried about the rising crime rate, it meant more police and stricter courts. To the racially biased, it meant keeping Blacks in their ghettoes.

Alabama Governor George Wallace, running as a third party candidate, won a lot of support when he promised to crush all demonstrations. To win, Nixon had to attract support from Wallace.

Win he did, but barely. Nixon won 43.7 percent of the vote to Humphrey's 42.7 percent and Wallace's 13.5 percent. (See map below.) Turnout was the lightest in years, suggesting that many voters had no liking for any of the candidates. Republicans gained a few seats in Congress but not enough to win control of either house. It was hardly a massive endorsement of Nixon or the Republicans. But it was a rejection of the Johnson policies.

THE ELUSIVE PEACE.

Despite his promise to spend his remaining months in office pursuing peace, President Johnson kept up a fairly hard line on the war. He even continued to bomb the southern part of North Vietnam for six months. *The North Vietnamese accepted his offer to negotiate, and peace talks opened in Paris in May 1968.*

At the end of the year, the two sides were stalemated. The difficulty was that the Vietcong guerrillas, who controlled substantial parts of South Vietnam, demanded a role in the government. The military governors in Saigon had little popular support. They had to keep fighting to stay in power.

The United States was in a similar dilemma. To win the war it would have to send a million troops into Southeast Asia and keep them there indefinitely. That was not politically possible. Withdrawing meant confessing that the tens of thousands of lives lost in Vietnam had been lost for noth-

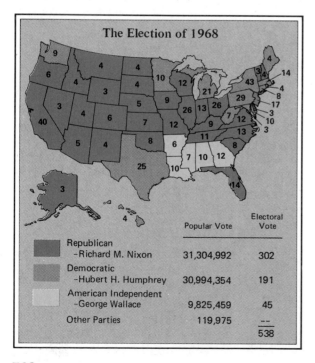

The Election of 1968

	Popular Vote	Electoral Vote
Republican —Richard M. Nixon	31,304,992	302
Democratic —Hubert H. Humphrey	30,994,354	191
American Independent —George Wallace	9,825,459	45
Other Parties	119,975	---
		538

ing. As the dreadful year drew to a close and Americans prepared for a change of Presidents, it seemed that there was no alternative but eternal war.

Section Review

1. Mapping: Using the map on page 768, locate the states won by George Wallace. Who do you think would have won those states if Wallace had not been a candidate?
2. Identify or explain: the Tet offensive, McCarthy's children's crusade, Robert Kennedy, Richard Daley, Spiro Agnew, George Wallace.
3. How did the war in Vietnam affect President Lyndon Johnson's political career?
4. On what issue did Richard Nixon focus his campaign for the Presidency in 1968? Why?

5. "Bring Us Together Again"

UNITY OR DIVISION? During the election campaign, Richard Nixon spotted a young girl carrying a placard saying "Bring us together again." It was a moving plea to end the division and disruption, the urban violence, and the hate-filled speeches. Nixon liked the slogan and adopted it. It was the theme of his victory speech the morning after the election.

At first it looked as if the new President intended just the opposite. He sent the Vice-President on a speaking tour to denounce student demonstrators. Agnew's acid statements added to the national din. The Justice Department cooperated with local police departments in a campaign to break up the Black Panthers, who talked of race war but did little. Shootouts in Panther headquarters in Chicago and other cities decimated Panther leadership.

DISMANTLING THE GREAT SOCIETY. Nixon wanted to dismantle the federal poverty programs, but agreed to a cautious approach when advisers told him the economy would be disrupted. Instead, he slashed 4 billion dollars from the budget, starving the poverty programs so much that several project heads resigned. Johnson's Office of Economic Opportunity was put out of business in 1972.

RESHAPING THE SUPREME COURT. When Chief Justice Earl Warren resigned in 1969, Nixon had the opportunity to redeem his promise to place a conservative on the Supreme Court. *His choice of Warren Burger, a highly respected judge from Minnesota, won approval.* When other vacancies occurred he named ultra-conservatives. The Senate rejected them. Nixon did not bring the nation together, but his administration won support from a wide range of people weary of violence and strife.

BEGINNING THE VIETNAM PULLOUT. It seemed that Nixon's Presidency, like Johnson's, would stand or fall on his handling of the Vietnam War. The secret plan for resolving the war, which Nixon announced during the election campaign, was probably never well developed. After taking office he realized he had only three choices: 1) continue the war at the present level (rejected because it led nowhere), 2) pull out quickly, and let the South Vietnamese take care of themselves (rejected because the sudden collapse of South Vietnam might trigger a political reaction at home), 3) begin a slow pullout, while trying to negotiate a settlement.

Nixon took the third course because the other alternatives were unacceptable. The heart of the policy was Vietnamization, or letting South Vietnam forces do most of the ground fighting while the United States supplied air cover. Vietnamization was the Kennedy-Johnson policy before the 1965

This antiwar moratorium in New York City in 1968 is one of many similar scenes during that turbulent year. Which groups seemed to be against the Vietnam War?

buildup. This time it would permit an American withdrawal.

In June 1969 Nixon flew to Midway Island to meet South Vietnamese President Nguyen Van Thieu (NWIN VAHN TYOO). With Thieu's reluctant agreement, he announced the withdrawal of 25,000 troops from Vietnam, the first reduction in the American commitment of military aid in 15 years of fighting.

THE NIXON DOCTRINE AND THE END OF CONTAINMENT. Following the first moon landing on July 20, 1969, President Nixon flew to Guam in the Pacific to greet the triumphant astronauts. He took advantage of a press conference there to explain his Vietnam policy in a global context. Reporters labeled this policy the Nixon Doctrine.

The United States did not plan to abandon Asia, the President announced, but it would engage in no more "brushfire" wars like Vietnam. Instead, Asian countries would have to take responsibility for their own defense, receiving economic and moral support from the United States.

The Nixon Doctrine seemed to be a rationale for the continued withdrawal from South Vietnam. By the end of the year, 115,000 troops had been brought home—about a quarter of the total American force. *The long-range meaning of the Nixon Doctrine was the end of containment.* No longer would the United States seek to defend a line ringing the Soviet Union and the People's Republic of China. The Cold War entered a less militant phase.

CONTINUING WAR RESISTANCE. The significance of the Nixon Doctrine was not evident in the fall of 1969. The troop withdrawal seemed pathetically slow, and the bombing of South Vietnamese jungles increased. An area the size of Massachusetts was sprayed with chemicals to strip it of foliage and expose Vietcong trails.

On October 15, 1969, more than a million Americans participated in a one-day work stoppage to protest the war. A month later a quarter of a million people descended on the nation's capital to stage a mass rally.

To take some of the steam out of the movement, President Nixon went on television to announce plans for total withdrawal of American troops. But he refused to reveal the timetable. The announcement improved his popularity rating in the opinion polls. And the antiwar movement began to lose its force. A government blunder in the spring of 1970—the invasion of Cambodia—brought it back to life.

INVASION OF CAMBODIA. Cambodia, a nation in the Indochina peninsula, had remained neutral. On March 18, 1970, a right-wing general seized control of the government. CIA involvement was widely suspected. In response, North Vietnam moved large numbers of troops into the defenseless country.

On April 27 President Nixon ordered a combined American-South Vietnamese invasion of Cambodia to remove the North Vietnamese. Public reaction was instantaneous. Students took to the streets, smashing everything in sight. Many colleges and universities had to close down.

COLLAPSE OF THE NEW LEFT. When classes began at university campuses that fall, there was a noticeable drop in tension. The New Left was in disarray, its members battling one another over fine points of ideology. Much of the student protest originated with the draft. When President Nixon revised the system (he did not abolish the draft, although that was the general impression), students lost interest in

On July 20, 1969, astronaut Neil Armstrong became the first person to set foot on the moon. This event was the crowning achievement of the American space program.

demonstrations. When antiwar leaders called meetings, a few pathetic radicals appeared. Police, better trained and equipped for crowd control by 1970, kept things peaceful. Like the ghetto riots, the student protest vanished.

Violence did not disappear. It merely shifted base. The antiwar movement had caused a rightist reaction. Spiro Agnew pointed the way with his denunciation of protesters. *Over the next two years a covert kind of violence characterized the Nixon administration. It led to Watergate.*

Section Review

1. Identify or explain: Warren Burger, Office of Economic Opportunity, Nguyen Van Thieu.
2. What was the Nixon Doctrine? Why did it signal an end to containment?
3. What blunder did the government make in the spring of 1970 in Southeast Asia? How did the nation respond?

Chapter 33 Review

Bird's-Eye View

Lyndon Johnson's stunning victory in 1964 enabled him to implement the key elements of his Great Society program. At the same time military moves in the Dominican Republic and in Vietnam created more anti-Americanism in Latin America and a deteriorating situation in Southeast Asia.

Many Americans—especially college and university students—began publicly to express their opposition to the war. By the end of 1967, Johnson's popularity was at an all-time low. Responsible for this were three things—the awful image of war people got from television newscasts, the credibility gap, and the great cost of the war in human and financial terms.

During the 1960's Americans manifested their criticism of and concern for American society in the civil rights movement and the women's liberation movement. The civil rights movement, which had begun as a nonviolent crusade, turned militant and sometimes violent as Black frustration mounted. Rioting occurred in several large cities, shifting the movement north. The violence persuaded Congress to step up its activities in civil rights.

The women's liberation movement was sparked by Betty Friedan's *The Feminine Mystique*. The movement made important gains, as government took steps to wipe out discrimination against women.

In 1968 Lyndon Johnson announced that he would not run for the Presidency again. Three Democratic candidates sought the nomination—Eugene McCarthy, Robert Kennedy, and Hubert Humphrey. Kennedy and Martin Luther King, Jr., were assassinated in the spring of 1968. Humphrey won the Democratic nomination. The Republican candidate was Richard Nixon. Nixon won the election by a very slight margin.

Nixon began dismantling Great Society programs, extracting Americans from Vietnam, and negotiating a settlement of the war. He proclaimed the Nixon Doctrine, a statement ending containment as the basis of United States foreign policy.

Ending the war and healing the wounds it caused were not accomplished quickly. In 1970 the administration's authorization of the invasion of Cambodia touched off a wave of protest.

Vocabulary

Define or identify each of the following:

coup d'etat	credibility gap	Tet offensive
free fire zone	SNCC	Medicare
teach-in	NOW	*The Feminine Mystique*

Review Questions

1. What decision forced President Johnson to abandon Great Society programs?
2. How was the Vietnam War escalated during the Johnson administration?

772

3. How did television affect American attitudes toward the Vietnam War?
4. What changes took place in the civil rights movement between 1965 and 1968? What factors accounted for these changes?
5. How did Betty Friedan influence the women's movement?
6. How did the Vietnam War influence the 1968 Presidential campaign?
7. Richard Nixon took the slogan "Bring Us Together Again" as the theme of his Presidential victory speech. Did Nixon's first years in the White House bring the nation together again? Explain.

Reviewing Social Studies Skills

1. Using the map on page 767, complete the following:
   a. Through which countries does the Mekong River flow?
   b. Describe the geographic location of Cambodia, Laos, Hanoi, and Saigon.
   c. List the countries through which the Ho Chi Minh trail passes.
   d. From which country was the Tet offensive launched?
2. Using the statistics on page 757, make a line graph showing, both in terms of dollars spent and troops committed, how American involvement in Vietnam escalated between 1965 and 1968.

Reading for Meaning

1. The title of Section 4 is "1968: An Ugly Year." Reread this section, and then write a paragraph explaining why, in your view, the authors chose this title.
2. The phrase credibility gap is used to describe one of the reasons Americans became disillusioned with their government over the Vietnam War. Define the phrase. Then define it again using dictionary definitions of credibility and gap. Do the two definitions differ? How? Finally, make a list of situations in everyday life in which a credibility gap might occur.
3. Eugene McCarthy declared his candidacy for the 1968 Presidential nomination with these words: "There comes a time when an honorable man simply has to raise the flag." Write a paragraph explaining what you think McCarthy meant. Why did he use the image of raising the flag?

Bibliography

Nicholas von Hoffman's *Mississippi Notebook* (David White) is a journalist's firsthand acount of student involvement in civil rights activities during the 1960's.

Alexander Kendrick's *The Wound Within: Americans in the Vietnam Years* (Little, Brown) describes the interaction of war and protest.

Barbara Deckard's *The Women's Movement* (Harper & Row) and Benjamin Muse's *The American Negro Revolution: From Nonviolence to Black Power, 1963–1967* (University of Indiana Press) discuss two of the most prominent movements of the 1960's.

773

Chapter 34

From Passion to Peace

A century ago being self-made was a badge of honor. People like Commodore Vanderbilt and Andrew Carnegie were imposing, confident, and self-assured precisely because they had made their fortunes.

Richard Nixon, too, was self-made. But his road to success left him deeply scarred. He built his congressional reputation in the Red Scare years of the early 1950's.

Eisenhower only tolerated him as Vice-President. His visible disdain nearly wrecked Nixon's chances of winning the nomination in 1960. Eisenhower told reporters he could think of no reason why Nixon ought to be President.

Nixon won the 1968 election only by carefully cultivating the image of a "new Nixon"—calm, politically moderate, and mature. Avoiding journalists, whom he still regarded as enemies, he campaigned in 1968 with carefully planned television appearances. They were basically taped interviews in which Nixon answered bland questions by friendly aides.

His chief political strategist, Attorney General John Mitchell, seemed to be the opposite sort of person. Perhaps that is why Nixon admired him. Mitchell had the steely-eyed self-assurance of a Vanderbilt or a Carnegie and the discipline and composure to overcome any emergency. Members of the White House staff called him El Supremo. He was the most important person in the administration, next to the President himself.

Two other aides were nearly as important as Mitchell—H. R. Haldeman and John Ehrlichman. Haldeman was White House chief of staff, the person who controlled appointments and access to the President. Ehrlichman, the domestic coordinator, offered advice on matters of domestic policy and conveyed decisions to department heads.

Nixon enjoyed power but detested public exposure. Haldeman and Ehrlichman erected what one aide described as a Berlin wall around the President, protecting him from legislators, lobbyists, and members of the cabinet. This arrangement enabled the President to concentrate on broad strategy, leaving details to department chiefs. It also isolated him from Congress and the country. His circle of advisers became secretive, resentful of criticism, and hostile toward outsiders.

Chapter Objectives

After you have finished reading this chapter, you should be able to:
1. Describe foreign policy under the Nixon administration.

2. List the events in the Watergate crisis that led to President Nixon's resignation.

3. Describe the domestic and foreign policy of the country after Nixon's resignation.

4. List the issues facing the United States in the 1980's.

The way the White House was run was a prescription for disaster. But before disaster struck, the administration achieved some remarkable successes in the field of diplomacy. Largely the work of Henry Kissinger, who began as Nixon's National Security Adviser and eventually became Secretary of State, foreign policy was an outstanding feature of the Nixon Presidency.

1. The Statecraft of Henry Kissinger

RISING TO THE TOP. A Jewish refugee from Nazi Germany, Henry Kissinger combined great talent and ambition. He was a professor of government at Harvard University and served occasionally as a State Department consultant in the 1960's. He was not widely known, so it was quite a surprise when Nixon summoned him to a private meeting shortly after the 1968 election.

Sharing a background of adversity, the two men got along well from the start. Each considered himself a realist in the world of diplomacy. At a second meeting Kissinger accepted the post of National Security Adviser. Because he had the President's respect, Kissinger became Nixon's chief foreign policy specialist. Secretary of State William Rogers, a lawyer with no diplomatic experience, was left to govern the State Department bureaucracy.

THE END OF THE COLD WAR. *The most important development on the international scene in the 1960's was the split between the Soviet Union and the People's Republic of China.* Since the late 1950's each had vied with the other to lead the Communist world. Each power based its claim on the belief that it was ideologically purer than the other. In the 1960's the rift widened. Border disputes became armed confrontations. By 1970 the two Communist giants had more weapons pointed at each other than at the United States.

The split meant that one of the key American assumptions about the Cold War was wrong. Communism was not a unified ideology that bound its followers in a single goal of world conquest. It was as fragmented and quarrelsome as any other economic doctrine. Chinese Communists were different from Soviet Communists. It was quite possible that North Vietnamese Communists were different from both.

A RETURN TO TRADITIONAL DIPLOMACY. Henry Kissinger recognized this and convinced Nixon of his point of view. The two planned to treat the Soviet Union and China not as ideological enemies but as rival powers, each with its own interests to protect. They decided to return to traditional diplomacy, balancing one power against another, pursuing limited goals with limited means, and not worrying about the forces of good and evil. *This policy meant the end of the Cold War as Americans had known it.* International rivalries continued. But they were rivalries between concerned nations, not natural enemies.

The end of ideological conflict opened many possibilities for diplomacy. On the one hand, a reduction of tensions or détente with the Soviet Union opened the way for discussions of how to limit the arms race.

In February 1972 Richard M. Nixon became the first American President to visit China. Because of his visit, Americans became increasingly interested in China, which had been cut off from the United States. President and Mrs. Nixon are shown reviewing Chinese troops.

On the other, contacts with the leaders of China became a possibility.

ARMS LIMITATION TALKS. Halting the nuclear arms race was the first priority. After the Cuban missile crisis, the Soviet Union made an all-out effort to catch up with the United States in intercontinental missiles. By 1970 the two powers were roughly equal. Each was able to blow up the other three or four times.

The lessening of tensions afforded an opportunity to slow the arms race. Nixon opened Strategic Arms Limitations Talks (SALT) with the Soviets in the fall of 1969.

The discussions dragged on for two years until the two sides reached agreement. In May 1972 President Nixon flew to Moscow to sign the treaty, which the press dubbed SALT I. Areas of disagreement were left to future negotiations, or SALT II talks, which resumed in the fall of 1977.

The SALT I treaty limited each side to 200 ABM's and froze the number of land-based intercontinental ballistic missiles. The Soviets were given an advantage in ICBM's because the United States had developed a way of placing multiple independently-targeted reentry vehicles (MIRVs) in each missile. Each side maintained overkill.

The Moscow summit and the signing of SALT I made détente a reality. Unfortunately, it did not end the arms race. Each side redoubled its efforts to develop weapons not covered by the agreement, leaving many problems for SALT II.

CHANGING RELATIONS WITH CHINA. Early in Nixon's term the President and Kissinger put out feelers to improve relations with China. Because the United States had no embassy in China, the President had to use third parties, such as Poland and Pakistan. Chinese Premier Chou

En-lai (JOE en-LIE), worrying about the Soviet menace and the revival of Japan, recognized the value of the United States as a counterweight in the Far East. China's Mao Tse-tung, although more anti-American, gradually came around to the Premier's view.

The first indication that the Chinese were becoming sociable to Americans came in April 1971. They invited an American table tennis team, then in Japan for a tournament, to visit China. The gesture was rich in meaning, for table tennis is China's national game. When the American team received a warm welcome, Nixon sent Kissinger on a secret mission to Peking to work out details for a Presidential visit. On July 15, 1971, the President stunned the nation with a television announcement that he would visit the People's Republic of China—once the United States' enemy—the following year.

NIXON'S CHINA VISIT. Nixon's visit to China in February 1972 was attended with enormous fanfare. A planeload of reporters accompanied him, and live television coverage was beamed to the United States by satellite.

The President's talks with Chinese leaders came to little, but the lack of substance didn't matter. *The importance of Nixon's visit was symbolic.* Calm discussion took the place of hysterical accusations. The United States and the People's Republic of China were rivals—even potential enemies—and they would remain so for many years. But now they could calmly talk over their differences.

It was a personal triumph that few others could have carried out. Détente with China had been possible years earlier. But no President had tried it for fear of public reaction. Nixon could, because no one could possibly suspect him of being "soft on communism." Thus, his overture to China provoked scarcely a murmur of public protest. One of the biggest reversals in diplomatic history was accepted as common sense. It was Nix-

on's greatest achievement, and he had Kissinger to thank.

VIETNAM: BEGINNING THE FINAL PULLOUT. The Nixon-Kissinger diplomacy of realism dictated a final withdrawal from Vietnam. It was a war that could not be won. Its continuance hampered negotiations elsewhere in the world. It was important that the withdrawal not appear to be a surrender. Nixon and Kissinger thought there had to be some kind of negotiated settlement. To abandon the war would risk a public reaction such as the one that had wrecked Truman's administration after the fall of China. Secret negotiations between Kissinger and North Vietnamese representatives began soon after Nixon's inauguration. They continued off and on for four years.

By the end of 1971, an additional 100,000 Americans were withdrawn from South Vietnam, cutting the original commitment by nearly half. Those who remained were seldom sent into battle.

RESUMPTION OF AIR STRIKES. In March 1972 North Vietnam launched an all-out attack, spearheaded by Soviet-built tanks. Nixon ordered air strikes deep into the North, the first since 1969. A fleet of 20 B-52's, each carrying bombs, leveled parts of Hanoi and Haiphong (hi-FONG), the country's main harbor.

AGREEMENT TO STOP FIGHTING. *In October 1972, on the eve of the Presidential election, Kissinger and the North Vietnamese finally came to terms.* Each yielded an important point. The North Vietnamese abandoned their demand for a coalition government in Saigon, thus leaving Thieu and his generals in power. The United States agreed to permit the North Vietnamese Army to remain in South Vietnam after the cease-fire. It was an agreement to call it quits, with the armies remaining in place. Although not the "peace with honor" Nixon called it, the settlement was quite acceptable to war-weary Americans. It helped secure Nixon's reelection.

THE CHRISTMAS BOMBING, 1972. Haggling over details, both in Saigon and in Hanoi, held up confirmation of the agreement. In December 1972 Nixon lost patience and unleashed B-52 attacks on the North, the most ferocious yet. The Christmas bombing caused an outcry around the world at American barbarity and a deep feeling of shame at home. However, the bombing impressed the North Vietnamese. A final cease-fire was signed on January 27, 1973. The remaining American troops departed shortly thereafter.

VIETNAM: THE COLLAPSE. Neither side complied with the peace settlement. The Thieu regime in Saigon sent troops into the countryside. The Vietcong raided progovernment villages. President Nixon violated the agreement by ordering air raids on Cambodia, where the war continued without letup.

The bombing of Cambodia prompted Congress to pass a resolution making August 15, 1973, a deadline for ceasing all American military activity in Southeast Asia. Since Roosevelt's moves on the eve of World War II, American Presidents had been making military and diplomatic commitments around the world without consulting Congress. Congress reasserted itself at last.

After two years of sporadic fighting, the Communists mounted a massive attack in the spring of 1975. Simultaneous attacks in South Vietnam, Laos, and Cambodia by a combination of local rebels and North Vietnamese regulars indicated considerable planning. The South Vietnamese Army committed most of its reserves in the opening battle. When the battle was lost, the army fled in disarray.

Entire provinces fell into Communist hands almost daily. In a few weeks it was all over. *On April 30, with Communist forces at the gates of Saigon, South Vietnam surrendered.* American ships and helicopters evacuated some Vietnamese who wanted to leave. Most of those who wanted to leave had been employed by the American government and feared retaliation. The United States also evacuated several thousand war orphans. The speed with which South Vietnam collapsed revealed how unpopular the regime was.

Americans took the collapse with amazing calm. Perhaps its speed helped. Even those who supported the war to the end believed that they had done all they could. Most Americans realized that no country can help another that cannot help itself.

Section Review

1. Identify or explain: détente, SALT, Chou En-lai, the Christmas bombing.
2. Why did the diplomacy of realism developed by Kissinger and Nixon end the Cold War?
3. Describe the background of the SALT I treaty, and list the provisions of the treaty.
4. List the steps that led to the final withdrawal of American troops from Vietnam.

2. The Politics of Fear

NIXON'S UNDOING. With all his faults, Richard Nixon came close to greatness. Except for Watergate and the series of blunders that accompanied it, historians would probably have considered his Presidency more than a modest success.

His foreign policy held great promise of bringing peace to the world. Those who credit Kissinger (whom Nixon elevated to Secretary of State in 1972) with diplomatic successes should remember that Nixon and Kissinger worked in close cooperation.

In domestic policy Nixon dismantled the poverty programs of the Great Society.

Even liberals were becoming disenchanted with the theory, popular since the New Deal, that any social problem could be solved with a federal appropriation. Critics may fault the Nixon administration for catering to business elements at the expense of every other group. But they can hardly fault the President for failing to undertake far-reaching domestic reform.

The nation was basically conservative in the 1970's. No election in the decade indicated any deep desire for social change. Nixon fitted the mood of the country. He would have left office with honor and modest popularity had he not stumbled over Watergate. His downfall was his own fault. Like the hero of a classical Greek tragedy, Richard Nixon's character flaws were his undoing.

BACKLASH FROM THE RIGHT. It began in the atmosphere of fear created by the clashes between students and police in the "Cambodia spring" of 1970. Some students believed a revolution was at hand. A few conservatives agreed with them. Law and order disciples reacted, and violence from the Left bred violence from the Right.

In May 1970 a group of New York City construction workers, angered by an antiwar demonstration in front of City Hall, attacked the students and broke up the gathering. Three days later 2,000 "hard hats" paraded down Wall Sreet. They chanted "All the way, U.S.A."

THE ADMINISTRATION VS. WAR CRITICS. Nixon worked to maintain a moderate position between the radicals of the Left and the Right. He believed there was a silent majority in the country—people who supported his views but were not as outspoken as the other groups.

Vice-President Spiro Agnew served as the spokesperson for this group and the major critic of the Left. In the 1970 fall congressional elections, Spiro Agnew campaigned for Republicans. His denunciations of war

critics had wide appeal. The Republicans picked up two Senate seats, and the Democrats gained 11 in the House. Considering that the party in control of the White House usually loses seats in an off-year election, the administration could count it a victory. Its hard-line attitude toward demonstrators seemed to have popular approval.

THE PENTAGON PAPERS. In June 1971 newspapers across the country began publishing secret military documents leaked to them by Daniel Ellsberg, a former employee of the Pentagon. The documents, dating from the Johnson administration, were a history of United States involvement in Vietnam. Although they did not involve the Nixon administration or any current government program, the government sought to have them suppressed. The Supreme Court denied the President's request. It ruled that he had failed to demonstrate that national security was at stake. The ruling was a stinging defeat for the administration and a blow to its credibility.

THE PLUMBERS. To Nixon the publication of The Pentagon Papers was an indignity. To prevent further government news leaks, he ordered the formation of a special task force, whose members became known as the Plumbers. *They were to identify government employees who might be providing embarrassing information to reporters.*

THE ENEMIES LIST. Later that summer White House aides Charles Colson and John Dean put together an "enemies" list. Besides such well-known critics of the war as baby specialist Dr. Benjamin Spock, the list included Black representatives to Congress, several university presidents, and even football quarterback Joe Namath.

The administration used the list to embarrass its critics. Government agencies, such as the Internal Revenue Service, harassed the people on the list. *Both the enemies list and the Plumbers' activities were abuses of government power.*

CREEP. Having squeaked through by a very narrow margin in 1968, President Nixon was determined to be reelected by a large majority in 1972. Rather than rely on the regular Republican party apparatus, his supporters formed a special Committee to Reelect the President (CRP, later dubbed CREEP).

The committee received enormous campaign donations from wealthy people who were concerned about the social upheavals of the 1960's. Heading CRP was former Attorney General John Mitchell. He brought with him some of the White House aides who had initiated the Plumbers and the enemies list. Before long CRP was using underhanded tactics.

THE WATERGATE BREAK-IN. On June 17, 1972, Howard Hunt and Gordon Liddy, former Plumbers, arranged for CRP's chief of security and four Cuban hirelings to break into the Democratic National Committee headquarters in the Watergate office-apartment complex in Washington, D.C. The burglary was discovered by a guard who notified police. The five burglars were arrested. They were indicted three months later, along with Liddy and Hunt. The Democrats, suspecting that the burglars had been after documents revealing political strategy, called it political espionage. They filed a million-dollar damage suit against the Committee to Reelect the President.

The White House denied any connection with the break-in. Nixon's press secretary, Ron Ziegler, called it a "third-rate burglary." *Within days, however, Nixon's principal aides, H. R. Haldeman and John Ehrlichman, began a massive effort to conceal the connection between the burglars and the Committee to Reelect the President.* CRP funds were used to pay the burglars' legal

expenses. And the accused were promised large sums to keep silent.

The effort was a success. Despite some heroic investigative efforts by *Washington Post* reporters Robert Woodward and Carl Bernstein, the public knew nothing of the connection between the President and the Watergate break-in before the November election. It is not certain whether Nixon knew about the burglary in advance. But he did know about the effort to conceal the role of CRP in the break-in. To cover up a crime is itself a crime. Therein lay Nixon's downfall.

THE ELECTION OF 1972. Nixon had no difficulty securing the Republican nomination. The Democratic nomination went to George McGovern, a liberal antiwar senator from South Dakota. *McGovern was never able to overcome the image that he was a "prairie Populist" bent on overturning the governmental apple cart.* Nixon won in a landslide, capturing 60.7 percent of the popular vote and carrying every state but Mas-

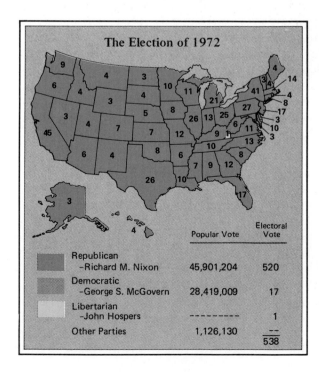

The Election of 1972

	Popular Vote	Electoral Vote
Republican —Richard M. Nixon	45,901,204	520
Democratic —George S. McGovern	28,419,009	17
Libertarian —John Hospers	----------	1
Other Parties	1,126,130	--
		538

sachusetts and the District of Columbia. (See map below.) Democrats maintained their huge majorities in Congress.

HIGH-HANDED GOVERNMENT. The election victory changed the White House mood. It became confidently aggressive. Nixon challenged the Democratic majority in Congress by announcing the termination of 112 Great Society programs. He also refused to spend 8.7 billion dollars appropriated by Congress in 1972 for various federal programs.

Whether the President had the right to impound money appropriated by Congress was an interesting constitutional question. A major battle between President and Congress was shaping up when, in the spring of 1973, sensational Watergate revelations gave the struggle a new dimension.

WATERGATE AGAIN. *The beginning of the end for Richard Nixon came on March 23, 1973.* Judge John Sirica, who had sentenced the seven convicted Watergate burglars, read in court a letter from one of the defendants, James McCord. McCord claimed that he had been pressured to lie at the trial. Shortly thereafter Nixon's legal adviser, John Dean, realizing that the administration's illegal activities had gone too far, began talking to FBI agents about the cover-up. The revelations of the *Washington Post* became more specific. Other newspapers and magazines started investigations of their own.

In an effort to still the growing outcry, President Nixon appeared on nationwide television on April 30 to announce the resignation of Attorney General Richard Kleindienst, John Dean, H. R. Haldeman, and John Ehrlichman. He still denied any wrongdoing and praised Haldeman and Ehrlichman as "two of the finest public servants it has been my privilege to know." The new Attorney General, Elliot Richardson, a widely respected Republican, was given the power to appoint a special prosecutor to in-

vestigate the whole Watergate affair. He chose Harvard law professor Archibald Cox.

THE TAPES. In May 1973 a special Senate investigating committee summoned John Dean and other members of the administration to testify. *Dean claimed that he had informed the President of the illegal cover-up in March.* When the President failed to investigate, Dean said, he went to the FBI.

There was no way to substantiate Dean's story until another witness, Alexander Butterfield, informed the committee that White House conversations were tape-recorded. The President apparently had had the system set up to help him in the writing of his memoirs after he left office.

Realizing that the tapes might reveal who was telling the truth, Nixon or Dean, both the Senate committee and Prosecutor Cox asked Nixon to submit those pertaining to the investigation. Nixon refused to surrender the tapes. When Cox persisted, Nixon fired him. Attorney General Richardson and his deputy resigned in protest.

The resignations (because they came on a weekend, reporters dubbed them "the Saturday night massacre") brought a deluge of protests. Nixon was forced to retreat. He announced the appointment of another special prosecutor, Leon Jaworski, and promised to let him carry on the investigation. He also agreed to surrender certain tapes.

THE RESIGNATION OF VICE-PRESIDENT AGNEW. For some months a separate investigation had been proceeding in Maryland, home of Spiro Agnew. *The Vice-President, it appeared, had accepted bribes while governor of Maryland and had compounded the crime by failing to report the income.* Rather than suffer trial, Agnew pleaded "no contest" to the charge of tax evasion and resigned as Vice-President on October 10, 1973. Nonetheless, he protested his innocence. Nixon replaced him with

Gerald Ford, Republican minority leader in the House of Representatives.

THE EVIDENCE OF THE TAPES. *The tapes Nixon surrendered substantiated the testimony of John Dean.* The Judiciary Committee of the House of Representatives was considering the possibility of impeaching the President. It asked for all the remaining relevant tapes. When the Supreme Court ordered the release of the tapes because they were evidence in a criminal investigation, Nixon was finished. The critical tape was a conversation between Nixon and Haldeman. They discussed the cover-up just six days after the Watergate break-in. *The tape proved that the President had known about Watergate all along.*

PRESIDENT NIXON RESIGNS. In televised hearings, a majority of the House Judiciary Committee solemnly declared themselves in favor of impeaching the President. There was little doubt that the entire House would agree. Senate Republican leaders told Nixon that he would be convicted in a Senate trial.

On August 8 President Nixon resigned. Gerald Ford, whom Nixon had appointed Vice-President months before, became President. Ford, in turn, named Nelson Rockefeller Vice-President. For the first time in its history, the country was led by a President and Vice-President who had not been elected.

HOW DID IT HAPPEN? When it was all over, Republican Senate leader Hugh Scott addressed a letter to James Madison. "Dear Sir," read the simple message. "It worked." All the complex machinery of checks and balances created by Madison and other founders when they wrote the Constitution had been severely tested. It worked to perfection.

The real issue in Watergate was the abuse of power, or the imperial Presi-

Senator Sam Ervin of North Carolina, on the right, and Senator Howard Baker of Tennessee, on the left, led the Senate committee on Watergate. Their efforts helped bring about President Nixon's resignation.

dency, as one scholar labeled it. Truman had begun the process, threatening both labor unions and business corporations with government force and sending troops into Korea without consulting Congress. Lyndon Johnson's use of the Tonkin Gulf Resolution as an excuse to do anything he wanted expanded the "imperial" power. Nixon's attacks on neutral Laos and Cambodia went one step further. The Cold War had made the American President all-powerful. Nixon's claim that he could withhold funds appropriated by Congress brought that fact home. His use of executive privilege to cover up evidence of his own guilt showed how dangerous such power was.

SECRET GOVERNMENT. Richard Nixon was not the first President to abuse his power. Nor was he the first to be excessively secretive. Secrecy had become a way of life for the government in the 1960's.

The army covered up errors in planning that cost millions of dollars and sometimes hundreds of lives by stamping its documents "Top Secret." When the air force conducted bombing raids over neutral Cambodia, it falsified reports to indicate that the planes had gone elsewhere. The CIA provided secret funds to overthrow governments unfriendly to the United States, as it did in Chile in 1973.

In such an environment the secret activities of Nixon's Plumbers were almost normal. The Cold War had corrupted the moral fiber of the nation. Watergate was the tip of the iceberg. It revealed that in addition to restoring the balance of power among the President, Congress, and the courts, it was necessary to elect officials who were committed to honest and open government.

Section Review

1. Mapping: Using the maps on pages 768 and 780, identify the states that did not vote for Nixon in 1968. How did Nixon's electoral victory in 1972 change the mood of the White House?
2. Identify or explain: the Plumbers, Cambodia spring, the silent majority, the enemies list, Leon Jaworski, CREEP.
3. Why did Senator George McGovern fail to win the Presidency in 1972?
4. Why was March 23, 1973, the beginning of the end for Richard Nixon?

3. A New Era Begins

A WELCOME CHANGE. Watergate was the last act in a decade of violence that had begun at Selma and Watts in 1964. Social disruption from the Left had been answered by repression from the Right. By 1974 the vast majority of Americans had enough of both. A calm settled over the nation in the mid-1970's. And it was a welcome change.

PRESIDENT GERALD FORD. Given the chaos that attended Nixon's downfall (a President and a Vice-President had resigned, and two former Cabinet members had been indicted for crimes, along with a half dozen of the President's top aides), the new President was of higher caliber than some disillusioned people expected. A long-time member of Congress from Michigan and leader of Republicans in the House, Ford was liked and respected by members of both political parties. Unassuming, open, and sociable by nature, he created a wholesome atmosphere in the White House. Public confidence in the Presidency was quickly restored. After Ford's first three weeks in office, a public-opinion poll indicated that 71 percent of the American people approved of his style of leadership.

PARDON FOR RICHARD NIXON. Ford lost some of the support in an initial effort to bind up the wounds resulting from Watergate. *In September 1974, he pardoned Richard Nixon of all crimes, although the ex-President had not been formally accused of any.* Ford acted partly out of sympathy for the ex-President, who was said to be in poor health and under severe strain. Ford also wished to end the agony of Watergate for the American people. Were Nixon indicted on criminal charges, his trial would have dragged on for months or years, leaving Americans more divided and bitter than ever.

Ford's act was well-intentioned, but the pardon angered many. Several of Nixon's top advisers were under indictment for the Watergate cover-up. The burglars were serving jail sentences. It seemed unjust to let Nixon bypass the judicial process. Some critics argued that the full truth of Watergate could be discovered only by putting the ex-President on the witness stand. The pardon meant that this could never be done.

AMNESTY FOR DRAFT EVADERS.
President Ford's amnesty plan for draft evaders of the Vietnam War further damaged his popularity. Before the selective service system ended, thousands of young men had evaded the draft by fleeing to Canada and other countries. The injustice of the war, they believed, justified their actions.

Prosecuting these people would prolong the national agony. Ford decided to offer them a conditional pardon. The pardon had to be earned by performing two years of alternative service in penal, custodial, or rehabilitation centers. Letting them return to the United States without penalty, the President reasoned, would be unfair to the many thousands of young men who had loyally served in the armed forces.

MORE NORMALCY.
Unpopular though these actions were, the protests soon died. With an almost audible sigh of relief, the nation settled into normalcy.

President Ford, a conservative at heart, fitted this mood perfectly. He had little of substance to recommend to Congress. He spent much of his brief term battling the Democrats over proposals for social welfare programs. He vetoed more bills in less time than any President in history. Many Americans approved of Ford's efforts to hold down budget deficits. Others criticized his failure to provide energetic and imaginative leadership.

PROBLEMS MOUNT.
To Ford's critics, the nation seemed to be drifting in a sea of problems. From 1972 until early 1975, the economy experienced the most serious slow-down since the 1930's. National growth slowed to a halt. And in some months it even slipped backward. In the depths of the recession, unemployment hovered around 10 percent. Among Blacks and young people it exceeded 30 percent. Compounding the distress was severe inflation. Prices rose about 10 percent per year, causing great hardship to persons living on fixed incomes and pensions.

The outbreak of another Arab-Israeli war in 1973 caused additional problems. The Arabs halted oil exports in an effort to exert pressure on Israel's allies. The fuel shortage caused a worldwide depression. And the reduction in trade intensified America's problems. *The oil shortage demonstrated how dependent on foreign oil the United States had become.*

Ford's response to these mounting troubles was neither bold nor imaginative. Although he vetoed congressional efforts to boost the economy by government spending, he offered no solutions of his own. For two years, the nation idled like a bedridden patient, healing its wounds. Despite numerous problems, there was little call for change.

The situation was not entirely Ford's fault, nor was it the result of a post-Watergate, postwar letdown. For many of the problems there were no obvious remedies. *The strange mixture of economic stagnation and inflation (requiring the invention of a word, "stagflation") was particularly troublesome.* Government spending to boost the economy risked causing worse inflation. Efforts to reduce inflation (by tightening the money supply, for instance) would further dampen the economy. Most of the remedies for the energy shortage—gasoline rationing, for instance—were political hot potatoes that no one dared handle.

THE ELECTION OF 1976. The mood of uncertain conservatism was evident throughout the election campaign of 1976. President Ford, hoping to win a term of his own, faced strong challenge from Ronald Reagan, the leader of the Republicans' conservative wing. Ford narrowly won the nomination. But the Reaganites dictated a platform that denounced many of Ford's policies, notably Kissinger's détente with the Soviet Union.

With Republicans tainted by Watergate, the Democrats' prospects seemed the brightest since 1964. A host of candidates entered the early primaries, but none caught the public fancy.

Then Jimmy Carter, a former naval officer, peanut farmer, and one-term governor of Georgia, won several early primaries and built momentum. Carter's appeal was that of an outsider who had no connection with Washington. He benefited greatly from the post-Watergate suspicion of politicians. He entered every open primary, lost only one, and arrived at the convention with enough votes to win nomination.

During the campaign—highlighted by the first Presidential debates since 1960—neither candidate promised easy remedies for the nation's problems. Both promised honest government but otherwise confined themselves to generalities. Carter's southern background restored that section to Democratic ranks. And he carried enough of the big eastern and midwestern states to win a slim majority—297 electoral votes to Ford's 241. (See map above.)

PRESIDENT JIMMY CARTER. Ford restored public confidence in the Presidency. *Carter dismantled some of the im-*

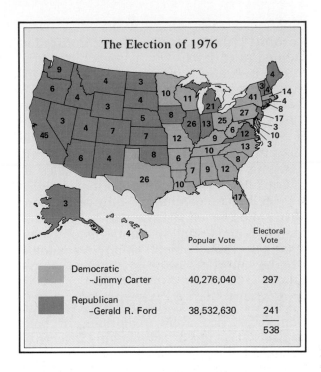

The Election of 1976

		Popular Vote	Electoral Vote
Democratic –Jimmy Carter		40,276,040	297
Republican –Gerald R. Ford		38,532,630	241
			538

perial trappings that surrounded the office. Carter set the tone with informality of manner and appearance. He cut the White House staff by a fourth (Ford had cut Nixon's staff by a fourth), and he took away their chauffeured limousines. The President sought to communicate directly with the people through "phone-in" press conferences and town meetings held in various parts of the country. He visited Americans in their homes and sometimes stayed overnight.

Much of this was a matter of creating a favorable public image. The effort might have been more successful if Carter had not erred in other ways. Carter went to Washington as an outsider, and to many in Congress and the press corps, he remained aloof. His closest advisers, several of whom came from his home state of Georgia, had little experience in government. Some, such as White House Chief of Staff Hamilton Jordan, were capable people who grew into their jobs. But acquiring knowledge and experience took time. While they were learning, the uncertain administration seemed to stumble.

The Bert Lance affair suggested that inexperience is not necessarily virtuous. A Georgia banker and friend of the President, Lance was appointed Director of the Office of Management and Budget. After the Comptroller of the Currency issued a report charging that Lance's banking policies in Georgia had been irregular, perhaps unethical, the Senate conducted an investigation. Carter proclaimed that he was proud of his friend. Maintaining his innocence, Lance resigned from office. Many wondered whether outsiders were any better than insiders.

CARTER AND CONGRESS. Although Democrats had solid majorities in both houses of Congress, President Carter had difficulty getting his programs enacted. In the spring of 1977 he announced a comprehensive energy program. He emphasized conservation of fuel by encouraging Americans to use more home insulation. He wanted to tax big gas-guzzling cars. And he wanted to allocate more federal money to energy research. Congress passed the least painful features of the program, such as tax incentives for home insulation. But it balked at increasing taxes and expenditures for energy. The administration failed to provide leadership. After two years of wrangling, Congress passed legislation that bore little resemblance to the President's energy programs.

CARTER AND MINORITIES. *Carter used his executive powers to help minorities and women.* He appointed three Hispanics to the White House staff as special assistants—Graciela Olivarez, Fabian Chávez, and Alex Mercuri. Andrew Young became the first Black to serve as United States Ambassador to the United Nations. Two women were appointed to cabinet posts—Patricia Roberts Harris, Secretary of Housing and Urban Development, and Juanita Kreps, Secretary of Commerce. Under Carter the number of women appointed federal judges more than doubled. The President also lobbied for the ratification of the Equal Rights Amendment.

THE ROLE OF ROSALYNN CARTER. Early in the administration, Rosalynn Carter emerged as a key adviser and personal envoy. Not since Jacqueline Kennedy or perhaps even Eleanor Roosevelt had the wife of a President played such an important role. Rosalynn Carter visited Latin America as the President's personal representative. She worked hard and successfully on behalf of legislation to benefit people suffering from mental illness. In the campaign of 1980, she traveled across the country, making campaign speeches. The partnership forged by America's first family symbolized the increased stature and respect earned by women in American society.

CARTER'S FOREIGN POLICY: A MIXED RECORD. President Carter's greatest achievement was the agreement between Israel's Prime Minister Menachem Begin and Egypt's President Anwar Sadat. Following a dramatic visit to Jerusalem by Sadat, Carter invited the two leaders to Camp David, Maryland. There the former enemies reached a historic agreement, which was followed, after Carter's tactful application of pressure, by the signing of a treaty in April 1979. Israel withdrew from the Sinai Peninsula, which it had seized during the Six-Day War of 1967. Egypt agreed to open the Suez Canal to Israel's ships. Much more remained to be done, particularly in regard to the displaced Palestinians. But a major step had been taken toward peace in the Middle East.

President Carter played a vital role in the Egyptian-Israeli negotiations, although some of the groundwork had been laid by Henry Kissinger during the Nixon-Ford years. Carter also inherited from Kissinger a

The signing of the peace treaty between Israel and Egypt is thought to be President Carter's most significant foreign policy achievement. How does it compare with Carter's handling of other foreign affairs and crises?

half-completed agreement with Panama on the future of the Panama Canal. The United States continued to lease the Canal Zone from Panama on a long-term basis. But nationalists were demanding it back. Carter resumed negotiations with Panama when he became President. In 1978 he signed a Panama Canal Treaty. The agreement called for Panamanian control of the canal by the year 2000. After that date, the United States would have the right to intervene to ensure the canal's neutrality.

The treaty was approved by the Senate after intense debate. The Panama Canal had long been a source of American pride. There were some who believed that it had been given away too easily. On the other hand, supporters of the treaty pointed out that the land had never belonged to the United States.

The SALT II negotiations were also inherited from the Nixon-Ford administrations. President Carter signed a strategic arms limitation treaty with the Soviet Union in May 1979. The agreement attempted to establish equality in missile systems between the two superpowers. SALT II ran into sharp criticism in the Senate and in the press. When the Soviets sent troops into Afghanistan toward the end of 1979, the President withdrew the treaty from the Senate.

THE LIMITED USE OF POWER. Jimmy Carter's foreign policy was influenced by the lessons of Vietnam. The Vietnam War had taught Americans the limits of power. It taught that even a strong military power cannot sustain a government against the will of its people without turning the country into a military garrison. It taught

787

the limits of technology: air power, sighted bombs, rockets, and napalm cannot bring a nation to heel. To President Carter these lessons meant the end of military adventures in the Third World.

The results, as with so many other things Jimmy Carter attempted, were mixed. A revolution in Nicaragua overthrew the Somoza family, which had ruled the country for generations. Carter refused to intervene. When the rebels won, he quickly extended diplomatic recognition to the new regime. Some feared that the rebels might be anti-American, Communist, or both. Nicaragua established a seemingly stable, democratic, and neutral government. Friendship with the United States emerged as a possibility. A revolution in Iran turned out less favorably.

THE HOSTAGE CRISIS. Iranian nationalists and Muslim religious leaders staged massive demonstrations against the pro-American Shah Mohammad Reza Pahlavi. The United States was faced with an anti-American revolution, whose leaders maintained ties with neither Soviet nor Chinese Communists. Carter adopted a hands-off policy. The revolution succeeded. The Shah fled Iran in early 1979.

After living for brief periods in several countries, the Shah was admitted to the United States for medical treatment. Iranian nationalists were furious. They broke into the United States embassy in Tehran on November 4, 1979. They occupied the embassy and seized the resident American diplomats, consular officials, and other Americans in the embassy.

The hostage crisis dominated the last year of Carter's Presidency. An attempt to rescue the hostages in April 1980 failed when helicopters broke down in the desert of Iran.

After 444 days of captivity, the 52 American hostages were freed from Iran. This sparked a celebration and a feeling of unity throughout the country. Here, a cheerful crowd in Washington, D.C., welcomes the freed Americans as they pass in a motorcade.

Feeling helpless and frustrated, many Americans began to think that the President's peaceful, low-key approach to problems was to blame.

Although this feeling of frustration may have contributed to Carter's defeat in the Presidential election, President Carter secured the release of the hostages on his last day in office, January 20, 1981.

Section Review

1. Identify or explain: the hostage crisis, SALT II, Juanita Kreps, Andrew Young, Presidential pardon.
2. What factors led to Carter's election in 1976?
3. Explain Carter's role in the Egyptian-Israeli peace treaty.

4. The Reagan Years

THE ELECTION OF 1980. Steadily rising prices plagued the nation throughout the Carter Presidency. Inflation seemed to defy solution. Any attempt to combat it disrupted other economic goals. In the spring of 1980 the Federal Reserve Board and the nation's banks raised interest rates to record levels in an effort to discourage buying. According to the theory, if Americans purchased fewer goods, prices would stop rising. Unable to borrow, people would buy less. By summer the economy was in a deep recession. Millions of people were out of work, and prices kept rising.

Americans were angry and frustrated. Nothing seemed to work well, either at home or abroad. As they had in the past, Americans blamed their troubles on the President. Carter's ratings in the polls declined steadily during 1979. At one point his rating was lower than Nixon's during Watergate. Carter's popularity recovered during the early stages of the hostage crisis. This enabled him to win the primaries in the

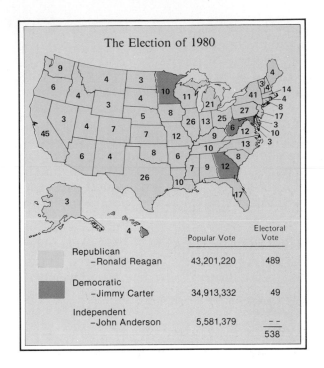

The Election of 1980

	Popular Vote	Electoral Vote
Republican —Ronald Reagan	43,201,220	489
Democratic —Jimmy Carter	34,913,332	49
Independent —John Anderson	5,581,379	--
		538

spring of 1980 and be renominated by the Democratic party. But in the fall of 1980 Carter's popularity dropped again.

Sensing that the country was in a mood for change, a host of Republicans had sought the nomination of their party. Ronald Reagan, who had made a strong showing against Gerald Ford in 1976, won the nomination.

In the election campaign Reagan succeeded in convincing the voters that he was a moderate, common-sense conservative. He carried all but six states and the District of Columbia. Even the South, Jimmy Carter's home base, voted Republican in 1980.

THE REAGAN PROGRAM. All politicians make campaign promises. Reagan's were more ambitious than most. He promised to increase defense spending and balance the budget. He promised to lessen inflation and stimulate the economy. To accomplish such goals Reagan based his economic program on "supply side" economics. A form of classical economic theory,

789

"supply side" economics is supposed to stimulate the production of goods by removing government regulations and controls. A bountiful supply of consumer goods will mean less pressure on prices. Increased production means more jobs and increased government revenues. The rise in government revenue, in turn, will ultimately enable the government to balance the budget despite increased defense expenditures. So much for the theory. In practice such changes take time. Whether it will work remains to be proved.

THE CONSERVATIVE MOOD. The election of Ronald Reagan reflected the mood of conservatism that has developed among Americans since the early 1970's. Although it means a less active role for the government, we cannot repeal the past. Many lessons of the past still challenge us. We shall close this story of American history with a brief look at America in the 1980's.

FOREIGN AFFAIRS. The Cold War of the 1940's and 1950's has ended. Great power rivalries will doubtless continue. Soviet-American or Chinese-American relations may worsen, but the conflict will not take the form of the Cold War. The spread of Communist ideology is no longer as worrisome as it was in the 1950's. Americans recognize that a Yugoslavian or a Polish Communist is not the same as a Soviet Communist. Americans also recognize the limits of United States power. They still believe in a strong army and navy and have supported increased defense expenditures in recent years. But they understand that the use of American military power must continue to be more restrained than it was in the Cold War years.

MINORITY RIGHTS. The civil rights issue, as it was once understood, has also changed. The movement originated in an effort to do away with official discrimination, protected and sometimes enforced by law, and it succeeded. Laws sanctioning segregation in schools and other public places have been nullified. Although laws prohibit most forms of discrimination, prejudice continues. But it no longer has the support of government.

In the 1970's, the issue facing Blacks and other minorities was not legal rights, but social rights — a decent standard of living and the leverage to influence society.

Because of earlier discrimination and a sluggish economy, many minorities have become trapped in a vicious circle of poor education, unemployment, and substandard housing. The civil rights movement in the 1970's took the form of government efforts to break the circle. Placing government-built, low-rent housing in the suburbs has helped in some cities. Other cities encouraged suburbanites to return to the central city by building apartment complexes. In the 1980's such efforts have been slowed by a shortage of government funds.

WOMEN. The women's movement took a new turn in the 1970's. The early militancy and the worst forms of discrimination had ended. Governments, educational institutions, and large corporations developed affirmative action programs. They promised to give employment preference to qualified

Ronald Reagan is sworn in as the 40th President of the United States. He has promised a new beginning for America.

Viewpoints to History

Changing Perspectives on Women in History

The portrayal of women in American history has been characterized by omission, or casual mention. The idea that women have a definite place in history and have always been involved in the making of history is relatively recent.

An example of omission is to be found in a set of volumes called *The American Nation Series.* One of the volumes, *The Federalist System,* written by John Spencer Basset, is representative of the series. Basset taught history to women at Smith College for about a quarter of a century starting in 1919. In the chapter on the state of society during the 18th century, people, inhabitants, Negroes, agriculture, dancing, inns, fried bacon, and corn bread are mentioned, but no women are referred to. Going through other chapters, one finds a reference to Martha Washington as a hostess. Nothing is found of Abigail Adams or Mercy Warren.

In 1922 Arthur Meir Schlesinger wrote *New Viewpoints in American History,* in which he commented on the absence of women in American history textbooks.

"An examination of the standard histories of the United States and of the history textbooks in use in our schools raises the pertinent question whether women have ever made a contribution to American national progress that is worthy of record. If the silence of the historian is taken to mean anything, it would appear that one half of our population have been negligible factors in our country's history."

Professor Schlesinger's comments had little immediate effect. Nearly 20 years later, Ralph H. Gabriel wrote *The Course of American Demo-cratic Thought: An Intellectual History Since 1815.* The period in question was one in which thousands of articles, pamphlets, and books on democracy, law, and justice were written by women. In the bibliography there is no work by a woman. Professor Gabriel did not give even a page to the women's declaration at Seneca Falls.

By 1957 historians were routinely including aspects of the role of women in American history. Richard Hofstadter was one of the authors of *The United States, the History of a Republic.* In the index there are 16 listings for women. Abigail Adams and Mercy Warren were not listed.

Although women were left out of history texts in the past, they are now the subject matter of many books. Statistics are being uncovered that show there were more professional women, more working women, more influential women than had ever been realized. Recent studies include Linda Kerber's *Women in the Revolution,* Nancy F. Cott's *The Bonds of Womanhood: "Women's Sphere" in New England, 1780–1835,* and Julie Roy Jeffrey's *Frontier Women: The Trans-Mississippi West, 1840–1880.* The titles suggest the rich variety of women's experience in the American past.

One of the newest American histories, *The Great Republic* by Bernard Bailyn and others, gives good coverage of women in American history. Although Mercy Warren is still unlisted, Abigail Adams is listed in the index among well over 30 entries under "women" or "feminism." In discussing the social feminist movement, Professor Bailyn writes:

"Working together in a new spirit of professionalism, the social feminists built staffs of dedicated administrators like Frances Perkins, the Goldmarcks, Pauline and Josephine, who would carry their crusade against child labor and social abuse into the 1920's."

The many contributions that women have made are well summarized by June Sochen in *Herstory: A Woman's View of American History* (1974).

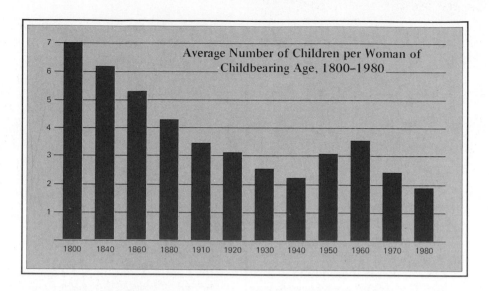

Average Number of Children per Woman of Childbearing Age, 1800–1980

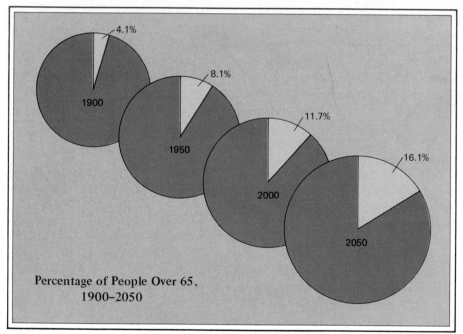

4.1%

8.1%

11.7%

16.1%

1900

1950

2000

2050

Percentage of People Over 65,
1900–2050

women and minorities. "Equal opportunity" laws passed by the state and federal governments have encouraged women to move into the labor force in ever-increasing numbers.

The employment of large numbers of women outside the home is having enormous social consequences. There is a continuing drop in the annual birthrate, which has been falling steadily since 1960. Employed women often marry late or not at all, and they usually have fewer children. Smaller families, in turn, are helping revitalize the cities. People fled to the suburbs, in part, to provide living space and fresh air for their children. Couples with a single child or

Many communities have programs that enable senior citizens to tutor young people after school.

none at all often remain in the city, where there are more cultural events and social activities.

THE AGED. Because people are living longer and having fewer children, the population is aging. A century ago, when large families were common, the average age of Americans was 20. In the 1950's, it was 30; by the year 2000, it will be about 35. By the year 2030, half the population will be of retirement age and will be eligible to collect Social Security.

To prevent the Social Security system from being swamped, it is likely that the retirement age will be raised by offering tax and other incentives to those who wish to work beyond the age of 65. What the social and political results will be when the aged are a majority can only be guessed.

THE ENVIRONMENT. The declining birth rate should have beneficial results for the environment. Concern for the quality of the environment was one of the most significant developments of the 1970's. President Carter shared this concern. He worked hard to obtain congressional approval of a bill to preserve the Alaskan wilderness. The law, passed in November 1980, set aside more than 40 million hectares (100 million acres) of pristine forest in Alaska. Lumbering, mining, and other forms of development are prohibited in some parts and limited in others. Future generations may feel that the Alaska Land Act was President Carter's finest legacy.

Unlike some problems facing Americans, preserving the environment will require world solutions. The regulation of oil tankers will require international treaties. Much of the earth's air pollution is due to poor agricultural methods in areas where overpopulation requires every inch of soil to be tilled. The result is erosion and dust storms. Hungry people must be fed. And hunger may be the biggest source of world friction in the coming decades. The elimination of hunger and the improvement of agricultural methods are world concerns.

These, then, are some of the problems and opportunities facing the American people in the 1980's. One thing the past has taught us is that the future will be full of surprises.

Section Review

1. Mapping: Using the maps on pages 785 and 789, make a list of the states Carter won in 1976 but lost in 1980.
2. How has the changed status of women affected American life? How will it affect life in the future?
3. What is the significance of the fact that the average age of Americans is growing higher all the time?
4. Why will environmental problems require world solutions?

Bird's-Eye View

One of the significant changes of the 1970's took place in the area of foreign affairs. The Cold War policy of containment gave way to the diplomacy of realism developed by President Richard M. Nixon and Secretary of State Henry Kissinger. Important results of this new diplomatic approach were the initiation of arms limitation talks with the Soviet Union, renewal of contacts with the People's Republic of China, and the end of American involvement in Southeast Asia, particularly involvement in the Vietnam conflict.

Although Nixon made signal achievements in the field of foreign policy, the same could not be said for his domestic record. Nixon and his advisers undertook a campaign of harassment against people who spoke out against the administration. Ultimately, the President's involvement in the Watergate cover-up led to his resignation from the Presidency on August 8, 1974.

Nixon was succeeded by Gerald Ford. Although Ford brought many good qualities and experience to the Presidency, he was unable to deal forcefully or imaginatively with the many problems facing the nation. One of his first acts was the pardon of Richard Nixon, an act that angered many. Ford's popularity was also undermined by his inability to cope with the serious recession of the mid-1970's and with the escalating energy crisis.

In the 1976 Presidential election, Ford was defeated by Jimmy Carter. Carter worked to make the Presidency more down to earth and informal and to restore contact between the White House and the people. He used the power of the executive department to bring women and minorities into government in greater numbers than any other President. Dissatisfaction with Carter's passive style of leadership, however, caused many to believe it was time for a change. Ronald Reagan, a Republican, became President in January 1981.

In the 1980's Americans are as aware of past trials and future troubles as they are of the nation's achievements and goals. Advances have been made in many important areas—the environment and rights for women and minorities—but much work remains to be done both in the United States and in the world.

Vocabulary

Define or identify each of the following:

détente	the Plumbers	stagflation
SALT I	Archibald Cox	supply side economics
Pentagon Papers	John Dean	Patricia Harris

Review Questions

1. Why was the split between the Soviet Union and the People's Republic of China important to the United States?
2. What was the significance of President Nixon's visit to China?

3. What steps were involved in the withdrawal of United States forces from Vietnam?
4. List three abuses of power that took place during Nixon's administration.
5. Why, when Watergate was over, did Senator Hugh Scott address a letter to James Madison saying, "Dear Sir, It worked."?
6. How did Gerald Ford restore America's confidence in the Presidency?
7. How was Carter's style different from previous Presidents'?
8. What issues face the United States in the 1980's?

Reviewing Social Studies Skills

1. Using the graphs on page 792, complete the following:
   a. What percentage of people were over 65 in 1900? In 1950? What will the percentage be in 2000? In 2050? What is the trend shown in this graph?
   b. What do you think is responsible for this trend?
2. Using the maps on pages 785 and 789, complete the following:
   a. How many more popular votes did Carter receive in 1976 than in 1980?
   b. How many electoral votes did Reagan receive?
   c. How many popular votes did Anderson receive?

Reading for Meaning

1. Using the information in this chapter, write a character sketch of former President Nixon. Does your characterization of Nixon agree with the ones developed by the authors?
2. The Committee to Reelect the President was often referred to by the nickname CREEP. What is the basis for this nickname? Who do you think coined it—committee members or people critical of the committee? Why?

Bibliography

Washington Post reporters Carl Bernstein and Bob Woodward, who first unraveled the Watergate mystery, have told their story in two splendid books, *All the President's Men* (Warner Books) and *The Final Days* (Simon and Schuster).

Jonathan Schell's *The Time of Illusion* (Random House) is the most balanced account of Nixon's highly controversial administration.

Unit 7 Review

Vocabulary

Define or identify each of the following:

Gross National Product	summit	coup d'état
unemployment rate	missile	SALT I
guerrilla warfare	blue-collar workers	Watergate
Third World	racketeer	Kissinger

Recalling the Facts

1. What factors contributed to the nation's general era of prosperity during the 1950's?
2. How was nonviolent protest used in the Black civil rights movement?
3. What did Eisenhower mean by the phrase "modern republicanism," and how was this concept reflected in his programs?
4. Explain the theory of massive retaliation.
5. List the military actions carried out during the Eisenhower administration.
6. How did the United States respond to *Sputnik I*?
7. What factors accounted for the great popularity of President Kennedy?
8. How did Kennedy respond to the arming of Cuba with Soviet missiles?
9. Describe the Alliance for Progress program and evaluate its effectiveness.
10. What social legislation was passed during the Johnson administration?
11. How did the nation react to the escalation of the Vietnam War during the Johnson administration?
12. Where did the 1968 urban riots take place? What caused them?
13. How did the Vietnam War end?
14. Explain Henry Kissinger's influence in his roles as foreign policy specialist and Secretary of State in the Nixon administration.
15. Why did Spiro Agnew and Richard Nixon resign from their elected offices of Vice-President and President?
16. What was President Ford's greatest contribution to the nation?
17. What factors contributed to the election of Jimmy Carter to the Presidency?

History Lab

1. Create a map history of the Black civil rights movement. First, make a large outline map of the United States. Then make a key, using a combination of labels, colors, and symbols to show the following: 1) the dates of and the places where important events took place; 2) the areas where the Black civil rights movement started, and the directions in which it spread.
2. Make a list of the qualities you believe a President of the United States should have. Rank these qualities in their order of importance, giving each one a numerical value. Then, rate the following

796

Presidents on your scale of values: Eisenhower, Kennedy, Johnson, Nixon, Ford, Carter, and Reagan. Which President scored highest?

Local History

1. Since the end of World War II, urban and suburban populations have shifted. How has your community been affected by these shifts in population?
2. Energy conservation is one of the nation's major priorities. What are the principal sources of energy in your area? What power source is used to generate your electricity? Where does it come from? What steps are being taken in your state and local community to conserve energy? What efforts has your family made to conserve energy?

Forming an Opinion

1. Both the United States and the Soviet Union have the capability of destroying one another with nuclear weapons. Furthermore, both rely on the threat of massive retaliation to ensure their security. The SALT talks are an attempt to control the number of weapons on each side. Do you think the concept of massive retaliation is a sound and effective means of maintaining peace? Are the attempts to restrict weapons a realistic approach to the problem? How can the United States ensure that these weapons will never be used? What would be the results of an all-out attack by either side?
2. When Gerald Ford pardoned Richard Nixon, he angered many Americans. The Nixon associates involved in the Watergate incident were tried and sent to jail. Do you think President Ford was right in pardoning Nixon? Should he have faced trial along with the others?

Time Line

Using the time line below, answer the following:
1. How many years were there between Stalin's death and the Cuban missile crisis?
2. What two events are related by their causes and their effects?
3. Identify the people mentioned on the time line who were assassinated. In what year did each assassination take place?
4. When was the war in Vietnam over for the United States?
5. What do you think will be the most critical events of the next 10 years?

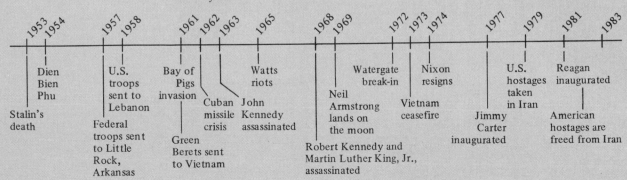

797

PRESIDENTS OF THE UNITED STATES

To the right of each portrait are the President's name,
his age on taking office, terms of office, party affiliation,
the name of the Vice-President, and the name of the President's wife.

1.
George Washington, 57
1789–1797
Federalist
John Adams
Martha Dandridge
   Washington

2.
John Adams, 61
1797–1801
Federalist
Thomas Jefferson
Abigail Smith Adams

3.
Thomas Jefferson, 57
1801–1809
Democratic-Republican
Aaron Burr
George Clinton
Martha Wayles Jefferson

4.
James Madison, 57
1809–1817
Democratic-Republican
George Clinton
Elbridge Gerry
Dolley Payne Madison

5.
James Monroe, 58
1817–1825
Democratic-Republican
Daniel D. Tompkins
Eliza Kortright Monroe

6.
John Quincy Adams, 57
1825–1829
Democratic-Republican
John C. Calhoun
Louisa Johnson Adams

7.
Andrew Jackson, 61
1829–1837
Democrat
John C. Calhoun
Martin Van Buren
Rachel Donelson Jackson

8.
Martin Van Buren, 54
1837–1841
Democrat
Richard M. Johnson
Hannah Hoes Van Buren

9.
*William Henry Harrison, 68
1841–1841
Whig
John Tyler
Anna Symmes Harrison

10.
John Tyler, 51
1841- 1845
Whig
. . . . .
Julia Gardiner Tyler

11.
James K. Polk, 49
1845–1849
Democrat
George M. Dallas
Sarah Childress Polk

12.
*Zachary Taylor, 64
1849–1850
Whig
Millard Fillmore
Margaret Smith Taylor

13.
Millard Fillmore, 50
1850–1853
Whig
. . . . .
Abigail Powers Fillmore

14.
Franklin Pierce, 48
1853–1857
Democrat
William R. King
Jane Appleton Pierce

15.
James Buchanan, 65
1857–1861
Democrat
John C. Breckinridge
(unmarried)

16.
**Abraham Lincoln, 52
1861–1865
Republican
Hannibal Hamlin
Andrew Johnson
Mary Todd Lincoln

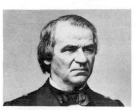

17.
Andrew Johnson, 56
1865–1869
Democrat
. . . . .
Eliza McCardle Johnson

18.
Ulysses S. Grant, 46
1869–1877
Republican
Schuyler Colfax
Henry Wilson
Julia Dent Grant

19.
Rutherford B. Hayes, 54
1877–1881
Republican
William A. Wheeler
Lucy Webb Hayes

20.
**James A. Garfield, 49
1881–1881
Republican
Chester A. Arthur
Lucretia Rudolph Garfield

21.
Chester A. Arthur, 50
1881–1885
Republican
. . . . .
Ellen Herndon Arthur

22.
Grover Cleveland, 47
1885–1889
Democrat
Thomas A. Hendricks
Frances Folsom Cleveland

23.
Benjamin Harrison, 55
1889–1893
Republican
Levi P. Morton
Caroline Scott Harrison

24.
Grover Cleveland, 55
1893–1897
Democrat
Adlai E. Stevenson
Frances Folsom Cleveland

25.
**William McKinley, 54
1897–1901
Republican
Garret A. Hobart
Theodore Roosevelt
Ida Saxton McKinley

26.
Theodore Roosevelt, 42
1901–1909
Republican
Charles W. Fairbanks
Edith Carow Roosevelt

27.
William H. Taft, 51
1909–1913
Republican
James S. Sherman
Helen Herron Taft

28.
Woodrow Wilson, 56
1913–1921
Democrat
Thomas R. Marshall
Edith Bolling Wilson

29.
*Warren G. Harding, 55
1921–1923
Republican
Calvin Coolidge
Florence Kling Harding

30.
Calvin Coolidge, 51
1923–1929
Republican
Charles G. Dawes
Grace Goodhue Coolidge

31.
Herbert C. Hoover, 54
1929–1933
Republican
Charles Curtis
Lou Henry Hoover

32.
*Franklin D. Roosevelt, 51
1933–1945
Democrat
John N. Garner
Henry A. Wallace
Harry S. Truman
Anna Eleanor Roosevelt

33.
Harry S. Truman, 60
1945–1953
Democrat
Alben Barkley
Bess Wallace Truman

34.
Dwight D. Eisenhower, 62
1953–1961
Republican
Richard M. Nixon
Mamie Doud Eisenhower

35.
**John F. Kennedy, 43
1961–1963
Democrat
Lyndon B. Johnson
Jacqueline Bouvier Kennedy

36.
Lyndon B. Johnson, 55
1963–1969
Democrat
Hubert H. Humphrey
Claudia (Ladybird) Taylor
   Johnson

37.
***Richard M. Nixon, 55
1969–1974
Republican
Spiro T. Agnew
Gerald R. Ford
Thelma (Pat) Ryan Nixon

38.
Gerald R. Ford, 61
1974–1977
Republican
Nelson A. Rockefeller
Elizabeth (Betty) Bloomer
   Ford

39.
James E. Carter, 52
1977–1981
Democrat
Walter F. Mondale
Rosalyn Smith Carter

40.
Ronald W. Reagan, 69
1981—
Republican
George Bush
Nancy Davis Reagan

*died while in office   **assassinated   ***resigned from office

THE
$\mathbf{S}$TATES

Order of entry	State	Date of entry	Area in sq. mi.*	Capital	Order of entry	State	Date of entry	Area in sq. mi.*	Capital
1	Delaware	1787	2,057	Dover	27	Florida	1845	58,560	Tallahassee
2	Pennsylvania	1787	45,333	Harrisburg	28	Texas	1845	267,339	Austin
3	New Jersey	1787	7,836	Trenton	29	Iowa	1846	56,290	Des Moines
4	Georgia	1788	58,876	Atlanta	30	Wisconsin	1848	56,154	Madison
5	Connecticut	1788	5,009	Hartford	31	California	1850	158,693	Sacramento
6	Massachusetts	1788	8,257	Boston	32	Minnesota	1858	84,068	St. Paul
7	Maryland	1788	10,577	Annapolis	33	Oregon	1859	96,981	Salem
8	South Carolina	1788	31,055	Columbia	34	Kansas	1861	82,264	Topeka
9	New Hampshire	1788	9,304	Concord	35	West Virginia	1863	24,181	Charleston
10	Virginia	1788	40,817	Richmond	36	Nevada	1864	110,540	Carson City
11	New York	1788	49,576	Albany	37	Nebraska	1867	77,227	Lincoln
12	North Carolina	1789	52,586	Raleigh	38	Colorado	1876	104,247	Denver
13	Rhode Island	1790	1,214	Providence	39	North Dakota	1889	70,665	Bismarck
14	Vermont	1791	9,609	Montpelier	40	South Dakota	1889	77,047	Pierre
15	Kentucky	1792	40,395	Frankfort	41	Montana	1889	147,138	Helena
16	Tennessee	1796	42,244	Nashville	42	Washington	1889	68,192	Olympia
17	Ohio	1803	41,222	Columbus	43	Idaho	1890	83,557	Boise
18	Louisiana	1812	48,523	Baton Rouge	44	Wyoming	1890	97,914	Cheyenne
19	Indiana	1816	36,291	Indianapolis	45	Utah	1896	84,916	Salt Lk. C.
20	Mississippi	1817	47,716	Jackson	46	Oklahoma	1907	69,919	Okla. City
21	Illinois	1818	56,400	Springfield	47	New Mex.	1912	121,666	Santa Fe
22	Alabama	1819	51,609	Montgomery	48	Arizona	1912	113,909	Phoenix
23	Maine	1820	33,215	Augusta	49	Alaska	1959	586,412	Juneau
24	Missouri	1821	69,686	Jefferson C.	50	Hawaii	1959	6,540	Honolulu
25	Arkansas	1836	63,104	Little Rock		District of Columbia	(1791)	67	
26	Michigan	1837	58,216	Lansing					

*1 square mile = 2.59 square kilometers.

AMAZING FACTS
ABOUT
OUR COUNTRY

• The Equal Rights Amendment was first drafted in 1923, almost 60 years ago.

• In 1931 Jane Addams, an American, became the first woman to receive the Nobel Peace Prize.

• In 1959 the New York City Council adopted a resolution supporting the formation of a committee to study the possibility of making New York City the 51st state.

• The largest flag in the world, the "Stars and Stripes," was flown in New York City as part of the Bicentennial celebration in 1976. It weighed 1.4 metric tonnes (1.5 tons) and measured 5,790 × 10,995 centimeters (193 × 366½ feet); each star was 330 centimeters (11 feet) in diameter!

• The entire area of Hawaii, the 50th state, was created by volcanic activity.

• The state of Virginia extends farther to the west than the state of West Virginia—152 kilometers (95 miles) to be precise!

• Texas is the only state that was governed by six different regimes—France, Spain, Mexico, the Republic of Texas, the Confederate States of America, and the United States of America.

• Only the states of Missouri and Tennessee are bordered by as many as eight states. Check a map and see!

• The state of Illinois is located both east and west of the Mississippi River.

• Do you know that one American colony was owned by another colony? The Gorges family owned Maine. In 1677 Massachusetts paid the family heirs 1,250 pounds (about 2,955 dollars) for their territory.

• Salt Lake City, Utah, far removed from the ocean, erected a monument to a sea gull! In 1848 the sudden appearance of a flock of gulls saved crops from being damaged by grasshoppers. The monument was named as a tribute to the city's fine feathered friends.

• Alaska, our largest state, has the smallest population.

• One of the least settled areas of the world is in our country: The state of Alaska has about 3.04 million hectares (7.6 million acres) of uninhabited land.

• The most popular place name in the United States is Washington. The nation's capital, one state, 29 counties, and 33 towns bear the name of our nation's first President.

• The mighty Mississippi River, which drains the entire central heartland of the United States, was once the only north-south "road" into the interior.

• The Mississippi-Missouri River ranks as the third longest river in the world—5,936 kilometers (3,710 miles).

• The third highest waterfall in the world is in the United States at Yosemite, California: 72,750 centimeters (2,425 feet).

• The second largest lake in the world is one of the Great Lakes, Lake Superior: 50,720 square kilometers (31,700 square miles) in area.

- California was originally thought to be an island. In 1535 Hernando Cortés, the Spanish conquistador, named the territory after "the island of California" described in a popular fairy tale.

- The first Thanksgiving lasted three days! Settlers asked their Indian ally Massasoit to join their harvest celebration. He did, accompanied by 90 uninvited friends.

- The original 13-star American flag first made its appearance during the early part of the American Revolution.

- "Yankee Doodle" is a well-known tune that was introduced in America by resident British troops before the beginning of the American Revolution.

- Sybil Ludington is known as the female Paul Revere. On April 26, 1777, she rode nearly twice the distance traveled by Revere to warn colonial soldiers of a British raid near Danbury, Connecticut.

- Andrew Jackson was the only United States president to have been a prisoner of war before becoming president. In 1781 he was captured by the British during the Revolutionary War.

- Only one official United States coin has never been minted. The mill was defined by Congress in 1786 as one tenth of a cent.

- The year 1816 was recorded as the "year in which there was no summer." On June 6, 1816, 25 centimeters (10 inches) of snow fell on New England.

- The U.S.S. Constitution won its nickname of Old Ironsides when British cannonballs literally bounced off its heavily-timbered sides during the War of 1812.

- In addition to being considered one of our greatest Presidents, Abraham Lincoln is distinguished for being the only chief executive to receive a patent before becoming President. Granted in 1849, it covered "an improved method of lifting vessels over shoals" by means of "adjustable buoyant chambers."

- Have you ever wondered whether skyscrapers would have been built if the modern elevator had not been invented? Henry Waterman of New York developed it in 1850.

- The first Black Vice-Presidential candidate was Frederick Douglass, who was nominated in 1872 by the National Woman Suffrage Association.

- There is a royal palace in the United States! Iolani Palace was built in Honolulu, Hawaii, in 1882 during the reign of King Kalakaua.

- Ellis Island, now part of the Statue of Liberty National Monument, was the point of entry for 20 million immigrants between 1892 and 1943.

- In order to see the sun rise in the United States at the earliest time of day, you would have to be at Mt. Katahdin, Maine.

- Do you know which state in the continental United States is the northernmost? It may surprise you to learn it is Minnesota.

- In Custer, South Dakota, an ambitious sculptor named Korczak Ziolkowski is carving a likeness of Sioux Chief Crazy Horse into the side of Thunderhead Mountain. When the sculpture of the chief astride his horse is completed, its size will be incredible: Four thousand people will be able to stand on the chief's arm!

- The walls of the Grand Canyon in Arizona record a geological period spanning more than 1 billion years.

- One of the most amazing physical phenomena of our country is in Yellowstone National Park in Wyoming: the largest geyser on the planet. It is called Old Faithful because it has erupted regularly since its discovery by westerners in 1870.

- The United States is 5,784,195 square kilometers (3,615,122 square miles) in area. It is outranked in size by the Soviet Union, Canada, and the People's Republic of China.

AMERICAN HISTORY
GAZETTEER

A gazetteer (gaz-uh-TIER) is a geographical dictionary that gives information about the location of a particular place, including the origin of the place name. Below is a gazetteer of place names important to the historical and geographical study of our country.

ALASKA (uh-LAS-kuh) • Located in extreme northwest North America; from an Aleutian word meaning "mainland," used to distinguish inhabitants of the mainland from the many nearby islanders; 49th state admitted to the United States.

BOSTON (BAWS-tun) • Capital city of Massachusetts, along the east coast of the state; named after a city in the county of Lincolnshire in England, a center of Puritan activity.

CHESAPEAKE (CHES-uh-PEEK) **Bay** • An inlet of the Atlantic Ocean, extending into Virginia and Maryland; from Algonkian word, possibly meaning "on the big bay."

CHICAGO (shuh-KAH-goe) • Second largest city in the United States, located at the southern end of Lake Michigan; from American Indian name meaning "skunk," "wild onion," or "powerful."

DENVER (DEN-ver) • Capital and largest city of Colorado, in the northcentral part of the state; named after Governor Denver of the Kansas Territory.

DETROIT (Dih-TROIT) • Largest city of Michigan, in southeastern part of the state; from French word meaning "strait," so named because it is located between Lake Erie and St. Clair Lake.

GALVESTON (GAL-vuh-stun) • A port city in southeastern Texas; named after Bernardo de Gálvez, a Spanish colonial leader and statesman.

GETTYSBURG (GET-eez-berg) • A small town in southern Pennsylvania; site of the 1863 Civil War battle; named after James Gettys, to whom the site was granted by William Penn.

HOUSTON (HYOO-stun) • A port city of Texas, located 40 kilometers (25 miles) northwest of Galveston Bay; named after Samuel Houston, Texas patriot and statesman.

KANSAS (KAN-zus) • Located in the central United States; 34th state admitted to the United States; from the old Sioux word *Kansa*, meaning "people of the south wind."

MINNESOTA (min-uh-SOE-tuh) • Located in the northern United States, bordering on Canada; 32nd state admitted to the United States; the state takes its name from the river, which took its name from the Sioux words meaning "cloudy water."

NATCHEZ (NACH-ez) • City on the Mississippi River, in southwestern Mississippi; probably from an American Indian word meaning "woods" or "timber."

OKEFENOKEE (oe-kuh-fuh-NOE-kee) **Swamp** • Mainly in southeast Georgia and partly in east Florida; makes up the bulk of the Okefenokee National Wildlife Refuge; name taken from the American Indian word meaning "land of trembling earth."

PUGET (PYOO-jet) **Sound** • An inlet of the Pacific Ocean, extending south into west Washington; named for Peter Puget, an officer in the expeditionary group led by Captain George Vancouver in 1792.

ROCHESTER (RAHCH-uh-ster) • A city in western New York State, on the Erie Canal; named by Colonel Nathaniel Rochester, Revolutionary War soldier and Maryland aristocrat, who owned much of the land.

SHENANDOAH (shen-uhn-DOE-uh) **River** • Located in northern Virginia, flows across northeast tip of West Virginia and empties into the Potomac River; from the Algonkian word meaning "spruce stream."

TAMPA (TAM-puh) • A seaport in westcentral Florida, located on northeast end of Tampa Bay; probably from Cree Indian word meaning "near it."

UTAH (YOO-taw) • Located in the westcentral United States; 45th state admitted to the United States; from the American Indian name *Ute*, or *Eutaw*, meaning "in the tops of the mountains," "high up," "the land of the sun," or "the land of plenty."

WABASH (WAW-bash) **River** • Located in Indiana and Illinois, flows across Indiana to form the Illinois-Indiana border and empties southwest into the Ohio River; from Miami Indian words *wahba* meaning "white" and *shik-ki* meaning "color bright."

YOSEMITE (yoe-SEM-ut-ee) **Valley** • Located in central California, in the Yosemite National Park; named for a local American Indian tribe whose name means "grizzly bear."

AMERICAN HISTORY
GLOSSARY

abolitionist one who strongly favors doing away with something he or she thinks is wrong—the name given to someone who opposed slavery

Agricultural Adjustment Act (1933) a law that authorized the Secretary of Agriculture to enter into agreements with farmers to limit production in the hope of raising prices

Alaska Land Act (1980) an act proposed by President Jimmy Carter in an attempt to preserve the Alaskan wilderness

Albany Plan (1754) a plan to unify the colonies in order to defeat the French in the French and Indian War; the plan was rejected by the colonists because they feared the dependence of one colony on another

Alien Enemies Act (1798) an act mainly directed at French immigrants; gave the President power to deport any alien considered suspect

aliens immigrants who have not become American citizens

Alliance for Progress (1961) a program through which the United States provided Latin America with funds to promote economic and social progress and democratic institutions

Allied Powers countries that joined in an alliance in support of one another; in World War I the major Allies were Russia, France, the British Commonwealth, Italy, and the U.S.; in World War II the major Allies were the U.S., Britain, and the Soviet Union

amendment a formal change in or an addition to a document, a bill, or a constitution

American Antislavery Society an organization founded by William Lloyd Garrison in 1833 to crusade for the abolition of slavery

American Colonization Society an organization founded in 1817; the members of this society hoped to solve the nation's racial problems by sending Blacks back to Africa

American Federation of Labor a national organization of trade unions formed in 1886 by Samuel Gompers that represented skilled workers in various trades or crafts

amnesty a general release from prosecution that the chief executive of a government issues for an offense; often granted to a large group of people

anarchy disorder and lawlessness that exists when there is no governmental authority

anthropologist one who studies human culture and its development

anti-Federalists people who in 1787–88 objected to the federal Constitution

anti-Semitism hostility toward Jews, often accompanied by social, economic, and political discrimination

appeasement a policy of making concessions to satisfy the demands made by a nation

appellate jurisdiction the right of higher courts to review cases appealed from lower courts; the right of the Supreme Court to review cases decided by lower courts

aristocracy the upper class or the privileged class of society by right of birth

assembly line a mass-production technique in which each worker has an assigned task that he or she repeats over and over

asset   an item of value that is owned

Atlanta Compromise   a summary of Booker T. Washington's philosophy that equality for Blacks must be earned; inferred from an address he made in Atlanta in 1895

atomic bomb   a devastating weapon that unleashed atomic energy; it was developed by the United States during World War II, dropped on Hiroshima and Nagasaki in 1945, and brought about the end of the war against Japan

Australian ballot   a secret ballot, developed in Australia, that lists candidates' names on a single sheet; after marking a choice in private, a voter deposits a ballot in a ballot box

autocracy   a government that lacks popular consent and shows little concern for popular rights

Axis Powers   a name derived from Mussolini's idea of a "Rome-Berlin axis."; an alliance during World War II of Germany, Italy, and Japan

B

bill of attainder   a law that declares an individual guilty of a crime without a trial

Bill of Rights   the first ten amendments to the Constitution; protects the rights of citizens

bipartisan   cooperation between Republican and Democratic parties, usually in the area of foreign affairs

Black Codes   laws established after the Civil War in the South, regulating the freed Blacks and providing for segregation in public facilities

blitzkrieg   the German word for lightning warfare; a method of attack used by the Germans in World War II, characterized by the rapid movement of highly mechanized armies in order to surprise or outflank an enemy force

blue-collar workers   wage earners whose jobs require manual labor

brinkmanship   a tactic developed by Secretary of State John Foster Dulles in 1954 that meant going to the brink or the verge of war, without getting into it, in order to achieve American objectives

***Brown* v. *Board of Education* (1954)**   a Supreme Court decision that declared that separate educational facilities were inherently unequal

Bull Moose party   a nickname for the Progressive party of which Theodore Roosevelt was the Presidential candidate in 1912

bureaucracy   a system of specialized departments in governments, corporations, institutions

capital   the wealth and property invested in business or industry for the purpose of making a profit

Carpetbaggers   northerners who either sought to take advantage of the war-torn South or to promote the cause of freed Blacks

cartel   an agreement among producers to limit production and fix prices

caucus   a closed meeting of party members in Congress

census   a national head count conducted every 10 years in the United States to ascertain the population of the states so that direct taxes and congressional representatives can be apportioned among the states

cheap money   inflated money that benefited debtors and hurt creditors

Civilian Conservation Corps (CCC)   created in 1933 (during the depression) for the purpose of teaching skills and offering employment to young Americans

Civil Rights Act of 1866 an act that guaranteed *federal* protection of certain rights for Blacks, including the right to travel and the right to assemble peaceably

Civil Rights Act of 1875 an act that prohibited discrimination by state governments or by businesses that served the public

Civil Rights Act of 1968 an act that prohibited discrimination in renting apartments and selling houses

civil service a system of selecting government employees on the basis of merit

Civil Works Administration (CWA) a federal agency established in 1933 to put jobless people on the federal payroll

Clayton Antitrust Act (1914) an act that outlawed certain activities that impaired free and fair competition

closed shop a working arrangement that is the result of an agreement between management and unions to hire only union members for particular jobs

coalition an alliance of people, parties, or countries for a specific reason or purpose

Committees of Correspondence committees created in the 1770's to help people in the various colonies stay in contact with one another

Common Sense a pamphlet published in 1776 by Thomas Paine that advocated freeing the colonies from British rule

Compromise of 1850 a series of bills designed by Henry Clay to settle disputes between North and South on the question of slavery

confederation a loose union of states in which each member retains many powers of government

Confiscation Acts (1862) acts that allowed the government to confiscate the property, including the slaves, of all persons in rebellion

against the United States

Congress of Industrial Organizations (CIO) an organization of labor unions formed in 1936 by expelled members of the A.F. of L.

Congress of Racial Equality (CORE) a civil rights organization founded in 1940 to carry out nonviolent, direct action to end discrimination against Blacks

congressional immunity legal status that prevents prosecution for statements made by representatives on the floor of Congress

containment a policy designed to hold the line against Soviet advances through economic aid and military alliances

Continental Divide the point in the Rocky Mountains that separates the rivers flowing east from the rivers flowing west

Copperheads a name given to northerners who opposed fighting the Civil War

corporate colony a colony run by a joint stock company

coup d'état the sudden overthrow of a government

customs duties taxes levied on goods imported from abroad; also known as tariffs

D

Dawes Allotment Act (1887) an act that offered 64 hectares (160 acres) of public land to every American Indian head of family and lesser amounts for orphaned children

D-Day June 6, 1944, the day the Allies invaded Normandy, France, and established a beachhead in Europe

Declaratory Act (1766) an act that reasserted the right of Parliament to pass laws for or to levy taxes on America "in all cases whatsoever"

807

de facto segregation   segregation that exists because of neighborhood residency patterns

deism   a religious viewpoint that maintains that God created a rational universe governed by natural law

demobilization   a return to a peacetime condition

democracy   a way of governing in which the people participate by voting and officeholding

depression   an economic condition marked by a decrease in trade, production, and employment

dictator   a ruler who often brutally and oppressively exercises absolute power

disfranchise   to prevent a person or a group of people from exercising the right to vote

dollar diplomacy   the name given by critics to President Taft's policy of financing a nation's debt and enforcing the Monroe Doctrine

domino theory   a post-World War II theory that predicts that after one country in Asia falls to communism, its neighbors will fall like a row of dominoes

doughface   a nickname for a northerner who sided with the South and supported slavery

Dred Scott decision (1857)   a Supreme Court ruling that declared that the federal government had no power to ban slavery in the territories

Eisenhower Doctrine (1957)   the United States' commitment to aid any nation in the Middle East that asked for help against an aggressor "controlled by international communism"

electoral college   originally a group of citizens, now party members elected by the voters of each state to cast ballots for the President and the Vice-President of the United States; each state has as many electors as it has senators and representatives in Congress

Emancipation Proclamation (1863)   a Civil War measure designed by President Lincoln to free the slaves belonging to persons in rebellion against the United States

embargo   a total cutoff of trade

emigrant   a person who departs from a country to settle elsewhere

eminent domain   the power of the state to take private property for public use

Espionage Act (1917)   an act that imposed fines and prison terms for acts of sabotage, spying, obstructing the draft, and speaking out against the sale of war bonds during World War I

estuary   an arm of the sea at the lower end of a river

exchange   a place where shares of stock, bonds, and other securities are traded

excise tax   a tax placed on goods produced within a country

executive branch   the branch of government headed by the President, who enforces the laws, commands the armed forces, and negotiates with foreign governments; includes the President's cabinet

ex-post facto law   a law that makes an act a crime after the act has been committed

extradition   the return of a person accused of a crime to the state or country where the crime was committed

F

Fair Deal the name given by President Truman to his domestic policies in 1948–49

farm tenancy the farming of land that farmers rent but do not own

fascism a political philosophy, movement, or government that exalts nation and race; based on centralized, dictatorial rule that imposes a severe economic and social order

federal a form of government that divides power between individual states and the central government

Federal Deposit Insurance Corporation (FDIC) a federal agency created in 1933 to restore faith in the banking system by insuring individual deposits in banks

Federal Emergency Relief Administration (FERA) a federal agency established in 1933 by Congress to make grants of money to the states

Federalists supporters of the Constitution who wanted the United States to have a strong central government

The Federalist Papers essays written by Alexander Hamilton, James Madison, and John Jay that explained and defended the Constitution

Federal Reserve Act of 1913 an act that left banking in private hands but provided federal control and supervision

Federal Trade Commission created in 1914 to investigate unfair business practices

filibuster an extended speech lasting hours, even days, in the Senate that is aimed at talking a bill to death

foreclosure seizure by a bank of property of a person who has failed to pay a loan

Fourteen Points Woodrow Wilson's outline for a World War I peace settlement; presented to Congress in 1918

Freedman's Bureau a federal agency set up during the Civil War to aid war refugees and freed Blacks.

free enterprise an economic system that permits private ownership of the means of production and distribution

"free soil" movement a group of people who did not want to abolish slavery, but who wanted to prevent its expansion

Fundamental Orders of Connecticut the first written constitution in America

G

Gadsden Purchase (1853) the purchase from Mexico of an area of land in Arizona south of the Gila River for 10 million dollars

gag rule a rule in the House of Representatives in effect between 1836 and 1844 that provided for the automatic tabling, without debate, of petitions on abolition

Geneva Summit Conference (1955) summit meeting of the leaders of the United States, the Soviet Union, Britain, and France at Geneva, Switzerland, to discuss the future of Germany and nuclear disarmament

ghost dance a Sioux dance ritual that was supposed to hasten the day of judgment and bring back the dead

Gold Reserve Act (1934) an act that prohibited American citizens from possessing gold or depositing it in foreign banks and stopped the exchange of paper notes for gold

Good Neighbor Policy Franklin D. Roosevelt's policy toward Latin America, which was based on the concept that "the neighbor who resolutely respects himself . . . respects the rights of others"

government bonds obligations under which a government promises to pay back money lent to it, plus interest, by a certain date

graduated income tax a tax system under which higher tax rates are levied as an individual's income increases

grandfather clause a provision of laws enacted by southern states to permit any male to register if his father or grandfather had voted in 1868—a condition only Whites met because no Blacks had been permitted to vote in 1868

grand jury an investigative panel composed of citizens that ascertains whether there is sufficient evidence to warrant an indictment

the Grange an organization of farmers founded in 1867 to educate farmers in methods of cultivation, to encourage them to form cooperative associations, and to help them fight the unfair business practices of railroads

Great Awakening a religious revival that swept across America in the early 18th century

Great Society President Lyndon Johnson's domestic program designed to end poverty and racial injustice; it included Medicare, federal aid to education, and civil rights legislation

Greenback party a political party formed in the mid-1870's by those who supported the printing of more paper money to provide farmers with cheap money to ease debt payments

greenbacks a name given to paper dollars issued by the Union during the Civil War; greenbacks were redeemable for gold at a future date

gross national product the dollar value of all goods and services produced in a nation

guerrilla warfare irregular methods of warfare, such as "hit-and-run" sabotage, pursued by small bands of fighters

headright system offering of land to encourage immigration to the colonies

holding company a corporation whose sole function is to hold, or own, the stock of one or more companies

Holocaust the extermination of about six million Jews by the Nazis in concentration camps during World War II

Homestead Act of 1862 an act that granted 64 hectares (160 acres) of government land to any head of family on condition that he or she live on it for five years

horizontal combination an organization combining companies in the same line of business in order to reduce competition

immigrant a person who comes to a country to take up permanent residence

impeachment a charge of misconduct brought against a public official; an accused person continues in office until tried and found guilty of the charge

imperial characteristic of action and policies undertaken for the purpose of establishing colonies and building an empire

impressment kidnapping of American sailors by the British before and during the War of 1812; sailors were often forced to serve on British ships

indentured servants individuals in servitude for a specified period of time

Indian Removal Act of 1830 an act that authorized the exchange of certain lands in the plains for Indian holdings in the East

810

Indian Reorganization Act (1934) an act designed to stop the practice of breaking up reservations and to restore local control by giving the American Indians a voice in their own destiny

industrial revolution the process through which a nation develops its simple rural economy into a complex technology requiring large investments in factories and machines

inflation the economic condition that exists when prices rise rapidly while purchasing power declines

initiative a draft of a bill sent to the legislature with a petition signed by a certain percentage of the voters in a state

injunction a court order designed to prevent a potential injury from occurring

intelligence (operation) the process of (the agency involved in) obtaining information about an enemy

Interstate Commerce Act (1887) an act that prohibited unjust and unreasonable rates, rebates, and other railroad abuses and created the Interstate Commerce Commission to enforce it

interstate highway system the most massive construction project in the nation's history; it was begun during the Eisenhower administration

Intolerable Acts (1774) measures enacted by Parliament to punish Massachusetts for the Boston Tea Party and to restore imperial authority in the American colonies

J

judiciary the branch of government composed of court officials who interpret the laws and resolve civil and criminal controversies

Judiciary Act of 1789 an act that created a pyramid of federal courts; it established the Supreme Court comprised of a Chief Justice and 5 associate justices and 2 circuit courts and 13 federal courts under the Supreme Court

jurisdiction authority of a court to try a case

K

kamikaze Japanese suicide pilots whose mission was to crash their planes into American ships during World War II

Kansas-Nebraska Act (1854) an act that divided the Nebraska territory into two territories—Nebraska and Kansas—and repealed a portion of the Missouri Compromise of 1820 that prohibited slavery north of the 36°30′ line

Kellogg-Briand Pact (1928) an agreement to outlaw war, which eventually was signed by 62 centuries but contained no powers for enforcement

Knights of Labor a national labor organization founded in 1869 that sought to create a universal union of workers—skilled and unskilled, Blacks and immigrants, women and men

Know-Nothing party a political party of the 1850s which was anti-Black and anti-immigrant; its members were so named because they refused to answer questions about their aims and activities

Ku Klux Klan a secret organization formed after the Civil War to terrorize both Blacks and sympathetic Whites; revived after World War I, it became a nationwide anti-Black organization

L

laissez faire a government policy of noninterference in business and industry

lame duck a rejected officeholder or a session of Congress that meets after an election but before the newly elected President and Congress are sworn into office

latitude distance, measured in degrees, north or south of the equator

League of Nations a general association of nations conceived after World War I that was formed to guarantee the political independence and the territorial integrity of great and small states alike

League of Women Voters an organization formed by Carrie Chapman Catt in 1920 to educate women about politics and to mobilize them to vote

Lend-Lease Act (1941) an act that authorized the President to lend American military equipment to Britain and other Allies

The Liberator a newspaper founded in 1831 to crusade for the abolition of slavery

Liberty party a political party of abolitionists formed in 1840; it concentrated on stamping out slavery in Washington, D.C., and in the western territories

local-color school a major literary form of the late 19th century whose practitioners described as precisely and as faithfully as possible the life of particular localities

Louisiana Purchase land bought in 1803 from Napoleon for 15 million dollars; it included an entire inland empire between the Mississippi River and the Continental Divide

Loyalists colonists who sympathized with the British during the American Revolution

lynching the killing of a suspect by a mob before he or she could be brought to trial

M

McCarthyism unethical tactics used by Senator Joseph McCarthy in the 1950's to expose people he claimed were Communists

Manifest Destiny an 1840's doctrine that proclaimed that the United States was destined to expand to the Pacific Ocean

Marbury v. *Madison* **(1803)** a Supreme Court ruling that established the principle of judicial review, making the Court the final authority in determining the constitutionality of laws

Marshall Plan (1947) a plan proposed by Secretary of State George Marshall under which 15 billion dollars in American aid was given to 17 countries from 1948 to 1952 to rebuild Western Europe, including Germany

massive retaliation a doctrine formulated by the United States in the 1950's that was designed to deter every act of Communist aggression by threatening to unleash nuclear weapons against the territory of the Soviet Union

Mayflower Compact (1620) an agreement, signed by the Pilgrims before leaving the *Mayflower,* to obey the laws they would make in the New World

Medicare a program passed by Congress in 1965 to provide national health insurance for the aged by paying hospital bills and some doctors' services

mercantilism an economic theory that maintained that profitable trade was in the national interest, and for this reason, a nation should sell more goods to its rivals than it bought from them

militia a force of citizen soldiers

minutemen a group of armed colonists at the time of the Revolution who were prepared to fight at a minute's notice

missile gap a term used in 1959 by Senate majority leader Lyndon Johnson to describe the extent to which America was behind the Soviet Union in developing missiles

monopoly a complete control over a product or a service exercised by a person, a company, or a country

Monroe Doctrine (1823) a policy stating that the United States would regard European intervention in the New World as "an unfriendly act"

mountain men trappers who lived year-round in the Rocky Mountain region

muckrakers journalists who published in the early 1900's accounts of their investigations of business fraud and political corruption

mugwumps a faction of the Republican party in the 1880's that wanted clean government and a professional civil service

National Association for the Advancement of Colored People (NAACP) an organization founded in 1909 to obtain equality for Blacks

national banks privately owned banks under the general supervision of the United States Treasury Department

National Industrial Recovery Act (NIRA) an act that created the National Recovery Administration (NRA) and the Public Works Administration (PWA) in 1933 to attack the depression

nationalism identifying with and feeling proud of one's nation

National Labor Relations Board a federal agency created in 1935 as a result of the National Labor Relations Act; it protects the right of workers to organize

National Labor Union a labor organization formed in 1866; it was the first attempt by trade organizations to forge nationwide labor unity

National Negro Congress an organization founded in 1935 to help promote the interests of Blacks in New Deal agencies

National Organization of Women (NOW) an organization formed in 1966 by Betty Friedan to promote legislation that would guarantee equality to women

National Recovery Act (NRA) an act designed to promote cooperation among industries in finding jobs for the unemployed and to raise wages; a part of the Industrial Recovery Act passed in 1933

National Security Act of 1947 an act that authorized the separation of the air force from the army and placed all the services under a new Department of Defense; created the Central Intelligence Agency and the National Security Council to advise the President on international relations and defense strategy

nativism an attitude or a policy that favors the native-born inhabitants of a country over immigrants

Nat Turner rebellion a rebellion of Black slaves led by Nat Turner in southern Virginia in 1831

Navigation Acts 17th century acts of Parliament that excluded foreign vessels from trading with the English colonies in order to strengthen the colonies' dependence on England and on one another

Neutrality Acts (1935 and 1937) laws that gave President Roosevelt power to impose an arms embargo "whenever he shall find that there exists a war"

New Deal program proposed by Franklin D. Roosevelt that was aimed at ending the depression

New Left radicals of the 1960s who were critical of American society, government, and foreign policy; a movement made up largely of college students

Nixon Doctrine (1969) a policy that maintained that Asian countries would have to take responsibility for their own defense, receiving only economic and moral support from the United States

Norris-La Guardia Anti-Injunction Act (1932) an act that outlawed yellow-dog contracts and prohibited the use of court injunctions to stop strikes

North Atlantic Treaty Organization (NATO) a formal alliance formed in 1949 among nations of Western Europe, the United States, and Canada

Northwest Ordinance of 1787 a law that provided for the creation of a government in the area north of the Ohio River

Nuclear Test Ban Treaty (1963) an agreement made with the Soviet Union that banned the atmospheric testing of nuclear bombs and provided for fallout-detection devices that could be monitored without on-site inspection

Office of Price Administration a federal agency that set ceiling prices on every important consumer good produced during World War II

Open Door Policy (1900) American policy that called for all nations to keep China's ports open to free trade and that aimed to preserve the territorial entity of China

Oregon crisis (1846) crisis created by the United States' announcement that the joint occupation with Britain of the Oregon country was over; the United States agreed to the British proposal to divide the territory between the two countries at the 49th parallel

original jurisdiction the right of the Supreme Court to try a case that has not been heard by a lower court

Panama Canal Treaty (1978) an agreement between the United States and Panama that called for the Panamanians to assume control of the canal by the year 2000, after which the United States would have the right to intervene only to ensure the canal's neutrality

partisan issue an issue associated with a particular political party

Pendleton Civil Service Act (1883) an act that created a bipartisan commission to administer competitive examinations for persons seeking government employment

Pinckney's treaty (1795) an agreement under which Spain gave up its territorial claims in the Southwest and accepted the 31st parallel as the northern boundary of Florida; it also allowed Americans to use the Mississippi and the port of New Orleans for a period of three years

platform a statement reflecting the beliefs and the policies of a political party, a candidate, or a group

Platt Amendment (1901) a declaration that asserted that the United States would exercise the right to send military forces into Cuba whenever the freedom of Cuban citizens was threatened by their own government

***Plessy* v. *Ferguson* (1896)** Supreme Court ruling that "separate but equal" accommodations on railroad cars did not deprive Blacks of their right to equal protection under the law

pocket veto a power exercised by the President when he does not sign a bill within the period specified by Congress

police action a term used by President Truman to explain the role played by United States' forces in Korea

poll tax a tax levied on individuals by southern states; proof of payment had to be presented before individuals were allowed to vote

popular sovereignty a doctrine that championed the right of the people to decide such issues as whether a territory should be free or slave

popular votes votes cast by the people of each state in a national election

Populism a political movement of the 1890's whose aim was to unite all working people in factories as well as on farms

Potsdam Conference the final wartime conference of Allied leaders in 1945 at which arrangements for dividing Germany and Austria into Soviet, British, French, and American zones were worked out

power of the purse a power by which colonial assemblies levied taxes and spent revenues

primary (also known as a nominating election) an election in which voters of each party choose their party's nominees for the general election

Progressivism a middle-class movement of the early 1900's that was directed toward making the American system work better by eliminating political corruption, monopolies, tariffs, and consumer fraud

propaganda the spreading of ideas, information, or rumors to further a particular cause or to damage an opposing cause

proprietary colony a colony authorized by a royal grant of land to a family, a person, or a group of people empowered to govern the colony in the name of the king who retained ownership

protective tariff high taxes levied on imported goods in order to protect American manufacturers from foreign competition

protectorate the guardianship of a small country by a larger country

Public Works Administration (PWA) a federal agency created by the passage of the National Industrial Recovery Act in 1933 to stimulate the construction industry

Pullman Strike a strike in 1894 by employees of the Pullman Palace Car Company that resulted in a bloody riot when federal troops intervened to suppress the work stoppage

Pure Food and Drug Act (1906) a law enacted to regulate the quality and purity of medicines and food

quorum the minimum number of members required to be present in each chamber of Congress to carry out business

realism a period in the late 19th and early 20th centuries when American art depicted life as it was

reapportionment the process of redefining the boundaries of election districts or of reallocating legislative seats among districts

rebate a refund of part of the rate charged for goods or services

recall a petition signed by voters calling for a special election in which the voters would pass judgment on an officeholder

receivership the assumption by an outside agency of responsibility for managing the finances of a bankrupt company

Reconstruction Acts four acts passed by Congress between 1867 and 1868 that established governments in the South after the Civil War; specified requirements for readmitting southern states, ordered the new governments to give the vote to Blacks, and ratified the 14th Amendment

Reconstruction Finance Corporation (1932) a federal agency created to lend money to financially troubled businesses to prevent bankruptcy

referendum an electoral device through which a legislature submits a measure directly to the voters for approval

reparations payments for war damages

republic a form of government in which the head of state is chosen by an elective process

royal colony a colony owned and ruled by a king or a queen

S

Scalawags southern Unionists who cooperated with reconstructionist governors either to serve their own interests or to revitalize the South

Second Agricultural Adjustment Act (1938) a law that contained a number of measures designed to cut back farm production; it also established the parity system

sectionalism an exaggerated concern for one's region and its problems that ignores the interests of the country as a whole

Securities and Exchange Commission (1934) a federal agency that was set up to oversee the stock exchanges and prevent dishonest practices

sedition action designed to generate opposition to or rebellion against a government

Sedition Act (1798) a law that made it a crime to criticize the President and Congress; it was intended to silence the Republican press during the Presidential election

Sedition Act (1918) a law that made it a crime to criticize the government's involvement in World War I

Selective Service Act of 1940 required that all men between the ages of 21 and 35 register for military service

Seminole War (1837—1841) violent resistance by the Seminole to a federal order relocating them to Oklahoma

Seneca Falls convention a meeting in 1848 that marked the inauguration of the women's rights movement in America

Servicemen's Readjustment Act (1944) a law, popularly called the G.I. Bill of Rights, that provided special unemployment benefits for veterans who could not find jobs; also offered low-interest loans and educational benefits

Sherman Antitrust Act (1890) a law that banned "every combination . . . or conspiracy in restraint of trade"

Sherman Silver Purchase Act (1890) an act that authorized the Treasury Department to purchase 4.5 million ounces of silver, paying for it with paper notes

Silver Democrats a segment of the Democratic party in the 1890's that favored free and unlimited coinage of silver

sit-down strikes strikes in which workers sit by their machines, sometimes for days, refusing to work and preventing others from taking over their jobs

slave codes regulations that kept the Black population in the colonies under control

Smith Act of 1940 a law that made it a

crime to advocate the overthrow of the government by force

Social Darwinism   the extension of the theory of evolution to human society; that is, hypothesizing that human society evolves through competition—those who are smarter or more hardworking survive and succeed

Socialist   an advocate of government ownership and control of the means of production and distribution

social mobility   movement from one class, rank, or status to another

Social Security Act of 1935   a law that created unemployment-insurance programs for specified periods of time and an old-age, or retirement, insurance program

sod-house frontier   land marked by the presence of sod houses built by settlers in the West

soil bank   a program adopted by the Eisenhower administration to help solve the problem of surplus crops; farmers were paid to take land out of production and "bank" it for the future in order to decrease surpluses

Sons of Liberty   citizen groups that led the agitation against Great Britain, 1765–1775

Southern Christian Leadership Conference   a civil rights organization formed in 1957 to encourage Blacks to break down the nation's racial barriers by peaceful means

sovereignty   authority of a state to govern

speculator   one who engages in risky financial deals with the hope of making a large profit

sphere of influence   a part of the world in which one country exercises strong political and economic influence

spoils system   the practice of rewarding political supporters with government jobs

Sputnik I   a Soviet satellite launched on October 4, 1957; it was the first artificial satellite that orbited Earth

Square Deal   a program proposed by Theodore Roosevelt that included compensation paid to workers for job-related injuries, regulation of child labor, protection for women workers, lower tariffs, regulation of big business, and a graduated income tax

stagflation   a word invented to describe an economic condition characterized by economic stagnation and soaring inflation

Stamp Act (1765)   an imperial tax put on goods produced in the colonies

Strategic Arms Limitations Talks (SALT)   negotiations initiated by President Nixon and Premier Brezhnev in 1969; ongoing talks between the United States and the Soviet Union to halt the nuclear arms race

subversion   the undermining of a government or its overthrow from within

suffrage   the legal right to vote

suffragist   one who advocated giving women the right to vote

summit   a meeting attended by the highest level of government officials, that is, the heads of government

"supply side" economics   an economic theory that suggests that removing government regulations and controls and enacting corporate and personal income tax cuts and other economic incentives will stimulate economic growth, create jobs, and increase government revenues

sweatshop   small factory where working conditions are poor and hours of labor are long

T

Taft-Hartley Act (1947)   a law, passed by Congress over President Truman's veto, that

prohibited various labor practices

tariffs   duties placed on goods to earn revenue or to protect domestic manufacturers from foreign competition

temperance   the curtailment or the prohibition of alcoholic beverages

tenements   dwellings for tenants (or renters) that were multifamily residences erected in rows

Tennessee Valley Authority (TVA)   a public authority that was created in 1933 as a public corporation to produce electric power cheaply and undertook flood control and other conservation projects

Third World   a term that describes the developing areas of the world that do not yet possess adequate resources to provide food, shelter, and energy for their citizens

Three-Fifths Compromise   an agreement reached during the Constitutional Convention concerning the counting of slaves for the purpose of determining the allocation of taxes and seats in Congress under the Constitution; each slave was to be counted as three fifths of a person for both purposes

Tonkin Gulf Resolution (1964)   a congressional declaration that gave President Johnson the authority to take all necessary measures to repel any armed attack against forces of the United States in Vietnam in order to prevent further aggression

totalitarianism   a system of government in which the individual serves the state, which controls all aspects of life

Townshend taxes (1767)   taxes on various colonial imports, the revenue from which was used to pay governors' salaries; the tax legislation eliminated the only power the colonists had been able to wield against the governors

trade union   an organization of skilled workers who form unions by craft or trade, rather than by factory unit

"Trail of Tears"   the long overland trek that the Cherokee was forced to take across Tennessee and Arkansas to Oklahoma in the winter of 1838–1839

Transcontinental Treaty (1819)   a treaty that resulted in the purchase of Florida from Spain by the United States; and it drew a transcontinental boundary from the Gulf of Mexico to the Pacific, delineating American and Spanish claims in the West

Treaty of Guadalupe Hidalgo (1848) a peace settlement between the United States and Mexico that required Mexico to give up all its claims to Texas and to sell the rest of the Southwest territory to the United States

Treaty of Paris (1783)   a treaty that gave Spain control of Florida and the western part of the Louisiana territory; ended the American Revolution

Treaty of Versailles   the peace settlement following World War I

Truman Doctrine (1947)   a pledge by the United States that it would assist "free peoples" to resist communism in Greece and Turkey

Un-American Activities Committee   a committee of the House of Representatives that held hearings from the 1940s to the 1960s to determine if the United States was in danger of subversion

Underground Railroad   an organized means by which slaves could escape from the South to Canada

United Nations   an international organization created to preserve peace after World War II

United States v. *Debs* **(1895)**   Supreme Court decision that upheld the use of injunctions in labor strikes

vertical combination an organization that brought all the steps of production, from raw materials to final sales, under the control of a corporation

veto the refusal to sign a bill

Vietnamization a policy that called for allowing South Vietnamese forces to do most of the fighting while the United States supplied air cover

VISTA the domestic Peace Corps, which was started in 1964; it sent young people into urban ghettos and rural shantytowns to work as teachers, medical aides, and service workers

Volstead Act (1919) prohibited the manufacture and the sale of beverages containing more than one half of one percent of alcohol

Voting Rights Act of 1965 suspended literacy tests and other tests used to discriminate against Blacks and directed the registration of Black voters by federal registrars in any state or county in the South in which the number of persons who voted in the election of 1964 was less than half the number of eligible voters

Wade-Davis Bill (1864) a bill that authorized Congress, not the President, to determine the conditions under which the Confederate states would be readmitted to the Union; President Lincoln refused to sign this bill, and it never became a law

Warsaw Pact an alliance system developed after World War II by the Soviet Union and the countries of eastern Europe

Whig party a political party formed in 1834 in opposition to the Jacksonian Democrats; it evolved into the modern-day Republican party

white-collar workers salaried employees whose jobs include clerical, professional, and other nonmanual occupations

wholesale price index a list of the prices of a nation's most important products that are tracked over a period of time; one indication of a nation's economic health

Women's Christian Temperance Union an organization founded by Frances Willard in 1879 to unite families and Protestantism in the crusade against alcohol

workers' compensation an insurance program that provides compensation for workers injured on the job

Works Progress Administration (WPA) a federal agency established in 1935 during the New Deal era that offered jobs to many people during the depression

writ of habeas corpus a court order demanding that a person who has been arrested be brought before a court so that a judge can determine whether he or she is being held lawfully

writs of assistance written court orders that enabled customs officials to conduct general searches

Yalta conference a meeting in February 1945 of allied leaders where the division of Germany and Austria were agreed upon in principle, and the Soviet Union agreed to enter the war against Japan

"yellow-dog" contract a pledge that a worker was required to sign, beginning in the 1890's, to certify that he or she had promised never to join a union as a condition of employment

INDEX

Italicized page numbers preceded by *p*, *m*, or *c* refer to a picture *(p)*, map *(m)*, or chart *(c)* on that page.

Boldface page numbers are pages on which a definition or explanation is given.

Abolitionist movement, 245, 251, 255–57, 297, 301, 319, 321; anti-slavery societies, 56–57, 109, 110; colonial, 56; emancipation, **110;** Harpers Ferry, 305–306; women and, 245. *See also* names.

Acheson, Dean, 672, *p672,* 674, 677, 678, 679, 684, 713

Adams, Abigail, 126, 791

Adams, John, 68, 104, *p118,* 126, 181, 182, 184–85, 205; Boston Massacre trial, 88; Continental Congress, 100–101, 104, 119; election, 179; presidency, 179, 180, 183; Vice-President, 175; XYZ Affair, 179–80, 181

Adams, John Quincy, *p206,* 206–208, 216, 218, 219, *m219,* 271; election, 217, *m217;* Gag Rule, 256; relationship with Jackson, 207, 218

Adams, Samuel, 88, 89, 90, 98

Adams, Sherman, 725, 729–30

Addams, Jane, 458, 462, 512, 515, 541

Advertising, 387, 392, 568, *p578*

Aeronautics: moon landing, 770, *p771;* space travel, 725–26, *p726,* 734, *p741,* 743, 770

Afghanistan: Soviet Union invasion of, 787

Africa, 10, 11, *m12–13,* 53, 189, *m189, p250,* 522, 567, 721, 734, 739, 744; ancient civilizations, 248, 249, *m249;* colonialism, 520, 554; colonization, freed slaves, 56, 57, 108; music, 576; slaves and slave trade, *m52,* 53, 249–50; World War II, 616, 635–36, *m641,* 675. *See also* Africans; countries.

Africans: colonial, 22, 42, *p55; colonial* population, 54; explorers, 52–53; indentured servants, 51–52, 53; slaves, 22, *m52,* 53, *p53, m54,* 55–58, 249–50 (*see also* Slaves and slavery; Slave trade). *See also* Africa; Blacks; Slaves and slavery.

Afro-Americans. *See* Blacks.

Aged, *c792,* 793

Agnew, Spiro T., 166, 768, 771, 779, 781–82

Agricultural Adjustment Acts: (1933), 594–95, *c595,* (1938), *c601,* 602

Agriculture, 213, 432–35, 793; banking credit, 435; barbed-wire, 427–28; barn raising, *p433;* colleges and, 460; colonial, 21, 22, 27, 39–40, *c45,* 61, *m63,* 74, 116; conservation, *see* Conservation; cultivation, 432–33; Department of, 436, 495, 594; depressions, 434–35, 589, 594–95, *p597;*

desert farming, 292, 497; droughts, 428–29, *p597;* 18th-century, *m63;* equipment and technology, 363, 432, 433–34; exports, 434; farm tenancy, *m434,* 434–35, *m588,* 602 (*see also* Farmers, tenancy); federal aid, 437; fences, 427–28, 432; grain elevator, **436;** grapes, 760; grasshoppers, 428–29; Great Britain, 213; Great Plains, 412, 423, 428–29, 432; Indians, 215, 421, 606; industry and, 213, 363, 432; Mexican Americans, *p750,* 760; migrant workers, 567, 749; New Deal, 594–95, *p595,* 597, *c601,* 602; occupations, *c404;* post-World War I, 563, 570; prices, 434, 570, 698; productivity, 434, 698; share-cropping, 353; soil bank, 698; South, 213, 214, *m246,* 246–48, 353, 435; specialization, 432–33; surpluses, 434, 497, 520, 570, 589, 595, 602, 698; transportation, 435 (*see also* Railroads); water, 428, 497. *See also* Farmers; Plantations and planters; crops; names of places; products.

Aguinaldo, Emilio, 527

Alabama, 191, 202, *m208,* 213, *m214,* 270, 308, 325, *c349,* 462, 701, 702, 754

Alamo, 226, 274–75, *m275, p275*

Alaska, 3; admission, 132; gold, 448; Land Act, 793; Russian, 208, 519

Albany, N.Y., 77, 79, *m80,* 112, *m112,* 262, *m262*

Albany Plan of Union, 79

Albemarle Sound, N.C., 39–40, *m44,* 263

Aldrich, Nelson, 494, 497, 498, 507

Alger, Horatio, 380

Algeria, 636, *m641*

Algiers, Afr., 189, *m189*

Algonkian tribe, 4, 8, 73

Alien Enemies Act, 181, 182, 184

Aliens, 181. *See also* Immigration and immigrants.

Allegheny Mountains, 79, 444

Allen, Ethan, *m101,* 101–102

Alliance for Progress, 741–43

Allied Powers, 539, 552, 553, 554, 556, 616, 682; U.S. loans, 540, 542; World War I, 539, 540, 542, *m543,* 544, 549, 550, *m550,* 551, 552, 611; World War II, 620, 621, 622, 624, 630, *m635,* 636–41, *m641,* 644, 645, 647, 653. *See also* countries; wars.

Altgeld, John P., 445, 453

Amendment(s). *See* Constitution, U.S.; subjects.

American Antislavery Society, 251, 256, 257

American Colonization Society, 255–56

American Communist party, 666, 674, 676

American Expeditionary Force (AEF), 549–50

American Federation of Labor (A. F. of L.), 405, 406–407, 508, 563, 564, 606, 607, 760; Blacks and, 406, 564; CIO merger, 729, 760; corruption, 729; craft union, 405; discrimination, 405; immigrants, 405–406; membership, 407; women, 406; World War I, 548. *See also* Strikes.

American Indians. *See* Indians, Middle America; Indians, North America; names; places.

American Samoa, 520, 526, *m527*

American Telephone and Telegraph Co., 396, 586

American Woman Suffrage Association, 459

Amnesty, 336, 784

Amnesty Proclamations: Lincoln, 336–37; Johnson, 340–41

Anarchists, 405

Anarchy, 130

Anglican, 64

Anglican Church. *See* Church of England.

Anthony, Susan B., 294, 396, 459, 513, 514

Anthropologists, 4

Anti-Ballistic Missile (ABM), 776

Antietam, battle of, *p316, m317,* 317–18, 321, 326, 327

Anti-Federalists, 136, 137, *m137,* 171, 172, 175

Anti-Saloon League, 511

Anti-Semitism, 471, **472**

Antitrust laws, 399–400, 508–509, 569, 594, 598

Antitrust legislation, 498, 598

Antiwar efforts, 758, 759, 765, *p770;* governmental, 612 (*see also* League of Nations; United Nations); public, 616–17, 758, 759, 761, 766, 771

Apache (Indians), *m416*

Appalachian Mts., *m75,* 76, 82, *m83,* 261, *m262*

Appeasement, 668, 681

Appellate jurisdiction, 151

Appomattox Court House, *m330,* 331

Arabs: Israel, 675, 722, 724, 784; nationalism, 721, 725; oil crises, 784; Palestine, 675; slavery and slave trade, 53; Soviet Union, 721, 724; World War I, 540

Arapaho, 366

Architecture, *p367,* 469; city planning, 480; colonial, 51, *p60, p64;* masonry buildings, 469; 19th-century, *p224, p381, p403,* 469, 480; skyscraper, 469; 20th-century, 690. *See also* names.

Arizona, 276, 298, *m298,* 528

Arkansas, *m214,* 270; cattle industry, 446; reconstruction, 336, *c349;* secession, *m309,* 312

Arkansas River, 14, 74, *m75, m192,* 273, 366

Armaments: bomb shelters, 727; Geneva Summit Conference, 720–21; inspection, 720–21, 731, 743; limitations, 204, 720, 743, 775, 776, 787; missiles, 726–27, 734, 736–37, 738–39, 776; naval limitation, 612; nuclear, 713–14, 720, 743, 776; race, 714, 726–27, 737, 775, 776

Armed forces, 591, 783; Bill of Rights on, 156; Blacks, 320–31, *p321, p524,* 551, *p551,* 632, 663; CCC, 631; Commander in Chief, 149; compulsory service, 784; Constitution on, 145, 156; Department of Defense, 657, 758; desegregation, 632, 663; discrimination in, 632, 663; discrimination in, national guard, 545–46, 623, 631, 632; draft, 545–46, 623, 631, 632; draft dodgers and resisters, 761, 784; G.I.'s, *p637, p653,* 653–54; Green Berets, 745; honors, *p633, p680;* intelligence, **634,** 657; Japanese Americans, 633, *p633;* Jews, 471; national guard, 145; National Security Act of 1947, 657; "new look," 713; post-World War I, 563; prisoners of war, 683; Rough Riders, 490, *p524,* 525, 528; Selective Service Act, 631; Spanish-American War, 527; spending, 713; veterans, 590–91, 653; Vietnam, *p759;* women, *p632;* World War I, 542, 545–46, 550, 551; World War II, 620, 623, 632

Armour, Phillip, 390–391

Arnold, Benedict, *m101,* 101–102, *p102,* 112, *m112,* 113, 120–21

Art, 318, *p328, p330, p338, p346, p414, p420, p426, p457,* 465–70, *p511, p519, p553, p564, p566, p653, p728;* African, *p54;* American, 468–70; American school, 81; Aztec, *m17;* cartoons, *p394, p398, p399, p484, p506, p533, p599, p637, p661;* Centennial Exposition, 396; Civil War, *p313, p328, p330, p337;* colonial, *p20;* English, *p29;* Indian (American), *p8;* museums, 468; occupations, *c404;* precolonial, *p21;* realism, *p391,* 465, *p466, p467,* 468;

820

128, 460; discrimination and segregation, 663, 699–701, 745, 747, 799; federal aid, 460, 654, 661, 740, 751; elementary, 238–39, 460; Germany, Nazi, *p615*; G.I. Bill, 653–54; graduate school, 460, 461, 568, 663; high school, 238; land grants, 366; occupations, *c404*, 695; parochial schools, 473, **740**, 755; Post-Civil War South, 334, 342–43; private, 238, 239; public, 238–39, 342, 350, 460, 654, 663; reconstruction, 334, 342–43; 350; self-taught, 64, 66; summer school, 471; teachers, 239, 242, 402; television, *p696*, 707, 749, 758, 767; tutors, 238; urban, 460; West, 366; women, 240, 241, 242–44, 402, 461. *See also* Colleges and Universities; Dewey, John; Morrill Land Grant Act; names; subjects.
Edwards, Jonathan, 69
Egypt, *m721*; Aswan Dam, 721, *m721*; Great Britain, 722; Israel, 723, 786, *p787*; Nasser, 721, 724; Suez Canal, 786; Suez crisis, 721–22, 723–24; World War II, 636
Eisenhower, Dwight D., 681, *p719*, 737, 740; Adams, 725, 729–30; arms race, 726–27; brinkmanship, 718–19; budget deficit, 698–99, 728; civil rights, 701, 703; containment, 713; defense, 698; disarmament, 720–21; Doctrine, 724–25; domino theory, 715, 716; election, 682, 683, *p683*, 722, *m722*, 724; farm surplus, 698; Formosa Straits, 718, 719, 727–28; Geneva Conference, 717; Geneva Summit Conference, 720–21; Korea, 682, 684; McCarthyism, 684–85, 690; massive retaliation, 713–14, 715, 717; "Modern Republicanism," 697, 698; N.A.T.O., 682; Paris Summit, 731; President, 690, 709, 724; presidential candidate, 681, 682, 683, *p683*; stroke, 725, 730; U-2 incident, 731; World War II, 636, 637, 638, 640, 641, 690
Elections, congressional: (1810), 198; (1866), *p344*, 344–45, (1894), 445–46, (1910), 498, (1918), 557–58, (1946), 656, (1958), 730
Elections, presidential, 148–49, 371; (1792), 175–76, (1796), 158, 179, (1800), 158, 183–84, (1804), 185, (1808), 198, (1824), 217, *m217*, (1828), 218–19, *m219*, (1832), 220, 223, (1836), 226, (1840), 227, *m227*, (1848), 292, (1856), 300, 301–302, (1860), 306, 307–308, *m308*, (1864), 338–39, (1868), *m348*, 348–49, (1872), 375, (1876), 375–76, *m376*, (1880), 376–77, *m377*, (1884), 378, *m378*, (1888), 379, (1892), 441, 442, *m442*, (1896), 448, *m448*, 523, (1904), 493–94, *m494*, (1912), 499, 505, *m505*, (1916), 543, 544, *m544*, (1920), 559,

567, *m567*, (1924), *m569*, 569, (1928), *m570*, 570–71, (1932), 591, *m591*, (1936), 600, (1940), 623, *m623*, (1944), 644, (1948), *p658*, 658–59, *m659*, 660, (1952), 682, *p683*, 683, (1956), 722, *m722*, 724, (1960), *m735*, 735–36, (1964), 750–51, (1968), 767–68, *m768*, (1972), *m780*, 780–81, (1976), 785, *m785*, (1980), 789, *m789*
Electoral college. *See* Electors and electoral system.
Electors and electoral system, 139, 148–49, 160, 161–62, 165, 217, *m217*, *m219*, 226, 487; Amendment (Twelfth), 148, 158–59; disputed elections, 376; ties, 158, 188
Electricity, 66, *p67*, 386–87, 569, 576, 577–78, 661; hydro-electricity, 721; New Deal programs, 597
Eliot, Charles W., 460
Elizabeth I, 18, 19, 28, *p28*, 29–30
Elliott, Robert Brown, 350, 355, *p355*
Ely, Richard T., 483, 489
Emancipation, 110, 256
Emancipation Proclamation, 321–22. *See also* Slaves and slavery.
Embargo Act, 197–98, *p198*
Emergency Banking Relief Act, *c595*
Emergency Quota Act, 574
Emerson, Ralph Waldo, 235–36, 238, 240
Emigrants, 32, 574
Employment, *c404*, 662–63; service, 694–95; women, 61, 268, 392, *p396*, *c404*, 459, 548, 572, 695, *c695*
Energy shortage, 784, 785; Carter and, 786
England. *See* Great Britain.
English Channel, 539, 620, 638
Entertainment. *See* Recreation.
Environment, 793; energy problems, 784, 705, 786; pollution, 756, 793; population trends, 792, *c792*, 793; resources, 786
Era of Good Feelings, 212, *c308*
Ericson, Leif, 9, 18
Erie Canal, 235, *m262*, *p263*, 263–64, 368
Erie Ring, 368–69, *p368*
Espionage Act, 549, 566
Estuary, 21
Europe, 176, 177, 196; age of exploration, 9–11, *m12–13*, 14, *m15*, 18–20; Civil War, 315, 323, 324; crusades, 10; depressions, 589, 612; exports to, 434; immigrants, *c574*, (*see also* Immigration); imperialism, 520, 526, 529–30; Latin America, 533–34; Marshall Plan, 670; peace movement, 541; post–World War I, *m557*; post–World War II, *m645*, 670; Reformation, 27–29; religious wars, 27; Renaissance, 10, 18, 31; Seven Years' War, *c77*; slaves and slave trade, 249; Spain's decline, 17–18; trade with Indians, 20, 31, 73; trade

with U.S., 611–12; Treaty of Versailles, 553–54, 555, 556; War of the Austrian Succession, *c77*; War of the League of Augsburg, *c77*; War of the Spanish Succession, *c77*; wars for empire, 77–82, 552; World War I, 538, 539–40, 542–43, *m543*, 549–50; World War II, 620, *m622*, 636, 638, *m641*, *m645*, 646. *See also* Monroe Doctrine; countries; subjects.
Evangelical churches, 69
Evers, Medgar, 747
Exchange, 369
Executive branch, 130, 135, 147–50, 171. *See also* President; Vice-President.
Expansionism, 520–21; Caribbean, 519–20, 530–32, *m531*; Far East, 518–19
Exploration, age of: African, 10, 11, 52–53; English, *m15*, 18–20, 21; French, *m15*, 73–76, *m75*; medieval trade routes, 9, 10; Netherlands, *m15*; Norse, 9, *m12–13*; Portuguese, 10–11, *m12–13*; relation with American Indians, 11, 14, 16; Spanish, 11, *m12–13*, 14, *m15*, 16. *See also* names; places.

Factory system, 267–68, 269, 388, 396–97, 401, 509, 520, 562, 577, 694; women, 268, *p269*. *See also* Industries and industrialization.
Fair Deal, 654, 660–63.
Fair Employment Practices Act, 654, 662, 663
Fair Labor Standards Act, *c601*, 601
Fanaticism, 615, 616
Far East, 518–19, *m527*, 674, 751; colonies, German, 554; expansionism, 518–19; World War II, *m635*. *See also* countries; subjects.
Farmers, 131, 212, 235, *p440*, 509, 698; agricultural revolution, 432–35; Alliances, 436, 111; banking credit, 435; Blacks, *p429*, 449, 461; cattle industry, 427; cooperative, 435, 436; desert, 292; education, 366, 432, 436; frontier, 366, 412, 428–29; homesteaders, 365–66, 420–21, 428–29, *p429*; Indians, 4, 421; legislation, 130, 436, 437, 509; lifestyle, 432, *p433*, *p439*, *p440*; loans, government, 435, 442, 509, 602; mail order business, 392; mechanization, 433–34; migrants, 427, 767, 769; migration to cities, 456; money problems, 434–35, 437–38; New Deal, 594–95, *c595*, 597, 602; 1920's, 570; organizations, 436, 441; parity, 602; plains, 412, 428–29; population, 434; post–Civil War, 363; productivity, 434, 698; protest, 436–39, 440; railroad, 435, 436, 437; revolt, 379; security, **435;** sodhouse, **383,** 428–29; technology, 363, 428–29, 433–34; tenancy, *m434*,

434–35, 461, *m588*, 602; Whiskey Rebellion, 177; women, 61, 432; World War I, 546, 563; World War II, 631. *See also* Agriculture; Railroad(s).
Fascism, 616, 617
Federal, 131
Federal Bureau of Investigation (F.B.I.), 677; Watergate, 781
Federal Convention, 135, *p135*; arguments, pro and con (primary sources), 135, 136; bill of rights rejected, 136; commerce compromise, 146; delegates, 134, 135, 136; federal government, 135–36; Great Compromise, 135; representation, 135–36; separation of powers, 135; slave representation, 135–36; slave trade, 146; slavery, 138; Virginia Plan, 135
Federal Deposit Insurance Corporation (FDIC), 593, *c595*
Federal Emergency Relief Administration, 593, *c595*
Federal Farm Board, 559
Federal Farm Loan Act, 509
Federal Housing Administration (FHA), *c595*
Federal Power Commission, 569
Federal Reserve System, 365, *p506*, 507
Federal Securities Act, *c595*
Federal system, 9
Federal Trade Commission, 504, 507–508, 569
"Federalist Papers, The," 136
Federalists, 136, 137, 172, 175, 176, 179, 180, 181, 182, 184–85, 195, 198, 199, 205; New England, 191, 197; party split, 182–83
Federal Government. *See* Government, U.S.; subjects.
Ferdinand, Franz, 538, *p539*
Field, Cyrus W., *c390*, 395
Filibuster, 663, 703
Fillmore, Millard, 293
Finney, Charles Grandison, 236–38
Fireside Chats, 592, 593, *p593*, 595, 623
Fishing: colonial, 43, *m63*
Fisk, Jim, 368–69, 370, 372
Florida, 11, 14, 19, 78, 81, 118, *m132*, 178–79, *m180*, *m192*, *m214*, 272, *m298*, *c349*, 376; Everglades, 273; purchase of, 207; West Florida, 191, *m208*
Food, 16, 572; Administration (World War I), 546; beef roundup, 427; colonial, 20, 21, 22, 90; exports, 434; Indians, 4, *c7*, 8, 16, 413, 414, 417; industry, 390–91; preservation of, 260–61, *c390*, 390–91; purity laws, *p484*, 495, *c601*; regulating, 494–95; wartime supplies, 424–26; World War I, 546, *p546*; World War II, 631, 632. *See also* Agriculture; names.
Force Acts, 221, 354·
Ford, Gerald, 789; appointment to Vice-President, 166, 782; background, 783; and Congress, 784;

Humphrey, Hubert, 660, 735, 741, 767, 768, *m768*
Hundred Days, 593, 598
Hungary, 556, *m557, m641, m645,* 724, 761; uprising, 722–23, *p723*
Huntington, Collis P., 367, 422
Hurons, 4, 73
Hutchinson, Anne, 36
Hutchinson, Thomas, 86, 88, 90
Hydrogen bomb, 713, 714

Iceland, 4, 9, 11, 624
Idaho, 413, 513
Illinois, *m199,* 266, 270, 271, 302, 304, 448; admitted, 132, *m208,* 213, *m214;* agriculture, 433; Mormons, 291, 292
Immigration and immigrants, 32, 235, 263, 266, *p267,* 448, 452–56, *m453, p454, p455,* 565, *c574;* advertising, 429; Alien Enemies Act, 181, 182, 184; colonial, 22, 41–42, 62; Constitution, 144; Contract Labor Law, 456; discrimination, 405, 406, 454–55, 456, 473, 566, 573, 574, 661, 756; Displaced Persons Act (1950), 661; Emergency Quota Act, 574; industry, 268, 454; labor unions, 269, 403, 405–406, 472, *p472;* melting pot, 473, 574; nationalities, 266, 452–53, *m453;* Naturalization Act, 181–82, 184; number, 452, *m453, c574;* quota system, 574; railroad, 422, *p422;* restrictions, 455, 528, 567, 573–74; settlement, frontier, 428, 429; settlement houses, 458, *p459;* steamship, 266–67; sweatshop, 453, **454;** Tweed Ring, 373–74, *p374,* 375. *See also* ethnic groups; names of countries.
Impeachment, 140, 141, 150, 151, **347;** Johnson, 141, 347; Nixon, 141, 782. *See also* House of Representatives; Senate.
Imperial, 520
Imperialism, 518–21, *m527,* 529–30. *See also* Expansionism; countries.
Imports: customs house, 376; duty, 170–71; taxed, 83, 146, 147
Impressment, 197; Civil War, 323
Inca (Indians), *m6*
Inchon, Korea, 679, *m679*
Income tax, 441, 503, 506, 631; amendment (Sixteenth), 161, 506
Indentured servants, 51–52, 53
Independence Hall, *p135*
India, 10, 11, 18, 717; World War II, 625, 634, *m635,* 636
Indian Affairs, Bureau of, 373
Indian Ocean, 10, *m635,* 636
Indian Reorganization Act, 606
Indiana, 563; admitted, 132, *m208,* 213, *m214;* Blacks, 293; Canals, 265; Tecumseh, 201; Territory, *m199,* 201
Indians, Middle America, 4, *m6;* art, *m17;* cultural region, 4, *c7;* naming of, 11; occupation, *c7;* relation with explorers, 14

Indians, North America, 4, *m6, p415;* Agency, 418; Algonkian, 4, 8, 73; allotment scheme, 418; "Americanization," 605; British and, 20, 113, 201; buffalo and, 366, 413–14, *p414;* cattle industry, 418, 423; Christianity, 277; choosing leaders, 9; citizenship, 160, 421; city dwellers, 4, *c7,* 8; colonial relations with, 2–3, 19, 20, 22, 26, 31, 35–37, 41, *p42; coureurs de bois* and, 74; culture, 4–5, 8–9, 270, 413, 418, 606; cultural region, *m6, c7;* Dawes Act, 418–20, 421, 605; desert farming, 292; discrimination, 160, 287; Dutch and, 9, 73; education, 606; explorers and, 11, 14, 16, 73–74; farmers, 4, 5, *c7,* 8, 215, 421; food gatherers, *c7;* French and, 9, 73–76, 78; French and Indian War, *c77, m80,* 80–81; frontier conflicts and wars, 35–37, 43–46, 82, *m83,* 200–201, 366, 413–15, 418 (*see also* names of places; tribes); fur trade, 31, 39, 41, 44, 73; Hiawatha, 8–9; hunters, 4, 5, *c7, p414;* Indian Affairs, Bureau of, 373; King William's War, *c77;* land claims and conflicts, 35–37, 43–46, 76, 82, *m83, m119,* 200–201, 213, 215–16, 270–73, 278, 366, *m416;* lands ceded to U.S., 200–201, *m270,* 415, 416, 420; lands, opened to settlers, 366; language, 4, 5, 8, 215; Lewis and Clark Expedition, 192–93; migration, 4, *m6;* mining, 413, 415–16; mound builders, 5; Muskogean, 4; New Deal, 605–606; nomadic, 8; Northwest Ordinance, 132; occupation, *c7;* oral tradition, 4; Pequot War, 35–37; Plains, 14, 273, 413–14, 423; political systems, 9; Pontiac's Conspiracy, 82, *m83;* poverty, 606; pride, 200–201; Proclamation of 1763, 82–83; railroads, 366, *p422;* relations with Whites, 200–201, 213, 215, 270, 366, 416, 418; religion, 4, 5, 8, 74, 201, 416–18; removal, *m270,* 270, *p271,* 271–73, *m416;* Removal Act of 1830, 271, *p271;* Reorganization Act, 616; reservations, *m119, m270,* 271, 366, 413, 414, 415, *m416,* 417, 418, 420, 606; Revolution, American, 113; slavery and slave trade, 14, 53; Spanish and, 14; suffrage, 185, 420, 421; trade with Europeans, 20, 31, 39, 73; treaties, 200; Treaty of Guadalupe Hidalgo, 284–85; tribes, major, *m6, m416;* War of 1812, 200–204; weapons, 4, *c7;* women, 8–9; World War I, 421, 632; World War II, 273. *See also* names.
Indicting, 195
Indochina, *m527;* Japan, 610, 625, 626
Indochina (French), 529, *m715,* 715–17
Indonesia, 715, *m715,* 717, *m718*
Industrial Revolution, 387–93,

402, 432. *See also* Industry; inventors; names; subjects.
Industry and industrialization, 267, 312, 363–66, 386–93, *m395,* 434, 460, 520, 572, 576–79; advertising, 387, 392, 568, *p578,* 693; assembly line, 363, 389–90, 391, *p397,* 576, 577, 631; automation, 694; business organization, 393–400 (*see also* forms); competition, 397, 398, 399, 400; chemical, 577; depressions, *see* Depressions; development, *m395;* energy source, 388 (*see also* forms); factory system, *see* Factory system; food and drug, 390–91; government regulation, 483; growth (horizontal), 397, 400, (vertical), 396–97, 400; immigrants, 268, 454; labor, *see* Labor unions; mass market, 391–92; 393; mass production, 363, 389–90, 499, 577, 578, 606; meat processing, 390–91, 495; New Deal, 594, *c595,* 597, 606–607; new materials (aluminum), 577, (fiberglass), 577, (plastic), 577, (nylon), 577; 19th-century, 267, 362, 387–93; occupations, *c404;* post-Civil War, 335, 353, 362, 363–66; post-World War I, 563–64, *p564,* 565, 568, 569; post-World War II, 654–55, 694, 695; power-driven machines, 268, 388, 401; price wars, 394, 400; profits, 393, 397, protective tariffs, 205, 363 (*see also* Tariffs); raw materials, 397; revolutions, industrial, 268, 387–93, 567–79; South, 353, technological revolution, 389–90; transportation and, 232, *c390,* 395, 435; trusts, *see* Trusts; urbanization, 456; vertical combination, 396–97, 400; wholesale price index, **397;** World War I, 546, 547–48; World War II, 624, 625, 626, 631. *See also* Business; Corporation(s); Holding companies; Industrial Revolution; Trusts; areas; industries; subjects.
Inflation, 31, *c654,* 654–55, 784, 785, 789
Inflationists, 438
Initiative, 487, 503
Injunction, 445, 508, 564, 655
Insurance programs, 600, *c601,* 661, 740, 755
Intelligence (operation), 634, 657
Intercontinental ballistic missile (ICBM), 726, 737, 776
Interior Department, 376, 568
Internal Revenue Bureau, 373, 779
International Ladies' Garment Workers Union, 406, 472
International Longshoremen's Union (ILU), 406, 472
International Workers of the World (Wobblies), 566
Internationalism, 647, 667–68, 669
Interstate commerce, 144, 146, 206, 437, 509, 601, 747; Act,

436–37; Commission, 437, 494, 569, 745
Interstate highway, 697–98, *m697,* 756
Intolerable Acts (1774), 90–91
Inventors and inventions, 144, 237, 246, 268, 278, 282, 363, 386–87, 388, *c390, p393,* 396, 432, 469, 577
Iowa, 270, 271, 298, 448; agriculture, 433, *p730*
Iran, 644, 717; hostage crisis, 788–89
Iraq, 717, 718
Irish immigrants, 42, 266, *p267,* 319, *p422,* 423, 452, *c453,* 540; Catholics, 378, 473. *See also* names.
Iron and iron industry, *m63,* 353, 388; development, *m395;* productions, *c388*
"Iron curtain," 652, 653, 672
Iroquois, *p8,* 8–9, 74, 113, 235; Confederation (Five Nations/Six Nations), 79; federal system (Five/Six Nations), 9; League (Five Nations), 73
Isabella (1474–1504), 11, 17
Islam. *See* Muslim; Religion.
Isolationism, 616, 618, 619, 647, 667–68, 669
Israel, 675, 717, 720, *m721;* Arabs, 675, 722, 784; Egypt, 722, 723, 786, *p787;* Sinai Peninsula, 723, 786
Isthmus of Panama, 21, 53, 286, 530–31, *m531,* 532
Italy, 9, 470, 672; Badoglio, 638; explorers, 11; immigrants, 453, *c453, p472,* 566, 574; Kellogg–Briand Pact, 612; League of Nations, 556; Mussolini and Fascism, 615–16; navy, 612; Rome-Berlin axis, 616; World War I, 539, *m543,* 552, *m557;* World War II, 620, *m622,* 626, 635, 637, 638, *m641, m645*
Iwo Jima, 643, *p643*

Jackson, Andrew, 216, 218, *p220, p225,* 226, 227, 235, 266, 275; and Adams, John Q., 207, 217, *m217;* democracy, 217, 219, 222–25; duel with Tom Benton, 227; Indian policies, 271, 272; "kitchen cabinet," 222–23; nullification issue, 219–20, 221; Presidency, 218–19, *m219,* 221; spoils system, 222; War of 1812, 200, 202
Jackson, Thomas (Stonewall), 316, *m317,* 327, *p328*
James I (1603–1625), 19–20, 22–23, 30, 31, 42
James River, 20, 21, 316, 319, 330, *m330*
James II (Duke of York, 1685–1688), 38–39, 41, 46, 66
Jamestown, Va., 2, *m19,* 19–20, 21, 22, 31, *m44, c45,* 46, 53
Japan, *m527;* airforce, 618, 619, 634, 643; Axis powers, 616, 626; China, 529–30, 612–13, 618, 777; discrimination, 633; Earhart, Amelia, 617; Gentlemen's Agreement, 574; Hiroshima, 649;

Picture Credits

Sources have been abbreviated as follows:
BASI—Collection of Business Americana, Smithsonian Institution; **Bettmann**—The Bettmann Archive; **CP**—Culver Pictures; **LC**—Library of Congress; **N-YHS**—New York Historical Society; **NYPL**—New York Public Library; **WW**—Wide World Photos

Cover: Clockwise from top left: Magnum Photos; Culver Pictures; Detail from Political Banner, 1839, New York State Historical Association; Owen Franken/Sygma; Culver Pictures; Detail from Pilgrims going to Church, New-York Historical Society; Detail from Unveiling of the Statue of Liberty, Museum of the City of New York; U.S. Signal Corps; HRW Photo by Russell Dian/New School for Social Research. Center: HRW Photo by Russell Dian/National Archives.

Table of Contents: ivT—NYPL, Picture Collection; ivBR—National Gallery of Canada; ivBL—Detail from Shaker Women Packing Medicines by Benson J. Lossing, Collection of the Henry E. Huntington Library. vT—Anne S. K. Brown Military Collection. vB—Detail from Congress Voting Independence by Robert Edge Pine, Historical Society of Pennsylvania. viT—Bettmann. viB—NYPL, Prints Division. vii—Detail from Genius of Freedom, 1874, Chicago Historical Society. viiiT—Photo Collection, Suzzallo Library, University of Washington. viiiB—LC. ixT—CP. ixB—CP. xT—Bettmann. xB—Detail from A GI's Homecoming by Norman Rockwell, Curtis Publishing Company © Norman Rockwell. xiT—Associated Press. xiB—Bonnie Breer/Photo Researchers. xii—WW.

Unit 1: 1—Eric Kroll, Taurus Photos. 5—Monkmeyer Press Photos. 8—Museum of the American Indian. 11—NYPL, Picture Collection. 17—American Museum of Natural History, New York. 20—LC. 21—British Museum. 23—Collection of Mr. and Mrs. Paul Mellon. 27—British Museum Library. 28—Woburn Abbey Collection, by kind permission of His Grace, the Duke of Bedford. 29—The Granger Collection. 30—Woolaroc Museum, Bartlesville, Oklahoma. 32—John Hancock Mutual Life Insurance Company. 34—Worcester Art Museum, Worcester, Massachusetts. 36—CP. 39—R. McGill Mackall. 40—LC. 41—NYPL, Picture Collection. 42—Thomas Gilcrease Institute of American History and Art, Tulsa, Oklahoma. 53—CP. 54—Museum of Primitive Art, New York. 55—National Maritime Museum, Greenwich, England. 56—Mother Bethel AME Church, Philadelphia, Pennsylvania. 57—Maryland Historical Society. 58—Historical Collection of the Insurance Company of North America. 59—N-YHS. 60—Library Company of Philadelphia. 61—Collection of the Henry E. Huntington Library, San Marino, California. 62—Shelburne Museum, Shelburne, Vermont. 64—Panaggio, Newport, Rhode Island. 67—Library Company of Philadelphia. 73—Le Vieux Lachine et le Massacre du 5 Août, 1689, by Désiré Girouard, 1889; NYPL. 76—National Gallery of Art. 78—CP. 79—NYPL. 81—National Gallery of Canada, Ottawa. 84—Worshipful Company of Fishmongers, Fleming. 85—NYPL, Rare Book Division. 86—LC. 87—Bettmann. 89—Bettmann.

Unit 2: 97—Eric Sanford. 100—Yale University Art Gallery. 102—Pictorial Field Book of the Revolution by Benson J. Lossing, 1851. 103 T—NYPL, Picture Collection. 103 B—Lexington Historical Society, Lexington, Massachusetts. 104—LC. 105—Historical Society of Pennsylvania. 109—Anne S. K. Brown Military Collection. 110—Metropolitan Museum of Art, Gift of John Stuart Kennedy, 1897. 113—National Gallery of Canada, Ottawa. 114—CP. 115—National Archives. 118—Henry Francis duPont Winterthur Museum, Wilmington, Delaware. 120—NYPL, Picture Collection. 125—M. E. Warren/Uniphoto. 126—CP. 127—Museum of Fine Arts, Boston. 129—Princeton University Library. 134—N-YHS. 135—Independence National Historic Park Collection, Philadelphia. 136—White House Historical Association. 152—N-YHS. 171—Janice E. Chabas. 172—NYPL, Picture Collection. 174—Maryland Historical Society. 175—Chase Manhattan Numismatic Collection. 176—Metropolitan Museum of Art, Gift of Edgar Williams and Bernice Chrysler Garbisch, 1963. 178—CP. 179—Brooklyn Museum. 183—LC. 185—White House Historical Association. 190—Architect of the Capitol's Office, Washington, D.C. 193—Detail from Lewis and Clark at Three Forks by Charles Russell, Montana Historical Society. 195—N-YHS. 198—N-YHS. 200—CP. 203—NYPL, Prints Division. 204—Pictorial History of the Negro in America by Langston Hughes and Milton Meltzer, 1968. Used by permission of Crown Publishers, Inc. 206—Museum of Fine Arts, Boston. 215—CP. 216—J. B. Speed Art Museum, Louisville, Kentucky. 220—CP. 221—Dartmouth College. 224—NYPL, Prints Division. 225—LC.

Unit 3: 233—Courtesy of The Cincinnati Historical Society. 236—Brooklyn Museum, lent by Mr. and Mrs. Alvin Mann. 238—LC. 241—CP. 242—Courtesy of American Heritage Publishing Company, Inc. 244—The Citizens and Southern National Bank, Macon, Georgia. 250—British Museum. 215—CP. 252—Bettmann. 253—N-YHS. 254—The Granger Collection. 256—Newberry Library, Chicago, Illinois. 263—N-YHS. 264—NYPL, Picture Collection. 267—CP. 269—NYPL, Prints Division. 271—Woolaroc Museum, Bartlesville, Oklahoma. 272—National Portrait Gallery, Smithsonian Institution, Washington, D.C.; lent by The National Museum of American Art. 274—NYPL. 275—Courtesy of Mrs. Bill Arthur and Mrs. Al Warner. 279—Metropolitan Museum of Art, Rogers Fund. 284—CP. 285—San Antonio Museum Association. 286—California State Library. 291—Church of Jesus Christ of Latter-Day Saints. 293—LC. 296—CP. 297—LC. 300—CP. 303—Brooklyn Museum, Gift of Miss Gwendolyn O. L. Conkling. 307—Chicago Historical Society. 313—Seventh Regiment Fund, Inc., New York. 314—LC. 316—LC. 319—N-YHS. 321—Historical Society of Pennsylvania. 322—LC. 323—LC. 324—CP. 325 L—Collection of Curtis Carroll Davis, Baltimore, Maryland. 325 R—The Granger Collection. 328—Collection of Mr. and Mrs. Charles J. Sinnott; Courtesy of Life. 330—Metropolitan Museum of Art, Gift of Mrs. Frank B. Porter. 337—LC. 338—White House Historical Association. 339—Harper's Weekly, April 29, 1865. 341—State Historical Society of Missouri. 343—CP. 344—NYPL, Picture Collection. 346—Harper's Weekly, November 16, 1867. 348 T—BASI. 352—The Granger Collection. 355—Detail from Genius of Freedom, 1874, Chicago Historical Society.

Unit 4: 361—LC. 364—Chicago Historical Society. 365—BASI. 367—CP. 370—CP. 374—Harper's Weekly, August 19, 1871. 378—Harper's Weekly, July 8, 1881. 381—Photo © Arnold Newman. 389—Bethlehem Steel Corporation, Bethlehem, Pennsylvania. 391—Museum of the City of New York. 392—Sears & Roebuck Catalog, 1897. 393—Bettmann. 394—N-YHS. 396—American Telephone and Telegraph Company. 397—LC. 398—The Verdict, January 22, 1900. 399—CP. 403—Bettmann. 406—CP. 411—Northern Pacific Railway Company. 414—National Gallery of Art. 415—Taft Museum, Cincinnati, Ohio. 417—Courtesy of the Buffalo Bill Historical Center, Cody, Wyoming. 420—United States Department of the Interior. 422—Photography Collection, Suzzallo Library, University of Washington, Seattle. 425—CP. 426—Mckay Collection, Montana Historical Society. 429—Nebraska State Historical Society. 433—The Massillon Museum, Massillon, Ohio. 437—LC. 439—CP. 440—CP. 443—Chicago Historical Society. 444—The Granger Collection. 447—Bettmann. 454—LC. 455—Bancroft Library, University of California. 457—Brooklyn Museum, Dick S. Ramsey Fund. 459—Henry Street Settlement, Urban Life Center. 461—Department of Manuscripts and University Archives, Cornell University. 463—NAACP. 464—NYPL, Schomburg Collection. 466 T—Whitney Museum of American Art. 466 B—Addison Gallery of American Art, Phillips Academy, Andover, Massachusetts. 467 TL—Art Institute of Chicago. 467 TR—Whitney Museum of American Art. 467 BL—Museum of Art, Carnegie Institute, Pittsburgh; Patrons Art Fund. 467 BR—Sandak. 472—Brown Brothers.

Unit 5: 481—Chicago Historical Society. 484—Bettmann. 485—Pelletier Library, Allegheny College. 488—State Historical Society of Wisconsin. 490—The Verdict, January 22, 1900. 493—N-YHS. 496—American Museum of Natural History. 498—Smithsonian Institution. 504—UPI. 506—CP. 508 Both—BASI. 510—The Granger Collection. 511—Smithsonian Institution. 512—CP. 514—NYPL, Picture Collection. 515 Both—Courtesy of Anne Tully Ruderman. 519—From The Japan Expedition 1852–1854, The Personal Journal of Commodore Matthew C. Perry. Edited by Roger Pineau. © Smithsonian Institution. 512—CP. 524—LC. 533—CP. 539—CP. 541—CP. 546—BASI. 548—National Archives. 550—United States Air Force Art Collection. 551—National Archives. 553—Whitney Museum of American Art. 554—Imperial War Museum, London. 559—Bettmann. 564—New School for Social Research; HRW Photo by Russell Dian. 565—Brown Brothers. 566—Courtesy of the Kennedy Galleries, Inc. 573 L—CP. 573 R—Collection of Louise Miller Smith, courtesy of American Heritage Publishing Company, Inc. 575—San Diego Museum of Art. 576—Frank Driggs. 577—BASI.

Unit 6: 585—Ewing Galloway. 590—Bettmann. 593—Philadelphia Inquirer, courtesy of American Heritage Publishing Company, Inc. 596—LC. 597—LC. 599—Esquire, 1938. 605—UPI. 613—Brown Brothers. 615—LC. 617—CP. 618—Hugo Jaeger/Life Magazine © Time, Inc. 621—Brown Brothers. 627—United States Navy Photo. 632—National Archives. 633—United States Army Photo. 637 Both—Bill Mauldin's Army, 1951. 639—United States Coast Guard Photo. 640—WW. 643—Lawrence Hedges/Uniphoto. 648 Both—Reprinted from The Book of Alfred Kantor by Alfred Kantor and John Wykert. 653—Curtis Publishing Company, © Norman Rockwell. 658—UPI. 661—The Herblock Book, 1952; Beacon Press. 662—UPI. 669—United States Army Photo. 671—Walter Sanders/Life Magazine © Time Inc. 672—United States Army Photo. 673—William Sewall. 675—Brown Brothers. 676—WW. 680—UPI. 683—Ralph Morse/Life Magazine © Time, Inc. 684—Robert Phillips/Black Star.

Unit 7: 691—P. Schmitt/Alpha Photos. 696—Bettmann. 700—WW. 702—UPI. 704 T—Courtesy of Allyn P. Robinson, owner. 704 B—The Museum of Modern Art, New York. 706—Messerschmidt/Alpha Photos. 708—WW. 714—UPI. 716—Robert Capa/Magnum Photos, Inc. 719—WW. 723—UPI. 726—© The New York Times Company, 1957. 728—Collection of Mr. and Mrs. Lewis Garlick. 730—Bob Henriques/Magnum Photos, Inc. 736—John F. Kennedy Library. 738—UPI. 741—Ralph Morse/Life Magazine © Time, Inc. 742—Paul Conklin, Peace Corps. 746—Associated Press. 748—Marvin E. Newman. 750—Marcia Keegan Photography. 756—WW. 759—Sygma. 760—WW. 764 T—Hirshhorn Museum, courtesy Scala. 764 BL—Leo Castelli Gallery. 764 BR—Hirshhorn Museum, courtesy Scala. 766—UPI. 770—Bonnie Freer/Photo Researchers, Inc. 771—Courtesy of NASA. 782—Wally McNamee/Woodfin Camp. 787—Sygma. 788—Louise Gubb/Gamma-Liaison. 790—WW. 793—Courtesy of Two Together program; HRW Photo by Russell Dian.

Presidents of the United States: in chronological order from top left—The White House; Essex Institute; Granger Collection; Bowdoin College Museum of Fine Arts; New York City Hall Gallery; Metropolitan Museum of Art; LC; LC; Chicago Historical Society; LC; LC; LC; LC; LC; LC; LC; LC; LC; LC; LC; Clinedinst Studio; LC; LC; LC; LC; LC; Harry S Truman Library; General Services Administration; WW; Lyndon B. Johnson Library; Holt, Rinehart and Winston; WW; The White House; Michael Evans/Gamma-Liaison.

840